Preface

Whether tackling quick or cryptic crosswords, every cruciverbalist has experienced the frustration that comes from staring in vain at those obstinately white squares. Even a clue as simple as 'River (5)' may pose insurmountable problems once the Loire, Rhine, Rhône and Seine have been ruled out and one's mind remains stubbornly blank. This book is designed for exactly those moments. Rather than scurrying for an atlas, or – as the case may be – a biographical dictionary, factfinder or other reference, beleaguered solvers can find a wealth of possible solutions in seconds by reaching for *Chambers Crossword Lists*.

This book draws on material from across the authoritative Chambers reference range, including the *Biographical Dictionary*, *Dictionary of Literary Characters*, *Book of Facts*, *Crossword Dictionary* and *Dictionary of World History*. Furthermore, it contains thousands of terms from *The Chambers Dictionary*, including many of the archaic, literary and obscure words so beloved of cryptic crossword compilers.

Over 170,000 possible solutions to quick or cryptic clues are arranged in 1,650 lists under more than 900 headwords in this third edition. The information is truly diverse, from actors to wizards, political parties to capital cities, deserts to racehorses and landmarks to sieges. Additional information is included for many of the entries, such as nationalities and dates for people, sources for literary characters and locations for geographical features. A detailed contents list and extensive cross-references ensure that the material may be quickly and easily found.

Chambers Crossword Lists makes an ideal companion volume to the popular *Chambers Crossword Dictionary*, and should prove to be an invaluable aid to crossword setters and solvers alike.

We welcome all comments and suggestions from members of the public, which will be considered for incorporation in future editions. These should be sent to The Editor, *Chambers Crossword Lists*, Chambers Harrap Publishers Ltd, 338 Euston Road, London NW1 3BH.

The publisher would like to thank all the people whose work has contributed to the present and past two editions of this title.

Introduction

Chambers Crossword Lists contains more than 170,000 possible solutions to quick and cryptic crossword clues. It draws on *The Chambers Dictionary*, *Chambers Biographical Dictionary*, *Chambers Dictionary of Literary Characters*, *Chambers Crossword Dictionary* and the other authoritative Chambers databases.

Word forms

The forms *-ize* and *-ization* are used throughout; users should be aware that the alternative *-ise* and *-isation* spelling may be required as the solution to some crossword clues.

Organization

Words and phrases have been sorted into more than 1,650 lists. These are arranged under 900 main headwords, each with one or more list.

Each list focuses on a specific category of information; for example, there is not simply one list of cities, but four: capital cities, ancient cities, former names of cities and cities and towns from around the world. This makes locating exact information much easier.

Within the lists, words and phrases are grouped firstly by length, that is by the total number of letters in each word or phrase, and then ordered alphabetically within these word-length sections:

rainbow

Colours of the rainbow:

03 red	**05** green	orange	yellow
04 blue	**06** indigo	violet	

Solvers should note that alphabetization of solutions is strictly by letter, and usual stylistic conventions may be disregarded. For example, 'Mc' will be found at 'Mc' rather than mingled with 'Mac'. Items which are prefaced with 'The' will be found at 'T' rather than at the first letter of the second word. 'Saint' is rendered as 'St' throughout except in people's names and, similarly, 'Mount' is rendered as 'Mt'. The number of letters given for items will therefore reflect this.

Alphabetization of headwords, however, is by word so that 'air force' and 'air travel' precede 'aircraft' and 'airport'. Headwords which are prefaced with 'The' are alphabetized by the first letter of the second word so that 'The Americas' is found at 'A' rather than at 'T'.

There are extensive cross-references to assist users in finding the correct solution. There is also a detailed contents list at the start of the volume.

Inclusion

The content of the lists is intended to strike a balance between comprehensiveness and the likelihood of the words and phrases actually occurring as the solutions to crossword clues. Consideration has been given to the differing needs of different kinds of crosswords, from concise to the more advanced cryptics, and nothing has been excluded simply on the grounds of obscurity. An effort has been made to include colourful vocabulary, such as dialect, literary and archaic terms.

Chambers
Crossword Lists

Over 170,000 solutions to every kind of crossword

Chambers

CHAMBERS
An imprint of Chambers Harrap Publishers Ltd
338 Euston Road, London NW1 3BH

Chambers Harrap is an Hachette UK company

© Chambers Harrap Publishers Ltd 2009, 2013

Chambers® is a registered trademark of Chambers Harrap Publishers Ltd

This third edition published by Chambers Harrap Publishers Ltd 2013
First published in 2005
Second edition published in 2009

Database right Chambers Harrap Publishers Ltd (makers)

A CIP catalogue record for this book is available from the British Library.

ISBN 978 1471 80169 3 / 978 1471 80170 9

10 9 8 7 6 5 4

www.chambers.co.uk

Designed by Chambers Harrap Publishers Ltd
Typeset in Optima and Frutiger by Cenveo® Publisher Services.
Printed and bound by CPI Group (UK) Ltd, Croydon, CR0 4YY

witch

Witches, witch doctors and wizards include:

03 hag	mganga	conjurer	**10** besom-rider
hex	shaman	magician	reim-kennar
04 mage	voodoo	marabout	**11** enchantress
05 Hecat	wisard	night-hag	gyre-carline
lamia	zendik	**09** enchanter	medicine man
magus	**07** angekok	galdragon	necromancer
sibyl	carline	occultist	thaumaturge
weird	sangoma	pythoness	**12** Weird Sisters
06 Hecate	warlock	sorceress	**13** thaumaturgist
magian	wise man	wise woman	
	08 angekkok	witch-wife	

Content

The lists include both historical and current information; for example, in the list of actors users will find not only contemporary figures like Sir Ian McKellen and Leonardo DiCaprio, but also notable actors from the past like Richard Burbage and Edward Alleyn.

Similarly, the lists may contain both real and fictional or legendary items. For example, the list of heroes and heroines includes the legendary Robin Hood, the literary D'Artagnan, the historical William Wallace, the cinematic Indiana Jones, and the comic strip Superman.

Common generic terms have been omitted from the items in the lists, to avoid unwieldy and unnecessary repetition. For example, the word 'abbey' has not been included in the names in the list of abbeys, and the word 'saw' has not been included in the list of saws.

Users should be aware that such generic terms may form part of the solution to crossword clues.

saw

Saws include:

03 jig	hand	**06** coping	**08** circular
rip	**05** bench	rabbet	crosscut
04 band	chain	scroll	**09** radial-arm
fret	panel	**07** compass	**11** power-driven
hack	tenon	pruning	

The reference material has been selected to be as wide-ranging in scope as possible. Users should note that:

- variant spellings have been included, for example *topi* and *topee* in the list of hats.

- numbers may be found in solutions in some instances, as numbers may be encountered or referenced in some form in cryptic puzzles. For example, the list of films includes *2001: A Space Odyssey* and *Apollo 13*.

- some items are included under a certain headword on the grounds of usefulness, even if they are not strictly types of the headword. For example, *Washington DC* is included in the list of US states; *tomato* is included in the list of vegetables and *Pluto* is included in the list of planets. Similarly, items which are related to the headword may be included; succulents in the list of cacti, for example.

The size of the standard crossword grid is 15 letters across and down. In order to maximize the number of useful solutions in this edition, a distinction has been made between finite and non-finite lists in the book. In finite lists (ie those involving a closed set of solutions, such as members of the Commonwealth), no limit has been imposed on the length of solutions. In non-finite lists (ie those involving an open set of solutions, such as board games), solutions have been edited to 15 letters.

An exception has been made for lists of artistic works as these are often longer than 15 letters in length, such as fables, films and novels. Another minor exception concerns the lists of twins and pairs of lovers, as each solution in these lists comprises two names. In these exceptional cases, solutions longer than 15 letters have been permitted.

In lists of musical works, long solutions of the variety *Symphony No 6 in F Major* have been edited and listed by nickname or shortened title; solvers may need to investigate the full title of a musical work elsewhere.

In lists of people, death dates were researched in July 2013.

Extra information

Some of the lists contain extra information in brackets, following the core information. For example:

- first names or nicknames are given following a listed surname for real people, often with the person's birth and death dates and nationality

- fictional characters have the source given, with the date of publication and author

- for geographical features, buildings and similar items, the location is given in brackets

- musical and literary works have the composer/author and date of first performance/publication

- abbreviations, codes and similar items have the expanded form

- archbishops and popes have the date of accession

- legendary or mythological figures and creatures have the source of the legend or myth given

- gods and goddesses have their domain of power given

- words and expressions from foreign languages have the English term given

- films have date of release given

- battles have dates

- some terms have the thing related to; for example phobias include the thing feared, adjectives relating to eating include the thing eaten, dependencies have the governing country, sporting competitions have the relevant sport, and anniversaries have the number

The exact nature of the extra bracketed material is usually not indicated, but should be clear. Where it differs to that which might be expected, this is indicated in the introductory line to the list.

Some lists may have extra bracketed material for some items but not others. For example, in a list of airports *Gatwick* will have (London), but extra information is not needed for *Glasgow*.

Additional bracketed information is not included in the count of the number of letters, although it may form part of the solution to some crossword clues. The regnal numbers of individual popes, emperors, kings and queens have been omitted from main items, but are given in the brackets.

Reference Lists

A

abbey

See also **religious order**

aborigine

accessory *see* **fashion**; **photography**

accommodation

Accommodation includes:

03	06		
cot	bedsit	quarters	outlodging
hut	billet	tenement	padding-ken
inn	bothie	**09** almshouse	Picts' house
kip	camper	apartment	pied-à-terre
pad	duplex	bedsitter	quarterage
04 camp	flotel	bunkhouse	shantytown
cell	grange	camper van	wheelhouse
crib	hostel	dharmsala	**11** agriturismo
digs	hostry	dormitory	appartement
ferm	insula	dosshouse	bachelor pad
flat	mia-mia	firehouse	bed and board
gaff	pondok	frat house	bridal suite
gite	refuge	full board	condominium
mews	shanty	guest-room	duplex house
room	studio	half board	head-station
tent	succah	homestead	pit-dwelling
tipi	sukkah	hospitale	youth hostel
unit	teepee	hospitium	**12** guest-chamber
weem	walk-up	houseboat	halfway house
yurt	wigwam	longhouse	hunting-lodge
zeta	**07** caravan	peel-house	lodging house
05 b and b	cottage	peel-tower	porter's lodge
block	flatlet	pele-house	private hotel
board	floatel	pele-tower	private house
bothy	hospice	penthouse	room and board
bower	hutment	pondokkie	rooming house
cabin	mansion	residence	self-catering
condo	parador	rooming-in	two-up, two-down
hotel	pension	single-end	**13** boarding-house
house	pousada	tanka boat	dwelling-house
igloo	shelter	timeshare	habitat module
lodge	taverna	tree house	sponging-house
manse	village	**10** casual ward	spunging-house
meuse	**08** barracks	dharmshala	**14** bedsitting-room
motel	crashpad	earth-house	loft conversion
rooms	hacienda	guardhouse	**15** bed and breakfast
split	home unit	guest house	duplex apartment
squat	hospital	habitation	fraternity house
suite	lodgings	habitaunce	hall of residence
tepee	minshuku	labour camp	married quarters
villa	paradise	mobile home	

See also **house**; **tent**

acid

Acids include:

03	thio	auric	malic
DHA	uric	boric	mucic
DNA	wood	fatty	osmic
RNA	**05** amino	folic	
04 EDTA		Lewis	**06** acetic

bromic
cholic
citric
domoic
erucic
formic
gallic
lactic
lauric
maleic
marine
nitric
oxalic
pectic
phenol
picric
quinic
sorbic
tannic
toluic
07 acrylic
alginic
benzoic
boracic
butyric
cerotic
chloric
chromic
fumaric
fusidic
malonic

nitrous
nucleic
plumbic
prussic
pteroic
pyruvic
sebacic
silicic
stearic
valeric
08 abscisic
ascorbic
aspartic
butanoic
carbamic
carbolic
carbonic
cinnamic
cresylic
ethanoic
glutamic
iopanoic
itaconic
linoleic
lysergic
manganic
margaric
molybdic
myristic
nonanoic
palmitic

periodic
retinoic
succinic
tantalic
tartaric
telluric
trans fat
09 aqua regia
cevitamic
hydrazoic
linolenic
methanoic
nalidixic
nicotinic
pentanoic
propanoic
propenoic
propionic
salicylic
sulphonic
sulphuric
10 aqua fortis
barbituric
carboxylic
dodecanoic
glutaminic
hyaluronic
margaritic
naphthenic
omega fatty
pelargonic

phosphonic
phosphoric
sulphurous
trans fatty
valerianic
11 arachidonic
ethanedioic
gibberellic
hydrobromic
hydrocyanic
pantothenic
permanganic
phosphorous
ribonucleic
12 alpha-hydroxy
hydrochloric
hydrofluoric
indoleacetic
octadecanoic
orthoboracic
terephthalic
13 indolebutyric
spirits of salt
thiosulphuric
tricarboxylic
14 essential fatty
peptide nucleic
15 acetylsalicylic
pteroylglutamic

See also **amino acid**

Act *see* **law**

acting

Actors include:

03 Cox (Brian; 1946– , Scottish)
Fox (Michael J; 1961– , Canadian)
Fry (Stephen; 1957– , English)
Law (Jude; 1973– , English)
Lee (Bruce; 1940–73, Chinese)
Lee (Christopher; 1922– , English)
Lee (Spike; 1957– , US)
Lom (Herbert; 1917–2012, Czech)
Sim (Alastair; 1900–76, Scottish)

04 Alda (Alan; 1936– , US)
Caan (James; 1939– , US)
Cage (Nicolas; 1964– , US)
Chan (Jackie; 1954– , Chinese)
Cook (Peter; 1937–95, English)
Dean (James; 1931–55, US)
Depp (Johnny; 1963– , US)
Ford (Harrison; 1942– , US)

Foxx (Jamie; 1967– , US)
Gere (Richard; 1949– , US)
Holm (Sir Ian; 1931– , English)
Hope (Bob; 1903–2003, English/US)
Hurt (John; 1940– , English)
Kean (Edmund; c.1789–1833, English)
Lowe (Rob; 1964– , US)
Marx (Chico; 1891–1961, US)
Marx (Groucho; 1895–1977, US)
Marx (Harpo; 1893–1964, US)
Marx (Zeppo; 1901–79, US)
Peck (Gregory; 1916–2003, US)
Penn (Sean; 1960– , US)
Pitt (Brad; 1963– , US)
Reed (Oliver; 1938–99, English)
Roth (Tim; 1961– , English)
Rush (Geoffrey; 1951– , Australian)

Sher (Sir Antony; 1949– , South African/
  British)
Tati (Jacques; 1908–82, French)
Thaw (John; 1942–2002, English)
Wood (Elijah; 1981– , US)

05 Allen (Woody; 1935– , US)
Arkin (Alan; 1934– , US)
Bacon (Kevin; 1958– , US)
Bates (Alan; 1934–2003, English)
Boyer (Charles; 1897–1978, French)
Brody (Adrien; 1973– , US)
Caine (Sir Michael; 1933– , English)
Candy (John; 1950–94, Canadian)
Chase (Chevy; 1943– , US)
Clift (Montgomery; 1920–66, US)
Conti (Tom; 1941– , Scottish)
Crowe (Russell; 1964– , Australian)
Dafoe (Willem; 1955– , US)
Damon (Matt; 1970– , US)
Dance (Charles; 1946– , English)
Firth (Colin; 1960– , English)
Flynn (Errol; 1909–59, Australian/US)
Fonda (Henry; 1905–82, US)
Fonda (Peter; 1939– , US)
Gabin (Jean; 1904–76, French)
Gable (Clark; 1901–60, US)
Grant (Cary; 1904–86, English/US)
Grant (Hugh; 1960– , English)
Grant (Richard E; 1957– , Swazi/British)
Hanks (Tom; 1956– , US)
Hardy (Oliver; 1892–1957, US)
Hauer (Rutger; 1944– , Dutch)
Hogan (Paul; 1939– , Australian)
Irons (Jeremy; 1948– , English)
Jet Li (1963– , Chinese)
Jones (Tommy Lee; 1946– , US)
Julia (Raul; 1940–94, Puerto Rican)
Kelly (Gene; 1912–96, US)
Kempe (Will; c.1550–c.1603, English)
Kline (Kevin; 1947– , US)
Leung (Tony; 1962– , Chinese)
Lewis (Jerry; 1926– , US)
Lloyd (Harold; 1893–1971, US)
Mason (James; 1909–84, English)
Miles (Bernard, Lord; 1907–91, English)
Mills (Sir John; 1908–2005, English)
Moore (Dudley; 1935–2002, English)
Moore (Roger; 1927– , English)
Neill (Sam; 1947– , New Zealand)
Niven (David; 1910–83, English)
Nolte (Nick; 1940– , US)
Pesci (Joe; 1943– , US)
Price (Vincent; 1911–93, US)
Quinn (Anthony; 1915–2001, Mexican/US)
Reeve (Christopher; 1952–2004, US)
Sheen (Charlie; 1965– , US)
Sheen (Martin; 1940– , US)
Sheen (Michael; 1969– , Welsh)

Smith (Mel; 1952– , English)
Smith (Will; 1968– , US)
Spall (Timothy; 1957– , English)
Stamp (Terence; 1939– , English)
Sydow (Max von; 1929– , Swedish)
Tracy (Spencer; 1900–67, US)
Wayne (John; 1907–79, US)

06 Alleyn (Edward; 1566–1626, English)
Beatty (Warren; 1937– , US)
Bogart (Humphrey; 1899–1957, US)
Brando (Marlon; 1924–2004, US)
Brooks (Mel; 1926– , US)
Burton (Richard; 1925–84, Welsh)
Cagney (James; 1899–1986, US)
Callow (Simon; 1949– , English)
Carrey (Jim; 1962– , Canadian)
Cleese (John; 1939– , English)
Coburn (James; 1928–2002, US)
Cooper (Gary; 1901–61, US)
Coward (Sir Noël; 1899–1973, English)
Crosby (Bing; 1904–77, US)
Cruise (Tom; 1962– , US)
Culkin (Macaulay; 1980– , US)
Curtis (Tony; 1925–2010, US)
De Niro (Robert; 1943– , US)
De Sica (Vittorio; 1902–74, Italian)
DeVito (Danny; 1944– , US)
Dillon (Matt; 1964– , US)
Duvall (Robert; 1931– , US)
Fields (W C; 1879–1946, US)
Finney (Albert; 1936– , English)
Gambon (Sir Michael; 1940– , Irish)
Garner (James; 1928– , US)
Gibson (Mel; 1956– , US/Australian)
Glover (Danny; 1947– , US)
Harris (Richard; 1930–2002, Irish)
Heston (Charlton; 1924–2008, US)
Hopper (Dennis; 1936–2010, US)
Howard (Leslie; 1893–1943, English)
Howard (Trevor; 1916–88, English)
Hudson (Rock; 1925–85, US)
Irving (Sir Henry; 1838–1905, English)
Jacobi (Sir Derek; 1938– , English)
Jolson (Al; 1886–1950, Russian/US)
Keaton (Buster; 1895–1966, US)
Keitel (Harvey; 1941– , US)
Kemble (Charles; 1775–1854, English)
Kemble (John Philip; 1757–1823, English)
Kemble (Stephen; 1758–1822, English)
Laurel (Stan; 1890–1965, English/US)
Ledger (Heath; 1979–2008, Australian)
Lemmon (Jack; 1925–2001, US)
Lugosi (Bela; 1882–1956, Hungarian/US)
Martin (Steve; 1945– , US)
Marvin (Lee; 1924–87, US)
Massey (Raymond; 1896–1983, Canadian/US)
Morley (Robert; 1908–92, English)
Murphy (Eddie; 1961– , US)

Murray (Bill; 1950– , US)
Neeson (Liam; 1952– , Northern Irish)
Newman (Paul; 1925–2008, US)
Oldman (Gary; 1959– , English)
O'Toole (Peter; 1932– , Irish)
Pacino (Al; 1940– , US)
Quayle (Sir Anthony; 1913–89, English)
Reagan (Ronald; 1911–2004, US)
Reeves (Keanu; 1964– , US)
Rooney (Mickey; 1920– , US)
Rourke (Mickey; 1956– , US)
Sharif (Omar; 1932– , Egyptian)
Sinden (Sir Donald; 1923– , English)
Slater (Christian; 1969– , US)
Spacey (Kevin; 1959– , US)
Spader (James; 1960– , US)
Suchet (David; 1946– , English)
Swayze (Patrick; 1954–2009, US)
Walken (Christopher; 1943– , US)
Welles (Orson; 1915–85, US)
Wilder (Gene; 1935– , US)
Willis (Bruce; 1955– , US)
Wolfit (Sir Donald; 1902–68, English)

07 Astaire (Fred; 1899–1987, US)
Auteuil (Daniel; 1950– , French)
Aykroyd (Dan; 1952– , Canadian)
Baldwin (Alec; 1958– , US)
Benigni (Roberto; 1952– , Italian)
Bennett (Alan; 1934– , English)
Berkoff (Steven; 1937– , English)
Blessed (Brian; 1936– , English)
Bogarde (Sir Dirk; 1921–99, English)
Branagh (Kenneth; 1960– , Northern Irish)
Bridges (Jeff; 1949– , US)
Bridges (Lloyd; 1913–98, US)
Bronson (Charles; 1922–2003, US)
Brosnan (Pierce; 1953– , Irish)
Brynner (Yul; 1915–85, Swiss/Russian/US)
Burbage (Richard; c.1567–1619, English)
Carlyle (Robert; 1961– , Scottish)
Chaplin (Charlie; 1889–1977, English)
Clooney (George; 1962– , US)
Connery (Sir Sean; 1930– , Scottish)
Costner (Kevin; 1955– , US)
Crystal (Billy; 1947– , US)
Cushing (Peter; 1913–94, English)
Douglas (Kirk; 1916– , US)
Douglas (Michael; 1944– , US)
Elliott (Denholm; 1922–92, English)
Everett (Rupert; 1960– , English)
Fiennes (Ralph; 1962– , English)
Freeman (Morgan; 1937– , US)
Garrick (David; 1717–79, English)
Gielgud (Sir John; 1904–2000, English)
Hackman (Gene; 1930– , US)
Hoffman (Dustin; 1937– , US)
Hopkins (Sir Anthony; 1937– , Welsh/US)
Hordern (Sir Michael; 1911–95, English)

Hoskins (Bob; 1942– , English)
Jackson (Samuel L; 1948– , US)
Jenkins (Richard; 1947– , US)
Karloff (Boris; 1887–1969, English)
Marceau (Marcel; 1923–2007, French)
Matthau (Walter; 1920–2000, US)
McQueen (Steve; 1930–80, US)
Mitchum (Robert; 1917–97, US)
Montand (Yves; 1921–91, Italian/French)
Nielsen (Leslie; 1926–2010, Canadian)
Olivier (Laurence, Lord; 1907–89, English)
Perkins (Anthony; 1932–92, English)
Plummer (Christopher; 1927– , Canadian)
Poitier (Sidney; 1924– , US)
Presley (Elvis; 1935–77, US)
Redford (Robert; 1937– , US)
Rickman (Alan; 1947– , English)
Robbins (Tim; 1958– , US)
Roscius (c.134–62 BC; Roman)
Russell (Kurt; 1951– , US)
Selleck (Tom; 1945– , US)
Sellers (Peter; 1925–80, English)
Shepard (Sam; 1943– , US)
Stewart (James; 1908–97, US)
Tennant (David; 1971– , Scottish)
Ustinov (Sir Peter; 1921–2004, English)
Van Dyke (Dick; 1925– , US)

08 Atkinson (Rowan; 1955– , English)
Barrault (Jean-Louis; 1910–94, French)
Belmondo (Jean-Paul; 1933– , French)
Coltrane (Robbie; 1950– , Scottish)
Crawford (Michael; 1942– , English)
Day-Lewis (Daniel; 1958– , English)
DiCaprio (Leonardo; 1974– , US)
Dreyfuss (Richard; 1947– , US)
Eastwood (Clint; 1930– , US)
Goldblum (Jeff; 1952– , US)
Guinness (Sir Alec; 1914–2000, English)
Harrison (Sir Rex; 1908–90, English)
Kingsley (Ben; 1943– , English)
Langella (Frank; 1938– , US)
Laughton (Charles; 1899–1962, English)
Macready (William Charles; 1793–1873,
  English)
McGregor (Ewan; 1971– , Scottish)
McKellen (Sir Ian; 1939– , English)
Rathbone (Basil; 1892–1967, South African/
  British)
Redgrave (Sir Michael; 1908–85, English)
Reynolds (Burt; 1936– , US)
Robinson (Edward G; 1893–1973,
  Romanian/US)
Scofield (Paul; 1922–2008, English)
Stallone (Sylvester; 1946– , US)
Stroheim (Erich von; 1885–1957, Austrian)
Travolta (John; 1954– , US)
Turturro (John; 1957– , US)
Van Damme (Jean-Claude; 1961– , Belgian)

von Sydow (Max; 1929– , Swedish)
Whitaker (Forest; 1961– , US)
Williams (Michael; 1935–2001, English)
Williams (Robin; 1951– , US)
Woodward (Edward; 1930–2009, English)

09 Barrymore (John; 1882–1942, US)
Barrymore (Lionel; 1878–1954, US)
Broadbent (Jim; 1949– , English)
Broderick (Matthew; 1963– , US)
Chevalier (Maurice; 1888–1972, French)
Courtenay (Sir Tom; 1937– , English)
Depardieu (Gérard; 1948– , French)
Fairbanks (Douglas, Jnr; 1909–2000, US)
Fairbanks (Douglas, Snr; 1883–1939, US)
Griffiths (Richard; 1947–2013, English)
Harrelson (Woody; 1961– , US)
Hawthorne (Sir Nigel; 1929–2001, English)
Lancaster (Burt; 1913–94, US)
Malkovich (John; 1953– , US)
Nicholson (Jack; 1937– , US)
Pleasence (Donald; 1919–95, English)

Valentino (Rudolph; 1895–1926, Italian/
US)

10 Cassavetes (John; 1929–89, US)
Chow Yun-Fat (1956– , Chinese)
Guttenberg (Steve; 1958– , US)
Sutherland (Donald; 1935– , Canadian)
Sutherland (Kiefer; 1966– , US)
Washington (Denzel; 1954– , US)

11 Mastroianni (Marcello; 1923–96, Italian)
von Stroheim (Erich; 1885–1957, Austrian)
Weissmuller (Johnny; 1903–84, Romanian/
US)

12 Attenborough (Richard, Lord; 1923– ,
English)
Downey Junior (Robert; 1965– , US)
Stanislavsky (Konstantin; 1863–1938,
Russian)

14 Schwarzenegger (Arnold; 1947– , Austrian/
US)
Seymour Hoffman (Philip; 1967– , US)

Actresses include:

03 Bow (Clara; 1905–65, US)
Cox (Courteney; 1964– , US)
Day (Doris; 1924– , US)
Loy (Myrna; 1905–93, US)

04 Ball (Lucille; 1910–89, US)
Cruz (Penélope; 1974– , Spanish)
Diaz (Cameron; 1972– , US)
Duse (Eleonora; 1859–1924, Italian)
Gish (Lillian; 1893–1993, US)
Gwyn (Nell; c.1650–87, English)
Hawn (Goldie; 1945– , US)
Hird (Dame Thora; 1911–2003, English)
Neal (Patricia; 1926–2010, US)
Rigg (Dame Diana; 1938– , English)
Ryan (Meg; 1962– , US)
Ward (Dame Geneviève; 1838–1922, US)
West (Mae; 1893–1980, US)
Wood (Natalie; 1938–81, US)
Wray (Fay; 1907–2004, US)
York (Susannah; 1941– , English)

05 Allen (Gracie; 1895–1964, US)
Berry (Halle; 1966– , US)
Brice (Fanny; 1891–1951, US)
Close (Glenn; 1947– , US)
Davis (Bette; 1908–89, US)
Davis (Geena; 1957– , US)
Davis (Judy; 1955– , Australian)
Dench (Dame Judi; 1934– , English)
Derek (Bo; 1956– , US)
Evans (Dame Edith; 1888–1976, English)
Field (Sally; 1946– , US)
Fonda (Jane; 1937– , US)
Gabor (Zsa Zsa; 1918– , Hungarian)

Garbo (Greta; 1905–90, Swedish/US)
Gonne (Maud; 1865–1953, Irish)
Horne (Lena; 1917–2010, US)
Jolie (Angelina; 1975– , US)
Kelly (Grace; 1929–82, US)
Lange (Jessica; 1949– , US)
Leigh (Janet; 1927–2004, US)
Leigh (Vivien; 1913–67, British)
Lenya (Lotte; 1898–1981, Austrian)
Lewis (Juliette; 1973– , US)
Lopez (Jennifer; 1969– , US)
Loren (Sophia; 1934– , Italian)
Mills (Hayley; 1946– , English)
Moore (Demi; 1962– , US)
Moore (Julianne; 1961– , US)
O'Hara (Maureen; 1920– , Irish)
Ryder (Winona; 1971– , US)
Smith (Dame Maggie; 1934– , English)
Smith (Liz; 1921– , English)
Stone (Sharon; 1958– , US)
Swank (Hilary; 1974– , US)
Tandy (Jessica; 1907–94, English/US)
Terry (Dame Ellen; 1848–1928, English)
Tomei (Marisa; 1964– , US)
Weisz (Rachel; 1971– , English)
Welch (Raquel; 1940– , US)

06 Adjani (Isabelle; 1955– , French)
Arnaud (Yvonne; 1892–1958, French)
Bacall (Lauren; 1924– , US)
Bardot (Brigitte; 1934– , French)
Bening (Annette; 1958– , US)
Bergen (Candice; 1946– , US)
Bisset (Jacqueline; 1944– , English)

Cheung (Maggie; 1964– , Chinese)
Curtis (Jamie Lee; 1958– , US)
Ekland (Britt; 1942– , Swedish)
Farrow (Mia; 1945– , US)
Fisher (Carrie; 1956– , US)
Foster (Jodie; 1962– , US)
Gong Li (1965– , Chinese)
Gordon (Hannah; 1941– , Scottish)
Grable (Betty; 1916–73, US)
Hannah (Daryl; 1960– , US)
Harlow (Jean; 1911–37, US)
Hedren (Tippi; 1931– , US)
Hiller (Dame Wendy; 1912–2003, English)
Hopper (Hedda; 1885–1966, US)
Hunter (Holly; 1958– , US)
Huston (Anjelica; 1951– , US)
Keaton (Diane; 1946– , US)
Kemble (Fanny; 1809–93, English)
Kidman (Nicole; 1967– , US/Australian)
Kinski (Nastassja; 1960– , German)
Kudrow (Lisa; 1963– , US)
Lamarr (Hedy; 1913–2000, Austrian)
Lamour (Dorothy; 1914–96, US)
Lumley (Joanna; 1946– , English)
Midler (Bette; 1945– , US)
Mirren (Helen; 1945– , English)
Monroe (Marilyn; 1926–62, US)
Moreau (Jeanne; 1928– , French)
Robson (Dame Flora; 1902–84, English)
Rogers (Ginger; 1911–95, US)
Spacek (Sissy; 1949– , US)
Streep (Meryl; 1949– , US)
Suzman (Janet; 1939– , South African/
 British)
Tautou (Audrey; 1978– , French)
Taylor (Dame Elizabeth; 1932–2011,
 English/US)
Temple (Shirley; 1928– , US)
Tomlin (Lily; 1939– , US)
Turner (Kathleen; 1954– , US)
Turner (Lana; 1920–95, US)
Weaver (Sigourney; 1949– , US)
Winger (Debra; 1955– , US)

07 Andress (Ursula; 1936– , Swiss)
Andrews (Dame Julie; 1935– , English)
Aniston (Jennifer; 1969– , US)
Bergman (Ingrid; 1915–82, Swedish)
Binoche (Juliette; 1964– , French)
Bullock (Sandra; 1964– , US)
Colbert (Claudette; 1903–96, French/US)
Deneuve (Catherine; 1943– , French)
Dunaway (Faye; 1941– , US)
Gardner (Ava; 1922–90, US)
Garland (Judy; 1922–69, US)
Grahame (Gloria; 1923–81, US)
Hepburn (Audrey; 1929–93, Belgian)
Hepburn (Katharine; 1907–2003, US)
Huppert (Isabelle; 1955– , French)

Jackson (Glenda; 1936– , English)
Johnson (Dame Celia; 1908–82, English)
Langtry (Lillie; 1853–1929, English)
Lombard (Carole; 1908–42, US)
Madonna (1958– , US)
Magnani (Anna; 1908–73, Italian)
Paltrow (Gwyneth; 1973– , US)
Roberts (Julia; 1967– , US)
Russell (Jane; 1921–2011, US)
Sevigny (Chloë; 1974– , US)
Seymour (Jane; 1951– , English)
Siddons (Sarah; 1755–1831, English)
Swanson (Gloria; 1897–1983, US)
Swinton (Tilda; 1960– , English)
Tierney (Gene; 1920–91, US)
Ullmann (Liv; 1939– , Norwegian)
Walters (Julie; 1950– , English)
Winslet (Kate; 1975– , English)
Winters (Shelley; 1920–2006, US)

08 Ashcroft (Dame Peggy; 1907–91, English)
Bancroft (Anne; 1931–2005, US)
Bankhead (Tallulah; 1903–68, US)
Basinger (Kim; 1953– , US)
Charisse (Cyd; 1922–2008, US)
Christie (Julie; 1940– , English)
Crawford (Joan; 1906–77, US)
Dietrich (Marlene; 1901–92, German/US)
Fontaine (Joan; 1917– , US)
Goldberg (Whoopi; 1949– , US)
Griffith (Melanie; 1957– , US)
Hathaway (Anne; 1982– , US)
Hayworth (Rita; 1918–87, US)
Lawrence (Gertrude; 1898–1952, English)
Lockwood (Margaret; 1911–90, English)
MacLaine (Shirley; 1934– , US)
Mercouri (Melina; 1923–94, Greek)
Minnelli (Liza; 1946– , US)
Pfeiffer (Michelle; 1958– , US)
Pickford (Mary; 1893–1979, Canadian/
 US)
Rampling (Charlotte; 1946– , English)
Redgrave (Vanessa; 1937– , English)
Sarandon (Susan; 1946– , US)
Shepherd (Cybill; 1950– , US)
Signoret (Simone; 1921–85, French)
Stanwyck (Barbara; 1907–90, US)
Thompson (Emma; 1959– , English)
Whitelaw (Billie; 1932– , English)
Woodward (Joanne; 1930– , US)

09 Barrymore (Drew; 1975– , US)
Bernhardt (Sarah; 1844–1923, French)
Blanchett (Cate; 1969– , Australian)
Cotillard (Marion; 1975– , French)
Johansson (Scarlett; 1984– , US)
Knightley (Keira; 1985– , English)
MacDowell (Andie; 1958– , US)
Mansfield (Jayne; 1933–67, US)

McDormand (Frances; 1957– , US)
Plowright (Joan; 1929– , English)
Streisand (Barbra; 1942– , US)
Thorndike (Dame Sybil; 1882–1976, English)
Zellweger (Renée; 1969– , US)
Zeta-Jones (Catherine; 1969– , Welsh)

10 Richardson (Miranda; 1958– , English)
Rossellini (Isabella; 1952– , US)

See also **comedy**

Rutherford (Dame Margaret; 1892–1972, English)
Woffington (Peg; 1720–60, Irish)

11 de Havilland (Olivia; 1916– , US)
Scott-Thomas (Kristin; 1960– , English)
Witherspoon (Reese; 1976– , US)

12 Bonham Carter (Helena; 1966– , English)
Lollobrigida (Gina; 1927– , Italian)

activist

Activists include:

04 Bono (1960– , Irish)
King (Martin Luther, Jnr; 1929–68, US)

05 Nader (Ralph; 1934– , US)
Parks (Rosa Lee; 1913–2005, US)

06 Gandhi (Mahatma; 1869–1948, Indian)
Geldof (Bob; 1954– , Irish)

07 Angelou (Maya; 1928– , US)
Chomsky (Noam; 1928– , US)
Guevara (Che; 1928–67, Argentine)

See also **aborigine**

Jackson (Jesse; 1941– , US)
Mandela (Nelson; 1918– , South African)
Mandela (Winifred 'Winnie'; 1934– , South African)

08 Malcolm X (1925–65, US)
Silkwood (Karen; 1946–1974, US)

09 Pankhurst (Christabel; 1880–1958, English)
Pankhurst (Emmeline; 1857–1928, English)
Pankhurst (Sylvia; 1882–1960, English)

administrative area

Administrative areas include:

04	06		09
city	county	enclave	pergunnah
town	oblast	pargana	territory
ward	parish	village	**11** conurbation
zila	region	**08** district	**12** constituency
zone	sector	division	municipality
05 shire	zillah	precinct	
state	**07** borough	province	
theme	commune	township	

See also **Australia; Austria; Belgium; Canada; Czech Republic; Denmark; Finland; France; Germany; Greece; India; Ireland; Italy; The Netherlands; Norway; Portugal; South Africa; Spain; Sweden; Switzerland; United Kingdom**

admiral

Admirals include:

04 Byng (George, Viscount Torrington; 1663–1733, English)
Hood (Samuel, Viscount; 1724–1816, English)
Howe (Richard, Earl; 1726–99, English)
Togo (Heihachiro, Count; 1848–1934, Japanese)

05 Blake (Robert; 1599–1657, English)
Croft (Admiral; *Persuasion*, 1818, Jane Austen)

Dewey (George; 1837–1917, US)
Doria (Andrea; c.1466–1560, Genoese)
Hawke (Edward, Lord; 1705–81, English)
Rooke (Sir George; 1650–1709, English)
Tromp (Maarten; 1598–1653, Dutch)

06 Beatty (David, Earl; 1871–1936, English)
Benbow (John; 1653–1702, English)
Darlan (Jean François; 1881–1942, French)
Dönitz (Karl; 1891–1980, German)
Fisher (John, Lord; 1841–1920, English)

Grasse (François, Comte de; 1722–88, French)
Halsey (William F, Jnr; 1884–1959, US)
Howard (Charles; 1536–1624, English)
Nelson (Horatio, Lord; 1758–1805, English)
Nimitz (Chester; 1885–1966, US)
Raeder (Erich; 1876–1960, German)
Rodney (George, Lord; 1719–92, English)
Ruyter (Michiel de; 1607–76, Dutch)
Vernon (Edward; 1684–1757, English)

07 Kanaris (Constantine; 1790–1877, Greek)
McClure (Sir Robert; 1807–73, Irish)
Tirpitz (Alfred von; 1849–1930, German)

Wrangel (Ferdinand, Baron von; 1794–1870, Russian)

08 Cochrane (Thomas; 1775–1860, Scottish)
Gorshkov (Sergei; 1910–88, Soviet)
Jellicoe (John, Earl; 1859–1935, English)

09 Artemisia (fl.5c BC, Greek)

10 Villeneuve (Pierre Charles; 1763–1806, French)

11 Collingwood (Cuthbert, Lord; 1750–1810, English)
Krusenstern (Adam Johann, Baron von; 1770–1846, Russian)
Mountbatten (Louis, Earl; 1900–79, English)

Africa

Countries in Africa:

04 Chad
Mali
Togo

05 Benin
Congo
Egypt
Gabon
Ghana
Kenya
Libya
Niger
Sudan

06 Angola
Guinea
Malawi
Rwanda
Uganda
Zambia

07 Algeria

Burundi
Comoros
Eritrea
Lesotho
Liberia
Morocco
Namibia
Nigeria
Senegal
Somalia
Tunisia

08 Botswana
Cameroon
Djibouti
Ethiopia
Tanzania
Zimbabwe

09 Cape Verde
Mauritius

Swaziland
The Gambia

10 Madagascar
Mauritania
Mozambique
Seychelles
South Sudan

11 Burkina Faso
Côte d'Ivoire
Sierra Leone
South Africa

12 Guinea-Bissau

13 Western Sahara

16 Equatorial Guinea

18 São Tomé and Príncipe

22 Central African Republic

28 Democratic Republic of the Congo

Cities and notable towns in Africa include:

03 Fez (Morocco)
Ife (Nigeria)

04 Kano (Nigeria)
Lomé (Togo)
Oran (Algeria)
Safi (Morocco)
Sfax (Tunisia)

05 Abuja (Nigeria)
Accra (Ghana)
Beira (Mozambique)
Dakar (Senegal)
Enugu (Nigeria)
Gweru (Zimbabwe)
Harer (Ethiopia)
Kitwe (Zambia)
Lagos (Nigeria)

Mopti (Mali)
Ndola (Zambia)
Oujda (Morocco)
Rabat (Morocco)
Ségou (Mali)
Thiès (Senegal)
Tunis (Tunisia)
Zaria (Nigeria)
Zomba (Malawi)

06 Agadès (Niger)
Agadir (Morocco)
Annaba (Algeria)
Asmara (Eritrea)
Bamako (Mali)
Bangui (Central African Republic)
Banjul (The Gambia)

Benoni (South Africa)
Bissau (Guinea-Bissau)
Bouaké (Côte d'Ivoire)
Butare (Rwanda)
Dodoma (Tanzania)
Douala (Cameroon)
Durban (South Africa)
Gondar (Ethiopia)
Harare (Zimbabwe)
Huambo (Angola)
Ibadan (Nigeria)
Ilesha (Nigeria)
Ilorin (Nigeria)
Kaduna (Nigeria)
Kigali (Rwanda)
Kumasi (Ghana)
Lobito (Angola)
Luanda (Angola)
Lusaka (Zambia)
Maputo (Mozambique)
Maseru (Lesotho)
Mekele (Ethiopia)
Meknès (Morocco)
Mutare (Zimbabwe)
Mwanza (Tanzania)
Nakuru (Kenya)
Niamey (Niger)
Skikda (Algeria)
Sokodé (Togo)
Sousse (Tunisia)
Soweto (South Africa)
Tamale (Ghana)

07 Abidjan (Côte d'Ivoire)
Algiers (Algeria)
Berbera (Somalia)
Calabar (Nigeria)
Conakry (Guinea)
Cotonou (Benin)
Kampala (Uganda)
Kananga (Congo, Democratic Republic of the)
Kenitra (Morocco)
Lobamba (Swaziland)
Maramba (Zambia)
Mbabane (Swaziland)
Mombasa (Kenya)
Moundou (Chad)
Nairobi (Kenya)
Nampula (Mozambique)
Oshogbo (Nigeria)
Tangier (Morocco)
Tétouan (Morocco)
Tlemcen (Algeria)
Yaoundé (Cameroon)

08 Abeokuta (Nigeria)
Bandundu (Congo, Democratic Republic of the)

Benguela (Angola)
Blantyre (Malawi)
Bulawayo (Zimbabwe)
Cape Town (South Africa)
Djibouti (Djibouti)
Freetown (Sierra Leone)
Gabarone (Botswana)
Hargeysa (Somalia)
Kairouan (Tunisia)
Kinshasa (Congo, Democratic Republic of the)
Lilongwe (Malawi)
Mafeteng (Lesotho)
Monrovia (Liberia)
N'Djamena (Chad)
Pretoria (South Africa)
Victoria (Seychelles)
Windhoek (Namibia)
Zanzibar (Tanzania)

09 Bujumbura (Burundi)
Kimberley (South Africa)
Kisangani (Congo, Democratic Republic of the)
Maiduguri (Nigeria)
Marrakesh (Morocco)
Mbuji-Mayi (Congo, Democratic Republic of the)
Mogadishu (Somalia)
Ogbomosho (Nigeria)
Port Louis (Mauritius)
Porto-Novo (Benin)
Toamasina (Madagascar)

10 Addis Ababa (Ethiopia)
Casablanca (Morocco)
Klerksdorp (South Africa)
Libreville (Gabon)
Lubumbashi (Congo, Democratic Republic of the)
Nouakchott (Mauritania)

11 Brazzaville (Congo)
Chitungwiza (Zimbabwe)
Constantine (Algeria)
Dar es Salaam (Tanzania)
Ouagadougou (Burkina Faso)
Pointe-Noire (Congo)
Vereeniging (South Africa)

12 Antananarivo (Madagascar)
Bloemfontein (South Africa)
Johannesburg (South Africa)
Port Harcourt (Nigeria)
Yamoussoukro (Côte d'Ivoire)

13 Bobo-Dioulasso (Burkina Faso)
Port Elizabeth (South Africa)

15 Sekondi-Takoradi (Ghana)

Africans include:

03 Ibo	Libyan	Beninese	Ethiopian
Kru	Malian	Egyptian	Sahrawian
Twi	Somali	Eritrean	Santoméan
04 Boer	Tuareg	Gabonese	São Toméan
Efik	Yoruba	Ghanaian	Tanzanian
Igbo	**07** Angolan	Liberian	**10** Djiboutian
Kroo	Basotho	Malagasy	Mozambican
Moor	Chadian	Malawian	Sahraouian
Susu	Gambian	Moroccan	Senegalese
Tshi	Guinean	Motswana	Zimbabwean
Zulu	Ivorian	Namibian	
05 Masai	Mosotho	Nigerian	**11** Cameroonian
Swazi	Rwandan	Nigerien	Cape Verdean
Temne	Sahrawi	Sahraoui	Mauritanian
Tonga	Swahili	Sudanese	**12** South African
06 Griqua	Ugandan	Togolese	**13** Equatoguinean
Herero	Zambian	Tunisian	Sierra Leonean
Kenyan	**08** Algerian	**09** Burkinabé	**14** Central African
Kikuyu	Batswana	Burundian	Guinea-Bissauan
		Congolese	

African landmarks include:

04 Giza (Egypt)
Nile (east/north-east Africa)

05 Congo (central/west Africa)
Luxor (Egypt)

06 Karnak (Egypt)
Sahara (north Africa)
Sphinx (Egypt)

07 Zambezi (south-east Africa)

08 Aswan Dam (Egypt)
Kalahari (south-west Africa)
Lake Chad (Cameroon/Chad)
Okavango (Angola/Namibia/Botswana)
Pyramids (Egypt)

09 Lake Nyasa (Malawi/Mozambique/Tanzania)
Masai Mara (Kenya)
River Nile (east/north-east Africa)
Serengeti (Tanzania)
Suez Canal (Egypt)

10 Lake Malawi (Malawi/Mozambique/Tanzania)
Lake Nasser (Egypt)

See also **South Africa**

River Congo (central/west Africa)
River Niger (west Africa)

11 Drakensberg (South Africa)
Great Sphinx (Egypt)
Kilimanjaro (Tanzania)
Luxor Temple (Egypt)

12 Aswan High Dam (Egypt)
Great Pyramid (Egypt)
Lake Victoria (Kenya/Tanzania/Uganda)
Sahara Desert (north Africa)
Zambezi River (south-east Africa)

13 Mt Kilimanjaro (Tanzania)
Okavango Delta (Botswana)
Table Mountain (South Africa)
Victoria Falls (Zimbabwe/Zambia)

14 Atlas Mountains (Algeria/Morocco/Tunisia)
Cape of Good Hope (South Africa)
Kalahari Desert (south-west Africa)
Lake Tanganyika (central/east Africa)

15 Great Rift Valley (east/south-east Africa)

agent *see* **spy**

agreement *see* **treaty**

agriculture

Agricultural equipment includes:

03 ard
ATV
axe
hoe
saw
04 fork
plow
rake
wain
05 baler
drill
flail
gambo
mower
share
spade
06 harrow
plough
ricker

ripple
scythe
shovel
sickle
tanker
tedder
07 combine
draw hoe
grubber
hayfork
hayrake
mattock
scuffle
sprayer
tractor
trailer
08 buckrake
chainsaw
hay knife
haymaker

scuffler
spreader
09 corn drill
drop-drill
harvester
irrigator
pitchfork
power lift
rotary hoe
Rotavator®
Rotovator®
scarifier
seed drill
whetstone
10 cropduster
cultivator
disc harrow
disc plough
earth-board
flail mower

seed-harrow
11 bale wrapper
broadcaster
chaff-cutter
chaff-engine
drill-harrow
hedgecutter
mole drainer
reaping hook
wheelbarrow
wheel plough
12 muckspreader
slurry tanker
13 fork-lift truck
potato planter
slurry sprayer
14 field sprinkler
front end loader
milking machine

Agriculturists include:

04 Coke (Thomas William; 1752–1842, English)
Tull (Jethro; 1674–1741, English)
05 Lawes (Sir John Bennet; 1814–1900, English)
Young (Arthur; 1741–1820, English)
06 Carver (George Washington; 1864–1943, US)
Farrer (William; 1845–1906, English)
07 Borlaug (Norman; 1914–2009, US)
Burbank (Luther; 1849–1926, US)

Russell (Sir John; 1872–1965, English)
Wallace (Harry; 1866–1924, US)
Wallace (Henry; 1836–1916, US)
Wallace (Henry A; 1888–1965, US)
08 Bakewell (Robert; 1725–95, English)
09 McCormick (Cyrus; 1809–84, US)
12 Boussingault (Jean-Baptiste; 1802–87, French)

See also **cattle**; **farm**

air force *see* military

air travel

Airports in the UK include:

04 Dyce (Aberdeen)
Lydd (Kent)
Wick (Caithness)
05 Luton (Bedfordshire)
Tiree (Hebrides)
06 Dundee
Exeter (Devon)
Jersey (Channel Islands)
Scatsa (Shetlands)
Tresco (Scilly Isles)
07 Bristol (Avon)
Cardiff

Gatwick (London)
Glasgow
Norwich (Norfolk)
Sandown (Isle of Wight)
St Mary's (Scilly Isles)
Swansea
Westray (Orkney)
08 Alderney (Channel Islands)
Coventry (West Midlands)
Fair Isle (Shetlands)
Guernsey (Channel Islands)
Heathrow (London)

Kirkwall (Orkney)
North Bay (Hebrides)
Penzance (Cornwall)
Plymouth (Devon)
Southend (Essex)
Stansted (London)
Sumburgh (Shetlands)
Teesside (Cleveland)
Tingwall (Shetlands)
09 Benbecula (Hebrides)
Blackpool (Lancashire)
Cambridge
Inverness
Newcastle
Prestwick (Ayrshire)
Robin Hood (Doncaster-Sheffield)
Stornoway (Hebrides)

Turnhouse (Edinburgh)
10 Baltasound (Shetlands)
Biggin Hill (Kent)
Grimsetter (Orkney)
Humberside
John Lennon (Liverpool)
London City
Manchester
Ronaldsway (Isle of Man)
11 Belfast City
Bournemouth (Dorset)
Glenegedale (Islay)
Southampton (Hampshire)
12 West Midlands (Birmingham)
13 Leeds-Bradford

Airports worldwide include:

03 JFK (USA)
Kos (Greece)
Moi (Kenya)
Nis (Serbia)
Zia (Bangladesh)
04 Agno (Switzerland)
Bole (Ethiopia)
Cebu (Philippines)
Cork (Ireland)
Doha (Qatar)
Elat (Israel)
Erie (USA)
Faro (Portugal)
Gaza (Israel)
Guam (Guam)
Hato (Netherlands
Antilles)
Linz (Austria)
Lomé (Togo)
Luqa (Malta)
Male (Maldives)
Nadi (Fiji)
Oran (Algeria)
Orly (France)
Pula (Croatia)
Riem (Germany)
Saab (Sweden)
Sale (Morocco)
Seeb (Oman)
Sfax (Tunisia)
Sola (Norway)
Vigo (Spain)
Yoff (Senegal)
05 Adana (Turkey)
Aminu (Nigeria)
Beira (Mozambique)
Berne (Switzerland)
Brnik (Slovenia)

Cairo (Egypt)
Dubai (United Arab
Emirates)
Elmas (Italy)
Hanoi (Vietnam)
Ibiza (Spain)
Ivato (Madagascar)
Izmir (Turkey)
Kimpo (South Korea)
Liège (Belgium)
Logan (USA)
Luano (Democratic
Republic of the Congo)
Lungi (Sierra Leone)
Luxor (Egypt)
Mahon (Menorca)
McCoy (USA)
Miami (USA)
Nauru (Nauru)
O'Hare (USA)
Osaka (Japan)
Palma (Majorca)
Perth (Australia)
Pleso (Croatia)
Praia (Cape Verde)
Rejon (Mexico)
Sanaa (Yemen)
Senou (Mali)
Sliac (Slovakia)
Sofia (Bulgaria)
Split (Croatia)
Sunan (North Korea)
Tampa (USA)
Turin (Italy)
Turku (Finland)
Vaasa (Finland)
Vagar (Faroe Islands)
Varna (Bulgaria)
Vigie (St Lucia)

06 Abadan (Iran)
Alborg (Denmark)
Asmara (Eritrea)
Balice (Poland)
Beirut (Lebanon)
Benina (Libya)
Bremen (Germany)
Bromma (Sweden)
Butmir (Bosnia and
Herzegovina)
Cairns (Australia)
Cancun (Mexico)
Cannon (USA)
Canton (USA)
Changi (Singapore)
Darwin (Australia)
Deurne (Belgium)
Dorval (Canada)
Douala (Cameroon)
Dublin (Ireland)
Dulles (USA)
El Alto (Bolivia)
El Paso (USA)
Findel (Luxembourg)
Geneva (Switzerland)
Gillot (Réunion)
Hahaya (Comoros)
Hanedi (Japan)
Harare (Zimbabwe)
Hassan (Morocco)
Ivanka (Slovakia)
Kalmar (Sweden)
Kamazu (Malawi)
Kigali (Rwanda)
Kjevik (Norway)
Komaki (Japan)
Košice (Slovakia)
Kotoka (Ghana)
Kuwait (Kuwait)

Lahore (Pakistan)
La Mesa (Honduras)
Linate (Italy)
Lisbon (Portugal)
Luanda (Angola)
Lusaka (Zambia)
Mactan (Philippines)
Malaga (Spain)
Maputo (Mozambique)
Maseru (Lesotho)
Medina (Saudi Arabia)
Melita (Tunisia)
Menara (Morocco)
Midway (USA)
Narita (Japan)
Nassau (The Bahamas)
N'Djili (Democratic
  Republic of the Congo)
Nejrab (Syria)
Newark (USA)
Niamey (Niger)
Odense (Denmark)
Okecie (Poland)
Orebro (Sweden)
Palese (Italy)
Paphos (Cyprus)
Penang (Malaysia)
Piarco (Trinidad)
Regina (Canada)
Riyadh (Saudi Arabia)
Ruzyne (Czech Republic)
Skanes (Morocco)
Skopje (Macedonia)
Snilow (Ukraine)
Spilve (Latvia)
Sturup (Sweden)
Subang (Malaysia)
Tacoma (USA)
Tirana (Albania)
Tucson (USA)
Vantaa (Finland)
V C Bird (Antigua)
Verona (Italy)
Wattay (Laos)
Yangon (Myanmar)
Yundum (The Gambia)
Zürich (Switzerland)

07 Alma Ata (Kazakhstan)
Almeria (Spain)
Arlanda (Sweden)
Atatürk (Turkey)
Baghdad (Iraq)
Bahrain (Bahrain)
Baneasa (Romania)
Bangkok (Thailand)
Barajas (Spain)
Beijing (China)
Billund (Denmark)

Blagnac (France)
Bourgas (Bulgaria)
Bradley (USA)
Buffalo (USA)
Calabar (Nigeria)
Calgary (Canada)
Cotonou (Benin)
Dalaman (Turkey)
D F Malan (South Africa)
Dhahran (Saudi Arabia)
Dresden (Germany)
Entebbe (Uganda)
Esbjerg (Denmark)
Faleolo (Samoa)
Fornebu (Norway)
G'Bessia (Guinea)
Granada (Spain)
Halifax (Canada)
Hopkins (USA)
Houston (USA)
Itazuke (Japan)
Karachi (Pakistan)
Kerkyra (Greece)
Key West (USA)
Kuching (Malaysia)
La Parra (Spain)
Larnaca (Cyprus)
Leipzig (Germany)
Lesquin (France)
Liepaja (Latvia)
Lincoln (USA)
Lubbock (USA)
Managua (Nicaragua)
Maxglan (Austria)
Memphis (USA)
Mirabel (Canada)
Morelos (Mexico)
Norfolk (USA)
Oakland (USA)
Okinawa (Japan)
Orlando (USA)
Otopeni (Romania)
Patenga (Bangladesh)
Polonia (Indonesia)
Pulkovo (Russia)
Roberts (Liberia)
San José (USA)
São Tomé (São Tomé and
  Príncipe)
Satolas (France)
Shannon (Ireland)
Sharjah (United Arab
  Emirates)
Sondica (Spain)
Spokane (USA)
St Louis (USA)
Tamatve (Madagascar)
Timehri (Guyana)

Tripoli (Libya)
Unokovo (Russia)
Uplands (Canada)
Vilnius (Lithuania)
Vitoria (Spain)
Wichita (USA)

08 Abu Dhabi (United Arab
  Emirates)
Adelaide (Australia)
Ain el Bay (Algeria)
Alicante (Spain)
Amarillo (USA)
Amborovy (Madagascar)
Arrecife (Canary Islands)
Ashkabad (Turkmenistan)
Asturias (Spain)
Auckland (New Zealand)
Belgrade (Serbia)
Borispol (Ukraine)
Boulogne (France)
Brasilia (Brazil)
Brisbane (Australia)
Bulawayo (Zimbabwe)
Carrasco (Uruguay)
Carthage (Tunisia)
Ciampino (Italy)
Columbus (USA)
Damascus (Syria)
Djibouti (Djibouti)
Edmonton (Canada)
El Dorado (Colombia)
Entzheim (France)
Esenboga (Turkey)
Ferihegy (Hungary)
Flesland (Norway)
Freeport (The Bahamas)
G Marconi (Italy)
Goleniow (Poland)
Hong Kong (Hong Kong)
Hongqiao (China)
Honolulu (USA)
Inezgane (Morocco)
Keflavik (Iceland)
Khartoum (Sudan)
La Aurora (Guatemala)
La Coruña (Spain)
Le Raizet (Guadeloupe)
Loshitsa (Belarus)
Mais Gate (Haiti)
Malpensa (Italy)
Matsapha (Swaziland)
Maya Maya (Congo)
McCarran (USA)
Mehrabad (Iran)
Merignac (France)
Mohamed V (Morocco)
Murmansk (Russia)
Nagasaki (Japan)

N'Djamena (Chad)
Pago Pago (Samoa)
Pamplona (Spain)
Paradisi (Greece)
Peretola (Italy)
Peshawar (Pakistan)
Portland (USA)
Provence (France)
Richmond (USA)
San Diego (USA)
Sangster (Jamaica)
San Pablo (Spain)
Santiago (Spain)
Schiphol (The Netherlands)
St Thomas (Virgin Islands)
Tontouta (New Caledonia)
Ulemiste (Estonia)
Valencia (Spain)
Victoria (Canada)
Winnipeg (Canada)

09 Anchorage (USA)
Archangel (Russia)
Arnos Vale (St Vincent)
Barcelona (Spain)
Ben Gurion (Israel)
Boukhalef (Morocco)
Bujumbura (Burundi)
Charleroi (Belgium)
Charlotte (USA)
Congonhas (Brazil)
Cuscatlan (El Salvador)
Des Moines (USA)
Dubrovnik (Croatia)
Eindhoven (The
  Netherlands)
Fiumicino (Italy)
Fort Myers (USA)
Guarulhos (Brazil)
Heraklion (Greece)
Hewanorra (St Lucia)
Islamabad (Pakistan)
Isle Verde (Puerto Rico)
James M Cox (USA)
Jose Marti (Cuba)
Kagoshima (Japan)
Kaohsiung (Taiwan)
Karpathos (Greece)
La Guardia (USA)
Las Palmas (Canary Islands)
Lindbergh (USA)
Llabanère (France)
Long Beach (USA)
Marco Polo (Italy)
Maupertus (France)
Mogadishu (Somalia)
Nashville (USA)
Nuremberg (Germany)
Octeville (France)

Peninsula (USA)
Port Bouet (Côte d'Ivoire)
Port Sudan (Sudan)
Queen Alia (Jordan)
Rotterdam (The
  Netherlands)
Sainte Foy (Canada)
San Giusto (Italy)
San Javier (Spain)
Santa Cruz (Canary Islands)
Santander (Spain)
Schwechat (Austria)
Stapleton (USA)
St Eufemia (Italy)
Thalerhof (Austria)
Timisoara (Romania)
Tribhuyan (Nepal)
Vancouver (Canada)
Viracopos (Brazil)
Zakynthos (Greece)

10 Alexandria (Egypt)
Belize City (Belize)
Birmingham (USA)
Charleston (USA)
Copenhagen (Denmark)
Côte d'Azure (France)
Crown Point (Tobago)
Domodedovo (Russia)
Dusseldorf (Germany)
Frejorgues (France)
Golden Rock (St Kitts)
Guararapes (Brazil)
Harrisburg (USA)
Hartsfield (USA)
Hellenikon (Greece)
Kansas City (USA)
Katunayake (Sri Lanka)
Kent County (USA)
King Khaled (Saudi Arabia)
Klagenfurt (Austria)
Kungsangen (Sweden)
Landvetter (Sweden)
Les Angades (Morocco)
Libreville (Gabon)
Little Rock (USA)
Los Angeles (USA)
Louis Botha (South Africa)
Louisville (USA)
Maastricht (The
  Netherlands)
Manchester (USA)
New Orleans (USA)
North Front (Gibraltar)
Nouadhibou (Mauritania)
Nouakchott (Mauritania)
Panama City (Panama)
Pochentong (Cambodia)
Punta Raisi (Sicily)

Rabiechowo (Poland)
Reina Sofia (Canary Islands)
Rochambeau (French
  Guiana)
San Antonio (USA)
Seychelles (Seychelles)
Sky Harbour (USA)
Townsville (Australia)
Trivandrum (India)
Truax Field (USA)
Washington (USA)
Wellington (New Zealand)
Will Rogers (USA)

11 Albuquerque (USA)
Capodichino (Italy)
Cologne-Bonn (Germany)
Dar es Salaam (Tanzania)
Dois de Julho (Brazil)
Ecterdingen (Germany)
Fuhlsbüttel (Germany)
Jorge Chavez (Peru)
Khoramaksar (Yemen)
Kranebitten (Austria)
Las Americas (Dominican
  Republic)
Narssarsuaq (Greenland)
Ninoy Aquino (Philippines)
Ouagadougou (Burkina
  Faso)
Owen Roberts (West
  Indies)
Pointe Noire (Congo)
Poprad Tatry (Slovakia)
Punta Arenas (Chile)
San Salvador (El Salvador)
Santa Isabel (Guinea)
Tallahassee (USA)
Tegucigalpa (Honduras)
Tito Menniti (Italy)
Tullamarine (Australia)
Vilo de Porto (Azores)

12 Albany County (USA)
Benito Juarez (Mexico)
Berline-Tegel (Germany)
Bishkek-Manas (Kyrgyzstan)
Christchurch (New
  Zealand)
Eduardo Gomes (Brazil)
Fontanarossa (Sicily)
Fort de France (Martinique)
Fuenterrabia (Spain)
Hancock Field (USA)
Indianapolis (USA)
Indira Gandhi (India)
Jackson Field (Papua New
  Guinea)
Jacksonville (USA)

Johannesburg (South Africa)
John F Kennedy (USA)
Jomo Kenyatta (Kenya)
Khwaja Rawash (Afghanistan)
Kota Kinabalu (Malaysia)
Monroe County (USA)
Norman Manley (Jamaica)
Osvaldo Veira (Guinea-Bissau)
Papola Casale (Italy)
Philadelphia (USA)
Point Salines (Grenada)
Ponta Delgado (Azores)
Port Harcourt (Nigeria)
Queen Beatrix (Netherlands Antilles)
Ras al Khaimah (United Arab Emirates)
Rio de Janeiro (Brazil)
Salgado Filho (Brazil)
Salt Lake City (USA)
San Francisco (USA)
Santos Dumont (Brazil)

Sheremetyevo (Russia)
Simon Bolivar (Ecuador)
Simon Bolivar (Venezuela)
Thessalonika (Greece)
13 Amilcar Cabral (Cape Verde)
Basle-Mulhouse (Switzerland)
Château Bougon (France)
Chiang Kai Shek (Taiwan)
Costa Smeralda (Sardinia)
Fuerteventura (Canary Islands)
Grantley Adams (Barbados)
Ho Chi Minh City (Vietnam)
King Abdul Aziz (Saudi Arabia)
Mariscal Sucre (Ecuador)
Peterson Field (USA)
Raleigh/Durham (USA)
Santa Caterina (Madeira)
14 Eppley Airfield (USA)

Fort Lauderdale (USA)
Galileo Galilei (Italy)
Henderson Field (Solomon Islands)
Juan Santamaria (Costa Rica)
Kingsford Smith (Australia)
Lester B Pearson (Canada)
Luis Muñoz Marin (Puerto Rico)
Novo-Alexeyevka (Georgia)
15 Augusto C Sandino (Nicaragua)
Charles de Gaulle (France)
Dallas/Fort Worth (USA)
Frankfurt am Main (Germany)
General Mitchell (USA)
Murtala Muhammed (Nigeria)
Sir Seretse Khama (Botswana)
Theodore Francis (USA)

Airlines include:

02 BA		Air India	**11** Continental
UA	El Al	Alitalia	**13** Air New Zealand
03 BEA	**05** Flybe	Emirates	Cathay Pacific
BMI	Pan Am	Loganair	Delta Airlines
JAL	**06** Iberia		**14** British Airways
KLM	Qantas	**09** Aer Lingus	British Midland
PIA	**07** easyJet	Air Canada	United Airlines
SAS	Monarch	Air France	Virgin Atlantic
TWA	Ryanair	Lufthansa	**15** Turkish Airlines
04 BOAC	**08** Aer Arann	**10** Air Jamaica	
	Aeroflot	Iceland Air	

Air travel terms include:

03 DVT	seat	**06** bumped	carrier
ETA	taxi	charge	charges
ETD	trip	closed	charter
FIM	visa	divert	check-in
hub	wait	flight	co-pilot
leg	x-ray	lounge	customs
PIR		no show	delayed
rep	**05** aisle	red-eye	descent
	board	runway	drop off
04 APEX	brace	ticket	economy
bags	cargo	window	e-ticket
bump	class		holding
desk	delay	**07** airline	inbound
exit	fleet	air rage	landing
fare	pilot	airside	layover
fees	plane	arm rest	legroom
gate	route	baggage	life cot
IATA	taxes	booking	luggage
open		captain	

net fare
net rate
network
on board
photo ID
standby
steward
take-off
transit
trolley
upgrade
voucher
08 act of god
aircraft
airmiles
airplane
APEX fare
approach
arrivals
boarding
cruising
departed
duty-free
empty leg
landside
life vest
long haul
magazine
manifest
outbound
overwing
passport
seat belt
security

stopover
tail wind
terminal
waitlist
09 aeroplane
aisle seat
cabin crew
club class
code share
concourse
franchise
itinerary
passenger
screening
short haul
surcharge
10 air hostess
air marshal
air steward
allowances
baggage tag
connection
departures
first class
flight deck
gate closed
life jacket
luggage tag
medium haul
on approach
open return
open ticket
red channel
safety card

stewardess
turbulence
window seat
11 airport code
blue channel
code sharing
connections
destination
fast bag drop
hand baggage
hand luggage
left luggage
overbooking
reservation
viewing area
12 baggage check
boarding card
boarding pass
cabin baggage
direct flight
economy class
force majeure
green channel
lost property
luggage label
plane spotter
return ticket
Schengen visa
Schengen zone
single ticket
super economy
trolley dolly
wait in lounge
13 airport lounge

blackout dates
budget airline
business class
emergency exit
excess baggage
frequent flier
frequent flyer
non-stop flight
open jaw ticket
seat row number
standard class
ultra-long haul
14 baggage handler
baggage reclaim
baggage trolley
cabin attendant
customs control
flat-bed service
luggage trolley
outsize baggage
overhead locker
representative
15 baggage carousel
cancellation fee
departure lounge
executive lounge
executive travel
flight attendant
in-flight service
oversize baggage
passport control
proof of identity
scheduled flight
travel documents

aircraft

Aircraft types include:

03 B-52
jet
MiG
Yak
04 Hawk
kite
Moth
STOL
VTOL
Zero
05 blimp
Comet
Eagle
jumbo
Piper
plane
Stuka
06 Airbus®

Boeing
bomber
Cessna
copter
Fokker
glider
Jaguar
Mirage
Nimrod
07 airship
air taxi
all-wing
balloon
biplane
Chinook
chopper
Dornier
fighter

gunship
Halifax
Harrier
Heinkel
Hellcat
jump-jet
Junkers
Learjet
Mustang
prop-jet
Tornado
Tristar
Typhoon
08 airliner
autogiro
autogyro
Blenheim
Catalina

Concorde
Henschel
Hercules
jumbo jet
Mosquito
seaplane
Sikorsky
skiplane
Spitfire
spy plane
superjet
triplane
turbojet
warplane
Zeppelin
09 aeroplane
amphibian
aquaplane

Boeing 747
delta-wing
dirigible
egg beater
fixed-wing
Focke-Wulf
freighter
Gipsy Moth
Helldiver
Hurricane
Lancaster
Lightning
monoplane
Sturmovik
swing-wing

Tiger Moth
turboprop
two-seater
10 Concordski
dive-bomber
Dreamliner
hang-glider
helicopter
microlight
multiplane
rotorcraft
rotor plane
Sunderland
Super Sabre
tankbuster

Wellington
whirlybird
11 battleplane
Beaufighter
de Havilland
Flying Tiger
interceptor
rocket plane
Starfighter
taildragger
Thunderbolt
Vickers Vimy
12 air ambulance
Lockheed Vega

single-seater
Sopwith Camel
troop-carrier
13 Avro Lancaster
hot-air balloon
Messerschmitt
Stealth Bomber
Superfortress
14 aerospace-plane
Flying Fortress
Mitsubishi Zero
Stratofortress
15 Bristol Blenheim
Hawker Hurricane

Aircraft parts include:

03 fin
rib
04 cowl
flap
hold
hood
prow
skid
wing
05 cabin
probe
pylon
radar
radio
stick
06 canopy
engine
fan-jet

intake
rudder
07 aileron
ammeter
blister
cockpit
cowling
fairing
hush kit
tail fin
trim tab
winglet
08 elevator
fuselage
gust-lock
intercom
joystick
longeron

main gear
tail boom
tailskid
turbojet
wing flap
09 altimeter
astrodome
autoflare
main plane
nose wheel
outrigger
propeller
tailplane
tail wheel
turboprop
10 boost gauge
flight deck
11 chronometer

gyro horizon
landing flap
landing gear
turbo-ram-jet
vertical fin
12 control stick
equilibrator
radio compass
rudder pedals
vertical tail
13 accelerometer
control column
undercarriage
14 horizontal tail
radar altimeter
15 landing-carriage
magnetic compass

Aircraft include:

04 R101
06 Bell X-1
07 *Voyager*
08 *Enola Gay*
See also **aviation**

09 *Winnie Mae*
10 *Hindenburg*
11 *Lucky Lady II*
Spruce Goose

Wright Flyer
Air Force One
12 *Graf Zeppelin*
Memphis Belle

15 *Spirit of St Louis*

airport *see* **air travel**

Albania *see* **Balkans**

alcohol *see* **drink**

algae

Algae and lichens include:

05 chara	Valonia	cup lichen	manna-lichen
usnea	**08** anabaena	Isokontae	Protococcus
06 archil	conferva	rock tripe	Valoniaceae
corkir	lecanora	spirogyra	**12** Cyanophyceae
crotal	lungwort	stonewort	Heterocontae
desmid	pond scum	**10** brown algae	reindeer moss
diatom	red algae	Charophyta	stromatolite
korkir	Roccella	Conjugatae	Ulotrichales
nostoc	sea ivory	cyanophyte	water flowers
volvox	stonerag	fallen star	
07 crottle	stoneraw	green algae	**13** chlamydomonas
cup moss	tree moss	heterocont	Protococcales
euglena	Ulothrix	heterokont	Schizophyceae
Graphis	wall moss	rock violet	witches' butter
oak lump	wartwort	water bloom	**14** blue-green algae
parella	**09** Characeae	**11** blanketweed	cyanobacterium
seaweed	chlorella	Iceland moss	dinoflagellate

See also **seaweed**

alloy *see* **metal**

alphabet

Alphabets and writing systems include:

03 ABC	runic	futhorc	cuneiform
IPA	**06** Arabic	futhork	ideograph
ITA	Brahmi	Glossic	logograph
04 kana	finger	linear A	syllabary
ogam	Glagol	linear B	**10** Chalcidian
05 Greek	Hebrew	**08** Cyrillic	devanagari
kanji	nagari	Georgian	estrangelo
Kufic	naskhi	Gurmukhi	pictograph
Latin	Pinyin	hiragana	**11** estranghelo
ogham	romaji	katakana	hieroglyphs
Roman	**07** Braille	phonetic	**14** Augmented Roman
runes	futhark	**09** Byzantine	**15** Initial Teaching

Letters of the Arabic alphabet:

02 ba	**03** ayn	mim	zay
fa	dad	nun	**04** alif
ha	dai	qaf	dhai
ra	jim	sad	shin
ta	kaf	sin	**05** ghayn
ya	kha	tha	
za	lam	waw	

Letters of the English alphabet:

02 ar	ef	en	oh
ay	el	es	wy
ee	em	ex	**03** bee

cee	ess	see	**06** haitch
cue	eye	tee	**07** double-u
dee	gee	vee	**09** double-you
eff	jay	you	
eks	kay	zed	
ell	kew	zee	
enn	pee	**05** aitch	

Letters of the Old English alphabet include:

03 ash	wen	ogam	**05** thorn
edh	wyn	wynn	
eth	**04** aesc	yogh	

Letters of the Greek alphabet:

02 mu	rho	delta	**07** digamma
nu	san	gamma	epsilon
pi	tau	kappa	omicron
xi	vau	koppa	upsilon
03 chi	**04** beta	omega	ypsilon
eta	iota	sigma	
phi	zeta	theta	
psi	**05** alpha	**06** lambda	

Letters of the Hebrew alphabet:

02 fe	tav	khaf	lamed
he	taw	koph	sadhe
pe	tet	qoph	tsadi
03 bet	vav	resh	tzade
heh	waw	sade	zayin
het	yod	shin	**06** daleth
kaf	**04** alef	teth	lamedh
mem	ayin	yodh	saddhe
nun	beth	**05** aleph	samech
peh	chaf	cheth	samekh
qof	heth	dalet	
sin	kaph	gimel	

Letters of the NATO phonetic alphabet:

04 echo	zulu	romeo	**07** charlie
golf	**05** alpha	tango	foxtrot
kilo	bravo	**06** juliet	uniform
lima	delta	quebec	whiskey
mike	hotel	sierra	**08** november
papa	india	victor	
xray	oscar	yankee	

American football

National Football League teams:

11 New York Jets	Detroit Lions	Miami Dolphins
St Louis Rams	**13** Dallas Cowboys	New York Giants
12 Buffalo Bills	Denver Broncos	**14** Atlanta Falcons
Chicago Bears	Houston Texans	Oakland Raiders

15 Baltimore Ravens
Cleveland Browns
Green Bay Packers
Seattle Seahawks
Tennessee Titans
16 Arizona Cardinals
Carolina Panthers

Kansas City Chiefs
Minnesota Vikings
New Orleans Saints
San Diego Chargers
17 Cincinnati Bengals
Indianapolis Colts
San Francisco 49ers

18 New England Patriots
Philadelphia Eagles
Pittsburgh Steelers
Tampa Bay Buccaneers
Washington Redskins
19 Jacksonville Jaguars

National Football League team nicknames include:

04 Jets (New York)
Rams (St Louis)
05 Bears (Chicago)
Bills (Buffalo)
Colts (Indianapolis)
Lions (Detroit)
06 Browns (Cleveland)
Chiefs (Kansas City)
Eagles (Philadelphia)
Giants (New York)
Niners (San Francisco)

Ravens (Baltimore)
Saints (New Orleans)
Texans (Houston)
Titans (Tennessee)
07 Bengals (Cincinnati)
Broncos (Denver)
Cowboys (Dallas)
Falcons (Atlanta)
Jaguars (Jacksonville)
Packers (Green Bay)
Raiders (Oakland)

Vikings (Minnesota)
08 Chargers (San Diego)
Dolphins (Miami)
Panthers (Carolina)
Patriots (New England)
Redskins (Washington)
Seahawks (Seattle)
Steelers (Pittsburgh)
09 Cardinals (Arizona)
10 Buccaneers (Tampa Bay)
11 Forty Niners (San Francisco)

American footballers include:

04 Camp (Walter; 1859–1925, US)
Rice (Jerry; 1962– , US)
05 Brown (Jim; 1936– , US)
Brown (Paul; 1908–91, US)
Elway (John; 1960– , US)
Favre (Brett; 1969– , US)
Halas (George; 1895–1983, US)
Owens (Terrell; 1973– , US)
Perry (Joe; 1927–2011, US)
Perry (William 'The Fridge'; 1962– , US)
Shula (Don; 1930– , US)
Smith (Emmitt; 1969– , US)
06 Blanda (George; 1927–2010, US)
Butkus (Dick; 1942– , US)
Graham (Otto; 1921–2003, US)
Grange (Red; 1903–91, US)
Hutson (Don; 1913–97, US)
Landry (Tom; 1924–2000, US)

Marino (Dan; 1961– , US)
Namath (Joe; 1943– , US)
Payton (Walter; 1954–99, US)
Rockne (Knute; 1888–1931, Norwegian/US)
Sayers (Gale; 1943– , US)
Taylor (Lawrence; 1959– , US)
Thorpe (Jim; 1888–1953, US)
Unitas (Johnny; 1933–2002, US)
07 Lambeau (Curly; 1898–1965, US)
Montana (Joe; 1956– , US)
Sanders (Barry; 1968– , US)
Sanders (Deion; 1967– , US)
Simpson (O J; 1947– , US)
08 Andersen (Morten; 1960– , Danish)
Harrison (Marvin; 1972– , US)
Lombardi (Vince; 1913–70, US)
Peterson (Adrian; 1985– , US)
09 Tarkenton (Fran; 1940– , US)

American football terms include:

03 AFC
NFC
NFL
04 ball
bomb
clip
down
draw
flag
muff
pass

play
punt
sack
snap
05 blitz
block
drive
field
guard
shift
sneak

spike
zebra
06 all-pro
bullet
center
chains
end run
fumble
huddle
pocket
prayer

punter
safety
spiral
tackle
umpire
07 audible
bootleg
defense
end zone
handoff
holding
lateral
lineman
offense
offside
pigskin
Pro Bowl
quarter
red zone
referee
rushing
shotgun
time out
traffic
X's and O's
08 face mask
fullback
gridiron
hail Mary
halfback
hang time
hash mark
linesman
overtime
pass rush
receiver
scramble
See also **sport**

split end
tailback
tight end
trenches
turnover
weak side
09 backfield
back judge
chain gang
chop block
end around
fair catch
field goal
franchise
line judge
pooch kick
reception
scrimmage
secondary
side judge
Super Bowl
take a knee
touchback
touchdown
10 completion
conversion
cornerback
extra point
field judge
Hall of Fame
linebacker
nickelback
nose tackle
onside kick
option play
play action
point after

screen pass
shovel pass
strong side
wobbly duck
11 all-American
counter play
curl pattern
dime defense
flea flicker
man coverage
neutral zone
post pattern
quarterback
running back
12 complete pass
defensive end
interception
naked bootleg
on the numbers
slant pattern
slot receiver
special teams
wide receiver
zone coverage
13 defensive back
Heisman trophy
nickel defense
14 climb the ladder
hurry-up offense
incomplete pass
outlet receiver
prevent defense
15 franchise player
line of scrimmage
no-huddle offense
primary receiver
thread the needle

The Americas

Countries in North, Central and South America:

04 Cuba
Peru
05 Chile
Haiti
06 Belize
Brazil
Canada
Guyana
Mexico
Panama
07 Bolivia
Ecuador

Grenada
Jamaica
St Lucia
Uruguay
08 Colombia
Dominica
Honduras
Paraguay
Suriname
09 Argentina
Costa Rica
Guatemala

Nicaragua
Venezuela
10 El Salvador
The Bahamas
15 St Kitts and Nevis
17 Antigua and Barbuda
Dominican Republic
Trinidad and Tobago
21 United States of America
25 St Vincent and the
Grenadines

Cities and notable towns in North America include:

04 Léon (Mexico)

05 Miami (USA)
Omaha (USA)
Tampa (USA)
Tulsa (USA)

06 Austin (USA)
Boston (USA)
Dallas (USA)
Denver (USA)
El Paso (USA)
Jalapa (Mexico)
London (Canada)
Mérida (Mexico)
Newark (USA)
Oaxaca (Mexico)
Ottawa (Canada)
Puebla (Mexico)
Québec (Canada)
St Paul (USA)
Toledo (USA)
Tucson (USA)

07 Atlanta (USA)
Buffalo (USA)
Calgary (Canada)
Chicago (USA)
Detroit (USA)
Houston (USA)
Memphis (USA)
Norfolk (USA)
Oakland (USA)
Phoenix (USA)

San José (USA)
Seattle (USA)
St Louis (USA)
Tampico (Mexico)
Toronto (Canada)
Zapopan (Mexico)

08 Acapulco (Mexico)
Campeche (Mexico)
Columbus (USA)
Culiacán (Mexico)
Edmonton (Canada)
Hamilton (Canada)
Hartford (USA)
Honolulu (USA)
Mexicali (Mexico)
Montréal (Canada)
Portland (USA)
San Diego (USA)
Veracruz (Mexico)
Victoria (Canada)
Winnipeg (Canada)

09 Baltimore (USA)
Charlotte (USA)
Chihuahua (Mexico)
Cleveland (USA)
Fort Worth (USA)
Kitchener (Canada)
Long Beach (USA)
Milwaukee (USA)
Monterrey (Mexico)
Nashville (USA)

Vancouver (Canada)

10 Cincinnati (USA)
Hermosillo (Mexico)
Kansas City (USA)
Los Angeles (USA)
Mexico City (Mexico)
New Orleans (USA)
Pittsburgh (USA)
Sacramento (USA)
Salina Cruz (Mexico)
San Antonio (USA)
Valladolid (Mexico)

11 Albuquerque (USA)
Guadalajara (Mexico)
Minneapolis (USA)
New York City (USA)
Scarborough (Canada)

12 Ciudad Juárez (Mexico)
Indianapolis (USA)
Jacksonville (USA)
Oklahoma City (USA)
Philadelphia (USA)
Salt Lake City (USA)
San Francisco (USA)
St Catharines (Canada)
Washington DC (USA)

13 Piedras Negras (Mexico)
San Luis Potosí (Mexico)
Virginia Beach (USA)

14 Ciudad Victoria (Mexico)

Cities and notable towns in Central America include:

04 León (Nicaragua)
Xela (Guatemala)

05 Colón (Panama)
David (Panama)
Limón (Costa Rica)

06 Masaya (Nicaragua)

07 Antigua (Guatemala)
Cartago (Costa Rica)
Granada (Nicaragua)
Heredia (Costa Rica)
La Ceiba (Honduras)
Liberia (Costa Rica)
Managua (Nicaragua)
San José (Costa Rica)

08 Santa Ana (El Salvador)

09 Choluteca (Honduras)

Escuintla (Guatemala)
Matagalpa (Nicaragua)
San Miguel (El Salvador)

10 Belize City (Belize)
Chinandega (Nicaragua)
El Progreso (Honduras)
Panama City (Panama)
Puntarenas (Costa Rica)

11 Mazatenango (Guatemala)
San Salvador (El Salvador)
Tegucigalpa (Honduras)

12 San Pedro Sula (Honduras)

13 Guatemala City (Guatemala)
Huehuetenango (Guatemala)

14 Quetzaltenango (Guatemala)

Cities and notable towns in South America include:

04 Cali (Colombia)
Lima (Peru)

05 Belém (Brazil)
Cuzco (Peru)

La Paz (Bolivia)
Natal (Brazil)

Oruro (Bolivia)
Pisco (Peru)
Quito (Ecuador)
Salto (Uruguay)
Sucre (Bolivia)
06 Bogotá (Colombia)
Callao (Peru)
Campos (Brazil)
Cúcuta (Colombia)
Cuenca (Ecuador)
El Alto (Bolivia)
Ibarra (Ecuador)
Maceio (Brazil)
Manaus (Brazil)
Mérida (Venezuela)
Olinda (Brazil)
Osasco (Brazil)
Potosí (Bolivia)
Recife (Brazil)
Santos (Brazil)
Vargas (Venezuela)
07 Aracajú (Brazil)
Caracas (Venezuela)
Cayenne (French Guiana)
Córdoba (Argentina)
Goiânia (Brazil)
Iquitos (Peru)
La Plata (Argentina)
Maracay (Venezuela)
Mendoza (Argentina)
Niterói (Brazil)
Rosario (Argentina)
Santa Fe (Argentina)

São Luis (Brazil)
08 Arequipa (Peru)
Asunción (Paraguay)
Brasilia (Brazil)
Campinas (Brazil)
Chiclayo (Peru)
Chimbote (Peru)
Contagem (Brazil)
Curitiba (Brazil)
Jaboatão (Brazil)
Londrina (Brazil)
Medellin (Colombia)
Mercedes (Uruguay)
Paysandú (Uruguay)
Riobamba (Ecuador)
Salvador (Brazil)
Santiago (Chile)
São Paulo (Brazil)
Sorocaba (Brazil)
Teresina (Brazil)
Trujillo (Peru)
Valencia (Venezuela)
09 Barcelona (Venezuela)
Cartagena (Colombia)
Fortaleza (Brazil)
Guarulhos (Brazil)
Guayaquil (Ecuador)
Maracaibo (Venezuela)
Ouro Preto (Brazil)
Santa Cruz (Bolivia)
10 Cochabamba (Bolivia)
Concepción (Chile)
Concepción (Paraguay)

Esmeraldas (Ecuador)
Georgetown (Guyana)
João Pessoa (Brazil)
Juiz de Fora (Brazil)
Las Piedras (Uruguay)
Montevideo (Uruguay)
Nova Iguaçu (Brazil)
Paramaribo (Suriname)
Santo André (Brazil)
São Gonçalo (Brazil)
Talcahuano (Chile)
Valparaíso (Chile)
Villarrica (Paraguay)
Vina del Mar (Chile)
11 Antofagasta (Chile)
Bucaramanga (Colombia)
Buenos Aires (Argentina)
Campo Grande (Brazil)
Mar del Plata (Argentina)
Pôrto Alegre (Brazil)
San Fernando (Trinidad and Tobago)
12 Barquisimeto (Venezuela)
Barranquilla (Colombia)
Rio de Janeiro (Brazil)
San Cristobal (Venezuela)
13 Belo Horizonte (Brazil)
Ciudad Bolívar (Venezuela)
Ciudad Guayana (Venezuela)
Duque de Caxias (Brazil)
Ribeirão Preto (Brazil)
14 Feira de Santana (Brazil)

Native American peoples include:

02 Ge	Hupa	Tygh	Huari
03 Fox	Inca	Yahi	Huron
Han	Innu	Yana	Jamul
Hoh	Iowa	Yuit	Jemez
Mam	Ipai	Yuki	Kamia
Ofo	Iswa	Yuma	Kanai
Ona	Itzá	Zuñi	Kansa
Sac	Kato		Karok
Ute	Koso	**05** Acoma	Kaska
Wea	Kuna	Ahtna	Keres
Zia	Maya	Aleut	Lenca
	Mono	Alsea	Lipan
04 Adai	Pima	Aztec	Maidu
Coos	Piro	Bidai	Makah
Cree	Pomo	Brule	Mayan
Crow	Sauk	Caddo	Me-wuk
Dene	Seri	Campo	Miwok
Erie	Suma	Carib	Moche
Hano	Tait	Comox	Modoc
Hare	Taos	Conoy	Nambe
Hopi	Tewa	Creek	Nazca
		Haida	

Olmec
Omaha
Opata
Otomi
Pecos
Petun
Pipil
Sahtu
Sarsi
Sioux
Sooke
Tache
Taino
Talio
Teton
Tigua
Tipai
Twana
Unami
Wappo
Wenro
Wiyot
Yaqui
Yuchi
Yupik
Yurok

06 Ahtena
Apache
Arawak
Atsina
Aymara
Babine
Beaver
Bororo
Calusa
Caniba
Cayapó
Cayuga
Cayuse
Celilo
Chatot
Chetco
Chiaha
Cocopa
Cupeño
Cusabo
Dakota
Dogrib
Galice
Haihai
Haisla
Iquito
Isleta
Jivaro
Jumano
Kiliwa
Kitsai
Klemtu

Konkow
Laguna
Lakota
Lassik
Lenape
Mandan
Micmac
Mi'kmaq
Mixtec
Mocama
Mohave
Mohawk
Mojave
Muisca
Munsee
Nakipa
Nakoda
Natick
Navaho
Navajo
Nisga'a
Nishka
Nootka
Oglala
Ohlone
Ojibwa
Oneida
Ottawa
Paipai
Paiute
Panoan
Papago
Patwin
Pawnee
Peigan
Piegan
Pueblo
Quapaw
Quiché
Salish
Samish
Sandia
Santee
Saponi
Sekani
Seneca
Skagit
Slavey
Stoney
Taensa
Tagish
Tanana
Tawasa
Tenino
Tlicho
Toboso
Tolowa
Toltec

Tongva
Tunica
Tupian
Tutelo
Wikeno
Wintun
Woccon
Yahgan
Yakama
Yamana
Yokuts
07 Abenaki
Akokisa
Anasazi
Aranama
Arapaho
Arikara
Atakapa
Bannock
Beothuk
Chibcha
Chilula
Chinook
Choctaw
Chumash
Ciboney
Clatsop
Cochiti
Esselen
Flatbow
Giamina
Guarani
Hasinai
Hidatsa
Ho-Chunk
Hohokam
Huastec
Huchnom
Huichol
Ingalik
Juaneño
Kitimat
Klallam
Klamath
Koasati
Kolchan
Koskimo
Koyukon
Kutchin
Kutenai
Kwatami
Lucayan
Luiseño
Mahican
Mapuche
Mattole
Mazatec
Mimbres

Mískito
Mohegan
Mohican
Monache
Nanaimo
Naskapi
Natchez
Neutral
Nisenan
Nomlaki
Nongatl
Oji-Cree
Picuris
Puelche
Quechan
Quechua
Quiripi
Saanich
Salinan
Sanpoil
Sechelt
Secotan
Selknam
Serrano
Shawnee
Shipibo
Shuswap
Siksika
Songish
Spokane
Tahltan
Takelma
Tamique
Tanaina
Tekesta
Tesuque
Timucua
Tlingit
Tonkawa
Totonac
Tulalip
Tümpisa
Waicuri
Wailaki
Walapai
Wanapum
Wawenoc
Whilkut
Wyandot
Yamasee
Yankton
Yaquina
Zapotec
08 Achomawi
Alacaluf
Atsugewi
Cahuilla
Calapuya

Chawasha	Paviotso	Karankawa	Chiricahua
Chehalis	Pocumtuk	Kaweshkar	Chitimacha
Chemakum	Puyallup	Kitanemuk	Chukchansi
Cherokee	Qahatika	Klickitat	Clatskanie
Cheyenne	Quileute	Mascouten	Fernandeño
Chippewa	Quinault	Menominee	Gabrieliño
Comanche	Sahaptin	Migueleño	Gros Ventre
Cowichan	Saraguro	Mundurucu	Halkomelem
Delaware	Seminole	Nanticoke	Holikachuk
Diaguita	Shoshone	Nipissing	Kwalhioqua
Diegueño	Sinkyone	Niskwalli	Laurentian
Flathead	Sliammon	Nisqually	Los Luceros
Fountain	Squamish	Paugusset	Makiritare
Guaicuru	Tarascan	Pennacook	Montagnais
Heiltsuk	Tasttine	Pensacola	Potawatomi
Hesquiat	Tataviam	Pentlatch	Shinnecock
Hitchiti	Tepehuan	Purepecha	Tarahumara
Hualapai	Tsetsaut	Saulteaux	Wallawalla
Illinois	Tsnungwe	Snohomish	Wet'suweten
Iroquois	Tsuu T'ina	Suquamish	**11** Assiniboine
Kalapuya	Tukanoan	Swinomish	Chasta Costa
Kawaiisu	Tuskegee	Tanacross	Chickamauga
Kickapoo	Umatilla	Tehuelche	Halchidhoma
Kimsquit	Waccamaw	Tillamook	Lushootseed
Kittitas	Yanomamo	Tlaxcalan	Muckleshoot
Konomihu	**09** Algonkian	Topachula	Souriquoian
Kootenay	Antoniaño	Tsimshian	Tubatulabal
Kumeyaay	Atacameño	Tupinamba	Unalachtigo
Kwakiutl	Atikamekw	Tuscarora	**12** Isleta del Sur
Kwantlem	Blackfoot	Unquachog	Kavelchadhom
Maliseet	Calapooia	Wappinger	Mississaugas
Maricopa	Chickasaw	Winnebago	Narragansett
Menomini	Chilcotin	Yanktonai	Nuu-chah-nulth
Minitari	Chilliwak	Yocha Dehe	Pend'Oreilles
Musqueam	Chimariko	**10** Algonquian	Rappahannock
Nez Percé	Chipewyan	Anishinabe	**13** Haudenosaunee
Nooksack	Clayoquot	Araucanian	Nawathinehena
Nottoway	Costanoan	Athabescan	Ponca Nebraska
Okanagan	Coushatta	Bella Bella	Susquehannock
Okanagon	Degexit'an	Bella Coola	Tlatlasikoala
Onondaga	Havasupai	Besawunena	
Panamint	Jicarilla	Chemehuevi	

South American landmarks include:

04 moai	pampas	Gran Chaco	Mt Aconcagua
05 Andes	Paraná	Itaipu Dam	Pico Bolívar
Colca	**07** Atacama	Patagonia	**12** Easter Island
llano	Ipanema	**10** Angel Falls	Lake Titicaca
Plata	Orinoco	Copacabana	Perito Moreno
Plate	**08** Cape Horn	Mato Grosso	Río de la Plata
selva	Cotopaxi	River Plate	**13** Atacama Desert
06 Amazon	Titicaca	Salto Ángel	Kaieteur Falls
Iguaçu	**09** Aconcagua	**11** Colca Canyon	**14** Cristo Redentor
Itaipu	Cartagena	Iguaçu Falls	Tierra del Fuego
Osorno	Galápagos	Machu Picchu	**15** Guiana Highlands

North American words and expressions include:

03 cot (camp bed)
gas (petrol)

04 bill (banknote)
crib (cot)
fall (autumn)
hood (car bonnet)
line (queue)
mono (glandular fever)
semi (articulated lorry)
vest (waistcoat)

05 bangs (fringe)
braid (plait)
broil (grill)
candy (sweets)
check (bill)
chips (crisps)
derby (bowler hat)
fries (chips)
jello (jelly)
jelly (jam)
klutz (stupid/clumsy person)
purse (handbag)
sedan (saloon car)
shade (window blind)
trunk (car boot)

06 box car (goods wagon)
catsup (ketchup)
closet (wardrobe)
cookie (biscuit)
diaper (nappy)
faucet (tap)
honcho (gaffer)
period (full stop)
rotary (roundabout)
subway (underground)
teller (cashier)
wrench (spanner)

07 antenna (aerial)
beltway (ring road)
blowout (puncture)
freeway (motorway)
garters (suspenders)
muffler (car silencer)
off ramp (motorway exit)
realtor (estate agent)
repo man (bailiff)
seltzer (soda water)
trailer (caravan)
zip code (postcode)

08 attorney (lawyer)
cilantro (coriander)
crawfish (crayfish)
eggplant (aubergine)
elevator (lift)

gasoline (petrol)
gas pedal (accelerator)
kerosene (paraffin)
men's room (gents' toilets)
overpass (flyover)
pacifier (baby's dummy)
pie dough (shortcrust pastry)
railroad (railway)
restroom (toilets)
scallion (spring onion)
sidewalk (pavement)
sneakers (trainers)
steerage (economy class)
stroller (pushchair)
trash can (dustbin)
vacation (holiday)
zucchini (courgette)

09 blueberry (bilberry)
cream puff (choux bun)
housecoat (dressing gown)
loose meat (minced meat)
thumbtack (drawing pin)
underpass (subway)

10 cornstarch (cornflour)
expressway (motorway)
flashlight (torch)
gas station (petrol station)
ground meat (minced meat)
heavy cream (double cream)
interstate (motorway)
light cream (single cream)
main street (high street)
nightstick (truncheon)
parking lot (car park)
phone booth (phone box)
pocketbook (handbag)
suspenders (braces)
turtle neck (polo neck)
undershirt (vest)
wading pool (paddling pool)
windshield (windscreen)

11 call collect (reverse the charges)
cotton candy (candy floss)
plastic wrap (cling film)

12 garbanzo bean (chickpea)
intersection (junction)
movie theater (cinema)
railroad ties (railway sleepers)
shopping cart (shopping trolley)
station wagon (estate car)
superhighway (motorway)

13 graham cracker (digestive biscuit)
traffic circle (roundabout)

14 divided highway (dual carriageway)
housing project (housing estate)

15 round trip ticket (return ticket)
school principal (head)

See also **Canada**; **Mexico**; **mythology**; **United States of America**

amino acid

Amino acids include:

04 dopa

06 glycin
leucin
lysine
serine
valine

07 alanine
glycine

leucine
proline

08 arginine
cysteine
tyrosine

09 glutamine
histidine
ornithine

threonine

10 asparagine
citrulline
domoic acid
isoleucine
methionine
tryptophan

11 tryptophane

12 aspartic acid
glutamic acid
phenylalanin

13 phenylalanine

14 glutaminic acid

amphibian

Amphibians include:

03 ask
eft
olm

04 frog
hyla
newt
pipa
toad

05 siren

06 peeper
taddie

07 axolotl
froglet
paddock
puddock
tadpole

08 bullfrog
cane-toad
frogling
mudpuppy
platanna
polliwig
polliwog
pollywig
pollywog
tree frog
tree toad

09 caecilian
green toad
marsh frog
Nototrema
pouch-toad
warty newt

10 alpine newt
Bosca's newt
clawed frog
clawed toad
common frog
common toad
edible frog
flying frog
hellbender
horned toad
marine toad
natterjack
ophiomorph
salamander
smooth newt

11 goliath frog
leopard frog
marbled newt

midwife toad
painted frog
palmate newt
parsley frog
Surinam toad
walking toad

12 platanna frog
springkeeper
spring peeper

14 common treefrog
fire salamander
labyrinthodont
mole salamander
natterjack toad

15 arrow-poison frog
Cape nightingale
common spadefoot

See also **animal**

anaesthetic

Anaesthetics include:

03 gas
PCP

05 ether
trike

06 eucain
Evipan®
spinal

07 Avertin®
cocaine

eucaine
urethan

08 ketamine
metopryl
procaine
stovaine
urethane

09 Fluothane®
halothane

lidocaine
Pentothal®

10 benzocaine
chloroform
lignocaine
nerve block
orthocaine
thiopental

11 Dutch liquid

laughing gas
thiopentone

12 cyclopropane
hexobarbital
nitrous oxide

13 hexobarbitone
phencyclidine

14 methyl chloride

15 tribromoethanol

analgesic

Analgesics include:

06 Calpol®	Panadol®	**09** Calprofen®	paracetamol
07 aspirin	quinine	co-codamol	pentazocine
codeine	salicin	ibuprofen	**12** indomethacin
Disprin®	**08** Cuprofen®	pethidine	salicylamide
Disprol®	fentanyl	**10** diclofenac	**13** carbamazepine
menthol	ketamine	**11** aminobutene	phencyclidine
metopon	morphine	Distalgesic®	
morphia	salicine	indometacin	**14** phenylbutazone
Nurofen®	stovaine		

anatomy

Anatomists include:

03 His (Wilhelm; 1831–1904, German)

04 Baer (Karl Ernst von; 1792–1876, German)
Bell (Sir Charles; 1774–1842, Scottish)
Dart (Raymond A; 1893–1988, South African)
Knox (Robert; 1791–1862, Scottish)
Roux (Wilhelm; 1850–1924, German)

05 Clark (Sir Wilfred le Gros; 1895–1971, English)
Graaf (Regnier de; 1641–73, Dutch)
Henle (Friedrich; 1809–85, German)
Hyrtl (Joseph; 1810–94, Austrian)
Monro (Alexander 'Primus'; 1697–1767, Scottish)
Monro (Alexander 'Secondus'; 1733–1817, Scottish)

06 Adrian (Edgar, Lord; 1889–1977, English)
Camper (Pieter; 1722–89, Dutch)
Cowper (William; 1666–1709, English)
Cuvier (Georges, Baron; 1769–1832, French)
Flower (Sir William Henry; 1831–99, English)
Hagens (Gunther von; 1945– , German)
Haller (Albrecht von; 1708–77, Swiss)
Harvey (William; 1578–1657, English)

Hunter (William; 1718–83, Scottish)
Pander (Christian Heinrich; 1794–1865, German)
Tobias (Phillip; 1925–2012, South African)

07 Baillie (Matthew; 1761–1823, Scottish)
Colombo (Matteo Realdo; 1516–59, Italian)
Galvani (Luigi; 1737–98, Italian)
Goodsir (John; 1814–67, Scottish)
Pecquet (Jean; 1622–74, French)

08 Alcmaeon (fl.520 BC; Greek)
Kölliker (Albert von; 1817–1905, Swiss)
Malpighi (Marcello; 1628–94, Italian)
Vesalius (Andreas; 1514–64, Belgian)

09 Bartholin (Caspar the Younger; 1655–1738, Danish)
Eustachio (Bartolommeo; 1520–74, Italian)
Fallopius (Gabriele; 1523–62, Italian)
Gegenbaur (Karl; 1826–1903, German)

10 Herophilus (c.335–c.280 BC, Greek)

11 Cruveilhier (Jean; 1791–1874, French)
Weidenreich (Franz; 1873–1948, German)

12 Papanicolaou (George Nicholas; 1883–1962, US)

13 Waldeyer-Hartz (Wilhelm; 1839–1921, German)

Terms used in anatomy include:

03 arm	chin	neck	chest
ear	crus	nose	digit
eye	foot	oral	elbow
hip	hand	shin	gland
jaw	head	vein	groin
leg	hock	womb	heart
toe	knee	**05** aorta	helix
04 anus	limb	aural	ileum
back	lobe	bowel	joint
bone	lung	brain	liver

lungs
mouth
nasal
navel
nerve
optic
ovary
pedal
penis
renal
spine
thumb
trunk
uvula
volar
vulva
wrist

06 artery
atrium
axilla
biceps
breast
buccal
carpal
carpus
crural
dental
dermal
distal
dorsal
finger
flexor
genial
gullet
kidney
lingua
lumbar
muscle
narial
narine
neural
neuron
ocular
penile
pleura
rectum
rectus
rotula
sacral
septum
soleus
spinal
spleen
temple

tendon
tensor
testis
thenar
throat
thymic
thymus
tongue
tonsil
tragus
uterus
uvular
vagina

07 abdomen
alveary
alveoli
auricle
bladder
buttock
cardiac
cnemial
cochlea
cranial
cranium
gastric
genital
glossal
glottal
glottis
gnathic
gristle
hepatic
jejunal
jejunum
jugular
kneecap
levator
lingual
mammary
membral
neurone
optical
osseous
patella
phalanx
pleural
pyloric
pylorus
ribcage
rotator
sternum
stomach
sublime
thyroid

triceps
urethra
uterine
vaginal
ventral

08 appendix
axillary
brachial
brachium
bronchus
cerebral
cervical
cochlear
coronary
duodenal
duodenum
extensor
foreskin
genitals
gingival
laryngal
ligament
mandible
muscular
opponent
pancreas
parietal
pectoral
perineal
perineum
prostate
proximal
shoulder
temporal
testicle
thoracic
vena cava
vertebra
voice-box
windpipe

09 abdominal
antihelix
bronchial
capillary
cartilage
coccygeal
coccygian
depressor
diaphragm
epidermal
epidermis
funny bone
genitalia

hamstring
labyrinth
lachrymal
lymph node
pulmonary
sartorial
sartorius
sphincter
tendinous
umbilical
umbilicus
ventricle
vertebral

10 Adam's apple
antitragus
cerebellum
encephalic
encephalon
epiglottal
epiglottis
intestinal
intestines
ligamental
mandibular
nociceptor
oesophagal
oesophagus
pancreatic
peritoneal
peritoneum
phalangeal
protractor
quadriceps
trochanter

11 diaphragmal
gall bladder
infracostal
intercostal
pericardium
solar plexus

12 adrenal gland

13 cartilaginous
diaphragmatic
Fallopian tube
gastrocnemius
lachrymal duct

14 Achilles tendon
Fallopian tubes
lachrymal gland
large intestine
pituitary gland
small intestine

See also **artery**; **bone**; **brain**; **ear**; **eye**; **face**; **gland**; **heart**; **hormone**; **immune system**; **mouth**; **muscle**; **nerve**; **organ**; **skin**; **teeth**; **vein**

anchor

Anchors include:

03 car	Bruce®	stream	mushroom
CQR	drift	**07** grapnel	**09** admiralty
ice	kedge	killick	stockless
sea	sheet	killock	yachtsman
04 navy	waist	stocked	**12** double fluked
rond	**06** drogue	weather	
05 bower	plough	**08** Danforth®	

ancient *see* **city**; **festival**

Ancient Egypt *see* Egypt

angel

Angels include:

05 Ariel	**06** Abdiel	Moloch	Michael
Eblis	Arioch	Zephon	Raphael
Iblis	Azrael	**07** Gabriel	Zadkiel
Satan	Belial	Israfel	**08** Ithuriel
Uriel	Mammon	Lucifer	**09** Beelzebub

Orders of angel:

05 angel	seraph	**08** dominion	**12** principality
power	throne	**09** archangel	
06 cherub	virtue	**10** domination	

angle

Angle types include:

05 acute	reflex	hour-angle	
right	**08** straight	**13** complementary	
06 obtuse	**09** conjugate	supplementary	

Angle measurements include:

04 hour	minute	arcsecond	minute of arc
05 grade	radian	steradian	second of arc
point	second	**10** revolution	**15** radian per second
06 degree	**09** arcminute	**11** degree of arc	

See also **measurement**

angling *see* fishing

animal

Animals include:

03			
ape	eland	gibbon	sealion
cat	horse	impala	wallaby
cow	hyena	jaguar	**08** aardvark
dog	koala	monkey	antelope
elk	lemur	ocelot	elephant
fox	llama	rabbit	hedgehog
gnu	moose	racoon	kangaroo
pig	mouse	walrus	mongoose
rat	otter	weasel	platypus
04 bear	panda	wombat	reindeer
bull	sheep	**07** buffalo	squirrel
deer	skunk	caribou	
goat	tiger	cheetah	**09** armadillo
hare	whale	dolphin	orang-utan
lion	zebra	gazelle	polar bear
mink	**06** baboon	giraffe	wolverine
mole	badger	gorilla	**10** chimpanzee
puma	beaver	hamster	giant panda
seal	cougar	leopard	rhinoceros
wolf	ermine	panther	**11** grizzly bear
05 bison	ferret	polecat	
camel	gerbil	raccoon	**12** hippopotamus

Adjectives relating to animals include:

05 apian (bee)
avian (bird)
avine (bird)
ovine (sheep)

06 bovine (cattle/ox)
canine (dog)
equine (horse)
feline (cat)
hippic (horse)
larine (gull)
lupine (wolf)
murine (mouse)
simian (ape/monkey)
ursine (bear)

07 acarine (mite)
anguine (snake)
asinine (ass/donkey)
caprine (goat)
cervine (deer)
corvine (crow)
hircine (goat)
leonine (lion)
milvine (kite)
otarine (seal)
pardine (leopard)

phocine (seal)
piscine (fish)
porcine (pig)
saurian (lizard)
sebrine (zebra)
taurine (bull)
tigrine (tiger)
turdine (thrush)
vespine (wasp)
vulpine (fox)

08 anserine (goose)
aquiline (eagle)
bubaline (buffalo)
cameline (camel)
elaphine (red deer)
ichthyic (fish)
lemurine (lemur)
leporine (hare)
limacine (slug)
ophidian (snake)
pavonine (peacock)
sciurine (squirrel)
soricine (shrew)
suilline (pig)
viperine (viper)
vituline (calf)

09 caballine (horse)
chelonian (tortoise/turtle)
colubrine (snake)
columbine (dove)
crotaline (rattlesnake)
falconine (falcon)
hirundine (swallow)
ichthyoid (fish)
musteline (badger/otter/
weasel)
ornithoid (bird)
viverrine (civet/ferret)
volucrine (bird)
vulturine (vulture)

10 erinaceous (hedgehog)
psittacine (parrot)
serpentine (snake)

11 accipitrine (hawk)
elephantine (elephant)
fringilline (finch)
lacertilian (lizard)

12 gallinaceous (fowl)
oryctolagine (rabbit)

13 rhopalocerous (butterfly)

14 papilionaceous (butterfly)

Collective nouns for animals include:

03 bed (clams/oysters)
cry (hounds)
gam (whales)
mob (kangaroos)
nid (pheasants)
nye (pheasants)
pod (seals/whales)

04 army (caterpillars/frogs)
bale (turtles)
band (gorillas)
bask (crocodiles)
bevy (larks/pheasants/quail/swans)
bury (rabbits)
cast (hawks)
cete (badgers)
dole (doves/turtles)
down (hares)
dray (squirrels)
erst (bees)
fall (woodcocks)
gang (buffalo/elk)
herd (buffalo/cattle/deer/elephants/goats/
   horses/kangaroos/oxen/seals/whales)
hive (bees)
host (sparrows)
husk (hares)
knot (toads)
leap (leopards)
mute (hares/hounds)
nest (ants/bees/pheasants/vipers)
nide (pheasants)
pace (asses)
pack (dogs/grouse/hounds/wolves)
romp (otters)
rout (wolves)
safe (ducks)
span (mules)
team (ducks/horses)
trip (goats/sheep)
turn (turtles)
wing (plovers)
yoke (oxen)
zeal (zebras)

05 bloat (hippopotami)
brace (ducks)
brood (chickens/hens)
charm (finches/goldfinches)
chirm (goldfinches)
cloud (gnats)
covey (partridges/quail)
crash (rhinoceros)
drift (hogs/swine)
drove (cattle/horses/oxen/sheep)
flock (birds/ducks/geese/sheep)
grist (bees)
horde (gnats)

hover (trout)
leash (foxes)
pride (lions)
route (wolves)
sedge (cranes)
shoal (fish)
siege (cranes/herons)
skein (geese)
skulk (foxes)
sloth (bears)
smack (jellyfish)
stand (flamingos)
stare (owls)
swarm (ants/bees/flies/locusts)
tower (giraffes)
tribe (goats)
troop (baboons/kangaroos/monkeys)
watch (nightingales)
wedge (swans)

06 ambush (tigers)
cackle (hyenas)
clutch (chickens)
colony (ants/bees/penguins/rats)
family (otters)
flight (birds)
gaggle (geese)
kennel (dogs)
kindle (kittens)
labour (moles)
litter (kittens/pigs)
murder (crows)
muster (peacocks/penguins)
parade (elephants)
parcel (penguins)
plague (locusts)
pounce (cats)
rafter (turkeys)
school (dolphins/fish/porpoises/whales)
scurry (squirrels)
shiver (sharks)
sleuth (bears)
spring (teal)
stable (horses)
streak (tigers)
string (horses/ponies)
tiding (magpies)
volery (birds)

07 bouquet (pheasants)
clowder (cats)
company (parrots)
descent (woodpeckers)
draught (fish)
prickle (porcupines)
rookery (rooks/seals)
sounder (swine)
turmoil (porpoises)

08 building (rooks)
    busyness (ferrets/flies)
    paddling (ducks)

09 intrusion (cockroaches)
    mustering (storks)
    obstinacy (buffalo)
    tittering (magpies)

10 exaltation (larks)

parliament (owls/rooks)
shrewdness (apes)
unkindness (ravens)

11 convocation (eagles)
    murmuration (starlings)
    ostentation (peacocks)
    pandemonium (parrots)

12 congregation (plovers)

Male animals include:

03 cob (swan)
    dog (dog/fox/wolf)
    hob (ferret)
    nun (smew)
    ram (sheep)
    tom (cat)
    tup (sheep)

04 boar (pig)
    buck (deer/goat/hare/rabbit)
    bull (cattle/elephant/moose/walrus/whale)
    cock (chicken/crab/lobster/salmon/sparrow)
    hart (deer)
    jack (ass/donkey)
    stag (deer)
    zobo (zho)
    zobu (zho)

05 billy (goat)
    drake (duck)
    drone (honey bee)
    dsobo (zho)

06 gander (goose)
    musket (sparrowhawk)
    old man (kangaroo)
    ramcat (cat)
    tarcel (hawk)
    tarsal (hawk)
    tarsel (hawk)
    tassel (hawk)
    tercel (hawk)

07 tassell (hawk)

08 seecatch (Aleutian fur seal)
    stallion (horse)

09 blackcock (black grouse)

10 turkey cock (guinea fowl/turkey)

11 tassell-gent (peregrine falcon)

12 tassel-gentle (peregrine falcon)
    tercel-gentle (peregrine falcon)
    tercel-jerkin (gerfalcon)
    throstle-cock (song-thrush)

Female animals include:

03 cow (cattle/elephant/elk/whale)
    doe (antelope/deer/hare/kangaroo/rabbit)
    ewe (sheep)
    hen (chicken)
    pen (swan)
    ree (ruff)
    sow (pig/badger)

04 gill (ferret)
    hind (deer)
    jill (ferret)
    jomo (zho)
    mare (horse)

05 bitch (dog/fox/wolf)
    dsomo (zho)
    jenny (ass/donkey)
    nanny (goat)
    queen (cat)

reeve (ruff)
vixen (fox)
zhomo (zho)

06 peahen (peacock)

07 greyhen (black grouse)
    lioness (lion)
    tigress (tiger)

08 water cow (water buffalo)

09 dolphinet (dolphin)
    guinea hen (guinea fowl)
    turkey hen (turkey)

10 leopardess (leopard)
    weasel coot (smew)

12 falcon-gentil (peregrine falcon)
    falcon-gentle (peregrine falcon)

Lairs, nests and homes of animals include:

03 den (bear/lion)
    nid (pheasant)
    pen (sheep)

sty (pig)

04 bike (wasp/wild bee)
    bink (wasp/wild bee)

byre (cow)
cage (squirrel)
coop (fowl)

drey (squirrel)
fold (sheep)
form (hare)
hive (bee)
hole (mouse)
holt (otter)
nest (bird/mouse/wasp)
sett (badger)

05 earth (fox)
eyrie (eagle)
lodge (beaver)
shell (snail)
06 burrow (rabbit)
warren (rabbit)
wurley (rat)
08 dovecote (pigeon)

fortress (mole)
vespiary (wasp)
09 formicary (ant)
11 formicarium (ant)
termitarium (termite)

Sounds made by animals include:

03 baa
bay
caw
coo
low
mew
moo
yap

04 bark
blat
bray
crow
hiss

hoot
howl
purr
roar
woof
yawp
yelp
yowl

05 bleat
cheep
chirp
cluck
croak

groin
growl
grunt
miaow
neigh
quack
snarl
tweet

06 bellow
cackle
gobble
heehaw
squawk

squeak
warble
whinny

07 chirrup
gruntle
screech
trumpet
twitter
whicker

09 caterwaul

Young animals include:

03 cub (bear/fox/lion/wolf)
elt (female pig)
fry (fish)
kid (antelope/goat)
kit (ferret/fox/polecat)
nit (louse)

04 brit (herring/sprat)
calf (cattle/elephant/whale)
colt (horse)
eyas (hawk)
fawn (deer)
foal (horse)
gilt (female pig)
grig (eel)
guga (gannet)
joey (kangaroo)
lamb (sheep)
maid (skate)
parr (salmon)
peal (sea trout)
peel (sea trout)
quey (cow)
sild (herring)
slip (pig)
yelt (female pig)

05 bunny (rabbit)
chick (chicken)
cuddy (coalfish)
elver (eel)
owlet (owl)

piper (pigeon)
poult (chicken)
puppy (dog/rat/seal)
scrod (cod/haddock)
shoat (pig)
shote (pig)
smolt (salmon)
sprod (salmon)
squab (chicken/pigeon/
  rook)
steer (ox)
whelp (dog)

06 alevin (fish)
cuddie (coalfish)
cygnet (swan)
eaglet (eagle)
eirack (hen)
finnac (sea trout)
gimmer (female sheep)
grilse (salmon)
heifer (cow)
hidder (male sheep)
kid-fox (fox)
kitten (cat)
lionet (lion)
mattie (herring)
mousie (mouse)
peeper (bird)
piglet (pig)
podley (coalfish)

pullet (chicken)
samlet (salmon)
scaury (gull)
theave (female sheep)
weaner (pig)

07 bull-pup (bulldog)
cheeper (fowl)
cockney (snapper fish)
codling (cod)
eanling (sheep)
eelfare (eel)
finnack (sea trout)
finnock (sea trout)
gosling (goose)
herling (sea trout)
hirling (sea trout)
leveret (hare)
pigling (pig)
sardine (pilchard)
scourie (gull)
scowrie (gull)
sillock (coalfish)
skegger (salmon)
sounder (boar)
spitter (deer)
tadpole (frog/toad)
wolfkin (wolf)

08 brancher (hawk)
cockerel (cock)
duckling (duck)

goatling (goat)
grey-fish (coalfish)
hernshaw (heron)
heronsew (heron)
jackfish (pike)
moor-poot (grouse)
moor-pout (grouse)
mousekin (mouse)

muir-poot (grouse)
muir-pout (grouse)
nestling (bird)
pea-chick (peafowl)
pickerel (pike)
porkling (pig)
squeaker (bird)
squealer (pig/pigeon)

wolfling (wolf)
yeanling (goat/sheep)
09 calf whale (whale)
fledgling (bird)
heronshaw (heron)
whale calf (whale)

Terms to do with animals include:

03 ear
egg
eye
fin
fur
leg
paw
pet
04 beak
bill
bite
claw
coat
crop
dock
foot
gill
gula
hair
hoof
horn
hump
jowl
loin
mane
mate
nose
prey
ribs
rump
tail
teat
tusk

wild
wing
wool
05 chine
crest
fangs
feral
moult
pouch
scale
shell
snout
spine
sting
teeth
trunk
udder
venom
06 antler
barrel
dewlap
forfex
jubate
mantle
muzzle
thorax
tongue
ungula
07 abdomen
antenna
feather
flehmen
flipper

gizzard
habitat
migrate
mimicry
pallium
pteryla
segment
withers
08 apatetic
coupling
ditokous
domestic
forefoot
forewing
halteres
hindfoot
hindwing
predator
shoulder
torquate
ungulate
whiskers
09 didelphic
gastraeum
marsupium
oviparous
prehallux
proboscis
pygostyle
syndactyl
taligrade
10 alloparent
aposematic

camouflage
digoneutic
epimeletic
gressorial
ovipositor
viviparous
webbed feet
11 compound eye
diphycercal
iteroparous
lateral line
search image
semelparous
swim bladder
unguligrade
waggle dance
12 dibranchiate
etepimeletic
forked tongue
longicaudate
longipennate
micropterous
13 electric organ
metamorphosis
perissodactyl
semioviparous
solidungulate
solidungulous
synaposematic
14 startle colours
15 prehensile thumb

See also **amphibian**; **ant**; **antelope**; **ape**; **bat**; **bear**; **beetle**; **bird**; **butterfly**; **calendar**; **carnivore**;
    cat; **cattle**; **chicken**; **crustacean**; **deer**; **dinosaur**; **disease**; **dog**; **duck**; **eel**; **falcon**; **farm**;
    fish; **fly**; **fur**; **game: hunting**; **goose**; **horse**; **hybrid**; **insect**; **invertebrate**; **jellyfish**;
    lizard; **mammal**; **marsupial**; **mollusc**; **monkey**; **moth**; **mythology**; **parasite**; **parrot**;
    pet; **pig**; **poison**; **poultry**; **primate**; **rabbit**; **reptile**; **rodent**; **ruminant**; **seal**; **shark**;
    sheep; **snake**; **spaniel**; **spider**; **swan**; **terrier**; **vermin**; **whale**; **worm**

anniversary

Wedding anniversaries:

03 fur (13th)
tin (10th)

04 gold (50th)
iron (6th)

jade (35th)
lace (8th/13th)

ruby (40th)
silk (12th)
wood (5th/6th)
wool (7th)
05 china (2nd/20th)
coral (35th)
fruit (4th)
glass (3rd)
ivory (14th)
linen (8th/12th)
paper (1st)
pearl (12th/30th)
steel (11th)

sugar (6th)
06 bronze (8th)
clocks (1st)
copper (7th)
cotton (2nd)
silver (25th)
willow (9th)
07 crystal (3rd/15th)
diamond (30th/60th)
emerald (55th)
flowers (4th)
leather (3rd/9th)

pottery (8th/9th)
watches (15th)
08 desk sets (7th)
platinum (20th/70th)
sapphire (45th)
textiles (13th)
09 aluminium (10th)
10 appliances (4th)
silverware (5th)
13 gold jewellery (14th)
16 diamond jewellery (10th)
fashion jewellery (11th)

See *also* **festival**; **religion**

ant

Ants include:

03 red
04 army
fire
leaf
wood

05 black
crazy
06 Amazon
driver
weaver

07 bulldog
forager
pharaoh
soldier
08 honeydew

09 black lawn
carpenter
harvester
10 leaf-cutter
12 red harvester

antelope

Antelopes include:

03 bok
doe
gnu
kid
kob
04 kudu
oryx
puku
suni
thar
topi
05 addax
bubal
chiru
eland
goral
nagor
nyala

oribi
sable
saiga
sasin
serow
06 bosbok
dik-dik
duiker
duyker
dzeren
impala
inyala
koodoo
lechwe
nilgai
nilgau
pygarg
reebok

07 blaubok
blesbok
bloubok
bubalis
chamois
chikara
gazelle
gemsbok
gerenuk
grysbok
madoqua
nylghau
sassaby
08 Antilope
bontebok
boschbok
bushbuck
palebuck
reedbuck

steenbok
tsessebe
09 blackbuck
sitatunga
situtunga
springbok
steinbock
tragelaph
waterbuck
10 Alcelaphus
hartebeest
ox-antelope
wildebeest
11 zebra duiker
12 goat-antelope
klipspringer
13 sable antelope

anthropology

Anthropologists include:

04 Boas (Franz; 1858–1942, US)
Buck (Sir Peter; 1879–1951, New Zealand)
Mead (Margaret; 1901–78, US)
05 Tylor (Sir Edward; 1832–1917, English)

06 Frazer (Sir J G; 1854–1941, Scottish)
Leakey (Louis; 1903–72, Kenyan/British)
Marett (R R; 1866–1943, British)
07 Goodall (Jane; 1934–　, English)

Métraux (Albert; 1902–63, US)
09 Heyerdahl (Thor; 1914–2002, Norwegian)
10 Malinowski (Bronislaw; 1884–1942, Polish/British)
11 Lévi-Strauss (Claude; 1908–2009, French)
14 Radcliffe-Brown (Alfred; 1881–1955, English)

antibiotic

Antibiotics include:

05 Cipro®
07 allicin
08 neomycin
nystatin
09 avoparcin
kanamycin
Neosporin®
polymyxin
quinolone
10 ampicillin

Aureomycin®
bacitracin
gramicidin
lincomycin
meticillin
penicillin
polymyxin B
rifampicin
Terramycin®
vancomycin
11 amoxicillin

amoxycillin
clindamycin
cloxacillin
cycloserine
doxorubicin
doxycycline
fusidic acid
methicillin
12 erythromycin
griseofulvin
streptomycin

tetracycline
trimethoprim
13 cephalosporin
ciprofloxacin
co-trimoxazole
metronidazole
spectinomycin
virginiamycin
15 chloramphenicol
oxytetracycline

antipope *see* **pope**

antique

Antiques terms include:

04 Goss
Ming
ring
T'ang
05 glaze
ivory
06 barock
dealer
empire
Gothic
lustre
patina
period
rococo
07 art deco

auction
barocco
baroque
ceramic
federal
impasto
opaline
pilgrim
pottery
Tiffany
08 filigree
Georgian
Jacobean
majolica
Sheraton

trecento
09 bone china
collector
Delftware
Edwardian
porcelain
Queen Anne
soft paste
stoneware
valuation
Victorian
10 art nouveau
millefiori
11 chinoiserie
Chippendale

cinquecento
haute époque
Hepplewhite
period piece
restoration
12 antiques fair
blanc de Chine
blue and white
reproduction
transitional
13 arts and crafts
willow pattern
15 churrigueresque

See also **furniture**

antiseptic

Antiseptics include:

03 TCP®
05 eupad
eusol
06 cresol
Dettol®
flavin
formol
phenol

Savlon®
thymol
07 benzoin
flavine
08 creasote
creosote
formalin
iodoform

09 cassareep
cassaripe
cetrimide
Germolene®
Listerine®
merbromin
zinc oxide
10 acriflavin

11 acriflavine
12 carbolic acid
methyl violet
13 chlorhexidine
crystal violet

flowers of zinc
gentian violet
silver nitrate
14 Dakin's solution
rubbing alcohol

sodium benzoate
sodium chlorate
15 hexachlorophane
hexachlorophene

ape

Apes include:

05 chimp
orang
pongo

06 bonobo
gibbon
07 gorilla

09 orang-utan
10 chimpanzee
11 orang-outang

15 pygmy chimpanzee

See also **primate**

Apocrypha *see* Bible

apostle

Apostles of Jesus Christ:

04 John
05 James
Judas
Peter
Simon
06 Andrew

Philip
Thomas
07 Matthew
08 Matthias
Thaddeus
11 Bartholomew

13 Judas Iscariot
14 Simon the Zealot
15 James of Alphaeus
17 Simon the Canaanite

apparatus *see* laboratory

apple

Apple varieties include:

03 Cox
04 Cox's
crab
snow
05 eater
06 biffin
codlin
cooker
eating
idared

pippin
russet
07 Baldwin
Bramley
codling
cooking
costard
crispin
ribston
Sturmer
wine-sap

08 Braeburn
Jonathan
McIntosh
pearmain
Pink Lady
queening
ribstone
sweeting
09 delicious
jenneting
king-apple

nonpareil
Royal gala
11 Granny Smith
McIntosh red
russet apple
12 Red Delicious
13 Ribston pippin
Sturmer Pippin
15 Golden Delicious

See also **fruit**

appliance *see* domestic appliance

aquarium *see* fish

Arab League

Arab League members:

04 Iraq	**06** Jordan	Tunisia
Oman	Kuwait	**08** Djibouti
05 Egypt	**07** Algeria	**09** Palestine
Libya	Bahrain	**10** Mauritania
Qatar	Comoros	**11** Saudi Arabia
Sudan	Lebanon	**18** United Arab Emirates
Syria	Morocco	
Yemen	Somalia	

Arabic *see* **alphabet**

arable *see* **crop**

arachnid *see* **spider**

arch

Arches include:

04 keel	lancet	**08** inverted	**10** proscenium
ogee	Norman	recessed	shouldered
skew	safety	**09** Ctesiphon	**11** discharging
05 round	tented	horseshoe	equilateral
Tudor	**07** pointed	parabolic	four-centred
06 convex	squinch	relieving	**12** basket handle
corbel	stilted	segmental	three-centred
Gothic	trefoil	triumphal	

archaeology

Archaeologists include:

04 Uhle (Max; 1856–1944, German)

05 Aston (Michael; 'Mick' 1946–2013, English)
Clark (Grahame; 1907–95, English)
Evans (Sir Arthur; 1851–1941, English)

06 Anning (Mary; 1799–1847, English)
Breuil (Henri; 1877–1961, French)
Carter (Howard; 1874–1939, English)
Childe (Gordon; 1892–1957, Australian)
Clarke (David L; 1937–76, English)
Daniel (Glyn; 1914–86, Welsh)
Hawkes (Jacquetta; 1910–96, English)
Kenyon (Dame Kathleen; 1906–78, English)
Kidder (A V; 1885–1963, US)
Layard (Sir Austen; 1817–94, English)
Leakey (Louis; 1903–72, Kenyan/British)
Leakey (Mary; 1913–96, English)
Petrie (Sir Flinders; 1853–1942, English)
Putnam (Frederic Ward; 1839–1915, US)

07 Binford (Lewis; 1931–2011, US)

Renfrew (Colin, Lord; 1937– , English)
Thomsen (Christian; 1788–1865, Danish)
Wheeler (Sir Mortimer; 1890–1976, English)
Woolley (Sir Leonard; 1880–1960, English)
Worsaae (J J A; 1821–85, Danish)

08 Breasted (J H; 1865–1935, US)
Cunliffe (Barry; 1939– , English)
Fiorelli (Giuseppe; 1823–96, Italian)
Koldewey (Robert; 1855–1925, German)
Mallowan (Sir Max; 1904–78, English)
Mariette (Auguste; 1821–81, French)
Marshall (Sir John; 1876–1958, English)

09 Andersson (Johan Gunnar; 1874–1960, Swedish)

10 Pitt-Rivers (Augustus; 1827–1900, English)
Schliemann (Heinrich; 1822–90, German)

11 Champollion (Jean François; 1790–1832, French)

Terms used in archaeology include:

03 ard
cup
dig
DMV
DNA
jar
jug
SAM
tor
urn

04 adze
berm
bowl
celt
cist
core
dyke
grid
kist
rath
site
tell
term
work

05 agger
armil
auger
blade
burin
cairn
ditch
flake
flask
flint
fogou
henge
hoard
mound
mummy
quoit
shard
sherd
stele
whorl

06 barrow
Beaker
bogman
crater
cursus
dolmen
dromos

dugout
eolith
juglet
kurgan
menhir
midden
mosaic
patina
raggle
strata
syrinx
trench
vallum

07 amphora
anomaly
armilla
Azilian
cave art
crannog
cup mark
geofact
handaxe
horizon
Iron Age
logboat
lynchet
neolith
obelisk
papyrus
rock art
sondage
spindle
stratum
talayot
tumulus

08 artefact
artifact
capstone
carbon-14
Chellean
cistvaen
cromlech
dene-hole
excavate
grattoir
Halstatt
hill fort
kistvaen
knapping
ley lines
megalith

palmette
palstave
post hole
potshard
potshare
potsherd
ring fort
Stone Age
Strepyan
tranchet
typology

09 Acheulean
Acheulian
arrowhead
bracteate
Bronze Age
C14 dating
cartouche
Cro-Magnon
crop-marks
earthwork
enclosure
fieldwork
hut-circle
hypocaust
longhouse
microlith
Neolithic
palafitte
potboiler
shell heap
Solutrean
Solutrian

10 Anglo-Saxon
assemblage
burnt earth
Clactonian
cup-and-ring
excavation
fire-plough
geophysics
grave goods
Gravettian
hieroglyph
inhumation
loom weight
Madelenian
megalithic
Mesolithic
Middle Ages
Mousterian

Neandertal
palaeolith
petroglyph
roundhouse
shadow mark
skeuomorph
tear bottle
wheelhouse

11 Aurignacian
burial mound
cross-dating
horned cairn
Magdalenian
Maglemosian
Neanderthal
New Stone Age
Old Stone Age
Perigordian
Reindeer Age
rock shelter
shell midden
spacer plate
stone circle

12 amphitheatre
archaeometry
carbon dating
field walking
interglacial
lake dwelling
maiden castle
palaeobotany
Palaeolithic
stratigraphy
Tardenoisian

13 kitchen-midden
Neandertal Man
standing stone
treasure trove
vitrified fort
wattle and daub

14 archaeozoology
clearance cairn
conchoidal ring
diatom analysis
extended burial
hunter-gatherer
Neanderthal Man
pollen analysis

15 linear earthwork
occupation level

archbishop

Archbishops of Canterbury, with date of accession:

03 Oda (942)

04 Lang (Cosmo Gordon; 1928)
Laud (William; 1633)
Pole (Reginald; 1556)
Tait (Archibald; 1868)
Wake (William; 1716)

05 Abbot (George; 1611)
Carey (George; 1991)
Deane (Henry; 1501)
Grant (Richard le; 1229)
Islip (Simon; 1349)
Juxon (William; 1660)
Kempe (John; 1452)
Moore (John; 1783)
Welby (Justin; 2013)

06 Anselm (1093)
Athelm (914)
Becket (Thomas à; 1162)
Benson (Edward; 1883)
Coggan (Donald; 1974)
Edmund (of Abingdon; 1234)
Fisher (Geoffrey; 1945)
Howley (William; 1828)
Hutton (Matthew; 1757)
Justus (624)
Lyfing (1013)
Morton (John; 1486)
Parker (Matthew; 1559)
Potter (John; 1737)
Ramsey (Michael; 1961)
Robert (of Jumieges; 1051)
Runcie (Robert; 1980)
Secker (Thomas; 1758)
Sumner (John; 1848)
Temple (Frederick; 1896)
Temple (William; 1942)
Walden (Roger; 1398)
Walter (Hubert; 1193)
Warham (William; 1503)

07 Aelfric (995)
Alphege (1005)
Arundel (Thomas; 1396/1399)
Baldwin (1184)
Corbeil (William de; 1123)
Cranmer (Thomas; 1533)
Dunstan (960)
Eadsige (1038)
Grindal (Edmund; 1576)
Herring (Thomas; 1747)
Langham (Simon; 1366)
Langton (Stephen; 1207)
Longley (Charles; 1862)
Meopham (Simon; 1328)

Nothelm (735)
Peckham (John; 1279)
Richard (of Dover; 1174)
Sheldon (Gilbert; 1663)
Sigeric (990)
Stigand (1052)
Sudbury (Simon; 1375)
Tatwine (731)
Tenison (Thomas; 1695)
Wulfred (805)

08 Aelfsige (959)
Bancroft (Richard; 1604)
Boniface (of Savoy; 1245)
Brithelm (959)
Ceolnoth (833)
Chichele (Henry; 1414)
Cuthbert (740)
Davidson (Randall; 1903)
d'Escures (Ralph; 1114)
Ethelgar (c.988)
Ethelred (870)
Honorius (627)
Jaenbert (765)
Lanfranc (1070)
Mellitus (619)
Plegmund (890)
Reynolds (Walter; 1313)
Sancroft (William; 1678)
Stafford (John; 1443)
Theobald (1139)
Theodore (668)
Whitgift (John; 1583)
Williams (Rowan; 2002)
Wulfhelm (923)

09 Augustine (597)
Berhtwald (693)
Bourchier (Thomas; 1454)
Bregowine (761)
Courtenay (William; 1381)
Deusdedit (655)
Ethelhard (793)
Ethelnoth (1020)
Feologeld (832)
Kilwardby (Robert; 1273)
Stratford (John de; 1333)
Tillotson (John; 1691)

10 Cornwallis (Frederick; 1768)
Laurentius (604)
Whittlesey (William; 1368)
Winchelsey (Robert; 1294)

11 Bradwardine (Thomas; 1349)

13 Manners-Sutton (Charles; 1805)

Archbishops of York, with date of accession:

03 Lee (Edward; 1531)

04 Bosa (678)
Chad (644)
Grey (Walter de; 1215)
Hope (David; 1995)
John (of Thoresby; 1352)
John (St, of Beverley; 705)
Lang (Cosmo Gordon; 1908)

05 Booth (Lawrence; 1476)
Booth (William; 1452)
Bowet (Henry; 1407)
Dawes (Sir William; 1714)
Heath (Nicholas; 1555)
Henry (of Newark; 1298)
Kempe (John; 1425)
Magee (William Connor; 1890)
Neile (Richard; 1632)
Piers (John; 1589)
Roger (of Pont-L'Eveque; 1154)
Scott (Thomas; 1480)
Sharp (John; 1691)
Young (Thomas; 1561)

06 Blanch (Stuart; 1975)
Bovill (Sewal de; 1256)
Ceadda (644)
Coggan (Donald; 1961)
Dolben (John; 1683)
Edwald (971)
Egbert (735)
Frewen (Accepted; 1660)
Gerard (1101)
Hutton (Matthew; 1595)
Hutton (Matthew; 1747)
Oswald (972)
Puttoc (Aelfric; 1023)
Ramsey (Michael; 1956)
Romeyn (John le; 1286)
Sandys (Edwin; 1577)
Savage (Thomas; 1501)
Scrope (Richard le; 1398)
Sterne (Richard; 1664)
Temple (William; 1929)
Thomas (I; 1070)
Thomas (II; 1109)
Thomas (of Corbridge; 1300)
Waldby (Robert; 1396)
Wolsey (Thomas; 1514)
Zouche (William le; 1342)

07 Arundel (Thomas; 1388)
Ealdred (1061)
Ealdulf (992)
Eanbald (I; 780)

Eanbald (II; 796)
Garbett (Cyril; 1942)
Giffard (Walter; 1265)
Gilbert (John; 1757)
Godfrey (of Kineton; 1258)
Godfrey (of Ludham; 1258)
Grindal (Edmund; 1570)
Habgood (John; 1983)
Herring (Thomas; 1743)
Holgate (Robert; 1545)
Longley (Charles; 1860)
Markham (William; 1777)
Matthew (Tobias; 1606)
Neville (Alexander; 1374)
Neville (George; 1465)
Oskytel (958)
Romanus (1286)
Sentamu (John; 2005)
Thomson (William; 1862)
Wigmund (837)
Wilfrid (I; 669)
Wilfrid (II; 718)
William (of Melton; 1317)

08 Cynesige (1051)
Drummond (Robert; 1761)
Harcourt (Edward Vernon; 1807)
Harsnett (Samuel; 1628)
Lamplugh (Thomas; 1688)
Lodeward (904)
Maclagan (William; 1891)
Musgrave (Thomas; 1847)
Paulinus (627)
Rotheram (Thomas; 1480)
Thurstan (1119)
Wickwane (William; 1279)
Williams (John; 1641)
Wulfhere (854)
Wulfsige (808)
Wulfstan (I; 931)
Wulfstan (II; 1003)

09 Ethelbald (900)
Ethelbert (767)
Ethelwold (971)
Monteigne (George; 1628)

10 Bainbridge (Christopher; 1508)
Blackburne (Lancelot; 1724)
Greenfield (William; 1306)

11 Fitzherbert (Henry; 1147)
Fitzherbert (William; 1143)
Hrotheweard (904)
Plantagenet (Geoffrey; 1181)

Other archbishops, with date of accession include:

04 Gray (Gordon; 1951)
Hume (Basil; 1976)
Tutu (Desmond; 1986)

05 Beran (Josef; 1946)
Glemp (Jozef; 1981)

06 Beaton (David; 1539)
Heenan (John Carmel; 1963)
Hilary (St; c.350)
Mannix (Daniel; 1917)

Trench (Richard Chenevix; 1864)
Ussher (James; 1625)

07 Mendoza (Pedro Gonzalez de; 1474)
Wiseman (Nicholas; 1850)

08 Adalbert (1043)
Makarios (1948)

10 Damaskinos (Dimitrios Papandreou; 1938)
Huddleston (Trevor; 1978)

archdiocese *see* diocese

archery

Archery types include:

03 run
ski

05 clout
field

06 flight
target

Archery terms include:

03 bow
end

04 back
bolt
boss
butt
face
fast
FITA
grip
limb
nock
pile

05 arrow
belly
cable
inner
notch
outer
point
riser
rover
scope
shaft

sight
wheel

06 anchor
archer
bowman
bracer
flight
handle
magpie
quiver
string
target
upshot

07 barebow
bow-hand
bowshot
longbow
nocking
release

08 armguard
bull's-eye
crossbow
draw hand

limb bolt

09 arrowhead
arrow rest
bowstring
finger tab
fletching
lower limb
upper limb

10 cable guard
classic bow
draw weight
recurve bow
stabilizer
target face

11 cock feather
compound bow
shooting peg

12 nocking point
shooting line

14 instinctive bow
marked distance
tensioning wire

15 mounting bracket

archipelago

Archipelagoes include:

04 Cuba (Caribbean Sea)
Fiji (South Pacific)
Sulu (South China Sea/Pacific Ocean)

05 Åland (Baltic Sea)
Gulag (USSR)

Japan (Pacific Ocean)
Malay (Indian Ocean/Pacific Ocean)
Malta (Mediterranean Sea)
Tonga (Pacific Ocean)

06 Arctic (Arctic Ocean)

Azores (Atlantic Ocean)
Chagos (Indian Ocean)
Kosrae (Pacific Ocean)
Tuvalu (Pacific Ocean)

07 Iles d'Or (Mediterranean Sea)
Mayotte (Indian Ocean)
Tuamotu (Pacific Ocean)

08 Bismarck (Papua New Guinea/Pacific Ocean)
Cyclades (Aegean Sea)
Kiribati (Pacific Ocean)
Maldives (Indian Ocean)
Moluccas (Pacific Ocean)
Svalbard (Arctic Ocean)

09 Alexander (Alaska/Pacific Ocean)
Antarctic (Southern Ocean)
Cape Verde (Atlantic Ocean)
Catherine (Alaska/Pacific Ocean)
Galápagos (Pacific Ocean)
Indonesia (Indian Ocean/Pacific Ocean)
Louisiade (Solomon Sea/Coral Sea)
Marquesas (Pacific Ocean)
North Land (Arctic Ocean)

10 Ahvenanmaa (Baltic Sea)
Seychelles (Indian Ocean)
The Bahamas (Caribbean Sea)
Vesterålen (Norwegian Sea/Arctic Ocean)
West Indies (Caribbean Sea)

11 Iles d'Hyères (Mediterranean Sea)
Line Islands (Pacific Ocean)
Philippines (Pacific Ocean)
Spitsbergen (Arctic Ocean)
Vesteraalen (Norwegian Sea/Arctic Ocean)

12 Kuril Islands (Pacific Ocean)
Novaya Zemlya (Kara Sea/Arctic Ocean)

See also **island**

Pearl Islands (Indian Ocean)
Spice Islands (Pacific Ocean)
Sunda Islands (Celebes Sea/South China Sea)

13 Aegean Islands (Aegean Sea)
Caicos Islands (Atlantic Ocean)
Canary Islands (Atlantic Ocean)
Ellice Islands (Atlantic Ocean)
Ionian Islands (Ionian Sea)
Tubuai Islands (Pacific Ocean)

14 Austral Islands (South Pacific)
Bijagos Islands (Guinea-Bissau/Atlantic Ocean)
Channel Islands (English Channel)
Franz Josef Land (Arctic Ocean)
Gilbert Islands (Pacific Ocean)
Leeward Islands (Caribbean Sea/Atlantic Ocean)
Lofoten Islands (Arctic Ocean)
Nicholas II Land (Arctic Ocean)
Oki Archipelago (Sea of Japan)
Papua New Guinea (Pacific Ocean)
Phoenix Islands (Pacific Ocean)
Solomon Islands (Solomon Sea/Pacific Ocean)
Tierra del Fuego (Atlantic Ocean/Pacific Ocean/Southern Ocean)
Visayan Islands (Visayan Sea/South China Sea)

15 Balearic Islands (Mediterranean Sea)
Friendly Islands (South Pacific)
Marshall Islands (Pacific Ocean)
Pitcairn Islands (Pacific Ocean)
Severnaya Zemlya (Arctic Ocean)
Wallis and Futuna (South Pacific)
Windward Islands (Caribbean Sea)

architecture

Architectural features include:

03 orb	neck	hance	torus
web	ogee	helix	tower
04 anta	ribs	mould	truss
apse	vase	nerve	vault
arch	void	ogive	**06** abacus
base	**05** antae	print	atrium
bell	attic	pylon	canton
boss	congé	quirk	caulis
cove	crown	scape	chevet
crop	flute	socle	cinque
cusp	gable	spire	cippus
cyma	gavel	stria	column
dado	glyph	talon	concha
drum	groin	tenia	congee
list	gutta	tondo	coping

corbel
corona
coving
crenel
dentil
façade
fascia
fillet
finial
flèche
fornix
frieze
haunch
impost
lierne
metope
patera
patten
pillar
podium
portal
reglet
regula
rosace
scotia
severy
striae
taenia
turret
wreath

07 aileron
annulet
balloon
bandrol
capital
cavetti
cavetto
conchae
corbeil
cornice
crocket
diglyph

doucine
echinus
fantail
festoon
fronton
fusarol
grecque
larmier
mullion
necking
nervure
pannier
parapet
Persian
pilotis
portico
rosette
solidum
squinch
surbase
tambour
telamon
tondino

08 abutment
accolade
apophyge
astragal
baguette
bandelet
banderol
bannerol
bellcote
buttress
canephor
cartouch
chapiter
chaptrel
ciborium
cincture
crenelle
diastyle
dipteral

dipteros
entresol
epistyle
frontoon
fusarole
gorgerin
imperial
intrados
mascaron
moulding
pediment
pilaster
prostyle
pulpitum
rockwork
sept-foil
skewback
spandrel
spandril
terminus
triglyph
tympanum
voussoir

09 apsidiole
archivolt
balection
banderole
bolection
cartouche
crossette
cul-de-four
decastyle
embrasure
embrazure
foliation
guilloche
hypostyle
mezzanine
modillion
octastyle
octostyle
peristyle

strap work
stylobate
tierceron
triforium
water leaf

10 acroterion
architrave
ball-flower
bratticing
cauliculus
chambranle
clearstory
clerestory
demicupola
ditriglyph
egg-and-dart
eye-catcher
feathering
jerkinhead
pendentive
quatrefoil
subarcuate
water table
weathering

11 brattishing
entablature
paternoster

12 egg-and-anchor
egg-and-tongue
frontispiece

13 chain moulding
Ctesiphon arch
interpilaster
quatrefeuille
vermiculation

14 Catherine-wheel
flying buttress
shouldered arch

Architectural styles include:

04 Adam
05 Greek
Saxon
06 Gothic
Norman
rococo
07 art deco
barocco

baroque
Italian
Lombard
mission
mudéjar
08 baronial
high tech
09 beaux arts

brutalism
Byzantine
Cape Dutch
decorated
Palladian
Queen Anne
10 art nouveau
Corinthian
Romanesque

11 Elizabethan
Renaissance
13 Gothic revival
international
neoclassicism
Perpendicular
post-modernism
15 churrigueresque

Architects include:

03 Ito (Toyo; 1941– , Japanese)
Lin (Maya; 1959– , US)
Oud (J J P; 1890–1963, Dutch)
Pei (I M; 1917– , US)

04 Adam (James; 1730–94, Scottish)
Adam (Robert; 1728–92, Scottish)
Adam (William; 1689–1748, Scottish)
Ando (Tadao; 1941– , Japanese)
Burn (William; 1789–1870, Scottish)
Drew (Dame Jane; 1911–96, English)
Hood (Raymond M; 1881–1934, US)
Hunt (Richard Morris; 1827–95, US)
Jahn (Helmut; 1940– , US)
Kahn (Louis I; 1901–74, US)
Kent (William; 1684–1748, English)
Loos (Adolf; 1870–1933, Austrian)
Nash (John; 1752–1835, English)
Otto (Frei; 1925– , German)
Shaw (Norman; 1831–1912, English)
Webb (Philip; 1831–1915, English)
Webb (Sir Aston; 1849–1930, English)
Wood (John; 1728–82, English)
Wood (John, the Elder; c.1705–54, English)
Wren (Sir Christopher; 1632–1723, English)

05 Aalto (Alvar; 1898–1976, Finnish)
Alsop (Will; 1947– , English)
Baker (Sir Herbert; 1862–1946, English)
Barry (Sir Charles; 1795–1860, English)
Bryce (David; 1803–76, Scottish)
Costa (Lucio; 1902–98, French/Brazilian)
Dance (George; 1700–68, English)
Dance (George; 1741–1825, English)
Doshi (Balkrishna; 1927– , Indian)
Dudok (Willem; 1884–1974, Dutch)
Engel (Carl Ludwig; 1778–1840, German/Finnish)
Gaudí (Antoni; 1852–1926, Spanish)
Gehry (Frank; 1929– , Canadian/US)
Gibbs (James; 1682–1754, Scottish)
Gilly (Friedrich; 1772–1800, German)
Hadid (Dame Zaha; 1950– , Iraqi)
Horta (Victor, Baron; 1861–1947, Belgian)
Jones (Inigo; 1573–1652, English)
Levau (Louis; 1612–70, French)
Mayne (Thom; 1944– , US)
McKim (Charles; 1847–1909, US)
Meier (Richard; 1934– , US)
Mills (Robert; 1781–1855, US)
Moore (Charles; 1925–93, US)
Nervi (Pier Luigi; 1891–1979, Italian)
Pelli (César; 1926– , US)
Piano (Renzo; 1937– , Italian)
Pugin (Augustus; 1812–52, English)
Rocha (Paulo Mendes da; 1928– , Brazilian)
Scott (M H Baillie; 1865–1945, English)

Scott (Sir George Gilbert; 1811–78, English)
Scott (Sir Giles Gilbert; 1880–1960, English)
Soane (Sir John; 1753–1837, English)
Speer (Albert; 1905–81, German)
Stern (Robert A M; 1939– , US)
Tange (Kenzo; 1913–2005, Japanese)
Utzon (Jørn; 1918–2008, Danish)
Velde (Henri van de; 1863–1957, Belgian)
Wyatt (James; 1746–1813, English)
Yeang (Ken; 1948– , Malaysian)

06 Breuer (Marcel; 1902–81, Hungarian/US)
Burton (Decimus; 1800–81, English)
Campen (Jacob van; 1595–1657, Dutch)
Casson (Sir Hugh; 1910–99, English)
Coates (Wells; 1895–1958, English)
Foster (Norman, Lord; 1935– , English)
Fowler (Sir Michael; 1929– , New Zealand)
Fuller (Buckminster; 1895–1983, US)
Geddes (Norman Bel; 1893–1958, US)
Geddes (Sir Patrick; 1854–1932, Scottish)
Giotto (c.1267–1337, Italian)
Graves (Michael; 1934– , US)
Howard (Sir Ebenezer; 1850–1928, English)
Keyser (Hendrik de; 1565–1621, Dutch)
Lasdun (Sir Denys; 1914–2001, English)
Ledoux (Claude Nicolas; 1736–1806, French)
Lescot (Pierre; c.1510–78, French)
Nouvel (Jean; 1945– , French)
Paxton (Sir Joseph; 1801–65, English)
Perret (Auguste; 1874–1954, French)
Pisano (Giovanni; c.1250–c.1320, Italian)
Pisano (Nicola; c.1225–c.1284, Italian)
Rogers (Richard, Lord; 1933– , English)
Safdie (Moshe; 1938– , Israeli/Canadian)
Serlio (Sebastiano; 1475–1554, Italian)
Smirke (Sir Robert; 1781–1867, English)
Spence (Sir Basil; 1907–76, Scottish)
Street (G E; 1824–81, English)
Stuart (James; 1713–88, English)
Tessin (Nicodemus the Elder; 1615–81, Swedish)
Tessin (Nicodemus the Younger; 1654–1728, Swedish)
Voysey (Charles; 1857–1941, English)
Wagner (Otto; 1841–1918, Austrian)
Wright (Frank Lloyd; 1867–1959, US)

07 Alberti (Leon Battista; 1404–72, Italian)
Asplund (Erik Gunnar; 1885–1940, Swedish)
Behrens (Peter; 1868–1940, German)
Berlage (H P; 1856–1934, Dutch)
Bernini (Gian Lorenzo; 1598–1680, Italian)
Bethune (Louise; 1856–1913, US)
Burnham (Daniel; 1846–1912, US)
Candela (Felix; 1910–97, Mexican)

Delorme (Philibert; c.1510–70, French)
Gabriel (Jacques-Ange; 1698–1782, French)
Garnier (Tony; 1869–1948, French)
Gilbert (Cass; 1859–1934, US)
Gropius (Walter; 1883–1969, US)
Guarini (Guarino; 1624–83, Italian)
Guimard (Hector; 1867–1942, French)
Holland (Henry; 1746–1806, English)
Ictinus (5cBC, Greek)
Imhotep (27cBC; Egyptian)
Johnson (Philip; 1906–2005, US)
L'Enfant (Pierre Charles; 1754–1825, US)
Lethaby (William; 1857–1931, English)
Lorimer (Sir Robert; 1864–1929, Scottish)
Lutyens (Sir Edwin; 1869–1944, English)
Maderna (Carlo; 1556–1629, Italian)
Maderno (Carlo; 1556–1629, Italian)
Mansard (François; 1598–1666, French)
Mansard (Jules; 1645–1708, French)
Mansart (François; 1598–1666, French)
Mansart (Jules; 1645–1708, French)
Neumann (Balthasar; 1687–1753,
  German)
Orcagna (c.1308–68, Italian)
Peruzzi (Baldassare; 1481–1536, Italian)
Poelzig (Hans; 1869–1936, German)
Renwick (James; 1818–95, US)
Thomson (Alexander 'Greek'; 1817–75,
  Scottish)
Venturi (Robert; 1925– , US)
Vignola (Giacomo da; 1507–73, Italian)

08 Bramante (Donato; 1444–1514, Italian)
Chambers (Sir William; 1726–96, Scottish)
Cullinan (Edward; 1931– , English)
Eisenman (Peter; 1932– , US)
Erickson (Arthur; 1924–2009, Canadian)
Figueroa (Leonardo de; c.1650–1730,
  Spanish)
Gwathmey (Charles; 1938–2009, US)
Hamilton (Thomas; 1784–1858, Scottish)
Hoffmann (Josef; 1870–1956, Austrian)
Jacobsen (Arne; 1902–71, Danish)
Leonardo (da Vinci; 1452–1519, Italian)
Lombardo (Pietro; c.1433–1515, Italian)
Makovecz (Imre; 1935–2011, Hungarian)
Miralles (Enric, 1955–2000, Spanish)
Niemeyer (Oscar; 1907–2012, Brazilian)
Palladio (Andrea; 1508–80, Italian)
Piranesi (Giambattista; 1720–78, Italian)
Playfair (William Henry; 1789–1857,
  Scottish)
Rietveld (Gerrit; 1888–1964, Dutch)

Saarinen (Eero; 1910–61, Finnish/US)
Saarinen (Eliel; 1873–1950, Finnish/US)
Schinkel (Karl Friedrich; 1781–1841,
  German)
Smythson (Robert; c.1535–1614, English)
Sottsass (Ettore, Jnr; 1917–2007, Italian)
Soufflot (Jacques Germain; 1709–80,
  French)
Stirling (James; 1926–92, Scottish)
Sullivan (Louis; 1856–1924, US)
Vanbrugh (Sir John; 1664–1726, English)

09 Blomfield (Sir Reginald; 1856–1942,
  English)
Borromini (Francesco; 1599–1667, Italian)
Chowdhury (Eulie; 1923– , Indian)
Cockerell (Charles Robert; 1788–1863,
  English)
Haussmann (Georges, Baron; 1809–91,
  French)
Hawksmoor (Nicholas; 1661–1736, English)
Labrouste (Henri; 1801–75, French)
Libeskind (Daniel; 1946– , US)
Mackmurdo (Arthur; 1851–1942, English)
Sansovino (1460–1529, Italian)
Sansovino (Jacopo; 1486–1570, Italian)
Vitruvius (1cAD, Roman)

10 Andronicus (1cBC, Greek)
Chermayeff (Serge; 1900–96, Russian/US)
Cyrrhestes (1cBC, Greek)
Darbyshire (Jane; 1948– , English)
Mackintosh (Charles Rennie; 1868–1928,
  Scottish)
Mendelsohn (Erich; 1887–1953, US)
Michelozzi (Michelozzo; 1396–1472,
  Italian)
Sanmichele (Michele; c.1484–1559, Italian)
Waterhouse (Alfred; 1830–1905, English)

11 Abercrombie (Sir Patrick; 1879–1957,
  English)
Butterfield (William; 1814–1900, English)
Callicrates (5cBC, Greek)
Churriguera (Don José; 1650–1725, Spanish)
Hertzberger (Herman; 1932– , Dutch)
Le Corbusier (1887–1965, French)

12 Brunelleschi (Filippo; 1377–1446, Italian)
Viollet-Le-Duc (Eugène; 1814–79, French)

14 Mies van der Rohe (Ludwig; 1886–1969,
  US)

15 Leonardo da Vinci (1452–1519, Italian)
Vitruvius Pollio (Marcus; 1cAD, Roman)

Terms used in architecture and building include:

03	CAD	jamb	**05**	Doric	groin
04	dado	plan		eaves	Ionic
	dome	roof		gable	model

ridge
Tudor
06 alcove
annexe
coving
dormer
duplex
façade
fascia
fillet
finial
frieze
Gothic
lintel
Norman
pagoda
plinth
reveal
rococo

See also **building**

scroll
soffit
stucco
Tuscan
07 baroque
cornice
festoon
fletton
fluting
mullion
pantile
parapet
rafters
Regency
rotunda
skywalk
08 baluster
capstone

dogtooth
dry-stone
fanlight
gargoyle
Georgian
pinnacle
sacristy
terrazzo
wainscot
09 bas relief
classical
decorated
Edwardian
elevation
gatehouse
Queen Anne
roughcast
skybridge

10 architrave
barge-board
Corinthian
drawbridge
flamboyant
groundplan
Romanesque
weathering
11 coping stone
cornerstone
Elizabethan
Flemish bond
12 Early English
French window
frontispiece
half-timbered
13 double glazing
14 casement window

area *see* **administrative area**

armour

Armour includes:

04 cush
gear
gere
jack
lame
mail
suit
tace
05 armet
brace
cuish
culet
curat
salet
tasse
visor
06 beaver
byrnie
casque
corium
couter
crinet
cuisse
curiet
faulds
gorget
greave
grille

gusset
helmet
jamber
morion
poleyn
rondel
salade
sallet
shield
taslet
tasset
tonlet
tuille
voider
07 ailette
barding
basinet
besagew
brasset
buckler
cap-à-pie
corslet
cuirass
harness
hauberk
jambeau
jambeux
jambier
lamboys

morrion
palette
placcat
placket
poitrel
puldron
sabaton
surcoat
ventail
08 aventail
bascinet
brassard
brassart
chaffron
chamfron
chausses
corselet
gauntlet
giambeux
jambeaux
jazerant
pauldron
pectoral
placcate
pouldron
shynbald
solleret
spaulder
vambrace

ventaile
ventayle
09 aventaile
backpiece
backplate
chain mail
chamfrain
garniture
habergeon
jesserant
mandilion
mandylion
nosepiece
rerebrace
vantbrace
vantbrass
10 body armour
cataphract
coat-armour
coat of mail
11 breastplate
genouillère
mentonnière
plate armour
scale armour
12 splint armour

army

Armies include:

02 AA	Red	**05** Sally	Salvation
SA	USA	**06** Church	**10** Blue Ribbon
TA	WLA	Tartan	Women's Land
03 AVR		**08** New Model	**11** Grande Armée
GAR	**04** BAOR	**09** Eurocorps	Territorial
IRA	INLA		

See also **military**; **regiment**

art

Arts and crafts include:

04 film	weaving	patchwork	psaligraphy
zari	**08** ceramics	sculpture	stitchcraft
05 batik	graphics	sketching	watercolour
video	knitting	woodcraft	woodcarving
06 fresco	painting	**10** basketwork	wood cutting
mosaic	pencraft	caricature	**12** animatronics
saikei	spinning	embroidery	architecture
07 carving	tapestry	enamelling	chalcography
collage	tsutsumu	needlework	illustration
crochet	**09** animation	xylography	stained glass
drawing	cloisonné	**11** calligraphy	**13** digital design
etching	engraving	lithography	graphic design
ikebana	jewellery	needlecraft	wood engraving
origami	marquetry	oil painting	**14** relief printing
pottery	metalwork	photography	screenprinting
	modelling	portraiture	

Schools, movements and styles of art include:

02 Op	netPop	Futurism	**10** arte povera
03 mec	Purism	graffiti	Automatism
PRB	Rayism	informel	bande noire
YBA	Rococo	Intimism	Biomorphic
04 BMPT	**07** Baroque	Japonism	Classicism
Brit	Bauhaus	kakemono	Conceptual
Brut	Dadaism	Luminism	Literalism
Dada	digital	OuPeinPo	Minimalism
Deco	Fauvism	Pont-Aven	Naturalism
funk	Kinetic	Rayonism	New Realism
Madí	New York	Tachisme	Romanesque
Merz	Nouveau	Venetian	Section d'Or
Nabi	Optical	**09** Die Brücke	Surrealism
05 Cobra	Orphism	Encaustic	troubadour
Hague	Plastic	Formalism	**11** anacronismo
Lyons	Realism	Intimisme	bad painting
Mosan	Tachism	Mannerism	Blaue Reiter
Naïve	**08** Abstract	Modernism	Caravaggism
video	Atticism	Nazarenes	Divisionism
Zebra	Barbizon	Rubénisme	Eclecticism
06 Cubism	Concrete	Symbolism	Glasgow Boys
fluxus	Feminist	Tenebrism	Macchiaioli
		Vorticism	Orientalism

Pointillism
Primitivism
Renaissance
Romanticism
spazialismo
Suprematism
Synchronism
12 Aestheticism

Hyperrealism
Magic Realism
Mir Iskusstva
non-figuratif
Non-objective
Photorealism
pittura colta
Quattrocento

second empire
Superrealism
13 Arts and Crafts
Expressionism
Impressionism
Neoclassicism
Neo-Plasticism
Post-Modernism

Social Realism
14 Action Painting
Constructivism
Post-Minimalism
Pre-Raphaelites
15 Camden Town
    Group
    nouveau réalisme

Artists, craftsmen and craftswomen include:

05 video
06 etcher
    limner
    master
    potter
    weaver
07 graphic
    painter
    printer
08 animator

designer
engraver
graffiti
pavement
sculptor
09 architect
carpenter
colourist
craftsman
goldsmith

10 blacksmith
cartoonist
conceptual
oil painter
11 coppersmith
craftswoman
draughtsman
illustrator
miniaturist
performance

portraitist
silversmith
web designer
12 caricaturist
lithographer
photographer
13 draughtswoman
screenprinter
14 watercolourist
15 graphic designer

Art materials and art terms include:

03 ink
04 term
    wash
05 cameo
    easel
    fitch
    liner
    sable
    smock
    turps
    video
06 badger
    crayon

fusain
pastel
pencil
relief
sketch
tusche
07 atelier
cartoon
digital
grainer
modello
organic
palette
scumble

torchon
08 abstract
alfresco
charcoal
gumption
intaglio
monotint
paintbox
pastille
terminus
09 lay-figure
maulstick
pen and ink

stretcher
10 delineavit
from nature
paintbrush
sketchbook
turpentine
11 perspective
trompe l'oeil
wash drawing
12 installation
underdrawing
13 social realism
15 oil of turpentine

See also **cartoon; Japan; paint; photography**

artery

Arteries include:

05 aorta (heart)
    renal (kidney)
    ulnar (arm)
06 radial (arm)
07 carotid (neck)
    coeliac (gut)
    femoral (thigh)

hepatic (liver)
splenic (spleen)
08 brachial (arm)
coronary (heart)
09 popliteal (leg)
pulmonary (lung)
spermatic (testes)

10 innominate (neck)
mesenteric (gut)
subclavian (upper body)
11 common iliac (groin)
14 anterior tibial (leg)
15 brachiocephalic (neck)
posterior tibial (leg)

See also **vein**

Arthurian legend *see* **legend**

Asia

Countries in Asia include:

04 Laos	Vietnam	**09** East Timor	Tajikistan
05 China	**08** Cambodia	Indonesia	Uzbekistan
India	Malaysia	Singapore	**11** Afghanistan
Japan	Maldives	**10** Bangladesh	Philippines
Nepal	Mongolia	Kazakhstan	**12** Turkmenistan
06 Bhutan	Pakistan	Kyrgyzstan	
Taiwan	Sri Lanka	North Korea	
07 Myanmar (Burma)	Thailand	South Korea	

Cities and notable towns in Asia include:

03 Osh (Kyrgyzstan)

04 Agra (India)
Baku (Azerbaijan)
Gifu (Japan)
Jixi (China)
Kobe (Japan)
Kota (India)
Kure (Japan)
Mary (Turkmenistan)
Naha (Japan)
Nara (Japan)
Oita (Japan)
Wuhu (China)
Wuxi (China)
Xian (China)
Zibo (China)

05 Adana (Turkey)
Ajmer (India)
Akita (Japan)
Baoji (China)
Benxi (China)
Bursa (Turkey)
Chiba (Japan)
Delhi (India)
Dhaka (Bangladesh)
Dukou (China)
Fukui (Japan)
Fuxin (China)
Gäncä (Azerbaijan)
Haeju (North Korea)
Hefei (China)
Herat (Afghanistan)
Hubli (India)
Iwaki (Japan)
Izmir (Turkey)
Jilin (China)
Jinan (China)
Kabul (Afghanistan)
Kandy (Sri Lanka)
Kochi (Japan)
Konya (Turkey)
Kyoto (Japan)

Masan (South Korea)
Nampo (North Korea)
Omiya (Japan)
Osaka (Japan)
Patan (Nepal)
Patna (India)
Poona (India)
Pusan (South Korea)
Sakai (Japan)
Semey (Kazakhstan)
Seoul (South Korea)
Surat (India)
Suwon (South Korea)
Taegu (South Korea)
Taraz (Kazakhstan)
Tokyo (Japan)
Ulsan (South Korea)
Urawa (Japan)
Wuhan (China)

06 Almaty (Kazakhstan)
Ankara (Turkey)
Anshan (China)
Anyang (China)
Aqtöbe (Kazakhstan)
Astana (Kazakhstan)
Baotou (China)
Batumi (Georgia)
Bhopal (India)
Cochin (India)
Dalian (China)
Daqing (China)
Datong (China)
Fushun (China)
Fuzhou (China)
Guilin (China)
Guntur (India)
Gyumri (Armenia)
Handan (China)
Harbin (China)
Hegang (China)
Himeji (Japan)
Hohhot (China)

Howrah (India)
Inchon (South Korea)
Indore (India)
Jaffna (Sri Lanka)
Jaipur (India)
Kanpur (India)
Khulna (Bangladesh)
Kulyab (Tajikistan)
Lahore (Pakistan)
Leshan (China)
Meerut (India)
Multan (Pakistan)
Mumbai (India)
Mysore (India)
Nagano (Japan)
Nagoya (Japan)
Nagpur (India)
Ningbo (China)
Quetta (Pakistan)
Raipur (India)
Rajkot (India)
Ranchi (India)
Sendai (Japan)
Sukkur (Pakistan)
Suzhou (China)
Taejon (South Korea)
Tainan (Taiwan)
T'aipei (Taiwan)
Toyama (Japan)
Urumqi (China)
Wonsan (North Korea)
Xiamen (China)
Xining (China)
Xuzhou (China)
Yantai (China)
Yichun (China)
Zigong (China)

07 Aligarh (India)
Andijon (Uzbekistan)
Asansol (India)
Baoding (China)
Beijing (China)

Bishkek (Kyrgyzstan)
Bukhara (Uzbekistan)
Chengdu (China)
Chennai (India)
Chifeng (China)
Chilung (Taiwan)
Chungho (Taiwan)
Colombo (Sri Lanka)
Dandong (China)
Fukuoka (Japan)
Ganzhou (China)
Guiyang (China)
Gwalior (India)
Hamhung (North Korea)
Huaibei (China)
Huainan (China)
Jessore (Bangladesh)
Jiamusi (China)
Jiaozuo (China)
Jinzhou (China)
Jodhpur (India)
Kaesong (North Korea)
Kaifeng (China)
Karachi (Pakistan)
Kayseri (Turkey)
Khoqand (Uzbekistan)
Kolkata (India)
Kunming (China)
Kutaisi (Georgia)
Kwangju (South Korea)
Lanzhou (China)
Liuzhou (China)
Lucknow (India)
Luoyang (China)
Madurai (India)
Matsudo (Japan)
Nanjing (China)
Nanning (China)
Nantong (China)
Niigata (Japan)
Okayama (Japan)
Qingdao (China)
Qiqihar (China)
Rustavi (Georgia)
Sapporo (Japan)
Shantou (China)
Shihezi (China)
Sialkot (Pakistan)
Sinuiju (North Korea)
Taiyuan (China)
Tbilisi (Georgia)
Thimphu (Bhutan)
Tianjin (China)
Tonghua (China)
Weifang (China)
Wenzhou (China)
Yakeshi (China)
Yerevan (Armenia)

Yichang (China)
Yingkou (China)
Zhuzhou (China)
08 Amritsar (India)
Ashgabat (Turkmenistan)
Bareilly (India)
Changsha (China)
Chimkent (Kazakhstan)
Chongjin (North Korea)
Dashoguz (Turkmenistan)
Durgapur (India)
Dushanbe (Tajikistan)
Ferghana (Uzbekistan)
Fukuyama (Japan)
Guwahati (India)
Hachioji (Japan)
Hakodate (Japan)
Hangzhou (China)
Hengyang (China)
Hong Kong (China)
Huangshi (China)
Hunjiang (China)
Ichikawa (Japan)
Istanbul (Turkey)
Jabalpur (India)
Kanazawa (Japan)
Kandahar (Afghanistan)
Kawasaki (Japan)
Khudzand (Tajikistan)
Kimchaek (North Korea)
Kolhapur (India)
Koriyama (Japan)
Kumamoto (Japan)
Kustanay (Kazakhstan)
Liaoyang (China)
Liaoyuan (China)
Ludhiana (India)
Maebashi (Japan)
Miyazaki (Japan)
Nagasaki (Japan)
Namangan (Uzbekistan)
Nanchang (China)
New Delhi (India)
Panchiao (Taiwan)
Pavlodar (Kazakhstan)
Peshawar (Pakistan)
Sargodha (Pakistan)
Shanghai (China)
Shaoguan (China)
Shenyang (China)
Shenzhen (China)
Shizuoka (Japan)
Sholapur (India)
Srinagar (India)
Sumqayit (Azerbaijan)
Taichung (Taiwan)
Tangshan (China)
Tashkent (Uzbekistan)

Vadodara (India)
Vanadzor (Armenia)
Varanasi (India)
Wakayama (Japan)
Warangal (India)
Xiangfan (China)
Xiangtan (China)
Xinxiang (China)
Yamagata (Japan)
Yangquan (China)
Yinchuan (China)
Yokohama (Japan)
Yokosuka (Japan)
09 Ahmadabad (India)
Allahabad (India)
Amagasaki (Japan)
Asahikawa (Japan)
Bangalore (India)
Bhaktapur (Nepal)
Bhavnagar (India)
Changchun (China)
Changzhou (China)
Chongqing (China)
Eskiçehir (Turkey)
Faridabad (India)
Fukushima (Japan)
Funabashi (Japan)
Gaziantep (Turkey)
Gorakhpur (India)
Guangzhou (China)
Hamamatsu (Japan)
Hiroshima (Japan)
Hyderabad (India)
Hyderabad (Pakistan)
Islamabad (Pakistan)
Jalalabad (Afghanistan)
Jalandhar (India)
Kagoshima (Japan)
Kaohsiung (Taiwan)
Karaganda (Kazakhstan)
Kathmandu (Nepal)
Kawaguchi (Japan)
Kyzyl-Kiya (Kyrgyzstan)
Matsuyama (Japan)
Moradabad (India)
Pingxiang (China)
Pyongyang (North Korea)
Samarkand (Uzbekistan)
Takamatsu (Japan)
Tokushima (Japan)
Toyohashi (Japan)
Ulan Bator (Mongolia)
Zhengzhou (China)
Zhenjiang (China)
10 Bahawalpur (Pakistan)
Balkanabat (Turkmenistan)
Chandigarh (India)

Chittagong (Bangladesh)
Coimbatore (India)
Diyarbakir (Turkey)
Faisalabad (Pakistan)
Gujranwala (Pakistan)
Jamshedpur (India)
Jingdezhen (China)
Kitakyushu (Japan)
Liupanshui (China)
Mudanjiang (China)
Przhevalsk (Kyrgyzstan)

Rawalpindi (Pakistan)
Sagamihara (Japan)
Trivandrum (India)
Utsunomiya (Japan)
Vijayawada (India)
11 Bhubaneswar (India)
Gandhinagar (India)
Kurgan-Tyube (Tajikistan)
Lianyungang (China)
Narayanganj (Bangladesh)
Qinhuangdao (China)

Zhangjiakou (China)
12 Higashiosaka (Japan)
Mazar-e-Sharif
(Afghanistan)
Pingdingshan (China)
Shijiazhuang (China)
Shuangyashan (China)
Türkmenbashi
(Turkmenistan)
13 Petropavlovsk (Kazakhstan)
Visakhapatnam (India)

Asians include:

03 Han	**06** Afghan	Kirghiz	**09** Bhutanese
Lao	Baluch	Laotian	Cambodian
04 Ainu	Gurkha	Manchoo	Malaysian
Cham	Indian	Maratha	Mongolian
Nair	Kazakh	Russian	Pakistani
Shan	Kyrgyz	Tadzhik	Sri Lankan
Sulu	Manchu	Tagálog	Taiwanese
Thai	Mongol	Turkish	**10** Indonesian
05 Bajau	Pathan	Turkmen	Myanmarese
Karen	Tadjik		Vietnamese
Kazak	Telugu	**08** Bruneian	**11** Azerbaijani
Nayar	**07** Baluchi	Canarese	Bangladeshi
Tajik	Burmese	Filipina	Kazakhstani
Tamil	Chinese	Filipino	North Korean
Uzbeg	Goanese	Japanese	Singaporean
Uzbek	Goorkha	Kanarese	South Korean
Vedda	Karenni	Mahratta	Tajikistani
		Nepalese	

Asian landmarks include:

05 Indus (China/India/Pakistan)

06 Mekong (south-east Asia)

07 Everest (China/Nepal)

08 Krakatoa (Indonesia)
Lake Sebu (Philippines)
Red River (China/Vietnam)

09 Angkor Wat (Cambodia)
Annapurna (Nepal)
Himalayas (central Asia)

See also **China**; **India**; **Japan**

Mt Everest (China/Nepal)

10 Gobi Desert (China/Mongolia)
River Indus (China/India/Pakistan)
Sagarmatha (China/Nepal)

11 Mekong River (south-east Asia)

12 Raffles Hotel (Singapore)

13 Kangchenjunga (India/Nepal)

14 Jaganath Temple (Nepal)

assassin *see* **murder**

assembly *see* **parliament**

asteroid

Asteroids include:

04 Eros	Iris	**05** Ceres	Metis
Hebe	Juno	Flora	Vesta

06 Apollo
   Cybele
   Davida

Europa
Hygiea
Icarus

Pallas
Psyche
Trojan

07 Eunomia

10 Interamnia

astrology

Terms used in astrology include:

02 IC
   MC
   ox
03 age
   air
   arc
   dog
   Leo
   orb
   pig
   rat
   sun
04 aura
   cast
   cusp
   fate
   fire
   goat
   Mars
   moon
   node
   star
   wood
05 Aries
   earth
   horse
   house

Libra
metal
Pluto
snake
tiger
trine
Venus
Virgo
water
06 apogee
   aspect
   astral
   Cancer
   dragon
   Gemini
   monkey
   occult
   oracle
   Pisces
   planet
   rabbit
   Saturn
   spirit
   Taurus
   trigon
   Uranus
   zodiac
07 Admetos

Apollon
destiny
element
equinox
fortune
Jupiter
Mercury
Neptune
rooster
Scorpio
sextile
transit
08 anaretic
   Aquarius
   forecast
   quartile
   quincunx
   quintile
   solstice
   star sign
   synastry
09 ascendant
   aspectual
   Capricorn
   celestial
   horoscope
   Imum Coeli
   influence

infortune
planetary
spiritual
10 astrologer
   birthchart
   descendant
   dispositor
   exaltation
   numerology
   opposition
   prediction
   retrograde
11 astrologian
   astrologist
   conjunction
   Medium Coeli
   progression
   Sagittarius
   satellitium
12 astroanalyst
   degree of fate
   planet-struck
   significator
13 constellation
14 acronycal place
   planet-stricken

See also **birth symbol**; **zodiac**

astronaut

Astronauts include:

04 Bean (Alan; 1932– , US)
   Ride (Sally; 1951–2012, US)

05 Foale (Michael; 1957– , English)
   Glenn (John; 1921– , US)
   Irwin (James; 1930–91, US)
   Scott (David; 1932– , US)
   Titov (Gherman; 1935–2000, Soviet)
   White (Edward; 1930–67, US)

06 Aldrin (Edwin 'Buzz'; 1930– , US)
   Conrad (Charles 'Pete'; 1930–99, US)
   Leonov (Aleksei; 1934– , Russian)
   Lovell (James 'Jim'; 1928– , US)

See also **space travel**

07 Chaffee (Roger; 1935–67, US)
   Collins (Eileen; 1956– , US)
   Collins (Michael; 1930– , US)
   Gagarin (Yuri; 1934–68, Soviet)
   Grissom (Gus; 1926–67, US)
   Schirra (Wally; 1923–2007, US)
   Sharman (Helen; 1963– , English)
   Shepard (Alan; 1923–98, US)

08 Mitchell (Edgar; 1930– , US)
   Williams (Sunita; 1965– , US)

09 Armstrong (Neil; 1930–2012, US)

10 Tereshkova (Valentina; 1937– , Russian)

astronomy

Astronomers and astrophysicists include:

04 Airy (Sir George; 1801–92, English)
Biot (Jean Baptiste; 1774–1862, French)
Gold (Thomas; 1920–2004, US)
Hale (George; 1868–1938, US)
Lyot (Bernard; 1897–1952, French)
Oort (Jan; 1900–92, Dutch)
Pond (John; 1767–1836, English)
Rees (Sir Martin; 1942– , English)
Ryle (Sir Martin; 1918–84, English)
Saha (Meghnad; 1894–1956, Indian)
Webb (James E; 1906–92, US)

05 Adams (John Couch; 1819–92, English)
Adams (Walter S; 1876–1956, US)
Baade (Walter; 1893–1960, US)
Baily (Francis; 1774–1844, English)
Bliss (Nathaniel; 1700–64, English)
Brahe (Tycho; 1546–1601, Danish)
Brown (John Campbell; 1947– , Scottish)
Dyson (Sir Frank; 1868–1939, English)
Gauss (Carl Friedrich; 1777–1855, German)
Hoyle (Sir Fred; 1915–2001, English)
Jeans (Sir James; 1877–1946, English)
Jones (Sir Harold Spencer; 1890–1960, English)
Milne (Edward; 1896–1950, English)
Moore (Sir Patrick; 1923–2012, English)
Reiss (Adam; 1969– , US)
Sagan (Carl; 1934–96, US)
Smith (Sir Francis Graham-; 1923– , English)
Vogel (Hermann; 1841–1907, German)

06 Bessel (Friedrich; 1784–1846, German)
Halley (Edmond; 1656–1742, English)
Hewish (Antony; 1924– , English)
Hubble (Edwin; 1889–1953, US)
Jansky (Karl; 1905–50, US)
Kepler (Johannes; 1571–1630, German)
Kuiper (Gerard; 1905–73, US)
Lovell (Sir Bernard; 1913–2012, English)
Olbers (Heinrich Wilhelm; 1758–1840, German)
Piazzi (Giuseppe; 1746–1826, Italian)
Roemer (Olaus; 1644–1710, Danish)

07 Babcock (Harold D; 1882–1968, US)
Barnard (Edward Emerson; 1857–1923, US)
Bradley (James; 1693–1762, English)
Cassini (Giovanni; 1625–1712, French)
Celsius (Anders; 1701–44, Swedish)
Galilei (Galileo; 1564–1642, Italian)
Galileo (1564–1642, Italian)
Hawking (Stephen; 1942– , English)
Huggins (Sir William; 1824–1910, English)
Korolev (Sergei; 1907–66, Soviet)

Langley (Samuel; 1834–1906, US)
Laplace (Pierre, Marquis de; 1749–1827, French)
Lockyer (Sir Norman; 1836–1920, English)
Maunder (E W; 1851–1924, English)
Michell (John; 1724–93, English)
Penrose (Sir Roger; 1931– , English)
Penzias (Arno; 1933– , US)
Ptolemy (c.90–168 AD, Egyptian)
Russell (Henry Norris; 1877–1957, US)
Sandage (Allan; 1926–2010, US)
Schmidt (Brian; 1967– , US)
Schmidt (Maarten; 1929– , US)
Seyfert (Carl; 1911–60, US)
Shapley (Harlow; 1885–1972, US)
Slipher (Vesto; 1875–1969, US)
Whipple (Fred; 1906–2004, US)
Woolley (Sir Richard; 1906–86, English)

08 Burbidge (Geoffrey; 1925–2010, English)
Burbidge (Margaret; 1923– , English)
Chandler (Seth Carlo; 1846–1913, US)
Christie (Sir William; 1845–1922, English)
Douglass (Andrew Ellicott; 1867–1962, US)
Friedman (Herbert; 1916–2000, US)
Herschel (Caroline; 1750–1848, German/British)
Herschel (Sir John; 1792–1871, English)
Herschel (Sir William; 1738–1822, British)
Lemaître (Georges; 1894–1966, Belgian)
Tombaugh (Clyde W; 1906–97, US)
Trumpler (Robert; 1886–1956, US)

09 Eddington (Sir Arthur; 1882–1944, English)
Fabricius (David; 1564–1617, German)
Flamsteed (John; 1646–1719, English)
Maskelyne (Nevil; 1732–1811, English)
Sosigenes (fl.c.40 BC, Egyptian)

10 Carrington (Richard; 1826–75, English)
Copernicus (Nicolas; 1473–1543, Polish)
Hipparchos (c.180–125 BC, Greek)
Perlmutter (Saul; 1959– , US)
Wolfendale (Sir Arnold; 1927– , English)

11 Bell Burnell (Dame Jocelyn; 1943– , Northern Irish)
Graham-Smith (Sir Francis; 1923– , English)
Hertzsprung (Ejnar; 1873–1967, Danish)
Tsiolkovsky (Konstantin; 1857–1935, Russian)

12 Schiaparelli (Giovanni; 1835–1910, Italian)

13 Chandrasekhar (Subrahmanyan; 1910–95, US)
Schwarzschild (Karl; 1873–1916, German)

Terms used in astronomy include:

03 GUT
NEO
sun

04 core
flux
moon
node
nova
star
Yagi

05 comet
coudé
epoch
giant
orbit
rings
umbra

06 apogee
blazar
corona
cosmos
galaxy
jansky
lander
meteor
nebula
parsec
planet
pulsar
quasar
spinar
syzygy

07 almanac
anomaly
azimuth
big bang
eclipse
Metonic

nocturn
perigee
transit

08 aphelion
asteroid
cosmical
ecliptic
emersion
evection
gas giant
inferior
infrared
Milky Way
nutation
parallax
prograde
red dwarf
red giant
red shift
subgiant
sunspots
totality
Tychonic
universe

09 air shower
astrodome
black body
black hole
coelostat
collapsar
ephemeris
exoplanet
great year
hour-angle
hypernova
immersion
magnitude
Oort cloud
polar axis

protostar
radio star
Roche lobe
satellite
shell star
supernova
telescope

10 aberration
almacantar
astrometry
binary star
black dwarf
brown dwarf
Copernican
cosmic rays
dark energy
dark matter
double star
inequality
Kuiper Belt
Local Group
luminosity
periastron
perihelion
retrograde
Roche limit
supergiant
white dwarf

11 Baily's beads
bright giant
declination
gegenschein
helium flash
magnetotail
neutron star
observatory
occultation
singularity
solar system

12 binary pulsar
cosmic string
Doppler shift
event horizon
galactic halo
heliocentric
main sequence
meteor shower
Metonic cycle
periselenium
perturbation
shepherd moon
spectral type
spiral galaxy
supercluster

13 accretion disk
celestial body
constellation
Olbers' paradox
Seyfert galaxy
solar constant
synodic period
X-ray astronomy

14 celestial poles
Chandler wobble
closed universe
equation of time
Hubble constant
radar astronomy
right ascension
space telescope

15 armillary sphere
celestial sphere
Cepheid variable
eclipsing binary
globular cluster
Hubble telescope
near-Earth object

See also **asteroid**; **astronaut**; **comet**; **constellation**; **galaxy**; **meteor**; **moon**; **observatory**;
planet; **satellite**; **space travel**; **star**

astrophysics *see* **astronomy**

athletics

Athletics events include:

04 100m
200m
400m
800m
dash
mile
shot

05 1,500m

3,000m
5,000m
field
relay
track

06 10,000m
discus
hammer

sprint

07 hurdles
javelin
shot put

08 10km walk
16lb ball
20km walk
22lb ball

50km walk
biathlon
high jump
long jump
marathon
tug-of-war

09 broad jump
caber toss

decathlon	pentathlon	400m hurdles	javelin throw
pole vault	tetrathlon	discus throw	steeplechase
sheaf toss	triple jump	fell running	**13** sprint hurdles
triathlon	**11** 100m hurdles	hammer throw	**14** hop, step and jump
10 16lb hammer	110m hurdles	high hurdles	**15** tossing the caber
22lb hammer	4×100m relay	race walking	
heptathlon	4×400m relay	**12** half marathon	

Athletes include:

03 Coe (Sebastian, Lord; 1956– , English)

04 Bolt (Usain; 1986– , Jamaican)
Budd (Zola; 1966– , South African)
Cram (Steve; 1960– , English)
Ewry (Ray; 1873–1937, US)
Koch (Marita; 1957– , German)
Mota (Rosa; 1958– , Portuguese)
Tyus (Wyomia; 1945– , US)

05 Balas (Iolanda; 1936– , Romanian)
Bubka (Sergey; 1963– , Ukrainian)
Defar (Meseret; 1983– , Ethiopian)
Ennis (Jessica; 1986– , English)
Etone (Françoise Mbango; 1976– , Cameroon)
Farah (Mohamed; 1983– , Somali/English)
Felix (Allyson; 1985– , US)
Jamal (Maryam Jusuf; 1984– , Bahraini)
Jones (Marion; 1975– , US)
Keino (Kip; 1940– , Kenyan)
Lewis (Carl; 1961– , US)
Lewis (Denise; 1972– , English)
Moses (Ed; 1955– , US)
Nurmi (Paavo; 1897–1973, Finnish)
Ottey (Merlene; 1960– , Jamaican/Slovenian)
Ovett (Steve; 1955– , English)
Owens (Jesse; 1913–80, US)
Pérec (Marie-José; 1968– , French)
Snell (Peter; 1938– , New Zealand)
Viren (Lasse; 1949– , Finnish)
Waitz (Grete; 1953– , Norwegian)
Wells (Allan; 1952– , Scottish)
Xiang (Liu; 1983– , Chinese)

06 Aouita (Said; 1960– , Moroccan)
Barber (Eunice; 1974– , French)
Beamon (Bob; 1946– , US)
Bekele (Kenenisa; 1982– , Ethiopian)
Bikila (Abebe; 1932–73, Ethiopian)
Borzov (Valeri; 1949– , Ukrainian)
Boston (Ralph; 1939– , US)
Clarke (Ron; 1937– , Australian)
Devers (Gail; 1966– , US)
Dibaba (Tirunesh; 1985– , Ethiopian)
Dvořák (Tomáš; 1972– , Czech)
Foster (Brendan; 1948– , English)
Greene (Maurice; 1974– , US)
Holmes (Dame Kelly; 1970– , English)
Kemboi (Ezekiel; 1982– , Kenyan)

Mutola (Maria; 1972– , Mozambican)
Oerter (Al; 1936–2007, US)
Peters (Mary; 1939– , Northern Irish)
Powell (Asafa; 1982– , Jamaican)
Slaney (Mary Decker; 1958– , US)
Wöckel (Bärbel; 1955– , German)
Yifter (Miruts, c.1938– , Ethiopian)

07 Backley (Steve; 1969– , English)
Edwards (Jonathan; 1966– , English)
Elliott (Herb; 1938– , Australian)
Fosbury (Dick; 1947– , US)
Freeman (Cathy; 1973– , Australian)
Gunnell (Sally; 1966– , English)
Jackson (Colin; 1967– , Welsh)
Johnson (Ben; 1961– , Canadian)
Johnson (Michael; 1967– , US)
Liddell (Eric; 1902–45, Scottish)
Rudolph (Wilma; 1940–94, US)
Shorter (Frank; 1947– , US)
Stecher (Renate; 1950– , German)
Wariner (Jeremy; 1984– , US)
Zatopek (Emil; 1922–2000, Czech)
Zelezny (Jan; 1966– , Czech)

08 Brownlee (Alistair; 1988– , English)
Brownlee (Jonathan; 1990– , English)
Christie (Linford; 1960– , English)
Crawford (Shawn 1978– , US)
Cuthbert (Betty; 1938– , Australian)
Guerrouj (Hicham el-; 1974– , Moroccan)
Kipketer (Wilson; 1970– , Kenyan/Danish)
McColgan (Liz; 1964– , Scottish)
Morcelli (Noureddine; 1977– , Algerian)
Ohuruogu (Christine; 1984– , English)
Phillips (Dwight; 1977– , US)
Thompson (Daley; 1958– , English)
Zaharias (Babe; 1914–56, US)

09 Bannister (Sir Roger; 1929– , English)
Boulmerka (Hassiba; 1968– , Algerian)
de la Hunty (Shirley; 1925–2004, Australian)
Drechsler (Heike; 1964– , German)
Ennis-Hill (Jessica; 1986– , English)
Jepkosgei (Janeth; 1983– , Kenyan)
Kazankina (Tatyana; 1951– , Russian)
O'Sullivan (Sonia; 1969– , Irish)
Radcliffe (Paula; 1973– , English)
Sanderson (Tessa; 1956– , English)
Špotáková (Babora; 1981– , Czech)

Szewinska (Irena; 1946–   , Polish)
Warmerdam (Cornelius 'Dutch'; 1915–2001, US)
Whitbread (Fatima; 1961–   , English)
10 Isinbayeva (Yelena; 1982–   , Russian)
Wang Junxia (1973–   , Chinese)
11 Kristiansen (Ingrid; 1956–   , Norwegian)
Newby-Fraser (Paula; 1962–   , South African)
Thorkildsen (Andreas; 1982–   , Norwegian)
12 Blankers-Koen (Fanny; 1918–2004, Dutch)
Gebrselassie (Haile; 1973–   , Ethiopian)
Grey-Thompson (Dame Tanni; 1969–   , Welsh)
Joyner-Kersee (Jackie; 1962–   , US)
13 Campbell-Brown (Veronica; 1982–   , Jamaican)
14 Griffith Joyner (Florence; 1959–98, US)

Athletics terms include:

02 PB	skip	qualify	plasticine
SB	step	red flag	**11** Fosbury flop
03 air	walk	shot put	heptathlete
bar	**05** baton	starter	photo finish
box	board	unpaced	season's best
dip	break		track record
hop	field	**08** deselect	western roll
lap	prize	distance	
leg	relay	gymkhana	**12** back straight
pit	track	straight	home straight
			long distance
04 bend	**06** blocks	**09** hitch kick	personal best
bore	circle	pacemaker	reaction time
fail	no jump	pancratic	take-over zone
foul	record	pole vault	wind-assisted
heat	runway	water jump	
jump	spikes	white flag	**13** following wind
kick	Tartan®	**10** disqualify	**14** crouching start
lane		false start	middle distance
race	**07** boxed in	finish line	staggered start

See also **Olympic Games**; **Paralympic Games**; **sport**

atmosphere

Atmospheric layers include:

09 exosphere	**10** ionosphere	tropopause	**12** plasmasphere
ionopause	mesosphere	**11** stratopause	stratosphere
mesopause	ozone layer	troposphere	thermosphere

atom

Subatomic particles include:

01 W	preon	nucleon	down quark
X	quark	pi meson	gravitron
Z	sigma	up quark	tau lepton
03 psi	**06** baryon	upsilon	**10** anti-proton
04 J/psi	B-meson	**08** electron	gauge boson
kaon	hadron	neutrino	truth quark
muon	lambda	neutrino (electron)	**11** anti-neutron
pion	lepton	neutrino (muon)	beauty quark
05 boson	parton	neutrino (tau)	bottom quark
gluon	photon	positron	**12** anti-neutrino
meson	proton	top quark	charmed quark
omega	**07** neutron	**09** antiquark	strange quark

aunt

Aunts include:

02 Em (*The Wonderful Wizard of Oz*, 1900, L Frank Baum)

03 Dot (*The Towers of Trebizond*, 1956, Rose Macaulay)

04 Doom (Ada; *Cold Comfort Farm*, 1932, Stella Gibbons)
Gray (Ruth; *Epitaph for George Dillon*, 1954, John Osborne and Anthony Creighton)
Jean (*Tingha and Tucker*, TV)
Monk (Lady; *Can You Forgive Her?*, 1864–65, Anthony Trollope)
Reed (Mrs; *Jane Eyre*, 1847, Charlotte Brontë)
Zita (*Wild Nights*, 1979, Emma Tennant)

05 Glegg (Mrs; *The Mill on the Floss*, 1860, George Eliot)
Hamps (Clara; *Clayhanger*, 1910, Arnold Bennett)
Julia (*Aunt Julia and the Scriptwriter*, 1977, Mario Vargas Llosa)
Livia (*Women Beware Women*, c.1621, Thomas Middleton)
March (*Little Women*, 1868, Louisa M Alcott)
Mildy (*Langton Tetralogy*, 1952–62, Martin Boyd)
Polly (*The Adventures of Tom Sawyer*, 1876, Mark Twain)
Sally
Scott (Vanessa; *Careful, He Might Hear You*, 1963, Sumner Locke Elliott)

06 Agatha (*The Family Reunion*, 1939, T S Eliot)
Baines (Lila; *Careful, He Might Hear You*, 1963, Sumner Locke Elliott)
Dahlia (*Carry On, Jeeves*, 1925, et seq, P G Wodehouse)
Fisher (Sylvie; *Housekeeping*, 1980, Marilynne Robinson)
Lizzie (*Philadelphia, Here I Come!*, 1965, Brian Friel)
Lowder (Mrs; *The Wings of the Dove*, 1902, Henry James)
Maylie (Rose; *Oliver Twist*, 1838, Charles Dickens)
Morton (Jean; *Tingha and Tucker*, TV)
Nellie (*The Dressmaker*, 1973, Beryl Bainbridge)
Poyser (Mrs; *Adam Bede*, 1859, George Eliot)
Pullet (Mrs; *The Mill on the Floss*, 1860, George Eliot)

Rayner (Claire; 1931–2010, English)
Sophie (*Act of Darkness*, 1983, Francis King)

07 Barbary (Miss; *Bleak House*, 1853, Charles Dickens)
Bertram (Augusta; *Travels with My Aunt*, 1969, Graham Greene)
Failing (Emily; *The Longest Journey*, 1907, E M Forster)
Flowers (Margaret; *The Magic Toyshop*, 1967, Angela Carter)
Forsyte (Ann; *The Forsyte Saga*, 1922, John Galsworthy)
Langton (Mildred; *Langton Tetralogy*, 1952–62, Martin Boyd)
Rickard (Miss; *No Laughing Matter*, 1967, Angus Wilson)
Spenser (Lucy; *Love Always*, 1985, Ann Beattie)

08 Charley's (*Charley's Aunt*, 1892, Brandon Thomas)
de Bourgh (Lady Catherine; *Pride and Prejudice*, 1813, Jane Austen)
Malaprop (Mrs; *The Rivals*, 1775, Richard Brinsley Sheridan)
Pontifex (Alethea; *The Way of All Flesh*, 1903, Samuel Butler)
Slingsby, (Helen; *Prufrock and Other Observations*, 1917, T S Eliot)
Trotwood (Betsey; *David Copperfield*, 1850, Charles Dickens)
Willowes (Lolly; *Lolly Willowes*, 1926, Sylvia Townsend Warner)
Wishfort (Lady; *The Way of the World*, 1700, William Congreve)

09 Bordereau (Miss; *The Aspern Papers*, 1888, Henry James)
Bracknell (Lady; *The Importance of Being Earnest*, 1895, Oscar Wilde)
McPherson (Cathy; *The Tax Inspector*, 1991, Peter Carey)
Poppyseed (Philomela; *Headlong Hall*, 1816, Thomas Love Peacock)
Stansbury (Jemima; *He Knew He Was Right*, 1869, Anthony Trollope)
Stephanie (*Too Late the Phalarope*, 1953, Alan Paton)
Yeobright (Mrs; *The Return of the Native*, 1878, Thomas Hardy)

10 Harrington (Polly; *Pollyanna*, 1913, Eleanor Porter)

12 Lonelyhearts (Miss; *Miss Lonelyhearts*, 1933, Nathanael West)

Austen, Jane (1775–1817)

Significant works include:

04 *Emma* (1816)
08 *Sanditon* (1925)
09 *Lady Susan* (1871)

10 *Persuasion* (1818)
   The Watsons (1871)
13 *Mansfield Park* (1814)

15 *Northanger Abbey* (1818)
17 *Pride and Prejudice* (1813)
19 *Sense and Sensibility* (1811)

Significant characters include:

04 Clay (Mrs)
05 Bates (Hetty)
   Croft (Admiral)
   Croft (Mrs)
   Darcy (Mr Fitzwilliam)
   Elton (Mr)
   Elton (Mrs)
   Lucas (Charlotte)
   Price (Fanny)
   Price (Mrs)
   Smith (Harriet)
   Smith (Mrs)
   Yates (Mr)
06 Bennet (Elizabeth)
   Bennet (Jane)
   Bennet (Lydia)
   Bennet (Mr)
   Bennet (Mrs)
   Elliot (Anne)
   Elliot (Elizabeth)
   Elliot (Mary)
   Elliot (Sir Walter)
   Elliot (William)
   Martin (Robert)

Norris (Mrs)
Steele (Lucy)
Taylor (Anne)
Thorpe (Isabella)
Thorpe (John)
Tilney (Captain Frederick)
Tilney (Eleanor)
Tilney (General)
Tilney (Henry)
Weston (Mr)
07 Bertram (Edmund)
   Bertram (Julia)
   Bertram (Lady)
   Bertram (Maria)
   Bertram (Sir Thomas)
   Bertram (Tom)
   Bingley (Charles)
   Brandon (Colonel)
   Collins (William)
   Fairfax (Jane)
   Ferrars (Edward)
   Ferrars (Mrs)
   Ferrars (Robert)
   Morland (Catherine)

Morland (James)
Russell (Lady)
Wickham (George)
08 Crawford (Henry)
   Crawford (Mary)
   Dashwood (Elinor)
   Dashwood (Fanny)
   Dashwood (John)
   Dashwood (Marianne)
   Dashwood (Mrs)
   de Bourgh (Lady Catherine)
   Jennings (Mrs)
   Musgrove (Charles)
   Musgrove (Henrietta)
   Musgrove (Louisa)
09 Churchill (Frank)
   Knightley (Mr George)
   Rushworth (Mr)
   Wentworth (Captain Frederick)
   Woodhouse (Emma)
   Woodhouse (Mr Henry)
10 Willoughby (John)

Australasia

Countries in Australasia and Oceania include:

04 Fiji (Melanesia)
   Guam (Federated States of Micronesia)
   Niue (Polynesia)
05 Nauru (Federated States of Micronesia)
   Palau (Federated States of Micronesia)
   Samoa (Polynesia)
   Tonga (Polynesia)
06 Tuvalu (Polynesia)
07 Tokelau (Polynesia)
   Vanuatu (Melanesia)
08 Kiribati (Federated States of Micronesia)
   Pitcairn (Polynesia)

09 Australia
10 New Zealand
11 Cook Islands (Polynesia)
12 New Caledonia (Melanesia)
13 American Samoa (Polynesia)
   Norfolk Island
14 Papua New Guinea (Melanesia)
   Solomon Islands (Melanesia)
15 French Polynesia (Polynesia)
   Marshall Islands (Federated States of Micronesia)

Cities and notable towns in Australasia and Oceania include:

04 Apia (Samoa)
   Suva (Fiji)
05 Perth (Australia)

06 Sydney (Australia)
07 Dunedin (New Zealand)
   Honiara (Solomon Islands)

Manukau (New Zealand)
08 Adelaide (Australia)
Auckland (New Zealand)
Brisbane (Australia)
Canberra (Australia)
Hamilton (New Zealand)

09 Melbourne (Australia)
Newcastle (Australia)
10 Wellington (New Zealand)
11 Port Moresby (Papua New Guinea)
12 Christchurch (New Zealand)

Australia

Australian states and territories, with abbreviations and regional capitals:

08 Tasmania (TAS; Hobart)
Victoria (VIC; Melbourne)
10 Queensland (QLD; Brisbane)
13 New South Wales (NSW; Sydney)

14 South Australia (SA; Adelaide)
16 Western Australia (WA; Perth)
17 Northern Territory (NT; Darwin)
26 Australian Capital Territory (ACT; Canberra)

Australian state residents' nicknames include:

08 Top Ender (Northern Territory)
09 croweater (South Australia)
gumsucker (Victoria)
Taswegian (Tasmania)
10 sandgroper (Western Australia)
11 Territorian (Northern Territory)

Vandemonian (Tasmania)
12 bananabender (Queensland)
13 Apple Islander (Tasmania)
14 Cabbage Patcher (Victoria)
15 Cabbage Gardener (Victoria)

Cities and notable towns in Australia include:

05 Perth	Hobart	Brisbane	Melbourne
06 Cairns	Sydney	Canberra	**12** Alice Springs
Darwin	**08** Adelaide	**09** Fremantle	

Australian electorates:

04 Bass	Lyons	Gwydir	Dickson
Cook	Makin	Hotham	Dunkley
Grey	Moore	Hughes	Fairfax
Holt	Oxley	Hunter	Forrest
Hume	Perth	Isaacs	Gilmore
Indi	Sturt	Lilley	Hasluck
Lowe	Wills	Mallee	Herbert
Lyne	**06** Barker	McEwan	Higgins
Mayo	Barton	Murray	Hinkler
Page	Batman	Parkes	Kennedy
Reid	Bonner	Pearce	Kooyong
Ryan	Bowman	Petrie	La Trobe
Swan	Calare	Rankin	Lindsay
05 Aston	Cowper	Sydney	Longman
Banks	Curtin	Wannon	Maranoa
Blair	Dawson	Watson	Menzies
Brand	Deakin	**07** Bendigo	Moreton
Bruce	Dobell	Berowra	O'Connor
Casey	Fadden	Boothby	Scullin
Corio	Farrer	Braddon	Solomon
Cowan	Fisher	Calwell	Tangney
Forde	Fowler	Canning	Throsby
Groom	Fraser	Chifley	Werriwa
Lalor	Gorton	Denison	Wide Bay

08 Adelaide	McMillan	Macarthur	Gellibrand
Ballarat	Mitchell	Mackellar	Kalgoorlie
Blaxland	Paterson	Macquarie	Leichhardt
Brisbane	Prospect	McPherson	New England
Canberra	Richmond	Melbourne	Parramatta
Charlton	Riverina	Moncrieff	**11** Capricornia
Chisholm	Stirling	Newcastle	Corangamite
Flinders	**09** Bennelong	Robertson	Maribyrnong
Franklin	Bradfield	Shortland	North Sydney
Greenway	Fremantle	Wakefield	**12** Port Adelaide
Griffith	Gippsland	Warringah	**14** Kingsford Smith
Jagajaga	Goldstein	Wentworth	Melbourne Ports
Kingston	Grayndler	**10** Cunningham	
Lingiari	Hindmarsh	Eden-Monaro	

Australian landmarks include:

05 Uluru	**10** Bondi Beach	Hunter Valley	Simpson Desert
08 Lake Eyre	Yarra River	Rialto Towers	**14** Australian Alps
Shark Bay	**11** Mt Kosciusko	**13** Barossa Valley	Nullarbor Plain
09 Ayers Rock	Murray River	Blue Mountains	Pinnacle Desert
Botany Bay	**12** Darling River	Bungle Bungles	Snowy Mountains
Pinnacles	Fraser Island	Devil's Marbles	Twelve Apostles
Purnululu	Gibson Desert	Flinders Range	Uluru-Kata Tjuta

See also **aborigine; Australasia; governor; prime minister**

Australian rules football

Australian rules football teams include:

07 Carlton	Essendon	Kangaroos	**12** Port Adelaide
Geelong	Hawthorn	Melbourne	**13** Brisbane Lions
St Kilda	Richmond	**11** Collingwood	**15** West Coast Eagles
08 Adelaide	**09** Fremantle	Sydney Swans	Western Bulldogs

Australian rules football team nicknames include:

04 Cats (Geelong)	Swans (Sydney)	Dockers (Fremantle)
05 Blues (Carlton)	**06** Demons (Melbourne)	Magpies (Collingwood)
Crows (Adelaide)	Eagles (West Coast)	**08** Bulldogs (Western
Hawks (Hawthorn)	Saints (St Kilda)	Bulldogs)
Lions (Brisbane)	Tigers (Richmond)	**09** Kangaroos (North
Power (Port Adelaide)	**07** Bombers (Essendon)	Melbourne)

Australian rules football players include:

04 Dyer (Jack; 1913–2003)	**07** Barassi (Ron; 1936–)
05 Carey (Wayne; 1971–)	Jackson (Mark 'Jacko'; 1959–)
06 Ablett (Gary, Jnr; 1984–)	Lockett (Tony 'Plugger'; 1966–)
Ablett (Gary, Snr; 1961–)	Whitten (Ted; 1933–95)
Blight (Malcolm; 1950–)	**08** Bartlett (Kevin; 1947–)
Bunton (Haydn, Jnr; 1937–)	Brereton (Dermot; 1964–)
Bunton (Haydn, Snr; 1911–55)	Brownlow (Charles 'Chas'; 1861–1924)
Capper (Warwick; 1963–)	Matthews (Leigh; 1952–)
Cazaly (Roy; 1893–1963)	Richards (Lewis 'Lou'; 1923–)
Farmer (Graham 'Polly'; 1935–)	**10** Jesaulenko (Alex 'Jezza'; 1945–)

Australian rules football terms include:

04 goal	time on	left wing	spear tackle
mark	umpire	**09** playfield	**12** boundary line
ruck	**07** dispose	right wing	centre bounce
wing	quarter	ruck rover	centre square
05 rover	ruckman	**10** back pocket	**13** fifty-metre arc
06 ball up	**08** free kick	centre line	forward pocket
behind	full back	goal square	half-back flank
centre	half back	**11** full forward	**14** centre half-back
tackle	handpass	half forward	

See also **sport**

Austria

Cities and notable towns in Austria include:

04 Graz	Wien	**08** Salzburg	**10** Klagenfurt
Linz	**06** Vienna	**09** Innsbruck	

Administrative divisions of Austria, with regional capitals:

04 Wien
05 Tirol (Innsbruck)
Tyrol (Innsbruck)
06 Styria (Graz)
Vienna
07 Kärnten (Klagenfurt)

08 Salzburg (Salzburg)
09 Carinthia (Klagenfurt)
10 Burgenland (Eisenstadt)
Steiermark (Graz)
Vorarlberg (Bregenz)
12 Lower Austria (Sankt Pölten)

Upper Austria (Linz)
14 Oberösterreich (Linz)
16 Niederösterreich (Sankt Pölten)

Austrian landmarks include:

07 Hofburg
Rathaus
08 Domplatz
09 Hellbrunn
10 Opera House
Schönbrunn

Untersberg
Wienerwald
11 Burgtheater
Stephansdom
Vienna Woods
Wolfgangsee

Zwölferhorn
12 Mozart's House
13 Grossglockner
Hohensalzburg
Kapuzinerberg
Linz Cathedral

Neusiedler See
Stift Nonnberg
14 Mozart-
Wohnhaus
15 Pasterze Glacier
Schloss Mirabell

author *see* **novel**

aviation

Aviators, aviation pioneers and aircraft designers include:

03 Ulm (Charles; 1898–1934, Australian)
04 Ader (Clément; 1841–1926, French)
Byrd (Richard E; 1888–1957, US)
Cody (Samuel; 1862–1913, US/British)
Fysh (Sir Hudson; 1895–1974, Australian)
Post (Wiley; 1900–35, US)
Udet (Ernst; 1896–1941, German)
05 Bader (Sir Douglas; 1910–82, English)
Balbo (Italo, Count; 1896–1940, Italian)
Brown (Sir Arthur; 1886–1948, Scottish)
Johns (Captain W E; 1893–1968, English)

Rolls (Charles; 1877–1910, English)
Scott (Sheila; 1927–88, English)
Smith (Sir Ross; 1892–1922, Australian)
06 Alcock (Sir John; 1892–1919, English)
Arnold (Henry 'Hap'; 1886–1950, US)
Auriol (Jacqueline; 1917–2000, French)
Batten (Jean; 1909–82, New Zealand)
Cayley (Sir George; 1773–1857, English)
Cessna (Clyde; 1879–1954, US)
Farman (Henri; 1874–1958, French)
Gibson (Guy; 1918–44, English)

Göring (Hermann; 1893–1946, German)
Harris (Sir Arthur 'Bomber'; 1892–1984, English)
Hughes (Howard; 1905–76, US)
Nobile (Umberto; 1885–1978, Italian)
Quimby (Harriet; 1882–1912, US)
Taylor (Sir Gordon; 1896–1966, Australian)
Wallis (Barnes; 1887–1979, English)
Wright (Orville; 1871–1948, US)
Wright (Wilbur; 1867–1912, US)
Yeager (Chuck; 1923– , US)

07 Balchen (Bernt; 1899–1973, US)
Bennett (Floyd; 1890–1928, US)
Blériot (Louis; 1872–1936, French)
Branson (Sir Richard; 1950– , English)
Cochran (Jacqueline; 1910–80, US)
Curtiss (Glenn; 1878–1930, US)
Dornier (Claudius; 1884–1969, German)
Douglas (Donald; 1892–1981, US)
Earhart (Amelia; 1897–1937, US)
Fossett (Steve; 1944–2007, US)
Giffard (Henri; 1825–82, French)
Goering (Hermann; 1893–1946, German)
Heinkel (Ernst; 1888–1958, German)
Hinkler (Bert; 1892–1933, Australian)
Johnson (Amy; 1903–41, English)
Korolev (Sergei; 1907–66, Soviet)
Markham (Beryl; 1902–86, English/African)
Piccard (Auguste; 1884–1962, Swiss)
Piccard (Bertrand; 1958– , Swiss)
Piccard (Jean; 1884–1963, Swiss/US)

Sopwith (Sir Thomas; 1888–1989, English)
08 Brabazon (John, Lord; 1884–1964, English)
Cheshire (Leonard, Lord; 1917–92, English)
Dassault (Marcel; 1892–1986, French)
Ilyushin (Sergei; 1894–1977, Russian)
Mitchell (Reginald; 1895–1937, English)
Mitchell (William; 1879–1936, US)
Mollison (James; 1905–59, Scottish)
Zeppelin (Ferdinand, Count von; 1838–1917, German)

09 Blanchard (Jean Pierre; 1753–1809, French)
Doolittle (Jimmy; 1896–1993, US)
Lindbergh (Charles; 1902–74, US)
McDonnell (James; 1899–1980, US)

10 Lindstrand (Per; 1953– , Swedish)
Richthofen (Manfred, Baron von; 1882–1918, German)
Tissandier (Gaston; 1835–99, French)

11 Montgolfier (Jacques; 1745–99, French)
Montgolfier (Joseph; 1740–1810, French)

12 Grahame-White (Claude, 1879–1959, English)
Rickenbacker (Eddie; 1890–1973, US)
Saint-Exupéry (Antoine de; 1900–44, French)
Santos-Dumont (Alberto; 1873–1932, Brazilian)

13 Messerschmitt (Willy; 1898–1978, German)

14 Kingsford Smith (Sir Charles; 1897–1935, Australian)

Terms to do with aviation include:

03 hop
04 dive
drag
flap
taxi
05 fly-by
pilot
plane
prang
06 airway
flight
hangar
runway
thrust
07 airline
air miss
airport
airprox

airship
captain
console
fly-past
landing
lift-off
spoiler
take-off
08 aircraft
airfield
airplane
airspace
airstrip
altitude
black box
nose dive
subsonic
windsock
wingspan

09 aeroplane
aerospace
crash dive
fixed-wing
fly-by-wire
jetstream
overshoot
parachute
sonic boom
test pilot
touchdown
10 air station
chocks away
flight crew
Mach number
solo flight
supersonic
test flight
undershoot

11 aeronautics
ground speed
loop-the-loop
night-flying
vapour trail
12 control tower
crash-landing
landing strip
maiden flight
sound barrier
13 ground control
jet propulsion
14 automatic pilot
flight recorder
holding pattern
15 mid-air collision

See also **air travel**; **aircraft**; **bomb**

award

Awards and prizes include:

04 Emmy	Grammy	Pulitzer	**11** Fields Medal
Tony	Orange	Stirling	Golden Globe
05 Bafta	Razzie	**09** Grand Jury	**12** Prix Goncourt
César	Turner	Grand Prix	**15** Golden Raspberry
Costa	**07** Academy	Man Booker	
Nobel	Olivier	Templeton	
Oscar	**08** Audience	**10** Golden Bear	
06 Booker	Palme d'Or	Golden Palm	

See also **literature**; **Nobel Prize**

B

Babylonian god, goddess *see* **mythology**

Bach, Johann Sebastian (1685–1750)

Significant works include:

10 *Magnificat* (Canticles; 1723, 1733)

11 *God Is My King* (1707)
Passacaglia (1717)
'Brandenburg' (Concertos; 1721)

13 *St John Passion* (1724)
St Mark Passion (1731)
The Art of Fugue (1750)

14 *Easter Oratorio* (1725)

15 *Die Kunst der Fuge* (1750)
Musical Offering (1747)

16 *St Matthew Passion* (1729)

17 *Christmas Oratorio* (1734)

18 'Goldberg Variations' (1741)
Musikalisches Opfer (1747)

bacteria

Bacteria include:

03 Hib
04 MRSA
05 C. diff
E. coli
06 coccus
vibrio
07 proteus
08 bacillus
gut flora
listeria
shigella
09 Azobacter
rhizobium
spirulina

treponema
10 C. difficile
gonococcus
Klebsiella
legionella
Leptospira
salmonella
11 acidophilus
Azotobacter
clostridium
eubacterium
pasteurella
Penicillium
pseudomonas
12 enterococcus

pneumococcus
thiobacillus
13 campylobacter
lactobacillus
mycobacterium
streptococcus
14 actinobacillus
Archaebacteria
Corynebacteria
staphylococcus
trichobacteria
Vibrio cholerae
Yersinia pestis
15 Escherichia coli
sulphur bacteria

Bacteriologists include:

04 Cohn (Ferdinand; 1828–98, German)
Gram (Hans; 1853–1938, Danish)
Koch (Robert; 1843–1910, German)
Roux (Émile; 1853–1933, French)

05 Avery (Oswald; 1877–1955, US)
Bassi (Agostino; 1773–1856, Italian)
Dubos (René; 1901–82, US)
Smith (Theobald; 1859–1934, US)
Twort (Frederick; 1877–1950, English)

06 Enders (John; 1897–1985, US)
Gaffky (Georg; 1850–1918, German)
Guérin (Camille; 1872–1961, French)
Hansen (Armauer; 1841–1912, Norwegian)

Warren (J Robin; 1937– , Australian)
Wright (Sir Almroth; 1861–1947, English)
Yersin (Alexandre; 1863–1943, French)

07 Behring (Emil von; 1854–1917, German)
Buchner (Hans; 1850–1902, German)
Ehrlich (Paul; 1854–1915, German)
Fleming (Amalia; 1909–86, Greek/British)
Fleming (Sir Alexander; 1881–1955,
Scottish)
Hérelle (Felix d'; 1873–1949, Canadian)
Löffler (Friedrich; 1852–1915, German)
Noguchi (Hideyo; 1876–1928, US)
Theiler (Max; 1899–1972, US)
Zinsser (Hans; 1878–1940, US)

08 Calmette (Albert; 1863–1933, French)
Haffkine (Waldemar; 1860–1930, Russian/
British)
Kitasato (Shibasaburo, Baron; 1852–1931,
Japanese)
Leishman (Sir William; 1865–1926, Scottish)

Marshall (Barry; 1951– , Australian)
Pfeiffer (Richard; 1858–1945, German)

10 Wassermann (August von; 1866–1925,
German)

11 Chamberland (Charles; 1851–1908, French)

badminton

Badminton terms include:

03 net	court	**06** racket	wood shot
set	drive	**07** doubles	**11** shuttlecock
04 bird	flick	racquet	**12** service court
kill	rally	singles	**13** underarm clear
05 clear	serve	**08** drop shot	
	smash		

See also **sport**

bag

Bags include:

03 bum	money	evening	suitcase
kit	**06** carpet	holdall	**09** briefcase
04 case	clutch	satchel	fanny pack
grip	duffel	**08** backpack	Gladstone
hand	flight	carry-all	haversack
pack	saddle	knapsack	moneybelt
sack	tucker	reticule	overnight
tote	valise	rucksack	**10** laptop case
wash	vanity	shopping	**11** attaché-case
05 ditty	**07** carrier	shoulder	

See also **container**

baking

Baked items include:

03 bun	**06** cookie	soufflé	shortcake
pie	Danish	stollen	**10** baked apple
04 cake	gateau	strudel	brandy snap
flan	muffin	tartlet	Brown Betty
loaf	parkin	tea cake	cheesecake
puff	pastry	tea loaf	Florentine
roll	quiche	**08** blackcap	shortbread
tart	sponge	en croûte	**11** baked Alaska
05 bread	square	flapjack	gingerbread
pasty	tiffin	meringue	hot cross bun
patty	waffle	tea bread	**12** bread pudding
plait	**07** bannock	traybake	Danish pastry
scone	biscuit	**09** bara brith	fruit cobbler
slice	brioche	batch loaf	fruit crumble
tarte	brownie	clafoutis	pain au raisin
torte	cobbler	clapbread	**13** sponge pudding
twist	lattice	croissant	**14** pain au chocolat
wafer	oatcake	drop scone	
	pancake		

See also **biscuit**; **bread**; **cake**; **dessert**; **food**

Balkans

Cities and notable towns in the Balkans include:

03 Niš (Serbia)
04 Iaşi (Romania)
05 Sibiu (Romania)
Sofia (Bulgaria)
Split (Croatia)
Tuzla (Bosnia and Herzegovina)
Varna (Bulgaria)
Volos (Greece)
Zadar (Croatia)
06 Athens (Greece)
Bitola (Macedonia)
Braila (Romania)
Braşov (Romania)
Burgas (Bulgaria)
Galati (Romania)
Mostar (Bosnia and Herzegovina)
Oradea (Romania)
Osijek (Croatia)
Patras (Greece)
Rijeka (Croatia)
Skopje (Macedonia)
Tirana (Albania)
Zagreb (Croatia)
07 Čakovec (Croatia)

Cetinje (Montenegro)
Craiova (Romania)
Maribor (Slovenia)
Novi Sad (Serbia)
Piraeus (Greece)
Plovdiv (Bulgaria)
Shkodër (Albania)
08 Belgrade (Serbia)
Botoşani (Romania)
Gostivar (Macedonia)
Ploieşti (Romania)
Priština (Kosovo)
Sarajevo (Bosnia and Herzegovina)
09 Banja Luka (Bosnia and Herzegovina)
Bucharest (Romania)
Constanta (Romania)
Heraklion (Greece)
Ljubljana (Slovenia)
Podgorica (Montenegro)
Timişoara (Romania)
10 Cluj-Napoca (Romania)
Kragujevac (Serbia)
11 Stara Zagora (Bulgaria)
12 Thessaloniki (Greece)

ballet

Ballets, with composer, choreographer and date of first performance, include:

05 *Manon* (Massenet; MacMillan; 1974)
Rodeo (Copland; de Mille; 1942)
Rooms (Hopkins; Sokolow; 1955)
06 *Boléro* (Ravel; Bejart; 1961)
Carmen (Bizet; Petit; 1949)
Façade (Walton; Ashton; 1931)
Hamlet (Tchaikovsky; Helpmann; 1942)
Jewels (Fauré, Stravinsky, Tchaikovsky; Balanchine; 1967)
La Luna (Bach; Béjart; 1991)
Ondine (Henze; Ashton; 1958)
Onegin (Tchaikovsky, Stolze; Cranko; 1965)
Parade (Satie; Massine; 1917)
07 *Giselle* (Adam; Coralli, Perro, Petipa; 1841)
Isadora (Bennett; MacMillan; 1981)
La Valse (Ravel; Nijinska; 1929)
Orpheus (Stravinsky; Balanchine; 1948)
Requiem (Fauré; MacMillan; 1976)
Rituals (Bartók; MacMillan; 1975)
08 *Coppélia* (Delibes; St Léon; 1870)
Le Renard (Stravinsky; Nijinska; 1922)
Les Noces (Stravinsky; Nijinska; 1923)
Mathilde (Wagner; Béjart; 1965)
Nocturne (Delius; Ashton; 1936)

Raymonda (Glazunov; Petipa; 1898)
Rhapsody (Rachmaninov; Ashton; 1980)
Serenade (Tchaikovsky; Balanchine; 1934)
Swan Lake (Tchaikovsky; Petipa, Ivanov; 1895)
09 *Anastasia* (Tchaikovsky, Martinu; MacMillan; 1971)
Checkmate (Bliss; de Valois; 1937)
Fancy Free (Bernstein; Robbins; 1944)
La Ventana (Lumbye, Holm; Bournonville; 1854)
Les Biches (Poulenc; Nijinska; 1924)
Mayerling (Liszt; MacMillan; 1978)
Spartacus (Khachaturian; Grigorovich; 1968)
The Burrow (Martin; MacMillan; 1958)
10 *Cinderella* (Prokofiev; Ashton; 1948)
Don Quixote (Minkus; Petipa; 1869)
La Bayadère (Minkus; Petipa; 1877)
La Sylphide (Løvenskjold; Bournonville; 1836)
Les Saisons (Glazunov; Petipa; 1900)
Petroushka (Stravinsky; Fokine; 1911)
Prince Igor (Borodin; Fokine; 1909)
The Masques (Poulenc; Ashton; 1933)

Variations (Stravinsky; Balanchine; 1966)

11 *Billy the Kid* (Copland; Loring; 1938)
Cain and Abel (Panufnik; MacMillan; 1968)
Jeu de Cartes (Stravinsky; Balanchine; 1937)
Las Hermanas (Martin; MacMillan; 1963)
Night Shadow (Rieti; Balanchine; 1946)
Summerspace (Feldman; Cunningham; 1958)
Symphony in C (Bizet; Balanchine; 1947)
The Firebird (Stravinsky; Fokine; 1910)
Voluntaries (Poulenc; Tetley; 1973)

12 *Harlequinade* (Drigo; Balanchine; 1965)
Illumination (Britten; Ashton; 1950)
Knight Errant (Strauss; Tudor; 1968)
Les Papillons (Schumann, Tcherepnin; Fokine; 1913)
Les Patineurs (Meyerbeer, Lambert; Ashton; 1937)
Les Sylphides (Chopin; Fokine; 1909)
Night Journey (Schuman; Graham; 1947)
Schéhérazade (Rimsky-Korsakov; Fokine; 1910)
The Judas Tree (Elias; MacMillan; 1992)

13 *Duo Concertant* (Stravinsky; Balanchine; 1972)
Ebony Concerto (Stravinsky; Carter; 1957)
Lady of Shallot (Sibelius; Ashton; 1931)
Les Rendezvous (Auber, Lambert; Ashton; 1933)
Les Vainqueurs (Wagner, Indian/Tibetan music; Béjart; 1969)
Pineapple Poll (Sullivan, Mackerras; Cranko; 1951)
Stoics Quartet (Mendelssohn; Burrows; 1991)
The Invitation (Seiber; MacMillan; 1960)
The Nutcracker (Tchaikovsky; Ivanov; 1892)

14 *Daphnis et Chloé* (Ravel; Fokine; 1912)
Legend of Joseph (Strauss; Fokine; 1914)
Legend of Judith (Mordecai; Graham; 1962)
Romeo and Juliet (Prokofiev; Lavrovsky; 1940)
Russian Soldier (Prokofiev; Fokine; 1942)
Scènes de Ballet (Stravinsky; Dolin; 1944)
Scotch Symphony (Mendelssohn; Balanchine; 1952)
Song of the Earth (Mahler; MacMillan; 1965)
Tales of Hoffman (Offenbach, Lanchberg; Darrell; 1973)
The Four Seasons (Verdi; MacMillan; 1975)
The Moor's Pavane (Purcell; Limón; 1949)
The Prodigal Son (Prokofiev; Balanchine; 1929)

15 *Apollon Musagète* (Stravinsky; Bolm; 1928)
A Wedding Bouquet (Berners; Ashton; 1937)
Concerto Barocco (Bach; Balanchine; 1940)

Fall River Legend (Gould; de Mille; 1948)
Ivan the Terrible (Prokofiev, Chulaki; Grigorovich; 1975)
The Rite of Spring (Stravinsky, Roerich; Nijinsky; 1913)

16 *Enigma Variations* (Elgar; Ashton; 1968)
La Fille Mal Gardée (French songs; Dauberval; 1789)
Lament of the Waves (Masson; Ashton; 1970)
Present Histories (Schubert; Tuckett; 1991)
The Rake's Progress (Gordon; de Valois; 1935)

17 *Appalachian Spring* (Copland; Graham; 1944)
Elite Syncopations (Joplin; MacMillan; 1974)
Le Spectre de la Rose (Weber; Fokine; 1911)
The Gods Go A-Begging (Handel; Balanchine; 1928)
The Lady and the Fool (Verdi, Mackerras; Cranko; 1954)
The Sleeping Beauty (Tchaikovsky; Petipa; 1890)

18 *A Month in the Country* (Chopin, Lanchbery; Ashton; 1976)
L'Après-midi d'un Faune (Debussy; Nijinsky; 1912)
Le Chant du Rossignol (Stravinsky; Massine; 1920)
Le Malade Imaginaire (Rota; Béjart; 1976)
Le Sacré du Printemps (Stravinsky, Roerich; Nijinsky; 1913)
The Seven Deadly Sins (Weill; Balanchine; 1933)

19 *La Boutique Fantasque* (Rossini, Respighi; Massine; 1919)
Symphonic Variations (Franck; Ashton; 1946)
The Four Temperaments (Hindemith; Balanchine; 1946)
The Taming of the Shrew (Scarlatti, Stolze; Cranko; 1969)
The Three-Cornered Hat (de Falla; Massine; 1919)

20 *Le Jeune Homme et la Mort* (Bach; Petit; 1946)
Symphonie Fantastique (Berlioz; Massine; 1936)

21 *A Midsummer Night's Dream* (Mendelssohn; Balanchine; 1962)
Monumentum pro Gesualdo (Stravinsky; Balanchine; 1960)
The Prince of the Pagodas (Britten; Cranko; 1957)

24 *Symphony in Three Movements* (Stravinsky; Balanchine; 1972)

26 *The Walk to the Paradise Garden* (Delius; Ashton; 1972)

Ballet companies include:

04 Maly
West
05 Jooss
Kirov
Royal
06 Boston
07 Bolshoi
Houston
Joffrey
Rambert
08 Hong Kong
National

Scottish
09 Miami City
Stuttgart
10 Australian
Borovansky
Gulbenkian
Paris Opéra
11 New York City
Royal Danish
12 Alicia Alonso
Pennsylvania
Royal Swedish

Sadler's Wells
San Francisco
Stanislavsky
13 Dutch National
Royal Winnipeg
14 London Festival
Western Theatre
15 Birmingham Royal
English National
Royal New Zealand

Ballet dancers include:

04 Bolm (Adolph; 1884–1951, Russian)
Bull (Deborah; 1963– , English)
Dean (Laura; 1945– , US)
Edur (Thomas; 1969– , Estonian)
Feld (Eliot; 1942– , US)
Gore (Walter; 1910–79, Scottish)
Grey (Dame Beryl; 1927– , English)
Kain (Karen; 1951– , Canadian)
Kaye (Nora; 1920–87, US)
Kent (Allegra, 1938– , US)
Kidd (Michael; 1919–2007, US)
Oaks (Agnes; 1969– , Estonian)

05 Bruce (Christopher; 1945– , English)
Bruhn (Erik; 1928–86, Danish)
Clark (Michael; 1962– , Scottish)
Dolin (Anton; 1904–83, English)
Gable (Christopher; 1940–98, English)
Genée (Dame Adelin; 1878–1970, Danish)
Grahn (Lucile; 1819–1907, Danish)
Grant (Alexander; 1925–2011, New Zealand)
Grisi (Carlotta; 1819–99, Italian)
Jooss (Kurt; 1901–79, German)
Laban (Rudolf von; 1879–1958, Hungarian)
Legat (Nikolai; 1869–1937, Russian)
Lifar (Serge; 1905–86, Russian/French)
Manen (Hans van; 1932– , Dutch)
Marin (Maguy; 1951– , French)
Mauri (Rosita; 1849–1923, Spanish)
Neary (Patricia; 1942– , US)
Panov (Valeri; 1938– , Russian)
Petit (Roland; 1924–2011, French)
Sallé (Marie; 1707–56, French)
Sleep (Wayne; 1948– , English)
Somes (Michael; 1917–94, English)
Spink (Ian; 1947– , Australian)
Tudor (Antony; 1908–87, English)
Verdy (Violette; 1933– , French)

06 Alonso (Alicia; 1921– , Cuban)
Ashley (Merrill; 1950– , US)
Ashton (Sir Frederick; 1904–88, English)

Béjart (Maurice; 1927–2007, French)
Blasis (Carlo; 1797–1878, Italian)
Bourne (Matthew; 1960– , English)
Cooper (Adam; 1971– , English)
Dowell (Sir Anthony; 1943– , English)
Dupond (Patrick; 1959– , French)
Fokine (Michel; 1880–1942, Russian/US)
Fracci (Carla; 1936– , Italian)
Franca (Celia; 1921–2007, English)
Gilpin (John; 1930–83, English)
Haydee (Marcia; 1939– , Brazilian)
Ivanov (Lev; 1834–1901, Russian)
Kylian (Jiri; 1947– , Czech)
Lander (Harald; 1905–71, Danish/French)
Murphy (Graeme; 1950– , Australian)
Panova (Galina; 1949– , Russian)
Perrot (Jules; 1810–94, French)
Petipa (Lucien; 1815–98, French)
Petipa (Marius; 1818–1910, French)
Sibley (Dame Antoinette; 1939– , English)
St-Léon (Arthur; 1821–71, French)
Tetley (Glen; 1926–2007, US)
Valois (Dame Ninette de; 1898–2001, Irish)
Wright (Sir Peter; 1926– , English)

07 Babilée (Jean; 1923– , French)
Bintley (David; 1957– , English)
Bujones (Fernando; 1955–2005, US)
Bussell (Darcey; 1969– , English)
Camargo (Maria Anna de; 1710–70, French)
Coralli (Jean; 1779–1854, French)
Dantzig (Rudi van; 1933–2012, Dutch)
Didelot (Charles-Louis; 1767–1837,
Swedish/French)
Durante (Viviana; 1967– , Italian)
Edwards (Leslie; 1916–2001, English)
Elssler (Fanny; 1810–84, Austrian)
Farrell (Suzanne; 1945– , US)
Fonteyn (Dame Margot; 1919–91, English)
Gielgud (Maina; 1945– , English)
Gregory (Cynthia; 1946– , US)

Guillem (Sylvie; 1965– , French)
Hawkins (Erick; 1909–94, US)
Joffrey (Robert; 1930–88, US)
Larrieu (Daniel; 1957– , French)
Lichine (David; 1910–72, Russian/US)
Markova (Dame Alicia; 1910–2004, English)
Martins (Peter; 1946– , Danish)
Massine (Léonide; 1896–1979, Russian)
Mordkin (Mikhail; 1880–1944, Russian/US)
Nureyev (Rudolf; 1938–93, Russian)
Osipova (Natalia; 1986– , Russian)
Pavlova (Anna; 1881–1931, Russian)
Rambert (Dame Marie; 1888–1982, Polish/ British)
Robbins (Jerome; 1918–98, US)
Seymour (Lynn; 1939– , Canadian/British)
Shearer (Moira; 1926–2006, Scottish)
Shearer (Sybil; 1918–2005, Canadian/US)
Spoerli (Heinz; 1941– , Swiss)
Ulanova (Galina; 1910–98, Russian)
Vestris (Auguste; 1760–1842, French)
08 Chauviré (Yvette; 1917– , French)
Cullberg (Birgit; 1908–99, Swedish)
d'Amboise (Jacques; 1934– , US)
Danilova (Alexandra; 1904–97, Russian/US)
Eglevsky (André; 1917–77, Russian/US)
Forsythe (William; 1949– , US)
Franklin (Frederic; 1914–2013, English)
Hamilton (Gordon; 1918–59, Australian)
Helpmann (Sir Robert; 1909–86, Australian)
Jasinski (Roman; 1907–91, Polish/US)
Kirkland (Gelsey; 1952– , US)
Lopukhov (Fyodor; 1886–1973, Russian)
Makarova (Natalia; 1940– , Russian)
McDonald (Elaine; 1943– , Scottish)
Messerer (Asaf; 1903–92, Russian)

Mitchell (Arthur; 1934– , US)
Moiseyev (Igor; 1906–2007, Russian)
Neumeier (John; 1942– , US)
Nijinska (Bronislava; 1891–1972, Russian)
Nijinsky (Vaslav; 1890–1950, Russian)
Stretton (Ross; 1952–2005, Australian)
Taglioni (Maria; 1804–84, Italian)
Villella (Edward; 1936– , US)
Zakharov (Rostislav; 1907–84, Russian)
09 Beauchamp (Pierre; 1636–1705, French)
Cecchetti (Enrico; 1850–1928, Italian)
Dai Ailian (1916–2006, Chinese)
Hightower (Rosella; 1920–2008, US)
Karsavina (Tamara; 1885–1978, Russian/ British)
Lavrovsky (Leonid; 1905–67, Russian)
Macmillan (Sir Kenneth; 1929–92, Scottish)
Saint-Léon (Arthur; 1821–71, French)
Schaufuss (Peter; 1949– , Danish)
Tallchief (Maria; 1925–2013, US)
Trefilova (Vera; 1875–1943, Russian)
Van Praagh (Dame Peggy; 1910–90, English)
10 Borovansky (Edouard; 1902–59, Czech)
Mukhamedov (Irek; 1960– , Russian)
Nemchinova (Vera; 1899–1984, Russian)
Rubinstein (Ida; 1885–1960, Russian)
Volochkova (Anastasia; 1976– , Russian)
11 Baryshnikov (Mikhail; 1948– , Russian/US)
Grigorovich (Yuri; 1927– , Russian)
Plisetskaya (Maya; 1925– , Russian)
12 Bessmertnova (Natalia; 1941–2008, Russian)
Bournonville (August; 1805–79, Danish)
Spessivtseva (Olga; 1895–1991, Russian/US)
13 Riabouchinska (Tatiana; 1917–2000, Russian/US)

Ballet choreographers include:

04 Bolm (Adolph; 1884–1951, Russian)
Dean (Laura; 1945– , US)
Feld (Eliot; 1942– , US)
Kidd (Michael; 1919–2007, US)
05 Bruce (Christopher; 1945– , English)
Clark (Michael; 1962– , Scottish)
Dolin (Anton; 1904–83, English)
Gades (Antonio; 1936–2004, Spanish)
Jooss (Kurt; 1901–79, German)
Laban (Rudolf von; 1879–1958, Hungarian)
Legat (Nikolai; 1869–1937, Russian)
Manen (Hans van; 1932– , Dutch)
Marin (Maguy; 1951– , French)
North (Robert; 1945– , US/British)
Petit (Roland; 1924–2011, French)
Sleep (Wayne; 1948– , English)
Spink (Ian; 1947– , Australian)

Tudor (Antony; 1908–87, English)
06 Alonso (Alicia; 1921– , Cuban)
Ashton (Sir Frederick; 1904–88, English)
Béjart (Maurice; 1927–2007, French)
Blasis (Carlo; 1797–1878, Italian)
Bourne (Matthew; 1960– , English)
Cranko (John; 1927–73, South African)
Fokine (Michel; 1880–1942, Russian/US)
Ivanov (Lev; 1834–1901, Russian)
Kylian (Jiri; 1947– , Czech)
Lander (Harald; 1905–71, Danish/French)
Murphy (Graeme; 1950– , Australian)
Perrot (Jules; 1810–94, French)
Petipa (Marius; 1818–1910, French)
St-Léon (Arthur; 1821–71, French)
Tetley (Glen; 1926–2007, US)
Valois (Dame Ninette de; 1898–2001, Irish)

07 Babilée (Jean; 1923– , French)
Bintley (David; 1957– , English)
Coralli (Jean; 1779–1854, French)
Dantzig (Rudi van; 1933–2012, Dutch)
Darrell (Peter; 1929–87, English)
Didelot (Charles-Louis; 1767–1837,
Swedish/French)
Hawkins (Erick; 1909–94, US)
Joffrey (Robert; 1930–88, US)
Larrieu (Daniel; 1957– , French)
Massine (Léonide; 1896–1979, Russian)
Noverre (Jean-Georges; 1727–1810,
French)
Robbins (Jerome; 1918–98, US)
Spoerli (Heinz; 1941– , Swiss)

08 Cullberg (Birgit; 1908–99, Swedish)
d'Amboise (Jacques; 1934– , US)
Forsythe (William; 1949– , US)
Helpmann (Sir Robert; 1909–86, Australian)
Lopukhov (Fyodor; 1886–1973, Russian)
McGregor (Wayne; 1970– , English)
Messerer (Asaf; 1903–92, Russian)

Mitchell (Arthur; 1934– , US)
Moiseyev (Igor; 1906–2007, Russian)
Neumeier (John; 1942– , US)
Nijinska (Bronislava; 1891–1972, Russian)
Nijinsky (Vaslav; 1890–1950, Russian)
Wheeldon (Christopher; 1973– , English)
Zakharov (Rostislav; 1907–84, Russian)

09 Beauchamp (Pierre; 1636–1705, French)
Cecchetti (Enrico; 1850–1928, Italian)
Dai Ailian (1916–2006, Chinese)
Dauberval (Jean; 1742–1806, French)
Hightower (Rosella; 1920–2008, US)
Lavrovsky (Leonid; 1905–67, Russian)
Macmillan (Sir Kenneth; 1929–92,
Scottish)
Ratmansky (Alexei; 1968– , Russian)
Saint-Léon (Arthur; 1821–71, French)

10 Balanchine (George; 1904–83, US)
Borovansky (Edouard; 1902–59, Czech)

11 Baryshnikov (Mikhail; 1948– , Russian/US)
Grigorovich (Yuri; 1927– , Russian)

12 Bournonville (August; 1805–79, Danish)

Ballet terms include:

03 bar
pas

04 jeté
plié
posé
tutu

05 adage
barre
battu
brisé
coupé
couru
fondu
gilet
passé
sauté
tendu

06 à terre
attack
ballon
chaîné
chassé
dégagé
devant
écarté
en face
en l'air
entrée
pointe
relevé
retiré

school
splits

07 allegro
à pointe
balancé
bourrée
bras bas
chaînés
ciseaux
company
coryphe
danseur
échappé
emboîté
en avant
fouetté
leotard
maillot
pas jeté
pointes
premier
sissone

08 assemblé
attitude
ballonné
ballotté
batterie
cabriole
capriole
coryphée
couronne

danseuse
demi bras
demi plié
en pointe
ensemble
figurant
fish dive
fouettés
glissade
lame duck
première
stulchak
sur place

09 arabesque
ballabile
ballabili
ballerina
battement
cou de pied
développé
élévation
en seconde
entrechat
figurante
pas de chat
pas de deux
pas de seul
pas de vals
petit jeté
pirouette
point shoe
posé coupé

promenade
régisseur
temps levé
variation

10 à la seconde
ballabiles
ballet shoe
bras croisé
changement
demi pointe
en première
en tournant
épaulement
foudroyant
grande jeté
pas de trois
pas de valse
port de bras
répétiteur
soubresaut
tour en l'air

11 changements
chassé passé
comprimario

See also **dance**

down-the-line
echaînement
en cinquième
en quatrième
en troisième
Laban system
pas ballonné
pas de basque
pas de quatre
petits tours
ports de bras

12 ballet-dancer
ballet-master
bluebird lift
choreography
danseur noble
gargouillade
labanotation
shoulder lift

13 ballet-dancing
corps de ballet
fifth position
first position
five positions

posé arabesque
sur les pointes
third position

14 ballet-mistress
divertissement
fourth position
grand battement
grand pas de deux
maître de ballet
petit battement
premier danseur
prima ballerina
second position
sur le cou-de-pied

15 attitude grecque
ballonné composé
changement battu
demi contretemps
entrechat quatre
full contretemps
posé in arabesque
principal dancer

Bartók, Béla (1881–1945)

Significant works include:

07 *Kossuth* (1903)

08 *Sonatina* (1915)
Suite No 1 (1905)
Suite No 2 (1907)

10 *Dance Suite* (1923)
Out of Doors (1926)

11 *Mikrokosmos* (1926; 1932–39)
Two Pictures (1910)

13 *Piano Rhapsody* (1904)
Romanian Dance (1911)

14 *Allegro Barbaro* (1911)
Cantata Profana (1930)
From Olden Times (1935)

15 *The Wooden Prince* (1917)

18 *Fourteen Bagatelles* (1908)
Romanian Folk Dances (1915)

20 *Duke Bluebeard's Castle* (1918)

21 *The Miraculous Mandarin* (1926)

28 *Fifteen Hungarian Peasant Songs*
(1914–18; 1933)

baseball

Major League baseball teams:

11 Chicago Cubs
New York Mets

12 Boston Red Sox
Tampa Bay Rays
Texas Rangers

13 Atlanta Braves
Detroit Tigers
Houston Astros

14 Cincinnati Reds
Florida Marlins

Minnesota Twins
New York Yankees
San Diego Padres

15 Chicago White Sox
Colorado Rockies
Seattle Mariners
Toronto Blue Jays

16 Baltimore Orioles
Cleveland Indians
Kansas City Royals

Los Angeles Angels
Milwaukee Brewers
Oakland Athletics
St Louis Cardinals

17 Los Angeles Dodgers
Pittsburgh Pirates

18 San Francisco Giants

19 Arizona Diamondbacks
Washington Nationals

20 Philadelphia Phillies

Major League baseball team nicknames include:

04 Cubs (Chicago)
Mets (New York)
Rays (Tampa Bay)
Reds (Cincinnati)

05 Twins (Minnesota)

06 Angels (Los Angeles)
Astros (Houston)
Braves (Atlanta)
Giants (San Francisco)
Padres (San Diego)

Red Sox (Boston)
Royals (Kansas City)
Tigers (Detroit)

07 Brewers (Milwaukee)
Dodgers (Los Angeles)
Indians (Cleveland)
Marlins (Florida)
Orioles (Baltimore)
Pirates (Pittsburgh)
Rangers (Texas)

Rockies (Colorado)
Yankees (New York)

08 Blue Jays (Toronto)
Mariners (Seattle)
Phillies (Philadelphia)
White Sox (Chicago)

09 Athletics (Oakland)
Cardinals (St Louis)
Nationals (Washington)

12 Diamondbacks (Arizona)

Baseball players and associated figures include:

03 Ott (Mel; 1909–58, US)

04 Cobb (Ty; 1886–1961, US)
Mack (Connie; 1862–1956, US)
Mays (Willie; 1931– , US)
Rose (Pete; 1941– , US)
Ruth (Babe; 1895–1948, US)
Ryan (Nolan; 1947– , US)
Sosa (Sammy; 1968– , Dominican)

05 Aaron (Hank; 1934– , US)
Bench (Johnny; 1947– , US)
Berra (Yogi; 1925– , US)
Boggs (Wade; 1958– , US)
Bonds (Barry; 1964– , US)
Gwynn (Tony; 1960– , US)
Paige (Satchel; 1906–82, US)
Spahn (Warren; 1921–2003, US)
Young (Cy; 1867–1955, US)

06 Gehrig (Lou; 1903–41, US)
Gibson (Bob; 1935– , US)
Gibson (Josh; 1911–47, US)
Koufax (Sandy; 1935– , US)
Mantle (Micky; 1931–95, US)
Musial (Stan; 1920–2013, US)
Rickey (Branch; 1881–1965, US)
Ripken (Cal, Jnr; 1960– , US)

Suzuki (Ichiro; 1973– , Japanese)
Wagner (Honus; 1874–1951, US)

07 Clemens (Roger; 1962– , US)
Gossage (Richard; 1951– , US)
Hoffman (Trevor; 1967– , US)
Hornsby (Rogers; 1896–1963, US)
Jackson (Reggie; 1946– , US)
Jackson ('Shoeless' Joe; 1888–1951, US)
Johnson (Randy; 1963– , US)
Johnson (Walter; 1887–1946, US)
McGwire (Mark; 1963– , US)
Stengel (Casey; 1890–1975, US)

08 Anderson (George 'Sparky'; 1934–2010, US)
Clemente (Roberto; 1932–72, Puerto Rican)
DiMaggio (Joe; 1914–99, US)
Robinson (Brooks; 1937– , US)
Robinson (Frank; 1935– , US)
Robinson (Jackie; 1919–72, US)
Sadaharu (Oh; 1940– , Japanese)
Williams (Ted; 1918–2002, US)

09 Alexander (Grover Cleveland; 1887–1950, US)
Henderson (Rickey; 1958– , US)
Mathewson (Christie; 1880–1925, US)

Baseball terms include:

03 ace
ERA
gap
hit
out
RBI
run
tag
top

04 balk
ball
base
bunt
cage

mitt
safe
save
walk

05 alley
at bat
bench
bloop
count
cycle
error
mound
pitch
plate

pop up
relay
steal

06 assist
batter
bottom
closer
cutter
double
fly out
hitter
inning
on deck
single

sinker
slider
strike
triple
wind-up

07 all-star
base hit
battery
bull pen
catcher
chopper
diamond
drive in
fly ball
home run
infield
pennant
pick off
pitcher
rundown
shutout
slugger
stretch

08 backstop
ballpark
baseline
change-up
fair ball
fastball
foul ball
foul pole
nightcap
no-hitter
outfield
pitch-out
set-up man
splitter
throw out

See also **sport**

09 curveball
cut-off man
earned run
first base
full count
gold glove
grand slam
ground out
hit-and-run
home plate
infielder
in the hole
left field
line drive
sacrifice
screwball
shortstop
strike out
third base
wild pitch

10 baserunner
batter's box
double play
first pitch
ground ball
Hall of Fame
outfielder
passed ball
right field
second base
strike zone
triple play

11 All-Star game
base on balls
basket catch
centre field
knuckleball
left fielder

major league
minor league
perfect game
pinch hitter
pinch runner
run batted in
triple crown
unearned run

12 breaking ball
complete game
double-header
extra innings
first baseman
load the bases
long reliever
on-deck circle
right fielder
switch hitter
third baseman
warning track

13 centre fielder
clean-up hitter
foul territory
lead-off hitter
relief pitcher
safety squeeze
second baseman
silver slugger

14 American League
backdoor slider
batting average
fielder's choice
middle reliever
National League
position player
suicide squeeze

15 starting pitcher

basketball

Basketball teams:

08 Utah Jazz

09 Miami Heat

11 Phoenix Suns

12 Atlanta Hawks
Chicago Bulls
Orlando Magic

13 Boston Celtics
Denver Nuggets
Indiana Pacers
New Jersey Nets

New York Knicks

14 Detroit Pistons
Houston Rockets
Milwaukee Bucks
Toronto Raptors

15 Dallas Mavericks
Sacramento Kings
San Antonio Spurs

16 Charlotte Bobcats
Los Angeles Lakers

Memphis Grizzlies

17 New Orleans Hornets
Philadelphia 76ers
Washington Wizards

18 Cleveland Cavaliers
Los Angeles Clippers

19 Golden State Warriors
Oklahoma City Thunder

20 Portland Trail Blazers

21 Minnesota Timberwolves

Basketball team nicknames include:

04 Heat (Miami)
Jazz (Utah)
Nets (New Jersey)
Suns (Phoenix)

05 Bucks (Milwaukee)
Bulls (Chicago)
Hawks (Atlanta)
Kings (Sacramento)
Magic (Orlando)
Spurs (San Antonio)

06 Knicks (New York)
Lakers (Los Angeles)
Pacers (Indiana)

07 Bobcats (Charlotte)
Celtics (Boston)
Hornets (New Orleans)
Nuggets (Denver)
Pistons (Detroit)
Raptors (Toronto)
Rockets (Houston)

Thunder (Oklahoma City)
Wizards (Washington)

08 Clippers (Los Angeles)
Warriors (Golden State)

09 Cavaliers (Cleveland)
Grizzlies (Memphis)
Mavericks (Dallas)

12 Timberwolves (Minnesota)
Trail Blazers (Portland)

13 Seventy-Sixers (Philadelphia)

Basketball players and associated figures include:

04 Bird (Larry; 1956– , US)
Nash (Stephen; 1974– , Canadian)

05 Belov (Sergei; 1944– , Russian)
Cousy (Bob; 1928– , US)
Lemon (Meadowlark; 1935– , US)
Mikan (George; 1924–2005, US)
O'Neal (Shaquille; 1972– , US)

06 Bryant (Kobe; 1978– , US)
Erving (Julius; 1950– , US)
Jordan (Michael; 1963– , US)
Malone (Karl; 1963– , US)
Miller (Cheryl; 1964– , US)
Pippen (Scottie; 1965– , US)
Rodman (Dennis; 1961– , US)

07 Barkley (Charles; 1963– , US)
Bradley (Bill; 1943– , US)
Iverson (Allen; 1975– , US)
Jackson (Phil; 1945– , US)
Johnson (Earvin 'Magic'; 1959– , US)
Russell (Bill; 1934– , US)

08 Auerbach (Arnold 'Red'; 1917–2006, US)
Nowitzki (Dirk; 1978– , German)
Olajuwon (Hakeem; 1963– , Nigerian/US)
Petrovic (Drazen; 1964–93, Croatian)
Stockton (John; 1962– , US)

09 Robertson (Oscar; 1938– , US)

11 Abdul-Jabbar (Kareem; 1947– , US)
Chamberlain (Wilt; 1936–99, US)

Basketball terms include:

03 key
NBA

04 dunk
hoop
trap

05 block
drive
guard
lay-up
pivot
steal
tap-in

06 assist
basket
box out
centre
post up
rim out
screen
tip-off

07 dribble
forward

foul out
kick out
low post
rebound
sky hook
time-out

08 alley oop
bank shot
charging
fadeaway
foul lane
foul line
hang time
high post
hook shot
inbounds
jump ball
jump hook
jump shot
sixth man
slam dunk
team foul
turnover

09 backboard
chest pass
fast break
field goal
free throw
perimeter
shot clock
violation

10 bounce pass
double pump
double team
foul circle
point guard
transition
travelling

11 goal-tending
pick and roll
zone defence

12 baseball pass
personal foul
power forward
small forward
triple double

13 double dribble
shooting guard
See also **sport**

	technical foul	three-point line
14	full-court press	

bat

Bats include:

03 red	vampire	pipistrelle
05 fruit	**08** big brown	**14** Kitti's hog-nosed
guano	**09** flying fox	**15** lesser horseshoe
hoary	leaf-nosed	Mexican freetail
06 yellow	**10** frog-eating	
07 mastiff	**11** little brown	

battle

Battles include:

04 Jena (1806)	Quebec (1759)	Hastings (1066)
Loos (1915)	Shiloh (1862)	Mafeking (1900)
Neva (1240)	Tobruk (1941–42)	Marathon (490 BC)
Nile (1798)	Towton (1461)	Monmouth (1778)
Zama (202 BC)	Verdun (1916)	Omdurman (1898)
05 Alamo (1836)	Wagram (1809)	Philippi (42 BC)
Anzio (1944)	**07** Antwerp (1918)	Poitiers (1356)
Boyne (1690)	Britain (1940)	Pyramids (1798)
Bulge (1944)	Bull Run (1861/1862)	Saratoga (1777)
Crécy (1346)	Cambrai (1916)	Spion Kop (1900)
Issus (333 BC)	Cassino (1944)	St Albans (1455)
Liège (1914)	Colenso (1899)	Waterloo (1815)
Maipó (1818)	Corunna (1809)	Yorktown (1781)
Maipú (1818)	Cowpens (1781)	**09** Agincourt (1415)
Marne (1914)	Dresden (1813)	Balaclava (1854)
Mylae (260 BC)	Dunkirk (1940)	Bay of Pigs (1961)
Pavia (1525)	Flodden (1513)	Chaeronea (338 BC)
Rhine (1945)	Iwo Jima (1944–45)	Contreras (1847)
Sedan (1870)	Jutland (1916)	Ebro River (1938)
Sluys (1340)	Leipzig (1813)	El Alamein (1943)
Somme (1916)	Lepanto (1571)	Gaugamela (331 BC)
Spurs (1513)	Leuctra (371 BC)	Leyte Gulf (1944)
Valmy (1792)	Marengo (1800)	Nicopolis (1396)
Varna (1828)	Okinawa (1945)	Otterburn (1388)
Ypres (1914/1915)	Plassey (1757)	Pharsalus (48 BC)
06 Actium (31 BC)	Salamis (5 C BC)	Pichincha (1822)
Amiens (1918)	Salerno (1943)	Ramillies (1706)
Arnhem (1944)	Thapsus (46 BC)	Sedgemoor (1685)
Cannae (216 BC)	**08** Atlantic (1940–43)	Seven Days (1862)
Harlaw (1411)	Ayacucho (1824)	Solferino (1859)
Kosovo (1389)	Blenheim (1704)	Spartacus (73–71 BC)
Lützen (1632)	Carabobo (1821)	Stormberg (1899)
Midway (1942)	Culloden (1746)	Trafalgar (1805)
Mohács (1526)	Edgehill (1642)	Vicksburg (1863)
Mycale (5 C BC)	Fontenoy (1745)	Worcester (1651)
Naseby (1645)	Formigny (1450)	**10** Aboukir Bay (1798)
Pinkie (1547)	Granicus (334 BC)	Adrianople (AD 78)

Austerlitz (1805)
Brandywine (1777)
Bunker Hill (1775)
Camperdown (1797)
Charleston (1780)
Chevy Chase (1388)
Cold Harbor (1864)
Copenhagen (1801/1807)
Gettysburg (1863)
Gravelotte (1870)
Majuba Hill (1881)
Malplaquet (1709)
Oudenaarde (1708)
Paardeberg (1900)
Petersburg (1864)

River Plate (1939)
Shrewsbury (1403)
Solway Moss (1542)
Stalingrad (1942–43)
Stillwater (1777)
Tannenberg (1914)
Tel-El-Kebir (1882)
Wilderness (1864)

11 Bannockburn (1314)
Guadalcanal (1942)
Halidon Hill (1333)
Hohenlinden (1800)
Marston Moor (1644)
Modder River (1899)
Navarino Bay (1827)

Pearl Harbor (1941)
Prestonpans (1745)
Sheriffmuir (1715)
Wounded Knee (1890)

12 Mons Graupius (AD 4)
Monte Cassino (1944)
Tet offensive (1968)

13 Bosworth Field (1485)
Cape St Vincent (1797)
Killiecrankie (1689)
Little Bighorn (1876)
Magersfontein (1899)
Passchendaele (1917)
Spanish Armada (1588)

14 Fredericksburg (1862)

See also **siege; war**

bay

Bays include:

03 Tor (England)
04 Acre (Brazil)
Clew (Ireland)
Daya (China)
Kiel (Germany)
Luce (Scotland)
Lyme (England)
Pigs (Cuba)
Tees (England)
05 Algoa (South Africa)
Blind (Canada)
Cloud (Canada)
Enard (Scotland)
Evans (Canada)
False (South Africa)
Fundy (Canada)
Hawke (New Zealand)
Shark (Australia)
Table (South Africa)
06 Baffin (Canada)
Bantry (Ireland)
Bengal (India/Bangladesh/
  Myanmar)
Biscay (France/Spain)
Botany (Australia)
Broken (Australia)
Colwyn (Wales)
Dingle (Ireland)
Dublin (Ireland)
Galway (Ireland)

Hervey (Australia)
Hudson (Canada)
Lubeck (Germany)
Mounts (England)
Naples (Italy)
Plenty (New Zealand)
Tasman (New Zealand)
Walvis (Namibia)
07 Bustard (Australia)
Chaleur (Canada)
Donegal (Ireland)
Dundalk (Ireland)
Fortune (Canada)
Halifax (Australia)
Hudson's (Canada)
Montego (Jamaica)
Moreton (Australia)
Pegasus (New Zealand)
Prudhoe (USA)
Thunder (Canada)
Thunder (USA)
Trinity (Canada)
Volcano (Japan)
08 Campeche (Mexico)
Cardigan (Wales)
Delaware (USA)
Georgian (Canada)
Hang-Chow (China)
Portland (Australia)
Quiberon (France)

San Pablo (USA)
St Bride's (Wales)
St Magnus (Scotland)
Tremadog (Wales)
Weymouth (England)
09 Admiralty (Antarctica)
Discovery (Australia)
Discovery (USA)
Encounter (Australia)
Frobisher (Canada)
Galveston (USA)
Geographe (Australia)
Hermitage (Canada)
Mackenzie (Canada)
Morecambe (England)
Notre Dame (Canada)
Placentia (Canada)
St George's (Canada)
10 Barnstaple (England)
Bridgwater (England)
Carmarthen (Wales)
Chesapeake (USA)
Conception (Canada)
Heligoland (Germany)
Providence (Canada)
Robin Hood's (England)
11 Port Jackson (Australia)
Port Phillip (Australia)
12 San Francisco (USA)

beach

Beaches include:

04 Gold (France)
Juno (France)
Long (USA)
Utah (France)

05 Bells (Australia)
Bondi (Australia)
Cable (Australia)
Miami (USA)
Omaha (France)

Sword (France)

06 Chesil (England)
Malibu (USA)
Sunset (USA)
Tahiti (French Polynesia)
Venice (USA)

07 Daytona (USA)
Ipanema (Brazil)
Pattaya (Thailand)

Waikiki (USA)

08 St Tropez (France)
Virginia (USA)

09 Blackpool (England)

10 Copacabana (Brazil)

11 Coney Island (USA)

13 Skeleton Coast (Namibia)

15 Surfers Paradise (Australia)

bean

Beans and pulses include:

03 dal
pea
soy
wax

04 dhal
fava
gram
lima
mung
navy
okra
snap
soya

05 aduki
black
broad

carob
green
pinto
sugar
tonka

06 adzuki
Boston
butter
chilli
cowpea
French
kidney
legume
lentil
locust
runner

string

07 alfalfa
edamame
fasolia
haricot
snow pea

08 black-eye
borlotti
chickpea
garbanzo
split pea
sugar pea

09 black-eyed
black gram
flageolet
green gram

mangetout
petit pois
pigeon pea
puy lentil
red kidney
red lentil

10 beansprout
cannellini
golden gram

11 dwarf runner
garbanzo pea
green lentil

12 black-eyed pea
marrowfat pea

13 scarlet runner
water chestnut

See also **food**; **vegetable**

bear

Bears include:

03 sea
sun

04 balu
cave
Pooh
Yogi

05 baloo
black
brown

Bruin
Great
honey
koala
Nandi
polar
sloth
Sooty
teddy

water
white

06 Little
native
Rupert
woolly

07 grizzly
Malayan

08 cinnamon

09 Ursa Major
Ursa Minor

10 giant panda
Paddington

13 Iorek Byrnison
Teddy Robinson
Winnie the Pooh

bed

Beds include:

01 Z

03 box
cot

day

04 boat
bunk

camp
crib
sofa

twin

05 berth
divan

futon
water
06 cradle
double
pallet
Put-u-up®
settee
single

sleigh
07 folding
hammock
trestle
truckle
trundle
08 bassinet
foldaway

king-size
mattress
platform
put-you-up
09 couchette
king-sized
lit bateau
palliasse

queen-size
shakedown
10 adjustable
four-poster
mid sleeper
queen-sized
11 high sleeper
12 chaise longue

Bedclothes include:

05 doona
duvet
quilt
sheet
06 pillow
07 bedroll
blanket
bolster

valance
08 coverlet
09 bed canopy
bedspread
comforter
eiderdown
throwover
10 duvet cover

pillowcase
pillow sham
pillowslip
quilt cover
11 counterpane
fitted sheet
sleeping bag
13 mattress cover

valanced sheet
Witney blanket
14 patchwork quilt
15 cellular blanket
electric blanket

See also **house**

beer

Beers include:

03 ale
dry
ice
IPA
keg
04 bock
mild
Pils
rice
05 abbey
black
fruit
green
guest
heavy
honey
Kriek
kvass
lager
March
plain
sahti
sixty
steam
stone
stout
wheat
06 bitter
Dunkel
eighty

export
gueuze
Helles
Kölsch
lambic
Märzen
old ale
porter
red ale
shandy
Vienna
07 Altbier
bottled
draught
Eisbock
pale ale
Pilsner
real ale
seventy
08 amber ale
brown ale
cream ale
Guinness®
home brew
Irish ale
light ale
Pilsener
Trappist
09 Framboise
frambozen

microbrew
milk stout
Rauchbier
snakebite
Weissbier
winter ale
10 barley wine
black lager
harvest ale
Hefeweizen
low-alcohol
malt liquor
sweet stout
Weisse Bier
Weizenbier
11 black-and-tan
12 bière de garde
Christmas ale
India Pale Ale
oatmeal stout
13 Hefe-Weissbier
sixty shilling
14 Berliner Weisse
eighty shilling
Kristall-Weizen
15 cask-conditioned
seventy shilling

Brewing terms include:

03 fox
   keg
   pin
   tun
04 back
   bigg
   butt
   cask
   head
   hoop
   hops
   lees
   malt
   mash
   stum
   wort
05 draff
   goods
   grain
   grist
   middy
   nappy
   round
   stave

   yeast
06 barley
   barrel
   bright
   browst
   cooper
   copper
   fining
   firkin
   infuse
   liquor
   mature
   multum
   straik
   sweets
   trough
   widget
07 beerage
   bummock
   draught
   extract
   ferment
   flowers
   gravity

   hogwash
   hop back
   hop boil
   malt tea
   mashman
   mash-tub
   mash-tun
   mash-vat
   real ale
   set mash
   zymurgy
08 blacking
   hogshead
   home-brew
   maltster
   molasses
   mucilage
   pale malt
   puncheon
   real beer
   sparging
09 amber malt
   blown malt
   brown malt

   cleansing
   isinglass
   kilderkin
   soft spile
   under-back
10 barleycorn
   black strap
   brewmaster
   malt-factor
   malt liquor
   mashing-tub
   saccharine
11 attenuation
   broad cooper
12 abroad cooper
   attemperator
   essentia bina
   final gravity
   microbrewery
13 brewers' pounds
   carbon dioxide
   saccharimeter
   saccharometer

See also **drink**

Beethoven, Ludwig van (1770–1827)

Significant works include:

06 'Choral' (Symphony; 1824)
   'Eroica' (Symphony; 1805)
   'Spring' (Sonata; 1801)

07 *Fidelio* (1805)
   'Emperor' (Concerto; 1811)

08 'Kreutzer' (Sonata; 1803)
   'Pastoral' (Symphony; 1808)

09 'Les Adieux' (Sonata; 1803)
   'Moonlight' (Sonata; 1801)
   'Waldstein' (Sonata; 1803)

10 *Grosse Fuge* (String Quartet; 1825)

   'Pathétique' (Sonata; 1798)

12 *Archduke Trio* (1811)
   'Appassionata' (Sonata; 1804)

13 *Missa Solemnis* (1824)
   'Hammerklavier' (Sonata; 1818)

14 *Egmont Overture* (1810)

16 *Leonora Overtures* (1805)

18 *Diabelli Variations* (1819–23)
   Rasumovsky Quartets (1806)

beetle

Beetles include:

03 dor
   may
   oil
04 bark
   dorr
   dung
   flea
   gold

   leaf
   musk
   pine
   rose
   rove
   stag
05 black
   click

   clock
   shard
   snout
   tiger
   water
06 batler
   carpet
   chafer

diving
dor-fly
elater
ground
larder
may bug
museum
sacred
scarab
sexton
spider
spring
weevil
07 blister
bruchid
burying
cadelle
carabid
carrion
diamond
gold-bug
goliath
hop-flea

hornbug
June bug
rose bug
08 bum-clock
cardinal
Colorado
darkling
glowworm
Hercules
Japanese
ladybird
longhorn
minotaur
skipjack
tortoise
wireworm
woodworm
09 cantharis
Christmas
clavicorn
dermestid
furniture
goldsmith

longicorn
tumblebug
whirligig
10 bloody-nose
bombardier
churchyard
cockchafer
deathwatch
pine-chafer
rhinoceros
rose chafer
scarabaean
scarabaeid
Spanish fly
tumbledung
turnip flea
11 bloody-nosed
coprophagan
grain weevil
typographer
13 argus tortoise
house longhorn

See also **insect**

Belgium

Cities and notable towns in Belgium include:

04 Gand	Ieper	Bruges	Oostende
Gent	Liège	Brugge	**09** Charleroi
Luik	Namur	Ostend	Zeebrugge
Mons	Ypres	**07** Antwerp	
05 Ghent	**06** Anvers	**08** Brussels	

Administrative divisions of Belgium, with regional capitals:

05 Liège (Liège)	**08** Limbourg (Hasselt)	**14** Flemish Brabant (Leuven)
Namur (Namur)	**10** Luxembourg (Arlon)	Walloon Brabant (Wavre)
07 Antwerp (Antwerp)	**12** East Flanders (Ghent)	
Hainaut (Mons)	West Flanders (Bruges)	

Belgian landmarks include:

05 Meuse	Notre Dame	Manneken Pis
Senne	**10** Grand Place	Royal Palace
07 Atomium	Jeaneke Pis	**12** Hôtel de Ville
Belfort	Market Hall	Rubens's House
Scheldt	Rubenshuis	**13** Brabo Fountain
08 Stadhuis	**11** Gravensteen	**14** Ghent Cathedral
09 Cloth Hall	Jeanneke Pis	Rue des Bouchers
Menin Gate	Maison du Roi	**15** Bruges Cathedral

See also **Low Countries**

belief

Beliefs include:

06 holism
malism
racism
07 animism
atheism
elitism
08 demonism
feminism
hedonism
humanism
nihilism

Satanism
09 pantheism
physicism
tritheism
10 liberalism
Manicheism
monotheism
polytheism
11 agnosticism
parallelism

supremacism
tetratheism
12 Manicheanism
13 ethnocentrism
individualism
structuralism
14 fundamentalism
traditionalism
tripersonalism
15 supernaturalism

Believers include:

03 Jew
04 Babi
Jain
Sikh
Sofi
Sufi
05 Babee
Hindu
Jaina
06 holist
Muslim
07 Alawite
animist
Bahaist
Genevan
Lollard
Scotist
08 Arminian
Buddhist
Calixtin
Catholic

demonist
Erastian
Glassite
humanist
Lutheran
Nazarean
Nazarene
Pelagian
Salesian
Satanist
Wesleyan
09 animalist
Calixtine
Christian
Confucian
Eutychian
Gregorian
Methodist
Nestorian
Origenist
pantheist
Sabellian

Simeonite
Wyclifite
10 Bergsonian
Berkeleian
Cameronian
Capernaite
Holy Roller
Marcionite
polytheist
Wycliffite
11 Sandemanian
Valentinian
12 Apollinarian
Southcottian
13 Hutchinsonian
Roman Catholic
Swedenborgian
14 fundamentalist
the Oxford group
15 supernaturalist

See also **Buddhism; Christianity; Hinduism; Islam; Judaism; missionary; philosophy; politics; priest; religion; Sikhism; theology**

berry

Berries include:

04 goji
05 lichi
06 lichee
litchi
lychee
07 bramble
leechee
08 bilberry
See also **fruit**

dewberry
goosegog
mulberry
tayberry
09 blaeberry
blueberry
cranberry
raspberry
shadberry

whimberry
10 blackberry
cloudberry
elderberry
gooseberry
loganberry
redcurrant
salal berry
strawberry

11 boysenberry
huckleberry
sallal berry
12 blackcurrant
serviceberry
whitecurrant
whortleberry

bet

Bets and betting systems include:

03 TAB

04 tote

06 double
parlay
roll-up
tierce
treble
triple

See also **gambling**

Yankee

07 à cheval
each way

08 ante-post
forecast
perfecta
quinella
trifecta

09 on the nose
quadrella

10 martingale
pari-mutuel
superfecta

11 accumulator
daily double

13 double or quits

Betjeman, Sir John (1906–84)

Significant works include:

09 *Mount Zion* (1931)

10 *High and Low* (1966)

12 *A Nip in the Air* (1974)
Continual Dew (1937)

14 *Collected Poems* (1958)

15 *Summoned by Bells* (1960)

16 *Ghastly Good Taste* (1933)

20 *New Bats in Old Belfries* (1945)

22 *A Few Late Chrysanthemums* (1954)

23 *Old Lights For New Chancels* (1940)

Bible

Versions of the Bible include:

02 AV
RV

03 NIV

05 Douai
Douay
Itala

Reims

06 Geneva
Gideon
Italic
Wyclif

07 Matthew

Peshito
Tyndale
Vulgate

08 Breeches
Peshitta
Peshitto

Wycliffe

09 Coverdale
King James

10 New English
Septuagint

14 Revised Version

Old Testament books of the Bible:

03 Job (Book of)

04 Amos (Book of)
Ezra (Book of)
Joel (Book of)
Ruth (Book of)

05 Hosea (Book of)
Jonah (Book of)
Kings (Books of)
Micah (Book of)
Nahum (Book of)

06 Daniel (Book of)
Esther (Book of)
Exodus (Book of)
Haggai (Book of)
Isaiah (Book of)
Joshua (Book of)
Judges (Book of)
Psalms (Book of)
Samuel (Books of)

07 Ezekiel (Book of)
Genesis (Book of)
Malachi (Book of)
Numbers (Book of)
Obadiah (Book of)

08 Habakkuk (Book of)
Jeremiah (Book of)
Jeremiah (Letter of)
Nehemiah (Book of)
Proverbs (Book of)

09 Leviticus (Book of)
Zechariah (Book of)
Zephaniah (Book of)

10 Chronicles (Books of)

11 Deuteronomy (Book of)

12 Ecclesiastes (Book of)
Lamentations

13 Song of Solomon

New Testament books of the Bible:

04 John (Gospel according to)
John (Letters of)
Jude (Letter of)
Luke (Gospel according to)
Mark (Gospel according to)

05 James (Letter of)
Peter (Letters of)
Titus (Letter of Paul to)

06 Romans (Letter of Paul to the)

07 Hebrews (Letter of Paul to the)
Matthew (Gospel according to)
Timothy (Letters of Paul to)

08 Philemon (Letter of Paul to)

09 Ephesians (Letter of Paul to the)
Galatians (Letter of Paul to the)

10 Colossians (Letter of Paul to the)
Revelation (Book of)

11 Corinthians (Letters of Paul to the)
Philippians (Letter of Paul to the)

13 Thessalonians (Letters of Paul to the)

17 Acts of the Apostles

18 Apocalypse of St John

Apocryphal books of the Bible include:

03 Bar
Esd
Jud
Sir
Sus
Tob

04 Macc
Wisd

05 Tobit (Book of)

06 Baruch (Book of)
Ecclus

Esdras (Books of)
Judith (Book of)

07 Pr of Man
Susanna (History of)

08 Bel and Dr
Manasseh (Prayer of)

09 Maccabees

14 Ecclesiasticus (Book of)

15 Bel and the Dragon
Wisdom of Solomon (Book of)

Biblical characters include:

03 Dan
Eve
Gad
Ham
Job
Lot

04 Abel
Adam
Ahab
Amos
Anna
Baal
Cain
Esau
Ezra
Jehu
Joel
John
Leah
Levi
Luke
Mark
Mary
Noah
Paul
Ruth

Saul
Seth
Shem

05 Aaron
Abner
Achan
Annas
Asher
Caleb
David
Enoch
Hagar
Herod
Hosea
Isaac
Jacob
James
Jesse
Jesus
Jonah
Judah
Magog
Micah
Moses
Nahum
Naomi

Peter
Rahab
Rhoda
Sarah
Sheba
Sihon
Silas
Simon
Titus
Tobit
Uriah

06 Andrew
Baruch
Christ
Daniel
Darius
Elijah
Elisha
Esther
Gideon
Hannah
Isaiah
Joseph
Joshua
Josiah
Judith

Martha
Miriam
Nathan
Nimrod
Philip
Pilate
Rachel
Reuben
Salome
Samson
Samuel
Simeon
Sisera
Thomas
Uzziah
Vashti

07 Abigail
Abraham
Absalom
Amaziah
Azariah
Cleopas
Delilah
Ephraim
Ezekiel
Gabriel

Goliath
Ishmael
Japheth
Jezebel
Lazarus
Malachi
Matthew
Micaiah
Michael
Obadiah
Rebecca
Rebekah
Solomon
Stephen
Susanna
Tabitha
Timothy
Zebedee
Zebulun

08 Barabbas
Barnabus
Benjamin
Caiaphas
Habbakuk
Hezekiah
Issachar
Jeremiah
Jeroboam
Jonathan
Manasseh
Matthias
Mordecai
Naphtali
Nehemiah
Rehoboam
Thaddeus
Zedekiah

09 Bathsheba
Nathanael
Nathaniel
Nicodemus
Priscilla
Zacchaeus
Zacharias
Zechariah
Zephaniah

10 Adam and Eve
Bartimaeus
Belshazzar
Methuselah
Simon Magus
Simon Peter
Theophilus

11 Bartholomew
Gog and Magog

Jehoshaphat
Jesus Christ
Melchizedek

12 Herod Agrippa
Herod Antipas
James the Less
Mephibosheth
Queen of Sheba

13 Herod the Great
Judas Iscariot
Mary Magdalene
Pontius Pilate
Simon of Cyrene

14 John the Baptist
Nebuchadnezzar
Simon the Zealot

Biblical places include:

03 Nod
04 Gaza
Rome
05 Babel
Egypt
Judah
Sodom
06 Canaan

Cyrene
Israel
Judaea
Mt Zion
Red Sea
07 Babylon
Calvary
Jericho
Mt Sinai

Nineveh
08 Bethesda
Dalmatia
Damascus
Golgotha
Gomorrah
Mt Ararat
Nazareth

09 Bethlehem
Jerusalem
Palestine
10 Alexandria
Gethsemane
11 River Jordan
12 Garden of Eden
Sea of Galilee

Biblical terms include:

02 NT
OT
03 ark
God
law
05 canon
flood
06 gospel
missal
Yahweh
07 epistle
evangel
gospels
hexapla

Jehovah
letters
Messiah
miracle
octapla
parable
08 epistles
good book
holy writ
Pharisee
prophets
writings
09 Apocrypha
Holy Bible

Holy Ghost
leviathan
Samaritan
10 Armageddon
evangelist
Holy Spirit
Pentateuch
Philistine
revelation
Scriptures
12 New Testament
Old Testament
13 Good Samaritan
14 holy Scriptures

See also **patriarch**; **plague**; **prophet**

bicycle

Bicycles include:

03 BMX
04 push
solo
05 hobby
racer
06 safety
tandem
07 chopper
Raleigh®
touring
08 draisene
draisine

exercise	tricycle	boneshaker	stationary
kangaroo	unicycle	dandy-horse	two-wheeler
mountain	**09** recumbent	fairy-cycle	velocipede
ordinary	**10** all-terrain	fixed-wheel	**13** penny farthing

Bicycle parts include:

03 hub	hub gear	disc brake	Woods® valve
04 bell	pannier	drum brake	**11** gear shifter
fork	rim tape	gear cable	lamp bracket
gear	toe clip	gear lever	Presta® valve
lamp	tool bag	gearwheel	roller chain
pump	top tube	inner tube	speedometer
tire	**08** aero bars	kickstand	
tyre	cassette	prop stand	**12** brake caliper
05 brake	chainset	reflector	coaster brake
chain	crankset	seat stays	diamond frame
crank	crossbar	tyre valve	spoke nipples
frame	down tube	wheel lock	steering head
pedal	head tube	**10** brake block	steering tube
spoke	mudguard	brake cable	stirrup guide
wheel	rim brake	brake lever	wheel bearing
06 dynamo	rod brake	chain guard	wheel spindle
fender	seat post	chain guide	**13** bottom bracket
hanger	seat tube	chain stays	clipless pedal
pulley	sprocket	chain wheel	freewheel unit
saddle	wheel nut	crank lever	handlebar stem
spokes	wheel rim	derailleur	Schrader® valve
07 bar ends	**09** brake shoe	drive train	shock absorber
carrier	chain link	handlebars	sprocket wheel
headset	chain ring	seat pillar	**14** drop handlebars
		stabilizer	side-pull brakes

See also **cycling**

biochemistry

Biochemists include:

02 Li (Choh Hao; 1913–87, US)

03 Dam (Henrik; 1895–1976, Danish)

04 Abel (John Jacob; 1857–1938, US)
Cech (Thomas; 1947– , US)
Cori (Carl; 1896–1984, US)
Cori (Gerty; 1896–1957, US)
Doty (Paul; 1920–2011, US)
Duve (Christian de; 1917–2013, Belgian)
Endo (Akira; 1933– , Japanese)
Funk (Casimir; 1884–1967, US)
Rose (William C; 1887–1984, US)
Wald (George; 1906–97, US)

05 Bloch (Konrad; 1912–2000, US)
Boyer (Herbert; 1936– , US)
Boyer (Paul D; 1918– , US)
Brown (Rachel Fuller; 1898–1980, US)
Chain (Sir Ernst B; 1906–79, British)
Cohen (Seymour S; 1917– , US)

Cohen (Stanley; 1922– , US)
Doisy (Edward A; 1893–1986, US)
Elion (Gertrude B; 1918–99, US)
Jacob (François; 1920–2013, French)
Kamen (Martin; 1913–2002, US)
Krebs (Sir Edwin G; 1918–2009, US)
Krebs (Sir Hans; 1900–81, German/British)
Lynen (Feodor; 1911–79, German)
Monod (Jacques; 1910–76, French)
Moore (Stanford; 1913–82, US)
Smith (Lester; 1904–92, English)
Smith (Michael; 1932–2000, Canadian)
Stein (William H; 1911–80, US)
Synge (Richard L M; 1914–94, English)
Tatum (Edward; 1909–75, US)

06 Asimov (Isaac; 1920–92, US)
Beadle (George; 1903–89, US)
Chance (Britton; 1913–2010, US)
Collip (James 'Bert'; 1892–1965, Canadian)

de Duve (Christian; 1917–2013, Belgian)
Domagk (Gerhard; 1895–1964, German)
Holley (Robert W; 1922–93, US)
Keilin (David; 1887–1963, Russian/British)
Leloir (Luis; 1906–87, Argentine)
Levene (Phoebus; 1869–1940, US)
Martin (Archer; 1910–2002, English)
Michel (Hartmut; 1948– , German)
Mullis (Kary B; 1944– , US)
Oparin (Aleksandr; 1894–1980, Russian)
Pardee (Arthur B; 1921– , US)
Perutz (Max; 1914–2002, Austrian/British)
Peters (Sir Rudolf Albert; 1889–1982, English)
Porter (Rodney R; 1917–85, English)
Sanger (Frederick; 1918– , English)
Steitz (Thomas; 1940– , US)
Sumner (James B; 1887–1955, US)
Walker (Sir John E; 1941– , English)
Yonath (Ada; 1939– , Israeli)

07 Abraham (Sir Edward; 1913–99, English)
Edelman (Gerald M; 1929– , US)
Emerson (Gladys Anderson; 1903–84, US)
Fischer (Edmond H; 1920– , US)
Folkers (Karl; 1906–97, US)
Hopkins (Sir Frederick; 1861–1947, English)
Khorana (H Gobind; 1922–2011, US)
Lipmann (Fritz; 1899–1986, US)
Needham (Joseph; 1900–95, English)
Okazaki (Reiji; 1930–75, Japanese)
Quastel (J H; 1899–1987, English)
Rodbell (Martin; 1925–98, US)
Schally (Andrew V; 1926– , US)
Sherman (Henry C; 1875–1955, US)
Stanley (Wendell M; 1904–71, US)

See also **chemistry**

Waksman (Selman; 1888–1973, US)
Warburg (Otto; 1883–1970, German)

08 Anfinsen (Christian B; 1916–95, US)
Blumberg (Baruch S; 1925–2011, US)
Chargaff (Erwin; 1905–2002, US)
Elvehjem (Conrad; 1901–62, US)
Hoagland (Mahlon; 1921–2009, US)
Kornberg (Arthur; 1918–2007, US)
Kornberg (Roger D; 1947– , US)
Kornberg (Sir Hans; 1928– , German/British)
McCollum (Elmer; 1879–1967, US)
Meyerhof (Otto; 1884–1951, US)
Mitchell (Peter; 1920–92, English)
Northrop (John H; 1891–1987, US)
Prusiner (Stanley B; 1942– , US)
Theorell (Hugo; 1903–82, Swedish)
Vigneaud (Vincent du; 1901–78, US)
Virtanen (Artturi; 1895–1973, Finnish)
Weinberg (Robert; 1942– , US)

09 Bergström (Sune; 1916–2004, Swedish)
Butenandt (Adolf; 1903–95, German)
Greengard (Paul; 1925– , US)
Hitchings (George H; 1905–98, US)
Michaelis (Leonor; 1875–1949, US)
Nirenberg (Marshall W; 1927–2010, US)

10 Samuelsson (Bengt I; 1934– , Swedish)
Sutherland (Earl W; 1915–74, US)

11 Hoppe-Seyler (Felix; 1825–95, German)

12 Euler-Chelpin (Hans von; 1873–1964, Swedish)
Ramakrishnan (Venkatraman; 1952– , Indian)
Schoenheimer (Rudolf; 1898–1941, US)
Szent-Györgyi (Albert von; 1893–1986, US)

14 Fraenkel-Conrat (Heinz; 1910–99, US)

biography

Biographers include:

04 Bold (Alan; 1943–98, Scottish)
Brod (Max; 1884–1968, Austrian)
Edel (Leon; 1907–97, US)

05 Croly (George; 1780–1860, Irish)
Gwynn (Stephen; 1864–1950, Irish)
Haley (Alex; 1921–92, US)
Lodge (Henry Cabot; 1850–1924, US)
Lucas (E V; 1868–1938, English)
Spark (Dame Muriel; 1918–2006, Scottish)
Weems (Mason Locke; 1759–1825, US)

06 Aubrey (John; 1626–97, English)
Martin (Sir Theodore; 1816–1909, Scottish)
Morley (John, Viscount; 1838–1923, English)
Motion (Andrew; 1952– , English)
Sparks (Jared; 1789–1866, US)
Symons (A J A; 1900–41, English)
Symons (Julian; 1912–94, English)

Wilson (A N; 1950– , English)

07 Ackroyd (Peter; 1949– , English)
Barnard (Marjorie; 1897–1987, Australian)
Bedford (Sybille; 1911–2006, German/British)
Bolitho (Hector; 1898–1977, New Zealand)
Boswell (James; 1740–95, Scottish)
Debrett (John; c.1750–1822, English)
Ellmann (Richard; 1918–87, US)
Forster (John; 1812–76, English)
Granger (James; 1723–76, English)
Holroyd (Michael; 1935– , English)
Lindsay (Philip; 1906–58, Australian)
Lubbock (Percy; 1879–1965, English)
Maurois (André; 1885–1967, French)
Pearson (Hesketh; 1887–1964, English)
Sherard (Robert; 1861–1943, English)
Sitwell (Sir Sacheverell; 1897–1988, English)

08 Berryman (John; 1914–72, US)
Chalmers (Alexander; 1759–1834, Scottish)
Lockhart (John Gibson; 1794–1854, Scottish)
Plutarch (c.46–c.120 AD, Greek)
Quennell (Sir Peter; 1905–93, English)
Sinclair (Sir Keith; 1922–93, New Zealand)

Spurling (Hilary; 1940– , English)
Strachey (Lytton; 1880–1932, English)
Van Doren (Carl; 1885–1950, US)
09 Aldington (Richard; 1892–1962, English)
Kingsmill (Hugh; 1889–1949, English)
Suetonius (c.69–c.140 AD, Roman)
15 Sebag Montefiore (Simon; 1965– , English)

biology

Biology fields include:

06 botany
07 bionics
ecology
zoology
08 biometry
cytology
genetics
genomics
mycology
taxonomy
virology
09 bionomics
Darwinism
evolution
histology
Mendelism

pathology
phycology
10 biometrics
biophysics
bioscience
embryology
enzymology
immunology
Lamarckism
morphology
physiology
proteomics
teratology
toxicology
11 aerobiology
agrobiology
biodynamics

cryobiology
cybernetics
stoichology
systematics
12 bacteriology
biochemistry
biogeography
biorhythmics
cytogenetics
human biology
hydrobiology
macroecology
microbiology
neo-Darwinism
neuroscience
organography
parasitology

pharmacology
photobiology
radiobiology
sociobiology
13 biopsychology
biotechnology
chronobiology
endocrinology
marine biology
palaeontology
14 biogeochemisty
bioinformatics
biomathematics
biometeorology
biosystematics
natural history
15 cellular biology

Biologists, marine biologists and naturalists include:

03 His (Wilhelm; 1831–1904, Swiss/German)
Ray (John; 1627–1705, English)
Say (Thomas; 1787–1834, US)
04 Axel (Richard; 1946– , US)
Baer (Karl Ernst von; 1792–1876, Estonian/German)
Bell (Thomas; 1792–1880, English)
Berg (Paul; 1926– , US)
Cory (Charles B; 1857–1921, US)
Fell (Dame Honor; 1900–86, English)
Hume (Allan; 1829–1912, Scottish)
Hunt (Tim; 1943– , English)
Katz (Sir Bernard; 1911–2003, German/British)
Klug (Sir Aaron; 1926– , English)
Koch (Ludwig; 1881–1974, German)
Loeb (Jacques; 1859–1924, German/US)
Lyon (Mary; 1925– , English)
Muir (John; 1838–1914, Scottish/US)
Obel (Matthias de L'; 1538–1616, Flemish)
Sars (Michael; 1805–69, Norwegian)
Savi (Paolo; 1798–1871, Italian)
Skou (Jens; 1918– , Danish)
Vogt (Peter; 1932– , German/US)
05 Arber (Werner; 1929– , Swiss)

Bacon (Francis, Viscount; 1561–1626, English)
Baird (Spencer; 1823–87, US)
Bates (Henry; 1825–92, English)
Beebe (William; 1877–1962, US)
Belon (Pierre; 1517–64, French)
Blyth (Edward; 1810–73, English)
Brehm (Alfred Edmund; 1829–84, German)
Bruce (Sir David; 1855–1931, Australian/British)
Cetti (Francesco; 1726–78, Italian)
Chase (Martha; 1927–2003, US)
Cohen (Stanley; 1922– , US)
Crick (Francis; 1916–2004, English)
David (Armand; 1826–1900, French)
Elton (Charles; 1900–91, English)
Evans (Alice; 1881–1975, US)
Golgi (Camillo; 1843–1926, Italian)
Gosse (Philip; 1810–88, English)
Hardy (Sir Alister; 1896–1985, English)
Huber (Robert; 1937– , German)
Lewis (Edward B; 1918–2004, US)
Lobel (Matthias de; 1538–1616, Flemish)
Luria (Salvador; 1912–91, Italian/US)
Lwoff (André; 1902–94, French)

Monod (Théodore; 1902–2000, French)
Neher (Erwin; 1944– , German)
Nurse (Sir Paul; 1949– , English)
Radde (Gustav; 1831–1903, Polish/German)
Rubin (Gerald; 1950– , US)
Sabin (Albert; 1906–93, Russian/US)
Scott (Sir Peter; 1909–89, English)
Selby (Prideaux John; 1788–1867, English)
Sharp (Phillip; 1944– , US)
Smith (Hamilton; 1931– , US)
Steno (Nicolaus; 1638–86, Danish)
Weiss (Robin; 1940– , English)
White (Gilbert; 1720–93, English)
Yalow (Rosalyn; 1921–2011, US)
Yonge (Charles Maurice; 1899–1986, English)

06 Akeley (Carl; 1864–1926, US)
Altman (Sidney; 1939– , Canadian)
Anning (Mary; 1799–1847, English)
Bishop (Michael; 1936– , US)
Blobel (Günter; 1936– , US)
Bonnet (Charles; 1720–93, Swiss)
Boveri (Theodor; 1862–1915, German)
Buffon (George-Louis, Comte de; 1707–88, French)
Cairns (H. John 1922– , English)
Carson (Rachel; 1907–64, US)
Castle (William; 1867–1962, US)
Chagas (Carlos; 1879–1934, Brazilian)
Claude (Albert; 1899–1983, Belgian)
Darwin (Charles; 1809–82, English)
Dayton (Paul K; 1941– , US)
Denton (Sir Eric; 1923–2007, English)
Finsch (Otto; 1839–1917, German)
Friend (Charlotte; 1921–87, US)
Geddes (Sir Patrick; 1854–1932, Scottish)
Gesner (Conrad; 1516–65, Swiss)
Häckel (Ernst; 1834–1919, German)
Hudson (W H; 1841–1922, Argentine/British)
Huxley (Hugh; 1924– , English)
Huxley (Sir Julian; 1887–1975, English)
Huxley (Thomas; 1825–95, English)
Isaacs (Alick; 1921–67, Scottish)
Kandel (Eric; 1929– , Austrian/US)
Mivart (St George; 1827–1900, English)
Morgan (Thomas Hunt; 1866–1945, US)
Müller (Otto; 1730–84, Danish)
Murray (Sir John; 1841–1914, Canadian)
Nansen (Fridtjof; 1861–1930, Norwegian)
Nocard (Edmond; 1850–1903, French)
Palade (George; 1912–2008, Romanian/US)
Pallas (Peter; 1741–1811, German)
Rathke (Martin Heinrich; 1793–1860, Polish/German)
Sloane (Sir Hans; 1660–1753, Northern Irish/British)
Turner (William; c.1510–68, English)

Ussing (Hans; 1911–2000, Danish)
Varmus (Harold; 1939– , US)
Watson (James; 1928– , US)
Wilson (Edward; 1872–1912, English)
Wilson (Edward O; 1929– , US)

07 Adamson (Joy; 1910–80, Austrian/British)
Agassiz (Elizabeth; 1822–1907, US)
Agassiz (Louis; 1807–73, US)
Andrews (Roy; 1884–1960, US)
Audouin (Jean Victor; 1797–1841, French)
Bastian (Henry; 1837–1915, English)
Beneden (Edouard; 1846–1910, Belgian)
Bombard (Alain; 1924–2005, French)
Boyd Orr (John, Lord; 1880–1971, Scottish)
Brenner (Sydney; 1927– , South African/British)
Britten (Roy; 1919–2012, US)
Davaine (Casimir; 1812–82, French)
Dawkins (Richard; 1941– , Kenyan/British)
Durrell (Gerald; 1925–95, English)
Epstein (Sir Anthony; 1921– , English)
Flavell (Richard; 1945– , British)
Flexner (Simon; 1863–1946, US)
Förster (Johann Reinhold; 1729–98, German)
Gilbert (Walter; 1932– , US)
Graells (Mariano de la Paz; 1809–98, Spanish)
Haeckel (Ernst; 1834–1919, German)
Haldane (J B S; 1892–1964, English/Indian)
Hershey (A D; 1908–97, US)
Jackson (Barbara, Baroness; 1914–81, English)
Kendrew (Sir John; 1917–97, English)
Lamarck (Jean; 1744–1829, French)
Lubbock (Sir John; 1834–1913, English)
McLaren (Dame Anne; 1927–2007, English)
Merriam (Clinton Hart; 1885–1942, US)
Montagu (George; 1753–1815, English)
Nathans (Daniel; 1928–99, US)
Nicolle (Charles; 1866–1936, French)
Nuttall (Thomas; 1786–1859, English/US)
Pasteur (Louis; 1822–95, French)
Ptashne (Mark; 1940– , US)
Roberts (Richard; 1943– , English)
Russell (Sir Frederick; 1897–1984, English)
Sanders (Howard; 1921–2001, US)
Sibbald (Sir Robert; 1641–1722, Scottish)
Spencer (Sir Baldwin; 1860–1929, English/Australian)
Stanier (Roger; 1916–82, Canadian)
Steller (Georg; 1709–46, German)
Steptoe (Patrick; 1913–88, English)
Stevens (Nettie; 1861–1912, US)
Swinhoe (Robert; 1836–77, Indian/British)
Van Niel (Cornelis; 1897–1985, Dutch)
Wallace (Alfred; 1823–1913, English)
Wyckoff (Ralph; 1897–1994, US)

08 Beverton (Raymond; 1922–95, English)
Brinster (Ralph; 1932– , US)
Brünnich (Morten Thrane; 1737–1827, Danish)
Chamisso (Adalbert von; 1781–1838, French/German)
Cousteau (Jacques; 1910–97, French)
Davidson (Eric; 1937– , US)
Delbrück (Max; 1906–81, German)
Drummond (Henry; 1851–97, Scottish)
Flemming (Walther; 1843–1905, German)
Harrison (Ross; 1870–1959, US)
Hartwell (Lee; 1939– , US)
Humboldt (Alexander, Baron von; 1769–1859, German)
Jeffreys (Sir Alec; 1950– , English)
Lacépède (Bernard de Laville, Comte de; 1756–1825, French)
Linnaeus (Carl; 1707–78, Swedish)
Li Shizen (1518–93, Chinese)
Margulis (Lynn; 1938–2011, US)
Meselson (Matthew; 1930–2011, US)
Milstein (Cesar; 1927–2002, Argentine/British)
Richmond (Sir Mark; 1931– , Australian/British)
Schimper (Karl; 1803–67, German)
Sielmann (Heinz; 1917–2006, German)
Swainson (William; 1789–1855, English)
Tonegawa (Susumu; 1939– , Japanese)
Tristram (Henry Baker; 1822–1906, English)
Weismann (August; 1834–1914, German)
Weissman (Charles; 1931– , Hungarian/Swiss)
Williams (Robley; 1908–95, US)

09 Baltimore (David; 1938– , US)
Berthelot (Sabin; 1794–1880, French)

Burroughs (John; 1837–1921, US)
Carpenter (William; 1813–85, English)
Collinson (Peter; 1694–1768, English)
Ehrenberg (Christian Gottfried; 1795–1876, German)
Lederberg (Joshua; 1925–2008, US)
MacArthur (Robert; 1930–72, US)
Schaudinn (Fritz; 1871–1906, German)
Wieschaus (Eric; 1947– , US)

10 Aldrovandi (Ulisse; 1522–1605, Italian)
Brongniart (Alexandre; 1770–1847, French)
Darlington (Cyril; 1903–81, English)
Felsenfeld (Gary; 1929– , US)
Leichhardt (Ludwig; 1813–c.1848, Prussian/Australian)
Montagnier (Luc; 1932– , French)
Richardson (Sir John; 1787–1865, Scottish)
Swammerdam (Jan; 1637–80, Dutch)
Tradescant (John, the Elder; 1570–c.1638, English)

11 Cretzschmar (Philipp Jakob; 1786–1845, German)
Deisenhofer (Johann; 1943– , US)
Goldschmidt (Richard; 1878–1958, German)
Leeuwenhoek (Antoni van; 1632–1723, Dutch)
Metchnikoff (Elie; 1845–1916, Russian)
Ramón y Cajal (Santiago; 1852–1934, Spanish)
Spallanzani (Lazaro; 1729–99, Italian)

12 Attenborough (Sir David; 1926– , English)
Maynard Smith (John; 1920–2004, English)
Wigglesworth (Sir Vincent Brian; 1899–1994, English)

14 Levi-Montalcini (Rita; 1909–2012, Italian)

Terms used in biology include:

02 ER	gland	globin	anatomy
GM	lysis	intron	chiasma
03 ADP	order	karyon	chimera
ATP	organ	kinase	diploid
DNA	sense	ligand	euploid
RNA	virus	mutant	guanine
04 cell	**06** allele	mutate	habitat
exon	anlage	myosin	haploid
gene	chiasm	operon	hormone
germ	cilium	phylum	kingdom
05 actin	coccus	ploidy	linkage
cilia	colony	purine	meiosis
clade	embryo	stasis	microbe
class	enzyme	tissue	mimicry
clone	family	uracil	mitosis
codon	fossil	vector	nucleus
genus	gamete	zygote	osmosis
	genome	**07** adenine	peptide

plasmid	**09** adenosine	symbiosis	pinocytosis
protein	amino acid	syncytium	pluripotent
somatic	anabolism	telophase	polypeptide
species	analogous	thymidine	replication
spindle	aneuploid	transfect	respiration
synapse	antisense	transform	transferase
thymine	apoptosis	**10** alpha helix	transfer RNA
tubulin	bacterium	beta barrel	translation
uridine	beta sheet	catabolism	unicellular
08 anaphase	biologist	centromere	**12** cell division
autosome	cell cycle	chemotaxis	conservation
bacillus	chromatin	chromosome	crossing over
bacteria	commensal	cryophilic	cytoskeleton
base pair	corpuscle	dimorphism	glycoprotein
botanist	cytoplasm	exocytosis	growth factor
chimaera	Darwinism	expression	invertebrate
cofactor	desmosome	extinction	messenger RNA
cultivar	diffusion	haptotaxis	mitochondria
cytidine	ecosystem	homologous	phagocytosis
cytosine	ectoplasm	interphase	phospholipid
ectoderm	eukaryote	Lamarckism	reproduction
endoderm	evolution	metabolism	thermophilic
enhancer	excretion	nucleoside	**13** animal kingdom
euploidy	flagellum	nucleotide	flora and fauna
genetics	food chain	parasitism	micro-organism
globulin	Golgi body	population	mitochondrion
integrin	guanosine	prokaryote	morphogenesis
ligation	haplotype	proteinase	multicellular
lysogeny	karyotype	protoplasm	proliferation
membrane	life cycle	pyrimidine	recombination
mesoderm	Mendelism	speciation	sex chromosome
metazoan	metaphase	vertebrate	tight junction
molecule	notochord	**11** conjugation	tissue culture
mutation	nutrition	cytokinesis	transcription
necrosis	organelle	endocytosis	**14** Golgi apparatus
organism	oxidation	gap junction	photosynthesis
parasite	pollution	genetic code	regulatory gene
promoter	protozoan	Haeckel's law	**15** animal behaviour
prophase	reduction	homeostasis	differentiation
receptor	repressor	kinetochore	nuclear membrane
ribosome	reticulum	leading edge	primitive streak
stem cell	secretion	living world	ribonucleic acid
telomere	selection	phosphatase	
wild type	stop codon		

See also **botany**; **cell**; **enzyme**

bird

Birds include:

03 ani	owl	dodo	gull
auk	roc	dove	hawk
daw	tit	duck	huia
emu	tui	emeu	huma
hen	**04** Aves	erne	ibis
jay	chat	fowl	kagu
kea	coot	fung	kite
moa	crow	guan	kiwi

knot	robin	quelea	horn owl
lark	snipe	raptor	jacamar
loom	squab	redcap	jackdaw
loon	stilt	roller	kamichi
lory	stint	sea-mew	kestrel
myna	stork	shrike	lapwing
nene	swift	simorg	leghorn
rail	twite	simurg	limpkin
rhea	vireo	siskin	mallard
rook	wader	takahe	manakin
ruff	**06** avocet	thrush	manikin
shag	avoset	tom-tit	manumea
skua	bantam	toucan	marabou
smee	barbet	trogon	may-bird
swan	budgie	turaco	minivet
taha	bulbul	turkey	moorhen
teal	canary	weaver	mudlark
tern	chough	whidah	oilbird
tody	condor	whydah	ortolan
wren	cuckoo	willet	ostrich
05 agami	curlew	yaffle	peacock
ariel	cushat	zoozoo	pelican
avian	darter	**07** antbird	penguin
booby	dipper	apteryx	phoenix
capon	drongo	babbler	pintail
chick	dunlin	barn owl	pochard
colly	falcon	bee-kite	pockard
crane	fulmar	bittern	poe-bird
dicky	gannet	bluecap	poultry
diver	godwit	blue jay	poy-bird
eagle	grouse	blue tit	quetzal
egret	hoopoe	bullbat	redbird
eider	houdan	bunting	redpoll
finch	jabiru	bushtit	redwing
fleet	jaçana	bustard	rooster
flier	kakapo	buzzard	ruddock
galah	kokako	catbird	sea dove
goose	leipoa	chicken	seagull
grebe	linnet	coal-tit	seriema
heron	magpie	cotinga	simurgh
hobby	martin	courlan	sirgang
junco	merlin	courser	sitella
liver	mesite	cowbird	skimmer
lowan	missel	creeper	skylark
macaw	motmot	dottrel	spadger
mynah	oriole	dun-bird	sparrow
noddy	osprey	dunnock	sunbird
ousel	ox-bird	egg-bird	swallow
pewee	parrot	emu wren	tanager
piper	peahen	fantail	tattler
pipit	peewee	fern-owl	tiercel
pitta	peewit	fig-bird	tinamou
poaka	petrel	finfoot	titlark
poker	pigeon	goshawk	touraco
potoo	plover	grackle	vulture
quail	puffin	halcyon	wagtail
raven	pukeko	harrier	warbler
reeve	pullet	hoatzin	waxbill

waxwing
wren tit
wrybill
wryneck

08 aasvogel
accentor
adjutant
aigrette
alcatras
antpitta
araponga
arapunga
bald-coot
bee-eater
bellbird
blackcap
bluebird
boatbill
bobolink
bobwhite
bushwren
cockatoo
cockerel
curassow
dabchick
dotterel
fernbird
fire-bird
fish-hawk
flamingo
gnatwren
great tit
grosbeak
guacharo
hawfinch
hernshaw
hoactzin
hornbill
kingbird
landrail
laverock
leafbird
lorikeet
lovebird
lyrebird
mannikin
marabout
megapode
myna bird
nightjar
notornis
nuthatch
ovenbird
oxpecker
palmchat
parakeet
percolin
pheasant

prunella
puffbird
rainbird
redshank
redstart
reed-bird
reedling
ricebird
ringtail
rock-bird
rock dove
rock lark
sand-lark
screamer
sea eagle
shoebill
sittella
snowbird
starling
sungrebe
tapacolo
tapaculo
tick bird
titmouse
troopial
troupial
umbrette
water-hen
wheatear
whimbrel
whinchat
whitecap
white-eye
wire bird
woodchat
woodcock
wood duck
woodlark

09 aepyornis
albatross
ant thrush
bald eagle
baldicoot
Baltimore
beccafico
beefeater
bergander
blackbird
blackgame
blackhead
black swan
blood-bird
bowerbird
brambling
broadbill
bullfinch
campanero
cassowary

cedar-bird
chaffinch
chickadee
cockatiel
cormorant
corncrake
eider duck
fairy tern
fieldfare
fig-pecker
flute-bird
francolin
frogmouth
gallinule
gerfalcon
gnateater
goldcrest
golden eye
goldfinch
goldspink
goosander
gowdspink
grassbird
guillemot
honey-bird
horned owl
impundulu
jack-snipe
kittiwake
little owl
mallemuck
merganser
meropidan
mollymawk
mound-bird
mousebird
mynah bird
nighthawk
nutpecker
organ-bird
ossifrage
paddy-bird
partridge
peregrine
phalarope
plume-bird
porphyrio
ptarmigan
razorbill
redbreast
rifle bird
rock pipit
sandpiper
satin bird
scrub bird
seedsnipe
sheldrake
snow finch

sooty tern
spoonbill
stonechat
sugar bird
thick knee
thornbill
trumpeter
turnstone
umber-bird
wheat bird
widow bird
willow tit
wind-hover

10 aberdevine
black robin
bluebreast
bluethroat
budgerigar
bush-shrike
butter-bird
chiff-chaff
crab plover
dickcissel
fledgeling
flycatcher
goatsucker
gobemouche
greenfinch
greenshank
guinea fowl
hammerhead
harpy eagle
honeyeater
honey guide
indigo bird
junglefowl
kingfisher
kookaburra
locust bird
magpie lark
mallee-bird
missel-bird
mutton bird
night-churr
night heron
night-raven
nutcracker
parson-bird
peckerwood
pratincole
Quaker-bird
rafter-bird
rain-plover
regent-bird
sanderling
sand grouse
sand martin
shearwater

sheathbill
sicklebill
song thrush
stone snipe
sun bittern
tropicbird
turtledove
tyrant bird
wattlebird
willow wren
woodhoopoe
woodpecker
woodpigeon
zebra finch

11 black grouse
brush turkey
buffalo-bird
butcherbird
button quail
Canada goose
cock-sparrow
diamond bird
dragoon-bird
frigate bird
gobe-mouches
golden eagle
hummingbird
indigo finch

Java sparrow
king-vulture
mockingbird
nightingale
plantcutter
purple finch
reed bunting
reed-sparrow
reed warbler
sea dotterel
snow bunting
song sparrow
sparrowhawk
stone curlew
storm petrel
thunderbird
tree-creeper
tree sparrow
vanga shrike
woodcreeper
wood-swallow

12 adjutant bird
bramble-finch
cardinal-bird
cow blackbird
crested swift
cuckoo-roller
cuckoo shrike

diving petrel
false sunbird
flowerpecker
golden plover
hedge sparrow
honey buzzard
honey creeper
missel-thrush
mistle-thrush
mound-builder
painted snipe
reed-pheasant
rifleman bird
ruffed grouse
sedge warbler
standard wing
umbrella bird
yellowhammer

13 archaeopteryx
barnacle goose
boatswain-bird
coachwhip-bird
cock-of-the-rock
crocodile bird
indigo bunting
owlet-nightjar
oyster-catcher
plantain-eater

secretary bird
short-eared owl
trumpeter swan
willow warbler
zebra parakeet

14 bird of paradise
black guillemot
brain-fever bird
horned screamer
New Zealand wren
plains wanderer
rhinoceros bird
shell parrakeet
sooty albatross
St Helena plover

15 American warbler
Baltimore oriole
bearded titmouse
blue-footed booby
green woodpecker
Montagu's harrier
passenger pigeon
peregrine falcon
pied butcherbird
purple gallinule
silky flycatcher

Birds of prey include:

03 owl
04 erne
hawk
kite
pern
05 eagle
hobby
06 falcon
lanner
merlin
osprey
raptor
07 barn owl
buzzard
goshawk
harrier

hawk owl
kestrel
red kite
08 bateleur
berghaan
duck-hawk
eagle owl
fish-hawk
Scops owl
sea eagle
spar-hawk
tawny owl
09 bald eagle
black kite
eagle-hawk
fish eagle
gyrfalcon

little owl
marsh hawk
peregrine
stone hawk
10 harpy eagle
Harris hawk
hen harrier
screech owl
spotted owl
tawny eagle
11 booted eagle
chicken hawk
Cooper's hawk
golden eagle
sparrowhawk
stone falcon

12 great grey owl
honey buzzard
long-eared owl
marsh harrier
13 American eagle
Iceland falcon
imperial eagle
lesser kestrel
pallid harrier
secretary bird
short-eared owl
14 short-toed eagle
15 Montagu's harrier
peregrine falcon
red-footed falcon

Seabirds include:

03 auk
cob
mew
04 cobb
guga
gull

shag
skua
tern
05 cahow
solan
06 fulmar

gannet
petrel
puffin
07 pickmaw
seagull
09 black tern

cormorant
great skua
guillemot
kittiwake
little auk
mallemuck
razorbill

swart-back	little tern	Sabine's gull	**13** Bermuda petrel
10 Arctic skua	saddleback	storm petrel	**14** black guillemot
Arctic tern	solan goose	**12** glaucous gull	long-tailed skua
common gull	**11** herring gull	Leach's petrel	Manx shearwater
common tern	Iceland gull	pomarine skua	**15** black-headed gull
little gull	roseate tern	sandwich tern	

Wading birds include:

03 ree	stilt	lapwing	turnstone
04 hern	stint	**08** dotterel	**10** greenshank
ibis	stork	flamingo	sanderling
knot	**06** avocet	redshank	**11** little stint
ruff	curlew	whimbrel	stone curlew
05 crake	dunlin	woodcock	**12** golden plover
crane	godwit	**09** dowitcher	great bustard
heron	plover	grey heron	ringed plover
reeve	**07** bittern	phalarope	**13** little bustard
snipe	bustard	sandpiper	oyster-catcher

Flightless birds include:

03 emu	rhea	takahe	notornis
04 dodo	weka	**07** ostrich	**09** cassowary
emeu	**06** kakapo	penguin	owl-parrot
kiwi	ratite	**08** great auk	solitaire

See also **falcon**; **farm**; **game: hunting**; **goose**; **mythology**; **parrot**; **poultry**; **swan**

birth symbol

Birth flowers:

04 rose (Jun)	**08** hawthorn (May)	**10** poinsettia (Dec)
05 aster (Sep)	larkspur (Jul)	**11** honeysuckle (Jun)
daisy (Apr)	primrose (Feb)	**12** morning glory (Sep)
holly (Dec)	snowdrop (Jan)	**13** chrysanthemum (Nov)
poppy (Aug)	sweet pea (Apr)	**15** lily of the valley (May)
06 cosmos (Oct)	**09** calendula (Oct)	
violet (Feb)	carnation (Jan)	
violet (Mar)	gladiolus (Aug)	
07 jonquil (Mar)	narcissus (Dec)	
	water lily (Jul)	

Birth stones:

04 opal (Oct)	**07** diamond (Apr)	**09** moonstone (Jun)
ruby (Jul)	emerald (May)	turquoise (Dec)
05 pearl (Jun)	peridot (Aug)	**10** aquamarine (Mar)
topaz (Nov)	**08** amethyst (Feb)	bloodstone (Mar)
06 garnet (Jan)	sapphire (Sep)	tourmaline (Oct)
zircon (Dec)	sardonyx (Aug)	**11** alexandrite (Jun)

See also **astrology**; **zodiac**

biscuit

Biscuits include:

03 dog
nut
sea
tea
04 kiss
Nice
puff
rice
rusk
ship
snap
tack
thin
Twix®
wine
05 Marie
ship's
wafer

water
06 cookie
HobNob
KitKat®
parkin
07 Bourbon
cracker
fig roll
Gold Bar
iced Gem®
Lincoln
oatcake
Penguin®
pretzel
ratafia
rich tea
saltine
08 biscotto

captain's
cracknel
flapjack
hardtack
macaroon
Zwieback
09 Abernethy
BreakAway®
cereal bar
chocolate
digestive
four-by-two
garibaldi
ginger nut
jaffa cake
party ring
petit four
shortcake

10 Bath Oliver
Blue Riband®
brandy snap
dunderfunk
florentine
gingersnap
malted milk
shortbread
Wagon Wheel®
11 brown George
fly cemetery
soda cracker
squashed fly
12 custard cream
jammie dodger
langue de chat
14 gingerbread man

See also **baking**; **cake**; **food**

bishop

Bishops include:

03 Odo (of Bayeux; c.1036–97, Bayeux)
05 Aidan (St; d.651, Lindisfarne)
Peter (St; 1 c AD, Rome)
06 Blaise (St; d.c.316 AD, Sebastea)
Ninian (St; c.390–c.432 AD, Old Welsh British)
Osmund (St; d.1099, Salisbury)
07 Ambrose (St; c.339–97 AD, Milan)
Carroll (John; 1735–1815, Baltimore)

Hadrian (1100–59, Albano)
Patrick (St; 5 c AD, Armagh)
08 Geoffrey (of Monmouth; c.1100–c.1154, St Asaph)
Holloway (Richard; 1933– , Edinburgh)
Nicholas (St; 4 c AD, Myra)
Sheppard (David; 1929–2005, Liverpool)
11 Elphinstone (William; 1431–1514, Ross, Aberdeen)

See also **archbishop**; **cathedral**; **diocese**; **religion**

black

Shades of black include:

03 jet
04 blae

coal
ebon

jeat
05 dwale

ebony
sable

See also **dye**; **pigment**

Blake, William (1757–1827)

Significant works include:

06 *Tiriel* (1789/1874)
07 *The Lamb* (1789)
08 *The Tyger* (1794)
09 *Jerusalem* (1804–20)

11 *The Sick Rose* (1794)
12 *The Song of Los* (1794)
13 *The Book of Thel* (1789)
15 *Europe, a Prophecy* (1794)

The Book of Ahania (1795)
The Book of Urizen (1794)
16 *America, a Prophecy* (1793)
Poetical Sketches (1783)
Songs of Innocence (1789)
17 *An Island in the Moon* (1784–85)

Songs of Experience (1794)
18 *Valam, or The Four Zoas* (1795–1804)
19 *The French Revolution* (1791)
26 *The Marriage of Heaven and Hell* (1790–93)
29 *Visions of the Daughters of Albion* (1793)

blemish

Blemishes include:

03 zit	scar	**07** blister	blackhead
04 acne	spot	freckle	carbuncle
boil	wart	pustule	chilblain
bump	**06** bunion	verruca	whitehead
corn	callus		
mole	naevus	**08** pockmark	**13** port-wine stain
scab	pimple	**09** birthmark	**14** strawberry mark

blend *see* **coffee**

blindness

Sight impairments include:

03 AMD	**10** nyctalopia	**14** far-sightedness
06 myopia	presbyopia	night blindness
08 glaucoma	**11** astigmatism	**15** colour blindness
trachoma	hemeralopia	long-sightedness
09 amaurosis	**12** purblindness	near-sightedness
cataracts	**13** hypermetropia	

blue

Shades of blue include:

04 anil	indigo	**09** caerulean	nattier blue
aqua	**07** caerule	royal blue	peacock-blue
bice	gentian	steel-blue	ultramarine
blae	ice-blue	turquoise	**12** air-force blue
cyan	jacinth	**10** aquamarine	dumortierite
navy	sea-blue	Berlin blue	electric blue
Saxe	sky-blue	cornflower	midnight blue
teal	watchet	kingfisher	Prussian blue
05 azure	**08** baby blue	Oxford blue	Wedgwood blue
perse	cerulean	periwinkle	**13** Cambridge blue
smalt	dark blue	petrol blue	robin's-egg blue
06 cerule	mazarine	powder blue	
cobalt	Nile blue	**11** duck-egg blue	
haüyne	sapphire	lapis lazuli	

See also **dye**; **pigment**

blues *see* **jazz**

Blyton, Enid (1897–1968)

Blyton series include:

05 Noddy   **11** Secret Seven   **14** The Faraway Tree

10 Famous Five   **12** Malory Towers

Significant characters, with appropriate gang, include:

03 Pam (Secret Seven)

04 Jack (Secret Seven)

05 Colin (Secret Seven)
Janet (Secret Seven)
Noddy
Peter (Secret Seven)
Timmy (Famous Five)

06 Amelia (Jane)
George (Secret Seven)

Kirrin (Anne; Famous Five)
Kirrin (Dick; Famous Five)
Kirrin (Georgina 'George'; Famous Five)
Kirrin (Julian; Famous Five)

07 Barbara (Secret Seven)
Big Ears
Scamper (Secret Seven)

13 The Famous Five

14 The Secret Seven

board game *see* game

boat *see* ship

bodily humour *see* humour

bomb

Bombs include:

02 V-1
V-2

03 car

04 aero
atom
buzz
dumb
mine
MOAB
nail
pipe
time

05 A-bomb
dirty
E-bomb
H-bomb

Mills
shell
smart
smoke
stink

06 binary
candle
cobalt
drogue
flying
fusion
letter
parcel
petrol
radium
rocket

07 bomblet
cluster
fission
grenade
megaton
missile
neutron
nuclear
plastic
tallboy
torpedo

08 bouncing
firebomb
hydrogen
landmine

09 doodlebug

Grand Slam

10 incendiary

11 blockbuster
daisy-cutter
depth charge
penetration
sensor fuzed
stun grenade
thermobaric

12 bunker buster
rifle grenade

13 fragmentation
thermonuclear

14 general purpose

15 Molotov cocktail

Bombers include:

03 B-10
B-17
B-19
B-52
MB-1

04 dive

05 Stuka

06 Gotha G
Harris
Sukhoi

07 Avenger

Heinkel
Junkers
stealth
suicide
Tupolev
Warthog

08 Mitchell

09 Lancaster
Liberator

13 Superfortress

14 Flying Fortress

See also missile; weapon

bone

Bones and joints include:

01 T

02 os

03 hip
jaw
luz
rib

04 back
coxa
knee
rump
shin
ulna

05 ankle
anvil
blade
cheek
costa
facet
femur
funny
hinge
hyoid
ilium
incus
jugal
malar
nasal
pivot
pubis
share
skull
spade

spine
talus
thigh
thumb
tibia
vomer
woven
wrist

06 breast
carpal
carpus
coccyx
collar
cuboid
fibula
hamate
hammer
pecten
pelvis
radial
radius
sacrum
saddle
spauld
stapes
tarsal
tarsus
zygoma

07 cranium
ethmoid
fibrous
gliding

humerus
ischium
kneecap
knuckle
malleus
mastoid
maxilla
ossicle
patella
phalanx
prootic
scapula
shackle
sternum
stirrup

08 clavicle
cortical
lamellar
lower jaw
mandible
palatine
parietal
periotic
pisiform
scaphoid
sesamoid
shoulder
sphenoid
splinter
synovial
temporal
turbinal

tympanic
upper jaw
vertebra

09 calcaneum
calcaneus
condyloid
ellipsoid
manubrium
navicular
occipital
pterygoid
trapezium
turbinate
zygomatic

10 astragalus
cancellous
innominate
metacarpal
metatarsal
premaxilla
trabecular

11 diarthrosis
intermedium

12 parasphenoid
pelvic girdle
synarthrosis

13 ball and socket
cartilaginous
shoulder-blade
zygomatic arch

14 amphiarthrosis

book

Books include:

03 pad

04 A to Z
bath
chap
cook
copy
days
hand
hymn
note
text
work
year

05 album
atlas
audio

board
cloth
comic
diary
e-book
guide
novel
pop-up
scrap
story

06 annual
gradus
hymnal
jotter
ledger
manual
missal

phrase
prayer
primer
sketch

07 almanac
fiction
Filofax®
journal
lexicon
omnibus
picture
psalter

08 exercise
grimoire
hardback
libretto

self-help
softback
thriller

09 anthology
biography
catalogue
children's
detective
directory
gazetteer
paperback
reference
thesaurus

10 bestseller
compendium
dictionary

large print	**11** coffee-table	travel guide	travel journal
lectionary	concordance	**12** encyclopedia	**15** pocket companion
manuscript	instruction	**13** penny dreadful	

Bookbinding terms include:

03 aeg	**08** backbone	half bound	wire binding
04 case	blocking	loose-leaf	wiro binding
head	casing-in	millboard	**12** all edges gilt
limp	doublure	paperback	binder's board
tail	drilling	signature	binder's brass
yapp	endpaper	soft-cover	cloth binding
05 bolts	fore edge	**10** back lining	flexi binding
hinge	hardback	binder's die	notch binding
spine	headband	front board	quarter bound
06 boards	open-flat	laminating	saddle-stitch
gather	shoulder	pasteboard	thread sewing
jacket	smashing	raised band	**13** back cornering
lining	stamping	side-stitch	blind blocking
Linson®	tailband	square back	spiral binding
sewing	**09** backboard	stab-stitch	unsewn binding
07 binding	book block	strawboard	wire stitching
buckram	casebound	varnishing	**14** library binding
drawn-on	debossing	whole bound	perfect binding
flyleaf	dust cover	**11** comb binding	**15** adhesive binding
headcap	embossing	ring binding	cloth-lined board
morocco	full bound	velo binding	hot foil stamping

See also **Bible**; **literature**; **non-fiction**; **novel**; **printing**; **publishing**; **science fiction**

boot

Boots include:

03 gum	wader	riding	climbing
top	welly	**07** blucher	finnesko
04 crow	**06** bootee	bottine	football
half	buskin	Chelsea	high shoe
jack	chukka	cracowe	larrigan
lace	finsko	finnsko	muckluck
moon	galosh	galoche	overshoe
snow	golosh	Hessian	**09** scarpetto
05 ankle	jemima	walking	**10** Doc Martens®
kamik	mucluc	**08** balmoral	wellington
thigh	mukluk	bootikin	**13** beetle-crusher

See also **footwear**

border

Borders and boundaries include:

07 Rubicon	no-man's-land	**13** Bamboo Curtain
09 Green Line	**11** Iron Curtain	**14** Mason-Dixon Line
10 Berlin Wall	Maginot Line	**15** cordon sanitaire

See also **wall**

borough *see* **London**; **New York**

Bosnia and Herzegovina *see* **Balkans**

botany

Botanists include:

03 Mee (Margaret; 1909–89, English)
Ray (John; 1627–1705, English)

04 Ball (John; 1818–89, Irish)
Bary (Anton de; 1831–88, German)
Cohn (Ferdinand; 1828–98, German)
Dahl (Anders; 1751–89, Swedish)
Gray (Asa; 1810–88, US)
Gray (Edward Whitaker; 1748–1806, English)
Gray (J E; 1800–75, English)
Gray (Samuel Frederick; 1766–1828, English)
Grew (Nehemiah; 1641–1712, English)
Mohl (Hugo von; 1805–72, German)
Ward (Nathaniel; 1791–1868, English)

05 Arber (Agnes; 1879–1960, English)
Ashby (Eric, Lord; 1904–92, Australian)
Banks (Sir Joseph; 1744–1820, English)
Blume (C L; 1796–1862, German)
Bower (Frederick; 1855–1948, English)
Braun (Lucy; 1889–1971, US)
Brown (Robert; 1773–1858, Scottish)
Davis (Peter; 1918–92, English)
Druce (G Claridge; 1850–1932, English)
Hales (Stephen; 1677–1761, English)
Sachs (Julius von; 1832–97, German)
Scott (Dukinfield Henry; 1854–1934, English)
Smith (Sir James Edward; 1759–1828, English)
Vries (Hugo de; 1848–1935, Dutch)

06 Alpino (Prospero; 1553–1616, Italian)
Aublet (Jean Baptiste Fusée; 1723–78, French)
Bailey (Liberty Hyde; 1858–1954, US)
Bauhin (Caspar; 1560–1624, Swiss)
Bauhin (Gaspard; 1560–1624, Swiss)
Biffen (Sir Rowland; 1874–1949, English)
Carver (George Washington; c.1860–1943, US)
Clarke (Charles Baron; 1832–1906, English)
Curtis (William; 1747–99, English)
Engler (Adolf; 1844–1930, German)
Farrer (Reginald; 1880–1920, English)
Gmelin (Johann Georg; 1709–55, German)
Gmelin (Samuel Gottlieb; 1745–74, German)
Godwin (Sir Harry; 1901–85, English)

Harvey (William Henry; 1811–66, Irish)
Hedwig (Johannes; 1730–99, German)
Hooker (Sir Joseph; 1817–1911, English)
Hooker (Sir William; 1785–1865, English)
Hudson (William; 1734–93, English)
Maiden (Joseph Henry; 1859–1925; Australian)
Mendel (Gregor; 1822–84, Austrian)
Müller (Sir Ferdinand von, Freiherr; 1825–96, German/Australian)
Nägeli (Karl Wilhelm von; 1817–91, Swiss)
Prance (Sir Ghillean; 1937– , English)
Spruce (Richard; 1817–93, English)
Stearn (William T; 1911–2001, English)
Torrey (John; 1796–1873, US)
Wilson (Ernest; 1876–1930, English)

07 Adanson (Michel; 1727–1806, French)
Agassiz (Louis; 1807–73, US)
Andrews (Roy Chapman; 1884–1960, US)
Bartram (John; 1699–1777, American)
Bellamy (David; 1933– , English)
Bentham (George; 1800–84, English)
Bigelow (Jacob; 1787–1879, US)
Britton (Nathaniel Lord; 1859–1934, US)
Camerer (Joachim; 1534–98, German)
Camerer (Rudolph; 1665–1721, German)
Correns (Carl; 1864–1933, German)
Douglas (David; 1799–1834, Scottish)
Forrest (George; 1873–1932, Scottish)
Gardner (George; 1812–49, Scottish)
Gilmour (John S L; 1906–86, English)
Haworth (Adrian H; 1766–1833, English)
Jackson (Benjamin Daydon; 1846–1927, English)
Jussieu (Antoine Laurent de; 1748–1836, French)
Jussieu (Bernard; c.1699–1777, French)
Lindley (John; 1799–1865, English)
Morison (Robert; 1620–83, Scottish)
Mueller (Sir Ferdinand von, Freiherr; 1825–96, German/Australian)
Pfeffer (Wilhelm; 1845–1920, German)
Siebold (Philipp Franz von; 1796–1866, German)
Stewart (Ralph R; 1890–1993, US)
Tansley (Sir Arthur; 1871–1955, English)
Vavilov (Nikolai I; 1887–1943, Russian)
Wallich (Nathaniel; 1786–1854, Danish)
Warming (Eugenius; 1841–1924, Danish)

08 Airy Shaw (Kenneth; 1902–85, English)
Blackman (Frederick F; 1866–1947, English)
Boissier (Pierre-Edmond; 1810–85, Swiss)
Candolle (Alphonse de; 1806–93, Swiss)
Candolle (Augustin Pyrame de; 1778–1841, Swiss)
Falconer (Hugh; 1808–65, Scottish)
Linnaeus (Carl; 1707–78, Swedish)
Saussure (Nicolas Théodore de; 1767–1845, Swiss)
Schimper (Andreas; 1856–1901, German)
Schimper (Wilhelm Philipp; 1808–80, German)
Senebier (Jean; 1742–1809, Swiss)
Sprengel (Christian Konrad; 1750–1816, German)
Stebbins (G Ledyard; 1906–2000, US)

09 Baulcombe (David; 1952– , English)
Blakeslee (Albert; 1874–1954, US)
Boerhaave (Hermann; 1668–1738, Dutch)
Cesalpino (Andrea; 1519–1603, Italian)

Cronquist (Arthur; 1919–92, US)
Endlicher (Stephan; 1804–49, Austrian)
Grisebach (August; 1814–79, German)
Rechinger (Karl Heinz; 1906–98, Austrian)
Salisbury (Edward James; 1886–1978, English)
Salisbury (Richard Anthony; 1781–1829, English)
Schleiden (Matthias; 1804–81, German)
Takhtajan (Armen; 1910–2009, Armenian)

10 Aldrovandi (Ulisse; 1522–1605, Italian)
Cunningham (Allan; 1791–1839, English)
Hofmeister (Wilhelm; 1824–77, German)
Pringsheim (Nathaniel; 1823–94, German)
Tournefort (Joseph Pitton de; 1656–1708, French)
Williamson (William; 1816–95, English)

11 Strasburger (Eduard; 1844–1912, German)

12 Schweinfurth (Georg August; 1836–1925, German)

bottle

Bottles include:

03 bed	flask	pooter	demijohn
gas	gourd	siphon	hip flask
ink	Klein	stubby	hot-water
pig	phial	syphon	magnetic
04 beer	scent	Woulfe	medicine
case	snuff	**07** amphora	screwtop
codd	water	ampulla	smelling
jack	**06** carafe	costrel	weighing
junk	carboy	feeding	**09** Aristotle
mick	cutter	flacket	
milk	feeder	pilgrim	**10** apothecary
tear	fiasco	pitcher	lachrymary
vial	flacon	squeezy	Winchester
wash	flagon	sucking	**11** vinaigrette
wine	hottie	torpedo	water bouget
05 bidon	inkpot	vinegar	**12** Bologna phial
cruet	lagena	washing	lachrymatory
cruse	magnum	**08** calabash	Thermos® flask
dumpy	poison	decanter	

See also **container**; **wine**

boundary *see* **border**

boxing

Professional boxing weight divisions:

09 flyweight

11 heavyweight
lightweight
strawweight

12 bantamweight
middleweight
welterweight

13 cruiserweight

featherweight
mini flyweight
minimum weight
14 light flyweight
super flyweight
15 junior flyweight
16 light heavyweight
super lightweight
17 junior lightweight

light middleweight
super bantamweight
super middleweight
super welterweight
18 junior bantamweight
junior middleweight
junior welterweight
super featherweight
19 junior featherweight

Boxers and associated figures include:

03 Ali (Muhammad; 1942– , US)
04 Baer (Max; 1909–59, US)
Benn (Nigel; 1964– , English)
Bowe (Riddick; 1967– , US)
Byrd (Chris; 1970– , US)
Clay (Cassius; 1942– , US)
King (Don; 1932– , US)
Ruiz (John; 1972– , US)
Ward (Andre; 1984– , US)
Watt (Jim; 1948– , Scottish)
05 Bruno (Frank; 1961– , English)
Duran (Roberto; 1951– , Panamanian)
Hamed ('Prince' Naseem; 1974– , English)
Lewis (Lennox; 1965– , Canadian/British)
Louis (Joe; 1914–81, US)
Lynch (Benny; 1913–46, Scottish)
Moore (Archie; 1913–98, US)
Peter (Samuel; 1980– , Nigerian)
Tyson (Mike; 1966– , US)
06 Cerdan (Marcel; 1916–49, French)
Cooper (Sir Henry; 1934–2011, English)
Dundee (Angelo; 1923–2012, US)
Eubank (Chris; 1966– , English)
Hearns (Tommy; 1958– , US)
Holmes (Larry; 1949– , US)
Liston (Sonny; 1932–70, US)
Monzon (Carlos; 1942–95, Argentine)
Norton (Ken; 1943– , US)
Rahman (Hasim; 1972– , US)
Sayers (Tom; 1826–65, English)
Spinks (Leon; 1953– , US)
Tunney (Gene; 1897–78, US)
Valuev (Nikolai; 1973– , Russian)

07 Chagaev (Ruslan; 1978– , Uzbekistani)
Collins (Steve; 1964– , Irish)
Corbett ('Gentleman' Jim; 1866–1933, US)
Dempsey (Jack; 1895–1983, US)
Foreman (George; 1949– , US)
Frazier (Joe; 1944–2011, US)
LaMotta (Jake; 1921– , US)
Leonard (Sugar Ray; 1956– , US)
Maskaev (Oleg; 1969– , Russian)
08 Brewster (Lamon; 1973– , US)
Buchanan (Ken; 1945– , Scottish)
Calzaghe (Joe; 1972– , English/Welsh)
Graziano (Rocky; 1922–90, US)
Marciano (Rocky; 1923–69, US)
McGuigan (Barry; 1961– , Irish)
Povetkin (Aleksandr; 1979– , Russian)
Robinson (Sugar Ray; 1920–89, US)
Whitaker (Pernell 'Sweet Pea'; 1964– , US)
09 Armstrong (Henry; 1912–88, US)
Holyfield (Evander; 1962– , US)
Honeyghan (Lloyd; 1960– , Jamaican/British)
Klitschko (Vitali; 1971– , Ukrainian)
Klitschko (Vladimir; 1976– , Ukrainian)
Patterson (Floyd; 1935–2006, US)
Schmeling (Max; 1905–2005, German)
Stevenson (Teofilo; 1952– , Jamaican/Cuban)
10 Liakhovich (Sergei; 1976– , Belarussian)
11 Fitzsimmons (Bob; 1862–1917, English/New
Zealand/US)
Gaydarbekov (Gaydarbek; 1976– ,
Russian)
Queensberry (Sir John Sholto Douglas,
Marquis of; 1844–1900, Scottish)

Boxing terms include:

03 jab
04 belt
bout
down
foul
hold
hook
lead

pull
ring
spar
05 apron
count
cross
feint
guard

judge
reach
round
weave
06 canvas
clinch
corner
one-two

07 caution
counter
warning
08 blocking
knockout
passbook
pugilism
shortarm
southpaw
speed bag
See also **sport**

uppercut
09 corner man
headguard
ring-rusty
10 eight-count
infighting
mouthpiece
outclassed
punch drunk

scoring hit
11 combination
Queensberry
rabbit punch
12 shadow boxing
13 neutral corner
split decision
14 out for the count
15 throw in the towel

boy *see* **name**

Brahms, Johannes (1833–97)

Significant works include:

12 Piano Quintet (1864)

13 *German Requiem* (1869)

14 Double Concerto (1887)
Tragic Overture (1886)
Zigeunerlieder (1888)

15 *Hungarian Dances* (1869)

16 *Four Serious Songs* (1896)

17 *Vier ernste Gesänge* (1896)

18 *Tragische Ouverture* (1881)

19 *Ein deutsches Requiem* (1869)

brain

Brain parts include:

04 pons
06 cortex
07 cinerea
08 amygdala
cerebrum
meninges
midbrain
thalamus
09 brainstem

forebrain
hindbrain
ventricle
10 Broca's area
cerebellum
grey matter
pineal body
spinal cord
11 frontal lobe
hippocampus

white matter
12 hypothalamus
limbic system
parietal lobe
Purkinje cell
temporal lobe
visual cortex
13 choroid plexus
mesencephalon
occipital lobe

olfactory bulb
optic thalamus
Wernicke's area
14 cerebral cortex
corpus callosum
left hemisphere
pituitary gland
15 right hemisphere
substantia nigra

bread

Bread and rolls include:

03 bap
cob
nan
rye
tea
04 azym
cake
corn
farl
loaf
milk
naan
pita

pone
puri
roti
soda
05 arepa
azyme
bagel
black
brown
cheat
fancy
horse
matza

matzo
pitta
plait
poori
ravel
white
06 damper
French
garlic
graham
Indian
injera
lavash

matzah
matzoh
panini
panino
simnel
stotty
wastel
07 bannock
bloomer
brioche
brownie
buttery
challah

chapati	ciabatta	burger bun	French loaf
currant	corn pone	cornbread	multigrain
ficelle	focaccia	croissant	stotty cake
granary	grissini	flatbread	unleavened
jannock	leavened	petit pain	vienna loaf
manchet	ravelled	schnecken	wholewheat
paratha	ryebread	shewbread	**11** cottage loaf
pretzel	schnecke	showbread	French stick
stottie	standard	sourdough	morning roll
wheaten	tortilla	wholemeal	potato bread
08 baguette	**09** bara brith	**10** breadstick	potato scone
barm cake	barmbrack	bridge roll	**12** pumpernickel
chapatti	batch loaf	finger roll	**13** farmhouse loaf

See also **baking**; **cake**; **food**

breakfast *see* **cereal**

Brecht, Bertolt (1898–1956)

Significant works include:

04 *Baal* (1922)
08 *Edward II* (1924)
10 *Coriolanus* (1959)
12 *Man Equals Man* (1926)
15 *Drums in the Night* (1922)
16 *The Life of Galileo* (1943)
The Measures Taken (1929–30)
17 *The Duchess of Malfi* (1946)
18 *The Threepenny Opera* (1928)

The Trial of Lukullus (1940)
21 *St Joan of the Stockyards* (1929–30)
The Good Woman of Setzuan (1938–41)
23 *Mr Puntila and His Man Matti* (1940)
The Caucasian Chalk Circle (1944–45)
26 *He Who Says Yes and He Who Says No* (1930)
27 *Mother Courage and Her Children* (1941)
The Resistible Rise of Arturo Ui (1941)
28 *Fear and Misery of the Third Reich* (1935)

Significant characters include:

02 Ta (Shui)
Te (Shen)
Ui (Arturo)
03 Gay (Gayly)
Sun (Yang)
04 Baal
Giri (Emanuele)
Roma (Ernesto)
05 Azdak
Brown (Tiger)

Eilif
Matti
06 Andrea
Givola (Giuseppe)
07 Galileo
Kattrin
Kazbeki (Arsen)
Peachum (Celia)
Peachum (Jonathan Jeremiah)

Peachum (Polly)
Puntila
08 Fierling (Anna)
Macheath
Shashava (Simon)
09 Abashwili (Michael)
Abashwili (Natella)
Vashnadze (Grusha)

10 The Florist
11 Dogsborough
Mac the Knife
Swiss Cheese
12 Low-Dive Jenny
Schweizerkas
The Fat Prince
13 Mother Courage
The Beggar King

breed *see* **cat**; **cattle**; **dog**; **horse**

brewing *see* **beer**

bridge

Bridge types include:

03 air	road	girder	floating
fly	rope	**07** bascule	humpback
04 arch	skew	flyover	overpass
beam	toll	lattice	**09** box girder
deck	wire	lifting	**10** cantilever
draw	**05** chain	pontoon	suspension
foot	pivot	railway	traversing
leaf	swing	through	**11** cable-stayed
over	**06** Bailey	viaduct	transporter
raft	flying	**08** aqueduct	

Bridges include:

03 Tay (Scotland)

04 Skye (Scotland)
Tyne (England)

05 Forth (Scotland)
Sighs (Italy)
Tower (England)

06 Humber (England)
Kintai (Japan)
London (England)
Rialto (Italy)
Severn (England)

07 Bifrost (Norse mythology)
Rainbow (USA)
Tsing Ma (China)
Yichang (China)

08 Bosporus (Turkey)
Brooklyn (USA)
Jiangyin (China)
Mackinac (USA)
Waterloo (England)

09 Evergreen (USA)
Forth Road (Scotland)

River Kwai (Thailand)

10 Bosporus II (Turkey)
Golden Gate (USA)
Höga Kusten (Sweden)
Ironbridge (England)
Kurushima-2 (Japan)
Kurushima-3 (Japan)
Millennium (England)
Pont du Gard (France)
Storebaelt (Denmark)

11 Brocade Sash (Japan)

12 Akashi-Kaikyo (Japan)
Pont d'Avignon (France)
Ponte Vecchio (Italy)

13 Great Belt East (Denmark)
Kita Bisan-Seto (Japan)
Millau Viaduct (France)
Sydney Harbour (Australia)

14 Ponte 25 de Abril (Portugal)
Quebec Railroad (Canada)

15 Minami Bisan-Seto (Japan)

See also **game**

bridle

Bridle parts include:

03 bit	**06** musrol	eye-flap	noseband
04 curb	pelham	snaffle	**09** headstall
05 cheek	**07** bridoon	**08** browband	**10** cheekpiece

British *see* **monarch**

Britten, Benjamin (1913–76)

Significant works include:

06 *Te Deum* (1936)
07 *Phaedra* (1976)
08 *Antiphon* (1956)
　　Gloriana (1953)
　　Mont Juic (1938)
　　Nocturne (1958)
09 *Billy Budd* (1951)
　　Lachrymae (various dates)
　　Night Mail (1936)
　　St Nicolas (1948)
10 *'Amo Ergo Sum'* (1949)
　　Paul Bunyan (1941)
　　War Requiem (1961)
　　Welcome Ode (1977)
11 *A Boy Was Born* (1934)
　　Curlew River (1964)
　　Missa Brevis (1959)
　　Noye's Fludde (1958)
　　Passacaglia (1945)
　　Peter Grimes (1945)
　　Sinfonietta (1933)
　　Winter Words (1953)
12 *On This Island* (1937)
　　Owen Wingrave (1971)
13 *Albert Herring* (1947)
　　Cello Symphony (1964)

Death in Venice (1973)
Hymn to St Peter (1955)
14 *Ballad of Heroes* (1939)
　　Festival Te Deum (1945)
　　Kinderkreuzzug (1969)
　　Scottish Ballad (1941)
　　Spring Symphony (1949)
　　The Little Sweep (1949)
　　The Prodigal Son (1968)
　　Voices for Today (1965)
15 *A Simple Symphony*
　　　(1934)
　　Five Flower Songs (1950)
　　Hymn to St Cecilia (1942)
　　Hymn to the Virgin (1931)
　　Let's Make an Opera
　　　(1949)
　　Prelude and Fugue (1943)
　　The Beggar's Opera (1948)
　　The Golden Vanity (1967)
16 *Les Illuminations* (1940)
17 *The Rape of Lucretia* (1946)
　　The Turn of the Screw (1954)
21 *A Midsummer Night's Dream* (1960)
22 *The Burning Fiery Furnace* (1966)
31 *Variations on a Theme of Frank Bridge* (1937)

broadcasting

Broadcasting terms include:

02 CB
　　OB
　　TV
03 BSC
　　DAB
　　DBS
　　mix
　　PAL
　　pan
　　Sky
04 FHSS
　　HDTV
　　live
　　NTSC
05 audio
　　bleep
　　cable
　　Dolby®
　　ident
　　NICAM
　　pilot

　　radio
　　rerun
　　SECAM
　　video
06 advert
　　anchor
　　Ceefax
　　filler
　　repeat
　　script
　　serial
　　series
　　studio
　　teaser
07 air play
　　airtime
　　airwave
　　CB radio
　　channel
　　dead air
　　digital
　　episode

　　God slot
　　hammock
　　link man
　　network
　　phone-in
　　sponsor
　　station
　　the pips
　　trailer
　　webcast
08 analogue
　　Freeview
　　national
　　newscast
　　news desk
　　on the air
　　playlist
　　producer
　　regional
　　roadshow
　　schedule
　　teletext

09 announcer
　　cablecast
　　frequency
　　interview
　　multicast
　　multiplex
　　off the air
　　prime time
　　satellite
　　simulcast
　　streaming
　　subtitles
　　syndicate
　　watershed
10 commentary
　　commercial
　　continuity
　　mixing desk
　　needle time
　　sportscast
　　telebridge

11 aspect ratio
commentator
rolling news
telestrator

12 Citizens' Band
transmission

13 advertisement
double pumping

narrowcasting
satellite dish
telerecording

14 high definition

15 commercial break
satellite linkup

See also **journalism**; **radio**; **television**

Brontë, Anne (1820–49)

Significant works include:

09 *Agnes Grey* (1845)

23 *The Tenant of Wildfell Hall* (1848)

Significant characters include:

04 Grey (Agnes)

06 Arthur
Graham (Mrs Helen)
Murray (Rosalie)

Weston (Rev Mr Edward)

07 Markham (Gilbert)

08 Lawrence (Frederick)

10 Huntingdon (Arthur)

Brontë, Charlotte (1816–55)

Significant works include:

07 *Shirley* (1849)

08 *Jane Eyre* (1847)

Villette (1853)

12 *The Professor* (1857)

Significant characters include:

04 Beck (Madame)
Eyre (Jane)
Home (Paulina 'Polly')
Reed (Eliza)
Reed (Georgiana)
Reed (John)
Reed (Mrs)

05 Burns (Helen)
Henri (Frances)
Lloyd (Dr)
Mason (Bertha)
Moore (Louis)
Moore (Robert Gerard)
Pelet (Monsieur)
Poole (Grace)
Pryor (Mrs)

Snowe (Lucy)
Yorke (Martin)
Yorke (Mr)

06 Farren (William)
Ingram (Miss Blanche)
Miller (Miss)
Oliver (Miss Rosamond)
Reuter (Zoraide)
Rivers (Diana)
Rivers (Mary)
Rivers (St John)
Sophie
Temple (Miss Maria)

07 Bretton (Dr John)
Keeldar (Shirley)
Nasmyth (Reverend)

Nunnely (Sir Philip)

08 Emmanuel (Monsieur Paul)
Fanshawe (Ginevra)
Helstone (Caroline)
Helstone (James)
Helstone (Mr)
Helstone (Reverend
Matthewson)

09 Rochester (Adele)
Rochester (Mr Edward
Fairfax)
Scatcherd (Miss)
Walravens (Madame)

10 Crimsworth (William)

12 Brocklehurst (Mr)

Brontë, Emily (1818–48)

Significant works include:

09 'Last Lines' (1846)

10 'Plead for Me' (1846)

13 'To Imagination' (1846)

16 *Wuthering Heights* (1847)

Significant characters include:

04 Dean (Ellen 'Nelly')

05 Green (Mr)

06 Joseph

Linton (Catherine)
Linton (Edgar)
Linton (Isabella)

Linton (Mr)
Linton (Mrs)
Zillah

08 Earnshaw (Catherine   Earnshaw (Hindley)   **10** Heathcliff
     'Cathy')   Earnshaw (Mr)   Heathcliff (Linton)
   Earnshaw (Frances)   Earnshaw (Mrs)
   Earnshaw (Hareton)   Lockwood (Mr)

brown

Shades of brown include:

03 bay	hazel	burnet	cinnamon
dun	honey	coffee	mahogany
tan	khaki	copper	mushroom
04 buff	mocha	ginger	nut-brown
drab	ochre	russet	philamot
ecru	rusty	sorrel	raw umber
fawn	sepia	walnut	**09** chocolate
pine	taupe	**07** biscuit	earth-tone
rust	tawny	caramel	**10** burnt umber
sand	tenné	chamois	café au lait
teak	umber	filemot	terracotta
05 beige	**06** auburn	oatmeal	**11** burnt sienna
camel	bister	oxblood	orange-tawny
cocoa	bistre	**08** brunette	**12** vandyke brown
dusky	bronze	chestnut	

See also **dye**; **pigment**

buccaneer *see* **piracy**

Buddhism

Buddhist groups, schools and orders include:

03 Zen	Sakyapa	Mahayana	Theravada
06 Tendai	Shingon	Nichiren	
	Tantric	Pure Land	**11** Vaibhashika
07 Gelugpa	Tibetan	**09** Nyingmapa	**13** Sarvastivadin
Kagyupa	**08** Hinayana	Sinhalese	

See also **religion**

building

Building types include:

03 inn	arena	mosque	low-rise
pub	cabin	museum	mansion
04 barn	hotel	pagoda	theatre
café	house	palace	**08** barracks
fort	store	prison	beach hut
mews	villa	school	bungalow
mill	**06** castle	stable	dovecote
pier	chapel	temple	fortress
riad	church	**07** chateau	gurdwara
shed	cinema	college	high-rise
shop	garage	cottage	hospital
silo	gazebo	factory	monument
05 abbey	mandir	library	outhouse

pavilion
showroom
skilling
skillion
windmill
09 apartment
boathouse
cathedral

farmhouse
gymnasium
mausoleum
monastery
multiplex
synagogue
warehouse
10 lighthouse

maisonette
restaurant
skyscraper
sports hall
tower block
university
11 condominium
observatory

office block
public house
summerhouse
12 block of flats
power station
14 apartment house
sliver building

Building materials include:

03 MDF
04 clay
sand
tile
wood
05 brick
glass
grout
slate
steel
stone
06 ashlar
cement
girder
gravel
gypsum

lintel
lumber
marble
mastic
mortar
pavior
siding
tarmac
thatch
timber
07 asphalt
bitumen
decking
drywall
fixings
granite
lagging

plaster
plastic
plywood
sarking
shingle
08 asbestos
cast iron
cladding
concrete
hard core
roof tile
wall tile
09 aggregate
aluminium
chipboard
clapboard
flagstone

floor tile
hardboard
sandstone
steel beam
10 glass fibre
insulation
matchboard
11 breeze block
paving stone
roofing felt
12 plasterboard
13 building block
wattle and daub
14 foam insulation
stainless steel

Buildings include:

05 Duomo (Italy)
07 BT Tower (England)
CN Tower (Canada)
Kremlin (Russia)
La Scala (Italy)
St Paul's (England)
UN Plaza (USA)
08 Casa Milà (Spain)
Cenotaph (England)
Pantheon (Italy)
St Peter's (Vatican City)
Taj Mahal (India)
The Shard (England)
09 Acropolis (Greece)
Coit Tower (USA)
Colosseum (Italy)
Notre Dame (France)
Old Bailey (England)
Parthenon (Greece)
Reichstag (Germany)
Taipei 101 (Taiwan)
The Louvre (France)
US Capitol (USA)
10 Guggenheim (Spain)

Guggenheim (USA)
Sears Tower (USA)
Tate Modern (England)
The Gherkin (England)
Trump Tower (USA)
White House (USA)
11 Canary Wharf (England)
Eden Project (England)
Eiffel Tower (France)
Musée d'Orsay (France)
Space Needle (USA)
The Alhambra (Spain)
The Panthéon (France)
The Pentagon (USA)
Tower Bridge (England)
12 Globe Theatre (England)
Great Pyramid (Egypt)
Mont St Michel (France)
The Parthenon (Greece)
Winter Palace (Russia)
13 Crystal Palace (England)
Dome of the Rock (Israel)
Musée du Louvre (France)
Somerset House (England)

Tower of London (England)
14 Balmoral Castle (Scotland)
Barbican Centre (England)
Blenheim Palace (England)
Centre Pompidou (France)
Hoover Building (England)
Millennium Dome
(England)
Pompidou Centre (France)
Sagrada Familia (Spain)
Wells Cathedral (England)
15 Ashmolean Museum
(England)
Banqueting House
(England)
Brandenburg Gate
(Germany)
Capitol Building (USA)
Edinburgh Castle (Scotland)
Lincoln Memorial (USA)
Post Office Tower (England)
Royal Opera House
(England)
Statue of Liberty (USA)
Westminster Hall (England)

See also **abbey**; **accommodation**; **architecture**; **castle**; **house**; **palace**; **religion**; **tent**

bulb

Plants grown from bulbs, corms, rhizomes and tubers include:

04 iris
ixia
lily
05 tulip
06 allium
crinum
crocus
dahlia
garlic
nerine
scilla
squill
07 anemone
jonquil
muscari
peacock
08 bluebell
camassia
curtonus
cyclamen
daffodil
endymion
galtonia

gladioli
harebell
hyacinth
snowdrop
sparaxis
09 colchicum
crocosmia
galanthus
gladiolus
heliconia
narcissus
snowflake
tiger lily
Titan arum
10 agapanthus
chionodoxa
fritillary
giant rouge
montbretia
ranunculus
snake's head
solfaterre
wand flower
11 acidanthera

African lily
erythronium
fritillaria
hippeastrum
lapeirousia
naked ladies
sternbergia
tiger flower
12 autumn crocus
ornithogalum
Solomon's seal
wild hyacinth
13 crown imperial
grape hyacinth
lily-of-the-Nile
striped squill
winter aconite
14 belladonna lily
chincherinchee
glory of the snow
Ithuriel's spear
15 dog's tooth violet
lily-of-the-valley

See also **plant**

Bulgaria *see* **Balkans**

burial ground *see* **cemetery**

Burns, Robert (1759–96)

Significant works include:

08 'To a Mouse' (1785)
10 'The Twa Dogs' (1785)
11 *Tam o'Shanter* (1791)
'Scots Wha Hae' (1793)
'The Holy Fair' (1785)
12 'Auld Lang Syne' (c.1788)
13 'The Banks o' Doon' (c.1791)
14 'Epistle to Davie' (1785)
'Where Helen Lies' (1788)
15 'Comin' Thro' the Rye' (c.1795)
'The Jolly Beggars' (1785)
'Ye Banks and Braes' (c.1791)
16 'Address to a Haggis' (1786)
'Address to the Deil' (1785)
'John Anderson My Jo' (1789)

'To a Mountain Daisy' (1776)
17 'A Man's a Man for A' That' (c.1795)
'Holy Willie's Prayer' (1785)
'Ye Jacobites by Name' (1791)
18 'Death and Dr Hornbook' (1785)
19 'Green Grow the Rashes O' (c.1784)
'The Lass o' Ballochmyle' (1786)
20 'Address to the Unco Guid' (1786)
21 'O Tibbie, I Hae Seen the Day' (c.1777)
22 'My Heart's in the Highlands' (c.1790)
23 'Man Was Made to Mourn: A Dirge' (1784)
'My Luve is Like a Red, Red Rose' (1794)
'The Cotter's Saturday Night' (1785)
24 'Ae Fond Kiss, and Then We Sever' (1791)

bushranger

business

Sony
05 Abbey
Alcan
Bayer
Boots
Canon
Corus
Exxon
Heinz
Intel
Nokia
Ricoh
Sharp
Shell
Tesco
Volvo
06 Adecco
Arriva
Boeing
Diageo
Dixons
Du Pont
Group 4
Hanson
L'Oréal
Nestlé
Pfizer
Texaco
Virgin
Wimpey
07 Arcadia
Aventis
Chevron
easyJet
Fujitsu
Harrods
Hitachi
Hyundai
Lafarge
Marconi
Matalan
Minerva
Pearson
Pepsico
Peugeot
Philips
Renault
Reuters
Safeway
Samsung
Siemens

Toshiba
Wal-Mart
W H Smith
08 Barclays
Burberry
Centrica
Chrysler
Coca-Cola
Goodyear
JP Morgan
Michelin
Olivetti
Rentokil
Rio Tinto
Unilever
Vodafone
Waitrose
09 Akzo Nobel
Carrefour
Home Depot
John Laing
Ladbrokes
Lloyds TSB
McDonald's
Microsoft
Morrisons
Schroders
Whitbread
10 BAE Systems
Bovis Homes
Electrolux
Exxon Mobil
Greene King
Honda Motor
J Sainsbury
Kingfisher
Mazda Motor
Mitsubishi
Nationwide
Pilkington
Prudential
Rolls-Royce
Sainsbury's
Somerfield
Stagecoach
Telefonica
Volkswagen
Walt Disney
11 AstraZeneca
Caterpillar
Isuzu Motors

Nippon Steel
Nissan Motor
Standard Oil
Suzuki Motor
Toyota Motor
William Hill
12 Allied Domecq
Capital Radio
DFS Furniture
Eastman Kodak
Groupe Danone
Hilton Hotels
Hyundai Motor
Merrill Lynch
Northern Rock
Philip Morris
Reed Elsevier
Sears Roebuck
Total Fina Elf
Toyota Tsusho
Union Carbide
Union Pacific
Western Union
13 Abbey National
Alcatel-Lucent
Anglo American
Balfour Beatty
Fuji Photo Film
General Motors
Harvey Nichols
J D Wetherspoon
Lever Brothers
Sanyo Electric
Taylor Woodrow
Travis Perkins
14 Akzo Nobel
Alfred McAlpine
British Airways
Credit Agricole
Hewlett-Packard
Virgin Atlantic
15 American Express
DaimlerChrysler
Deutsche Telekom
General Electric
GlaxoSmithKline
Legal and General
Marks and Spencer
National Express
News Corporation

Businesspeople, industrialists, magnates and entrepreneurs include:

03 Day (Sir Graham; 1933–   , Canadian)
Fay (Sir Michael; 1949–   , New Zealand)
Fry (Joseph; 1728–87, English)

04 Bata (Tomas; 1876–1932, Czechoslovakian)
Benz (Karl; 1844–1929, German)
Bond (Alan; 1938–   , Australian)

Boot (Sir Jesse; 1850–1931, English)
Cook (Thomas; 1808–92, English)
Coty (François; 1874–1934, French)
Dale (David; 1739–1806, Scottish)
Egan (Sir John; 1939– , English)
Ford (Henry; 1863–1947, US)
Ford (Henry II; 1917–87, US)
Jobs (Steven; 1955–2011, US)
King (John, Lord; 1917–2005, English)
Mond (Alfred, Lord Melchett; 1868–1930, English)
Mond (Ludwig; 1839–1909, German/British)
Shah (Eddy; 1944– , English)
Tate (Sir Henry; 1819–99, English)
Wang (An; 1920–90, US/Chinese)

05 Allan (Sir Hugh; 1810–82, Canadian)
Arden (Elizabeth; c.1880–1966, US)
Astor (John, Lord; 1886–1971, Anglo-US)
Astor (William Waldorf, Lord; 1848–1919, Anglo-US)
Bevan (Edward; 1856–1921, English)
Bezos (Jeff; 1964– , US)
Bosch (Carl; 1874–1940, German)
Brown (Sir John; 1816–96, English)
Cross (Charles; 1855–1935, English)
Dawes (Charles G; 1865–1951, US)
Elder (Sir Thomas; 1818–97, Australian)
Fayed (Mohamed al-; 1933– , Egyptian)
Firth (Mark; 1819–80, English)
Fleck (Alexander, Lord; 1889–1968, Scottish)
Forte (Charles, Lord; 1908–2007, Scottish)
Frick (Henry; 1849–1919, US)
Gates (Bill; 1955– , US)
Getty (J Paul; 1892–1976, US)
Grade (Michael, Lord; 1943– , English)
Green (Sir Philip; 1952– , English)
Guest (Sir Josiah; 1785–1852, Welsh)
Heinz (Henry John; 1844–1919, US)
Honda (Soichiro; 1906–91, Japanese)
Krupp (Alfred; 1812–87, German)
Krupp (Friedrich; 1854–1902, German)
Laker (Sir Freddie; 1922–2006, English)
Lyons (Sir Joseph; 1848–1917, English)
Marks (Simon, Lord; 1888–1964, English)
Nobel (Alfred; 1833–96, Swedish)
Rolls (Charles; 1877–1910, English)
Royce (Sir Henry; 1863–1933, English)
Sieff (Israel, Lord; 1889–1972, English)
Sugar (Alan; 1947– , English)
Trump (Donald; 1946– , US)
Zeiss (Carl; 1816–88, German)

06 Amdahl (Gene; 1922– , US)
Ansett (Sir Reg; 1909–81, Australian)
Austin (Herbert, Lord; 1866–1941, English)
Bedaux (Charles; 1886–1944, US)
Beilby (Sir George Thomas; 1850–1924, Scottish)

Boeing (William Edward; 1881–1956, US)
Butlin (Billy; 1899–1980, English)
Conran (Sir Terence; 1931– , English)
Cunard (Sir Samuel; 1787–1865, Canadian)
Davies (David; 1818–90, Welsh)
Dunlop (John Boyd; 1840–1921, Scottish)
du Pont (Eleuthère Irénée; 1771–1834, French/US)
du Pont (Pierre Samuel; 1870–1954, US)
Fairey (Sir Richard; 1887–1956, English)
Frasch (Hermann; 1851–1914, US)
Fugger (Johannes; 1348–1409, German)
Gamble (Josias; 1776–1848, Irish)
Geneen (Harold; 1910–97, US)
Girard (Stephen; 1750–1831, US)
Grange (Kenneth; 1929– , English)
Hammer (Armand; 1899–1990, US)
Hanson (James, Lord; 1922–2004, English)
Hilton (Conrad; 1887–1979, US)
Hoover (William Henry; 1849–1932, US)
Hughes (Howard; 1905–76, US)
Hulton (Sir Edward; 1906–88, English)
Mellon (Andrew; 1855–1937, US)
Mittal (Lakshmi; 1950– , Indian/British)
Morgan (J Pierpont; 1837–1913, US)
Morita (Akio; 1921–99, Japanese)
Necker (Jacques; 1732–1804, French)
Packer (Kerry; 1937–2005, Australian)
Taylor (Frederick W; 1856–1915, US)
Turner (Ted; 1938– , US)

07 Agnelli (Giovanni; 1866–1945, Italian)
Angliss (Sir William; 1865–1957, Australian)
Baldwin (Matthias; 1795–1866, US)
Barclay (Robert; 1843–1913, English)
Bourdon (Eugène; 1808–84, French)
Branson (Sir Richard; 1950– , English)
Bugatti (Ettore; 1882–1947, Italian)
Burrell (Sir William; 1861–1958, Scottish)
Cadbury (George; 1839–1922, English)
Cadbury (John; 1801–89, English)
Chandos (Oliver Lyttelton, Lord; 1893–1972, English)
Citroën (André; 1878–1935, French)
Cornell (Ezra; 1807–74, US)
De L'Isle (William Philip Sidney, Lord; 1909–91, English)
Enderby (Samuel; fl.1830–39, English)
Hackett (Deborah Vernon; 1887–1965, Australian)
Hancock (Lang; 1909–92, Australian)
Iacocca (Lee; 1924– , US)
Kennedy (Joseph P; 1888–1969, US)
Maxwell (Robert; 1923–91, English)
Murdoch (Rupert; 1931– , Australian/US)
Onassis (Aristotle; 1906–75, Greek)
Roddick (Anita; 1942–2007, English)
Seebohm (Henry; 1832–95, English)

Sotheby (John; 1740–1807, English)
Tiffany (Charles; 1812–1902, US)
Wolfson (Sir Isaac; 1897–1991, Scottish)

08 Baillieu (William Lawrence; 1859–1936, Australian)
Birchall (Derek; 1930–95, English)
Birdseye (Clarence; 1886–1956, US)
Brierley (Sir Ron; 1937– , New Zealand)
Buckland (Henry Seymour Berry, Lord; 1877–1928, Welsh)
Carnegie (Andrew; 1835–1918, Scottish/US)
Christie (James; 1730–1803, English)
Dassault (Marcel; 1892–1986, French)
Drummond (George; 1687–1766, Scottish)
Edwardes (Sir Michael; 1930– , South African/British)
Gillette (King Camp; 1855–1932, US)
Giugiaro (Giorgio; 1938– , Italian)
Guinness (Sir Benjamin Lee; 1798–1868, Irish)
McNamara (Robert; 1916–2009, US)
Michelin (André; 1853–1931, French)
Nuffield (William Morris, Lord; 1877–1963, English)
Olivetti (Adriano; 1901–60, Italian)
Paphitis (Theo; 1959– , Greek Cypriot)
Paterson (William; 1658–1719, Scottish)
Pulitzer (Joseph; 1847–1911, Hungarian/US)
Rathenau (Walther; 1867–1922, German)
Rowntree (Joseph; 1836–1925, English)
Sinclair (Sir Clive; 1940– , English)
Zaharoff (Sir Basil; 1850–1936, French)

09 Arkwright (Sir Richard; 1732–92, English)
Armstrong (William, Lord; 1810–1900, English)
Barr Smith (Robert; 1824–1915, Australian)
Bernstein (Sidney, Lord; 1899–1993, English)

Carothers (Wallace; 1896–1937, US)
Cockerill (John; 1790–1840, English)
Courtauld (Samuel; 1876–1947, English)
Finlayson (James; 1772–1852, Scottish)
Finniston (Monty; 1912–91, Scottish)
Firestone (Harvey S; 1868–1938, US)
Göransson (Göran; 1819–1900, Swedish)
Greenspan (Alan; 1926– , US)
Sainsbury (Alan, Lord; 1902–98, English)
Selfridge (Harry Gordon; 1858–1947, US/British)
Woolworth (Frank Winfield; 1852–1919, US)

10 Abramovich (Roman; 1966– , Russian)
Berlusconi (Silvio; 1936– , Italian)
Chardonnet (Hilaire, Comte de; 1839–1924, French)
Guggenheim (Meyer; 1828–1905, US)
Gulbenkian (Calouste; 1869–1955, British/Turkish)
Leverhulme (William Hesketh Lever, Lord; 1851–1925, English)
Pilkington (Sir Alastair; 1920–95, English)
Rothermere (Harold Harmsworth, Lord; 1868–1940, Irish)
Rothschild (Meyer; 1744–1812, German)
Vanderbilt (Cornelius; 1794–1877, US)

11 Beaverbrook (Max, Lord; 1879–1964, Canadian/British)
Haji-Ioannou (Stelios; 1967– , Greek Cypriot/British)
Harvey-Jones (Sir John; 1924–2008, English)
Rockefeller (John D; 1839–1937, US)

12 Benediktsson (Einar; 1864–1940, Icelandic)
Gyllenhammar (Pehr Gustaf; 1935– , Swedish)

Terms used in business include:

03 CBI
IPO
JIT
PLC
SKU
USP
04 FMCG
soho
05 angel
06 assets
buy-out
dot com
margin
mark-up
merger
tender
07 duopoly

synergy
08 blue chip
demerger
monopoly
offshore
oligarch
price war
takeover
trade war
unit cost
09 break even
corporate
franchise
oligopoly
10 bottom line
closed shop
dot com boom

downsizing
high street
just in time
loss leader
offshoring
sole trader
subsidiary
11 acquisition
corporation
fixed assets
golden hello
minimum wage
niche market
partnership
supply chain
white knight
12 above the line
below the line

black economy
brand loyalty
conglomerate
core business
deregulation
distribution
entrepreneur
liquid assets
micromanager
productivity
profit margin
retail sector

13 acid test ratio
asset sweating
consumer goods

listed company
multinational
mutual society
organic growth
parent company
privatization
protectionism
purchase order
quoted company
restructuring

14 asset stripping
capitalization
holding company
limited company
vertical market

15 barriers to entry
bricks and mortar
building society
clicks and mortar
demutualization
differentiation
diversification
golden handcuffs
golden handshake
golden parachute
nationalization
supply and demand
turnkey solution
wholesale sector

See also **economics**; **finance**

butterfly

Butterflies include:

03 map
04 blue
wall
05 argus
comma
elfin
heath
satyr
white
06 apollo
copper
hermit
morpho
pierid
psyche
07 admiral
cabbage
monarch
Papilio
peacock
ringlet
satyrid
skipper

thistle
Ulysses
vanessa
08 birdwing
cardinal
grayling
hesperid
milk-weed
09 brimstone
cleopatra
Hesperian
holly blue
metalmark
nymphalid
orange-tip
wall brown
wood white
10 brown argus
common blue
fritillary
gatekeeper
hairstreak
red admiral

11 large copper
meadow-brown
painted lady
Scotch argus
small copper
swallowtail
12 cabbage-white
dingy skipper
Essex skipper
marbled-white
white admiral
13 chalkhill blue
clouded yellow
mourning cloak
purple emperor
tortoiseshell
15 black hairstreak
brown hairstreak
green hairstreak
grizzled skipper
heath fritillary
Lulworth skipper
marsh fritillary
mountain ringlet

See also **insect**; **moth**

Byron, George Gordon, Lord (1788–1824)

Significant works include:

04 *Cain* (1821)
Lara (1814)
05 *Beppo* (1818)
07 *Don Juan* (1819–24)
Manfred (1817)
Mazeppa (1819)

09 *The Giaour* (1813)
The Island (1823)
10 *Prometheus* (1816)
The Corsair (1814)
12 *Maid of Athens* (1810)
Sardanapalus (1821)

13 *Lament of Tasso* (1817)
   Marino Faliero (1821)
   The Two Foscari (1821)

14 *Heaven and Earth* (1823)
   Hebrew Melodies (1815)
   The Age of Bronze (1823)

15 *Hours of Idleness* (1807)
   Prophecy of Dante (1821)

16 *The Bride of Abydos* (1813)

   'She Walks in Beauty' (1814)

20 *The Prisoner of Chillon* (1816)
   The Vision of Judgement (1822)

21 *So, We'll Go No More a Roving* (1817)

22 *The Deformed Transformed* (1824)

23 *Childe Harold's Pilgrimage*
   (1812/1816/1818)
   Poems on Various Occasions (1807)

30 *English Bards and Scotch Reviewers* (1809)

Byzantine empire

Byzantine emperors and empresses, with regnal dates:

03 Leo (II; AD 74)
   Leo (III, the Isaurian; 717–41)
   Leo (I, the Great; AD 57–74)
   Leo (IV, the Khazar; 775–80)
   Leo (VI, the Wise; 886–912)
   Leo (V, the Armenian; 813–20)
   Zoë (1042)

04 John (II Comnenus; 1118–43)
   John (III Ducas-Vatatzes; 1222–54)
   John (I Tzimisces; 969–76)
   John (IV Lascaris; 1258–61)
   John (VI Cantacuzene; 1347–55)
   John (VIII Palaeologus; 1425–48)
   John (VII Palaeologus; 1390)
   John (V Palaeologus; 1341–47/1355–
   76/1379–90)
   Zeno (AD 76–91)

05 Basil (II; 976–1025)
   Basil (I, the Macedonian; 867–86)
   Irene (the Athenian; 797–802)
   Isaac (I Comnenus; 1057–59)
   Isaac (II Angelus; 1185–95/1203–04)

06 Jovian (AD 63–64)
   Julian (the Apostate; AD 61–63)
   Justin (I; 518–27)
   Justin (II; 565–78)
   Manuel (I Comnenus; 1143–80)
   Manuel (II Palaeologus; 1391–1425)
   Phocas (602–10)
   Valens (AD 64–78)

07 Alexius (I Comnenus; 1081–1118)
   Alexius (III Angelus-Comnenus; 1195–1203)
   Alexius (IV Angelus; 1203–04)
   Alexius (V; 1204)
   Eudocia (1067)
   Marcian (AD 50–57)
   Michael (I Angelus; 1204–15)
   Michael (II Comnenus-Ducas; 1237–71)
   Michael (III, the Drunkard; 842–67)
   Michael (II, the Amorian; 820–29)
   Michael (I Rhangabe; 811–13)
   Michael (IV, the Paphlagonian; 1034–41)

Michael (V Calaphates; 1041–42)
Michael (VII Ducas; 1071–78)
Michael (VIII Palaeologus; 1261–82)
Michael (VI Stratioticus; 1056–57)
Romanus (II; 959–63)
Romanus (III Argyrus; 1028–34)
Romanus (I Lecapenus; 919–44)
Romanus (IV Diogenes; 1068–71)

08 Arcadius (AD 95–408)
   Constans (II; 641–68)
   Leontius (695–98)
   Mezezius (668–69)
   Theodora (1042)
   Theodore (I Comnenus-Lascaris; 1208–22)
   Theodore (II Ducas-Lascaris; 1254–58)
   Tiberius (II Constantine; 578–82)
   Tiberius (III; 698–705)

09 Alexander (912–13)
   Heraclius (610–41)
   Justinian (II; 685–95/705–11)
   Justinian (I, the Great; 527–65)

10 Anastasius (I; AD 91–518)
   Anastasius (II; 713–15)
   Andronicus (I Comnenus; 1183–85)
   Andronicus (III Palaeologus; 1328–41)
   Andronicus (II Palaeologus; 1282–1328)
   Andronicus (IV Palaeologus; 1376–79)
   Artavasdus (742–43)
   Basiliscus (AD 75–76)
   Nicephorus (742–43)
   Nicephorus (I; 802–11)
   Nicephorus (III Botaniates; 1078–81)
   Nicephorus (II Phocas; 963–69)
   Stauracius (811)
   Theodosius (II; AD 08–50)
   Theodosius (III, of Adramytium; 715–17)
   Theodosius (I, the Great; AD 79–95)
   Theophilus (829–42)

11 Constantine (I, the Great; AD 30–37)
   Constantine (IV; 654–85)
   Constantine (IX Monomachus; 1042–55)
   Constantine (V Copronymus; 720–41/741–75)

Constantine (VI; 775–97)
Constantine (VIII Porphyrogenitus; 1025–28)
Constantine (VII Porphyrogenitus; 913–59)
Constantine (X Ducas; 1059–67)
Constantine (XI Palaeologus; 1448–53)
Constantius (AD 37–61)
Heracleonas (641)
Philippicus (711–13)
12 Zeno Tarasius (AD 74–75)
13 Isaac Comnenus (1184–91)

Theophylactus (811–13)
15 Maurice Tiberius (582–602)
17 John Comnenus-Ducas (1237–42/1242–44)
Zoë Porphyrogenita (1042)
19 Manuel Comnenus-Ducas (1230–37)
20 Heraclius Constantine (641)
21 Theodore Comnenus-Ducas (1224–30)
22 Theodora Porphyrogenita (1056)

C

The Cabinet *see* **government**

cactus

Cacti include:

04 crab
toad

05 dildo
nopal

06 barrel
cereus
cholla
Easter
mescal
old man
orchid
peanut
peyote

07 jointed
old lady
opuntia

See also **plant**

rainbow
saguaro

08 dumpling
gold lace
hedgehog
rat's tail
snowball
starfish
Turk's cap

09 bunny ears
Christmas
goat's horn
gold charm
Indian fig
mistletoe
sea-urchin

10 cotton-pole
sand dollar
silver ball
strawberry
zygocactus

11 grizzly bear
mammillaria
prickly pear
scarlet ball
silver torch

12 golden barrel

13 Bristol beauty
schlumbergera

14 drunkard's dream

15 queen of the night
snowball cushion

cake

Cakes, pastries and puddings include:

03 bun
cup
fig
oat
pan
pie
tea

04 baba
flan
fool
plum
rock
seed
tart

05 angel
bombe
bride
bundt
cream
crêpe
fairy

fruit
fudge
Genoa
jelly
lardy
layer
pound
queen
scone
short
sweet
tipsy
torte
yeast

06 banana
carrot
cheese
coffee
Dundee
Eccles
éclair
gateau

ginger
girdle
junket
marble
mousse
muffin
parkin
simnel
sponge
trifle
waffle
yum-yum

07 baklava
Banbury
bannock
Bath bun
brioche
brownie
crumble
crumpet
currant
fig roll

fritter
iced bun
jam roll
jam tart
Madeira
Pavlova
plum pie
Pomfret
ratafia
rum baba
saffron
savarin
soufflé
stollen
strudel
sultana
tartlet
tea loaf
wedding
Yule log

08 apple pie
birthday
black bun
date roll
doughnut
flummery
macaroon
malt loaf
meringue
mince pie
mooncake
pecan pie
sandwich
syllabub
tiramisu
turnover
whim-wham

09 angel food
banana-nut
cherry-pie
chocolate
Christmas
cranachan
cream horn
cream puff
drop scone
fruit tart
lamington
lemon tart
madeleine
panettone
Sally Lunn
sweetmeat
Swiss roll

10 banana loaf
Battenburg
Chelsea bun
key lime pie
panna cotta
Pontefract
pumpkin pie
shoofly pie
tarte tatin
toasted tea
upside-down

11 baked Alaska
banana bread
banoffee pie
choux pastry
cinnamon bun
crème brulée
custard tart
gingerbread
hot cross bun

jam roly-poly
lady's finger
Linzertorte
plum pudding
profiterole
rice pudding
Sachertorte
sago pudding
spotted dick
treacle tart

12 apfel strudel
apple fritter
Bakewell tart
chocolate log
crème caramel
custard slice
Danish pastry
figgy pudding
hasty pudding
mille-feuille
plum porridge
tarte au sucre

13 apple dumpling
apple turnover
Scotch pancake
sponge pudding
summer pudding

14 apple charlotte
charlotte russe
chocolate fudge
steamed pudding
Victoria sponge

15 black-cap pudding
chocolate éclair
queen of puddings
strawberry short

See also **baking**; **biscuit**; **dessert**; **food**

calendar

Calendars include:

05	Baha'i					09	arbitrary
	Hindu	06	Coptic	07	Chinese		Gregorian
	lunar		Hebrew		Islamic		lunisolar
	Roman		Jewish		Persian		

Animals representing years in the Chinese calendar:

02	ox		cock		snake	07	buffalo
03	dog		goat		tiger		chicken
	pig		hare	06	dragon		rooster
	rat	05	horse		monkey		serpent
04	boar		sheep		rabbit		

Months of the Hindu calendar:

04 Magh	Kartik	08 Jyaistha	Margasirsa
05 Magha	07 Ashadha	Karttika	12 Margashirsha
Pausa	Chaitra	Phalguna	13 Dvitiya Asadha
Paush	Jaystha	Vaisakha	14 Dvitiya Sravana
06 Asadha	Phalgun	Vaishakh	
Ashvin	Shravan	09 Bhadrapad	
Asvina	Sravana	10 Bhadrapada	

Months of the Islamic calendar:

05 Rabi I	06 Rabi II	Ramadan	Muharram
Rajab	Shaban	Shawwal	10 Dhu al-Qadah
Safar	07 Jumada I	08 Jumada II	11 Dhu al-Hijjah

Months of the Jewish calendar:

02 Ab	Nisan	Kislev	07 Chislev
Av	Sivan	Shebat	Heshvan
04 Abib	Tebet	Shevat	09 Adar Sheni
Adar	Tevet	Tammuz	10 Adar Rishon
Elul	Tisri	Tebeth	11 Marcheshvan
Iyar	06 Hesvan	Tishri	
05 Iyyar	Kisleu	Veadar	

See also **day**; **month**; **religion**; **season**; **time**; **year**

Cambridge University *see* **college**

camera

Camera parts include:

02 AF	film holder	focus control
04 lens	mirror lens	focusing hood
05 blind	object lens	focusing ring
spool	pentaprism	focus setting
06 mirror	take-up reel	frame counter
07 lens cap	viewfinder	light control
shutter		reflex viewer
08 AF lenses	11 compact lens	rewind handle
aperture	data display	13 accessory shoe
card door	film advance	exposure meter
film gate	fisheye lens	film transport
magazine	leaf shutter	iris diaphragm
zoom lens	lens release	long-focus lens
09 autofocus	program card	mirror shutter
data panel	rewind crank	release button
diaphragm	take-up spool	telephoto lens
meter cell	viewing lens	wide-angle lens
spool knob	12 cable release	14 battery chamber
10 card window	card on/off key	shutter release
	compound lens	15 autofocus sensor
	flash contact	registration pin
	flash setting	

Camera types include:

02 TV

03 APS
SLR
TLR

04 cine
disc
film
Fuji®
view

05 Canon®
Kodak®
Leica®
Nikon®
plate
press
sound
still
video

06 Konica®
Pentax®

reflex
Rollei®
stereo
Super 8®
Webcam

07 bellows
compact
digital
Minolta®
Olympus®
pinhole
Yashica®

08 dry-plate
Polaroid®
Praktica®
security
wet-plate

09 automatic
binocular
camcorder
half-plate

miniature
panoramic
Rolliflex®
single use
Steadicam®

10 box Brownie®
disposable
Instamatic®
sliding box

11 large-format

12 quarter-plate
subminiature
surveillance

13 camera obscura
daguerreotype
folding reflex
point-and-press

14 twin-lens reflex

15 cinematographic

See also **photography**

Canada

Cities and notable towns in Canada include:

06 Ottawa
Quebec
Regina

07 Calgary
Halifax
Toronto

08 Edmonton
Montreal
Victoria

Winnipeg

09 Saskatoon
Vancouver

Canadian provinces and territories, with abbreviations and regional capitals:

03 NWT

06 Quebec (QC; Quebec City)

07 Alberta (AB; Edmonton)
Nunavut (NU; Iqaluit)
Ontario (ON; Toronto)

08 Manitoba (MB; Winnipeg)

10 Nova Scotia (NS; Halifax)

12 New Brunswick (NB; Fredericton)
Saskatchewan (SK; Regina)

14 Yukon Territory (YT; Whitehorse)

15 British Columbia (BC; Victoria)

18 Prince Edward Island (PE; Charlottetown)

20 Northwest Territories (NT; Yellowknife)

23 Newfoundland and Labrador (NL; St John's)

Canadian landmarks include:

06 Mt Thor

07 CN Tower
Mt Logan
Niagara
Rockies
Sky Dome

08 Lake Erie

09 Hudson Bay
Lake Huron
Mt Seymour

10 Great Lakes
St Lawrence

11 Lake Ontario

12 Lake Superior
Niagara Falls

13 Algonquin Park
Parc Olympique

14 Horseshoe Falls
Rocky Mountains

See also **prime minister**

canal

Canals include:

04 Erie (US)
Kiel (Germany)
Suez (Egypt)
05 Grand (Italy)

06 Panama (Panama)
Rideau (Canada)
07 Corinth (Greece)
Midland (Germany)

Welland (Canada)
10 Caledonian (Scotland)
Mittelland (Germany)
11 Welland Ship (Canada)

canonical hour

Canonical hours include:

04 none
sext
05 lauds
nones

prime
terce
06 matins
tierce

07 complin
orthros
vespers
08 compline

evensong

Canterbury *see* **archbishop**

Canterbury Tales *see* **Chaucer, Geoffrey**

cape

Capes include:

03 Cod (USA)
Dra (Morocco)
Icy (USA)
Low (Canada)
Nao (Spain)
Ray (Canada)
04 Arid (Australia)
Cruz (Cuba)
East (New Zealand)
Fear (USA)
Fria (Namibia)
Frio (Brazil)
Gata (Spain)
Horn (Chile)
Howe (Australia)
Pine (Canada)
Pole (USA)
Race (Canada)
Rojo (Mexico)
Vert (Senegal)
York (Australia/Greenland)
05 Adare (Antarctica)
Beata (Dominican Republic)
Canso (Canada)
Corse (France)
Creus (Spain)
Cross (Namibia)
Falso (Dominican Republic)
Gaspé (Canada)
Jaffa (Australia)
Mount (Sierra Leone)

North (Canada/New Zealand/Norway)
Otway (Australia)
Parry (Canada)
Sable (USA/Canada)
Sandy (Australia)
South (Papua New Guinea)
St Ann (Sierra Leone)
Tappi (Japan)
Weggs (Canada)
Wrath (Scotland)
06 Arkona (Germany)
Arnhem (Australia)
Barren (Australia)
Blanca (Argentina)
Codera (Venezuela)
Comino (Italy)
Cretin (Papua New Guinea)
Egmont (New Zealand)
Engaño (Philippines)
Fartak (Yemen)
Freels (Canada)
Linaro (Italy)
Muroto (Japan)
Norman (Canada)
Orange (Brazil)
Palmas (Liberia)
Recife (South Africa)
Samana (Dominican Republic)
St John (Canada)
St Mary (The Gambia)
07 Agulhas (South Africa)

Bolinao (Philippines)
Catoche (Mexico)
Charles (USA)
Chidley (Canada)
Comorin (India)
Delgado (Mozambique)
Falaise (Vietnam)
Hallett (Antarctica)
Isabela (Dominican Republic)
Kennedy (USA)
Leeuwin (Australia)
Lévêque (Australia)
L'Eveque (New Zealand)
Lookout (USA)
Mondego (Portugal)
Negrais (Myanmar)
Ortegal (Spain)
Rachado (Malaysia)
San Blas (USA)
Timiris (Mauritania)
Tortosa (Spain)
Vincent (USA)

08 Anguille (Canada)
Bathurst (Canada)
Colville (New Zealand)
de Hornos (Chile)
des Irois (Haiti)
Espichel (Portugal)
Farewell (New Zealand/Greenland)
Farquhar (Australia)
Foulwind (New Zealand)
Fournier (New Zealand)
Gerhards (Papua New Guinea)
Good Hope (South Africa)
Hatteras (USA)
Lisburne (USA)
Lucrezia (Cuba)
Matapalo (Costa Rica)
Melville (Australia/Philippines)
Mesurado (Liberia)
Newenham (USA)
Norvegia (Antarctica)
Palliser (New Zealand)
Romanzof (USA)

Saunders (New Zealand)
Stephens (New Zealand)
St George (Canada)
Suckling (Papua New Guinea)
Vaticano (Italy)
West Howe (Australia)

09 Canaveral (USA)
Carbonara (Italy)
Dame Marie (Haiti)
de la Hague (France)
dos Bahías (Argentina)
Madeleine (Canada)
Mendocino (USA)
North West (Australia)
Nunap Isua (Greenland)
Patterson (Australia)
South East (Australia)
Southwest (New Zealand)
St Nicolas (Haiti)
St Vincent (Portugal)
Trafalgar (Spain)
Van Diemen (Australia)

10 Corrientes (Mexico/Cuba/Colombia)
de São Roque (Brazil)
Finisterre (Spain)
Kidnappers (New Zealand)
Kormakitis (Cyprus)
Providence (Canada/South Africa/New
    Zealand)
Tarkhankut (Ukraine)
Tormentine (Canada)

11 Londonderry (Australia)
Naturaliste (Australia)
Sierra Leone (Sierra Leone)
Spartivento (Italy)
Three Points (Ghana)
Tribulation (Australia)

12 Breton Island (Canada)
Hopes Advance (Canada)

13 Prince of Wales (USA)

14 Henrietta Maria (Canada)
Maria van Diemen (New Zealand)

capital *see* **Australia; Austria; Belgium; Canada; city; Czech Republic; Denmark; Finland; France; Germany; Greece; India; Ireland; Italy; The Netherlands; Norway; Portugal; Spain; Sweden; Switzerland; United States of America**

captain

Captains include:

04 Ahab (Captain; *Moby Dick*, 1851, Hermann
    Melville)
Cook (Captain James; 1728–79, English)
Hook (Captain; *Peter Pan*, 1911, J M Barrie)

Kidd (Captain William; c.1645–1701,
    Scottish)
Nemo (Captain; *20,000 Leagues under the
    Sea*, 1872, Jules Verne)

05 Bligh (Captain William; 1754–1817, English)
Flint (Captain J; *Treasure Island*, 1883,
Robert Louis Stevenson)
Johns (Captain W E; 1893–1968, English)
Queeg (Captain Philip; *The Caine Mutiny*,
1951, Herman Wouk)
Smith (Captain John; 1580–1631, English)
Swing (Captain; nom de plume of Swing
Rioters, 1830–31, England)

07 Corelli (Captain Antonio; *Captain Corelli's
Mandolin*, 1994, Louis de Bernières)
Marryat (Captain Frederick; 1792–1848,
English)

Sparrow (Captain Jack; Pirates of the
Caribbean films, 2003–07)

08 Bobadill (Captain; *Every Man in His
Humour*, 1598–1616, Ben Jonson)
Hastings (Captain Arthur; Poirot novels
and short stories, 1920–75, Agatha
Christie)
MacHeath (Captain; *The Beggar's Opera*,
1728, John Gay)

09 Singleton (Captain; *Adventures of Captain
Singleton*, 1720, Daniel Defoe)

10 Hornblower (Captain Horatio; Hornblower
novels, 1937–67, C S Forester)

car *see* **motoring**

cardinal

Cardinals include:

03 Sin (Jaime; 1928–2005, Philippine)

04 Gray (Gordon; 1910–93, Scottish)
Hume (Basil; 1923–99, English)
Pole (Reginald; 1500–58, English)
Retz (Jean François de; 1614–79, French)

05 Chigi (Fabio; 1599–1667, Italian)

06 Beaton (David; 1494–1546, Scottish)
Borgia (Rodrigo; 1431–1503, Spanish)
Fisher (St John; 1469–1535, English)
Heenan (John; 1905–75, English)
Medici (Giovanni de'; 1499–1565, Italian)
Newman (John Henry; 1801–90, English)
O'Brien (Keith; 1938– , Scottish)
Rovere (Francesco della; 1414–84, Italian)
Stuart (Henry, Duke of York; 1725–1807,
British)
Wolsey (Thomas; c.1475–1530, English)

07 Bethune (David; 1494–1546, Scottish)
Langham (Simon; d.1376, English)
Langton (Stephen; c.1150–1228, English)
Mazarin (Jules; 1602–61, French)

See also **archbishop**; **religion**

Mendoza (Pedro Gonzalez de; 1428–95,
Spanish)
Pandulf (d.1226, Italian)
Vaughan (Herbert; 1832–1903, English)
Winning (Thomas; 1925–2001, Scottish)
Wiseman (Nicholas; 1802–65, English)
Ximenes (1436–1517, Spanish)

08 Alberoni (Giulio; 1664–1752, Spanish/
Italian)
Aubusson (Pierre d'; 1423–1503, French)
Beaufort (Henry; 1377–1447, English)
Stepinac (Aloysius; 1898–1960, Yugoslav)

09 Richelieu (Armand Jean du Plessis, Duc de;
1585–1642, French)
Wyszynski (Stefan; 1901–81, Polish)

10 Bellarmine (Robert; 1542–1621, Italian)
Breakspear (Nicolas; 1100–59, English)
Mindszenty (József; 1892–1975,
Hungarian)

13 Murphy-O'Connor (Cormac; 1932– ,
English)

cards *see* **game**

Caribbean

Cities and notable towns in the Caribbean include:

06 Havana (Cuba)
Nassau (The Bahamas)

07 Holguín (Cuba)
San Juan (Puerto Rico)

08 Camagüey (Cuba)

Castries (St Lucia)
Gonaïves (Haiti)
Kingston (Jamaica)
Santiago (Dominican Republic)

10 Cap-Haïtien (Haiti)

Port-de-Paix (Haiti)
11 Port of Spain (Trinidad and Tobago)
San Fernando (Trinidad and Tobago)

12 Port-au-Prince (Haiti)
Santo Domingo (Dominican Republic)
14 Santiago de Cuba (Cuba)

carnivore

Carnivores include:

03 cat
dog
owl

04 bear
frog
hawk
kite
lion
newt
orca
puma
seal
skua
wolf

05 adder
civet
cobra
dingo
eagle
heron
hyena
mamba
otter
shark
stoat
stork
tiger
viper
whale

06 condor
coyote
falcon
ferret
hyaena
jackal
jaguar
lizard
osprey
python
taipan
walrus
weasel

07 barn owl
buzzard
cheetah
dolphin
kestrel
leopard
panther
pelican
penguin
polecat
sea lion
vulture
wildcat

08 anaconda
brown owl
eagle-owl

snowy owl
tawny owl

09 albatross
alligator
bald eagle
black bear
blue whale
brown bear
crocodile
polar bear

10 copperhead
salamander
screech owl
sperm whale
tiger shark
whale shark

11 electric eel
golden eagle
grizzly bear
killer whale
rattlesnake
sparrowhawk

14 boa constrictor

15 great white shark
hammerhead shark
peregrine falcon

See also **bear**; **bird**; **cat**; **dinosaur**; **dog**; **insectivorous plant**; **meat**; **reptile**; **shark**; **snake**

carpet

Carpets and rugs include:

03 rag
red
rya

04 kali

05 Dutch
kelim
kilim
magic

pilch
stair
throw

06 hearth
hooked
khilim
Kirman
numdah

prayer
Turkey
Wilton

07 bergama
flokati
Persian
Turkish

08 bergamot

Brussels

09 Axminster
sheepskin

10 travelling

11 Bessarabian
buffalo robe

13 Kidderminster

See also **house**

carriage

Carriages include:

03 cab	T-cart	chariot	rickshaw
gig	**06** berlin	dogcart	rockaway
04 arba	calash	droshky	sociable
baby	chaise	hackney	stanhope
drag	drosky	phaeton	victoria
dray	go-cart	pillbox	
ekka	hansom	ricksha	**09** britschka
mail	herdic	tilbury	cabriolet
pony	landau	vettura	wagonette
rath	pochay	vis-à-vis	
trap	purdah	**08** barouche	**10** four-in hand
05 araba	spider	britzska	post chaise
aroba	spring	brougham	
bandy	surrey	carriole	**11** family coach
buggy	**07** britska	carryall	hurly-hacket
coupé	britzka	clarence	village cart
ratha	cariole	jump-seat	
sulky	caroche	po'chaise	**13** désobligeante
			mourning coach
			spider phaeton

Carroll, Lewis (1832–98)

Significant works include:

14 *Phantasmagoria* (1869)
Rhyme? And Reason? (1883)
Sylvie and Bruno (1889)

20 *The Hunting of the Snark* (1876)

22 *Through the Looking-Glass* (1872)

23 *Sylvie and Bruno Concluded* (1893)

24 *Euclid and his Modern Rivals* (1879)

28 *Alice's Adventures in Wonderland* (1865)

Significant characters include:

05 Alice	Tweedledee	**13** Father William
07 The Baby	Tweedledum	The Jabberwock
The Cook	**11** The Dormouse	The Mock Turtle
08 The Snark	The Red Queen	The White Queen
09 The Walrus	**12** Humpty Dumpty	**14** The Caterpillar
10 The Duchess	The Carpenter	The Cheshire Cat
The Gryphon	The Mad Hatter	The White Knight
The Red King	The March Hare	The White Rabbit
	The White King	**15** The King of Hearts

cartography *see* **geography**

cartoon

Cartoon characters include:

03 Ren	Stan	Jerry
Tom	**05** Alice	Kenny
04 Bart	Bluto	Louey
Fred	Dewey	Marge
Huey	Dumbo	Mr Men
Kyle	Goofy	Robin
Lisa	Homer	Rocky

Snowy
Wally
06 Batman
Beavis
Boo Boo
Calvin
Daphne
Droopy
Hobbes
Maggie
Obelix
Popeye
Shaggy
Snoopy
Stimpy
Thelma
Tintin
Top Cat
07 Asterix
Cartman
Custard
Dilbert
Gnasher
Muttley
Old Bill
Penfold
Roobarb
08 Andy Capp
Butthead
Garfield
Krazy Kat

Olive Oyl
Super Man
Superted
Tank Girl
The Joker
Yogi Bear
09 Betty Boop
Bugs Bunny
Chip 'n' Dale
Daffy Duck
Daisy Duck
Dastardly
Dick Tracy
Elmer Fudd
Marmaduke
Oor Wullie
Pepe le Pew
Scooby Doo
Spider Man
Sylvester
The Broons
Tweety Pie
10 Bullwinkle
Donald Duck
Doonesbury
Judge Dredd
Road Runner
Scrappy Doo
The Far Side
The Riddler
11 Bart Simpson

Betty Rubble
Danger Mouse
Felix the Cat
Flash Gordon
Fred Bassett
Korky the Cat
Lisa Simpson
Mickey Mouse
Minnie Mouse
The Simpsons
Wile E Coyote
12 Barney Rubble
Charlie Brown
Desperate Dan
Homer Simpson
Little Misses
Marge Simpson
Ren and Stimpy
13 Dick Dastardly
Maggie Simpson
Modesty Blaise
Rupert the Bear
Scrooge McDuck
14 Foghorn Leghorn
Fred Flintstone
The Pink Panther
15 Calvin and Hobbes
Dennis the Menace
Penelope Pitstop
Steamboat Willie
Wilma Flintstone

Cartoonists include:

02 HB (1797–1868, Irish)

03 Low (Sir David; 1891–1963, New Zealand/British)

04 Arno (Peter; 1904–68, US)
Bell (Steve; 1951– , English)
Capp (Al; 1909–79, US)
Cohl (Emile; 1857–1938, French)
Ding (1876–1962, US)
Kane (Bob; 1915–98, US)
Matt (1964– , English)
Nast (Thomas; 1840–1902, US)
Rémi (Georges; 1907–83, Belgian)
Tidy (Bill; 1933– , English)
Trog (1924– , Canadian/British)

05 Adams (Scott; 1957– , US)
Avery (Tex; 1908–80, US)
Block (Herbert L; 1909–2001, US)
Busch (Wilhelm; 1832–1908, German)
Dirks (Rudolph; 1877–1968, US)
Doyle (John; 1797–1868, Irish)
Emett (Rowland; 1906–90, English)
Giles (Carl Giles; 1916–95, English)

Gould (Chester; 1900–85, US)
Halas (John; 1912–95, Hungarian/British)
Hanna (William; 1910–2001, US)
Hergé (1907–83, Belgian)
Jones (Chuck; 1912–2002, US)
Kelly (Walt; 1913–73, US)
Lantz (Walter; 1900–94, US)
McCay (Winsor; 1867–1934, US)
Segar (Elzie; 1894–1938, US)
Silas (1867–1934, US)
Vicky (1913–66, German/British)
Weisz (Victor; 1913–66, German/British)
Yeats (Jack B; 1870–1957, Irish)
Young (Chic; 1901–73, US)

06 Addams (Charles; 1912–88, US)
Browne (Tom; 1870–1910, English)
Caniff (Milt; 1907–88, US)
Caplin (Alfred Gerald; 1909–79, US)
Disney (Walt; 1901–66, US)
Fawkes (Walter; 1924– , Canadian/British)
Fisher (Bud; 1885–1954, US)
Gibson (Charles Dana; 1867–1944, US)
Graham (Alex; 1917–91, Scottish)

Iwerks (Ub; 1901–71, US)
Jaffee (Al; 1921– , US)
Larson (Gary; 1950– , US)
Miller (David Wiley; 1951– , US)
Scarfe (Gerald; 1936– , English)
Schulz (Charles M; 1922–2000, US)
Searle (Ronald; 1920–2011, English)
Siegel (Jerry; 1914–96, US)
Smythe (Reg; 1917–98, English)
Strube (Sidney; 1891–1956, English)
Studdy (George Edward; 1878–1948, English)
Uderzo (Albert; 1927– , French)
Wilson (Roy; 1900–65, English)

07 Barbera (Joseph; 1911–2006, US)
Bateman (H M; 1887–1970, Australian)
Courtet (Emile; 1857–1938, French)
Darling (Jay Norwood; 1876–1962, US)
Dowling (Stephen; 1904–86, English)
Godfrey (Bob; 1921–2013, Australian/British)
Hampson (Frank; 1918–85, English)
Hassall (John; 1868–1948, English)
Raymond (Alex; 1909–56, US)
Rushton (Willie; 1937–96, English)
Shepard (E H; 1879–1976, English)
Shuster (Joseph; 1914–92, US)
Tenniel (Sir John; 1820–1914, English)

Thurber (James; 1894–1961, US)
Trudeau (Garry; 1948– , US)
Watkins (Dudley D; 1907–69, English)
Webster (Tom; 1890–1962, English)

08 Goldberg (Rube; 1883–1970, US)
Groening (Matt; 1954– , US)
Herblock (1909–2001, US)
Herriman (George; 1880–1944, US)
Hoffnung (Gerard; 1925–59, German/British)
Kurtzman (Harvey; 1924–93, US)
Robinson (Heath; 1872–1944, English)

09 Batchelor (Joy; 1914–91, English)
Baxendale (Leo; 1930– , English)
du Maurier (George; 1834–96, French/British)
Feininger (Lyonel; 1871–1956, US)
Fleischer (Max; 1883–1972, US)
Lancaster (Sir Osbert; 1908–86, English)
Pritchett (Matthew; 1964– , English)
Sambourne (Edward Linley; 1844–1910, English)
Watterson (Bill; 1958– , US)

10 Raemaekers (Louis; 1869–1956, Dutch)

12 Bairnsfather (Bruce; 1888–1959, British)
Hanna-Barbera (US)

case *see* **grammar**

castle

Castle parts include:

04 berm	corbel	barbican	inner wall
keep	crenel	bartizan	**10** drawbridge
moat	donjon	brattice	murder hole
ward	merlon	buttress	portcullis
05 ditch	turret	crosslet	watchtower
fosse	**07** bastion	loophole	**11** battlements
motte	dungeon	stockade	curtain wall
mound	parados	wall walk	outer bailey
scarp	parapet	**09** arrow-slit	**12** crenellation
tower	postern	courtyard	lookout tower
06 bailey	rampart	embrasure	**13** enclosure wall
chapel	**08** approach	gatehouse	

British and Irish castles include:

03 Doe (Ireland)	Drum (Scotland)	Trim (Ireland)
Eye (England)	Etal (England)	Ward (Northern Ireland)
Lea (Ireland)	Hume (Scotland)	York (England)
Mey (Scotland)	Leap (Ireland)	**05** Aydon (England)
04 Birr (Ireland)	Peel (Isle of Man)	Ayton (Scotland)
Clun (England)	Piel (England)	Black (Ireland)
Coch (Wales)	Raby (England)	Blair (Scotland)
Deal (England)	Ross (Ireland)	Bowes (England)

Burgh (England)
Cabra (Ireland)
Cahir (Ireland)
Carew (Wales)
Chirk (Wales)
Clara (Ireland)
Coity (Wales)
Conna (Ireland)
Conwy (Wales)
Coole (Northern Ireland)
Corfe (England)
Cregg (Ireland)
Croft (England/Wales)
Doune (Scotland)
Dover (England)
Drogo (England)
Duart (Scotland)
Elcho (Scotland)
Ewloe (Wales)
Ferns (Ireland)
Flint (Wales)
Fyvie (Scotland)
Green (Northern Ireland)
Gylen (Scotland)
Hever (England)
Hurst (England)
Knock (Scotland)
Leeds (England)
of Mey (Scotland)
Powis (Wales)
Salem (Ireland)
Skibo (Scotland)
Slade (Ireland)
Slane (Ireland)
Sween (Scotland)
Tully (Northern Ireland)
Upnor (England)
White (Wales)
y Bere (Wales)

06 Bangor (Northern Ireland)
Belsay (England)
Bodiam (England)
Bolton (England)
Brodie (Scotland)
Brough (England)
Bungay (England)
Cadzow (Scotland)
Camber (England)
Carlow (Ireland)
Carnew (Ireland)
Cawdor (Scotland)
Conway (Ireland)
Dalkey (Ireland)
Dangan (Ireland)
Darver (Ireland)
Dublin (Ireland)
Duffus (Scotland)
Dunmoe (Ireland)

Durham (England)
Edzell (Scotland)
Floors (Scotland)
Fraser (Scotland)
Glamis (Scotland)
Glinsk (Ireland)
Grange (Ireland)
Gregan (Ireland)
Hailes (Scotland)
Howard (England)
Howard (Ireland)
Huntly (Scotland)
Hylton (England)
Kellie (Scotland)
Kilkea (Ireland)
Ludlow (England)
Lynchs (Ireland)
Maiden (England)
Mallow (Ireland)
Matrix (Ireland)
Minard (Ireland)
Morton (Scotland)
Muness (Scotland)
Nenagh (Ireland)
Newark (England/
 Scotland)
Norham (England)
Nunney (England)
Oakham (England)
Ogmore (Wales)
Orford (England)
Ormond (Ireland)
Oxwich (Wales)
Parkes (Ireland)
Raglan (Wales)
Rheban (Ireland)
Ripley (England)
Rushen (Isle of Man)
Sandal (England)
Shanid (Ireland)
Slains (Scotland)
Strome (Scotland)
Sutton (Ireland)
Swords (Ireland)
Tioram (Scotland)
Totnes (England)
Toward (Scotland)
Walmer (England)
Wiston (Wales)

07 Alnwick (England)
Appleby (England)
Arundel (England)
Ashford (Ireland)
Ashtown (Ireland)
Athenry (Ireland)
Athlone (Ireland)
Audleys (Northern Ireland)
Balfour (Northern Ireland)

Balloch (Scotland)
Barnard (England)
Beeston (England)
Belfast (Northern Ireland)
Belvoir (England)
Berwick (England)
Blarney (Ireland)
Braemar (Scotland)
Bramber (England)
Bremore (Ireland)
Brodick (Scotland)
Bullock (Ireland)
Caister (England)
Calshot (England)
Cardiff (Wales)
Chester (England)
Clifden (Ireland)
Cloghan (Ireland)
Compton (England)
Crathes (Scotland)
Culzean (Scotland)
Denbigh (Wales)
Desmond (Ireland)
Dinefwr (Wales)
Donamon (Ireland)
Donegal (Ireland)
Dundrum (Northern
 Ireland)
Dunsany (Ireland)
Dunster (England)
Eastnor (England)
Farnham (England)
Fethard (Ireland)
Granagh (Ireland)
Harlech (Wales)
Hemyock (England)
Jordan's (Northern Ireland)
Kanturk (Ireland)
Kelburn (Scotland)
Kielder (England)
Kilteel (Ireland)
Kisimul (Scotland)
Lachlan (Scotland)
Lackeen (Ireland)
Langley (England)
Leixlip (Ireland)
Lisheen (Ireland)
Lismore (Ireland)
Loughor (Wales)
Lydford (England)
Macroom (Ireland)
Markree (Ireland)
McGrath (Ireland)
Menzies (Scotland)
Mingary (Scotland)
Moydrum (Ireland)
Moygara (Ireland)
Newport (Wales)

Newtown (Ireland)
Old Wick (Scotland)
Penrhyn (Wales)
Penrith (England)
Peveril (England)
Prudhoe (England)
Redwood (Ireland)
Roscrea (Ireland)
Scotney (England)
Sizergh (England)
Skipsea (England)
Skipton (England)
Stalker (Scotland)
St Mawes (England)
Sudeley (England)
Swansea (Wales)
Threave (Scotland)
Torosay (Scotland)
Tutbury (England)
Warwick (England)
Weeting (England)
Weobley (Wales)
Wigmore (England)
Windsor (England)

08 Aberdour (Scotland)
Altidore (Ireland)
Ardvreck (Scotland)
Armadale (Scotland)
Askeaton (Ireland)
Auckland (England)
Ballybur (Ireland)
Balmoral (Scotland)
Balvaird (Scotland)
Balvenie (Scotland)
Bamburgh (England)
Barmeath (Ireland)
Bastille (France)
Berkeley (England)
Bolsover (England)
Bothwell (Scotland)
Bronllys (Wales)
Brougham (England)
Broughty (Scotland)
Bunratty (Ireland)
Burleigh (Scotland)
Campbell (Scotland)
Carlisle (England)
Chepstow (Wales)
Clonmore (Ireland)
Corgarff (Scotland)
Crichton (Scotland)
Delgatie (Scotland)
Dirleton (Scotland)
Drimnagh (Ireland)
Drishane (Ireland)
Drummond (Scotland)
Dryslwyn (Wales)
Dunashad (Ireland)

Dunollie (Scotland)
Dunottar (Scotland)
Dunrobin (Scotland)
Dunvegan (Scotland)
Dunyvaig (Scotland)
Egremont (England)
Elsinore (Denmark)
Eynsford (England)
Gallarus (Ireland)
Glenquin (Ireland)
Goodrich (England)
Grosmont (Wales)
Hadleigh (England)
Hastings (England)
Helmsley (England)
Hertford (England)
Humewood (Ireland)
Jedburgh (Scotland)
Kidwelly (Wales)
Kilcasan (Ireland)
Kilchurn (Scotland)
Kilclief (Northern Ireland)
Kilkenny (Ireland)
Killaghy (Ireland)
Killiane (Ireland)
Kisimull (Scotland)
Lawrence (England)
Leamaneh (Ireland)
Listowel (Ireland)
Loch Doon (Scotland)
Longtown (England)
Lulworth (England)
Malahide (Ireland)
Maynooth (Ireland)
Menstrie (Scotland)
Monmouth (Wales)
Neidpath (Scotland)
Noltland (Scotland)
Old Sarum (England)
Oranmore (Ireland)
Pembroke (Wales)
Pevensey (England)
Portland (England)
Portumna (Ireland)
Rhuddlan (Wales)
Richmond (England)
Rothesay (Scotland)
Shankill (Ireland)
Skipness (Scotland)
Southsea (England)
Stirling (Scotland)
Stokesay (England)
Tamworth (England)
Tintagel (England)
Tiverton (England)
Tolquhon (Scotland)
Tretower (Wales)
Urquhart (Scotland)

Wolvesey (England)
Yarmouth (England)

09 Ardgillan (Ireland)
Athlumney (Ireland)
Baldongan (Ireland)
Ballyhack (Ireland)
Ballymoon (Ireland)
Ballymote (Ireland)
Beaumaris (Wales)
Bickleigh (England)
Blackness (Scotland)
Blackrock (Ireland)
Bolebroke (England)
Cardoness (Scotland)
Carsluith (Scotland)
Caulfield (Northern Ireland)
Chipchase (England)
Cilgerran (Wales)
Claypotts (Scotland)
Criccieth (Wales)
Cromwell's (England)
Crookston (Scotland)
Culcreuch (Scotland)
Dartmouth (England)
Dolbadarn (Wales)
Dolforwyn (Wales)
Dumbarton (Scotland)
Dundonald (Scotland)
Dungarvan (Ireland)
Dunguaire (Ireland)
Dun Na Sead (Ireland)
Dunnottar (Scotland)
Dunsinane (Scotland)
Dunsoghly (Ireland)
Edinburgh (Scotland)
Edlingham (England)
Ferriters (Ireland)
Findlater (Scotland)
Garryhill (Ireland)
Gleninagh (Ireland)
Guildford (England)
Hedingham (England)
Hermitage (Scotland)
Highclere (England)
Hunginton (Ireland)
Inveraray (Scotland)
Inverness (Scotland)
Johnstown (Ireland)
Kilbolane (Ireland)
Kilcolgan (Ireland)
Kildrummy (Scotland)
Kimbolton (England)
King Johns (Ireland)
Knappogue (Ireland)
Lancaster (England)
Laugharne (Wales)
Lauriston (Scotland)
Lemaneagh (Ireland)

Llawhaden (Wales)
Lochleven (Scotland)
Lochmaben (Scotland)
Lochranza (Scotland)
Middleham (England)
Monkstown (Ireland)
Muncaster (England)
Newcastle (Wales)
O Donovans (Ireland)
Pendennis (England)
Pickering (England)
Powderham (England)
Restormel (England)
Rochester (England)
Rockfleet (Ireland)
Roscommon (Ireland)
Scalloway (Scotland)
Shankhill (Ireland)
Sherborne (England)
Skenfrith (Wales)
Spofforth (England)
St Andrews (Scotland)
Tantallon (Scotland)
Tonbridge (England)
Tynemouth (England)
Warkworth (England)

10 Auchindoun (Scotland)
Aughnanure (Ireland)
Ballinafad (Ireland)
Ballyhealy (Ireland)
Ballynahow (Ireland)
Balrothery (Ireland)
Bridgnorth (England)
Caernarfon (Wales)
Caernarvon (Wales)
Caerphilly (Wales)
Carmarthen (Wales)
Castle Acre (England)
Castlemore (Ireland)
Craigievar (Scotland)
Cubbie Row's (Scotland)
Dardistown (Ireland)
Deddington (England)
Donnington (England)
Drumlanrig (Scotland)
Foulksrath (Ireland)
Glenbuchat (Scotland)
Highcliffe (England)
Huntington (Ireland)
Inverlochy (Scotland)
Jewel Tower (England)
Kenilworth (England)
Kinnersley (England)

See also **fortification; tower**

Kirkistown (Northern Ireland)
Launceston (England)
Liscarroll (Ireland)
Maclellan's (Scotland)
Montgomery (Wales)
Okehampton (England)
Old Wardour (England)
Pontefract (England)
Rathcoffey (Ireland)
Rockingham (England)
St Briavel's (England)
St Quentin's (Wales)
Strancally (Ireland)
Tinnahinch (Ireland)
Tullynally (Ireland)

11 Ballaghmore (Ireland)
Ballyhannan (Ireland)
Ballyragget (Ireland)
Barryscourt (Ireland)
Berkhamsted (England)
Bolingbroke (England)
Carisbrooke (England)
Carnasserie (Scotland)
Castell Coch (Wales)
Charleville (Ireland)
Chillingham (England)
Conisbrough (England)
Craigmillar (Scotland)
Craignethan (Scotland)
Dolwyddelan (Wales)
Eilean Donan (Scotland)
Enniscorthy (Ireland)
Farnham Keep (England)
Ferniehirst (Scotland)
Fotheringay (England)
Framlingham (England)
Grimsthorpe (England)
King Charles (England)
Kirby Muxloe (England)
Lindisfarne (England)
Llansteffan (Wales)
Ludgershall (England)
Narrow Water (Northern Ireland)
Parkavonear (Ireland)
Portchester (England)
Rathfarnham (Ireland)
Rathmacknee (Ireland)
Ravenscraig (Scotland)
Robertstown (Ireland)
Scarborough (England)
Tattershall (England)
Thirlestane (Scotland)

12 Acton Burnell (England)
Baconsthorpe (England)
Ballybrittan (Ireland)
Ballycarbery (Ireland)
Ballyloughan (Ireland)
Ballynahinch (Ireland)
Berry Pomeroy (England)
Caerlaverock (Scotland)
Carreg Cennen (Wales)
Carrigafoyle (Ireland)
Castell y Bere (Wales)
Castlemartyr (Ireland)
Castle Rising (England)
Christchurch (England)
Coulter Motte (Scotland)
Dunstaffnage (Scotland)
Dunstanburgh (England)
Huntingtower (Scotland)
King Charles's (England)
Kinnaird Head (Scotland)
Lullingstone (England)
Marmion Tower (England)
Mountfitchet (England)
New Buckenham (England)
Sherborne Old (England)
St Catherine's (England)
Tyrrellspass (Ireland)

13 Ballinacarrig (Ireland)
Ballindalloch (Scotland)
Carrickfergus (Northern Ireland)
Carrigaphooca (Ireland)
Chiddingstone (England)
Cloughouthter (Ireland)
Druchtag Motte (Scotland)
Knaresborough (England)
Moreton Corbet (England)
Rathnageeragh (Ireland)

14 Ashby de la Zouch (England)
Ballynacarriga (Ireland)
Boarstall Tower (England)
Carrigogunnell (Ireland)
Clifford's Tower (England)
Falkland Palace (Scotland)

15 Carrickabraghey (Ireland)
Kilmallock Kings (Ireland)
Longthorpe Tower (England)
St Leonard's Tower (England)
St Michael's Mount (England)
Warkworth Castle

cat

Cat types include:

03 bob	**06** cougar	leopard	**12** mountain lion
04 lion	jaguar	**08** domestic	Scottish wild
lynx	kodkod	mountain	**13** little spotted
puma	margay	**09** Geoffroy's	**14** clouded leopard
05 feral	ocelot	**10** jaguarundi	
tiger	pampas	**11** snow leopard	
	07 cheetah		

Cat breeds include:

03 rex	ragdoll	Selkirk Rex
04 Manx	Siamese	Turkish Van
05 Korat	Tiffany	**11** Egyptian Mau
tabby	**08** Balinese	Foreign Blue
06 Angora	Burmilla	Russian Blue
Bengal	Devon Rex	silver tabby
Birman	Snowshoe	**12** Foreign White
Bombay	Tiffanie	Scottish Fold
Cymric	**09** Himalayan	**13** domestic tabby
Havana	Maine Coon	Tortoiseshell
LaPerm	Singapura	Turkish Angora
Ocicat	Tonkinese	**15** British longhair
Somali	**10** Abyssinian	Exotic shorthair
07 Burmese	Carthusian	Japanese Bobtail
Persian	chinchilla	Norwegian Forest
	Cornish Rex	

Cats include:

03 Gus (*Old Possum's Book of Practical Cats*, 1939, T S Eliot)
Tom (*Tom & Jerry*, 1967– , MGM cartoon)

04 Bast (Egyptian mythology)
Jess (*Postman Pat*, 1981– , children's TV animation)

05 Dinah (*Alice in Wonderland*, 1865, Lewis Carroll)
Felix (*Feline Follies*, 1919, Otto Messmer)
Korky (*The Dandy*, 1937– , D C Thomson, comic)

06 Arthur (pet food ad, UK TV)
Bastet (Egyptian mythology)
Ginger (*The Tale of Ginger and Pickles*, 1909, Beatrix Potter)
Kaspar (cat statue, The Savoy Hotel, London)
Top Cat (*Top Cat*, 1961, Hanna-Barbera animation)
Ubasti (Egyptian mythology)

07 Bagpuss (1974, UK children's TV)
Custard (*Roobarb*, 1974–2005, Grange Caveley, BBC cartoon)
Simpkin (*The Tailor of Gloucester*, 1903, Beatrix Potter)

08 Beerbohm (Globe Theatre, UK, longest serving mouser)
Garfield (*Garfield*, 1978– , Jim Davis, comic strip)
Humphrey (house cat at 10 Downing Street)
Krazy Kat (1913–44, George Herriman, comic strip)
Macavity (*Old Possum's Book of Practical Cats*, 1939, T S Eliot)

09 Mehitabel (*Archy and Mehitabel*, 1916– , Don Marquis, newspaper column)
Mrs Norris (Harry Potter series, 1997–2007, J K Rowling)
Sylvester (*Sylvester & Tweety Pie*, 1945–66, Looney Tunes & Merrie Melodies cartoons)
Thomasina (*Thomasina: The Cat who thought she was God*, 1957, Paul Gallico)
Tom Kitten (*Tale of Tom Kitten*, 1907, Beatrix Potter)

10 El Brooshna (Judao-Christian mythology)
Heathcliff (*Heathcliff*, 1973, George Gately, comic strip)

11 Cat in the Hat (1957, Dr Seuss)

Cheshire Cat (*Alice in Wonderland*, 1865, Lewis Carroll)
Crookshanks (Harry Potter series, 1997–2007, J K Rowling)
Korky the Cat (*The Dandy*, 1937– , D C Thomson, comic)
Puss in Boots (pantomime)

13 Skimbleshanks (*Old Possum's Book of Practical Cats*, 1939, T S Eliot)

14 Bustopher Jones (*Old Possum's Book of Practical Cats*, 1939, T S Eliot)
Mr Mistoffelees (*Old Possum's Book of Practical Cats*, 1939, T S Eliot)
Old Deuteronomy (*Old Possum's Book of Practical Cats*, 1939, T S Eliot)
The Cat in the Hat (1957, Dr Seuss)

Terms to do with cats include:

03 AOV
gib
mew
mog
paw
pet

04 bowl
claw
coat
comb
fawn
flea
fuff
hiss
mink
purr
puss
show
spay
spit
tail
tick
waul

05 black
breed
brush
cameo
cream
ebony
Felis
feral
groom
honey
ID tag
kitty
leash

mange
miaow
miaul
moggy
mouse
pussy
queen
ruddy
sable
smoke
tabby
white
wrawl

06 albino
basket
bronze
calico
catnep
catnip
cat toy
collar
declaw
dilute
feline
gib-cat
golden
hybrid
kitten
litter
mitted
moggie
mouser
neuter
ramcat
shaded
silver
Tib-cat

tomcat

07 allergy
Baudron
bobtail
cat-flap
catling
catmint
cattery
odd-eyed
patched
spotted

08 bi-colour
blue-eyed
brindled
cinnamon
crossing
domestic
dominant
gold-eyed
good luck
hairball
lavender
outcross
platinum
purebred
whiskers
wirehair

09 amber-eyed
blue-cream
caterwaul
cat litter
champagne
green-eyed
grimalkin
lynx point
marmalade

micro-chip
nine lives
pedigreed
purebreed
recessive
sealpoint

10 cat-carrier
cat-fancier
chinchilla
copper-eyed
flame point
flea collar
lilac point
litter tray
long-haired
smoke-white
tabby-white

11 ailurophile
ailurophobe
colourpoint
lilac-tortie
short-haired

12 ailurophilia
ailurophobia
ailurophobic
cat scratcher
silver-tipped

13 straight-eared
tortoiseshell
toxoplasmosis

14 chocolate point
scratching post

15 any other variety
seal-tortie point

cathedral

Cathedrals in the UK include:

03 Ely
05 Derby
Isles
Leeds
Ripon

Truro
Wells
06 Bangor
Brecon
Dundee

Durham
Exeter
Oxford
07 Arundel
Bristol

Cardiff
Chester
Clifton
Dornoch
Glasgow

Lincoln	Coventry	Lichfield	Chichester
Newport	Hereford	Liverpool	Gloucester
Norwich	Llandaff	Newcastle	Manchester
Salford	Plymouth	Rochester	Nottingham
St Asaph	St Albans	Salisbury	Portsmouth
St John's	St Davids	Sheffield	Shrewsbury
St Mary's	**09** Blackburn	Southwark	Winchester
St Paul's	Brentwood	St Andrews	**11** Northampton
Swansea	Edinburgh	Wakefield	York Minster
Wrexham	Guildford	Worcester	**12** Christ Church
08 Aberdeen	Inverness	**10** Birmingham	Peterborough
Bradford	Lancaster	Canterbury	**13** Middlesbrough
Carlisle	Leicester	Chelmsford	St Edmundsbury

Cathedrals worldwide include:

04 Lund (Sweden)

05 Duomo (Italy)
    Milan (Italy)

06 Aachen (Germany)
    Rheims (France)

See also **church**

07 Cologne (Germany)
    Córdoba (Spain)
    Orvieto (Italy)
    St Mark's (Italy)

08 Chartres (France)
    Florence (Italy)

St Basil's (Russia)
St Peter's (Vatican City)

09 Notre-Dame (France)

10 Strasbourg (France)

11 Hagia Sophia (Turkey)

cattle

Cattle breeds include:

02 zo	wagyu	Friesian	**10** Africander
03 dso	white	Galloway	beefmaster
dzo	zhomo	gelbvieh	Brown Swiss
gir	**06** ankole	Guernsey	Canadienne
gur	dexter	Hereford	Lincoln Red
gyr	Durham	Highland	Murray grey
zho	Jersey	Holstein	Piemontese
04 dzho	Salers	illawara	Simmenthal
jomo	Sussex	Limousin	South Devon
tuli	watusi	longhorn	Tarentaise
zebu	**07** beefalo	Shetland	Welsh Black
zobo	brahman	**09** Afrikaner	**11** Belgian Blue
zobu	brahmin	braunvieh	Chillingham
05 Angus	brangus	Charolais	Piedmontese
black	cattabu	Corriente	**12** British White
Devon	cattalo	Romagnola	Simmenthaler
dsobo	Latvian	shorthorn	**13** Aberdeen Angus
dsomo	red poll	Simmental	droughtmaster
Kerry	**08** Alderney	Teeswater	Texas longhorn
Luing	Ayrshire	Ukrainian	**14** Belted Galloway
sanga	Chianina	white park	Santa Gertrudis

See also **animal**; **meat**

cave

Caves include:

04 Zitu (Spain)	**09** G E S Malaga (Spain)	Jean Bernard (France)
06 Berger (France)	Snezhnaya (Georgia)	**14** Lamprechtsofen (Austria)
Vqerdi (Spain)	**10** Schneeloch (Austria)	Pierre-St-Martin (France)
08 Badalona (Spain)	**11** Batmanhöhle (Austria)	Sistema Huautla (Mexico)

ceilidh *see* **dance**

celebration

Celebrations include:

04 fête	wedding	homecoming
gala	**08** birthday	retirement
05 feast	festival	**11** anniversary
party	hen night	christening
06 May Day	marriage	coming-of-age
07 banquet	**09** centenary	harvest-home
baptism	Labour Day	**12** thanksgiving
ceilidh	reception	**13** commemoration
jubilee	stag night	**15** harvest festival
name-day	**10** bar mitzvah	Independence Day
reunion	bat mitzvah	
tribute	graduation	

See also **anniversary**; **ceremony**; **festival**; **holiday**

cell

Cells include:

01 B	**06** animal	Sertoli
T	cancer	somatic
03 egg	collar	voltaic
PEC	diaxon	**08** akaryote
red	gamete	basophil
rod	goblet	daughter
sex	Hadley	galvanic
wet	killer	gonidium
04 cone	memory	gonocyte
fuel	mother	monocyte
germ	neuron	myoblast
HeLa	oocyte	neoblast
mast	plasma	parietal
ovum	target	platelet
stem	tumour	Purkinje
05 blood	**07** cadmium	red blood
guard	Daniell	retinula
nerve	gravity	sclereid
plant	helper T	selenium
solar	initial	tracheid
sperm	neurone	zooblast
water	primary	**09** acidophil
white	Schwann	adipocyte

antipodal
astrocyte
coenocyte
corpuscle
fibrocyte
haemocyte
hybridoma
idioblast
Leclanché
leucocyte
leukocyte
macrocyte
microcyte
myofibril
phagocyte
photocell
prokaryon
sclereide
secondary
spermatid
syncytium
thymocyte
tracheide
10 choanocyte

cnidoblast
enterocyte
eosinophil
fibroblast
gametocyte
hepatocyte
histiocyte
histoblast
leucoblast
leukoblast
lymphocyte
macrophage
melanocyte
myeloblast
neuroblast
neutrophil
osteoblast
osteoclast
spherocyte
suppressor
thread-cell
white blood
11 B lymphocyte
erythrocyte

granulocyte
lymphoblast
megaloblast
odontoblast
poikilocyte
thrombocyte
T lymphocyte
12 chondroblast
erythroblast
haematoblast
red corpuscle
reticulocyte
spermatocyte
spermatozoid
spermatozoon
13 chromatophore
natural killer
photoelectric
spermatoblast
14 blood corpuscle
spermatogonium
white corpuscle

See also **immune system**

Celtic god, goddess *see* **mythology**

cemetery

Cemeteries and burial places include:

07 Mt Holly (US)
Nunhead (England)

08 Brompton (England)
Highgate (England)
Mt Olivet (Canada/US)
Panthéon (France)

09 Abney Park (England)
Arlington (US)

10 El Escorial (Spain)
La Almudena (Spain)
Montmartre (France)

San Michele (Italy)
Weissensee (Germany)

11 Kensal Green (England)
West Norwood (England)

12 Golders Green (England)
Les Invalides (France)
Montparnasse (France)
Père Lachaise (France)
Tower Hamlets (England)

13 Mount of Olives (Israel)

15 Island of the Dead (Italy/Australia)

See also **World Heritage site**

Central and South American god, goddess *see* **mythology**

cereal

Cereals include:

03 oat
rye
tef
zea

04 corn
oats
rice
sago

teff
05 bajra
emmer
maize

spelt
wheat
06 barley
bulgur

millet	amelcorn	sweetcorn	**12** common millet
07 bulghur	couscous	triticale	**13** bulrush millet
sorghum	semolina	**10** Indian corn	foxtail millet
08 amaranth	**09** buckwheat	Kaffir corn	Italian millet

Breakfast cereals include:

05 Alpen®	Weetabix®	Puffed Wheat®
06 muesli	**09** Grape Nuts®	Sultana Bran®
Weetos®	Just Right®	**12** Country Crisp®
07 All Bran®	Ready Brek®	Raisin Wheats®
08 Cheerios®	Shreddies®	Rice Krispies®
Clusters®	**10** Bran Flakes®	**13** Frosted Flakes®
Coco Pops®	cornflakes	Fruit and Fibre®
Frosties®	Quaker Oats®	Golden Grahams®
Fruitbix®	Raisin Bran®	Honey Nut Loops®
Fruitful®	Sugar Puffs®	Shredded Wheat®
porridge	**11** Common Sense®	**14** Nestlé Clusters®
Ricicles®	Fruit'n'Fibre®	**15** Cinnamon Grahams®
Special K®	Oatso Simple®	

See also **crop**; **food**

ceremony

Ceremonies include:

05 amrit	capping	nuptials	initiation
doseh	chanoyu	**09** committal	**11** christening
tangi	chuppah	matrimony	fire-walking
06 maundy	matsuri	**10** bar mitzvah	**12** confirmation
nipter	wedding	bat mitzvah	
07 baptism	**08** marriage	graduation	

See also **celebration**; **Japan**

chair

Chairs include:

03 arm	king's	sag bag	**08** captain's
lug	night	sledge	electric
pew	potty	swivel	fauteuil
04 Bath	sedan	throne	prie-dieu
camp	stool	wicker	recliner
cane	wheel	**07** beanbag	wainscot
deck	**06** basket	Berbice	**09** director's
easy	carver	bergère	**10** boatswain's
form	curule	commode	fiddle-back
head	dining	guérite	frithstool
high	estate	kitchen	ladder-back
push	jampan	lounger	**11** Cromwellian
wing	Morris	nursing	gestatorial
05 bench	pouffe	rocking	**12** ducking-stool
elbow	rocker	Windsor	

See also **furniture**; **house**

channel

Channels include:

03 Kii (Japan)
04 Foxe (Canada)
05 Bashi (Taiwan/Philippines)
Bungo (Japan)
Kaiwi (USA)
Kauai (USA)
Lamma (Hong Kong)
Minas (Canada)
Minch (Scotland)
North (Northern Ireland/Scotland/Canada)
06 Akashi (Japan)
Kalohi (USA)
Manche (France)
Queens (Australia)
07 Babuyan (Philippines)
Bristol (England)
English (England/France)
Jamaica (Haiti)
Massawa (Ethiopia)
Pailolo (USA)
Sandwip (Bangladesh)
St Lucia (St Lucia/Martinique)
Yucatán (Cuba/Mexico)
08 Dominica (Dominica/Martinique)
See also **television**

La Manche (France)
Nicholas (Cuba/The Bahamas)
Santaren (Cuba/The Bahamas)
Sicilian (Italy)
St Andrew (Canada)
The Minch (Scotland)
09 Balintang (Philippines)
Capricorn (Australia)
East Lamma (Hong Kong)
Geographe (Australia)
Kaulakahi (USA)
Northwest (Australia)
Old Bahama (Cuba/The Bahamas)
Skagerrak (Denmark/Norway)
St George's (Wales/Ireland)
West Lamma (Hong Kong)
10 Alalakeiki (USA)
Alenuihaha (USA)
McClintock (Canada)
Mozambique (Mozambique)
North Minch (Scotland)
11 Little Minch (Scotland)
12 Kealaikahiki (USA)
Santa Barbara (USA)

character *see* **Austen, Jane; Bible; Blyton, Enid; Brecht, Bertolt; Brontë Anne; Brontë Charlotte; Brontë Emily; Carroll, Lewis; cartoon; Chaucer, Geoffrey; Chekhov, Anton; Christie, Dame Agatha; Defoe, Daniel; Dickens, Charles; Dostoevsky, Fyodor; Doyle, Sir Arthur Conan; Dumas, Alexandre; Eliot, George; fairy tale; Gilbert, Sir W S; Hardy, Thomas; Hemingway, Ernest; Homer; Ibsen, Henrik; James Bond; James, Henry; Joyce, James; Kipling, Rudyard; Lawrence, D H; legend; literature; Molière; Morrison, Toni; Mozart, Wolfgang Amadeus; Murdoch, Dame Iris; mythology; O'Neill, Eugene; opera; Orwell, George; pantomime; Racine, Jean-Baptiste; Rowling, J K; Scott, Sir Walter; Shakespeare, William; Stevenson, Robert Louis; Tolkien, J R R; Tolstoy, Count Leo; Trollope, Anthony; Twain, Mark; Verdi; Giuseppe; Voltaire; Wells, H G; Wilde, Oscar; Wodehouse, Sir P G; Woolf, Virginia; Zola, Émile**

charity

Charities include:

03 BHF	**05** CAFOD	Barnardo's
DEC	NSPCC	Macmillan
FOE	Oxfam	**10** Greenpeace
NCH	RSPCA	Marie Curie
RBL	Scope	**11** Comic Relief
04 PDSA	**06** Mencap	Help the Aged
RNIB	**07** Amnesty	**12** Christian Aid
RNLI	**08** Red Cross	**13** National Trust
RSPB	**09** ActionAid	Salvation Army
WRVS		

Wellcome Trust | **14** Cancer Research | Save the Children
Woodland Trust | **15** Leonard Cheshire | St John Ambulance

Charity fundraising events include:

06 fun run | swimathon | sponsored swim
raffle | **10** jumble sale | sponsored walk
08 telethon | **12** slave auction | **14** charity auction
09 radiothon | **13** coffee morning | **15** bring-and-buy sale

Chaucer, Geoffrey (c.1345–1400)

Significant works include:

14 *The House of Fame* (c.1378) | *Troilus and Criseyde* (c.1385–89)
16 *Book of the Duchess* (1369) | **20** *The Legend of Good Women* (c.1385–87)
18 *The Canterbury Tales* (c.1387–1400) | **21** *The Parliament of Fowles* (1380)

The Canterbury Tales comprise:

12 'The Cook's Tale' | 'The Man of Law's Tale'
'The Monk's Tale' | 'The Merchant's Tale'
13 'The Clerk's Tale' | 'The Pardoner's Tale'
'The Friar's Tale' | 'The Prioress's Tale'
'The Reeve's Tale' | 'The Summoner's Tale'
14 'The Knight's Tale' | 'The Tale of Melibee'
'The Miller's Tale' | **17** 'The Physician's Tale'
'The Parson's Tale' | 'The Second Nun's Tale'
'The Squire's Tale' | **18** 'The General Prologue'
15 'The Shipman's Tale' | 'The Nun's Priest's Tale'
16 'The Franklin's Tale' | 'The Tale of Sir Thopas'
'The Manciple's Tale' | 'The Wife of Bath's Tale'
 | **20** 'The Canon's Yeoman's Tale'

Significant characters include:

03 May | Criseyde | **11** The Franklin
05 Emily | Griselda | The Manciple
06 Arcite | Pandarus | The Man of Law
Damien | The Canon | The Merchant
Thopas (Sir) | The Friar | The Pardoner
07 Alisoun | The Reeve | The Prioress
Bailley (Harry) | **09** Arveragus | The Summoner
Dorigen | Constance | **12** Chaunticleer
January (Old) | Eglantyne (Madame) | The Carpenter
Palamon | Pertelote | The Physician
The Cook | The Knight | The Second Nun
The Dyer | The Miller | **13** The Nun's Priest
The Host | The Parson | The Wife of Bath
The Monk | The Squire | **14** The Haberdasher
Troilus | The Weaver |
08 Aurelius | The Yeoman |
 | **10** The Shipman |

cheese

Cheeses include:

03 ewe
Oka

04 Brie
curd
Edam
feta
goat
skyr
Yarg

05 Caboc
Carré
Derby
Gouda
quark

06 Cantal
chèvre
Dunlop
junket
Orkney
paneer
Romano
Tilsit

07 Boursin
Cheddar
crottin
crowdie
Fontina
Gruyère
kebbock
kebbuck
Limburg
Münster

ricotta
sapsago
Stilton®

08 bel paese
Cheshire
Churnton
Emmental
halloumi
Huntsman
manchego
Parmesan
pecorino
raclette
Taleggio
vacherin

09 Amsterdam
Blue Vinny
Cambozola®
Camembert
chevreton
Emmenthal
Ilchester
Jarlsberg®
Killarney
Leicester
Limburger
Lymeswold®
mouse-trap
Port Salut
processed
provolone
reblochon

Roquefort
sage Derby

10 blue cheese
Caerphilly
Danish blue
dolcelatte
Dorset Blue
Emmentaler
Gloucester
Gorgonzola
hard cheese
Lancashire
mascarpone
mozzarella
Neufchâtel
Red Windsor
soft cheese
stracchino
vegetarian

11 Coulommiers
cream cheese
Petit Suisse
Pont l'Évêque
Saint-Paulin
Wensleydale

12 Blue Cheshire
fromage frais
Monterey Jack
Philadelphia®
Red Leicester

13 Bleu d'Auvergne
cottage cheese

See also **dairy**

chef

Chefs, restaurateurs and cookery writers include:

03 Hom (Ken; 1949– , US)

04 Diat (Louis; 1885–1957, French/US)
Dods (Meg; 1781–1857, Scottish)
Kerr (Graham; 1934– , English/New Zealand)
Roux (Albert; 1935– , French)
Roux (Michel; 1941– , French)
Spry (Constance; 1886–1960, English)

05 Beard (James; 1903–85, US)
Blanc (Raymond; 1949– , French)
Brown (David; 1951– , Scottish)
Brown (Hilary; 1952– , Scottish)
Child (Julia; 1912–2004, US)
David (Elizabeth; 1913–92, English)
Floyd (Keith; 1943–2009, English)

Leith (Prue; 1940– , English)
Nairn (Nick; 1959– , Scottish)
Sardi (Vincent; 1885–1969, Italian/US)
Savoy (Guy; 1953– , French)
Smith (Delia; 1941– , English)
Soyer (Alexis; 1809–58, French)
Stein (Rick; 1947– , English)
White (Marco Pierre; 1961– , English)

06 Appert (Nicolas; 1749–1841, French)
Beeton (Mrs Isabella; 1836–65, English)
Bocuse (Paul; 1926– , French)
Carême (Marie Antoine; 1784–1833, French)
Farmer (Fannie; 1857–1915, US)
Fisher (M F K; 1908–92, US)

Franey (Pierre; 1921–96, French/US)
Harvey (Fred; 1835–1901, US)
Lawson (Nigella; 1960– , English)
Little (Alistair; 1950– ,English)
Oliver (Jamie; 1975– , English)
Ramsay (Gordon; 1967– , Scottish)
Rhodes (Gary; 1960– , English)
Slater (Nigel; 1958– , English)
Turner (Brian; 1946– , English)
Wilson (David; 1938– , Scottish)

07 Cradock (Fanny; 1909–94, English)
Eriksen (Gunn; 1956– , Norwegian/
Scottish)
Grigson (Jane; 1928–90, English)
Grigson (Sophie; 1959– , English)
Guérard (Michel; 1933– , French)
Jaffrey (Madhur; 1933– , Indian/US)
Ladenis (Nico; 1934– , Kenyan)
Novelli (Jean-Christophe; 1961– , French)
Vickery (Philip; 1961– , English)

08 Dimbleby (Josceline; 1943– , English)

Grossman (Loyd; 1950– , US)
Harriott (Ainsley; 1957– , English)
Mosimann (Anton; 1947– , Swiss)
Paterson (Jennifer; 1928–99, English)
Robuchon (Joël; 1945– , French)
Rombauer (Irma; 1877–1962, US)

09 Carluccio (Antonio; 1937– , Italian)
Claiborne (Craig; 1920–2000, US)
Delmonico (Lorenzo; 1813–81, Swiss/US)
Escoffier (Auguste; c.1847–1935, French)
Heathcote (Paul; 1960– , English)
Johnstone (Isobel; 1781–1857, Scottish)
Locatelli (Giorgio; 1962– , Italian)
McCartney (Linda; 1941–98, US/British)
Prudhomme (Paul; 1940– , US)

10 Blumenthal (Heston; 1966– , English)

13 Dickson Wright (Clarissa; 1946– , English)

14 Brillat-Savarin (Anthelme; 1755–1826,
French)

15 Worrall Thompson (Antony; 1952– , English)

Chekhov, Anton (1860–1904)

Significant works include:

06 *Ivanov* (1887)

07 *The Bear* (1890)

10 *The Seagull* (1896)

Uncle Vanya (1896)

11 *The Proposal* (1889)

12 *The Wood Demon* (1889)

15 *The Three Sisters* (1901)

16 *The Cherry Orchard* (1904)

Significant characters include:

04 Anna
Olga

05 Irina
Masha
Sasha
Sonya
Vanya

06 Astrov (Michael)
Helena
Ivanov (Nikolai)
Yelena

07 Lebedev (Sasha)
Treplev (Konstantin 'Kostaya' Gavrilovich)

08 Abramson (Sarah)
Arkadina (Irina Nikolayevna)
Lopakhin (Ermolai Alexeyevitch)
Ranevsky (Lubov Andreyevna 'Madame')
Trigorin (Boris Alexeyevich)

09 Voynitsky (Ivan 'Vanya')

10 Zarechnaya (Nina Mikhailovna)

11 Serebryakov (Alexander)

chemistry

Chemical elements, their symbols and atomic numbers include:

03 tin (Sn, 50)

04 gold (Au, 79)
iron (Fe, 26)
lead (Pb, 82)
neon (Ne, 10)
zinc (Zn, 30)

05 argon (Ar, 18)
boron (B, 5)
radon (Rn, 86)

xenon (Xe, 54)

06 barium (Ba, 56)
carbon (C, 6)
cerium (Ce, 58)
cobalt (Co, 27)
copper (Cu, 29)
curium (Cm, 96)
erbium (Er, 68)
helium (He, 2)

indium (In, 49)
iodine (I, 53)
nickel (Ni, 28)
osmium (Os, 76)
oxygen (O, 8)
radium (Ra, 88)
silver (Ag, 47)
sodium (Na, 11)

07 arsenic (As, 33)

bismuth (Bi, 83)
bohrium (Bh, 107)
bromine (Br, 35)
cadmium (Cd, 48)
caesium (Cs, 55)
calcium (Ca, 20)
dubnium (Db, 105)
fermium (Fm, 100)
gallium (Ga, 31)
hafnium (Hf, 72)
hahnium (Ha)
hassium (Hs, 108)
holmium (Ho, 67)
iridium (Ir, 77)
krypton (Kr, 36)
lithium (Li, 3)
mercury (Hg, 80)
niobium (Nb, 41)
rhenium (Re, 75)
rhodium (Rh, 45)
silicon (Si, 14)
sulphur (S, 16)
terbium (Tb, 65)
thorium (Th, 90)
thulium (Tm, 69)
uranium (U, 92)
yttrium (Y, 39)

08 actinium (Ac, 89)
antimony (Sb, 51)

astatine (At, 85)
chlorine (Cl, 17)
chromium (Cr, 24)
europium (Eu, 63)
fluorine (F, 9)
francium (Fr, 87)
hydrogen (H, 1)
lutetium (Lu, 71)
nitrogen (N, 7)
nobelium (No, 102)
platinum (Pt, 78)
polonium (Po, 84)
rubidium (Rb, 37)
samarium (Sm, 62)
scandium (Sc, 21)
selenium (Se, 34)
tantalum (Ta, 73)
thallium (Tl, 81)
titanium (Ti, 22)
tungsten (W, 74)
unumbium (Uub, 112)
vanadium (V, 23)

09 aluminium (Al, 13)
americium (Am, 95)
berkelium (Bk, 97)
beryllium (Be, 4)
germanium (Ge, 32)
lanthanum (La, 57)
magnesium (Mg, 12)

manganese (Mn, 25)
neodymium (Nd, 60)
neptunium (Np, 93)
palladium (Pd, 46)
plutonium (Pu, 94)
potassium (K, 19)
ruthenium (Ru, 44)
strontium (Sr, 38)
tellurium (Te, 52)
ytterbium (Yb, 70)
zirconium (Zr, 40)

10 dysprosium (Dy, 66)
gadolinium (Gd, 64)
lawrencium (Lr, 103)
meitnerium (Mt, 109)
molybdenum (Mo, 42)
phosphorus (P, 15)
promethium (Pm, 61)
rontgenium (Rg, 111)
seaborgium (Sg, 106)
technetium (Tc, 43)

11 californium (Cf, 98)
einsteinium (Es, 99)
mendelevium (Md, 101)

12 darmstadtium (Ds, 110)
praseodymium (Pr, 59)
protactinium (Pa, 91)

13 rutherfordium (Rf, 104)

Chemical compounds include:

03 PVC
04 DEET
soap
urea
06 phenol
07 ammonia
borazon
chloral
ethanol
styrene

toluene
08 atrazine
kerosene
methanol
paraffin
09 bromoform
carbazole
10 chloramine
chloroform
12 benzaldehyde

borosilicate
13 carbon dioxide
chlorhexidine
chlorobromide
14 carbon monoxide
chloral hydrate
15 organophosphate
sodium hydroxide

Chemists include:

03 Lee (Yuan T; 1936– , Taiwanese/US)
04 Abel (Sir Frederick; 1827–1902, English)
Auer (Karl, Baron von Welsbach; 1858–1929, Austrian)
Cram (Donald J; 1919–2001, US)
Curl (Robert F, Jnr; 1933– , US)
Davy (Sir Humphry; 1778–1829, English)
Dorn (Friedrich; 1848–1916, German)
Ertl (Gerhard; 1936– , German)
Fenn (John B; 1917–2010, US)
Gahn (Johan Gottlieb; 1745–1818, Swedish)
Hall (Charles; 1863–1914, US)

Heck (Richard; 1931– , US)
Hess (Germain Henri; 1802–50, Swiss/Russian)
Hope (Thomas Charles; 1766–1844, Scottish)
Keir (James; 1735–1820, Scottish)
Kipp (Petrus Jacobus; 1808–64, Dutch)
Kopp (Hermann; 1817–92, German)
Kuhn (Richard; 1900–67, Austrian/German)
Lehn (Jean-Marie; 1939– , French)
Levi (Primo; 1919–87, Italian)
Mond (Ludwig; 1839–1909, German/British)
Nöth (Heinrich; 1928– , German)

Olah (George A; 1927– , Hungarian/US)
Pope (Sir William Jackson; 1870–1939, English)
Swan (Sir Joseph; 1828–1914, English)
Todd (Alexander, Lord; 1907–97, Scottish)
Urey (Harold C; 1893–1981, US)

05 Abegg (Richard; 1869–1910, German)
Abney (Sir William; 1844–1920, English)
Alder (Kurt; 1902–58, German)
Allen (Sir Geoffrey; 1928– , English)
Baumé (Antoine; 1728–1804, French)
Bevan (Edward; 1856–1921, English)
Birch (Arthur; 1915–95, Australian)
Black (Joseph; 1728–99, Scottish)
Bosch (Carl; 1874–1940, German)
Boyle (Robert; 1627–91, Irish)
Brown (Herbert C; 1912–2004, English/US)
Clark (William Mansfield; 1884–1964, US)
Corey (Elias; 1928– , US)
Cross (Charles; 1855–1935, English)
Curie (Marie; 1867–1934, Polish/French)
Curie (Pierre; 1859–1906, French)
Dakin (Henry; 1880–1952, English)
Davis (Raymond, Jnr; 1914–2006, US)
Debye (Peter; 1884–1966, Dutch/US)
Dewar (Michael; 1918–97, Indian/British)
Dewar (Sir James; 1842–1923, Scottish)
Diels (Otto; 1876–1954, German)
Dufay (Charles; 1698–1739, French)
Dumas (Jean Baptiste; 1800–84, French)
Eigen (Manfred; 1917– , German)
Ernst (Richard R; 1933– , Swiss)
Ewins (A J; 1882–1957, English)
Fleck (Alexander, Lord; 1889–1968, Scottish)
Flory (Paul J; 1910–85, US)
Frémy (Edmond; 1814–94, French)
Fukui (Kenichi; 1918–98, Japanese)
Genth (Frederick A; 1820–93, German/US)
Haber (Fritz; 1868–1934, German)
Hales (Stephen; 1677–1761, English)
Henry (William; 1774–1836, English)
Hirst (Sir Edmund; 1898–1975, English)
Hooke (Robert; 1635–1703, English)
Karle (Isabella; 1921– , US)
Kolbe (Hermann; 1818–84, German)
Kroto (Sir Harold; 1939– , English)
Le Bel (Joseph Achille; 1847–1930, French)
Lewis (Gilbert N; 1875–1946, US)
Libby (Willard F; 1908–80, US)
Lowry (Martin; 1874–1936, English)
Marsh (James; 1789–1846, English)
Mayow (John; 1640–79, English)
Meyer (Lothar; 1830–95, German)
Meyer (Viktor; 1848–97, German)
Natta (Giulio; 1903–79, Italian)
Nobel (Alfred; 1833–96, Swedish)
Pople (Sir John; 1925–2004, English)
Pregl (Fritz; 1869–1930, Austrian)

Runge (Friedlieb Ferdinand; 1795–1867, German)
Soddy (Frederick; 1877–1965, English)
Stahl (Georg; 1660–1734, German)
Stock (Alfred; 1876–1946, German)
Taube (Henry; 1915–2005, Canadian/US)
Tsien (Roger Y; 1952– , US)
Vogel (Hermann Wilhelm; 1834–98, German)
Waage (Peter; 1833–1900, Norwegian)
Wiley (Harvey Washington; 1844–1930, US)
Wurtz (Adolphe; 1817–84, French)

06 Baeyer (Adolf von; 1835–1917, German)
Balard (Antoine Jérôme; 1802–76, French)
Barton (Sir Derek; 1918–98, English)
Becher (Johann Joachim; 1635–82, German)
Beilby (Sir George; 1850–1924, Scottish)
Benson (Sidney; 1918–2011, US)
Brandt (Georg; 1694–1768, Swedish)
Bunsen (Robert; 1811–99, German)
Calvin (Melvin; 1911–97, US)
Claude (Georges; 1870–1960, French)
Cotton (F Albert; 1930–2007, US)
Couper (Archibald Scott; 1831–92, Scottish)
Cullen (William; 1710–90, Scottish)
Dalton (John; 1766–1844, English)
Draper (John William; 1811–82, English/US)
Dulong (Pierre; 1785–1838, French)
Eyring (Henry; 1901–81, US)
Fajans (Kasimir; 1887–1975, Polish/US)
Frasch (Hermann; 1851–1914, German/US)
Gmelin (Leopold; 1788–1853, German)
Graebe (Karl; 1841–1927, German)
Graham (Thomas; 1805–69, Scottish)
Gregor (William; 1761–1817, English)
Grubbs (Robert H; 1942– , US)
Harden (Sir Arthur; 1865–1940, English)
Hassel (Odd; 1897–1981, Norwegian)
Hevesy (George de; 1885–1966, Hungarian)
Hückel (Erich; 1896–1980, German)
Ingold (Sir Christopher; 1893–1970, English)
Karrer (Paul; 1889–1971, Russian/Swiss)
Kirwan (Richard; 1733–1812, Irish)
Kossel (Albrecht; 1853–1927, German)
Lémery (Nicolas; 1645–1715, French)
Liebig (Justus von; 1803–73, German)
Marcus (Rudolph A; 1923– , Canadian/US)
Mendel (Lafayette; 1872–1935, US)
Mercer (John; 1791–1866, English)
Miller (Stanley L; 1930–2007, US)
Morley (E W; 1838–1923, US)
Müller (Franz, Baron von Reichenstein; 1740–1825, Austrian)
Müller (Paul; 1899–1965, Swiss)
Nernst (Walther; 1864–1941, German)
Niepce (Nicéphore; 1765–1833, French)
Noyori (Ryoji; 1938– , Japanese)
Odling (William; 1829–1921, English)

Orfila (Mathieu; 1787–1853, French)
Paneth (Fritz; 1887–1958, Austrian)
Parkes (Alexander; 1813–90, English)
Perkin (Sir William Henry, Snr; 1838–1907, English)
Porter (George, Lord; 1920–2002, English)
Prelog (Vladimir; 1906–98, Swiss)
Proust (Joseph Louis; 1754–1826, French)
Ramsay (Sir William; 1852–1916, Scottish)
Raoult (François Marie; 1830–1901, French)
Rideal (Sir Eric; 1890–1974, English)
Roscoe (Sir Henry; 1833–1915, English)
Solvay (Ernest; 1838–1922, Belgian)
Spence (Peter; 1806–83, Scottish)
Suzuki (Akira; 1930– , Japanese)
Thorpe (Sir Edward; 1845–1925, English)
Tilden (Sir William Augustus; 1842–1926, English)
Tizard (Sir Henry; 1885–1959, English)
Traube (Moritz; 1826–94, German)
Tsvett (Mikhail S; 1872–1919, Russian)
Tswett (Mikhail S; 1872–1919, Russian)
Urbain (Georges; 1872–1938, French)
Walker (Sir James; 1863–1935, Scottish)
Werner (Alfred; 1866–1919, French/Swiss)
Wittig (Georg; 1897–1987, German)
Wöhler (Friedrich; 1800–82, German)
Zewail (Ahmed H; 1946– , Egyptian)

07 Abelson (Philip H; 1913–2004, US)
Acheson (Edward Goodrich; 1856–1931, US)
Andrews (Thomas; 1813–85, Irish)
Bergius (Friedrich; 1884–1949, German)
Bergman (Torbern; 1735–84, Swedish)
Borodin (Aleksandr; 1833–87, Russian)
Buchner (Eduard; 1860–1917, German)
Cadogan (Sir John; 1930– , Welsh)
Calvert (Frederick Crace; 1819–73, English)
Castner (Hamilton Young; 1848–99, US)
Chalfie (Martin; 1947– , US)
Chaptal (Jean, Comte de Chanteloupe; 1756–1832, French)
Charles (Jacques; 1746–1823, French)
Chauvin (Yves; 1930– , French)
Coulson (C A; 1910–74, English)
Crookes (Sir William; 1832–1919, English)
Crutzen (Paul J; 1933– , Dutch)
Curtius (Theodor; 1857–1928, German)
Dainton (Frederick, Lord; 1914–97, English)
Daniell (John; 1790–1845, English)
Ekeberg (Anders; 1767–1813, Swedish)
Faraday (Michael; 1791–1867, English)
Fischer (Emil; 1852–1919, German)
Fischer (Ernst Otto; 1918–2007, German)
Fischer (Hans; 1881–1945, German)
Friedel (Charles; 1832–99, French)
Gadolin (Johan; 1760–1852, Finnish)
Giauque (William F; 1895–1982, Canadian/US)
Gilbert (Sir Henry; 1817–1901, English)

Gomberg (Moses; 1866–1947, Russian/US)
Guthrie (Samuel; 1782–1848, US)
Hammett (Louis P; 1894–1987, US)
Haworth (Sir Norman; 1883–1950, English)
Helmont (Jan van; 1579–1644, Flemish)
Hittorf (Johann; 1824–1914, German)
Hodgkin (Dorothy; 1910–94, Egyptian/British)
Hofmann (August Wilhelm von; 1818–92, German)
Kendall (Edward C; 1886–1972, US)
Khorana (H Gobind; 1922–2011, Indian/US)
Kipping (Frederick Stanley; 1863–1949, English)
Knowles (William S; 1917–2012, US)
Kobilka (Brian; 1955– , US)
Laurent (Auguste; 1807–53, French)
Leblanc (Nicholas; 1724–1806, French)
Macquer (Pierre Joseph; 1718–84, French)
Moissan (Henri; 1852–1907, French)
Moscíki (Igancy; 1867–1946, Polish)
Negishi (Ei-ichi; 1935– , Japanese)
Norrish (Ronald G W; 1897–1978, English)
Ostwald (Wilhelm; 1853–1932, Latvian/German)
Pasteur (Louis; 1822–95, French)
Pauling (Linus; 1901–94, US)
Piccard (Jean Felix; 1884–1963, Swiss/US)
Polanyi (John; 1929– , German/Canadian)
Polanyi (Michael; 1891–1976, Hungarian/British)
Richter (Hieronymous; 1824–98, German)
Richter (Jeremias; 1762–1807, German)
Roberts (John D; 1918– , US)
Rowland (F Sherwood; 1927–2012, US)
Ruzicka (Leopold; 1887–1976, Croatian/Swiss)
Scheele (Carl; 1742–86, Swedish)
Schrock (Richard R; 1945– , US)
Seaborg (Glenn; 1912–99, US)
Semenov (Nikolai; 1896–1986, Soviet)
Sharman (Helen; 1963– , English)
Shriver (D F; 1934– , US)
Smalley (Richard E; 1943–2005, US)
Sobrero (Ascanio; 1812–88, Italian)
Tennant (Charles; 1768–1838, Scottish)
Tennant (Smithson; 1761–1815, English)
Thénard (Louis Jacques; 1777–1857, French)
Travers (Morris; 1872–1961, English)
Wallach (Otto; 1847–1931, German)
Wieland (Heinrich; 1877–1957, German)
Windaus (Adolf; 1876–1959, German)
Winkler (Clemens; 1838–1904, German)
Ziegler (Karl; 1898–1973, German)

08 Anderson (John Stuart; 1908–90, English)
Avogadro (Amedeo; 1776–1856, Italian)
Bartlett (Neil; 1932–2008, English)
Beckmann (Ernst Otto; 1853–1923, German)
Birchall (Derek; 1930–95, English)
Brønsted (Johannes; 1879–1947, Danish)

Butlerov (Aleksandr; 1828–86, Russian)
Caventou (Joseph; 1795–1877, French)
Chevreul (Michel Eugène; 1786–1889, French)
Coolidge (William D; 1873–1975, US)
Courtois (Bernard; 1777–1838, French)
Djerassi (Carl; 1923– , Austrian/US)
Fourcroy (Antoine François, Comte de; 1755–1809, French)
Gerhardt (Charles; 1816–56, French)
Grignard (Victor; 1871–1935, French)
Guldberg (Cato; 1836–1902, Norwegian)
Hadfield (Sir Robert; 1858–1940, English)
Hantzsch (Arthur; 1857–1935, German)
Harcourt (Sir William Vernon; 1789–1871, English)
Herzberg (Gerhard; 1904–99, German/Canadian)
Hoffmann (Roald; 1937– , Polish/US)
Ipatieff (Vladimir N; 1867–1952, Russian/US)
Kjeldahl (Johan; 1849–1900, Danish)
Klaproth (Martin; 1743–1817, German)
Kornberg (Roger D; 1947– , US)
Langmuir (Irving; 1881–1957, US)
Lapworth (Arthur; 1872–1941, Scottish)
Lipscomb (William; 1919–2011, US)
Lonsdale (Dame Kathleen; 1903–71, Irish)
Lovelock (James; 1919– , English)
Marggraf (Andreas; 1709–82, German)
Mulliken (Robert S; 1896–1986, US)
Muspratt (James; 1793–1886, Irish/British)
Newlands (John; 1837–98, English)
Pedersen (Charles; 1904–90, US)
Pimentel (George; 1922–89, US)
Regnault (Henri Victor; 1810–78, French)
Richards (Sir Rex; 1922– , English)
Richards (Theodore W; 1868–1928, US)
Robinson (Sir Robert; 1886–1975, English)
Sabatier (Paul; 1854–1941, French)
Sefström (Nils; 1765–1829, Swedish)
Sidgwick (Nevil; 1873–1951, English)
Silliman (Benjamin; 1779–1864, US)
Silliman (Benjamin; 1816–85, US)
Smithson (James; 1765–1829, English)
Sørensen (Søren; 1868–1939, Danish)
Sprengel (Hermann; 1834–1906, German/British)
Svedberg (Theo; 1884–1971, Swedish)
Takamine (Jokichi; 1834–1922, Japanese/US)
Tiselius (Arne; 1902–71, Swedish)
van't Hoff (Jacobus H; 1852–1911, Dutch)
Voelcker (Augustus; 1822–84, German)
Weizmann (Chaim; 1874–1952, Russian/Israeli)
Woodward (Robert B; 1917–79, US)
Wüthrich (Kurt; 1938– , Swiss)

09 Armstrong (Henry; 1848–1937, English)
Arrhenius (Svante; 1859–1927, Swedish)
Baekeland (Leo; 1863–1944, Belgian/US)
Beilstein (Friedrich; 1838–1906, German/Russian)

Bernstein (Richard; 1923–90, US)
Berthelot (Marcellin; 1827–1907, French)
Berzelius (Jöns Jacob; 1779–1848, Swedish)
Carothers (Wallace; 1896–1937, US)
Cavendish (Henry; 1731–1810, English)
Chabaneau (François; 1754–1842, French)
Cornforth (Sir John; 1917– , Australian)
Crum Brown (Alexander; 1838–1922, Scottish)
Frankland (Sir Edward; 1825–99, English)
Fresenius (Karl Remigius; 1818–97, German)
Gay-Lussac (Joseph Louis; 1778–1850, French)
Harington (Sir Charles; 1897–1972, British)
Heyrovský (Jaroslav; 1890–1967, Czech)
Lavoisier (Antoine; 1743–94, French)
Leclanché (Georges; 1839–82, French)
Lefkowitz (Robert; 1943– , US)
Macintosh (Charles; 1766–1843, Scottish)
Nieuwland (Julius; 1878–1936, US)
Pelletier (Pierre Joseph; 1788–1842, French)
Priestley (Joseph; 1733–1804, English)
Prigogine (Ilya, Vicomte; 1917–2003, Russian/Belgian)
Roozeboom (Hendrick; 1854–1907, Dutch)
Schönbein (Christian; 1799–1868, German)
Sharpless (K Barry; 1941– , US)
Shechtman (Dan; 1941– , Israeli)
Shimomura (Osamu; 1928– , Japanese)
Stromeyer (Friedrich; 1776–1835, German)
Vauquelin (Nicolas-Louis; 1763–1829, French)
Wilkinson (Sir Geoffrey; 1921–96, English)
Wollaston (William; 1766–1828, English)
Zsigmondy (Richard; 1865–1929, Austrian)

10 Berthollet (Claude Louis, Comte de; 1749–1822, French)
Bodenstein (Max; 1871–1942, German)
Brongniart (Alexandre; 1770–1847, French)
Cannizzaro (Stanislao; 1826–1910, Italian)
Chardonnet; (Hilaire, Comte de; 1839–1924, French)
Chittenden (Russell; 1856–1943, US)
Döbereiner (Johann; 1780–1849, German)
Herschbach (Dudley R; 1932– , US)
Hildebrand (Joel; 1881–1983, US)
Ingenhousz (Jan; 1730–99, Dutch)
Ingen-Housz (Jan; 1730–99, Dutch)
MacDiarmid (Alan G; 1927–2007, New Zealand/US)
Mendeleyev (Dmitri; 1834–1907, Russian)
Merrifield (Bruce; 1921–2006, US)
Reichstein (Tadeus; 1897–1996, Polish/Swiss)
Staudinger (Hermann; 1881–1965, German)

11 Boisbaudran (Paul Lecoq de; 1838–1912, French)
Eschenmoser (Albert; 1925– , Swiss)
Goldschmidt (Hans; 1861–1923, German)
Goldschmidt (V M; 1888–1947, Swiss/Norwegian)
Hinshelwood (Sir Cyril; 1897–1967, English)

Hoppe-Seyler (Felix; 1825–95, German)
Le Châtelier (Henri; 1850–1936, French)
Mège Mouriés (Hippolyte; 1817–80, French)
Pettenkofer (Max von; 1818–1901, German)
Poggendorff (Johann; 1796–1877, German)
Unverdorben (Otto; 1806–73, German)
Willstätter (Richard; 1872–1942, German)

12 Boussingault (Jean Baptiste; 1802–87, French)

Christiansen (Jens Anton; 1888–1969, Danish)
Lennard-Jones (Sir John; 1894–1954, English)
Mitscherlich (Eilhard; 1794–1863, German)

14 Longuet-Higgins (H C; 1923–2004, English)
Vernon Harcourt (William; 1789–1871, English)

15 Guyton de Morveau (Louis Bernard, Baron; 1737–1816, French)

Terms used in chemistry include:

02 IR
pH

03 cis
gas
ion
sol

04 acid
atom
base
bond
mass
mole
salt
weak

05 assay
block
cycle
ester
group
IUPAC
lipid
order
phase
polar
redox
shell
trans
yield

06 alkali
alkane
alkene
buffer
chiral
Dalton
dilute
dipole
fusion
halide
isomer
ketone
ligand
liquid
matter
period

phenyl
pi bond
proton
solids
strong
symbol

07 alchemy
chelate
chemist
colloid
crystal
density
element
entropy
fission
formula
halogen
isotope
lattice
mixture
neutral
neutron
nucleus
orbital
organic
polymer
product
racemic
reagent
soluble
solvent
valency

08 analysis
aromatic
catalyst
chemurgy
compound
cracking
denature
dialysis
effusion
electron
emulsion
end point

enthalpy
fixation
half life
hydroxyl
inert gas
lone pair
meniscus
miscible
molecule
noble gas
nonpolar
physical
reactant
reaction
solution

09 aliphatic
allotrope
anhydrous
bioenergy
catalysis
corrosion
diffusion
electrode
empirical
homologue
hydration
hydroxide
indicator
inorganic
insoluble
ionic bond
oxidation
reduction
saturated
side chain
sigma bond
structure
substance
synthesis
titration

10 amphoteric
atomic mass
combustion
complex ion

curly arrow
double bond
enantiomer
exothermic
free energy
hydrolysis
immiscible
ion channel
ionotropic
latent heat
litmus test
neutralize
reversible
single bond
suspension
triple bond
zwitterion

11 alkali metal
biomolecule
crystallize
diffraction
electrolyte
endothermic
equilibrium
evaporation
free radical
ground state
homogeneous
hydrocarbon
hygroscopic
ion exchange
ionic radius

litmus paper
phase change
precipitate
respiration
sublimation

12 atomic number
atomic radius
atomic weight
band spectrum
beta particle
biochemistry
chemical bond
chlorination
concentrated
condensation
covalent bond
deliquescent
desalination
dissociation
distillation
efflorescent
electrolysis
excited state
fermentation
fluorescence
heat capacity
heterocyclic
hydrogen bond
line spectrum
masking agent
melting point
metallic bond

rate constant
reaction rate
spectroscopy
stereoisomer

13 alpha particle
chain reaction
critical point
decomposition
fractionation
freezing point
heterogeneous
hybridization
periodic table
quantum number
radioactivity
stoichiometry

14 Avogadro number
Brownian motion
buffer solution
chromatography
covalent radius
saponification

15 atomic structure
aufbau principle
chemical element
collision theory
electrospinning
optical activity
transition metal
transition state
van der Waals bond

See also **biochemistry**; **environment**; **Nobel Prize**; **salt**

cherry

Cherry varieties include:

04 wild
05 morel
See also **fruit**

07 morello
10 blackheart

maraschino

chess

Chess pieces include:

04 king   rook
     pawn   **05** queen

06 bishop   knight
     castle

Chess players and computers include:

03 Tal (Mikhail; 1936–92, Soviet)

04 Euwe (Max; 1901–81, Dutch)

05 Anand (Viswanathan; 1969–   , Indian)
     Short (Nigel; 1965–   , English)

06 Karpov (Anatoli; 1951–   , Russian)

Lasker (Emanuel; 1868–1941, German)
Morphy (Paul; 1837–84, US)
Polgar (Judit; 1976–   , Hungarian)
Polgar (Zsuzsa; 1969–   , Hungarian)
Thomas (Sir George; 1881–1972, Turkish/
     British)

Timman (Jan; 1951– , Dutch)
Xie Jun (1970– , Chinese)

07 Fischer (Bobby; 1943–2008, US)
Kramnik (Vladimir; 1975– , Russian)
Smyslov (Vasili; 1921– , Russian)
Spassky (Boris; 1937– , Russian)
Topalov (Veselin; 1975– , Bulgarian)

08 Alekhine (Alexander; 1892–1946, French)
Deep Blue
Kasparov (Garry; 1963– , Russian)

Korchnoi (Viktor; 1931– , Russian)
Philidor (François André; 1726–95, French)
Staunton (Howard; 1810–74, English)
Steinitz (Wilhelm; 1836–1900, Czech)

09 Botvinnik (Mikhail; 1911–95, Soviet)
Khalifman (Alexander; 1966– , Russian)
Petrosian (Tigran; 1929–84, Soviet)

10 Capablanca (José; 1888–1942, Cuban)
Ponomariov (Ruslan; 1983– , Ukrainian)

13 Chiburdanidze (Maya; 1961– , Russian)

Chess terms include:

03 man	**06** attack	squeeze	**10** fianchetto
pin	bishop	**08** back rank	good bishop
row	castle	castling	major piece
04 bind	centre	diagonal	middle game
FIDE	double	exchange	minor piece
fork	gambit	kingside	passed pawn
king	knight	opponent	**11** counterplay
move	master	queening	grandmaster
pawn	patzer	zugzwang	zwischenzug
play	square	**09** bad bishop	**12** backward pawn
rook	**07** chequer	checkmate	problem child
05 black	defence	Elo rating	**13** counter attack
board	develop	en passant	fifty move rule
check	endgame	fool's mate	**14** lightning chess
flank	en prise	miniature	perpetual check
march	j'adoube	promotion	**15** knight's progress
piece	opening	queenside	
queen	promote	stalemate	
white	retract		

chicken

Chickens include:

06 Ancona	Hamburg	Welsummer	**11** Spanish fowl
bantam	leghorn	wyandotte	**12** Plymouth Rock
Cochin	Minorca	**10** Andalusian	**14** Rhode Island Red
houdan	**08** Hamburgh	Australorp	
sultan	Langshan	chittagong	
07 Dorking	**09** Orpington	jungle fowl	

See also **bird**

chief rabbi

Chief rabbis, with dates of office:

04 Hart (Aaron; 1704–56)
Lyon (Hart; 1758–64)

05 Adler (Hermann; 1891–1911)
Adler (Nathan; 1845–91)
Hertz (J H; 1913–46)
Sacks (Jonathan, Lord; 1991–2013)

06 Brodie (Israel; 1948–65)
Mirvis (Ephraim; 2013–)

09 Hirschell (Solomon; 1802–42)

10 Jakobovits (Immanuel, Lord; 1966–91)

12 Tevele Schiff (David; 1765–91)

See also **religion**

children *see* **literature; novel**

China

Cities and notable towns in China include:

04 Xi'an	Guilin	Nanking	Victoria
05 Lhasa	Peking	Taiyuan	09 Chongqing
Wuhan	07 Beijing	Tianjin	Guangzhou
	Kunming	08 Shanghai	
06 Canton	Nanjing	Shenyang	

Chinese landmarks include:

03 Han	08 Badaling	12 Imperial City
04 Wuyi	Gaochang	Potala Palace
05 Wei He	Shenzhen	Summer Palace
06 Harbin	09 Great Wall	Victoria Peak
Mt Wuyi	Huangshan	13 Forbidden City
Suzhou	Ming Tombs	Jokhang Temple
Urumqi	Mt Tai Shan	14 Imperial Palace
07 Chengdu	Tiananmen	Maitreya Buddha
Qianmen	10 Lama Temple	Peninsula Hotel
Tai Shan	Pearl River	Temple of Heaven
The Bund	11 Man Mo Temple	Terracotta Army
Tiantan	Mt Huangshan	15 Confucius Temple
Xi Jiang	Three Gorges	Tiananmen Square
Yangtze	Yellow River	

Imperial dynasties and periods include:

03 Han	Ming	10 Eastern Han
Jin	Qing	Eastern Jin
Qin	Song	Western Han
Sui	Sung	Western Jin
Xia	Tang	11 Eastern Chou
Yin	Yuan	Western Chou
04 Ch'in	Zhou	13 Three Kingdoms
Chou	05 Shang	Warring States

See also **Asia**

Chinese *see* **calendar**

choreography *see* **ballet**

Christianity

Christian churches and denominations include:

04 Copt	Gnostic	09 Adventist
05 Amish	Opus Dei	Calvinist
06 Coptic	Puritan	Methodist
Jesuit	08 Anglican	Unitarian
Quaker	Catholic	10 Anabaptist
07 Baptist	Lutheran	Protestant

11 Evangelical
Pentecostal
12 Episcopalian
Presbyterian

13 Greek Orthodox
Roman Catholic
Salvation Army
14 Society of Jesus

15 Christadelphian
Church of England
Church of Ireland
Eastern Orthodox

See also **reformer**; **religion**

Christie, Dame Agatha (1890–1976)

Significant works include:

04 *N or M?* (1941)

05 *Poems* (1973)

07 *Curtain* (1975)
Nemesis (1971)
Verdict (1958)

08 *Akhnaton* (1973)

09 *Double Sin* (1961)
The Burden (1956)
The Clocks (1963)
The Hollow (1946)
Third Girl (1966)

10 *Sad Cypress* (1940)
Spider's Web (1954)
The Big Four (1927)

11 *Black Coffee* (1930)
Dumb Witness (1937)
Giant's Bread (1930)
Rule of Three (1962)
The Under Dog (1951)
Towards Zero (1944)

12 *Crooked House* (1949)
Endless Night (1967)
Murder Is Easy (1939)
The Mousetrap (1952)
The Pale Horse (1961)

13 *Dead Man's Folly* (1956)
Fiddlers Three (1972)
Postern of Fate (1973)
The ABC Murders (1936)
The Golden Ball (1971)

14 *Death on the Nile* (1937)
Five Little Pigs (1943)
Hallowe'en Party (1969)
Regatta Mystery (1939)
Sleeping Murder (1976)
Three Blind Mice (1950)

15 *After the Funeral* (1953)
An Autobiography (1977)
At Bertram's Hotel (1965)
Cards on the Table (1936)
Evil Under the Sun (1941)
Lord Edgware Dies (1933)
Mrs McGinty's Dead (1952)
Murder in the Mews (1937)
Partners in Crime (1929)

Peril at End House (1932)
Taken at the Flood (1948)
The Hound of Death (1933)
The Moving Finger (1942)
The Road of Dreams (1924)
Three-Act Tragedy (1934)

16 *A Pocket Full of Rye* (1953)
Death in the Clouds (1935)
Sparkling Cyanide (1945)

17 *4.50 from Paddington* (1957)
Absent in the Spring (1944)
A Caribbean Mystery (1964)
Ordeal by Innocence (1958)
Poirot's Early Cases (1974)
Star Over Bethlehem (1965)
They Came to Baghdad (1951)

18 *A Murder Is Announced* (1950)
Cat Among the Pigeons (1959)
Death Comes As the End (1944)
Destination Unknown (1954)
Hickory Dickory Dock (1955)
One, Two, Buckle My Shoe (1940)
Poirot Investigates (1924)
The Secret Adversary (1922)
The Unexpected Guest (1958)
Unfinished Portrait (1934)

19 *A Daughter's a Daughter* (1952)
Murder in Mesopotamia (1936)
The Body in the Library (1942)
The Murder on the Links (1923)
The Mysterious Mr Quin (1930)
The Secret of Chimneys (1925)
The Sittaford Mystery (1931)
The Thirteen Problems (1932)
They Do It with Mirrors (1952)

20 *And Then There Were None* (1939)
Appointment With Death (1938)
Come, Tell Me How You Live (1946)
Elephants Can Remember (1972)
Passenger to Frankfurt (1970)
The Labours of Hercules (1947)
The Listerdale Mystery (1934)
The Man in the Brown Suit (1924)
The Rose and the Yew Tree (1948)
The Seven Dials Mystery (1929)
Why Didn't They Ask Evans? (1934)

21 *Miss Marple's Final Cases* (1979)

22 *Parker Pyne Investigates* (1934)
The Murder at the Vicarage (1930)

23 *By the Pricking of My Thumbs* (1968)
Hercule Poirot's Christmas (1938)

The Murder of Roger Ackroyd (1926)

24 *Murder on the Orient Express* (1934)
The Mystery of the Blue Train (1928)
Witness for the Prosecution (1953)

27 *The Mysterious Affair at Styles* (1920)

29 *The Mirror Crack'd from Side to Side* (1962)

33 *The Adventure of the Christmas Pudding* (1960)

Significant characters include:

04 Japp (Chief Inspector)
Pyne (Parker)
Quin (Mr Harley)
Race (Colonel Johnny)
West (Raymond)

05 Lemon (Miss Felicity)
Slack (Inspector)

06 Bantry (Colonel Arthur)

Bantry (Mrs Dolly)
Battle (Superintendent)
Marple (Miss Jane)
Oliver (Mrs Ariadne)
Poirot (Hercule)

07 Ackroyd (Roger)
Haydock (Dr)

08 Hastings (Captain Arthur)

09 Beresford (Tommy)
Beresford (Tuppence)
Lempriere (Joan)
Protheroe (Colonel)

10 Clithering (Sir Henry)

13 Satterthwaite (Mr)

Christmas

Gifts for the Twelve Days of Christmas:

09 gold rings (5th)
10 French hens (3rd)
11 turtle doves (2nd)
12 calling birds (4th)

geese a-laying (6th)
pipers piping (11th)
13 ladies dancing (9th)
lords a-leaping (10th)

maids a-milking (8th)
14 swans a-swimming (7th)
16 drummers drumming (12th)
20 partridge in a pear tree (1st)

Santa's reindeer:

05 Comet
Cupid
Vixen

06 Dancer
Dasher
Donner

07 Blitzen
Prancer
Rudolph

Terms to do with Christmas include:

03 ivy
04 bell
card
crib
gift
king
Magi
Mary
Noël
putz
snow
star
Xmas

05 angel
carol
glogg
goose
holly
Jesus
punch

robin
waits
06 bauble
Befana
candle
donkey
Joseph
Kinara
manger
mummer
piñata
sleigh
stable
tinsel
turkey
wreath

07 chimney
cracker
glüwein
holiday

Lapland
pageant
present
Rudolph
Scrooge
snowman
stollen
wassail
wise man
Yule log

08 daft days
junkanoo
mince pie
Papa Noël
reindeer
shepherd
stocking
Yuletide

09 Bethlehem
chestnuts

John Canoe
Julinisse
level-coil
mistletoe
North Pole
panettone
pantomime
10 Babouschka
decoration
mulled wine
poinsettia
round robin

Santa Claus
St Nicholas
Twelfth Day
watch night
11 advent crown
carol singer
fairy lights
plum pudding
12 Advent candle
Midnight Mass
nativity play
Queen's Speech

Twelfth Night
13 Christmas cake
Christmas card
Christmas tree
Lord of Misrule
wrapping paper
14 advent calendar
Christmas bonus
Christmas party
white Christmas
15 Ebenezer Scrooge
Father Christmas

church

Church and cathedral parts include:

03 pew
04 apse
arch
font
nave
rood
tomb
05 aisle
altar
choir
crypt
porch
slype
spire
stall
stoup
tower
vault
06 adytum
arcade
atrium
belfry
chapel
chevet
corona
parvis

portal
pulpit
sedile
shrine
squint
vestry
07 almonry
chancel
frontal
gallery
lectern
lucarne
narthex
piscina
reredos
steeple
tambour
08 cloister
credence
crossing
keystone
parclose
pinnacle
predella
sacellum
sacristy

transept
09 antechoir
bell tower
graveyard
organ loft
sacrarium
sanctuary
sepulchre
stasidion
triforium
10 ambulatory
baptistery
bell screen
clerestory
diaconicon
fenestella
frithstool
misericord
presbytery
retrochoir
rood screen
12 chapterhouse
confessional
deambulatory
14 ringing chamber
schola cantorum

See also **cathedral; cemetery; religion**

cicada

Cicadas include:

05 Myer's
06 red-eye
09 Union Jack

10 blue prince
11 black prince
floury baker

greengrocer
green Monday
masked devil

12 floury miller
yellow Monday
13 double drummer

cigar, cigarette *see* tobacco

cinema

Cinema and theatre names include:

03 ABC
MGM
Rex
Rio
UCI
UGC
04 Gala
IMAX
Ritz
Roxy
05 Byron
Cameo
Forum
Grand
Kings
Metro
Odeon
Orion
Plaza
Regal
Royal
Scala
Tower
06 Albany
Apollo
Cannon
Casino
Curzon
Empire
Gaiety
Marina
Palace
Queens

Regent
Rialto
Robins
Tivoli
Virgin
07 Arcadia
Astoria
Capitol
Carlton
Central
Century
Circuit
Classic
Coronet
Embassy
Essoldo
Gaumont
Granada
La Scala
Locarno
Mayfair
Orpheum
Paragon
Phoenix
Picardy
08 Alhambra
Broadway
Charlton
Cineplex
Citizens
Colonial
Dominion
Electric

Everyman
Festival
Imperial
Landmark
Majestic
Memorial
Pavilion
The Cameo
Windmill
09 Alexandra
Cineworld
Filmhouse
Hollywood
Palladium
Paramount
Playhouse
10 Ambassador
Hippodrome
Lighthouse
Vue Cinemas
11 Her Majesty's
His Majesty's
New Victoria
Ster Century
12 Metropolitan
Picturedrome
Picturehouse
Thefilmworks
13 Picture Palace
Warner Village
14 Electric Palace
15 Screen on the Hill

See also **film**; **theatre**

Cinque Port

Cinque Ports and Limbs include:

03 Rye
04 Deal
limb
Lydd
05 baron
Dover
Hythe

07 Margate
08 Hastings
head port
portsmen
Ramsgate
Sandwich
09 Faversham

New Romney
Tenterden
10 Folkestone
Lord Warden
Winchelsea
13 confederation
15 corporate member

circle

Circles include:

03 lap
orb

04 ball
band
belt
coil
corn
crop
curl
disc
eddy
gyre
halo
hoop
hour
loop
oval
ring
turn

tyre

05 crown
cycle
dress
globe
grand
great
magic
mural
orbit
pitch
plate
polar
round
stone
upper
wheel

06 Arctic
circus

cordon
discus
girdle
rundle
saucer
sphere
spiral
tropic
vortex
wreath

07 annulet
annulus
circuit
compass
coronet
ellipse
equator
roundel
traffic

transit
turning
vicious

08 epicycle
gyration
meridian
rotation
roundure
striking
virtuous

09 Antarctic
perimeter
whirlpool
whirlwind

10 almacantar
almucantar
Circassian
revolution

13 circumference

See also **shape**

circus

Circus terms include:

03 boo
fun
lot
wig

04 band
Bozo
cage
clap
gags
jeff
Joey
lion
mime
nose
pole
pony
rein
ring
spec
tent
whip
zany

05 antic
arena
blues
camel
cheer
clown
comic

crowd
dwarf
freak
funny
grift
horse
laugh
llama
rubes
straw
towny
Tramp
trick

06 August
big top
canvas
dancer
exotic
hoop-la
houdah
howdah
humour
jester
juggle
make-up
parade
pie car
risley
squirt

stilts
tumble

07 acrobat
Auguste
balance
balloon
buffoon
butcher
caravan
costume
doniker
juggler
leotard
peanuts
Pierrot
popcorn
rigging
sawdust
speeler
spieler
trapeze
tumbler

08 Alley-Oop
Allez Oop
applause
audience
backyard
bale ring
ballyhoo

blowdown
calliope
carnival
children
chivaree
conjurer
conjuror
drum roll
elephant
guy lines
high wire
laughter
magician
mechanic
ring-side
shivaree
sideshow
tear down
unicycle

09 aerialist
bandwagon
charivari
clown suit
fire-eater
lion tamer
menagerie
rosinback
safety net
strongman

tightrope
tom-walker
Whiteface

10 acrobatics
acrobatism
Billy Smart
candy floss
circus hand
cloud swing
clown alley
custard pie
impresario
ringmaster
roustabout
somersault
spectators
trick-rider

See also **clown**

unicyclist

11 Arabian pony
carpet clown
cotton candy
entertainer
funambulate
funambulist
greasepaint
rope dancing
straightman
tent raising

12 escape artist
funambulator
liberty horse
Ringling Bros®
roll up! roll up!
stiltwalking

trick cyclist

13 bareback rider
contortionist
entertainment
equestrian act
Neat Whiteface
sleight-of-hand
trapeze artist

14 character clown
Cirque du Soleil
Joseph Grimaldi

15 Barnum and Bailey
Comedy Whiteface
European Auguste
jerry-come-tumble
three-ring circus

CIS

Commonwealth of Independent States members:

06 Russia
07 Armenia
Belarus

Georgia
Moldova
Ukraine

10 Azerbaijan
Kazakhstan
Kyrgyzstan

Tajikistan
Uzbekistan
12 Turkmenistan

city

Capital cities include:

04 Apia (Samoa)
Baku (Azerbaijan)
Dili (East Timor)
Doha (Qatar)
Juba (South Sudan)
Kiev (Ukraine)
Lima (Peru)
Lomé (Togo)
Malé (Maldives)
Oslo (Norway)
Riga (Latvia)
Rome (Italy)
Suva (Fiji)

05 Abuja (Nigeria)
Accra (Ghana)
Amman (Jordan)
Berne (Switzerland)
Cairo (Egypt)
Dakar (Senegal)
Dhaka (Bangladesh)
Hanoi (Vietnam)
Kabul (Afghanistan)
Koror (Palau)
La Paz (Bolivia)
Minsk (Belarus)
Paris (France)
Praia (Cape Verde)

Quito (Ecuador)
Rabat (Morocco)
Sana'a (Yemen)
Seoul (South Korea)
Sofia (Bulgaria)
Sucre (Bolivia)
Tokyo (Japan)
Tunis (Tunisia)
Vaduz (Liechtenstein)

06 Ankara (Turkey)
Asmara (Eritrea)
Astana (Kazakhstan)
Athens (Greece)
Bamako (Mali)
Bangui (Central African Republic)
Banjul (The Gambia)
Beirut (Lebanon)
Berlin (Germany)
Bissau (Guinea-Bissau)
Bogotá (Colombia)
Dodoma (Tanzania)
Dublin (Ireland)
Harare (Zimbabwe)
Havana (Cuba)
Kigali (Rwanda)
Lisbon (Portugal)
London (UK)

Luanda (Angola)
Lusaka (Zambia)
Madrid (Spain)
Majuro (Marshall Islands)
Malabo (Equatorial Guinea)
Manama (Bahrain)
Manila (Philippines)
Maputo (Mozambique)
Maseru (Lesotho)
Monaco (Monaco)
Moroni (Comoros)
Moscow (Russia)
Muscat (Oman)
Nassau (The Bahamas)
Niamey (Niger)
Ottawa (Canada)
Prague (Czech Republic)
Riyadh (Saudi Arabia)
Roseau (Dominica)
Skopje (Macedonia)
T'aipei (Taiwan)
Tarawa (Kiribati)
Tehran (Iran)
Tirana (Albania)
Vienna (Austria)
Warsaw (Poland)
Zagreb (Croatia)

07 Abidjan (Côte d'Ivoire)
Algiers (Algeria)
Baghdad (Iraq)
Bangkok (Thailand)
Beijing (China)
Bishkek (Kyrgyzstan)
Caracas (Venezuela)
Colombo (Sri Lanka)
Conakry (Guinea)
Cotonou (Benin)
El Aaiún (Western Sahara)
Honiara (Solomon Islands)
Jakarta (Indonesia)
Kampala (Uganda)
Managua (Nicaragua)
Mbabane (Swaziland)
Nairobi (Kenya)
Nicosia (Cyprus)
Palikir (Federated States of
Micronesia)
San José (Costa Rica)
São Tomé (São Tomé and
Príncipe)
St John's (Antigua and
Barbuda)
Tallinn (Estonia)
T'bilisi (Georgia)
Thimphu (Bhutan)
Tripoli (Libya)
Vilnius (Lithuania)
Yaoundé (Cameroon)

Yerevan (Armenia)
08 Abu Dhabi (United Arab
Emirates)
Ashgabat (Turkmenistan)
Asunción (Paraguay)
Belgrade (Serbia)
Belmopan (Belize)
Brasília (Brazil)
Brussels (Belgium)
Budapest (Hungary)
Canberra (Australia)
Cape Town (South Africa)
Castries (St Lucia)
Chisinau (Moldova)
Damascus (Syria)
Djibouti (Djibouti)
Dushanbe (Tajikistan)
Freetown (Sierra Leone)
Funafuti (Tuvalu)
Gaborone (Botswana)
Helsinki (Finland)
Khartoum (Sudan)
Kingston (Jamaica)
Kinshasa (Democratic
Republic of the Congo)
Laayoune (Western Sahara)
Lilongwe (Malawi)
Monrovia (Liberia)
N'Djamena (Chad)
New Delhi (India)
Port-Vila (Vanuatu)
Pretoria (South Africa)
Pristina (Kosovo)
Santiago (Chile)
Sarajevo (Bosnia and
Herzegovina)
Tashkent (Uzbekistan)
Valletta (Malta)
Victoria (Seychelles)
Windhoek (Namibia)

09 Amsterdam (The
Netherlands)
Bucharest (Romania)
Bujumbura (Burundi)
Islamabad (Pakistan)
Kathmandu (Nepal)
Kingstown (St Vincent and
the Grenadines)
Ljubljana (Slovenia)
Mogadishu (Somalia)
Naypyidaw (Myanmar)
Nuku'alofa (Tonga)
Phnom Penh (Cambodia)
Podgorica (Montenegro)
Port Louis (Mauritius)
Porto Novo (Benin)
Pyongyang (North Korea)

Reykjavík (Iceland)
San Marino (San Marino)
Singapore (Singapore)
St George's (Grenada)
Stockholm (Sweden)
Ulan Bator (Mongolia)
Vientiane (Laos)

10 Addis Ababa (Ethiopia)
Basseterre (St Kitts and
Nevis)
Bratislava (Slovakia)
Bridgetown (Barbados)
Copenhagen (Denmark)
Georgetown (Guyana)
Kuwait City (Kuwait)
Libreville (Gabon)
Luxembourg (Luxembourg)
Mexico City (Mexico)
Montevideo (Uruguay)
Nouakchott (Mauritania)
Panama City (Panama)
Paramaribo (Suriname)
Wellington (New Zealand)

11 Brazzaville (Congo)
Buenos Aires (Argentina)
Kuala Lumpur (Malaysia)
Ouagadougou (Burkina
Faso)
Port Moresby (Papua New
Guinea)
Port of Spain (Trinidad and
Tobago)
San Salvador (El Salvador)
Tegucigalpa (Honduras)
Vatican City (Vatican City)

12 Antananarivo (Madagascar)
Bloemfontein (South Africa)
Port-au-Prince (Haiti)
Santo Domingo
(Dominican Republic)
Tel Aviv-Jaffa (Israel)
Washington, DC (USA)
Yamoussoukro (Côte
d'Ivoire)

13 Guatemala City
(Guatemala)
Yaren District (Nauru)

14 Andorra la Vella (Andorra)

Ancient cities include:

02 Ur	Petra	Ephesus	**09** Byzantium
04 Acre	Saida	Megiddo	Cartagena
Axum	Sidon	Miletus	Epidaurus
Ebla	Tikal	Mycenae	Sukhothai
Nuzi	Uxmal	Nineveh	**10** Alexandria
Rome	**06** Athens	Paestum	Angkor Thom
Susa	Byblos	Plataea	Carchemish
Troy	Cyrene	Pompeii	Heliopolis
Tula	Jabneh	Samaria	Hierapolis
Tyre	Jamnia	Sybaris	Monte Albán
Uruk	Napata	Vergina	Persepolis
05 Aksum	Nippur	**08** Carthage	**11** Chichén Itzá
Argos	Sardis	Damascus	Herculaneum
Bosra	Shiloh	Hattusas	Machu Picchu
Bursa	Sparta	Hattusha	Polonnaruwa
Copán	Thebes	Kerkuane	Teotihuacán
Cuzco	Ugarit	Palenque	**12** Anuradhapura
Eridu	**07** Antioch	Pergamon	**13** Halicarnassus
Hatra	Babylon	Pergamum	**14** Constantinople
Huari	Bukhara	Sigiriya	
Mitla	Corinth	Tashkent	
Moche	El Tajín	Thysdrus	

Former names of cities include:

03 Edo (Tokyo)
04 York (Toronto)
05 Gorky (Nizhniy Novgorod)
    Keijo (Seoul)
    Tihwa (Urumqi)
06 Angora (Ankara)
    Berlin (Kitchener)
    Bombay (Mumbai)
    Bytown (Ottawa)
    Danzig (Gdansk)
    Madras (Chennai)
    Mukden (Shenyang)
    Peking (Beijing)
    Ryojun (Lüshun)
    Saigon (Ho Chi Minh City)
    Siking (Xian)
    Smyrna (Izmir)
07 Batavia (Jakarta)
    Benares (Varanasi)
    Bezmein (Abadan)
    Breslau (Wroclaw)
    Changan (Xian)
    Hanyang (Seoul)
    Kalinin (Tver)
    Songjin (Kimchaek)
08 Bathurst (Banjul)
    Calcutta (Kolkata)
    Fengtian (Shenyang)

    Fort Lamy (N'Djamena)
    Kishinev (Chisinau)
    Lyallpur (Faisalabad)
    Titograd (Podgorica)
09 Jesselton (Kota Kinabalu)
    Kingstown (Dún Laoghaire)
    Leninabad (Khujand)
    Leningrad (St Petersburg)
    Petrograd (St Petersburg)
    Salisbury (Harare)
    Tsaritsyn (Volgograd)
10 Gottwaldov (Zlín)
    Konigsberg (Kaliningrad)
    Kristiania (Oslo)
    Luluabourg (Kananga)
    Nova Lisboa (Huambo)
    Port Arthur (Lüshun)
    Queenstown (Cobh)
    Stalingrad (Volgograd)
    Sverdlovsk (Yekaterinburg)
    Titov Veles (Veles)
11 Christiania (Oslo)
    Livingstone (Maramba)
    Santa Isabel (Malabo)
    Stalinogród (Katowice)
    Sunda Kelapa (Jakarta)
12 Léopoldville (Kinshasa)
    New Amsterdam (New York)

Stanleyville (Kisangani)
13 Aleksandropol (Gyumri)
Karl-Marx-Stadt (Chemnitz)

14 Ciudad Trujillo (Santo Domingo)
Constantinople (Istanbul)

Cities and notable towns include:

02 Bo	Jixi	Tyre	Chita
LA	Kano	Umeå	Colón
NY	Kiel	Vasa	Conwy
03 Åbo	Kobe	Vigo	Cowes
Ayr	Köln	Waco	Crewe
Ely	Kota	Wick	Cuzco
Fès	Labé	Wien	Davao
Fez	La-sa	Wuhu	Davos
Gao	León	Wuxi	Delft
Hué	Linz	Xi'an	Delhi
Lae	Lódz	York	Derby
Niš	Lugo	Zibo	Dijon
NYC	Luik	Zörs	Dover
Pau	Lund	05 Adana	Duala
Qom	Lvov	Agaña	Dubai
Ufa	Metz	Ahvaz	Dukou
Ulm	Mold	Åland	Eilat
Vac	Mons	Al Ayn	Elche
Zug	Naas	Aosta	Essen
04 Acre	Naha	Aqaba	Eupen
Aden	Nara	Argos	Évora
Agra	Nice	Århus	Fiume
Ajme	Nuuk	Arica	Frome
Amoy	Oban	Arles	Fuxin
Bari	Oita	Arras	Genoa
Bath	Omsk	Aspen	Ghent
Bonn	Oran	Aswan	Gijón
Brno	Oulu	Ávila	Gomel
Bury	Pécs	Baden	Gorky
Caen	Pegu	Banff	Gouda
Cali	Perm	Baoji	Gweru
Cebu	Pisa	Basle	Hagen
Como	Pula	Basra	Haifa
Cork	Pune	Beira	Halle
Dazu	Rand	Belém	Hefei
Deal	Reno	Benxi	Hohot
Edam	Rhyl	Blida	Honan
Elat	Ruse	Blyth	Ichun
Eton	Ryde	Boise	Ieper
Faro	Safi	Bondi	Iwaki
Gand	Sale	Borga	Izmir
Gent	Salt	Bouar	Jaffa
Gifu	Sfax	Braga	Jedda
Graz	Sian	Breda	Jilin
Györ	Sion	Brest	Jinan
Homs	Soul	Bursa	Jinja
Hove	St-Lô	Busan	Kaédi
Hull	Suez	Cádiz	Kandy
Iasi	Sumy	Canea	Karaj
Icel	Tema	Cavan	Kazan
Ipoh	Thun	Ceuta	Kelso
Jima	Tula	Chiba	Kirov

Kitwe	Rouen	Agadir	Cuenca
Kochi	Rovno	Albany	Dalian
Konya	Rugby	Ålborg	Dallas
Köseg	Sakai	Aleppo	Da Nang
Kursk	Salem	Amiens	Danzig
Kyoto	Salta	Annaba	Daqing
Lagos	Sebha	Annecy	Darhan
Leeds	Ségou	Anshan	Darwin
Lewes	Sidon	Anvers	Datong
Lhasa	Siena	Anyang	Dayton
Liège	Skien	Arezzo	Denver
Lille	Sochi	Armagh	Dieppe
Limbe	Sopot	Arnhem	Douala
Luton	Split	Arusha	Dudley
Luxor	Suita	Ashdod	Duluth
Lyons	Surat	Atbara	Dundee
Mâcon	Suwon	At Taif	Durban
Mainz	Taegu	Austin	Durham
Malmö	Talca	Avarua	Durrës
Masan	Tampa	Baguio	El Gîza
Mecca	Tanga	Bangor	El Paso
Medan	Tanta	Bangui	Eugene
Miami	Tempe	Baotou	Evreux
Milan	Thane	Bastia	Exeter
Mitla	Thiès	Bengpu	Fatima
Mopti	Thule	Bergen	Fresno
Mosul	Tokyo	Bhopal	Frunze
Namen	Tomar	Bilbao	Fu-chou
Namur	Tomsk	Biloxi	Fushun
Nancy	Torun	Bitola	Fuzhou
Nasik	Tours	Bochum	Galway
Natal	Trier	Bolton	Gdansk
Ndola	Troon	Bombay	Gdynia
Nîmes	Truro	Bootle	Geneva
Ohrid	Tulsa	Boston	Gitega
Omagh	Tunja	Brasov	Grodno
Omaha	Turin	Bremen	Grozny
Omiya	Turku	Bruges	Guelph
Oryol	Tzu-po	Brugge	Guilin
Osaka	Udine	Burgos	Guimar
Otley	Ulsan	Buxton	Gujrat
Oujda	Urawa	Cairns	Guntur
Padua	Utica	Calais	Ha'apai
Parma	Vaasa	Callao	Hamina
Patan	Varna	Calmar	Handan
Patna	Vejle	Camden	Han-kou
Pavia	Vlorë	Campos	Harbin
Penza	Wells	Cancún	Harlem
Perth	Wigan	Cannes	Harlow
Plzen	Worms	Canton	Hebron
Ponce	Wuhan	Carlow	Hegang
Poole	Ypres	Casper	Himeji
Poona	Zadar	Chania	Hobart
Pusan	Zaria	Chi-nan	Howrah
Reims	Zarqa	Chonju	Huelva
Resit	**06** Aachen	Cochin	Ibadan
Ripon	Aarhus	Cracow	Ichang
Ronda	Agadez	Crosby	Inchon

Indore	Nagano	Sintra	Whitby
Jaffna	Nagoya	Skikda	Widnes
Jaipur	Nagpur	Sliema	Woking
Jarash	Nantes	Slough	Xiamen
Jarrow	Napier	Smyrna	Xining
Jeddah	Naples	Sokodé	Xuzhou
Jiddah	Narvik	Sousse	Yangku
Jilong	Newark	Soweto	Yantai
Juneau	Ningbo	Sparta	Yeovil
Kalmar	Nouméa	St Ives	Yichun
Kaluga	Odense	St John	Yunnan
Kankan	Odessa	St-Malo	Zabrze
Kanpur	Oldham	St Paul	Zigong
Kaolan	Olinda	Stroud	Zinder
Kassel	Oporto	Stuart	Zürich
Kaunas	Örebro	Suchow	Zwolle
Kendal	Osasco	Sukkur	**07** Aberfan
Khulna	Osijek	Suzhou	Airdrie
Kirkby	Ostend	Sydney	Ajaccio
Kirkuk	Oviedo	Szeged	Aligarh
Kosice	Oxford	Tabriz	Alma-Ata
Kraków	Padang	Tacoma	Alnwick
Kumasi	Paphos	Tadmur	Antibes
Kurgan	Pátrai	Taejon	Antioch
Lahore	Phuket	Tahoua	Antwerp
Lanark	Piatra	Tainan	Aracaju
Leiden	Pierre	Tamale	Atlanta
Le Mans	Pilsen	Tambov	Augusta
Leshan	Porvoo	Tarbes	Auxerre
Leuven	Potosí	Tarsus	Avignon
Leyden	Poznan	Ta-t'ung	Baalbek
London	Presov	Teruel	Badajoz
Lübeck	Puebla	Thurso	Bairiki
Lublin	Quebec	Tipasa	Banares
Ludlow	Queluz	Tobruk	Banbury
Lugano	Quetta	Toledo	Bandung
Maceio	Raipur	Toluca	Baoding
Madras	Rajkat	Topeka	Barnaul
Makale	Rajkot	Torbay	Barossa
Málaga	Ranchi	Toulon	Bayamón
Malang	Recife	Toyama	Bedford
Manaus	Redcar	Toyota	Beeston
Mantua	Reggio	Tralee	Beijing
Matrah	Regina	Trento	Belfast
Medina	Rennes	Treves	Benares
Meerut	Rheims	Tromsø	Bendigo
Mekele	Rijeka	Troyes	Berbera
Meknès	Ryazan	Tsinan	Bergama
Meshed	Saigon	Tubruq	Bergamo
Mobile	Salala	Tucson	Bexhill
Mukden	Samara	Tyumen	Bizerta
Multan	Santos	Urumqi	Blarney
Mumbai	Schwyz	Vannes	Bologna
Muncie	Sefadu	Vargas	Bolzano
Munich	Sendai	Venice	Boulder
Murcia	Shiraz	Verona	Bourges
Mysore	Silves	Viborg	Braemar
Nablus	Sining	Weimar	Brescia

Bristol	Geelong	Le Havre	Orleans
Bryansk	Glasgow	Leipzig	Ostrava
Buffalo	Goiânia	Lerwick	Pahsien
Burnley	Gosport	Liberia	Paisley
Cáceres	Granada	Limoges	Palermo
Calgary	Grimsby	Lincoln	Panshan
Calicut	Guiyang	Lipetsk	Pattaya
Caracas	Gwalior	Liuzhou	Peebles
Cardiff	Gwangju	Livorno	Penrith
Catania	Haerbin	Logroño	Perugia
Chalcis	Halifax	Louvain	Phoenix
Changan	Hamburg	Lucerne	Piraeus
Cheadle	Hamhumg	Lucknow	Pistoia
Cheddar	Hamhung	Lugansk	Pitesti
Chelsea	Hanover	Lumbini	Plovdiv
Chengde	Harwich	Luoyang	Poltava
Chengdu	Henzada	Machida	Popayán
Cheng-tu	Heredia	Madison	Portree
Chennai	Houston	Madurai	Potsdam
Chester	Huaibei	Malvern	Preston
Chicago	Huainan	Manzini	Prizren
Chifeng	Ipswich	Maracay	Qingdao
Chi-lung	Iquique	Marburg	Qiqihar
Chongju	Iquitos	Margate	Quimper
Chungho	Irkutsk	Mashhad	Raleigh
Clonmel	Isfahan	Massawa	Randers
Coblenz	Ivanovo	Matlock	Rangoon
Coimbra	Izhevsk	Matsudo	Ravenna
Cologne	Jackson	Melilla	Reading
Concord	Jericho	Memphis	Redwood
Córdoba	Jiamusi	Mendoza	Reigate
Corinth	Jiaozuo	Mildura	Roanoke
Corinto	Jinzhou	Mindelo	Rosario
Corunna	Jodhpur	Miskolc	Rostock
Crawley	Kaesong	Mitsiwa	Rotorua
Dandong	Kaifeng	Mogilev	Roubaix
Detroit	Kalinin	Mombasa	Runcorn
Devizes	Kananga	Morpeth	Sagunto
Donegal	Karachi	Münster	Salamis
Donetsk	Kassala	Nanjing	Salerno
Douglas	Kayseri	Nanking	Salford
Dresden	Keelung	Nanning	Sandown
Dundalk	Kenitra	Nantong	San José
Dunedin	Keswick	Newbury	Santa Fe
Dunkirk	Kharkov	Newport	São Luis
Durango	Kherson	Newquay	Sapporo
Entebbe	Koblenz	New Ross	Saransk
Erdenet	Kolding	New York	Saratov
Esbjerg	Kolkata	Niigata	Sassari
Evesham	Kuching	Niterói	Seattle
Exmouth	Kunming	Norfolk	Segovia
Falkirk	Kutaisi	Norwich	Setúbal
Fareham	Lansing	Novi Sad	Seville
Ferrara	Lanzhou	Oakland	Shannon
Foochow	La Plata	Okayama	Shantou
Fukuoka	Larnaca	Okinawa	Shihezi
Funchal	Latakia	Olympia	Shikoku
Ganzhou	Leghorn	Orlando	Shkodër

Sialkot	Zwickau	Columbia	Iowa City
Sinuiju	**08** Aberdeen	Columbus	Istanbul
Songnam	Acapulco	Contagem	Jabalpur
Spokane	Adelaide	Coventry	Jaboatoa
Spoleto	Akureyri	Culiacán	Kairouan
Staines	Alajuela	Curitiba	Kanazawa
Stanley	Albacete	Dartford	Kandahar
St Denis	Alicante	Dearborn	Karlsbad
St Louis	Amarillo	Debrecen	Katowice
Sudbury	Amritsar	Djakarta	Kawasaki
Sumgait	Arbroath	Dortmund	Keflavik
Swansea	Arequipa	Drogheda	Kemerovo
Swindon	Auckland	Duisburg	Kilkenny
Taiyuan	Augsburg	Dumfries	Kirkwall
Tampere	Aviemore	Dunhuang	Kismaayo
Tampico	Ayia Napa	Dunleary	Klosters
Tangier	Ballarat	Durgapur	Kolhapur
Táranto	Banghazi	Dzhambul	Konstanz
Taunton	Bareilly	Ebbw Vale	Koriyama
Tel Aviv	Barnsley	Edmonton	Kuei-yang
Telford	Bathurst	El Kharga	Kumamoto
Tétouan	Bayreuth	Elsinore	Laâyoune
Tianjin	Beauvais	Europort	La Laguna
Tijuana	Belgorod	Falmouth	Las Vegas
Tilburg	Benghazi	Florence	Lausanne
Tilbury	Benguela	Flushing	Legoland
Tlemcen	Benidorm	Freeport	Leskovac
Tonghua	Besançon	Fribourg	Liaoyang
Toronto	Bhadgaon	Fujisawa	Liaoyuan
Torquay	Biarritz	Fukuyama	Limassol
Tournai	Bismarck	Gaoxiong	Limerick
Trenton	Blantyre	Gisborne	Llanelli
Trieste	Bobruysk	Gorlovka	Londrina
Tucumán	Bordeaux	Grantham	Longford
Ulan-Ude	Boulogne	Grasmere	Lüderitz
Uppsala	Bradford	Greenock	Ludhiana
Utrecht	Braganza	Grenoble	Lyallpur
Ventnor	Brighton	Guernica	Makassar
Vicenza	Brindisi	Hachioji	Mandalay
Vitebsk	Brisbane	Haiphong	Mannheim
Vitosha	Bulawayo	Hakodate	Marbella
Walsall	Burgundy	Hamilton	Mariupal
Warwick	Cagliari	Hangchow	Mariupol
Watford	Calcutta	Hangzhou	Mayaguez
Weifang	Campinas	Hannover	Mazatlán
Wenzhou	Carlisle	Hartford	Medellín
Wexford	Cebu City	Hastings	Mercedes
Wichita	Changsha	Hengyang	Mexicali
Windsor	Chartres	Hereford	Mogilyov
Wrexham	Chemnitz	Hertford	Montreal
Wroclaw	Chepstow	Hirakata	Montreux
Wuhsien	Cheyenne	Holyhead	Montrose
Yakeshi	Chiclayo	Holywell	Mufulira
Yichang	Chimbote	Hong Kong	Mulhouse
Yingkou	Chimkent	Honolulu	Murmansk
Yonkers	Ching-tao	Huangshi	Myingyan
Zermatt	Chongjin	Hunjiang	Nagasaki
Zhuzhou	Clevedon	Ichikawa	Namangan

Nanchang
Nazareth
Newhaven
New Haven
Nijmegen
Novgorod
Nuneaton
Nürnberg
Oak Ridge
Omdurman
Oostende
Orenburg
Oswestry
Pago Pago
Pamplona
Panchiao
Pasadena
Pavlodar
Penzance
Peshawar
Piacenza
Ploiesti
Plymouth
Poitiers
Portland
Portrush
Port Said
Pristina
Ramsgate
Rancagua
Randstad
Redditch
Richmond
Road Town
Rochdale
Rockford
Roskilde
Rosslare
Sabadell
Salonica
Salonika
Saltillo
Salvador
Salzburg
San Diego
Santa Ana
Santarém
São Paulo
Satu Mare
Savannah
Schwerin
Semarang
Shanghai
Shanklin
Shaoguan
Shenyang
Shizuoka
Sholapur

Silk Road
Simbirsk
Skegness
Smolensk
Solihull
Solingen
Sorocaba
Southend
Srinagar
Stafford
St Albans
Stamford
St David's
St Gallen
St Helens
St Helier
Stirling
St Moritz
Stockton
Strabane
St-Tropez
Subotica
Suicheng
Surabaya
Swan Hill
Syracuse
Szczecin
Taganrog
Taichung
Tamworth
Tangshan
Teesside
Teresina
Thetford
Thonburi
Tiberias
Tientsin
Timbuktu
Titograd
Tolyatti
Tongeren
Toulouse
Toyohasi
Toyonaka
Trujillo
Tsingtao
Tübingen
Uleaborg
Ullapool
Vadodara
Valencia
Valletta
Varanasi
Veracruz
Vila Real
Vinnitsa
Vittoria
Vladimir

Voronezh
Wakayama
Wallasey
Wallsend
Warangal
Weymouth
Winnipeg
Worthing
Würzburg
Xiangfan
Xiangtan
Xinxiang
Yangchow
Yangquan
Yangzhou
Yinchuan
Yin-hsien
Yokohama
Yokosuko
Yorktown
Yukosuko
Zakopane
Zanzibar
Zhitomir

09 Adis Abeba
Ahmadabad
Alba Iulia
Albufeira
Aldershot
Algeciras
Allahabad
Amagasaki
Ambleside
Anchorage
Annapolis
Archangel
Asahikawa
Astrakhan
Audenarde
Aylesbury
Bakhtaran
Baltimore
Bangalore
Barcelona
Beersheba
Berbérati
Bethlehem
Bhavnagar
Bialystok
Blackburn
Blackpool
Bossangoa
Botany Bay
Brunswick
Bydgoszcz
Cambridge
Cartagena
Castlebar

Changchun
Changzhou
Charleroi
Charlotte
Chengchow
Cherbourg
Chernobyl
Chiang Mai
Chihuahua
Choluteca
Chongqing
Chungking
Cleveland
Colwyn Bay
Constance
Constanta
Davao City
Des Moines
Doncaster
Dordrecht
Dubrovnik
Dudelange
Dumbarton
Dungannon
Dunstable
Eastleigh
Edinburgh
Eindhoven
Eskisehir
Esztergom
Fairbanks
Famagusta
Faridabad
Fishguard
Fleetwood
Fortaleza
Fort Worth
Frankfort
Frankfurt
Fremantle
Funabashi
Galveston
Gateshead
Gaziantep
Gippsland
Gold Coast
Gorakhpur
Gravesend
Greenwich
Groningen
Guangzhou
Guarulhos
Guayaquil
Guildford
Hallstatt
Hamamatsu
Harrogate
Haslemere

Helsingør	Middleton	Sundsvall	Cluj-Napoca
Heraklion	Milwaukee	Surakarta	Coatbridge
Hilversum	Monterrey	Takamatsu	Cochabamba
Hiroshima	Moradabad	Takatsuki	Coimbatore
Humpty Doo	Morecambe	Tarragona	Colchester
Hyderabad	Mullingar	Tenkodogo	Concepción
Immingham	Nashville	T'ien-ching	Darjeeling
Innsbruck	Neuchâtel	Timisoara	Darlington
Inverness	Newcastle	Toamasina	Diyarbakir
Ismailiya	Newmarket	Togliatti	Dorchester
Jalandhar	Nikolayev	Toowoomba	Düsseldorf
Jamestown	Nuremberg	Trondheim	Dzerzhinsk
Jerusalem	Ogbomosho	Tullamore	Eastbourne
Johnstone	Osnabrück	Ulyanovsk	El Mansoura
Jönköping	Palembang	Vancouver	Faisalabad
Kagoshima	Pamporovo	Velingrad	Felixstowe
Kamchatka	Perpignan	Vicksburg	Folkestone
Kaohsiung	Peterhead	Volgograd	Fray Bentos
Karaganda	Pingxiang	Wakefield	Galashiels
Karlsruhe	Pontianak	Walvis Bay	George Town
Kawaguchi	Port Natal	Waterford	Gillingham
Killarney	Port Sudan	Wiesbaden	Glenrothes
Kimberley	Pressburg	Wimbledon	Gloucester
King's Lynn	Prestwick	Wolfsburg	Goose Green
Kirkcaldy	Princeton	Worcester	Gothenburg
Kisangani	Qinghai Hu	Wuppertal	Gujranwala
Kishinyov	Querétaro	Xiangyang	Haddington
Kitchener	Riverside	Yaroslavl	Harrisburg
Kitzbühel	Rochester	Zamboanga	Hartlepool
Kórinthos	Rotherham	Zaozhuang	Heidelberg
Kozhikode	Rotterdam	Zhengzhou	Hermosillo
Krasnodar	Rovaniemi	Zhenjiang	Hildesheim
Krivoy Rog	Salisbury	Zrenjanin	Huntingdon
Kurashiki	Samarkand	**10** Alexandria	Huntsville
Kuybyshev	San Miguel	Baton Rouge	Jamshedpur
Kwang-chow	Santa Cruz	Belize City	Jingdezhen
Lancaster	Santander	Birkenhead	João Pessoa
Las Cruces	Saragossa	Birmingham	Juiz de Fora
Leicester	Saskatoon	Bridgeport	Kakopetria
Lexington	Shanchung	Bridgwater	Kalgoorlie
Lichfield	Sheerness	Broken Hill	Kansas City
Liverpool	Sheffield	Caernarvon	Kenilworth
Llangefni	Sioux City	Caerphilly	Khabarovsk
Long Beach	South Bend	Canterbury	Kilmarnock
Lowestoft	Southport	Carmarthen	Kitakyushu
Lymington	Southwark	Carnoustie	Kompong Som
Magdeburg	St Andrews	Carson City	Lake Placid
Mahajanga	Stavanger	Casablanca	Las Piedras
Maidstone	Stavropol	Chandigarh	Launceston
Makeyevka	St-Étienne	Charleston	Leeuwarden
Mamoudzan	Stevenage	Cheboksary	Letchworth
Manizales	St-Nazaire	Chelmsford	Linlithgow
Mansfield	Stockport	Cheltenham	Little Rock
Maracaibo	Stornoway	Cheng-hsien	Liupanshui
Maralinga	St-Quentin	Chichester	Livingston
Marrakesh	Stranraer	Chittagong	Llangollen
Matsuyama	Stuttgart	Cienfuegos	Los Angeles
Melbourne	Sukhothai	Cincinnati	Louisville

Lubumbashi
Luluabourg
Maastricht
Maidenhead
Manchester
Marseilles
Medjugorje
Miami Beach
Monte Carlo
Montego Bay
Montgomery
Montpelier
Mostaganem
Motherwell
Mudanjiang
New Orleans
Nottingham
Nouadhibou
Nova Iguacu
Oranjestad
Oudenaarde
Palmerston
Petersburg
Pittsburgh
Pontefract
Portishead
Portsmouth
Providence
Quezon City
Quinnipiac
Rawalpindi
Regensburg
Sacramento
Sagamihara
San Antonio
San Ignacio
Santa Marta
Santo André
São Gonçalo
Scunthorpe
Sebastopol
Shepparton
Shreveport
Shrewsbury
Simferapol
Simferopol
Sioux Falls
Södertälje
Strasbourg
Sunderland
Sverdlovsk
Talcahuano
Tammerfors
Tananarive
Thunder Bay
Townsville
Trivandrum
Trowbridge

Tsaochuang
Utsunomiya
Valladolid
Valparaíso
Vijayawada
Viña del Mar
Vlissingen
Wadi Medani
Wagga Wagga
Warrington
Washington
Whitehorse
Wilmington
Winchester
Windermere
Winterthur
Wittenberg
Wollongong
Workington
Yogyakarta
Yoshkar Ola
Zaporozhye

11 Aberystwyth
Albuquerque
Antofagasta
Bahía Blanca
Banjarmasin
Basingstoke
Bhilai Nagar
Bognor Regis
Bournemouth
Brandenburg
Bremerhaven
Bridlington
Broadstairs
Brownsville
Bucaramanga
Campo Grande
Carcassonne
Charlestown
Chattanooga
Chelyabinsk
Cherepovets
Cirencester
Cleethorpes
Cockermouth
Coney Island
Conisbrough
Constantine
Cumbernauld
Dar es Salaam
Differdange
Downpatrick
Dunfermline
Enniskillen
Farnborough
Fort William
Francistown

Fraserburgh
Fredericton
Glastonbury
Grangemouth
Guadalajara
Guisborough
Hälsingborg
Helsingborg
Helsingfors
High Wycombe
Johor Baharu
Juan-les-Pins
Kaliningrad
Kampong Saom
Karlovy Vary
Kompong Saom
Komsomolosk
Krasnoyarsk
Lianyungang
Londonderry
Lossiemouth
Makhachkala
Mar del Plata
Medicine Hat
Medway Towns
Minneapolis
Montpellier
Narayanganj
Newport News
New York City
Nishinomiya
Nizhny Tagil
Northampton
Novosibirsk
Palm Springs
Pointe-Noire
Polonnaruwa
Port Augusta
Porto Alegre
Prestonpans
Punta Arenas
Qinhuangdao
Resistencia
Rockhampton
Rostov-on-Don
Saarbrücken
Scarborough
Southampton
Spanish Town
Springfield
Stourbridge
Szombathely
Tallahassee
Trincomalee
Tselinograd
Vladivostok
Westminster
White Plains

Wu-lu-k'o-mu-shi
Yellowknife
Zhangjiakou

12 Alice Springs
Anuradhapura
Atlantic City
Barquisimeto
Barranquilla
Beverly Hills
Bloemfontein
Buenaventura
Caloocan City
Chesterfield
Christchurch
Ciudad Juárez
East Kilbride
Great Malvern
Higashiosaka
Hubli-Dharwar
Huddersfield
Indianapolis
Jacksonville
Johannesburg
Keetmanshoop
Kota Kinabalu
Kristianstad
Léopoldville
Lisdoonvarna
Loughborough
Luang Prabang
Ludwigshafen
Macclesfield
Magnitogorsk
Mazar-e-Sharif
Milton Keynes
New Amsterdam
Nizhniy Tagil
Novokuznetsk
Oklahoma City
Petaling Jaya
Peterborough
Philadelphia
Pingdingshan
Pointe-à-Pitre
Ponta Delgada
Port Harcourt
Puerto Cortes
Rio de Janeiro
Rostov-na-Donu
Salt Lake City
San Cristobal
San Francisco
San Pedro Sula
San Sebastian
Santa Barbara
Schaffhausen
Shijiazhuang
Shuangyashan

Sidi bel Abbès
Skelmersdale
South Shields
Speightstown
Stanleyville
St Catherines
Stoke-on-Trent
St Petersburg
Tel Aviv-Jaffa
Tennant Creek
Thessaloníki
Trichinopoly
Ujung Pandang
Villahermosa
West Bromwich
Williamsburg
Winston-Salem
13 Aix-en-Provence
Belo Horizonte
Bobo-Dioulasso

Charlottetown
Ciudad Guayana
Duque de Caxias
Ellesmere Port
Epsom and Ewell
Great Yarmouth
Ho Chi Minh City
Jefferson City
Kidderminster
Kirkcudbright
Kirkintilloch
Leamington Spa
Lytham St Anne's
Middlesbrough
Ordzhonikidze
Port Elizabeth
Portlaoighise
Quezaltenango
Ribeirão Prêto
San Bernardino

San Luis Potosí
Semipalatinsk
Sihanoukville
Veliko Turnovo
Virginia Beach
Visakhapatnam
Wolverhampton
Yekaterinburg
Zamboanga City
Zlatni Pyasaci
14 Andorra-la-Vella
Dnepropetrovsk
Elisabethville
Feira de Santana
Hemel Hempstead
Henley-on-Thames
Louangphrabang
Santiago de Cuba
Shihchiachuang
Stockton-on-Tees

Székesfehérvár
Tunbridge Wells
Ust-Kamenogorsk
Voroshilovgrad
15 Barrow-in-Furness
Burton-upon-Trent
Charlotte Amalie
Charlottesville
Chester-le-Street
Clermont-Ferrand
Colorado Springs
Frankfurt am Main
Netzahaulcoyotl
Nizhniy Novgorod
Palma de Mallorca
Palmerston North
Sekondi-Takoradi
Shoubra el-Kheima
Sutton Coldfield
Weston-super-Mare

See also **Africa**; **The Americas**; **Asia**; **Australasia**; **Australia**; **Austria**; **Balkans**; **Belgium**; **Canada**; **Caribbean**; **China**; **Czech Republic**; **Denmark**; **Europe**; **Finland**; **France**; **Germany**; **Greece**; **India**; **Ireland**; **Italy**; **Japan**; **Low Countries**; **Mexico**; **Middle East**; **The Netherlands**; **New Zealand**; **Norway**; **Portugal**; **Russia**; **South-east Asia**; **Spain**; **Sweden**; **Switzerland**; **town**; **United Kingdom**; **United States of America**

clan *see* **Scottish**

Clare, John (1793–1864)

Significant works include:

03 'I Am!' (c.1840)
05 'Decay'
11 'The Flitting' (1832)
12 *The Rural Muse* (1835)
'Remembrances' (c.1832)

18 *The Village Minstrel* (1821)
'An Invite, to Eternity'
20 *The Shepherd's Calendar* (1827)
37 *Poems Descriptive of Rural Life and Scenery* (1820)

classical *see* musician

classification

Classifications of living organisms include:

05 class
genus
order

06 domain
empire
family

phylum
07 kingdom
species

08 division

Kingdoms, domains and empires include:

05 fungi
06 monera
plants

07 animals
archaea
08 bacteria

protista
10 eubacteria
eukaryotes

11 prokaryotes
14 archaebacteria

Classes of living organisms include:

04 Aves	**09** Arachnida	**11** Cephalopoda
07 Insecta	Bryopsida	**12** Malacostraca
08 Amphibia	Pinopsida	**13** Magnoliopsida
Bivalvia	**10** Gastropoda	
Mammalia	Liliopsida	

cleaning

Cleaning products include:

04 soap	shower gel	**12** disinfectant
06 bleach	sugar soap	**13** paint-stripper
polish	**10** bubble bath	washing powder
07 shampoo	soap powder	**14** scouring powder
solvent	turpentine	
09 detergent	**11** white spirit	**15** washing-up liquid

clerical vestment

Clerical vestments include:

03 alb	mitre	chimere	scapular
04 cope	scarf	maniple	skullcap
cowl	stole	pallium	surplice
hood	**06** mantle	soutane	yarmulka
05 amice	rochet	tallith	**09** dog-collar
cotta	tippet	tunicle	**10** Geneva gown
ephod	wimple	**08** chasuble	**11** Geneva bands
frock	**07** biretta	dalmatic	**14** clerical collar
habit	cassock	mozzetta	

climbing *see* mountaineering

cloak

Cloaks include:

04 capa	galabea	galabiah
05 amice	galabia	gallabea
grego	jellaba	gallabia
jelab	korowai	himation
manta	manteel	mantelet
pilch	mantlet	mantilla
sagum	paenula	palliate
shawl	pelisse	**09** djellabah
talma	pluvial	gabardine
06 abolla	rocklay	gaberdine
capote	rokelay	gallabeah
dolman	sarafan	gallabiah
domino	**08** capuchin	gallabieh
poncho	cardinal	gallabiya
visite	djellaba	**10** gallabiyah
07 chlamys	galabeah	gallabiyeh

| paludament | **11** buffalo robe | **12** mousquetaire |
| roquelaure | | paludamentum |

clock

Clocks and watches include:

03 fob	**06** atomic	pendant	**09** repeating
Tim	cuckoo	sundial	**10** travelling
04 ring	mantel	**08** analogue	**11** chronograph
stop	quartz	carriage	chronometer
05 alarm	**07** bracket	longcase	grandfather
wrist	digital	speaking	grandmother

Clock and watch parts include:

03 bob	pendulum	wheel train
eye	set lever	winding key
key	top plate	**11** barrel pivot
LCD	**09** back plate	bottom plate
peg	case screw	bridge screw
pin	clock face	centre wheel
04 case	cock screw	check spring
dial	crown gear	clutch lever
face	fusee stop	crutch screw
gear	hour wheel	entry pallet
hook	main wheel	escape wheel
pawl	rating nut	fourth wheel
stem	regulator	hinged bezel
05 bezel	return bar	lever bridge
click	steady pin	minute track
cover	stop screw	minute wheel
fusee	stud screw	motion works
gears	**10** balance cap	pallet screw
glass	banking pin	pendulum rod
jewel	bottom door	ratchet pawl
strap	castle gear	wheel bridge
wheel	click screw	**12** balance pivot
06 anchor	click wheel	balance wheel
arbour	clock train	barrel arbour
barrel	cover plate	cannon pinion
bridge	crown wheel	detent spring
chaton	dial washer	dial foot hole
clutch	escapement	escape pinion
collet	exit pallet	keyless works
crutch	front plate	pallet arbour
pallet	fusee chain	pull-out piece
pillar	fusee pivot	ratchet screw
pinion	hand collet	ratchet wheel
screws	hour marker	safety roller
wheels	mainspring	**13** anti-shock unit
winder	minute hand	balance spring
07 back box	pallet cock	bottom door key
battery	pallet fork	hour hand screw
ratchet	second hand	impulse roller
08 dial foot	third wheel	lenticular bob
hour hand	train wheel	quartz crystal
	watch glass	

regulator boot
set lever screw
setting bridge
tension spring
winding pinion

14 escape movement
fusee stop screw
quartz movement
regulator index

15 balance assembly
minute wheel cock
minute wheel post
pallet cock screw

clothes

Clothes include:

03 aba
bra
PJs
tie
top

04 501s®
abba
belt
body
cape
gown
kilt
muff
sari
slip
sock
suit
sulu
toga
veil
vest

05 abaya
burka
cloak
cords
dhoti
dress
frock
glove
hoody
ihram
jeans
kanzu
Levis®
lungi
pants
parka
ruana
scarf
shawl
shift
shirt
shrug
skirt
smock
stole
teddy
thong
tunic

06 basque
bikini
blouse
bodice
boorka
bow tie
boxers
braces
briefs
caftan
corset
cravat
denims
dirndl
fleece
garter
girdle
hoodie
jersey
jilbab
jubbah
jumper
kaross
kimono
mitten
poncho
samfoo
sarong
shorts
slacks
tabard
tights
T-shirt

07 catsuit
crop top
doublet
g-string
hosiery
jammies
jimjams
leotard
muffler
necktie
nightie
overall
panties
pyjamas
singlet
sweater

tank top
twinset
uniform
vest top
wet suit
yashmak
Y-fronts

08 bathrobe
bedsocks
breeches
camisole
cardigan
culottes
earmuffs
flannels
guernsey
hipsters
hot pants
jodhpurs
jumpsuit
leggings
lingerie
negligee
pashmina
pinafore
polo neck
pullover
swimsuit
tee-shirt
trousers

09 balaclava
bed-jacket
brassière
coveralls
dishdasha
dress suit
dungarees
hair shirt
housecoat
jockstrap
long johns
mini skirt
outerwear
pantihose
petticoat
plus-fours
polo shirt
salopette
separates

shahtoosh
shell suit
Sloppy Joe
stockings
tracksuit
underwear
waistcoat

10 boiler suit
Capri pants
cargo pants
cummerbund
dinner-gown
drainpipes
dress shirt
flying suit
leg warmers
lounge suit
nightdress
nightshirt
romper suit
rugby shirt

string vest
suspenders
sweat-shirt
turtleneck
underpants
wife-beater

11 bell-bottoms
board shorts
boiled shirt
boxer-shorts
eveningwear
leisure suit
morning suit
pencil skirt
thermal vest
trouser suit

12 body stocking
camiknickers
divided skirt
dressing-gown
evening dress

palazzo pants
pedal-pushers
shirtwaister

13 Bermuda shorts
cycling shorts
liberty bodice
pinafore skirt
shalwar-kameez
suspender belt

14 bathing costume
combat trousers
double-breasted
French knickers
board shorts
jogging bottoms
single-breasted
swimming trunks
three-piece suit

15 swimming costume

See also **boot**; **clerical vestment**; **cloak**; **coat**; **dress**; **fashion**; **fur**; **hat**; **scarf**; **tie**; **underwear**

cloud

Clouds include:

06 cirrus (Ci)
07 cumulus (Cu)
stratus (St)
11 altocumulus (Ac)

altostratus (As)
12 cirrocumulus (Cc)
cirrostratus (Cs)
cumulonimbus (Cb)

nimbostratus (Ns)
13 stratocumulus (Sc)

clown

Clowns include:

04 Bozo (Bob Bell, 1922–97, US)
Coco (Nicolai Poliakoff, 1900–74, Latvian)
Hobo
Joey (Joseph Grimaldi, 1779–1837, English)
07 Pierrot (Commedia del Arté)
08 Grimaldi (Joseph; 1779–1837, English)
Owl-glass (German folklore)

Trinculo (The Tempest, 1623, William
Shakespeare)
09 Owle-glass (German folklore)
10 Howleglass (German folklore)
Owlspiegle (German folklore)
11 Little Tramp (Charlie Chaplin, 1889–1977,
English)

club

Club names include:

03 MCC
Ski
04 Arts
Turf
05 Buck's
Naval
06 Alpine

Cotton
Drones
Kennel
Kitcat
Pratt's
Queen's
Reform
Rotary

Savage
Savile
White's
07 Almack's
Authors'
Boodle's
Brooks's
Canning

Carlton
Country
Farmers
Garrick
Groucho
Kiwanis
Leander
Railway
Variety
08 Hell-fire
National
Oriental
Portland
09 Athenaeum

Beefsteak
East India
Green Room
Lansdowne
Wig and Pen
10 Caledonian
City Livery
Crockford's
Flyfishers'
Hurlingham
Oddfellows
Roehampton
Travellers
11 Army and Navy

Arts Theatre
Chelsea Arts
12 Anglo-Belgian
City of London
London Rowing
New Cavendish
Thames Rowing
13 Royal Air Force
14 American Women's
City University
15 National Liberal
Royal Automobile
Victory Services

Club types include:

03 fan
job
04 book
glee
golf
05 field
goose
slate

strip
yacht
youth
06 bridge
health
tennis
07 country
pudding

singles
09 Christmas
warehouse
10 investment
12 Darby and Joan

Clubs include:

03 bar
04 cosh
mace

polt
05 staff
stick

06 cudgel
07 bourdon
08 bludgeon

trunnion
09 blackjack
truncheon

See also **golf**

coat

Coats include:

03 box
car
fur
mac
04 baju
buff
cape
jack
jump
maxi
midi
over
pink
rain
sack
tail
05 acton
cimar

cymar
drape
dress
frock
gilet
great
grego
jupon
lammy
loden
parka
sayon
wamus
06 achkan
Afghan
anorak
Basque
blazer

bolero
cagoul
covert
dolman
duffel
duster
fleece
jacket
jerkin
kagool
kagoul
kirtle
lammie
reefer
riding
sacque
sports
tabard
taberd

trench
tuxedo
Zouave
07 Barbour®
blanket
blouson
cagoule
cutaway
kagoule
Mae West
matinée
morning
overall
snorkel
surtout
swagger
vareuse
zamarra

zamarro
08 Burberry®
camisole
gambeson
haqueton
mackinaw
sherwani
09 bed jacket
gabardine
gaberdine
hacqueton
macintosh
Mao-jacket

newmarket
pea-jacket
petticoat
redingote
shortgown
10 body-warmer
bumfreezer
bush jacket
carmagnole
claw-hammer
Eton jacket
flak jacket
half-kirtle
life jacket

mackintosh
mess jacket
roundabout
windjammer
11 biker jacket
puffa jacket
shell jacket
swallowtail
Windbreaker®
windcheater
12 bomber jacket
combat jacket
dinner jacket

donkey jacket
lumberjacket
monkey jacket
Prince Albert
pyjama jacket
safari jacket
sports jacket
straitjacket
13 hacking jacket
matinee jacket
Norfolk jacket
reefing-jacket
14 shooting jacket

cocktail

Cocktails include:

04 Sour
05 Bronx
06 eggnog
Gimlet
Mai tai
mimosa
mojito
Rickey
Rob Roy
07 Bellini
Collins
Martini®
negroni
pink gin

Sazerac®
Sidecar
Slammer
Stinger
08 Acapulco
Brown Cow
Bullshot
Daiquiri
Pink Lady
salty dog
snowball
09 buck's fizz
Kir Royale
long vodka
Manhattan

Margarita
pisco sour
Rusty Nail
Sea Breeze
whisky mac
White Lady
10 Bloody Mary
blue lagoon
Caipirinha
Horse's Neck
margharita
Moscow Mule
piña colada
Tom Collins
whisky sour

11 black velvet
gin-and-tonic
gloom raiser
Screwdriver
12 Black Russian
Cosmopolitan
Old Fashioned
White Russian
13 Planter's Punch
14 American Beauty
Singapore Sling
tequila slammer
Tequila Sunrise
15 Brandy Alexander

See also **drink**

code *see* **air travel; country; United States of America; vehicle**

coffee

Coffee roasts and blends include:

04 Java
05 decaf
06 filter
ground

Kenyan
07 Arabica
instant
09 Colombian

dark roast
macchiato
10 Costa Rican
light roast
percolated

11 French roast
12 Blue Mountain
13 decaffeinated

Coffees include:

05 black
Irish
latte
milky
Mocha

white
06 filter
Gaelic
07 Turkish

08 café noir
espresso
09 Americano
cafetière
demitasse

10 café au lait
café filtre
cappuccino
11 skinny latte

See also **drink**

coin

Coins include:

02 as	louis	tickey	xeraphin
03 bit	mohur	toonie	zecchino
bob	mopus	**07** austral	**09** dandiprat
cob	noble	cardecu	dupondius
dam	obang	carolus	fourpenny
écu	paolo	crusado	gold crown
hao	piece	drachma	half-crown
mil	plack	guilder	half groat
moy	rider	handsel	halfpenny
rap	royal	ha'penny	luck-penny
sol	sceat	jacobus	Maple Leaf
sou	scudo	millime	ninepence
zuz	scute	moidore	quadruple
04 anna	semis	Pfennig	rix-dollar
bean	soldo	pistole	rose noble
cash	stamp	pollard	sovereign
dime	taler	quarter	yellow-boy
doit	tical	ruddock	zwanziger
dump	ticky	sextant	**10** broadpiece
fals	toman	solidus	chervonets
jane	unite	spanker	half-dollar
jiao	**06** aureus	thrimsa	half florin
joey	bawbee	thrymsa	half guinea
lion	bezant	xerafin	Krugerrand
mite	boddle	**08** cardecue	lucky-piece
mule	copper	decussis	sestertius
obol	denier	denarius	silverling
para	double	doubloon	touch-piece
quid	escudo	ducatoon	**11** bonnet-piece
real	florin	farthing	contorniate
rial	gilder	gazzetta	double eagle
ryal	guinea	Groschen	pocket-piece
05 angel	gulden	half anna	sixpenny bit
baisa	hansel	half mark	spade guinea
bodle	heller	imperial	sword-dollar
brock	kobang	johannes	tetradrachm
brown	lepton	louis d'or	**12** antoninianus
crown	loonie	maravedi	double-header
daler	mancus	millième	silver dollar
daric	nickel	napoleon	unicorn-shell
dinar	obolus	picayune	**13** brass farthing
ducat	Paduan	portague	half sovereign
eagle	pagoda	portigue	sixpenny piece
gerah	sceatt	quadrans	threepenny bit
groat	sequin	semuncia	**14** three-farthings
khoum	stater	sesterce	three-halfpence
koban	stiver	shilling	**15** threepenny piece
liard	talent	sixpence	
livre	tanner	skilling	
	thaler	solidare	

See also **currency**

cold meat *see* meat

collar

Collars include:

03 dog
04 Eton

flea
roll
ruff
wing
05 horse
ox-bow
shawl
steel
storm
whisk

06 bertha
choker
collet
gorget
jampot
rabato
rebato
07 brecham
partlet
rebater
stick-up

tie-neck
vandyke
08 carcanet
clerical
granddad
mandarin
Peter Pan
polo neck
rabatine
turn-down

09 holderbat
piccadell
piccadill
10 chevesaile
piccadillo
piccadilly
11 falling band
12 mousquetaire

collection

Collectors and enthusiasts include:

05 gamer (computer games)
07 gourmet (good food)
08 neophile (novelty/new things)
zoophile (animals)
09 antiquary (antiques)
cinephile (cinema)
ex-librist (bookplates)
logophile (words)
oenophile (wine)
philomath (learning)
xenophile (foreigners)
10 arctophile (teddy bears)
audiophile (broadcast sound)
cartophile (cigarette cards)
discophile (gramophone records)
ephemerist (ephemera)
gastronome (good food/wine)
hippophile (horses)
monarchist (the monarchy)
11 ailurophile (cats)
balletomane (ballet)
bibliophile (books)
canophilist (dogs)
cynophilist (dogs)
etymologist (words)
notaphilist (banknotes, cheques)
numismatist (coins/medals)
oenophilist (wine)
philatelist (stamps)

scripophile (bond/share certificates)
technophile (technology)
toxophilite (archery)
12 ailourophile (cats)
cartophilist (cigarette cards)
coleopterist (beetles)
Dantophilist (Dante)
deltiologist (postcards)
entomologist (insects)
incunabulist (early printed books)
ophiophilist (snakes)
phillumenist (matches/matchboxes)
stegophilist (climbing buildings for sport)
13 arachnologist (spiders/arachnids)
campanologist (bell-ringing)
chirographist (handwriting)
chrysophilite (gold)
documentalist (documents)
lepidopterist (butterflies)
ornithologist (birds)
scripophilist (bond/share certificates)
tegestologist (beer mats)
timbrophilist (stamps)
14 cruciverbalist (crosswords)
pteridophilist (ferns)
tegestollogist (beer mats)
15 conservationist (countryside)
paroemiographer (proverbs)
stigmatophilist (tattooing/body piercing)

collective noun *see* animal

college

Cambridge University colleges and halls:

05	Clare		St John's	**10**	Hughes Hall
	Jesus		Trinity		Peterhouse
	King's		Wolfson	**11**	Fitzwilliam
06	Darwin	**08**	Emmanuel		Trinity Hall
	Girton		Homerton	**12**	Sidney Sussex
	Queens'		Pembroke		St Catharine's
	Selwyn		Robinson	**13**	Corpus Christi
07	Christ's	**09**	Churchill		Lucy Cavendish
	Downing		Clare Hall	**16**	Gonville and Caius
	New Hall		Magdalene		
	Newnham		St Edmund's		

Oxford University colleges and private halls:

03	New		St John's	**10**	Somerville
05	Green		Trinity		University
	Jesus		Wolfson	**11**	Campion Hall
	Keble	**08**	All Souls		Regent's Park
	Oriel		Hertford	**12**	Christ Church
06	Exeter		Magdalen		St Benet's Hall
	Merton		Nuffield		St Catherine's
	Queen's		Pembroke		St Edmund Hall
	Wadham		St Hilda's		Wycliffe Hall
07	Balliol		St Peter's	**13**	Corpus Christi
	Kellogg	**09**	Brasenose	**14**	Greyfriars Hall
	Linacre		Mansfield	**15**	Blackfriars Hall
	Lincoln		St Antony's		St Stephen's House
	St Anne's		Templeton	**16**	Harris Manchester
	St Cross		The Queen's		Lady Margaret Hall
	St Hugh's		Worcester		

See also **university**

colour

Colours include:

03	jet		rose		lilac		canary
	red		ruby		mauve		cerise
	tan		rust		milky		cherry
04	anil		sage		ochre		cobalt
	blue	**05**	amber		peach		copper
	ecru		beige		sepia		indigo
	fawn		black		slate		maroon
	gold		brown		taupe		orange
	grey		coral		topaz		purple
	jade		cream		umber		salmon
	navy		ebony		white		silver
	pink		green	**06**	auburn		violet
	plum		khaki		bottle		yellow
	puce		lemon		bronze	**07**	apricot

avocado
crimson
emerald
gentian
magenta
saffron
scarlet
08 burgundy
charcoal

chestnut
cinnamon
eau de nil
lavender
magnolia
mahogany
sapphire
09 aubergine
chocolate

tangerine
turquoise
vermilion
10 aquamarine
chartreuse
cobalt blue
11 burnt sienna
lemon yellow

French colour names with English translation:

04 bleu (blue)
brun (brown)
gris (grey)
noir (black)

rose (pink)
vert (green)
blanc (white)
05 jaune (yellow)

rouge (red)
06 orange (orange)

German colour names with English translation:

03 Rot (red)
04 Blau (blue)
Gelb (yellow)
Grau (grey)

Grün (green)
Rosa (pink)
05 Braun (brown)
Weiss (white)

06 Orange (orange)
07 Schwarz (black)

Italian colour names with English translation:

03 blu (blue)
04 nero (black)
rosa (pink)

05 rosso (red)
verde (green)
06 bianco (white)
giallo (yellow)

grigio (grey)
07 arancia (orange)
azzurro (blue)
marrone (brown)

Spanish colour names with English translation:

04 azul (blue)
gris (grey)
rojo (red)
rosa (pink)

05 negro (black)
verde (green)
06 blanco (white)

marrón (brown)
07 naranja (orange)
08 amarillo (yellow)

See also **black; blue; brown; dye; green; grey; orange; pigment; pink; purple; rainbow; red; white; yellow**

comedy

Comedy types include:

03 gag
low
pun
wit
04 high
joke
sick
05 black
farce
Greek
06 humour
modern
satire

sitcom
visual
07 musical
stand-up
08 romantic
09 burlesque
satirical
situation
slapstick
10 comic opera
sketch show
television
theatrical

11 alternative
comedy drama
Pythonesque
restoration
tragicomedy
12 Chaplinesque
neoclassical
13 practical joke
Shakespearian
15 comedy of humours
comedy of manners
improvisational

Comedians include:

03 Dee (Jack; 1962– , English)
Fry (Stephen; 1957– , English)
Lom (Herbert; 1917–2012, Czech)
Loy (Myrna; 1905–93, US)
Sim (Alastair; 1900–76, Scottish)
Wax (Ruby; 1953– , US)

04 Ball (Lucille; 1910–89, US)
Barr (Roseanne; 1952– , US)
Carr (Alan; 1977– , English)
Cook (Peter; 1937–95, English)
Dodd (Ken; 1927– , English)
Gold (Jimmy; 1886–1967, Scottish)
Hill (Benny; 1924–92, English)
Hill (Harry; 1964– , English)
Hope (Bob; 1903–2003, English/US)
Hudd (Roy; 1936– , English)
Idle (Eric; 1943– , English)
Kaye (Danny; 1913–87, US)
Leno (Dan; 1860–1904, English)
Marx (Chico; 1891–1961, US)
Marx (Groucho; 1895–1977, US)
Marx (Harpo; 1893–1964, US)
Marx (Zeppo; 1901–79, US)
Reid (Beryl; 1919–96, English)
Sims (Joan; 1930–2001, English)
Tati (Jacques; 1908–82, French)
Wall (Max; 1908–90, English)
Wise (Ernie; 1925–99, English)
Wood (Victoria; 1953– , English)

05 Abbot (Russ; 1947– , English)
Allen (Dave; 1936–2005, Irish)
Allen (Woody; 1935– , US)
Askey (Arthur; 1900–82, English)
Benny (Jack; 1894–1974, US)
Brand (Jo; 1957– , English)
Brown (Janet; 1924–2011, Scottish)
Bruce (Lenny; 1925–66, US)
Burns (George; 1896–1996, US)
Cosby (Bill; 1937– , US)
Elton (Ben; 1959– , English)
Emery (Dick; 1917–83, English)
Fyffe (Will; 1885–1947, Scottish)
Hardy (Jeremy; 1961– , English)
Hardy (Oliver; 1892–1957, US)
Henry (Lenny; 1958– , English)
Hicks (Bill; 1961–94, US)
Inman (John; 1935–2007, English)
James (Sid; 1913–76, South African/British)
Jones (Terry; 1942– , Welsh)
Kempe (Will; c.1550–c.1603, English)
Large (Eddie; 1941– , Scottish)
Lewis (Jerry; 1926– , US)
Lloyd (Harold; 1893–1971, US)
Moore (Dudley; 1935–2002, English)
Oddie (Bill; 1941– , English)
Palin (Michael; 1943– , English)
Pryor (Richard; 1940–2005, US)

Robey (Sir George; 1869–1954, English)
Sayle (Alexei; 1952– , English)
Smith (Mel; 1952– , English)
Sykes (Eric; 1923–2012, English)

06 Abbott (Bud; 1898–1974, US)
Bailey (Bill; 1964– , English)
Barker (Ronnie; 1929–2005, English)
Baxter (Stanley; 1926– , Scottish)
Brooks (Mel; 1926– , US)
Cleese (John; 1939– , English)
Coborn (Charles; 1852–1945, English)
Coogan (Steve; 1965– , English)
Cooper (Tommy; 1922–84, Welsh)
Dawson (Les; 1934–93, English)
Fields (W C; 1880–1946, US)
French (Dawn; 1957– , English)
Fulton (Rikki; 1924–2004, Scottish)
Garden (Graeme; 1943– , Scottish)
Henson (Leslie; 1891–1957, English)
Higson (Charlie; 1958– , English)
Howerd (Frankie; 1917–92, English)
Izzard (Eddie; 1962– , Yemeni/British)
Jordan (Dorothy; 1762–1816, Irish)
Keaton (Buster; 1895–1966, US)
Lauder (Sir Harry; 1870–1950, Scottish)
Laurel (Stan; 1890–1965, English/US)
Laurie (Hugh; 1959– , English)
Little (Syd; 1942– , English)
Martin (Steve; 1945– , US)
Mayall (Rik; 1958– , English)
Merton (Paul; 1957– , English)
Midler (Bette; 1945– , US)
Miller (Max; 1895–1963, English)
Murphy (Eddie; 1961– , US)
Murray (Bill; 1950– , US)
Norton (Graham; 1963– , Irish)
O'Grady (Paul; 1955– , English)
Proops (Greg; 1959– , US)
Reeves (Vic; 1959– , English)
Rivers (Joan; 1933– , US)
Tilley (Vesta; 1864–1952, English)
Ullman (Tracey; 1959– , English)
Wilder (Gene; 1933– , US)
Wisdom (Sir Norman; 1915–2010, English)

07 Aykroyd (Dan; 1952– , US)
Baddiel (David; 1964– , English)
Bentine (Michael; 1921–96, English)
Bremner (Rory; 1961– , English)
Burnett (Carol; 1933– , US)
Carrott (Jasper; 1945– , English)
Chaplin (Charlie; 1889–1977, English)
Chapman (Graham; 1941–89, English)
Corbett (Ronnie; 1930– , Scottish)
Deayton (Angus; 1956– , English)
Durante (Jimmy; 1893–1980, US)
Edwards (Jimmy; 1920–88, English)
Enfield (Harry; 1961– , English)

Everett (Kenny; 1944–95, English)
Feldman (Marty; 1933–82, English)
Gervais (Ricky; 1961– , English)
Gilliam (Terry; 1940– , US)
Hancock (Tony; 1924–68, English)
Handley (Tommy; 1892–1949, English)
Jacques (Hattie; 1924–80, English)
Langdon (Harry; 1884–1944, US)
Manning (Bernard; 1930–2007, English)
Mathews (Charles; 1776–1835, English)
Mathews (Charles J; 1803–78, English)
Matthau (Walter; 1920–2000, US)
Newhart (Bob; 1929– , US)
Ó Briain (Dara; 1972– , Irish)
Roscius (c.134–62 BC, Roman)
Rushton (Willie; 1937–96, English)
Secombe (Sir Harry; 1921–2001, Welsh)
Sellers (Peter; 1925–80, English)
Silvers (Phil; 1912–85, US)
Skinner (Frank; 1957– , English)
Stewart (Andy; 1933–94, Scottish)
Tarbuck (Jimmy; 1940– , English)
Tarlton (Richard; d.1588, English)
Toksvig (Sandi; 1959– , Danish/British)
Trinder (Tommy; 1909–89, English)
Ustinov (Sir Peter; 1921–2004, English)

08 Atkinson (Rowan; 1955– , English)
Coltrane (Robbie; 1950– , Scottish)
Connolly (Billy; 1942– , Scottish)
Coquelin (Benoît Constant; 1841–1909, French)
Costello (Lou; 1908–50, US)
Grimaldi (Joseph; 1779–1837, English)

Guilbert (Yvette; c.1869–1944, French)
Marshall (Penny; 1942– , US)
Milligan (Spike; 1918–2002, Irish)
Mitchell (Warren; 1926– , English)
Mortimer (Bob; 1959– , English)
Naughton (Charles; 1887–1976, Scottish)
Robinson (Sir Anthony 'Tony'; 1946– , English)
Roseanne (1952– , US)
Saunders (Jennifer; 1958– , English)
Seinfeld (Jerry; 1954– , US)
Sessions (John; 1953– , Scottish)
Tarleton (Richard; d.1588, English)
The Goons
Williams (Kenneth; 1926–88, English)
Williams (Robin; 1951– , US)

09 Edmondson (Adrian; 1957– , English)
Fernandel (1903–71, French)
Grossmith (George; 1847–1912, English)
Humphries (Barry; 1934– , Australian)
Morecambe (Eric; 1926–84, English)
Rhys Jones (Griff; 1953– , Welsh)
Whitfield (June; 1925– , English)

10 The Goodies
Whitehouse (Paul; 1959– , Welsh)

11 Monty Python
Terry-Thomas (1911–90, English)

12 Brooke-Taylor (Tim; c.1940– , English)

14 Laurel and Hardy
Little and Large

15 Naughton and Gold
The Marx Brothers
The Three Stooges

See also **humour**

comet

Comets include:

04	West		Newton		Seki-Lines
	Wolf	**07**	Bennett	**10**	De Chéseaux
05	Cruls		Humason		Flauergues
	Encke		Tebbutt		Great Comet
	Kirch	**08**	Daylight	**11**	Arend-Roland
	Mrkos		Hale-Bopp		Swift-Tuttle
	Tycho		Kohoutek	**12**	Pons-Winnecke
06	Donati	**09**	Hyakutake	**14**	Tago-Sato-Kosaka
	Halley		Ikeya-Seki	**15**	IRAS-Araki-Alcock
	Lexell		Morehouse		

comic

Comics include:

03	Viz		Bunty		The Dandy	The Topper
04	Judy		Dandy		The Eagle	
05	Beano	**08**	The Beano	**09**	The Beezer	

See also **newspaper**

command

Commands include:

03	hie		whoa		huddup
	hup	05	be off	07	give way
	hye		enter	09	stand easy
04	easy		gee up	10	quick march
	halt	06	come by	12	be off with you
	high		entrez	15	stand and deliver
	mush		gee hup		

See also **shout**

commander

Commanders include:

03	aga		captain		taxiarch		trierarch
	mir		general		tetrarch		
04	agha		prefect	09	chieftain	11	encomendero
	meer		warlord		chiliarch		turcopolier
06	sardar	08	governor		imperator		
	sirdar		hipparch		polemarch	13	generalissimo
07	admiral		phylarch		privateer		
			risaldar		seraskier		

See also **admiral**; **field marshal**; **general**; **governor**; **king**; **president**; **prime minister**; **queen**

commonwealth

Commonwealth members:

05	Ghana		Namibia	10	Bangladesh
	India		Nigeria		Mozambique
	Kenya		St Lucia		New Zealand
	Malta		Vanuatu		Seychelles
	Nauru	08	Barbados		The Bahamas
	Samoa		Botswana	11	Sierra Leone
	Tonga		Cameroon		South Africa
06	Belize		Dominica	13	United Kingdom
	Brunei		Kiribati	14	Papua New Guinea
	Canada		Malaysia		Solomon Islands
	Cyprus		Maldives	15	St Kitts and Nevis
	Guyana		Pakistan	16	Brunei Darussalam
	Malawi		Sri Lanka	17	Antigua and Barbuda
	Rwanda		Tanzania		Trinidad and Tobago
	Tuvalu	09	Australia	21	St Christopher and Nevis
	Uganda		Mauritius	25	St Vincent and the
	Zambia		Singapore		Grenadines
07	Grenada		Swaziland		
	Jamaica		The Gambia		
	Lesotho				

See also **CIS**

communication

Communications include:

02 IM	gossip	Intelsat	voice mail
IT	letter	intercom	**10** communiqué
TV	notice	Internet	dictaphone
03 fax	poster	junk mail	loud-hailer
MMS	report	magazine	pay-per-view
Net	speech	mailshot	television
PDA	tannoy	pamphlet	typewriter
SMS	the net	postcard	**11** advertising
04 memo	**07** bleeper	telegram	chain letter
news	Braille	teletext	satellite TV
note	cable TV	wireless	Telemessage®
post	Digibox®	**09** broadband	teleprinter
wire	journal	catalogue	text message
word	leaflet	digital TV	the Internet
05 cable	message	facsimile	**12** announcement
e-mail	Prestel®,	grapevine	broadcasting
media	webcast	mass media	conversation
pager	website	megaphone	press release
pay TV	**08** access TV	Morse code	sign language
press	aerogram	newsflash	walkie-talkie
radar	brochure	newspaper	World Wide Web
radio	bulletin	publicity	**13** video-on-demand
Skype®	circular	satellite	word processor
telex	computer	semaphore	**14** correspondence
video	dialogue	statement	subscription TV
06 Blu-ray®	dispatch	telephone	

company *see* **business; dance**

compass

Compass points:

01 E	S by W	south by east
N	W by N	south by west
S	W by S	west by north
W	west	west by south
02 NE	**05** NE by E	
NW	NE by N	**13** east-north-east
SE	north	east-south-east
SW	NW by N	west-north-west
03 ENE	NW by W	west-south-west
ESE	SE by E	**14** north-north-east
NNE	SE by S	north-north-west
NNW	south	south-south-east
SSE	SW by S	south-south-west
SSW	SW by W	**15** north-east by east
WNW	**09** north-east	north-west by west
WSW	north-west	south-east by east
04 east	south-east	south-west by west
E by N	south-west	**16** north-east by north
E by S	**11** east by north	north-west by north
N by E	east by south	south-east by south
N by W	north by east	south-west by south
S by E	north by west	

competition *see* sport

complementary medicine *see* medicine

composer

Composers include:

03 Bax (Sir Arnold; 1883–1953, English)
Cui (César; 1835–1918, Russian)
Gál (Hans; 1890–1987, Austrian)
Puw (Guto; 1971– , Welsh)
Suk (Joseph; 1875–1935, Czech)

04 Adam (Adolphe; 1803–56, French)
Adès (Thomas; 1971– , English)
Arne (Thomas; 1710–78, English)
Bach (C P E; 1714–88, German)
Bach (Johann Christian; 1735–82, German)
Bach (Johann Christoph Friedrich; 1732–95, German)
Bach (Johann Sebastian; 1685–1750, German)
Bach (Wilhelm Friedemann; 1710–84, German)
Bart (Lionel; 1930–99, English)
Berg (Alban; 1885–1935, Austrian)
Blow (John; 1649–1708, English)
Bull (John; c.1563–1628, English)
Bush (Alan; 1900–95, English)
Byrd (William; 1543–1623, English)
Cage (John; 1912–92, US)
Cary (Tristram; 1925–2008, Australian)
Foss (Lukas; 1922–2009, US)
Gade (Niels; 1817–90, Danish)
Haba (Alois; 1893–1972, Czech)
Hahn (Reynaldo; 1874–1947, Venezuelan/French)
Hill (Alfred; 1870–1960, Australian)
Indy (Vincent d'; 1851–1931, French)
Ives (Charles; 1874–1954, US)
King (Carole; 1942– , US)
Lalo (Édouard; 1823–92, French)
Löwe (Karl; 1796–1869, German)
Nono (Luigi; 1924–90, Italian)
Orff (Carl; 1895–1982, German)
Pärt (Arvo; 1935– , Estonian/Austrian)
Peri (Jacopo; 1561–1633, Italian)
Raff (Joachim; 1822–82, Swiss)
Rota (Nino; 1911–79, Italian)
Shaw (Martin; 1876–1958, English)
Weir (Judith; 1954– , Scottish)
Wolf (Hugo; 1860–1903, Austrian)
Wood (Charles; 1866–1926, Irish)
Wood (Haydn; 1882–1959, English)

05 Adams (John; 1947– , US)
Alkan (1813–88, French)
Aquin (Louis Claude d'; 1694–1772, French)

Auber (Daniel-François-Esprit; 1782–1871, French)
Auric (Georges; 1899–1983, French)
Balfe (Michael William; 1808–70, English)
Banks (Don; 1923–80, Australian)
Beach (Mrs H H A; 1867–1944, US)
Berio (Luciano; 1925–2003, Italian)
Bizet (Georges; 1838–75, French)
Blake (Eubie; 1883–1983, US)
Bliss (Sir Arthur; 1891–1975, English)
Bloch (Ernest; 1880–1959, Swiss/US)
Boito (Arrigo; 1842–1918, Italian)
Boyce (William; 1711–79, English)
Brian (Havergal; 1876–1972, English)
Bruch (Max; 1838–1920, German)
Cilea (Francesco; 1866–1950, Italian)
Darke (Harold; 1888–1976, English)
Dufay (Guillaume; c.1400–74, French)
Dukas (Paul; 1865–1935, French)
Durey (Louis; 1888–1979, French)
Einem (Gottfried von; 1918–96, Austrian)
Elgar (Sir Edward; 1857–1934, English)
Falla (Manuel de; 1876–1946, Spanish)
Fasch (Johann Friedrich; 1688–1758, German)
Fauré (Gabriel; 1845–1924, French)
Field (John; 1782–1837, Irish)
Finzi (Gerald; 1901–56, English)
Friml (Rudolf; 1879–1972, US)
Glass (Philip; 1937– , US)
Gluck (Christoph; 1714–87, German)
Goehr (Alexander; 1932– , German/British)
Gould (Morton; 1913–96, US)
Grieg (Edvard; 1843–1907, Norwegian)
Grofé (Ferde; 1892–1972, US)
Harty (Sir Hamilton; 1880–1941, Northern Irish)
Haydn (Joseph; 1732–1809, Austrian)
Haydn (Michael; 1737–1806, Austrian)
Henze (Hans Werner; 1926–2012, German)
Holst (Gustav; 1874–1934, English)
Ibert (Jacques; 1890–1962, French)
Kagel (Mauricio; 1931–2008, Argentine)
Lawes (Henry; 1596–1662, English)
Lehár (Franz; 1870–1948, Hungarian)
Liszt (Franz; 1811–86, Hungarian)
Lloyd (George; 1913–98, English)
Locke (Matthew; c.1621–77, English)
Loewe (Karl; 1796–1869, German)
Lully (Jean Baptiste; 1632–87, French)

Meale (Richard; 1932–2009, Australian)
Moore (Thomas; 1779–1852, Irish)
Novák (Vitezslav; 1870–1949, Czech)
Nyman (Michael; 1944– , English)
Ogdon (John; 1937–89, English)
Parry (Sir Hubert; 1848–1918, English)
Ravel (Maurice; 1875–1937, French)
Reger (Max; 1873–1916, German)
Reich (Steve; 1936– , US)
Roman (Johan Helmich; 1694–1758, Swedish)
Rorem (Ned; 1923– , US)
Rózsa (Miklós; 1907–95, Hungarian)
Satie (Erik; 1866–1925, French)
Scott (Cyril; 1879–1970, English)
Scott (Francis George; 1880–1958, Scottish)
Smyth (Dame Ethel; 1858–1944, English)
Sousa (John Philip; 1854–1932, US)
Spohr (Ludwig; 1784–1859, German)
Still (William Grant; 1895–1978, US)
Suppé (Franz von; 1819–95, Austrian)
Swann (Donald; 1923–94, Welsh)
Tovey (Sir Donald Francis; 1873–1940, English)
Tubin (Eduard; 1905–82, Estonian/Swedish)
Verdi (Giuseppe; 1813–1901, Italian)
Weber (Carl Maria von; 1786–1826, German)
Weill (Kurt; 1900–50, German/US)
Widor (Charles Marie; 1845–1937, French)
Wirén (Dag; 1905–86, Swedish)

06 Albert (Eugen d'; 1864–1932, German)
Alford (Kenneth; 1881–1945, English)
Alfvén (Hugo; 1872–1960, Swedish)
Antill (John; 1904–86, Australian)
Arnold (Sir Malcolm; 1921–2006, English)
Avison (Charles; c.1710–70, English)
Barber (Samuel; 1910–81, US)
Bartók (Béla; 1881–1945, Hungarian)
Bishop (Sir Henry R; 1786–1855, English)
Boulez (Pierre; 1925– , French)
Brahms (Johannes; 1833–97, German)
Bridge (Frank; 1879–1941, English)
Brumby (Colin; 1933– , Australian)
Carter (Elliott, Jnr; 1908–2012, US)
Carver (Robert; c.1484–c.1568, Scottish)
Chávez (Carlos; 1899–1978, Mexican)
Chopin (Frédéric; 1810–49, Polish)
Clarke (Jeremiah; c.1674–1707, English)
Coates (Eric; 1886–1957, English)
Cowell (Henry; 1897–1965, US)
Czerny (Karl; 1791–1857, Austrian)
Daquin (Louis Claude; 1694–1772, French)
Davies (Sir Henry Walford; 1869–1941, Welsh)
Delius (Frederick; 1862–1934, English)
Dessau (Paul; 1894–1979, German)
Dieren (Bernard van; 1884–1936, Dutch)
Duparc (Henri; 1848–1933, French)
Dussek (Jan Ladislav; 1760–1812, Czech)
Dvořák (Antonín; 1841–1904, Czech)
Eisler (Hanns; 1898–1962, German)

Enesco (Georges; 1881–1955, Romanian)
Finger (Godfrey; fl.1685–1717, Czech)
Flotow (Friedrich, Freiherr von; 1812–83, German)
Foulds (John; 1880–1939, English)
Franck (César; 1822–90, French)
García (Manuel; 1775–1832, Spanish)
German (Sir Edward; 1862–1936, English)
Glinka (Mikhail; 1804–57, Russian)
Godard (Benjamin; 1849–95, French)
Gounod (Charles; 1818–93, French)
Grétry (André; 1741–1813, French)
Gurney (Ivor; 1890–1937, English)
Halévy (Fromental; 1799–1862, French)
Handel (George Frideric; 1685–1759, German/English)
Hanson (Howard; 1896–1981, US)
Hanson (Raymond; 1913–76, Australian)
Harper (Edward; 1941–2009, English)
Harris (Roy; 1898–1979, US)
Harris (Sir William; 1883–1973, English)
Hérold (Ferdinand; 1791–1833, French)
Hiller (Johann Adam; 1728–1804, German)
Hummel (Johann Nepomuk; 1778–1837, Austrian)
Jongen (Joseph; 1873–1953, Belgian)
Kodály (Zoltán; 1882–1967, Hungarian)
Koppel (Herman D; 1908–98, Danish)
Krenek (Ernst; 1900–91, Austrian/US)
Lamond (Frederic; 1868–1948, Scottish)
Lassus (Orlandus; c.1532–94, Dutch)
Lecocq (Charles; 1832–1918, French)
Liadov (Anatoli; 1855–1914, Russian)
Ligeti (Györgi; 1923–2006, Hungarian/Austrian)
Linley (Thomas; 1732–95, English)
Lyadov (Anatoli; 1855–1914, Russian)
Mahler (Gustav; 1860–1911, Czech/Austrian)
Marais (Marin; 1656–1728, French)
Martin (Frank; 1890–1974, Swiss)
Mennin (Peter; 1923–83, US)
Moeran (E J; 1894–1950, English)
Morley (Thomas; 1557–1603, English)
Mozart (Wolfgang Amadeus; 1756–91, Austrian)
Nathan (Isaac; 1790–1864, Australian)
Ó Riada (Seán; 1931–71, Irish)
Piston (Walter; 1894–1976, US)
Pleyel (Ignaz; 1757–1831, Austrian)
Previn (André; 1929– , German/US)
Quantz (Johann Joachim; 1697–1773, German)
Rameau (Jean Philippe; 1683–1764, French)
Reicha (Antonín; 1770–1836, Czech)
Rubbra (Edmund; 1901–86, English)
Schütz (Heinrich; 1585–1672, German)
Searle (Humphrey; 1915–82, English)
Seiber (Mátyás; 1905–60, Hungarian/British)
Sitsky (Larry; 1934– , Australian)
Stoker (Richard; 1938– , English)

Straus (Oscar; 1870–1954, Austrian/French)
Tallis (Thomas; c.1505–85, English)
Thomas (Ambroise; 1811–96, French)
Turina (Joaquín; 1882–1949, Spanish)
Varèse (Edgard; 1885–1965, French/US)
Vogler (Georg Joseph; 1749–1814, German)
Wagner (Richard; 1813–83, German)
Wagner (Siegfried; 1869–1930, German)
Walton (Sir William; 1902–83, English)
Webern (Anton von; 1883–1945, Austrian)
Wesley (Samuel; 1766–1837, English)
Wilson (Thomas; 1927–2001, Scottish)

07 Allegri (Gregorio; 1582–1652, Italian)
Arriaga (Juan Crisóstomo; 1806–26, Spanish)
Babbitt (Milton; 1916–2011, US)
Bainton (Edgar; 1880–1956, English)
Bantock (Sir Granville; 1868–1946, English)
Bellini (Vincenzo; 1801–35, Italian)
Bennett (Sir Richard Rodney; 1936–2012, English)
Bennett (Sir William Sterndale; 1816–75, English)
Bentzon (Niels Viggo; 1919–2000, Danish)
Berlioz (Hector; 1803–69, French)
Berners (Gerald, Lord; 1883–1950, English)
Berwald (Franz; 1796–1868, Swedish)
Borodin (Aleksandr; 1833–87, Russian)
Britten (Benjamin, Lord; 1913–76, English)
Bruneau (Alfred; 1857–1934, French)
Cabezón (Antonio de; 1500–66, Spanish)
Caccini (Giulio; c.1550–1618, Italian)
Campion (Thomas; 1567–1620, English)
Casella (Alfredo; 1883–1947, Italian)
Cavalli (Francesco; 1602–76, Italian)
Copland (Aaron; 1900–90, US)
Corelli (Arcangelo; 1653–1713, Italian)
Debussy (Claude; 1862–1918, French)
Delibes (Léo; 1836–91, French)
di Lasso (Orlando; c.1532–94, Dutch)
Dowland (John; 1563–1626, English)
Dunhill (Thomas; 1877–1946, English)
Duruflé (Maurice; 1902–86, French)
Farnaby (Giles; c.1563–1640, English)
Fricker (Peter; 1920–90, English)
Galuppi (Baldassaro; 1706–85, Italian)
Gerhard (Roberto; 1896–1970, Spanish/British)
Gibbons (Orlando; 1583–1625, English)
Górecki (Henryk; 1933–2010, Polish)
Herbert (Victor; 1859–1924, Irish/US)
Howells (Herbert; 1892–1983, English)
Ireland (John; 1879–1962, English)
Janáček (Leoš; 1854–1928, Czech)
Joachim (Joseph; 1831–1907, Hungarian)
Knussen (Oliver; 1952– , English)
Lambert (Constant; 1905–51, English)
Leclair (Jean Marie; 1697–1764, French)
Lilburn (Douglas; 1915–2001, New Zealand)
Lutyens (Elizabeth; 1906–83, English)
MacCunn (Hamish; 1868–1916, Scottish)

Maderna (Bruno; 1920–73, Italian)
Martinu (Bohuslav; 1890–1959, Czech)
Mathias (William; 1934–92, Welsh)
McGuire (Edward; 1948– , Scottish)
Menotti (Gian-Carlo; 1911–2007, Italian/US)
Milhaud (Darius; 1892–1974, French)
Nicolai (Otto; 1810–49, German)
Nielsen (Carl; 1865–1931, Danish)
Nikisch (Arthur; 1855–1922, Hungarian)
Nørgård (Per; 1932– , Danish)
Novello (Ivor; 1893–1951, Welsh)
Novello (Vincent; 1781–1861, English)
Okeghem (Johannes; c.1430–97, Flemish)
Pepusch (Johann Christoph; 1667–1752, German)
Poulenc (Francis; 1899–1963, French)
Puccini (Giacomo; 1858–1924, Italian)
Purcell (Henry; 1659–95, English)
Quilter (Roger; 1877–1953, English)
Riegger (Wallingford; 1885–1961, US)
Rodrigo (Joaquín; 1901–99, Spanish)
Romberg (Sigmund; 1887–1951, US)
Rossini (Gioacchino; 1792–1868, Italian)
Roussel (Albert; 1869–1937, French)
Salieri (Antonio; 1750–1825, Italian)
Schmidt (Franz; 1874–1939, Austrian)
Schuman (William; 1910–92, US)
Shankar (Ravi; 1920–2012, Indian)
Simpson (Robert; 1921–97, English)
Smeaton (Bruce; 1938– , Australian)
Smetana (Bedrich; 1824–84, Czech)
Sorabji (Kaikhosru; 1892–1988, English)
Sowerby (Leo; 1895–1968, US)
Stamitz (Carl; 1745–1801, German)
Stamitz (Johann; 1717–57, Bohemian)
Stanley (John; 1713–86, English)
Steiner (Max; 1888–1971, US)
Strauss (Johann, the Elder; 1804–49, Austrian)
Strauss (Johann, the Younger; 1825–99, Austrian)
Strauss (Richard; 1864–1949, German)
Taneyev (Sergei; 1856–1915, Russian)
Tartini (Giuseppe; 1692–1770, Italian)
Tavener (Sir John; 1944– , English)
Thomson (Virgil; 1896–1989, US)
Tippett (Sir Michael; 1905–98, English)
Tomkins (Thomas; 1572–1656, English)
Vivaldi (Antonio; 1678–1741, Italian)
Warlock (Peter; 1894–1930, English)
Wellesz (Egon; 1885–1974, Austrian)
Xenakis (Iannis; 1922–2001, Romanian/French)
Zwilich (Ellen Taaffe; 1939– , US)

08 Albinoni (Tomasso; 1671–1751, Italian)
Bairstow (Sir Edward; 1874–1946, English)
Barsanti (Francesco; 1690–1775, Italian)
Benedict (Sir Julius; 1804–85, German)
Berkeley (Michael, Lord; 1948– , English)
Berkeley (Sir Lennox; 1903–89, English)
Blomdahl (Karl-Birger; 1916–68, Swedish)

Boughton (Rutland; 1878–1960, English)
Bruckner (Anton; 1824–96, Austrian)
Carr-Boyd (Ann; 1938– , Australian)
Catalani (Alfredo; 1854–93, Italian)
Chabrier (Emmanuel; 1841–94, French)
Chausson (Ernest; 1855–99, French)
Chisholm (Erik; 1904–65, Scottish)
Cimarosa (Domenico; 1749–1801, Italian)
Clementi (Muzio; 1752–1832, Italian)
Cornyshe (William; c.1465–1523, English)
Couperin (François; 1668–1733, French)
Dohnanyi (Ernst von; 1877–1960, Hungarian)
Gabrieli (Andrea; c.1533–86, Italian)
Gabrieli (Giovanni; c.1555–1612, Italian)
Giordano (Umberto; 1867–1948, Italian)
Glazunov (Aleksandr; 1865–1936, Russian)
Godowsky (Leopold; 1870–1938, US)
Goldmark (Carl; 1830–1915, Hungarian)
Goossens (Sir Eugène; 1893–1962, English)
Goudimel (Claude; c.1514–72, French)
Grainger (Percy; 1882–1961, Australian/US)
Hamilton (Iain; 1922–2000, Scottish)
Henschel (Sir George; 1850–1934, Polish/
  British)
Herrmann (Bernard; 1911–75, US)
Hoffmann (E T A; 1776–1822, German)
Holliger (Heinz; 1939– , Swiss)
Honegger (Arthur; 1892–1955, French)
Ketèlbey (Albert William; 1875–1959, English)
Koechlin (Charles; 1867–1950, French)
Korngold (Erich Wolfgang; 1897–1957,
  Czech/US)
Leighton (Kenneth; 1929–88, English)
Maconchy (Dame Elizabeth; 1907–94, English)
Marcello (Benedetto; 1686–1739, Italian)
Marshall (William; 1748–1833, Scottish)
Mascagni (Pietro; 1863–1945, Italian)
Massenet (Jules; 1842–1912, French)
Messager (André; 1853–1929, French)
Messiaen (Olivier; 1908–92, French)
Monckton (Lionel; 1861–1924, English)
Musgrave (Thea; 1928– , Scottish)
Ockeghem (Johannes; c.1430–97, Flemish)
Panufnik (Sir Andrej; 1914–94, Polish/British)
Pfitzner (Hans; 1869–1949, German)
Philidor (François André; 1726–95, French)
Pizzetti (Ildebrando; 1880–1968, Italian)
Respighi (Ottorino; 1879–1936, Italian)
Richards (Henry Brinley; 1819–85, Welsh)
Riisager (Knudäge; 1897–1975, Danish)
Sallinen (Aulis; 1935– , Finnish)
Sarasate (Pablo; 1844–1908, Spanish)
Schnabel (Artur; 1882–1951, Austrian)
Schubert (Franz; 1797–1828, Austrian)
Schumann (Clara; 1819–96, German)
Schumann (Robert; 1810–56, German)
Scriabin (Aleksandr; 1872–1915, Russian)
Sessions (Roger; 1896–1985, US)
Sibelius (Jean; 1865–1957, Finnish)

Skriabin (Aleksandr; 1872–1915, Russian)
Spontini (Gasparo; 1774–1851, Italian)
Stanford (Sir Charles Villiers; 1852–1924, Irish)
Sullivan (Sir Arthur; 1842–1900, English)
Svendsen (Johan; 1840–1911, Norwegian)
Telemann (Georg Philipp; 1681–1767,
  German)
Victoria (Tomás Luis de; 1548–1611, Spanish)
Willaert (Adrian; c.1490–1562, Flemish)
Williams (John; 1932– , US)
09 Balakirev (Mili; 1836–1910, Russian)
Beethoven (Ludwig van; 1770–1827, German)
Bernstein (Elmer; 1922–2004, US)
Bernstein (Leonard; 1918–90, US)
Boïeldieu (François Adrien; 1775–1834, French)
Bononcini (Giovanni Maria; 1642–78, Italian)
Boulanger (Lili; 1893–1918, French)
Boulanger (Nadia; 1887–1979, French)
Butterley (Nigel; 1935– , Australian)
Buxtehude (Diderik; c.1637–1707, Danish)
Carissimi (Giacomo; 1605–74, Italian)
Cavalieri (Emilio de'; c.1550–1602, Italian)
Cherubini (Luigi; 1760–1842, Italian)
Conyngham (Barry; 1944– , Australian)
Cornelius (Peter; 1824–74, German)
Donizetti (Gaetano; 1797–1848, Italian)
Dunstable (John; c.1390–1453, English)
Dutilleux (Henri; 1916–2013, French)
Froberger (Johann Jakob; 1616–67, German)
Goldsmith (Jerry; 1929–2004, US)
Gruenberg (Louis; 1884–1964, US)
Hindemith (Paul; 1895–1963, German)
Hoddinott (Alun; 1929–2008, Welsh)
Holbrooke (Josef; 1878–1958, English)
Järnefelt (Armas; 1869–1958, Swedish)
MacDowell (Edward; 1861–1908, US)
Mackenzie (Sir Alexander; 1847–1935,
  Scottish)
Malipiero (Francesco; 1882–1973, Italian)
Merikanto (Aarre; 1893–1958, Finnish)
Meyerbeer (Giacomo; 1791–1864, German)
Morricone (Ennio; 1928– , Italian)
Musorgski (Modest; 1835–81, Russian)
Musorgsky (Modest; 1835–81, Russian)
Offenbach (Jacques; 1819–80, German)
Pachelbel (Johann; c.1653–1706, German)
Paisiello (Giovanni; 1740–1816, Italian)
Pergolesi (Giovanni Battista; 1710–36, Italian)
Prokofiev (Sergei; 1891–1953, Russian)
Scarlatti (Alessandro; 1659–1725, Italian)
Scarlatti (Domenico; 1685–1757, Italian)
Schmelzer (Johann Heinrich; 1623–80,
  Austrian)
Schnittke (Alfred; 1934–98, Russian)
Schönberg (Arnold; 1874–1951, Austrian/US)
Shchedrin (Rodion; 1932– , Russian)
Stevenson (Ronald; 1928– , Scottish)
Stradella (Alessandro; c.1642–82, Italian)
Takemitsu (Toru; 1930–96, Japanese)

Tortelier (Paul; 1914–90, French)
Whitehead (Gillian; 1941– , New Zealand)
Zemlinsky (Alexander von; 1871–1942,
　Austrian)

10 Birtwistle (Sir Harrison; 1934– , English)
Boccherini (Luigi; 1743–1805, Italian)
Buononcini (Giovanni Maria; 1642–78, Italian)
Campenhout (François von; 1779–1849, Belgian)
Ferrabosco (Alfonso; 1543–88, Italian)
Ferrabosco (Alfonso; c.1575–1628, English)
Ferrabosco (Domenico Maria; 1513–74, Italian)
Kabalevsky (Dmitri; 1904–87, Russian)
Monteverdi (Claudio; 1567–1643, Italian)
Mussargsky (Modest; 1835–81, Russian)
Mussorgsky (Modest; 1835–81, Russian)
Myaskovsky (Nikolai; 1881–1950, Russian)
Paderewski (Ignacy Jan; 1860–1941, Polish)
Palestrina (Giovanni Pierluigi da; c.1525–94,
　Italian)
Penderecki (Krzysztof; 1933– , Polish)
Ponchielli (Amilcare; 1834–86, Italian)
Praetorius (Michael; 1571–1621, German)
Rawsthorne (Alan; 1905–71, English)
Rubinstein (Anton; 1829–94, Russian)
Saint-Saëns (Camille; 1835–1921, French)
Schoenberg (Arnold; 1874–1951, Austrian/US)
Sculthorpe (Peter; 1929– , Australian)
Skalkottas (Nikolaos; 1904–49, Greek)
Stravinsky (Igor; 1882–1971, Russian/US)
Sutherland (Margaret; 1897–1984,
　Australian)
Tcherepnin (Nikolai; 1873–1945, Russian)
Villa-Lobos (Heitor; 1887–1959, Brazilian)
Waldteufel (Emile; 1837–1915, French)
Weinberger (Jaromir; 1896–1967, Czech)
Williamson (Malcolm; 1931–2003, Australian)
Wordsworth (William Brocklesby; 1908–88,
　English)

11 Butterworth (George; 1885–1916, English)
Charpentier (Gustave; 1860–1956, French)
Dittersdorf (Karl Ditters von; 1739–99, Austrian)

Frescobaldi (Girolamo; 1583–1643, Italian)
Goldschmidt (Berthold; 1903–96, German/
　British)
Gubaydulina (Sofiya; 1931– , Russian)
Humperdinck (Engelbert; 1854–1921, German)
Leoncavallo (Ruggiero; 1858–1919, Italian)
Lutoslawski (Witold; 1913–94, Polish)
Mendelssohn (Felix; 1809–47, German)
Moussorgsky (Modest; 1835–81, Russian)
Rachmaninov (Sergei; 1873–1943, Russian)
Rakhmaninov (Sergei; 1873–1943, Russian)
Ravenscroft (Thomas; 1592–1640, English)
Reizenstein (Franz; 1911–68, German)
Stockhausen (Karlheinz; 1928–2007, German)
Tailleferre (Germaine; 1892–1983, French)
Tchaikovsky (Pyotr Ilyich; 1840–93, Russian)
Thalben-Ball (Sir George; 1896–1987,
　Australian/British)
Theodorakis (Mikis; 1925– , Greek)
Thorpe Davie (Cedric; 1913–83, Scottish)
Weingartner (Felix; 1863–1942, Austrian)
Wolf-Ferrari (Ermanno; 1876–1948, Italian)

12 Dallapiccola (Luigi; 1904–75, Italian)
Dargomizhsky (Aleksandr; 1813–69, Russian)
Shostakovich (Dmitri; 1906–75, Russian)

13 Khatchaturian (Aram; 1903–78, Russian)
Maxwell Davies (Sir Peter; 1934– , English)
Rouget de Lisle (Claude Joseph; 1760–1836,
　French)

14 Glanville-Hicks (Peggy; 1912–90, Australian)
Jaques-Dalcroze (Émile; 1865–1951, Swiss)
Josquin des Prez (c.1440–1521, Franco-Flemish)
Josquin Desprez (c.1440–1521, Franco-
　Flemish)
Peterson-Berger (Wilhelm; 1867–1942,
　Swedish)
Rimsky-Korsakov (Nikolai; 1844–1908, Russian)

15 Coleridge-Taylor (Samuel; 1875–1912,
　English)
Vaughan Williams (Ralph; 1872–1958,
　English)

Masters of the King's/Queen's Music, with date of appointment:

03 Bax (Sir Arnold; 1883–1953, English; 1942)

05 Bliss (Sir Arthur; 1891–1975, English; 1953)
Boyce (William; 1710–79), English; 1755)
Elgar (Sir Edward; 1857–1934, English; 1924)
Grabu (Louis; ?–after 1693, Catalan; 1666)
Green (Maurice; 1696–1755, English; 1735)

06 Cramer (Franz (François); 1772–1848,
　English; 1834)
Cusins (Sir William; 1833–93, English; 1870)
Davies (Sir Henry Walford; 1869–1941,
　Welsh; 1934)
Eccles (John; 1668–1735, English; 1700)
Kramer (Christian; ?–1834, German; 1829)

Lanier (Nicholas; 1588–1666, English; 1626, 1660)
Shield (William; 1748–1829, English; 1817)

07 Parratt (Sir Walter; 1841–1924, English; 1893)
Parsons (Sir William; 1745/6–1817, English;
　1786)
Stanley (John; 1712–86, English; 1779)

08 Anderson (George; c.1793–1876, English;
　1848)
Staggins (Nicholas; 1650–1700, English; 1674)

10 Williamson (Malcolm; 1931–2003,
　Australian; 1975)

13 Maxwell Davies (Sir Peter; 1934– , English; 2004)

See also **Bach, Johann Sebastian; Bartók, Béla; Beethoven, Ludwig van; Brahms, Johannes; Britten, Benjamin; Debussy, Claude; Dvořák, Antonín; Gilbert, Sir W S and Sullivan, Sir Arthur; Handel, George Frideric; Haydn, Joseph; libretto; Mahler, Gustav; Mozart, Wolfgang Amadeus; music; Prokofiev, Sergei; Puccini, Giacomo; Purcell, Henry; Ravel, Maurice; Rossini, Gioacchino; Schoenberg, Arnold; Schubert, Franz; Schumann, Robert; Shostakovich, Dmitri; song; Strauss, Richard; Stravinsky, Igor; Tchaikovsky, Pyotr Ilyich; Verdi, Giuseppe; Wagner, Richard**

composition *see* music

compound *see* chemistry

computer

Computers include:

03 HAL		VIKI	06 UNIVAC	09 The Matrix
IBM	05 Eddie	08 Apple Mac®	11 Deep Thought
Mac®	ENIAC	Colossus	12 Commodore Pet
SAL	Holly	Deep Blue	
04 iMac®	iBook®	Spectrum	

Computer programming languages include:

01 C++	04 HTML	COBOL	07 FORTRAN
C	Java	06 Delphi	10 Postscript
02 VB	Perl	Pascal	11 Visual Basic
03 AWK	05 BASIC	Python	

Computer scientists and pioneers include:

04 Bell (Gordon; 1934–   , US)
Brin (Sergey; 1973–   , Russian/US)
Bush (Vannevar; 1890–1974, US)
Cray (Seymour; 1925–96, US)
Hoff (Ted; 1937–   , US)
Hurd (Cuthbert; 1911–96, US)
Jobs (Steve; 1955–2011, US)
Page (Lawrence; 1973–   , US)
Wang (An; 1920–90, US)
Zuse (Konrad; 1910–95, German)

05 Aiken (Howard Hathaway; 1900–73, US)
Bezos (Jeff; 1964–   , US)
Burks (Arthur; 1915–2008, US)
Gates (Bill; 1955–   , US)
Mazor (Stanley; 1941–   , US)
Olsen (Ken; 1926–2011, US)
Sugar (Sir Alan; 1947–   , English)

06 Amdahl (Gene; 1922–   , US)
Backus (John; 1924–2007, US)
Comrie (L J; 1893–1950, New Zealand)
Eckert (J Presper; 1919–95, US)
Faggin (Federico; 1941–   , Italian/US)
Hopper (Grace Murray; 1906–92, US)
Huskey (Harry; 1916–   , US)
Michie (Donald; 1923–2007, Burmese/British)
Milner (Robin; 1934–2010, English)
Turing (Alan; 1912–54, English)

Wilkes (Sir Maurice V; 1913–2010, English)

07 Babbage (Charles; 1791–1871, English)
Gosling (James; 1955–   , Canadian)
Hartree (Douglas; 1897–1958, English)
Kilburn (Tom; 1921–2001, English)
Mauchly (John W; 1907–80, US)
Shannon (Claude; 1916–2001, US)
Stibitz (George R; 1904–95, US)
Wheeler (David; 1927–2004, English)
Wozniak (Steve; 1950–   , US)

08 Lovelace (Ada, Countess of; 1815–52, English)
Sinclair (Sir Clive; 1940–   , English)
Stallman (Richard; 1953–   , US)
Strachey (Christopher; 1916–75, English)
Torvalds (Linus; 1969–   , Finnish)
Williams (Sir Frederic; 1911–77, English)

09 Atanasoff (John Vincent; 1903–95, US)
Engelbart (Douglas; 1925–   , US)
Forrester (Jay; 1918–   , US)
Goldstine (Herman H; 1913–2004, US)
Hollerith (Herman; 1860–1929, US)
Wilkinson (James H; 1919–86, English)

10 Berners-Lee (Tim; 1955–   , English)
Fairclough (Sir John; 1930–2003, English)
Michaelson (Sidney; 1925–91, English)
Stroustrup (Bjarne; 1950–   , Danish)
Von Neumann (John; 1903–57, Hungarian/US)

Computing terms include:

02 CD
PC
VR

03 bit
bot
bug
bus
CD-R
CPU
CSS
DOS
DTP
DVD
FAQ
FTP
GUI
hit
LAN
P2P
PDF
RAM
rip
ROM
RTF
VDU
WAN

04 BIOS
boot
byte
card
CD-RW
chip
data
disk
dump
file
game
hack
Help
HTML
icon
ISDN
leet
menu
port
SGML
worm

05 ASCII
BASIC
cache
CD-ROM
COBOL
JANET®
login
log on
macro

modem
mouse
pixel
shell
virus

06 access
applet
backup
binary
bitmap
buffer
cursor
DVD-ROM
editor
export
format
hacker
import
joypad
laptop
log off
memory
output
plug-in
reboot
screen
script
server
tablet
toggle
window

07 darknet
default
dequeue
desktop
enqueue
FORTRAN
gigabit
hacking
hotspot
install
monitor
network
package
palmtop
Pentium®
pointer
printer
program
rootkit
scanner
servlet
sidebar
toolbar
Unicode
upgrade
WYSIWYG

zip disk

08 autosave
cold boot
core dump
cracking
databank
database
e-journal
firewall
FireWire®
function
gigabyte
graphics
handheld
hard disk
hardware
joystick
keyboard
kilobyte
light pen
megabyte
metafile
mouse mat
notebook
password
phishing
platform
protocol
rollover
software
template
terabyte
terminal
touchpad
user name
warm boot
wireless
Wordstar®

09 character
debugging
digitizer
directory
disk drive
drill down
e-business
e-commerce
hard drive
hyperlink
hypertext
interface
leetspeak
mainframe
megapixel
mouseover
newsgroup
overclock
scrolling

sound card
timestamp
trackball
transcode
utilities
video card
workspace

10 aggregator
cable modem
floppy disk
keylogging
message box
multimedia
peer-to-peer
peripheral
rewritable
serial port
server farm
text mining
virtualize

11 application
compact disc
compression
cut and paste
floppy drive

Memory Stick®
motherboard
optical disk
proxy server
screen saver
shellscript
silicon chip
spreadsheet
Trojan horse
WordPerfect®
workstation

12 circuit board
client-server
computer game
graphics card
installation
laser printer
magnetic disk
magnetic tape
minicomputer
nanocomputer
parallel port
reverse proxy
search engine
spellchecker
subdirectory

user-friendly
virus checker

13 character code
file extension
ink-jet printer
interoperable
microcomputer
nanocomputing
telecommuting
user interface

14 backing storage
external memory
grammar checker
internal memory
microprocessor
read only memory
rich text format
virtualization
virtual machine
virtual reality
word processing

15 denial of service
operating system
read-write memory
wide area network

Types of computer software include:

02 IE®
MS
XP

03 CAD
DOS
ERP
GUI
IDE
OS X®
SQL
Sun

04 game
Sage
Unix®
Word®
worm

05 Adobe
Apple
Corel
Flash®
Linux
Lotus
Mac OS®
MS-DOS®
Opera
Skype®
virus
Vista®

06 adware

Apache
Claris®
driver
iTunes®
Novell
Office®
Oracle®
Safari®
server
system
window

07 Acrobat®
badware
browser
Firefox
malware
Mozilla
Notepad®
Outlook®
Pegasus
program
spyware
utility
Windows®

08 business
compiler
database
debugger
embedded

firewall
firmware
freeware
function
platform
Symantec
template

09 algorithm
antivirus
interface
Microsoft
Photoshop®
procedure
processor
shareware
teachware
transcode

10 aggregator
courseware
middleware
OpenOffice
open-source
PowerPoint®
simulation
source code
text editor
web browser

11 abandonware
application

educational
Flash Player
office suite
programming
proprietary
spreadsheet
Thunderbird
Trojan horse

WordPerfect®
12 closed-source
    computer game
    device driver
    public domain
13 documentation
    word processor

14 data processing
    Outlook Express®
    system software
    word processing
15 computer program
    operating system
    programming tool

See also **chess; Internet; key; scanner; social media; video game**

concept *see* **science**

condition *see* **disease; psychology**

conductor

Conductors include:

04 Adès (Thomas; 1971– , English)
Böhm (Karl; 1894–1981, Austrian)
Hahn (Reynaldo; 1874–1947, Venezuelan/
    French)
Muti (Riccardo; 1941– , Italian)
Wood (Sir Henry; 1869–1944, English)

05 Boult (Sir Adrian; 1889–1983, English)
Bülow (Hans, Baron von; 1830–94,
    German)
Busch (Fritz; 1890–1951, German)
Davis (Sir Colin; 1927–2013, English)
Elgar (Sir Edward; 1857–1934, English)
Hallé (Sir Charles; 1819–95, Prussian/
    British)
Harty (Sir Hamilton; 1880–1941, Northern
    Irish)
Kempe (Rudolf; 1910–76, German)
Lloyd (George; 1913–98, English)
Masur (Kurt; 1927– , German)
Meale (Richard; 1932– , Australian)
Mehta (Zubin; 1936– , Indian/US)
Ozawa (Seiji; 1935– , Japanese/US)
Rizzi (Carlo; 1960– , Italian)
Solti (Sir Georg; 1912–97, Hungarian/
    British)
Sousa (John Philip; 1854–1932, US)
Spohr (Ludwig; 1784–1859, German)
Szell (George; 1897–1970, US)

06 Abbado (Claudio; 1933– , Italian)
Boulez (Pierre; 1925– , French)
Bridge (Frank; 1879–1941, English)
Casals (Pablo; 1876–1973, Spanish)
Cortot (Alfred; 1877–1962, French)
Daniel (Paul; 1958– , English)
Dessau (Paul; 1894–1979, German)
Dorati (Antal; 1906–88, US)
Galway (James; 1939– , Northern Irish)

Gibson (Sir Alexander; 1926–95, Scottish)
Glover (Jane; 1949– , English)
Groves (Sir Charles; 1915–92, English)
Heinze (Sir Bernard; 1894–1982, Australian)
Hickox (Richard; 1948–2008, English)
Jochum (Eugen; 1902–87, German)
Levine (James; 1943– , US)
Maazel (Lorin; 1930– , US)
Maazel (Lorin; 1930– , US)
Mahler (Gustav; 1860–1911, Czech/
    Austrian)
Previn (André; 1929– , German/US)
Rattle (Sir Simon; 1955– , English)
Reiner (Fritz; 1888–1963, US)
Sacher (Paul; 1906–99, Swiss)
Volkov (Ilan; 1976– , Israeli)
Wagner (Siegfried; 1869–1930, German)
Walter (Bruno; 1876–1962, German/US)

07 Bainton (Edgar; 1880–1956, English)
Beecham (Sir Thomas; 1879–1961, English)
Fiedler (Arthur; 1894–1979, US)
Gergiev (Valery; 1953– , Russian)
Giulini (Carlo Maria; 1914–2005, Italian)
Godfrey (Sir Dan; 1868–1939, English)
Haitink (Bernard; 1929– , Dutch)
Karajan (Herbert von; 1908–89, Austrian)
Kleiber (Erich; 1890–1956, Argentine)
Knussen (Oliver; 1952– , English)
Kubelik (Rafael; 1914–96, Swiss)
Lambert (Constant; 1905–51, English)
Maderna (Bruno; 1920–73, Italian)
Malcolm (George; 1917–97, English)
Monteux (Pierre; 1875–1964, US)
Nicolai (Otto; 1810–49, German)
Nikisch (Arthur; 1855–1922, Hungarian)
Ormandy (Eugene; 1899–1985, US)
Richter (Hans; 1843–1916, Hungarian)

Sargent (Sir Malcolm; 1895–1967, English)
Smetana (Bedrich; 1824–84, Czech)
Strauss (Johann, the Elder; 1804–49, Austrian)
Strauss (Johann, the Younger; 1825–99, Austrian)
Strauss (Richard; 1864–1949, German)
Swensen (Joseph; 1960– , US)
08 Atherton (David; 1944– , English)
Goossens (Eugène; 1845–1906, Belgian)
Goossens (Sir Eugène; 1893–1962, English)
Henschel (Sir George; 1850–1934, Polish/British)
Jurowski (Vladimir; 1972– , Russian)
Ketèlbey (Albert William; 1875–1959, English)
Marriner (Sir Neville; 1924– , English)
Panufnik (Sir Andrej; 1914–94, Polish/British)
Tuckwell (Barry; 1931– , Australian)
Zukerman (Pinchas; 1948– , Israeli)
09 Ashkenazy (Vladimir; 1937– , Russian/Icelandic)
Barenboim (Daniel; 1942– , Argentine/Israeli)
Bernstein (Leonard; 1918–90, US)
Boulanger (Nadia; 1887–1979, French)
See also **musician**

Järnefelt (Armas; 1869–1958, Swedish)
Klemperer (Otto; 1885–1973, German)
Leinsdorf (Erich; 1912–93, US)
Mackerras (Sir Charles; 1925– , Australian)
Mravinsky (Yevgeni; 1903–88, Russian)
Runnicles (Donald; 1954– , Scottish)
Schönberg (Arnold; 1874–1951, Austrian/US)
Stokowski (Leopold; 1882–1977, English/US)
Tortelier (Paul; 1914–90, French)
Toscanini (Arturo; 1867–1957, Italian)
Zemlinsky (Alexander von; 1871–1942, Austrian)
10 Barbirolli (Sir John; 1899–1970, English)
Schoenberg (Arnold; 1874–1951, Austrian/US)
Villa-Lobos (Heitor; 1887–1959, Brazilian)
11 Furtwängler (Wilhelm; 1886–1954, German)
Lutoslawski (Witold; 1913–94, Polish)
Mitropoulos (Dimitri; 1896–1960, US)
Weingartner (Felix; 1863–1942, Austrian)
12 Koussevitzky (Serge; 1874–1951, Russian/US)
Rostropovich (Mstislav; 1927–2007, Russian)
Shostakovich (Maxim; 1938– , US)

confectionery *see* **sweet**

constellation

Constellations include:

03		
03 Ara	Swan	Orion
Cup	Vela	Pyxis
Fly	Wolf	Sails
Fox	**05** Altar	Table
Leo	Aries	Twins
Net	Arrow	Virgo
Ram	Cetus	Whale
04 Apus	Clock	**06** Antlia
Bull	Crane	Aquila
Crab	Draco	Archer
Crow	Eagle	Auriga
Crux	Easel	Boötes
Dove	Hydra	Caelum
Grus	Indus	Cancer
Hare	Lepus	Carina
Harp	Level	Chisel
Keel	Libra	Corvus
Lion	Lupus	Crater
Lynx	Mensa	Cygnus
Lyra	Musca	Dorado
Pavo	Norma	Dragon

Fishes
Fornax
Gemini
Hydrus
Indian
Lizard
Octans
Octant
Pictor
Pisces
Puppis
Scales
Scutum
Shield
Taurus
Toucan
Tucana
Virgin
Volans

07 Air Pump
Centaur
Cepheus
Columba
Dolphin
Furnace
Giraffe
Lacerta
Peacock
Pegasus
Perseus
Phoenix
Sagitta
Sea Goat
Serpens
Serpent
See also **star**

Sextans
Sextant
Unicorn

08 Aquarius
Circinus
Equuleus
Eridanus
Great Dog
Hercules
Herdsman
Leo Minor
Scorpion
Scorpius
Sculptor
Triangle

09 Andromeda
Capricorn
Centaurus
Chameleon
Compasses
Delphinus
Great Bear
Little Dog
Monoceros
Ophiuchus
Reticulum
Swordfish
Telescope
Ursa Major
Ursa Minor
Vulpecula

10 Canis Major
Canis Minor
Cassiopeia

Chamaeleon
Charioteer
Flying Fish
Horologium
Little Bear
Little Lion
Microscope
Sea Serpent
Ship's Stern
Triangulum
Water Snake

11 Capricornus
Hunting Dogs
Little Horse
Sagittarius
Telescopium
Water Bearer
Winged Horse

12 Microscopium
Southern Fish

13 Berenice's Hair
Canes Venatici
Coma Berenices
Northern Crown
River Eridanus
Serpent Bearer
Southern Cross
Southern Crown

14 Bird of Paradise
Camelopardalis
Corona Borealis

15 Corona Australis
Mariner's Compass
Piscis Austrinus

container

Containers include:			
03 bag	case	purse	**07** cistern
bin	cask	trunk	dustbin
box	dish		pannier
can	drum	**06** barrel	pitcher
cup	pack	basket	tumbler
jar	pail	beaker	
jug	sack	bottle	**08** canister
keg	tank	bucket	cauldron
mug	tube	carton	cylinder
pan	vase	casket	lunch box
pot	well	hamper	suitcase
tin		kettle	tea caddy
tub	**05** basin	locker	tea chest
urn	chest	packet	waste bin
vat	churn	punnet	
	crate	teapot	**09** water-butt
04 bath	crock	trough	
bowl	glass	tureen	

See also **bag**; **bottle**; **wine**

continent

Continents of the world:

04 Asia	**07** America	**11** Australasia
06 Africa	Oceania	**12** North America
Europe	**10** Antarctica	South America

contraceptive

Contraceptives include:

03 cap	safe	johnnie	**10** Lippes loop
IUD	**06** condom	the pill	protective
IVD	johnny	**08** Dutch cap	**11** Depo-Provera®
04 coil	rubber	minipill	
IUCD	sheath	**09** birth pill	**12** female condom
loop	Vimule®	diaphragm	French letter
pill	**07** Femidom®	prolactin	prophylactic

convent *see* **religious order**

cookery

Cooking methods include:

03 fry	grill	flambé	scramble
04 bake	poach	pan-fry	
boil	roast	simmer	**09** casserole
sear	sauté		char-grill
stew	steam	**07** deep-fry	fricassee
05 broil	sweat	parboil	microwave
brown	toast	stir-fry	oven-roast
curry	**06** braise	**08** barbecue	spit-roast
	coddle	pot-roast	**10** flame-grill

Cookery utensils include:

03 pan	peeler	skillet
wok	pestle	skimmer
04 fork	shears	spatula
05 corer	sifter	steamer
ladle	skewer	terrine
mouli	stoner	
sieve	tureen	**08** blini pan
tongs	zester	breadbin
whisk		colander
06 baster	**07** blender	crêpe pan
bun tin	cake tin	cruet set
grater	cleaver	egg-timer
juicer	cocotte	grill pan
karahi	flan tin	ham stand
mincer	grinder	herb mill
mortar	loaf tin	mandolin
	milk pan	pie plate
	ramekin	saucepan

scissors
stockpot
tea caddy
teaspoon
wine rack

09 bain marie
blowtorch
brochette
can-opener
casserole
corkscrew
dough hook
egg slicer
fish knife
fish slice
fondue set
frying pan
gravy boat
mezzaluna
muffin tin
paella pan
pie funnel
processor
punch bowl
sharpener
soup spoon
spice rack
toast rack

10 breadboard
bread knife
butter dish
cook's knife
egg coddler
egg poacher
fish kettle
jelly mould
knife block
liquidizer
mixing bowl
nutcracker
pasta ladle

pasta maker
pepper mill
quiche dish
rice cooker
rolling pin
slow cooker
steak knife
storage jar
table knife
tablespoon
tea infuser
waffle iron
wine cooler

11 baking sheet
boning knife
butter knife
cheese board
cheese knife
chestnut pan
cooling rack
garlic press
lemon reamer
melon baller
oil drizzler
omelette pan
oyster knife
paring knife
pastry board
pastry brush
potato ricer
roasting pan
sandwich tin
soufflé dish
tea strainer
thermometer
tomato knife
wooden spoon

12 biscuit press
bottle opener
butter curler
canelle knife

carving knife
cheese slicer
deep-fat fryer
dessert spoon
egg separator
fish tweezers
flour dredger
heat diffuser
icing syringe
madeleine tin
measuring jug
nutmeg grater
palette knife
pastry cutter
potato masher
pudding basin
pudding mould
salad spinner
serving spoon
yoghurt maker

13 butcher's block
chopping-board
cocktail knife
draining spoon
food processor
ice-cream scoop
Kitchen Devils®
kitchen scales
lemon squeezer
preserving pan

14 gravy separator
measuring spoon
pressure cooker
straining spoon
vegetable brush
vegetable knife

15 asparagus cooker
grapefruit knife
meat thermometer
mortar and pestle
sharpening steel

Cookery styles include:

04 Thai

05 Greek
halal
Irish
mezze
rural
tapas
vegan
Welsh

06 French
fusion
German

Indian
kosher
Tex-Mex

07 African
British
Chinese
Eastern
English
Italian
Mexican
seafood
Spanish

Turkish

08 American
fast food
Japanese
Scottish

09 Cantonese
Caribbean
Malaysian
Provençal

10 cordon bleu
Far Eastern

gluten-free
Indonesian
Pacific Rim
vegetarian

11 home cooking
lean cuisine

12 haute cuisine

13 Mediterranean
Middle Eastern

14 cuisine minceur

15 nouvelle cuisine

Foreign cookery and food terms include:

03 jus	bhoona	piccata	usukuchi
04 dhal	bisque	pierogi	vindaloo
ghee	blintz	polenta	yaki-nori
meze	bonito	poutine	yakitori
miso	byesar	ravioli	zarzuela
naan	canapé	ripiene	**09** antipasto
puri	coulis	risotto	bain marie
roux	dim sum	sag aloo	ballotine
sake	ditali	sashimi	carbonara
soba	eliche	schlada	charmoula
sugo	flambé	seviche	cochiglie
taco	fondue	soufflé	colcannon
05 ancho	hoisin	tempura	concassée
balti	hummus	terrine	enchilada
bhaji	kibbeh	timbale	entrecôte
blini	Kung Po	tostada	fricassée
cajun	masala	vongole	jambalaya
crêpe	moglai	**08** au gratin	pastitsio
dashi	paella	bouillon	picadillo
gelée	pakora	briouate	rogan josh
halva	paneer	brunoise	spaghetti
humus	panini	bucatini	**10** avgolemono
keema	pullao	chupatti	cacciatore
korai	ragoût	couscous	cannelloni
korma	samosa	crostini	fettuccine
kulfi	tagine	dolmades	feuilletté
mirin	tamari	escalope	jardinière
murgh	wasabi	farfalle	nasi goreng
panko	wonton	gazpacho	parmigiana
penne	**07** baklava	jalfrezi	quesadilla
phall	biriani	julienne	salsa verde
pilaf	brinjal	kleftiko	sauerkraut
pilau	buñuelo	linguini	**11** beurre manié
ponzu	dhansak	lumaconi	chimichanga
purée	fusilli	macaroni	garam masala
raita	gemelli	mesquite	hors d'oeuvre
sauté	gnocchi	moussaka	katsuobushi
shoyu	granite	shashlik	orecchiette
sushi	gratiné	sukiyaki	panch phoran
tapas	hoummos	tandoori	ratatouille
tarka	lumache	tapenade	smorgåsbord
tikka	merguez	teriyaki	tagliatelli
torte	nam prik	tonkatsu	**12** taramasalata
06 anelli	pak choi	tortilla	**13** cresti di gallo
bargar	parfait	tzatziki	**14** capelli d'angelo
	pasanda	umeboshi	

Cookery terms include:

03 Aga	cook	**05** baste	devil
dip	cure	brown	dress
gut	dice	carve	glaze
hob	mash	chill	grate
ice	oven	chump	knead
04 chef	rise	curry	mince
chop	whip	daube	mould

press
purée
score
shave
smoke
steep
stuff
whisk

06 batter
blanch

de-bone
entrée
fillet
fondue
infuse
kosher
leaven
recipe
reduce
season
spread

07 deglaze
de-scale
garnish
nibbles
proving
starter
tandoor
topping

08 cookbook
devilled

marinade
marinate
preserve

09 antipasto
percolate
reduction
tenderize

10 caramelize

11 amuse bouche
hors d'oeuvre

See also **chef**; **curry**; **food**

corm *see* **bulb**

cosmetics

Cosmetics include:

05 rouge
toner

07 blusher
bronzer
mascara
perfume

08 cleanser
eyeliner
face mask
face pack
lip gloss

lip liner
lipstick
panstick

09 concealer
eye shadow
face cream
lightener

10 eyelash dye
face powder
foundation
kohl pencil

maquillage
nail polish

11 greasepaint
loose powder
moisturizer
nail varnish

13 eyebrow pencil
pancake make-up
pressed powder

14 false eyelashes

cotton

Cotton fabrics include:

04 aida
duck
jean

05 chino
denim
dhoti
drill
jaspé
jeans
kanga
piqué
surat
toile

06 Bengal
calico
canvas
chintz
coutil
dhooti
diaper
dimity
humhum
jersey

khanga
madras
moreen
muslin
nankin
Oxford
pongee
sateen
T-cloth

07 batiste
buckram
challis
duvetyn
fustian
galatea
gingham
jaconet
kitenge
Mexican
nankeen
percale
printer
silesia

08 chambray
corduroy
coutille
cretonne
drilling
frocking
lambskin
marcella
nainsook
organdie
osnaburg
shantung
thickset

09 cottonade
huckaback
longcloth
percaline
sailcloth
satin jean
swans-down
velveteen

10 Balbriggan
candlewick

monk's cloth
seersucker
winceyette

11 cheesecloth
flannelette
mutton cloth
nettle-cloth

Oxford cloth
sponge cloth

13 casement cloth

council *see* **United Kingdom**

country

Countries of the world include:

03 UAE
USA
04 Chad
Cuba
Fiji
Iran
Iraq
Laos
Mali
Oman
Peru
Togo
05 Benin
Chile
China
Congo
Egypt
Gabon
Ghana
Haiti
India
Italy
Japan
Kenya
Libya
Malta
Nauru
Nepal
Niger
Palau
Qatar
Samoa
Spain
Sudan
Syria
Tonga
Wales
Yemen
06 Angola
Belize
Bhutan
Brazil
Canada
Cyprus
France
Greece

Guinea
Guyana
Israel
Jordan
Kosovo
Kuwait
Latvia
Malawi
Mexico
Monaco
Norway
Panama
Poland
Russia
Serbia
Rwanda
Sweden
Taiwan
Turkey
Tuvalu
Uganda
Zambia
07 Albania
Algeria
Andorra
Armenia
Austria
Bahrain
Belarus
Belgium
Bolivia
Burundi
Comoros
Croatia
Denmark
Ecuador
England
Eritrea
Estonia
Finland
Georgia
Germany
Grenada
Hungary
Iceland
Ireland

Jamaica
Lebanon
Lesotho
Liberia
Moldova
Morocco
Myanmar
Namibia
Nigeria
Romania
Senegal
Somalia
St Lucia
Tunisia
Ukraine
Uruguay
Vanuatu
Vietnam
08 Barbados
Botswana
Bulgaria
Cambodia
Cameroon
Colombia
Djibouti
Dominica
Ethiopia
Honduras
Kiribati
Malaysia
Maldives
Mongolia
Pakistan
Paraguay
Portugal
Scotland
Slovakia
Slovenia
Sri Lanka
Suriname
Tanzania
Thailand
Zimbabwe
09 Argentina
Australia
Cape Verde

Costa Rica
East Timor
Guatemala
Indonesia
Lithuania
Macedonia
Mauritius
Nicaragua
San Marino
Singapore
Swaziland
The Gambia
Venezuela

10 Azerbaijan
Bangladesh
El Salvador
Kazakhstan
Kyrgyzstan
Luxembourg
Madagascar
Mauritania
Montenegro
Mozambique
New Zealand
North Korea

Seychelles
South Korea
South Sudan
Tajikistan
The Bahamas
Uzbekistan

11 Afghanistan
Burkina Faso
Côte d'Ivoire
Philippines
Saudi Arabia
Sierra Leone
South Africa
Switzerland
Vatican City

12 Great Britain
Guinea-Bissau
Turkmenistan
Turkmenistan
United States

13 Czech Republic
Liechtenstein
United Kingdom
Western Sahara

14 Papua New Guinea
Solomon Islands
The Netherlands

15 Marshall Islands
Northern Ireland
St Kitts and Nevis

16 Brunei Darussalam
Equatorial Guinea

17 Antigua and Barbuda
Dominican Republic
Trinidad and Tobago

18 São Tomé and Príncipe
United Arab Emirates

20 Bosnia and Herzegovina

21 United States of America

22 Central African Republic

25 St Vincent and the
Grenadines

27 Federated States of
Micronesia

28 Democratic Republic of the
Congo

Country codes include:

03 ABW (Aruba)
AFG (Afghanistan)
AGO (Angola)
AIA (Anguilla)
ALB (Albania)
AND (Andorra)
ANT (Netherlands Antilles)
ARE (United Arab Emirates)
ARG (Argentina)
ARM (Armenia)
ASM (American Samoa)
ATA (Antarctica)
ATF (French Southern and Antarctic
Territories)
ATG (Antigua and Barbuda)
AUS (Australia)
AUT (Austria)
AZE (Azerbaijan)
BDI (Burundi)
BEL (Belgium)
BEN (Benin)
BFA (Burkina Faso)
BGD (Bangladesh)
BGR (Bulgaria)
BHR (Bahrain)
BHS (The Bahamas)
BIH (Bosnia and Herzegovina)
BLR (Belarus)
BLZ (Belize)

BMU (Bermuda)
BOL (Bolivia)
BRA (Brazil)
BRB (Barbados)
BRN (Brunei Darussalam)
BTN (Bhutan)
BVT (Bouvet Island)
BWA (Botswana)
CAF (Central African Republic)
CAN (Canada)
CCK (Cocos Islands)
CHE (Switzerland)
CHL (Chile)
CHN (China)
CIV (Côte d'Ivoire)
CMR (Cameroon)
COD (Democratic Republic of the Congo)
COG (Congo)
COK (Cook Islands)
COL (Colombia)
COM (Comoros)
CPV (Cape Verde)
CRI (Costa Rica)
CUB (Cuba)
CXR (Christmas Island)
CYM (Cayman Islands)
CYP (Cyprus)
CZE (Czech Republic)
DEU (Germany)

DJI (Djibouti)
DMA (Dominica)
DNK (Denmark)
DOM (Dominican Republic)
DZA (Algeria)
ECU (Ecuador)
EGY (Egypt)
ERI (Eritrea)
ESH (Western Sahara)
ESP (Spain)
EST (Estonia)
ETH (Ethiopia)
FIN (Finland)
FJI (Fiji)
FLK (Falkland Islands)
FRA (France)
FRO (Faroe Islands)
FSM (Federated States of Micronesia)
GAB (Gabon)
GBR (United Kingdom)
GEO (Georgia)
GHA (Ghana)
GIB (Gibraltar)
GIN (Guinea)
GLP (Guadeloupe)
GMB (The Gambia)
GNB (Guinea-Bissau)
GNQ (Equatorial Guinea)
GRC (Greece)
GRD (Grenada)
GRL (Greenland)
GTM (Guatemala)
GUF (French Guiana)
GUM (Guam)
GUY (Guyana)
HGK (Hong Kong)
HND (Honduras)
HRV (Croatia)
HTI (Haiti)
HUN (Hungary)
IDN (Indonesia)
IMN (Isle of Man)
IND (India)
IOT (British Indian Ocean Territory)
IRL (Ireland)
IRN (Iran)
IRQ (Iraq)
ISL (Iceland)
ISR (Israel)
ITA (Italy)
JAM (Jamaica)
JOR (Jordan)
JPN (Japan)
KAZ (Kazakhstan)
KEN (Kenya)
KGZ (Kyrgyzstan)
KHM (Cambodia)
KIR (Kiribati)

KNA (St Kitts and Nevis)
KOR (South Korea)
KWT (Kuwait)
LAO (Laos)
LBN (Lebanon)
LBR (Liberia)
LBY (Libya)
LCA (St Lucia)
LIE (Liechtenstein)
LKA (Sri Lanka)
LSO (Lesotho)
LTU (Lithuania)
LUX (Luxembourg)
LVA (Latvia)
MAC (Macao)
MAR (Morocco)
MCO (Monaco)
MDA (Moldova)
MDG (Madagascar)
MDV (Maldives)
MEX (Mexico)
MHL (Marshall Islands)
MKD (Macedonia)
MLI (Mali)
MLT (Malta)
MMR (Myanmar)
MNE (Montenegro)
MNG (Mongolia)
MOZ (Mozambique)
MRT (Mauritania)
MSR (Montserrat)
MTQ (Martinique)
MUS (Mauritius)
MWI (Malawi)
MYS (Malaysia)
MYT (Mayotte)
NAM (Namibia)
NCL (New Caledonia)
NER (Niger)
NFK (Norfolk Island)
NGA (Nigeria)
NIC (Nicaragua)
NIU (Niue)
NLD (The Netherlands)
NOR (Norway)
NPL (Nepal)
NRU (Nauru)
NZL (New Zealand)
OMN (Oman)
PAK (Pakistan)
PAN (Panama)
PCN (Pitcairn Island)
PER (Peru)
PHL (Philippines)
PLW (Palau)
PNG (Papua New Guinea)
POL (Poland)
PRI (Puerto Rico)

PRK (North Korea)
PRT (Portugal)
PRY (Paraguay)
PYF (French Polynesia)
QAT (Qatar)
REU (Réunion)
ROU (Romania)
RUS (Russia)
RWA (Rwanda)
SAU (Saudi Arabia)
SDN (Sudan)
SEN (Senegal)
SGP (Singapore)
SHN (St Helena)
SJM (Svalbard and Jan Mayen Islands)
SLB (Solomon Islands)
SLE (Sierra Leone)
SLV (El Salvador)
SMR (San Marino)
SOM (Somalia)
SPM (St Pierre and Miquelon)
SRB (Serbia)
SSD (South Sudan)
STP (São Tomé and Príncipe)
SUR (Suriname)
SVK (Slovakia)
SVN (Slovenia)
SWE (Sweden)
SWZ (Swaziland)
SYC (Seychelles)
SYR (Syria)
TCA (Turks and Caicos Islands)

TCD (Chad)
TGO (Togo)
THA (Thailand)
TJK (Tajikistan)
TKL (Tokelau)
TKM (Turkmenistan)
TLS (East Timor)
TON (Tonga)
TTO (Trinidad and Tobago)
TUN (Tunisia)
TUR (Turkey)
TUV (Tuvalu)
TWN (Taiwan)
TZA (United Republic of Tanzania)
UGA (Uganda)
UKR (Ukraine)
URY (Uruguay)
USA (United States of America)
UZB (Uzbekistan)
VAT (Vatican City)
VCT (St Vincent and the Grenadines)
VEN (Venezuela)
VGB (British Virgin Islands)
VIR (United States Virgin Islands)
VNM (Vietnam)
VUT (Vanuatu)
WLF (Wallis and Futuna)
WSM (Samoa)
YEM (Yemen)
ZAF (South Africa)
ZMB (Zambia)
ZWE (Zimbabwe)

Former country names include:

04 Siam (Thailand)
USSR (Armenia/Azerbaijan/Belarus/
Estonia/Georgia/Kazakhstan/Kyrgyzstan/
Latvia/Lithuania/Moldova/Russia/
Tajikistan/Turkmenistan/Ukraine/
Uzbekistan)

05 Burma (Myanmar)
Zaire (Democratic Republic of the Congo)

06 Bengal (Bangladesh)
Ceylon (Sri Lanka)
Persia (Iran)
Urundi (Burundi)

07 Dahomey (Benin)
Formosa (Taiwan)

08 Rhodesia (Zimbabwe)

09 Abyssinia (Ethiopia)
Indochina (Cambodia/Vietnam)
Kampuchea (Cambodia)
Nyasaland (Malawi)

10 Basutoland (Lesotho)
Ivory Coast (Côte d'Ivoire)

Senegambia (The Gambia/Senegal)
Tanganyika (Tanzania)
Upper Volta (Burkina Faso)
Yugoslavia (Bosnia and Herzegovina/
Croatia/Kosovo/Macedonia/Montenegro/
Serbia/Slovenia)

11 Dutch Guiana (Suriname)
French Sudan (Mali)
New Hebrides (Vanuatu)
Ubangi Shari (Central African Republic)

12 Bechuanaland (Botswana)
French Guinea (Guinea)
Ruanda-Urundi (Burundi/Rwanda)

13 British Guiana (Guyana)
Ellice Islands (Tuvalu)
Khmer Republic (Cambodia)
Spanish Guinea (Equatorial Guinea)
Spanish Sahara (Western Sahara)
Trucial States (United Arab Emirates)

14 Czechoslovakia (Czech Republic/Slovakia)
French Togoland (Togo)
Gilbert Islands (Kiribati)

15 British Honduras (Belize)
British Togoland (Ghana)

Dutch East Indies (Indonesia)
South West Africa (Namibia)

Local country names include:

03 Lao (Laos)

04 Éire (Ireland)
Misr (Egypt)
'Uman (Oman)
Viti (Fiji)

05 Belau (Palau)
Eesti (Estonia)
Ellas (Greece)
Ertra (Eritrea)
Nihon (Japan)
Norge (Norway)
Suomi (Finland)
Tchad (Chad)

06 België (Belgium)
Bharat (India)
Brasil (Brazil)
Chosun (North Korea)
España (Spain)
Guinée (Guinea)
Guyane (French Guiana)
Hanguk (South Korea)
Ísland (Iceland)
Italia (Italy)
Kibris (Cyprus)
Kipros (Cyprus)
Lubnan (Lebanon)
México (Mexico)
Naoero (Nauru)
Nippon (Japan)
Polska (Poland)
Srbija (Serbia)
Suisse (Switzerland)
Svizra (Switzerland)
T'ai-wan (Taiwan)

07 Algérie (Algeria)
Al-Urdun (Jordan)
Al-Yaman (Yemen)
As-Sudan (Sudan)
Comores (Comoros)
Danmark (Denmark)
Druk Yul (Bhutan)
Føroyar (Faroe Islands)
Latvija (Latvia)
Lietuva (Lithuania)
Rossiya (Russia)
Schweiz (Switzerland)
Suriyah (Syria)
Sverige (Sweden)
Türkiye (Turkey)
Ukraïna (Ukraine)

Viêt Nam (Vietnam)

08 Al-Jaza'ir (Algeria)
Al-Kuwayt (Kuwait)
Aotearoa (New Zealand)
Belgique (Belgium)
Cameroun (Cameroon)
Crna Gora (Montenegro)
Grønland (Greenland)
Hayastan (Armenia)
Hrvatska (Croatia)
Ityop'iya (Ethiopia)
Svizzera (Switzerland)
Tunisiya (Tunisia)
Zhong Guo (China)

09 Al-Bahrayn (Bahrain)
Al Maghrib (Morocco)
Balgarija (Bulgaria)
Cabo Verde (Cape Verde)
Færøerne (Faroe Islands)
Kâmpuchéa (Cambodia)
Mongol Uls (Mongolia)
Pilipinas (Philippines)
Qazaqstan (Kazakhstan)
Shqipëria (Albania)
Slovenija (Slovenia)
Slovensko (Slovakia)

10 Azerbaycan (Azerbaijan)
Makedonija (Macedonia)
Mauritanie (Mauritania)
Moçambique (Mozambique)
Muritaniya (Mauritania)
Österreich (Austria)
Özbekistan (Uzbekistan)
Sak'art'velo (Georgia)
Soomaaliya (Somalia)
Timor-Leste (East Timor)

11 Deutschland (Germany)
Guiné-Bissau (Guinea-Bissau)
Prathet Thai (Thailand)

12 Madagasikara (Madagascar)
Magyarorszag (Hungary)
Timor Lorosa'e (East Timor)

13 Dhivehi Raajje (Maldives)

14 Ceská Republika (Czech Republic)
Dawlat Israqa'il (Israel)
Die Nederlanden (The Netherlands)
Medinat Yisra'el (Israel)

15 Kalaallit Nunaat (Greenland)
Umbuso weSwatini (Kingdom of Swaziland)

See also **Africa**; **The Americas**; **Arab League**; **Asia**; **Australasia**; **Australia**; **Austria**; **Belgium**;

Canada; China; CIS; commonwealth; Czech Republic; Denmark; dependency; Europe; Finland; France; Germany; Greece; India; Ireland; Italy; Japan; Mexico; NATO; The Netherlands; New Zealand; Norway; OPEC; Portugal; Russia; Spain; Sweden; Switzerland; United Kingdom; United Nations; United States of America

country and western

Country and western musicians and singers include:

04 Cash (Johnny; 1932–2003, US)
Lynn (Loretta; 1935– , US)

05 Cline (Patsy; 1932–63, US)
Jones (George; 1931–2013, US)
Pride (Charley; 1938– , US)
Raitt (Bonnie; 1949– , US)

06 Atkins (Chet; 1924–2001, US)
Brooks (Garth; 1962– , US)
Denver (John; 1943–97, US)
Harris (Emmylou; 1947– , US)
Lovett (Lyle; 1956– , US)

Nelson (Willie; 1933– , US)
Parton (Dolly; 1946– , US)
Rogers (Kenny; 1938– , US)

07 Francis (Connie; 1938– , US)
Haggard (Merle; 1937– , US)
Wynette (Tammy; 1942–98, US)

08 Griffith (Nanci; 1954– , US)
Jennings (Waylon; 1937–2002, US)
Ronstadt (Linda; 1946– , US)
Williams (Hank; 1923–53, US)

county *see* **town; United Kingdom**

course *see* **golf**

court

Courts include:

03 ICC

04 High
Lyon
moot
open

05 burgh
civil
Crown
prize
trial
World
youth

06 appeal
Arches
church
claims
county
family

See also **law**

Honour
police
record

07 appeals
assizes
borough
circuit
Diplock
divorce
federal
justice
Probate
Session
sheriff
Supreme

08 coroner's
criminal
district
juvenile

kangaroo
Requests
superior
tribunal

09 children's
Exchequer
Faculties
municipal
Old Bailey
Piepowder
the Arches

10 Commercial
commissary
Divisional
Piepowders
Protection

11 Arbitration
Common Bench

Common Pleas
High Justice
magistrates'
police-court
Prerogative
small claims

12 court-martial
House of Lords
Privy Council

13 first instance

14 Criminal Appeal
High Commission
High Justiciary

15 Central Criminal
European Justice
Lord Chancellor's

Coward, Sir Noël (1899–1973)

Significant works include:

08 *Hay Fever* (1925)
Operette (1938)
Sail Away (1961)

09 *Cavalcade* (1931)
Quadrille (1952)
The Vortex (1924)

10 *Easy Virtue* (1926)
Sigh No More (1945)

11 *Bitter Sweet* (1929)

12 *Blithe Spirit* (1941)
Fallen Angels (1925)
Private Lives (1930)
13 *Words and Music* (1932)
14 *Brief Encounter* (1945)

In Which We Serve (1942)
Nude With Violin (1956)
Peace in Our Time (1947)
Relative Values (1951)
This Happy Breed (1939)
15 *Design for Living* (1933)

I'll Leave It to You (1920)
Present Laughter (1939)
This Year of Grace (1928)
17 *Conversation Piece* (1934)
Waiting in the Wings (1960)

Significant characters include:

05 Bliss (David)
Bliss (Judith)
Bliss (Simon)
Bliss (Sorel)
Chase (Elyot)
Chase (Sybil)
Clara
06 Arcati (Madame)

Harvey (Dr Alec)
Jesson (Laura)
Prynne (Amanda)
Prynne (Victor)
Tyrell (Sandy)
07 Arundel (Myra)
Coryton (Jackie)
Gibbons (Ethel)

Gibbons (Frank)
Kinross (Captain)
08 Greatham (Richard)
09 Condomine (Charles)
Condomine (Elvira)
Condomine (Ruth)
Lancaster (Florence)
Lancaster (Nicky)

craft *see* **art**

cricket

Cricket teams include:

04 Kent
05 Essex
06 Durham
Surrey
Sussex
08 Somerset
Victoria

09 Glamorgan
Hampshire
Middlesex
Yorkshire
10 Derbyshire
Lancashire
Queensland
12 Warwickshire

13 New South Wales
14 Leicestershire
South Australia
Worcestershire
15 Gloucestershire
Nottinghamshire
16 Northamptonshire
Western Australia

Cricket team nicknames include:

05 Bears (Warwickshire)
Blues (New South Wales)
Bulls (Queensland)
Foxes (Leicestershire)
Hawks (Hampshire)
06 Eagles (Essex)
Royals (Worcestershire)
Sabres (Somerset)
Sharks (Sussex)
Tigers (Tasmania)
07 Dragons (Glamorgan)
Dynamos (Durham)

Outlaws (Nottinghamshire)
Phoenix (Yorkshire)
08 Phantoms (Derbyshire)
Redbacks (South Australia)
Warriors (Western Australia)
09 Brown Caps (Surrey)
Crusaders (Middlesex)
Lightning (Lancashire)
Spitfires (Kent)
10 Gladiators (Gloucestershire)
Steelbacks (Northamptonshire)
11 Bushrangers (Victoria)

Cricketers and associated figures include:

03 Dev (Kapil; 1959– , Indian)
Fry (C B; 1872–1956, English)
04 Ames (Les; 1905–90, English)
Bedi (Bishen; 1946– , Indian)
Bird (Harold 'Dickie'; 1933– , English)

Hall (Wes; 1937– , Barbadian)
Hick (Graeme; 1966– , Zimbabwean/British)
Lara (Brian; 1969– , Trinidadian)
Lock (Tony; 1929–95, English)
Lord (Thomas; 1755–1832, English)

05 Allen (Sir Gubby; 1902–89, English)
Amiss (Dennis; 1943– , English)
Crowe (Martin; 1962– , New Zealand)
Evans (Godfrey; 1920–99, English)
Gibbs (Lance; 1934– , Guyanese)
Gooch (Graham; 1953– , English)
Gough (Darren; 1970– , English)
Gower (David; 1957– , English)
Grace (W G; 1848–1915, English)
Greig (Tony; 1946– , South African/British)
Healy (Ian; 1964– , Australian)
Hobbs (Sir Jack; 1882–1963, English)
Knott (Alan; 1946– , English)
Laker (Jim; 1922–86, English)
Lawry (Bill; 1937– , Australian)
Lloyd (Clive; 1944– , Guyanese/British)
Marsh (Rodney; 1947– , Australian)
Pilch (Fuller; 1804–70, English)
Walsh (Courtney; 1962– , Jamaican)
Warne (Shane; 1969– , Australian)
Waugh (Mark; 1965– , Australian)
Waugh (Steve; 1965– , Australian)

06 Arlott (John; 1914–91, English)
Bailey (Trevor; 1923–2011, English)
Benaud (Richie; 1930– , Australian)
Border (Allan; 1955– , Australian)
Botham (Ian; 1955– , English)
Cronje (Hansie; 1969–2002, South African)
Dexter (Ted; 1935– , English)
Donald (Allan; 1966– , South African)
Dravid (Rahul; 1973– , Indian)
Edrich (Bill; 1916–86, English)
Garner (Joel; 1952– , Barbadian)
Hadlee (Sir Richard; 1948– , New Zealand)
Haynes (Desmond; 1956– , Barbadian)
Hutton (Sir Len; 1916–90, English)
Jessop (Gilbert; 1874–1955, English)
Lillee (Dennis; 1949– , Australian)
Miller (Keith; 1919–2004, Australian)
Rhodes (Wilfred; 1877–1973, English)
Sobers (Sir Garfield; 1936– , Barbadian)
Thorpe (Graham; 1969– , English)
Titmus (Fred; 1932–2011, English)
Turner (Glenn; 1947– , New Zealand)
Warner (Sir Pelham 'Plum'; 1873–1963, Trinidadian/British)

07 Ambrose (Curtley; 1963– , Antiguan)
Boycott (Geoffrey; 1940– , English)
Bradman (Sir Don; 1908–2001, Australian)
Compton (Denis; 1918–97, English)
Cowdrey (Colin, Lord; 1932–2000, English)
Denness (Mike; 1940–2013, Scottish)
De Silva (Aravinda; 1965– , Sri Lankan)

Gatting (Mike; 1957– , English)
Hammond (Wally; 1903–65, English)
Holding (Michael; 1954– , Jamaican)
Hussain (Nasser; 1968– , Indian/British)
Jardine (Douglas; 1900–58, English)
Larwood (Harold; 1904–95, English)
McGrath (Glenn; 1970– , Australian)
Pataudi (Mansur Ali, Nawab of, Jnr; 1941– , Indian)
Pollock (Graeme; 1944– , South African)
Roberts (Andy; 1951– , Antiguan)
Simpson (Bobby; 1936– , Australian)
Stewart (Alec; 1963– , English)
Thomson (Jeff; 1950– , Australian)
Trueman (Fred; 1931–2006, English)
Tufnell (Philip; 1966– , English)
Worrell (Frank; 1924–67, Barbadian)

08 Atherton (Michael; 1968– , English)
Chappell (Greg; 1948– , Australian)
Chappell (Ian; 1943– , Australian)
Flintoff (Andrew; 1977– , English)
Gavaskar (Sunil; 1949– , Indian)
Johnston (Brian; 1912–94, English)
Kapil Dev (1959– , Indian)
Lindwall (Ray; 1921–96, Australian)
Marshall (Malcolm; 1958–99, Barbadian)
Richards (Barry; 1945– , South African)
Richards (Sir Vivian; 1952– , Antiguan)

09 deFreitas (Phillip; 1966– , English)
D'Oliveira (Basil; 1931–2011, South African/British)
Greenidge (Gordon; 1951– , Barbadian)
Imran Khan (1952– , Pakistani)
Pietersen (Kevin; 1980– , South African)
Ranatunga (Arjuna; 1963– , Sri Lankan)
Sutcliffe (Herbert; 1894–1978, English)
Tendulkar (Sachin; 1973– , Indian)

10 Azharuddin (Mohammad; 1963– , Indian)
Barrington (Ken; 1930–81, English)
Lillywhite (William; 1792–1854, English)
Wasim Akram (1966– , Pakistani)

11 Constantine (Sir Learie; 1901–71, West Indian)
Heyhoe Flint (Rachael, Baroness 1939– , English)
Illingworth (Ray; 1932– , English)
Trescothick (Marcus; 1975– , English)
Zaheer Abbas (1947– , Pakistani)

12 Javed Miandad (1957– , Pakistani)
Muralitharan (Muttiah 'Murali'; 1972– , Sri Lankan)

13 Chandrasekhar (Bhagwat; 1945– , Indian)
Mohammed Hanif (1934– , Pakistani)

Cricket deliveries include:

06 doosra
googly

teesra
yorker

07 bouncer
swinger

08 bodyline   off break   off-cutter
    Chinaman
    fastball   **09** inswinger   **10** outswinger
    leg break   leg-cutter   **11** daisy-cutter

Cricket terms include:

01 b	tice	googly	infield
c	tonk	ground	innings
M	walk	howzat	inswing
w	wide	leg bye	knock up
02 by	work	length	last man
CC	**05** block	long on	leg side
in	break	maiden	leg slip
lb	c and b	middle	leg spin
nb	catch	mid off	long hop
no	cover	no ball	long leg
on	dolly	not out	long off
ro	drive	nurdle	offside
03 bat	extra	onside	off spin
box	field	opener	on drive
bye	gaper	play on	on the up
CCC	glide	rabbit	paceman
cut	guard	rubber	put down
ECB	gully	runner	shooter
ICC	Jaffa	run out	spinner
lbw	knock	scorer	striker
leg	mid on	screen	stumped
MCC	pitch	seamer	sweeper
net	plumb	seam up	swinger
ODI	point	single	Windies
off	quilt	sledge	wrong'un
pad	shoot	splice	**08** backlift
peg	short	square	backward
run	silly	strike	bodyline
six	skier	stumps	boundary
ton	skyer	swerve	Chinaman
04 bail	snick	the leg	delivery
ball	spell	tickle	fielding
blob	stand	timber	flannels
bowl	stump	umpire	follow-on
deep	sweep	whites	for keeps
draw	swing	wicket	full toss
duck	throw	willow	gazunder
edge	track	yorker	half-cock
four	yahoo	**07** air shot	hat trick
go in	**06** appeal	batsman	how's that
grub	beamer	batting	king pair
hook	bowled	bouncer	leg break
meat	bowler	century	leg guard
Oval	bumper	creeper	long slip
over	carpet	declare	long stop
pair	caught	dismiss	misfield
poke	cherry	dot ball	off break
pull	crease	fielder	off drive
seam	eleven	fine leg	off guard
slip	extras	flipper	on strike
tail	fizzer	fly slip	outfield
	glance	grubber	over rate

pavilion
short leg
sledging
stumping
the Ashes
thigh pad
third man
throw out
uncapped

09 batswoman
big hitter
blockhole
deep field
dolly girl
fieldsman
gardening
hit wicket
inswinger
left guard
leg before
leg-cutter
leg theory
long field
mid-wicket
off-cutter
overpitch
overthrow
See also **sport**

powerplay
short slip
square cut
square leg
stonewall
test match
tip and run

10 all-rounder
cover drive
cover point
draw stumps
extra cover
fast bowler
golden duck
half-volley
inside edge
leg spinner
maiden over
off spinner
outswinger
pace bowler
right guard
scoreboard
seam bowler
silly mid-on
silly point
skittle out

spin bowler
spring line
take a guard
take strike
twelfth man

11 clean bowled
daisy-cutter
diamond duck
fast bowling
fieldswoman
grass-cutter
ground staff
half-century
limited-over
net practice
one-day match
outside edge
pace-bowling
pinch-hitter
seam bowling
sight screen
silly mid-off
spin bowling
swing bowler

12 carry your bat
middle and leg

middle and off
return crease
reverse sweep
reverse swing
scoring board
single-wicket
twenty-twenty
wicketkeeper

13 bowling crease
break one's duck
county cricket
keep your end up
maiden century
night-watchman
popping crease
pyjama cricket

14 off the back foot
sit on the splice
take out your bat

15 bodyline bowling
bowl a maiden over
carry out your bat
caught and bowled
leather on willow
leg before wicket
square leg umpire

crime

Crimes include:

03 ABH
GBH

04 rape

05 arson
fraud
theft

06 bigamy
hijack
murder
piracy

07 assault
battery
bribery
forgery
larceny
mugging
perjury

robbery
treason

08 banditry
burglary
homicide
poaching
sabotage
stalking

09 blackmail
extortion
hate crime
joy-riding
pilfering
terrorism
vandalism

10 corruption
cybercrime

kidnapping

11 drug dealing
hooliganism
shoplifting
trespassing

12 drink-driving
embezzlement
manslaughter

13 assassination
drug smuggling
honour killing
housebreaking
identity theft

14 counterfeiting
insider dealing
insider trading

15 computer hacking

Criminal types include:

03 lag

04 hood
thug

05 crook

thief

06 bandit
forger
gunman
killer

mugger
pirate
rapist
robber
vandal

07	brigand		perjurer		fire-raiser
	burglar		receiver		highwayman
	hoodlum		saboteur		paedophile
	mobster		smuggler		pickpocket
	poacher		swindler		shoplifter
	rustler	09	buccaneer		trespasser
	stalker		cracksman	11	armed robber
08	arsonist		embezzler		blackmailer
	assassin		kidnapper		bogus caller
	batterer		larcenist		drink-driver
	bigamist		racketeer		kerb-crawler
	car-thief		ram-raider		safecracker
	gangster		strangler		war criminal
	hijacker		terrorist	12	drug smuggler
	jailbird	10	bootlegger		extortionist
	joyrider		cat burglar		housebreaker
	murderer		dope pusher		sexual abuser
	pederast		drug dealer	13	counterfeiter

Criminals and outlaws include:

03 Nym (*The Merry Wives of Windsor*, 1597, William Shakespeare)

04 Wild (Jonathan; *The Life of Jonathan Wild the Great*, 1743, Henry Fielding)

05 Biggs (Ronald; 1929– , English)
Blood (Thomas; c.1618–80, Irish)
Curry (Kid; 1865–1903, US)
Fagin (*Oliver Twist*, 1838, Charles Dickens)
James (Jesse; 1847–82, US)
Kelly (Ned; 1855–80, Australian)
Nancy (*Oliver Twist*, 1838, Charles Dickens)
Sikes (Bill; *Oliver Twist*, 1838, Charles Dickens)
Tweed (William M; 1823–78, US)

06 Barrow (Clyde; 1909–34, US)
Bonney (William H; 1859–81, US)
Capone (Al; 1899–1947, US)
Dalton (Robert; 1867–92, US)
Manuel (Peter; 1931–58, Scottish)
Meehan (Patrick; 1927–94, Scottish)

Parker (Bonnie; 1911–34, US)
Pistol (*The Merry Wives of Windsor*, 1597, William Shakespeare)
Rob Roy (1671–1734, Scottish)
Vidocq (Eugène; 1775–1857, French)

07 Cassidy (Butch; 1866–?1908, US)
Ireland (William Henry; 1777–1835, English)
Luciano (Lucky; 1897–1962, Italian/US)
Raffles (*The Amateur Cracksman*, 1899, E W Hornung)

08 Bardolph (*Henry IV Part I*, 1596/7, William Shakespeare)
Moriarty (Professor; *The Final Problem*, 1892–93, Arthur Conan Doyle)
Sheppard (Jack; 1702–24, English)

09 Dillinger (John; 1903–34, US)
Robin Hood (c.1250–c.1350, English)

11 Billy the Kid (1859–81, US)
Sundance Kid (1870–?1908, US)

See also **highwayman**; **murder**; **police**

critic *see* **literature**

Croatia *see* **Balkans**

crop

Arable crops include:

03	pea		corn		oats		swede
	rye		flax		rice		wheat
	yam		hemp				
			kale	05	colza	06	barley
04	bean		milo		maize		kharif

millet	lucerne	soya bean	sweetcorn
potato	oilseed	teosinte	triticale
turnip	popcorn	**09** milo maize	**10** fodder beet
07 alfalfa	sorghum	sugar beet	**11** oilseed rape
cassava	soy bean	sugar cane	sweet potato
linseed	**08** mung bean	sunflower	**12** mangel wurzel

See also **agriculture**; **cereal**; **farm**

cross

Crosses include:

01 T	Rouen	capital	Southern
03 Red	**06** ansate	Cornish	St Peter's
tau	botoné	Maltese	swastika
04 ankh	Celtic	Russian	Victoria
high	fleury	saltire	**09** encolpion
Iron	fylfot	Weeping	Jerusalem
ring	Geneva	**08** Buddhist	preaching
rood	George	capuchin	St Andrew's
rose	market	cardinal	St George's
rosy	moline	crosslet	**10** St Anthony's
05 fiery	Norman	crucifix	**11** patriarchal
Greek	potent	Lorraine	**13** Constantinian
Latin	Y-cross	military	**14** archiepiscopal
papal	**07** Avelian	pectoral	
	Calvary	quadrate	

See also **religion**; **symbol**

crossword

Crosswords and crossword setters include:

03 Phi	**05** Afrit	**07** Columba	Pasquale
04 Apex	Rufus	Cyclops	**09** Araucaria
Azed	Wynne (Arthur)	Fidelio	Beelzebub
Duck		Quixote	Bunthorne
Mass	**06** Aelred	Spurius	Cinephile
Monk	Crispa	Ximenes	Virgilius
Paul	Custos	**08** Everyman	**10** Enigmatist
Shed	Gemini	Giovanni	Torquemada
	Portia	Mephisto	

crust

Parts of the Earth's crust include:

03 sal	sima	mantle
04 sial	**06** craton	

crustacean

Crustaceans include:

04 crab	**06** gilgie	partan
05 krill	hermit	scampi
prawn	jilgie	scrawl
yabby	marron	shrimp

squill
yabbie
07 camaron
copepod
daphnia
dog-crab
fiddler
limulus
lobster
pagurid
pea-crab
pill bug
08 barnacle
crawfish
crayfish
crevette
king crab
land crab
ochidore
pagurian
09 centipede
devil-crab
fish louse
ghost crab
king prawn
langouste
millipede

phyllopod
schizopod
sea slater
shore crab
soft-shell
stone crab
water flea
woodlouse
10 acorn-shell
edible crab
hermit crab
mitten-crab
robber crab
sandhopper
seed shrimp
spider crab
stomatopod
tiger prawn
velvet-crab
velvet worm
whale louse
11 brine shrimp
calling-crab
coconut crab
common prawn
Dublin prawn
fairy shrimp

fiddler crab
langoustine
rock lobster
soldier crab
spectre crab
tiger shrimp
12 common shrimp
mantis shrimp
mussel shrimp
saucepan-fish
sentinel crab
spiny lobster
squat lobster
13 acorn-barnacle
common lobster
goose barnacle
horseshoe crab
noble crayfish
Norway lobster
opossum shrimp
spectre shrimp
tadpole shrimp
velvet-fiddler
14 Dublin Bay prawn
skeleton shrimp
woolly-hand crab

currency

Currencies, with country and smaller units, include:

03 kip (Laos: at)
lat (Latvia: santims)
lek (Albania: qindarka)
leu (Moldova: bani, Romania: bani)
lev (Bulgaria: stotinki)
som (Kyrgyzstan: tyjyn)
sum (Uzbekistan: tiyin)
won (North Korea: chon, South Korea: jeon)
yen (Japan: sen)

04 baht (Thailand: satang)
birr (Ethiopia: cents)
cedi (Ghana: pesewas)
dong (Vietnam: hao/xu)
dram (Armenia: lumas)
euro (Andorra/Austria/Belgium/Cyprus/
Estonia/Finland/France/Germany/Greece/
Ireland/Italy/Kosovo/Luxembourg/Malta/
Monaco/Montenegro/The Netherlands/
Portugal/San Marino/Slovakia/Slovenia/
Spain/Vatican City: cents)
kina (Papua New Guinea: toea)
kuna (Croatia: lipa)
kyat (Myanmar: pyas)
lari (Georgia: tetri)
lira (Turkey: kurus)

loti (Lesotho: lisente)
peso (Argentina/Chile/Colombia/Cuba/
Dominican Republic/Mexico/Philippines:
centavos)
pula (Botswana: thebe)
rand (South Africa: cents)
real (Brazil: centavos)
rial (Iran/Oman: baisas, Qatar: dirhams)
riel (Cambodia: sen)
taka (Bangladesh: poisha)
tala (Samoa: sene)
vatu (Vanuatu: centimes)
yuan (China: jiao/fen)

05 colón (Costa Rica: centimos, El Salvador:
centavos)
denar (Macedonia: deni)
dinar (Algeria: centimes, Bahrain/Iraq/
Jordan/Kuwait: fils, Libya: dirhams, Sudan:
pounds, Tunisia: millimes)
dobra (São Tomé and Príncipe: centimos)
franc (Benin/Burkina Faso/Burundi/Cameroon/
Central African Republic/Chad/Comoros/
Democratic Republic of the Congo/Congo/
Côte d'Ivoire/Djibouti/Equatorial Guinea/
Gabon/Guinea/Guinea-Bissau/Mali/

Niger/Rwanda/Senegal/Togo: centimes,
Liechtenstein/Switzerland: centimes/rappen)
krona (Iceland: aurar, Sweden: ore)
krone (Denmark/Norway: ore)
leone (Sierra Leone: cents)
litas (Lithuania: centas)
manat (Azerbaijan: gopik, Turkmenistan: tenesi)
naira (Nigeria: kobo)
nakfa (Eritrea: cents)
pound (Egypt/Lebanon/Syria: piastres, UK:
pence)
riyal (Saudi Arabia: qursh/halala, Yemen: fils)
rupee (India: paise, Mauritius/Seychelles/Sri
Lanka: cents, Nepal: paise/pice, Pakistan:
paisa)
tenge (Kazakhstan: tiyn)
zloty (Poland: groszy)

06 ariary (Madagascar: iraimbilanja)
balboa (Panama: centesimos)
dalasi (The Gambia: butut)
dirham (Morocco: centimes, United Arab
Emirates: fils, West Sahara: centimes)
dollar (Antigua and Barbuda/Australia/The
Bahamas/Barbados/Belize/Brunei/Canada/
Dominica/East Timor/Ecuador/El Salvador/
Fiji/Grenada/Guyana/Jamaica/Kiribati/
Liberia/Marshall Islands/Federated States of
Micronesia/Namibia/Nauru/New Zealand/
Palau/St Kitts and Nevis/St Lucia/St Vincent/
Solomon Islands/Suriname/Trinidad and
Tobago/Tuvalu/USA/Zimbabwe: cents,
Singapore: ringgit/cents)
forint (Hungary: filler)
gourde (Haiti: centimes)

koruna (Czech Republic: haleru)
kwacha (Malawi: tambala, Zambia: ngwee)
kwanza (Angola: lwei)
maloti (Lesotho: lisente)
pa'anga (Tonga: seniti)
rouble (Belarus/Russia:kopeks)
rupiah (Indonesia: sen)
shekel (Israel: agora)
somoni (Tajikistan: dirams)
tugrik (Mongolia: mongo)
tugrug (Mongolia: mongo)

07 afghani (Afghanistan: puls)
bolivar (Venezuela: centimos)
cordoba (Nicaragua: centavos, reales)
guarani (Paraguay: centimos)
hyrvnia (Ukraine: kopiykas)
lempira (Honduras: centavos)
metical (Mozambique: centavos)
new peso (Uruguay: centimos)
ouguiya (Mauritania: khoums)
quetzal (Guatemala: centavos)
ringgit (Malaysia: cents)
rufiyaa (Maldives: laarees)

08 new dinar (Serbia: paras)
ngultrum (Bhutan: chetrum)
nuevo sol (Peru: cents)
renminbi (China: jiao/fen)
shilling (Kenya/Somalia/Tanzania/Uganda: cents)
sterling (UK)

09 boliviano (Bolivia: centavos)
lilangeni (Swaziland: cents)
new dollar (Taiwan: cents)

10 emalangeni (Swaziland: cents)

Former currencies include:

04 lira (Italy/Malta)
mark (Germany)
punt (Ireland)

05 franc (France/Belgium/Luxembourg)
kroon (Estonia)
pound (Cyprus)
sucre (Ecuador)
tolar (Slovenia)
zaïre (Democratic Republic of the Congo)

06 escudo (Portugal)
Koruna (Slovakia)
markka (Finland)
peseta (Spain)

07 drachma (Greece)
guilder (The Netherlands)

09 schilling (Austria)

11 Deutschmark (Germany)

Currency abbreviations, with unit and country, include:

03 AUD (dollar; Australia)
CAD (dollar; Canada)
CHF (franc; Switzerland)
CNY (renminbi yuan; China)
DKK (krone; Denmark)
EUR (euro; Euro member countries)
GBP (pound; UK)
HKD (dollar; Hong Kong)
HUF (forint; Hungary)

See also **coin**

INR (rupee; India)
JPY (yen; Japan)
MXN (peso; Mexico)
NOK (krone; Norway)
NZD (dollar; New Zealand)
RUB (rouble; Russia)
SEK (krona; Sweden)
SGD (dollar; Singapore)
USD (dollar; USA)
ZAR (rand; South Africa)

curry

Curries include:

05 balti	penang	pasanda	tandoori
bhuna	**07** biriani	red thai	vindaloo
korma	biryani	rendang	**09** chettinad
06 ceylon	dhansak	**08** biriyani	green thai
madras	dopiaza	jalfrezi	rogan josh
masala	hanglay	kashmiri	**10** yellow thai
pathia	malayan	massaman	**11** tikka masala

See also **herb**

cut *see* **meat**

cutlery

Cutlery items include:

04 fork	salt spoon	**11** butter knife
05 knife	soup spoon	carving fork
ladle	**10** bread knife	cheese knife
spoon	caddy spoon	corn holders
spork	cake server	**12** apostle spoon
08 fish fork	chopsticks	carving knife
teaspoon	pickle fork	dessertspoon
09 fish knife	steak knife	salad servers
fish slice	sugar tongs	**14** vegetable knife
	tablespoon	

cutter

Cutters include:

03 axe	lopper	poll-axe	secateurs
saw	meat-ax	sparthe	**10** coal-cutter
sax	piolet	twibill	cork-cutter
04 adze	poleax	**08** battle-ax	guillotine
bill	scythe	billhook	putty-knife
celt	shears	chainsaw	spokeshave
05 blade	sickle	clippers	**11** chaff-cutter
knife	sparth	palstaff	coup de poing
mower	**07** chopper	palstave	glass-cutter
plane	cleaver	partisan	grass-cutter
razor	coulter	scissors	Lochaber axe
sword	cutlass	shredder	paper-cutter
06 chisel	fretsaw	stone axe	straw-cutter
colter	gisarme	Strimmer®	**12** cookie-cutter
culter	hacksaw	tomahawk	hedgetrimmer
dagger	halberd	**09** battle-axe	Jeddart staff
ice axe	hatchet	double-axe	marble-cutter
jigsaw	meat-axe	holing-axe	**13** mowing machine
labrys	poleaxe	lawnmower	pinking shears

See also **dagger**; **knife**; **sword**

cycling

Cyclists include:

03 Hoy (Sir Chris; 1976– , Scottish)

04 Gaul (Charly; 1932–2005, Luxembourg)

05 Binda (Alfredo; 1902–76, Italian)
Bobet (Louison; 1925–83, French)
Coppi (Fausto; 1919–60, Italian)
Kelly (Sean; 1956– , Irish)
Moser (Francesco; 1951– , Italian)
Zabel (Erik; 1970– , German)

06 Boonen (Thomas; 1980– , Belgian)
Burton (Beryl; 1937–96, English)
Fignon (Laurent; 1960– , French)
Harris (Reg; 1920–92, English)
LeMond (Greg; 1961– , US)
Merckx (Eddy; 1945– , Belgian)
O'Grady (Stuart; 1973– , Australian)

07 Bartali (Gino; 1914–2000, Italian)
Bettini (Paolo; 1974– , Italian)
Hinault (Bernard; 1954– , French)
Museeuw (Johan; 1965– , Belgian)
Pantani (Marco; 1970–2004, Italian)
Pereiro (Óscar; 1977– , Spanish)
Queally (Jason; 1970– , English)

Simpson (Tom; 1938–67, English)
Ullrich (Jan; 1973– , German)
Van Looy (Rik; 1933– , Belgian)
Wiggins (Sir Bradley; 1980– , Belgian)

08 Anquetil (Jacques; 1934–87, French)
Beaumont (Mark; 1983– , Scottish)
Boardman (Chris; 1968– , English)
Contador (Alberto; 1982– , Spanish)
Indurain (Miguel; 1964– , Spanish)
Maertens (Freddy; 1953– , Belgian)
Opperman (Sir Hubert; 1904–96, Australian)
Poulidor (Raymond; 1936– , French)
Virenque (Richard; 1969– , Moroccan/French)

09 Armstrong (Lance; 1971– , US)
Zoetemelk (Joop; 1946– , Dutch)

10 Bahamontes (Federico; 1928– , Spanish)
Cancellara (Fabian; 1981– , Swiss)
van Moorsel (Leontien Ziljaard-; 1970– , Dutch)

11 De Vlaeminck (Roger; 1947– , Belgian)
Freire Gómez (Óscar; 1976– , Spanish)

13 Longo-Ciprelli (Jeannie; 1958– , French)

Cycling terms include:

02 GC

03 UCI

04 pavé

05 bidon
block
break
bunch
cleat
climb
clips
drops
field
hoods
prime
stage

06 attack
bridge
Keirin
lapped
sprint

07 banking
cadence
chasers
climber
echelon
lead-out

Madison
musette
peloton
rouleur
skid lid

08 aero bars
drafting
kermesse
paceline
pole line
road bike
road race
soigneur
sprinter
toe-clips

09 breakaway
chainring
criterium
disc wheel
freewheel
handsling
mass start
monocoque
repechage
sprockets
stage race
time trial

track bike
track race
velodrome

10 broom wagon
chainwheel
dérailleur
domestique
fixed-wheel
neutralize
points race
stand still
team sprint

11 bunch sprint
flamme rouge
green jersey
neutral zone
pursuit race
scratch race

12 bonification
voiture balai
yellow jersey

13 measuring line
slipstreaming
sprinters' lane
sprinters' line
starting block

team time trial
time-trial bike
14 clipless pedals
See also **bicycle**; **sport**

contre-la-montre
feeding station
neutral support

polka-dot jersey

Czech Republic

Cities and notable towns in the Czech Republic include:

04 Brno	**06** Pilsen	**08** Karlsbad
Telc	Prague	**09** Kutná Hora
05 Plzen	**07** Budweis	**12** Ceské Krumlov
Praha	Olomouc	**15** Ceské Budejovice
	Ostrava	

Administrative divisions of the Czech Republic, with regional capitals:

06 Prague
09 Jihocesky (Ceské Budejovice)
10 Západoesky (Plzen)
11 East Bohemia (Hradec Králové)
Severocesky (Usti nad Labem)
Stredocesky (Prague)
West Bohemia (Plzen)

12 Jihomoravsky (Brno)
North Bohemia (Usti nad Labem)
North Moravia (Ostrava)
South Bohemia (Ceské Budejovice)
South Moravia (Brno)
13 Vychodoceskya (Hradec Králové)
14 Central Bohemia (Prague)
Severomoravsky (Ostrava)

Czech landmarks include:

06 Loreta	**11** Petrin Tower	Moravian Karst
Vltava	Powder Tower	**14** Cesky Sternberk
07 Josefov	Pražský Hrad	House of Two Suns
Mihulka	Tyrov Castle	Infant of Prague
08 Berounka	Zlata Koruna	Koneprusy Caves
Hradcany	**12** Cernin Palace	Litomyšl Castle
Spilberk	Prague Castle	Rozmberk Castle
09 Karlstejn	**13** Brno Cathedral	Tugendhat Villa
Koneprusy	Charles Bridge	**15** Bretfield Palace
Vyssi Brod	Jesuit College	Karlstejn Castle
10 Telc Castle	Mikulov Castle	Krivoklat Castle

D

dagger

04 dirk
kris

05 skean
skene

06 anlace
bodkin

07 anelace
dudgeon
handjar
jambiya

hanjar
kirpan

khanjar
poniard

08 baselard
jambiyah
puncheon
skean-dhu

skene-dhu
stiletto

10 misericord
skene-occle

11 misericorde

See also **knife**; **weapon**

dairy

04 ghee
milk
whey

05 cream
curds
quark

06 beurre
butter
cheese
yogurt

07 UHT milk
yoghurt

08 ice cream
yoghourt

09 butter oil
goat's milk
milk shake
sour cream
whole milk

10 buttermilk
milk powder

11 double cream
semi-skimmed
single cream
skimmed milk
soured cream

12 clotted cream
crème fraîche

fromage frais
long-life milk
powdered milk

13 condensed milk
full cream milk
low-fat yoghurt
whipping cream

14 evaporated milk
sterilized milk
unsalted butter

15 clarified butter
homogenized milk
semi-skimmed milk

See also **cheese**

Dalai Lama

11 Gedun Gyatso (1475–1542)
Gedun Truppa (1391–1475)
Sonam Gyatso (1543–88)

12 Jampel Gyatso (1758–1804)
Kezang Gyatso (1708–57)
Luntok Gyatso (1806–15)
Tenzin Gyatso (1935–   )

See also **religion**

Trinle Gyatso (1856–75)
Yonten Gyatso (1589–17)

13 Khedrup Gyatso (1838–56)
Thupten Gyatso (1876–1933)

15 Tsang-yang Gyatso (1683–1706)
Tshultrim Gyatso (1816–37)

20 Ngawang Lobzang Gyatso (1617–82)

dam

Dams include:

04 Guri (Venezuela)
Hume (Australia)
Mica (Canada)

05 Aswan (Egypt)
Ertan (China)
Nurek (Tajikistan)
Rogun (Tajikistan)

06 Bratsk (Russia)
Hoover (USA)
Inguri (Georgia)
Itaipu (Brazil/Paraguay)
Kariba (Zambia/Zimbabwe)
Vaiont (Italy)

07 Benmore (New Zealand)
Boulder (USA)
Tarbela (Pakistan)

08 Akosombo (Ghana)

Chapetón (Argentina)
Gezhouba (China)

09 Aswan High (Egypt)
Mauvoisin (Switzerland)
Owen Falls (Uganda)

10 Glen Canyon (USA)

11 Afsluitdijk (The Netherlands)
Grand Coulee (USA)
La Esmeralda (Colombia)
Three Gorges (China)

13 Alberto Lleras (Colombia)
Alvaro Obregon (Mexico)
Grande Dixence (Switzerland)
Manuel M Torres (Mexico)

14 Afsluitdijk Sea (The Netherlands)

15 Sayano-Shushensk (Russia)

dance

Dances include:

03 bop
hay
hey
jig
war

04 barn
jive
rain
reel
shag

05 conga
crunk
krunk
mambo
polka
round
rumba
salsa
samba
skank
stomp
sword
tango
twist
waltz

06 Balboa
bolero
can-can
cha-cha
hustle
minuet
morris

pavane
valeta
veleta

07 beguine
foxtrot
gavotte
hoe-down
lancers
mazurka
milonga
morrice
musette
one-step
tordion
two-step

08 boogaloo
cakewalk
excuse-me
fandango
flamenco
galliard
habanera
hay-de-guy
hey-de-guy
hornpipe
krumping
lindy hop
merengue
Playford
the twist

09 bossa nova
cha-cha-cha

clogdance
écossaise
jitterbug
paso doble
passepied
Paul Jones
quadrille
quickstep
rock 'n' roll
roundelay

10 charleston
corroboree
Gay Gordons
hokey-cokey
slow rhythm
tarantella
turkey-trot

11 black bottom
Lambeth Walk
morris dance
schottische
varsovienne

12 boogie-woogie
mashed potato
Virginia reel

13 eightsome reel
Highland fling
Viennese waltz

14 strip the willow

15 military two-step
St Bernard's waltz

Dance types include:

03 lap	disco	social	flamenco
tap	Irish	square	Highland
04 clog	Latin	street	robotics
folk	limbo		skanking
jazz	salsa	**07** bogling	**10** belly-dance
line	swing	ceilidh	breakdance
05 belly	**06** ballet	country	**11** traditional
break	hip-hop	morrice	**12** contemporary
ceroc	modern	old-time	**13** Latin-American
	morris	**08** ballroom	

Dance functions include:

03 hop	**05** disco	shindig	**10** thé dansant
04 ball	**06** social	**08** hunt ball	**11** charity ball
prom	**07** ceilidh	tea dance	dinner dance
rave	knees-up	**09** barn dance	**14** fancy dress ball

Dance steps include:

03 dig	stamp	**08** back step	**10** ball-change
dip	stomp	crab walk	chainé turn
fan	strut	flat step	change step
set	Suzi-Q	four-step	charleston
04 buck	three	hair comb	chassé turn
chop	twist	headspin	come-around
chug	whisk	heel pull	Cuban walks
clip		heel turn	cucarachas
comb	**06** aerial	hook turn	inside turn
dame	breaks	neck wrap	jackhammer
drag	bronco	pas-de-bas	rubber legs
draw	chassé	push spin	spiral turn
drop	circle	rock step	texas tommy
ocho	jockey	shedding	triple step
riff	paddle	spot turn	**11** alemana turn
spin	riffle	swingout	impetus turn
turn	shimmy	throwout	natural turn
vine	uprock	time step	outside turn
whip		windmill	pas de basque
	07 box step		quarter turn
05 abajo	fan kick	**09** allemagne	reverse turn
brush	feather	applejack	setting step
catch	jig step	crazy legs	
corté	locking	cross over	**12** last shedding
cramp	lollies	cross turn	shake and turn
flare	popping	dile que no	under-arm turn
galop	pop turn	grapevine	
glide	rocking	lindy turn	**13** double-shuffle
grind	scuffle	pas de deux	fall off the log
hitch	shuffle	poussette	first shedding
pivot	six-step	promenade	
scuff	swivels	quick stop	**14** change of places
seven	toprock	sugarfoot	kick-ball-change
spike	twinkle	sugarpush	transition step
			travelling step

dandy

03 Lee (Gypsy Rose; 1914–70, US)

04 Bird (Bonnie; 1914–95, US)
Dunn (Douglas; 1942– , US)
Holm (Hanya; 1893–1992, German/US)
Kemp (Lindsay; 1939– , Scottish)
Monk (Meredith; 1943– , Peruvian/US)
Page (Ruth; 1899–1991, US)

05 Ailey (Alvin, Jnr; 1931–89, US)
Baker (Josephine; 1906–75, French)
Cohan (Robert; 1925– , US/British)
Fagan (Garth; 1940– , Jamaican)
Falco (Louis; 1942–93, US)
Gades (Antonio; 1936–2004, Spanish)
Kelly (Gene; 1912–96, US)
Limón (José; 1908–72, Mexican/US)
North (Robert; 1945– , US/British)
Reitz (Dana; 1948– , US)
Shawn (Ted; 1891–1972, US)
Sleep (Wayne; 1948– , English)
Takei (Kei; 1939– , Japanese)
Tharp (Twyla; 1941– , US)

06 Bausch (Pina; 1940– , German)
Childs (Lucinda; 1940– , US)
Clarke (Martha; 1944– , US)
Davies (Siobhan; 1950– , English)
Duncan (Isadora; 1877–1927, US)
Dunham (Katherine; 1909– , US)
Fenley (Molissa; 1954– , US)
Fuller (Loie; 1862–1928, US)
Gordon (David; 1936– , US)
Graham (Martha; 1894–1991, US)
Horton (Lester; 1906–53, US)

See also **ballet**

Montez (Lola; 1818–61, Irish/US)
Morris (Mark; 1956– , US)
Paxton (Steve; 1939– , US)
Primus (Pearl; 1919–94, Trinidadian/US)
Rainer (Yvonne; 1934– , US)
Rogers (Ginger; 1911–95, US)
Wigman (Mary; 1886–1973, German)

07 Astaire (Adele; 1898–1981, US)
Astaire (Fred; 1899–1987, US)
Bennett (Michael; 1943–87, US)
Carlson (Carolyn; 1943– , US)
de Mille (Agnes; 1905–93, US)
Jamison (Judith; 1943– , US)
Sokolow (Anna; 1912–2000, US)
Wagoner (Dan; 1932– , US)
Weidman (Charles; 1901–75, US)

08 Armitage (Karole; 1954– , US)
Charisse (Cyd; 1921–2008, US)
Hayworth (Rita; 1918–87, US)
Humphrey (Doris; 1895–1958, US)
Nikolais (Alwin; 1910–93, US)
Petronio (Stephen; 1956–, US)

09 Argentina (La; 1890–1936, Argentine/
Spanish)
Schlemmer (Oskar; 1888–1943, German)

10 Cunningham (Merce; 1919– 2009, US)
Saint Denis (Ruth; 1879–1968, US)

11 Mistinguett (1874–1956, French)

13 De Keersmaeker (Anne Teresa; 1960– ,
Belgian)

dandy

04 Nash (Richard 'Beau'; 1674–1762, Welsh)

05 Crisp (Quentin; 1908–99, English)
Wilde (Oscar; 1854–1900, Irish)

06 Coward (Noël; 1899–1973, English)

See also **Wilde, Oscar**

08 Beerbohm (Max; 1872–1956, English)
Brummell (George 'Beau'; 1778–1840,
English)

12 Yankee Doodle (Dandy; *Little Johnny Jones*,
1904, George M Cohan)

Dante Alighieri (1265–1321)

07 *Inferno* (c.1307–21)

08 *Eclogues* (c.1319)
Paradiso (c.1307–21)

10 *Il convivio* (c.1304)
On Monarchy (c.1313)

Purgatorio (c.1307–21)
The Banquet (c.1304)
The New Life (c.1292)

11 *De monarchia* (c.1313)
La vita nuova (c.1292)

14 *Divina Commedia* (c.1307–21)
15 *The Divine Comedy* (c.1307–21)
19 *De vulgari eloquentia* (1304)

25 *Concerning the Common Speech* (1304)
29 *On the Eloquence of the Vernacular* (1304)

darts

Darts players include:

04 King (Mervyn; 1966– , English)
Lowe (John; 1945– , English)
Part (John; 1966– , Canadian)
05 Adams (Martin; 1956– , English)
06 Beaton (Steve; 1964– , English)
George (Bobby; 1945– , English)
Stompe (Co; 1962– , Dutch)
Taylor (Phil; 1960– , English)
Wilson (Jocky; 1951–2012, Scottish)
07 Bristow (Eric; 1957– , English)

Fordham (Andy; 1962– , English)
Klaasen (Jelle; 1984– , Dutch)
Webster (Mark; 1983– , Welsh)
08 Anderson (Bob; 1947– , English)
Gulliver (Trina; 1969– , English)
09 Barneveld (Raymond van; 1967– , Dutch)
Lazarenko (Cliff; 1952– , English)
Priestley (Dennis; 1950– , English)
12 Dobromyslova (Anastasia; 1984– , Russian)

Darts terms include:

03 bed	shaft	treble	**09** bounce-out
04 bull	**06** barrel	**07** maximum	cover shot
bust	double	outshot	double top
oche	finish	**08** bull's eye	**12** hold the throw
stem	flight	checkout	with the darts
tops	game on	dartitis	**13** break the throw
05 outer	marker	game shot	**15** against the darts
	spider		

See also **sport**

daughter

Daughters include:

04 Anne (Princess; 1950– , English)
Hero (*Much Ado About Nothing*, 1598, William Shakespeare)
Kate (*The Taming of the Shrew*, 1593, William Shakespeare)
Page (Anne; *The Merry Wives of Windsor*, 1597/8, William Shakespeare)
05 Freud (Anna; 1895–1982, Austrian/British)
Lloyd (Emily; 1971– , English)
Mills (Hayley; 1946– , English)
O'Neal (Tatum; 1963– , US)
Regan (*King Lear*, 1605–6, William Shakespeare)
06 Bhutto (Benazir; 1953–2007, Pakistani)
Bianca (*The Taming of the Shrew*, 1593, William Shakespeare)
Fatima (c.605–33, Arab)
Fisher (Carrie; 1956– , US)
Forbes (Emma; 1965– , English)
Gandhi (Indira; 1917–84, Indian)

Imogen (*Cymbeline*, 1610, William Shakespeare)
Juliet (*Romeo and Juliet*, 1595, William Shakespeare)
Marina (*Pericles*, 1607, William Shakespeare)
07 Electra (Greek mythology)
Forsyte (Fleur; *The Forsyte Saga*, 1922, John Galsworthy)
Goneril (*King Lear*, 1605–6, William Shakespeare)
Jessica (*The Merchant of Venice*, 1596–7, William Shakespeare)
Lavinia (*Titus Andronicus*, 1592, William Shakespeare)
Miranda (*The Tempest*, 1611, William Shakespeare)
Ophelia (*Hamlet*, 1600–1, William Shakespeare)
Perdita (*The Winter's Tale*, 1609, William Shakespeare)
Presley (Lisa Marie; 1968– , US)

08 Cordelia (*King Lear*, 1605–6, William
Shakespeare)
Lovelace (Ada; 1816–52, English)
Minnelli (Liza; 1946– , US)
Williams (Shirley; 1930– , English)

09 Cassandra (Greek mythology)
du Maurier (Daphne; 1907–89, English)
Katharina (*The Taming of the Shrew*, 1593,
William Shakespeare)

McCartney (Stella; 1972– , English)
Pankhurst (Christabel; 1880–1958, English)

10 Beckinsale (Kate; 1974– , English)
Richardson (Joely; 1965– , English)
Richardson (Natasha; 1963–2009, English)
Rossellini (Isabella; 1952– , Italian)

13 Princess Royal (1950– , English)

day

Days of the week:

06	Friday	**07**	Tuesday	**09**	Wednesday
	Monday	**08**	Saturday		
	Sunday		Thursday		

French day names with English translation:

05	jeudi (Thursday)	**06**	samedi (Saturday)	vendredi (Friday)
	lundi (Monday)	**08**	dimanche (Sunday)	
	mardi (Tuesday)		mercredi (Wednesday)	

German day names with English translation:

06	Montag (Monday)		Sonntag (Sunday)	**10**	Donnerstag (Thursday)
07	Freitag (Friday)	**08**	Dienstag (Tuesday)		
	Samstag (Saturday)		Mittwoch (Wednesday)		

Italian day names with English translation:

06	lunedì (Monday)		martedì (Tuesday)	**09**	mercoledì (Wednesday)
	sabato (Saturday)		venerdì (Friday)		
07	giovedì (Thursday)	**08**	domenica (Sunday)		

Latin day names with English translation:

09	Jovis dies (Thursday)	**10**	Martis dies (Tuesday)	**12**	Mercurii dies (Wednesday)
	Lunae dies (Monday)	**11**	Saturni dies (Saturday)		
	Solis dies (Sunday)		Veneris dies (Friday)		

Spanish day names with English translation:

05	lunes (Monday)		sábado (Saturday)	**09**	miércoles (Wednesday)
06	jueves (Thursday)	**07**	domingo (Sunday)		
	martes (Tuesday)		viernes (Friday)		

Named days include:

09	Fat Monday		Meal Monday		Egg Saturday
	Fig Sunday		Pack Monday		Fat Thursday
	Low Sunday		Palm Sunday		Hock Tuesday
	Red Friday		Whit Monday		Wakes Monday
10	Care Sunday		Whit Sunday	**12**	Advent Sunday
	Good Friday	**11**	Bible Sunday		Ash Wednesday
	Hock Monday		Black Friday		Black Tuesday
	Holy Friday		Black Monday		Bloody Monday

Bloody Sunday
Caring Sunday
Collop Monday
Easter Monday
Easter Sunday
Golden Friday
Holy Saturday
Holy Thursday
Plough Monday

Stir-up Sunday
13 Black Saturday
Carling Sunday
Easter Tuesday
Handsel Monday
Mid-Lent Sunday
Passion Sunday
Shrove Tuesday
Trinity Sunday

14 Easter Saturday
Fastens Tuesday
Maundy Thursday
Pancake Tuesday
Rogation Sunday
Shrift Thursday
15 Mothering Sunday
Pulver Wednesday
Refection Sunday

See also **Christmas**

death

Terms to do with death include:

03 die
DOA
end
RIP
urn
war
04 bier
cist
deid
doom
dust
hell
lily
loss
mort
obit
pall
pyre
sati
soul
toll
tomb
wake
will
05 angel
ashes
bardo
black
cairn
decay
dirge
dying
elegy
éloge
elogy
fatal
ghost
grave
Hades
haunt
inter
Lethe

mourn
shiva
shoot
skull
tangi
vigil
widow
worms
06 Azrael
bedral
behead
burial
candle
chadar
coffin
corpse
demise
die out
entomb
eulogy
exequy
finish
fossor
grieve
hearse
heaven
heroon
lament
lethal
martyr
monody
mortal
murder
obital
orphan
rosary
shibah
shivah
shroud
solemn
suttee
wreath

07 autopsy
banshee
bargest
bederal
bereave
butcher
carcass
carrion
coroner
cortège
cremate
crucify
disease
elogist
elogium
epicede
epitaph
funeral
ghostly
inquest
karoshi
keening
mastaba
mourner
obitual
passing
penalty
quietus
requiem
suicide
widower
08 bale-fire
barghest
casualty
cemetery
cenotaph
ceremony
clinical
contract
dead-fire
deathbed
death row
deceased

disinter
dispatch
eulogium
exequial
fatality
funebral
funerary
funereal
grieving
hara-kiri
homicide
hypogeum
interred
last post
lethally
long home
mortbell
mortuary
mournful
mourning
necropsy
necrosis
necrotic
obituary
paradise
post-obit
predator
sin-eater
soul-scat
soul-scot
soul-shot
suicidal
terminal
unhearse
yahrzeit
09 afterlife
anabiosis
barghaist
cataplexy
committal
cremation
damnation
dead march

dead thraw
death-bell
death duty
death mask
death rate
death-song
deathtrap
death wish
departure
disentomb
dormition
epicedium
funebrial
graveside
graveyard
headstone
homicidal
hypogaeum
interment
last enemy
last rites
mass grave
matricide
mausoleum
mortality
mortcloth
mortician
necrology
necrotize
obsequial
obsequies
passing on
patricide
plague-pit

purgatory
sacrifice
sepulchre
sepulture
taphonomy
testament
thanatoid
tombstone
transport
year's mind

10 ante mortem
apparition
catafalque
ceremonial
death knell
death squad
death-token
death-wound
defunction
euthanasia
expiration
fratricide
gravestone
grim reaper
in extremis
loss of life
month's mind
necrolatry
necrophile
necrophobe
necropolis
obituarist
pall-bearer

play possum
posthumous
post mortem
predecease
sororocide
strae death
undertaker

11 bereavement
crematorium
death-notice
death rattle
death-stroke
eternal rest
fratricidal
funeral home
grave-digger
grave robber
hic sepultus
last honours
lethiferous
mortiferous
necrophilia
necrophobia
necrophobic
passing away
passing bell
requiem mass
rest in peace
rigor mortis
sarcophagus
suicide pact
thanatology
thanatopsis

12 burial ground
commorientes
danse macabre
death warrant
debt of nature
disinterment
last farewell
mercy killing
mourning band
mourning ring
necrographer
necrophagous
necrophiliac
passage grave
pollice verso
posthumously
resting place
the other side
transmigrate

13 burial society
mourning cloak
mourning coach
mourning piece
mourning-stuff
natural causes
thanatography
thanatophobia

14 extreme unction
funeral parlour
mourning border

15 funeral director
resurrectionist

See also **execution**

Debussy, Claude (1862–1918)

Significant works include:

04 *Jeux* (1913)

05 *La Mer* (1905)

06 *Images* (1905–12)
Khamma (1912)

07 *Zuleima* (1885–86)

08 *Estampes* (1903)
Préludes (various)

09 *Nocturnes* (1899)

11 *Clair de lune* (1882)
Pour le piano (1901)

12 *L'Isle joyeuse* (1904)

13 *En blanc et noir* (1915)

15 *Etudes pour piano* (1915)
L'Enfant prodigue (1884)

Sonata for violin (1917)

16 *Mazurka pour piano* (1890)

20 *Children's Corner Suite* (1908)

26 *Prélude à l'après-midi d'un faune* (1894)

decoration *see* **military**

deer

Deer include:

03 elk
hog
red

04 axis
mule
roe

musk
pudu
rusa

sika

05 moose
water

06 chital
fallow
forest
sambar
sambur
tufted
wapiti

07 barking
brocket
caribou
jumping
muntjac
muntjak

08 cariacou

carjacou
Irish elk
reindeer
Virginia

09 barasinga

10 barasingha

Père David's

11 black-tailed
white-tailed

12 Chinese water
Indian sambar

13 Indian muntjac

See also **animal**; **game: hunting**

Defoe, Daniel (1660–1731)

Significant works include:

06 *Roxana* (1724)
12 *Moll Flanders* (1722)
14 *Robinson Crusoe* (1719)
17 *Augusta Triumphans* (1728)
23 *A Journal of the Plague Year* (1722)

28 *Roxana, or The Fortunate Mistress* (1724)
31 *The Shortest Way with the Dissenters* (1702)
36 *The Farther Adventures of Robinson Crusoe* (1720)
The Great Law of Subordination Considered (1724)

Significant characters include:

04 Jack (Colonel)
Jemy
06 Crusoe (Robinson)

Friday (Man)
Roxana
08 Flanders (Moll)

09 Singleton (Captain)

delivery *see* **cricket**

Denmark

Cities and notable towns in Denmark include:

05 Århus
06 Aarhus
Ålborg
Odense

07 Aalborg
Esbjerg
Kolding
Randers

09 København
10 Copenhagen

Administrative divisions of Denmark, with regional capitals:

03 Fyn (Odense)
04 Ribe (Ribe)
05 Århus
Vejle (Vejle)
06 Aarhus
Viborg (Viborg)
08 Bornholm (Rønne)

Roskilde (Roskilde)
09 København
Storstrøm (Nykøbing Falster)
10 Copenhagen
Ringkøbing (Ringkøbing)
11 Nordjylland (Aalborg)

West Zealand (Sorø)
12 North Jutland (Aalborg)
South Jutland (Aebeurace)
13 Frederiksborg (Hillerød)
Sønderjylland (Aebeurace)
Vestjaelland (Sorø)

Danish landmarks include:

06 Nyhavn
Tivoli
07 Jelling
Strøget
08 Legoland
09 Møns Klint

Rundetårn
10 Round Tower
Trelleborg
11 Christiansø
Egeskov Slot
Folketinget

Oresundbron
Slotsholmen
12 Ålborg Castle
Vor Frue Kirke
13 Egeskov Castle
Little Mermaid

Mermaid Statue
Oresund Bridge
Radhus Pladset

Ribe Cathedral
Rosenborg Slot
14 Århus Cathedral

Kronborg Castle
15 Ålborg Cathedral
Odense Cathedral

department *see* **France; government**

dependency

Dependencies include:

04 Guam (USA)
Niue (New Zealand)
05 Aruba (The Netherlands)
07 Bermuda (UK)
Curaçao (The Netherlands)
Mayotte (France)
Réunion (France)
Tokelau (New Zealand)
08 Anguilla (UK)
St Helena (UK)
09 Gibraltar (UK)
Greenland (Denmark)
Isle of Man (British Crown)
St Maarten (The Netherlands)
10 Guadeloupe (France)
Martinique (France)
Montserrat (UK)
Puerto Rico (USA)

11 Cook Islands (New Zealand)
12 Cocos Islands (Australia)
Faroe Islands (Denmark)
French Guiana (France)
New Caledonia (France)
South Georgia (UK)
13 American Samoa (USA)
Cayman Islands (UK)
Dutch Antilles (The Netherlands)
Norfolk Island (Australia)
14 Channel Islands (British Crown)
Keeling Islands (Australia)
Ross Dependency (New Zealand)
15 Christmas Island (Australia)
Falkland Islands (UK)
French Polynesia (France)
Pitcairn Islands (UK)
US Virgin Islands (USA)

desert

Deserts include:

04 Gobi (Mongolia/China)
Thar (India/Pakistan)
05 Kavir (Iran)
Namib (Namibia)
Ordos (China)
Sturt (Australia)
06 Gibson (Australia)
Mojave (USA)
Nubian (Sudan)
Sahara (Africa)

Syrian (Asia)
07 Alashan (China)
Arabian (Asia)
Atacama (Chile)
Kara Kum (Turkmenistan)
Simpson (Australia)
Sonoran (USA)
Ustyurt (Kazakhstan)
08 Kalahari (Africa)
Kyzyl-Kum (Kazakhstan)

09 Dzungaria (China)
10 Betpak-Dala (Kazakhstan)
Chihuahuan (Mexico)
Great Basin (USA)
Great Sandy (Australia)
Patagonian (Argentina)
Takla Makan (China)
13 Great Victoria (Australia)
14 Bolson de Mapimi (Mexico)

designer *see* **fashion; furniture**

despot

Despots include:

04 Amin (Idi; 1925–2003, Ugandan)
05 Timur (the Lame; 1336–1405, Turkic/Mongol)
06 Caesar (Julius; c.101–44 BC, Roman)
Führer (Der; 1889–1945, Austrian/German)
Hitler (Adolf 'Der Führer'; 1889–1945,
Austrian/German)

Stalin (Joseph; 1879–1953, Russian)
07 Papa Doc (1907–71, Haitian)
08 Duvalier (François 'Papa Doc'; 1907–71,
Haitian)
09 Ceaușescu (Nicolae; 1918–89, Romanian)
Mao Zedong (1893–1976, Chinese)

Tamerlane (1336–1405, Turkic/Mongol)
10 Mao Tse-tung (1893–1976, Chinese)
11 Robespierre (Maximilien de; 1758–94, French)

Tamburlaine (1336–1405, Turkic/ Mongol)
15 Ivan the Terrible (1530–84, Russian)

dessert

Desserts and puddings include:

03 pie
04 flan
    tart
05 bombe
    jelly
    kugel
    kulfi
    salad
06 mousse
    mud pie
    sorbet
    sundae
    trifle
    yogurt
07 baklava
    cobbler
    compote
    crumble
    parfait
    pavlova
    soufflé

    tapioca
    tartufo
    yoghurt
08 Eton mess
    ice cream
    pandowdy
    plum-duff
    syllabub
    tiramisu
    vacherin
    yoghourt
09 clafoutis
    cranachan
10 blancmange
    Brown Betty
    cheesecake
    egg custard
    frangipane
    panna cotta
    peach Melba
    zabaglione

11 baked Alaska
    banana split
    banoffee pie
    crème brûlée
    Eve's pudding
    milk pudding
    plum pudding
    rice pudding
    spotted dick
12 crème caramel
    crêpe suzette
    fruit crumble
    profiteroles
13 fruit cocktail
    millefeuilles
    summer pudding
14 charlotte russe
15 clootie dumpling
    queen of puddings
    roly-poly pudding

See also **baking**; **cake**; **food**

detective

Detectives include:

03 Zen (Aurelio; *Ratking*, 1988, et seq, Michael Dibdin)
04 Bony (Napoleon Bonaparte; *The Barrakee Mystery*, 1931, et seq, Arthur Upfield)
    Chan (Charlie; *The House without a Key*, 1925, et seq, Earl Derr Biggers)
    Cuff (Richard; *The Moonstone*, 1868, Wilkie Collins)
    Dean (Sam; *Blood Rights*, 1989, et seq, Mike Phillips)
    Gray (Cordelia; *An Unsuitable Job for a Woman*, 1972, et seq, P D James)
    Vane (Harriet; *Strong Poison*, 1930, et seq, Dorothy L Sayers)
05 Brown (Father; *The Innocence of Father Brown*, 1911, G K Chesterton)
    Drake (Paul; *The Case of the Velvet Claws*, 1933, et seq, Erle Stanley Gardner)
    Duffy (Nicholas; *Duffy*, 1980, et seq, Dan Kavanagh)

Dupin (C Auguste; 'The Mystery of Marie Roget', 1842–43, et seq, Edgar Allan Poe)
Ghote (Inspector Ganesh; *The Perfect Murder*, 1964, et seq, H R F Keating)
Grant (Alan; *A Shilling for Candles: The Story of a Crime*, 1936, et seq, Josephine Tey)
Mason (Perry; *The Case of the Velvet Claws*, 1933, et seq, Erle Stanley Gardner)
Morse (Inspector; *Last Bus To Woodstock*, 1975, et seq, Colin Dexter)
Queen (Ellery; *The Roman Hat Mystery*, 1929, et seq, Ellery Queen)
Rebus (John; *Knots and Crosses*, 1987, et seq, Ian Rankin)
Spade (Sam; *The Maltese Falcon*, 1930, et seq, Dashiell Hammett)
Vance (Philo; *The Benson Murder Case*, 1926, et seq, S S Van Dine)
Wolfe (Nero; *Fer-de-lance*, 1934, et seq, Rex Stout)

06 Alleyn (Roderick; *A Man Lay Dead*, 1934, et seq, Ngaio Marsh)
Archer (Lew; *The Moving Target*, 1949, et seq, Ross MacDonald)
Essrog (Lionel; *Motherless Brooklyn*, 1999, Jonathan Lethem)
Hanaud (Inspector; *At the Villa Rose*, 1910, et seq, A E W Mason)
Holmes (Sherlock; *A Study in Scarlet*, 1887, et seq, Arthur Conan Doyle)
Marple (Miss Jane; *Murder at the Vicarage*, 1930, et seq, Agatha Christie)
Pascoe (Peter; *A Clubbable Woman*, 1970, et seq, Reginald Hill)
Poirot (Hercule; *The Mysterious Affair at Styles*, 1920, et seq, Agatha Christie)
Silver (Miss Maude; *Pilgrim's Rest*, 1948, et seq, Patricia Wentworth)
Vidocq (Eugène François; 1775–1857, French)
Watson (Dr John; *A Study in Scarlet*, 1887, et seq, Arthur Conan Doyle)
Wimsey (Lord Peter; *Whose Body?*, 1923, et seq, Dorothy L Sayers)

07 Appleby (John; *Death at the President's Lodging*, 1936, et seq, Michael Innes)
Cadfael (Brother; *A Morbid Taste for Bones*, 1977, et seq, Ellis Peters)
Campion (Albert; *The Crime at Black Dudley*, 1929, et seq, Margery Allingham)
Charles (Nick; *The Thin Man*, 1934, Dashiell Hammett)
Dalziel (Andy; *A Clubbable Woman*, 1970, et seq, Reginald Hill)
Fansler (Kate; *Sweet Death, Kind Death*,

1984, et seq, Amanda Cross)
Laidlaw (Jack; *Laidlaw*, 1977, et seq, William McIlvanney)
Maigret (Jules; *The Death of M Gallet*, 1931, Georges Simenon)
Marlowe (Philip; *The Big Sleep*, 1939, et seq, Raymond Chandler)
Milhone (Kinsey; *A is for Alibi*, 1986, et seq, Sue Grafton)
Moseley (Hoke; *Miami Blues*, 1984, et seq, Charles Willeford)
Wexford (Reginald; *From Doon with Death*, 1964, et seq, Ruth Rendell)
Whicher (Jonathan 'Jack'; 1814–81, English)

08 Lestrade (Inspector; *A Study in Scarlet*, 1887, et seq, Arthur Conan Doyle)
Ramotswe (Precious; *The No 1 Ladies' Detective Agency*, 1998, et seq, Alexander McCall Smith)

09 Bonaparte (Napoleon; *The Barrakee Mystery*, 1931, et seq, Arthur Upfield)
Dalgliesh (Adam; *Cover Her Face*, 1962, et seq, P D James)
Hawksmoor (Nicholas; *Hawksmoor*, 1985, Peter Ackroyd)
Pinkerton (Allan; 1819–84, Scottish/US)
Scarpetta (Kay; *Postmortem*, 1990, et seq, Patricia Cornwell)

10 Van Der Valk (Piet; *Love in Amsterdam*, 1962, et seq, Nicolas Freeling)
Warshawski (V I; *Indemnity Only*, 1982, et seq, Sara Paretsky)

13 Continental Op (*Red Harvest*, 1929, Dashiell Hammett)

device

Devices include:

02 PC	lighter	hairdryer
04 iPod®	printer	hole punch
iron	stapler	magnifier
Xbox®	Walkman®	MP3 player
05 clock	**08** barbecue	pedometer
Dyson®	CD player	staple gun
phone	computer	stopwatch
razor	egg timer	telephone
torch	epilator	tin opener
watch	nail file	**10** calculator
	scissors	coin sorter
06 camera	tweezers	data logger
heater		fax machine
Hoover®	**09** cafetière	ice scraper
juicer	can opener	overlocker
scales	cell phone	percolator
shaver	corkscrew	wine cooler
	DVD player	
07 foot spa	fan heater	**11** answerphone
Game Boy®	flip phone	baby monitor

camera phone
electric fan
manicure set
mobile phone
patio heater
PlayStation®
thermometer
video camera
12 bottle opener
curling tongs

dehumidifier
games console
kitchen timer
nail clippers
steam cleaner
stitch ripper
13 eyelash curler
floor polisher
remote control
sewing machine

smoke detector
staple remover
vacuum cleaner
video recorder
14 clamshell phone
eyelash curlers
needle threader
personal stereo
Swiss army knife
15 electric blanket

See also **computer**; **domestic appliance**; **electricity**; **optics**; **rhetoric**; **scanner**

diamond

Diamonds include:

04 Agra
Hope
Shah
05 Jacob
Mouna
Nepal
Nizam
Sancy
06 Gruosi
Nassak
Regent
07 Allnatt

Ashberg
Eugénie
Jubilee
Lesotho
Paragon
Tiffany
08 Cullinan
Deepdene
Idol's Eye
Kimberly
Koh-I-Noor
Nur-Ul-Ain
Red Cross

09 Amsterdam
Beau Sancy
Blue Heart
Centenary
Darya-i Nur
Earth Star
Excelsior
Graff Blue
Hortensia
10 Florentine
Ocean Dream
Portuguese
11 Premier Rose

Spoonmaker's
Wittelsbach
12 Dresden Green
Incomparable
Porter Rhodes
Taylor-Burton
13 Golden Jubilee
Star of the East
14 Archduke Joseph
Millennium Star
Star of the South
15 Heart of Eternity

diary

Diarists include:

03 Lee (Lorelei; *Gentlemen Prefer Blondes*, 1925, Anita Loos)

04 Byrd (William; 1674–1744, American)
Gide (André; 1869–1951, French)
Mole (Adrian; *The Secret Diary of Adrian Mole Aged 13¾*, 1982, et seq, Sue Townsend)
Ooka (Shohei; 1909–88, Japanese)

05 Birde (William; 1674–1744, American)
Frank (Anne; 1929–45, German)
Grant (Elizabeth; 1797–1885, Scottish)
Jones (Bridget; *Bridget Jones's Diary*, 1996, et seq, Helen Fielding)
Pasek (Jan Chryzostom; c.1636–1701, Polish)
Pepys (Samuel; 1633–1703, English)
Reyes (Alfonso; 1889–1959, Mexican)
Scott (Robert Falcon; 1868–1912, English)
Torga (Miguel; 1907–90, Portuguese)

06 Burney (Fanny; 1752–1840, English)
Evelyn (John; 1620–1706, English)

Pooter (Charles; *The Diary of a Nobody*, 1892, George and Weedon Grossmith)

07 Andrews (Pamela; *Pamela*, 1740–41, Samuel Richardson)
Carlyle (Jane Welsh; 1801–66, Scottish)
Chesnut (Mary; 1823–86, US)
Creevey (Thomas; 1768–1838, English)
Kilvert (Francis; 1840–79, English)
Shields (Rev Robert; 1918–2007, US)

08 Greville (Charles; 1794–1865, English)
Melville (James; 1556–1614, Scottish)
Robinson (Henry Crabb; 1775–1867, English)

09 Schreiber (Lady Charlotte; 1812–95, Welsh)
Slaveykov (Petko; 1827–95, Bulgarian)

11 Lichtenberg (Georg Christoph; 1742–99, German)
Thermopolis (Mia; *The Princess Diaries*, 2000, et seq, Meg Cabot)

12 Bashkirtseva (Marya; 1860–84, Russian)

Dickens, Charles (1812–70)

Significant works include:

09 *Hard Times* (1854)
The Chimes (1844)

10 *Bleak House* (1852–53)

11 *Oliver Twist* (1837–38)

12 *Barnaby Rudge* (1841)
Dombey and Son (1846–48)
Little Dorrit (1855–57)
Nobody's Fault (1855–57)

13 *American Notes* (1842)
Sketches by Boz (1833–68)
The Haunted Man (1848)

14 *Christmas Books* (1843–49)
Pickwick Papers (1836–37)

15 *A Christmas Carol* (1843)
Our Mutual Friend (1865)
The Battle of Life (1846)

16 *A Tale of Two Cities* (1859)

Christmas Stories (1859–67)
David Copperfield (1849–50)
Martin Chuzzlewit (1843–44)
Nicholas Nickleby (1838–39)

17 *Great Expectations* (1860–61)
Pictures from Italy (1846)

19 *The Old Curiosity Shop* (1840–41)

21 *The Cricket on the Hearth* (1845)
The Parish Boy's Progress (1837–38)

22 *Hard Times for These Times* (1854)
The Mystery of Edwin Drood (1870)

23 *A Child's History of England* (1851–53)

33 *Dealings with the Firm of Dombey and Son* (1846–48)

36 *The Posthumous Papers of the Pickwick Club* (1836–37)

Significant characters include:

02 Jo

03 Bud (Rosa)
Cly (Roger)
Gay (Walter)
Joe
Tox (Miss Lucretia)

04 Bray (Madeline)
Bray (Walter)
Cute (Alderman)
Dick (Mr)
Em'ly (Little)
Fang (Mr)
Fern (Will)
Gamp (Mrs Sarah 'Sairey')
Hawk (Sir Mulberry)
Heep (Uriah)
Hugh
Humm (Anthony)
Jupe (Signor)
Jupe (Sissy)
Omer (Mr)
Prig (Betsey)
Riah
Tigg (Montague)
Tope (Mr)
Tope (Mrs)
Veck (Margaret 'Meg')
Veck (Toby 'Trotty')
Wade (Miss)
Wegg (Silas)
Wren (Jenny)

05 Allen (Arabella)

Allen (Benjamin)
Bates (Charley)
Biddy
Brass (Sally)
Brass (Sampson)
Brown (Mrs)
Casby (Christopher)
Chick (Mrs Louisa)
Clare (Ada)
Daisy (Solomon)
Doyce (Daniel)
Drood (Edwin)
Fagin
Filer (Mr)
Flite (Miss)
Gills (Solomon)
Gowan (Henry)
Gride (Arthur)
Guppy (William)
Hexam (Charley)
Hexam (Gaffer Jesse)
Hexam (Lizzie)
Kenge (Mr)
Krook (Mr)
Lorry (Mr Jarvis)
Lupin (Mrs)
Miggs (Miss)
Molly
Nancy
Noggs (Newman)
Pinch (Ruth)
Pinch (Tom)
Pross (Miss)

Pross (Solomon)
Quilp (Betsey)
Quilp (Daniel)
Rudge (Barnaby)
Rudge (Mr)
Rudge (Mrs Mary)
Sikes (Bill)
Slyme (Chevy)
Smike
Toots (Mr)
Twist (Oliver)
Venus (Mr)
Voles (Mr)

06 Badger (Bayham)
Bagnet (Mr)
Bagnet (Mrs)
Bailey (Benjamin)
Bailey (Young)
Barkis (Mr)
Barsad (John)
Beadle (Harriet 'Tattycoram')
Bitzer
Boffin (Mr Nicodemus)
Boffin (Mrs)
Bowley (Sir Joseph)
Bucket (Mr)
Bumble (Mr)
Bunsby (Captain Jack)
Buzfuz (Serjeant)
Carker (Harriet)
Carker (James)

Carker (John)
Carton (Sydney)
Codlin (Harris 'Short')
Codlin (Thomas)
Corney (Mrs)
Cuttle (Captain Edward 'Ned')
Darnay (Charles)
Dartle (Rosa)
Dennis (Ned)
Deputy
Dombey (Edith)
Dombey (Florence)
Dombey (Mr Paul)
Dombey (Paul)
Dorrit (Amy)
Dorrit (Edward 'Tip')
Dorrit (Fanny)
Dorrit (Frederick)
Dorrit (William)
Dowler (Mr)
Endell (Martha)
Feenix (Lord)
Fizkin (Horatio)
Gordon (Lord George)
Graham (Mary)
Guster
Harmon (John)
Hawdon (Captain)
Higden (Betty)
Howler (Rev Melchisedech)
Hunter (Mrs Leo)
Hutley (Jem)
Jarley (Mrs)
Jasper (Mr John)
Jingle (Alfred)
Lammle (Alfred)
Magnus (Peter)
Maldon (Jack)
Maylie (Mrs)
Maylie (Rose)
Merdle (Mr)
Merdle (Mrs)
Nipper (Susan)
Orlick (Dolge)
Pancks (Mr)
Pegler (Mrs)
Pirrip (Philip 'Pip')
Pocket (Herbert)
Pocket (Matthew)
Puffer (Princess)
Redlaw (Mr)
Rigaud
Sapsea (Mr Thomas)
Sawyer (Bob)
Sleary (Mr)
Strong (Dr)
Strong (Mrs Annie)

Tapley (Mark)
Tartar (Mr)
Toodle (Polly)
Toodle (Robin)
Tupman (Tracy)
Varden (Dolly)
Varden (Gabriel)
Warden (Michael)
Weller (Mrs)
Weller (Mr Tony)
Weller (Sam)
Wilfer (Bella)
Wilfer (Reginald)
Willet (Joe)
Willet (John)
Winkle (Nathaniel)
Wopsle (Mr)

07 Barbara
Barbary (Miss)
Bardell (Mrs Martha)
Blimber (Doctor)
Boldwig (Captain)
Britain (Benjamin)
Browdie (John)
Chester (Edward)
Chester (Sir John, formerly Mr)
Chivery (Young John)
Chuffey (Mr)
Cleaver (Fanny)
Clennam (Arthur)
Clennam (Mrs)
Creakle (Mr)
Crewler (Sophy)
Dawkins (Jack)
Dedlock (Lady)
Dedlock (Sir Leicester)
Deedles
Defarge (Ernest)
Defarge (Madame Thérèse)
Drummle (Bentley)
Durdles
Estella
Gabelle (Theophile)
Gargery (Joe)
Gargery (Mrs Joe)
Garland (Mr Abel)
Garland (Mrs Abel)
Gaspard
General (Mrs)
Granger (Edith)
Gridley (Mr)
Jaggers (Mr)
Jeddler (Dr Anthony)
Jeddler (Grace)
Jeddler (Marion)
Jellyby (Caroline 'Caddy')
Jellyby (Mrs)

Jiniwin (Mrs)
Jobling (Tony)
Jorkins (Mr)
Kenwigs (Mr)
Kenwigs (Mrs)
Leeford (Edward 'Monks')
Lewsome (Mr)
Manette (Dr Alexandre)
Manette (Lucie)
Marwood (Alice)
Meagles (Minnie 'Pet')
Meagles (Mr)
Meagles (Mrs)
Mowcher (Miss)
Nadgett (Mr)
Neckett
Neckett (Charlotte)
Newcome (Clemency)
Nubbles (Christopher 'Kit')
Nupkins (George)
Pipchin (Mrs)
Plummer (Bertha)
Plummer (Caleb)
Plummer (Edward)
Podsnap (Mr John)
Rachael
Rachael (Mrs)
Scrooge (Ebenezer)
Skewton (The Hon Mrs)
Slammer (Doctor)
Slowboy (Tilly)
Slumkey (The Hon Samuel)
Snagsby (Mr)
Snawley (Mr)
Snubbin (Serjeant)
Sparsit (Mrs)
Spenlow (Dora)
Spenlow (Mr Francis)
Squeers (Wackford)
Stryver (Mr)
Tiny Tim
Todgers (Mrs)
Trotter (Job)
Wackles (Sophy)
Wemmick (John)

08 Bagstock (Major Joseph)
Boythorn (Lawrence)
Brownlow (Mr)
Carstone (Richard)
Chadband (Rev Mr)
Claypole (Noah)
Clickett ('The Orfling')
Cratchit (Bob)
Crummles (Mrs Vincent)
Crummles (Mr Vincent)
Cruncher (Jeremiah 'Jerry')
Datchery (Dick)
Fielding (May)

Finching (Flora)
Fledgeby (Fascination)
Gashford (Mr)
Gummidge (Mrs)
Haredale (Emma)
Haredale (Mr Geoffrey)
Havisham (Miss)
Hortense (Mademoiselle)
Jarndyce (John)
La Creevy (Miss)
Landless (Helena)
Landless (Neville)
Littimer
Magwitch (Abel)
Micawber (Mrs Emma)
Micawber (Mr Wilkins)
Montague (Tigg)
Nickleby (Kate)
Nickleby (Mrs)
Nickleby (Nicholas)
Nickleby (Ralph)
Peggotty (Clara)
Peggotty (Daniel)
Peggotty (Ham)
Petowker (Miss Henrietta)
Pickwick (Samuel)
Plornish (Mrs Thomas)
Plornish (Mr Thomas)
Skimpole (Harold)
Snitchey (Jonathan)
Sparkler (Edmund)
Stiggins (The Rev Mr)
Traddles (Thomas)
Trotwood (Miss Betsey)
Westlock (John)
Wrayburn (Eugene)

09 Billickin (Mrs)
Blackpool (Stephen)
Bounderby (Josiah)
Cheeryble (Charles)
Cheeryble (Edwin)
Compeyson
Gradgrind (Louisa)
Gradgrind (Thomas)

Gradgrind (Tom)
Grewgious (Mr Hiram)
Harthouse (James)
Headstone (Bradley)
Lightwood (Mortimer)
Lillyvick (Mr)
Mantalini (Madame)
Mantalini (Mr Alfred)
Murdstone (Jane)
Murdstone (Mr Edward)
Old Martin
Pardiggle (Mrs)
Pecksniff (Charity)
Pecksniff (Mercy)
Pecksniff (Seth)
Potterson (Abbey)
Riderhood (Roger 'Rogue')
Rokesmith (John)
Smallweed (Grandfather
  Joshua)
Smorltork (Count)
Snodgrass (Augustus)
Summerson (Esther)
Swiveller (Richard 'Dick')
Tackleton (Mr)
Tappertit (Simon 'Sim')
The Fat Boy
Trabb's boy
Veneering (Mr Hamilton)
Veneering (Mrs)
Verisopht (Lord Frederick)
Wickfield (Agnes)
Wickfield (Mr)
Woodcourt (Allan)

10 Cavalletto (John Baptist)
Chuzzlewit (Anthony)
Chuzzlewit (Jonas)
Chuzzlewit (Martin)
Chuzzlewit ('Old' Martin)
Crisparkle (Revd Septimus)
Flintwinch (Affery)
Flintwinch (Jeremiah)
Heathfield (Alfred)
Little Nell

MacStinger (Mrs)
Rouncewell (Mr)
Rouncewell (Mr George)
Rouncewell (Mrs)
Sowerberry (Mr)
Sowerberry (Mrs)
Steerforth (Mr James)
Tattycoram
The Wardles
Turveydrop (Mr)
Turveydrop (Prince)
Twinkleton (Miss)
Wititterly (Mr Henry)
Wititterly (Mrs)

11 Copperfield (David)
Copperfield (Mrs Clara)
Dismal Jemmy
Grandfather
Linkinwater (Tim)
Peerybingle (John)
Peerybingle (Mrs Mary
  'Dot')
Pumblechook (Uncle)
Slackbridge
Snevellicci (Miss)
St Evremonde (Marquis de)
Sweedlepipe (Paul 'Poll')
The Bachelor
Tulkinghorn (Mr)

12 Bailey Junior
Grip the Raven
Honeythunder (Mr Luke)
Little Dorrit
Marley's Ghost
The Barnacles
The Fezziwigs

13 M'Choakumchild (Mr)
Rob the Grinder

14 Chickenstalker (Mrs Anne)
The Marchioness

15 The Artful Dodger

diet

Diets include:

02 GI	Ornish	body boost
03 FIT	**07** banting	herbalife
Hay	LA Shape	Hollywood
04 VLCD	raw food	juice fast
zone	**08** beetroot	low sodium
05 F-plan	Pritikin	omega zone
06 Atkins	Slim-Fast	Perricone
low fat	**09** blood type	Scarsdale
		10 fit for life

grapefruit
Jenny Craig
Mayo Clinic
ready to eat
revival soy
South Beach
superfoods
vegetarian
11 cabbage soup

high protein
hip and thigh
macrobiotic
somersizing
The Hamptons
thin for life
12 Beverly Hills
protein power
sugar busters

13 food combining
radiant health
Slimming World
14 Richard Simmons
very low calorie
Weight Watchers
15 metabolic typing
nutrisystem plan
Rosemary Conley's

dinosaur

Dinosaurs include:

04 T Rex
06 raptor
08 coelurus
sauropod
theropod
09 hadrosaur
iguanodon
oviraptor
10 allosaurus
anatotitan
barosaurus
diplodocus
megalosaur
ophiacodon
torosaurus
utahraptor
11 apatosaurus

ceteosaurus
coelophysis
coelurosaur
deinonychus
dromaeosaur
polacanthus
prosauropod
saurischian
stegosaurus
triceratops
tyrannosaur
12 ankylosaurus
brontosaurus
camptosaurus
ceratosaurus
megalosaurus
ornithischia
ornithomimus

plateosaurus
psittacosaur
titanosaurus
velociraptor
13 atlantosaurus
brachiosaurus
compsognathus
corythosaurus
dwarf allosaur
edmontosaurus
herrerasaurus
ornitholestes
styracosaurus
tyrannosaurus
14 leaellynasaura
psittacosaurus
15 cryolophosaurus
parasaurolophus

diocese

Dioceses and archdioceses of the UK, with denomination, include:

03 Ely (Anglican)
04 York (Anglican)
05 Derby (Anglican)
Derry (Catholic)
Leeds (Catholic)
Truro (Anglican)
06 Armagh (Anglican/Catholic)
Bangor (Anglican)
Connor (Anglican)
Durham (Anglican)
Exeter (Anglican)
Hallam (Catholic)
London (Anglican)
Oxford (Anglican)
07 Brechin (Anglican)
Bristol (Anglican)
Cardiff (Catholic)
Chester (Anglican)
Clifton (Catholic)
Clogher (Anglican/Catholic)

Dromore (Catholic)
Dunkeld (Catholic)
Glasgow (Catholic)
Kilmore (Catholic)
Lincoln (Anglican)
Menevia (Catholic)
Norwich (Anglican)
Paisley (Catholic)
Salford (Catholic)
St Asaph (Anglican)
Wrexham (Catholic)
08 Aberdeen (Catholic)
Bradford (Anglican)
Carlisle (Anglican)
Coventry (Anglican)
Galloway (Catholic)
Hereford (Anglican)
Llandaff (Anglican)
Monmouth (Anglican)
Plymouth (Catholic)
St Albans (Anglican)

St Davids (Anglican)
09 Blackburn (Anglican)
Brentwood (Catholic)
Edinburgh (Anglican)
Guildford (Anglican)
Lancaster (Catholic)
Leicester (Anglican)
Lichfield (Anglican)
Liverpool (Anglican/
Catholic)
Newcastle (Anglican)
Rochester (Anglican)
Salisbury (Anglican)
Sheffield (Anglican)
Southwark (Anglican/
Catholic)
Southwell (Anglican)
Wakefield (Anglican)
Worcester (Anglican)
10 Birmingham (Anglican/
Catholic)

Canterbury (Anglican)
Chelmsford (Anglican)
Chichester (Anglican)
East Anglia (Catholic)
Gloucester (Anglican)
Manchester (Anglican)
Motherwell (Catholic)
Nottingham (Catholic)
Portsmouth (Anglican/
Catholic)

Shrewsbury (Catholic)
Winchester (Anglican)

11 Northampton (Catholic)
Sodor and Man (Anglican)
Westminster (Catholic)

12 Bath and Wells (Anglican)
Peterborough (Anglican)

13 Down and Connor
(Catholic)

Middlesbrough (Catholic)

Ripon and Leeds (Anglican)

14 Derry and Raphoe
(Anglican)

Down and Dromore
(Anglican)

See also **archbishop**; **religion**

director

Film and theatre directors and producers include:

03 Cox (Brian; 1946– , Scottish)
Lee (Ang; 1954– , Taiwanese)
Lee (Spike; 1957– , US)
May (Elaine; 1932– , US)
Ozu (Yasujiro; 1903–63, Japanese)
Ray (Satyajit; 1921–92, Indian)
Wai (Wong Kar; 1956– , Chinese)
Woo (John; 1948– , Chinese)

04 Alda (Alan; 1936– , US)
Axel (Gabriel; 1918– , Danish)
Bond (Edward; 1934– , English)
Coen (Ethan; 1958– , US)
Coen (Joel; 1954– , US)
Eyre (Sir Richard; 1943– , English)
Ford (John; 1895–1973, US)
Gray (Simon; 1936–2008, English)
Hall (Sir Peter; 1930– , English)
Hare (Sir David; 1947– , English)
Hart (Moss; 1904–61, US)
Hill (George Roy; 1921–2002, US)
Lang (Fritz; 1890–1976, Austrian/US)
Lean (Sir David; 1908–91, English)
Nunn (Sir Trevor; 1940– , English)
Papp (Joseph; 1921–91, US)
Reed (Sir Carol; 1906–76, English)
Roeg (Nicolas; 1928– , English)
Tati (Jacques; 1908–82, French)
Todd (Mike; 1909–58, US)
Weir (Peter; 1944– , Australian)
Wise (Robert; 1914–2005, US)

05 Allen (Woody; 1935– , US)
Barba (Eugenio; 1936– , Italian)
Boyle (Danny; 1956– , English)
Brook (Peter; 1925– , English)
Capra (Frank; 1897–1991, Italian/US)
Carné (Marcel; 1909–96, French)
Clair (René; 1898–1981, French)
Craig (Gordon; 1872–1966, English)
Cukor (George; 1899–1983, US)
Dante (Joe; 1946– , US)
Demme (Jonathan; 1944– , US)
Fosse (Bob; 1927–87, US)

Gance (Abel; 1889–1981, French)
Hands (Terry; 1941– , English)
Hawks (Howard; 1896–1977, US)
Ivory (James; 1928– , US)
Kazan (Elia; 1909–2003, Turkish/US)
Kelly (Gene; 1912–96, US)
Korda (Sir Alexander; 1893–1956,
Hungarian/British)
Leigh (Mike; 1943– , English)
Leone (Sergio; 1922–89, Italian)
Lloyd (Phyllida; 1957– , English)
Losey (Joseph; 1909–84, US)
Lucas (George; 1944– , US)
Lumet (Sidney; 1924–2011, US)
Lynch (David; 1946– , US)
Malle (Louis; 1932–95, French)
Mamet (David; 1947– , US)
Marsh (Dame Ngaio; 1899–1982, New
Zealand)
Mayer (Louis B; 1885–1957, US)
Miles (Bernard, Lord; 1907–91, English)
Noble (Adrian; 1950– , English)
Pabst (G W; 1895–1967, German)
Perry (Antoinette; 1888–1946, US)
Roach (Hal; 1892–1992, US)
Scott (Ridley; 1937– , English)
Stein (Peter; 1937– , German)
Stone (Oliver; 1946– , US)
Vadim (Roger; 1928–2000, French)
Varda (Agnès; 1928– , Belgian/French)
Verdy (Violette; 1933– , French)
Vidor (King; 1894–1982, US)
Wajda (Andrzej; 1926– , Polish)
Wells (John; 1936–98, English)
Wolfe (George C; 1954– , US)
Wyler (William; 1902–81, German/US)

06 Abbott (George; 1887–1995, US)
Altman (Robert; 1925–2006, US)
Ang Lee (1954– , Taiwanese)
Artaud (Antonin; 1896–1948, French)
Arzner (Dorothy; 1900–79, US)
August (Bille; 1948– , Danish)

Badham (John; 1939–   , US)
Barton (John; 1928–   , English)
Beatty (Warren; 1937–   , US)
Besson (Luc; 1959–   , French)
Brecht (Bertolt; 1898–1956, German)
Brooks (Mel; 1926–   , US)
Bryden (Bill; 1942–   , Scottish)
Buñuel (Luis; 1900–83, Spanish)
Burton (Tim; 1960–   , US)
Callow (Simon; 1949–   , English)
Cooney (Ray; 1932–   , English)
Copeau (Jacques; 1879–1949, French)
Corman (Roger; 1926–   , US)
Curtiz (Michael; 1888–1962, Hungarian)
Cusack (Cyril; 1910–93, Irish)
Daldry (Stephen; 1961–   , English)
Davies (Howard; 1945–   , English)
Davies (Terence; 1945–   , English)
De Sica (Vittorio; 1902–74, Italian)
Devine (George; 1910–65, English)
Dexter (John; 1925–90, English)
Disney (Walt; 1901–66, US)
Donner (Richard; 1930–   , US)
Dunlop (Frank; 1927–   , English)
Dybwad (Johanne; 1867–1950, Norwegian)
Ephron (Nora; 1941–2012, US)
Forbes (Bryan; 1926–   , English)
Forman (Miloš; 1932–   , Czech/US)
Frears (Stephen; 1941–   , English)
Fugard (Athol; 1932–   , South African)
Gibson (Mel; 1956–   , US/Australian)
Godard (Jean-Luc; 1930–   , French)
Godber (John; 1956–   , English)
Haydee (Marcia; 1939–   , Brazilian)
Herzog (Werner; 1942–   , German)
Hopper (Dennis; 1936–2010, US)
Howard (Ron; 1954–   , US)
Hughes (Howard; 1905–76, US)
Huston (John; 1906–87, US)
Jarman (Derek; 1942–94, English)
Jordan (Neil; 1950–   , Irish)
Jouvet (Louis; 1887–1951, French)
Kantor (Tadeusz; 1915–90, Polish)
Kasdan (Lawrence; 1949–   , US)
Landis (John; 1950–   , US)
Lupino (Ida; 1918–95, English)
Mendes (Sam; 1965–   , English)
Miller (George; 1945–   , Australian)
Miller (Jonathan; 1934–   , English)
Moreau (Jeanne; 1928–   , French)
Murnau (F W; 1888–1931, German)
Ophüls (Max; 1902–57, German/French)
Parker (Alan; 1944–   , English)
Powell (Michael; 1905–90, English)
Prince (Hal; 1928–   , US)
Prowse (Philip; 1937–   , Scottish)
Quayle (Sir Anthony; 1913–89, English)
Reiner (Carl; 1922–   , US)

Renoir (Jean; 1894–1979, French/US)
Rohmer (Eric; 1920–2010, French)
Siegal (Don; 1912–91, US)
Usigli (Rodolfo; 1905–79, Mexican)
Warhol (Andy; 1928–87, US)
Warner (Deborah; 1959–   , English)
Warner (Jack; 1892–1978, Canadian/US)
Welles (Orson; 1915–85, US)
Wilder (Billy; 1906–2002, US)
Wilson (Robert; 1941–   , US)
Zanuck (Darryl F; 1902–79, US)

07 Akerman (Chantal; 1950–   , Belgian)
Aldrich (Robert; 1918–83, US)
Asquith (Anthony; 1902–68, English)
Belasco (David; 1853–1931, US)
Benigni (Roberto; 1952–   , Italian)
Bennett (Alan; 1934–   , English)
Bennett (Michael; 1943–87, US)
Bergman (Ingmar; 1918–2007, Swedish)
Berkoff (Steven; 1937–   , English)
Bigelow (Kathryn; 1952–   , US)
Boorman (John; 1933–   , English)
Branagh (Kenneth; 1960–   , Northern Irish)
Bresson (Robert; 1901–99, French)
Cameron (James; 1954–   , Canadian)
Campion (Jane; 1954–   , New Zealand)
Chabrol (Claude; 1930–2010, French)
Chaikin (Joseph; 1935–2003, US)
Chaplin (Charlie; 1889–1977, English)
Clavell (James; 1924–94, Australian/US)
Clurman (Harold; 1901–80, US)
Cocteau (Jean; 1889–1963, French)
Coppola (Francis Ford; 1939–   , US)
Costner (Kevin; 1955–   , US)
De Mille (Cecil B; 1881–1959, US)
De Palma (Brian; 1940–   , US)
Douglas (Bill; 1934–91, Scottish)
Douglas (Michael; 1944–   , US)
Fellini (Federico; 1920–93, Italian)
Fincher (David; 1962–   , US)
Fleming (Tom; 1927–2010, Scottish)
Fleming (Victor; 1883–1949, US)
Forsyth (Bill; 1946–   , Scottish)
Gaumont (Léon; 1864–1946, French)
Gilliam (Terry; 1940–   , US)
Goldwyn (Samuel; 1882–1974, US)
Guthrie (Sir Tyrone; 1900–71, English)
Hartley (Hal; 1959–   , US)
Heiberg (Gunnar; 1857–1929, Norwegian)
Holland (Agnieszka; 1948–   , Polish)
Jackson (Peter; 1961–   , New Zealand)
Joffrey (Robert; 1930–88, US)
Kaufman (George S; 1889–1961, US)
Kaufman (Philip; 1936–   , US)
Kubrick (Stanley; 1928–99, US)
McBride (Jim; 1941–   , US)
McGrath (John; 1935–2002, English)
Nichols (Mike; 1931–   , German/US)

Olivier (Laurence, Lord; 1907–89, English)
Poitier (Sidney; 1924– , US)
Pollack (Sydney; 1934–2008, US)
Redford (Robert; 1937– , US)
Resnais (Alain; 1922– , French)
Robbins (Tim; 1958– , US)
Russell (Ken; 1927–2011, English)
Sellars (Peter; 1958– , US)
Sennett (Mack; 1880–1960, Canadian/US)
Stiller (Mauritz; 1883–1928, Finnish/
Swedish)
Sturges (Preston; 1898–1959, US)
Sturges (Preston; 1898–1959, US)
van Sant (Gus; 1952– , US)
Wenders (Wim; 1945– , German)
08 Anderson (Lindsay; 1923–94, Indian/British)
Anderson (Paul Thomas; 1970– , US)
Barrault (Jean-Louis; 1910–94, French)
Berkeley (Busby; 1895–1976, US)
Bjørnson (Bjørnstjerne; 1832–1910,
Norwegian)
Bogdanov (Michael; 1938– , English)
Brustein (Robert; 1927– , US)
Carrière (Jean-Claude; 1931– , French)
Clements (Sir John; 1910–88, English)
Crawford (Cheryl; 1902–86, US)
Eastwood (Clint; 1930– , US)
Friedkin (William; 1939– , US)
Griffith (D W; 1875–1948, US)
Houseman (John; 1902–88, Romanian/
English/US)
Jarmusch (Jim; 1953– , US)
Jeffries (Lionel; 1926–2010, English)
Kurosawa (Akira; 1910–98, Japanese)
Levinson (Barry; 1942– , US)
Lubitsch (Ernst; 1892–1947, German)
Luhrmann (Baz; 1962– , Australian)
Lyubimov (Yuri; 1917– , Russian/Hungarian)
Marshall (Penny; 1942– , US)
Merchant (Ismail; 1936–2005, Indian)
Minnelli (Vincente; 1913–86, US)
Mitchell (Arthur; 1934– , US)
Ninagawa (Yukio; 1935– , Japanese)
Pasolini (Pier Paolo; 1922–75, Italian)
Piscator (Erwin; 1893–1966, German)
Polanski (Roman; 1933– , French/Polish)
Pudovkin (Vsevolod; 1893–1953, Russian)
Schepisi (Fred; 1939– , Australian)
Scorsese (Martin; 1942– , US)
Selznick (David O; 1902–65, US)
Sjöström (Victor; 1879–1960, Swedish)
Stroheim (Erich von; 1885–1957, Austrian)
Truffaut (François; 1932–84, French)
Visconti (Luchino; 1906–76, Italian)
von Trier (Lars; 1956– , Danish)
Zemeckis (Robert; 1952– , US)
09 Alexander (Bill; 1948– , English)

Almodóvar (Pedro; 1951– , Spanish)
Antonioni (Michelangelo; 1912–2007, Italian)
Armstrong (Gillian; 1952– , Australian)
Carpenter (John; 1948– , US)
Chen Kaige (1954– , Chinese)
Fernández (Emilio; 1904–86, Mexican)
Greenaway (Peter; 1942– , English)
Grotowski (Jerzy; 1933–99, Polish)
Hitchcock (Sir Alfred; 1899–1980, English)
Malkovich (John; 1953– , US)
Meyerhold (Vsevolod; 1874–c.1940,
Russian)
Minghella (Anthony; 1947–2008, English)
Mizoguchi (Kenji; 1898–1956, Japanese)
Mountford (Charles P; 1890–1976,
Australian)
Peckinpah (Sam; 1925–84, US)
Plowright (Joan; 1929– , English)
Preminger (Otto; 1906–86, Austrian/US)
Spielberg (Steven; 1946– , US)
Stevenson (Robert; 1905–86, English)
Strasberg (Lee; 1901–82, Austrian/US)
Streisand (Barbra; 1942– , US)
Tarantino (Quentin; 1963– , US)
Tavernier (Bertrand; 1941– , French)
Von Trotta (Margarethe; 1942– , German)
Wanamaker (Sam; 1919–93, US)
Zinnemann (Fred; 1907–97, Austrian)
10 Bertolucci (Bernardo; 1941– , Italian)
Cronenberg (David; 1943– , Canadian)
Eisenstein (Sergei; 1898–1948, Russian)
Fassbinder (Rainer Werner; 1946–82,
German)
Greengrass (Paul; 1955– , English)
Kaurismäki (Aki; 1957– , Finnish)
Kiarostami (Abbas; 1940– , Iranian)
Kieslowski (Krzysztof; 1941–96, Polish)
Littlewood (Joan; 1914–2002, English)
Makhmalbaf (Mohsen; 1957– , Iranian)
Mankiewicz (Joseph L; 1909–93, US)
Mnouchkine (Ariane; 1938– , French)
Rossellini (Roberto; 1906–77, Italian)
Saint-Denis (Michel; 1897–1971, French)
Soderbergh (Steven; 1963– , US)
Sucksdorff (Arne E; 1917–2001, Swedish)
Vakhtangov (Yevgeni; 1883–1922, Russian)
Wertmuller (Lina; 1928– , Italian)
Zeffirelli (Franco; 1923– , Italian)
Zetterling (Mai; 1925–94, Swedish)
Zhang Yimou (1951– , Chinese)
11 Bogdanovich (Peter; 1939– , US)
Dingelstedt (Franz von; 1814–81, German)
Mackendrick (Alexander; 1912–93, US)
Pressburger (Emeric; 1902–88, Hungarian)
Riefenstahl (Leni; 1902–2003, German)
Roddenberry (Gene; 1921–91, US)
Schlesinger (John; 1926–2003, English)

12 Attenborough (Richard, Lord; 1923– , English)
Espert Romero (Nuria; 1935– , Spanish)
Stanislavsky (1863–1938, Russian)
Von Sternberg (Josef; 1894–1969, Austrian)

13 Aguilera Malta (Demetrio; 1909–81, Ecuadorean)
Gutiérrez Alea (Tomás; 1928–96, Cuban)
Stafford-Clark (Max; 1941– , English)

disease

Diseases and medical conditions include:

02
CF
ME
MS
TB

03
CFS
CJD
DVT
flu
FMS
IBS
PID
PKU
PMS
PMT
PVS
tic
TSS

04
acne
AIDS
ARDS
clap
cold
coma
gout
kuru
Lyme
mono
rash
SARS

05
boils
colic
crabs
croup
favus
heart
hives
lupus
mumps
polio
rigor
ulcer
warts
Weil's
worms

06
angina
apnoea
asthma
autism
cancer
chorea

Crohn's
dropsy
eczema
emesis
goitre
Grave's
hernia
herpes
myopia
oedema
otitis
Paget's
quinsy
rabies
scurvy
sprain
squint
stroke
thrush
tumour
typhus

07
abscess
allergy
anaemia
anthrax
anxiety
aphasia
aphonia
atrophy
Batten's
bird flu
Bright's
bulimia
cholera
coeliac
kissing
leprosy
lockjaw
malaria
Marburg
measles
myalgia
mycosis
myiasis
rickets
rubella
sarcoma
scabies
tetanus
typhoid

vertigo

08
Addison's
adynamia
alopecia
aneurism
aneurysm
anorexia
avian flu
beriberi
botulism
bursitis
cachexia
club foot
cold sore
coxalgia
Cushing's
cynanche
cystitis
dementia
diabetes
dyschroa
embolism
epilepsy
exanthem
fibroids
fracture
furuncle
gangrene
glaucoma
Hodgkin's
impetigo
jaundice
kala-azar
kyphosis
listeria
lordosis
lymphoma
melanoma
Ménière's
migraine
myositis
necrosis
orchitis
pyelitis
Raynaud's
rhinitis
ringworm
sciatica
shingles
smallpox

stenosis
syphilis
tapeworm
Tay-Sachs
tinnitus
trachoma
venereal
viraemia

09 arthritis
arthrosis
Asperger's
bilharzia
black lung
brown lung
cataracts
chlamydia
chlorosis
cirrhosis
cri du chat
distemper
dysentery
dyspraxia
eclampsia
emphysema
enteritis
exanthema
Fujian flu
halitosis
hepatitis
infection
influenza
ketonuria
king's evil
leukaemia
neoplasia
nephritis
nephrosis
neuralgia
paralysis
parotitis
pertussis
pneumonia
psoriasis
pyorrhoea
scoliosis
siderosis
silicosis
sinusitis
sunstroke
Sydenham's
toothache
Tourette's
urticaria
varicella

10 acromegaly
Alzheimer's
amoebiasis
asbestosis

Bell's palsy
Black Death
bronchitis
byssinosis
chickenpox
common cold
depression
dermatitis
diphtheria
gallstones
gingivitis
gonorrhoea
haemolysis
heat stroke
hyperaemia
laryngitis
Lassa fever
meningitis
metastasis
myasthenia
narcolepsy
ornithosis
orthopnoea
paraplegia
Parkinson's
rheumatism
salmonella
syringitis
tendonitis
thrombosis
titubation
trench foot

11 anaphylaxis
brain damage
brucellosis
cholestasis
cleft palate
consumption
dehydration
dengue fever
farmer's lung
green monkey
haemophilia
haemorrhage
heart attack
Huntington's
hydrophobia
hyperemesis
hyperplasia
hypersomnia
hypertrophy
hypotension
listeriosis
mastoiditis
motor neuron
myocarditis
peritonitis
pharyngitis

pneumonitis
proteinuria
psittacosis
rhinorrhoea
sarcoidosis
septicaemia
septic shock
slipped disc
spina bifida
tennis elbow
tonsillitis
trench fever
yellow fever

12 appendicitis
athlete's foot
autoimmunity
cor pulmonale
desquamation
encephalitis
encocarditis
exophthalmia
fibromyalgia
foot-and-mouth
haematemesis
heart failure
hyperalgesia
hyperpyrexia
hypersthenia
hypertension
Legionnaires'
liver failure
lymphangitis
malnutrition
motor neurone
osteoporosis
pericarditis
quadraplegia
rhinorrhagia
scarlet fever
tuberculosis
typhoid fever

13 acoustic shock
bronchiolitis
bubonic plague
cerebral palsy
coronary heart
Down's syndrome
dysmenorrhoea
elephantiasis
endometriosis
gastroparesis
German measles
hyperlipaemia
hypoglycaemia
kidney failure
leishmaniasis
malabsorption
microfracture

mononucleosis
osteomyelitis
poliomyelitis
Rett's syndrome
Reye's syndrome
schizophrenia
toxoplasmosis
varicose veins
West Nile virus
whooping cough

14 angina pectoris
break-bone fever
conjunctivitis

cystic fibrosis
glandular fever
housemaid's knee
hypercalcaemia
hyperglycaemia
hyperkeratosis
hypernatraemia
leukocytopenia
long QT syndrome
Marfan syndrome
osteoarthritis
pneumoconiosis
rheumatic fever
river blindness

sleepy sickness
thyrotoxicosis

15 anorexia nervosa
atherosclerosis
bipolar disorder
gastro-enteritis
Gulf War syndrome
hyperadrenalism
hyperthyroidism
manic depression
Marfan's syndrome
phenylketonuria
schistosomiasis

Disease symptoms include:

04 pain
rash

05 cramp
fever
hives

06 aching
lesion
tremor

07 anxiety
fatigue
fitting
itching

08 bruising
coughing
deafness
fainting
headache
insomnia
numbness

sickness
sneezing
swelling
tingling
vomiting
weakness

09 blindness
diarrhoea
dizziness
heartburn
impotence
lassitude
nosebleed
paralysis
stiffness
twitching

10 congestion
depression
flatulence
irritation

sore throat
tenderness

11 convulsions
indigestion
loss of voice
trapped wind

12 constipation
incontinence
inflammation
irritability
loss of libido
muscle cramps

13 loss of hearing
stomach cramps
swollen glands

14 loss of appetite
pins and needles

15 high temperature
loss of sensation

Animal diseases include:

03 BSE
FMD
gid
orf

04 gape
gout
loco
roup
wind

05 bloat
braxy
farcy
frush
hoove
pearl
surra
vives

06 canker

Johne's
mad cow
Marek's
nagana
rabies
spavie
spavin
sturdy

07 anthrax
blue ear
dourine
hard pad
measles
mooneye
moorill
murrain
roaring
rubbers
scrapie

yellows

08 bovine TB
fowl-pest
glanders
pullorum
scaly-leg
seedy-toe
sheep-pox
staggers
swayback
swine-pox
wildfire
wire-heel

09 Aujeszky's
blackhead
distemper
Newcastle
scratches
sheep scab

spauld-ill
St Hubert's
strangles
10 blue tongue
louping-ill
ornithosis
rinderpest
sallenders
swamp fever
swine fever

Texas fever
water-brain
11 blood-spavin
brucellosis
mad staggers
myxomatosis
parrot fever
psittacosis
12 black-quarter
bush sickness

cattle-plague
foot-and-mouth
furunculosis
gall-sickness
13 grass sickness
grass staggers
leptospirosis
14 sleepy staggers
15 Rift Valley fever
stomach staggers

Plant diseases include:

04 bunt
curl
rust
smut
05 ergot
06 blight
blotch
canker
mildew
mosaic
red rot

07 ferrugo
oak wilt
ring rot
rosette
soft rot
yellows
08 blackleg
black rot
clubroot
crown rot
Dutch elm

leaf curl
loose-cut
wheat eel
white rot
09 crown gall
potato rot
tulip root
10 fire-blight
leaf mosaic
silver leaf
sooty mould

vine-mildew
11 anthracnose
wheat mildew
12 finger-and-toe
peach-yellows
potato blight
13 powdery mildew
14 psyllid yellows
sudden oak death

See also **fever; inflammation; poison; skin; tumour**

dish *see* **food; pasta; potato; seafood**

district *see* **London; New York; Paris; United Kingdom**

diver *see* **swimming**

divination

Divination and fortune-telling techniques include:

04 dice
05 runes
tarot
06 I Ching
sortes (book opening)
07 dowsing (divining rod)
scrying (crystal gazing)
08 geomancy (shapes)
myomancy (mice)
taghairm (lying in a bullock's hide behind a
waterfall)
zoomancy (animals)
09 aeromancy (atmospheric phenomena)
astrology (stars and planets)
belomancy (arrows)
ceromancy (dropping melted wax in water)
gyromancy (walking in a circle and falling
from giddiness)

oenomancy (wine)
palmistry (hand)
pyromancy (fire)
sortilege (drawing lots)
tea leaves
theomancy (oracles)
tripudium (feeding birds)
10 axinomancy (an axe poised upon a stake, or
an agate upon a red-hot axe)
capnomancy (smoke)
cartomancy (playing cards)
chiromancy (reading the hand)
cleromancy (lot)
dukkeripen
hieromancy (sacrificial objects)
hydromancy (water)
lithomancy (stones)
numerology (numbers)
spodomancy (ashes)

11 bibliomancy (book opening)
 botanomancy (plants)
 crithomancy (strewing meal over sacrificial animals)
 gastromancy (sounds from the belly, or by large-bellied glasses)
 hepatoscopy (animal livers)
 oneiromancy (dreams)
 onychomancy (fingernails)
 rhabdomancy (rod, especially divining for water or ore)
 tephromancy (ashes, especially those left after a sacrifice)

12 clairvoyance
 coscinomancy (sieve and shears)

 lampadomancy (flame)
 omphalomancy (number of future children from the knots in the navel-string)
 ornithomancy (birds)
 radiesthesia (various)
 scapulomancy (cracks in a burning shoulder blade)

13 Book of Changes
 crystal gazing
 dactyliomancy (ring)
 fortune cookie
 omoplatoscopy (cracks in a burning shoulder blade)

14 crystallomancy (transparent bodies)

DIY

DIY terms include:

03 MDF
04 coat
 glue
 nail
05 joint
 screw
 tools
06 cement
 pre-mix
 router
 sawing
 tiling
 washer
 wiring
07 carving

 Evo-Stik
 planing
 roofing
 sanding
 sealant
 welding
08 Araldite®
 concrete
 drilling
 flooring
 fretwork
 grouting
 mitre box
 overalls
 painting

 plumbing
 Rawlplug®
 staining
 Swarfega®
 woodwork
09 carpentry
 hammering
 lubricant
 metalwork
 polishing
 Polyfilla®
 soldering
 sugar soap
 superglue
 wallpaper

10 decorating
 multimeter
 plastering
 tile cutter
 varnishing
 wood filler
11 mains tester
 masking tape
 stencilling
 white spirit
13 safety goggles
14 insulating tape
 loft conversion
15 silicone sealant

See also **insulator**

doctor

Doctor types include:

02 GP
 MO
03 vet
05 locum

06 intern
07 dentist
08 houseman
 resident

09 registrar
10 consultant
12 family doctor
14 hospital doctor

medical officer

Doctors include:

04 Aziz (Dr; *A Passage to India*, 1924, E M Forster)
 Cook (Frederick A; 1865–1940, US)
 Davy (Edward; 1806–85, English/Australian)
 Drew (Charles; 1904–50, US)
 Gall (Franz Joseph; 1758–1828, German)
 Gray (Edward Whitaker; 1748–1806, English)

 Grew (Nehemiah; 1641–1712, English)
 Hall (Marshall; 1790–1857, English)
 Hill (Charles, Lord; 1904–89, English)
 King (Sir Truby; 1858–1938, New Zealand)
 Knox (Robert; *The Anatomist*, 1930, James Bridie)
 Koch (Robert; 1843–1910, German)
 Lind (James; 1716–94, Scottish)

Long (Crawford; 1815–78, US)
Razi (ar-; c.865–923/932, Persian)
Redi (Francesco; 1626–97, Italian)
Ross (Sir Ronald; 1857–1932, Indian/British)
Rush (Benjamin; 1745–1813, American)
Slop (Dr; *The Life and Opinions of Tristram Shandy*, 1759–67, Laurence Sterne)
Ward (Nathaniel; 1791–1868, English)

05 Blane (Sir Gilbert; 1749–1834, Scottish)
Borde (Andrew; c.1490–1549, English)
Brown (John; c.1735–88, Scottish)
Bruce (Sir David; 1855–1931, Scottish)
Caius (Dr; *The Merry Wives of Windsor*, 1597/8, William Shakespeare)
Caius (John; 1510–73, English)
Ellis (Havelock; 1859–1939, English)
Fanon (Frantz; 1925–61, French West Indian)
Fludd (Robert; 1574–1637, English)
Frank (Johann Peter; 1745–1821, German)
Galen (c.130–c.201 AD, Greek)
Graaf (Regnier de; 1641–73, Dutch)
Hayem (Georges; 1841–1920, French)
Hench (Philip S; 1896–1965, US)
Henry (William; 1774–1836, English)
Jones (Henry; 1831–99, English)
Kolff (Willem J; 1911–2009, Dutch/US)
Lange (Carl; 1834–1900, Danish)
Leete (Dr; *Looking Backward: 2000–1887*, 1888, Edward Bellamy)
Lower (Richard; 1631–91, English)
Mayer (Robert von; 1814–78, German)
Minot (George R; 1885–1950, US)
Osler (Sir William; 1849–1919, Canadian/British)
Paget (Sir James; 1814–99, English)
Pinch (Dr; *The Comedy of Errors*, 1594, William Shakespeare)
Pinel (Philippe; 1745–1826, French)
Plarr (Edouardo; *The Honorary Consul*, 1973, Graham Greene)
Prout (William; 1785–1850, English)
Remak (Robert; 1815–65, German)
Rider (Edward; *The Doctor's Family*, 1863, Margaret Oliphant)
Selye (Hans; 1907–82, Austrian/Canadian)
Skoda (Joseph; 1805–81, Austrian)
Smith (Thomas Southwood; 1788–1861, English)
Spock (Benjamin; 1903–98, US)
Steno (Nicolaus; 1638–86, Danish)
Tyson (Edward; 1651–1708, English)
Young (Thomas; 1773–1829, English)

06 Alpino (Prospero; 1553–1616, Italian)
Aselli (Gasparo; 1582–1626, Italian)
Bárány (Robert; 1876–1936, Austrian)
Bauhin (Caspar; 1560–1624, Swiss)

Bauhin (Gaspard ; 1560–1624, Swiss)
Becher (Johann Joachim; 1635–82, German)
Bichat (Marie; 1771–1802, French)
Boorde (Andrew; c.1490–1549, English)
Bowman (Sir William; 1816–92, English)
Bright (Richard; 1789–1858, English)
Bright (Timothy; c.1551–1615, English)
Browne (Sir Thomas; 1605–82, English)
Celsus (Aulus; 1 CAD, Roman)
Chagas (Carlos; 1879–1934, Brazilian)
Crofts (James; *The Small House at Allington*, 1864, Anthony Trollope)
Cullen (William; 1710–90, Scottish)
Curran (Dr; *The Ante-Room*, 1934, Kate O'Brien)
Darwin (Erasmus; 1731–1802, English)
Dawson (Bertrand, *Viscount*; 1864–1945, English)
Fernel (Jean; 1497–1558, French)
Finlay (Dr; *Country Doctor*, 1935, A J Cronin)
Finsen (Niels; 1860–1904, Danish)
Firmin (George; *A Shabby Genteel Story*, 1840, W M Thackeray)
Forman (Simon; 1552–1611, English)
Garrod (Sir Archibald; 1857–1936, English)
Gesner (Conrad; 1516–65, Swiss)
Gorgas (William; 1854–1920, US)
Graves (Robert; 1796–1853, Irish)
Halevi (Jehuda; 1075–1141, Spanish)
Hansen (Gerhard; 1841–1912, Norwegian)
Harvey (William; 1578–1657, English)
Hedwig (Johannes; 1730–99, German)
Iannis (Dr; *Captain Corelli's Mandolin*, 1994, Louis de Bernières)
Jacobi (Mary Putnam; 1842–1906, English/US)
Jacobs (Aletta; 1851–1929, Dutch)
Jekyll (Dr; *The Strange Case of Dr Jekyll and Mr Hyde*, 1886, Robert Louis Stevenson)
Jenner (Edward; 1749–1823, English)
Jenner (Sir William; 1815–98, English)
Magiot (Dr; *The Comedians*, 1966, Graham Greene)
Manson (Sir Patrick; 1844–1922, Scottish)
Mesmer (Franz; 1734–1815, Austrian)
Murphy (William P; 1892–1987, US)
Savart (Félix; 1791–1841, French)
Sloane (Sir Hans; 1660–1753, Northern Irish/British)
Thomas (E Donnall; 1920– , US)
Thorne (Thomas; *Dr Thorne*, 1858, Anthony Trollope)
Turner (William; c.1510–68, English)
Walker (Mary Edwards; 1832–1919, US)
Watson (John; *A Study in Scarlet*, 1887, Arthur Conan Doyle)
Willis (Thomas; 1621–73, English)

07 Addison (Thomas; 1793–1860, English)
Allbutt (Sir Thomas Clifford; 1836–1925, English)
Baillie (Matthew; 1761–1823, Scottish)
Beddoes (Thomas; 1760–1808, English)
Bigelow (Jacob; 1787–1879, US)
Bombard (Alain; 1924–2005, French)
Bretton (John; *Villette*, 1853, Charlotte Brontë)
Camerer (Rudolph; 1665–1721, German)
Cardano (Girolamo; 1501–76, Italian)
Carmody (Dr; *Black Jack*, 1968, Leon Garfield)
Carroll (James; 1854–1907, English/US)
Ctesias (5c BC, Greek)
Cushing (Harvey; 1869–1939, US)
Cuticle (Cadwallader; *White-Jacket*, 1850, Herman Melville)
Davaine (Casimir Joseph; 1812–82, French)
Edelman (Talbot; *Daughter Buffalo*, 1972, Janet Frame)
Eijkman (Christiaan; 1858–1930, Dutch)
Gilbert (William; 1544–1603, English)
Glauber (Johann Rudolph; 1604–70, German)
Guthrie (Samuel; 1782–1848, US)
Helmont (Jan van; 1579–1644, Flemish)
Hodgkin (Thomas; 1798–1866, English)
Imhotep (27c BC, Egyptian)
Jeddler (Anthony; *The Battle of Life*, 1846, Charles Dickens)
Laënnec (René; 1781–1826, French)
Laveran (Charles; 1845–1922, French)
Linacre (Thomas; c.1460–1524, English)
MacEwen (Sir William; 1848–1924, Scottish)
Macquer (Pierre Joseph; 1718–84, French)
Manette (Alexandre; *A Tale of Two Cities*, 1859, Charles Dickens)
Motlana (Nthato; 1925–2008, South African)
Nicolle (Charles; 1866–1936, French)
Pringle (Sir John; 1707–82, Scottish)
Sanchez (Francisco; c.1550–1623, Portuguese or Spanish)
Shonjen (Dr; 'The Good Anna', 1909, Gertrude Stein)
Sibbald (Sir Robert; 1641–1722, Scottish)
Siebold (Philipp von; 1796–1866, German)
Slammer (Dr; *Pickwick Papers*, 1837, Charles Dickens)
Sylvius (Franciscus; 1614–72, German)
Winston (Robert, Lord; 1940– , English)

08 Alcmaeon (fl.520 BC, Greek)
Anderson (Elizabeth Garrett; 1836–1917, English)
Aretaeus (fl.100 AD, Greek)
Avenzoar (c.1072–1162, Spanish)
Averroës (1126–98, Spanish)
Avicenna (980–1037, Persian)

Barnardo (Thomas; 1845–1905, Irish)
Billings (John Shaw; 1838–1913, US)
Birkbeck (George; 1776–1841, English)
Campbell (Jeff; 'Melanctha', 1909, Gertrude Stein)
Copeland (Benedict; *The Heart is a Lonely Hunter*, 1940, Carson McCullers)
Cournand (André F; 1895–1988, French/US)
Culpeper (Nicholas; 1616–54, English)
Duchenne (Guillaume; 1806–75, French)
Fishbein (Morris; 1889–1976, US)
Grenfell (Sir Wilfred; 1865–1940, English)
Hamilton (Alice; 1869–1970, US)
Heberden (William; 1710–1801, English)
Jeffries (John; 1744–1819, American)
Jex-Blake (Sophia; 1840–1912, English)
Linnaeus (Carl; 1707–78, Swedish)
Lombroso (Cesare; 1836–1909, Italian)
Magendie (François; 1783–1855, French)
Mitchell (Silas Weir; 1829–1914, US)
Monygham (Dr; *Nostromo*, 1904, Joseph Conrad)
Morgagni (Giovanni Battista; 1682–1771, Italian)
Mori Ogai (1862–1922, Japanese)
Prichard (James Cowles; 1786–1848, English)
Renaudot (Théophraste; 1586–1653, French)
Richards (Dickinson W; 1895–1973, US)
Sefström (Nils; 1765–1829, Swedish)
Servetus (Michael; 1511–53, Spanish)
Sherlock (Dame Sheila; 1918–2001, Irish/British)
Stoppard (Miriam; 1937– , English)
Sydenham (Thomas; 1624–89, English)
Tournier (Paul; 1898–1986, Swiss)
Villemin (Jean-Antoine; 1827–92, French)

09 Altounyan (Roger; 1922–87, Syrian/British)
Arbuthnot (John; 1667–1735, Scottish)
Armstrong (John; c.1709–79, Scottish)
Averrhoës (1126–98, Spanish)
Bartholin (Caspar, the Elder; 1585–1629, Swedish/Danish)
Bartholin (Erasmus; 1625–98, Danish)
Bartholin (Thomas, the Elder; 1616–80, Danish)
Biandrata (Giorgio; c.1515–c.1590, Italian)
Blackwell (Elizabeth; 1821–1910, English/US)
Blackwell (Emily; 1826–1910, English/US)
Blandrata (Giorgio; c.1515–c.1590, Italian)
Boerhaave (Hermann; 1668–1738, Dutch)
Cesalpino (Andrea; 1519–1603, Italian)
Dutrochet (Henri; 1776–1847, French)
Elliotson (John; 1791–1868, English)
Emin Pasha (1840–92, German)
Fabricius (Johannes; 1587–c.1615, Dutch)
Greatorex (Valentine; 1629–83, Irish)

Guillotin (Joseph; 1738–1814, French)
Hahnemann (Samuel; 1755–1843, German)
Kennicott (Will; *Main Street*, 1920, Sinclair Lewis)
Kingsford (Anna; 1846–88, English)
Long Ghost (*Omoo*, 1847, Herman Melville)
MacKenzie (Sir James; 1853–1925, Scottish)
Macnamara (Dame Jean; 1899–1968, Australian)
Parkinson (James; 1755–1824, English)
Pitcairne (Archibald; 1652–1713, Scottish)
Radcliffe (John; 1650–1714, English)
Ramazzini (Bernardini; 1633–1714, Italian)
Withering (William; 1741–99, English)

10 Arrowsmith (Martin; *Arrowsmith*, 1925, Sinclair Lewis)
Blenkinsop (Dr; *The Doctor's Dilemma*, 1906, George Bernard Shaw)
Bretonneau (Pierre; 1778–1862, French)
Camerarius (Rudolph Jacob; 1665–1721, German)
Fracastoro (Girolamo; 1483–1553, Italian)
Goldberger (Joseph; 1874–1929, Hungarian/US)
Greatrakes (Valentine; 1629–83, Irish)
Kübler-Ross (Elisabeth; 1926–2004, US)
L'Esperance (Elise; 1878–1959, US)
Mackarness (Richard; 1916–96, English)
Montessori (Maria; 1870–1952, Italian)
Paracelsus (1493–1541, German)

See also **medical**; **surgery**

Quackleben (Quentin; *St Ronan's Well*, 1823, Sir Walter Scott)
Sanctorius (1561–1636, Italian)
Wunderlich (Carl; 1815–77, German)

11 Antommarchi (Francesco; 1780–1838, French)
Asclepiades (fl.1cBC, Greek)
Auenbrugger (Leopold; 1722–1809, Austrian)
Cretzschmar (Philipp Jakob; 1786–1845, German)
Dioscorides (Pedanius; c.40–c.90 AD, Greek)
Hippocrates (c.460–377/359 BC, Greek)
Nostradamus (1503–66, French)
Ramón y Cajal (Santiago; 1852–1934, Spanish)
Summerskill (Edith, Baroness; 1901–80, English)

12 Kincaid-Smith (Priscilla; 1926– , South African/Australian)

13 Prunesquallor (Alfred; *Titus Groan*, 1946, Mervyn Peake)
Turner-Warwick (Dame Margaret; 1924– , English)

14 Doctor of Physic (the; *The Canterbury Tales*, c.1387–1400, Geoffrey Chaucer)
Paulus Aegineta (7c, Greek)

15 Kay-Shuttleworth (Sir James; 1804–77, English)
Sextus Empiricus (2cAD, Greek)

dog

Dog types include:

02	pi	04	corn		watch		hearing
03	gun		rach		water		leading
	hot		wild		zorro		mongrel
	lap	05	guard	06	kennet		tracker
	pet		guide		pariah		truffle
	pie		house		police	08	huntaway
	pye		pooch		ranger		turnspit
	sea		rache		ratter	09	retriever
	top		ratch		sleeve	10	sheep-biter
	toy		sheep		yellow		shin-barker
	war		under	07	harrier	11	sleuth-hound

Dog breeds include:

03	gun		kuri		corgi
	lab		Peke		dhole
	Pom		tosa		dingo
	pug	05	akita		husky
04	chow		boxer		hyena

laika
spitz
06 badger
bandog
beagle
bitser
borzoi
briard
collie
poodle
saluki
Scotty
setter
vizsla
Westie
07 basenji
bouvier
bulldog
bush dog
coondog
griffon
lurcher
Maltese
mastiff
pointer
Samoyed
Scottie
Shar-Pei
sheltie
shih tzu
sloughi
spaniel
terrier
volpino
whippet
08 Airedale
Alsatian

chow-chow
coach dog
Doberman
elkhound
foxhound
keeshond
komondor
labrador
Landseer
malamute
papillon
Pekinese
Sealyham
sheepdog
warrigal
09 boar-hound
chihuahua
coonhound
dachshund
Dalmatian
Eskimo dog
Great Dane
greyhound
Kerry blue
Lhasa Apso
Pekingese
red setter
retriever
schnauzer
St Bernard
wolfhound
10 bloodhound
fox-terrier
Iceland-dog
Maltese dog
otter hound
Pomeranian
raccoon dog

Rottweiler
sausage dog
schipperke
spotted dog
St Bernard's
11 Afghan hound
basset-hound
bichon frise
bull-mastiff
bull-terrier
carriage dog
Irish setter
Jack Russell
kangaroo dog
King Charles
wishtonwish
12 Border collie
cairn terrier
heelermoppet
Irish terrier
Japanese tosa
Newfoundland
West Highland
13 affenpinscher
bearded collie
Boston terrier
cocker spaniel
Dandie Dinmont
Scotch terrier
14 English terrier
German Shepherd
Irish wolfhound
pit bull terrier
Tibetan terrier
15 golden retriever
Scottish terrier
springer spaniel

Dogs include:

03 Lad (*Lad: A Dog*, 1965, A P Terhune)
04 Lucy (Blue Peter dog, 1998–2011)
Nana (*Peter Pan*, 1904, J M Barrie)
Odie (*Garfield*, 1978– , Jim Davis, comic
    strip)
Shep (Blue Peter dog, 1971–78)
Spot (Spot the Dog series, 1980– , Eric Hill)
Toby (Punch and Judy)
Toto (*The Wonderful Wizard of Oz*, 1900, L
    Frank Baum)
05 Balto (1919–33, Alaskan husky)
Butch (*Tom & Jerry*, 1967– , MGM
    cartoon)
Flush (*Flush: A Biography*, 1933, Virginia
    Woolf)
Goofy (1932– , Disney animation)

Laika (first dog in space, d.1957)
Petra (Blue Peter dog, 1962–77)
Pluto (1930– , Disney animation)
Pongo (*The Hundred and One Dalmatians*,
    1956, Dodie Smith)
Sadie (explosives sniffer dog)
Snowy (*Tintin*, 1929–83, Herge)
Timmy (The Famous Five series, 1942–63,
    Enid Blyton)
06 Buster (explosives sniffer dog)
Droopy (1943–58, Tex Avery, MGM cartoon)
Gelert (Welsh mythology)
Gromit (Wallace & Gromit series, Aardman
    Animations)
Hector (*Hector's House*, 1960s, UK
    children's TV)

Lassie (*Lassie Come Home*, 1940, Eric Knight)
Missis (*The Hundred and One Dalmatians*, 1956, Dodie Smith)
Nipper (RCA 'His Master's Voice' logo)
Sirius (star)
Snoopy (*Peanuts*, 1950–2000, Charles Shulz)
07 Charley (*Travels with Charley*, 1962, John Steinbeck)
Gnasher (*The Beano*, 1938– , D C Thomson, comic)
Perdita (*The Hundred and One Dalmatians*, 1956, Dodie Smith)
Roobarb (*Roobarb*, 1974–2005, Grange Caveley, BBC cartoon)
08 Bullseye (*Oliver Twist*, 1838, Charles Dickens)

Cerberus (Greek mythology)
Dogmatix (Asterix series, 1959– , René Goscinny & Albert Uderzo)
09 Rin Tin Tin (1930–33, US radio and TV)
Scooby Doo (*Scooby Doo*, 1969– , Hanna-Barbera cartoon)
10 Deputy Dawg (1959–72, Terrytoons cartoon)
Fred Basset (1963– , Alex Graham, newspaper comic strip)
12 Real Huntsman (fl.1949–51, US greyhound)
13 Master McGrath (1866–77, Irish greyhound)
Mick the Miller (1926–39, Irish greyhound)
15 Greyfriars Bobby (d.1872)
The Littlest Hobo (1963–65/1979–85, Canadian TV series)

Terms to do with dogs include:

03 bay, cur, paw, pet, pup, red, tan, yap, yip

04 bark, bite, blue, bone, bowl, burr, claw, coat, fang, fawn, flea, gold, heel, hock, howl, mutt, pied, rach, rake, roan, ruby, sick, spay, tail, tick, tike, tyke, woof, yaff, yowl

05 bitch, blaze, brach, breed, brush, Canis, cobby, cream, flews, groom, growl, hound, leash, liver, mange, pinto, pooch, puppy, rache, ratch, spitz, whelp, whine, worry

06 basket, bitser, bow wow, canine, collar, docked, fallow, gun dog, hamble, kennel, lapdog, muzzle, neuter, ranger, ratter, setter, shaggy, silver, touser, towser, toy dog, woolly, yapper

07 apricot, brindle, doggles, dogsled, dropper, grizzle, harness, lurcher, mongrel, pastern, rose ear, scumber, skummer, sniffer, starter, utility, walkies, wheaten, whiffet, wolf dog, yapster, huntaway, mahogany, markings, mottling, pedigree, purebred, ring tail, sheepdog, shock dog, turnspit, watchdog, water dog

08 brindled, curl tail, domestic, flecking, forelegs, guard dog, guide dog

09 button ear, cave canem, chocolate, crop-eared, dog jacket, dog racing, dog sledge, dogsleigh, kennelman, miniature, outer coat, police dog, poop scoop, purebreed, retriever, sleeve dog, steel grey, tricolour, undercoat

10 canophobia, choke chain, dog biscuit, dog carrier, dog-fancier, dog handler, feathering

flea collar	tracker dog	sleuth-hound	hindquarters
hearing dog	truffle dog	trendle-tail	smooth-haired
long-haired	**11** black-and-tan	trindle-tail	
scent hound	canophilist	trundle-tail	**13** pooper-scooper
shin-barker	puppy-walker	**12** double coated	
sight hound	short-haired	forequarters	

See also **hybrid**; **spaniel**; **terrier**

doll

Dolls include:

		gollywog
03 kid	ethnic	**09** miniature
rag	fabric	porcelain
wax	Hamble	tachibina
04 baby	kewpie	Tiny Tears®
mama	modern	**10** bobblehead
05 China	moppet	matryoshka
cloth	ningyo	Raggedy Ann
Dutch	poppet	topsy-turvy
metal	puppet	**11** composition
paper	voodoo	gosho ningyo
Paris	wooden	Holly Hobbie®
Sindy®	**07** fashion	papier-mâché
vinyl	jointed	Polly Pocket®
06 artist	kachina	**12** reproduction
Barbie®	kokeshi	**15** Cabbage Patch Kid®
bisque	nesting	frozen Charlotte
blow-up	rag baby	
Daruma	Russian	

07 fashion — **08** golliwog

See also **toy**

dolphin see **whale**

domain see **classification**

domestic appliance

Domestic appliances include:

	washer	**10** coffee mill
03 Aga®	**07** blender	deep-freeze
hob	fan oven	dishwasher
Vax®	freezer	humidifier
04 iron	griddle	liquidizer
oven	ionizer	percolator
spit	toaster	rotisserie
05 grill	**08** barbecue	slow cooker
mixer	gas stove	steam press
radio	hotplate	television
stove	wireless	waffle iron
06 cooker	**09** deep fryer	**11** tumble-drier
fridge	Dutch oven	washer-drier
Hoover®	DVD player	**12** kitchen range
juicer	steam iron	refrigerator
kettle		

stereo system
trouser press
13 carpet sweeper
electric grill
floor polisher
food processor
fridge-freezer

ice-cream maker
microwave oven
sandwich maker
vacuum cleaner
video recorder
14 electric cooker
juice extractor

upright cleaner
washing machine
15 carpet shampooer
cylinder cleaner

See also **house**

Dostoevsky, Fyodor (1821–81)

Significant works include:

08 *Poor Folk* (1846)
The Idiot (1868)
09 *The Devils* (1871–72)
The Double (1846)
11 *The Raw Youth* (1875)
White Nights (1847)
13 *The Adolescent* (1875)
17 *The House of the Dead* (1860)
18 *Crime and Punishment* (1866)
20 *Notes from Underground* (1864)

The Brothers Karamazov (1879–80)
23 *Notes from the Underground* (1864)
24 *The Insulted and the Injured* (1861)
25 *The Village of Stepanchikovo* (1859)
26 *Notes from the House of the Dead* (1860)
30 *Winter Notes on Summer Impressions* (1863)
42 *The Village of Stepanchikovo and Its Inhabitants* (1859)

Significant characters include:

05 Rodia
Sonia
06 Dounia
Rodion
07 Myshkin (Prince Leo Nikolayevich)
Rodenka
08 Ivanovna (Katerina)
Nastasya
Petrovna (Varvara)
Rogozhin (Parfyon)
09 Karamazov (Alexei

'Alyosha' Fyodorovich)
Karamazov (Dmitri Fyodorovich)
Karamazov (Fyodor Pavlovich)
Karamazov (Ivan Fyodorovich)
Petrovich (Alexander)
Stavrogin (Nikolai)
10 Fillipnova (Nastasya)
Marmeladov (Sofya 'Sonia' Semyonovna)

11 Raskolnikov (Avdotya 'Dounia' Romanovna)
Raskolnikov (Rodion/ Rodya/Rodenka/Rodka Romanovitch)
Stepanovich (Peter)
Trofimovich (Stephan)
12 Svidrigaïlov (Arkady Ivanovitch)
13 Prince Myshkin
14 Underground Man

double agent *see* **spy**

Doyle, Sir Arthur Conan (1859–1930)

Significant works include:

08 *Sir Nigel* (1906)
Waterloo (1907)
11 *Micah Clarke* (1889)
Rodney Stone (1896)
12 *The Lost World* (1912)
White Company (1891)
13 *The Sign of Four* (1890)
15 *A Study in Scarlet* (1887)

19 *The War in South Africa* (1902)
24 *The History of Spiritualism* (1926)
25 *The Hound of the Baskervilles* (1901–02)
26 *The Memoirs of Sherlock Holmes* (1892–94)
28 *The Exploits of Brigadier Gerard* (1896)
29 *The Adventures of Sherlock Holmes* (1891–93)

drama

Significant characters include:

06 Clarke (Micah)
Gerard (Brigadier Etienne)
Holmes (Sherlock)
Watson (Dr John H)
08 Lestrade (Inspector G)

Moriarty (Professor James)
10 Challenger (Professor George Edward)
11 Baskerville (Sir Charles)
Baskerville (Sir Henry)
Baskerville (Sir Hugo)

drama *see* **play**

dress

Dresses include:

03 mob
04 ball
coat
maxi
sack
sari
tent
05 shift
shirt
smock
tasar
06 caftan

dirndl
jumper
kaftan
kimono
muu-muu
sheath
tusser
07 bathing
chemise
evening
gym slip
kitenge
matinée

tussore
wedding
08 ball-gown
cocktail
gym tunic
negligée
pinafore
princess
sundress
09 cheongsam
farandine
going-away

minidress
slammakin
trollopee
10 dinner-gown
empire-line
farrandine
slammerkin
wraparound
11 décolletage
Dolly Varden
riding habit
12 shirtwaister

dressing *see* **salad**

drink

Alcoholic drinks include:

03 ale
gin
kir
rum
rye
04 arak
beer
grog
hock
mead
ouzo
port
sake
vino
wine
05 cider
G and T
lager
perry
Pimm's®
plonk
stout
vodka
06 arrack

bishop
brandy
bubbly
Cognac
eggnog
grappa
mimosa
porter
poteen
Scotch
shandy
sherry
whisky
07 absinth
alcopop
aquavit
Bacardi®
bourbon
Campari
Gordon's®
liqueur
Marsala
Martell®
Martini®

pink gin
red wine
retsina
sangria
sloe gin
spirits
tequila
vin rosé
whiskey
08 absinthe
advocaat
Armagnac
Calvados
cold duck
Guinness®
hot toddy
schnapps
Smirnoff®
vermouth
vin blanc
vin rouge
09 badminton
Beefeater®
champagne

cocktails
Laphroaig®
snakebite
white wine
Wincarnis®

10 ginger wine
Remy Martin®

11 black-and-tan
boilermaker
Courvoisier®
gin-and-tonic
Glenfiddich®
Irish coffee
Jack Daniel's®

12 Famous Grouse®

Glenmorangie®
malternative

13 peach schnapps
Scotch and soda

14 Bombay Sapphire®

Non-alcoholic drinks include:

03 pop
tea

04 Coke®
milk
soda

05 Assam
cocoa
float
julep
latte
mixer
Pepsi®
tonic
water

06 coffee
Indian
Irn-Bru®
Ribena®
squash
tisane

07 beef tea
cordial
limeade
Perrier®

seltzer

08 café noir
China tea
Coca-Cola®
Earl Grey
egg cream
espresso
expresso
fruit tea
green tea
Horlicks®
lemonade
lemon tea
Lucozade®
Ovaltine®
root beer
smoothie

09 Aqua Libra®
ayahuasco
Canada Dry®
cherryade
cream soda
ginger ale
herbal tea
milk shake

mint-julep
orangeade
soda water

10 café au lait
café filtre
cappuccino
fizzy drink
fruit juice
ginger beer
rosehip tea
still water
tonic water
Vichy water

11 barley water
bitter lemon
camomile tea

12 hot chocolate
mineral water
sarsaparilla

13 peppermint tea
Turkish coffee

14 sparkling water

15 lapsang souchong

Drinks of the gods include:

06 amrita
nectar

08 ambrosia

Special drinks include:

03 ava

04 kava

05 haoma

soma

09 ayahuasca
ayahuasco

See also **beer**; **cocktail**; **coffee**; **liqueur**; **spirit**; **tea**; **water**; **whisky**; **wine**

drug

Drugs include:

01 Q

03 AZT

05 Intal®
NSAID
Taxol®
Zyban®

06 opiate
Prozac®
statin
sulpha
Valium®
Viagra®

Zantac®

07 antacid
aspirin
codeine
heparin
insulin

Nurofen®	ibuprofen	paracetamol
quinine	macrolide	propranolol
Relenza®	methadone	vasodilator
Ritalin®	oestrogen	**12** ACE-inhibitor
Seroxat®	stimulant	chlorambucil
steroid	tamoxifen	methotrexate
Tamiflu®	temazepam	progesterone
triptan	**10** antibiotic	sleeping pill
08 Antabuse®	anxiolytic	streptomycin
diazepam	chloroform	sulphonamide
diuretic	chloroquin	tetracycline
hyoscine	dimorphine	**13** antibacterial
methadon	interferon	anticoagulant
morphine	penicillin	antihistamine
narcotic	ranitidine	streptokinase
neomycin	salbutamol	tranquillizer
orlistat	**11** allopurinol	**14** anticonvulsant
Rohypnol®	amoxicillin	antidepressant
sedative	amyl nitrate	azidothymidine
warfarin	anaesthetic	bronchodilator
09 aciclovir	beta-blocker	corticosteroid
acyclovir	chloroquine	erythropoietin
analgesic	cyclosporin	hallucinogenic
cortisone	haloperidol	hydrocortisone
digitalis	ipecacuanha	**15** chloramphenicol
Herceptin®	neuroleptic	vasoconstrictor

Illegal drugs include:

01 E	**05** crack	**08** cannabis
03 ice	crank	ketamine
LSD	dagga	laudanum
PCP	jelly	methadon
pot	opium	morphine
tab	smack	Rohypnol®
04 acid	speed	Special K
barb	upper	**09** angel dust
blow	**06** downer	dance drug
coke	heroin	marijuana
dope	peyote	methadone
dove	popper	peace pill
gage	**07** cocaine	temazepam
hash	crystal	**11** amphetamine
hemp	ecstasy	barbiturate
meth	fantasy	purple heart
pill	guaraná	**12** date-rape drug
Tina	pep pill	**13** phencyclidine
weed	roofies	

See also **analgesic; antibiotic; medicine; narcotic**

duck

Ducks include:

04 blue	smee	surf
musk	smew	teal

wood

05 eider
Pekin
ruddy
scaup

06 burrow
hareld
herald
magpie
Peking
runner
scoter
smeath
smeeth
spirit
tufted
velvet

See also **bird**

07 wigeon
crested
gadwall
mallard
moulard
muscovy
old wife
pintail
pochard
steamer

08 garganey
hookbill
mandarin
old squaw
shelduck

09 Cuthbert's
goldeneye

goosander
harlequin
merganser
sheldrake
shielduck
shoveller

10 bufflehead
canvasback
long-tailed
ring-necked

11 ferruginous
St Cuthbert's
white-headed

12 common scoter
Indian runner
velvet scoter

13 ruddy shelduck

Dumas, Alexandre (1802–70)

Significant works include:

07 *Anthony* (1831)
Olympia (1851)

09 *My Memoirs* (1852–55)

11 *Queen Margot* (1845)

13 *Ten Years Later* (1848–50)
The Black Tulip (1850)

14 *The Mouth of Hell* (1851)

15 *Isabel of Bavaria* (1835)
The Tower of Nesle (1832)

16 *The Company of Jéhu* (1857)
The War of the Women (1844–46)
Twenty Years After (1845)

17 *The Queen's Necklace* (1849–50)

18 *The Lady of Monsoreau* (1845)

The Regent's Daughter (1844)
The Three Musketeers (1844)

19 *Henri III and His Court* (1829)
Memoirs of a Physician (1846–8)
The Bastard of Mauléon (1846–47)
The Countess de Charny (1852–55)

20 *The Whites and the Blues* (1867–68)

21 *The Count of Monte Cristo* (1845–46)

22 *Pauline: A Tale of Normandy* (1838)
The Knight of the Red House (1845–46)
The Vicomte de Bragelonne (1848–50)

27 *The Memoirs of Dr Joseph Balsamo*
(1846–48)
The Woman with the Velvet Collar (1850)

Significant characters include:

04 Anne (Queen)

05 Faria (Abbé)
Kitty
Raoul

06 Busoni (The Abbé)
Dantès (Edmond)
Margot (Queen)
Michon (Marie)
Milady

07 Fouquet (Nicolas)

Grimaud
Mazarin (Cardinal)
Mondego (Fernand)

08 Danglars (Monsieur, later
Baron)
de Winter (Lady 'Milady')
Louis XIV
Mercedes
Planchet

09 de Morcerf (Albert)

Louis XIII
Richelieu (Cardinal)

10 Bragelonne (Vicomte de)
Buckingham (George
Villiers, Duke of)

11 de Villefort (Monsieur
Gérard)
Monte Cristo (The Count of)

13 Anne of Austria (Queen)

Musketeers include:

05 Athos

06 Aramis

07 Porthos

09 D'Artagnan

Dvořák, Antonín (1841–1904)

Significant works include:

05 *Vanda* (1876)

06 *Alfred* (1938)
    Armida (1904)

07 *Jacobin* (1889)
    Rusalka (1901)

08 *Dimitrij* (1882)
    'American' (String Quartet; 1894)
    'New World' (Symphony; 1893)

09 *St Ludmila* (Oratorio; 1886)

10 *Humoresque* (1894)

11 *Requiem Mass* (1891)

14 *Dumky Piano Trio* (1891)
    Slavonic Dances (1878/1887)

15 *Josef Kajetan Tyl* (1882)
    Kate and the Devil (1899)
    'From the New World' (Symphony; 1893)

17 'The Bells of Zlonice' (Symphony; 1936)

dwarf

Snow White's seven dwarfs:

03 Doc	Happy	Sleepy	**07** Bashful
05 Dopey	**06** Grumpy	Sneezy	

dye

Dyes include:

04 anil	fustic	flavine	turnsole
wald	indigo	magenta	**09** cochineal
weld	kamala	mauvein	nigrosine
woad	korkir	mauvine	primuline
	madder	para-red	safranine
05 chica	mauvin	ponceau	Saxon blue
eosin	orcein	saffron	Turkey red
henna	orchel		Tyrian red
mauve	orchil	**08** amaranth	
		fuchsine	**10** carthamine
06 anatto	**07** alkanet	mauveine	Saxony blue
archil	annatto	orchella	tartrazine
corkir	azurine	orchilla	
flavin	cudbear	safranin	**12** Tyrian purple

See also **pigment**

dynasty

Dynasties include:

02 Yi	Sung	Valois	Habsburg
03 Jin	Tang	Wettin	Ilkhanid
Qin	Vasa	Zangid	
Sui	Yuan	**07** 'Abbasid	**09** Jagiellon
	Zhou	Ayyubid	**10** Qarakhanid
04 Asen		Chakkri	**11** Plantagenet
Avis	**05** Ch'ing	Fatimid	
Chin	Piast	Romanov	**12** Hohenstaufen
Lodi	Qajar	Safavid	Hohenzollern
Ming	Shang	Tughlaq	
Qing		**08** Capetian	**14** Petrovic-Njegos
Song	**06** Chakri		
	Sayyid		

See also **China**

E

ear

Earth's crust see crust

eating

See also **animal**

economics

Spence (A Michael; 1943– , US)
Struve (Pyotr Berngardovich; 1870–1944, Russian)
Tawney (R H; 1880–1962, English)
Turgot (Anne Robert Jacques; 1727–81, French)
Veblen (Thorstein; 1857–1929, US)
Wilson (James; 1805–60, Scottish)

07 Abalkin (Leonid Ivanovich; 1930–2011, Russian)
Akerlof (George A; 1940– , US)
Bagehot (Walter; 1826–77, English)
Diamond (Peter; 1940– , US)
Douglas (Sir Roger Owen; 1937– , New Zealand)
Eyskens (Gaston; 1905–88, Belgian)
Fawcett (Henry; 1833–84, English)
Heckman (James J; 1944– , US)
Hurwicz (Leonard; 1917–2008, Russian/US)
Jackson (Barbara Mary Ward, Baroness; 1914–81, English)
Kalecki (Michal; 1899–1970, Polish)
Kaufman (Henry; 1927– , German/US)
Krugman (Robin; 1953– , US)
Kuznets (Simon Smith; 1901–85, Ukrainian/US)
Leacock (Stephen Butler; 1869–1944, Canadian)
Malthus (Thomas Robert; 1766–1834, English)
Mundell (Robert A; 1932– , Canadian)
Myerson (Roger; 1951– , US)
Peacock (Sir Alan Turner; 1922– , Scottish)
Quesnay (François; 1694–1774, French)
Ricardo (David; 1772–1823, English)
Robbins (Lionel Charles Robbins, Baron; 1898–1984, English)
Russell (George William; 1867–1935, Irish)
Sargent (Thomas; 1943– , US)
Scholes (Myron S; 1941– , US)
Schultz (Theodore William; 1902–98, US)
Shapley (Lloyd; 1923– , US)
Stigler (George Joseph; 1911–91, US)
Toynbee (Arnold; 1852–83, English)
Vickrey (William Spencer; 1914–96, Canadian)
Volcker (Paul Adolph; 1927– , US)
Walters (Sir Alan; 1926–2009, English)

08 Anderson (James; 1739–1808, Scottish)
Brentano (Lujo; 1844–1931, German)
Buchanan (James McGill; 1919–2013, US)
Bulgakov (Sergei Nikolayevich; 1871–1944, Russian)
Crawford (Sir John Grenfell; 1910–85, Australian)

Crowther (Geoffrey Crowther, Baron; 1907–72, English)
Friedman (Milton; 1912–2006, US)
Haavelmo (Trygve Magnus; 1911–99, Norwegian)
Harsanyi (John C; 1920–2000, Hungarian/US)
Koopmans (Tjalling Charles; 1910–85, Dutch/US)
Leontief (Wassily; 1906–99, Russian/US)
Marshall (Alfred; 1842–1924, English)
McFadden (Daniel L; 1937– , US)
Mirrlees (Sir James Alexander; 1936– , Scottish)
Petrokov (Nikolai Yakovlevich; 1937– , Russian)
Primakov (Yevgeny Maksimovich; 1929– , Russian)
Robinson (Joan Violet; 1903–83, English)
Schiller (Karl; 1911–94, German)
Shatalin (Stanislav Sergeyevich; 1934–97, Soviet)
Stiglitz (Joseph E; 1943– , US)
von Mises (Ludwig; 1881–1973, Austrian)
Youngson (Alexander John; 1918–2004, Scottish)

09 Alexander (Sir Kenneth John Wilson; 1922–2001, Scottish)
Beveridge (William Henry Beveridge, 1st Baron; 1879–1963, Indian/British)
Bogomolov (Oleg Timofeyevich; 1927– , Russian)
Edgeworth (Francis Ysidro; 1845–1926, Irish)
Galbraith (J K; 1908–2006, Canadian/US)
Markowitz (Harry M; 1927– , US)
Mortensen (Dale; 1939– , US)
Rodbertus (Johann Karl; 1805–75, German)
Samuelson (Paul Anthony; 1915–2009, US)
Schelling (Thomas C; 1921– , US)
Tinbergen (Jan; 1903–94, Dutch)

10 Aganbegyan (Abel Gazevich; 1932– , Armenian/Russian)
Delfim Neto (Antônio; 1929– , Brazilian)
Modigliani (Franco; 1918–2003, Italian/US)
Pissarides (Christopher; 1948– , Cypriot)
Schumpeter (Joseph Alois; 1883–1950, Austrian/US)
Williamson (Oliver; 1932– , US)

11 Balcerowicz (Leszek; 1947– , Polish)
Kantorovich (Leonid Vitalevich; 1912–86, Soviet)
Zaslavskaya (Tatyana Ivanovna; 1927– , Russian)

Terms used in economics include:

03 EMU	PEP	FTSE
GDP	WTO	GATT
GNP	**04** boom	OECD
IMF	debt	**05** asset

funds
share
slump
stock
trust
yield

06 budget
cartel
credit
mature
NASDAQ®
tariff
trader

07 annuity
autarky
buy-back
capital
deficit
embargo
futures
pension
product
savings
The City

08 cash flow
consumer
discount
dividend
e-economy
interest
leverage
monetary
monopoly
mortgage
producer
scarcity
taxation
tax haven
trade gap

09 cash ratio
commodity
deflation
excise tax
green fund
income tax
inflation

liability
liquidity
oligopoly
recession
reflation
skills gap
stamp duty
trademark
unit trust

10 bear market
bull market
capitalism
depression
excise duty
fiscal drag
fiscal year
new economy
old economy
price index
tax evasion
trade cycle
trade union
Wall Street

11 acquisition
CAT standard
Central Bank
devaluation
gold reserve
grey economy
liquid asset
money supply
open economy
overheating
reserve bank
stagflation
stakeholder
stock market
transaction

12 black economy
common market
consumer good
credit crunch
debt overhang
discount rate
economic rent
fixed capital
gold standard

human capital
marginal cost
merchant bank
mixed economy
price control
productivity
public sector
siege economy
stop-go policy
tiger economy
trade barrier
trade deficit
unemployment

13 budget deficit
business cycle
clearing-house
credit squeeze
Dow-Jones index
equity finance
financial year
free-trade area
hidden economy
liquidization
listed company
market economy
Phillips curve
private sector
protectionism
shadow economy
socio-economic
stock exchange
the Square Mile

14 balance of trade
command economy
commercial bank
corporation tax
disequilibrium
economy of scale
planned economy
single currency
working capital

15 Dow-Jones average
foreign exchange
marginal revenue
rationalization
reserve currency
supply and demand

See also **finance; Nobel Prize**

education

> *Educational establishments include:*

03 CTC	**07** academy	university	upper school
04 poly	college	**11** city academy	**12** beacon school
05 kindy	**08** seminary	faith school	infant school
06 kinder	**10** high school	polytechnic	kindergarten

middle school	**13** convent school	**14** boarding school	finishing school
public school	grammar school	business school	secondary modern
summer-school	nursery school	combined school	secondary school
Sunday school	primary school	**15** community school	voluntary school
	private school		

Terms used in education include:

03 NQT	head boy	professor	scholarship
NVQ	lecture	streaming	statemented
PTA	prefect	test paper	student loan
YTS	proctor	timetable	**12** exercise book
04 GCSE	student	top-up fees	literacy hour
SATs	subject	**10** curriculum	student grant
05 pupil	teacher	discipline	**13** baccalaureate
study	truancy	eleven-plus	catchment area
06 A-level	**08** governor	graduation	matriculation
bursar	half-term	playground	modular course
campus	head girl	quadrangle	qualification
course	homework	school term	Standard Grade
degree	literacy	SMART® board	**14** adult education
finals	numeracy	whiteboard	common entrance
intake	playtime	**11** certificate	parent governor
matron	register	coeducation	work experience
module	syllabus	double-first	**15** course of studies
Ofsted	textbook	dyscalculia	higher education
O-level	**09** break time	examination	refresher course
report	classroom	head teacher	teacher training
thesis	enrolment	Higher Grade	
07 diploma	final exam	Higher Still	
	opting out	invigilator	

See also **college**; **qualification**; **school**; **teaching**; **university**

eel

Eels and similar fish include:

03 hag	lance	launce	sandling
sea	moray	murena	**09** sand lance
04 grig	murry	murray	wheatworm
lant	siren	murrey	**10** spitchcock
sand	snake	**07** hagfish	
snig	wheat	muraena	
tuna	**06** conger	**08** Anguilla	
05 elver	gulper	electric	
	gunnel		

Egypt

Ancient Egyptian rulers:

05 Khufu (26c BC)

06 Ahmose (I; 16c BC)
Ahmose (II; 6c BC)
Cheops (26c BC)

07 Ptolemy (III, Euergetes; c.285–222 BC)
Ptolemy (II, Philadelphus; 308–246 BC)
Ptolemy (I, Soter; c.367–283 BC)
Ptolemy (IV, Philopator; d.205 BC)
Ptolemy (V, Epiphanes; c.210–180 BC)

Ptolemy (VIII, Euergetes II; d.116 BC)
Ptolemy (VI, Philometor; d.145 BC)
Ptolemy (XII Neos Dionysos; 1c BC)
Rameses (III; 1198–1167 BC)
Rameses (II, 'the Great'; 1304–1237 BC)

08 Berenice (I; fl.c.317–c.275 BC)
Berenice (III; d.c.80 BC)
Berenice (IV; d.55 BC)
Thutmose (I; fl.1493–1482 BC)
Thutmose (III; d.1426 BC)

Thutmose (IV; fl.1400–1390 BC)

09 Akhenaten (14c BC)
Amenhotep (II; 15c BC)
Amenhotep (III; c.1411–c.1375 BC)
Amenhotep (IV; 14c BC)
Cleopatra (69–30 BC)
Nefertiti (14c BC)
Sesostris (I; c.1980–1935 BC)

Sesostris (II; c.1906–1887 BC)
Sesostris (III; c.1887–1849 BC)
Tuthmosis (I; fl.1493–1482 BC)
Tuthmosis (III; d.1426 BC)
Tuthmosis (IV; fl.1400–1390 BC)

10 Hatshepsut (c.1540–c.1481 BC)

11 Tut'ankhamun (d.c.1340 BC)

See also **mythology**

electorate *see* **Australia; New Zealand**

electricity

Electrical components and devices include:

04 fuse

05 cable

06 socket

07 adaptor
ammeter
battery
conduit
fusebox

08 armature
neon lamp

test lamp

09 light bulb

10 lampholder
multimeter
transducer
two-pin plug

11 ceiling rose
earthed plug
fuse carrier
transformer

12 dimmer switch
three-pin plug

13 extension lead

14 bayonet fitting
circuit breaker
dry-cell battery
insulating tape
three-core cable
voltage doubler

15 copper conductor
fluorescent tube

Electricity and electronics terms include:

02 AC
DC

03 amp
ohm

04 cell
gate
volt
watt

05 anode
diode
Dolby®
farad
henry
NICAM®
valve

06 ampere
dynamo
OR gate
switch
triode
woofer

07 AND gate
battery
cathode

circuit
coulomb
EOR gate
NOR gate
siemens
tweeter
voltaic

08 galvanic
NAND gate
polarity
resistor
rheostat
solenoid

09 amplifier
capacitor
condenser
electrode
generator
impedance
logic gate
microchip
reactance
thyristor

10 alternator
commutator

grid system
inductance
oscillator
resistance
thermistor
transistor
truth table

11 capacitance
eddy current
electrolyte
Faraday cage
isoelectric
loudspeaker
silicon chip
thermionics
transformer

12 conductivity
electron tube
flicker noise
galvanometer
oscilloscope
power station

13 digital signal
direct current
electromagnet

isoelectronic
semiconductor
14 analogue signal
band-pass filter

bioelectricity
cathode-ray tube
induced current
15 Foucault current

mutual induction
nanoelectronics
optoelectronics
turboalternator

See also **power station**

element *see* **chemistry; metal**

Elgar, Sir Edward (1857–1934)

Significant works include:

05 *Elegy* (1909)

07 *Polonia* (1915)
Romance (1878, 1910)
Sospiri (1914)

08 *Carillon* (1914)
Falstaff (1902–13)

09 *Cockaigne* (1901)
Froissart (1890)
Une Idylle (1883)

10 *Caractacus* (Cantata; 1898)
In the South (1899)
King Arthur (1923)
Promenades (1878)
The Kingdom (Oratorio; 1906)

11 *Beau Brummel* (1928)

Sea Pictures (1897)
Severn Suite (1930)
The Apostles (Oratorio; 1903)

12 *Nursery Suite* (1931)

13 *Cello Concerto* (1919)
Coronation Ode (1902)
Dream Children (1902)
Imperial March (1897)
La Capricieuse (1891)

14 *Le Drapeau Belge* (1917)
The Black Knight (Cantata; 1892)
The Light of Life (Oratorio; 1896)
The Music Makers (1912)
The Wand of Youth (1906)
Violin Concerto (1909)

15 *Pageant of Empire* (1924)

Eliot, George (1819–80)

Significant works include:

06 'Agatha' (1869)
Romola (1862–3)

07 'Armgart' (1871)

08 *Adam Bede* (1859)

11 *Middlemarch* (1871–2)
Silas Marner (1861)

12 'Brother Jacob' (1864)

13 *Daniel Deronda* (1874–6)
'The Lifted Veil' (1859)

15 'The Spanish Gypsy' (1868)

16 *Brother and Sister* (1869)
'The Legend of Jubal' (1870)

17 *The Mill on the Floss* (1860)

19 *Felix Holt, the Radical* (1866)

20 *Scenes of Clerical Life* (1858)

26 'O May I Join the Choir Invisible' (1867)

29 *Impressions of Theophrastus Such* (1879)

Significant characters include:

04 Bede (Adam)
Cass (Dunstan)
Cass (Godfrey)
Holt (Felix)
Kenn (Dr)
Lyon (Esther)

05 Calvo (Baldassarre)
Crewe (Mr)
Deane (Lucy)
Eppie

Garth (Caleb)
Garth (Mary)
Glegg (Mrs)
Guest (Stephen)
Jakin (Bob)
Sarti (Caterina)
Tessa
Tryan (Rev Edgar)
Vincy (Fred)
Vincy (Rosamond)

Wakem (Philip)

06 Barton (Milly)
Barton (Rev Amos)
Brooke (Arthur)
Brooke (Celia)
Brooke (Dorothea)
Denner
Gilfil (Maynard)
Jermyn (Matthew)
Marner (Silas)

Melema (Tito)
Morris (Dinah)
Poyser (Martin)
Poyser (Mrs)
Pullet (Mrs)
Romola
Sorrel (Hetty)
Wybrow (Captain Anthony)

07 Chettam (Sir James)
Deronda (Daniel)
Harleth (Gwendolen)
Klesmer (Herr)
Lydgate (Tertius)

Raffles (John)

08 Casaubon (Rev Edward)
Dempster (Janet)
Dempster (Robert)
Ladislaw (Will)
Lammeter (Nancy)
Lapidoth (Mirah)
Lapidoth (Mordecai)
Transome (Harold)
Transome (Mrs)
Tulliver (Maggie)
Tulliver (Mr Jeremy)
Tulliver (Mrs Elizabeth 'Bessy')

Tulliver (Tom)
Winthrop (Dolly)

09 Bulstrode (Harriet)
Bulstrode (Nicholas)

10 Grandcourt (Henleigh)
Savonarola (Girolamo)

11 Cadwallader (Elinor)
Charles VIII
Donnithorne (Arthur)
Machiavelli (Niccolò)

12 Featherstone (Peter)

Eliot, T S (1888–1965)

Significant works include:

05 *Poems* (1919)
07 *The Rock* (1934)
12 *Ash-Wednesday* (1930)
Four Quartets (1943)
The Hollow Men (1925)
The Waste Land (1922)
13 *The Sacred Wood* (1920)
14 *Poetry and Drama* (1951)
16 *On Poetry and Poets* (1957)
Sweeney Agonistes (1932)
The Cocktail Party (1949)
The Family Reunion (1939)
17 *Elizabethan Essays* (1934)

The Elder Statesman (1959)
19 *For Lancelot Andrewes* (1928)
The Journey of the Magi (1927)
20 *Murder in the Cathedral* (1935)
The Confidential Clerk (1954)
26 *The Idea of a Christian Society* (1939)
28 *Prufrock and Other Observations* (1917)
The Love Song of J Alfred Prufrock (1917)
29 *Old Possum's Book of Practical Cats* (1939)
32 *Notes Towards a Definition of Culture* (1948)
34 *The Use of Poetry and the Use of Criticism* (1933)

emblem

Floral and plant emblems include:

04 rose (England)
06 wattle (Australia)
07 thistle (Scotland)
waratah (New South Wales, Australia)
08 daffodil (Wales)
shamrock (Ireland)
09 maple leaf (Canada)

maple tree (Canada)
10 fleur-de-lis (France)
fleur-de-lys (France)
silver fern (New Zealand)
11 common heath (Victoria, Australia)
kangaroo paw (Western Australia)

12 golden wattle (Australia)
13 royal bluebell (Australian Capital Territory)
14 Cooktown orchid (Queensland, Australia)
15 Sturt's desert pea (South Australia)

embroidery

Embroidery stitches include:

04 back
moss
stem
tent
05 chain
cross

satin
07 blanket
bullion
chevron
feather
running

08 fishbone
straight
09 half-cross
lazy-daisy
10 French knot

longstitch
11 herringbone
12 long-and-short
Swiss darning

empire

Empires and kingdoms include:

04 Cush
Inca
Kush
Moab
05 Akkad
Alban
Media
Mogul

Roman
06 Mughal
Naples
07 Argolis
Assyria
Bohemia
British
Chinese

Galicia
Ottoman
Persian
08 Dalriada
Japanese
Lombardy
Sardinia
09 Abyssinia

Byzantine
Holy Roman
10 New Kingdom
Old Kingdom
11 Northumbria
13 Middle Kingdom
15 Austro-Hungarian

Emperors include:

04 Otto (II; 955–83, Holy Roman)
Otto (III; 980–1002, Holy Roman)
Otto (I, the Great; 912–73, Holy Roman)
Otto (IV; c.1178–1218, Holy Roman)
Paul (1754–1801, Russian)
Pu Yi (1906–67, Chinese)

05 Akbar (the Great; 1542–1605, Mughal)
Babur (1483–1530, Mughal)
Boris (c.1551–1605, Russian)
Henry (III; 1017–56, Holy Roman)
Henry (IV; 1050–1106, Holy Roman)
Henry (V; 1081–1125, Holy Roman)
Henry (VI; 1165–97, Holy Roman)
Henry (VII; c.1274–1313, Holy Roman)
Louis (IV, the Bavarian; c.1283–1347, Holy Roman)
Murad (1612–40, Ottoman)
Peter (1672–1725, Russian)

06 Conrad (II; c.990–1039, Holy Roman)
Joseph (I; 1678–1711, Holy Roman)
Joseph (II; 1741–90, Holy Roman)
Rudolf (I; 1218–91, Holy Roman)
Rudolf (II; 1552–1612, Holy Roman)

07 Agustín (de Itúrbide; 1783–1824, Mexican)
Akihito (1933–   , Japanese)
Charles (II, the Fat; 839–88, Holy Roman)
Charles (I, the Bald; 823–77, Holy Roman)
Charles (IV; 1316–78, Holy Roman)
Charles (V; 1500–58, Holy Roman)
Francis (I; 1708–65, Holy Roman)

Francis (II; 1768–1835, Holy Roman)
Leopold (I; 1640–1705, Holy Roman)
Leopold (II; 1747–92, Holy Roman)

08 Hirohito (1901–89, Japanese)
Jahangir (1569–1627, Mughal)
Matthias (1557–1619, Holy Roman)
Napoleon (1769–1821, French)
Süleyman (1494–1566, Ottoman)

09 Alexander (1777–1825, Russian)
Aurangzeb (1618–1707, Mughal)
Ferdinand (I; 1503–64, Holy Roman)
Ferdinand (II; 1578–1637, Holy Roman)
Ferdinand (III; 1608–57, Holy Roman)
Frederick (I, Barbarossa; c.1123–1190, Holy Roman)
Frederick (II; 1194–1250, Holy Roman)
Frederick (III; 1415–93, Holy Roman)
Montezuma (1466–1520, Aztec)
Mutsuhito (1852–1912, Japanese)
Shah Jahan (1592–1666, Mughal)
Sigismund (1368–1437, Holy Roman)
Yoshihito (1879–1926, Japanese)

10 Kublai Khan (1214–94, Chinese/Mongol)
Maximilian (I; 1459–1519, Holy Roman)
Maximilian (II; 1527–76, Holy Roman)
Meiji Tenno (1852–1912, Japanese)

11 Charlemagne (747–814, Frankish)

12 Chandragupta (c.350–c.250 BC, Indian)

13 Haile Selassie (1891–1975, Ethiopian)

Empresses include:

02 Lü (d.180 BC, Chinese)

03 Zoë (980–1050, Roman)

04 Anna (1693–1740, Russian)
Cixi (1835–1908, Chinese)

05 Irene (c.752–803, Byzantine)
Livia (58 BC–AD 29, Roman)

06 Helena (St; c.255–330 AD, Roman)
Tz'u Hsi (1835–1908, Chinese)

Wu Chao (625–705, Chinese)
Wu Zhao (625–705, Chinese)

07 Eugénie (1826–1920, Spanish)

08 Adelaide (St; 931–99, Holy Roman)
Cunegund (St; c.978–1033, German)
Faustina (d.140/141 AD, Roman)
Nur Jahan (d.1645, Mughal)
Theodora (c.500–548, Byzantine)
Victoria (1819–1901, British; Empress of India)

09 Agrippina (the Younger; AD 5–59, Roman)
Alexandra (1872–1918, German; Empress of Russia)
Catherine (1684–1727, Russian)
Catherine (the Great; 1729–96, Russian)
Elizabeth (1709–62, Russian)
Joséphine (1763–1814, French)
Kunigunde (St; c.978–1033, German)
Messalina (c.25–c.48 AD, Roman)

Old Buddha (1835–1908, Chinese)
Theophano (c.955–991, Byzantine/Holy Roman)

11 Marie Louise (1791–1847, French)

12 Anna Ivanovna (1693–1740, Russian)
Maria Theresa (1717–80, Holy Roman)

13 Livia Drusilla (58 BC–AD 29, Roman)

See also **Byzantine empire**; **despot**; **Inca empire**; **Rome**

engine

Engines include:

03 air	**05** steam	Wankel	**09** aerospike
gas	water	**07** orbital	turboprop
ion	**06** diesel	turbine	**10** stationary
jet	donkey	V-engine	**11** atmospheric
oil	petrol	**08** compound	sleeve-valve
04 aero	Petter	Stirling	**13** fuel-injection
beam	radial	traction	reciprocating
heat	rocket	turbojet	**15** linear aerospike
	rotary		

Engine parts include:

04 pump	**08** camshaft	crankshaft	ignition coil
sump	flywheel	inlet valve	starter motor
05 choke	radiator	petrol pump	timing pulley
06 con-rod	rotor arm	piston ring	turbocharger
gasket	**09** air filter	thermostat	**13** camshaft cover
piston	drive belt	timing belt	connecting rod
tappet	oil filter	**11** carburettor	cylinder block
07 fan belt	rocker arm	rocker cover	inlet manifold
oil pump	spark plug	**12** cylinder head	power-steering
oil seal	**10** alternator	exhaust valve	**15** exhaust manifold
push-rod	cooling fan	fuel injector	

engineering

Engineers include:

03 Cui (César Antonovich; 1835–1918, Russian)
Fox (Sir Charles; 1810–74, English)

04 Ader (Clément; 1841–1926, French)
Arup (Sir Ove Nyquist; 1895–1988, English)
Barr (Archibald; 1855–1931, Scottish)
Bell (Alexander Graham; 1847–1922, Scottish/US)
Bell (Henry; 1767–1830, Scottish)
Benz (Karl Friedrich; 1844–1929, German)
Bush (Vannevar; 1890–1974, US)
Eads (James Buchanan; 1820–87, US)
Eyde (Samuel; 1866–1940, Norwegian)
Fink (Albert; 1827–97, German/US)

Ford (Henry; 1863–1947, US)
Gibb (Sir Alexander; 1872–1958, Scottish)
Hirn (Gustave Adolphe; 1815–90, French)
Lear (William Powell; 1902–78, US)
Otto (Nikolaus August; 1832–91, German)
Page (Sir Frederick Handley; 1885–1962, English)
Shen (Gua; 1031–95, Chinese)
Shen (Kua; 1031–95, Chinese)
Thom (Alexander; 1894–1985, Scottish)
Todt (Fritz; 1891–1942, German)
Wang (Ching; d.83 AD, Chinese)
Wang (Jing; d.83 AD, Chinese)
Watt (James; 1736–1819, Scottish)

05 Adams (William Bridges; 1797–1872, English)
Arrol (Sir William; 1839–1913, Scottish)
Baird (John Logie; 1888–1946, Scottish)
Baker (Sir Benjamin; 1840–1907, English)
Benet (Juan; 1927–93, Spanish)
Bouch (Sir Thomas; 1822–80, English)
Braun (Wernher von; 1912–77, German/US)
Burns (John Elliot; 1858–1943, English)
Clark (Josiah Latimer; 1822–98, English)
Clerk (Sir Dugald; 1854–1932, Scottish)
Dalén (Nils Gustav; 1869–1937, Swedish)
Darby (Abraham; 1750–91, English)
Dodge (Grenville Mellen; 1831–1916, US)
Ellet (Charles; 1810–62, US)
Ewing (Sir Alfred; 1855–1935, Scottish)
Fowke (Francis; 1823–65, Northern Irish/British)
Gooch (Sir Daniel; 1816–89, English)
Grove (Sir George; 1820–1900, English)
Grubb (Sir Howard; 1844–1931, Irish)
Kilby (Jack S; 1923–2005, US)
Laval (Carl Gustaf Patrik de; 1845–1913, Swedish)
Leith (Emmett Norman; 1927–2005, US)
Locke (Joseph; 1805–60, English)
Maxim (Sir Hiram Stevens; 1840–1916, US/British)
Milne (John; 1850–1913, English)
Nervi (Pier Luigi; 1891–1979, Italian)
North (John Dudley; 1893–1968, English)
Noyce (Robert Norton; 1927–90, US)
Olsen (Kenneth Harry; 1926–2011, US)
Olson (Harry Ferdinand; 1901–82, US)
Pitot (Henri; 1695–1771, French)
Prony (Gaspard Clair François Marie Riche, Baron de; 1755–1839, French)
Reber (Grote; 1911–2002, US)
Reith (John Charles Walsham Reith, 1st Baron; 1889–1971, Scottish)
Rolls (Charles Stewart; 1877–1910, English)
Royce (Sir Henry; 1863–1933, English)
Ruska (Ernst August Friedrich; 1906–88, German)
Smith (James; 1789–1850, Scottish)
Smith (William; 1769–1839, English)
Tesla (Nikola; 1856–1943, Croatian/US)
Vicat (Louis Joseph; 1786–1861, French)
White (Canvass; 1790–1834, US)
Woolf (Arthur; 1766–1837, English)

06 Allais (Maurice; 1911–2010, French)
Ammann (Othmar Hermann; 1879–1965, US)
Ayrton (William Edward; 1847–1908, English)
Bailey (Sir Donald Coleman; 1901–85, English)
Besson (Jacques; c.1535–c.1575, French)

Bidder (George Parker; 1806–78, English)
Brunel (Isambard Kingdom; 1806–59, English)
Brunel (Sir Marc Isambard; 1769–1849, French)
Carnot (Sadi; 1796–1832, French)
Cayley (Sir George; 1773–1857, English)
Chappe (Claude; 1763–1805, French)
Cierva (Juan de la; 1895–1936, Spanish)
Claude (Georges; 1870–1960, French)
Coanda (Henri; 1885–1972, Romanian)
Cubitt (Sir William; 1785–1861, English)
Cugnot (Nicolas Joseph; 1725–1804, French)
Diesel (Rudolf Christian Karl; 1858–1913, German)
Donkin (Bryan; 1768–1855, English)
Eckert (J Presper; 1919–95, US)
Edison (Thomas Alva; 1847–1931, US)
Eiffel (Gustave; 1832–1923, French)
Finley (James; 1762–1828, US)
Fokker (Anthony; 1890–1939, Dutch/US)
Forbes (George; 1849–1936, Scottish)
Fowler (Sir John; 1817–98, English)
Froude (William; 1810–79, English)
Fuller (Buckminster; 1895–1983, US)
Fulton (Robert; 1765–1815, US)
Gramme (Zénobe Théophile; 1826–1901, Belgian)
Hinton (Christopher Hinton, Baron; 1901–83, English)
Hudson (Sir William; 1896–1978, New Zealand)
Jansky (Karl Guthe; 1905–50, US)
Jazari (Ibn al-Razzaz al-; fl.c.1200, Islamic)
Jessop (William; 1745–1814, English)
Kármán (Theodore von; 1881–1963, Hungarian/US)
La Hire (Philippe de; 1640–1718, French)
Lenoir (Jean Joseph Étienne; 1822–1900, French)
Le Play (Frédéric; 1806–82, French)
McAdam (John Loudon; 1756–1836, Scottish)
Murray (Matthew; 1765–1826, English)
Napier (Robert; 1791–1876, Scottish)
Navier (Claude Louis Marie Henri; 1785–1836, French)
Nipkow (Paul; 1860–1940, German)
Oatley (Sir Charles; 1904–96, English)
Pelton (Lester Allen; 1829–1918, US)
Pierce (John Robinson; 1910–2002, US)
Pisano (Nicola; c.1225–c.1284, Italian)
Preece (Sir William Henry; 1834–1913, Welsh)
Rennie (George; 1791–1866, Scottish)
Rennie (John; 1761–1821, Scottish)
Rennie (Sir John; 1794–1874, Scottish)

Rumsey (James; 1743–92, US)
Savery (Thomas; c.1650–1715, English)
Séguin (Marc; 1786–1875, French)
Slater (Samuel; 1768–1835, English/US)
Sperry (Elmer Ambrose; 1860–1930, US)
Stevin (Simon; 1548–1620, Flemish)
Taylor (Frederick W; 1856–1915, US)
Vauban (Sébastien le Prestre de; 1633–1707, French)
Wallis (Sir Barnes Neville; 1887–1979, English)
Wankel (Felix; 1902–88, German)
Wright (Benjamin; 1770–1842, US)
Wright (Orville; 1871–1948, US)
Wright (Wilbur; 1867–1912, US)

07 Baldwin (Matthias William; 1795–1866, US)
Balfour (George; 1872–1941, Scottish)
Belidor (Bernard Forest de; 1698–c.1761, French)
Blondel (Nicolas François; 1618–86, French)
Boulton (Matthew; 1728–1809, English)
Brassey (Thomas; 1805–70, English)
Brinell (Johann August; 1849–1925, Swedish)
Bulleid (Oliver Vaughan Snell; 1882–1970, New Zealand/British)
Candela (Felix; 1910–97, Spanish/Mexican)
Carlson (Chester Floyd; 1906–68, US)
Carrier (Willis Haviland; 1876–1950, US)
Citroën (André Gustave; 1878–1935, French)
Colding (Ludvig August; 1815–88, Danish)
Corliss (George Henry; 1817–88, US)
Culmann (Karl; 1821–81, German)
Daimler (Gottlieb Wilhelm; 1834–1900, German)
Daubrée (Gabriel Auguste; 1814–96, French)
Dornier (Claude; 1884–1969, German)
Duddell (William du Bois; 1872–1917, English)
Eastman (George; 1854–1932, US)
Eckener (Hugo; 1868–1954, German)
Egerton (Francis, 3rd Duke of Bridgewater; 1736–1803, English)
Everest (Sir George; 1790–1866, Welsh)
Fleming (Sir John Ambrose; 1849–1945, English)
Fleming (Sir Sandford; 1827–1915, Scottish/Canadian)
Francis (James Bicheno; 1815–92, English/US)
Freeman (Sir Ralph; 1880–1950, English)
Garstin (Sir William Edmund; 1849–1925, English)
Gautier (Hubert; 1660–1737, French)
Giffard (Henri; 1825–82, French)
Gilruth (Robert Rowe; 1913–2000, US)

Goddard (Robert Hutchings; 1882–1945, US)
Gresley (Sir Nigel; 1876–1941, English)
Grumman (Leroy Randle; 1895–1982, US)
Heinkel (Ernst Heinrich; 1888–1958, German)
Hoffman (Samuel Kurtz; 1902–95, US)
Houston (Edwin J; 1847–1914, US)
Junkers (Hugo; 1859–1935, German)
Keldysh (Mstislav Vsevolodovich; 1911–78, Russian)
Korolev (Sergei Pavlovich; 1907–66, Soviet)
Latrobe (Benjamin Henry; 1764–1820, English/US)
Lesseps (Ferdinand, Vicomte de; 1805–94, French)
Metcalf (John; 1717–1810, English)
Metford (William Ellis; 1824–99, English)
Midgley (Thomas, Jnr; 1889–1944, US)
Murdock (William; 1754–1839, Scottish)
Nasmyth (James; 1808–90, Scottish)
Neilson (James Beaumont; 1792–1865, Scottish)
Panhard (René; 1841–1908, French)
Parsons (Sir Charles Algernon; 1854–1931, Irish)
Perkins (Jacob; 1766–1849, US)
Porsche (Ferdinand; 1875–1951, German)
Poulsen (Valdemar; 1869–1942, Danish)
Ramelli (Agostino; c.1531–c.1610, Italian)
Rankine (William John MacQuorn; 1820–72, Scottish)
Ricardo (Sir Harry Ralph; 1885–1974, English)
Roberts (Richard; 1789–1864, Welsh)
Roberts (Sir Gilbert; 1899–1978, English)
Russell (John Scott; 1808–82, Scottish)
Scheutz (Edvard Georg Raphael; 1821–81, Swedish)
Schwarz (Harvey Fisher; 1905–88, US)
Scruton (Kit; 1911–90, English)
Siemens (Ernst Werner von; 1816–92, German)
Siemens (Sir William; 1823–83, German/British)
Smeaton (John; 1724–94, English)
Sopwith (Sir Thomas Octave Murdoch; 1888–1989, English)
Sprague (Frank Julian; 1857–1934, US)
Stanier (Sir William Arthur; 1876–1965, English)
Stanley (William; 1858–1916, US)
Stevens (John; 1749–1838, US)
Stevens (Robert Livingston; 1787–1856, US)
Swinton (Alan Archibald Campbell; 1863–1930, Scottish)
Telford (Thomas; 1757–1834, Scottish)
Thomson (Elihu; 1853–1937, US)

Thomson (James; 1822–92, Scottish)
Thomson (Robert William; 1822–73, Scottish)
Tupolev (Andrei Nikolayevich; 1888–1972, Soviet)
Whittle (Sir Frank; 1907–96, English)
08 Anderson (Sir Robert Rowand; 1834–1921, Scottish)
Aspinall (Sir John Audley Frederick; 1851–1937, English)
Beeching (Richard Beeching, Baron; 1913–85, English)
Bertrand (Henri Gratien, Comte; 1773–1844, French)
Bessemer (Sir Henry; 1813–98, English)
Brindley (James; 1716–72, English)
Chadwick (Roy; 1893–1947, English)
Crampton (Thomas Russell; 1816–88, English)
Crompton (Rookes Evelyn Bell; 1845–1940, English)
De Forest (Lee; 1873–1961, US)
Drummond (Dugald; 1840–1912, Scottish)
Drummond (Thomas; 1797–1840, Scottish)
Edgerton (Harold Eugene; 1903–90, US)
Ericsson (John; 1803–89, US)
Ericsson (Nils; 1802–70, Swedish)
Ferguson (Harry George; 1884–1960, Irish)
Ferranti (Sebastian Ziani de; 1864–1930, English)
Gilbreth (Frank Bunker; 1868–1924, US)
Goethals (George Washington; 1858–1928, US)
Goldmark (Peter Carl; 1906–77, Hungarian/US)
Griffith (Sir Richard John; 1784–1878, Irish)
Guericke (Otto von; 1602–86, German)
Hamilton (Sir James Arnot; 1923–2012, Scottish)
Hartnett (Sir Laurence John; 1898–1986, English/Australian)
Hawkshaw (Sir John; 1811–91, English)
Huntsman (Benjamin; 1704–76, English)
Ilyushin (Sergei Vladimirovich; 1894–1977, Soviet)
Kennelly (Arthur Edwin; 1861–1939, Indian/US)
Leonardo (da Vinci; 1452–1519, Italian)
Maillart (Robert; 1872–1940, Swiss)
Maudslay (Henry; 1771–1831, English)
McNaught (William; 1813–81, Scottish)
Mitchell (Reginald Joseph; 1895–1937, English)
Perronet (Jean Rodolphe; 1708–94, French)
Poncelet (Jean Victor; 1788–1867, French)
Rastrick (John Urpeth; 1780–1856, English)
Reynolds (Osborne; 1842–1912, English)
Roebling (John Augustus; 1806–69, US)
Sangallo (Antonio Giamberti da, the

Younger; 1485–1546, Italian)
Sikorsky (Igor Ivan; 1889–1972, Russian/US)
Sinclair (Sir Clive Marles; 1940– , English)
Stirling (Patrick; 1820–95, Scottish)
Terzaghi (Karl; 1883–1963, Czech/US)
Tredgold (Thomas; 1788–1829, English)
Vignoles (Charles Blacker; 1793–1875, Irish)
Williams (Sir Frederic Calland; 1911–77, English)
Zeppelin (Count Ferdinand von; 1838–1917, German)
09 Armstrong (Edwin Howard; 1890–1954, US)
Bradfield (John Job Crew; 1867–1943, Australian)
Clapeyron (Benoît Paul Émile; 1799–1864, French)
Cockerell (Sir Christopher Sydney; 1910–99, English)
Desbarres (Joseph Frederick Wallet; 1722–1824, English)
Fairbairn (Sir William; 1789–1874, Scottish)
Fessenden (Reginald Aubrey; 1866–1932, Canadian/US)
Finniston (Monty; 1912–91, Scottish)
Forrester (Jay Wright; 1918– , US)
Göransson (Göran Fredrik; 1819–1900, Swedish)
Grünewald (Matthias; c.1475–1528, German)
Hackworth (Timothy; 1786–1850, English)
Issigonis (Sir Alec; 1906–88, Turkish/British)
Kettering (Charles Franklin; 1876–1958, US)
MacCready (Paul; 1925–2007, US)
Pickering (William Hayward; 1910–2004, New Zealand/US)
Steinmetz (Charles Proteus; 1865–1923, German/US)
Stevenson (Robert; 1772–1850, Scottish)
Swinburne (Sir James Swinburne, 9th Baronet; 1858–1958, Scottish)
Symington (William; 1763–1831, Scottish)
Trésaguet (Pierre Marie Jérôme; 1716–96, French)
Vaucanson (Jacques de; 1709–82, French)
Vermuyden (Sir Cornelius; c.1595–c.1683, Dutch/English)
Waterston (John James; 1811–83, Scottish)
Whitworth (Sir Joseph; 1803–87, English)
10 Artachaies (fl.c.500 BC, Persian)
Bazalgette (Sir Joseph William; 1819–91, English)
Churchward (George Jackson; 1857–1933, English)
Dornberger (Walter Robert; 1895–1980, German/US)
Fourneyron (Benoît; 1802–67, French)
Freyssinet (Marie Eugène Léon; 1879–1962, French)

Hennebique (François; 1842–1921, French)
Hodgkinson (Eaton; 1789–1861, English)
Hornblower (Jonathan Carter; 1753–1815, English)
Hounsfield (Sir Godfrey Newbold; 1919–2004, English)
Laithwaite (Eric Roberts; 1921–97, English)
Lanchester (Frederick William; 1868–1946, English)
Leeghwater (Jan Adrianszoon; 1575–1650, Dutch)
Lilienthal (Otto; 1849–96, German)
Sanmichele (Michele; c.1484–1559, Italian)
Stephenson (George; 1781–1848, English)
Stephenson (Robert; 1803–59, English)
Timoshenko (Stepan Prokofyevich; 1878–1972, Russian/US)
Trevithick (Richard; 1771–1833, English)
van der Meer (Simon; 1925–2011, Dutch)

11 Biringuccio (Vannoccio Vincenzio Agustino Luca; 1480–1539, Italian)

Castigliano (Alberto; 1847–84, Italian)
De Havilland (Sir Geoffrey; 1882–1965, English)
Kouwenhoven (William Bennett; 1886–1975, US)
Montgolfier (Joseph Michel; 1740–1810, French)
Reichenbach (Georg Friedrich von; 1772–1826, German)
Walschaerts (Égide; 1820–1901, Belgian)

12 Alexanderson (Ernst Frederick Werner; 1878–1975, Swedish/US)
Bunau-Varilla (Philippe Jean; 1859–1940, French)
Grahame-White (Claude; 1879–1959, English)
Westinghouse (George; 1846–1914, US)

13 Messerschmitt (Willy; 1898–1978, German)

15 Crates of Chalkis (fl.335–325 BC, Greek)
Leonardo da Vinci (1452–1519, Italian)
Vitruvius Pollio (Marcus; 1c AD, Roman)

Terms used in engineering include:

03 BSF
BSW
TDC

05 brace
gland
lever
O-ring
rotor
wedge
winch

06 flange
gasket
pinion
strain
thrust
torque

07 bearing
carbide
damping
density
fulcrum
galling
kinetic
pitting
S-N curve
statics
torsion
turbine

08 acoustic
dynamics
flatness
flow rate

pressure
split pin

09 axial load
corrosion
ductility
hydraulic
pneumatic
resonance
stability

10 arc welding
cantilever
compressor
deflection
efficiency
elasticity
TIG welding
turbulence
yield point

11 compression
deformation
DIN standard
laminar flow
Miner's rules
oscillation
shear stress
tensile load
Wöhler curve

12 aerodynamics
case-hardened
elastic range
electrolysis
external load

face flatness
face pressure
fatigue limit
geodesic dome
heat transfer
metal fatigue
sandblasting
spring washer

13 bearing stress
clamping force
dropping point
fluid dynamics
rack and pinion
radial bearing
sleeve bearing
tensile stress
thrust bearing
top dead centre
torque density
yield strength

14 Galvanic series

15 brake horse power
breakaway torque
compressive load
dynamic friction
low-cycle fatigue
tensile strength
tuned mass damper
tungsten carbide
Vickers hardness
Whitworth thread

English *see* **alphabet**; **football**; **monarch**; **town**; **United Kingdom**

entertainment

Entertainments include:

03 DVD	cinema	carnival	television
zoo	circus	festival	
04 fête	**07** airshow	gymkhana	**11** discothèque
05 dance	cabaret	waxworks	variety show
disco	concert	**09** burlesque	wall of death
opera	karaoke	floor show	**12** computer game
radio	musical	magic show	Punch-and-Judy
revue	pageant	music hall	show business
rodeo	recital	nightclub	**13** firework party
video	show biz	pantomime	**14** laser-light show
06 casino	theatre	video game	**15** greyhound racing
	08 barbecue	**10** puppet show	

Entertainers include:

02 DJ	Pierrot	pierrette	**12** chat-show host
04 bard	tumbler	presenter	escapologist
fool	**08** comedian	puppeteer	exotic dancer
Joey	conjuror	strong man	game-show host
05 actor	go-go girl	**10** comedienne	impersonator
clown	gracioso	disc jockey	snake charmer
comic	jongleur	go-go dancer	stand-up comic
mimic	magician	knockabout	street singer
06 artist	minstrel	mime artist	trick cyclist
august	musician	mind-reader	vaudevillean
busker	showgirl	pole dancer	vaudevillian
cowboy	stripper	ringmaster	**13** contortionist
dancer	**09** bunny girl	rope-walker	impressionist
jester	chanteuse	unicyclist	thimblerigger
mummer	ecdysiast	wire-dancer	trapeze artist
player	fire-eater	**11** belly dancer	ventriloquist
singer	harlequin	chansonnier	**14** pavement artist
07 acrobat	hypnotist	equilibrist	sword-swallower
actress	ice-skater	funambulist	**15** jerry-come-tumble
artiste	lap dancer	illusionist	song-and-dance
auguste	lion tamer	storyteller	act
juggler	performer	table-dancer	tightrope walker

Entertainment places include:

03 pub	cinema		niterie
zoo	circus		stadium
04 club	museum		theatre
dogs	nitery		**08** ballroom
fair	**07** cabaret		carnival
hall	funfair		dog track
05 arena	gallery		flesh pot
disco	hot spot		**09** bandstand
06 big top	ice rink		bingo hall
casino	marquee		dance hall

music hall
nightclub
strip club
10 auditorium
fairground
opera house

social club
11 boîte de nuit
concert hall
discothèque
public house
skating rink

12 amphitheatre
bowling alley
cattle market
13 leisure centre
15 amusement arcade

See also **clown**; **fair**; **fool**; **soap opera**; **television**

enthusiast *see* collection

entrepreneur *see* business

environment

Environmental problems include:

06 litter

07 drought

08 acid rain
landfill
oil slick
oil spill

09 pollution

10 extinction
fossil fuel
toxic waste

11 soil erosion

12 air pollution

nuclear waste

13 climate change
deforestation
global dimming
global warming
water shortage

14 light pollution
ozone depletion
water pollution

15 desertification
greenhouse gases

See also **chemistry**; **forest**; **fuel**; **gas**

enzyme

Enzymes include:

05 DNase
lyase
renin
RNase

06 cytase
kinase
ligase
lipase
papain
pepsin
rennin
zymase

07 amylase
emulsin
erepsin
inulase
lactase
maltase
oxidase
pepsine
plasmin
trypsin
uricase

08 bromelin
catalase
ceramide
elastase

esterase
lysozyme
nuclease
permease
protease
thrombin

09 amylopsin
aromatase
bromelain
cellulase
coagulase
hydrolase
invertase
isomerase
peptidase
reductase
urokinase

10 insulinase
luciferase
peroxidase
polymerase
sulphatase
telomerase
tyrosinase

11 collagenase
glutaminase
histaminase

hydrogenase
lecithinase
nitrogenase
phosphatase
transferase
transposase

12 alpha amylase
asparaginase
chymotrypsin
endonuclease
fibrinolysin
ribonuclease
transaminase

13 decarboxylase
dehydrogenase
DNA polymerase
neuraminidase
penicillinase
phosphorylase
RNA polymerase
streptokinase
thrombokinase
transcriptase

14 cholinesterase
thromboplastin

equestrian sport

Equestrians and showjumpers include:

03 Hoy (Andrew; 1959– , Australian)
Hoy (Bettina; 1962– , German)
Law (Leslie; 1965– , English)

04 Anne (Princess; 1950– , English)
King (Mary; 1961– , English)
Leng (Virginia; 1955– , British)
Tait (Blyth; 1961– , New Zealand)
Todd (Mark; 1956– , New Zealand)

05 Green (Lucinda; 1953– , English)
Meade (Richard; 1938– , Welsh)
Smith (Harvey; 1938– , English)

06 Astley (Philip; 1742–1814, English)

Broome (David; 1940– , Welsh)
D'Inzeo (Raimondo; 1925– , Italian)
Klimke (Reiner; 1936–99, German)
Lennon (Dermott; 1969– , Irish)
Smythe (Pat; 1928–96, English)

07 Fox-Pitt (William; 1969– , English)
Skelton (Nick; 1957– , English)
Winkler (Hans-Günther; 1926– , German)

08 Grunsven (Anky van; 1968– , Dutch)
Phillips (Mark; 1948– , English)
Phillips (Zara; 1981– , English)
Whitaker (John; 1955– , English)
Whitaker (Michael; 1960– , English)

Equestrian sport terms include:

03 aid
04 gait
gate
jump
lath
lead
rail
trot
walk
wall
whip
05 baulk
cones

fault
groom
06 canter
gallop
manège
piaffe
07 jump-off
longeur
passage
refusal
reining
routine

08 dressage
half pass
marathon
movement
obstacle
vaulting
vertical
09 grand prix
pirouette
puissance
time fault
water jump
10 clean round

lead change
natural aid
resistance
11 figure eight
showjumping
12 cross country
disobedience
steeplechase
13 half pirouette
14 roads and tracks
15 carriage driving
endurance riding

See also **horse**; **racing: horse racing**

equipment *see* **agriculture**; **laboratory**; **medical**; **office**; **photography**; **plumbing**; **sport**

espionage

Terms to do with espionage include:

03 bug
FBI
FSB
GRU
KGB
MI5
MI6
spy
04 burn
cell
code
GCHQ
mole
ring
05 agent
angel

blown
clean
cover
plant
spial
spook
06 beagle
cipher
defect
Enigma
secret
setter
shadow
target
07 apparat
Cold War

hacking
handler
mission
sleeper
08 blowback
briefing
codename
dead drop
emissary
informer
intrigue
mouchard
09 black list
blind date
informant
pseudonym

safe house
spymaster
top secret
10 cover story
dead letter
infiltrate
signal site
tradecraft
undercover
11 case officer
chicken feed
clandestine
double agent
penetration
12 brush contact
code-cracking

cold approach	interception	cryptographer	**14** cloak and dagger
cryptanalyst	surveillance	intelligencer	reconnaissance
intelligence	**13** call-out signal	Secret Service	

See also **spy**

essay

Essayists include:

04 Greg (William Rathbone; 1809–81, English)
Hunt (Leigh; 1784–1859, English)
Lamb (Charles; 1775–1834, English)
Lynd (Robert; 1879–1949, Irish)
Rodó (José Enrique; 1872–1917, Uruguayan)

05 Bacon (Francis; 1561–1626, English)
Lucas (Edward Verrall; 1868–1938, English)
Pater (Walter Horatio; 1839–94, English)
Smith (Sydney; 1771–1845, English)
White (E B; 1899–1985, US)

06 Borges (Jorge Luis; 1899–1986, Argentine)
Breton (André; 1896–1966, French)
Orwell (George; 1903–50, English)
Ruskin (John; 1819–1900, English)
Steele (Sir Richard; 1672–1729, Irish)

07 Addison (Joseph; 1672–1719, English)
Calvino (Italo; 1923–85, Italian)
Carlyle (Thomas; 1795–1881, Scottish)
Chapone (Hester; 1727–1801, English)
Emerson (Ralph Waldo; 1803–82, US)

Hayward (Abraham; 1802–84, English)
Hazlitt (William; 1778–1830, English)
Lazarus (Emma; 1849–87, US)
Meynell (Alice Christiana Gertrude; 1847–1922, English)
Montagu (Lady Mary Wortley; 1689–1762, English)
Thoreau (Henry David; 1817–62, US)

08 Beerbohm (Sir Max; 1872–1956, English)
Macaulay (Thomas Babington, Lord; 1800–59, English)

09 De Quincey (Thomas; 1785–1859, English)
Dickinson (Lowes; 1862–1932, English)
Montaigne (Michel Eyquem de; 1533–92, French)

10 Chesterton (G K; 1874–1936, English)
Crèvecoeur (Michel Guillaume Jean de; 1735–1813, US)

12 Quiller-Couch (Sir Arthur; 1863–1944, English)

Europe

Countries in Europe, with European Union membership:

02 UK (EU)

05 Italy (EU)
Malta (EU)
Spain (EU)

06 Cyprus (EU)
France (EU)
Greece (EU)
Kosovo
Latvia (EU)
Monaco
Norway
Poland (EU)
Russia
Serbia
Sweden (EU)
Turkey

07 Albania

Andorra
Austria (EU)
Belarus
Belgium (EU)
Croatia
Denmark (EU)
Estonia (EU)
Finland (EU)
Germany (EU)
Hungary (EU)
Iceland
Ireland (EU)
Moldova
Romania (EU)
Ukraine

08 Bulgaria (EU)
Portugal (EU)

Slovakia (EU)
Slovenia (EU)

09 Lithuania (EU)
Macedonia
San Marino

10 Luxembourg (EU)
Montenegro

11 Switzerland
Vatican City

13 Czech Republic (EU)
Liechtenstein
United Kingdom (EU)

14 The Netherlands (EU)

20 Bosnia and Herzegovina

Cities and notable towns in Northern Europe include:

04 Cork (Ireland)
Lund (Sweden)
Oslo (Norway)

Riga (Latvia)
York (England)

05 Århus (Denmark)

Derby (England)
Espoo (Finland)
Leeds (England)

Malmö (Sweden)
Narva (Estonia)
Tartu (Estonia)
Turku (Finland)
06 Ålborg (Denmark)
Bergen (Norway)
Dublin (Ireland)
Dundee (Scotland)
Kaunas (Lithuania)
London (England)
Odense (Denmark)
Örebro (Sweden)
Vantaa (Finland)
07 Belfast (Northern Ireland)
Bristol (England)
Cardiff (Wales)
Glasgow (Scotland)

Liepaja (Latvia)
Swansea (Wales)
Tallinn (Estonia)
Tampere (Finland)
Uppsala (Sweden)
Vilnius (Lithuania)
08 Aberdeen (Scotland)
Bradford (England)
Coventry (England)
Helsinki (Finland)
Klaipeda (Lithuania)
Limerick (Ireland)
Plymouth (England)
Šiauliai (Lithuania)
Västerås (Sweden)
09 Edinburgh (Scotland)
Jönköping (Sweden)

Leicester (England)
Linköping (Sweden)
Liverpool (England)
Reykjavík (Iceland)
Sheffield (England)
Stavanger (Norway)
Stockholm (Sweden)
Trondheim (Norway)
Waterford (Ireland)
10 Birmingham (England)
Copenhagen (Denmark)
Daugavpils (Latvia)
Gothenburg (Sweden)
Manchester (England)
Norrköping (Sweden)
Nottingham (England)
11 Southampton (England)

Cities and notable towns in Western Europe include:

04 Bonn (Germany)
Caen (France)
Graz (Austria)
Kiel (Germany)
Linz (Austria)
Metz (France)
Nice (France)
05 Arles (France)
Basle (Switzerland)
Berne (Switzerland)
Dijon (France)
Essen (Germany)
Lille (France)
Lyons (France)
Mainz (Germany)
Nancy (France)
Nîmes (France)
Paris (France)
Reims (France)
Tours (France)
06 Aachen (Germany)
Berlin (Germany)
Bochum (Germany)
Bremen (Germany)
Geneva (Switzerland)
Kassel (Germany)
Munich (Germany)
Nantes (France)
Rennes (France)
Toulon (France)
Vienna (Austria)
Zürich (Switzerland)
07 Avignon (France)

Cologne (Germany)
Dresden (Germany)
Hamburg (Germany)
Hanover (Germany)
Leipzig (Germany)
Limoges (France)
Lucerne (Switzerland)
Orleans (France)
Potsdam (Germany)
08 Augsburg (Germany)
Chemnitz (Germany)
Dortmund (Germany)
Duisburg (Germany)
Lausanne (Switzerland)
Mannheim (Germany)
Poitiers (France)
Salzburg (Austria)
Toulouse (France)
09 Innsbruck (Austria)
Magdeburg (Germany)
Nuremberg (Germany)
Osnabrück (Germany)
Stuttgart (Germany)
Wiesbaden (Germany)
Wuppertal (Germany)
10 Düsseldorf (Germany)
Klagenfurt (Austria)
Luxembourg (Luxembourg)
Marseilles (France)
Strasbourg (France)
11 Montpellier (France)
15 Clermont-Ferrand (France)
Frankfurt am Main (Germany)

Cities and notable towns in Eastern Europe include:

03 Ufa (Russia)

04 Brno (Czech Republic)
Györ (Hungary)
Kiev (Ukraine)
Lódz (Poland)
Lvov (Ukraine)
Omsk (Russia)
Orsk (Russia)
Pécs (Hungary)
Perm (Russia)
Tula (Russia)

05 Brest (Belarus)
Chita (Russia)
Gomel (Belarus)
Kazan (Russia)
Kursk (Russia)
Minsk (Belarus)
Penza (Russia)
Plzeň (Czech Republic)
Rovno (Ukraine)
Tomsk (Russia)

06 Gdansk (Poland)
Grozny (Russia)
Hrodna (Belarus)
Košice (Slovakia)
Kraków (Poland)
Lublin (Poland)
Moscow (Russia)
Odessa (Ukraine)
Poznan (Poland)
Prague (Czech Republic)
Samara (Russia)
Szeged (Hungary)
Warsaw (Poland)

07 Barnaul (Russia)
Donetsk (Ukraine)
Irkutsk (Russia)
Kharkov (Ukraine)
Kherson (Ukraine)
Luhansk (Ukraine)
Miskolc (Hungary)
Olomouc (Czech Republic)
Ostrava (Czech Republic)
Poltava (Ukraine)
Rybinsk (Russia)
Saratov (Russia)

Ulan-Ude (Russia)
Vitebsk (Belarus)
Wroclaw (Poland)
Yakutsk (Russia)

08 Budapest (Hungary)
Chisinau (Moldova)
Debrecen (Hungary)
Gorlovka (Ukraine)
Katowice (Poland)
Kemerovo (Russia)
Mahilyow (Belarus)
Mariupol (Ukraine)
Murmansk (Russia)
Orenburg (Russia)
Smolensk (Russia)
Szczecin (Poland)
Tiraspol (Moldova)
Vinnitsa (Ukraine)
Voronezh (Russia)

09 Archangel (Russia)
Astrakhan (Russia)
Bydgoszcz (Poland)
Krasnodar (Russia)
Krivoy Rog (Ukraine)
Makeyevka (Ukraine)
Nikolayev (Ukraine)
Volgograd (Russia)
Yaroslavl (Russia)

10 Bratislava (Slovakia)
Khabarovsk (Russia)
Simferopol (Ukraine)
Zaporozhye (Ukraine)

11 Chelyabinsk (Russia)
Kaliningrad (Russia)
Komsomolosk (Russia)
Krasnoyarsk (Russia)
Novosibirsk (Russia)
Rostov-on-Don (Russia)
Vladivostok (Russia)

12 Magnitogorsk (Russia)
Novokuznetsk (Russia)
St Petersburg (Russia)

13 Yekaterinburg (Russia)

14 Dnepropetrovsk (Ukraine)

15 Nizhniy Novgorod (Russia)

Cities and notable towns in Southern Europe include:

04 Bari (Italy)
Pisa (Italy)
Rome (Italy)

05 Genoa (Italy)
Milan (Italy)
Padua (Italy)

Palma (Majorca)
Siena (Italy)
Turin (Italy)

06 Bilbao (Spain)
Lisbon (Portugal)
Madrid (Spain)

Málaga (Spain)
Modena (Italy)
Murcia (Spain)
Naples (Italy)
Oporto (Portugal)
Venice (Italy)

Verona (Italy)
07 Bologna (Italy)
Catania (Italy)
Coimbra (Portugal)
Granada (Spain)
Messina (Italy)
Palermo (Italy)

Ravenna (Italy)
Setúbal (Portugal)
Seville (Spain)
08 Braganza (Portugal)
Florence (Italy)
Valencia (Spain)
09 Barcelona (Spain)

Las Palmas (Gran Canaria)
Santander (Spain)
Saragossa (Spain)
10 Valladolid (Spain)
11 Vatican City (Vatican City)

Europeans include:

04 Balt	Briton	Andorran	Slovakian
Brit	German	Austrian	Slovenian
Dane	Nordic	Croatian	Ukrainian
Esth	Sabine	Dutchman	**10** Anglo-Saxon
Finn	Salian	Estonian	Belarusian
Flem	Teuton	Irishman	Dutchwoman
Lapp	Zyrian	Moldovan	Englishman
Pict	**07** Belgian	Romanian	Irishwoman
Pole	Bosnian	Scotsman	Lithuanian
Scot	Cypriot	Siberian	Macedonian
Serb	Fleming	Silurian	Monégasque
Slav	Iberian	Spaniard	Portuguese
Turk	Italian	Welshman	Welshwoman
05 Angle	Latvian	**09** Britisher	**11** Belarussian
Croat	Lombard	Bulgarian	Frenchwoman
Czech	Maltese	Englander	Montenegrin
Greek	Manxman	Englisher	Sammarinese
Latin	Monacan	Frenchman	**12** Englishwoman
Swede	Russian	Hungarian	Luxembourger
Swiss	Samnite	Icelander	Scandinavian
Vlach	Serbian	Manxwoman	**13** Herzegovinian
06 Almain	Walloon	Norwegian	**15** Liechtensteiner
Basque	**08** Albanian	Sardinian	

European landmarks include:

04 Alps (France/Switzerland/Italy/Austria)
05 Rhine (Switzerland/France/Germany/The
Netherlands)
06 Danube (Germany/Austria/Slovakia/
Hungary/Croatia/Serbia/Bulgaria/
Romania/Moldova)
Geysir (Iceland)
Tatras (Poland)
08 Ardennes (France/Belgium/Luxembourg)
Pyrenees (France/Spain/Andorra)

Strokkur (Iceland)
09 Auschwitz (Poland)
10 Bran Castle (Romania)
Julian Alps (Slovenia)
Lake Geneva (France/Switzerland)
11 Simplon Pass (Switzerland/Italy)
13 Lake Constance (Germany/Switzerland/
Austria)
15 Rock of Gibraltar (Gibraltar)

See also **parliament**; **party**

evangelism *see* **missionary**

event *see* **athletics**; **gymnastics**; **Olympic Games**; **Paralympic Games**; **skiing**

execution

Execution methods include:

06 noyade
07 burning
gassing
hanging
stoning
See also **death**

08 lynching
shooting
09 beheading
10 garrotting
guillotine

the gallows
11 crucifixion
firing squad
stringing up
12 decapitation

13 electric chair
electrocution
15 lethal injection

exercise

Exercises include:

04 yoga
05 Medau
Tae-Bo®
06 cardio
chin-up
qigong
t'ai chi

07 aquafit
chi kung
jogging
keep fit
Pilates
08 aerobics
09 boxercise

Yogalates®
hatha yoga
10 aquarobics
daily dozen
dancercise
11 Callanetics

12 body-building
calisthenics
step aerobics
13 callisthenics
cross-training
physical jerks
15 circuit training

Terms to do with exercise include:

04 burn
06 cardio
warm-up
07 aerobic
See also **sport**; **yoga**

workout
08 warm down
09 anaerobic
Swiss ball

endurance
low impact
10 resistance
stretching

13 high intensity
14 cardiovascular

exploration

Explorers and navigators include:

03 Cam (15c, Portuguese)
Cão (15c, Portuguese)
Rae (John; 1813–93, Scottish)

04 Anza (Juan Bautista de; 1735–88, Mexican/
Spanish)
Back (Sir George; 1796–1878, English)
Beke (Charles Tilstone; 1800–74, English)
Byrd (Richard Evelyn; 1888–1957, US)
Cano (Juan Sebastian del; d.1526, Basque)
Cook (Frederick Albert; 1865–1940, US)
Cook (James; 1728–79, English)
Dias (Bartolomeu; c.1450–1500,
Portuguese)
Diaz (Bartolomeu; c.1450–1500,
Portuguese)
Eyre (Edward John; 1815–1901, English)
Gama (Vasco da; c.1469–1525, Portuguese)
Gray (Robert; 1755–1806, US)
Grey (Sir George; 1812–98, Portuguese/
British)
Hall (Charles Francis; 1821–71, US)
Hume (Hamilton; 1797–1873, Australian)
Kane (Elisha Kent; 1820–57, US)

Park (Mungo; 1771–1806, Scottish)
Pike (Zebulon Montgomery; 1779–1813,
US)
Polo (Marco; 1254–1324, Venetian)
Ross (Sir James Clark; 1800–62, Scottish)
Ross (Sir John; 1777–1856, Scottish)
Soto (Fernando de; c.1500–1542, Spanish)
Soto (Hernando de; c.1500–1542, Spanish)

05 Adams (Will; 1564–1620, English)
Baker (Sir Samuel White; 1821–93, English)
Barth (Heinrich; 1821–65, German)
Beebe (William; 1877–1962, US)
Boone (Daniel; 1735–1820, US)
Bruce (James; 1730–94, Scottish)
Burke (Robert O'Hara; 1820–61, Irish)
Cabot (John; 1425–c.1500, Italian)
Cabot (Sebastian; 1474–1557, Venetian)
Clark (William; 1770–1838, US)
Davis (John; c.1550–1605, English)
Davys (John; c.1550–1605, English)
Drake (Sir Francis; c.1540–1596, English)
Fuchs (Sir Vivian Ernest; 1908–99, English)
Giles (Ernest; 1835–97, English/Australian)

Gosse (William Christie; 1842–81, English/
Australian)
Grant (James Augustus; 1827–92, Scottish)
Hanno (5c BC; Carthaginian)
Hayes (Isaac Israel; 1832–81, US)
Hedin (Sven Anders; 1865–1952, Swedish)
Laing (Alexander Gordon; 1793–1826,
Scottish)
Laird (MacGregor; 1808–61, Scottish)
Lewis (Meriwether; 1774–1809, US)
Monod (Théodore André; 1902–2000,
French)
Monts (Pierre du Gua, Sieur de;
c.1560–c.1630, French)
Nares (Sir George Strong; 1831–1915,
Scottish)
Newby (Eric; 1919–2006, English)
Oates (Lawrence Edward Grace; 1880–
1912, English)
Parry (Sir William Edward; 1790–1855,
English)
Pavie (Auguste Jean Marie; 1847–1925,
French)
Peary (Robert Edwin; 1856–1920, US)
Radde (Gustav Ferdinand Richard; 1831–
1903, Polish/German)
Scott (Robert Falcon; 1868–1912, English)
Smith (Jedediah Strong; 1799–1831, US)
Speke (John Hanning; 1827–64, English)
Stein (Sir Aurel; 1862–1943, Hungarian/
British)
Sturt (Charles; 1795–1869, Indian/British)
Wager (Lawrence Rickard; 1904–65,
English)
Wills (William John; 1834–61, English/
Australian)
06 Aublet (Jean Baptiste Christophe Fusée;
1723–78, French)
Baffin (William; c.1584–1622, English)
Baikie (William Balfour; 1825–64, Scottish)
Balboa (Vasco Núñez de; 1475–1519,
Spanish)
Behaim (Martin; 1440–1507, German)
Bering (Vitus Jonassen; 1681–1741, Danish)
Brazza (Pierre Savorgnan de; 1852–1905,
Brazilian/French)
Burton (Sir Richard Francis; 1821–90,
English)
Cabral (Pedro Álvarez; c.1467–c.1520,
Portuguese)
Carson (Kit; 1809–68, US)
De Long (George Washington; 1844–81, US)
Denham (Dixon; 1786–1828, English)
Elcano (Juan Sebastian del; d.1526, Basque)
Fraser (Simon; 1776–1862, American/
Canadian)
Greely (Adolphus Washington; 1844–1935,
US)

Hearne (Samuel; 1745–92, English)
Hudson (Henry; c.1550–1611, English)
Joliet (Louis; 1645–1700, French)
Lander (Richard; 1803–34, English)
Mawson (Sir Douglas; 1882–1958, English/
Australian)
Müller (Sir Ferdinand Jakob Heinrich von,
Freiherr; 1825–96, German/Australian)
Nansen (Fridtjof; 1861–1930, Norwegian)
Philby (Harry St John Bridger; 1885–1960,
Sri Lanka/British)
Pinzón (Vicente Yáñez; c.1460–c.1524,
Spanish)
Quiros (Pedro Fernandez de; 1565–1615,
Portuguese)
Ralegh (Sir Walter; 1552–1618, English)
Rogers (Woodes; c.1679–1732, English)
Rohlfs (Gerhard; 1831–96, German)
Sabine (Sir Edward; 1788–1883, Irish)
Selous (Frederick Courtenay; 1851–1917,
English)
Stuart (John McDouall; 1815–66, Scottish/
Australian)
Tasman (Abel Janszoon; 1603–c.1659,
Dutch)
Torres (Luis Vaez de; fl.1605–13, Spanish)
Uemura (Naomi; 1942–84, Japanese)
Wallis (Samuel; 1728–95, English)
Wilson (Edward Adrian; 1872–1912,
English)
07 Andrews (Roy Chapman; 1884–1960, US)
Balchen (Bernt; 1899–1973, Norwegian/US)
Ballard (Robert Duane; 1942– , US)
Barents (Willem; d.1597, Dutch)
Belzoni (Giovanni Battista; 1778–1823,
Italian)
Borough (Steven; 1525–84, English)
Borough (William; 1536–99, English)
Cabrera (Pedro Álvarez; c.1467–c.1520,
Portuguese)
Cameron (Verney Lovett; 1844–94, English)
Cartier (Jacques; 1491–1557, French)
Chesney (Francis Rawdon; 1789–1872, Irish)
Dampier (William; 1652–1715, English)
Fawcett (Percy Harrison; 1867–1925,
English)
Fiennes (Sir Ranulph Twisleton-Wykeham;
1944– , English)
Fleming (Peter; 1907–71, English)
Forrest (John Forrest, 1st Baron; 1847–1918,
Australian)
Frémont (John Charles; 1813–90, US)
Gardner (George; 1812–49, Scottish)
Garnier (Francis; 1839–73, French)
Gilbert (Sir Humphrey; 1537–83, English)
Gregory (Augustus Charles; 1819–1905,
English/Australian)
Gregory (John Walter; 1864–1932, English)

Hawkins (Sir John; 1532–95, English)
Hawkyns (Sir John; 1532–95, English)
Herbert (Sir Wally; 1934–2007, English)
Hillary (Sir Edmund Percival; 1919–2008, New Zealand)
Jolliet (Louis; 1645–1700, French)
La Salle (René Robert Cavelier, Sieur de; 1643–87, French)
McClure (Sir Robert John Le Mesurier; 1807–73, Irish)
Moresby (John; 1830–1922, English)
Mueller (Sir Ferdinand Jakob Heinrich von, Freiherr; 1825–96, German/Australian)
Raleigh (Sir Walter; 1552–1618, English)
Rüppell (Eduard; 1794–1884, German)
Simpson (Myrtle Lillias; 1931– , Scottish)
Simpson (Sir George; 1792–1860, Scottish/Canadian)
Stanley (Sir Henry Morton; 1841–1904, Welsh/US/British)
Steller (Georg Wilhelm; 1709–46, German)
Thomson (Joseph; 1858–95, Scottish)
Weddell (James; 1787–1834, English)
Wilkins (Sir George Hubert; 1888–1958, Australian)
Wrangel (Ferdinand Petrovich, Baron von; 1794–1870, Russian)

08 Amundsen (Roald Engelbreth Gravning; 1872–1928, Norwegian)
Cárdenas (Garcia Lopez de; mid-16c, Spanish)
Carteret (Philip; d.1796, English)
Columbus (Christopher; 1451–1506, Genoese)
Coronado (Francisco Vázquez de; 1510–54, Spanish)
Cousteau (Jacques Yves; 1910–97, French)
Eriksson (Leif; fl.1000, Icelandic)
Filchner (Wilhelm; 1877–1957, German)
Flaherty (Robert Joseph; 1884–1951, US)
Flinders (Matthew; 1774–1814, English)
Foucauld (Charles Eugène, Vicomte de; 1858–1916, French)
Franklin (Sir John; 1786–1847, English)
Johnston (Sir Harry H; 1858–1927, English)
Kotzebue (Otto von; 1787–1846, Russian)
Linnaeus (Carolus; 1707–78, Swedish)
Magellan (Ferdinand; c.1480–1521, Portuguese)
Malaurie (Jean; 1922– , French)
Marchand (Jean-Baptiste; 1863–1934, French)
Mitchell (Sir Thomas Livingstone; 1792–1855, Scottish)
Orellana (Francisco de; c.1500–1549, Spanish)
Ridgeway (John; 1938– , English)
Schwatka (Frederick; 1849–92, US)

Scoresby (William; 1789–1857, English)
Standish (Myles; c.1584–1656, English)
Sverdrup (Otto; 1855–1930, Norwegian)
Thesiger (Sir Wilfred Patrick; 1910–2003, English)
Thompson (David; 1770–1857, English/Canadian)
Thorfinn (fl.1000, Icelandic)
Thunberg (Carl Peter; 1743–1828, Swedish)
Vespucci (Amerigo; 1451–1512, Italian/Spanish)
Vlamingh (Willem Hesselsz de; fl.1690s, Dutch)
Williams (Roger; c.1604–1683, American)

09 Andersson (Karl Johan; 1827–67, Swedish)
Champlain (Samuel de; 1567–1635, French)
Drygalski (Erich Dagobert von; 1865–1949, German)
Eiríksson (Leif; fl.1000, Icelandic)
Ellsworth (Lincoln; 1880–1951, US)
Emin Pasha (1840–92, German)
Fernández (Juan; c.1536–c.1604, Spanish)
Frobisher (Sir Martin; c.1535–1594, English)
Heyerdahl (Thor; 1914–2002, Norwegian)
Karesefni (Thorfinn; fl.1000, Icelandic)
Lancaster (Sir James; c.1554–1618, English)
La Pérouse (Jean François de Galaup, Comte de; 1741–88, French)
Mackenzie (Sir Alexander; 1764–1820, Scottish)
MacMillan (Donald Baxter; 1874–1970, US)
Marquette (Jacques; 1637–75, French)
Rasmussen (Knud Johan Victor; 1879–1933, Danish)
Vancouver (George; 1757–98, English)
Verendrye (Pierre Gaultier de Varennes, Sieur de la; 1685–1749, French)
Verrazano (Giovanni da; c.1480–1527, Italian)
Warburton (Peter Egerton; 1813–89, English/Australian)

10 Charlevoix (Pierre François Xavier de; 1682–1761, French)
Clapperton (Hugh; 1788–1827, Scottish)
Cunningham (Allan; 1791–1839, English)
Erik the Red (10c, Norwegian)
Huntington (Ellsworth; 1876–1943, US)
Leichhardt (Ludwig; 1813–c.1848, Prussian/Australian)
Oglethorpe (James Edward; 1696–1785, English)
Richardson (Sir John; 1787–1865, Scottish)
Shackleton (Sir Ernest Henry; 1874–1922, Irish/British)
Stefánsson (Vilhjalmur; 1879–1962, Canadian)
van der Post (Sir Laurens Jan; 1906–96, South African)

Willoughby (Sir Hugh; d.c.1554, English)
11 Livingstone (David; 1813–73, Scottish)
   Matthiessen (Peter; 1927–   , US)
   Ponce de León (Juan; 1460–1521, Spanish)
12 Borchgrevink (Carsten Egeberg; 1864–1934, Norwegian)
   Bougainville (Louis Antoine de; 1729–1811, French)
   Leif the Lucky (fl.1000, Icelandic)
   Nordenskjöld (Otto; 1869–1928, Swedish)
   Schweinfurth (Georg August; 1836–1925, German)

See also **sailing**

Younghusband (Sir Francis Edward; 1863–1942, Indian/British)
14 Bellingshausen (Fabian Gottlieb, von; 1778–1852, Russian)
   Blashford-Snell (Colonel John; 1936–   , English)
   Dumont d'Urville (Jules Sébastien César; 1790–1842, French)
   Hanbury-Tenison (Robin; 1936–   , English)
15 Doudart de Lagrée (Ernest-Marie-Louis de Gonzague; 1823–68, French)

explosive

Explosives include:

03	RDX		tonite		melinite		xyloidine
	TNT	07	ammonal		roburite	11	nitrocotton
04	ANFO		cordite		xyloidin	14	nitrocellulose
	TATP		dunnite	09	cyclonite		nitroglycerine
06	amatol		lyddite		gelignite		trinitrotoluol
	dualin	08	cheddite		guncotton	15	trinitrotoluene
	Semtex®		dynamite		gunpowder		

eye

Eye parts include:

03	rod		eyelid	08	chorioid	12	chorioid coat
04	cone		macula	09	blind spot		lacrimal duct
	iris		retina		optic disc		ocular muscle
	lens		sclera	10	optic nerve	13	aqueous humour
05	fovea	07	choroid	11	ciliary body		sclerotic coat
	pupil		eyeball		conjunctiva	14	vitreous humour
	white		eyelash		lower eyelid	15	anterior chamber
06	areola		papilla		upper eyelid		hyaloid membrane
	cornea		vitreum				

See also **blindness**

fable

28 'The Beetle Who Went on His Travels' (Hans Christian Andersen)
'The Camel and the Floating Sticks' (La Fontaine)
'The Eagle and Assembly of Animals' (John Gay)
'The Hunter, the Fox and the Leopard' (Bidpai)
'The Rich Man and the Bundle of Wood' (Bidpai)

'The Setting-Dog and the Partridge' (John Gay)
'The Tyrant Who Became a Just Ruler' (Bidpai)

29 'The Bleacher, the Crane and the Hawk' (Bidpai)

30 'The Lion, the Tiger and the Traveller' (John Gay)

Fable writers include:

03 Ade (George; 1866–1944, US)
Fay (András; 1786–1864, Hungarian)
Gay (John; 1685–1732, English)

04 Esop (6c BC, Greek)
Ruiz (Juan; c.1283–c.1350, Spanish)

05 Aesop (6c BC, Greek)
Boner (Ulrich; 1300–49, Swiss)
Torga (Miguel; 1907–90, Portuguese)

06 Bidpai (c.4c AD, Indian)
Dryden (John; 1631–1700, English)
Halévy (Léon; 1802–83, French)
Krylov (Ivan; 1768–1844, Russian)
Ramsay (Allan; c.1685–1758, Scottish)
Tessin (Carl-Gustaf; 1695–1770, Swedish)

07 Arreola (Juan José; 1918–2001, Mexican)

Babrius (fl.c.2c AD, Greek)
Fénelon (François; 1651–1715, French)
Gellert (Christian Fürchtegott; 1715–69, German)
Iriarte (Tomás de; 1750–91, Spanish)
Kipling (Rudyard; 1865–1936, English)
Sologub (Fyodor; 1863–1927, Russian)

08 Andersen (Hans Christian; 1805–75, Danish)
de France (Marie; fl.c.1160–c.1190, French)
Phaedrus (c.15 BC–c.50 AD, Macedonian)
Saltykov (Michail; 1826–89, Russian)

09 Furetière (Antoine; 1619–88, French)

10 La Fontaine (Jean de; 1621–95, French)

15 Iriarte y Oropesa (Tomas de; 1750–91, Spanish)

fabric

Fabrics include:

03 kid
net
rep
say

04 aida
baft
ciré
cord
felt
harn
ikat
jean
lace
lamé
lawn
leno
repp
silk
tapa
wool

05 batik
beige
Binca®
camel
chino

crape
crepe
crêpe
denim
dhoti
doily
doyly
drill
duroy
gauze
gazar
gunny
linen
lisle
llama
loden
Lurex®
Lycra®
moire
ninon
nylon
Orlon®
panne
piqué
plush
rayon

satin
scrim
serge
sheer
suede
surah
tabby
tamin
tammy
tappa
terry
Tibet
toile
tulle
tweed
twill
union
voile
wigan

06 alpaca
angora
armure
barège
Bengal
bouclé

broché
burlap
calico
camlet
canvas
chintz
cloqué
coburg
cotton
coutil
crepon
cubica
cyprus
Dacron®
damask
dévoré
doyley
Dralon®
duffel
durrie
faille
fleece
gloria
harden
herden
hurden

jersey	hessian	mazarine	shahtoosh
kersey	holland	moleskin	sharkskin
kincob	hopsack	oilcloth	sheepskin
linsey	jaconet	organdie	stockinet
madras	kidskin	pashmina	towelling
merino	leather	plaiding	velveteen
mohair	morocco	pleather	wire gauze
moreen	nacarat	quilting	**10** Balbriggan
muslin	nankeen	sarsenet	brocatelle
Oxford	oil silk	shagreen	candlewick
plissé	organza	shalloon	florentine
poplin	orleans	shantung	hop-sacking
ratine	paisley	spun silk	matellasse
samite	percale	suedette	mousseline
sateen	rabanna	swanskin	mummy-cloth
shoddy	raschel	Terylene®	needlecord
Tactel®	ratteen	waxcloth	paper-cloth
tamine	raw silk	whipcord	parramatta
Thibet	sagathy	**09** Alcantara®	peau de soie
tissue	satinet	astrakhan	polycotton
tricot	schappe	baldachin	seersucker
tusser	spandex	bombasine	sicilienne
velour	tabaret	bombazine	Tattersall
velvet	taffeta	calamanco	winceyette
vicuña	ticking	Carmelite	**11** cheesecloth
07 alepine	veiling	Chantilly	flannelette
baracan	velours	Crimplene®	Harris tweed®
batiste	Viyella®	crinoline	marquisette
brocade	webbing	folk-weave	Oxford cloth
buckram	woolsey	fur fabric	stockinette
cambric	worsted	gabardine	**12** brilliantine
challis	zanella	gaberdine	Brussels lace
chamois	**08** barathea	georgette	butter-muslin
chiffon	barracan	grenadine	cavalry twill
cypress	bayadère	grosgrain	crêpe-de-chine
doeskin	buckskin	haircloth	leathercloth
drabbet	cashmere	horsehair	Milanese silk
droguet	chambray	huckaback	Shetland wool
drugget	chenille	kalamkari	**13** casement cloth
duvetyn	corduroy	matelassé	crocodile skin
façonné	coutille	Moygashel®	mourning-stuff
flannel	cretonne	organzine	satin sheeting
foulard	diamanté	paramatta	**14** heather mixture
fustian	duvetine	petersham	terry towelling
galatea	duvetyne	polyester	
gingham	gossamer	sackcloth	
Gore-Tex®	jacquard	sailcloth	
heather	marcella	satinette	

See also **cotton**

face

Face parts include:

03 ear	lip	iris	nose
eye	**04** brow	jowl	skin
gum	chin	lips	**05** beard
jaw	hair	neck	cheek

mouth	temple	freckle	philtrum
pupil	tongue	jawbone	**09** cheekbone
teeth	**07** earlobe	nostril	moustache
06 eyelid	eyeball	unibrow	
sclera	eyebrow	wrinkle	**10** complexion
septum	eyelash	**08** monobrow	double chin

See also **ear**; **eye**; **hair**; **mouth**

facial hair *see* hair

fair

Fairground attractions include:

06 hoop-la	**10** bumper cars	**11** Ferris wheel	merry-go-round
07 Dodgems®	coconut shy	wall of death	tunnel of love
08 carousel	ghost train	**12** bouncy castle	**13** helter-skelter
waltzers	swing boats	chair-o-planes	rollercoaster

fairy tale

Fairy tales include:

07 *Aladdin* (Arabian Nights)
Ali Baba (Arabian Nights)
The Bell (Hans Christian Andersen)

08 *Momo Taro* (Japan)
Peter Pan (J M Barrie)
Rapunzel (Brothers Grimm)
Snowdrop (Brothers Grimm)
The Angel (Hans Christian Andersen)
The Daisy (Hans Christian Andersen)
The Raven (Brothers Grimm)
Tom Thumb (Brothers Grimm)

09 *Ashputtel* (Brothers Grimm)
Bluebeard (Charles Perrault)
Briar Rose (Brothers Grimm)
Pinocchio (Carlo Collodi)
The Shadow (Hans Christian Andersen)
The Storks (Hans Christian Andersen)

10 *Cinderella* (Charles Perrault)
Clever Hans (Brothers Grimm)
Goldilocks (traditional)
Hans in Luck (Brothers Grimm)
The Fir Tree (Hans Christian Andersen)
The Rose-Elf (Hans Christian Andersen)
Thumbelina (Hans Christian Andersen)

11 *Clever Elsie* (Brothers Grimm)
Hop o' my Thumb (Charles Perrault)
Little Thumb (Hans Christian Andersen)
Mother Elder (Hans Christian Andersen)
Mother Goose (Charles Perrault)
Puss in Boots (Charles Perrault)
The Old House (Hans Christian Andersen)
The Red Shoes (Hans Christian Andersen)

12 *Holger Danske* (Hans Christian Andersen)
Little Red-Cap (Brothers Grimm)
The Elderbush (Hans Christian Andersen)
The Goose Girl (Brothers Grimm)
The Snow Queen (Hans Christian Andersen)
The Tinderbox (Hans Christian Andersen)
The Wild Swans (Hans Christian Andersen)
Urashima Taro (Japan)

13 *Chicken Licken* (traditional)
The Frog Prince (Brothers Grimm)
The Golden Bird (Brothers Grimm)
The Neighbours (Hans Christian Andersen)
The Tin Soldier (Hans Christian Andersen)
The White Snake (Brothers Grimm)
The Wizard of Oz (L Frank Baum)

14 *Babes in the Wood* (Brothers Grimm)
Sleeping Beauty (Charles Perrault)
The Flying Trunk (Hans Christian Andersen)
The Golden Goose (Brothers Grimm)
The Juniper Tree (Brothers Grimm)
The Nightingale (Hans Christian Andersen)
The Seven Ravens (Brothers Grimm)
The Water of Life (Brothers Grimm)

15 *Dick Whittington* (traditional)
Hansel and Gretel (Brothers Grimm)
Rumpelstiltskin (Brothers Grimm)
The Elfin Hillock (Hans Christian Andersen)
The Little Lovers (Hans Christian Andersen)
The Ugly Duckling (Hans Christian Andersen)

16 *Sindbad the Sailor* (Arabian Nights)
Sweetheart Roland (Brothers Grimm)

The Little Mermaid (Hans Christian Andersen)
The Little Peasant (Brothers Grimm)
The Old Street-Lamp (Hans Christian Andersen)

17 *Beauty and the Beast* (traditional)
Little Ida's Flowers (Hans Christian Andersen)
The Miser in the Bush (Brothers Grimm)
The Twelve Huntsmen (Brothers Grimm)
The Young Swineherd (Hans Christian Andersen)

18 *Jack the Giant-Killer* (traditional)
The Brave Tin Soldier (Hans Christian Andersen)
The Little Match Girl (Hans Christian Andersen)
The Three Little Pigs (traditional)

19 *Jack and the Beanstalk* (traditional)
Little Red Riding Hood (Charles Perrault, Brothers Grimm)
Snow White and Rose Red (Brothers Grimm)
The Dog and the Sparrow (Brothers Grimm)
The Garden of Paradise (Hans Christian Andersen)
The Robber Bridegroom (Brothers Grimm)

20 *The Brave Little Tailor* (Brothers Grimm)
The Goloshes of Fortune (Hans Christian Andersen)
The Princess and the Pea (Hans Christian Andersen)
The Princess on the Bean (Hans Christian Andersen)

21 *The Emperor's New Clothes* (Hans Christian Andersen)
The Pied Piper of Hamelin (Brothers Grimm, Robert Browning)

22 *Aladdin and the Magic Lamp* (Arabian Nights)

Little Claus and Big Claus (Hans Christian Andersen)
The Fisherman and his Wife (Brothers Grimm)
The Travelling Companion (Hans Christian Andersen)
The Travelling Musicians (Brothers Grimm)
The Valiant Little Tailor (Brothers Grimm)
The Wonderful Wizard of Oz (L Frank Baum)

23 *The Elves and the Shoemaker* (Brothers Grimm)
The Three Billy Goats Gruff (traditional)

24 *Dick Whittington and his Cat* (traditional)
The Adventures of Pinocchio (Carlo Collodi)
The Town Musicians of Bremen (Brothers Grimm)

25 *Ali Baba and the Forty Thieves* (Arabian Nights)
The Shepherdess and the Sweep (Hans Christian Andersen)
The Straw, the Coal, and the Bean (Brothers Grimm)
The Three Princes of Serendip (Persian traditional)

26 *Goldilocks and the Three Bears* (traditional)
Snow White and the Seven Dwarfs (Brothers Grimm)
The King of the Golden Mountain (Brothers Grimm)
The Swineherd and the Princess (Hans Christian Andersen)
The Twelve Dancing Princesses (Brothers Grimm)

28 *The Mouse, the Bird, and the Sausage* (Brothers Grimm)

Fairy tale characters include:

03 Cat *(The Little Red Hen)*
Cat *(The Musicians of Bremen)*
Dog *(The Little Red Hen)*
Dog *(The Musicians of Bremen)*

04 Duck *(The Little Red Hen)*
Jack *(Jack and the Beanstalk)*
John *(Peter Pan)*
Liza *(Peter Pan)*
Nana *(Peter Pan)*
Nibs *(Peter Pan)*

05 Beast *(Beauty and the Beast)*
Curly *(Peter Pan)*
Wendy *(Peter Pan)*

06 Beauty *(Beauty and the Beast)*
Conrad *(The Goose Girl)*
Donkey *(The Musicians of Bremen)*

Falada *(The Goose Girl)*
Gretel *(Hansel and Gretel)*
Hansel *(Hansel and Gretel)*

07 Michael *(Peter Pan)*
Rooster *(The Musicians of Bremen)*
Rose Red *(Snow White and Rose Red)*
The King *(Puss in Boots)*
The King *(Rumpelstiltskin)*
The Ogre *(Jack and the Beanstalk)*
The Ogre *(Puss in Boots)*
The Wolf *(Little Red Riding Hood)*
Tootles *(Peter Pan)*

08 Baby Bear *(Goldilocks and the Three Bears)*
Foxy Loxy *(Chicken Licken)*
Geppetto *(Pinocchio)*
Peter Pan *(Peter Pan)*
Rapunzel *(Rapunzel)*

Slightly *(Peter Pan)*
The Elves *(The Elves and the Shoemaker)*
The Giant *(Jack and the Beanstalk)*
The Queen *(Snow White and the Seven Dwarfs)*
The Troll *(The Three Billy Goats Gruff)*
The Twins *(Peter Pan)*
Tom Thumb *(Tom Thumb)*

09 Daddy Bear *(Goldilocks and the Three Bears)*
Good Fairy *(Sleeping Beauty)*
Mummy Bear *(Goldilocks and the Three Bears)*
Pinocchio *(Pinocchio)*
Snow White *(Snow White and Rose Red)*
Snow White *(Snow White and the Seven Dwarfs)*
The Miller *(Puss in Boots)*
The Miller *(Rumpelstiltskin)*
The Mirror *(Snow White and the Seven Dwarfs)*
The Prince *(Cinderella)*
The Prince *(Rapunzel)*
The Prince *(Sleeping Beauty)*

10 Cinderella *(Cinderella)*
Ducky Lucky *(Chicken Licken)*
Goldilocks *(Goldilocks and the Three Bears)*
Henny Penny *(Chicken Licken)*
Stepmother *(Hansel and Gretel)*
The Emperor *(The Emperor's New Clothes)*
Thumbelina *(Thumbelina)*
Tinker Bell *(Peter Pan)*

11 Captain Hook *(Peter Pan)*

Grandmother *(Little Red Riding Hood)*
Pedlar Woman *(Snow White and the Seven Dwarfs)*
Puss in Boots *(Puss in Boots)*
The Huntsman *(Snow White and the Seven Dwarfs)*
The Lost Boys *(Peter Pan)*
The Princess *(Puss in Boots)*
The Princess *(The Princess and the Pea)*
Ugly Sisters *(Cinderella)*
Wicked Fairy *(Sleeping Beauty)*
Wicked Witch *(Hansel and Gretel)*

12 Goosey Loosey *(Chicken Licken)*
The Goose Girl *(The Goose Girl)*
The Shoemaker *(The Elves and the Shoemaker)*

13 Band of Robbers *(The Musicians of Bremen)*
Chicken Licken *(Chicken Licken)*
Red Riding Hood *(Little Red Riding Hood)*

14 Fairy Godmother *(Cinderella)*
The Golden Goose *(The Golden Goose)*
The Seven Dwarfs *(Snow White and the Seven Dwarfs)*

15 Alice Fitzwarren *(Dick Whittington)*
Dick Whittington *(Dick Whittington)*
Fairy Godmothers *(Sleeping Beauty)*
Mr and Mrs Darling *(Peter Pan)*
Rumpelstiltskin *(Rumpelstiltskin)*
The Little Red Hen *(The Little Red Hen)*
The Rich Merchant *(Beauty and the Beast)*
The Ugly Duckling *(The Ugly Duckling)*
Three Little Pigs *(The Three Little Pigs)*

Fairies include:

04 Moth *(A Midsummer Night's Dream*, 1595, William Shakespeare)
Ozma (Princess; *The Marvellous Land of Oz*, 1904, et seq, L Frank Baum)
Puck *(A Midsummer Night's Dream*, 1595, William Shakespeare)

05 Ariel *(The Tempest*, 1611, William Shakespeare)

06 Cobweb *(A Midsummer Night's Dream*, 1595, William Shakespeare)
Oberon *(A Midsummer Night's Dream*, 1595, William Shakespeare)

07 Titania *(A Midsummer Night's Dream*, 1595, William Shakespeare)

08 Iolanthe *(Iolanthe*, 1882, Gilbert and Sullivan)

10 Maleficent *(Sleeping Beauty* (film), 1959)
Tinkerbell *(Peter Pan*, 1904, J M Barrie)

11 Mustardseed *(A Midsummer Night's Dream*, 1595, William Shakespeare)

12 Peaseblossom *(A Midsummer Night's Dream*, 1595, William Shakespeare)
The Blue Fairy *(Pinocchio* (film), 1940)

13 Nac Mac Feegles *(The Wee Free Men*, 2003, Sir Terry Pratchett)

14 Fairy Godmother *(Cinderella/Sleeping Beauty*, fairy tales)
Sugar Plum Fairy *(The Nutcracker*, 1892, Tchaikovsky)

15 Robin Goodfellow *(A Midsummer Night's Dream*, 1595, William Shakespeare)

See also **mythology**; **pantomime**; **Shakespeare, William**

falcon

Falcons include:

05 hobby	**07** Iceland	jerfalcon	falcon-gentle
saker	kestrel	peregrine	tassel-gentle
06 gentle	**08** duck-hawk	stone hawk	tercel-gentle
lanner	**09** gerfalcon	**11** tassell-gent	tercel-jerkin
merlin	gyrfalcon	**12** falcon-gentil	

family

Family members include:

02 ex	nanny	sibling	stepmother
ma	niece	stepdad	step-parent
pa	uncle	stepmum	stepsister
03 dad	**06** cousin	stepson	twin-sister
mom	ex-wife	**08** daughter	**11** first cousin
mum	father	godchild	foster-child
son	godson	grandkid	god-daughter
04 aunt	grampa	grandson	grandfather
gran	granny	**09** ex-husband	grandmother
heir	mother	godfather	grandparent
mama	nephew	godmother	great nephew
nana	parent	great aunt	half-brother
papa	sister	stepchild	stepbrother
twin	spouse	**10** grandchild	twin-brother
wife	**07** brother	great niece	**12** foster-parent
05 daddy	grandad	great uncle	second cousin
mummy	husband	half-sister	stepdaughter
nanna	partner	stepfather	**13** grand-daughter

See also **aunt**; **daughter**; **father**; **genealogy**; **mother**; **relative**; **son**; **uncle**

fantasy *see* **science fiction**

farm

Farms and farming types include:

03 dry	**05** croft	salmon	intensive
ley	dairy	turkey	**10** collective
pig	mixed	**07** factory	plantation
04 deer	store	organic	**11** cattle ranch
fish	trash	ostrich	monoculture
hill	trout	poultry	subsistence
stud	**06** arable	**09** extensive	**12** sheep station
wind	estate	free-range	smallholding

Farm animals include:

02 ox	pig	calf	lamb
03 ass	ram	cock	mare
cow	sow	duck	mule
ewe	**04** boar	foal	**05** goose
hen	bull	goat	horse

llama	donkey	ostrich	wild boar
sheep	rabbit	rooster	**09** billy goat
06 alpaca	turkey	**08** cockerel	
cattle	**07** chicken	stallion	

Farming terms include:

03 CAP	shear	**08** abbatoir	pesticide
dip	straw	breeding	ploughing
hay	swill	cash crop	sharecrop
mir	**06** arable	farm cart	side-dress
pen	braird	farm hand	slaughter
sow	eat off	hacienda	**10** cereal crop
04 bale	fallow	hay-wagon	fertilizer
barn	farmer	hill farm	interplant
byre	fodder	home farm	irrigation
cart	furrow	land army	winter crop
crap	grieve	land girl	**11** agriculture
crop	manure	mulesing	zero-grazing
ferm	shamba	outfield	**12** crop rotation
hind	silage	root crop	foot and mouth
peon	slurry	steading	tenant farmer
reap	**07** grazing	township	vermiculture
wick	harvest	**09** after-crop	**13** goodman's croft
05 baler	holding	break crop	green manuring
breer	kibbutz	catch-crop	tattie howking
croft	kolkhoz	cover crop	tattie lifting
dairy	milking	deadstock	tattie picking
field	organic	farmhouse	**14** drip irrigation
gambo	orra man	free range	slaughterhouse
plant	pasture	green crop	**15** animal husbandry
ranch	tractor	intercrop	
		livestock	

See also **agriculture**; **cattle**; **cereal**; **chicken**; **crop**; **disease**; **duck**; **horse**; **meat**; **pig**; **poultry**; **rabbit**; **sheep**

fashion

Fashion accessories include:

03 bag	stole	parasol	scrunchie
cap	watch	sunnies	stockings
fur	**06** gloves	**08** hairband	victorine
hat	poncho	hair clip	**10** evening bag
04 belt	tights	headband	legwarmers
boot	tippet	palatine	spectacles
wrap	**07** glasses	pashmina	sunglasses
05 purse	handbag	pelerine	**13** body jewellery
scarf	hosiery	pelerine	evening gloves
shawl	mittens	umbrella	leather gloves
shoes	muffler	**09** headscarf	
		jewellery	

Fashion designers and labels include:

03 YSL	DKNY
04 Choo (Jimmy; 1952– , Malaysian/British)	fcuk
Dior (Christian; 1905–57, French)	Joop!

Joop (Wolfgang; 1944– , German)
Lang (Helmut; 1956– , Austrian)
Muir (Jean; 1928–95, English)

05 Amies (Sir Hardy; 1909–2003, English)
Chloé
D and G
Dolce (Domenico; 1958– , Italian)
Farhi (Nicole; 1946– , French/British)
Fendi
Gucci
Karan (Donna; 1948– , US)
Kenzo (1940– , Japanese)
Klein (Anne; 1923–74, US)
Klein (Calvin; 1942– , US)
Ozbek (Rifat; 1954– , Turkish)
Patou (Jean; 1880–1936, French)
Prada
Prada (Miuccia; 1949– , Italian)
Pucci (Emilio, Marchese di Barsento;
  1914–92, Italian)
Quant (Mary; 1934– , English)
Ricci (Nina; 1883–1970, Italian)
Smith (Sir Paul; 1946– , English)
Worth (Charles Frederick; 1825–95, English)

06 Armani
Armani (Giorgio; 1935– , Italian)
Ashley (Laura; 1925–85, Welsh)
Cardin (Pierre; 1922– , French)
Chanel (Coco; 1883–1971, French)
Conran (Jasper; 1959– , English)
Conran (Shirley; 1932– , English)
Hermes
Jacobs (Marc; 1963– , US)
Lauren (Ralph; 1939– , US)
Miu Miu
Miyake (Issey; 1938– , Japanese)
Poiret (Paul; 1879–1944, French)
Rhodes (Zandra; 1940– , English)
Sander (Jil; 1943– , German)
Ungaro (Emanuel; 1933– , French)

07 Balmain (Pierre; 1914–82, French)
Blahnik (Manolo; 1942– , Spanish/British)
Fassett (Kaffe; 1937– , US)
Gabbana (Stefano; 1962– , Italian)
Hamnett (Katharine; 1952– , English)
Jackson (Betty; 1949– , English)
Lacoste
Lacroix (Christian; 1951– , French)
Laroche (Guy; 1923–89, French)

See also **clothes**

Max Mara
McQueen (Alexander; 1970–2010, English)
Missoni (Ottavio; 1921–2013, Italian)
Versace (Donatella; 1955– , Italian)
Versace (Gianni; 1946–97, Italian)
Vuitton (Louis; 1821–1892, French)

08 Burberry
Chalayan (Hussein; 1970– , Turkish
  Cypriot)
Galliano (John; 1961– , Gibraltarian/
  British)
Gaultier (Jean-Paul; 1952– , French)
Givenchy (Hubert de; 1927– , French)
Hartnell (Sir Norman; 1901–78, English)
Hilfiger (Tommy; 1951– , US)
Hugo Boss
Kawakubo (Rei; 1942– , Japanese)
Molyneux (Edward; 1891–1974, English)
Moschino
Moschino (Franco; 1950–94, Italian)
Oldfield (Bruce; 1950– , English)
Richmond (John; 1960– , English)
Ted Baker
Westwood (Vivienne; 1941– , English)
Yamamoto (Yohji; 1943– , Japanese)

09 Claiborne (Liz; 1929–2007, Belgian/US)
Courrèges (André; 1923– , French)
de la Renta (Oscar; 1932– , Dominican/
  US)
Hulanicki (Barbara; 1936– , Polish/British)
Lagerfeld (Karl-Otto; 1938– , German)
McCartney (Stella; 1972– , English)
Mortensen (Erik; 1926–98, Danish)
Paul Smith
Valentino (1933– , Italian)

10 Balenciaga (Cristóbal; 1895–1972,
  Spanish)
Mainbocher (c.1890–1976, US)
Vanderbilt (Gloria; 1924– , US)

11 Calvin Klein
Cath Kidston
Laura Ashley

12 Louis Vuitton
Saint Laurent (Yves; 1936–2008, French)
Schiaparelli (Elsa; 1890–1973, Italian/
  French)

13 Dolce e Gabbana
Tommy Hilfiger

fast

Fast-days and fasting periods include:

04 Lent (Christian)
06 Ashura (Islam)

Friday (Christian)
07 Ramadan (Islam)

08 Moharram (Islam)
Muharram (Islam)

Muharrem (Islam)
Ramadhan (Islam)
Tisha Bov (Judaism)

09 Ember days (Christian)

See also **festival**

Tisha Baav (Judaism)
Tisha be'Ab (Judaism)
Tisha Be'Av (Judaism)
Tishah b'Ab (Judaism)

Tishah B'Av (Judaism)
Yom Kippur (Judaism)

10 Holy Friday (Christian)

12 Golden Friday (Christian)

fast food *see* food; restaurant

fastener

Fasteners include:

03 tie	loop	eyelet	**09** paperclip
zip	nail	holder	press stud
04 bond	stud	staple	**10** collar stud
clip	**05** catch	stitch	hook-and-eye
frog	clasp	toggle	**11** Bulldog® clip
hasp	hinge	Velcro®	Chelsea clip
hook	latch	zipper	treasury tag
knot	rivet	**07** padlock	**13** alligator clip
lace	screw	**08** cufflink	crocodile clip
link	**06** button	shoelace	
lock	cotter	split pin	

fate

The Greek Fates:

06 Clotho   **07** Atropos   **08** Lachesis

The Norse Fates:

03 Urd   **05** Skuld   **08** Verdande

father

Fathers include:

04 Amis (Sir Kingsley; 1922–95, English)
Bush (George; 1924–   , US)
Lear (King; *King Lear*, 1605–06, William
Shakespeare)
Pitt (William; 1708–78, English)

05 Dumas (Alexandre; 1802–70, French)
Ghost (*Hamlet*, 1600–01, William
Shakespeare)
Isaac (Bible)
Jacob (Bible)
Mills (Sir John; 1908–2005, English)
Nehru (Jawaharlal 'Pandit'; 1889–1964,
Indian)

06 Bhutto (Zulfikar Ali; 1928–79, Pakistani)

07 Abraham (Bible)
Capulet (Lord; *Romeo and Juliet*, 1595,
William Shakespeare)
Chatham (William Pitt, Earl of; 1708–78,
English)

Kennedy (Joseph P; 1888–1969, US)
Leontes (*The Winter's Tale*, 1609, William
Shakespeare)
Shylock (*The Merchant of Venice*, 1596–97,
William Shakespeare)
Simpson (Homer; *The Simpsons*, TV)

08 Campbell (Sir Malcolm; 1885–1949,
English)
Dimbleby (Richard; 1913–65, English)
King Lear (*King Lear*, 1605–06, William
Shakespeare)
Polonius (*Hamlet*, 1600–01, William
Shakespeare)
Pontifex (Theo; *The Way of All Flesh*, 1903,
Samuel Butler)
Prospero (*The Tempest*, 1611, William
Shakespeare)

09 Antiochus (*Pericles*, c.1608, William
Shakespeare)

Dumas père (1802–70, French)

10 Clayhanger (Darius; *Clayhanger*, 1910, Arnold Bennett)

11 Rockefeller (John D; 1839–1937, US)

12 Pitt the Elder (William; 1708–78, English)

14 Uther Pendragon (Arthurian legend)

female animal *see* animal

feminism

Feminists include:

04 Daly (Mary; 1928–2010, US)
Hite (Shere; 1943– , US)
Mott (Lucretia; 1793–1880, US)
Shaw (Anna Howard; 1847–1919, US)
Wolf (Naomi; 1962– , US)

05 Abzug (Bella; 1920–98, US)
Astor (Nancy; 1879–1964, US/British)
Beale (Dorothea; 1831–1906, English)
Greer (Germaine; 1939– , Australian)
Stone (Lucy; 1818–93, US)

06 Callil (Carmen; 1938– , Australian)
Cixous (Hélène; 1937– , French)
Faludi (Susan; 1960– , US)
Friday (Nancy; 1937– , US)
Fuller (Margaret; 1810–50, US)
Gilman (Charlotte Perkins; 1860–1935, US)
Grimké (Sarah; 1792–1873, US)
Orbach (Susie; 1946– , English)
Paglia (Camille; 1947– , US)
Rankin (Jeannette; 1880–1973, US)
Stopes (Marie; 1880–1958, Scottish)
Weldon (Fay; 1931– , English)

07 Anthony (Susan B; 1820–1906, US)
Davison (Emily; 1872–1913, English)
Dworkin (Andrea; 1946–2005, US)
Egerton (Sarah; 1670–1723, English)
Fawcett (Dame Millicent; 1847–1929, English)
Friedan (Betty; 1921–2006, US)
Goldman (Emma; 1869–1940, US)
Kennedy (Helena, Baroness; 1950– , Scottish)
Lenclos (Ninon de; 1620–1705, French)
Steinem (Gloria; 1934– , US)

08 Beauvoir (Simone de; 1908–86, French)
Brittain (Vera; 1893–1970, English)
MacPhail (Agnes; 1890–1954, Canadian)
Rathbone (Eleanor; 1872–1946, English)

09 Blackwell (Elizabeth; 1821–1910, US)
Pankhurst (Adela; 1885–1961, English)
Pankhurst (Christabel; 1880–1958, English)
Pankhurst (Emmeline; 1857–1928, English)
Pankhurst (Sylvia; 1882–1960, English)

11 Burgos Seguí (Carmen de; c.1870–1932, Spanish)

14 Wollstonecraft (Mary; 1759–97, Anglo-Irish)

fencing

Fencing terms include:

03 bib	piste	quinte	coquille
cut	prime	remise	plastron
hit	punto	thrust	tac-au-tac
04 bout	sabre	tierce	traverse
épée	sixte	touché	
foil	touch	**07** barrage	**09** disengage
pass	volte	counter	repechage
pink	**06** attack	en garde	**10** flanconade
volt	button	on guard	imbroccata
ward	come in	passado	time-thrust
05 allez	doigté	reprise	**11** corps à corps
appel	faible	riposte	punto dritto
carte	flèche	seconde	**12** colichemarde
feint	foible	septime	counter-parry
forte	octave	stop hit	punto reverso
lunge	parade	**08** back edge	punto riverso
parry	puncto	balestra	**14** counter-riposte
	quarte		

See also **sport**

fern

Ferns include:

03 lip
man
oak

04 blue
felt
fork
hard
lady
male
sago
seed
tara
tree

05 beech
brake
chain
coral
crown
glory
holly
marsh
ponga
punga
royal
scale
sword
water

06 azolla
bamboo
Boston

button
ladder
lunary
nardoo
osmund
ribbon
shield
silver
tongue

07 bladder
bracken
bristle
buckler
Byfield
cabbage
Dickie's
elkhorn
emerald
foxtail
Goldie's
leather
osmunda
ostrich
parsley
rockcap
tatting
walking
wall rue
woodsia

08 aspidium
barometz

bear's paw
ceterach
cinnamon
climbing
goldback
hairy lip
licorice
moonwort
northern
pillwort
polypody
soft tree
staghorn

09 asparagus
asplenium
bird's nest
black tree
fairy moss
flowering
hare's foot
rhizocarp
rock brake
rusty-back
sensitive
snow brake

10 Asian chain
broad beech
common rasp
golden male
hard shield
Korean rock

maidenhair
soft shield
spleenwort
woolly tree

11 hart's tongue
interrupted
nephrolepis
rabbit's foot
shuttlecock
silver balls
walking leaf

12 broad buckler
elephant's ear
golden Boston
Hawaiian tree
Japanese felt
resurrection
Wallich's wood

13 crested ribbon
European chain
hen-and-chicken
Japanese holly
narrow buckler
prickly shield
scolopendrium
squirrel's foot

14 brittle bladder
Japanese tassel

15 Japanese painted
Mrs Frizell's lady

See also **plant**

festival

Ancient festivals and celebrations include:

03 Bon (mid-Jul)

04 Holi (Spring)
Lots (one month before Passover)
Noel (Winter)
Yule (Winter)

05 Purim (one month before Passover)
Saman (1 Nov)
Weeks (50 days after Passover)
Wesak (Apr/May)

06 Advent (four weeks before Christmas)
Diwali (Oct/Nov)
Easter (Spring)
Floria (28 Apr to 3 May)
Lammas (1 Aug)
May Day (1 May)
Oimelc (1 Feb)

Opalia (19 Dec)
Pesach (Spring)
Plebii (4–17 Nov)

07 Beltane (1 May)
Equiria (27 Feb/14 Mar/15 Oct)
Feralia (21/22 Feb)
Fugalia (24 Feb)
Imbolic (1 Feb)
Lady Day (25 Mar)
Lemuria (9–13 May)
Navrati (Sep/Oct)
Palilia (21 Apr)
Parilia (21 Apr)
Ramadan (moveable)
Samhain (1 Nov)
Sukkoth (Autumn)
Sullani (26 Oct to 1 Nov)

Theseia (Oct)
Vinalia (23 Apr)

08 Agonalia (9 Jan/17 Mar/21 May/11 Dec)
Cerealia (Apr)
Fasching (Feb)
Faunalia (13 Feb/13 Oct/5 Dec)
Floralia (28 Apr to 3 May)
Hanukkah (Winter)
Hogmanay (New Year)
Homstrom (end of Winter)
Hull Fair (Oct)
Id ul-Adha (moveable)
Id ul-Fitr (moveable)
Lucia Day (13 Dec)
Lugnasad (2 Aug)
Mahayana (mid-Jul)
Matralia (11 Jun)
Nit de foc (Mar)
Passover (Spring)
Samhuinn (1 Nov)
Setsubun (3/4 Feb)
Shabuoth (50 days after Passover)
Stow Fair (May/Oct)
Tanabata (7 Jul)
Vestalia (9 Jun)

09 Baishakhi (13/14 Apr)
Boxing Day (26 Dec)
Christmas (25 Dec)
Floralies (Summer)
Hallowe'en (31 Oct)
Hallowmas (1 Nov)
Ides of Mar (15 Mar)
Liberalia (17 Mar)
Ludi Magni (Sep)
Lugnasadh (2 Aug)
Magalesia (4–10 Apr)
Magha-puja (Feb)
Mardi Gras (Feb/Mar)
Martinmas (11 Nov)
Nemoralia (13 Aug)
Paganalia (24–26 Jan)
Pentecost (50 days after Pesach)
Puanepsia (Autumn)
Robigalia (25 Apr)
Thargelia (late May)
Ullambana (15th day of the 7th lunar
  month)
Up-Helly-Aa (Jan/Feb)
Wakes Week (Summer)
Yom Kippur (Autumn)

10 Allhallows (1 Nov)
Ambarvalia (29 May)
Barnet Fair (Sep)
Fordicidia (15 Apr)
Fornicalia (17 Feb)
Good Friday (Spring)
Larentalia (Dec)

La Tomatina (Aug)
Lee Gap Fair (24 Aug/17 Sep)
Ludi Romani (5–19 Sep)
Lupercalia (15 Feb)
Matronalia (1 Mar)
Mother's Day (Spring)
Neptunalia (23 Jul)
Palm Sunday (Sunday before Easter Day)
Pancake Day (Feb/Mar)
Parentalia (13–21 Feb)
Portunalia (17 Aug)
Quirinalia (17 Feb)
Regifugium (24 Feb)
Saturnalia (17–23 Dec)
Swan Upping (Jul)
Terminalia (23 Feb)
Volcanalia (23 Aug)

11 All Fools' Day (1 Apr)
All Souls' Day (2 Nov)
Bacchanalia (Mar)
Carmentalia (11 and 15 Jan)
Epulum Jovis (13 Nov)
Hina Matsuri (3 Mar)
Lady Luck Day (5 Apr)
Oktoberfest (Oct)
Oskhophoria (Autumn)
Panathenaea (Jul)
Quinquatrus (19–21 Mar)
Semo Sanctus (Jun)
St David's Day (1 Mar)
Tabernacles (Autumn)

12 All Saints' Day (1 Nov)
Armilustrium (19 Oct)
Ascension Day (40 days after Easter)
Ash Wednesday (Feb/Mar)
Barranquilla (Spring)
Day of the Dead (2 Nov)
Doll Festival (3 Mar)
Holy Wells Day (2 Mar)
Kanda Matsuri (mid-May)
Ludi Merceruy (15 May)
Mahashivrati (Jan/Feb)
Meditrinalia (11 Oct)
Nutters Dance (Easter Saturday)
Rosh Hashanah (Autumn)
St Andrew's Day (30 Nov)
St George's Day (23 Apr)
Thanksgiving (Nov)
Tubilustrium (23 Mar)
Twelfth Night (5 Jan)
Well-dressing (Ascension Day to Sep)

13 April Fool's Day (1 Apr)
Haxey Hood Game (5/6 Jan)
Ludi Consualia (21 Aug)
Ludi Martiales (12 May)
Midsummer's Eve (late Jun)
Raksha Bandhan (Jul/Aug)

Shrove Tuesday (Feb/Mar)
St Patrick's Day (17 Mar)
The Furry Dance (Spring)
Water Festival (13–15 Apr)
Widecombe Fair (Sep)

14 Chinese New Year (Jan/Feb)
Maundy Thursday (Mar/Apr)
St Nicholas's Day (6 Dec)
Vinalia Rustica (19 Aug)

Walpurgis Night (30 Apr–1 May)

15 Festival of Light (2 Aug)
Harvest Festival (Autumn)
Ludi Apollinares (5 Jul)
Mahavira Jayanti (Oct/Nov)
Mothering Sunday (4th Sunday of Lent)
Priddy Sheep Fair (mid-Aug)
St Valentine's Day (14 Feb)

Modern festivals and celebrations include:

05 VE Day (8 May)
VJ Day (14 Aug)
WOMAD (Jul/Aug)

08 Anzac Day (25 Apr)
Earth Day (22 Apr)
Labor Day (Sep)

09 Canada Day (1 Jul)
Labour Day (1 May)

10 Burns Night (25 Jan)

11 Bastille Day (14 Jul)
Cinco de Mayo (5 May)
Glastonbury (end Jun)

Republic Day (various)
Waitangi Day (6 Feb)

12 Armistice Day (11 Nov)
Australia Day (26 Jan)
Bonfire Night (5 Nov)
Groundhog Day (2 Feb)

13 New Zealand Day (6 Feb)

14 Guy Fawkes' Night (5 Nov)
Remembrance Day (11 Nov or nearest
Sunday)

15 Edinburgh Fringe (Aug)
Independence Day (4 Jul)

See also **celebration**; **fast**; **holiday**; **religion**

fever

Fevers include:

01 Q
03 hay
tap
04 ague
camp
gaol
gold
jail
Rock
ship
tick
worm
05 brain
cabin
dandy
Lassa
Malta
marsh
stage
swamp
swine
Texas
06 dengue

dumdum
hectic
jungle
parrot
plague
rabbit
spring
trench
typhus
valley
yellow
07 biliary
enteric
gastric
malaria
measles
ratbite
sandfly
scarlet
splenic
spotted
typhoid
verruga

08 childbed
kala-azar
undulant
09 breakbone
calenture
East Coast
glandular
phrenitis
puerperal
relapsing
remittent
rheumatic
10 blackwater
Rift Valley
scarlatina
yellow Jack
12 African coast
13 cerebrospinal
leptospirosis
Mediterranean
14 kissing disease
15 acute rheumatism

See also **disease**

fiction

Fictional places include:

02 Ix (*Dune*, 1965, et seq, Frank Herbert)
Oz (*The Wonderful Wizard of Oz*, 1900, L Frank Baum)

04 Alph (*Kubla Khan*, 1816, Samuel Taylor Coleridge)
Rhun (*The Lord of the Rings*, 1954–55, J R R Tolkien)

05 Arnor (*The Lord of the Rings*, 1954–55, J R R Tolkien)
Holby (*Casualty/Holby City*, TV)
Moria (*The Lord of the Rings*, 1954–55, J R R Tolkien)
Rohan (*The Lord of the Rings*, 1954–55, J R R Tolkien)

06 Canley (*The Bill*, TV)
Dibley (*The Vicar of Dibley*, TV)
Gondor (*The Lord of the Rings*, 1954–55, J R R Tolkien)
Laputa (*Gulliver's Travels*, 1726, Jonathan Swift)
Lorien (*The Lord of the Rings*, 1954–55, J R R Tolkien)
Mordor (*The Lord of the Rings*, 1954–55, J R R Tolkien)
Narnia (*The Chronicles of Narnia*, 1950–56, C S Lewis)
Titipu (*The Mikado*, 1885, Gilbert and Sullivan)
Utopia (*Utopia*, 1516, Sir Thomas More)
Vulcan (*Star Trek*, TV/film)
Wessex (various novels, Thomas Hardy)
Xanadu (*Kubla Khan*, 1816, Samuel Taylor Coleridge)

07 Avonlea (*Anne of Green Gables*, 1908, L M Montgomery)
Bedrock (*The Flintstones*, TV)
Camelot (Arthurian legend)
Erewhon (*Erewhon*, 1872, Samuel Butler)
Eriador (*The Lord of the Rings*, 1954–55, J R R Tolkien)
Eurasia (*1984*, 1949, George Orwell)
Midwich (*The Midwich Cuckoos*, 1957, John Wyndham)
Mole End (*The Wind in the Willows*, 1908, Kenneth Grahame)
Sun Hill (*The Bill*, TV)
Toyland (*Noddy Goes to Toyland*, 1949, et seq, Enid Blyton)
Walford (*Eastenders*, TV)

08 Ambridge (*The Archers*, radio)
Blefuscu (*Gulliver's Travels*, 1726, Jonathan Swift)

Calormen (*The Chronicles of Narnia*, 1950–56, C S Lewis)
Earthsea (*A Wizard of Earthsea*, 1968, et seq, Ursula Le Guin)
Hobbiton (*The Lord of the Rings*, 1954–55, J R R Tolkien)
Lilliput (*Gulliver's Travels*, 1726, Jonathan Swift)
Llaregyb (*Under Milk Wood*, 1954, Dylan Thomas)
Mirkwood (*The Lord of the Rings*, 1954–55, J R R Tolkien)
Stepford (*The Stepford Wives*, 1972, Ira Levin)
Sylvania (*Duck Soup*, 1933)
Tartarus (Greek mythology)
The Shire (*The Lord of the Rings*, 1954–55, J R R Tolkien)
Toad Hall (*The Wind in the Willows*, 1908, Kenneth Grahame)

09 Barataria (*The Gondoliers*, 1889, Gilbert and Sullivan)
Brigadoon (*Brigadoon*, 1947)
Discworld (*The Colour of Magic*, 1983, et seq, Terry Pratchet)
Emmerdale (*Emmerdale*, TV)
Freedonia (*Duck Soup*, 1933)
Hollyoaks (*Hollyoaks*, TV)
Rivendell (*The Lord of the Rings*, 1954–55, J R R Tolkien)
River Alph (*Kubla Khan*, 1816, Samuel Taylor Coleridge)
Ruritania (*The Prisoner of Zenda*, 1894, Anthony Hope)
Shangri-La (*Lost Horizon*, 1933, James Hilton)
Summer Bay (*Home and Away*, TV)
Venusberg (*Venusberg*, 1932, Anthony Powell)
Westworld (*Westworld*, 1973)

10 Archenland (*The Chronicles of Narnia*, 1950–56, C S Lewis)
Barchester (various novels, Anthony Trollope)
Borchester (*The Archers*, radio)
Moominland (*The Little Trolls and the Great Flood*, 1945, et seq, Tove Jansson)
Shieldinch (*River City*, TV)
Vanity Fair (*Pilgrim's Progress*, 1678/84, John Bunyan)
Wonderland (*Alice's Adventures in Wonderland*, 1865, Lewis Carroll)

11 Airstrip One (*1984*, 1949, George Orwell)

Barsetshire (various novels, Anthony Trollope)
Borsetshire (*The Archers*, radio)
Brobdingnag (*Gulliver's Travels*, 1726, Jonathan Swift)
Diagon Alley (*Harry Potter and the Philosopher's Stone*, 1997, et seq, J K Rowling)
Emerald City (*The Wonderful Wizard of Oz*, 1900, L Frank Baum)
Gormenghast (*Titus Groan*, 1946, et seq, Mervyn Peake)
Middle-Earth (*The Lord of the Rings*, 1954–55, J R R Tolkien)
Skull Island (*King Kong*, 1933)
The Wild Wood (*The Wind in the Willows*, 1908, Kenneth Grahame)
12 Albert Square (*Eastenders*, TV)
Celesteville (*The Story of Babar the Little Elephant*, 1931, et seq, Jean de Brunhoff)
Erinsborough (*Neighbours*, TV)
Glubbdubdrib (*Gulliver's Travels*, 1726, Jonathan Swift)
Jurassic Park (*Jurassic Park*, 1990, Michael Crichton)

See also **film**; **superhero**; **television**

Ramsay Street (*Neighbours*, TV)
Sleepy Hollow (*The Legend of Sleepy Hollow*, 1819, Washington Irving)
Tralfamadore (*Slaughterhouse-Five*, 1969, Kurt Vonnegut)
Weatherfield (*Coronation Street*, TV)
13 Celestial City (*Pilgrim's Progress*, 1678/84, John Bunyan)
Christminster (various novels, Thomas Hardy)
Montego Street (*River City*, TV)
14 Brookside Close (*Brookside*, TV)
Doubting-Castle (*Pilgrim's Progress*, 1678/84, John Bunyan)
Hogwarts School (*Harry Potter and the Philosopher's Stone*, 1997, et seq, J K Rowling)
Never-Never Land (*Peter Pan*, 1904, J M Barrie)
Nightmare Abbey (*Nightmare Abbey*, 1818, Thomas Love Peacock)
Treasure Island (*Treasure Island*, 1883, Robert Louis Stevenson)
15 Baskerville Hall (*The Hound of the Baskervilles*, 1902, Arthur Conan Doyle)

field marshal

Field marshals include:

04 Haig (Douglas, Earl; 1861–1928, Scottish)
05 Lucan (George Bingham, Earl of; 1800–88, English)
Monty (Bernard Viscount, Montgomery; 1887–1976, English)
06 French (Sir John; 1852–1925, English)
Raglan (Fitzroy Somerset, Lord; 1788–1855, English)
07 Allenby (Edmund Hynman, Viscount; 1861–1936, English)
Roberts (Frederick, Earl; 1832–1914, English)

08 Ironside (William, Lord; 1880–1959, Scottish)
Wolseley (Garnet Joseph, Viscount; 1833–1913, Irish/British)
09 Robertson (Sir William; 1860–1933, English)
10 Alanbrooke (Alan Francis Brooke, Viscount; 1883–1963, French/British)
Auchinleck (Sir Claude John Eyre; 1884–1981, English)
Kesselring (Albert; 1885–1960, German)
Montgomery (Bernard, Viscount 'Monty'; 1887–1976, English)

fighter

Fighters include:

05 boxer	**07** matador	wrestler	**10** rejoneador
pugil	picador	**09** gladiator	**11** bullfighter
06 fencer	sworder	kick boxer	digladiator
hitman	**08** pugilist	spadassin	**12** banderillero
knight	toreador	swordsman	prizefighter

See also **boxing**; **fencing**; **wrestling**

figure of speech *see* **rhetoric**

film

Film types include:

03 spy
war

04 blue
cult
epic
noir

05 adult
anime
buddy
crime
farce
heist
short
spoof
vogue
weepy
wuxia

06 action
auteur
biopic
B-movie
comedy
Disney
erotic
family
horror
murder
police
remake
rom-com
serial
silent
weepie

07 Carry-on
cartoon
classic
dramedy
fantasy
musical
neo-noir
new wave

passion
realist
robbery
slasher
telepic
tragedy
war hero
western

08 animated
disaster
escapist
film noir
gangster
newsreel
romantic
space-age
thriller

09 adventure
Bollywood
burlesque
chopsocky
detective
film à clef
flashback
Hitchcock
Hollywood
James Bond
love story
low-budget
machinima
melodrama
political
road movie
satirical
skin flick
Spielberg
whodunnit

10 avant-garde
bonkbuster
gay-lesbian
neo-realist

period epic
snuff movie
surrealist
tear-jerker
travelogue

11 black comedy
blockbuster
cliff-hanger
documentary
kitchen sink
period drama
tragicomedy
underground

12 cinéma-vérité
Ealing comedy
ethnographic
fly-on-the-wall
mockumentary
pornographic
rockumentary
social comedy

13 comic-book hero
expressionist
multiple-story
murder mystery
nouvelle vague
sexploitation
sexual fantasy
social problem

14 blaxploitation
Charlie Chaplin
comedy thriller
police thriller
rites of passage
romantic comedy
science-fiction
sword-and-sandal

15 cowboy and Indian
romantic tragedy
screwball comedy

Films include:

02 *If...* (1963)

03 *Big* (1988)
Cal (1984)
Hud (1963)
JFK (1991)
Kes (1970)
Ran (1985)

04 *Antz* (1998)
Argo (2012)

Babe (1995)
Bird (1988)
Diva (1981)
Dr No (1962)
Gigi (1958)
Heat (1995)
Jaws (1975)
MASH (1970)
Milk (2008)
Reds (1981)

Rope (1948)
X-Men (2000)

05 *Alfie* (1966/2004)
Alien (1973)
Angel (1982)
Bambi (1942)
Bugsy (1992)
Crash (1996/2004)
Dumbo (1941)
Fargo (1996)
Ghost (1990)
Giant (1956)
Greed (1924)
Klute (1971)
Marty (1955)
Naked (1993)
Rocky (1976)
Shane (1953)
Shrek (2001)
Texas (1941)

06 *Aliens* (1986)
Amélie (2001)
Avatar (2009)
Batman (1989)
Ben-Hur (1959)
Blow-Up (1966)
Brazil (1985)
Casino (1995)
Ed Wood (1994)
Gandhi (1982)
Go West (1940)
Grease (1978)
Heimat (1984)
Kundun (1997)
Lolita (1962)
Mad Max (1979)
Marnie (1964)
Misery (1990)
Patton (1970)
Psycho (1960)
The Fly (1986)
The Kid (1921)
Top Gun (1986)
Top Hat (1935)

07 *Aladdin* (1992)
Amadeus (1984)
Big Fish (2003)
Bullitt (1968)
Cabaret (1972)
Charade (1963)
Darling (1965)
Das Boot (1981)
Dead Man (1995)
Die Hard (1988)
Dracula (1931/1958/1974/1979/1992)
Jezebel (1938)
L'Âge d'Or (1930)
Matador (1986)

Memento (2000)
Platoon (1986)
Poor Cow (1968)
Rain Man (1988)
Rebecca (1940)
Robocop (1987)
Serpico (1973)
Sunrise (1927)
The Dead (1987)
The Mask (1994)
The Omen (1976)
The Robe (1953)
Titanic (1997)
Tootsie (1982)
Traffic (2000)
Twister (1996)
Vertigo (1958)
Witness (1985)

08 *Apollo 13* (1995)
Badlands (1973)
Body Heat (1981)
Born Free (1966)
Cape Fear (1962/1991)
Cast Away (2000)
Chocolat (2000)
Clockers (1995)
Duck Soup (1933)
Election (1999)
Fantasia (1940)
Fearless (1993)
Gaslight (1944)
Gun Crazy (1950)
High Noon (1952)
Insomnia (2002)
Key Largo (1948)
Kill Bill (2003/2004)
King Kong (1933/1976/2005)
La Strada (1954)
Life of Pi (2012)
Mamma Mia (2008)
Mona Lisa (1986)
Papillon (1973)
Rashomon (1951)
Red River (1948)
Ridicule (1996)
Riff Raff (1991)
Rio Bravo (1959)
Rushmore (1998)
Saboteur (1942)
Salvador (1986)
Scarface (1932/1983)
Showboat (1936)
Star Wars (1977)
The Birds (1963)
The Field (1990)
The Piano (1993)
The Sting (1973)
The Thing (1951)

The Tramp (1915)
Toy Story (1995)
War Horse (2011)

09 *12 Monkeys* (1995)
A Bug's Life (1998)
Annie Hall (1977)
Betty Blue (1986)
Black Swan (2010)
Cat Ballou (1965)
Chinatown (1974)
City of God (2002)
Cleopatra (1963)
Decameron (1971)
Dick Tracy (1937/1945/1990)
Down By Law (1986)
Easy Rider (1969)
Excalibur (1981)
Funny Face (1957)
Funny Girl (1968)
Genevieve (1953)
Get Shorty (1995)
Gladiator (2000)
GoldenEye (1996)
Home Alone (1990)
Limelight (1952)
Local Hero (1983)
Love Story (1970)
Manhattan (1979)
Moonraker (1979)
Nashville (1975)
Ninotchka (1939)
Nosferatu (1922/1979)
Notorious (1946)
Octopussy (1983)
Pinocchio (1940)
Rio Grande (1950)
Robin Hood (1922/1973)
Sea of Love (1989)
Sexy Beast (2001)
Short Cuts (1993)
Spartacus (1959)
Spider-Man (2002)
Stand by Me (1986)
Straw Dogs (1971)
Talk to Her (2002)
The Artist (2011)
The Damned (1969)
The Devils (1971)
The Player (1992)
The Reader (2008)
Vera Drake (2004)
Viridiana (1961)
Walkabout (1970)
White Heat (1949)
Woodstock (1970)

10 *Adaptation* (2002)
Bagdad Café (1987)
Barton Fink (1991)

Blue Velvet (1986)
Braveheart (1995)
Breathless (1960)
Caravaggio (1986)
Casablanca (1942)
Chicken Run (2000)
City Lights (1931)
Cry Freedom (1987)
Dirty Harry (1971)
East of Eden (1955)
Eraserhead (1977)
Fort Apache (1948)
Frost/Nixon (2008)
Goldfinger (1964)
GoodFellas (1990)
Grand Hotel (1932)
High Sierra (1941)
Jules et Jim (1962)
Men in Black (1997)
Metropolis (1927)
Moonstruck (1987)
Mrs Miniver (1942)
My Fair Lady (1964)
My Left Foot (1989)
Now, Voyager (1942)
Out of Sight (1998)
Paris, Texas (1983)
Peeping Tom (1959)
Pépé le Moko (1936)
Raging Bull (1980)
Rear Window (1954)
Rumble Fish (1983)
Run Lola Run (1998)
Safety Last (1923)
Stagecoach (1939)
Taxi Driver (1976)
The Big Easy (1987)
The Getaway (1972/1994)
The Hustler (1961)
The Insider (1999)
The Leopard (1963)
The Mission (1986)
The Postman (1994)
The Servant (1963)
The Shining (1980)
The Snapper (1993)
The Tin Drum (1979)
The Wild One (1954)
Tokyo Story (1953)
Topsy-Turvy (1999)
Unforgiven (1992)
Videodrome (1983)
Wall Street (1987)
Whale Rider (2002)

11 *A Few Good Men* (1992)
All About Eve (1950)
American Pie (1999)
Beetlejuice (1988)

Belle de Jour (1967)
Blade Runner (1982)
Blood Simple (1984)
Bugsy Malone (1976)
Carlito's Way (1993)
Citizen Kane (1941)
Dark Victory (1939)
Dead Ringers (1988)
Deliverance (1972)
Donnie Darko (2001)
Don't Look Now (1973)
Elmer Gantry (1960)
Finding Nemo (2003)
Forrest Gump (1994)
Gosford Park (2001)
Heaven's Gate (1981)
Intolerance (1916)
Jungle Fever (1991)
La Dolce Vita (1959)
Life is Sweet (1990)
Lost Highway (1997)
Mars Attacks! (1996)
Mary Poppins (1964/1967)
Mean Streets (1973)
Modern Times (1936)
Monsters, Inc (2001)
Moulin Rouge (2001)
My Name is Joe (1998)
Mystic River (2003)
Notting Hill (1999)
Out of Africa (1985)
Plein Soleil (1960)
Pretty Woman (1990)
Public Enemy (1931)
Pulp Fiction (1994)
The 400 Blows (1959)
The Big Chill (1983)
The Big Sleep (1946)
The Departed (2006)
The Evil Dead (1983)
The Exorcist (1973)
The Fugitive (1948/1993)
The Gold Rush (1925)
The Graduate (1967)
The Ice Storm (1997)
The King and I (1956)
The Lion King (1994)
The Music Man (1962)
The Quiet Man (1952)
The Red Shoes (1948)
The Third Man (1949)
Thunderball (1965)
Touch of Evil (1958)
Unbreakable (2000)
Wayne's World (1992)
Wild at Heart (1990)
Yellow Earth (1984)
12 *About Schmidt* (2000)

Amores Perros (2000)
Atlantic City (1980)
A View to a Kill (1985)
Bad Education (2004)
Blood and Sand (1922/1941/1989)
Brighton Rock (1947)
Casino Royale (1954/1967/2006)
Cool Hand Luke (1967)
Days of Heaven (1978)
Delicatessen (1991)
Donnie Brasco (1997)
Eyes Wide Shut (1999)
Fitzcarraldo (1982)
Frankenstein (1931)
Ghostbusters (1984)
Gregory's Girl (1980)
Groundhog Day (1993)
Hidden Agenda (1990)
Intermission (2003)
Jurassic Park (1993)
Lethal Weapon (1987)
Man on the Moon (1999)
Night on Earth (1991)
Philadelphia (1993)
Pierrot Le Fou (1965)
Prizzi's Honor (1985)
Roman Holiday (1953)
Rome, Open City (1945)
Salaam Bombay! (1988)
Seven Samurai (1954)
Sleepy Hollow (1999)
The Apartment (1960)
The Go-Between (1971)
The Godfather (1972)
The Iron Horse (1924)
The Last Waltz (1978)
The Lost World (1925)
The Naked City (1948)
The Sacrifice (1986)
The Searchers (1956)
The Two Towers (2002)
The Wicker Man (1973)
The Wild Bunch (1969)
Whisky Galore! (1949)
Withnail and I (1987)
13 *Apocalypse Now* (1979)
Babette's Feast (1987)
Basic Instinct (1992)
Batman Forever (1995)
Batman Returns (1992)
Broadcast News (1987)
Burnt by the Sun (1994)
Death in Venice (1971)
December Bride (1990)
Die Another Day (2002)
Doctor Zhivago (1965)
Dr Strangelove (1964)
Dumb and Dumber (1994)

Educating Rita (1983)
Eight and a Half (1963)
Field of Dreams (1989)
Happy Together (1997)
Hard Day's Night (1964)
His Girl Friday (1940)
Horse Feathers (1932)
Les Misérables (2012)
Licence to Kill (1989)
Live and Let Die (1973)
Manon de Source (1986)
Mildred Pierce (1945)
Raining Stones (1993)
Reservoir Dogs (1992)
'Round Midnight (1986)
Scent of a Woman (1992)
Some Like It Hot (1959)
Sophie's Choice (1982)
The Crying Game (1992)
The Dam Busters (1955)
The Deer Hunter (1978)
The Dirty Dozen (1967)
The Fisher King (1991)
The Hurt Locker (2009)
The Jazz Singer (1927)
The Jungle Book (1942)
The Longest Day (1962)
The Right Stuff (1983)
The Sixth Sense (1999)
The Terminator (1984)
To Catch a Thief (1955)
Trainspotting (1996)
Watership Down (1978)
West Side Story (1961)
Wings of Desire (1987)
Zorba the Greek (1964)

14 A Day at the Races (1937)
American Beauty (1999)
American Gigolo (1980)
American Psycho (2000)
Animal Crackers (1930)
As Good as it Gets (1997)
Black Narcissus (1947)
Blazing Saddles (1974)
Bonnie and Clyde (1967)
Brief Encounter (1946)
Bringing Up Baby (1938)
Central Station (1998)
Chariots of Fire (1981)
Cinema Paradiso (1989)
Dial M for Murder (1954)
Empire of the Sun (1987)
Enter the Dragon (1973)
Erin Brockovich (2000)
Five Easy Pieces (1970)
Fools of Fortune (1990)
Gangs of New York (2002)
Goodbye Mr Chips (1939/1969)

In a Lonely Place (1950)
In Which We Serve (1942)
Jean de Florette (1986)
LA Confidential (1997)
Land and Freedom (1995)
Les Diaboliques (1956)
Lord of the Rings (2001/2002/2003)
Michael Collins (1996)
Midnight Cowboy (1969)
Minority Report (2002)
Muriel's Wedding (1994)
Prospero's Books (1991)
Raising Arizona (1987)
Schindler's List (1993)
Secrets and Lies (1996)
The Big Lebowski (1998)
The Commitments (1991)
The Elephant Man (1980)
The Great Escape (1963)
The King of Kings (1927/1961)
The King's Speech (2010)
The Ladykillers (1955/2004)
The Last Emperor (1987)
The Life of Brian (1979)
The Little Foxes (1941)
The Lost Weekend (1945)
The Mask of Zorro (1998)
The Music Lovers (1971)
The Night Porter (1974)
The Seventh Seal (1957)
Un Chien Andalou (1928)
Woman of the Year (1942)
Zabriskie Point (1969)

15 A Passage to India (1984)
Back to the Future (1985)
Crocodile Dundee (1986)
Dog Day Afternoon (1975)
Do the Right Thing (1989)
Double Indemnity (1944)
Fanny by Gaslight (1944)
Fatal Attraction (1987)
Forbidden Planet (1956)
For Your Eyes Only (1981)
Full Metal Jacket (1987)
Gone With the Wind (1939)
Good Will Hunting (1997)
Independence Day (1996)
Ivan the Terrible (1944)
Life Is Beautiful (1997)
Meet Me in St Louis (1944)
Midnight Express (1978)
Miller's Crossing (1990)
Mulholland Drive (2001)
Nothing Personal (1995)
On the Waterfront (1954)
Oscar and Lucinda (1997)
Quantum of Solace (2008)
Return of the Jedi (1983)

Road to Perdition (2002)
Singin' in the Rain (1952)
Sunset Boulevard (1950)
Tarzan the Ape Man (1932)
The African Queen (1951)
The Bicycle Thief (1948)
The Conversation (1974)
The House of Mirth (2000)
The King of Comedy (1983)
The Lady Vanishes (1938/1979)
Thelma and Louise (1991)
The Piano Teacher (2001)
The Sound of Music (1965)
This is Spinal Tap (1984)
Three Colours: Red (1994)

16 A Clockwork Orange (1971)
All About My Mother (1999)
American Graffiti (1973)
An Angel at my Table (1990)
A Night at the Opera (1935)
A Night to Remember (1958)
Cat on a Hot Tin Roof (1958)
Cyrano de Bergerac (1990)
Dead Poet's Society (1989)
Eat Man Drink Woman (1994)
Frankie and Johnny (1991)
How the West was Won (1962)
Husbands and Wives (1992)
Ladybird Ladybird (1994)
Last Tango in Paris (1972)
Lawrence of Arabia (1962)
Lilies of the Field (1963)
Night of the Hunter (1955)
North by Northwest (1959)
Revenge of the Sith (2005)
Strictly Ballroom (1992)
Superman: The Movie (1978)
The Cincinnati Kid (1965)
The Grapes of Wrath (1940)
The Great Dictator (1940)
The Maltese Falcon (1941)
The Phantom Menace (1999)
The Princess Bride (1987)
The Quiet American (1958/2002)
The Scarlet Letter (1926/1934/1995)
The Seven Year Itch (1955)
The Spy Who Loved Me (1977)
The Straight Story (1999)
This Sporting Life (1963)
Three Colours: Blue (1993)
To Have and Have Not (1944)
Triumph of the Will (1936)
Wild Strawberries (1957)
Wuthering Heights (1939/1970/1992)
You Only Live Twice (1967)

17 2001: A Space Odyssey (1968)
A Fistful of Dollars (1964)

A Man for all Seasons (1966)
American Splendour (2003)
An American in Paris (1951)
Arsenic and Old Lace (1944)
Attack of the Clones (2002)
Birdman of Alcatraz (1962)
Broadway Danny Rose (1984)
Dangerous Liaisons (1988)
Death and the Maiden (1994)
Dr Jekyll and Mr Hyde (1931/1941)
Fanny and Alexander (1982)
Glengarry Glen Ross (1992)
Heavenly Creatures (1995)
Hiroshima mon amour (1959)
It's a Wonderful Life (1946)
Lost in Translation (2003)
Million Dollar Baby (2004)
Mr Deeds Goes to Town (1936)
Passport to Pimlico (1949)
Pride and Prejudice (1940/2003)
Saving Private Ryan (1998)
Strangers on a Train (1951)
Terms of Endearment (1983)
The Age of Innocence (1993)
The Birth of a Nation (1915)
The Hudsucker Proxy (1994)
The Man who Never Was (1955)
The Thief of Baghdad (1924/1940)
The Wedding Banquet (1993)
Three Colours: White (1994)
Tomorrow Never Dies (1997)
When Harry Met Sally (1989)
Yankee Doodle Dandy (1942)

18 A Month in the Country (1984)
Au Revoir Les Enfants (1987)
Battleship Potemkin (1925)
Being John Malkovich (1999)
Coal Miner's Daughter (1980)
Diamonds are Forever (1971)
Edward Scissorhands (1990)
From Here to Eternity (1953)
From Russia With Love (1963)
Good Morning Vietnam (1987)
Intolerable Cruelty (2003)
It Happened One Night (1934)
McCabe and Mrs Miller (1971)
Mississippi Burning (1988)
Never Say Never Again (1983)
No Country for Old Men (2007)
Raise the Red Lantern (1991)
Rebel Without a Cause (1955)
Sleepless in Seattle (1993)
Slumdog Millionaire (2008)
The Company of Wolves (1984)
The Godfather Part II (1974)
The Last Picture Show (1971)
The Lavender Hill Mob (1951)
The Living Daylights (1987)

The Man without a Past (2002)
The Return of the King (2003)
The Royal Tenenbaums (2001)
The Thirty-Nine Steps (1935/1959/1978)
The Towering Inferno (1974)
To Kill a Mockingbird (1962)

19 *All That Heaven Allows* (1955)
All the President's Men (1976)
All This and Heaven Too (1940)
A Short Film about Love (1988)
Breakfast at Tiffany's (1961)
Bullets over Broadway (1994)
Farewell my Concubine (1993)
Hannah and her Sisters (1986)
How Green was my Valley (1941)
Last Year in Marienbad (1961)
Les Enfants du Paradis (1945)
My Darling Clementine (1946)
Only Angels Have Wings (1939)
Picnic at Hanging Rock (1975)
Raiders of the Lost Ark (1980)
Sense and Sensibility (1995)
sex, lies, and videotape (1989)
Shoot the Piano Player (1960)
The French Connection (1971)
The Magnificent Seven (1960)
The Man Who Wasn't There (2001)
The World is Not Enough (1999)

20 *Aguirre, the Wrath of God* (1972)
Angels with Dirty Faces (1938)
Children of a Lesser God (1986)
Chitty Chitty Bang Bang (1968)
My Big Fat Greek Wedding (2002)
Night of the Living Dead (1968)
O Brother, Where Art Thou (2000)
She Wore a Yellow Ribbon (1949)
Stranger than Paradise (1984)
The Empire Strikes Back (1980)
The Man who Knew Too Much (1934/1956)
The Motorcycle Diaries (2003)
The Mutiny on the Bounty (1962)
The Philadelphia Story (1940)
The Poseidon Adventure (1972)
The Pride of the Yankees (1942)
The Purple Rose of Cairo (1985)
The Silence of the Lambs (1991)
The Thomas Crown Affair (1968/1999)
The Travelling Players (1975)

21 *A Matter of Life and Death* (1946)
A Nightmare on Elm Street (1984)
Born on the Fourth of July (1989)
ET The Extra-Terrestrial (1982)
Gunfight at the OK Corral (1957)
Kind Hearts and Coronets (1949)
Monsieur Hulot's Holiday (1953)
My Beautiful Laundrette (1985)
The Passion of Joan of Arc (1928)

22 *An Officer and a Gentleman* (1982)
A Short Film about Killing (1987)
Crimes and Misdemeanours (1989)
Once upon a Time in America (1984)
The Best Years of Our Lives (1946)
The Fellowship of the Ring (2001)
The Manchurian Candidate (1962) (2004)
The Man with the Golden Gun (1974)
The Shawshank Redemption (1994)

23 *Four Weddings and a Funeral* (1994)
Ghost Dog: Way of the Samurai (1999)
Guess Who's Coming to Dinner (1967)
Interview with the Vampire (1994)
Mr Smith Goes to Washington (1939)
The Bridge on the River Kwai (1957)
The Draughtsman's Contract (1982)
The Enigma of Kaspar Hauser (1975)
The Good, the Bad and the Ugly (1966)
The Magnificent Ambersons (1942)
The Return of Martin Guerre (1982)

24 *Pat Garrett and Billy the Kid* (1973)
Robin Hood: Prince of Thieves (1991)
The Adventures of Robin Hood (1938)
The Double Life of Veronique (1991)
The Texas Chainsaw Massacre (1974/2003)

25 *Fear and Loathing in Las Vegas* (1998)
Leningrad Cowboys Go America (1989)
One Flew Over the Cuckoo's Nest (1975)
The Inn of the Sixth Happiness (1958)
Who's Afraid of Virginia Woolf? (1966)

26 *Alice Doesn't Live Here Anymore* (1974)
Crouching Tiger, Hidden Dragon (2000)
Invasion of the Body Snatchers (1956/1978)
Monty Python and the Holy Grail (1975)
On Her Majesty's Secret Service (1969)
Snow White and the Seven Dwarfs (1937)
The Postman Always Rings Twice
  (1946/1981)
What Ever Happened to Baby Jane? (1962)

27 *The Man Who Shot Liberty Valance* (1962)
The Nightmare Before Christmas (1993)
The Treasure of the Sierra Madre (1948)

29 *Bill and Ted's Excellent Adventure* (1988)
Butch Cassidy and the Sundance Kid (1969)
Close Encounters of the Third Kind (1977)
Harry Potter and the Goblet of Fire (2005)
Indiana Jones and the Last Crusade (1989)
Saturday Night and Sunday Morning (1961)
The Life and Death of Colonel Blimp (1943)

30 *Indiana Jones and the Temple of Doom*
  (1984)
The Curious Case of Benjamin Button
  (2008)

31 *Harry Potter and the Sorcerer's Stone* (2001)

32 *Harry Potter and the Half-Blood Prince*

(2009)

The Discreet Charm of the Bourgeoisie (1972)

33 *Employees Leaving the Lumière Factory* (1895)

Harry Potter and the Chamber of Secrets (2002)

The Cook, the Thief, His Wife and Her Lover (1989)

34 *Harry Potter and the Order of the Phoenix* (2007)

Harry Potter and the Philosopher's Stone (2001)

Harry Potter and the Prisoner of Azkaban (2004)

Women on the Verge of a Nervous Breakdown (1988)

Film characters include:

02 ET (*ET The Extra-Terrestrial*, 1982)

03 Ash (*Alien*, 1979)
HAL (*2001: A Space Odyssey*, 1968)
Joe ('Josephine'; *Some Like It Hot*, 1959)
Neo (*The Matrix*, 1999, et seq)
Rae (Norma; *Norma Rae*, 1979)
Sam (*Casablanca*, 1942)

04 Abra (*East of Eden*, 1955)
Blue (Bubba; *Forrest Gump*, 1994)
Blue (Mr; *Reservoir Dogs*, 1991)
Bond (James; *Dr No*, 1962, et seq)
Book (John; *Witness*, 1985)
Buck (Joe; *Midnight Cowboy*, 1969)
Dory (*Finding Nemo*, 2003)
Evil (Doctor; *Austin Powers: International Man of Mystery*, 1997, et seq)
Gale (Dorothy; *The Wizard of Oz*, 1939)
Gump (Forrest; *Forrest Gump*, 1994)
Hall (Annie; *Annie Hall*, 1977)
Hill (Henry; *Goodfellas*, 1990)
Hunt (Ethan; *Mission Impossible*, 1996, et seq)
Iris (*Taxi Driver*, 1976)
Kane (Charles Foster; *Citizen Kane*, 1941)
Kane (Marshal Will; *High Noon*, 1952)
Kane (Sugar; *Some Like It Hot*, 1959)
Kent (Clark; *Superman*, 1978, et seq)
Kint (Roger 'Verbal'; *The Usual Suspects*, 1995)
Lane (Lois; *Superman*, 1978, et seq)
Lapp (Rachel; *Witness*, 1985)
Leia (Princess; *Star Wars*, 1977, et seq)
Léon (*Léon*, 1994)
Lime (Harry; *The Third Man*, 1949)
Lund (Isla, *Casablanca*, 1942)
Neff (Walter; *Double Indemnity*, 1944)
Nemo (*Finding Nemo*, 2003)
Pink (Mr; *Reservoir Dogs*, 1991)
Rink (Jett; *Giant*, 1956)
Ryan (Jack; *Patriot Games*, 1992, et seq)
Shaw (Raymond; *The Manchurian Candidate*, 1962/2004)
Solo (Han; *Star Wars*, 1977, et seq)
Soze (Keyser; *The Usual Suspects*, 1995)
Spud (*Trainspotting*, 1995)
Tony (*West Side Story*, 1961)
Toto (*The Wizard of Oz*, 1939)

Vega (Vincent; *Pulp Fiction*, 1994)
Ward (Vivian; *Pretty Woman*, 1990)
Yoda (*Star Wars*, 1977, et seq)
Zorg (*Betty Blue*, 1986)

05 Baloo (*The Jungle Book*, 1967)
Barry (Father; *On the Waterfront*, 1954)
Bates (Norman; *Psycho*, 1960)
Batty (Roy; *Blade Runner*, 1982)
Betty (*Betty Blue*, 1986)
Billy (*Easy Rider*, 1969)
Boggs (Kim; *Edward Scissorhands*, 1990)
Booth (Frank; *Blue Velvet*, 1986)
Brown (Cosmo; *Singin' in the Rain*, 1952)
Brown (Doctor Emmett; *Back to the Future*, 1985)
Brown (Mr; *Reservoir Dogs*, 1992)
Brown (Oda Mae; *Ghost*, 1990)
Dobbs (Fred C; *The Treasure of the Sierra Madre*, 1947)
Doyle (Jimmy 'Popeye'; *The French Connection*, 1971)
Exley (Edmund 'Ed'; *LA Confidential*, 1997)
Fiona (Princess; *Shrek*, 2001, et seq)
Foley (Axel; *Beverly Hills Cop*, 1984, et seq)
Gekko (Gordon; *Wall Street*, 1987)
Hatch (Mary; *It's a Wonderful Life*, 1947)
Jerry ('Daphne'; *Some Like It Hot*, 1959)
Jones (Indiana; *Raiders of the Lost Ark*, 1980, et seq)
Klute (John; *Klute*, 1971)
Kurtz (Colonel Walter E; *Apocalypse Now*, 1979)
Lewis (Edward; *Pretty Woman*, 1990)
Marco (Bennet; *The Manchurian Candidate*, 1962/2004)
Maria (*Metropolis*, 1927)
Maria (*West Side Story*, 1961)
McFly (Marty; *Back to the Future*, 1985, et seq)
Mills (Detective David; *Seven*, 1995)
Ocean (Danny; *Ocean's Eleven*, 2001, et seq)
Riggs (Martin; *Lethal Weapon*, 1987, et seq)
Rizzo (Betty; *Grease*, 1978)
Rizzo (Ratso; *Midnight Cowboy*, 1969)
Rocco (Johnny; *Key Largo*, 1948)
Russo (Buddy 'Cloudy'; *The French Connection*, 1971)
Saito (Colonel; *The Bridge on the River*

Kwai, 1957)
Sayer (Rose; *The African Queen*, 1951)
Shaft (John; *Shaft*, 1971/2000)
Shrek (*Shrek*, 2001, et seq)
Simba (*The Lion King*, 1994)
Spade (Sam; *The Maltese Falcon*, 1941)
Stark (Jim; *Rebel Without a Cause*, 1955)
Swann (Elizabeth; *Pirates of the Caribbean*, 2003, et seq)
Tibbs (Detective Virgil; *In the Heat of the Night*, 1967, et seq)
Trask (Caleb; *East of Eden*, 1955)
Vance (Susan; *Bringing Up Baby*, 1938)
Wayne (Bruce; *Batman*, 1989, et seq)
Wheat (Sam; *Ghost*, 1990)
White (Mr; *Reservoir Dogs*, 1991)
White (Wendell 'Bud'; *LA Confidential*, 1997)
Woody (*Toy Story*, 1995, et seq)
Wyatt (*Easy Rider*, 1969)
Zucco (Danny; *Grease*, 1978)

06 Allnut (Charlie; *The African Queen*, 1951)
Bailey (George; *It's a Wonderful Life*, 1947)
Balboa (Rocky; *Rocky*, 1976, et seq)
Bannon (Hud; *Hud*, 1962)
Barrow (Clyde; *Bonnie and Clyde*, 1967)
Barton (Judy; *Vertigo*, 1958)
Batman (*Batman*, 1989, et seq)
Begbie (*Trainspotting*, 1995)
Bickle (Travis; *Taxi Driver*, 1976)
Blaine (Rick; *Casablanca*, 1942)
Blonde (Mr; *Reservoir Dogs*, 1991)
Bowles (Sally; *Cabaret*, 1972)
Bowman (Mission Commander David; *2001: A Space Odyssey*, 1968)
Carter (Jack; *Get Carter*, 1971)
Casper (Billy; *Kes*, 1969)
Connor (Sarah; *The Terminator*, 1984, et seq)
Conway (Jimmy; *Goodfellas*, 1990)
Croker (Charlie; *The Italian Job*, 1969)
Curran (Jenny; *Forrest Gump*, 1994)
Cypher (*The Matrix*, 1999)
Daniel (Bree; *Klute*, 1971)
Darrow (Ann; *King Kong*, 1933/2005)
DeVito (Tommy; *Goodfellas*, 1990)
DuBois (Blanche; *A Streetcar Named Desire*, 1951)
Durden (Tyler; *Fight Club*, 1999)
Elkins (Alfie; *Alfie*, 1965/2004)
Elster (Madeleine; *Vertigo*, 1958)
Gerard (Deputy Marshal Samuel; *The Fugitive*, 1993)
Gittes (J J; *Chinatown*, 1974)
Glinda (*The Wizard of Oz*, 1939)
Harper (Willa; *The Night of the Hunter*, 1955)
Hudson (Blanche; *What Ever Happened to Baby Jane?*, 1962)
Hudson (Jane; *What Ever Happened to Baby Jane?*, 1962)

Iselin (Eleanor Shaw; *The Manchurian Candidate*, 1962/2004)
Jensen (Molly; *Ghost*, 1990)
Kambei (*Seven Samurai*, 1954)
Kenobi (Obi-Wan; *Star Wars*, 1977, et seq)
Kimble (Dr Richard; *The Fugitive*, 1993)
Lamont (Lina; *Singin' in the Rain*, 1952)
Laszlo (Victor; *Casablanca*, 1942)
Lecter (Dr Hannibal; *The Silence of the Lambs*, 1991, et seq)
Malloy (Terry; *On the Waterfront*, 1954)
Manero (Tony; *Saturday Night Fever*, 1977, et seq)
Marlin (*Finding Nemo*, 2003)
Marvel (Professor; *The Wizard of Oz*, 1939)
Mowgli (*The Jungle Book*, 1967)
Olsson (Sandy; *Grease*, 1978)
Orange (Mr; *Reservoir Dogs*, 1991)
Parker (Bonnie; *Bonnie and Clyde*, 1967)
Pierce (Mildred; *Mildred Pierce*, 1945)
Powell (Preacher Harry; *The Night of the Hunter*, 1955)
Powers (Austin; *Austin Powers: International Man of Mystery*, 1997, et seq)
Rabbit (Jessica; *Who Framed Roger Rabbit*, 1988)
Rabbit (Roger; *Who Framed Roger Rabbit*, 1988)
Renton (*Trainspotting*, 1995)
Ripley (Ellen; *Alien*, 1979, et seq)
Rubini (Marcello; *La Dolce Vita*, 1960)
Selden (Kathy; *Singin' in the Rain*, 1952)
Serizy (Séverine; *Belle de Jour*, 1967)
Shears (Commander; *The Bridge on the River Kwai*, 1957)
Singer (Alvy; *Annie Hall*, 1977)
Sylvia (*La Dolce Vita*, 1960)
Taylor (George; *Planet of the Apes*, 1967)
Taylor (Lieutenant Dan; *Forrest Gump*, 1994)
Temple (Nora; *Key Largo*, 1948)
Turner (Will; *Pirates of the Caribbean*, 2003, et seq)
Warden (Major; *The Bridge on the River Kwai*, 1957)

07 Babbitt (Charlie; *Rain Man*, 1988)
Babbitt (Raymond; *Rain Man*, 1988)
Blondie (*The Good, the Bad, and the Ugly*, 1966)
Burnham (Lester; *American Beauty*, 1999)
Clayton (Michael; *Michael Clayton*, 2007)
Daniels (Melanie; *The Birds*, 1963)
Deckard (Rick; *Blade Runner*, 1982)
DeLarge (Alex; *A Clockwork Orange*, 1971)
Desmond (Norma; *Sunset Boulevard*, 1950)
Dillard (Preston; *Jezebel*, 1938)
Edwards (Ethan; *The Searchers*, 1956)
Forrest (Alex; *Fatal Attraction*, 1987)
Higgins (Professor Henry; *My Fair Lady*, 1964)
Kendall (Eve; *North by Northwest*, 1959)

Kilgore (Lieutenant Colonel Bill; *Apocalypse Now*, 1979)
Krueger (Freddy; *A Nightmare on Elm Street*, 1984, et seq)
La Motta (Jake; *Raging Bull*, 1980)
MacGuff (Juno; *Juno*, 2007)
Marlowe (Philip; *The Big Sleep*, 1946)
Marsden (Julie; *Jezebel*, 1938)
Maximus (*Gladiator*, 2000)
McClane (John; *Die Hard*, 1988, et seq)
McCloud (Frank; *Key Largo*, 1948)
Miniver (Kay; *Mrs Miniver*, 1942)
Montana (Tony; *Scarface*, 1983)
Montoya (Inigo; *The Princess Bride*, 1987)
Poulain (Amélie; *Amélie*, 2001)
Ratched (Nurse; *One Flew Over the Cuckoo's Nest*, 1975)
Serpico (Frank; *Serpico*, 1973)
Sick Boy (*Trainspotting*, 1995)
Sparrow (Captain Jack; *Pirates of the Caribbean*, 2003, et seq)
Spicoli (Jeff; *Fast Times at Ridgemont High*, 1982)
Travers (Jerry; *Top Hat*, 1935)
Tremont (Dale; *Top Hat*, 1935)
Trinity (*The Matrix*, 1999, et seq)
Valiant (Eddie; *Who Framed Roger Rabbit*, 1988)
Vallens (Dorothy; *Blue Velvet*, 1986)
Ventura (Ace; *Ace Ventura: Pet Detective*, 1994, et seq)
Westley (*The Princess Bride*, 1987)
Willard (Captain Benjamin L; *Apocalypse Now*, 1979)

08 Barbossa (Captain; *Pirates of the Caribbean*, 2003, et seq)
Beaumont (Jeffrey; *Blue Velvet*, 1986)
Benedict (Jordan 'Bick'; *Giant*, 1956)
Benedict (Leslie Lynnton; *Giant*, 1956)
Braddock (Benjamin; *The Graduate*, 1967)
Callahan (Harry; *Dirty Harry*, 1971, et seq)
Calloway (Major; *The Third Man*, 1949)
Channing (Margo; *All About Eve*, 1950)
Clouseau (Inspector Jacques; *The Pink Panther*, 1963, et seq)
Corleone (Don Vito; *The Godfather*, 1972)
Corleone (Michael; *The Godfather*, 1972, et seq)
Corleone (Santino 'Sonny'; *The Godfather*, 1972)
Dufresne (Andy; *The Shawshank Redemption*, 1994)
Ferguson (John 'Scottie'; *Vertigo*, 1958)
Freemont (Lisa Carol; *Rear Window*, 1954)
Friendly (Johnny; *On the Waterfront*, 1954)
Greenway (Aurora; *Terms of Endearment*, 1983, et seq)
Hirayama (Shukichi; *Tokyo Story*, 1953)

King Kong (*King Kong*, 1933/2005)
Kowalski (Stanley; *A Streetcar Named Desire*, 1951)
Kowalski (Stella; *A Streetcar Named Desire*, 1951)
Lockwood (Don; *Singin' in the Rain*, 1952)
Mathilda (*Léon*, 1994)
McMurphy (Randle Patrick; *One Flew Over the Cuckoo's Nest*, 1975)
Mitchell (Pete 'Maverick'; *Top Gun*, 1986)
Morpheus (*The Matrix*, 1999, et seq)
Murtaugh (Roger; *Lethal Weapon*, 1987, et seq)
Robinson (Mrs; *The Graduate*, 1967)
Somerset (Detective-Lieutenant William; *Seven*, 1995)
Starling (Clarice; *The Silence of the Lambs*, 1991, et seq)
Superman (*Superman*, 1978, et seq)
Torrance (Jack; *The Shining*, 1980)
von Trapp (Captain Gaylord; *The Sound of Music*, 1965)

09 Breedlove (Garrett; *Terms of Endearment*, 1983, et seq)
Buttercup (*The Princess Bride*, 1987)
Chewbacca (*Star Wars*, 1977, et seq)
Cornelius (*Planet of the Apes*, 1967)
Darth Maul (*Star Wars Episode I: The Phantom Menace*, 1999)
Doolittle (Eliza; *My Fair Lady*, 1964)
Gallagher (Dan; *Fatal Attraction*, 1987)
Golightly (Holly; *Breakfast at Tiffany's*, 1961)
Gunderson (Marge; *Fargo*, 1996)
Hunsecker (J J; *Sweet Smell of Success*, 1957)
Jefferies (L B 'Jeff'; *Rear Window*, 1954)
Kutschera (Maria Augusta; *The Sound of Music*, 1965)
Nicholson (Colonel; *The Bridge on the River Kwai*, 1957)
Plainview (Daniel; *There Will Be Blood*, 2007)
Skywalker (Anakin; *Star Wars Episode I: The Phantom Menace*, 1999, et seq)
Skywalker (Luke; *Star Wars*, 1977, et seq)
Thornhill (Roger; *North by Northwest*, 1959)
Vincennes (Jack; *LA Confidential*, 1997)
Winnfield (Jules; *Pulp Fiction*, 1994)
Yakushova (Nina 'Ninotchka' Ivanova; *Ninotchka*, 1939)

10 Agent Smith (*The Matrix*, 1999, et seq)
Darth Vader (*Star Wars*, 1977, et seq)
Terminator (*The Terminator*, 1984, et seq)

11 Dietrichson (Phyllis; *Double Indemnity*, 1944)

Humperdinck (Prince; *The Princess Bride*, 1987)
McCallister (Kevin; *Home Alone*, 1990, et seq)
Rockatansky (Max; *Mad Max*, 1979, et seq)
Strangelove (Dr; *Dr Strangelove or How I Learned to Stop Worrying and Love the Bomb*, 1964)

12 O'Shaughnessy (Brigid; *The Maltese Falcon*, 1941)

Padmé Amidala (Queen; *Star Wars Episode I: The Phantom Menace*, 1999, et seq)
Scissorhands (Edward; *Edward Scissorhands*, 1990)

13 Buzz Lightyear (*Toy Story*, 1995, et seq)
de la Cheyniest (Christine; *La règle du jeu*, 1939)

Film and cinema terms include:

02 3–D	blimp	cowboy	costume
PG	cameo	critic	credits
VO	crane	dailys	cutaway
03 ACE	début	Ealing	dailies
AFI	Dolby®	editor	Dogme 95
ASA	dolly	extras	drive-in
BFI	drama	fade-in	edit out
CGI	extra	freeze	fade-out
cue	flick	gaffer	fantasy
cut!	focus	goodie	film set
CVD	foley	helmer	footage
dub	foyer	insert	heroine
DVD	frame	kidult	ingenue
hit	genre	majors	jump-cut
mix	goody	master	key grip
NFT	hammy	option	lip sync
pan	image	prevue	manager
POV	matte	remake	matinée
R18	mogul	retake	miscast
SFX	morph	review	montage
	movie	rom-com	Moviola®
04 16mm	oater	rushes	musical
35mm	Oscar®	screen	narrate
70mm	pitch	script	noirish
BBFC	prize	sequel	out-take
boom	props	slow-mo	popcorn
cast	sci-fi	splice	prequel
clip	score	studio	preview
edit	set-up	Super 8®	release
epic	short	talkie	reshoot
grip	shots	ticket	showbiz
hero	sound	turkey	stand-in
IMAX®	stunt	weepie	starlet
lens	tie-in	X-rated	sunlamp
porn	usher	zoom in	talkies
reel	video	**07** 180° rule	trailer
take	weepy	actress	trilogy
tilt	**06** action!	advance	TV movie
wipe	auteur	backlit	villain
wrap	baddie	backlot	Western
05 actor	biopic	best boy	whip pan
agent	blow up	billing	zoom out
anime	B-movie	bit part	**08** aperture
award	camera	bootleg	arc light
baddy	censor	cartoon	arthouse
BAFTA	cinema	classic	audition
BECTU	comedy	close-up	bankable

blocking
Brat Pack
cassette
ceremony
cine film
cineplex
Cinerama®
composer
contract
dialogue
director
dissolve
dramatic
emulsion
ensemble
exposure
exterior
festival
film buff
filmgoer
film noir
film star
head room
intercut
in the can
key light
lead role
location
male lead
McGuffin
morphing
on-screen
outgross
pictures
porn star
première
printing
rough cut
scenario
schedule
sequence
soundman
sprocket
stuntman
subtitle
suspense
synopsis
telefilm
thriller
timecode
to camera
wardrobe
Wild West
wrangler
zoom shot

09 angle shot
animation
archetype
auteurism

back story
billboard
blue movie
Bollywood
box office
call sheet
cameraman
cartridge
Celluloid®
chopsocky
cinematic
cinephile
colourize
copyright
crane shot
detective
directrix
docudrama
dolly grip
dolly shot
dope sheet
Dutch tilt
exhibitor
film-maker
film still
film stock
filmstrip
flashback
franchise
Hollywood
indie film
letterbox
MacGuffin
melodrama
multiplex
off-camera
off-screen
post-synch
projector
publicist
publicity
rack focus
recording
recordist
red carpet
road movie
shoot-'em-up
showbizzy
skinflick
slapstick
snuff film
soft focus
spotlight
Steadicam®
storyline
subtitled
superstar
swing gang
theme song

theme tune
time-lapse
title role
treatment
video grab
voice-over
wrap party
xenon lamp

10 action film
action hero
adaptation
blue screen
body double
buddy movie
Capraesque
cartoonist
censorship
chick flick
cinema-goer
ciné vérité
claymation
colour film
continuity
cowboy shot
crowd scene
dénouement
developing
double bill
featurette
female lead
film rights
fullscreen
head-on shot
horror film
horse opera
Kleig light
Klieg light
leading man
movie house
movie-maker
on location
pixilation
screenplay
screen test
second unit
seventh art
silent film
sleeper hit
slow-motion
snuff movie
sound mixer
soundstage
soundtrack
space opera
star system
stop-motion
storyboard
stuntwoman
tear-jerker

that's a wrap!
ultra-rapid
walk-on part
widescreen

11 art director
aspect ratio
black comedy
blockbuster
canted angle
certificate
CinemaScope®
cliffhanger
comedy drama
cutting room
cyber cinema
day-for-night
Disneyesque
distributor
documentary
dolly tracks
Europudding
fade-to-black
feature film
femme fatale
filmography
foley artist
freeze-frame
hairstylist
intertitles
lap dissolve
leading lady
martial arts
matinée idol
merchandise
mise en scène
mood montage
pixillation
pornography
protagonist
release date
reverse shot
running time
set designer
slasher film
sound effect
split screen
star-studded
synchronize
Technicolor®
title design

12 Academy Award®
Biblical epic
bird's-eye shot
bird's-eye view
boom operator
camera loader
casting couch
choreography

chromakeying
cinemathèque
cinéma vérité
clapperboard
co-production
credit titles
crosscutting
director's cut
eyeline match
film magazine
flashforward
Hitchcockian
magic lantern
make-up artist
maltese cross
method acting
movie theatre
overcranking
picture house
post-synching
quota quickie
reverse angle
rockumentary
screenwriter
script doctor
scriptwriter
shallow focus
short subject

show business
shutter speed
silver screen
slasher movie
sneak preview
splatter film
swashbuckler
tracking shot
working title

13 black and white
character part
choreographer
cinematically
ciné projector
clapper loader
continuity man
deepfocus shot
dialogue coach
diegetic sound
digital camera
disaster movie
dream sequence
Expressionism
feature-length
French New Wave
grande vedette
in development

location scout
medium close-up
merchandizing
motion picture
nouvelle Vague
preproduction
projectionist
shot selection
splatter movie
undercranking
variable focus

14 anamorphic lens
available light
back-projection
blaxploitation
cinematography
continuity girl
courtroom drama
digital editing
full-length shot
hand-held camera
knee-length shot
medium long shot
opening credits
opening weekend
post-production
production crew

property master
ripple dissolve
science-fiction
shooting script
special effects
supporting role
travelling shot

15 background noise
behind the scenes
casting director
cinematographer
cinematographic
comedy of
    manners
incidental music
location manager
non-speaking role
panoramic camera
point of view shot
screwball comedy
semidocumentary
shot composition
shot/reverse shot
stop-frame camera
supporting actor
sword and sorcery
swords and sandal

See also **cinema**; **director**; **James Bond**

finance

Terms used in finance include:		
03 ATM	bourse	e-banking
bid	broker	equities
CTF	bubble	Eurobond
EMU	buy-out	leverage
EPS	listed	new issue
FSA	Nasdaq	offshore
ISA	Nikkei	par value
PEP	quoted	sub-prime
RPI	Sensex	takeover
SIB	**07** annuity	Talisman
VCT	auction	TechMARK
04 OFEX	Big Bang	**09** allotment
stag	bullion	bell curve
05 bears	capital	commodity
bonds	futures	debenture
bulls	gearing	debit card
CREST	placing	endowment
gilts	**08** base rate	flotation
LIFFE	blue chip	focus fund
SERPS	break fee	gazumping
SIPPS	cash flow	hedge fund
TESSA	churning	inflation
yield	clawback	liquidity
06 bidder	dawn raid	loan stock
	dividend	ombudsman

portfolio
unit trust
10 bear market
boiler room
bonus issue
bucket shop
bull market
Bundesbank
CAC 40 index
call option
charge card
credit card
day trading
grey market
kerb market
mutual fund
prospectus
redemption
remortgage
securities
settlement
11 Chinese wall
common stock
derivatives
equity bonds
fund manager
golden share
index linked
like for like
liquidation
Lloyds names
managed bond

market maker
rights issue
share option
stockbroker
tracker fund
underwriter
white knight
12 affinity card
amortization
balance sheet
banker's draft
bridging loan
concert party
contract note
depreciation
glamour stock
interest rate
microfinance
offer for sale
orphan assets
share dealing
traded option
umbrella fund
13 Bank of England
best execution
corporate bond
dividend cover
equity markets
final dividend
fixed interest
listed company
mutual society

ordinary share
pension scheme
precipice bond
privatization
stock exchange
term insurance
14 bearer security
bid-offer spread
capitalization
deferred shares
double witching
inheritance tax
insider dealing
Lloyds of London
negative equity
offer-bid spread
triple witching
unlisted shares
unquoted shares
windfall shares
15 bed and breakfast
beneficial owner
building society
capital gains tax
demutualization
golden handcuffs
guaranteed stock
interim dividend
investment trust
preference share
secondary market
with-profits bond

See also **business**; **economics**

Finland

Cities and notable towns in Finland include:

04 Oulu
Pori
05 Espoo
Lahti

Turku

Vaasa

06 Vantaa

07 Tampere

08 Helsinki

09 Rovaniemi

Administrative divisions of Finland, with regional capitals:

04 Oulu (Oulu)
05 Åland (Mariehamn)
07 Lapland (Rovaniemi)

14 Eastern Finland (Mikkeli)
Western Finland (Turku)
15 Southern Finland (Hämeenlinna)

Finnish landmarks include:

05 Manta
07 Ateneum
Lapland
10 Seurasaari
11 Havis Amanda

Korkeasaari
Lenin Museum
Suomenlinna
Turku Castle
12 Åland Islands
Lake District

Pispala Ridge
Senaatintori
Senate Square
13 Finlandia Hall
Lake Näsijärvi
Lake Pyhäjärvi

Luostarinmäki
Pyynikki Ridge
Ravadasköngäs
14 Kalevala Church
Turku Cathedral
15 Church in the Rock

fireplace

Fireplaces include:

04 kiln	stove	firebox	**10** backboiler
oven	**06** boiler	furnace	**11** incinerator
05 forge	hearth	gas fire	wood burning
grate	**07** bonfire	**08** campfire	**12** electric fire
ingle	brazier	open fire	**13** paraffin stove

firework

Fireworks include:

04 cake	fisgig	sparkler	**11** firecracker
mine	fizgig	whizbang	firewriting
pioy	maroon	**09** firedrake	jumping-jack
05 devil	petard	girandola	roman candle
flare	rocket	girandole	tourbillion
gerbe	**07** cracker	sky-rocket	**14** Catherine wheel
peeoy	serpent	throw-down	Chinese cracker
pioye	volcano	waterfall	indoor firework
shell	**08** flip-flop	whizz-bang	**15** Pharaoh's serpent
squib	fountain	**10** golden rain	Waterloo cracker
wheel	pinwheel	Indian fire	
06 banger	slap-bang	tourbillon	

firth

Firths include:

03 Tay (Scotland)	Moray (Scotland)	**08** Cromarty (Scotland)
04 Lorn (Scotland)		Pentland (Scotland)
Wide (Scotland)	**06** Beauly (Scotland)	Stronsay (Scotland)
05 Clyde (Scotland)	Solway (England/Scotland)	Szczecin (Poland)
Forth (Scotland)	Thames (New Zealand)	**09** Inverness (Scotland)
Lorne (Scotland)	**07** Dornoch (Scotland)	**14** North Ronaldsay (Scotland)
	Westray (Scotland)	

fish

Fish include:

02 ai	bley	luce	tang
id	brit	moki	tuna
03 ahi	carp	opah	wels
ayu	cero	orfe	**05** ablet
bar	chad	pike	basse
bib	char	pope	blain
cod	chub	pout	bleak
dab	dace	rudd	bream
eel	dare	ruff	brill
gar	dart	scad	charr
ide	dory	scat	cisco
ray	fugu	scup	cobia
sar	gade	seer	coley
04 barb	goby	seir	danio
bass	hake	shad	Doras
blay	hoki	sild	doree
	ling	sole	

elops
grunt
guppy
lance
loach
lythe
manta
molly
perai
perch
pirai
platy
pogge
roach
ruffe
sargo
saury
shark
skate
smelt
sprat
squid
tench
tetra
torsk
trout
tunny
wahoo
whelk
whiff
zebra

06 anabas
angler
barbel
bigeye
blenny
bonito
bowfin
brassy
bumalo
burbot
callop
caplin
caribe
conger
conner
cottid
cottus
cunner
dentex
doctor
dorado
gadoid
goramy
gulper
gunnel
gurami
gurnet

inanga
jerker
kipper
launce
louvar
mahsir
maigre
marlin
meagre
medaka
minnow
mullet
murena
piraña
piraya
plaice
puffer
remora
robalo
roughy
runner
saithe
salmon
sander
sardel
sargos
sargus
sea cat
serran
shanny
shiner
skelly
sparid
sucker
tailor
tarpon
tautog
turbot
vendis
wrasse
zander
zingel

07 alewife
anchovy
azurine
batfish
bergylt
bloater
box-fish
bummalo
cabezon
candiru
capelin
catfish
cavalla
cavally
chimera
cichlid

clupeid
codfish
cowfish
crucian
crusian
dogfish
dolphin
drummer
escolar
garfish
garpike
gemfish
goldeye
gourami
grouper
growler
grunion
grunter
gudgeon
gurnard
haddock
halibut
herring
hogfish
houting
ice fish
inconnu
ink-fish
kahawai
lamprey
lampuki
mahseer
medacca
mooneye
morwong
mudfish
muraena
oar fish
octopus
old wife
panchax
pig-fish
pinfish
piranha
pollack
pollock
pomfret
pompano
pupfish
rat-tail
redfish
red moki
sandeel
sardine
sculpin
sea bass
seacock
sea pike

silurid
sleeper
snapper
sockeye
sparoid
sunfish
topknot
torpedo
vendace
vendiss
whiting

08 albacore
anableps
arapaima
atherine
bandfish
billfish
bloodfin
blowfish
bluefish
boarfish
bonefish
brisling
bullhead
carangid
characid
characin
chimaera
chimerid
clupeoid
coalfish
corkwing
cow-pilot
devil ray
dragonet
drumfish
eagle ray
fallfish
file fish
flathead
flounder
forktail
four-eyes
frogfish
gambusia
gilt-head
goat fish
goldfish
grayling
greeneye
grey-fish
hair-tail
halfbeak
hardhead
John Dory
kabeljou
kingfish
luderick

lumpfish
mackerel
manta ray
menhaden
milkfish
monkfish
moonfish
moray eel
mulloway
nannygai
pilchard
pipefish
rascasse
redbelly
rock bass
rockfish
rockling
rosefish
saibling
sailfish
sardelle
scopelid
scuppaug
sea bream
seahorse
sea perch
sea raven
sea robin
sea snail
skipjack
stingray
sturgeon
surffish
tilefish
toadfish
tuna fish
weakfish
wolffish

09 amber-fish
amberjack
angelfish
argentine
barracuda
black bass
blackfish
blindfish
carangoid
chaetodon
clingfish
conger-eel
coral-fish
coryphene
crab-eater
cramp-fish
Dover sole
globe fish
goldsinny

golomynka
goose-fish
grass carp
greenling
grenadier
hornyhead
hottentot
kabeljouw
killifish
lemon sole
mud minnow
neon tetra
pilot fish
queenfish
red mullet
red salmon
rock perch
round fish
sand smelt
scombroid
scopeloid
selachian
sheatfish
snailfish
snakehead
spadefish
spearfish
stargazer
steenbras
stone bass
stonefish
sweetfish
sweetlips
swine-fish
swordfish
swordtail
tiger fish
toothfish
topminnow
trumpeter
trunkfish
tunny fish
whitebait
whitebass
wreck fish

10 angler fish
archerfish
arctic char
barracouta
barramundi
bitterling
Bombay duck
bottle-fish
candlefish
cockabully
coffer-fish
craigfluke

cuttlefish
cycloidian
damselfish
demoiselle
dragon-fish
flutemouth
flying fish
golden orfe
grey mullet
groundling
hammer-fish
hammerhead
jellied eel
lancet fish
largemouth
lizardfish
lumpsucker
Maori chief
mossbunker
nettle-fish
ocean perch
paddlefish
parrot-fish
pikeminnow
puffer fish
rabbitfish
red snapper
ribbonfish
rock salmon
rock turbot
rudderfish
sacred fish
scorpaenid
sea swallow
serrasalmo
sheathfish
sheep's-head
silverfish
smallmouth
squeteague
stone loach
suckerfish
tiger shark
torpedo ray
whale shark

11 anemone fish
bellows-fish
blue whiting
buffalo fish
cutlass fish
Dolly Varden
dolphin fish
electric eel
electric ray
Eurypharynx
lake herring
lantern fish

lophobranch
moorish idol
muskellunge
oxyrhynchus
peacock-fish
pelican-fish
salmon trout
sea hedgehog
sea scorpion
silversides
snail darter
stickleback
sucking fish
surgeon fish
triggerfish
trumpetfish
walking fish
whistle fish
whiting pout

12 basking shark
father-lasher
fighting fish
four-eyed fish
mosquito fish
orange roughy
paradise fish
parrot-wrasse
rainbow trout
scabbard fish
scorpion fish
sea porcupine
sergeant fish
skipjack tuna
smooth blenny
squirrel fish
St Peter's fish
whiptail hake

13 armed bullhead
butterfly fish
Chinook salmon
climbing perch
horse mackerel
labyrinth fish
northern porgy
porcupine fish
Sergeant Baker
sergeant-major
sockeye salmon
yellow fin tuna

14 blueback salmon

15 great white shark
hammerhead shark
Spanish mackerel

Aquarium fish include:

04 barb

05 danio
    guppy
    loach
    tetra
    zebra

06 discus
    goramy
    gurami

07 catfish
    crucian
    crusian
    fantail

    gourami
    koi carp
    piranha

08 goldfish

09 angelfish
    clownfish
    neon tetra
    tiger barb

10 clown loach
    golden barb
    zebra danio

11 Jack Dempsey

12 cardinal fish
    dwarf cichlid
    dwarf gourami
    sucking loach

13 comet goldfish
    common hatchet
    Malawi cichlid

14 common goldfish
    kissing gourami
    red-finned shark
    walking catfish

15 fantail goldfish

See also **eel**; **poison**

fishing

Fishing flies include:

03 bob
    dry
    wet

04 harl

    herl
    tail

05 sedge

06 doctor

    hackle
    palmer
    salmon

07 watchet

09 hairy Mary
    Jock Scott

10 cock-a-bondy

Fishing and angling terms include:

03 dub
    fly
    gig
    jig
    net
    rod
    set
    tag
    tie

04 bait
    barb
    bite
    boat
    bunt
    cast
    drag
    gimp
    haaf
    hook
    lead
    line
    lure
    reel
    sean
    trot
    whip

05 alder
    angle

    baker
    braid
    catch
    clean
    creel
    drail
    dress
    poach
    seine
    snell
    trace
    troll

06 angler
    antron
    bobber
    bullet
    coarse
    dibble
    dip net
    dry-fly
    fly-rod
    gentle
    gillie
    leader
    norsel
    sagene
    sinker
    tackle
    waders

    wet-fly

07 angling
    bycatch
    catworm
    chromer
    drifter
    drop-fly
    dropper
    flybook
    flyline
    fly reel
    ghillie
    gill net
    harpoon
    keepnet
    monofil
    piscary
    plummet
    pout net
    setline
    spinner

08 backcast
    buzzbait
    drift net
    give line
    hand line
    roll cast
    trotline

09 brandling
    drabbling
    egg sinker
    false cast
    halieutic
    indicator
    leger bait
    leger line
    night-line
    piscatory
    propeller

10 bait bucket
    baitrunner
    casting arc
    casting-net
    double haul
    fly casting
    fly fishing
    halieutics
    landing net
    ledger bait
    ledger line
    line grease
    multiplier
    net-fishing
    sea-fishing
    treble hook
    weigh sling

11 forward cast
game fishing
haaf-fishing
line-fishing
paternoster
sinking line
spinner bait

spinning rod
surfcasting

12 black-fishing
drifter float
drift fishing
floating line

monofilament
night crawler
night-fishery
shooting line
trout-fishing
unhooking mat
whale-fishing

13 bottom-fishing
coarse fishing
ground-angling
salmon-fishing

14 baitcasting rod

15 catch-and-release

flag

Flag types include:

03 red

04 blue
jack

05 black
house
peter
pilot
whiff

whift

06 banner
burgee
cornet
ensign
fanion
pennon
prayer

signal
yellow

07 bunting
colours
pennant

08 banderol
gonfalon
standard

streamer
vexillum

09 blackjack
chequered
oriflamme
tricolour

10 quarantine

11 swallow tail

Flags include:

05 Union

07 Saltire

08 Crescent
Old Glory
Red Cross

09 Blue Peter
dannebrog
Red Dragon

Red Duster
Red Ensign
Rising Sun
Tricolour
Union Jack

10 Blue Ensign
Jolly Roger
Yellow Jack

11 Olympic Flag
Red Crescent
White Ensign

12 Stars and Bars

13 Royal Standard

15 Cross of St George
Hammer and Sickle
Stars and Stripes

flightless bird *see* bird

flower

Flower parts include:

05 calyx
ovary
ovule
petal
sepal
spike
stalk
style

torus
umbel

06 anther
carpel
corymb
pistil
raceme

spadix
stamen
stigma

07 corolla
nectary
panicle
pedicel

08 filament
thalamus

09 capitulum
dichasium
gynoecium

10 receptacle

11 monochasium

Garden flowers include:

04 aloe
flag
iris
lily
pink
rose
sego

05 aster

calla
camas
daisy
lotus
lupin
pansy
phlox
poppy

stock
tulip
viola
yucca

06 allium
azalea
camash
camass

crinum
crocus
dahlia
nerine
Nuphar
orchid
salvia
Scilla

smilax
squill
violet
zinnia

07 alyssum
anemone
begonia
campion
candock
cowslip
day-lily
freesia
fuchsia
lobelia
may-lily
nemesia
peacock
petunia
primula
quamash
Tritoma
verbena

08 arum lily
asphodel
bluebell
curtonus
cyclamen
daffodil
dianthus
foxglove
galtonia
gardenia
geranium
gladioli

gloriosa
harebell
hyacinth
marigold
martagon
Nenuphar
Phormium
pond lily
primrose
snowdrop
sweet pea
trillium
Turk's cap

09 amaryllis
aubrietia
calendula
calla lily
candytuft
carnation
crocosmia
digitalis
gladiolus
grass tree
herb Paris
hollyhock
Kniphofia
narcissus
nicotiana
regal lily
Richardia
snowflake
sunflower
tiger lily
torch lily

10 agapanthus
aspidistra
busy lizzie
Canada lily
chionodoxa
coneflower
cornflower
delphinium
Easter lily
fritillary
giant rouge
nasturtium
orange-lily
poinsettia
polyanthus
ragged-lady
snake's head
snapdragon
solfaterre
sweet briar
wallflower
wand flower

11 acidanthera
African lily
antirrhinum
cabbage tree
Convallaria
erythronium
forget-me-not
gillyflower
hippeastrum
lapeirousia
love-in-a-mist
Madonna lily

naked ladies
red-hot poker
rose campion
spatterdock
sternbergia
tiger flower

12 devil-in-a-bush
flower of Jove
Hemerocallis
Ornithogalum
rose geranium
sarsaparilla
Solomon's seal
sweet william
Turk's cap lily
victoria lily
wild hyacinth
Zantedeschia

13 African violet
butcher's broom
carrion-flower
chrysanthemum
crown imperial
eglantine rose
grape hyacinth
lily of the Nile
striped squill
winter aconite

14 belladonna lily
glory of the snow
Ithuriel's spear

15 dog's tooth violet
lily of the valley
star of Bethlehem

Wild flowers include:

05 clary
daisy
poppy

06 clover
oxslip
teasel
violet
yarrow

07 ale hoof
bistort
campion
comfrey
cowslip
dog rose
goldcup
heather

08 bluebell

crowfoot
dog daisy
foxglove
harebell
lungwort
primrose
rock rose
self-heal
toadflax
wild iris

09 Aaron's rod
birth-wort
broomrape
buttercup
celandine
columbine
edelweiss
goldenrod

horsetail
moneywort
stonecrop
water lily
wild pansy

10 crane's bill
goatsbeard
heartsease
lady's smock
marguerite
masterwort
oxeye daisy
pennyroyal
wild endive
wild orchid

11 ragged robin
wild chicory

wood anemone

12 common mallow
cuckoo flower
great mullein
lady's slipper
solomon's seal
white campion
yellow rocket

13 butter-and-eggs
field cow-wheat
shepherd's club
wild gladiolus

14 black-eyed susan
bladder campion
common toadflax
multiflora rose

15 New England aster

See also **birth symbol**; **emblem**; **hybrid**; **lily**; **orchid**; **plant**

fly

Flies include:

03 bee	pium	cuckoo	Spanish
bot	sand	forest	vinegar
day	**05** alder	motuca	**08** glossina
dor	birch	muscid	ruby-tail
gad	black	mutuca	scorpion
hop	crane	pomace	sheep ked
ked	drone	robber	simulium
may	flesh	stable	tachinid
med	froth	tipula	
04 beet	fruit	tsetse	**09** cantharis
blow	horse	turnip	ichneumon
boat	house	tzetse	screw-worm
bulb	hover	tzetze	
bush	march	warble	**10** bluebottle
cleg	midge	**07** blister	Cecidomyia
corn	onion	brommer	drosophila
deer	sedge	cabbage	spittle bug
dung	snake	cluster	**11** biting midge
fire	snipe	diptera	buffalo gnat
frit	water	dolphin	cabbage-root
gnat	wheat	harvest	greenbottle
gout	**06** blowie	Hessian	**12** cheesehopper
kade	caddis	lantern	**13** cheese skipper
lamp	carrot	sciarid	spittle insect
meat		smother	

See also **fishing**; **insect**

folk

Folk music groups include:

06 Pogues	Corries	**10** The Corries	**12** Capercaillie
Runrig	**09** Dubliners	The Weavers	Steeleye Span
07 Clannad	The Pogues	**11** Lindisfarne	**13** The Chieftains

Folk musicians and singers include:

03 Gow (Niel; 1727–1807, Scottish)

04 Baez (Joan; 1941– , US)
Bain (Aly; 1946– , Scottish)
Ives (Burl; 1909–95, US)
Vega (Suzanne; 1959– , US)

05 Bragg (Billy; 1947– , English)
Dylan (Bob; 1941– , US)
Makem (Tommy; 1932–2007, Northern Irish)
Moore (Christy; 1945– , Irish)
Sharp (Cecil James; 1859–1924, English)
Simon (Paul; 1941– , US)
Waits (Tom; 1949– , US)

06 Carthy (Martin; 1941– , English)
Clancy (Tom, 1924–90, Irish)
Fisher (Archie; 1939– , Scottish)

Foster (Stephen Collins; 1826–64, US)
Fraser (Marjory Kennedy; 1857–1930, Scottish)
Imlach (Hamish; 1940–96, Indian/British)
Mackay (Charles; 1814–89, Scottish)
Martyn (John; 1948– , English)
McLean (Don; 1945– , US)
McTell (Ralph; 1944– , English)
Nairne (Carolina; 1766–1845, Scottish)
Paxton (Tom; 1937– , US)
Seeger (Pete; 1919– , US)

07 Burgess (John Davie; 1934–2005, Scottish)
Cassidy (Eva; 1963–96, US)
Collins (Judy; 1939– , US)
Dickson (Barbara; 1947– , Scottish)
Donegan (Lonnie; 1931–2002, Scottish)
Donovan (1946– , Scottish)

Elliott (Ramblin' Jack; 1931– , US)
Gaughan (Dick; 1948– , Scottish)
Guthrie (Woody; 1912–67, US)
MacColl (Ewan; 1915–89, Scottish)
Redpath (Jean; 1937– , Scottish)
Skinner (James Scott; 1843–1927, Scottish)
Thomson (George; 1757–1851)
08 Marshall (William; 1748–1833, Scottish)
Mitchell (Joni; 1943– , Canadian)
Morrison (Van; 1945– , Northern Irish)

See also **pop**

O'Donnell (Daniel; 1961– , Irish)
Rafferty (Gerry; 1947– , Scottish)
Thompson (Richard; 1949– , English)
09 Henderson (Hamish; 1919–2002, Scottish)
Leadbelly (1888–1949, US)
Robertson (Jeannie; 1908–75, Scottish)
10 Wainwright (Loudon, III; 1946– , US)
Williamson (Roy; 1936–90, Scottish)
11 Sainte-Marie (Buffy; 1941/42– , US)

food

Foods include:			
03 dal	Quorn®	ragout	soufflé
dip	raita	salami	stovies
pie	ramen	samosa	Tabasco®
poi	rösti	scampi	tartare
04 cake	salad	subgum	tempura
dhal	salmi	tahina	terrine
hash	salsa	tamale	timbale
luau	satay	tsamba	tostada
mash	sauce	**07** biryani	**08** amaretti
mint	sushi	biscuit	barbecue
olio	tikka	borscht	bechamel
soss	toast	bourbon	biriyani
soup	wafer	burrito	biscotto
stew	Wimpy®	chorizo	brandade
taco	**06** bhajee	chowder	calamari
tofu	Big Mac®	chutney	chillada
wrap	borsch	compote	chop suey
05 apple	burgoo	corn dog	chow mein
bacon	canapé	cracker	coleslaw
balti	caviar	crowdie	consommé
bhaji	cheese	fajitas	coq au vin
boxty	cookie	falafel	couscous
brose	cou-cou	felafel	dog's-body
broth	faggot	fritter	dressing
champ	fajita	friture	empanada
chips	fondue	gnocchi	feijoada
curry	gratin	goulash	fishcake
dolma	haggis	gravlax	flapjack
grits	hot dog	lasagne	frittata
gumbo	hotpot	mesclun	gado-gado
kebab	hummus	mustard	gazpacho
kofta	kimchi	oatcake	halloumi
laksa	kipper	polenta	kedgeree
latke	mousse	ramakin	macaroon
maror	paella	ramekin	moussaka
pasta	pakora	rarebit	nut roast
pesto	panada	ratafia	olive oil
pilau	panini	risotto	omelette
pilaw	parkin	sashimi	porridge
pilow	pilaff	sausage	pot-roast
pizza	quiche	seafood	raclette

ramequin
sandwich
souvlaki
tandoori
teriyaki
tortilla
tzatziki
vindaloo
yakitori
zwieback
09 casserole
cassoulet
colcannon
condiment
crab stick
cranberry
digestive
enchilada
fricassee
galantine
Garibaldi
ginger nut
gravadlax
guacamole
hamburger
howtowdie
Irish stew
jambalaya
macédoine

meatballs
nut cutlet
petit four
reistafel
rijstafel
souvlakia
succotash
tabbouleh
vol-au-vent
10 brandy snap
bush tucker
cannelloni
cottage pie
crispbread
enchiladas
fish-finger
Florentine
ginger snap
Greek salad
green salad
mayonnaise
minestrone
mixed grill
peperonata
quesadilla
rijstaffel
salad cream
salmagundi
salmagundy

sauerkraut
shortbread
stroganoff
white sauce
11 baba ganoush
caesar salad
cockaleekie
frankfurter
French fries
fritto misto
gefilte fish
hollandaise
horseradish
imam bayildi
potato salad
ratatouille
rumblethump
saltimbocca
sauerbraten
smorgasbord
soda cracker
vichyssoise
vinaigrette
winter salad
12 cream cracker
eggs Benedict
fish and chips
langue de chat
mulligatawny

pease pudding
pissaladière
red wine sauce
rumblethumps
Russian salad
shepherd's pie
taramasalata
Waldorf salad
water biscuit
welsh rarebit
13 aubergine roll
bouillabaisse
fisherman's pie
prawn cocktail
salade niçoise
toad-in-the-hole
tomato ketchup
14 chilli con carne
French dressing
macaroni cheese
pickled herring
Scotch woodcock
white wine sauce
Worcestershire
15 balsamic vinegar
bubble and squeak
stuffed mushroom
Wiener schnitzel

Dishes include:

03 dal
pie
04 flan
fool
hash
pâté
puff
soup
stew
tart
05 adobo
crêpe
curry
daube
grill
jelly
kebab
pasty
patty
pilau
pizza
roast
salad
tapas

06 bhajee
burger
fondue
fu yung
gratin
mousse
paella
pastry
quiche
ragout
samosa
sorbet
tamale
trifle
waffle
07 chowder
cobbler
compôte
crumble
fajitas
fritter
galette
goulash
lasagne

pad thai
pancake
parfait
pavlova
platter
pudding
risotto
rissole
soufflé
stir-fry
terrine
08 barbecue
chop suey
chow mein
cocktail
consommé
dolmades
dumpling
ice cream
kedgeree
meringue
moussaka
omelette
pot-roast

syllabub
turnover
09 casserole
cassoulet
charlotte
croquette
empanadas
enchilada
fricassée
galantine
macédoine
paupiette
porchetta
turducken
10 blancmange
blanquette
chaud-froid
cheesecake
spring roll
stroganoff
11 hors-d'oeuvre
ratatouille

See also **baking**; **bean**; **biscuit**; **bread**; **cake**; **cereal**; **cheese**; **cookery**; **curry**; **dairy**; **dessert**; **eating**; **fruit**; **herb**; **meal**; **meat**; **mushroom**; **nut**; **pasta**; **pastry**; **pepper**; **restaurant**; **salad**; **sauce**; **sausage**; **seafood**; **soup**; **spread**; **sugar**; **sweet**; **vegetable**

fool

Lavache (*All's Well that Ends Well*)
08 Dogberry (*Much Ado About Nothing*)
Trinculo (*The Tempest*)

09 Autolycus (*A Winter's Tale*)
Thersites (*Troilus and Cressida*)
10 Touchstone (*As You Like It*)

football

English league football teams:

04 Bury
06 Fulham
Yeovil
07 Arsenal
Burnley
Chelsea
Everton
Reading
Walsall
Watford
Wrexham
08 Barnsley
Hull City
Millwall
Port Vale
Rochdale
09 Blackpool
Brentford
Liverpool
Luton Town
Stoke City
10 Aston Villa
Darlington
Gillingham
Portsmouth
Sunderland
11 Bournemouth
Bristol City
Cardiff City
Chester City

Derby County
Grimsby Town
Ipswich Town
Leeds United
Lincoln City
Norwich City
Notts County
Southampton
Swansea City
Swindon Town
12 Boston United
Bradford City
Chesterfield
Coventry City
Leyton Orient
Oxford United
13 Bristol Rovers
Crystal Palace
Leicester City
Mansfield Town
Middlesbrough
Torquay United
West Ham United
Wigan Athletic
14 Birmingham City
Cheltenham Town
Crewe Alexandra
Manchester City
Oldham Athletic
Plymouth Argyle
Shrewsbury Town

Southend United
Tranmere Rovers
15 Blackburn Rovers
Bolton Wanderers
Cambridge United
Doncaster Rovers
Newcastle United
Northampton Town
Preston North End
Rotherham United
Sheffield United
Stockport County
16 Charlton Athletic
Colchester United
Hartlepool United
Huddersfield Town
Macclesfield Town
Manchester United
Milton Keynes Dons
Nottingham Forest
Scunthorpe United
Tottenham Hotspur
17 Queen's Park Rangers
18 Peterborough United
Rushden and Diamonds
Sheffield Wednesday
West Bromwich Albion
21 Brighton and Hove Albion
Kidderminster Harriers
22 Wolverhampton Wanderers

Scottish league football teams:

05 Clyde
06 Celtic
Dundee
Gretna
07 Falkirk
Rangers
08 Aberdeen
Arbroath
East Fife
Montrose
St Mirren
09 Ayr United
Dumbarton
Elgin City
Hibernian

Peterhead
Stranraer
10 Kilmarnock
Livingston
Motherwell
Queen's Park
Ross County
11 Brechin City
Cowdenbeath
Raith Rovers
St Johnstone
12 Albion Rovers
Dundee United
13 Airdrie United
Alloa Athletic

Stenhousemuir
14 Berwick Rangers
Forfar Athletic
Greenock Morton
Partick Thistle
Stirling Albion
15 Queen of the South
17 East Stirlingshire
Heart of Midlothian
18 Hamilton Academical
19 Dunfermline Athletic
26 Inverness Caledonian
Thistle

European football teams include:

04 Ajax (The Netherlands)
05 Lazio (Italy)
 Malmö (Sweden)
 Parma (Italy)
 Porto (Portugal)
06 Alavés (Spain)
 AS Roma (Italy)
 Bastia (France)
 Monaco (France)
 Napoli (Italy)
 Torino (Italy)
07 AC Milan (Italy)
 Antwerp (Belgium)
 Benfica (Portugal)
 Cologne (Germany)
 Español (Spain)
 FC Porto (Portugal)
 Hamburg (Germany)
 Schalke (Germany)
08 Bordeaux (France)
 Juventus (Italy)
 Mallorca (Spain)
 Mechelen (Belgium)
 Salzburg (Austria)
 Tom Tomsk (Russia)
 Valencia (Spain)
09 Barcelona (Spain)
 Feyenoord (The Netherlands)
 FK Austria (Austria)
 Marseille (France)
 Sampdoria (Italy)
 St Etienne (France)
 Stuttgart (Germany)
 SV Hamburg (Germany)
 TSV Munich (Germany)
10 Anderlecht (Belgium)
 Bellinzona (Switzerland)
 Club Bruges (Belgium)
 Club Brugge (Belgium)

 Dynamo Kiev (Ukraine)
 Fiorentina (Italy)
 Inter Milan (Spain)
 Real Madrid (Spain)
11 Bate Borisov (Belarus)
 FC Magdeburg (Germany)
 Ferencvaros (Hungary)
 Galatasaray (Turkey)
 Hajduk Split (Croatia)
 Litex Lovech (Bulgaria)
 MTK Budapest (Hungary)
 Rapid Vienna (Austria)
 Ujpest Dozsa (Hungary)
 Wisla Krakow (Poland)
12 Banik Ostrava (Czech Republic)
 Bayern Munich (Germany)
 Dinamo Zagreb (Croatia)
 Gornik Zabrze (Poland)
 Moscow Dynamo (Russia)
 PSV Eindhoven (The Netherlands)
 Real Zaragoza (Spain)
 Stade de Reims (France)
 Valenciennes (France)
 Werder Bremen (Germany)
13 Carl Zeiss Jena (Germany)
 Dynamo Tbilisi (Georgia)
 IFK Gothenburg (Sweden)
 Nordsjaelland (Denmark)
 Panathinaikos (Greece)
 Standard Liège (Belgium)
14 Athletic Bilbao (Spain)
 Atletico Madrid (Spain)
 Paris St Germain (France)
 Sporting Lisbon (Portugal)
 Twente Enschede (The Netherlands)
15 Bayer Leverkusen (Germany)
 Red Bull Salzburg (Austria)
 Red Star Belgrade (Serbia)
 Shakhtar Donetsk (Ukraine)
 Steaua Bucharest (Romania)

Football club nicknames include:

02 O's (Leyton Orient)
 R's (Queen's Park Rangers)
 U's (Cambridge United/Colchester United/
 Oxford United)
03 Ton (Greenock Morton)
04 Bees (Barnsley/Brentford)
 Boro (Middlesborough)
 City (Brechin City/Elgin City)
 Dale (Rochdale)
 Dons (Aberdeen/Wimbledon)
 Gers (Rangers)
 Jags (Partick Thistle)

 Owls (Sheffield Wednesday)
 Pars (Dunfermline Athletic)
 Pool (Hartlepool United)
 Posh (Peterborough United)
 Rams (Derby County)
 Reds (Liverpool/Nottingham Forest/Stirling
 Albion)
 Sons (Dumbarton)
 Well (Motherwell)
05 Arabs (Dundee United)
 Bhoys (Celtic)
 Binos (Stirling Albion)

Blues (Birmingham City/Chelsea/Stranraer/
  Wycombe Wanderers)
Foxes (Leicester City)
Gills (Gillingham)
Gulls (Torquay United)
Irons (Scunthorpe United)
Lions (Millwall)
Loons (Forfar Athletic)
Shire (East Stirlingshire)
Spurs (Tottenham Hotspur)
Stags (Mansfield Town)
Swans (Swansea City)
Wasps (Alloa Athletic)

06 Accies (Hamilton Academical)
Albion (Stirling Albion)
Bairns (Falkirk)
Blades (Sheffield United)
County (Ross County)
Eagles (Crystal Palace)
Fifers (East Fife)
Hibees (Hibernian)
Killie (Kilmarnock)
Latics (Oldham Athletic/Wigan Athletic)
Pompey (Portsmouth)
Robins (Bristol City/Cheltenham Town/
  Swindon Town/Wrexham)
Rovers (Blackburn Rovers/Doncaster Rovers/
  Raith Rovers/Tranmere Rovers)
Royals (Reading)
Saints (Southampton/St Johnstone)
Tigers (Hull City)
Whites (Leeds United)
Wolves (Wolverhampton Wanderers)

07 Addicks (Charlton Athletic)
Baggies (West Bromich Albion)
Bantams (Bradford City)
Buddies (St Mirren)
Clarets (Burnley)
Glovers (Yeovil Town)
Gunners (Arsenal)
Hammers (West Ham United)
Hatters (Luton Town/Stockport County)
Hornets (Watford)
Magpies (Newcastle United/Notts County)
Pirates (Bristol Rovers)
Potters (Stoke City)
Quakers (Darlington)
Red Imps (Lincoln City)
Shakers (Bury)
Silkmen (Macclesfield Town)
Spiders (Queen's Park)

Terrors (Dundee United)
Toffees (Everton)

08 Blue Toon (Peterhead)
Bully Wee (Clyde)
Canaries (Norwich City)
Cherries (Bournemouth)
Citizens (Manchester City)
Cobblers (Northampton Town)
Diamonds (Airdrie United/Rushden and
  Diamonds)
Harriers (Kidderminster Harriers)
Jam Tarts (Heart of Midlothian)
Mariners (Grimsby Town)
Pilgrims (Boston United/Plymouth Argyle)
Saddlers (Walsall)
Seagulls (Brighton and Hove Albion)
Sky Blues (Coventry City)
Terriers (Huddersfield Town)
Trotters (Bolton Wanderers)
Valiants (Port Vale)
Villains (Aston Villa)
Warriors (Stenhousemuir)

09 Black Cats (Sunderland)
Bluebirds (Cardiff City)
Borderers (Berwick Rangers)
Chairboys (Wycombe Wanderers)
Cottagers (Fulham)
Cumbrians (Carlisle United)
Dark Blues (Dundee)
Honest Men (Ayr United)
Red Devils (Manchester United)
Seasiders (Blackpool)
Shrimpers (Southend United)
Spireites (Chesterfield)
Throstles (West Bromich Albion)
Wee Rovers (Albion Rovers)

10 Blue Brazil (Cowdenbeath)
Doonhamers (Queen of the South)
Lilywhites (Preston North End)
Livvy Lions (Livingston)
Minstermen (York City)
Railwaymen (Crewe Alexandra)
Teddy Bears (Rangers)

11 Gable Endies (Montrose)
Red Lichties (Arbroath)
Tractor Boys (Ipswich Town)

12 Caley Thistle (Inverness Caledonian Thistle)
Merry Millers (Rotherham United)

13 Blue and Whites (Blackburn Rovers)

14 Black and Whites (Elgin City/Gretna)

Football stadia include:

03 JJB (Wigan Athletic)

04 City (Livingston)
Deva (Chester City)

05 Abbey (Cambridge United)
Ibrox (Rangers)

06 Bescot (Walsall)

Reebok (Bolton Wanderers)
07 Anfield (Liverpool)
Ballast (Hamilton Academical)
Balmoor (Peterhead)
Firhill (Partick Thistle)
Fir Park (Motherwell)
Oakwell (Barnsley)
St Mary's (Southampton)

08 Belle Vue (Doncaster Rovers)
Deepdale (Preston North End)
Emirates (Arsenal)
Dens Park (Dundee)
Firs Park (East Stirlingshire)
Gigg Lane (Bury)
Home Park (Plymouth Argyle)
Madejski (Reading)
McAlpine (Huddersfield Town)
Memorial (Bristol Rovers)
Millmoor (Rotherham United)
Molineux (Wolverhampton Wanderers)
Moss Rose (Macclesfield Town)
Nene Park (Rushden and Diamonds)
Spotland (Rochdale)
Turf Moor (Burnley)
Vale Park (Port Vale)
Withdean (Brighton and Hove Albion)

09 Britannia (Stoke City)
Broadwood (Clyde)
Cappielow (Greenock Morton)
Ewood Park (Blackburn Rovers)
Field Mill (Mansfield Town)
Forthbank (Stirling Albion)
Gay Meadow (Shrewsbury Town)
Glebe Park (Brechin City)
Huish Park (Yeovil)
Layer Road (Colchester United)
Links Park (Montrose)
Ochilview (Falkirk)
Pittodrie (Aberdeen)
Plainmoor (Torquay United)
Pride Park (Derby County)
Riverside (Middlesbrough)
Roots Hall (Southend United)
Rugby Park (Kilmarnock)
Sixfields (Northampton Town)
Stair Park (Stranraer)
St Andrews (Birmingham City)
The Kassam (Oxford United)
The New Den (Millwall)
The Valley (Charlton Athletic)
Upton Park (West Ham United)
Villa Park (Aston Villa)

10 Aggborough (Kidderminster Harriers)
Ashton Gate (Bristol City)
Caledonian (Inverness Caledonian Thistle)
Carrow Road (Norwich City)
Celtic Park (Celtic)

City Ground (Nottingham Forest)
Easter Road (Hibernian)
Elland Road (Leeds United)
Loftus Road (Queen's Park Rangers)
London Road (Peterborough United)
Meadow Lane (Notts County)
Ninian Park (Cardiff City)
Sincil Bank (Lincoln City)
Stark's Park (Raith Rovers)
The Walkers (Leicester City)
Vetch Field (Swansea City)
York Street (Boston United)

11 Bayview Park (East Fife)
Bramall Lane (Sheffield United)
Central Park (Cowdenbeath)
Cliftonhill (Albion Rovers)
East End Park (Dunfermline Athletic)
Edgeley Park (Stockport County)
Fratton Park (Portsmouth)
Griffin Park (Brentford)
Hampden Park (Queen's Park Rangers)
Old Trafford (Manchester United)
Portman Road (Ipswich Town)
Prenton Park (Tranmere Rovers)
Priestfield (Gillingham)
Raydale Park (Gretna)
Station Park (Forfar Athletic)
St James' Park (Newcastle United)
Whaddon Road (Cheltenham Town)

12 Blundell Park (Grimsby Town)
Boundary Park (Oldham Athletic)
Brisbane Road (Leyton Orient)
County Ground (Swindon Town)
Gayfield Park (Arbroath)
Glanford Park (Scunthorpe United)
Goodison Park (Everton)
Hillsborough (Sheffield Wednesday)
Selhurst Park (Crystal Palace)
Somerset Park (Ayr United)
St Mirren Park (St Mirren)
The Hawthorns (West Bromwich Albion)
Valley Parade (Bradford City)
Vicarage Road (Watford)
Victoria Park (Hartlepool United/Ross County)

13 Borough Briggs (Elgin City)
Craven Cottage (Fulham)
Highfield Road (Coventry City)
McDiarmid Park (St Johnstone)
New Broomfield (Airdrie United)
Ochilview Park (Stenhousemuir)
Reynolds Arena (Darlington)
Tannadice Park (Dundee United)
The Alexandria (Crewe Alexandria)
White Hart Lane (Tottenham Hotspur)

14 Bloomfield Road (Blackpool)
Kenilworth Road (Luton Town)

National Hockey (Milton Keynes Dons)
Palmerston Park (Queen of the South)
Recreation Park (Alloa Athletic)
Shielfield Park (Berwick Rangers)

Stadium of Light (Sunderland)
Stamford Bridge (Chelsea)
15 The Fitness First (Bournemouth)
Tynescastle Park (Heart of Midlothian)

Footballers and associated figures include:

03 Law (Denis; 1940– , Scottish)

04 Best (George; 1946–2005, Northern Irish)
Dean (Dixie; 1907–80, English)
Didi (1928–2001, Brazilian)
Figo (Luis; 1972– , Portuguese)
Hall (Sir John; 1933– , English)
Owen (Michael; 1979– , English)
Pelé (1940– , Brazilian)
Rush (Ian; 1961– , Welsh)
Zico (1953– , Brazilian)
Zoff (Dino; 1942– , Italian)
Zola (Gianfranco; 1966– , Italian)

05 Adams (Tony; 1966– , English)
Banks (Gordon; 1937– , English)
Busby (Sir Matt; 1909–94, Scottish)
Carey (Johnny; 1919–95, Irish)
Giggs (Ryan; 1973– , Welsh)
Greig (John; 1942– , Scottish)
Henry (Thierry; 1977– , French)
Hurst (Sir Geoff; 1941– , English)
James (Alex; 1901–53, Scottish)
Moore (Bobby; 1941–93, English)
Revie (Don; 1927–89, English)
Rimet (Jules; 1871–1956, French)
Rossi (Paulo; 1956– , Italian)
Stein (Jock; 1922–85, Scottish)

06 Baggio (Roberto; 1967– , Italian)
Baresi (Franco; 1960– , Italian)
Barnes (John; 1963– , Jamaican/British)
Baxter (Jim; 1939–2001, Scottish)
Bosman (Jean-Marc; c.1964– , Belgian)
Clough (Brian; 1935–2004, English)
Cruyff (Johan; 1947– , Dutch)
Finney (Sir Tom; 1922– , English)
Ginola (David; 1967– , French)
Graham (George; 1944– , Scottish)
Gullit (Ruud; 1962– , Dutch)
Hoddle (Glenn; 1957– , English)
Keegan (Kevin; 1951– , English)
Lawton (Tommy; 1919–96, English)
McColl (R S; 1876–1959, Scottish)
Mercer (Joe; 1914–90, English)
Müller (Gerd; 1945– , German)
Puskas (Ferenc; 1927–2006, Hungarian)
Ramsey (Sir Alf; 1920–99, English)
Robson (Bryan; 1957– , English)
Robson (Sir Bobby; 1933–2009, English)
Rooney (Wayne; 1985– , English)
Seaman (David; 1963– , English)
St John (Ian; 1938– , Scottish)

Wenger (Arsene; 1949– , French)
Wright (Billy; 1924–94, English)
Wright (Ian; 1963– , English)
Yashin (Lev; 1929–90, Russian)
Zidane (Zinedine; 1972– , French)

07 Ardiles (Osvaldo 'Ossie'; 1952– , Argentine)
Beckham (David; 1975– , English)
Bremner (Billy; 1942–97, Scottish)
Butcher (Terry; 1958– , English)
Cantona (Eric; 1966– , French)
Capello (Fabio; 1946– , Italian)
Charles (John; 1931–2004, Welsh)
Di Canio (Paolo; 1968– , Italian)
Edwards (Duncan; 1936–58, English)
Eusebio (1942– , Mozambican/Portuguese)
Greaves (Jimmy; 1940– , English)
Lampard (Frank; 1978– , English)
Lineker (Gary; 1960– , English)
Macleod (Ally; 1931–2004, Scottish)
Mannion (Wilf; 1918–2000, English)
McCoist (Ally; 1962– , Scottish)
McNeill (Billy; 1940– , Scottish)
Paisley (Bob; 1919–96, English)
Platini (Michel; 1955– , French)
Rivaldo (1972– , Brazilian)
Ronaldo (1976– , Brazilian)
Shankly (Bill; 1913–81, Scottish)
Shearer (Alan; 1970– , English)
Shilton (Peter; 1949– , English)
Souness (Graeme; 1953– , Scottish)
Toshack (John; 1949– , Welsh)
Walcott (Theo; 1989– , English)

08 Bergkamp (Dennis; 1969– , Dutch)
Charlton (Jack; 1935– , English)
Charlton (Sir Bobby; 1937– , English)
Dalglish (Kenny; 1951– , Scottish)
Eriksson (Sven-Göran; 1948– , Swedish)
Ferguson (Sir Alex; 1941– , Scottish)
Fontaine (Just; 1933– , French)
Jennings (Pat; 1945– , Northern Irish)
Maradona (Diego; 1960– , Argentine)
Matthaus (Lothar; 1961– , German)
Matthews (Sir Stanley; 1915–2000, English)
Mourinho (José; 1963– , Portuguese)
Rivelino (Roberto; 1946– , Brazilian)

09 Di Stefano (Alfredo; 1926– , Argentine)
Garrincha (1933–83, Brazilian)
Gascoigne (Paul; 1967– , English)
Greenwood (Ron; 1921–2006, English)
Johnstone (Jimmy; 1944–2006, Scottish)

Klinsmann (Jürgen; 1964– , German)
Lofthouse (Nat; 1925–2011, English)
Van Basten (Marco; 1964– , Dutch)
10 Schmeichel (Peter; 1963– , Danish)

11 Beckenbauer (Franz; 1945– , German)
12 Blanchflower (Danny; 1926–93, Northern Irish)

Football terms include:

03 box	soccer	left back	relegation
cap	tackle	linesman	sending off
lob	treble	midfield	silver goal
net	volley	near post	substitute
04 back	winger	outfield	suspension
dive	**07** booking	play-offs	**11** bicycle kick
foul	caution	set piece	goalkeeping
goal	dribble	transfer	half-way line
half	far post	wall pass	keepie-uppie
head	forward	wingback	obstruction
hole	kick-off	**09** extra time	offside trap
loan	offside	five-a-side	penalty area
mark	own goal	formation	penalty kick
pass	penalty	give-and-go	penalty spot
post	play-off	goalmouth	six-yard area
save	red card	promotion	straight red
shot	referee	right back	time wasting
trap	stopper	touchline	**12** back-pass rule
wall	sweeper	**10** centre back	Bosman ruling
05 bench	throw-in	centre half	centre circle
chest	whistle	centre spot	overhead kick
pitch	**08** back heel	corner flag	stoppage time
06 assist	crossbar	corner kick	**13** centre forward
corner	dead ball	goalkeeper	dangerous play
double	defender	goalscorer	technical area
futsal	free kick	golden goal	**14** direct free kick
goalie	friendly	half volley	fourth official
handle	full back	injury time	goal difference
header	goal kick	man marking	relegation zone
keeper	goal line	midfielder	**15** eighteen-yard box
libero	half time	off-the-ball	two-footed tackle
one-two	hand ball	penalty box	
	hat-trick	possession	

See also **American football**; **Australian rules football**; **sport**

footwear

Footwear includes:

04 boot	brogue	trainer
clog	casual	**08** boat shoe
mule	galosh	deck shoe
pump	lace-up	flip-flop
shoe	loafer	moccasin
05 jelly	Oxford	overshoe
sabot	patten	pantofle
tacky	sandal	plimsoll
thong	slip-on	snowshoe
wader	**07** gumboot	snow-shoe
welly	slipper	**09** court-shoe
06 bootee	sneaker	court shoe

rugby boot
slingback
wedge heel
10 ballet shoe
combat boot
Doc Martens®
espadrille
hiking-boot
kitten heel

kitten-heel
riding boot
riding-boot
tennis shoe
11 bowling shoe
Chelsea boot
Hush Puppies®
walking-boot
12 climbing-boot

football boot
platform heel
stiletto heel
13 beetle-crusher
14 beetle-crushers
brothel creeper
wellington boot
15 brothel-creepers

Footwear parts include:

04 heel
lace
last
lift
sole
vamp
welt
05 inlay
round
shank
upper
waist

06 buckle
button
collar
eyelet
insole
lining
middle
throat
toe box
toe cap
tongue
07 counter

midsole
outsole
quarter
top lift
08 platform
09 back-strap
back-strip
vamp wings
wedge heel
10 middle sole
shankpiece
sock lining

Footwear makes include:

03 Kit
Pod
YSL
04 Arco
Bata
DKNY
Dune
Ecco
Etro
Fila
Gola
Nike
Puma
Tod's
Vans
05 Asics
Bally
Chloe
Edina
Faith
Fendi
Gucci
Guess
Hi-Tec
Kenzo
Levi's
Loake
Marni
Prada

Sacha
Schuh
Umbro
06 Adidas
Camper
Chipie
Clarks
Diesel
Dolcis
Dunlop
Esprit
Miu Miu
Mizuno
Reebok
Rieker
Van Dal
07 Buffalo
Carvela
Church's
Dockers
Ellesse
Energie
Kickers
Lacoste
Missoni
Moshulu
Padders
Salomon
Versace

08 Burberry
Converse
Mephisto
Moschino
Skechers
Ted Baker
09 Dr Martens
Dr Scholl's
Fly London
Jil Sander
Jimmy Choo
Kangaroos
LK Bennett
Miss Sixty
Paul Smith
Red or Dead
Slazenger
Start-rite
Wranglers
10 Aquascutum
Blundstone
Bruno Magli
Helmut Lang
Kurt Geiger
Patrick Cox
Pepe London
Timberland
11 Acupuncture
Birkenstock

Caterpillar
Hush Puppies
Ralph Lauren
12 Lulu Guinness
See also **boot**

Pierre Cardin
13 Christian Dior
Dolce e Gabbana
Manolo Blahnik

14 Sergio Tacchini
15 Alberta Ferretti
Irregular Choice

force *see* **police**

forecast *see* **ship; weather**

forest

Forests and woods include:

04 bush	mallee	mangrove	lignum-scrub
gapó	maquis	**09** chaparral	lignum-swamp
05 brush	pinery	deciduous	mallee scrub
igapò	**07** coastal	evergreen	moist forest
monte	garigue	greenwood	**12** vàrzea forest
selva	lowland	**10** coniferous	**13** ancient forest
taiga	macchie	peat forest	gallery forest
urman	wetland	rainforest	mangrove swamp
06 boreal	**08** caatinga	**11** cloud forest	savanna forest
jungle	garrigue	heath forest	**14** moist evergreen
	littoral		

See also **environment**

Formula One *see* **racing: motor racing**

fortification

Fortifications include:

04 bawn	Vauban	**09** barricade
fort	**07** barrier	earthwork
gate	bastion	fieldwork
keep	bulwark	fortalice
moat	citadel	gabionade
wall	defence	gatehouse
05 ditch	flanker	razor wire
fence	moineau	**10** barbed wire
hedge	outwork	bridgehead
limes	pillbox	trou de loup
tower	rampart	**11** crémaillère
06 abatis	sandbag	**13** cheval-de-frise
castle	**08** buttress	Martello tower
glacis	cavalier	**14** motte-and-bailey
laager	fortress	**15** circumvallation
sconce	palisade	contravallation
trench	stockade	

See also **castle**

fortune-telling *see* **divination**

fossil

Fossils include:

04 bone	baculite	steinkern	sharks' teeth
cast	dinosaur	trilobite	trace fossil
05 amber	echinoid	10 cast fossil	12 Burgess shale
shell	nautilus	gastrolith	paleontology
06 burrow	skeleton	snakestone	stratigraphy
07 bivalve	09 belemnite	11 ichnofossil	stromatolite
crinoid	coccolith	microfossil	13 palaeontology
08 ammonite	coprolite	mould fossil	petrification
	fish teeth	resin fossil	

France

Cities and notable towns in France include:

04 Caen	Reims	Rennes	Toulouse
Lyon	Rouen	Rheims	09 Cherbourg
Nice	Tours	07 Avignon	10 Marseilles
05 Arles	06 Amiens	Dunkirk	Strasbourg
Dijon	Calais	Limoges	11 Carcassonne
Lille	Cannes	Orléans	Montpellier
Lyons	Le Mans	08 Bordeaux	
Paris	Nantes		

French regions, with regional capitals:

05 Corse (Ajaccio)

06 Alsace (Strasbourg)
Centre (Orléans)
Guyane (Cayenne)

07 Corsica (Ajaccio)
Picardy (Amiens)

08 Auvergne (Clermont-Ferrand)
Bretagne (Rennes)
Brittany (Rennes)
Burgundy (Dijon)
Limousin (Limoges)
Lorraine (Nancy)
Picardie (Amiens)

09 Aquitaine (Bordeaux)
Bourgogne (Dijon)
La Réunion (Saint-Denis)

10 Guadeloupe (Basse-Terre)
Martinique (Fort-de-France)
Rhône-Alpes (Lyons)

11 Île de France (Paris)

12 Franche-Comté (Besançon)
Midi-Pyrénées (Toulouse)

13 Lower Normandy (Caen)
Pays de la Loire (Nantes)
Upper Normandy (Rouen)

14 Basse-Normandie (Caen)
Haute-Normandie (Rouen)

15 Nord-Pas-de-Calais (Lille)
Poitou-Charentes (Poitiers)

16 Champagne-Ardenne (Reims)

19 Languedoc-Roussillon (Montpellier)

22 Provence-Alpes-Côte d'Azur (Marseilles)

French departments, with prefectures:

03 Ain (Bourg-en-Bresse)
Lot (Cahors)
Var (Toulon)

04 Aube (Troyes)
Aude (Carcassonne)
Cher (Bourges)
Eure (Évreux)
Gard (Nîmes)

Gers (Auch)
Jura (Lons-le-Saunier)
Nord (Lille)
Oise (Beauvais)
Orne (Alençon)
Tarn (Albi)

05 Aisne (Laon)
Doubs (Besançon)

Drôme (Valence)
Indre (Châteauroux)
Isère (Grenoble)
Loire (Saint-Étienne)
Marne (Châlons-en-Champagne)
Meuse (Bar-le-Duc)
Paris (Paris)
Rhône (Lyon)
Somme (Amiens)
Yonne (Auxerre)

06 Allier (Moulins)
Ariège (Foix)
Cantal (Aurillac)
Creuse (Guéret)
Guyane (Cayenne)
Landes (Mont-de-Marsan)
Loiret (Orléans)
Lozère (Mende)
Manche (Saint-Lô)
Nièvre (Nevers)
Sarthe (Le Mans)
Savoie (Chambéry)
Vendée (La Roche-sur-Yon)
Vienne (Poitiers)
Vosges (Épinal)

07 Ardèche (Privas)
Aveyron (Rodez)
Bas-Rhin (Strasbourg)
Corrèze (Tulle)
Côte-d'Or (Dijon)
Essonne (Évry)
Gironde (Bordeaux)
Hérault (Montpellier)
Mayenne (Laval)
Moselle (Metz)

08 Ardennes (Charleville-Mézières)
Calvados (Caen)
Charente (Angoulême)
Dordogne (Périgueux)
Haut-Rhin (Colmar)
Morbihan (Vannes)
Val-d'Oise (Cergy-Pontoise)
Vaucluse (Avignon)

Yvelines (Versailles)

09 Finistère (Quimper)
La Réunion (Saint-Denis)
Puy-de-Dôme (Clermont-Ferrand)

10 Corse-du-Sud (Ajaccio)
Deux-Sèvres (Niort)
Eure-et-Loir (Chartres)
Guadeloupe (Basse-Terre)
Haute-Corse (Bastia)
Haute-Loire (Le Puy-en-Velay)
Haute-Marne (Chaumont)
Haute-Saône (Vesoul)
Loir-et-Cher (Blois)
Martinique (Fort-de-France)
Val-de-Marne (Créteil)

11 Côtes-d'Armor (Saint-Brieuc)
Hautes-Alpes (Gap)
Haute-Savoie (Annecy)
Haute-Vienne (Limoges)
Pas-de-Calais (Arras)

12 Haute-Garonne (Toulouse)
Hauts-de-Seine (Nanterre)
Indre-et-Loire (Tours)
Lot-et-Garonne (Agen)
Maine-et-Loire (Angers)
Saône-et-Loire (Mâcon)
Seine-et-Marne (Melun)

13 Ille-et-Vilaine (Rennes)
Seine-Maritime (Rouen)
Tarn-et-Garonne (Montauban)

14 Alpes-Maritimes (Nice)
Bouches-du-Rhône (Marseille)
Hautes-Pyrénées (Tarbes)

15 Loire-Atlantique (Nantes)
Seine-Saint-Denis (Bobigny)

16 Charente-Maritime (La Rochelle)
Meurthe-et-Moselle (Nancy)

18 Pyrénées-Orientales (Perpignan)

19 Pyrénées-Atlantiques (Pau)
Territoire-de-Belfort (Belfort)

20 Alpes-de-Haute-Provence (Digne-les-Bains)

French landmarks include:

04	Alps		Vosges		10	Mer de Glace		13	Arc de Triomphe
	Jura	07	Garonne			Pont du Gard			Fontainebleau
05	Loire		Lascaux			Versailles			Fontenay Abbey
	Meuse	08	Auvergne		11	Canal du Midi			Lyon Cathedral
	Rhône		Cévennes			Chenonceaux			Massif Central
	Saône		Dordogne			Eiffel Tower			Millau Viaduct
	Seine		Provence		12	Grand Trianon		14	Aiguille du Midi
	Somme		Pyrenees			Les Invalides			Suisse Normande
06	Carnac	09	Mont Blanc			Mont St Michel		15	Amiens Cathedral
	Landes		Notre Dame			Petit Trianon			Rheims Cathedral

French

French boys' names include:

03 Luc	Henri	Michel	Olivier
04 Jean	Jules	Pascal	Patrice
Léon	Louis	Pierre	Thibaut
Rémi	Serge	Xavier	Thierry
Rémy	06 Claude	07 Antoine	Vincent
René	Didier	Édouard	08 Frédéric
Yves	Gaston	Étienne	Matthieu
05 Alain	Gérard	Georges	Philippe
André	Honoré	Gustave	Stéphane
Denis	Jérôme	Jacques	Thibault
Émile	Marcel	Laurent	09 Guillaume

French girls' names include:

04 Fifi	Janine	Racquel	Claudette
Gigi	Jeanne	Sidonie	Dominique
05 Aimée	Nicole	08 Bertille	Françoise
Fleur	Simone	Brigitte	Gabrielle
Marie	Yvette	Charlize	Geneviève
06 Amélie	Yvonne	Danielle	Ghislaine
Ariane	07 Blanche	Francine	Madeleine
Denise	Camille	Juliette	Modestine
Eloise	Chantal	Michelle	Véronique
Evette	Colette	Villette	10 Antoinette
Evonne	Margaux	09 Angelique	Jacqueline
Hélène	Monique	Charmaine	

French words and expressions include:

04 élan (flair; flamboyance)

05 à deux (for two)
adieu (goodbye)
blasé (dulled to enjoyment)
coupé (two-door motor-car with sloping roof)
doyen (most distinguished member by virtue of seniority, experience and often also excellence)
ennui (world-weary listlessness)
outré (beyond what is customary or proper; eccentric)

06 au fait (knowledgeable or familiar with something)
au pair (a girl who performs domestic duties for board, lodging and pocket money)
cliché (a hackneyed phrase or concept)
déjà vu (an illusion of having experienced something before)
de trop (superfluous; in the way)
risqué (audaciously bordering on the unseemly)

07 affaire (liaison, intrigue)
à la mode (in fashion, fashionable)
atelier (a workshop; an artist's studio)
chagrin (melancholy or vexation at disappointment)
chambré (at room temperature)
en route (let us go)
entente (a friendly agreement between nations)
faux pas (a social blunder)
peloton (main group of riders in a cycle race)
vis-à-vis (in relation to)

08 à la carte (from the menu)
ambiance (surroundings, atmosphere, environment)
après-ski (evening amusements after skiing)
barrette (woman's hairclip or ornament)
cul-de-sac (a road closed at one end)
derrière (the buttocks)
film noir (a movement in cinema)
idée fixe (an obsession)
mot juste (the word which fits the context exactly)
prix fixe (used of a meal in a restaurant offered at a set price for a restricted choice)

09 au courant (aware of current events)
au naturel (naked)
banquette (long upholstered seat)
beau monde (fashionable society)
bel esprit (a brilliant or witty person)
bête noire (a bugbear; something one especially dislikes)
bon vivant (one who lives well, particularly enjoying good food and wine)
bon voyage (have a safe and pleasant journey)
bourgeois (a member of the middle class; conventional, conservative)
c'est la vie (denotes fatalistic resignation)
coup d'état (a violent overthrow of a government)
décolleté (with neck uncovered; low-cut dress)
de rigueur (compulsory)
grand prix (any of several international motor races; any competition of similar importance in other sports)
haut monde (high society)
n'est-ce pas? (is it not so?)
recherché (particularly choice)
sangfroid (self possession; coolness under stress)
vin du pays (a locally produced wine for everyday consumption)
volte-face (a sudden and complete change in opinion or in views expressed)

10 aide-de-camp (an officer who acts as a confidential personal assistant)
avant-garde (those in the forefront of an artistic movement)
cordon bleu (food cooked to a very high standard)
déshabillé (state of being only partially dressed, or of being casually dressed)
pied à terre (a flat kept for temporary or occasional accommodation)
table d'hôte (a set meal at a fixed price)

11 aide-mémoire (a reminder)
amuse-bouche (an appetizer)
au contraire (on the contrary)
belle époque (the time of gracious living immediately preceding World War I)
billets-doux (love letters)
chef d'oeuvre (a masterpiece)
coup de grâce (a finishing blow to end pain)
femme fatale (an irresistibly attractive

woman who brings difficulties or disasters on men; a siren)
fin de siècle (decadent)
prêt-à-porter (ready to wear)
raison d'être ('reason for existence')
savoir faire (knowing what to do and how to do it in any situation)
tour de force (feat of strength or skill)
trompe l'oeil ('an appearance of reality' in painting, architecture, etc)

12 ancien régime (an outdated political system or ruling elite)
bateau-mouche (sightseeing boat on the River Seine in Paris)
carte blanche (freedom of action)
cause célèbre (a very notable or famous trial)
c'est la guerre (denotes fatalistic resignation)
cinéma vérité (realism in films)
coup de foudre (love at first sight)
fait accompli (already done or settled, and therefore irreversible)
force majeure (an unforeseeable or uncontrollable course of events, excusing one from fulfilling a contract; a legal term)
haute couture (fashionable, expensive dress designing and tailoring)
je ne sais quoi (an indefinable something)
laissez-faire (a general principle of non-interference)
ménage à trois (a household comprising a husband and wife and the lover of one of them)
nouveau riche (one who has only lately acquired wealth, without acquiring good taste)
s'il vous plaît (please)

13 belles-lettres (literary studies or writings)
éminence grise (someone exerting power through their influence over a superior)
nouvelle vague (a movement in the French cinema)

14 crème de la crème (the very best)
double entendre (ambiguity, normally with indecent connotations)
enfant terrible (a person whose behaviour is indiscreet, embarrassing to his associates)
noblesse oblige (rank imposes obligations)

15 chargé-d'affaires (an ambassador's deputy)
nouvelle cuisine (a style of simple French cookery)

See also **day**; **month**; **number**; **shop**

Frost, Robert (1874–1963)

Significant works include:

07 'Birches' (1916)
09 *A Boy's Will* (1913)
11 'Mending Wall' (1914)
12 *A Witness Tree* (1942)
    New Hampshire (1923)

13 *In the Clearing* (1962)
    North of Boston (1914)
15 'The Road Not Taken' (1916)
16 *Mountain Interval* (1916)
21 'The Death of the Hired Man' (1914)

fruit

Fruits include:

03 bel	medlar	mulberry	elderberry
fig	narras	physalis	gooseberry
haw	orange	pitahaya	granadilla
hip	papaya	plantain	grapefruit
04 bael	pawpaw	rambutan	loganberry
bhel	pitaya	sebesten	redcurrant
date	pomelo	sunberry	salal berry
kiwi	quince	tamarind	sour cherry
lime	squash	**09** beach plum	spiceberry
noni	tomato	blueberry	strawberry
pear	wampee	carambola	watermelon
plum	**07** acerola	cherimoya	**11** blood orange
sloe	apricot	cranberry	boysenberry
Ugli®	avocado	greengage	Jaffa orange
yuzu	bramble	Juneberry	pomegranate
05 apple	chayote	kiwi fruit	sallal berry
carob	genipap	nectarine	sharon fruit
grape	kumquat	persimmon	sweet cherry
guava	mineola	pineapple	**12** blackcurrant
lemon	rhubarb	raspberry	buffalo-berry
mango	satsuma	rose apple	custard apple
melon	soursop	sapodilla	passion fruit
naras	tangelo	saskatoon	serviceberry
olive	**08** bilberry	shadberry	whitecurrant
peach	date-plum	star-apple	winter cherry
06 banana	dewberry	star fruit	**13** kangaroo-apple
cherry	goosegog	tangerine	sapodilla plum
damson	kalumpit	**10** blackberry	Seville orange
loquat	mandarin	breadfruit	**14** Cape gooseberry
lychee	minneola	clementine	pink grapefruit

See also **apple**; **berry**; **cherry**; **hybrid**; **melon**; **orange**; **pear**; **plum**

fuel

Fuels include:

03 gas	derv	eldin	diesel
LPG	logs	fagot	elding
MOX	peat	vraic	faggot
oil	slug	**06** benzol	gas oil
RDF	SURF	billet	hydyne
04 coal	wood	borane	petrol
coke	**05** argol	butane	smudge
			Sterno®

07 astatki
benzine
benzole
biofuel
Coalite®
eilding
gasahol
gasohol
mesquit
methane
propane
synfuel

08 calor gas®
charcoal
firewood
flex-fuel
gasoline
kerosene
kerosine
kindling
mesquite
paraffin
tan balls
triptane

09 acetylene
biodiesel
Campingaz®
cane-trash
diesel oil
hydrazine
red diesel

10 anthracite
atomic fuel
bioethanol
fossil fuel

natural gas
Orimulsion®

11 electricity
North Sea gas
nuclear fuel

12 buffalo chips
nitromethane
nuclear power

13 smokeless fuel

14 aviation spirit

See also **environment; gas**

fungus

Fungi include:

04 rust
scab
smut

05 ergot
morel
yeast

06 blight

07 candida

chytrid

08 botritis
brown rot
fusarium
mushroom

09 black spot
grey mould
toadstool

10 saprophyte

slime mould
sooty mould

11 downy mildew
penicillium
slime fungus

12 brewer's yeast
potato blight

13 chytrid fungus
powdery mildew

See also **mushroom**

fur

Furs include:

03 fox

04 flix
gris
mink
vair

05 budge
civet
fitch
genet
grise
otter
sable
skunk

06 beaver
ermine
marten
nutria
ocelot
rabbit
racoon
zorino

07 blue fox
caracal
caracul
crimmer
fitchet

fitchew
genette
karakul
krimmer
minever
miniver
muskrat
opossum
raccoon

08 cony-wool
kolinsky
moleskin
musquash

ponyskin
sealskin
sea otter
zibeline

09 broadtail
silver fox
wolverene
wolverine
zibelline

10 chinchilla

11 beech marten
Persian lamb
stone marten

furnishing

Furnishings include:

03 mat
rug

04 lamp
lino

05 blind
duvet

throw
tiles

06 carpet
mirror
pelmet
pillow

07 bath mat
beanbag
blanket
curtain
cushion
doormat

picture
valance

08 bed linen
linoleum
mattress
painting

tapestry	hearth rug	**10** bath pillow	wall hanging
09 bedspread	lampshade	carpet tile	**12** standard lamp
duckboard	panelling	Roman blind	**13** shower curtain
head board	wallpaper	**11** roller blind	Venetian blind

furniture

Furniture includes:

03 bed	sofa bed	overmantel
cot	tallboy	secretaire
04 bunk	whatnot	truckle bed
desk	**08** armchair	vanity unit
sofa	bar chair	**11** coffee table
05 chair	bedstead	dining chair
chest	bookcase	dining table
couch	cupboard	mantelpiece
divan	end table	room-divider
stool	hatstand	studio couch
suite	recliner	swivel chair
table	toy chest	**12** bedside table
trunk	tub chair	chaise-longue
wagon	wall unit	chesterfield
06 buffet	wardrobe	china cabinet
bureau	water bed	computer desk
carver	**09** bed-settee	folding table
coffer	card table	gateleg table
cradle	coatstand	kitchen chair
daybed	easy chair	kitchen table
fender	fireplace	magazine rack
lowboy	footstool	nest of tables
mirror	hallstand	rocking chair
pouffe	high-chair	Welsh dresser
settee	lamp table	**13** dressing table
waggon	sideboard	four-poster bed
07 armoire	side table	umbrella stand
beanbag	washstand	**14** chest of drawers
bunkbed	wine table	display cabinet
cabinet	**10** blanket box	extending table
camp-bed	chiffonier	refectory table
commode	dumb-waiter	**15** bathroom cabinet
dresser	encoignure	butcher's trolley
ottoman	escritoire	occasional chair
playpen	firescreen	occasional table

Furniture styles include:

04 Adam	Windsor	**10** Art Nouveau	**12** Gainsborough
buhl	**08** Colonial	Mackintosh	Transitional
06 boulle	Georgian	provincial	Vernis Martin
Empire	Sheraton	**11** Anglo-Indian	**13** Anglo-Colonial
Gothic	**09** Charles II	Biedermeier	Arts and Crafts
rococo	Edwardian	Chippendale	Dutch Colonial
Shaker	Queen Anne	Cromwellian	Louis Philippe
07 Art Deco	Shibayama	Hepplewhite	Louis-Quatorze
Baroque	Victorian	Louis-Quinze	**14** William and Mary
Regency	William IV	Restoration	

Furniture makers and designers include:

04 Buhl (André Charles; 1642–1732, French)
Elfe (Thomas; 1719–75, American)
Gray (Eileen; 1878–1976, Irish)
Heal (Sir Ambrose; 1872–1959, English)

05 Aalto (Alvar; 1898–1976, Finnish)
Bevan (Charles; c.1820s–1883, English)
Eames (Charles; 1907–1978, US)
Eames (Ray; 1912–88, US)
Ednie (John; 1876–1934, Scottish)
Klint (Kaare; 1888–1954, Danish)
Logan (George; 1866–1939, Scottish)
Phyfe (Duncan; 1768–1854, US)
Scott (Mackay Hugh Baillie; 1865–1945, English)
Stead (Tim; 1952–2000, English)

06 Batley (H W; fl.1872–1910, British)
Boulle (André Charles; 1642–1732, French)
Burges (William; 1827–81, English)
Conran (Sir Terence; 1931–   , English)
Gimson (Ernest William; 1864–1919, English)
Godwin (Edward; 1833–86, English)
Migeon (Pierre; 1701–58, French)
Seddon (J P; 1827–1906, English)
Starck (Philippe; 1949–   , French)
Taylor (E A; 1874–1951, Scottish)
Thonet (Michael; 1796–1871, German)
Voysey (C F A; 1857–1941, English)
Walton (George; 1867–1933, Scottish)

07 Beneman (Guillaume; 1684–1764, French)
Lethaby (W R; 1857–1931, English)
Macnair (J Herbert; 1868–1955, Scottish)
Ruhlman (Jacques-Émile; 1879–1933, French)

08 Barnsley (Ernest; 1863–1926, English)
Barnsley (Sidney; 1865–1926, English)
Eastlake (Charles; 1836–1906, English)
Jacobsen (Arne; 1902–71, Danish)
Montigny (Philippe-Claude; 1734–1800, French)
Riesener (Jean Henri; 1734–1806, French)
Rietveld (Gerrit; 1888–1964, Dutch)
Saarinen (Eero; 1910–61, US)
Sheraton (Thomas; 1751–1806, English)
Tredgold (Thomas; 1788–1829, English)

09 Hitchcock (Lambert; 1795–1852, US)

10 Chermayeff (Serge; 1900–96, US)
Mackintosh (Charles Rennie; 1868–1928, Scottish)

11 Chippendale (Thomas; 1718–79, English)
Hepplewhite (George; d.1786, English)
Le Corbusier (1887–1965, Swiss/French)

12 Riemerschmid (Richard; 1868–1957, German)

Terms to do with furniture include:

03 leg	drawer	moulding
oak	Empire	pediment
04 Adam	finial	rewarewa
buhl	ormolu	sabre leg
cane	period	Sheraton
ogee	plinth	
pine	rococo	**09** bonnet top
toon	sapele	coachwood
	veneer	Edwardian
05 apron	walnut	Japanning
beech		marquetry
bombé	**07** antique	panelling
boule	bun foot	Queen Anne
ebony	fitment	roundwood
inlay	fluting	saddlebag
ivory	pad foot	slip cover
kiaat	paw foot	spade foot
repro	reeding	Victorian
shelf		whitewood
suite	**08** cabriole	
	flatpack	**10** block front
06 boulle	fretwork	calamander
caster	harewood	distressed
castor	mahogany	encoignure

oxbow front
ribbon back
rosemaling
scroll foot
shield back
upholstery

11 ball-and-claw
Biedermeier
cabriole leg
Chippendale

claw-and-ball
collapsible
haute époque
Hepplewhite
marqueterie
overstuffed

12 French polish
reproduction
self-assembly
vernis martin

13 mother-of-pearl
tortoiseshell
unit furniture

14 barley-sugar leg
dental moulding
Marlborough leg

15 serpentine front
three-piece suite

See also **antique; office**

fury

The Furies:

06 Alecto
Megara

09 Tisiphone

G

galaxy

gallery *see* museum

gambling

06 bookie
casino
chip in
fan-tan
fulham
gaming
jetton
lay off
motser
policy
punter

07 baccara
flutter
lottery
tipster

08 baccarat
levanter
long shot
outsider

See also **bet**

play-debt
roulette
teetotum

09 blackjack
bookmaker
dog racing
favourite
place a bet
vingt-et-un

10 bouillotte
punto banco
put-and-take
put money on
sweepstake

11 blind hookey
card-sharper
find the lady
go one better
horse racing

numbers game
puncto banco
rouge-et-noir
slot machine

12 break the bank
card counting
debt of honour
pitch-and-toss
scoop the pool

13 hedge one's bets
shoot the works
spread betting

14 shove-halfpenny
three-card trick
wheel of fortune

15 cash in one's chips
disorderly house
greyhound racing
make a clean sweep

game

Games include:

03 loo
nap
nim
taw

04 brag
crib
dice
faro
I-spy
ludo
mora
pool
ruff
skat
snap
tray
vint

05 bowls
chess
clubs
craps
darts
gleek
halma
jacks
Jenga®
lurch
morra
noddy
ombre
poker
rummy

whist

06 basset
boston
bridge
Cluedo®
clumps
crambo
écarté
euchre
fan-tan
hazard
niffer
piquet
quinze
squail

07 baccara
bezique
bowling
canasta
cooncan
fusball
hangman
kalooki
mah-jong
mancala
marbles
muggins
old maid
picquet
pinball
pinocle
pontoon

primero
purpose
ring taw
snooker
traybit

08 all-fives
all-fours
baccarat
card game
charades
checkers
chequers
cribbage
dominoes
draughts
foosball
forfeits
fussball
gin rummy
kalookie
Kim's game
Klondike
Klondyke
mah-jongg
Monopoly®
Napoleon
patience
penneech
penneeck
penuchle
ping pong
pinochle

reversis
roulette
sardines
Scrabble®
tredille

09 air hockey
bagatelle
bagatelle
billiards
blackjack
board game
draw poker
floor game
Hacky Sack®
honeypots
hopscotch
jingo-ring
lanterloo
newmarket
pair-royal
Pelmanism
penny ante
quadrille
Simon says
solitaire
solo whist
spoilfive
stud poker
table game
tic-tac-toe

tredrille
twenty-one
vingt-et-un

10 backgammon
Balderdash®
Black Maria
bouillotte
criss-cross
fivestones
handy-dandy
hot-cockles
jackstraws
lansquenet
Pictionary®
spillikins
target game

11 battleships
beetle drive
bumble-puppy
catch-the-ten
chemin de fer
hide-and-seek
sancho-pedro
span-counter
speculation
table tennis
tiddlywinks
troll-my-dame

12 consequences
one-and-thirty

partner whist
pitch-and-toss
shove ha'penny
span-farthing

13 auction bridge
blindman's buff
clock patience
happy families
jingling match
musical chairs
pass the parcel
postman's knock
spin the bottle
table football
table skittles
ten-pin bowling

14 contract bridge
fives-and-threes
follow-my-leader
hunt-the-slipper
hunt-the-thimble
nine men's morris
shove-halfpenny
snip-snap-snorum
Trivial Pursuit®

15 Chinese checkers
Chinese chequers
Chinese whispers
duplicate bridge
puss in the corner

Board games include:

02 go

04 ludo
Risk®
siga

05 chess
darts
goose
halma
lurch
marls
nyout
senet
shogi
Sorry®

06 Boggle®
Cluedo®
gobang
gomuku
merels
merils
morals
morris
tables
tabula

uckers

07 Cranium®
mah-jong
mancala
marrels
merells
pachisi
petteia
reverse
reversi
Yahtzee®

08 checkers
chequers
cribbage
Dingbats®
draughts
miracles
Monopoly®
parchesi
Rummikub®
Scrabble®

09 bagatelle
Buccaneer®
Operation®

Parcheesi®
solitaire
tic-tac-toe

10 backgammon
Go for Broke®
latrunculi
Mastermind®
Pictionary®

11 battleships
fox and geese
Frustration®

12 pente grammai

13 concentration
table skittles
The Game of Life®

14 nine men's morris
Trivial Pursuit®

15 Chinese checkers
Chinese chequers
duodecim scripta
fivepenny morris
ninepenny morris
three men's morris

Card games include:

03 don
nap
pig
war

04 brag
bust
faro
fish
golf
king
loba
may I?
phat
pits
push
rook
scat
skat
snap
solo
spit
tunk
tute
ugly

05 blitz
cheat
cinch
crash
flush
knack
nerts
pairs
pedro
pitch
poker
ronda
rummy
samba
shoot
speed
tarok
tarot
whist

06 big two
boodle
bridge
casino
church
crates
cuckoo
dakota
deuces
écarté
euchre
fan tan
five up

go fish
hearts
henway
kaiser
knaves
oh hell!
palace
pepper
piquet
pounce
red dog
sevens
spades
spoons
squeal
stitch
switch
tarock
taroky
trumps
turtle
valets

07 auction
authors
bezique
bone ace
canasta
clabber
last one
old maid
pontoon
quartet
setback
spitzer
whipsaw

08 ace-deuce
all fives
all fours
anaconda
baccarat
bid whist
blackout
carousel
cribbage
drunkard
elevator
gin rummy
high five
Michigan
Napoleon
patience
pinochle
Pope Joan
sequence
shanghai
Welsh don

09 abyssinia
bid euchre
blackjack
catch five
golden ten
king pedro
king rummy
let it ride
newmarket
Pelmanism
poker bull
president
quadrille
racehorse
solitaire
solo whist
stud poker
tic-tac-toe
tile rummy
vingt-et-un

10 black maria
buck euchre
capitalism
Chinese ten
cincinnati
crazy nines
dirty clubs
German solo
parliament
preference
ride the bus
sheepshead
strip poker
three in one
Wall Street

11 cat and mouse
chase the ace
chemin de fer
chicken foot
crazy eights
English stud
find the lady
French tarot
French whist
German whist
high-low-jack
Indian poker
Mexican stud
nine-card don
Oklahoma gin
racing demon
Russian bank
six-card brag
speculation
Texas hold 'em

12 Chinese poker

devil's bridge
draw dominoes
five-card brag
five card draw
four-card brag
high card pool
kings corners
Mexican sweat
Mexican train
nine-card brag
one and thirty
pick a partner
ruff and trump
Russian poker
shoot pontoon

13 concentration
contract rummy

contract whist
happy families
knockout whist
lame-brain Pete
Michigan rummy
Romanian whist
sergeant major
seven-card brag
Shanghai rummy
three-card brag

14 Caribbean poker
contract bridge
five hundred rum
fives and threes
follow the queen
good, better, best
Jack the shifter

Liverpool rummy
Minnesota whist
rich man, poor man
ruff and honours
second hand high
spite and malice
spit in the ocean
three-card monte
trust-don't trust

15 back alley bridge
cut-throat euchre
double solitaire
nomination whist
railroad canasta
stealing bundles

Party games include:

06 bridge
Who Am I?®

07 mummies
statues
Twister®

08 charades
Kim's game
lucky dip
sardines

09 dead lions
fuzzy duck
poor pussy
Simon says

10 ducky ducky

memory game
wink murder

11 general post
hide-and-seek
truth or dare

12 consequences
musical bumps
treasure hunt

13 blindman's buff
chocolate game
musical chairs
pass the orange
pass the parcel
postman's knock

sleeping lions
spin-the-bottle
stuck in the mud
winking murder

14 British bulldog
follow-my-leader
hunt the thimble
musical statues
pass the balloon
sleeping pirate

15 Chinese whispers
egg and spoon race
murder in the dark
ring-a-ring-a-roses
three-legged race

Terms to do with games include:

02 go
03 bat
bid
die
run
set
win
04 base
beat
card
deal
dice
draw
goal

half
hand
lose
move
pass
play
shot
suit
team
tile
turn
05 board
bonus
cheat

court
field
match
piece
pitch
prize
round
rules
score
stick
table
throw
trick
trump

06 attack
gambit
player
tactic
07 counter
defence
doubles
forfeit
singles
08 opponent
role play
strategy
tie-break
10 tiebreaker

See also **chess**; **Monopoly®**; **video game**

game: hunting

Game animals include:

03 elk	hyena	giraffe	squirrel
fox	moose	leopard	wild boar
04 bear	snipe	muntjac	**09** crocodile
boar	tiger	red deer	
deer	zebra	roe deer	**10** fallow deer
lion	**06** badger	**08** antelope	**12** hippopotamus
stag	rabbit	elephant	mountain lion
wolf	**07** buffalo	kangaroo	
05 bison	caribou	sika deer	

Game birds include:

04 coot	moorhen		waterfowl
duck	ostrich		**10** guinea fowl
guan	pintail		tufted duck
teal	pochard		wild turkey
05 goose			wood grouse
quail	**08** pheasant		woodpigeon
scaup	shoveler		
	woodcock		**11** black grouse
06 curlew	**09** blackcock		Canada goose
grouse	blackgame		common snipe
plover	goldeneye		hazel grouse
wigeon	jack snipe		
07 gadwall	partridge		**12** capercaillie
greyhen	ptarmigan		capercailzie
greylag	red grouse		golden plover
mallard	scaup duck		**15** pink-footed goose

See also **poultry**

garden

Garden types include:

03 hop	water	winter	rosarium
tea	**06** alpine	**07** botanic	**09** allotment
04 beer	arbour	cottage	arboretum
herb	border	hanging	botanical
knot	bottle	Italian	flower bed
lawn	flower	kitchen	raised bed
rest	indoor	orchard	shrubbery
rock	market	rockery	terrarium
roof	physic	rose bed	window box
rose	rosary		
sink	rosery	**08** Japanese	**10** ornamental
	sunken	kailyard	rose arbour
05 fruit	walled	pleasure	**13** vegetable plot

Gardening tools include:

03 axe	rake	gloves	**07** fan rake
hoe	**05** Flymo®	scythe	hatchet
04 fork	spade	shears	kneeler
pots	**06** cloche	trowel	loppers

netting
pruners
trellis
wellies
08 chainsaw
clippers
hosepipe
shredder
Strimmer®

09 cold frame
fruit cage
garden saw
lawn edger
lawnmower
lawn raker
sack truck
secateurs
sprinkler
water butt

10 compost bin
cultivator
fertilizer
garden cart
lawn roller
soil tester
weedkiller
11 brushcutter
incinerator
lawn aerator

watering can
wheelbarrow
12 drop spreader
grass trimmer
hedge trimmer
potting table
13 garden sprayer
lawn scarifier
14 rotary spreader

Gardens include:

03 Kew (England)
04 Ness (England)
05 Lawai (USA)
Ninfa (Italy)
Stowe (England)
06 Het Loo (The Netherlands)
Monet's (France)
Suzhou (China)
Wisley (England)
07 Alnwick (England)
Bodnant (Wales)
Boxwood (USA)
Byodoin (Japan)
Giverny (France)
Heligan (England)
Kane'ohe (USA)
Motsuji (Japan)
Mt Usher (Ireland)
Nemours (USA)
Rousham (England)
Ryoanji (Japan)
Urakuen (Japan)
08 Aalsmeer (The Netherlands)
Alhambra (Spain)
Bagh-e Fin (Iran)
Bartram's (USA)
Biltmore (USA)
Blenheim (England)
Butchart (Canada)
Charbagh (India)
Claymont (USA)
Ermitage (Germany)
Hopewood (Australia)
Hyde Hall (England)
Korakuen (Japan)
La Granja (Spain)
Longwood (USA)
Mt Vernon (USA)
Nanzenji (Japan)
Pleasure (China)
Rikugien (Japan)
Rosedown (USA)
Rosemoor (England)

Sankeien (Japan)
Vaucluse (Australia)
09 Arley Hall (England)
Ascog Hall (Scotland)
Bagatelle (France)
Claremont (England)
Kenrokuen (Japan)
Keukenhof (The Netherlands)
Landriana (Italy)
Lingering (China)
Lion Grove (China)
Lodge Park (Ireland)
Majorelle (Morocco)
Maplelawn (Canada)
Mirabelle (Austria)
Newby Hall (England)
Sanssouci (Germany)
Stourhead (England)
Tuileries (France)
Upton Grey (England)
10 Afton Villa (USA)
Buen Retiro (Spain)
Chatsworth (England)
El Escorial (Spain)
Generalife (Spain)
Harlow Carr (England)
Hatley Park (Canada)
Holker Hall (England)
Isola Bella (Italy)
Kensington (England)
La Mortella (Italy)
Levens Hall (England)
Monticello (USA)
Schönbrunn (Austria)
Sen No Rikyu (Japan)
Versailles (France)
Villa d'Este (Italy)
Villa Lante (Italy)
Winterthur (USA)
11 Chanticleer (USA)
Eden Project (England)
Great Dixter (England)
Ji Chang Yuan (China)
Leonardslee (England)

Naranjestan (Iran)
Old Westbury (USA)
Parc Monceau (France)
Powerscourt (Ireland)
Villa Madama (Italy)
Wallenstein (Germany)

12 Castle Howard (England)
Chiddingfold (New Zealand)
Hampton Court (England)
Hidcote Manor (England)
Jingshan Park (China)
Katsura Rikyu (Japan)
Orto Botanico (Italy)
Ritsurin Koen (Japan)
Royal Botanic (Australia/England/Scotland)
Sissinghurst (England)

Studley Royal (England)
Villa Adriana (Italy)

13 Dumbarton Oaks (USA)
Harewood House (England)
Orange Botanic (Australia)
Vaux le Vicomte (France)

14 Benmore Botanic (Scotland)
Biddulph Grange (England)
Drummond Castle (Scotland)
Hua Ching Palace (China)
Middleton Place (USA)
Stone Lion Grove (China)
Wakehurst Place (England)
Younger Botanic (Scotland)

15 Arnold Arboretum (USA)

Gardeners include:

03 Don (Monty; 1955– , English)

04 Cane (Percy; 1881–1976, English)
Emes (William; 1730–1803, English)
Kent (William; 1684–1748, English)
Page (Russell; 1906–85, English)
Peto (Harold Ainsworth; 1854–1933, English)
Wise (Henry; 1653–1738, English)

05 Banks (Sir Joseph; 1744–1820, English)
Brown (Lancelot 'Capability'; 1715–83, English)
Enshu (Kobori; 1579–1647, Japanese)
Gavin (Diarmuid; 1964– , Irish)
Klein (Carol; 1945– , English)
Marot (Daniel; 1661–1752, French)
Monet (Claude; 1840–1926, French)
Roper (Lanning; 1912–83, US)
Swift (Joe; 1965– , English)
Wilde (Kim; 1960– , English)

06 Copijn (Hendrik; 1842–1923, Dutch)
Evelyn (John; 1620–1706, English)
Farrer (Reginald; 1880–1920, English)
Gerard (John; 1545–1612, English)
Gilpin (William Sawrey;1762–1845, English)
Hanmer (Sir Thomas; fl.1659; English)
Hooker (Sir William Jackson; 1785–1865, English)
Ingram (Collingwood 'Cherry'; 1880–1981, English)
Jekyll (Gertrude; 1843–1932, English)
London (George; d.1714, English)
Loudon (John Claudius; 1783–1843, Scottish)
Mawson (Thomas; 1861–1933, English)
Miller (Philip; 1691–1771, Scottish)
Mollet (André; d.c.1665, French)
Paxton (Sir Joseph; 1801–65, English)
Repton (Humphrey; 1752–1818, English)

Soseki (Muso; 1275–1351, Japanese)

07 Bartram (John; 1699–1777, American)
Blaikie (Thomas; 1751–1838, Scottish)
Clusius (Carolus; 1526–1609, Flemish)
Compton (Edward; d.1977, English)
de Thame (Rachel; 1961– , English)
Duchêne (Achille; 1866–1947, French)
Farrand (Beatrix; 1872–1959, US)
Forsyth (William; 1737–1804, Scottish)
Hanbury (Sir Thomas; 1832–1907; English)
L'Ecluse (Charles de; 1526–1609, Flemish)
Le Nôtre (André; 1613–1700, French)
Thrower (Percy; 1913–88, English)
Walling (Edna Margaret; 1896–1973, English/Australian)

08 Aislabie (John; d.1742, English)
Beaumont (Guillaume; fl.1680s/90s, French)
Buczacki (Stefan; 1945– , British)
Hamilton (Geoff; 1936–96 , English)
Hessayon (David G; 1928– , English)
Jellicoe (Sir Geoffrey; 1900–96, English)
Johnston (Lawrence; 1871–1958, US)
Nesfield (William Andrews; 1793–1881, English)
Robinson (William; 1838–1935, Irish)

09 Backhouse (James; 1794–1869, English)
Blomfield (Sir Reginald; 1856–1942, English)
Bridgeman (Charles; d.1738, English)
Forestier (Jean-Claude Nicolas; 1861–1930, French)

10 Aberconway (Henry Duncan, Lord; 1879–1953, English)
Blackburne (John; 1694–1786, English)
Titchmarsh (Alan; 1949– , English)

Tradescant (John, the Elder; 1570–c.1638, English)

Tradescant (John, the Younger; 1608–62, English)

11 Abercrombie (John; 1726–1806, English)

13 Sackville-West (Vita; 1892–1962, English)

Gardening terms include:

03 bed

04 bulb
clay
loam
plot
roji
seed
soil
tree
weed

05 bower
graft
hardy
hedge
mulch
plant
shrub

06 annual
arbour
hoeing
hybrid
manure
raking

07 climber
compost
cutting
digging

growing
herbary
olitory
organic
potager
produce
pruning
staking
topiary
topsoil
weeding

08 chinampa
dividing
gardener
layering
planting
thinning
watering

09 deciduous
evergreen
germinate
leaf-mould
perennial
pesticide
plantsman
pleasance

10 composture
coniferous

fertilizer
greenhouse
hardy plant
sharawadgi
sharawaggi

11 crazy paving
cultivation
green manure
ground cover
hydroponics
landscaping
plantswoman
potting shed
propagation
tender plant
tree surgeon
tree surgery

12 bedding plant
conservatory
horticulture
hybrid vigour

13 double digging
growing season
horticultural
plantie-cruive
transplanting

15 window gardening

See also **flower; insecticide; park**

gas

Gases include:

02 CS

04 neon
tear
town

05 ether
marsh
nerve
niton
ozone

radon
xenon

06 butane
helium
ketene
nitrox

07 ammonia
krypton
methane

mustard
natural
propane

08 cyanogen
ethylene
firedamp
laughing

09 acetylene
black damp

chokedamp

10 chloroform

12 nitrous oxide

13 carbon dioxide
dimethylamine

14 carbon monoxide

See also **fuel**

gate

Gates include:

03 New (Israel)

04 Dung (Israel)
Iron (Spain)
Land (Croatia)
Lion (Greece)
Nola (Italy)
Zion (Israel)

05 Black (England)
Black (*The Lord of the Rings*, J R R Tolkien)
Delhi (Pakistan)
Green (Poland)
Jaffa (Israel)
Lion's (Israel)
Menin (Belgium)
Roman (Croatia)
Sarno (Italy)
Sheep (ancient world/ Bible)
Water (Belgium)

06 Alcalá (Spain)
Appian (ancient world)
Bhatti (Pakistan)
Bridge (Croatia)
Double (Israel)
Golden (Israel)
Golden (Russia)
Golden (Ukraine)
Hebron (Israel)
Herod's (Israel)
Ishtar (ancient world)
Marine (Italy)
Nocera (Italy)
Sanmon (Japan)
Sather (USA)
Scaean (*The Iliad*)
Single (Israel)

Sunset (Japan)
Toledo (Spain)
Triple (Israel)
Upland (Poland)

07 Balawat (ancient world)
Colline (ancient world)
Gennath (ancient world/ Bible)
Harbour (Croatia)
Karamon (Japan)
Kashmir (India)
Monk Bar (England)
Nicanor (ancient world/ Bible)
Paisley (England)
Shankly (England)
Stabian (Italy)
St Rocco (Croatia)
Swedish (Latvia)
Tallinn (Estonia)
Thunder (Japan)
Victory (Egypt)
Zuwayla (Egypt)

08 Asinaria (Italy)
Conquest (Egypt)
Damascus (Israel)
Hadrian's (Greece)
Kashmiri (Pakistan)
Landport (England)
Maggiore (Italy)
Memorial (Gates; England)
Pinciana (Italy)
Rashomon (Japan)
Raushnai (Pakistan)
San Paolo (Italy)
Traitors' (England)
Vesuvius (Italy)

09 Bab Agnaou (Morocco)
Beautiful (ancient world/ Bible)
Bukdaemun (South Korea)
Great East (South Korea)
Namdaemun (South Korea)
Ostiensis (ancient world)

10 Bootham Bar (England)
Dongdaemun (South Korea)
Gate of Dawn (Lithuania)
gate of horn (Greek mythology)
Grand Torii (Japan)
Great North (South Korea)
Great South (South Korea)
Porta Nigra (Germany)
St Vincent's (Spain)
Sungnyemun (South Korea)
Waterpoort (Belgium)

11 Brandenburg (Germany)
Gate of China (China)
gate of ivory (Greek mythology)
Gate of Light (Pakistan)
Herculaneum (Italy)
Kaminarimon (Japan)
Walmgate Bar (England)

12 Heunginjimun (South Korea)
St John's Abbey (England)

13 Micklegate Bar (England)
San Sebastiano (Italy)

14 Gateway of India (India)
The Gates of Hell (sculpture, Rodin)

See also **Germany; London; sculpture**

gauge

Gauges include:

03 oil

04 plug
rain
ring
slip
snap
tide
tyre
wind

wire

05 block
broad
drill
limit
paper
steam
taper
water

06 feeler
radius
strain
vacuum

07 Bourdon
counter
cutting
loading
marking

mortise

08 gauge rod
pressure

10 gauge glass
gauge wheel
micrometer

See also **measurement**

gem

Gemstones include:

03 jet	zircon	carnelian	chrysolite
04 jade	**07** cat's eye	cornelian	rhinestone
onyx	citrine	demantoid	rose quartz
opal	crystal	malachite	serpentine
ruby	diamond	marcasite	spinel ruby
05 agate	emerald	moonstone	tourmaline
amber	peridot	morganite	**11** alexandrite
beryl	**08** amethyst	soapstone	chrysoberyl
coral	fire opal	tiger's eye	chrysoprase
pearl	sapphire	turquoise	lapis lazuli
topaz	sunstone	uvarovite	spessartite
06 garnet	**09** cairngorm	**10** aquamarine	**13** cubic zirconia
jasper	carbuncle	bloodstone	mother-of-pearl
		chalcedony	white sapphire

See also **diamond**

genealogy

Terms to do with genealogy include:

03 DSP	soundex	**10** ahnentafel
IGI	surname	descendant
née	testate	family name
04 AGRA	trustee	family tree
clan	widower	forefather
deed	witness	generation
heir	**08** ancestor	maiden name
late	ancestry	onomastics
race	bachelor	progenitor
will	base-born	succession
05 issue	bequeath	**11** beneficiary
trace	cadastra	genealogist
widow	canon law	record agent
06 census	deceased	**12** burial record
degree	decedent	census record
estate	emigrant	cousin-german
legacy	forebear	Domesday Book
relict	maternal	illegitimate
07 archive	paternal	primogenitor
bastard	pedigree	vital records
bequest	relation	**13** Christian name
consort	spinster	consanguinity
descent	theogony	died sine prole
divorce	**09** ascendant	pedigree chart
epitaph	given name	primary record
kinship	immigrant	primogeniture
lineage	indenture	**14** cemetery record
peerage	intestate	common ancestor
probate	necrology	marriage record
progeny	offspring	**15** secondary record
removed	sine prole	vital statistics
	testament	

See also **family**

general

Generals include:

03 Dix (John A; 1798–1879, US)
Doe (Samuel K; 1951–90, Liberian)
Lee (Robert E; 1807–70, US)
Ney (Michel; 1769–1815, French)

04 Alba (Ferdinand Alvarez de Toledo, Duke of; 1508–82, Spanish)
Alva (Ferdinand Alvarez de Toledo, Duke of; 1508–82, Spanish)
Asad (Hafez al-; 1928–2000, Syrian)
Dyer (Reginald; 1864–1927, British)
Haig (Alexander; 1924–2010, US)
Jehu (842–815 BC, Hebrew)
Jodl (Alfred; 1890–1946, German)
Juin (Alphonse; 1888–1967, French)
Pope (John; 1822–92, US)
Prem (Tinsulanonda; 1920–, Thai)

05 Assad (Hafez al-; 1928–2000, Syrian)
Booth (William; 1829–1912, English)
Bragg (Braxton; 1817–76, US)
Clive (Robert, Lord; 1725–74, English)
Davis (Benjamin Oliver; 1877–1970, US)
Deane (Richard; 1610–53, English)
Eanes (António Ramalho; 1935– , Portuguese)
Gates (Horatio; 1728–1806, American)
Gough (Sir Hubert; 1870–1963, Irish)
Grant (Ulysses S; 1822–85, US)
Ramos (Fidel; 1928– , Philippine)
Salan (Raoul; 1899–1984, French)
Scott (Winfield; 1786–1866, US)
Soult (Nicolas Jean de Dieu; 1769–1851, French)
Wolfe (James; 1727–59, English)

06 Aëtius (Flavius; c.390–454 AD, Roman)
Anders (Wladyslaw; 1892–1970, Polish)
Aranda (Pedro Pablo Abarca y Bolea, Conde de; 1718–99, Spanish)
Arnold (Benedict; 1741–1801, American)
Buller (Sir Redvers; 1839–1908, English)
Butler (Benjamin Franklin; 1818–93, US)
Caesar (Julius; 100/102–44 BC, Roman)
Church (Sir Richard; 1785–1873, Irish)
Custer (George Armstrong; 1839–76, US)
Davout (Louis Nicolas; 1770–1823, French)
De Bono (Emilio; 1866–1944, Italian)
Douhet (Giulio; 1869–1930, Italian)
Dunois (Jean d'Orléans, Comte de; 1403–68, French)
Fabius (Caius Fabius; fl.304 BC, Roman)
Fabius (Quintus Fabius Rullianus; 4c BC, Roman)
Franco (Francisco; 1892–1975, Spanish)
Geisel (Ernesto; 1908–96, Brazilian)

Gordon (Charles; 1833–85, English)
Joffre (Joseph; 1852–1931, French)
Jomini (Henri, Baron de; 1779–1869, French)
Kearny (Philip; 1814–62, US)
Kearny (Stephen Watts; 1794–1848, US)
Kléber (Jean Baptiste; 1753–1800, French)
Leslie (Alexander, Earl of Leven; c.1580–1661, Scottish)
Marion (Francis; c.1732–95, American)
Marius (Gaius; 157–86 BC, Roman)
Moreau (Jean Victor; 1761–1813, French)
Morgan (John Hunt; 1825–64, US)
Napier (Sir Charles; 1782–1853, English)
Narses (c.478–573 AD, Byzantine)
Outram (James; 1803–63, English)
Patton (George S; 1885–1945, US)
Putnam (Rufus; 1738–1824, American)
Rommel (Erwin; 1891–1944, German)
Scipio (the Younger; 185–129 BC, Roman)
Sharon (Ariel; 1928– , Israeli)
Spaatz (Carl A; 1891–1974, US)
Suchet (Louis Gabriel, Duc d'Albufera da Valencia; 1770–1826, French)
Thomas (George Henry; 1816–70, US)
Zhukov (Georgi; 1896–1974, Soviet)

07 Agrippa (Marcus Vipsanius; c.63–12 BC, Roman)
Atatürk (Mustapha Kemal; 1881–1938, Turkish)
Berwick (James Fitzjames, Duke of; 1670–1734, French)
Bouillé (François Claude Amour, Marquis de; 1739–1800, French)
Bradley (Omar N; 1893–1981, US)
Carmona (Antonio; 1869–1951, Portuguese)
Delgado (Humberto; 1906–65, Portuguese)
Duilius (Gaius; fl.260 BC, Roman)
Eyadéma (Gnassingbé; 1937–2005, Togolese)
Fairfax (Thomas, Lord; 1612–71, English)
Hampton (Wade; c.1751–1835, American)
Katsura (Taro; 1847–1913, Japanese)
Lambert (John; 1619–84, English)
Lincoln (Benjamin; 1733–1810, American)
Masséna (André; 1758–1817, French)
Obregón (Alvaro; 1880–1928, Mexican)
Paullus (Lucius Aemilius; d.216 BC, Roman)
Pickett (George E; 1825–75, US)
Regulus (Marcus Atilius; d.c.250 BC, Roman)
Ridgway (Matthew B; 1895–1993, US)
Sherman (William T; 1820–91, US)
Spínola (António de; 1910–96, Portuguese)

08 Agricola (Gnaeus Julius; 40–93 AD, Roman)
Anderson (Sir Kenneth; 1891–1959, Indian/British)

Badoglio (Pietro; 1871–1956, Italian)
Billiere (Sir Peter de la; 1934– , English)
Bourmont (Louis de Ghaisnes, Comte de; 1773–1846, French)
Brisbane (Sir Thomas Makdougall; 1773–1860, Scottish)
Camillus (Marcus Furius; 447–365 BC, Roman)
Cárdenas (Lázaro; 1895–1970, Mexican)
Cardigan (James Thomas Brudenell, Earl of; 1797–1868, English)
de Gaulle (Charles; 1890–1970, French)
Guderian (Heinz; 1888–1953, German)
Hamilton (Sir Ian Standish Monteith; 1853–1947, English)
Hannibal (247–182 BC, Carthaginian)
Johnston (Albert Sidney; 1803–62, US)
Johnston (Joseph E; 1807–91, US)
Josephus (Flavius; 37–c.100 AD, Jewish)
Kolingba (André; 1936–2010, Central African Republic)
Kornilov (Lavr Georgiyevich; 1870–1918, Russian)
Marshall (George C; 1880–1959, US)
Montrose (James Graham, Marquis of; 1612–50, Scottish)
Nearchus (4c BC, Macedonian)
Pershing (John J; 1860–1948, US)
Samsonov (Aleksandr Vasilevich; 1859–1914, Russian)
Schuyler (Philip John; 1733–1804, American)
Seleucus (I Nicator; c.358–281 BC, Macedonian)
Timoleon (d.c.337 BC, Greek)

09 Alekseyev (Mikhail Vasilevich; 1857–1918, Russian)
Alexander (Sir Harold, Earl; 1891–1969, Irish)
Antigonus (d.301 BC, Macedonian)
Antonescu (Ion; 1882–1946, Romanian)
Aristides (c.550–c.467 BC, Athenian)
Boulanger (Georges; 1837–91, French)
Brownrigg (Sir Robert; 1759–1833, English)
Doubleday (Abner; 1819–93, US)
Dumouriez (Charles François; 1739–1823, French)
Faidherbe (Louis; 1818–89, French)
Flaminius (Gaius; d.217 BC, Roman)
Hasdrubal (d.207 BC, Carthaginian)
Lemnitzer (Lyman L; 1899–1988, US)
MacArthur (Douglas; 1880–1964, US)

Marcellus (Marcus Claudius; c.268–208 BC, Roman)
McClellan (George Brinton; 1826–85, US)
Menshikov (Aleksandr Sergeyevich; 1789–1869, Russian)
Miltiades (the Younger; c.550–489 BC, Athenian)
Montholon (Charles Tristan, Marquis de; 1783–1853, French)
Musharraf (Pervaiz; 1943– , Pakistani)
Omar Pasha (1806–71, Ottoman)
Santander (Francisco de Paula; 1792–1840, Colombian)
Townshend (George, Viscount and Marquess; 1724–1807, English)
Townshend (Sir Charles Vere Ferrers; 1861–1924, English)

10 Abercromby (Sir Ralph; 1734–1801, Scottish)
Beauregard (P G T; 1818–93, US)
Belisarius (505–65, Byzantine)
Christison (Sir Philip; 1893–1993, Scottish)
Cunningham (Sir Alan Gordon; 1887–1983, Irish/British)
Eisenhower (Dwight D; 1890–1969, US)
Empecinado (El; 1775–1825, Spanish)
Hardie Boys (Sir Michael; 1931– , New Zealand)
Lysimachus (d.281 BC, Macedonian)
Oglethorpe (James Edward; 1696–1785, English)
Peng Dehuai (1899–1974, Chinese)
Schlieffen (Alfred, Count von; 1833–1913, Prussian)
Timoshenko (Semyon; 1895–1970, Russian)

11 Baden-Powell (Robert, Lord; 1857–1941, English)
Beauharnais (Eugène de; 1781–1824, French)
Epaminondas (c.418–362 BC, Theban)
Jiang Jieshi (1887–1975, Chinese)
Schwarzkopf (H Norman; 1934–2012, US)

12 Smith-Dorrian (Sir Horace; 1858–1930, English)

13 Chiang Kai-shek (1887–1975, Chinese)
Primo de Rivera (Miguel, Marqués de Estella; 1870–1930, Spanish)
Schwarzenberg (Karl Philipp, Prince of; 1771–1820, Austrian)

14 Osman Nuri Pasha (1832–1900, Turkish)

genetics

Geneticists include:

04 Ford (Edmund Brisco; 1901–88, English)
05 Brown (Michael S; 1941– , US)

Crick (Francis Harry Compton; 1916–2004, English)

Jones (Steve; 1944– , Welsh)
Leder (Philip; 1934– , US)
Ochoa (Severo; 1905–93, US)
Sager (Ruth; 1918–97, US)
Snell (George Davis; 1903–96, US)
Vries (Hugo de; 1848–1935, Dutch)
06 Beadle (George Wells; 1903–89, US)
Benzer (Seymour; 1921–2007, US)
Biffen (Sir Rowland; 1874–1949, English)
Bodmer (Sir Walter; 1936– , English)
Boveri (Theodor; 1862–1915, German)
Cantor (Charles; 1942– , US)
Clarke (Bryan; 1932– , English)
Fisher (Sir Ronald Aylmer; 1890–1962, English)
Galton (Sir Francis; 1822–1911, English)
Gurdon (Sir John; 1933– , English)
Harris (Sir Henry; 1925– , Australian/British)
Mendel (Gregor; 1822–84, Austrian)
Morgan (Thomas Hunt; 1866–1945, US)
Müller (Hermann Joseph; 1890–1967, US)
Venter (Craig; 1946– , US)
Watson (James Dewey; 1928– , US)
Wright (Sewall; 1889–1988, US)
Zinder (Norton; 1928–2012, US)
07 Bateson (William; 1861–1926, English)
Borlaug (Norman; 1914–2009, US)
Collins (Francis S; 1950– , US)
Correns (Carl; 1864–1933, German)
Gehring (Walter; 1939– , Swiss)

Hopwood (Sir David; 1933– , English)
Lysenko (Trofim Denisovich; 1898–1976, Soviet)
McLaren (Dame Anne; 1927–2007, English)
Penrose (Lionel Sharples; 1898–1972, English)
Vavilov (Nikolai Ivanovich; 1887–1943, Russian)
08 Auerbach (Charlotte; 1899–1994, German)
Franklin (Rosalind; 1920–58, English)
Lewontin (Richard; 1929– , US)
Palmiter (Richard; 1942– , US)
Sheppard (Philip MacDonald; 1921–76, English)
Yamanaka (Shinya; 1962– , Japanese)
Yanofsky (Charles; 1925– , US)
09 Ashburner (Michael; 1942– , English)
Baltimore (David; 1938– , US)
Goldstein (Joseph Leonard; 1940– , US)
Johanssen (Wilhelm; 1857–1927, Danish)
Lederberg (Joshua; 1925–2008, US)
10 Darlington (Cyril Dean; 1903–81, English)
Dobzhansky (Theodosius; 1900–75, US)
Kettlewell (Bernard; 1907–79, English)
McClintock (Barbara; 1902–92, US)
Pontecorvo (Guido; 1907–99, Italian/British)
Sturtevant (Alfred Henry; 1891–1970, US)
Waddington (C H; 1905–75, English)
Weatherall (Sir David; 1933– , English)
12 Maynard Smith (John; 1920–2004, English)

Terms used in genetics include:

02 GM

03 DNA
egg
RNA

04 base
gene
mRNA
tRNA

05 clone
codon
helix
sperm

06 allele
gamete
genome
hybrid
intron
parent
uracil

vector
zygote

07 adenine
diploid
guanine
meiosis
mitosis
thymine

08 autosome
cytosine
dominant
genetics
heredity
mutation
promoter
sequence

09 amino acid
behaviour
haplotype
homologue

inversion
karyotype
offspring
paralogue
recessive
repressor
transgene
variation

10 adaptation
chromosome
generation
geneticist
homozygous
nucleosome
nucleotide
orthologue
polymerase
speciation

11 double helix
epigenetics

genetic code
inheritance
nucleic acid
polypeptide
X-chromosome
Y-chromosome

12 cell division
F1 generation
F2 generation
heterozygous
mitochondria
reproduction

13 DNA sequencing
fertilization
mitochondrion
recombination
transcription
translocation

15 self-replication

geography

Geographical regions include:

04 veld	pampas	occident	wilderness
05 basin	steppe	savannah	**11** countryside
coast	tundra	woodland	
heath	**07** outback	**09** Antarctic	**13** rural district
plain	prairie	grassland	urban district
06 Arctic	riviera	green belt	**14** developed world
desert	seaside	marshland	**15** developing world
forest	tropics	scrubland	
jungle	**08** lowlands	wasteland	
orient	midlands	**10** Third World	

Geographical features include:

03 alp	brook	desert
bar	butte	forest
bay	canal	graben
bog	chasm	ice cap
cay	cliff	island
col	coast	lagoon
cwm	creek	mantle
fen	crust	pampas
key	delta	rapids
ria	esker	ravine
sea	fault	riegel
04 arch	fiard	steppe
bank	fiord	strait
bush	fjard	stream
cape	fjord	trench
cave	gorge	tundra
core	heath	valley
cove	horst	**07** caldera
dike	inlet	cerrado
dune	karst	channel
dyke	kopje	estuary
gulf	levée	fissure
hill	lough	glacier
lake	marsh	hillock
loch	nappe	iceberg
mesa	oasis	ice fall
moor	ocean	ice floe
mull	plate	isthmus
pass	point	moraine
pole	river	mud flat
pond	scree	plateau
reef	shore	pothole
rock	sound	prairie
spit	stack	savanna
veld	swamp	sea arch
wadi	veldt	terrace
wady		volcano
05 abyss	**06** arroyo	wetland
atoll	barrow	**08** blowhole
basin	canyon	crevasse
beach	cirque	headland
	corrie	
	crater	

ice field	tidal flat	swallow hole
ice sheet	waterfall	**12** abyssal plain
ice shelf	**10** barrier bar	barrier beach
moorland	blanket bog	fold mountain
mountain	block field	oceanic crust
ocean bed	cold desert	oceanic plate
sand dune	escarpment	oceanic ridge
savannah	fault plane	subcontinent
seamount	fault scarp	
sea stack	finger lake	**13** barrier island
09 chaparral	floodplain	block mountain
continent	ocean basin	glacial trough
coral reef	ocean floor	glacial valley
grassland	promontory	hanging valley
hot desert	rainforest	mangrove swamp
ice stream	rift valley	monsoon forest
island arc	**11** archipelago	mountain range
ox-bow lake	barrier reef	shore platform
peninsula	block stream	tectonic plate
quicksand	coastal dune	U-shaped valley
salt marsh	glacial lake	valley glacier
stream bed	ocean trench	**14** tropical forest
string bog	rock glacier	**15** paternoster lake

Geographers and cartographers include:

03 Dee (John; 1527–1608, English)

04 Cary (John; c.1754–1835, English)
Mela (Pomponius; fl.40 AD, Latin)

05 Adair (John; c.1655–c.1722, Scottish)
Barth (Heinrich; 1821–65, German)
Cabot (Sebastian; 1474–1557, Venetian)
Darby (Sir Clifford; 1909–92, Welsh)
Guyot (Arnold; 1807–84, US)
Hedin (Sven; 1865–1952, Swedish)
Imhof (Eduard; 1895–1986, Swiss)
Penck (Albrecht; 1858–1945, German)
Sauer (Carl; 1889–1975, US)
Speed (John; 1542–1629, English)
Stamp (Sir Dudley; 1898–1966, English)

06 Batuta (1304–68, Arab)
Behaim (Martin; 1440–1507, German)
Bowman (Isaiah; 1878–1950, US)
Clüver (Phillip; 1580–1622, German)
Edrisi (c.1100–64, Arab)
Gmelin (Johann Georg; 1709–55, German)
Harvey (David; 1935– , English)
Idrisi (c.1100–64, Arab)
Ritter (Karl; 1779–1859, German)
Saxton (Christopher; 1542/44–c.1611, English)
Strabo (c.60 BC–c.21 AD, Greek)

07 Gilbert (G K; 1843–1918, US)
Haggett (Peter; 1933– , English)
Hakluyt (Richard; c.1552–1616, English)
Hondius (Jodocus; 1563–1612, Flemish)

Markham (Sir Clements; 1830–1916, English)
Ogilvie (Alan; 1887–1954, Scottish)
Ptolemy (c.90–168 AD, Egyptian)
Wallace (Alfred Russel; 1823–1913, English)

08 Büsching (Anton Friedrich; 1724–93, German)
Filchner (Wilhelm; 1877–1957, German)
Humboldt (Alexander, Baron von; 1769–1859, German)
Mercator (Gerardus; 1512–94, Flemish)
Ortelius (Abraham Ortel; 1527–98, Flemish)
Robinson (Arthur; 1915–2004, US)

09 Cluverius (Phillip; 1580–1622, German)
Grisebach (A H R; 1814–79, German)
Kropotkin (Prince Peter; 1842–1921, Russian)
Mackinder (Sir Halford John; 1861–1947, English)
Muqaddasi (945–88, Arab)
Pausanias (2c AD, Greek)

10 Arrowsmith (Aaron; 1750–1823, English)
Hartshorne (Richard; 1899–1992, US)
Huntington (Ellsworth; 1876–1943, US)
Richthofen (Ferdinand, Baron von; 1833–1905, German)
Wooldridge (Sydney; 1900–63, English)

11 Bartholomew (John George; 1860–1920, Scottish)
Christaller (Walter; 1893–1969, German)

Hägerstrand (Torsten; 1916–2004, Swedish)
Ibn Battutah (1304–68, Arab)
Kingdon-Ward (Frank; 1885–1958, English)
12 Eratosthenes (c.276–194 BC, Greek)
Leo Africanus (c.1494–c.1552, Arab)

13 Waldseemüller (Martin; c.1480–c.1521, German)
15 Eudoxus of Cnidus (408–353 BC, Greek)
Vidal de la Blache (Paul; 1845–1918, French)

Terms used in geography include:

04 arid
crag
tail
05 shott
taiga
07 aggrade
equator
glacial
hachure
08 alluvium
altitude
landmass
landslip
latitude

meridian
prograde
09 accretion
antipodes
base level
billabong
deviation
ethnology
landslide
longitude
metroplex
relief map
10 coordinate
demography

glaciation
landlocked
topography
11 cartography
chorography
conurbation
demographic
hydrography
triangulate
vulcanology
13 Ordnance Datum
shield volcano
14 plate tectonics
roche moutonnée

See also **bay**; **beach**; **cape**; **cave**; **channel**; **compass**; **desert**; **firth**; **gulf**; **island**; **lake**; **mountain**; **ocean**; **passage**; **peninsula**; **plain**; **river**; **sea**; **sound**; **strait**; **volcano**; **waterfall**

geology

Geological time periods include:

04 Lias (Epoch/Series)
Malm (Epoch/Series)
06 Albian (Stage)
Antian (Stage)
Aptian (Stage)
Arenig (Epoch/Series)
Danian (Stage)
Dogger (Epoch/Series)
Emsian (Stage)
Eocene (Epoch/Series)
Ludlow (Epoch/Series)
Recent (Epoch/Series)
Viséan (Epoch/Series)
07 Anglian (Stage)
Ashgill (Epoch/Series)
Caradoc (Epoch/Series)
Hoxnian (Stage)
Miocene (Epoch/Series)
Neogene (Period)
Permian (Period)
Riphean (Era)
Vendian (Era)
Wenlock (Epoch/Series)
08 Aalenian (Stage)
Aphebian (Era)

Archaean (Eon)
Bajocian (Stage)
Cambrian (Period)
Cenozoic (Era)
Chattian (Stage)
Devonian (Period)
Eifelian (Stage)
Frasnian (Stage)
Givetian (Stage)
Holocene (Epoch/Series)
Jurassic (Period)
Langhian (Stage)
Llanvirn (Epoch/Series)
Lutetian (Stage)
Mesozoic (Era)
Namurian (Epoch/Series)
Pliocene (Epoch/Series)
Rhaetian (Stage)
Rupelian (Stage)
Silesian (Period)
Silurian (Period)
Tertiary (Sub-era)
Thurnian (Stage)
Toarcian (Stage)
Tremadoc (Epoch/Series)
Triassic (Period)

Turonian (Stage)
Ypresian (Stage)
Zanclian (Stage)

09 Barremian (Stage)
Bartonian (Stage)
Bathonian (Stage)
Baventian (Stage)
Callovian (Stage)
Campanian (Stage)
Coniacian (Stage)
Cromerian (Stage)
Devensian (Stage)
Dinantian (Period)
Flandrian (Stage)
Gedinnian (Stage)
Llandeilo (Epoch/Series)
Ludhamian (Stage)
Messinian (Stage)
Oligocene (Epoch/Series)
Oxfordian (Stage)
Pastonian (Stage)
Ryazanian (Stage)
Santonian (Stage)
Siegenian (Stage)
Thanetian (Stage)
Tortonian (Stage)
Waltonian (Stage)
Zechstein (Epoch/Series)

10 Aquitanian (Stage)
Beestonian (Stage)
Cenomanian (Stage)
Cretaceous (Period)
Hettangian (Stage)
Ipswichian (Stage)
Llandovery (Epoch/Series)
Ordovician (Period)
Palaeocene (Epoch/Series)
Palaeogene (Period)
Palaeozoic (Era)

Placenzian (Stage)
Priabonian (Stage)
Quaternary (Period)
Sinemurian (Stage)
Stephanian (Epoch/Series)
Wolstonian (Stage)

11 Burdigalian (Stage)
Famerianian (Stage)
Hauterivian (Stage)
Phanerozoic (Eon)
Pleistocene (Epoch/Series)
Portlandian (Stage)
Precambrian (Eon)
Proterozoic (Eon)
Tournaisian (Epoch/Series)
Valanginian (Stage)
Westphalian (Epoch/Series)

12 Kimmeridgian (Stage)
Rotliegendes (Epoch/Series)
Serravallian (Stage)

13 Carboniferous (Period)
Lower Cambrian (Epoch/Series)
Lower Devonian (Epoch/Series)
Lower Jurassic (Epoch/Series)
Lower Triassic (Epoch/Series)
Maastrichtian (Stage)
Mississippian (Period)
Pennsylvanian (Period)
Pliensbachian (Stage)
Upper Cambrian (Epoch/Series)
Upper Devonian (Epoch/Series)
Upper Jurassic (Epoch/Series)
Upper Triassic (Epoch/Series)

14 Middle Cambrian (Epoch/Series)
Middle Devonian (Epoch/Series)
Middle Jurassic (Epoch/Series)
Middle Triassic (Epoch/Series)

15 Lower Cretaceous (Epoch/Series)
Upper Cretaceous (Epoch/Series)

Terms used in geology include:

02 aa

03 bar
cwm
mya
ore

04 clay
dome
dune
fold
lava
limb
lode
Moho
till

trap
tuff
vein
wadi

05 agate
atoll
basin
butte
chert
delta
epoch
esker
fault
fiord

fjord
focus
gorge
gully
guyot
horst
joint
Karst
lahar
levee
magma
plain
P-wave
ridge
S-wave

talus
06 albite
arkose
arroyo
basalt
bolson
canyon
cirque
corrie
debris
gabbro
geyser
gneiss
graben
mantle
oolite
quartz
runoff
schist
scoria
stress
tephra
trench
uplift

07 aquifer
barchan
bauxite
bed-load
blowout
breccia
caldera
drumlin
glacier
granite
hogback
igneous
isograd
lapilli
meander
mineral
moraine
orogeny
outwash
plateau
pothole
vesicle
volcano

08 A-horizon
alluvium
backwash
basement

See also **crust**; **rock**

B-horizon
C-horizon
feldspar
fumarole
isostasy
leaching
lopolith
monolith
mountain
obsidian
oilfield
oil shale
pahoehoe
pediment
regolith
rhyolite
syncline
xenolith

09 alabaster
batholith
carbonate
deflation
epicentre
flood tide
hot spring
intrusion
laccolith
landslide
limestone
Mohs scale
monadnock
monocline
oxidation
peneplain
rock cycle
rockslide
sandstone
slip fault
striation
tableland
viscosity
volcanism

10 anthracite
astrobleme
block fault
cinder cone
deposition
depression
earthquake
flood plain
kettle hole
mineralogy

rift valley
subsidence
topography
travertine
water table
weathering

11 alluvial fan
central vent
exfoliation
geosyncline
groundwater
maar volcano
metamorphic
normal fault
sublimation
swallow hole
thrust fault
volcanic ash

12 artesian well
coastal plain
fringing reef
magma chamber
pyroclastics
stratigraphy
unconformity
volcanic bomb
volcanic cone
volcanic dome
volcanic pipe

13 angle of repose
barrier island
drainage basin
geomorphology
hanging valley
recumbent fold
shield volcano
stratovolcano
U-shaped valley
V-shaped valley

14 bituminous coal
eustatic change
lateral moraine
longshore drift
stratification
subduction zone
transform fault
wave-cut terrace

15 million years ago
sedimentary rock
strike-slip fault
terminal moraine

German

German boys' names include:

03 Jan	Sven	**06** Dieter	Mathias
Max	Swen	Jürgen	Steffen
Uwe	**05** Bernd	Markus	Stephan
04 Dirk	Erich	Niklas	Torsten
Eric	Fritz	Stefan	**08** Kristian
Erik	Jonas	Tobias	Matthias
Jens	Klaus	Ulrich	Thorsten
Jörg	Lukas	**07** Andreas	Wolfgang
Ralf	Ralph	Dominik	

German girls' names include:

04 Elke	Petra	Sigrun	Birgitta
Irma	Trudi	Steffi	Brunhild
Lili	**06** Angela	Ulrika	Christin
05 Berta	Astrid	Ursula	Gretchen
Erika	Birgit	**07** Bettina	**09** Brunhilde
Gerda	Dagmar	Jolanda	Elisabeth
Heidi	Frieda	Kristin	Franziska
Helga	Ingrid	**08** Adelheid	Hildegard
Hilde	Liesel	Angelika	**10** Wilhelmina
Lotti	Monika		

German words and expressions include:

04 echt (denotes authenticity, typicality)
Flak (abuse, criticism)
über (prefix used to mean ultimate, above all)

05 Angst (anxiety; anguish)
Blitz (lightning; also short for Blitzkrieg)
Geist (spirit)
kaput (broken; destroyed)
Reich (empire)
Stasi (former East German secret police)
U-Boot (submarine)

06 abseil (to descend a vertical face using rope)
ersatz (fake; substitute)
Führer (leader; dictator)
Kaiser (emperor)
Kitsch (something trashy)
Landau (type of carriage)
Panzer (military tank)
Umlaut (two dots indicating change in vowel sound)

07 Achtung (Attention!)
Bauhaus (architectural school and style)
Gestalt (original whole or unit)
Gestapo (former Nazi secret state police)
Pilsner (beer from Pilsen in Czech Republic)
Pretzel (hard, salted biscuit)
Strudel (type of pastry/dessert)

08 Autobahn (motorway)

Dummkopf (blockhead; idiot)
Hausfrau (housewife)
Kohlrabi (vegetable)
Pinscher (breed of dog)
Schnapps (distilled alcoholic drink)
spritzer (drink of wine and soda water)
Zugzwang (compulsion to make bad move, especially in chess)

09 Alpenhorn (musical instrument)
Anschluss (annexation of Austria in WWII)
Bratwurst (type of sausage)
Bundestag (German parliament)
Dachshund (breed of dog)
Edelweiss (type of flowering plant)
gemütlich (amiable; comfortable; cosy)
Hamburger (meat patty said to have originated in Hamburg)
Leitmotiv (recurrent theme in a literary or musical work)
Luftwaffe (air force)
nicht wahr? (isn't that so?)
Reichstag (German parliament)
Schnauzer (breed of dog)
Schnitzel (meat cutlet)
Wehrmacht (former German armed forces)
zeitgeist (spirit of the age)

10 Alpenstock (walking stick)
Blitzkrieg (a sudden overwhelming attack by ground and air forces)

Bundesbank (German Federal bank)
Gesundheit (your health, said to someone who has just sneezed)
Hinterland (remote area beyond coast)
Jugendstil ('youth style'; the German term for art nouveau)
Lebensraum ('room to live', ie justification for expansionism)
Lederhosen (leather trousers)
Meerschaum (tobacco pipe made from mineral of the same name)
Ostpolitik (former political stance of Western Germany towards the Communist bloc)
Rottweiler (breed of dog)
Sauerkraut (cabbage preserved in salt)
Übermensch (superman)
Volkswagen (people's car)
Wanderlust (desire to wander)
wunderkind (child prodigy)

11 Frankfurter (type of sausage originally from Frankfurt)
Kulturkampf (cultural battle, ie Church vs State)
Poltergeist (ghost that makes noises and moves objects)

Realpolitik (politics based on practical considerations)
und so weiter (and so forth)
Weltschmerz (sympathy with universal misery; utter pessimism)

12 Doppelgänger (double; look-alike)
eile mit Weile ('make speed with leisure')
Gastarbeiter (an immigrant worker, especially one who does menial work)
Glockenspiel (musical instrument)
Kindergarten (children's nursery)
Machtpolitik (power politics)
Pumpernickel (dark rye bread)

13 Bildungsroman (novel dealing with a character's formative years)
Kristallnacht (anti-Jewish pogrom of 9–10 Nov 1938)
Schadenfreude (enjoyment of another's misfortune)
Sturm und Drang (literary movement)

14 Weltanschauung (way of looking at the world)

15 Götterdämmerung (the downfall of any once powerful system)

See also **day**; **month**; **number**

Germany

Cities and notable towns in Germany include:

04 Bonn	Munich	Leipzig	Stuttgart
05 Essen	Weimar	**08** Würzburg	**10** Düsseldorf
Trier	**07** Cologne	**09** Frankfurt	**15** Frankfurt am Main
06 Berlin	Hamburg	Nuremberg	

Administrative divisions of Germany, with regional capitals:

06 Berlin (Berlin)	**11** Brandenburg (Potsdam)	**18** Nordrhein-Westfalen (Düsseldorf)
Bremen (Bremen)	**13** Niedersachsen (Hannover)	
Hessen (Wiesbaden)	Sachsen-Anhalt (Magdeburg)	**21** Mecklenburg-Vorpommern (Schwerin)
07 Bavaria (Munich)	**14** Rheinland-Pfalz (Mainz)	
Hamburg (Hamburg)	**16** Baden-Württemberg (Stuttgart)	
Sachsen (Dresden)		
08 Saarland (Saarbrücken)	**17** Schleswig-Holstein (Kiel)	
09 Thüringen (Erfurt)		

German landmarks include:

04 Elba	Danube	**09** Helgoland
Elbe	**07** Brocken	Linderhof
Main	Moselle	Reichenau
Oder	Rathaus	Reichstag
05 Rhine		Starnberg
06 Dachau	**08** Residenz	**10** Buchenwald

Heidelberg
Tiergarten
Wies Church
11 Berliner Dom
Black Forest
Fernsehturm
Königsplatz
Mariensäule
Rhine valley
Trostbrücke
12 Bavarian Alps

Frauenkirche
Museumsinsel
13 Bonn Cathedral
Colditz Castle
Festspielhaus
Harz Mountains
Moselle valley
14 Alexanderplatz
Essen Cathedral
Gemäldegalerie
Herrenchiemsee

Neuschwanstein
Potsdamer Platz
Trier Cathedral
Unter den Linden
Wartburg Castle
15 Aachen Cathedral
Auerbach's Keller
Brandenburg Gate
East Side Gallery
Munich Cathedral
Speyer Cathedral

giant

Giants include:

03 Gog
Oni
04 Bali
Bana
Bres
Caca
Corb
Ériu
Gaia
Gerd
Gorm
Grid
Hrod
Kari
Loki
Otus
Rhea
Ymir
05 Aegir
Arges
Argus
Atlas
Balor
Banba
Baugi
Cacus
Fodla
Gjalp
Greip
Gymir
Hymir
Jotun
Magog
Orion
Pan Gu
Skadi
Talos
Theia
Thrym
06 Albion
Anakim

Bestla
Cronus
Echion
Elatha
Fachan
Fafnir
Fasolt
Geryon
Hagrid
Phoebe
Tethra
Tethys
Themis
Thiazi
Titans
Tityus
Typhon
07 Antaeus
Ashuras
Brontes
Cyclops
Daityas
Ethlinn
Geirrod
Gilling
Goliath
Iapetus
Klytius
Oceanus
Olvaldi
Purusha
Suttung
Telemos
Telemus
Windigo
Zipacna
08 Angrboda
Bolthorn
Briareus
Cethlenn
Cyclopes
Eurytion

Firbolgs
Gigantes
Gogmagog
Hrungnir
Hyperion
Jarnsaxa
Morgante
Nephilim
Panoptes
Steropes
Upelluri
09 Angerboda
Aurgelmir
Bergelmir
Enceladus
Fomorians
Gandareva
Gargantua
Grantorto
Menoetius
Mnemosyne
Olentzero
10 Angerbotha
Buarainech
Epimetheus
Pantagruel
Paul Bunyan
Polyphemus
Prometheus
Ysbaddaden
11 Finn MacCool
Galligantus
Gog and Magog
Hiranyaksha
Thrudgelmir
Utgardaloki
12 Vafthruthnir
14 Hiranyakashipu
15 Cerne Abbas Giant
Fionn MacCumhail

gift *see* **Christmas**

Gilbert, Sir W S (1836–1911) and Sullivan, Sir Arthur (1842–1900)

Significant works include:

07 *Thespis* (1871)

08 *Iolanthe* (1882)
Patience (1881)

09 *Ruddigore* (1887)
The Mikado (1885)

11 *HMS Pinafore* (1878)
Princess Ida (1884)

The Sorcerer (1877)
Trial by Jury (1875)

12 *The Grand Duke* (1896)

13 *The Gondoliers* (1889)
Utopia, Limited (1893)

19 *The Yeomen of the Guard* (1888)

20 *The Pirates of Penzance* (1879)

Significant characters include:

03 Ada
Ida (Princess)

04 Arac
Daly (Dr)
Gama (King)
Hebe
Inez
Jane (Lady)
Kate
Ko-Ko
Lisa
Luiz
Ruth
Zara (Princess)

05 Cyril
Mabel
Point (Jack)
Sophy (Lady)
Tessa
Wells (John Wellington)

06 Angela
Apollo
Becket (Bob)
Bolero (Don Alhambra del)
Giulia
Ludwig
Maybud (Rose)
Meryll (Leonard)
Meryll (Sergeant)

Notary
Peep-Bo
Porter (Rt Hon Sir Joseph)
Psyche (Lady)
Willis (Private)
Yum-Yum

07 Antonio
Blanche (Lady)
Bobstay (Bill)
Casilda
Deadeye (Dick)
Fairfax (Colonel)
Florian
Giorgio
Katisha
Pooh-Bah

08 Annibale
Corcoran (Captain Sir Edward)
Dummkopf (Ernest)
Fiametta
Frederic
Gianetta
Hilarion
Iolanthe
Jellicoe (Julia)
Nanki-Poo
Oakapple (Richard)
Oakapple (Robin)
Palmieri (Giuseppe)

Palmieri (Marco)
Patience
Pish-Tush
Shadbolt (Wilfred)
Strephon
Vittoria

09 Bunthorne (Reginald)
Francesco
Grosvenor (Archibald)
Plaza-Toro (Duke of)
Rackstraw (Ralph)
Sangazure (Aline)
Sangazure (Lady)

10 Ben Hashbaz
Carruthers (Dame)
Hildebrand (King)
Monte Carlo (Prince of)
Murgatroyd (Sir Despard)
Murgatroyd (Sir Ruthven)
Pirate King
Tannhäuser (Dr)

11 Mad Margaret
Pointdextre (Alexis)
Pointdextre (Sir Marmaduke)

12 Cholmondeley (Sir Richard)

14 Von Krakenfeldt (Baroness)

15 Little Buttercup

girl *see* **name**

gland

Glands include:

05 lymph
ovary

06 cortex

pineal
thymus

07 adrenal

eccrine
mammary

medulla

parotid
thyroid

08 apocrine

exocrine	testicle	lachrymal	pituitary
pancreas	**09** endocrine	lymph node	sebaceous
prostate	holocrine	merocrine	**11** parathyroid

glass

Glass sizes include:

03 pot	**05** bobby	**07** butcher
six	middy	sleever
ten	seven	**08** half pint
04 pint	**06** handle	schooner

gods *see* **drink; Hinduism; mythology**

Goethe, Johann Wolfgang von (1749–1832)

Significant works include:

05 *Faust* (1808/1832)

06 'Autumn' (1775)
Egmont (1788)
Stella (1776)

07 *Clavigo* (1774)
'May Song' (1775)
Novelle (1828)
Pandora (1810)
Satyros (1817)

09 'Achilleis' (1808)
'To the Moon' (1778)

10 *Prometheus* (1830)
'The Erl-King' (1782)

11 *The Agitated* (1817)
'Tour in Italy' (1816–17)

12 'Reineke Fuchs' (1794)
Roman Elegies (1795)
Siege of Mainz (1820–21)

13 'Alexis and Dora' (1797)
'Reynard the Fox' (1794)
The Lover's Whim (1779)
Torquato Tasso (1790)

14 *Erwin and Elmire* (1775)
'French Campaign' (1820–21)
'New Love, New Life' (1775–76)
Poetry and Truth (1811–33)
The Accomplices (1776)

The Gross-Cophta (1791)

16 'To Coachman Kronos' (1789)
Trilogy of Passion (1827)
West-Eastern Divan (1819)

17 *Iphigenia in Tauris* (1787)
'The Bride of Corinth' (1798)
The Burgher-General (1793)

18 'Hermann and Dorothea' (1797)
The Natural Daughter (1803)
'Welcome and Farewell' (1775)

19 *Götz von Berlichingen* (1773)

21 *Claudine von Villa Bella* (1788)
'Only He Who Knows Longing' (1795–96)
The Elective Affinities (1809)
'The Wanderer's Night Song' (1776)
'The Wanderer's Storm Song' (1772)

22 'The Sorcerer's Apprentice' (1798)

23 'Spirit Song over the Waters' (1779)

24 *The Metamorphosis of Plants* (1790)
The Sorrows of Young Werther (1774)

25 *Wilhelm Meister's Wanderings* (1821)

29 *Wilhelm Meister's Apprenticeship* (1795)

32 *Wilhelm Meister's Theatrical Mission* (1795–96)

34 'Winter Journey over the Hartz Mountains' (1777)

golf

Golf clubs include:

04 iron	cleek	bulger
wood	spoon	driver
05 baffy	wedge	jigger
blade	**06** brassy	mashie

putter

07 blaster
brassie
midiron
niblick

08 long iron

09 midmashie

sand wedge
short iron

10 mashie iron

11 belly putter
driving iron
fairway wood
spade mashie

12 putting-cleek

13 mashie niblick
pitching wedge
two-ball putter

15 pitching niblick

Golf courses include:

04 Deal (England)
Eden (England)

05 Troon (Scotland)

06 Manito (USA)
Merion (USA)
Skokie (USA)

07 Balgove (Scotland)
Buffalo (USA)
Hoylake (England)
Jubilee (Scotland)
Medinah (USA)
Newport (USA)
Oak Hill (USA)
Oakmont (USA)
Oak Tree (USA)
Prince's (Scotland)
Sahalee (USA)

08 Bethesda (USA)
Birkdale (England)
Blue Hill (USA)
Glen View (USA)
Portland (USA)
Sandwich (England)
Valhalla (USA)

09 Aronimink (USA)
Baltimore (USA)
Baltusrol (USA)
Bellerive (USA)
Brookline (USA)
Englewood (USA)
Hazeltine (USA)
Inverness (USA)
Minikahda (USA)
Muirfield (Scotland)
New Course (Scotland)
Old Course (Scotland)
Onwentsia (USA)
Pinehurst (USA)
Prestwick (Scotland)
St Andrews (Scotland)
The Belfry (Scotland)
Turnberry (Scotland)

10 Canterbury (USA)
Carnoustie (Scotland)
Garden City (USA)
Royal Troon (Scotland)
Shoal Creek (USA)
Tanglewood (USA)
Winged Foot (USA)

11 Cherry Hills (USA)
Kemper Lakes (USA)
Miami Valley (USA)
Musselburgh (Scotland)
Olympic Club (USA)
Pebble Beach (USA)
Strathtyrum (Scotland)

12 Crooked Stick (USA)
Laurel Valley (USA)
Oakland Hills (USA)

13 Northwood Club (USA)
Olympia Fields (USA)
Royal Birkdale (England)
Royal Portrush (Northern Ireland)
Southern Hills (USA)

14 Keller Golf Club (USA)
Myopia Hunt Club (USA)
NCR Country Club (USA)
Pelham Golf Club (USA)

15 Augusta National (USA)
Chicago Golf Club (USA)
Shinnecock Hills (USA)

Golfers include:

03 Els (Ernie; 1969– , South African)
Wie (Michelle; 1989– , US)

04 Berg (Patty; 1918–2006, US)
Daly (John; 1966– , US)
Love (Davis, III; 1964– , US)
Lyle (Sandy; 1958– , Scottish)
Park (Willie, Jnr; 1864–1925, Scottish)
Park (Willie, Snr; 1834–1903, Scottish)
Webb (Karrie; 1974– , Australian)

05 Braid (James; 1870–1950, Scottish)
Faldo (Nick; 1957– , English)
Furyk (James 'Jim'; 1970– , US)
Hagen (Walter; 1892–1969, US)
Hogan (Ben; 1912–97, US)
Jones (Bobby; 1902–71, US)
Locke (Bobby; 1917–87, South African)
Lopez (Nancy; 1957– , US)
Singh (Vijay; 1963– , Fijian)
Snead (Sam; 1912–2002, US)
Woods (Tiger; 1976– , US)

06 Alliss (Peter; 1931– , English)
Cotton (Sir Henry; 1907–87, English)
Curtis (Ben; 1977– , US)
Davies (Laura; 1963– , English)
Garcia (Sergio; 1980– , Spanish)
Goosen (Retief; 1969– , South African)
Langer (Bernhard; 1957– , German)
Morris (Old Tom; 1821–1908, Scottish)
Morris (Young Tom; 1851–75, Scottish)
Nelson (Byron, Jnr; 1912–2006, US)
Norman (Greg; 1955– , Australian)
Ogilvy (Geoff; 1977– , Australian)
O'Meara (Mark; 1957– , US)
Palmer (Arnold; 1929– , US)
Player (Gary; 1936– , South African)
Taylor (J H; 1871–1963, English)
Vardon (Harry; 1870–1937, British)
Watson (Tom; 1949– , US)

07 Cabrera (Angel; 1969– , Argentine)
Charles (Bob; 1936– , New Zealand)

Couples (Fred; 1959– , US)
Creamer (Paula; 1986– , US)
Jacklin (Tony; 1944– , English)
Johnson (Zack; 1976– , US)
McIlroy (Rory; 1989– , N. Irish)
Sarazen (Gene; 1902–99, US)
Strange (Curtis; 1955– , US)
Thomson (Peter; 1929– , Australian)
Trevino (Lee; 1939– , US)
Woosnam (Ian; 1958– , Welsh)
Zoeller (Fuzzy; 1951– , US)

08 Anderson (Willie; 1897–1910, Scottish/US)
Campbell (Michael; 1969– , New Zealand)

Hamilton (Todd; 1965– , US)
Immelman (Trevor; 1979– , South African)
Nicklaus (Jack; 1940– , US)
Olazábal (José-María; 1966– , Spanish)
Torrance (Sam; 1953– , Scottish)
Westwood (Lee; 1973– , English)
Zaharias (Babe; 1914–56, US)

09 Mickelson (Phil; 1970– , US)
Sorenstam (Annika; 1970– , Swedish)

10 Harrington (Padraig; 1971– , Irish)

11 Ballesteros (Seve; 1957–2011, Spanish)
Montgomerie (Colin; 1963– , Scottish)

Golf terms include:

03 cup
cut
fat
lie
par
pin
tee
toe
top

04 away
card
chip
club
draw
drop
fade
flag
fore
heel
hook
iron
loft
plug
pull
push
putt
sole
thin
trap
turn
wood
yips

05 apron
baffy
bogey
break
carry
divot
drive
eagle
flier

green
gutty
hosel
lay up
links
Major
pitch
punch
rough
shaft
shank
skins
skull
slice
spoon
swing
tap-in
wedge

06 balata
birdie
blades
borrow
bounce
bunker
caddie
chip-in
dimple
dog leg
dormie
driver
fringe
gimmie
hazard
honour
jigger
mashie
Nassau
putter
relief
socket
stance

stymie
tee box
tee off

07 address
air shot
blaster
brassie
fairway
gallery
get down
Haskell
hole out
low side
midiron
niblick
pin high
putt out
scratch
tee shot
twosome

08 approach
back nine
bestball
club face
clubhead
duck hook
first cut
flop shot
fourball
foursome
free drop
handicap
high side
lob wedge
long iron
mulligan
overclub
Road Hole
Ryder Cup
sand save
sand trap

whipping

09 albatross
backswing
Crow's Nest
downswing
featherie
flagstick
front nine
grand slam
hole in one
matchplay
medalplay
overshoot
pitch mark
Rae's Creek
sand wedge
short game
short iron
sink a putt
stone dead
sweet spot

See also **sport**

tee marker
the Maiden
underclub
up-and-down

10 Amen Corner
betterball
bump and run
cavity back
fore caddie
greensomes
hanging lie
Hell Bunker
Stableford
stimpmeter
strokeplay
unplayable
Vardon grip

11 belly putter
casual water
compression
driving iron

fairway wood
gutta-percha
leaderboard
out of bounds
pin position
pitch and run
provisional
stroke index
Valley of Sin

12 approach shot

13 Challenge Tour
explosion shot
mashie niblick
pitching wedge
preferred lies
Texas scramble
two-ball putter

14 Eisenhower Tree

15 cross-handed grip
overlapping grip

goose

Geese include:

04 bean
kelp
nene
snow
swan

05 Brent
pygmy

Ross's

06 Andean
Canada
Embden
upland

07 Chinese
emperor

greylag
Orinoco

08 barnacle
Egyptian
Hawaiian
Toulouse

09 bar-headed

10 blue-winged
pink-footed
spur-winged

11 red-breasted
ruddy-headed

12 white-fronted

government

Government systems include:

05 junta

06 empire

07 kingdom

08 monarchy
republic

09 autocracy

communism
democracy
despotism
theocracy

10 absolutism
federation
hierocracy

plutocracy

11 triumvirate

12 commonwealth
dictatorship

UK government departments include:

02 DH

03 BIS
CPS
CSA
DCA
DfE
DfT
DWP

FCO
FSA
MoD
MoJ
NIO
PCO
SEU

04 BERR

DCLG
DCMS
DECC
DFID
DIUS
HMRC

05 DEFRA

08 Treasury

09 Exchequer	Home Office	Law Commission
Met Office	**11** Wales Office	**14** Scotland Office
10 HM Treasury	**13** Cabinet Office	**15** Audit Commission

UK government Cabinet positions:

13 Lord Privy Seal
Prime Minister

19 Deputy Prime Minister

22 First Lord of the Treasury

23 Leader of the House of Lords

24 Chancellor of the Exchequer
Secretary of State for Wales

25 Leader of the House of Commons
Lord President of the Council
Secretary of State for Health

26 Minister for the Civil Service
Secretary of State for Defence

27 Chief Secretary to the Treasury
Secretary of State for Scotland

28 Secretary of State for Education
Secretary of State for Transport

29 Minister for Women and Equalities

34 Secretary of State for Northern Ireland

Secretary of State for Work and Pensions

36 Secretary of State for the Home
Department

39 Secretary of State for Culture, Media and
Sport

41 Secretary of State for Energy and Climate
Change

43 Secretary of State for International
Development
Secretary of State for Justice and Lord
Chancellor

46 Secretary of State for Business, Innovation
and Skills

48 Secretary of State for Communities and
Local Government
Secretary of State for Foreign and
Commonwealth Affairs

49 Secretary of State for Environment, Food and
Rural Affairs

US government departments include:

02 ED	DOC	FBI	**04** ONAP
OA	DOD	FDA	OSTP
VA	DOE	FSA	USDA
03 BEA	DOI	HHS	USTR
BIA	DOJ	HUD	WHMO
CEA	DOL	IRS	**05** USCIS
CEQ	DOS	NSA	**06** Senate
CIA	DOT	NSC	**08** Congress
DHS	DPC	OHS	**10** White House
DIA	EOP	OMB	

See also **legislation**; **office**; **parliament**; **politics**; **republic**

governor

Types of governor include:

03 Ban	**06** eparch	nomarch	**09** beglerbeg
bey	exarch	podestà	castellan
dey	legate	voivode	proconsul
04 khan	satrap	**08** burgrave	**10** adelantado
naik	tuchun	ethnarch	proveditor
vali	**07** alcaide	hospodar	**11** stadtholder
05 hakim	catapan	pentarch	
mudir	harmost	subahdar	

Colonial governors of New South Wales:

04 King (Captain Philip Gidley; 1758–1808)

05 Bligh (Captain William; 1754–1817)
Gipps (Sir George; 1791–1847)

06 Bourke (Major-General Richard; 1777–1855)
Hunter (Captain John; 1737–1821)

07 Darling (Lieutenant-General Ralph; 1772–1858)
Denison (Sir William; 1804–71)
FitzRoy (Sir Charles; 1796–1858)
Phillip (Captain Arthur; 1738–1814)

08 Brisbane (Sir Thomas; 1777–1855)

09 Macquarie (Colonel Lachlan; 1762–1824)

Governors-general of Australia, with dates of office

04 Kerr (Sir John; 1974–77)
Slim (Field-Marshal Sir William; 1953–60)

05 Bryce (Ms Quentin; 2008–   )
Casey (Richard Gardiner, Baron; 1961–65)
Cowen (Sir Zelman; 1977–82)
Deane (Sir William; 1996–2001)

06 Denman (Thomas, Baron; 1911–14)
Dudley (William Humble Ward, Earl of; 1908–11)
Gowrie (Alexander Hore-Ruthven, Baron, 1936–45)
Hayden (William; 1989–96)
Isaacs (Sir Isaac; 1931–36)
McKell (Sir William; 1947–53)

07 De L'Isle (William, Viscount; 1961–65)

Forster (Henry William, Baron; 1920–25)
Hasluck (Sir Paul; 1969–74)
Jeffery (Major-General Michael; 2003–08)
Stephen (Sir Ninian; 1982–89)

08 Hopetoun (John Adrian Louis Hope, Earl of)
Tennyson (Hallam, Baron; 1902–03)

09 Dunrossil (William, Viscount; 1960–61)
Northcote (Henry, Baron; 1904–08)

10 Gloucester (Prince Henry, Duke of; 1945–47)
Stonehaven (Sir John Lawrence Baird, Baron; 1925–31)

12 Hollingworth (Dr Peter; 2001–03)

13 Munro-Ferguson (Sir Ronald; 1914–20)

Governors of New Zealand:

04 Grey (Sir George, 1848–53, 1861–68)

05 Bowen (Sir George Ferguson, 1868–73)

06 Browne (Colonel Thomas Robert Gore, 1855–61)
Gordon (Sir Arthur Hamilton, 1880–82)
Hobson (Sir William, 1841–42)
Onslow (Earl of, 1889–92)

07 FitzRoy (Sir Robert, 1843–45)
Glasgow (Earl of, 1892–97)

Jervois (William Francis Drummond, 1883–89)
Plunket (Lord, 1904–10)

08 Normanby (Marquess of, 1875–79)
Ranfurly (Earl of, 1897–1904)
Robinson (Sir Hercules George Robert, 1879–80)

09 Fergusson (Sir James, 1873–74)
Islington (Lord; 1910–12)
Liverpool (Earl of, 1912–17)

Governors-general of New Zealand, with dates of office

06 Cobham (Charles George Lyttleton; 1957–62)
Galway (Earl of; 1935–41)
Newall (Cyril Louis Norton; 1941–46)
Norrie (Lord; 1952–57)
Reeves (Paul Alfred; 1985–90)
Tizard (Catherine; 1990–96)

07 Beattie (David Stuart; 1980–85)
Porritt (Arthur Espie; 1967–72)

08 Blundell (Edward Denis; 1972–77)
Freyberg (Bernard Cyril; 1946–52)

Holyoake (Keith Jacka; 1977–80)
Jellicoe (John Henry Rushworth; 1920–24)

09 Bledisloe (Charles Bathurst; 1930–35)
Fergusson (Bernard; 1962–67)
Fergusson (Charles; 1924–30)
Liverpool (Earl of; 1917–20)
Mateparae (Sir Jerry, 2011–   )
Satyanand (Anand, 2006–11)

10 Cartwright (Silvia, 2001–06)
Hardie Boys (Michael; 1996–2001)

grace

The Three Graces:

06 Aglaia	**10** Euphrosyne
Thalia	

grade *see* nurse

grammar

Parts of speech include:

01 a	prep	**08** singular	preposition
n	verb	**09** adjective	**12** abbreviation
v	**06** adnoun	gerundive	interjection
02 vb	adverb	**10** common noun	**13** auxiliary verb
vi	gerund	connective	**14** transitive verb
vt	plural	copulative	**15** definite article
03 adj	prefix	participle	relative pronoun
adv	suffix	proper noun	
art	**07** article	**11** conjunction	
04 noun	pronoun	phrasal verb	

Grammatical cases include:

06 dative	ablative	inessive	comitative
essive	adessive	locative	nominative
	allative	vocative	possessive
07 elative	genitive	**09** objective	subjective
08 abessive	illative	**10** accusative	**11** translative

Grammatical tenses include:

02 pt	present	past perfect	present simple
03 pat	**08** preterit	**12** future simple	simple present
04 past	**09** imperfect	gnomic aorist	**14** past continuous
06 aorist	preterite	past historic	present perfect
future	**10** pluperfect	simple future	**15** paragogic future
07 perfect	**11** conditional	**13** future perfect	

Grand Prix *see* racing: motor racing

grape *see* wine

grass

Grasses include:

03 rye	oats	couch	
04 bent	reed	maize	
cane	rice	paddy	
corn	**05** arrow	wheat	
knot	beard	**06** bamboo	
moor	brome	barley	

fescue
marram
meadow
melick
millet
pampas
rattan
switch
twitch
07 esparto
papyrus

See also **plant**

quaking
sacaton
sorghum
timothy
wild oat
08 cat's-tail
dog's-tail
kangaroo
ryegrass
09 buckwheat
cocksfoot

marijuana
sugar cane
10 Italian rye
11 vernal grass
12 Kentucky blue
squirrel-tail
13 meadow foxtail
15 English ryegrass
Italian ryegrass

Great Lakes *see* lake

Greece

Cities and notable towns in Greece include:

05 Volos
06 Athens
Lárisa

Patras
07 Corinth
Knossos

Larissa
Piraeus
08 Iráklion

09 Heraklion
11 Peristérion
12 Thessaloníki

Administrative divisions of Greece, with regional capitals:

05 Crete (Heraklion)
Kríti (Heraklion)
06 Attica (Athens)
Attikí (Athens)
Epirus (Ioannina)
Ípiros (Ioannina)
08 Thessaly (Larissa)
09 Thessalía (Larissa)
10 West Greece (Patras)
11 Iónioi Nísoi (Corfu)
North Aegean (Mytilene)
Peleponnese (Tripolis)
South Aegean (Hermoupolis)

Stereá Ellás (Lamia)
12 Dhytikí Ellás (Patras)
Pelopónnisos (Tripolis)
13 Central Greece (Lamia)
Ionian Islands (Corfu)
Nótion Aiyaíon (Hermoupolis)
West Macedonia (Kozani)
14 Vóreion Aiyaíon (Mytilene)
16 Central Macedonia (Thessaloníki)
17 Dhytikí Makedhonía (Kozani)
Kedrikí Makedhonía (Thessaloníki)
22 East Macedonia and Thrace (Comotini)
28 Anatolikí Makedhonía kaí Thráki (Comotini)

Greek landmarks include:

05 Agora
Delos
Thera
Thíra
06 Delphi
Rhodes

07 Heraion
Metéora
Mt Athos
Mystras
Olympia
Theseum

09 Acropolis
Epidaurus
Mt Olympus
Parthenon
Santoríni
11 Mt Parnassus

12 Samaria Gorge
Tower of Winds
13 Palace of Minos

Greeks include:

04 Esop (6c BC, author)
05 Aesop (6c BC, author)
Galen (c.130–c.201 AD, physician)
Homer (c.8c BC, poet)

Plato (c.428–c.348 BC, philosopher)
06 Euclid (fl.300 BC, mathematician)
Lucian (c.117–c.180 AD, satirist)
Pindar (c.518–c.438 BC, poet)

Sappho (c.610–c.580 BC, poet)
Thales (c.620–c.555 BC, philosopher)

07 Hypatia (c.370–415 AD, philosopher)
Pytheas (of Marseilles; 4c BC, navigator)

08 Damocles (4c BC, courtier)
Epicurus (c.341–270 BC, philosopher)
Plotinus (c.205–270 AD, philosopher)
Plutarch (c.46–c.120 AD, historian)
Polybius (c.205–c.123 BC, historian)
Socrates (469–399 BC, philosopher)
Xenophon (c.435–c.354 BC, historian)

09 Aeschylus (c.525–c.456 BC, playwright)
Aristotle (384–322 BC, philosopher and scientist)
Euripides (484/480–406 BC, playwright)
Herodotus (c.485–425 BC, historian)
Sophocles (c.496–405 BC, playwright)

10 Archimedes (c.287–212 BC, mathematician)
Democritus (c.460–c.370 BC, philosopher)
Empedocles (fl.c.450 BC, philosopher and poet)
Heraclitus (d.460 BC, philosopher)
Hipparchos (c.180–125 BC, astronomer and mathematician)
Hipparchus (c.180–125 BC, astronomer and mathematician)
Praxiteles (4c BC, sculptor)
Protagoras (c.490–c.420 BC, philosopher)
Pythagoras (c.580–500 BC, philosopher)
Theocritus (c.310–250 BC, poet)
Thucydides (c.460–c.400 BC, historian)
Xenophanes (c.570–c.480 BC, philosopher)

11 Hippocrates (c.460–377/359 BC, physician)

12 Aristophanes (c.448–c.385 BC, playwright)
Theophrastus (c.372–c.286 BC, philosopher)

See also **Balkans**; **fable**; **history**; **Homer**; **mathematics**; **philosophy**; **play**; **poetry**

Greek see **alphabet**; **fate**; **Greece**; **muse**; **mythology**

green

Shades of green include:

04 jade
lime
sage
teal
vert

05 lovat
olive

06 reseda

sludge

07 avocado
celadon
corbeau
emerald

08 eau de Nil
pea-green
sap-green

sea green
viridian

09 moss green
Nile green
pistachio
turquoise

10 apple-green
aquamarine

chartreuse
rifle green
terre verte

11 bottle green
forest green

12 Lincoln green

14 turquoise-green

See also **party**; **pigment**

grey

Shades of grey include:

03 ash

04 drab

05 liard
liart
lyart
pearl
perse

slate

steel
stone
taupe

06 isabel
pewter
silver

07 grizzle

08 blue-grey
charcoal
dove grey
feldgrau
graphite
gridelin

platinum

09 field grey

10 dapple-grey
dove-colour
Payne's grey
pigeon grey

gulf

Gulfs include:

04 Aden (Yemen)
Huon (Papua New Guinea)
Lion (France)
Moro (Philippines)

Oman (Oman)
Riga (Latvia/Estonia)
Siam (Thailand/Cambodia)
Suez (Egypt)

05 Ancud (Chile)
Aqaba (Jordan)
Cádiz (Spain)
Davao (Philippines)
Dulce (Costa Rica)
Gabes (Tunisia)
Gaeta (Italy)
Genoa (Italy)
Kutch (India)
Lions (France)
Maine (USA/Canada)
Panay (Philippines)
Papua (Papua New Guinea)
Penas (Chile)
Ragay (Philippines)
Saros (Turkey)
Sidra (Libya)
Sirte (Libya)
Tunis (Tunisia)

06 Aegina (Greece)
Alaska (USA)
Cambay (India)
Chania (Crete, Greece)
Darien (Panama)
Gdansk (Poland)
Guinea (Africa)
Kavala (Greece)
Mannar (India/Sri Lanka)
Mexico (Mexico)
Naples (Italy)
Nicoya (Costa Rica)
Orosei (Italy)
Panama (Panama)
Parita (Panama)
Patras (Greece)
St Malo (France)
Tonkin (China/Vietnam)
Triste (Venezuela)
Venice (Italy)

07 Almeria (Spain)
Arabian (Middle East)
Asinara (Italy)
Boothia (Canada)
Bothnia (Sweden/Finland)
Cazones (Cuba)
Corinth (Greece)
Edremit (Turkey)
Exmouth (Australia)
Finland (Finland/Estonia)
Fonseca (Honduras)
Hauraki (New Zealand)
Kachchh (India)
Lepanto (Greece)
Obskaya (Russia)
Persian (Middle East)
Salerno (Italy)

San Blas (Panama)
Saronic (Greece)
Spencer (Australia)
Taranto (Italy)
The Gulf (Middle East)
Trieste (Italy)
Udskaya (Russia)

08 Amundsen (Canada)
Batabano (Cuba)
Cagliari (Italy)
Campeche (Mexico)
Chiriqui (Panama)
Honduras (Honduras)
Khambhat (India)
Liaotung (China)
Lingayen (Philippines)
Martaban (Myanmar)
Mosquito (Panama)
Oristano (Italy)
Papagayo (Costa Rica)
San Jorge (Argentina)
Taganrog (Russia/Ukraine)
Thailand (Thailand/Cambodia)
Valencia (Spain)

09 Buor-Khaya (Russia)
Corcovado (Chile)
Dvinskaya (Russia)
Guayaquil (Ecuador)
Queen Maud (Canada)
San Matias (Argentina)
San Miguel (Panama)
St Florent (Corsica, France)
St Vincent (Australia)
Van Diemen (Australia)
Venezuela (Venezuela)

10 California (Mexico)
Chaunskaya (Russia)
Cheshskaya (Russia)
Coronation (Canada)
Kyparissia (Greece)
Policastro (Italy)
St Lawrence (Canada)
Tazovskaya (Russia)
Thermaikos (Greece)

11 Carpentaria (Australia)
Guacanayabo (Cuba)
Manfredonia (Italy)
Pechorskaya (Russia)
Strymonikos (Greece)
Tehuantepec (Mexico)

12 los Mosquitos (Panama)
Penzhinskaya (Russia)

13 Baydaratskaya (Russia)
Santa Catalina (USA)

15 Joseph Bonaparte (Australia)

gun

Guns include:

02	MG		fusil	07	bazooka		starting
03	air		Lewis		carbine		Sterling
	gas		Maxim		chopper	09	Archibald
	gat		rifle		gatling		Big Bertha
	ray		siege		Long Tom		flintlock
	six		spear		machine		harquebus
	Uzi		tommy		pounder	10	black Maria
04	AK-47	06	airgun		scatter		demi-cannon
	Bren		Archie	08	air rifle		six shooter
	burp		Bofors		amusette		submachine
	Colt®		cannon		arquebus		Winchester®
	hand		mortar		elephant	11	blunderbuss
	pump		musket		falconet		four-pounder
	punt		needle		firelock		half-pounder
	shot		pistol		howitzer		Kalashnikov
	sten		pom-pom		magazine	12	fowling-piece
	stun		Purdey®		pederero		mitrailleuse
05	baton		Quaker		petronel		three-pounder
	field		turret		revolver		

See also **weapon**

gymnastics

Gymnastics events include:

04	ball		vault		uneven bars	13	horizontal bar
	beam	07	high bar	11	balance beam	14	asymmetric bars
05	clubs	08	tumbling		pommel horse		floor exercises
	floor	10	horse vault	12	parallel bars		side horse vault
	rings				trampolining		sports aerobics

Gymnasts include:

03 Kim (Nellie; 1957– , Russian)
Ono (Takashi; 1931– , Japanese)

06 Korbut (Olga; 1956– , Belarussian)
Liukin (Nastia; 1989– , Russian/US)
Miller (Shannon; 1977– , US)
Retton (Mary Lou; 1968– , US)

07 Johnson (Shawn; 1992– , US)
Scherbo (Vitaly; 1972– , Belarussian)
Yang Wei (1980– , Chinese)

08 Comaneci (Nadia; 1961– , Romanian)
Ditiatin (Aleksandr; 1957– , Russian)
Kanayeva (Yevgeniya; 1990– , Russian)
Latynina (Larissa; 1935– , Ukrainian)
Shakhlin (Boris; 1932–2008, Ukrainian)

09 Andrianov (Nikolai; 1952– , Russian)
Cáslavská (Vera; 1942– , Czech)

10 Boginskaya (Svetlana; 1973– , Belarussian)
Turischeva (Lyudmila; 1952– , Russian)

Gymnastics terms include:

04	beam	05	cross		twist
	Endo		flair		vault
	nail		floor	06	aerial
	pike		giant		bridge
	rudi		rings		Cuervo
	tuck		salto		Kovacs
			stick		

layout

07 element
flyaway
Gaylord
Gienger
Stalder

08 dismount
flic-flac
rotation
round-off
straddle
whip back

09 all-around
apparatus

See also **sport**

cartwheel
execution
handstand
hip circle
leg circle
pirouette
Tsukahara
Yurchenko

10 double back
handspring
somersault
uneven bars

11 balance beam
double twist

pommel horse
Swedish fall

12 back walkover
compulsories
parallel bars

13 back-in, full-out
front walkover
full-in, back-out
half-in, half-out
horizontal bar
inverted cross

14 asymmetric bars
back handspring

15 front handspring

H

hair

Hairstyles include:

02 DA	weave	pageboy	undercut
03 bob	**06** curled	pigtail	**09** duck's arse
bun	fringe	shingle	hair-piece
wig	mullet	tonsure	Hoxton fin
04 Afro	pouffe	topknot	pompadour
crop	toupee	**08** bouffant	sideburns
perm	**07** beehive	combover	**10** backcombed
shed	bunches	corn rows	dreadlocks
05 bangs	chignon	Eton crop	Marcel wave
braid	cowlick	frisette	sideboards
plait	crewcut	ponytail	**11** French pleat
quiff	crimped	ringlets	**13** hair extension
	Mohican	skinhead	

Terms to do with hair include:

03 bob	pouf		rinse
cue	tête		roots
cut	tint		sandy
dod	tips		serum
dye	tong		shade
gel	trim		shaft
jel	tuft		shine
not	wavy		short
pow	wiry		slick
wax	**05** baldy		slide
wig	bangs		snood
04 bald	black		tease
body	blond		thick
clip	bluey		toner
coif	braid		toque
comb	brown		tress
crop	brush		**06** auburn
curl	crimp		bagwig
down	curly		baldie
fine	foils		barber
friz	frizz		barnet
grey	hairy		blonde
grip	heare		bobble
hank	henna		bodkin
kesh	layer		brunet
lank	meche		coarse
lice	moult		colour
lock	moust		crease
mane	mousy		crinal
must	muist		fillet
nott	queue		flaxen
perm	quiff		fringe

frizzy
ginger
greasy
haffet
haffit
hairdo
hearie
kangha
lacker
mousey
mousse
peruke
pomade
pompom
pompon
pouffe
ribbon
roller
silver
styler
tangle
tettix
tie-wig
titian
toorie
tourie
wigged

07 balding
bandeau
blow-dry
bristle
carroty
cowlick
crinate
crinite
crinose
flaught
flyaway
foretop
frizzle
frizzly
greying
haircut
hair gel
hair net
hair oil
hennaed
hirsute
keratin
lacquer
melanin
parting
periwig
peruked
pileous
pin curl
pompoon
rat-tail

redhead
ringlet
shampoo
streaks
stylist
texture
tonsure
topknot
tow-head
tressed
undight
upstare
upswept
weaving
wet-look
xerasia

08 alopecia
ash-blond
back-comb
back-hair
baldpate
barrette
bar slide
bleached
bouffant
brunette
canities
chestnut
clippers
coiffeur
coiffure
combover
cordless
cow's lick
crinated
dandruff
demi-wave
diffuser
elflocks
fixature
follicle
forelock
full-head
grizzled
hair band
hairless
hairline
hair-wave
half-head
headring
lovelock
peroxide
rat's-tail
receding
roulette
scissors
scrunchy
side comb

sidelock
split end
straight
strammel
strummel
volumize
wig block
wig-maker

09 accessory
Alice band
ash-blonde
bandoline
bleaching
blue rinse
Brylcreem®
capillary
chevelure
coiffeuse
colourant
curlpaper
finger-dry
fright wig
hairbrush
hairdryer
hairpiece
hair slide
hairspray
hairstyle
hair-waver
headdress
hirsutism
Kirbigrip®
lowlights
madarosis
mop-headed
papillote
redheaded
scalp lock
scrunchie
tow-headed
trichosis
water wave

10 bad hair day
bald-headed
bathing cap
cockernony
curled-pate
detangling
extensions
fair-haired
fair-headed
finger wave
hair-powder
hairsetter
highlights
leiotrichy
long-haired
manageable

perruquier
piliferous
pocket-comb
scrunch-dry
transplant
trichology
widow's peak

11 banana slide
bottle-blond
conditioner
crinigerous
flame-haired
hairdresser
hairstylist
redding-comb
redding-kame

side-parting
tow-coloured
white-haired
white-headed

12 bottle-blonde
brilliantine
Cain-coloured
close-cropped
crimping-iron
curling tongs
cymotrichous
feather razor
hair restorer
leiotrichous
straightener
trichologist

13 centre-parting
corkscrew curl
deep condition
Judas-coloured
lissotrichous
pepper-and-salt
permanent wave
platinum-blond
straighteners

14 shoulder-length

15 deep conditioner
full-bottomed wig
permanent colour
strawberry blond
styling products

Terms to do with facial hair include:

05 beard
pluck
razor

06 goatee
tweeze
waxing

07 epilate
goateed
shaving
stubble

08 bumfluff

depilate
stubbled
sugaring
tweezers

09 depilator
moustache
sideburns

10 aftershave
depilation
depilatory
face-fungus
pogonotomy

shaving gel

11 clean-shaven
shaving foam
shaving-soap

12 electrolysis
shaving-brush
shaving-stick
side whiskers

13 eyebrow pencil
eyelash curler

15 designer stubble

hall *see* **college**

Handel, George Frideric (1685–1759)

Significant works include:

04 *Nero* (1705)
Saul (1739)

05 *Serse* (1738)
Silla (1713)
Teseo (1713)

06 *Admeto* (1726)
Alcina (1735)
Almira (1705)
Daphne (1708)
Esther (1718)
Samson (1743)
Semele (1744)
Xerxes (1738)

07 *Amadigi* (1715)
Athalia (1733)
Deborah (1733)
Jephtha (1752)

Messiah (1742)
Orlando (1733)
Rinaldo (1711)
Rodrigo (1707)
Solomon (1749)

08 *Deidamia* (1741)
Florindo (1706)
Hercules (1745)
Theodora (1750)

09 *Agrippina* (1709)
Ariodante (1735)
Radamisto (1720)
Tamerlano (1724)

10 *Alessandro* (1726)
Floridante (1721)
Water Music (1717)

11 *Pastoral Ode* (1740)

12 *Giulio Cesare* (1724)
Il Pastor Fido (1712/1734)

13 *Israel in Egypt* (1739)

14 *Acis and Galatea*
(1718/1732)
Concerti Grossi (1739)
Grand Concertos (1739)
La Resurrezione (1708)
Zadok the Priest (1727)

15 *Alexander's Feast* (1736)
Judas Maccabaeus (1747)

16 *The Power of Musick*
(1736)

17 *Il Trionfo del Tempo* (1707)
Tolomeo re di Egitto (1728)

Hardy, Thomas (1840–1928)

Significant works include:

10 *A Laodicean* (1881)
Human Shows (1925)

11 *Two on a Tower* (1882)
Wessex Poems (1898)
Wessex Tales (1888)
Winter Words (1928)

14 *Jude the Obscure* (1895)
The Well-Beloved (1897)
The Woodlanders (1887)

15 *A Pair of Blue Eyes* (1873)
Moments of Vision (1917)
The Trumpet-Major (1880)

17 *Desperate Remedies* (1871)

18 *A Group of Noble Dames* (1890)

Life's Little Ironies (1894)

19 *The Hand of Ethelberta* (1876)
Time's Laughingstocks (1909)

20 *Late Lyrics and Earlier* (1922)
The Poor Man and the Lady (unpublished)
The Return of the Native (1878)

21 *Satires of Circumstance* (1914)
Tess of the D'Urbervilles (1891)
Under the Greenwood Tree (1872)

22 *Far from the Madding Crowd* (1874)
The Mayor of Casterbridge (1886)

24 *Poems of the Past and Present* (1901)

36 *The Famous Tragedy of the Queen of Cornwall* (1923)

Significant characters include:

03 Day (Fancy)
Day (Geoffrey)
Oak (Gabriel)
Vye (Eustacia)

04 Caro (Avice)
Donn (Arabella)
Troy (Sergeant Francis 'Frank')
Venn (Diggory)

05 Brook (Rhoda)
Clare (Angel)
Dewey (Reuben)
Dewey (Richard 'Dick')
Graye (Cytherea)
Grebe (Barbara)
Power (Paula)
Robin (Fanny)
Smith (Stephen)
South (Marty)
Trewe (Robert)

06 Fawley (Jude)

Knight (Henry)
Newson (Elizabeth-Jane)

07 Farfrae (Donald)
Garland (Anne)
Le Sueur (Lucetta)
Loveday (John)
Loveday (Robert 'Bob')
Manston (Aeneas)
Maybold (Parson)
Melbury (George)
Melbury (Grace)
Wildeve (Damon)

08 Boldwood (William)
Charmond (Felice)
Derriman (Festus)
Everdene (Bathsheba)
Henchard (Michael)
Newberry (Lizzy)
Ollamoor (Wat 'Mop')
Pierston (Jocelyn)
St Cleeve (Swithin)

Willowes (Edmond)

09 Aldclyffe (Miss)
Bridehead (Susanna Florence Mary 'Sue')
Chickerel (Ethelberta)
Fitzpiers (Edred)
Marchmill (Ella)
Stockdale (Richard)
Swancourt (Elfride)
Yeobright (Clement 'Clym')
Yeobright (Mrs)
Yeobright (Thomasin 'Tamsin')

10 Father Time
Phillotson (Richard)
Springrove (Edward)

11 Constantine (Lady Viviette)
D'Urberville (Alec)
Durbeyfield (Tess)
Winterborne (Giles)

12 Uplandtowers (Earl of)

hare *see* **rabbit**

hat

Hats, headdresses and helmets include:

03			
cap	tin	hood	tête
fez	top	kell	tile
lum		kepi	tire
pot	**04** chip	plug	topi
red	doek	silk	
sun	hard	sola	**05** armet
taj	hive	tall	beret

Bronx
busby
crush
derby
gibus
mitre
mutch
pixie
salet
shako
straw
tammy
terai
tiara
topee
toque
tower
tuque

06 basher
basnet
beanie
beaver
bicorn
big-gin
boater
bobble
bonnet
bowler
Breton
casque
castor
chapka
cloche
cocked
cockle
coolie
cornet
fedora
heaume
helmet
hennin
kalpak
mob cap

modius
morion
panama
pileus
pinner
sailor
sallet
shovel
slouch
toorie
topper
trilby
turban
witch's

07 basinet
bicorne
biretta
bycoket
Christy
commode
coronet
Cossack
flat cap
Homburg
kufiyeh
leghorn
montero
morrion
murrion
petasus
picture
pillbox
plateau
pork-pie
Ramilie
scarlet
skid lid
ski mask
steeple
Stetson®
sundown
tarbush
tricorn

08 balmoral
bearskin
bongrace
burganet
burgonet
chaperon
Christie
coiffure
fontange
fool's cap
gimme cap
head tire
kaffiyeh
keffiyeh
knapscal
mushroom
nightcap
Ramilies
Ramillie
ship tire
skullcap
sombrero
stephane
tarboosh
tarboush
thrummed
tricorne
yarmulka

09 Balaclava
billycock
broad-brim
cock's-comb
dunce's cap
Dunstable
forage cap
glengarry
headpiece
jockey cap
knapscull
knapskull
muffin-cap
peaked cap
porringer

Ramillies
school cap
sou'wester
stovepipe
sun bonnet
tarpaulin
ten-gallon
war bonnet

10 balibuntal
blue-bonnet
chimney pot
cockernony
college cap
hunting-cap
Kilmarnock
pith helmet
poke bonnet
sola helmet

11 baseball cap
cabbage-tree
chapeau-bras
crash helmet
deerstalker
Dolly Varden
kamelaukion
mortarboard
pickelhaube
smoke helmet
stocking cap
Tam o' Shanter
trencher cap

12 cheesecutter
fore-and-after
hummle bonnet
Scotch bonnet
steeple-crown
toorie bonnet

13 feather bonnet

14 Kilmarnock cowl
pressure helmet

15 Balaclava helmet

See also **clothes**

Haydn, Joseph (1732–1809)

Significant works include:

03 'Hen' (Symphony; 1785)

04 'Bear' (Symphony; 1786)
'Bird' (String Quartet; 1781)
'Fire' (Symphony; c.1778)
'Hunt' (Symphony; 1781)
'Joke' (String Quartet; 1781)
'Lark' (String Quartet; 1790)

05 'Clock' (Symphony; 1794)

'Feuer' (Symphony; c.1778)
'Queen' (Symphony; 1785)
'Razor' (String Quartet; 1788)
'Rider' (String Quartet; 1793)

06 'Laudon' (Symphony; c.1778)
'Le Midi' (Symphony; c.1761)
'Le Soir' (Symphony; c.1761)
'London' (Symphony; 1795)

'Midday' (Symphony; c.1761)
'Oxford' (Symphony; 1791)
'Trauer' (Symphony; c.1771)

07 'Emperor' (String Quartet; 1797)
'Evening' (Symphony; c.1761)
'La Reine' (Symphony; 1785)
'Le Matin' (Symphony; c.1761)
'Mercury' (Symphony; c.1771)
'Miracle' (Symphony; 1792)
'Morning' (Symphony; c.1761)
'Passion' (Symphony; 1768)
'Sunrise' (String Quartet; 1797)

08 'Alleluia' (Symphony; 1765)
'Drum Roll' (Symphony; 1795)
'Farewell' (Symphony; 1772)
'Imperial' (Symphony; c.1780)
'La Chasse' (Symphony; 1781)
'Military' (Symphony; 1794)
'Mourning' (Symphony; c.1771)
'Surprise' (Symphony; 1791)

10 'Horn Signal' (Symphony; 1765)
'La Passione' (Symphony; 1768)

'La Roxelane' (Symphony; c.1780)
'L'Imperiale' (Symphony; c.1780)
'Palindrome' (Symphony; 1772)
The Seasons (1801)

11 'Il distratto' (Symphony; 1774)
'Philosopher' (Symphony; 1764)
Stabat Mater (1767)
The Creation (1798)

12 *Die Schöpfung* (1798)
Emperor's Hymn (1797)
'Lamentations' (Symphony; c.1770)
'Lamentazione' (Symphony; c.1770)
'Maria Theresa' (Symphony; c.1768)
'Maria Therese' (Symphony; c.1768)
'Schoolmaster' (Symphony; 1774)

14 'In Nomine Domini' (Symphony; 1786)

15 *Die Jahreszeiten* (1801)
'Tempora Mutantur' (Symphony; 1775)

17 *The Seven Last Words* (1796)

21 *Die sieben letzten Worte* (1796)

head cloth *see* scarf

headdress *see* hat

Heaney, Seamus (1939–2013)

Significant works include:

05 *North* (1975)
07 *Beowulf* (1999)
09 *Field Work* (1979)
10 *Human Chain* (2010)

11 *Eleven Poems* (1965)
12 *Wintering Out* (1972)
14 *Preoccupations* (1980)
15 *Door into the Dark* (1969)

17 *District and Circle* (2006)
18 *Death of a Naturalist* (1966)

heart

Heart parts include:

04 vein
05 aorta
valve
06 artery
atrium
AV node
muscle
SA node
07 auricle
08 vena cava

09 sinus node
ventricle
10 epicardium
left atrium
myocardium
11 aortic valve
endocardium
mitral valve
pericardium
right atrium

13 bicuspid valve
carotid artery
left ventricle
14 ascending aorta
pulmonary valve
Purkinje fibres
Purkinje system
right ventricle
sino-atrial node
tricuspid valve
15 papillary muscle

Hebrew *see* alphabet

helmet *see* hat

Hemingway, Ernest (1899–1961)

Significant works include:

09 *In Our Time* (1925)
14 *A Moveable Feast* (1964)
15 *A Farewell to Arms* (1929)
 Men without Women (1927)
 Selected Letters (1981)
 The Sun Also Rises (1926)
17 *Winner Take Nothing* (1933)

18 *The Old Man and the Sea* (1952)
19 *Death in the Afternoon* (1932)
 For Whom the Bell Tolls (1940)
 The Torrents of Spring (1926)
21 *The Green Hills of Africa* (1935)
23 *Three Stories and Ten Poems* (1923)
29 *Across the River and into the Trees* (1950)

Significant characters include:

05 Adams (Nick)
 Harry
 Henry (Frederic)
 Maria
 Pablo

 Pilar
06 Ashley (Lady Brett)
 Barnes (Jake)
 Jordan (Robert)
 Morgan (Harry)

07 Barkley (Catherine)
 Manolin
08 Macomber (Francis)
 Macomber (Margot)
 Santiago

heraldry

Terms to do with heraldry include:

02 or
04 arms
 lion
 orle
 pall
 pile
 semé
 urdé
 vert
05 azure
 badge
 crest
 eagle
 eisen
 field
 gules
 motto
 sable
 tawny
 tenné

 undee
06 argent
 bezant
 blazon
 canton
 centre
 charge
 dexter
 emblem
 ensign
 helmet
 impale
 mullet
 murrey
 sejant
 shield
 volant
 wivern
07 annulet
 bordure

 cendrée
 chevron
 dormant
 griffin
 gyronny
 lozenge
 martlet
 passant
 phoenix
 quarter
 rampant
 regalia
 roundel
 saltire
 statant
 tierced
 unicorn
 urinant
08 addorsed
 antelope
 caboched

 couchant
 insignia
 mantling
 sanguine
 sinister
 tincture
09 carnation
 displayed
 hatchment
10 camelopard
 cinquefoil
 coat of arms
 cockatrice
 emblazonry
 escutcheon
 fleur-de-lis
 quatrefoil
 supporters
11 bleu celeste
 compartment

herb

Herbs and spices include:

03 bay
04 balm
 dill
 mace
 mint
 sage
05 anise

 basil
 caper
 clove
 cumin
 curry
 thyme
06 borage
 cassia

 chilli
 chives
 cloves
 fennel
 garlic
 ginger
 hyssop
 lovage

nutmeg	saffron	tarragon
pepper	vanilla	turmeric
savory	**08** allspice	**09** chamomile
sesame	angelica	coriander
sorrel	bergamot	fenugreek
07 catmint	camomile	hypericum
chervil	cardamom	lemon balm
comfrey	cardamon	**10** gaillardia
mustard	cardamum	**11** St John's wort
oregano	cinnamon	**12** caraway seeds
paprika	lavender	**13** cayenne pepper
parsley	marjoram	
pimento	rosemary	

herbal tea *see* **tea**

heroism

Heroes and heroines include:

04 Bond (James; *Casino Royale*, 1953, et seq, Ian Fleming)
Dare (Dan; comic/film)
Hood (Robin; English legend)

05 Bruce (Robert; 1274–1329, Scottish)
Croft (Lara; video game/film)
Jason (Greek mythology)
Jones (Indiana; *Raiders of the Lost Ark*, 1981, et seq)
Kelly (Ned; 1855–80, Australian)
Zorro (TV/film)

06 Arthur (c.6c; Arthurian legend)
Barton (Dick; radio)
Batman (comic/TV/film)
Lassie (film/TV)
Ripley (Ellen; *Alien*, 1979, et seq)
Rogers (Buck; comic/film)
Sharpe (Richard; *Sharpe's Eagle*, 1981, et seq, Bernard Cornwell)
Tarzan (TV/film)

07 Beowulf (Scandinavian legend)
Biggles (*The Camels Are Coming*, 1932, et seq, Captain W E Johns)
Darling (Grace; 1815–42, English)
Deirdre (Irish legend)
Glyn Dwr (Owain; c.1350–c.1416, Welsh)
Ivanhoe (*Ivanhoe*, 1820, Sir Walter Scott)
Wallace (William; 1272–1305, Scottish)

08 Boadicea (d.61 AD, British)
Boudicca (d.61 AD, British)
Lancelot (English legend)

See also **legend**; **mythology**

Superman (comic/film)

09 Churchill (Sir Winston; 1874–1965, English)
D'Artagnan (*The Three Musketeers*, 1844, Alexandre Dumas)
Glendower (Owain; c.1350–c.1416, Welsh)
Joan of Arc (1412–31, French)
Macdonald (Flora; 1722–90, Scottish)
MacGregor (Rob Roy; 1671–1734, Scottish)
Rin Tin Tin (film/TV)
Schindler (Oskar; 1908–74, German)
Snow White (Grimm Brothers fairytale)
Spiderman (comic/film)

10 Cinderella (European folklore)
Cú Chulainn (Irish legend)
Hornblower (Horatio; *The Happy Return*, 1937, et seq, C S Forester)
Little John (English legend)
Lone Ranger (TV/film)
Richthofen (Manfred von, 'the Red Baron'; 1892–1918, German)

11 Finn MacCool (Irish legend)
Nightingale (Florence; 1820–1910, Italian/British)
Wilberforce (William; 1759–1833; English)
Wonderwoman (comic/film)

14 Finn MacCumhail (Irish legend)

15 Three Musketeers (*The Three Musketeers*, 1844, Alexandre Dumas)

highwayman

Highwaymen include:

04 King (Tom; 18c, English)
05 Duval (Claude; 1643–70, English)
06 Turpin (Dick; 1706–39, English)
07 Brennan (Willie; d.1804, Irish)
Nevison (John/William; 1648–84, English)
08 MacHeath (*The Beggar's Opera*, 1728, John

Gay/*The Threepenny Opera*, 1958, Kurt Weill/Bertolt Brecht)
09 Abershawe (Jerry; 1773–95, English)
Swift Nick (1648–84, English)
12 Mack the Knife (*The Beggar's Opera*, 1728, John Gay/*The Threepenny Opera*, 1958, Kurt Weill/Bertolt Brecht)

hill *see* **mountain**; **Rome**

Hinduism

Hindu groups, movements and denominations include:

06 Aghori
07 Saivism
Saktism
Smartha
08 Lingayat
Shaivism

Shaktism
Tantrism
09 Vedantism
10 Bhakti Yoga
Radha Soami
Siddha Yoga

11 Hare Krishna
Vaishnavism
12 Swaminarayan
15 Kashmir Shaivism
Shaiva Siddhanta

Hindu gods include:

04 Agni (fire)
Kama (lust/desire)
Rama (incarnation of Vishnu)
Siva (creation/destruction)
Soma (speech)
Yama (death)
05 Indra (storms/war)
Kurma (incarnation of Vishnu)
Rudra (destructive aspect of Shiva)
Shani (bringer of bad luck)
Shiva (creation/destruction)
Surya (sun)
06 Brahma (creation)
Ganesa (elephant-headed son of Shiva)
Ganesh (elephant-headed son of Shiva)
Garuda (bird that carries Shiva)
Iswara (nature/soul)

Narada (incarnation of Vishnu)
Pushan (enlightenment)
Ravana (demon king)
Skanda (war/son of Shiva)
Varuna (sea)
Vishnu (creation)
07 Ganesha (elephant-headed son of Shiva)
Hanuman (monkey)
Krishna (incarnation of Vishnu)
08 Ganapati (elephant-headed son of Shiva)
Nataraja (aspect of Shiva as the Lord of Dance)
09 Kartikeya (war)
Lakshmana (half-brother of Rama)
Narasimha (incarnation of Vishnu)
10 Jagannatha (incarnation of Vishnu)

Hindu goddesses include:

03 Uma (destruction/wife of Shiva)
04 Kali (destruction; wife of Shiva)
Sita (Rama's wife)
05 Aditi (all existence)
Durga (Shiva's wife)
Gauri (purity)
Radha (love; consort of Krishna)

Sakti (female principle of power and energy)
06 Shakti (female principle of power and energy)
07 Lakshmi (wealth/good luck)
Parvati (Shiva's wife)
09 Sarasvati (mother/art/learning/music)

See also **calendar**; **religion**

history

Trevelyan (G M; 1876–1962, English)

10 Baldinucci (Filippo; 1624–96, Italian)
Burckhardt (Jacob; 1818–97, Swiss)
Dio Cassius (c.150–c.235 AD, Roman)
Thucydides (c.460–c.400 BC, Greek)

11 Schlesinger (Arthur M; 1888–1965, US)

Tocqueville (Alexis de; 1805–59, French)
Trevor-Roper (Hugh, Lord Dacre; 1914–2003, English)

12 Guicciardini (Francesco; 1483–1540, Italian)

15 Diodorus Siculus (1c BC, Greek)

Terms used in history include:

02 AD	empire	**11** anachronism
BC	period	Eurocentric
03 age	source	oral history
AUC	treaty	**13** modern history
war	**07** dynasty	primary source
05 reign	**08** evidence	**14** ancient history
siege	monarchy	**15** secondary source
06 battle	**10** chronology	

See also **archaeology**; **Rome**

hobby

Hobbies and pastimes include:

05 batik	knitting	pyrography
chess	knotting	renovating
06 acting	lacework	upholstery
am-dram	lapidary	wine-making
baking	marbling	**11** archaeology
bonsai	painting	beadworking
hiking	quilling	bell-ringing
poetry	quilting	book-binding
raffia	spinning	calligraphy
07 camping	tapestry	card playing
CB radio	**09** astrology	cat breeding
collage	astronomy	cross-stitch
cookery	decoupage	dog breeding
crochet	gardening	dressmaking
dancing	genealogy	home brewing
drawing	marquetry	model-making
macramé	millinery	model trains
mosaics	model cars	needlepoint
origami	philately	numismatics
pottery	rug-making	ornithology
quizzes	sketching	paper crafts
reading	strawwork	papier-mâché
singing	toy-making	photography
tatting	train sets	wine-tasting
topiary	**10** beekeeping	woodcarving
weaving	board games	woodworking
writing	crosswords	**12** amateur radio
08 antiques	doll-making	basketmaking
basketry	embroidery	candle-making
cat shows	kite-flying	games playing
dog shows	lace-making	phillumenism
draughts	phillumeny	**13** bungee jumping
feng shui	pub quizzes	egg decorating

toy collecting
14 book collecting
coin collecting
cruciverbalism
doll collecting

flower pressing
herpetoculture
metal detecting
15 aquarium keeping
ballroom dancing

flower arranging
jewellery making
model aeroplanes
stamp collecting

See also **collection**; **crossword**

hockey

Hockey terms include:

01 D
03 hit
04 ball
feet
push
05 flick
scoop
06 aerial
tackle
07 dribble
free hit

red card
striker
sweeper
08 back line
bully-off
left back
left half
left wing
09 corner hit
drag flick
field goal
green card

right back
right half
right wing
10 centre half
centre pass
goal circle
goalkeeper
inside left
long corner
yellow card
11 field player
hockey stick

inside right
obstruction
short corner
12 penalty flick
reverse stick
13 centre forward
penalty corner
penalty stroke
14 shooting circle
striking circle

holiday

National holidays include:

07 Flag Day
08 Anzac Day
Unity Day
09 Labour Day
Women's Day
10 Culture Day
Freedom Day

Martyrs' Day
Mothers' Day
Victory Day
11 Bastille Day
National Day
Republic Day
12 Armistice Day

Australia Day
Children's Day
Discovery Day
Thanksgiving
13 King's Birthday
Liberation Day
Revolution Day

14 Armed Forces Day
Queen's Birthday
Remembrance Day
Unification Day
15 Constitution Day
Emancipation Day
Independence Day

See also **religion**

Homer (c.8c BC)

Significant characters include:

04 Aias *(Iliad)*
Ajax *(Iliad)*
Ares *(Iliad)*
Hera *(Iliad)*
Iris *(Iliad)*
Zeus *(Iliad)*
05 Arete *(Odyssey)*
Argos *(Odyssey)*
Circe *(Odyssey)*
Dione *(Iliad)*
Dolon *(Iliad)*
Hades *(Iliad)*
Helen *(Iliad)*
Paris *(Iliad)*
Priam *(Iliad)*

06 Aeneas *(Iliad)*
Aeolus *(Odyssey)*
Apollo *(Iliad)*
Athena *(Iliad)*
Hector *(Iliad)*
Hecuba *(Iliad)*
Hektor *(Iliad)*
Hekuba *(Iliad)*
Hermes *(Iliad)*
Nestor *(Iliad)*
Thetis *(Iliad)*
Tydeus *(Iliad)*
07 Antenor *(Iliad)*
Argives *(Iliad)*
Artemis *(Iliad)*

Atrides *(Odyssey)*
Briseis *(Iliad)*
Calchas *(Iliad)*
Chryses *(Iliad)*
Danaans *(Iliad)*
Eumaeus *(Odyssey)*
Glaucos *(Iliad)*
Glaucus *(Iliad)*
Glaukos *(Iliad)*
Helenos *(Iliad)*
Kalchas *(Iliad)*
Laertes *(Odyssey)*
Machaon *(Iliad)*
Phoenix *(Iliad)*
Telamon *(Iliad)*

Trojans *(Iliad)*
Tydides *(Iliad)*
Xanthos *(Iliad)*

08 Achaeans *(Iliad)*
Achilles *(Iliad)*
Alcinous *(Odyssey)*
Antinous *(Odyssey)*
Astyanax *(Iliad)*
Chryseis *(Iliad)*
Diomedes *(Iliad)*
Eupithes *(Odyssey)*
Melantho *(Odyssey)*
Menelaos *(Iliad)*
Menelaus *(Iliad)*
Nausicaa *(Odyssey)*

Odysseus *(Iliad/Odyssey)*
Pandarus *(Iliad)*
Penelope *(Odyssey)*
Poseidon *(Iliad)*
Sarpedon *(Iliad)*
Tiresias *(Odyssey)*

09 Agamemnon *(Iliad)*
Anticleia *(Odyssey)*
Aphrodite *(Iliad)*
Automedon *(Iliad)*
Cassandra *(Iliad)*
Euphorbus *(Iliad)*
Eurycleia *(Odyssey)*
Eurypylus *(Iliad)*
Idomeneus *(Iliad)*

Myrmidons *(Iliad)*
Patroclus *(Iliad)*
Patroklos *(Iliad)*

10 Alexandros *(Iliad)*
Andromache *(Iliad)*
Antilochos *(Iliad)*
Eurymachus *(Odyssey)*
Hephaestus *(Iliad)*
Melanthius *(Odyssey)*
Philoetius *(Odyssey)*
Polyphemus *(Odyssey)*
Poulydamas *(Iliad)*
Telemachus *(Odyssey)*

12 Clytemnestra *(Iliad)*

13 Aias the Lesser *(Iliad)*

honour

Honours include:

02 GC
KG
VC

03 CBE
CGC
DBE
DSC
DSO

GBE
KBE
MBE
OBE

09 Iron Cross

10 Bronze Star
Grand Cross

knighthood
Silver Star

11 George Cross
Purple Heart

12 Order of Lenin
Order of Merit

13 Croix de Guerre

Legion of Merit
Medal for Merit
Medal of Honour
Victoria Cross
Victoria Medal

14 Légion d'Honneur

See also **military**

hormone

Hormones include:

05 kinin
06 orexin
07 gastrin
ghrelin
insulin
relaxin
08 abscisin
androgen
autacoid

estrogen
florigen
glucagon
oxytocin
secretin
thyroxin
09 adrenalin
cortisone
melatonin
oestrogen

pituitrin
prolactin
thyroxine
10 adrenaline
calcitonin
hypocretin
11 thyrotropin
vasopressin
12 androsterone

melanotropin
noradrenalin
progesterone
somatostatin
somatotropin
testosterone
thyrotrophin
14 erythropoietin
glucocorticoid

horse

Horse and pony breeds include:

03 Don
04 Arab
Barb
Fell
05 Dales
Iomud
Lokai
Pinto
Shire

Toric
Waler
Welsh
06 Auxois
Breton
Brumby
Exmoor
Morgan
Nonius

Tersky
07 Comtois
Criollo
Finnish
Furioso
Hackney
Hispano
Jutland
Masuren

Muraköz
Murgese
Mustang
Salerno

08 Budyonny
Danubian
Dartmoor
Friesian
Highland
Holstein
Kabardin
Karabair
Karabakh
Lusitano
Palomino
Paso Fino
Poitevin
Shetland
Welsh Cob

09 Akhal-Teké
Alter-Réal
Anglo-Arab
Appaloosa
Ardennias
Brabançon
Calabrese

Connemara
Falabella
Groningen
Kladruber
Knabstrup
Kustanair
Maremmana
New Forest
New Kirgiz
Oldenburg
Percheron
Sardinian
Tchenaran
Trakehner

10 Andalusian
Boulonnais
Clydesdale
Einsiedler
Freiberger
Gelderland
Hanoverian
Lipizzaner
Mangalarga
Shagya Arab

11 Anglo-Norman
Døle Trotter

Irish Hunter
Mecklenburg
Przewalski's
Trait du Nord
Württemberg

12 Cleveland Bay
Dutch Draught
East Friesian
French Saddle
Irish Draught
Metis Trotter
North Swedish
Orlov Trotter
Suffolk Punch
Thoroughbred

13 East Bulgarian
Frederiksborg
French Trotter
German Trotter
Welsh Mountain

14 American Saddle
Latvian Harness
Plateau Persian

15 American Quarter
American Trotter
Swedish Halfbred

Points of a horse include:

03 ear
eye
hip

04 back
chin
dock
face
head
heel
hock
hoof
knee
lips
mane
neck
nose
poll
ribs
rump
shin
tail

05 atlas

belly
canon
cheek
chest
crest
croup
elbow
ergot
flank
girth
loins
mouth
thigh

06 breast
cannon
gaskin
haunch
muzzle
sheath
stifle
temple
throat

07 abdomen
brisket
buttock
coronet
crupper
fetlock
forearm
hind leg
pastern
quarter
shannon
tendons
withers

08 chestnut
forefoot
forehead
forelock
lower jaw
lower lip
nostrils
shoulder
under lip
upper lip

windpipe

09 hamstring
hock joint
nasal peak

10 chin groove
point of hip
wall of foot

11 back tendons
point of hock
stifle joint

12 fetlock joint
hindquarters
hollow of heel
point of elbow

13 dock of the tail
flexor tendons
jugular groove
root of the tail

14 Achilles tendon
crest of the neck

15 point of shoulder

A horse's tack includes:

03 bit

05 arson

cinch
girth

hames
reins

06 bridle
cantle

collar	housing	breeching	shabracque
halter	stirrup	hackamore	throatlash
numnah	**08** backband	headstall	
pommel	blinders	saddlebag	**11** bearing rein
saddle	blinkers	saddlebow	saddlecloth
traces	noseband	saddlepad	saddle-girth
07 alforja	shabrack	surcingle	throatlatch
bridoon	**09** bellyband	**10** martingale	**13** saddle blanket
crupper		saddletree	

Horses include:

03 Pie (The; *National Velvet*, 1935, Enid Bagnold)

04 Bree (*The Horse and His Boy*, 1954, C S Lewis)
Hwin (*The Horse and His Boy*, 1954, C S Lewis)

05 Arion (Greek mythology)
Arkle (racehorse; b.1957)
Binky (*The Colour of Magic*, 1985, et seq, Terry Pratchett)
Boxer (*Animal Farm*, 1945, George Orwell)
Misty (*Misty of Chincoteague*, 1947, et seq, Marguerite Henry)
Scout (*The Lone Ranger*, 1949–57, TV series)

06 Balius (Greek mythology)
Bayard (French folklore)
Diablo (*The Cisco Kid*, 1950–56, TV series)
Flicka (*My Friend Flicka*, 1941, Mary O'Hara)
Red Rum (racehorse; b.1965)
Silver (*The Lone Ranger*, 1949–57, TV series)
Stormy (*Stormy, Misty's Foal*, 1965, Marguerite Henry)

07 Burmese (Queen Elizabeth II's horse)
Capulet (*Twelfth Night*, 1601, William Shakespeare)
Eclipse (racehorse; 18c)
Galathe (*Troilus and Cressida*, 1602, William Shakespeare)
Lisette (Baron de Marbot's horse)
Llamrai (Arthurian legend)
Llamrei (Arthurian legend)
Marengo (Napoleon Bonaparte's horse)

Pegasus (Greek mythology)
Phantom (*Zorro*, 1957–59, TV series)
Roheryn (*The Lord of the Rings*, 1954–55, J R R Tolkien)
Shergar (racehorse; b.1978)
Tornado (*Zorro*, 1957–59, TV series)
Trigger (Roy Rogers's horse)
Xanthus (Greek mythology)

08 Champion (*Champion the Wonder Horse*, 1955–6, TV series)
Comanche (Captain Myles Keogh's horse)
Hengroen (Arthurian legend)
Mister Ed (*Mister Ed*, 1961–66, TV series)
Sleipnir (Scandinavian mythology)
Snowmane (*The Lord of the Rings*, 1954–55, J R R Tolkien)

09 Black Bess (Dick Turpin's horse)
Gringolet (Arthurian legend)
Incitatus (Emperor Caligula's horse)
Rosinante (Don Quixote's horse)
Rozinante (Don Quixote's horse)
Shadowfax (*The Lord of the Rings*, 1954–55, J R R Tolkien)
Traveller (General Robert E Lee's horse)

10 Bucephalus (Alexander the Great's horse; d.326 BC)
Copenhagen (Duke of Wellington's horse)
Seabiscuit (racehorse; b.1934)

11 Black Beauty (*Black Beauty*, 1877, Anna Sewell)
White Surrey (King Richard III's horse)

12 Desert Orchid (racehorse; b.1979)
Little Sorrel (General Jackson's horse)

Terms to do with horses include:

03 bay	buck	walk	nappy
cob	colt	**05** break	pinto
dun	foal	forge	steed
hie	gait	gee up	**06** bronco
hup	grey	groom	brumby
nag	mare	hands	canter
shy	roan	lunge	equine
04 bolt	stud	mount	gallop
	trot		

hippic	hacking	stallion	**11** riding habit
livery	nosebag	**09** horseshoe	**12** broken-winded
manège	paddock	roughshod	draught horse
riding	passade	**10** blood horse	pony-trekking
stable	piebald	draft horse	thoroughbred
07 astride	**08** chestnut	en cavalier	**13** champ at the bit
blanket	dismount	equestrian	mounting block
gelding	horse box	heavy horse	put out to grass
giddy-up	skewbald	side-saddle	**14** strawberry roan

See also **animal**; **bridle**; **equestrian sport**; **racing: horse racing**

horse racing *see* **racing: horse racing**

host *see* **quiz**

hotel

Hotels and hotel chains include:

03 Dom (Germany)

04 Ibis

05 Adlon (Germany)
Grand (Austria/England)
Hyatt
Lotti (France)
Peace (China)
Savoy (England)

06 Alcron (Czech Republic)
Brown's (England)
Gritti (Italy)
Hilton
Pierre (USA)
Sacher (Austria)

07 Astoria (Russia)
Cadogan (England)
Carlton
Chelsea (USA)
Crillon (France)
De Paris (Monaco)
Empress (Canada)
George V (France)
Hassler (Italy)
Le Royal (Cambodia)
Meikles (Zimbabwe)
Norfolk (Kenya)
Peabody (USA)
Pujiang (China)
Raffles (Singapore)
Sofitel
St James (England)
The Ritz (England)
Thistle
Windsor (Australia)

08 Cipriani (Italy)

Du Palais (France)
Elephant (Germany)
El Minzah (Morocco)
Fairmont
Imperial (Austria/Japan)
Landmark
Marriott
Metropol (Russia)
New Grand (Japan)
Palliser (Canada)
Radisson
Sheraton
The Plaza (USA)

09 Algonquin (USA)
Claridge's (England)
Copthorne
Esplanade (Croatia)
Kingsgate
Lancaster (France)
Le Bristol (France)
Le Meurice (France)
Metropole (Belgium)
Old Course (Scotland)
Park Hyatt (Japan)
Royal York (Canada)
Splendido (Italy)
Taft Hotel (*The Graduate*, 1967)

10 Astor House (China)
Bates Motel (*Psycho*, 1960)
Gleneagles (Scotland)
Holiday Inn
Hotel du Lac (*Hotel du Lac*, 1984, Anita
   Brookner)
Lake Palace (India)
La Mamounia (Morocco)
Millennium

Pera Palace (Turkey)
Rocco Forte
The Langham (England)
Villa D'Este (Italy)

11 Ambos Mundos (Cuba)
Best Western
Del Coronado (USA)
Dolder Grand (Switzerland)
Four Seasons
Mount Nelson (South Africa)
Old Cataract (Egypt)
Palace Praha (Czech Republic)
The Balmoral (Scotland)
The Berkeley (England)
The Park Lane (England)
The Scotsman (Scotland)

12 Alvear Palace (Argentina)
Fawlty Towers (TV series)
Le Beauvallon (France)
Nevsky Palace (Russia)
Strand Palace (England)
The Connaught (England)
The Peninsula (Hong Kong)

13 Ashford Castle (Ireland)

Knickerbocker (USA)
Overlook Hotel (*The Shining*, 1980)
Rambagh Palace (India)
The Ambassador (USA)
The Dorchester (England)
The Shelbourne (Ireland)
Trianon Palace (France)
Victoria Falls (Zimbabwe)
Waldorf Hilton (England)

14 Bayerischer Hof (Germany)
Chateau Laurier (Canada)
Frankfurter Hof (Germany)
Grand Hotel Pupp (Czech Republic)
Grosvenor House (England)
Hotel Splendide (*Casino Royale*, 2006)
Landmark London (England)
Moana Surfrider (USA)
Nacional de Cuba (Cuba)
Prince de Galles (France)
The Shakespeare (England)
Waldorf Astoria (USA)

15 Beverly Wilshire (USA)
Heartbreak Hotel (song, Elvis Presley)
Hotel California (song, The Eagles)
The Lanesborough (England)

See also **London**; **New York**; **Paris**

hour

Hours include:

04 rush	**06** dinner	working	visiting
05 flexi	golden	**08** business	witching
happy	office	eleventh	
lunch	waking	midnight	
small	**07** trading	unsocial	

See also **canonical hour**; **time**

house

House types include:

03 hut	chalet	detached	villa home
04 flat	datcha	hacienda	villa unit
hall	duplex	log cabin	**10** granny flat
semi	grange	terraced	maisonette
weem	mia-mia	vicarage	pied-à-terre
	pondok	**09** apartment	ranch house
05 croft	prefab	but and ben	state house
igloo	shanty	farmhouse	
lodge	studio	homestead	**11** condominium
manor	wurley	parsonage	**12** council house
manse	**07** cottage	penthouse	semi-detached
shack	mansion	single-end	
villa	rectory	town house	**14** chalet bungalow
06 bedsit	**08** bungalow	treehouse	**15** thatched cottage

House parts include:

04 dado
door
hall
loft
roof

05 attic
beams
grate
ingle
joist
newel
porch
slate
study
walls

06 alcove
boiler
cellar
coving
hallan

hearth
larder
lounge
pantry
socket
stairs
switch
thatch
window
wiring

07 balcony
bedroom
ceiling
chimney
cornice
en-suite
kitchen
landing
laundry
parlour

parquet
rafters
transom

08 baluster
banister
bathroom
dado rail
doorbell
radiator
skylight

09 bay window
cloakroom
fireplace
water tank

10 balustrade
chambranle
dining room
family room
floorboard

insulation
living room

11 ceiling rose
curtain rail
drawing room
mantelpiece
sitting room
utility room
window ledge

12 chimney piece
dormer window
light fitting

13 chimneybreast
double glazing
skirting board

14 central heating

15 air conditioning
built-in wardrobe
immersion heater

Household items include:

03 bin
mop

04 comb
hook
pram
vase

05 broom
brush
diary
match
potty
range
towel

06 basket
candle
duster
pet bed
sponge

07 ashtray
coaster
dustpan
flannel
key rack
key ring

wash bag

08 aquarium
bassinet
birdcage
calendar
coat hook
dish rack
fish tank
hat stand
hip flask
ornament
place mat
shoe rack
soap dish
suitcase
tealight
tea towel
waste bin
wine rack

09 cat basket
dishcloth
dog basket
door wedge
fireguard

hairbrush
hearth rug
highchair
memo board
phone book
pushchair
sponge bag
stair gate
stepstool
towel rail
washboard
washcloth

10 baby bottle
baby walker
coathanger
laundry bag
letter rack
oven gloves
photo album
photo frame
stepladder
storage box
toothbrush

11 address book

candlestick
changing mat
first aid kit
paperweight
toilet brush

12 clothes airer
clothes-brush
clothes horse
ironing board
magazine rack
perambulator
picnic basket
Thermos® flask

13 feather duster
laundry basket
satellite dish
soap dispenser
umbrella stand
washing-up bowl

14 hot water bottle

15 draught excluder
photograph album
photograph frame

See also **accommodation**; **opera**; **tent**

Hughes, Ted (1930–98)

Significant works include:

04 *Crow* (1970)

05 *River* (1983)

Wodwo (1967)

07 *Orghast* (1971)

08 *Lupercal* (1960)
    Moortown (1979)
09 *Cave Birds* (1975)
11 *Season Songs* (1974)

14 *Remains of Elmet* (1979)
15 *Birthday Letters* (1998)
16 *The Hawk in the Rain* (1957)

Hugo, Victor (1802–85)

Significant works include:

04 *Odes* (1822)
07 *Hernani* (1830)
    Ruy Blas (1838)
08 *Cromwell* (1827)
13 *Les Châtiments* (1853)
    Les Misérables (1862)
    Les Orientales (1829)
14 *Odes et Ballades* (1826)
16 *Notre-Dame de Paris* (1831)

17 *Les Contemplations* (1856)
    Quatrevingt-treize (1874)
18 *Les Voix intérieures* (1837)
19 *La Légende des siècles* (1859–83)
    Les Feuilles d'automne (1831)
20 *Les Rayons et les ombres* (1840)
21 *Les Chants du crépuscule* (1835)
22 *Les Travailleurs de la mer* (1866)
23 *The Hunchback of Notre Dame* (1831)

humour

Humour includes:

03 dry	**07** gallows	**09** satirical	**11** barrack-room
04 sick	surreal	slapstick	Pythonesque
05 black	**08** farcical	**10** lavatorial	**12** Chaplinesque

Bodily humours include:

05 blood	phlegm	**10** melancholy
06 choler	**09** black bile	yellow bile

See also **comedy**

hybrid

Hybrids include:

02 zo	oxlip	tangelo	**10** clementine
03 dso	tigon	tea rose	loganberry
dzo	topaz		polyanthus
zho	**06** oxslip	**08** citrange	**11** boysenberry
04 dzho	**07** beefalo	limequat	bull-mastiff
mule	Bourbon	noisette	Jacqueminot
OEIC	cattabu	sunberry	Lonicera fly
Ugli®	cattalo	tayberry	marionberry
05 hinny	Jersian	**09** perpetual	miracle rice
liger	lurcher	tiger tail	**13** polecat-ferret
	plumcot	triticale	

See also **dog**; **fruit**; **mythology**

hydrocarbon

Hydrocarbons include:

03 wax	ethane	heptane	isoprene
05 halon	hexane	methane	pristane
06 aldrin	indene	olefine	stilbene
alkane	nonane	pentane	09 butadiene
alkene	octane	propane	10 benzpyrene
alkyne	olefin	styrene	mesitylene
butane	picene	terpene	11 hatchettite
cetane	pyrene	08 camphane	naphthalene
decane	retene	camphene	12 cyclopropane
	07 benzene	diphenyl	

I

Ian Fleming *see* James Bond

Ibsen, Henrik (1828–1906)

Significant works include:

05 *Brand* (1866)

06 *Ghosts* (1881)

08 *Catiline* (1850)
Peer Gynt (1867)

11 *A Doll's House* (1879)
Hedda Gabler (1890)
Little Eyolf (1894)
Love's Comedy (1862)
Rosmersholm (1886)
The Wild Duck (1884)

13 *The Pretenders* (1863)

14 *The Burial Mound* (1850)

16 *The Master Builder* (1892)
When We Dead Awaken (1899)

17 *The Lady from the Sea* (1888)

18 *An Enemy of the People* (1882)
Emperor and Galilean (1873)
John Gabriel Borkman (1896)

19 *The Pillars of Society* (1877)

Significant characters include:

04 Aase
Gynt (Peer)
Rank (Dr)

05 Brack (Judge)
Ekdal (Hedvig)
Ekdal (Hjalmar)
Werle (Gregers)
Werle (Haakon)

06 Alving (Mrs Helene)
Alving (Oswald)
Gabler (Hedda)
Helmer (Nora)
Helmer (Torvald)
Tesman (Jörgen)
Tesman (Miss Juliane)
Tesman (Mrs Hedda)

07 Elvsted (Mrs)
Lövborg (Ejlert)
Manders (Pastor)
Solveig

08 Krogstad (Nils)

09 Engstrand (Regine)

12 the Troll King

ice

Ice includes:

03 dry
pan
sea

04 floe
grew
grue
hail
pack

rime
slob
snow

05 black
brash
crust
drift
field

shelf
shell
sleet
virga

06 anchor
frazil
ground
icicle

stream

07 glacier
hummock
pancake
verglas

10 silver thaw

13 tickly-benders

See also **snow**

ice hockey

Ice hockey players and associated figures include:

03 Orr (Bobby; 1948– , Canadian)

04 Hand (Tony; 1967– , Scottish)
Howe (Gordie; 1928– , Canadian)
Hull (Bobby; 1939– , Canadian)
Hull (Brett; 1964– , Canadian)

Jagr (Jaromir; 1972– , Czech)

05 Hasek (Dominik; 1965– , Czech)
Shore (Eddie; 1902–85, Canadian)

06 Bowman (Scotty; 1933– , Canadian)
Iginla (Jarome; 1977– , Canadian)

Malkin (Evgeni; 1986– , Russian)
Mikita (Stan; 1940– , Czech/Canadian)
Plante (Jacques; 1929–86, Canadian)

07 Gretzky (Wayne; 1961– , Canadian)
Lafleur (Guy; 1951– , Canadian)
Lemieux (Mario; 1965– , Canadian)
Richard (Maurice; 1921–2000, Canadian)
Sawchuk (Terry; 1929–70, Canadian/US)

Tretiak (Vladislav; 1952– , Russian)

08 Beliveau (Jean; 1931– , Canadian)
Esposito (Phil; 1942– , Canadian)
Forsberg (Peter; 1973– , Swedish)
Ovechkin (Alexander; 1985– , Russian)

09 Kharlamov (Valery; 1948–81, Russian)
Kovalchuk (Ilya; 1983– , Russian)

Ice hockey terms include:

04 cage
puck

05 check
icing
stick
zones

06 boards
period
sin-bin

07 face-off
forward
offside
penalty
red line

shut-out
Zamboni

08 blue line
boarding
defender
five-hole
linesman
one-timer
overtime
slap shot
slashing
spearing

09 blueliner
bodycheck

centreman
netminder
power play

10 centre line
cross-check
defenceman
goaltender
penalty box

11 penalty shot
short-handed
sudden-death

12 icing the puck
penalty bench

13 defending zone

See also **sport**

ice skating

Ice skaters include:

04 Dean (Christopher; 1958– , English)
Koss (Johann Olav; 1968– , Norwegian)
Kwan (Michelle; 1980– , US)
Meng (Wang; 1985– , Chinese)
Witt (Katarina; 1965– , German)
Yang (Yang 'A'; 1975– , Chinese)

05 Baiul (Oksana; 1977– , Ukrainian)
Blair (Bonnie; 1964– , US)
Curry (John; 1949–94, English)
Heiss (Carol; 1940– , US)
Henie (Sonja; 1912–69, Norwegian/US)
Kania (Karin; 1961– , German)
Syers (Madge; 1882–1917, English)

06 Button (Dick; 1929– , US)
Hamill (Dorothy; 1956– , US)

07 Arakawa (Shizuka; 1981– , Japan)
Boitano (Brian; 1963– , US)
Cousins (Robin; 1957– , English)
Fleming (Peggy; 1948– , US)
Grinkov (Sergei; 1967–95, Russian)

Harding (Tonya; 1971– , US)
Marinin (Maxim; 1977– , Russian)
Rodnina (Irina; 1949– , Russian)
Salchow (Ulrich; 1877–1949, Swedish)
Torvill (Jayne; 1957– , English)
Yagudin (Alexei; 1980– , Russian)

08 Browning (Kurt; 1966– , Canadian)
Dijkstra (Sjoukje; 1942– , Dutch)
Dmitriev (Artur; 1968– , Russian)
Eldredge (Todd; 1971– , US)
Gordeeva (Ekaterina; 1971– , Russian)
Hamilton (Scott; 1958– , US)
Kazakova (Oksana; 1975– , Russian)
Kerrigan (Nancy; 1969– , US)
Lipinski (Tara; 1982– , US)
Petrenko (Viktor; 1969– , Ukrainian)

09 Plushenko (Evgeny; 1982– , Russian)
Yamaguchi (Kristi; 1971– , US)

10 Ahn Hyun-Soo (1985– , Korean)
Ballangrud (Ivar; 1904–69, Norwegian)
Totmianina (Tatiana; 1981– , Russian)

Ice skating terms include:

04 Axel
edge
flip
loop
Lutz

05 blade
pairs
skate
waltz

06 figure
Mohawk
rocker
walley

07 bracket

See also **sport**

Choctaw
Salchow
sit spin
toe jump
toe loop
toe pick

08 ice dance
Ina Bauer
stag leap

09 camel spin
crossover
free dance

10 inside edge

11 death spiral

flying camel
layback spin
outside edge
spread eagle
upright spin

12 headless spin
speed skating

13 Biellmann spin
figure skating
flying sit spin
free programme

14 short programme

15 compulsory dance
set pattern dance

ideology *see* politics

illegal drug *see* drug

immune system

Immune system components include:

05 T-cell
06 NK cell
spleen

07 antigen

08 antibody
lysosome
lysozyme

09 commensal
histamine
leucocyte

leukocyte
lymph node
phagocyte
white pulp

10 interferon
lymphocyte
memory cell
plasma cell

11 B-lymphocyte
helper T-cell

killer T-cell
T-lymphocyte

12 receptor site

13 cytotoxic cell
dendritic cell
immune complex

14 germinal centre
immunoglobulin

15 lymphatic system

imprint *see* publishing

Inca empire

Inca emperors, with regnal dates:

07 Huascar (1525–32)

08 Inca Roca (dates unknown)

09 Atahualpa (1532–33)
Inca Urcon (dates unknown)

10 Manco Capac (dates unknown)
Mayta Capac (dates unknown)
Sayri Tupac (1545–60)
Sinchi Roca (dates unknown)
Tupac Amaru (1571–72)

11 Huayna Capac (1493–1525)

Topa Huallpa (1533)

12 Yahuar Huacac (dates unknown)

13 Capac Yupanqui (dates unknown)
Viracocha Inca (dates unknown)

14 Lloque Yupanqui (dates unknown)

16 Titu Cusi Yupanqui (1560–71)
Topa Inca Yupanqui (1471–93)

17 Manco Inca Yupanqui (1533–45)

21 Pachacuti Inca Yupanqui (1438–71)

incarnation

Incarnations of Vishnu include:

04 Rama

05 Kurma

06 Narada

07 Krishna

09 Jugannath
Narasimha

10 Jagannatha
Juggernaut

See also **Hinduism; mythology; religion**

India

Cities and notable towns in India include:

04 Agra

05 Delhi
Poona
Simla

06 Bombay

Jaipur
Kanpur
Madras
Mumbai
Mysore

Nagpur
Shimla

07 Chennai
Kolkata
Lucknow

08 Calcutta
New Delhi

09 Ahmadabad
Bangalore
Hyderabad

Indian states and union territories:

03 Goa

05 Assam
Behar
Bihar
Delhi

06 Kerala
Orissa
Punjab
Sikkim

07 Gujarat
Haryana
Manipur
Mizoram

Tripura

08 Nagaland

09 Jharkhand
Karnataka
Meghalaya
Rajasthan
Tamil Nadu

10 Chandigarh
West Bengal

11 Daman and Diu
Lakshadweep
Maharashtra

Pondicherry
Punducherry
Uttaranchal

12 Chhattisgarh
Uttar Pradesh

13 Andhra Pradesh
Madhya Pradesh

15 Himachal Pradesh
Jammu and Kashmir

16 Arunachal Pradesh

17 Andaman and Nicobar

19 Dadra and Nagar Haveli

Indian landmarks include:

06 Ganges

07 Raj Ghat
Red Fort

08 Taj Mahal

09 India Gate

10 Thar Desert

11 Brahmaputra

12 Golden Temple

14 Imperial Palace

15 Parliament House

See also **Asia**

industrialist *see* business

inflammation

Inflammations include:

03 RSI (tendons and joints of the hands and lower arms)
sty (eye)

04 acne (sebaceous follicles)
boil
bubo (lymph nodes)
stye (eye)

05 croup (larynx and trachea)
felon (sore)
mange (animal skin)

06 ancome (finger or toe)
angina (throat)
bunion (big toe)
canker (horse's feet)

garget (throat or udder in cows or swine)
grease (horse's heels)
iritis (iris of the eye)
otitis (ear)
quinsy (tonsils)
thrush (frog of a horse's foot)
ulitis (gum)

07 abscess
cecitis (caecum)
colitis (colon)
ileitis (ileum)
pink-eye (conjunctiva)
sycosis (hair follicles)
tylosis (eyelids)
uveitis (iris, ciliary body and choroid)
whitlow (finger or toe)

08 adenitis (glands)
aortitis (aorta)
bursitis (bursa)
caecitis (caecum)
carditis (heart)
cynanche (tonsils)
cystitis (inner lining of the bladder)
mastitis (breast or udder)
metritis (uterus)
myelitis (bone marrow)
neuritis (nerves)
orchitis (testicle)
ovaritis (ovary)
prunella (tonsils)
pyelitis (pelvis of the kidney)
rectitis (rectum)
rhinitis (mucous membrane of the nose)
uteritis (womb)
uvulitis (uvula)
vulvitis (vulva)
windburn (skin)

09 arteritis (artery)
arthritis (joint)
balanitis (glans penis in mammals)
barotitis (ear)
carbuncle (skin and subcutaneous tissues)
ceratitis (cornea)
cheilitis (lips/corners of the mouth)
conchitis (concha)
enteritis (intestines)
fasciitis (plantar fascia of the foot)
frostbite
gastritis (stomach lining)
glossitis (tongue)
hepatitis (liver)
keratitis (cornea)
laminitis (horse's lamina)
nephritis (kidneys)
onychitis (soft parts about the nail)
phlebitis (wall of a vein)
phrenitis (brain)

proctitis (rectum)
retinitis (retina)
sinusitis (sinus)
splenitis (spleen)
squinancy (tonsils)
strumitis (thyroid gland)
synovitis (synovial membrane)
typhlitis (blind-gut)
vaginitis (vagina)

10 alveolitis (alveoli in the lungs)
antiaditis (tonsils)
bronchitis (lining of the bronchial tubes)
cellulitis (subcutaneous body tissue)
cephalitis (brain)
cerebritis (cerebrum)
cervicitis (neck of the womb)
chondritis (cartilage)
dermatitis (skin)
duodenitis (duodenum)
erysipelas (skin)
fibrositis (fibrous tissue)
gingivitis (gums)
hysteritis (uterus)
intertrigo (skin)
laryngitis (larynx)
meningitis (meninges)
myringitis (eardrum)
oophoritis (ovary)
papillitis (head of the optic nerve)
paronychia (finger or toe)
sore throat (throat)
stomatitis (mucous membrane of the mouth)
syringitis (Eustachian tube)
tendinitis (tendon)
tonsilitis (tonsil)
tracheitis (trachea)
tympanitis (membrane of the ear)
ureteritis (ureter)
urethritis (urethra)
valvulitis (valve of the heart)
vasculitis (blood vessel)

11 blepharitis (eyelid)
choroiditis (choroid)
mad staggers (animal brain)
mastoiditis (air cells of the mastoid
   processes)
myocarditis (myocardium)
parotiditis (parotid gland)
periostitis (periosteum)
peritonitis (peritoneum)
pharyngitis (mucous membrane of the
   pharynx)
pneumonitis (alveoli)
prickly heat (sweat glands)
prostatitis (prostate gland)
salpingitis (tube, especially a Fallopian tube)
shin splints (muscles around the shinbone)

spondylitis (synovial joints of the backbone)
staphylitis (uvula)
tennis elbow (elbow)
thoroughpin (horse's hock joint)
thyroiditis (thyroid gland)
tonsillitis (tonsil)

12 appendicitis (appendix)
crystallitis (crystalline lens)
encephalitis (brain)
endocarditis (endocardium)
endometritis (endometrium)
lymphangitis (lymphatic vessel)
panarthritis (all the structures of a joint)
pancreatitis (pancreas)
pericarditis (pericardium)
perineuritis (perineurium)
polymyositis (several muscles at the same time)
polyneuritis (several nerves)
sacroiliitis (sacroiliac joint)
vestibulitis (labyrinth and cochlea of the inner ear)

13 arachnoiditis (arachnoid membrane)

See also **disease**; **skin**

cholecystitis (gall bladder)
epicondylitis (tissues beside the epicondyle of the humerus)
jogger's nipple (nipple)
labyrinthitis (inner ear)
perigastritis (outer surface of the stomach)
perihepatitis (peritoneum covering the liver)
perinephritis (perinephrium)
periodontitis (tissues surrounding the teeth)
perityphlitis (caecum or blind-gut)
tenosynovitis (tendon)
tenovaginitis (fibrous wall of the sheath surrounding a tendon)

14 conjunctivitis (conjunctiva)
diverticulitis (one or more diverticula)
housemaid's knee (knee)
lobar pneumonia (lung lobe)
sleepy staggers (animal brain)

15 diaphragmatitis (diaphragm)
gastroenteritis (lining of the stomach and intestines)
panophthalmitis (whole eye)

ingredient *see* **salad**

insect

Insects include:

03 ant
bee
bug
fly
ked
nit

04 cleg
flea
frit
gnat
kade
moth
pium
wasp
zimb

05 aphid
aphis
cimex
culex
emmet
louse
midge
ox-bot
roach
sauba
sedge
vespa

06 bedbug
bee fly
beetle
bembex
bembix
bum-bee
capsid
chigoe
chigre
chinch
cicada
cicala
coccid
cootie
day-fly
dor-fly
drongo
earwig
gadfly
gru-gru
hop-fly
hornet
jigger

locust
maggot
mantis
may bug
mayfly
medfly
motuca
muscid
mutuca
nasute
psylla
red ant
sawfly
sow bug
thrips
tipula
tsetse
tzetse
tzetze
weevil

07 antlion
army ant
beet-fly
blowfly
boat-fly

brommer
bulb fly
bull ant
bush-fly
buzzard
chalcid
chigger
cornfly
cricket
deer fly
diptera
duck-ant
dung-fly
fig wasp
fire ant
fritfly
gallfly
gold-bug
goutfly
grayfly
hive bee
June bug
katydid
lace bug
ladybug
lamp fly
meat-fly
pill bug
pismire
rose bug
sciarid
soldier
termite
vedalia
wood ant

08 alder-fly
berry bug
birch fly
black fly
bombycid
bookworm
cercopid
cornworm
crane fly
drone fly
ephemera
firebrat
flesh-fly
froth-fly
fruit fly
gall wasp
glossina
glow-worm
greenfly
groo-groo
honey ant
honey bee
horntail

horsefly
housefly
hoverfly
lacewing
ladybird
Maori bug
mason bee
mealy bug
mosquito
onion fly
ox-warble
reduviid
ruby-tail
ruby-wasp
sand wasp
sauba ant
sedge fly
sheep ked
simulium
snake fly
snipe fly
stink bug
stonefly
tachinid
water fly
wheat fly
white ant
whitefly
wood wasp
woodworm

09 amazon ant
ambush bug
ant weaver
bark-louse
bird-louse
booklouse
bumblebee
butterfly
caddis fly
campodeid
cantharis
capsid bug
carpet bug
carrot fly
chinch bug
cochineal
cockroach
coffee bug
Croton bug
cuckoo bee
cuckoo fly
damselfly
doodlebug
dragonfly
driver ant
ephemerid
forest-fly
golden-eye

humble-bee
ichneumon
leaf miner
mason wasp
may beetle
mining bee
mud dauber
nut-weevil
paper wasp
pomace-fly
robber fly
shield bug
squash bug
stable fly
strawworm
tsetse fly
turnip fly
tzetse fly
tzetze fly
velvet ant
warble fly
wax insect
wood-borer
woodlouse

10 blister fly
bluebottle
boll weevil
bulldog ant
cabbage-fly
cicadellid
cluster fly
cockchafer
corn thrips
corn weevil
digger-wasp
dolphin-fly
drosophila
frog-hopper
grapelouse
harvest bug
harvest-fly
Hessian fly
kissing bug
lantern fly
leaf-cutter
leaf insect
Pharaoh ant
phylloxera
pond skater
potter wasp
silverfish
smother-fly
spittlebug
springtail
vinegar-fly
web spinner
wheat midge

11 backswimmer
biting louse
biting midge
bristletail
buffalo gnat
bush cricket
caterpillar
chalcid wasp
coleopteran
coleopteron
froth-hopper
grasshopper
greenbottle
honeypot ant
mole cricket
neuropteran
Pharaoh's ant
scale insect
scorpion fly
snout beetle
stick insect

trombiculid
umbrella-ant
vine-fretter
walking leaf
walking twig
12 buzzard-clock
carpenter-ant
carpenter-bee
cheesehopper
desert locust
European flea
groundhopper
harvest louse
house cricket
ichneumon fly
lightning bug
San Jose scale
screw-worm fly
sucking louse
trichopteran
walking stick

walking straw
water boatman
water strider
yellow jacket
13 blister beetle
cheese skipper
daddy longlegs
diamond-beetle
green lacewing
leatherjacket
praying insect
praying mantis
spectre insect
spittle insect
water measurer
water scorpion
14 cabbage-root fly
European hornet
15 cochineal insect
migratory locust

Insect parts include:

03 eye
jaw
leg
rib
04 coxa
gula
head
horn
legs
palp
rasp
vein
wing
05 chela
colon
costa
femur
media
nerve
notum
scape
sting
tibia
06 air-sac
antlia
arista
cercus
feeler

glossa
labium
ligula
median
mentum
palpus
proleg
radius
scapus
scutum
sheath
somite
squama
stilet
stylet
tarsus
tegmen
tegula
tergum
thorax
unguis
venule
07 abdomen
aculeus
antenna
clypeus
cuticle
elytron
elytrum

maxilla
nervure
ocellus
pedicel
phalanx
pleuron
segment
sternum
strigil
terebra
torulus
08 antennae
cheliped
false leg
forewing
frenulum
gnathite
hindwing
labellum
mandible
onychium
ovariole
peduncle
pronotum
pygidium
spiracle
sternite
subcosta
tympanum

wing case
09 mouthpart
prescutum
proboscis
propodeon
prothorax
pulvillus
scutellum
sectorial
sensillum
subcostal
submentum
tentorium
underwing
10 acetabulum
epicuticle
haustellum
integument
mesothorax
metathorax
ovipositor
paraglossa
trochanter
11 compound eye
retinaculum
13 sclerodermite
14 proventriculus

See also **ant**; **beetle**; **butterfly**; **cicada**; **fly**; **moth**; **poison**

insecticide

Insecticides include:

02 Bt	safrole	rotenone	dimethoate
03 BHC	**08** camphene	**09** chlordane	Paris green
DDT	carbaryl	Gammexane®	piperazine
05 timbó	chlordan	Malathion®	**15** organophosphate
zineb	chromene	parathion	
06 aldrin	diazinon	pyrethrum	
derris	dieldrin	toxaphene	
07 cinerin	flyspray	**10** carbofuran	
	nicotine		

See also **poison**

insectivorous plant

Insectivorous plants include:

06 sundew	**09** cobra lily	sun pitcher	Venus flytrap
07 pitcher	corkscrew	waterwheel	**13** Albany pitcher
rainbow	monkey cup	**11** bladderwort	Venus's flytrap
08 dewy pine	**10** butterwort	**12** marsh pitcher	**15** tropical pitcher

institute

Institutes include:

02 IA (Institute of Aging)
IM (Institute of Management)
WI (Women's Institute)

03 BFI (British Film Institute)
CGI (City and Guilds of London Institute)
CIB (Chartered Institute of Bankers)
CMI (Chartered Management Institute)
EMI (European Monetary Institute)
ICA (Institute of Chartered Accountants; Institute of Contemporary Art)
MIT (Massachusetts Institute of Technology)

04 NICE (National Institute of Clinical Excellence)

RIBA (Royal Institute of British Architects)
RNIB (Royal National Institute of Blind People)
RNID (Royal National Institute for Deaf People)
RTPI (Royal Town Planning Institute)

05 C and G (City and Guilds of London Institute)
UMIST (University of Manchester Institute of Science and Technology)
UWIST (University of Wales Institute of Science and Technology)

07 Caltech (California Institute of Technology)

See also **charity; university**

instrument *see* **laboratory; measurement; music; musician; optics; science; torture**

insulator

Insulators include:

03 lag	tea cosy	**10** dielectric	**14** insulating tape
04 mica	**08** rock wool	**11** vermiculite	Willesden paper
07 bushing	**09** Pink Batts®	**12** friction tape	

International Vehicle Registration code *see* **vehicle**

Internet

02

.ac	.de	.je	.no
.ad	.dj	.jm	.np
.ae	.dk	.jo	.nr
.af	.dm	.jp	.nu
.ag	.do	.ke	.nz
.ai	.dz	.kg	.om
.al	.ec	.kh	.pa
.am	.ee	.ki	.pe
.an	.eg	.km	.pf
.ao	.eh	.kn	.pg
.aq	.er	.kp	.ph
.ar	.es	.kr	.pk
.as	.et	.kw	.pl
.at	.eu	.ky	.pm
.au	.fi	.kz	.pn
.aw	.fj	.la	.pr
.az	.fk	.lb	.ps
.ba	.fm	.lc	.pt
.bb	.fo	.li	.pw
.bd	.fr	.lk	.py
.be	.ga	.lr	.qa
.bf	.gd	.ls	.re
.bg	.ge	.lt	.ro
.bh	.gf	.lu	.ru
.bi	.gg	.lv	.rw
.bj	.gh	.ly	.sa
.bm	.gi	.ma	.sb
.bn	.gl	.mc	.sc
.bo	.gm	.md	.sd
.br	.gn	.mg	.se
.bs	.gp	.mh	.sg
.bt	.gq	.mk	.sh
.bv	.gr	.ml	.si
.bw	.gs	.mm	.sj
.by	.gt	.mn	.sk
.bz	.gu	.mo	.sl
.ca	.gw	.mp	.sm
.cc	.gy	.mq	.sn
.cd	.hk	.mr	.so
.cf	.hm	.ms	.sr
.cg	.hn	.mt	.st
.ch	.hr	.mu	.sv
.ci	.ht	.mv	.sy
.ck	.hu	.mw	.sz
.cl	.id	.mx	.tc
.cm	.ie	.my	.td
.cn	.il	.mz	.tf
.co	.im	.na	.tg
.cr	.in	.nc	.th
.cu	.io	.ne	.tj
.cv	.iq	.nf	.tk
.cx	.ir	.ng	.tm
.cy	.is	.ni	.tn
.cz	.it	.nl	.to

.tp	.us	.wf	.com
.tr	.uy	.ws	.edu
.tt	.uz	.ye	.gov
.tv	.va	.yt	.int
.tw	.vc	.yu	.mil
.tz	.ve	.za	.net
.ua	.vg	.zm	.org
.ug	.vi	.zw	.pro
.uk	.vn		.sci
.um	.vu	**03** .biz	.soc

Internet terms include:

02 IE®

03 AOL
ISP
Net
tab
URL
Web
WWW

04 back
feed
host
link
page
post
spam
VoIP
Wi-Fi®

05 add-on
cloud
e-mail
flame
forum
Gmail
Opera
pop-up
Skype®
troll
WiMAX
Yahoo

06 botnet
browse
cookie
filter
flamer
Google
mash-up
on-line
Safari®
search
the Net
the Web

upload
webify
window

07 browser
crawler
deep web
favicon
Firefox
history
hotmail
Mozilla
offline
Outlook®
Pegasus
podcast
profile
refresh
restore
session
setting
vishing
vodcast
webinar
webmail
web page
webring
web site
webzine

08 bookmark
download
e-journal
Explorer®
flame war
home page
Internet
Netscape
netspeak
pharming
phishing
rollover

09 broadband
e-business

e-commerce
flamebait
hyperlink
hypertext
interface
IP address
microsite
permalink
podcaster
vodcaster
web design

10 aggregator
cyberspeak
domain name
favourites
netiquette
podcasting
podcatcher
vodcasting
web browser

11 application
deep linking
Flash Player
podcatching
proxy server
the Internet
Thunderbird
Voice over IP

12 Google Chrome
public domain
search engine
skyscraper ad
webification
webliography
World Wide Web

14 electronic mail
Mozilla Firefox
Outlook Express®

15 denial of service

See also **computer; social media; video game**

invention

Inventors include:

01 I (Hsing; 682–727, Chinese)

02 Su (Song; 1020–1101, Chinese)
Su (Sung; 1020–1101, Chinese)
Yi (Xing; 682–727, Chinese)

03 Hoe (Richard; 1812–86, US)
Kay (John; 1704–c.1780, English)
Lee (James; 1831–1904, Scottish/US)
Sax (Adolphe; 1814–94, Belgian)
Zai (Lun; c.50–118 AD, Chinese)

04 Abel (Sir Frederick; 1827–1902, English)
Bell (Alexander Graham; 1847–1922, Scottish/US)
Bell (Patrick; 1799–1869, Scottish)
Benz (Karl; 1844–1929, German)
Biró (Laszlo; 1899–1985, Hungarian/ Argentine)
Böhm (Theobald; 1794–1881, German)
Bush (Vannevar; 1890–1974, US)
Cohl (Emile; 1857–1938, French)
Colt (Samuel; 1814–62, US)
Davy (Sir Humphry; 1778–1829, English)
Eads (James; 1820–87, US)
Gray (Elisha; 1835–1901, US)
Gray (Gustave Le; 1820–82, French)
Hein (Piet; 1905–96, Danish)
Hood (Thomas; 1799–1845, English)
Howe (Elias; 1819–67, US)
Ives (Frederick; 1856–1937, US)
Jobs (Steve; 1955–2011, US)
Kyan (John; 1774–1850, Irish)
Land (Edwin; 1909–91, US)
Lear (William; 1902–78, US)
Lyot (Bernard; 1897–1952, French)
Moon (William; 1818–94, English)
Otis (Elisha; 1811–61, US)
Paul (Lewis; d.1759, English)
Swan (Sir Joseph; 1828–1914, English)
Tiro (Marcus Tullius; 1C AD, Roman)
Tsai (Lun; c.50–118 AD, Chinese)
Tull (Jethro; 1674–1741, English)
Very (Edward; 1847–1910, US)
Watt (James; 1736–1819, Scottish)
Yale (Linus; 1821–68, US)

05 Adams (William Bridges; 1797–1872, English)
Baird (John Logie; 1888–1946, Scottish)
Basov (Nikolai; 1922–2001, Russian)
Beach (Moses; 1800–68, US)
Boehm (Theobald; 1794–1881, German)
Boyle (Robert; 1627–91, Irish)
Chang (Heng; 78–139 AD, Chinese)
Clegg (Samuel; 1781–1861, English)
Cooke (Sir William Fothergill; 1806–79, English)
Creed (Frederick; 1871–1957, Scottish)
Cyril (St; 827–69, Greek)
Deere (John; 1804–86, US)
Dunne (John William; 1875–1949, English)
Dyson (James; 1947– , English)
Evans (Oliver; 1755–1819, US)
Gregg (John Robert; 1867–1948, US)
Hertz (Heinrich; 1857–94, German)
Hyatt (John Wesley; 1837–1920, US)
Kelly (William; 1811–88, US)
Kilby (Jack S; 1923–2005, US)
König (Friedrich; 1774–1833, German)
Manby (George William; 1765–1854, English)
Maxim (Sir Hiram; 1840–1916, US/British)
Monge (Gaspard; 1746–1818, French)
Morey (Samuel; 1762–1843, US)
Morse (Samuel; 1791–1872, US)
Nobel (Alfred; 1833–96, Swedish)
Olson (Harry F; 1901–82, US)
Peale (Charles Willson; 1741–1827, US)
Pupin (Michael; 1858–1935, US)
Rubik (Ernö; 1944– , Hungarian)
Smith (Sir Francis Pettit; 1808–74, English)
Sousa (John Philip; 1854–1932, US)
Tesla (Nikola; 1856–1943, US)
Volta (Alessandro, Count; 1745–1827, Italian)
Wynne (Arthur; 1862–1945, English)
Zeiss (Carl; 1816–88, German)

06 Ampère (André Marie; 1775–1836, French)
Appert (Nicolas; 1749–1841, French)
Aspdin (Joseph; 1779–1855, English)
Ayrton (William; 1847–1908, English)
Baylis, (Trevor; 1937– , English)
Berger (Hans; 1873–1941, German)
Besson (Jacques; c.1535–c.1575, French)
Bodmer (Johann Georg; 1786–1864, Swiss)
Bramah (Joseph; 1748–1814, English)
Bright (Timothy; c.1551–1615, English)
Brunel (Isambard Kingdom; 1806–59, English)
Brunel (Sir Marc; 1769–1849, French)
Bunsen (Robert; 1811–99, German)
Chappe (Claude; 1763–1805, French)
Church (William; c.1778–1863, US)
Cooper (Peter; 1791–1883, US)
Curtis (Charles; 1860–1953, US)
Diesel (Rudolf; 1858–1913, German)
Donald (Ian; 1910–87, Scottish)
Donkin (Bryan; 1768–1855, English)
Dunlop (John Boyd; 1840–1921, Scottish)
Eckert (J Presper; 1919–95, US)

Edison (Thomas Alva; 1847–1931, US)
Fairey (Sir Richard; 1887–1956, English)
Frisch (Otto; 1904–79, Austrian/British)
Fuller (Richard Buckminster; 1895–1983, US)
Gurney (Sir Goldsworthy; 1793–1875, English)
Hansom (Joseph; 1803–82, English)
Haynes (Elwood; 1857–1925, US)
Hedley (William; 1779–1843, English)
Hornby (Frank; 1863–1936, English)
Hubble (Edwin; 1889–1953, US)
Hughes (D E; 1831–1900, English/US)
Hussey (Obed; 1792–1860, US)
Kaplan (Viktor; 1876–1934, Austrian)
Lenoir (Jean Joseph Étienne; 1822–1900, French)
Lister (Samuel, Lord; 1815–1906, English)
Mauser (P P von; 1838–1914, German)
McAdam (John; 1756–1836, Scottish)
Meikle (Andrew; 1719–1811, Scottish)
Murray (Matthew; 1765–1826, English)
Napier (John; 1550–1617, Scottish)
Newton (Sir Isaac; 1642–1727, English)
Oatley (Sir Charles; 1904–96, English)
Parkes (Alexander; 1813–90, English)
Pascal (Blaise; 1623–62, French)
Pelton (Lester; 1829–1918, US)
Pitman (Sir Isaac; 1813–97, English)
Rumsey (James; 1743–92, US)
Savery (Thomas; c.1650–1715, English)
Schick (Jacob; 1878–1937, US)
Singer (Isaac; 1811–75, US)
Sperry (Elmer; 1860–1930, US)
Stroud (William; 1860–1938, English)
Talbot (William Fox; 1800–77, English)
Walker (John; c.1781–1859, English)
Wallis (Sir Barnes; 1887–1979, English)
Wright (Orville; 1871–1948, US)
Wright (Wilbur; 1867–1912, US)

07 Acheson (Edward; 1856–1931, US)
Babbage (Charles; 1791–1871, English)
Babbitt (Isaac; 1799–1862, US)
Bednorz (J Georg; 1950– , German)
Bentham (Sir Samuel; 1757–1831, English)
Bigelow (Erastus; 1814–79, US)
Bourdon (Eugène; 1808–84, French)
Byrgius (Justus; 1552–1633, Swiss)
Carlson (Chester; 1906–68, US)
Carrier (Willis H; 1876–1950, US)
Corliss (George H; 1817–88, US)
Curtiss (Glenn; 1878–1930, US)
Daimler (Gottlieb; 1834–1900, German)
Drebbel (Cornelis; c.1572–1633, Dutch/British)
Eastman (George; 1854–1932, US)
Faraday (Michael; 1791–1867, English)
Forsyth (Alexander John; 1769–1843, Scottish)

Francis (James Bicheno; 1815–92, English/US)
Gatling (Richard; 1818–1903, US)
Gaumont (Léon; 1864–1946, French)
Giffard (Henri; 1825–82, French)
Goddard (Robert; 1882–1945, US)
Hancock (Thomas; 1786–1865, English)
Hartley (David; 1732–1813, English)
Holland (John; 1840–1914, Irish/US)
Huygens (Christiaan; 1629–93, Dutch)
Jacuzzi (Candido; 1903–86, Italian/US)
Janssen (Zacharias; 1580–1638, Dutch)
Laënnec (René; 1781–1826, French)
Lanston (Tolbert; 1844–1913, US)
Lumière (Auguste; 1862–1954, French)
Lumière (Louis; 1865–1948, French)
Marconi (Guglielmo, Marchese; 1874–1937, Italian)
Mauchly (John W; 1907–80, US)
Maxwell (James Clerk; 1831–79, Scottish)
Maybach (Wilhelm; 1846–1929, German)
Metford (William; 1824–99, English)
Midgley (Thomas, Jnr; 1889–1944, US)
Panhard (René; 1841–1908, French)
Pasteur (Louis; 1822–95, French)
Perkins (Jacob; 1766–1849, US)
Pullman (George; 1831–97, US)
Roberts (Richard; 1789–1864, Welsh)
Roebuck (John; 1718–94, English)
Ronalds (Sir Francis; 1788–1873, English)
Scheutz (Georg; 1785–1873, Swedish)
Sprague (Frank; 1857–1934, US)
Stanley (Francis; 1849–1918, US)
Starley (James; 1831–81, English)
Stevens (John; 1749–1838, US)
Stevens (Robert L; 1787–1856, US)
Swinton (Alan Campbell; 1863–1930, Scottish)
Swinton (Sir Ernest; 1868–1951, Indian/British)
Thomson (Elihu; 1853–1937, US)
Thomson (Robert; 1822–73, Scottish)
Whitney (Eli; 1765–1825, US)
Whittle (Sir Frank; 1907–96, English)

08 Berliner (Émile; 1851–1929, US)
Berthoud (Ferdinand; 1727–1807, Swiss)
Bessemer (Sir Henry; 1813–98, English)
Bickford (William; 1774–1834, English)
Birdseye (Clarence; 1886–1956, US)
Bogardus (James; 1800–74, US)
Browning (John M; 1855–1926, US)
Chalmers (James; 1782–1853, Scottish)
Coolidge (William D; 1873–1975, US)
Crompton (Samuel; 1753–1827, English)
Daguerre (Louis; 1789–1851, French)
De Forest (Lee; 1873–1961, US)
Ericsson (John; 1803–89, Swedish/US)
Ferguson (Harry; 1884–1960, Irish)

Ferguson (Patrick; 1744–80, Scottish)
Ferranti (Sebastian Ziani de; 1864–1930, English)
Franklin (Benjamin; 1706–90, US)
Geissler (Heinrich; 1814–79, German)
Gillette (King Camp; 1855–1932, US)
Goldmark (Peter; 1906–77, Hungarian/US)
Goodyear (Charles; 1800–60, US)
Harrison (John; 1693–1776, English)
Huntsman (Benjamin; 1704–76, English)
Janszoon (Laurens; c.1370–1440, Dutch)
Maudslay (Henry; 1771–1831, English)
McNaught (William; 1813–81, Scottish)
Newcomen (Thomas; 1663–1729, English)
Sandwich (John Montagu, Earl of; 1718–92, English)
Schawlow (Arthur L; 1921–99, US)
Sinclair (Sir Clive; 1940– , English)
Sprengel (Hermann; 1834–1906, German/British)
Stirling (Robert; 1790–1878, Scottish)
Thompson (John T; 1860–1940, US)
Zamenhof (Ludwig; 1859–1917, Polish)
Zeppelin (Count Ferdinand von; 1838–1917, German)

09 Applegath (Augustus; 1788–1871, English)
Arkwright (Sir Richard; 1732–92, English)
Armstrong (Edwin H; 1890–1954, US)
Armstrong (William, Lord; 1810–1900, English)
Blanchard (Jean Pierre; 1753–1809, French)
Burroughs (William Seward; 1855–98, US)
Butterick (Ebenezer; 1826–1903, US)
Carothers (Wallace; 1896–1937, US)
Cockerell (Sir Christopher; 1910–99, English)
Ctesibius (2c BC, Greek)
de Mestral (George; 1907–90, Swiss)
Elkington (George; 1801–65, English)
Fessenden (Reginald; 1866–1932, Canadian/US)
Fleischer (Max; 1883–1972, Austrian/US)
Greathead (James Henry; 1844–96, South African/British)
Gutenberg (Johannes; 1400–68, German)
Heathcoat (John; 1783–1861, English)
Hollerith (Herman; 1860–1929, US)
Hotchkiss (Benjamin B; 1826–85, US)
MacCready (Paul; 1925–2007, US)

Macintosh (Charles; 1766–1843, Scottish)
Macmillan (Kirkpatrick; 1813–78, Scottish)
McCormick (Cyrus; 1809–84, US)
Muybridge (Eadweard; 1830–1904, English/US)
Nicholson (William; 1753–1815, English)
Pinchbeck (Christopher; c.1710–1783, English)
Remington (Philo; 1816–89, US)
Schickard (Wilhelm; 1592–1635, German)
Symington (William; 1763–1831, Scottish)
Vaucanson (Jacques de; 1709–82, French)
Whitehead (Robert; 1823–1905, English)
Whitworth (Sir Joseph; 1803–87, English)
Wilkinson (John; 1728–1808, English)
Worcester (Edward Somerset, Earl of; 1601–67, English)

10 Archimedes (c.287–212 BC, Greek)
Berners-Lee (Tim; 1955– , English)
Cartwright (Edmund; 1743–1823, English)
Cristofori (Bartolommeo; 1655–1731, Italian)
Fahrenheit (Gabriel; 1686–1736, German)
Fourneyron (Benoît; 1802–67, French)
Hargreaves (James; c.1720–1778, English)
Laithwaite (Eric; 1921–97, English)
Lanchester (Frederick; 1868–1946, English)
Lilienthal (Otto; 1849–96, German)
Pilkington (Sir Alastair; 1920–95, English)
Senefelder (Aloys; 1771–1834, German)
Stephenson (George; 1781–1848, English)
Torricelli (Evangelista; 1608–47, Italian)
Trevithick (Richard; 1771–1833, English)

11 Cristofaloi (Bartolommeo; 1655–1731, Italian)
Desaguliers (J T; 1683–1744, French/British)
Mège Mouriés (Hippolyte; 1817–80, French)
Montgolfier (Jacques; 1745–99, French)
Montgolfier (Joseph; 1740–1810, French)
Reichenbach (Georg von; 1772–1826, German)

12 Alexanderson (Ernst; 1878–1975, Swedish/US)
Friese-Greene (William; 1855–1921, English)
Mergenthaler (Ottmar; 1854–99, German/US)
Stringfellow (John; 1799–1883, English)

invertebrate

Invertebrates include:

05 coral	**06** chiton	**07** bivalve
fluke	insect	crinoid
hydra	spider	mollusc
leech	sponge	sea lily

sea wasp
08 arachnid
flatworm
nematode
sea pansy
starfish
tapeworm
09 arthropod
centipede
earthworm
gastropod
jellyfish
millipede

planarian
roundworm
sea spider
sea urchin
spoonworm
trilobite
water bear
10 cephalopod
crustacean
echinoderm
sand dollar
sea anemone
tardigrade

11 annelid worm
brittle star
chaetognath
feather star
globigerina
sea cucumber
12 box jellyfish
coelenterate
Venus's girdle
13 crown-of-thorns
horseshoe crab
sea gooseberry
15 dead-men's fingers

See also **ant**; **beetle**; **butterfly**; **crustacean**; **insect**; **jellyfish**; **mollusc**; **moth**; **spider**; **worm**

Ireland

Cities and notable towns in Ireland include:

04 Cork	**06** Dublin	**07** Dundalk	Limerick
05 Sligo	Galway	**08** Drogheda	**09** Waterford

Administrative divisions of Ireland, with regional capitals:

04 Cork
Leix (Portlaoise)
Mayo (Castlebar)
05 Cavan
Clare (Ennis)
Kerry (Tralee)
Louth (Dundalk)
Meath (Trim)
Sligo

06 Carlow
Dublin
Galway
Offaly (Tullamore)
07 Donegal (Lifford)
Kildare (Naas)
Leitrim (Carrick)
Wexford
Wicklow

08 Kilkenny
Laoighis (Portlaoise)
Limerick
Longford
Monaghan
09 Roscommon
Tipperary (Clonmel)
Waterford
Westmeath (Mullingar)

Ancient Irish provinces:

06 Ulster	**08** Connacht
07 Munster	Leinster

Irish landmarks include:

03 Lee
05 Boyne
06 Liffey
07 Shannon
09 Bantry Bay
Connemara

Dublin Bay
Temple Bar
10 Sligo Abbey
11 Ferns Castle
12 Abbey Theatre
Blarney Stone

Dublin Castle
13 Ha'penny Bridge
14 O'Connell Street
Trinity College
15 Dingle Peninsula

See also **mythology**; **United Kingdom**

Irish

Irish boys' names include:

03 Kit	**04** Colm	Elva	Euan
Pat	Edel	Eoin	Ewan

Ewen	Duane	Ultan	Seamas
Finn	Dwane	**06** Arthur	Seamus
Liam	Elvis	Cathal	Shamus
Neal	Kelly	Ciaran	Tyrone
Neil	Kerry	Connor	**07** Brendan
Owen	Kevan	Declan	Christy
Rory	Kevin	Eamonn	Desmond
Ryan	Neale	Eamunn	Feargal
Sean	Niall	Finbar	Finbarr
05 Aidan	Oscar	Fingal	Killian
Aiden	Paddy	Fintan	Padraic
Barry	Ronan	Kieran	Padraig
Cahal	Shane	Kieron	Patrick
Colum	Shaun	Kilian	Shannon
Conor	Shawn	Lorcan	**08** Ruaidhri

Irish girls' names include:

03 Ena	Ethna	Ailish	Bronach
Una	Ethne	Dervla	Bronagh
04 Aine	Fionn	Dympna	Caitlin
Cait	Kelly	Eileen	Clodagh
Erin	Kiera	Eithna	Colleen
Kath	Maeve	Eithne	Deirdre
Kyra	Maire	Finola	Dymphna
Maev	Maude	Garret	Grainne
Maud	Maura	Grania	Mairead
Mona	Moira	Granya	Maureen
Nola	Moyra	Noreen	Shannon
Nora	Niamh	Roisin	Shelagh
Sine	Norah	Sheila	Siobhan
Tara	Nuala	Sinead	
05 Brona	Rowan	Sorcha	**08** Kathleen
Ciara	**06** Aileen	**07** Aisling	**09** Fionnuala

Islam

Muslim groups and denominations include:

04 Shia	**07** Alawite	**08** Senoussi
05 Ibadi	dervish	**10** Karmathian
Shiah	Mevlevi	**11** Black Muslim
Sunni	Senussi	**15** whirling dervish
06 Senusi	Sonnite	
Shiite	Sunnite	

See also **calendar**; **religion**

island

Islands and island groups include:

03 Cos (Aegean Sea)	**04** Aran (Atlantic Ocean)
Fyn (Baltic Sea)	Bali (Indian Ocean)
Ios (Aegean Sea)	Coll (Atlantic Ocean)
Man (Irish Sea)	Cook (Pacific Ocean)
Rab (Mediterranean Sea)	Corn (Caribbean Sea)
Rum (Sea of the Hebrides)	Cuba (Caribbean Sea)

Eigg (Sea of the Hebrides)
Elba (Tyrrhenian Sea/Mediterranean Sea)
Fiji (Pacific Ocean)
Gozo (Mediterranean Sea)
Guam (Pacific Ocean)
Herm (English Channel)
Holy (North Sea)
Iona (Atlantic Ocean)
Java (Java Sea/Indian Ocean)
Jura (Atlantic Ocean)
Line (Pacific Ocean)
Long (Atlantic Ocean)
Mahe (Indian Ocean)
Maui (Pacific Ocean)
Muck (Sea of the Hebrides)
Mull (Sea of the Hebrides/Atlantic Ocean)
Nias (Indian Ocean)
Niue (Pacific Ocean)
Oahu (Pacific Ocean)
Rota (Pacific Ocean)
Sado (Sea of Japan)
Sark (English Channel)
Skye (Sea of the Hebrides/Atlantic Ocean)
Wake (Pacific Ocean)

05 Arran (Atlantic Ocean)
Barra (Atlantic Ocean)
Bioko (Atlantic Ocean)
Bonin (Pacific Ocean)
Capri (Tyrrhenian Sea/Mediterranean Sea)
Chios (Aegean Sea)
Cocos (Indian Ocean)
Coney (Atlantic Ocean)
Corfu (Ionian Sea)
Crete (Aegean Sea/Mediterranean Sea)
Éfaté (Coral Sea/Pacific Ocean)
Ellis (Atlantic Ocean)
Faroe (Atlantic Ocean/Arctic Ocean)
Handa (Atlantic Ocean)
Hondo (East China Sea)
Hydra (Aegean Sea)
Ibiza (Mediterranean Sea)
Islay (Atlantic Ocean)
Kauai (Pacific Ocean)
Kuril (Pacific Ocean)
Lanai (Pacific Ocean)
Lundy (Celtic Sea/Atlantic Ocean)
Luzon (South China Sea/Pacific Ocean)
Malta (Mediterranean Sea)
Melos (Aegean Sea)
Nauru (Pacific Ocean)
Naxos (Aegean Sea)
North (Tasman Sea/Pacific Ocean)
Öland (Baltic Sea)
Orust (North Sea)
Palau (Pacific Ocean)
Paros (Aegean Sea)
Pearl (Indian Ocean)
Pemba (Indian Ocean)

Samoa (Pacific Ocean)
Samos (Aegean Sea)
South (Tasman Sea/Pacific Ocean)
Sunda (Celebes Sea/South China Sea)
Timor (Timor Sea/Indian Ocean)
Tiree (Sea of the Hebrides/Atlantic Ocean)
Tonga (Pacific Ocean)
Wight (English Channel)

06 Aegean (Aegean Sea)
Aegina (Aegean Sea)
Andros (Atlantic Ocean)
Azores (Atlantic Ocean)
Baffin (Labrador Sea/Arctic Ocean)
Bikini (Pacific Ocean)
Borneo (South China Sea/Celebes Sea)
Caicos (Atlantic Ocean)
Canary (Atlantic Ocean)
Chagos (Indian Ocean)
Comino (Mediterranean Sea)
Cyprus (Mediterranean Sea)
Devil's (Atlantic Ocean)
Easter (Pacific Ocean)
Euboea (Aegean Sea)
Flores (Pacific Ocean)
Flotta (Atlantic Ocean)
Hainan (South China Sea)
Harris (Atlantic Ocean)
Hawaii (Pacific Ocean)
Honshu (Pacific Ocean/East China Sea/Sea
    of Japan)
Icaria (Aegean Sea)
Ionian (Ionian Sea)
Jersey (English Channel)
Kodiak (Pacific Ocean)
Komodo (Flores Sea/Indian Ocean)
Kosrae (Pacific Ocean)
Kyushu (East China Sea/Pacific Ocean)
Lesbos (Aegean Sea)
Limnos (Aegean Sea/Mediterranean Sea)
Midway (Pacific Ocean)
Orkney (North Sea/Atlantic Ocean)
Patmos (Aegean Sea)
Penghu (South China Sea)
Rhodes (Aegean Sea/Mediterranean Sea)
Scilly (Atlantic Ocean)
Sicily (Mediterranean Sea)
Skiros (Aegean Sea)
Staffa (Sea of the Hebrides/Atlantic Ocean)
Staten (Atlantic Ocean)
Tahiti (Pacific Ocean)
Taiwan (China Sea/Pacific Ocean)
Tinian (Philippine Sea/Pacific Ocean)
Tobago (Caribbean Sea/Atlantic Ocean)
Tubuai (Pacific Ocean)
Tuvalu (Pacific Ocean)
Virgin (Caribbean Sea/Atlantic Ocean)

07 Anjouan (Indian Ocean)

Antigua (Caribbean Sea/Atlantic Ocean)
Bahrain (Persian Gulf)
Barbuda (Caribbean Sea/Atlantic Ocean)
Bermuda (Atlantic Ocean)
Bonaire (Caribbean Sea)
Cabrera (South China Sea)
Celebes (Celebes Sea/Molucca Sea/Java Sea/
  Banda Sea)
Channel (English Channel)
Chatham (Pacific Ocean)
Comoros (Indian Ocean)
Corsica (Mediterranean Sea)
Curaçao (Caribbean Sea)
Frisian (North Sea)
Gilbert (Pacific Ocean)
Gotland (Baltic Sea)
Grenada (Atlantic Ocean)
Iceland (Greenland Sea/Atlantic Ocean)
Ireland (Irish Sea/Atlantic Ocean)
Iwo Jima (Pacific Ocean)
Jamaica (Caribbean Sea)
La Digue (Indian Ocean)
Leeward (Caribbean Sea/Atlantic Ocean)
Lofoten (Arctic Ocean)
Loyalty (Coral Sea/Pacific Ocean)
Madeira (Atlantic Ocean)
Majorca (Mediterranean Sea)
Mayotte (Indian Ocean)
Menorca (Mediterranean Sea)
Mikonos (Aegean Sea)
Mindoro (South China Sea/Sulu Sea)
Minorca (Mediterranean Sea)
Molokai (Pacific Ocean)
Nicobar (Indian Ocean)
Norfolk (Pacific Ocean)
Okinawa (East China Sea)
Palawan (South China Sea/Sulu Sea)
Phoenix (Pacific Ocean)
Praslin (Indian Ocean)
Rathlin (Atlantic Ocean)
Réunion (Indian Ocean)
Salamis (Aegean Sea/Mediterranean Sea)
Siberut (Indian Ocean)
Society (Pacific Ocean)
Solomon (Solomon Sea/Pacific Ocean)
Stewart (Tasman Sea/Pacific Ocean)
St Kilda (Atlantic Ocean)
St Lucia (Caribbean Sea/Atlantic Ocean)
Sumatra (Indian Ocean)
Surtsey (Atlantic Ocean)
Tokelau (Pacific Ocean)
Vanuatu (Coral Sea/Pacific Ocean)
Visayan (Pacific Ocean)
Wrangel (Chukchi Sea/East Siberian Sea/
  Arctic Ocean)
Zealand (Baltic Sea)

08 Alderney (English Channel)
Aleutian (Bering Sea)

Anglesey (Irish Sea)
Anguilla (Caribbean Sea)
Balearic (Mediterranean Sea)
Barbados (Caribbean Sea/Atlantic Ocean)
Bornholm (Baltic Sea)
Colonsay (Atlantic Ocean)
Coral Sea (Coral Sea/Pacific Ocean)
Cyclades (Aegean Sea)
Dominica (Caribbean Sea/Atlantic Ocean)
Falkland (Atlantic Ocean)
Guernsey (English Channel)
Hawaiian (Pacific Ocean)
Hebrides (Atlantic Ocean)
Hokkaido (Sea of Japan/Sea of Okhotsk/
  Pacific Ocean)
Hong Kong (South China Sea)
Jan Mayen (Arctic Ocean)
Johnston (Pacific Ocean)
Kiribati (Pacific Ocean)
Lord Howe (Pacific Ocean)
Maldives (Indian Ocean)
Mallorca (Mediterranean Sea)
Marshall (Pacific Ocean)
Mindanao (Philippine Sea/Sulu Sea/Pacific
  Ocean)
Moluccas (Pacific Ocean)
Pitcairn (Pacific Ocean)
Sakhalin (Sea of Okhotsk/Pacific Ocean)
Sandwich (Pacific Ocean)
São Tiago (Atlantic Ocean)
Sardinia (Mediterranean Sea)
Shetland (Atlantic Ocean)
Skiathos (Aegean Sea)
Sri Lanka (Indian Ocean)
St Helena (Atlantic Ocean)
Sulawesi (Banda Sea/Java Sea/Molucca Sea)
Svalbard (Arctic Ocean)
Tasmania (Indian Ocean/Pacific Ocean)
Tenerife (Atlantic Ocean)
Trinidad (Caribbean Sea/Atlantic Ocean)
Victoria (Atlantic Ocean; Arctic Ocean)
Viti Levu (Pacific Ocean)
Westmann (Atlantic Ocean)
Windward (Caribbean Sea/Atlantic Ocean)
Zanzibar (Indian Ocean)

09 Admiralty (Bismarck Sea)
Ascension (Atlantic Ocean)
Australia (Tasman Sea/Coral Sea/Pacific
  Ocean/Indian Ocean)
Benbecula (Atlantic Ocean)
Cape Verde (Atlantic Ocean)
Christmas (Indian Ocean)
Ellesmere (Arctic Ocean)
Galápagos (Pacific Ocean)
Greenland (Atlantic Ocean/Arctic Ocean)
Halmahera (Pacific Ocean)
Indonesia (Indian Ocean/Pacific Ocean)
Irian Jaya (Indian Ocean/Pacific Ocean)

Isle of Man (Irish Sea)
Kárpathos (Aegean Sea/Mediterranean Sea)
Lanzarote (Atlantic Ocean)
Las Palmas (Atlantic Ocean)
Macquarie (Pacific Ocean)
Manhattan (Atlantic Ocean)
Marquesas (Pacific Ocean)
Mascarene (Indian Ocean)
Mauritius (Indian Ocean)
Melanesia (Pacific Ocean)
Nantucket (Atlantic Ocean)
New Guinea (Coral Sea/Solomon Sea/Pacific Ocean)
North Uist (Sea of the Hebrides/Atlantic Ocean)
Rodrigues (Indian Ocean)
Santorini (Aegean Sea)
Singapore (South China Sea)
South Uist (Sea of the Hebrides/Atlantic Ocean)
Stromboli (Tyrrhenian Sea)
Vanua Levu (Pacific Ocean)
Zacynthus (Ionian Sea/Mediterranean Sea)

10 Ahvenanmaa (Baltic Sea)
Basse-Terre (Caribbean Sea/Atlantic Ocean)
Cape Breton (Atlantic Ocean)
Cephalonia (Ionian Sea/Mediterranean Sea)
Dodecanese (Aegean Sea)
Formentera (Mediterranean Sea)
Heligoland (North Sea)
Hispaniola (Caribbean Sea/Atlantic Ocean)
Ile d'Oléron (Atlantic Ocean)
Kalimantan (Celebes Sea)
Kiritimati (Pacific Ocean)
Madagascar (Indian Ocean)
Martinique (Caribbean Sea/Atlantic Ocean)
Micronesia (Pacific Ocean)
Montserrat (Caribbean Sea)
New Britain (Solomon Sea/Bismarck Sea/ Pacific Ocean)
New Ireland (Solomon Sea/Bismarck Sea/ Pacific Ocean)
Puerto Rico (Caribbean Sea/Atlantic Ocean)
Samothrace (Aegean Sea)

Seychelles (Indian Ocean)
The Bahamas (Caribbean Sea)
Vesterålen (Norwegian Sea/Arctic Ocean)
West Indies (Caribbean Sea)

11 Gran Canaria (Atlantic Ocean)
Grand Bahama (Atlantic Ocean)
Grand Cayman (Caribbean Sea)
Grande-Terre (Indian Ocean)
Guadalcanal (Pacific Ocean)
Iles d'Hyères (Mediterranean Sea)
Iles du Salut (Atlantic Ocean)
Isla Cozumel (Caribbean Sea)
Isle of Wight (English Channel)
Scilly Isles (Atlantic Ocean)
South Orkney (North Sea/Atlantic Ocean)

12 Bougainville (Pacific Ocean)
Grande Comore (Indian Ocean)
Great Britain (North Sea/Irish Sea/Atlantic Ocean)
Isla de Pascua (Pacific Ocean)
Newfoundland (Atlantic Ocean)
Novaya Zemlya (Kara Sea/Arctic Ocean)
Prince Edward (Atlantic Ocean)
South Georgia (Atlantic Ocean)

13 American Samoa (Pacific Ocean)
British Virgin (Caribbean Sea)
Inner Hebrides (Atlantic Ocean)
Isla Contadora (Pacific Ocean)
Isles of Scilly (Atlantic Ocean)
New Providence (Atlantic Ocean)
Outer Hebrides (Atlantic Ocean)
South Shetland (Atlantic Ocean)

14 Oki Archipelago (Sea of Japan)
Papua New Guinea (Pacific Ocean)
Tierra del Fuego (Atlantic Ocean/Pacific Ocean/Southern Ocean)
Tristan da Cunha (Atlantic Ocean)
Turks and Caicos (Atlantic Ocean)

15 French Polynesia (Pacific Ocean)
Lewis with Harris (Atlantic Ocean)
Martha's Vineyard (Atlantic Ocean)
Wallis and Futuna (Pacific Ocean)

See also **archipelago**

Italian

Italian words and expressions include:

04 ciao (hello; bye)
05 prego (you're welcome)
salve (hello)
06 grazie (thanks)
stucco (ornamental plasterwork)
07 al dente (culinary term denoting cooked but firm)

barista (espresso coffee machine operator)
08 al fresco (in the open air)
intaglio (engraving)
seraglio (a harem or place of confinement)
09 a cappella (sung without instrumental accompaniment)
antipasto (appetizer)

paparazzo (photographer who pursues celebrities)

sgraffito (decoration achieved by scratching through to subsurface)

sotto voce (in an undertone; aside)

10 buongiorno (good morning)

Cosa Nostra (the Mafia)

prima donna (leading female singer in an opera)

11 arrivederci (good-bye)

che sarà sarà (what will be will be)

chiaroscuro (painting in which only light and shade are represented)

gran turismo (a car designed for high speed touring in luxury)

la dolce vita (a life of wealth, pleasure and self-indulgence)

12 così fan tutte (all women are like that)

lingua franca (a language chosen as a medium of communication among speakers of different languages)

See also **day**; **month**; **number**

Italy

Cities and notable towns in Italy include:

04	Pisa		Milan		Venice	**08** Florence
	Rome		Turin	**07**	Bologna	
05	Genoa	**06**	Naples		Palermo	

Administrative divisions of Italy, with regional capitals:

05	Lazio (Rome)		Campania (Naples)
06	Marche (Ancona)		Lombardy (Milan)
	Molise (Campobasso)		Piedmont (Turin)
	Puglia (Bari)		Piemonte (Turin)
	Sicily (Palermo)		Sardegna (Cagliari)
	Umbria (Perugia)		Sardinia (Cagliari)
	Veneto (Venice)	**09**	Lombardia (Milan)
07	Abruzzi (L'Aquila)	**10**	Basilicata (Potenza)
	Liguria (Genoa)	**11**	Valle d'Aosta (Aosta)
	Sicilia (Palermo)	**13**	Emilia-Romagna (Bologna)
	Toscana (Florence)	**17**	Trentino-Alto Adige (Bozen/Trient)
	Tuscany (Florence)	**19**	Friuli-Venezia Giulia (Trieste)
08	Calabria (Catanzaro)		

Italian landmarks include:

02	Po	**07**	La Scala		Dolomites		Rialto Bridge
04	Arno		Pompeii		Lake Garda	**13**	Bridge of Sighs
	Como	**08**	Lake Como	**10**	Grand Canal		Sistine Chapel
	Etna		Maggiore		Mt Vesuvius		St Mark's Square
	Lido		Pantheon	**11**	Doge's Palace		Uffizi Gallery
05	David		St Peter's		Herculaneum		Vatican Palace
	Forum		Vesuvius		Vatican City	**14**	Palazzo Vecchio
	Garda	**09**	Appian Way	**12**	Lake Maggiore		Piazza San Marco
	Tiber		Campanile		Leaning Tower		St Peter's Square
06	Mt Etna		Colosseum		Ponte Vecchio		Via Appia Antica

IVR code *see* **vehicle**

Ivy League *see* **university**

J

James Bond

Characters in James Bond films include:

01 M	**08** Hugo Drax	Kissy Suzuki
Q	Max Zorin	Paris Carver
03 Aki	Nick Nack	Pola Ivanova
Zao	Red Grant	Pussy Galore
04 Bibi	Whitaker	Rosie Carver
Jaws	**09** Kristatos	Tiffany Case
Jinx	Le Chiffre	Tiger Tanaka
05 Irina	Octopussy	**12** Andrea Anders
Mr Big	Rosa Klebb	Domino Derval
Naomi	Solitaire	Ernst Blofeld
06 Bianca	Stromberg	Plenty O'Toole
Fields	**10** Fiona Volpe	Stacey Sutton
Mathis	Goldfinger	Xenia Onatopp
May Day	Honey Ryder	**13** Corinne Dufour
Oddjob	Kara Milovy	Dominic Greene
Renard	Lupe Lamora	Holly Goodhead
TeeHee	Pam Bouvier	Mary Goodnight
Wai Lin	Raoul Silva	**14** Christmas Jones
07 Blofeld	Scaramanga	Melina Havelock
Camille	Vesper Lynd	Miss Moneypenny
Columbo	**11** Anya Amasova	Tracy Di Vicenzo
Mr White	Elektra King	**15** Auric Goldfinger
Sanchez	Emilio Largo	Natalya Simonova
Stamper	Felix Leiter	Patricia Fearing
	Helga Brandt	Tatiana Romanova

James, Henry (1843–1916)

Significant works include:

09 *In the Cage* (1898)

11 *Daisy Miller* (1879)
The American (1877)

12 *Terminations* (1895)
The Two Magics (1898)
Watch and Ward (1871)

13 *The Awkward Age* (1899)
The Bostonians (1886)
The Golden Bowl (1904)
The Other House (1896)
The Tragic Muse (1890)

14 *Roderick Hudson* (1875)
The Ambassadors (1903)

What Maisie Knew (1897)

15 *Portrait of a Lady* (1881)
The Aspern Papers (1888)
The Reverberator (1888)

16 *The American Scene* (1907)
Washington Square (1881)

17 *The Turn of the Screw* (1898)
The Wings of the Dove (1902)

18 *A Small Boy and Others* (1913)
The Spoils of Poynton (1897)

21 *Notes of a Son and Brother* (1914)

22 *The Princess Casamassima* (1886)

Significant characters include:

03 Wix (Mrs)	Miles	Brydon (Spencer)
04 Croy (Kate)	Pupin (Monsieur)	Claude (Sir)
Erme (Gwendolen)	Quint (Peter)	Gereth (Mrs)
Mark (Lord)	Stant (Charlotte)	Gereth (Owen)
05 Acton (Robert)	Vetch (Anastasius)	Hudson (Roderick)
Brand (Mr)	Vetch (Fleda)	Jessel (Miss)
Deane (Drayton)	Young (Felix)	Lowder (Mrs Maud)
Flora	**06** Archer (Isabel)	Miller (Daisy, properly
Merle (Madame Serena)	Aspern (Jeffrey)	Annie P)

Newman (Christopher)
Nioche (Noémie)
Osmond (Gilbert)
Osmond (Pansy)
Pocock (Sarah)
Ransom (Basil)
Sloper (Catherine)
Sloper (Dr Austin)
Theale (Milly)
Verver (Adam)
Verver (Maggie)

07 Amerigo (Prince)
Corvick
Densher (Merton)
Eugenia (Baroness Münster)
Farange (Beale)
Farange (Ida)
Farange (Maisie)
Gostrey (Maria)

Marcher (John)
Newsome (Chadwick 'Chad')
Newsome (Mrs)
Pynsent (Miss 'Pinnie')
Tarrant (Verena)
Vereker (Hugh)

08 Birdseye (Miss)
De Cintré (Claire)
Goodwood (Caspar)
Muniment (Paul)
Overmore (Miss)
Robinson (Hyacinth)
Strether (Lewis Lambert)
Touchett (Ralph)
Townsend (Morris)
Waymarsh
Wingrave (Owen)

09 Bordereau (Miss Juliana)
Bordereau (Miss Tina)
Brigstock (Mona)
De Vionnet (Madame)
Stackpole (Henrietta)
Stringham (Mrs Susan)
the editor
Warburton (Lord)
Wentworth (Charlotte)
Wentworth (Clifford)
Wentworth (Gertrude)

10 Brookenham (Nanda)
Chancellor (Olive)
Giovanelli (Mr)

11 Casamassima (Princess)
the narrator

12 the governess
Winterbourne (Frederick)

Japan

Cities and notable towns in Japan include:

04 Kobe	Osaka	**07** Sapporo	Yokohama
Nara	Tokyo	**08** Kawasaki	**09** Hiroshima
05 Kyoto	**06** Nagoya	Nagasaki	

Japanese landmarks include:

03 Ise	Horyu-ji	**10** Sea of Japan
05 Kokyo	Todaiji	**11** Genbaku Dome
Nikko	Tosho-gu	Itsukushima
06 Mt Fuji	**08** Miyajima	Shirakawa-go
Mt Koya	**09** Inland Sea	**12** Southern Alps
Ryukyu	Japan Alps	**14** Imperial Palace
07 Asakusa	Yakushima	**15** Shirakami-Sanchi

Japanese art forms include:

02 no	Imari	ukiyo-e	**08** kakemono
03 noh	kendo	**07** bunraku	kakiemon
04 raku	**06** gagaku	chanoyu	tsutsumu
05 haiku	kabuki	ikebana	**11** linked verse
Hizen	nogaku	nihonga	tea ceremony
	saikei	origami	

See also **Asia**

jazz

Jazz includes:

03 bop	jive	funky	**06** fusion
hot	soul	kwela	groove
04 acid	trad	modal	modern
Afro	**05** bebop	spiel	**07** classic
cool	blues	swing	hard bop

New Wave	**09** Afro-Cuban	**10** avant-garde	**11** barrelhouse
post-bop	bossa nova	improvised	third stream
ragtime	Dixieland	mainstream	traditional
08 free-form	gutbucket	neo-classic	**12** boogie-woogie
high life	West Coast	New Orleans	

Jazz and blues musicians and singers include:

03 Guy (Buddy; 1936– , US)
Ory (Kid; 1886–1973, US)

04 Bley (Carla; 1938– , US)
Byrd (Charlie; 1925–99, US)
Cole (Nat 'King'; 1919–65, US)
Cray (Robert; 1953– , US)
Getz (Stan; 1927–91, US)
Kidd (Carol; 1944– , Scottish)
King (B B; 1925– , US)
Kirk (Roland; 1936–77, US)
Lacy (Steve; 1934–2004, US)
Monk (Thelonious; 1917–82, US)
Pass (Joe; 1929–94, US)
Pine (Courtney; 1964– , English)
Shaw (Artie; 1910–2004, US)

05 Ayler (Albert; 1936–70, US)
Baker (Chet; 1929–88, US)
Basie (Count; 1904–84, US)
Brown (Sandy; 1929–75, Indian/Scottish)
Cooke (Sam; 1931–64, US)
Corea (Chick; 1941– , US)
Davis (Miles; 1926–91, US)
Dodds (Johnny; 1892–1940, US)
Ellis (Don; 1934–78, US)
Evans (Bill; 1929–80, US)
Evans (Gil; 1912–88, Canadian)
Handy (W C; 1873–1958, US)
Hines (Earl; 1903–83, US)
James (Elmore; 1918–63, US)
Jones (Elvin; 1927–2004, US)
Jones (Norah; 1979– , US)
Jones (Quincy; 1933– , US)
Krupa (Gene; 1909–73, US)
Laine (Dame Cleo; 1927– , English)
Lewis (John; 1920–2001, US)
Melly (George; 1926–2007, English)
Roach (Max; 1924–2007, US)
Scott (Ronnie; 1927–96, English)
Shepp (Archie; 1937– , US)
Smith (Bessie; 1894–1937, US)
Smith (Tommy; 1967– , Scottish)
Solal (Martial; 1927– , Algerian/French)
Sun Ra (1914–93, US)
Tatum (Art; 1910–56, US)
Tormé (Mel; 1925–99, US)
Tyner (McCoy; 1938– , US)
Weber (Eberhard; 1940– , German)
Young (Lester; 1909–59, US)

06 Barber (Chris; 1930– , English)

Bechet (Sidney; 1897–1959, US)
Blakey (Art; 1919–90, US)
Burton (Gary; 1943– , US)
Carter (Betty; 1929–98, US)
Cherry (Don; 1936–95, US)
Clarke (Kenny; 1914–85, US)
Dolphy (Eric; 1928–64, US)
Domino (Fats; 1928– , US)
Dorsey (Tommy; 1905–56, US)
Garner (Errol; 1921–77, US)
Gordon (Dexter; 1923–90, US)
Herman (Woody; 1913–87, US)
Hodges (Johnny; 1906–70, US)
Hooker (John Lee; 1920–2001, US)
Joplin (Janis; 1943–70, US)
Joplin (Scott; 1868–1917, US)
Kenton (Stan; 1912–79, US)
Miller (Glenn; 1904–44, US)
Mingus (Charles; 1922–79, US)
Morton (Jelly Roll; 1890–1941, US)
Oliver (King; 1885–1938, US)
Parker (Charlie; 1920–55, US)
Portal (Michel; 1935– , US)
Powell (Bud; 1924–66, US)
Rainey ('Ma'; 1886–1939, US)
Silver (Horace; 1928– , US)
Simone (Nina; 1933–2003, US)
Surman (John; 1944– , English)
Taylor (Cecil; 1933– , US)
Tharpe (Sister Rosetta; 1915–73, US)
Tracey (Stan; 1926– , English)
Walker (T-Bone; 1910–75, US)
Waller (Fats; 1904–43, US)
Waters (Ethel; 1896–1977, US)
Waters (Muddy; 1915–83, US)

07 Bennett (Tony; 1926– , US)
Broonzy (Big Bill; 1893–1958, US)
Brubeck (Dave; 1920–2012, US)
Charles (Ray; 1930–2004, US)
Clapton (Eric; 1945– , English)
Coleman (Ornette; 1930– , US)
Collins (Albert; 1932–93, US)
Goodman (Benny; 1909–86, US)
Hampton (Lionel; 1909–2002, US)
Hancock (Herbie; 1940– , US)
Hawkins (Coleman; 1904–69, US)
Holiday (Billie; 1915–59, US)
Hopkins (Lightnin'; 1912–82, US)
Ibrahim (Abdullah; 1934– , South African)
Jackson (Milt; 1923–99, US)

Jarrett (Keith; 1945–   , US)
Johnson (James P; 1894–1955, US)
Johnson (J J; 1924–2001, US)
Johnson (Robert; 1911–38, US)
Metheny (Pat; 1954–   , US)
Mezzrow (Mezz; 1899–1972, US)
Peyroux (Madeleine; 1974–   , US)
Rollins (Sonny; 1930–   , US)
Shorter (Wayne; 1933–   , US)
Vaughan (Sarah; 1924–90, US)
Webster (Ben; 1909–73, US)
Winding (Kai; 1922–83, Danish/US)

08 Adderley (Cannonball; 1928–75, US)
Barbieri (Gato; 1934–   , Argentine)
Calloway (Cab; 1907–94, US)
Coltrane (John; 1926–67, US)
Eldridge (Roy; 1911–89, US)
Franklin (Aretha; 1942–   , US)
Garbarek (Jan; 1947–   , Norwegian)
Gershwin (George; 1898–1937, US)
Gorelick (Kenneth 'Kenny G'; 1956–   , US)
Johnston (Lonny; 1889–1970, US)
Marsalis (Wynton; 1961–   , US)
Mulligan (Gerry; 1927–96, US)
Peterson (Oscar; 1925–2007, Canadian)
Tristano (Lennie; 1919–78, US)
Williams (Mary Lou; 1910–81, US)

See also **pianist**

Williams (Tony; 1945–97, US)

09 Armstrong (Louis; 1901–71, US)
Christian (Charlie; 1916–42, US)
Dankworth (John; 1927–2010, English)
Ellington (Duke; 1899–1974, US)
Gillespie (Dizzy; 1917–93, US)
Grappelli (Stéphane; 1908–97, French)
Henderson (Fletcher; 1897–1952, US)
Henderson (Joe; 1937–2001, US)
Jefferson (Blind Lemon; 1897–1929, US)
Leadbelly (1888–1949, US)
Lunceford (Jimmie; 1902–47, US)
Lyttelton (Humphrey; 1921–2008, English)
Reinhardt (Django; 1910–53, Belgian)
Teagarden (Jack; 1905–64, US)
Westbrook (Mike; 1936–   , English)

10 Fitzgerald (Ella; 1917–96, US)
Howlin' Wolf (1910–76, US)
McLaughlin (John; 1942–   , English)
Montgomery (Wes; 1923–68, US)
Thielemans (Toots; 1922–   , Belgian)
Washington (Dinah; 1924–63, US)

11 Beiderbecke (Bix; 1903–31, US)

14 Ørsted Pedersen (Niels-Henning; 1946–2005, Danish)

jellyfish

Jellyfish include:

03 box
04 bell
blue
moon
pink
05 brown
crown
warty
06 barrel
common
helmet
jimble
purple
saucer
Tamoya
07 acaleph
aurelia
blubber

compass
Nomura's
sea wasp
snottie
stalked
thimble
08 acalephe
Black Sea
blue fire
clinging
football
fried egg
09 Arctic red
fire jelly
flower hat
hair jelly
irukandji
lion's mane
root-mouth

sea nettle
10 blue button
cannonball
cassiopeia
dustbin-lid
freshwater
sea blubber
upside-down
11 blue blubber
mushroom cap
sea mushroom
12 jelly blubber
mauve stinger
white-spotted
13 Mediterranean
purple stinger
15 Arctic lion's mane

Jew *see* **Judaism**

jewellery

Jewellery includes:

04 prop
ring
stud

05 beads
bindi
cameo
chain
tiara

06 amulet
anklet
bangle
brooch
choker
corals
diadem

hatpin
locket
pearls
tiepin
torque

07 armilla
coronet
earring
necklet
pendant
rivière
sautoir
toe ring

08 bracelet
cufflink

necklace
negligee
nose ring
wristlet

09 medallion
navel ring

10 signet ring

11 mangalsutra
wedding ring

12 eternity ring

13 charm bracelet
solitaire ring

14 engagement ring

15 belly-button ring

jockey *see* **racing: horse racing**

joint *see* **bone; meat**

journalism

Journalists, broadcast journalists, editors and newsreaders include:

03 Day (Sir Robin; 1923–2000, English)
Mee (Arthur; 1875–1943, English)

04 Adie (Kate; 1945– , English)
Bell (Martin; 1938– , English)
Birt (John, Lord; 1944– , English)
Coty (François; 1874–1934, French)
Foot (Michael; 1913–2010, English)
Ford (Anna; 1943– , English)
Gall (Sandy; 1927– , Scottish)
Hogg (Sarah, Baroness; 1946– , English)
Jane (Fred T; 1865–1916, English)
Mair (Eddie; 1965– , Scottish)
Marr (Andrew; 1959– , Scottish)
Neil (Andrew; 1949– , Scottish)
Rook (Jean; 1931–91, English)
Self (Will; 1961– , English)
Snow (Jon; 1947– , English)
Snow (Peter; 1938– , Irish)
Wade (Rebekah; 1968– , English)
Wark (Kirsty; 1955– , Scottish)

05 Astor (William, Viscount; 1848–1919, US/
British)
Brown (Helen Gurley; 1922–2012, US)
Buerk (Michael; 1946– , English)
Cooke (Alistair; 1908–2004, English/US)
Dacre (Paul; 1948– , English)
Ensor (Sir Robert; 1877–1958, English)
Evans (Sir Harold; 1928– , English)

Frost (Sir David; 1939–2013, English)
Green (Charlotte; 1956– ; English)
James (Clive; 1939– , Australian)
Junor (Sir John; 1919–98, English)
Laski (Marghanita; 1915–88, English)
Levin (Bernard; 1928–2004, English)
Lewis (Martyn; 1945– , Northern Irish)
Reith (John, Lord; 1889–1971, Scottish)
Scott (C P; 1846–1932, English)
Twain (Mark; 1835–1910, US)
Tynan (Kenneth; 1927–80, English)
Waugh (Auberon; 1939–2001, English)
Wolfe (Tom; 1931– , US)
Woods (Donald; 1933–2001, South African)
Young (Toby; 1963– , English)

06 Baring (Maurice; 1874–1946, English)
Barron (Brian; 1940– , English)
Bierce (Ambrose; 1842–1914, US)
Burnet (Sir Alastair; 1928– , English)
Craven (John; 1941– , English)
Deedes (Bill, Lord; 1913–2007, English)
Gallup (George; 1901–84, US)
Gordon (John; 1890–1974, Scottish)
Greene (Sir Hugh; 1910–87, English)
Hislop (Ian; 1960– , English)
Hulton (Sir Edward; 1906–88, English)
Hutton (Will; 1950– , English)
Isaacs (Sir Jeremy; 1932– , Scottish)

Martin (Kingsley; 1897–1969, English)
Massie (Allan; 1938– , Scottish)
Morgan (Charles; 1894–1958, English)
Morgan (Piers; 1965– , English)
Morris (Jan; 1926– , English)
Murrow (Edward R; 1908–65, US)
O'Brien (Conor Cruise; 1917–2008, Irish)
Packer (Sir Frank; 1906–74, Australian)
Parker (Dorothy; 1893–1967, US)
Paxman (Jeremy; 1950– , English)
Pilger (John; 1939– , Australian)
Rayner (Claire; 1931–2010, English)
Reuter (Paul, Baron von; 1816–99, German/
  British)
Rippon (Angela; 1944– , English)
Stuart (Moira; c.1950– , English)
Suchet (John; 1944– , English)
Wilkes (John; 1727–97, English)

07 Alagiah (George; 1955– , Sri Lankan/British)
Barclay (Sir David; 1934– , English)
Barclay (Sir Frederick; 1934– , English)
Barclay (William; 1907–78, Scottish)
Boycott (Rosie; 1951– , English)
Bradlee (Ben; 1921– , US)
Brunson (Michael; 1940– , English)
Buckley (William F, Jnr; 1925–2008, US)
Bushell (Garry; 1955– , English)
Cameron (James; 1911–85, Scottish)
Cobbett (William; 1763–1835, English)
Dunnett (Sir Alastair; 1908–98, Scottish)
Edwards (Huw; 1961– , Welsh)
Fairfax (John; 1804–77, Australian)
Fleming (Peter; 1907–71, English)
Goodman (Elinor; 1946– , English)
Hellyer (A G L; 1902–93, English)
Ingrams (Richard; 1937– , English)
Jackson (Dame Barbara, Baroness; 1914–81,
  English)
Johnson (Boris; 1964– , English)
Kennedy (Helena, Baroness; 1950– ,
  Scottish)
Kennedy (Sir Ludovic; 1919–2009, Scottish)
Leeming (Jan; 1942– , English)
Malcolm (Derek; 1932– , English)
Mencken (H L; 1880–1956, US)
Perkins (Brian; 1943– , New Zealand/British)
Rowland (Tiny; 1917–98, British)
Simpson (John; 1944– , English)
Sissons (Peter; 1942– , English)
Stanley (Sir Henry; 1841–1904, Welsh/US/
  British)

08 Burchill (Julie; 1959– , English)
Cronkite (Walter, Jnr; 1916–2009, US)
Dimbleby (David; 1938– , English)
Dimbleby (Jonathan; 1944– , English)
Dimbleby (Richard; 1913–65, English)
Douglass (Frederick; 1817–95, US)
Drawbell (James; 1899–1979, Scottish)
Gellhorn (Martha; 1908–98, US)
Hanrahan (Brian; 1949– , English)
Hobhouse (Leonard; 1864–1929, English)
Horrocks (Sir Brian; 1895–1985, English)
Humphrys (John; 1943– , Welsh)
Lippmann (Walter; 1889–1974, US)
McCarthy (John; 1957– , English)
McDonald (Sir Trevor; 1939– , Trinidadian)
Naughtie (James; 1951– , Scottish)
Nevinson (Henry; 1856–1941, English)
Rees-Mogg (William, Lord; 1928–2012,
  English)
Robinson (Henry Crabb; 1775–1867, English)
Thompson (Hunter S; 1937–2005, US)
Woodward (Bob; 1943– , US)

09 Bernstein (Carl; 1944– , US)
Bosanquet (Reginald; 1932–84, English)
Hopkinson (Sir Tom; 1905–90, English)
Macdonald (Gus, Lord; 1940– , Scottish)
MacGregor (Sue; 1941– , English)
Mackenzie (Kelvin; 1946– , English)
Magnusson (Magnus; 1929–2007, Icelandic/
  Scottish)
Magnusson (Sally; 1955– , Scottish)
Plekhanov (Georgi; 1856–1918, Russian)
Streicher (Julius; 1885–1946, German)
Trethowan (Sir Ian; 1922–90, English)

10 Delescluze (Charles; 1809–71, French)
Desmoulins (Camille; 1760–94, French)
Greenslade (Roy; 1946– , English)
Guru-Murthy (Krishnan; 1970– , English)
Harmsworth (Alfred, Viscount Northcliffe;
  1865–1922, Irish/British)
McIlvanney (Hugh; 1933– , Scottish)
Muggeridge (Malcolm; 1903–90, English)
Rothermere (Harold Harmsworth, Viscount;
  1868–1940, English)
Rusbridger (Alan; 1953– , English)
Waterhouse (Keith; 1929–2009, English)
Worsthorne (Sir Peregrine; 1923– , English)

11 Northcliffe (Alfred Harmsworth, Viscount;
  1865–1922, Irish/British)

12 Street-Porter (Janet; 1944– , English)

Terms used in journalism include:		
03 cub	tip	deck
cut	**04** blat	desk
NPA	bump	kill
run	copy	leak

news
op-ed

05 angle
blatt
blurb
break
extra
gonzo
local
media
pitch
quote
radio
scoop
squib
story
tie in

06 anchor
Balaam
byline
column
editor
hourly
impact
kicker
leader
leg-man
rookie
source

07 advance
article
caption
compact
editing
feature
journal

kill fee
spoiler
subhead
tabloid
topical
writing

08 causerie
follow-up
headline
magazine
masthead
national
newshawk
news item
reporter
revision
stringer

09 broadcast
columnist
editorial
exclusive
freelance
freesheet
front-page
interview
newshound
newspaper
paragraph
pull quote
redletter
reportage
scare-head
scare-line
soundbite
statement
stop-press
strapline

10 background
broadsheet
centrefold
credit line
daily paper
journalese
journalist
leaderette
multimedia
newsreader
periodical
publishing
retraction
standfirst
television

11 city article
Fleet Street
Sunday paper

12 breaking news
centre spread
extra-special
gossip-writer
press council
press release
scare-heading

13 correspondent
human interest
middle article

14 banner headline
blind interview
current affairs
leading article

15 cyber-journalist
photojournalism
press conference

See also **news**; **newspaper**

Joyce, James (1882–1941)

Significant works include:

07 *The Dead* (1914)
Ulysses (1922)

09 *Dubliners* (1914)

11 *Stephen Hero* (1944)

12 *Chamber Music* (1907)

13 *Finnegans Wake* (1939)
Pomes Penyeach (1927)

31 *A Portrait of the Artist as a Young Man* (1916)

Significant characters include:

04 Issy

05 Bloom (Leopold)
Bloom (Molly 'Marion Tweed')
Duffy (James)

Maria

06 Conroy (Gabriel)
Conroy (Gretta)

07 Dedalus (Stephen 'Kinch')

08 Mulligan (Malachi 'Buck')

09 Earwicker (Humphrey Chimpden)

10 Plurabelle (Anna Livia)

12 Shaun the Post

13 Shem the Penman

Judaism

Jewish groups, movements and denominations include:

- **06** Reform
- **07** Haredim
  Hasidim
  Karaism
  Liberal
- **08** Chasidim
  Hasidism
  Masortes
  Orthodox
- **09** Massortes
- Sephardim
- **10** Ashkenazim
  Humanistic
- **11** Progressive
- **12** Conservative
- **13** Jewish Renewal
- **14** Modern Orthodox

See also **calendar**; **religion**

judge

Judges include:

- **04** Coke (Sir Edward; 1552–1634, English)
- **05** Allen (Florence E; 1884–1966, US)
  Burgh (Hubert de; d.1243, English)
  Minos (Greek mythology)
- **06** Aeacus (Greek mythology)
  Burger (Warren; 1907–95, US)
  Cullen (William, Lord; 1935– , Scottish)
  Gideon (biblical Israelite)
  Irvine (Alexander 'Derry', Lord; 1940– ,
  Scottish)
  Mackay (James, Lord; 1927– , Scottish)
  Taylor (Peter, Lord; 1930–97, English)
  Warren (Earl; 1891–1974, US)
- **07** Brennan (William J; 1906–97, US)
  Denning (Alfred, Lord; 1899–1999, English)
  Erskine (Thomas, Lord; 1750–1823, Scottish)
  O'Connor (Sandra Day; 1930– , US)
  Scarman (Leslie, Lord; 1911–2004, English)

- **08** Gardiner (Gerald, Lord; 1900–90, English)
  Ginsburg (Ruth Bader; 1933– , US)
  Hailsham (Quintin Hogg, Viscount;
  1907–2001, English)
  Jeffreys (George, Lord; 1648–89, English)
  Marshall (John; 1755–1835, US)
  Marshall (Thurgood; 1908–93, US)
- **09** Rehnquist (William; 1924–2005, US)
  Vyshinsky (Andrei; 1883–1954, Soviet)
- **10** Elwyn-Jones (Frederick, Lord; 1909–89,
  Welsh)
  Odio Benito (Elizabeth; 1939– , Costa
  Rican)
- **11** Butler-Sloss (Dame Elizabeth; 1933– ,
  English)
  Montesquieu (Charles-Louis de Secondat,
  Baron de; 1689–1755, French)
- **12** Rhadamanthus (Greek mythology)

K

karate

Keats, John (1795–1821)

key

03 alt	**04** ctrl	shift	**07** control
del	home	**06** delete	num lock
end	pg dn	escape	**08** caps lock
esc	pg up	insert	page down
ins	**05** alt gr	page up	
tab	enter	return	**09** backspace

See also **lock**; **music**

king

Common kings' names include:

04 Erik	Peter	Rudolf	Kristian
Ivan	**06** Albert	**07** Alfonso	**09** Alexander
John	Conrad	Charles	Antiochus
Karl	Darius	Francis	Christian
Olaf	Edmund	Kenneth	Ferdinand
05 David	Edward	Leopold	Frederick
Henri	George	Ptolemy	Theodoric
Henry	Harald	Richard	**10** Artaxerxes
James	Harold	William	**11** Constantine
Louis	Philip	**08** Frederik	

Kings include:

03 Aed (d.878, Scotland)
Ban (Arthurian legend, Benwick)
Ida (d.559, Bernicia)
Ine (d.c.726, West Saxon)
Lot (Arthurian legend, Orkney)
Lud (British legend, Britain)
Zog (I; 1895–1961, Albania)

04 Agis (IV; c.263–241 BC, Sparta)
Ahab (9c BC, Israel)
Cnut ('the Great'; c.995–1035, England/
    Denmark/Norway)
Dubh (d.966, Scotland)
Duff (d.966, Scotland)
Edwy (c.941–959, England)
Fahd (1923–2005, Saudi Arabia)
Ivan (III, 'the Great'; 1440–1505, Russia)
Ivan (IV, 'the Terrible'; 1530–84, Russia)
Jehu (842–815 BC, Israel)
John (Lackland; 1167–1216, England)
John (*King John*, 1590/1, William Shakespeare)
Lear (British legend, Britain)
Lear (*King Lear*, c.1605–06, William
    Shakespeare)
Lear (*Lear*, 1973, Edward Bond)
Mark (Celtic mythology, Cornwall)
Offa (d.796, Mercia)
Olav (V; 1903–91, Norway)
Otto (I, 'the Great'; 912–73, Germany)
Paul (I; 1901–64, Greece)
Quin (Auberon; *The Napoleon of Notting
    Hill*, 1904, G K Chesterton)

Saud (1902–69, Saudi Arabia)

05 Brian (c.926–1014, Ireland)
Bruce (Robert; 1274–1329, Scotland)
Capet (Hugo; c.938–996, France)
Carol (I; 1839–1914, Romania)
Carol (II; 1893–1953, Romania)
Creon (Greek mythology, Thebes)
Culen (d.971, Scotland)
David (11c BC, Israel)
David (I; c.1080–1153, Scotland)
David (II; 1324–71, Scotland)
Edgar (944–75, England)
Edgar (1074–1107, Scotland)
Edred (c.923–55, England)
Edwin (St; c.585–633, Northumbria)
Giric (d.889, Scotland)
Gyges (d.c.648 BC, Lydia)
Henry (I; 1068–1135, England)
Henry (II; 1133–89, England)
Henry (III; 1207–72, England)
Henry (IV; c.1366–1413, England)
Henry (V; 1387–1422, England)
Henry (V; *Henry V*, 1599, William
    Shakespeare)
Henry (VI; 1421–71, England)
Henry (VI; *Henry VI, Parts I, II, III*, early
    1590s, William Shakespeare)
Henry (VII; 1457–1509, England)
Henry (VII; *Henry VI Part III*, early 1590s,
    William Shakespeare)
Henry (VIII; 1491–1547, England)

Henry (VIII; *Henry VIII*, c.1613, William Shakespeare/John Fletcher)
Herod ('the Great'; c.74–4 BC, Judea)
Hiero (I; d.467/466 BC, Syracuse)
Ixion (Greek mythology, Thessaly)
James (I, of England; *The Fortunes of Nigel*, 1822, Sir Walter Scott)
James (I; 1394–1437, Scotland)
James (I; 1566–1625, England)
James (II; 1430–60, Scotland)
James (II; 1633–1701, England/Ireland)
James (III; 1452–88, Scotland)
James (IV; 1473–1513, Scotland)
James (V; 1512–42, Scotland)
James (VI/I; 1566–1625, Scotland/England)
James (VII/II; 1633–1701, Scotland, England/Ireland)
Laius (Greek mythology, Thebes)
Louis (XIV, 'the Sun King'; 1638–1715, France)
Louis (XV; 1710–74, France)
Louis (XVI; 1754–93, France)
Media (*Mardi*, 1849, Herman Melville)
Midas (Greek mythology, Phrygia)
Minos (Greek mythology, Crete)
Pepin (III, 'the Short'; c.715–768, Franks)
Peter (*The Lion, the Witch and the Wardrobe*, 1950, C S Lewis)
Priam (Greek mythology, Troy)
Priam (*Troilus and Cressida*, 1601/2, William Shakespeare)
Svein (I Haraldsson, 'Fork-Beard'; d.1014, Denmark/England)

06 Aeetes (Greek mythology, Colchis)
Agenor (Greek mythology, Tyre)
Ahmose (I; 16c BC, Egypt)
Ahmose (II; 6c BC, Egypt)
Alaric (I; c.370–410 AD, Visigoths)
Alaric (II; 450–507 AD, Visigoths)
Albert (I; 1875–1934, Belgians)
Albert (II; 1934– , Belgians)
Alfred ('the Great'; 849–99, Wessex)
Alonso (*The Tempest*, 1611, William Shakespeare)
Arthur (Arthurian legend, Britain)
Arthur ('Morte d'Arthur', 1842, Alfred, Lord Tennyson)
Attila (c.406–453 AD, Huns)
Atreus (Greek mythology, Argos)
Baliol (Edward de; c.1283–1364, Scotland)
Baliol (John de; c.1250–1315, Scotland)
Bladud (British legend, Britain)
Canute (c.995–1035, England/Denmark/Norway)
Cheops (26c BC, Memphis)
Clovis (465–511 AD, Franks)
Donald (I; d.862, Scotland)
Donald (II; d.900, Scotland)
Donald (III, 'Bane'; 1033–1100, Scotland)

Duncan (*Macbeth*, c.1606, William Shakespeare)
Duncan (I; c.1010–40, Scotland)
Duncan (II; c.1060–94, Scotland)
Eadgar (944–75, England)
Edmund (*The Lion, the Witch and the Wardrobe*, 1950, C S Lewis)
Edmund (I; 921–46, English)
Edmund (II, 'Ironside'; c.990–1016, England)
Edmund (St; c.841–870, East Anglia)
Edward (c.870–c.924, Wessex)
Edward (I; 1239–1307, England)
Edward (II; 1284–1327, England)
Edward (II, St, 'the Martyr'; c.963–978, England)
Edward (II; *Edward II*, 1594, Christopher Marlowe)
Edward (III; 1312–77, England)
Edward (III, 'the Confessor'; c.1003–66, England)
Edward (IV; 1442–83, England)
Edward ('the Elder'; d.924, England)
Edward (V; 1470–83, England)
Edward (VI; 1537–53, England/Ireland)
Edward (VII; 1841–1910, Great Britain/Ireland)
Edward (VIII; 1894–1972, Great Britain/Northern Ireland)
Egbert (d.839, Britain)
Faisal (1905–75, Saudi Arabia)
Faisal (I; 1885–1933, Iraq)
Faisal (II; 1935–58, Iraq)
Farouk (I; 1920–65, Egypt)
George (I; 1660–1727, Great Britain/Ireland)
George (II; 1683–1760, Great Britain/Ireland)
George (III; 1738–1820, Great Britain/Ireland/Hanover)
George (III; *The Madness of George III*, 1991, Alan Bennett)
George (IV; 1762–1830, Great Britain/Ireland/Hanover)
George (V; 1819–78, Hanover)
George (V; 1865–1936, Great Britain/Northern Ireland)
George (VI; 1895–1952, Great Britain/Northern Ireland)
Gustav (V; 1858–1950, Sweden)
Gustav (VI; 1882–1973, Sweden)
Haakon (VII; 1872–1957, Norway)
Harald (V; 1937– , Norway)
Harold (I Knutsson, 'Harefoot'; d.1040, England)
Harold (II; c.1022–66, England)
Hassan (II; 1929–99, Morocco)
Indulf (d.962, Scotland)
Josiah (649–609 BC, Judah)
Khalid (1913–82, Saudi Arabia)
Letsie (III; 1963– , Lesotho)

Lulach (1032–58, Scotland)
Magnus (*The Apple Cart*, 1929, George Bernard Shaw)
Oberon (*A Midsummer Night's Dream*, c.1594, William Shakespeare)
Oberon (European mythology, fairies)
Oileus (Greek mythology, Locris)
Oswald (St; c.605–642, Northumbria)
Peleus (Greek mythology, Phythia)
Philip (*King John*, 1590/1, William Shakespeare)
Philip (I, 'the Handsome'; 1478–1506, Castile)
Philip (III, 'the Bold'; 1245–85, France)
Philip (IV; 'the Fair'; 1268–1314, France)
Robert (II; 1316–90, Scotland)
Robert (III; c.1340–1406, Scotland)
Robert (III; *The Fair Maid of Perth*, 1828, Sir Walter Scott)
Sargon (II; d.705 BC, Assyria)
Tereus (Greek mythology, Thrace)
Xerxes (I; c.520–465 BC, Persia)

07 Aragorn (*The Lord of the Rings*, 1954–55, J R R Tolkien)
Arbaces (*A King and No King*, 1611, Francis Beaumont/John Fletcher)
Baldwin (II; d.1131, Jerusalem)
Baldwin (III; c.1130–62, Jerusalem)
Balliol (Edward de; c.1283–1364, Scotland)
Balliol (John de; c.1250–1315, Scotland)
Boabdil (d.c.1493, Granada)
Cecrops (Greek mythology, Athenians)
Cepheus (Greek mythology, Ethiopians)
Charles (I; 1600–49, Great Britain/Ireland)
Charles (II; 1630–85, Great Britain/Ireland)
Charles (II; *Peveril of the Peak*, 1823, Sir Walter Scott)
Charles (II; *Woodstock*, or *The Cavalier*, 1826, Sir Walter Scott)
Charles (VI; *Henry V*, 1599, William Shakespeare)
Croesus (6c BC, Lydia)
Dingaan (d.1843, Zululand)
Eumenes (II; d.159 BC, Pergamon)
Guthorm (d.890, East Anglia)
Hussein (1935–99, Jordan)
Ibn Saud (1880–1953, Saudi Arabia)
Kenneth (I; d.858, Scots)
Kenneth (II; d.995, Scotland)
Kenneth (III; d.1005, Scotland)
Latinus (Roman mythology, Latins)
Leontes (*The Winter's Tale*, 1611, William Shakespeare)
Leopold (I; 1790–1865, Belgium)
Leopold (II; 1835–1909, Belgium)
Leopold (III; 1901–83, Belgium)
Macbeth (c.1005–57, Scotland)
Macbeth (*Macbeth*, c.1606, William Shakespeare)

Malcolm (I; d.954, Scotland)
Malcolm (II; c.954–1034, Scotland)
Malcolm (III, 'Canmore'; c.1031–93, Scotland)
Malcolm (IV; 'the Maiden'; c.1141–65, Scotland)
Michael (1921– , Romania)
Pandion (Greek mythology, Athens)
Perseus (c.213–c.165 BC, Macedonia)
Polybus (Greek mythology, Corinth)
Ptolemy (I, Soter; c.367–283 BC, Egypt)
Ptolemy (II, Philadelphus; 308–246 BC, Egypt)
Ptolemy (VI, Philometor; d.145 BC, Egypt)
Ptolemy (VIII, Euergetes II; d.116 BC, Egypt)
Ptolemy (XII, Neos Dionysos; 1c BC, Egypt)
Pyrrhus (c.319–272 BC, Epirus)
Rameses (II; 1304–1237 BC, Egypt)
Richard (*Ivanhoe*, 1819, Sir Walter Scott)
Richard (I, 'the Lion Heart'; 1157–99, England)
Richard (II; *Richard II*, c.1595, William Shakespeare)
Richard (II; 1367–1400, England)
Richard (III; 1452–85, England)
Romulus (d.c.715 BC, Rome)
Solomon (c.962–922 BC, Israel)
Stephen (c.1097–1154, England)
Stephen (I; c.977–1038, Hungary)
Telamon (Greek mythology, Salamis)
Theoden (*The Lord of the Rings*, 1954–55, J R R Tolkien)
Umberto (I; 1844–1900, Italy)
Umberto (II; 1904–83, Italy)
Wilhelm (I; 1797–1888, Prussia)
Wilhelm (II; 1859–1941, Prussia)
William (I, 'the Conqueror'; 1027–87, England)
William (I; 1143–1214, Scotland)
William (II, 'Rufus'; c.1056–1100, England)
William (II/III, of Orange; 1650–1702, Great Britain/Ireland)
William (IV; 1765–1837, Great Britain)

08 Acrisius (Greek mythology, Argos)
Baudouin (I; 1930–93, Belgians)
Birendra (1945–2001, Nepal)
Cambyses (II; d.522 BC, Medes/Persians)
Cetewayo (c.1826–1884, Zululand)
Chosroes (d.579, Persia)
Chosroes (d.628, Persia)
Claudius (*Hamlet*, 1601/2, William Shakespeare)
Clotaire (II; 584–629, Franks)
Eteocles (Greek mythology, Thebes)
Ethelred (I; d.871, Wessex)
Ethelred (II, 'the Unready'; c.968–1016, England)
Gaiseric (c.390–477 AD, Vandals/Alans)
Genseric (c.390–477 AD, Vandals/Alans)
Gorboduc (British legend, Britain)

Jeroboam (I; 10c BC, Israel)
Jeroboam (II; 8c BC, Israel)
Jugurtha (d.104 BC, Numidia)
Leonidas (d.c.480 BC, Sparta)
Lycurgus (Greek mythology, Thrace)
Manasseh (7c BC, Judah)
Menelaus (Greek mythology, Sparta)
Mohammed (VI; 1963– , Morocco)
Napoleon (II; 1811–32, Rome)
Pentheus (Greek mythology, Thebes)
Philippe (1960– , Belgians)
Sihamoni (Norodom; 1953– , Cambodia)
Sihanouk (Norodom; 1922–2012,
  Cambodia)
Sisyphus (Greek mythology, Corinth)
Tantalus (Greek mythology, Sipylus)
Thutmose (I; fl.1493–1482 BC, Egypt)

09 Agamemnon (Greek mythology, Argos)
Agesilaus (444–360 BC, Sparta)
Akhenaten (14c BC, Egypt)
Alexander (I; 1888–1934, Serbs, Croats/
  Slovenes/Yugoslavia)
Alexander (I; c.1077–1124, Scotland)
Alexander (II; 1198–1249, Scotland)
Alexander (III; 1241–86, Scotland)
Amenhotep (II; 15c BC, Egypt)
Amenhotep (III; c.1411–c.1375 BC, Egypt)
Antiochus (*Pericles*, c.1608, William
  Shakespeare)
Archelaus (d.399 BC, Macedonia)
Athelstan (c.895–939, Anglo-Saxon)
Bonaparte (Jérôme; 1784–1860,
  Westphalia)
Bonaparte (Joseph; 1768–1844, Naples/
  Sicily/Spain)
Bonaparte (Louis; 1778–1846, Holland)
Cadwallon (d.634, Gwynedd)
Cassander (c.358–297 BC, Macedonia)
Cetshwayo (c.1826–1884, Zululand)
Cleomenes (I; d.490 BC, Sparta)
Cleomenes (III; c.260–219 BC, Sparta)
Cuchulain ('Cuchulain's Fight with the Sea',
  1893, W B Yeats)
Cymbeline (*Cymbeline*, 1609/10, William
  Shakespeare)
Ermanaric (fl.c.375 AD, Ostrogoths)
Ethelbald (d.860, England)
Ethelbert (d.616/618, Kent)
Ethelbert (d.866, England)
Ethelwulf (d.c.858, Wessex)
Ferdinand (*Love's Labour's Lost*, c.1594,
  William Shakespeare)
Frederick (I, Barbarossa; c.1123–90,
  Germany/Italy)
Gilgamesh (Sumerian mythology, Uruk)
Gyanendra (1947– , Nepal)
Hammurabi (d.c.1750 BC, Babylon)
Humanitas (Rex; *Ane Pleasant Satyre of the
  Thrie Estaitis*, 1540, Sir David Lindsay)

Masinissa (238–149 BC, Numidia)
Nadir Shah (1688–1747, Persia)
Perithous (Greek mythology, Lapiths)
Polixenes (*The Winter's Tale*, 1611, William
  Shakespeare)
Pygmalion (Greek mythology, Cyprus)
Rajasinha (II; 1629–87, Kandy)
Sesostris (Egyptian mythology, Egypt)
Simonides (*Pericles*, c.1608, William
  Shakespeare)
Taufa'ahau (Tupou IV; 1918–2006, Tonga)
Theoderic ('the Great'; c.455–526 AD,
  Ostrogoths)
Theodoric (I; d.451 AD, Visigoths)
Theodoric (II; d.466 AD, Visigoths)
Tuthmosis (I; fl.1493–1482 BC, Egypt)
Vortigern (fl.425–c.450 AD, Britain)
Wenceslas (St; c.907–929, Bohemia)
Zahir Shah (Mohammed; 1914–2007,
  Afghanistan)

10 Aethelstan (c.895–939, Anglo-Saxon)
Conchobhar (Celtic mythology, Ulster)
Erechtheus (Greek mythology, Athens)
Esarhaddon (d.669 BC, Assyria)
Fisher King (Arthurian legend)
Juan Carlos (I; 1938– , Spain)
Lysimachus (d.281 BC, Thrace)
Moshoeshoe (II; 1938–96, Lesotho)
Ozymandias ('Ozymandias', 1820, Percy
  Bysshe Shelley)
Wenceslaus (St; c.907–929, Bohemia)

11 Charlemagne (747–814, Franks)
Constantine (I; d.877, Scotland)
Constantine (II; d.952, Scotland)
Constantine (II; d.997, Scotland)
Constantine (II; 1940– , Greece)
Franz Joseph (1830–1916, Hungary)
Hardacanute (1018–42, Denmark/England)
Hardicanute (1018–42, Denmark/England)
Mithridates (VI; c.132–63 BC, Pontus)
Sennacherib (d.681 BC, Assyria)
Tut'ankhamun (d.c.1340 BC, Egypt)

12 Ancus Marcius (640–616 BC, Rome)
Ashurbanipal (7c BC, Assyria)
Boris Godunov (c.1551–1605, Russia)
Herod Agrippa (I; 10 BC–44 AD, Judea)
Sardanapalus (*Sardanapalus: A Tragedy*,
  1821, Lord Byron)

13 Carl XVI Gustaf (1946– , Sweden)
Chulalongkorn (Phra Paramindr Maha;
  1853–1910, Siam)
Edgar Atheling (c.1060–c.1125, England)
Hussein ibn 'Ali (1856–1931, Hejaz)
Knut Sveinsson (c.995–1035, England/
  Denmark/Norway)
Louis Philippe (1773–1850, French)
Numa Pompilius (8c–7c BC; Rome)

14 Cassivellaunus (1 c BC, Catuvellauni)
Harald Gormsson ('Blue-Tooth'; c.910–985,
Denmark)
Nebuchadnezzar (II; d.562 BC, Babylon)
Servius Tullius (fl.578–535 BC, Rome)
Uther Pendragon (Arthurian legend, Britain)
See also **legend; Rome**

Victor Emmanuel (III; 1869–1947, Italy)
15 Ptolemy Dionysus (*Caesar and Cleopatra*,
1898, George Bernard Shaw)
Tullus Hostilius (d.642 BC; Rome)
Willem-Alexander (1967– , The
Netherlands)

kingdom *see* **classification; empire**

Kipling, Rudyard (1865–1936)

Significant works include:

02 *If* (1910)
03 *Kim* (1901)
06 'Red Dog' (1895)
08 'Quiquern' (1895)
10 'Tiger! Tiger!' (1894)
11 'How Fear Came' (1895)
'Kaa's Hunting' (1894)
Stalky and Co (1899)
The Day's Work (1898)
The Naulahka (1891–92)
12 *The Seven Seas* (1896)
'The White Seal' (1894)
13 *Life's Handicap* (1891)
Soldiers Three (1888)
The Jungle Book (1894)
'The King's Ankus' (1895)
14 *Many Inventions* (1893)
'Rikki-Tikki-Tavi' (1894)
Songs from Books (1912)
The Five Nations (1903)
'The Undertakers' (1895)
15 'Mowgli's Brothers' (1894)
Puck of Pook's Hill (1906)
Schoolboy Lyrics (1881)
The Years Between (1919)
Wee Willie Winkie (1888)
16 *Debits and Credits* (1926)
'The Spring Running' (1895)
17 *Limits and Renewals* (1932)
Rewards and Fairies (1910)
Something of Myself (1937)
'The Elephant's Child' (1902)
18 *Barrack Room Ballads* (1890)
Captains Courageous (1897)

'Letting in the Jungle' (1895)
The Light That Failed (1890)
19 *Actions and Reactions* (1909)
Departmental Ditties (1886)
'Her Majesty's Servants' (1894)
The Second Jungle Book (1895)
20 'The Recall Recessional' (1894)
'Toomai of the Elephants' (1894)
21 *A Diversity of Creatures* (1917)
'How the Alphabet Was Made' (1902)
'How the Camel Got His Hump' (1902)
22 *Plain Tales from the Hills* (1888)
Traffics and Discoveries (1904)
23 'How the Whale Got His Throat' (1902)
'The Butterfly That Stamped' (1902)
'The Miracle of Purun Bhagat' (1902)
24 'How the Leopard Got His Spots' (1902)
25 'The Cat That Walked by Himself' (1902)
26 'How the Rhinoceros Got His Skin' (1902)
27 'How the First Letter Was Written' (1902)
'The Beginning of the Armadillos' (1902)
'The Crab That Played with the Sea' (1902)
'The Sing-Song of Old Man Kangaroo' (1902)
28 *Soldiers Three: In Black and White* (1888)
30 *Just So stories for Little Children* (1902)
Wee Willie Winkie: Under the Deodars (1888)
32 *Thy Servant a Dog and Other Dog Stories*
(1930)
33 *Land and Sea Tales for Scouts and Guides*
(1923)
Soldiers Three: The Story of the Gadsbys
(1888)
Wee Willie Winkie: The Phantom Rickshaw
(1888)

Significant characters include:

03 Dan
Kaa
Una

04 Puck
05 Akela
Baloo

Jukes (Morrowbie)
M'Turk ('Turkey')
O'Hara (Kimball

'Kim')
06 Beetle
Cheyne (Harvey)

Deever (Danny)
Lungri
Mowgli
Stalky
Toomai
07 Learoyd (Private)

08 Bagheera
Gunga Din
Hauksbee (Mrs)
Mulvaney (Private)
Ortheris (Private)
09 Gunga Dass

Shere Khan
10 Strickland
14 Rikki-Tikki-Tavi
15 Hobden the Hedger

kitchen

Kitchen parts include:

03 Aga®	tiles	twin tub	**11** tumble dryer
bin	U-bend	worktop	water filter
gas		**08** cupboard	**12** breakfast bar
hob	**06** boiler	hotplate	butcher block
04 lino	box-bed	wine rack	chest freezer
oven	chairs	**09** sideboard	extractor fan
ring	cooker	spin dryer	refrigerator
sink	drawer		service hatch
taps	fridge	**10** ceramic hob	**13** draining board
unit	gas hob	deep-freeze	fridge-freezer
05 grill	larder	dishwasher	microwave oven
pipes	pantry	halogen hob	**14** ice compartment
range	stools	rotisserie	peninsular unit
shelf	trivet	slow cooker	pressure cooker
stove	**07** freezer	splashback	washing machine
table	griddle	white goods	waste compactor
	trammel		

knife

Knives include:

02 da	fruit	dagger	Stanley®
03 dah	gully	gulley	whittle
hay	kukri	oyster	**08** bistoury
pen	panga	parang	chopping
04 bolo	paper	pocket	scalping
case	putty	sheath	skean-dhu
chiv	skean	trench	skene-dhu
dirk	skene	**07** bayonet	tranchet
fish	spade	carving	**09** butterfly
jack	steak	catling	jockteleg
moon	table	drawing	Swiss army
simi	**06** barong	dudgeon	toothpick
05 bowie	butter	hunting	**10** skene-occle
bread	carver	leather	**11** snickersnee
clasp	chakra	machete	switchblade
craft	cradle	palette	**13** Kitchen Devils®
cutto	cuttle	pruning	pusser's dagger
flick	cuttoe	scalpel	

See also **dagger**; **sword**

knight

Knights include:

04 grey
05 black
white
06 Bayard
carpet
errant
See also **legend**

kemper
ritter
07 paladin
08 bachelor
banneret
cavalier

douzeper
vavasour
09 chevalier
doucepere
valvassor
10 kempery-man

11 hospitaller
14 knight-bachelor
Knights Templar
preux chevalier

knitting

Knitting terms include:

03 rib
row
04 Aran
purl
wire
wool
05 chart
pearl
plain
06 cast on
chunky
intake
marker
narrow
needle
stitch
two-ply

07 bind off
cast off
chevron
four-ply
layette
tension
twin rib
08 ball band
Fair Isle
intarsia
pavilion
three-ply
09 box stitch
double rib
fingering
garter rib
honeycomb

single rib
10 chain cable
double knit
French heel
mistake rib
moss panels
moss stitch
rice stitch
row counter
seed stitch
slip stitch
Swiss check
tricoteuse
11 basketweave
cable needle
cable stitch
chain stitch
diagonal rib

drop a stitch
plain stitch
Roman stripe
thumb method
12 basket stitch
braided cable
garter stitch
lattice cable
stitch holder
13 fisherman's rib
stocking frame
14 circular needle
double knitting
knitting needle
stocking stitch
15 knitting machine
knitting pattern

knot

Knots include:

03 bow
tie
04 bend
flat
loop
love
reef
wale
wall
05 blood
chain
hitch
plait
thief
thumb
turle
06 Domhof

granny
lover's
prusik
square
07 bowline
Gordian
running
seizing
weaver's
Windsor
08 overhand
slipknot
spade-end
surgeon's
true-love
09 half hitch
lark's head

sheet bend
swab hitch
Turk's head
10 clove hitch
common bend
fisherman's
Flemish eye
sheepshank
true-lover's
11 carrick bend
donkey hitch
double blood
Englishman's
Hunter's bend
timber hitch
12 marling hitch
rolling hitch

simple sennit
weaver's hitch
13 drummer's chain
figure of eight
slippery hitch
14 Blackwall hitch
common whipping
double Cairnton
double-overhand
double-overhang
Englishman's tie
fisherman's bend
Matthew Walker's
running bowline

L

label see fashion

laboratory

Laboratory apparatus includes:

05 clamp	burette	stop clock	conical flask
flask	cuvette	**10** centrifuge	fume cupboard
slide	dropper	desiccator	heating block
stand	pipette	ice machine	test tube rack
still	spatula	microscope	Woulfe bottle
U-tube	stirrer	PCR machine	**13** bubble chamber
06 beaker	**08** crucible	Petri plate	Büchner funnel
Bunsen	cylinder	watchglass	top-pan balance
funnel	fume hood	**11** boiling tube	**14** Kipp's apparatus
Gilson®	glove box	filter flask	**15** Erlenmeyer flask
mortar	test tube	filter paper	evaporating dish
pestle	**09** autoclave	fume chamber	laminar flow hood
retort	condenser	thermometer	Liebig condenser
tripod	Petri dish	**12** Bunsen burner	volumetric flask
trough	power pack	cloud chamber	
07 bell jar	steam bath		

See also **science**

lace

Lace includes:

03 net	bobbin	pearlin	**09** bobbin net
04 bone	pillow	tatting	Chantilly
gold	thread	torchon	reticella
05 blond	trolly	trolley	**10** Colbertine
filet	**07** footing	**08** bobbinet	mignonette
jabot	galloon	Brussels	**12** Valenciennes
orris	guipure	dentelle	
point	Honiton	duchesse	
06 blonde	Mechlin	pearling	

lair see animal

lake

The Great Lakes:

04 Erie	**07** Ontario	Superior
05 Huron	**08** Michigan	

Lakes, lochs and loughs include:

03 Awe (Scotland)
Van (Turkey)

04 Abbé (Djibouti/Ethiopia)
Biwa (Japan)
Bled (Switzerland)
Chad (Chad/Niger/Nigeria)
Como (Italy)
Derg (Ireland)
Earn (Scotland)
Erie (USA/Canada)
Eyre (Australia)
Kivu (Democratic Republic
of the Congo/Rwanda)
Ness (Scotland)
Tana (Ethiopia)

05 Foyle (Ireland)
Garda (Italy)
Great (Australia)
Huron (USA/Canada)
Kyoga (Uganda)
Leven (Scotland)
Mjøsa (Norway)
Morar (Scotland)
Neagh (Ireland)
Nyasa (Mozambique/
Malawi/Tanzania)
Ohrid (Albania/FYR
Macedonia)
Onega (Russia)
Patos (Brazil)
Poopó (Bolivia)
Tahoe (Canada)
Taupo (New Zealand)
Traun (Austria)
Volta (Ghana)

06 Albert (Democratic
Republic of the Congo/
Uganda)
Baikal (Russia)
Corrib (Ireland)
Crater (USA)
Edward (Democratic
Republic of the Congo/
Uganda)

Finger (USA)
Geneva (France/
Switzerland)
Izabal (Guatemala)
Ladoga (Russia)
Lomond (Scotland)
Malawi (Mozambique/
Malawi/Tanzania)
Müritz (Germany)
Nasser (Egypt/Sudan)
Nelson (USA)
Peipsi (Estonia/Russia)
Peipus (Estonia/Russia)
Rudolf (Kenya/Ethiopia)
Saimaa (Finland)
Skadar (Montenegro/
Albania)
Taimyr (Russia)
Taymyr (Russia)
Te Anau (New Zealand)
Vänern (Sweden)
Zurich (USA)

07 Aral Sea (Kazakhstan/
Uzbekistan)
Balaton (Hungary)
Bourget (France)
Chapala (Mexico)
Dead Sea (Israel/Jordan)
Katrine (Scotland)
Lucerne (Switzerland; USA)
Ontario (USA/Canada)
Rannoch (Scotland)
Scutari (Montenegro/
Albania)
Torrens (Australia)
Turkana (Kenya/Ethiopia)
Vättern (Sweden)

08 Attersee (Austria)
Balkhash (Kazakhstan)
Bodensee (Austria/
Germany/Switzerland)
Chiemsee (Germany)
Issyk Kul (Kyrgyzstan)
Lac Léman (France/

Switzerland)
Maggiore (Italy/Switzerland)
Manitoba (Canada)
Michigan (USA)
Päijänne (Finland)
Poyang Hu (China)
Sniardwy (Poland)
Superior (USA/Canada)
Tiberias (Israel)
Titicaca (Bolivia/Peru)
Tonlé Sap (Cambodia)
Victoria (Tanzania/Uganda/
Kenya)
Winnipeg (Canada)

09 Athabasca (Canada)
Constance (Austria/
Germany/Switzerland)
Great Bear (Canada)
Great Salt (USA)
Kammersee (Austria)
Maracaibo (Venezuela)
Neuchâtel (Switzerland)
Nicaragua (Nicaragua)
Trikhonís (Greece)
Ullswater (England)
Willandra (Australia)
Zeller See (Germany)

10 Caspian Sea (Russia/
Azerbaijan/Iran/
Turkmenistan/Kazakhstan)
Great Slave (Canada)
Okeechobee (USA)
Tanganyika (Burundi/
Democratic Republic
of the Congo/Tanzania/
Zambia)
Windermere (England)
Wörther See (Austria)

11 Great Bitter (Egypt)

12 Derwent Water (England)
Kielder Water (England)
Winnipegosis (Canada)

13 Bassenthwaite (England)
Coniston Water (England)

landmark *see* **Africa; Asia; Australia; Austria; Belgium; Canada; China; Czech Republic; Denmark; Europe; Finland; France; Germany; Greece; India; Ireland; Italy; Japan; London; Mexico; Middle East; The Netherlands; New York; New Zealand; Norway; Paris; Portugal; Russia; Spain; Sweden; Switzerland; United Kingdom; United States of America**

language

Languages include:

02 Wu	Greek	Berber
03 ASL	Hakka	Bihari
BSL	Hausa	Bokmål
Edo	Hindi	Burman
Gan	husky	Canuck
Giz	Inuit	Celtic
Ibo	Ionic	Chadic
Kru	Iraqi	Coptic
Lao	Irish	Creole
Mam	Karen	Cymric
Mon	Kazak	Dakota
Yue	Khmer	Danish
04 Ainu	Ladin	Danisk
Chad	Latin	Djerma
Cham	Malay	Eskimo
Crow	Maori	Fantee
Dari	Masai	Fijian
Efik	Mayan	French
Erse	Mende	Gaelic
Fang	Norse	German
Fula	Oriya	Gothic
Gaul	Osage	Gullah
Ge'ez	Oscan	Hattic
Hopi	Osean	Hebrew
Igbo	Punic	Herero
Inca	Sango	Innuit
Krio	Saxon	Kalmyk
Kroo	Scots	Kanaka
Lapp	Shona	Kazakh
Manx	Sioux	Kikuyu
Maya	Sotho	Korean
Motu	Suomi	Kyrgyz
Nupe	Swiss	Ladino
Pali	Taino	Lakota
Shan	Tajik	Lydian
Sulu	Tamil	Magyar
Thai	Temne	Manchu
Urdu	Tetum	Micmac
Xosa	Uzbek	Minbei
Zend	Vedic	Minnan
Zulu	Welch	Minoan
05 Attic	Welsh	Mixtec
Azeri	Wolof	Mohawk
Aztec	Xhosa	Mongol
Bantu	Xiang	Navaho
Cajun	Yakut	Navajo
Carib	Yupik	Nepali
Creek	**06** Afghan	Ojibwa
Croat	Arabic	Ostiak
Czech	Aymara	Ostyak
Doric	Bahasa	Palaic
Dutch	Baluch	Pashto
Fanti	Bangla	Polish
Farsi	Basque	Romani

Romany
Samoan
Sepedi
Shelta
Sherpa
Slovak
Somali
Tartar
Telugu
Temnel
Tongan
Wendic
Yoruba

07 Amharic
Aramaic
Arapaho
Armoric
Ashanti
Avestan
Avestic
Ayamará
Baluchi
Bambara
Barotse
Basotho
Bengali
Bislama
Bosnian
British
Burmese
Calmuck
Catalan
Chaldee
Chechen
Chinese
Chinook
Comoran
Cornish
Crioulo
Dhivehi
Ebonics
English
Euskara
Euskera
Finnish
Flemish
Frisian
Gallego
Guaraní
Haitian
Hittite
Iranian
isiXosa
isiZulu
Italian
Kalmuck
Kannada
Kikongo

Kirghiz
Kirundi
Kurdish
Laotian
Lappish
Latvian
Lingala
Makaton
Malinke
Maltese
Manchoo
Marathi
Mexican
Miskito
Mohegan
Mohican
Mordvin
Morisco
Nahuatl
Nauruan
Nynorsk
Palauan
Persian
Punjabi
Quechua
Quichua
Riksmål
Russian
Semitic
Serbian
Sesotho
Siamese
Sinhala
SiSwati
Slovene
Sorbian
Sosetho
Spanish
Swahili
Swedish
Tagálog
Tibetan
Turkish
Turkmen
Umbrian
Walloon
Wendish
Yiddish
Zapotec

08 Akkadian
Albanian
Armenian
Assamese
Assyrian
Balinese
Bohemian
Canarese
Chaldaic

Cherkess
Cherokee
Cheyenne
Chichewa
Croatian
Demotiki
Dzongkha
Egyptian
Estonian
Etruscan
Fanagalo
Galician
Georgian
Gujarati
Gujerati
Hawaiian
Illyrian
isiXhosa
Japanese
Javanese
Kanarese
Kashmiri
Khoikhoi
Kwakiutl
Lusatian
Malagash
Malagasy
Mandarin
Mandinka
Menomini
Moldovan
Phrygian
Pilipino
Polabian
Romanian
Romansch
Rumanian
Sanskrit
Scottish
Scythian
Setswana
Slavonic
Sumerian
Tahitian
Tigrinya
Tuvaluan
Volscian
Xitsonga
Yanomami

09 Aborigine
Afrikaans
Algonquin
Bulgarian
Cantonese
Castilian
Dalmatian
Ethiopian
Hottentot

Hungarian	Ukrainian	**11** Anglo-French
Icelandic	Varangian	Anglo-Indian
I-Kiribati	**10** Aethiopian	Anglo-Romani
Inuktitut	Anglo-Irish	Azerbaijani
Kiswahili	Anglo-Saxon	Belarussian
Malayalam	Babylonian	Belorussian
Maldivian	beach-la-mar	Celtiberian
Marquesan	Belarusian	Kazakhstani
Menominee	Circassian	Kinyarwanda
Norwegian	High German	Marshallese
Nostratic	Hindustani	**12** ancient Greek
Old French	Indonesian	Byelorussian
Provençal	isiNdebele	Katharevousa
Putonghua	Lithuanian	Sranang Tongo
Sardinian	Macedonian	**13** Middle English
Shikomoro	Malayalaam	**14** Bahasa Malaysia
Sindebele	Old English	Church Slavonic
Sinhalese	Phoenician	Lëtzebuergesch
Slovenian	Portuguese	**15** Bahasa Indonesia
Tamazight	Serbo-Croat	
Tshivenda	Vietnamese	

Invented languages include:

03 Ido	**07** Volapük	**09** Esperanto	**11** Interglossa
Neo	**08** Mobspeak	**10** cyberspeak	Interlingua
06 Novial	Newspeak	Occidental	**12** Idiom Neutral

Terms used in linguistics include:

03 ASR	brogue	**08** idiolect	**11** doublespeak
NLP	creole	localism	linguistics
04 cant	jargon	standard	non-standard
05 argot	patois	**09** etymology	orthography
idiom	pidgin	phonetics	post-lingual
lingo	syntax	semantics	regionalism
slang	tongue	**10** journalese	**12** lexicography
usage	**07** dialect	vernacular	lingua franca
06 accent	grammar	vocabulary	**13** colloquialism

Types of diacritics include:

03 ayn	asper	lenis	umlaut
04 ayin	breve	tilde	**07** cedilla
hook	grave	**06** accent	**09** diaeresis
	hacek	macron	
05 acute	hamza	ogonek	**10** circumflex

See also **alphabet**; **The Americas**; **French**; **German**; **grammar**; **Italian**; **Latin**; **punctuation**; **rhetoric**; **rhyme**; **Spanish**; **word**

Latin

Latin words and expressions include:

03 sic (used in printed matter to show that the original is faithfully reproduced even if incorrect)

04 idem (the same)
pace (indicating polite disagreement)
stet ('let it stand' – an instruction used in printed matter to restore after marking for deletion)

05 ad hoc (for this special purpose)
circa (approximately)
id est (that is, that is to say)
per se (by itself, in itself)

06 gratis (free of charge)
ibidem (used in footnotes to indicate that the same book has been cited previously)
passim (dispersed through a book)

07 alumnus (a former pupil or student)
a priori (deductive reasoning)
de facto (in fact, actually)
erratum (an error in writing or printing)
floruit (denotes a period during which a person lived)
in vitro (in the test tube)
sub rosa (in secret, privately)

08 ab initio (from the beginning)
addendum (supplementary material for a book)
emeritus (holding a position on an honorary basis only)
et cetera (and the rest)
ex gratia (of a payment, one that is made as a favour, without any legal obligation)
gravitas (seriousness)
infra dig (below one's dignity)
mea culpa (an admission of fault and an expression of repentance)
nota bene (observe well, note well)
subpoena (a writ commanding attendance in court)

09 ad nauseam (disgustingly endless or repetitive)
alma mater (one's former school, college, or university)
carpe diem (seize the day)
et tu, Brute ('you too, Brutus' – Caesar's alleged exclamation when he saw Brutus amongst his assassins)
ex officio (by virtue of office or position)
inter alia (among other things)
ipso facto (thereby)
per capita (per head of the population)

status quo (the existing condition)
sub judice (under consideration by a judge or a court of law)
vox populi (public or popular opinion)

10 anno Domini (in the year of the Lord)
ante-bellum (denotes a period before a specific war, especially the American Civil War)
ex cathedra (from the chair of office)
in absentia (in absence, used for occasions when the recipient would normally be present)
in extremis (at the point of death; in desperate circumstances)
magnum opus (a person's greatest achievement, especially a literary work)
post mortem (an examination of a body in order to determine the cause of death)
prima facie (a legal term for evidence that is assumed to be true unless disproved by other evidence)
quid pro quo (something given or taken as equivalent to another, often as retaliation)
sine qua non (an indispensable condition)
tabula rasa (a mind not yet influenced by outside impressions and experience)

11 ad infinitum (denotes endless repetition)
memento mori (an object, such as a skull, or anything to remind one of mortality)
non sequitur (a remark that has no relation to what has gone before)
tempus fugit (time flies)

12 ante meridiem (between midnight and noon)
caveat emptor (let the buyer beware)
compos mentis (being sane)
habeas corpus (maintains the right of the subject to protection from unlawful imprisonment)
post meridiem (between noon and midnight)

13 camera obscura (a light-free chamber in which an image of outside objects is thrown upon a screen)
deus ex machina (a contrived solution to a difficulty in a plot)
exempli gratia (by way of example)
modus operandi (the characteristic methods employed by a particular criminal)

14 annus mirabilis (a remarkably successful or auspicious year)
in loco parentis (in place of a parent)
pro bono publico (something done for no fee)
terra incognita (an unknown land)

15 annus horribilis (a dreadful year)
    curriculum vitae (a summary of someone's educational qualifications and work experience)
    delirium tremens (a condition caused by alcoholism)

persona non grata (one who is not welcome or favoured)

See also **day**; **month**; **number**

law

Scientific and other laws include:

04 Ohm's
    Oral
    Sod's

05 lemon
    Roman
    Salic

06 Boyle's

    Hooke's
    Mosaic
    Snell's
    Stoke's

07 Dalton's
    Hubble's
    Kepler's

    Murphy's
    natural

08 Charles's

09 Avogadro's

10 Parkinson's

13 inverse square

Laws and Acts include:

04 DORA (1914)

07 Riot Act (1714)
    Test Act (1673)

08 Corn Laws (1815)
    Poor Laws (1562–1601)
    Stamp Act (1765)
    Sugar Act (1764)

10 Act of Union (1707, 1800)
    Magna Carta (1215)
    Patriot Act (2001)
    Reform Acts (various)

11 Abortion Act (1967)
    Equal Pay Act (1970)
    Scotland Act (1998)

12 Bill of Rights (1689)
    Homestead Act (1862)
    Terrorism Act (2000)

13 Act of Congress (various)
    Enclosure Acts (various)
    Parliament Act (1911/1949)

14 Act of Supremacy (1534)
    Cat and Mouse Act (1913)

    Civil Rights Act (1964)
    Corporation Act (1661)
    Declaratory Act (1766)
    Human Rights Act (1998)
    Native Title Act (1993)
    Taft-Hartley Act (1947)

15 Act of Parliament (various)
    Act of Settlement (1701)
    Act of Succession (1534)
    Habeas Corpus Act (1679)

Lawyer types include:

02 QC

05 avoué
    brief
    judge

06 avocat
    jurist

07 bencher
    coroner
    counsel
    justice
    mukhtar
    sheriff
    shyster

08 advocate

    attorney
    green-bag
    Law Lords
    man of law
    Recorder

09 barrister
    lawmonger
    solicitor

10 legal eagle

11 conveyancer
    crown lawyer
    pettifogger

12 circuit judge
    jurisconsult

    Lord Advocate

13 attorney at law
    Crown attorney
    district judge
    Queen's Counsel
    sheriff depute

14 criminal lawyer
    deputy recorder
    High Court judge
    Lord Chancellor
    public defender
    Vice-Chancellor

15 ambulance-chaser
    Attorney-General

Lawyers include:

04 Hill (Anita; 1956– , US)
    John (Otto; 1909–97, German)
    Reno (Janet; 1938– , US)

05 Baird (Vera; 1951– , English)
    Booth (Cherie; 1954– , English)
    Finch (Atticus; *To Kill a Mockingbird*, 1960,

Harper Lee)
Judge (Lord Igor; 1941– , Maltese/British)
Mason (Perry; *The Case of the Velvet Claws*,
  1933, et seq, Erle Stanley Gardner)
Mills (Dame Barbara; 1940–2011, English)
Nader (Ralph; 1934– , US)
Obama (Barack; 1961– , US)
Obama (Michelle; 1964– , US)
Slovo (Joe; 1926–95, South African)
Stark (Willie; *All the King's Men*, 1946,
  Robert Penn Warren)
Vance (Cyrus R; 1917–2002, US)

06 Bailey (F Lee; 1933– , US)
Butler (Benjamin F; 1818–93, US)
Carton (Sydney; *A Tale of Two Cities*, 1859,
  Charles Dickens)
Darrow (Clarence; 1857–1938, US)
Devlin (Patrick, Lord; 1905–92, English)
Harker (Jonathan; *Dracula*, 1897, Bram Stoker)
Harman (Harriet; 1950– , English)
Holmes (Oliver Wendell; 1841–1935, US)
Martin (Richard; 1754–1834, Irish)

07 Acheson (Dean; 1893–1971, US)

Clinton (Bill; 1946– , US)
Clinton (Hillary; 1947– , US)
Haldane (Richard, Viscount; 1856–1928,
  Scottish)
Kennedy (Helena, Baroness; 1950– ,
  Scottish)
Mondale (Walter F; 1928– , US)
O'Connor (Sandra Day; 1930– , US)
Peachum (Thomas; *The Beggar's Opera*,
  1728, John Gay)

08 Gonzales (Alberto; 1955– , US)
Marshall (Thurgood; 1908–93, US)
Mortimer (Sir John; 1923–2009, English)
Scotland (Baroness Patricia; 1955– , British)

09 La Guardia (Fiorello H; 1882–1947, US)
Shawcross (Hartley, Lord; 1902–2003, English)

10 Birkenhead (Frederick Edwin Smith, Earl of;
  1872–1930, English)

11 Hore-Belisha (Leslie, Lord; 1893–1957,
  English)

12 Guicciardini (Francesco; 1483–1540, Italian)

14 Brillat-Savarin (Anthelme; 1755–1826, French)

Legal terms include:

02 JP	**06** appeal	hearing	freehold
QC	arrest	inquest	hung jury
03 bar	bigamy	inquiry	innocent
DPP	charge	Law Lord	judgment
sue	client	lawsuit	juvenile
04 bail	demand	mandate	legal aid
deed	equity	penalty	mortgage
dock	estate	perjury	offender
fine	guilty	probate	prisoner
jury	lawyer	pursuer	receiver
oath	legacy	sheriff	reprieve
plea	pardon	statute	sanction
will	parole	summons	sentence
writ	patent	tenancy	subpoena
05 alibi	remand	verdict	tribunal
asset	repeal	warrant	**09** accessory
bench	the bar	witness	acquittal
brief	waiver		affidavit
by-law	**07** accused	**08** act of God	agreement
claim	alimony	adultery	annulment
felon	amnesty	advocate	barrister
grant	caution	civil law	common law
judge	charter	claimant	copyright
juror	codicil	contract	court case
lease	convict	covenant	defendant
party	coroner	criminal	endowment
proof	custody	defender	fee simple
proxy	damages	easement	indemnity
title	defence	eviction	intestacy
trial	divorce	evidence	judgement
		executor	

judiciary
leasehold
liability
not guilty
not proven
plaintiff
precedent
probation
solicitor
testimony
trademark
10 accomplice
allegation
civil union

confession
conveyance
decree nisi
indictment
injunction
liquidator
magistrate
settlement
11 adjournment
arbitration
extradition
foreclosure
inheritance
local search

maintenance
plea bargain
plead guilty
proceedings
prosecution
ward of court
12 age of consent
Bill of Rights
constitution
court martial
cross-examine
Lord Advocate
misadventure
notary public

13 King's evidence
public inquiry
Queen's Counsel
young offender
14 decree absolute
Lord Chancellor
plead not guilty
Queen's evidence
15 Act of Parliament
Attorney-General
clerk of the court
contempt of court
power of attorney

See also **astronomy**; **chemistry**; **judge**; **legislation**; **physics**

Lawrence, D H (1885–1930)

Significant works include:

06 *Amores* (1916)

07 *Pansies* (1929)

08 *Kangaroo* (1923)

09 *Aaron's Rod* (1922)

10 *Apocalypse* (1931)
The Rainbow (1915)

11 *The Lost Girl* (1920)
Women in Love (1920)

12 *Boy in the Bush* (1924)

13 *Sons and Lovers* (1913)
The Trespasser (1912)

14 *Etruscan Places* (1932)
Sea and Sardinia (1921)

15 *The White Peacock* (1911)
Twilight in Italy (1916)

16 *England, My England* (1922)
Mornings in Mexico (1927)
The Plumed Serpent (1926)

18 *Love Poems and Others* (1913)
The Prussian Officer (1914)

19 *The Woman Who Rode Away* (1928)

20 *Lady Chatterley's Lover* (1928)

21 *Birds, Beasts and Flowers* (1923)
Look! We Have Come Through! (1917)

24 *Fantasia of the Unconscious* (1922)

26 *Movements in European History* (1921)

31 *Psychoanalysis and the Unconscious* (1921)

Significant characters include:

05 Cicio
Crich (Gerald)
Dawes (Baxter)
Dawes (Clara)
Lilly (Rawdon)
March (Ellen)
Morel (Gertrude)
Morel (Paul)
Morel (Walter)

06 Birkin (Rupert)
Colley (Ben 'Kangaroo')
Egbert
Lensky (Anna)
Lensky (Lydia)

Leslie (Kate)
McNair (Siegmund)
Saxton (George)
Sisson (Aaron)
Somers (Harriet)
Somers (Richard)
St Mawr
07 Banford (Jill)
Grenfel (Henry)
Leivers (Miriam)
Mellors (Oliver)
Roddice (Hermione)
08 Brangwen (Gudrun)
Brangwen (Tom)

Brangwen (Ursula)
Brangwen (Will)
Callcott (Jack)
Cipriano (Don)
Houghton (Alvina)
09 Beardsall (Lettie)
10 Carrington (Lou)
Chatterley (Lady Constance
'Connie')
Chatterley (Sir Clifford)
Skrebensky (Anton)
15 Prussian Officer (the)

lawyer *see* **law**

layer *see* **atmosphere**

leaf

Leaf parts include:

03 tip	**06** margin	stipule	**09** epidermis
04 vein	midrib	stomata	footstalk
05 blade	sheath		leaf-stalk
sinus	stipel	**08** leaf axil	**11** axillary bud
stoma	**07** lacinia	leaf cell	chloroplast
	petiole	phyllode	

Leaf shapes include:

04 oval	crenate		subulate
05 acute	dentate	**09** acuminate
lobed	falcate		mucronate
ovate	hastate		orbicular
06 cusped	obovate		runcinate
entire	palmate		sagittate
linear	peltate	**10** lanceolate
lyrate	pinnate		pinnatifid
oblong	ternate		spathulate
07 acerose	**08** digitate		trifoliate
ciliate	elliptic	**13** doubly dentate
cordate	reniform	**15** abruptly pinnate

See also **disease**

leather

Leathers include:

03 kid	split	kipskin	**09** crocodile
taw	suede	morocco	lacquered
04 buff	waxed	pigskin	sheepskin
butt	white	saffian	slinkskin
calf	**06** chammy	**08** buckskin	snakeskin
fair	chrome	cabretta	**10** artificial
fell	Nubuck®	calfskin	checklaton
napa	patent	capeskin	shecklaton
pelt	Rexine®	cheverel	**11** aqualeather
roan	Russia	cheveril	cuir-bouilli
shoe	shammy	cordovan	cuir-bouilly
wash	skiver	cordwain	schecklaton
yuft	spruce	deerskin	whitleather
05 grain	**07** chamois	goatskin	**13** French morocco
Mocha	cowhide	japanned	Levant morocco
nappa	dogskin	lambskin	**14** Persian morocco
neat's	hog-skin	maroquin	
plate	kidskin	shagreen	

legal *see* **law**

legend

Legends include:

05 El Cid (Spain)
Faust (Germany)

06 Roland (France)

07 Aladdin (Arabia/Europe)
Ali Baba (Arabia)
Beowulf (Scandinavia)
Don Juan (Spain)

08 El Dorado (Spain/South America)
Kalevala (Finland)
St George (Britain)
The Eddas (Scandinavia/Iceland)

09 Bluebeard (France)
Elder Edda (Scandinavia/Iceland)
Prose Edda (Scandinavia/Iceland)
Robin Hood (Britain)
St Brendan (Ireland)
The Fianna (Ireland)

10 Blackbeard (Britain/USA)
Cúchulainn (Ireland)
Kalevipoeg (Estonia)

Lady Godiva (Britain)
Paul Bunyan (USA)
Poetic Edda (Scandinavia/Iceland)

11 Captain Kidd (Britain/USA)
Esplanadian (Spain)
Magic Carpet (Asia)
Puss in Boots (France)
William Tell (Switzerland)
Younger Edda (Scandinavia/Iceland)

12 Blarney Stone (Ireland)
Song of Roland (France)
The Holy Grail (Middle East/Europe)
The Three Sons (Ireland)
Völsunga Saga (Iceland)

13 Arabian Nights (Middle East)
Conán the Brave (Ireland)
Niebelunglied (Germany)

14 Flying Dutchman (The Netherlands)
Vlad the Impaler (Transylvania)

15 Johnny Appleseed (USA)

Characters in the Robin Hood legend include:

07 Sheriff	Friar Tuck	Maid Marian	Will Scarlet
08 Merry Men	Robin Hood	Prince John	**13** Guy of Gisborne
09 Alan A Dale	**10** Little John	**11** King Richard	Much the Miller

Knights of the Round Table in Arthurian legend:

06 Sir Cai
Sir Kay

07 Sir Bors

08 Sir Lucan
Sir Owain
Sir Safer
Sir Yvain

09 Sir Bedwyr
Sir Degore
Sir Gareth
Sir Gawain
Sir Safere

10 King Arthur
Sir Alymere
Sir Dagonet
Sir Gaheris

Sir Galahad
Sir Gawaine
Sir Geraint
Sir Lamorak
Sir Lionell
Sir Mordred
Sir Pelleas
Sir Tristam
Sir Tristan

11 Sir Aglovale
Sir Agravain
Sir Aristant
Sir Bedivere
Sir Florence
Sir Lancelot
Sir Perceval

Sir Percival
Sir Tristram

12 Sir Agravaine
Sir Bleoberis
Sir Palomedes
Sir Percivale

14 Sir Bors de Ganis
Sir Constantine

15 La Cote Male Taile
Sir Brunor le Noir
Sir Ector de Maris

16 Sir Lancelot Du Lac

17 Sir Launcelot Du Lac
Sir Le Bel Desconneu

22 Sir Palamedes the Saracen

Other characters in Arthurian legend include:

03 Ban
Lot
04 Elen
Mark
Urre
05 Alice
Amant
Balan
Balin
Balyn
Belin
Brine
Cador
David
Dinas
Eliot
Gayus
Harry
Hebes
Howel
Isoud
Labor
Lovel
Mador
Nimue
Nymue
Pinel
Tirre
Torre
Ulfin
Uther
06 Andred
Blamor
Bliant
Brisen
Bromel
Castor
Clegis
Elaine
Elamet
Elayne
Fergus
Iseult
Isolde
Lucius
Melias
Melion
Meliot
Melwas
Merlin
Modred
Nacien
Ozanna
Pellam
Pelles

Phelot
Ulfius
Uriens
07 Accolon
Aliduke
Anguish
Annowre
Argante
Baudwin
Bernard
Caradoc
Carados
Clarrus
Claudas
Dinadan
Dodinas
Eliazar
Evelake
Faramon
Gaheret
Galihud
Griflet
Hurlame
Igraine
Jacound
Jordans
Ladinas
Lanceor
Launfal
Lavaine
Lynette
Marhaus
Myrddyn
Nentres
Nimiane
Patrise
Peredur
Persant
Ragnell
Rivalin
Selises
Tarquin
Tolleme
Turquin
Walwain
Ygaerne
08 Anfortas
Angharad
Anglides
Astamore
Bersules
Brastias
Childric
Galahaut
Gingalin

Guenever
Hellawes
Ironside
Kehydius
Lambegus
Lyonesse
Margawse
Meliodas
Menaduke
Morgawse
Nerovens
Ontzlake
Palmerin
Parsifal
Pecchere
Pellinor
Petipase
Selivant
Tryamour
Villiars
09 Achefleur
Alisander
Arondight
Bragwaine
Brandiles
Elizabeth
Epinogrus
Estorause
Galihodin
Grail King
Guinevere
Pellinore
Sagramore
Tramtrist
10 Bagdemagus
Curselaine
Dame Brisen
Fisher King
Gouvernail
Guanhamara
Maimed King
Meliagaunt
Plenorious
Segwarides
Sentraille
11 Bellengerus
Brandegoris
Constantine
Galahantine
Leodegrance
Meliagrance
Morgan le Fay
Wounded King
12 Colgrevaunce
La Beale Isoud

Suppinabiles
13 Accolon of Gaul
Blamor de Ganis
Dame Bragwaine
Elaine le Blank
Elayne the Fair
Lady of Shalott

Lady of the Lake
Melias de Lisle
Persant of Inde
Pinel le Savage
Urre of Hungary
14 Duke of Tintagel
Elayne Sans Pere

Mador de la Porte
Meliot de Logris
Uther Pendragon
15 Cador of Cornwall
Damsel of the Lake
Dodinas le Savage
Hebes le Renoumes

Terms to do with Arthurian legend include:

03 Usk
04 Bath
Gaul
York
05 Arroy
Badon
06 Albion
Avalon
Camlan
Eildon
Logres
Meliot
Orkney
Thanet
07 Avelion
brachet
Camelot
Camlann
Carleon
Chester
Tarabel
08 Brittany
Caerleon
Caliburn
Camelerd
Camelide
Cornwall
Lyonesse
Tintagel
09 Badon Hill
See also **mythology**

Boscastle
Camelford
Cameliard
Excalibur
Holy Grail
Llyn Dinas
loadstone
Red Dragon
Roche Rock
Seat Royal
white hart
white stag
10 Black Cross
Cader Idris
Caledfwlch
Grail Table
Llyn Barfog
North Umber
Round Table
Stonehenge
Tintagalon
Winchester
11 Arthur's Seat
Cadbury Hill
Castle Taruc
Chalice Well
Craig y Dinas
Glastonbury
Grantmesnle
Merlin's Cave
12 Alderley Edge

Arthur's Cross
Dozemary Pool
Fescamp Abbey
Isle of Avalon
Perilous Seat
Seat Perilous
Vale of Avalon
13 Bleeding Lance
Cadbury Castle
City of Legions
Questing Beast
Ship of Damsels
Ship of Fairies
Siège Perilous
The Waste Lands
14 Bamburgh Castle
Caerleon Castle
Dolorous Stroke
enchanted rings
Glastonbury Tor
Island of Avalon
Northumberland
St Govan's Chapel
Tintagel Castle
15 Caerleon upon Usk
Slaughterbridge
St Michael's Mount
Sword in the Stone
The Giant's castle
The Tristan Stone
Valley of Delight

legislation

Terms to do with legislation include:

02 Cm
03 Act
aye
law
04 Bill
06 repeal
Treaty
08 Decision

Division
09 Amendment
directive
Public Act
10 Commission
devolution
Green Paper
guillotine

Public Bill
referendum
regulation
White Paper
11 legislation
Report Stage
Royal Assent
12 First Reading

House of Lords
Personal Bill
Third Reading
13 Command Papers
European Union
See also **law**; **politics**

Letters Patent
Second Reading
14 Committee Stage
Government Bill
House of Commons

15 Act of Parliament
Pre-Budget Report
Programme Motion

letter *see* **alphabet**

lettuce

Lettuce varieties include:

03 cos

04 flat

05 lamb's

round

06 frisée

07 cabbage

Chinese
iceberg
romaine

08 Batavian

09 little gem

10 butterhead
lollo rosso

See also **salad**

lexicography

Lexicographers and associated figures include:

04 Bopp (Franz; 1791–1867, German)
Fick (August; 1833–1916, German)

05 Aasen (Ivar; 1813–96, Norwegian)
Grant (William; 1863–1946, Scottish)
Kimhi (David; c.1160–1235, French)
March (Francis Andrew; 1825–1911, US)
Pliny (Gaius 'the Elder'; 23–79 AD, Roman)
Sapir (Edward; 1884–1939, US)
Skeat (Walter William; 1835–1912, English)
Smith (Benjamin Eli; 1857–1912, US)
Smith (Sir William; 1813–93, English)

06 Bailey (Nathan; d.1742, English)
Benfey (Theodor; 1809–81, German)
Bierce (Ambrose; 1842–1914, US)
Blount (Thomas; 1618–79, English)
Brewer (E Cobham; 1810–97, English)
Cooper (Thomas; c.1517–94, English)
Cooper (Thomas; c.1517–94, English)
Florio (John; c.1533–1625, English)
Fowler (H W; 1858–1933, English)
Freund (Wilhelm; 1806–94, German)
Hornby (A S; 1898–1978, English)
Kimchi (David; c.1160–1235, French)
Littré (Émile; 1801–81, French)
Murray (Sir James; 1837–1915, Scottish)
Onions (C T; 1873–1965, English)
Robert (Paul; 1910–80, French)
Trench (Richard Chenevix; 1807–86, Irish)
Walker (John; 1732–1807, English)
Wright (Joseph; 1855–1930, English)

07 Adelung (Johann Christoph; 1732–1806,
German)

Bradley (Henry; 1845–1923, English)
Chomsky (Noam; 1928– ; US)
Craigie (Sir William; 1867–1957, Scottish)
Curtius (Georg; 1820–85, German)
Diderot (Denis; 1713–84, French)
Johnson (Samuel; 1709–84, English)
Lönnrot (Elias; 1802–84, Finnish)
Mencken (H L; 1880–1956, US)
Simpson (John; 1953– , English)
Vámbéry (Arminius; 1832–1913, Hungarian)
Ventris (Michael; 1922–56, English)
Webster (Noah; 1758–1843, US)
Whitney (William Dwight; 1827–94, US)

08 Bosworth (Joseph; 1789–1876, English)
Calepino (Ambrogio; 1440–1510, Italian)
Chambers (Ephraim; c.1680–1740, English)
Chambers (Robert; 1802–71, Scottish)
Chambers (William; 1800–83, Scottish)
Jamieson (John; 1759–1838, Scottish)
Larousse (Pierre; 1817–75, French)
Saussure (Ferdinand de; 1857–1913, Swiss)

09 Ainsworth (Robert; 1660–1743, English)
Furetière (Antoine; 1619–88, French)
Furnivall (Frederick James; 1825–1910,
English)
Jespersen (Otto; 1860–1943, Danish)
Partridge (Eric; 1894–1979, New Zealand/
British)
Worcester (Joseph E; 1784–1865, US)

10 Amarasimha (probably 6c; Sanskrit)
Burchfield (Robert; 1923–2004, English)

13 Aguilo i Fuster (Marian; 1825–97, Spanish)

libertine *see* **womanizer**

libretto

Librettists and lyricists include:

04 Bart (Lionel; 1930–99, English)
Hart (Lorenz; 1895–1943, US)
Jouy (Étienne; 1764–1846, French)
Rice (Sir Tim; 1944– , English)
Stow (Randolph; 1935–2010, Australian)
Vega (Ventura de la; 1807–65, Argentine/
Spanish)

05 Boito (Arrigo; 1842–1918, Italian)
Piave (Francesco; 1810–76; Italian)
Rolli (Paolo; 1687–1765, Italian)
Swann (Donald; 1923–94, Welsh)

06 Berlin (Irving; 1888–1989, US)
Fields (Dorothy; 1904–74, US)
Lerner (Alan Jay; 1918–86, US)
Malouf (David; 1934– , Australian)
Porter (Cole; 1891–1964, US)

Scribe (Eugène; 1791–1861, French)

07 Crozier (Eric; 1914–94, English)
Da Ponte (Lorenzo; 1749–1838, Italian)
Elmslie (Kenward; 1929– , US)
Gilbert (Sir W S; 1836–1911, English)
Harwood (Gwen; 1920–95, Australian)
Ryskind (Morrie; 1895–1985, US)
Sedaine (Michel-Jean; 1719–97, French)

08 Ferretti (Jacopo; 1784–1852, Italian)
Gershwin (Ira; 1896–1983, US)
Meredith (William Morris; 1919–2007, US)
Sondheim (Stephen; 1930– , US)

09 Benserade (Isaac de; 1613–91, French)
Delavigne (Casimir; 1793–1843, French)

11 Hammerstein (Oscar, II; 1895–1960, US)

See also **composer**; **opera**; **song**

lichen *see* **algae**

lie

Lies include:

03 fib	story	untruth	**10** concoction
04 cram	**06** unfact	whopper	fairy story
flam	**07** cretism	**08** white lie	taradiddle
whid	fiction	**09** fairy tale	**11** fabrication
05 fable	leasing	falsehood	pseudologia
porky	romance	mendacity	tarradiddle

lily

Lilies include:

03 day	**06** camash	gloriosa	
may	camass	hyacinth	
04 aloe	Canada	martagon	
arum	crinum	nenuphar	
pond	Easter	Phormium	
sego	Nuphar	trillium	
05 calla	scilla	Turk's cap	
camas	smilax	victoria	
lotus	**07** candock	**09** amaryllis	
regal	Madonna	grass tree	
tiger	quamash	herb-Paris	
torch	Tritoma	kniphofia	
yucca	**08** asphodel	of the Nile	
	galtonia	Richardia	

10 agapanthus
   aspidistra
   belladonna
   fritillary
11 cabbage-tree

Convallaria
of the valley
red-hot poker
spatterdock
12 Annunciation

Hemerocallis
Solomon's seal
zantedeschia
13 butcher's broom
15 star of Bethlehem

liqueur

Liqueurs include:

04 ouzo (aniseed/liquorice)
05 Aurum® (brandy/orange/saffron)
   noyau (fruit kernels/almond)
06 Averna (herbs/roots)
   Glayva® (heather honey/orange peel)
   Izarra® (armagnac/herbs)
   Kahlúa® (coffee)
   kirsch (cherry)
   kümmel (cumin/caraway seeds)
   Malibu® (white rum/coconut)
   Midori® (melon)
   Nocino (green walnuts)
   pastis (aniseed/liquorice)
   Pernod® (aniseed/liquorice)
   Ponche (brandy/fruit/spices)
   Ricard® (aniseed/liquorice)
   Strega® (saffron/herbs)
07 Amarula® (marula fruit/cream)
   Baileys® (whiskey/cream)
   curaçao (bitter orange peel)
   ratafia (fruit kernels)
   sambuca (aniseed/elderberry)
08 absinthe (aniseed/herbs)
   advocaat (egg)
   amaretto (almond/apricot)
   anisette (anise)
   Drambuie® (whisky/heather honey)
   Galliano® (anise/liquorice/vanilla)
   prunelle (sloe/wild plum)

See also **spirit**

rum shrub (rum/sugar/citrus)
Tia Maria® (cask-aged rum/coffee bean/
   spices)
09 Cointreau® (bitter orange peel)
   Irish Mist® (cognac/honey/herbs)
   mirabelle (plum)
   Triple sec (grape brandy/ bitter orange peel)
   Van der Hum (brandy/tangerine/spices)
10 Chartreuse® (orange/herbs/spices)
   Frangelico® (hazelnut)
   limoncello (lemon)
   maraschino (cherry)
11 Benedictine (orange/herb/spices)
   Vana Tallinn (rum/vanilla)
12 cherry brandy (cherry)
   crème de cacao (chocolate)
   Goldschlager® (Scotch whisky/aniseed)
   Grand Marnier® (orange)
   Jägermeister (Irish whiskey/herbs/roots/fruit)
   kirschwasser (wild cherry)
   Parfait Amour (rose petal/vanilla/almond)
13 Cherry Heering (cherry)
   crème de cassis (blackcurrant)
   crème de menthe (peppermint)
   Cuarenta y Tres (vanilla/citrus)
   eau des creoles (mammee-apple flowers)
15 Southern Comfort® (American whiskey/
   peaches/orange)

literature

Literature and story types include:

03 spy
04 epic
   love
   myth
   saga
   tale
   yarn
05 crime
   drama
   essay

fable
fairy
farce
ghost
novel
prose
sci-fi
short
spiel
squib
triad

verse
06 comedy
   horror
   legend
   masque
   parody
   poetry
   postil
   satire
   thesis

07 Aga saga
bedtime
epistle
faction
fantasy
fiction
lampoon
mystery
novella
parable
polemic
romance
tragedy
trilogy
western

08 allegory
anecdote
chick lit
folk tale
libretto
pastiche
tall tale
thriller
treatise

09 adventure
anti-novel
biography
children's

criticism
detective
dime novel
fairytale
interlude
melodrama
novelette
saga novel
shaggy-dog
whodunnit

10 bonkbuster
magnum opus
non-fiction
photonovel
river novel
roman à clef
short story
travelogue
yellowback

11 black comedy
blockbuster
Gothic novel
interactive
pulp fiction
roman à thèse
roman fleuve
terror novel
thesis novel

three-decker

12 bodice-ripper
classic novel
crime fiction
double-decker
graphic novel
Mills and Boon®
nouveau roman
novelization
outside novel
problem novel
spine-chiller
swashbuckler

13 autobiography
belles-lettres
Bildungsroman
penny dreadful
roman à tiroirs
travel writing

14 science fiction
sex-and-shopping

15 epistolary novel
historical novel
non-fiction novel
picaresque novel
shilling shocker

Literary prizes include:

10 Nobel Prize (worldwide)

11 Booker Prize (UK)
Orange Prize (UK)

12 Baileys Prize (UK)
Prix Goncourt (France)

13 Carnegie Medal (UK)

Pulitzer Prize (US)

14 Man Booker Prize (UK)

15 Costa Book Awards (UK)

Literary critics include:

04 Beer (John; 1926– , English)
Bell (Clive; 1881–1964, English)
Blum (Léon; 1872–1950, French)
Frye (Northrop; 1912–91, Canadian)

05 Carey (John; 1934– , English)
Hicks (Granville; 1901–82, US)
Kazin (Alfred; 1915–88, US)
Lodge (David; 1935– , English)
Stead (C K; 1932– , New Zealand)

06 Arnold (Matthew; 1822–88, English)
Empson (Sir William; 1906–84, English)
Leavis (F R; 1895–1978, English)
Leavis (Q D; 1906–81, English)
Lukacs (Georg; 1885–1971, Hungarian)
Ransom (John; 1888–1974, US)
Sontag (Susan; 1933–2005; US)
Wilson (Edmund; 1895–1972, US)

07 Ackroyd (Peter; 1949– , English)

Alvarez (A; 1929– , English)
Barthes (Roland; 1915–80, French)
Daiches (David; 1912–2005, Scottish)
Derrida (Jacques; 1930–2004, French)
Hoggart (Richard; 1918– , English)
Kermode (Sir Frank; 1919–2010, Manx)
Wimsatt (William, Jnr; 1907–75, US)

08 Bradbury (Sir Malcolm; 1932–2000, English)
Eagleton (Terry; 1943– , British)
Longinus (c.1CAD, Greek)
Nicolson (Sir Harold; 1886–1968, English)
Richards (I A; 1893–1979, English)
Trilling (Lionel; 1905–75, US)
Williams (Raymond; 1921–88, Welsh)

10 Saintsbury (George; 1845–1933, English)

11 Matthiessen (F O; 1902–50, US)
Sainte-Beuve (Charles Augustin; 1804–69, French)

Literary characters include:

02 Pi (*Life of Pi*, 2002, Yann Martel)

03 Jim (Lord; *Lord Jim*, 1900, Joseph Conrad)
Kim (*Kim*, 1901, Rudyard Kipling)
Lee (Lorelei; *Gentlemen Prefer Blondes*, 1925, Anita Loos)
Pip (*Great Expectations*, 1861, Charles Dickens)
Una (*The Faerie Queene*, 1590–96, Sir Edmund Spenser)

04 Ahab (Captain; *Moby-Dick*, 1851, Herman Melville)
Bede (Adam; *Adam Bede*, 1859, George Eliot)
Bond (James; *Casino Royale*, 1954, et seq, Ian Fleming)
Budd (Billy; *Billy Budd, Foretopman*, 1924, Herman Melville)
Dent (Arthur; *The Hitch-Hiker's Guide to the Galaxy*, 1979, et seq, Douglas Adams)
Eyre (Jane; *Jane Eyre*, 1847, Charlotte Brontë)
Finn (Phineas; *Phineas Finn: The Irish Member*, 1869, Anthony Trollope)
Fogg (Phileas; *Around the World in Eighty Days*, 1873, Jules Verne)
Gamp (Sarah; *Martin Chuzzlewit*, 1844, Charles Dickens)
Gray (Charlotte; *Charlotte Gray*, 1998, Sebastian Faulks)
Gray (Dorian; *The Picture of Dorian Gray*, 1891, Oscar Wilde)
Haze (Dolores; *Lolita*, 1955, Vladimir Nabokov)
Heep (Uriah; *David Copperfield*, 1850, Charles Dickens)
Hood (Robin; *Ivanhoe*, 1819, Sir Walter Scott)
Hyde (Mr; *The Strange Case of Dr Jekyll and Mr Hyde*, 1886, Robert Louis Stevenson)
Mole (Adrian; *The Secret Diary of Adrian Mole, aged 13¾*, 1982, et seq, Sue Townsend)
Ridd (John; *Lorna Doone*, 1869, R D Blackmore)
Slop (Doctor; *The Life and Opinions of Tristram Shandy*, 1759–67, Laurence Sterne)
Tigg (Montague; *Martin Chuzzlewit*, 1844, Charles Dickens)
Trim (Corporal; *The Life and Opinions of Tristram Shandy*, 1759–67, Laurence Sterne)
Troy (Sergeant Francis; *Far from the Madding Crowd*, 1874, Thomas Hardy)
Tuck (Friar; *Ivanhoe*, 1819, Sir Walter Scott)

Wilt (Henry; *Wilt*, 1976, et seq, Tom Sharpe)

05 Athos (*The Three Musketeers*, 1844, Alexandre Dumas père)
Avery (Shug; *The Color Purple*, 1983, Alice Walker)
Bates (Miss; *Emma*, 1816, Jane Austen)
Bloom (Leopold; *Ulysses*, 1922, James Joyce)
Bloom (Molly; *Ulysses*, 1922, James Joyce)
Boxer (*Animal Farm*, 1945, George Orwell)
Brown (Father; *The Innocence of Father Brown*, 1911, G K Chesterton)
Celie (*The Color Purple*, 1983, Alice Walker)
Chips (Mr; *Goodbye, Mr Chips*, 1934, James Hilton)
Clare (Angel; *Tess of the D'Urbervilles*, 1891, Thomas Hardy)
Darcy (Fitzwilliam; *Pride and Prejudice*, 1813, Jane Austen)
Darcy (Mark; *Bridget Jones's Diary*, 1996, *Bridget Jones: The Edge of Reason*, 1999, Helen Fielding)
Doone (Lorna; *Lorna Doone*, 1869, R D Blackmore)
Drood (Edwin; *The Mystery of Edwin Drood*, 1870, Charles Dickens)
Geste (Beau; *Beau Geste*, 1924, P C Wren)
Jones (Bridget; *Bridget Jones's Diary*, 1996, *Bridget Jones: The Edge of Reason*, 1999, Helen Fielding)
Jones (Tom; *The History of Tom Jones*, 1749, Henry Fielding)
Kipps (Arthur; *Kipps*, 1904, H G Wells)
Kurtz (*Heart of Darkness*, 1902, Joseph Conrad)
Loman (Willy; *Death of a Salesman*, 1949, Arthur Miller)
Lucky (*Waiting for Godot*, 1955, Samuel Beckett)
Mitty (Walter; *The Secret Life of Walter Mitty*, 1939, James Thurber)
Moore (Mrs; *A Passage to India*, 1924, E M Forster)
Mosca (*Volpone, or The Fox*, 1606, Ben Jonson)
Nancy (*Oliver Twist*, 1838, Charles Dickens)
O'Hara (Kimball; *Kim*, 1901, Rudyard Kipling)
O'Hara (Scarlett; *Gone with the Wind*, 1936, Margaret Mitchell)
Polly (Alfred; *The History of Mr Polly*, 1910, H G Wells)
Porgy (*Porgy*, 1925, DuBose Heyward)
Pozzo (*Waiting for Godot*, 1955, Samuel Beckett)

Price (Fanny; *Mansfield Park*, 1814, Jane Austen)

Quilp (Daniel; *The Old Curiosity Shop*, 1841, Charles Dickens)

Rebus (Inspector John; *Knots and Crosses*, 1987, et seq, Ian Rankin)

Rudge (Barnaby; *Barnaby Rudge*, 1841, Charles Dickens)

Satan (*Paradise Lost*, 1667, *Paradise Regained*, 1671, John Milton)

Sharp (Becky; *Vanity Fair*, 1848, W M Thackeray)

Sikes (Bill; *Oliver Twist*, 1838, Charles Dickens)

Slope (Reverend Obadiah; *Barchester Towers*, 1857, Anthony Trollope)

Smike (*Nicholas Nickleby*, 1839, Charles Dickens)

Smith (Winston; *1984*, 1949, George Orwell)

Spade (Sam; *The Maltese Falcon*, 1930, et seq, Dashiell Hammett)

Stubb (*Moby-Dick*, 1851, Herman Melville)

Tarka (the Otter; *Tarka the Otter*, 1927, Henry Williamson)

Trent (Little Nell; *The Old Curiosity Shop*, 1841, Charles Dickens)

Twist (Oliver; *Oliver Twist*, 1838, Charles Dickens)

06 Aramis (*The Three Musketeers*, 1844, Alexandre Dumas père)

Archer (Isabel; *The Portrait of a Lady*, 1881, Henry James)

Archer (Newland; *The Age of Innocence*, 1920, Edith Wharton)

Arthur (King; 'Morte d'Arthur', 1842, Alfred, Lord Tennyson)

Barkis (Mr; *David Copperfield*, 1850, Charles Dickens)

Belial (*Paradise Lost*, 1667, John Milton)

Bennet (Elizabeth; *Pride and Prejudice*, 1813, Jane Austen)

Bourgh (Lady Catherine de; *Pride and Prejudice*, 1813, Jane Austen)

Bovary (Emma; *Madame Bovary*, 1857, Gustave Flaubert)

Brodie (Miss Jean; *The Prime of Miss Jean Brodie*, 1961, Muriel Spark)

Brooke (Dorothea; *Middlemarch*, 1871–72, George Eliot)

Bumble (Mr; *Oliver Twist*, 1838, Charles Dickens)

Bumppo (Natty; *The Pioneers*, 1823, et seq, James Fenimore Cooper)

Butler (Rhett; *Gone with the Wind*, 1936, Margaret Mitchell)

Carton (Sydney; *A Tale of Two Cities*, 1859, Charles Dickens)

Dombey (Paul; *Dombey and Son*, 1848, Charles Dickens)

Dorrit (Amy; *Little Dorrit*, 1857, Charles Dickens)

Dorrit (William; *Little Dorrit*, 1857, Charles Dickens)

DuBois (Blanche; *A Streetcar Named Desire*, 1947, Tennessee Williams)

Gamgee (Sam; *The Lord of the Rings*, 1954–55, J R R Tolkien)

Gatsby (Jay; *The Great Gatsby*, 1925, F Scott Fitzgerald)

Gawain (Sir; 'Sir Gawain and the Green Knight', 14c, anon)

Gollum (*The Hobbit*, 1937, *The Lord of the Rings*, 1954–55, J R R Tolkien)

Hannay (Richard; *The Thirty-Nine Steps*, 1915, et seq, John Buchan)

Holmes (Sherlock; *A Study in Scarlet*, 1887, et seq, Arthur Conan Doyle)

Jeeves (Reginald; *The Inimitable Jeeves*, 1924, et seq, P G Wodehouse)

Jekyll (Doctor Henry; *The Strange Case of Dr Jekyll and Mr Hyde*, 1886, Robert Louis Stevenson)

Little (Vernon Gregory; *Vernon God Little*, 2003, D B C Pierre)

Lolita (*Lolita*, 1955, Vladimir Nabokov)

Marley (Jacob; *A Christmas Carol*, 1843, Charles Dickens)

Marner (Silas; *Silas Marner*, 1861, George Eliot)

Marple (Jane; *Murder at the Vicarage*, 1930, et seq, Agatha Christie)

Moreau (Doctor; *The Island of Doctor Moreau*, 1896, H G Wells)

Omnium (Duke of; *Can You Forgive Her?*, 1864–65, et seq, Anthony Trollope)

Pickle (Peregrine; *The Adventures of Peregrine Pickle*, 1751, Tobias Smollett)

Pinkie (*Brighton Rock*, 1938, Graham Greene)

Pliant (Dame; *The Alchemist*, 1610, Ben Jonson)

Poirot (Hercule; *The Mysterious Affair at Styles*, 1920, et seq, Agatha Christie)

Rabbit (*Rabbit, Run*, 1960, et seq, John Updike)

Random (Roderick; *The Adventures of Roderick Random*, 1748, Tobias Smollett)

Rob Roy (*Rob Roy*, 1817, Sir Walter Scott)

Salmon (Susie; *The Lovely Bones*, 2002, Alice Sebold)

Sawyer (Bob; *Pickwick Papers*, 1837, Charles Dickens)

Shandy (Tristram; *The Life and Opinions of Tristram Shandy*, 1759–67, Laurence Sterne)

Subtle (*The Alchemist*, 1610, Ben Jonson)

Tarzan (*Tarzan of the Apes*, 1914, et seq, Edgar Rice Burroughs)

Tyrone (James; *Long Day's Journey into Night*, 1956, Eugene O'Neill)

Varden (Dolly; *Barnaby Rudge*, 1841, Charles Dickens)

Wadman (Widow; *The Life and Opinions of Tristram Shandy*, 1759–67, Laurence Sterne)

Watson (Doctor John; *A Study in Scarlet*, 1887, et seq, Arthur Conan Doyle)

Weller (Samuel; *Pickwick Papers*, 1837, Charles Dickens)

Wimsey (Lord Peter; *Whose Body?*, 1923, et seq, Dorothy L Sayers)

Wopsle (Mr; *Great Expectations*, 1861, Charles Dickens)

Yahoos (*Gulliver's Travels*, 1726, Jonathan Swift)

07 Andrews (Pamela; *Pamela*, 1740–41, Samuel Richardson)

Baggins (Bilbo; *The Hobbit*, 1937, *The Lord of the Rings*, 1954–55, J R R Tolkien)

Baggins (Frodo; *The Lord of the Rings*, 1954–55, J R R Tolkien)

Beowulf (*Beowulf*, 7c/8c, anon)

Biggles (*The Camels Are Coming*, 1932, et seq, Captain W E Johns)

Bramble (Matthew; *The Expedition of Humphry Clinker*, 1771, Tobias Smollett)

Bromden (Chief; *One Flew over the Cuckoo's Nest*, 1962, Ken Kesey)

Clinker (Humphry; *The Expedition of Humphry Clinker*, 1771, Tobias Smollett)

Corelli (Captain Antonio; *Captain Corelli's Mandolin*, 1994, Louis de Bernières)

Crackit (Toby; *Oliver Twist*, 1838, Charles Dickens)

Danvers (Mrs; *Rebecca*, 1938, Daphne Du Maurier)

Dawkins (Jack; *Oliver Twist*, 1838, Charles Dickens)

Dedalus (Stephen; *A Portrait of the Artist as a Young Man*, 1916, et seq, James Joyce)

Deronda (Daniel; *Daniel Deronda*, 1876, George Eliot)

Despair (Giant; *The Pilgrim's Progress*, Part I 1678, Part II 1684, John Bunyan)

Don Juan (*Don Juan*, 1819–24, George Gordon Byron, 6th Lord Byron)

Dorigen ('The Franklin's Tale' in *The Canterbury Tales*, c.1387–1400, Geoffrey Chaucer)

Dracula (Count; *Dracula*, 1897, Bram Stoker)

Estella (*Great Expectations*, 1861, Charles Dickens)

Fairfax (Jane; *Emma*, 1816, Jane Austen)

Gandalf (*The Hobbit*, 1937, *The Lord of the Rings*, 1954–55, J R R Tolkien)

Gargery (Joe; *Great Expectations*, 1861, Charles Dickens)

Grendel (*Beowulf*, 7c/8c, anon)

Harding (Reverend Septimus; *The Warden*, 1855, et seq, Anthony Trollope)

Harlowe (Clarissa; *Clarissa*, 1748, Samuel Richardson)

Higgins (Professor Henry; *Pygmalion*, 1913, George Bernard Shaw)

Hopeful (*The Pilgrim's Progress*, Part I 1678, Part II 1684, John Bunyan)

Humbert (Humbert; *Lolita*, 1955, Vladimir Nabokov)

Ishmael (*Moby-Dick*, 1851, Herman Melville)

Jaggers (Mr; *Great Expectations*, 1861, Charles Dickens)

Jellyby (Mrs; *Bleak House*, 1853, Charles Dickens)

Jenkins (Nicholas; *A Question of Upbringing*, 1921, et seq, Anthony Powell)

Le Fever (Lieutenant; *The Life and Opinions of Tristram Shandy*, 1759–67, Laurence Sterne)

Maigret (Jules; *The Death of Monsieur Gallet*, 1931, et seq, Georges Simenon)

Marlowe (Philip; *The Big Sleep*, 1939, et seq, Raymond Chandler)

Mellors (Oliver; *Lady Chatterley's Lover*, 1928, D H Lawrence)

Newsome (Chad; *The Ambassadors*, 1903, Henry James)

Obadiah (*The Life and Opinions of Tristram Shandy*, 1759–67, Laurence Sterne)

Olenska (Countess Ellen; *The Age of Innocence*, 1920, Edith Wharton)

Orlando (*Orlando*, 1928, Virginia Woolf)

Peachum (Thomas; *The Beggar's Opera*, 1728, John Gay)

Porthos (*The Three Musketeers*, 1844, Alexandre Dumas père)

Prefect (Ford; *The Hitch-Hiker's Guide to the Galaxy*, 1979, et seq, Douglas Adams)

Proudie (Doctor; *Barchester Towers*, 1857, et seq, Anthony Trollope)

Raffles (*The Amateur Cracksman*, 1899, *The Black Mask*, 1901, *The Thief in the Night*, 1905, E W Hornung)

Rebecca (*Ivanhoe*, 1819, Sir Walter Scott)

Scrooge (Ebenezer; *A Christmas Carol*, 1843, Charles Dickens)

Shalott (Lady of; 'The Lady of Shalott', 1833, Alfred, Lord Tennyson)

Slumkey (Samuel; *Pickwick Papers*, 1837, Charles Dickens)

Squeers (Wackford; *Nicholas Nickleby*, 1839, Charles Dickens)

Surface (Charles; *The School for Scandal*, 1777, Richard Brinsley Sheridan)

Surface (Joseph; *The School for Scandal*, 1777, Richard Brinsley Sheridan)

Tiny Tim (*A Christmas Carol*, 1843, Charles Dickens)

Wemmick (Mr; *Great Expectations*, 1861, Charles Dickens)

Wickham (George; *Pride and Prejudice*, 1813, Jane Austen)

Witches (The Three; *Macbeth*, c.1606, William Shakespeare)

Wooster (Bertie; *The Inimitable Jeeves*, 1924, et seq, P G Wodehouse)

Would-be (Sir Politic; *Volpone, or The Fox*, 1606, Ben Jonson)

08 Absolute (Captain; *The Rivals*, 1775, Richard Brinsley Sheridan)

Anderson (Pastor Anthony; *The Devil's Disciple*, 1897, George Bernard Shaw)

Backbite (Sir Benjamin; *The School for Scandal*, 1777, Richard Brinsley Sheridan)

Bedivere (Sir; 'Morte d'Arthur', 1842, Alfred, Lord Tennyson)

Casaubon (Reverend Edward; *Middlemarch*, 1871–72, George Eliot)

Cratchit (Bob; *A Christmas Carol*, 1843, Charles Dickens)

Criseyde (*Troilus and Criseyde*, c.1385–89, Geoffrey Chaucer)

Dalloway (Mrs Clarissa; *The Voyage Out*, 1915, *Mrs Dalloway*, 1925, Virginia Woolf)

Dashwood (Elinor; *Sense and Sensibility*, 1811, Jane Austen)

Dashwood (Marianne; *Sense and Sensibility*, 1811, Jane Austen)

de Winter (Max; *Rebecca*, 1938, Daphne Du Maurier)

de Winter (Rebecca; *Rebecca*, 1938, Daphne Du Maurier)

Estragon (*Waiting for Godot*, 1955, Samuel Beckett)

Everdene (Bathsheba; *Far from the Madding Crowd*, 1874, Thomas Hardy)

Faithful (*The Pilgrim's Progress*, Part I 1678, Part II 1684, John Bunyan)

Fezziwig (Mr; *A Christmas Carol*, 1843, Charles Dickens)

Flanders (Moll; *Moll Flanders*, 1722, Daniel Defoe)

Flashman (*Tom Brown's Schooldays*, 1857, et seq, Thomas Hughes)

Gloriana (*The Faerie Queene*, 1590–96, Sir Edmund Spenser)

Griselda (Patient; 'The Clerk's Tale' in *The Canterbury Tales*, c.1387–1400, Geoffrey Chaucer)

Gulliver (Lemuel; *Gulliver's Travels*, 1726, Jonathan Swift)

Havisham (Miss; *Great Expectations*, 1861, Charles Dickens)

Hiawatha (*The Song of Hiawatha*, 1855, Henry Wadsworth Longfellow)

Hrothgar (*Beowulf*, 7c/8c, anon)

Jarndyce (John; *Bleak House*, 1853, Charles Dickens)

Kowalski (Stanley; *A Streetcar Named Desire*, 1947, Tennessee Williams)

Kowalski (Stella; *A Streetcar Named Desire*, 1947, Tennessee Williams)

Ladislaw (Will; *Middlemarch*, 1871–72, George Eliot)

Lancelot (Sir; 'The Lady of Shalott', 1833, Alfred, Lord Tennyson)

Lestrade (Inspector; *A Study in Scarlet*, 1887, et seq, Arthur Conan Doyle)

MacHeath (Captain; *The Beggar's Opera*, 1728, John Gay)

Magwitch (Abel; *Great Expectations*, 1861, Charles Dickens)

Malaprop (Mrs; *The Rivals*, 1775, Richard Brinsley Sheridan)

McMurphy (Randle Patrick; *One Flew over the Cuckoo's Nest*, 1962, Ken Kesey)

Micawber (Wilkins; *David Copperfield*, 1850, Charles Dickens)

Moriarty (Dean; *On the Road*, 1957, Jack Kerouac)

Moriarty (Professor James; *The Memoirs of Sherlock Holmes*, 1892–93, Arthur Conan Doyle)

Napoleon (*Animal Farm*, 1945, George Orwell)

Nickleby (Nicholas; *Nicholas Nickleby*, 1839, Charles Dickens)

Nostromo (*Nostromo*, 1904, Joseph Conrad)

Paradise (Sal; *On the Road*, 1957, Jack Kerouac)

Peggotty (Clara; *David Copperfield*, 1850, Charles Dickens)

Pickwick (Samuel; *Pickwick Papers*, 1837, Charles Dickens)

Queequeg (*Moby-Dick*, 1851, Herman Melville)

Ramotswe (Precious; *The No 1 Ladies' Detective Agency*, 1998, et seq, Alexander McCall Smith)

Snowball (*Animal Farm*, 1945, George Orwell)

Starbuck (*Moby-Dick*, 1851, Herman Melville)

Svengali (*Trilby*, 1894, George Du Maurier)

Tashtego (*Moby-Dick*, 1851, Herman Melville)

The Clerk (*The Canterbury Tales*, c.1387–1400, Geoffrey Chaucer)

The Friar (*The Canterbury Tales*, c.1387–1400, Geoffrey Chaucer)

The Reeve (*The Canterbury Tales*, c.1387–1400, Geoffrey Chaucer)

Trotwood (Betsey; *David Copperfield*, 1850, Charles Dickens)

Tulliver (Maggie; *The Mill on the Floss*, 1860, George Eliot)

Twitcher (Jemmy; *The Beggar's Opera*, 1728, John Gay)

Vladimir (*Waiting for Godot*, 1955, Samuel Beckett)

09 Archimago (*The Faerie Queene*, 1590–96, Sir Edmund Spenser)

Bounderby (Josiah; *Hard Times*, 1854, Charles Dickens)

Britomart (*The Faerie Queene*, 1590–96, Sir Edmund Spenser)

Bulstrode (Nicholas; *Middlemarch*, 1871–72, George Eliot)

Caulfield (Holden; *The Catcher in the Rye*, 1951, J D Salinger)

Cheeryble (Charles; *Nicholas Nickleby*, 1839, Charles Dickens)

Christian (*The Pilgrim's Progress*, Part I 1678, Part II 1684, John Bunyan)

Churchill (Frank; *Emma*, 1816, Jane Austen)

Constance ('The Man of Law's Tale' in *The Canterbury Tales*, c.1387–1400, Geoffrey Chaucer)

D'Artagnan (*The Three Musketeers*, 1844, Alexandre Dumas père)

Doolittle (Eliza; *Pygmalion*, 1913, George Bernard Shaw)

Golightly (Holly; *Breakfast at Tiffany's*, 1958, Truman Capote)

Gradgrind (Thomas; *Hard Times*, 1854, Charles Dickens)

Grandison (Sir Charles; *Sir Charles Grandison*, 1754, Samuel Richardson)

Knightley (George; *Emma*, 1816, Jane Austen)

Lismahago (Obadiah; *The Expedition of Humphry Clinker*, 1771, Tobias Smollett)

Lochinvar (*Marmion*, 1808, Sir Walter Scott)

Minnehaha (*The Song of Hiawatha*, 1855, Henry Wadsworth Longfellow)

Pecksniff (Seth; *Martin Chuzzlewit*, 1844, Charles Dickens)

Pendennis (Arthur; *The History of Pendennis*, 1848–50, *The Newcomes*, 1853–55, W M Thackeray)

Pollyanna (*Pollyanna*, 1913, *Pollyanna Grows Up*, 1915, Eleanor H Porter)

Rochester (Edward Fairfax; *Jane Eyre*, 1847, Charlotte Brontë)

Scudamour (Sir; *The Faerie Queene*, 1590–96, Sir Edmund Spenser)

The Knight (*The Canterbury Tales*, c.1387–1400, Geoffrey Chaucer)

The Miller (*The Canterbury Tales*, c.1387–1400, Geoffrey Chaucer)

The Squire (*The Canterbury Tales*, c.1387–1400, Geoffrey Chaucer)

Van Winkle (Rip; 'Rip Van Winkle', 1819, Washington Irving)

Woodhouse (Emma; *Emma*, 1816, Jane Austen)

Yossarian (Captain John; *Catch-22*, 1961, Joseph Heller)

Zenocrate (*Tamburlaine the Great: Parts I and II*, 1587–90, Christopher Marlowe)

10 Big Brother (*1984*, 1949, George Orwell)

Challenger (Professor; *The Lost World*, 1912, et seq, Arthur Conan Doyle)

Chatterley (Lady Constance; *Lady Chatterley's Lover*, 1928, D H Lawrence)

Chuzzlewit (Martin; *Martin Chuzzlewit*, 1844, Charles Dickens)

Evangelist (*The Pilgrim's Progress*, Part I 1678, Part II 1684, John Bunyan)

Great-heart (Mr; *The Pilgrim's Progress*, Part I 1678, Part II 1684, John Bunyan)

Heathcliff (*Wuthering Heights*, 1848, Emily Brontë)

Hornblower (Horatio; *The Happy Return*, 1937, et seq, C S Forester)

Houyhnhnms (*Gulliver's Travels*, 1726, Jonathan Swift)

Little Nell (*The Old Curiosity Shop*, 1841, Charles Dickens)

The Tar Baby (*Tar Baby*, 1981, Toni Morrison)

11 Copperfield (David; *David Copperfield*, 1850, Charles Dickens)

D'Urberville (Alec; *Tess of the D'Urbervilles*, 1891, Thomas Hardy)

Durbeyfield (Tess; *Tess of the D'Urbervilles*, 1891, Thomas Hardy)

Mutabilitie (*The Faerie Queene*, 1590–96, Sir Edmund Spenser)

Pumblechook (Mr; *Great Expectations*, 1861, Charles Dickens)

The Franklin (*The Canterbury Tales*, c.1387–1400, Geoffrey Chaucer)

The Man of Law (*The Canterbury Tales*, c.1387–1400, Geoffrey Chaucer)

The Merchant (*The Canterbury Tales*, c.1387–1400, Geoffrey Chaucer)

The Pardoner (*The Canterbury Tales*, c.1387–1400, Geoffrey Chaucer)

The Prioress (*The Canterbury Tales*, c.1387–1400, Geoffrey Chaucer)

The Summoner (*The Canterbury Tales*, c.1387–1400, Geoffrey Chaucer)

12 Blatant Beast (*The Faerie Queene*, 1590–96, Sir Edmund Spenser)

Chaunticleer ('The Nun's Priest's Tale' in *The Canterbury Tales*, c.1387–1400, Geoffrey Chaucer)

Frankenstein (Victor; *Frankenstein, or, The Modern Prometheus*, 1818, Mary Shelley)

Lilliputians (*Gulliver's Travels*, 1726, Jonathan Swift)

Osbaldistone (Francis; *Rob Roy*, 1817, Sir Walter Scott)

Rip Van Winkle ('Rip Van Winkle', 1819, Washington Irving)

The Pied Piper (of Hamelin; 'The Pied Piper of Hamelin', in *Dramatic Romances*, 1845, Robert Browning)

13 The Wife of Bath (*The Canterbury Tales*, c.1387–1400, Geoffrey Chaucer)

14 Worldly Wiseman (Mr; *The Pilgrim's Progress*, Part I 1678, Part II 1684, John Bunyan)

15 The Artful Dodger (*Oliver Twist*, 1838, Charles Dickens)

Valiant-for-Truth (*The Pilgrim's Progress*, Part I 1678, Part II 1684, John Bunyan)

Characters from children's literature include:

03 BFG (*The BFG*, 1982, Roald Dahl)

Eva (Little; *Uncle Tom's Cabin, or, Life Among the Lowly*, 1851–52, Harriet Beecher Stowe)

Fox (Brer; *Uncle Remus*, 1880, Joel Chandler Harris)

Kaa (*The Jungle Book*, 1894, Rudyard Kipling)

Pan (Peter; *Peter Pan*, 1904, J M Barrie)

Roo (*Winnie-the-Pooh*, 1926, et seq, A A Milne)

Tom (Uncle; *Uncle Tom's Cabin, or, Life Among the Lowly*, 1851–52, Harriet Beecher Stowe)

04 Carr (Katy; *What Katy Did*, 1872, et seq, Susan Coolidge)

Finn (Huckleberry; *The Adventures of Tom Sawyer*, 1876, et seq, Mark Twain)

Gunn (Ben; *Treasure Island*, 1883, Robert Louis Stevenson)

Hook (Captain; *Peter Pan*, 1904, J M Barrie)

Long (Tom; *Tom's Midnight Garden*, 1958, Philippa Pearce)

Lucy (*The Lion, the Witch and the Wardrobe*, 1950, et seq, C S Lewis)

Mole (*The Wind in the Willows*, 1908, Kenneth Grahame)

Pooh (*Winnie-the-Pooh*, 1926, et seq, A A Milne)

Toad (Mr; *The Wind in the Willows*, 1908, Kenneth Grahame)

Wart (*The Sword in the Stone*, 1958, et seq, T H White)

05 Akela (*The Jungle Book*, 1894, Rudyard Kipling)

Alice (*Alice's Adventures in Wonderland*, 1865, Lewis Carroll)

Aslan (*The Lion, the Witch and the Wardrobe*, 1950, et seq, C S Lewis)

Baloo (*The Jungle Book*, 1894, Rudyard Kipling)

Fiver (*Watership Down*, 1972, Richard Adams)

Flint (Captain; *Swallows and Amazons*, 1930, et seq, Arthur Ransome)

Hatty (*Tom's Midnight Garden*, 1958, Philippa Pearce)

Hazel (*Watership Down*, 1972, Richard Adams)

Heidi (*Heidi*, 1880, Johanna Spyri)

Kanga (*Winnie-the-Pooh*, 1926, et seq, A A Milne)

March (Amy; *Little Women*, 1868, et seq, Louisa M Alcott)

March (Beth; *Little Women*, 1868, et seq, Louisa M Alcott)

March (Jo; *Little Women*, 1868, et seq, Louisa M Alcott)

March (Meg; *Little Women*, 1868, et seq, Louisa M Alcott)

Parry (Will; *The Subtle Knife*, 1997, *The Amber Spyglass*, 2000, Philip Pullman)

Peter (*Heidi*, 1880, Johanna Spyri)

Peter (*The Lion, the Witch and the Wardrobe*, 1950, et seq, C S Lewis)

Peter (*The Railway Children*, 1906, E Nesbit)

Ratty (*The Wind in the Willows*, 1908, Kenneth Grahame)

Remus (Uncle; *Uncle Remus*, 1880, Joel Chandler Harris)

Susan (*The Lion, the Witch and the Wardrobe*, 1950, et seq, C S Lewis)

Topsy (*Uncle Tom's Cabin, or, Life Among the Lowly*, 1851–52, Harriet Beecher Stowe)

Wendy (*Peter Pan*, 1904, J M Barrie)

Wonka (Willy; *Charlie and the Chocolate Factory*, 1964, *Charlie and the Great Glass Elevator*, 1973, Roald Dahl)

06 Arable (Fern; *Charlotte's Web*, 1952, E B White)

Badger (*The Wind in the Willows*, 1908, Kenneth Grahame)

Beaker (Tracey; *The Story of Tracey Beaker*, 1991, Jacqueline Wilson)

Bucket (Charlie; *Charlie and the Chocolate Factory*, 1964, *Charlie and the Great Glass Elevator*, 1973, Roald Dahl)

Bunter (Billy; *Billy Bunter of Greyfriars School*, 1949, et seq, Frank Richards)

Craven (Colin; *The Secret Garden*, 1911, Frances Hodgson Burnett)

Crusoe (Robinson; *Robinson Crusoe*, 1719, *The Farther Adventures of Robinson Crusoe*, 1720, *The Serious Reflections ... of Robinson Crusoe*, 1720, Daniel Defoe)

Dickon (*The Secret Garden*, 1911, Frances Hodgson Burnett)

Edmund (*The Lion, the Witch and the Wardrobe*, 1950, et seq, C S Lewis)

Eeyore (*Winnie-the-Pooh*, 1926, et seq, A A Milne)

Friday (Man; *Robinson Crusoe*, 1719, *The Farther Adventures of Robinson Crusoe*, 1720, *The Serious Reflections ... of Robinson Crusoe*, 1720, Daniel Defoe)

Gollum (*The Hobbit*, 1937, *The Lord of the Rings*, 1954–55, J R R Tolkien)

Hagrid (Rubeus; *Harry Potter and the Philosopher's Stone*, 1997, et seq, J K Rowling)

Legree (Simon; *Uncle Tom's Cabin, or, Life Among the Lowly*, 1851–52, Harriet Beecher Stowe)

Lennox (Mary; *The Secret Garden*, 1911, Frances Hodgson Burnett)

Little (Stuart; *Stuart Little*, 1945, E B White)

Malfoy (Draco; *Harry Potter and the Philosopher's Stone*, 1997, et seq, J K Rowling)

Mowgli (*The Jungle Book*, 1894, Rudyard Kipling)

Piglet (*Winnie-the-Pooh*, 1926, et seq, A A Milne)

Potter (Harry; *Harry Potter and the Philosopher's Stone*, 1997, et seq, J K Rowling)

Rabbit (Brer; *Uncle Remus*, 1880, Joel Chandler Harris)

Thatcher (Becky; *The Adventures of Tom Sawyer*, 1876, et seq, Mark Twain)

Sawyer (Tom; *The Adventures of Tom Sawyer*, 1876, et seq, Mark Twain)

Silver (Long John; *Treasure Island*, 1883, Robert Louis Stevenson)

Sophie (*The BFG*, 1982, Roald Dahl)

Tigger (*The House at Pooh Corner*, 1928, A A Milne)

Walker (John; *Swallows and Amazons*, 1930, et seq, Arthur Ransome)

Walker (Roger; *Swallows and Amazons*, 1930, et seq, Arthur Ransome)

Walker (Susan; *Swallows and Amazons*, 1930, et seq, Arthur Ransome)

Walker (Titty; *Swallows and Amazons*, 1930, et seq, Arthur Ransome)

07 Baggins (Bilbo; *The Hobbit*, 1937, *The Lord of the Rings*, 1954–55, J R R Tolkien)

Biggles (*The Camels are Coming*, 1932, et seq, Captain W E Johns)

Brer Fox (*Uncle Remus*, 1880, Joel Chandler Harris)

Diamond (*At the Back of the North Wind*, 1871, George Macdonald)

Dorothy (*The Wonderful Wizard of Oz*, 1900, L Frank Baum)

Gandalf (*The Hobbit*, 1937, *The Lord of the Rings*, 1954–55, J R R Tolkien)

Granger (Hermione; *Harry Potter and the Philosopher's Stone*, 1997, et seq, J K Rowling)

Hawkins (Jim; *Treasure Island*, 1883, Robert Louis Stevenson)

Phyllis (*The Railway Children*, 1906, E Nesbit)

Poppins (Mary; *Mary Poppins*, 1934, P L Travers)

Roberta (*The Railway Children*, 1906, E Nesbit)

Shirley (Anne; *Anne of Green Gables*, 1908, et seq, L M Montgomery)

Weasley (Ron; *Harry Potter and the Philosopher's Stone*, 1997, et seq, J K Rowling)

William (*Just William*, 1922, et seq, Richmal Crompton)

08 Bagheera (*The Jungle Book*, 1894, Rudyard Kipling)

Belacqua (Lyra; *Northern Lights*, 1995, *The Subtle Knife*, 1997, *The Amber Spyglass*, 2000, Philip Pullman)

Blackett (Nancy; *Swallows and Amazons*, 1930, et seq, Arthur Ransome)

Blackett (Peggy; *Swallows and Amazons*, 1930, et seq, Arthur Ransome)

Jennings (*Jennings Goes to School*, 1950, et seq, Anthony Buckeridge)

Peterkin (*The Coral Island*, 1857, R M Ballantyne)

Peter Pan (*Peter Pan*, 1904, J M Barrie)

09 Charlotte (*Charlotte's Web*, 1952, E B White)

Mad Hatter (*Alice's Adventures in Wonderland*, 1865, Lewis Carroll)

Shere Khan (*The Jungle Book*, 1894, Rudyard Kipling)

The Pauper (*The Prince and the Pauper*, 1882, Mark Twain)

The Prince (*The Prince and the Pauper*, 1882, Mark Twain)

The Walrus (*Through the Looking-Glass, and What Alice Found There*, 1872, Lewis Carroll)

Tiger Lily (*Through the Looking-Glass, and What Alice Found There*, 1872, Lewis Carroll)

Voldemort (Lord; *Harry Potter and the Philosopher's Stone*, 1997, et seq, J K Rowling)

10 Brer Rabbit (*Uncle Remus*, 1880, Joel Chandler Harris)

Dumbledore (Albus; *Harry Potter and the Philosopher's Stone*, 1997, et seq, J K Rowling)

Fauntleroy (Little Lord; *Little Lord Fauntleroy*, 1885, Frances Hodgson Burnett)

The Red King (*Through the Looking-Glass, and What Alice Found There*, 1872, Lewis Carroll)

Tinkerbell (*Peter Pan*, 1904, J M Barrie)

Tweedledee (*Through the Looking-Glass, and What Alice Found There*, 1872, Lewis Carroll)

Tweedledum (*Through the Looking-Glass, and What Alice Found There*, 1872, Lewis Carroll)

11 The Dormouse (*Alice's Adventures in Wonderland*, 1865, Lewis Carroll)

The Red Queen (*Through the Looking-Glass, and What Alice Found There*, 1872, Lewis Carroll)

White Rabbit (*Alice's Adventures in Wonderland*, 1865, Lewis Carroll)

12 Humpty-Dumpty (*Through the Looking-Glass, and What Alice Found There*, 1872, Lewis Carroll)

Longstocking (Pippi; *Pippi Longstocking*, 1945, Astrid Lindgren)

Silvertongue (Lyra; *Northern Lights*, 1995, *The Subtle Knife*, 1997, *The Amber Spyglass*, 2000, Philip Pullman)

The Carpenter (*Through the Looking-Glass, and What Alice Found There*, 1872, Lewis Carroll)

The Mad Hatter (*Alice's Adventures in Wonderland*, 1865, Lewis Carroll)

The March Hare (*Alice's Adventures in Wonderland*, 1865, Lewis Carroll)

The Red Knight (*Through the Looking-Glass, and What Alice Found There*, 1872, Lewis Carroll)

The Scarecrow (*The Wonderful Wizard of Oz*, 1900, L Frank Baum)

Wilbur the Pig (*Charlotte's Web*, 1952, E B White)

13 The Jabberwock (*Through the Looking-Glass, and What Alice Found There*, 1872, Lewis Carroll)

The Mock Turtle (*Alice's Adventures in Wonderland*, 1865, Lewis Carroll)

The Tin Woodman (*The Wonderful Wizard of Oz*, 1900, L Frank Baum)

Winnie-the-Pooh (*Winnie-the-Pooh*, 1926, et seq, A A Milne)

14 Rikki-Tikki-Tavi (*The Jungle Book*, 1894, Rudyard Kipling)

The White Rabbit (*Alice's Adventures in Wonderland*, 1865, Lewis Carroll)

15 The Cowardly Lion (*The Wonderful Wizard of Oz*, 1900, L Frank Baum)

Literary terms include:

03 act	**05** aside	novel
lay	canon	paean
ode	canto	story
04 acto	elegy	style
bard	essay	tanka
Edda	fable	theme
epic	farce	voice
foil	frame	**06** accent
foot	genre	ballad
iamb	haiku	bathos
mood	idyll	chorus
myth	irony	climax
plot	meter	comedy
saga	motif	dactyl
tone	motiv	legend
	muses	

masque
oeuvre
parody
pathos
rococo
satire
sequel
sestet
simile
sonnet
stanza

07 analogy
ballade
baroque
cadence
caesura
canzone
conceit
couplet
Dadaism
diction
eclogue
epigram
episode
epistle
epithet
euphony
fabliau
fantasy
georgic
imagery
imagism
lampoon
memoirs
novella
parable
paradox
persona
polemic
preface
prosody
realism
romance
rondeau
setting
spondee
subplot
tragedy
trilogy
trochee

08 abstract
acrostic
allegory
allusion
analogue
anapaest
anecdote

anti-hero
aphorism
apologue
bestiary
chick lit
conflict
dialogue
didactic
dystopia
epigraph
epilogue
epiphany
epitasis
euphuism
exemplum
foreword
futurism
Gruppe 47
hamartia
humanism
lapidary
limerick
metaphor
metonymy
mock epic
narrator
oxymoron
pastoral
prologue
protasis
quatrain
samizdat
scansion
sub-genre
suspense
The Group
thriller
travesty
trouvère

09 absurdism
Agrarians
ambiguity
anthology
anti-novel
apocrypha
archetype
assonance
Beat Poets
biography
burlesque
cacophony
character
chronicle
complaint
Decadents
Dionysian
euphemism
fairytale

flashback
folk tales
free verse
Gilded Age
grotesque
hyperbole
inference
Lake Poets
La Pléiade
leitmotiv
lyric poem
mannerism
melodrama
modernism
monologue
narrative
pantheism
Platonism
soliloquy
symbolism
terza rima
vers libre
Zeitgeist

10 antagonist
antimasque
antithesis
Apollonian
apostrophe
avant-garde
blank verse
bonkbuster
classicism
conclusion
consonance
dénouement
dissonance
enjambment
epistolary
exposition
incunabula
in media res
Lake School
manuscript
naturalism
nom de plume
pure poetry
raisonneur
resolution
rhyme-royal
roman à clef
short story
stereotype
synecdoche
tetrameter
tragic flaw
troubadour
utopianism

11 Age of Reason
black comedy
catastrophe
comic relief
courtly love
dream vision
epic theatre
Festschrift
fin de siècle
generation X
gothic novel
Greek chorus
hagiography
Jacobean Age
lyric poetry
Minnesinger
mise en scène
noble savage
poète maudit
primitivism
protagonist
pulp fiction
rhyme-scheme
romanticism
The Apostles
The Movement
thesis novel
tragicomedy
Weltschmerz

12 aestheticism
Age of Johnson
alliteration
Beat Movement
bodice-ripper
concrete poem
Doppelgänger
epithalamion
epithalamium

Jindyworobak
magic realism
nouveau roman
novel of ideas
nursery rhyme
onomatopoeia
Poet Laureate
rising action
synaesthesia
three unities
urban realism
utopian novel

13 Angry Young Men
autobiography
belles-lettres
Bildungsroman
carpe diem poem
Cavalier Poets
deus ex machina
dream allegory
expressionism
falling action
foreshadowing
Georgian Poets
heroic couplet
Kunstlerroman
narrative poem
neoclassicism
new journalism
nonsense verse
Parnassianism
poetic justice
poetic licence
postmodernism
social realism
structuralism
Sturm und Drang
vers de société

versification

14 Art for Art's Sake
Celtic Twilight
concrete poetry
deconstruction
dramatic poetry
dystopian novel
existentialism
figure of speech
Horatian satire
hypertext novel
Lost Generation
novel of manners
Pre-Raphaelites
Restoration Age
revenge tragedy
science fiction
tragedy of blood
understatement
verisimilitude
Weltanschauung

15 Bloomsbury Group
chansons de geste
comedy of manners
Erziehungsroman
Graveyard School
historical novel
occasional verse
pathetic fallacy
personification
picaresque novel
teatro grottesco

See also **Austen, Jane; Blyton, Enid; Brontë, Anne; Brontë, Charlotte; Brontë, Emily; Carroll, Lewis; Chaucer, Geoffrey; Christie, Dame Agatha; Defoe, Daniel; Dickens, Charles; Dostoevsky, Fyodor; Doyle, Sir Arthur Conan; Dumas, Alexandre; Eliot, George; fable; Hardy, Thomas; Hemingway, Ernest; James, Henry; Joyce, James; Kipling, Rudyard; Lawrence, D H; legend; miser; Morrison, Toni; Murdoch, Dame Iris; mythology; Nobel Prize; non-fiction; novel; Orwell, George; play; poetry; Potter, Beatrix; prosody; Proust, Marcel; Rowling, J K; science fiction; Scott, Sir Walter; Shakespeare, William; Stevenson, Robert Louis; Tolkien, J R R; Tolstoy, Count Leo; Trollope, Anthony; Twain, Mark; Voltaire; Wells, H G; Wodehouse, Sir P G; Woolf, Virginia; writing; Zola, Émile**

lizard

Lizards include:

03 eft	wall	Draco	night
04 gila	worm	fence	skink
sand	**05** anole	gecko	snake
seps	blind	guana	varan

06	agamid		worrel		slowworm		horned toad
	beaded		zonure		stellion	11	chisel-tooth
	dragon	07	bearded		sungazer		gila monster
	flying		frilled		teguexin		
	goanna		monitor		wall newt	12	flying dragon
	horned		perenty	09	chameleon		girdle-tailed
	iguana		serpent		galliwasp		Komodo dragon
	Komodo		stellio	10	blue-tongue	13	bearded dragon
	Moloch	08	basilisk		chamaeleon	14	Bornean earless
	worral		perentie		glass snake		

loch *see* **lake**

lock

Locks include:

03	pad		Chubb®		mortise
	rim		wagon	08	cylinder
04	dead	06	safety	10	night latch
	Yale®		spring	11	combination
05	child	07	mortice		

Lock parts include:

03	bit		keyway		latch bolt
	key		spring	10	escutcheon
	pin		staple		latch lever
04	bolt	07	key card		push-button
	hasp		keyhole	11	mortise bolt
	knob		spindle		spindle hole
	rose	08	cylinder		strike plate
	sash		dead bolt	12	cylinder hole
05	latch		sash bolt	13	latch follower
06	barrel	09	face-plate		

London

London boroughs:

05	Brent		Enfield	10	Hillingdon
06	Barnet		Hackney		Wandsworth
	Bexley		Lambeth	12	Tower Hamlets
	Camden	08	Haringey	13	Waltham Forest
	Ealing		Havering	17	City of Westminster
	Harrow		Hounslow	18	Barking and Dagenham
	Merton		Lewisham		Kingston upon Thames
	Newham	09	Greenwich		Richmond upon Thames
	Sutton		Islington	20	Hammersmith and Fulham
07	Bromley		Redbridge		Kensington and Chelsea
	Croydon		Southwark		

Other districts of London include:

03 Bow	Kilburn	Stanmore
Kew	Mayfair	Surbiton
Lee	Mile End	Sydenham
04 Bank	Mitcham	Tolworth
Oval	Neasden	Uxbridge
Soho	Norwood	Vauxhall
05 Acton	Old Ford	Victoria
Angel	Olympia	Walworth
Erith	Peckham	Wanstead
Hayes	Pimlico	Waterloo
Penge	Selsdon	Woodford
06 Arkley	Stepney	Woolwich
Balham	The City	**09** Abbey Wood
Barnes	Tooting	Addington
Debden	Wapping	Barnsbury
Eltham	Welling	Battersea
Epping	Wembley	Bayswater
Euston	West End	Beckenham
Fulham	West Ham	Becontree
Hendon	Yeading	Belgravia
Heston	**08** Alperton	Blackwall
Hoxton	Bankside	Brentford
Ilford	Barbican	Brimsdown
Kenton	Brockley	Canonbury
Leyton	Brompton	Chalk Farm
Malden	Chiswick	Chingford
Morden	Coulsdon	Colindale
Pinner	Crayford	Crouch End
Poplar	Dagenham	Docklands
Purley	Deptford	Fitzrovia
Putney	Edmonton	Foots Cray
Temple	Elmstead	Gant's Hill
Waddon	Finchley	Gidea Park
07 Aldgate	Finsbury	Gipsy Hill
Archway	Grays Inn	Goodmayes
Barking	Hanworth	Gospel Oak
Beckton	Hatch End	Greenford
Belmont	Heathrow	Green Park
Borough	Highbury	Hampstead
Brixton	Highgate	Harefield
Catford	Holloway	Harlesden
Chelsea	Homerton	Harringay
Clapham	Hyde Park	Herne Hill
Cranham	Ickenham	Isleworth
Dalston	Kingston	Kidbrooke
Dulwich	Mill Hill	Kingsbury
East End	Mortlake	Kingsland
East Ham	New Cross	Limehouse
Edgware	Nine Elms	Maida Vale
Elm Park	Northolt	Mark's Gate
Feltham	Osterley	Newington
Hampton	Perivale	Northwood
Hanwell	Plaistow	Orpington
Holborn	Richmond	Park Royal
Hornsey	Shadwell	Petts Wood
	Southall	Plumstead

South Bank
Southgate
Stockwell
St Pancras
Stratford
Streatham
Tottenham
Tower Hill
Tulse Hill
Upminster
Whetstone
White City
Whitehall
Willesden
Wimbledon
Wood Green

10 Addiscombe
Albany Park
Arnos Grove
Beddington
Bellingham
Bermondsey
Blackheath
Bloomsbury
Brent Cross
Camberwell
Chase Cross
Collier Row
Creekmouth
Dollis Hill
Earls Court
Earlsfield
Embankment
Farringdon
Forest Gate
Forest Hill
Goddington
Green Lanes
Haggerston
Harlington
Harold Hill
Harold Wood
Horse Ferry
Isle of Dogs
Kennington
Kensington
King's Cross
Manor House
Marylebone
Mottingham

Paddington
Piccadilly
Queensbury
Raynes Park
Seven Dials
Seven Kings
Shad Thames
Shoreditch
Silvertown
Smithfield
Teddington
Thamesmead
Totteridge
Twickenham
Wallington
Wealdstone

11 Bedford Park
Belsize Park
Bexleyheath
Blackfriars
Bounds Green
Brondesbury
Canada Water
Canary Wharf
Canning Town
Chessington
Clerkenwell
Cockfosters
Cricklewood
East Dulwich
Fortis Green
Gunnersbury
Hammersmith
Highams Park
Holland Park
Kensal Green
Kentish Town
Leytonstone
Lincoln's Inn
Little Italy
Ludgate Hill
Muswell Hill
Notting Hill
Pentonville
Regent's Park
Rotherhithe
Snaresbrook
St John's Wood
Surrey Quays
Tufnell Park

Walthamstow
Westminster
Whitechapel

12 Bethnal Green
Billingsgate
Bromley-by-Bow
Charing Cross
City of London
Colliers Wood
Covent Garden
Crossharbour
Epping Forest
Finsbury Park
Golders Green
Hatton Garden
Havering Park
London Bridge
London Fields
Palmers Green
Parsons Green
Pool of London
Primrose Hill
Seven Sisters
Sloane Square
Stamford Hill
Swiss Cottage

13 Ardleigh Green
Chadwell Heath
Crystal Palace
Harmondsworth
Knightsbridge
Ladbroke Grove
Lancaster Gate
North Woolwich
Petticoat Lane
Shepherd's Bush
Thornton Heath
Tottenham Hale
Wanstead Flats
Winchmore Hill

14 Angel Islington
Becontree Heath
Hackney Marshes
Stoke Newington
Tottenham Green
Wormwood Scrubs

15 Alexandra Palace
Leicester Square
Westbourne Green

London streets include:

06 Strand

07 Aldgate
Aldwych
The Mall

Westway

08 Kingsway
Long Acre
Millbank

Minories
Pall Mall
Park Lane
York Road

09 Bow Street
Cheapside
Drury Lane
Haymarket
King's Road
Maida Vale
Queensway
Tower Hill
Whitehall

10 Bond Street
Dean Street
Eaton Place
Euston Road
Fetter Lane
Fulham Road
London Wall
Onslow Road
Piccadilly
Queen's Gate
Soho Square
Vine Street

11 Baker Street
Eaton Square
Edgware Road
Fleet Street
Goswell Road
Gower Street
High Holborn
Lambeth Road
Leather Lane
Ludgate Hill
Old Kent Road
Pimlico Road

Savoy Street
Warwick Road

12 Albany Street
Belgrave Road
Birdcage Walk
Brompton Road
Cannon Street
Chancery Lane
Cromwell Road
Gray's Inn Road
Hatton Garden
Jermyn Street
Oxford Street
Regent Street
Sloane Square
Sloane Street
Tooley Street

13 Bayswater Road
Bedford Square
Berwick Street
Carnaby Street
Downing Street
Garrick Street
Gerrard Street
Grosvenor Road
Knightsbridge
Lombard Street
Ludgate Circus
New Bond Street
New Fetter Lane
Newgate Street
Old Bond Street
Petticoat Lane

Portland Place
Portman Square
Russell Square
Wardour Street

14 Belgrave Square
Berkeley Square
Coventry Street
Earl's Court Road
Earnshaw Street
Exhibition Road
Gloucester Road
Holborn Viaduct
Horseferry Road
Hyde Park Square
Kensington Road
Marylebone Road
Mayfair Gardens
Portobello Road
Stamford Street

15 Albemarle Street
Blackfriars Road
Clerkenwell Road
Grosvenor Square
Horse Guards Road
Leicester Square
Liverpool Street
New Bridge Street
Pentonville Road
Southwark Street
St John's Wood Road
Trafalgar Square
Whitechapel Road

London landmarks include:

03 ICA
Kew

04 City
Eros
Oval
Soho

05 Lord's
V and A

06 Big Ben
Lloyds
Temple
Thames

07 Harrods
Mayfair
St Paul's
The City
The Mall

08 Bow bells
Cenotaph

Gray's Inn
Hyde Park
Liberty's
Monument
St Bride's

09 Chinatown
Cutty Sark
George Inn
Green Park
Guildhall
London Eye
London Zoo
Old Bailey
Rotten Row
Royal Mews
South Bank
Staple Inn
The Temple
Trocadero

10 Albert Hall

Camden Lock
Cock Tavern
Earl's Court
HMS Belfast
Jewel Tower
Kew Gardens
Marble Arch
Selfridge's
Serpentine
Tate Modern
the Gherkin

11 Apsley House
Canary Wharf
Golden Hinde
Lincoln's Inn
OXO building
Queen's House
Regent's Park
River Thames
St John's Gate

St Margaret's
St Mary-Le-Bow
Tate Britain
Tower Bridge

12 Charterhouse
Covent Garden
Design Museum
Dickens House
Guards Museum
Hatton Garden
Hay's Galleria
London Bridge
Mansion House
Spencer House
statue of Eros
St James's Park
Telecom Tower
Temple Church
Traitors' Gate

13 Admiralty Arch
Bank of England

British Museum
Carnaby Street
Clarence House
Gabriel's Wharf
Geffrye Museum
Greenwich Park
Lambeth Palace
London Dungeon
Nelson's Column
Petticoat Lane
Queen's Gallery
Royal Exchange
Science Museum
Somerset House
Tower of London
Wesley's Chapel

14 Albert Memorial
Barbican Centre
British Library
Hayward Gallery
Hermitage Rooms
Lancaster House

London Aquarium
Madame Tussaud's
Millennium Dome
Museum of London
Portobello Road
Speakers' Corner
St Clement Danes
St James's Palace
Waterloo Bridge
Wellington Arch

15 Bankside Gallery
Banqueting House
Brompton Oratory
Burlington House
Cabinet War Rooms
Dr Johnson's House
National Gallery
Royal Albert Hall
Royal Opera House
Temple of Mithras
Trafalgar Square
Westminster Hall

London Underground lines:

06 Circle (yellow)

07 Central (red)
Jubilee (grey)

08 Bakerloo (brown)
District (green)
Northern (black)
Victoria (sky blue)

10 East London (orange)
Piccadilly (navy blue)

12 Metropolitan (maroon)

15 Waterloo and City (jade green)

18 Hammersmith and City (pink)

21 Docklands Light Railway (sea green and white)

London Underground stations:

04 Bank (Central/Docklands Light Railway/ Northern/Waterloo and City)
Oval (Northern)

05 Angel (Northern)

06 Balham (Northern)
Cyprus (Docklands Light Railway)
Epping (Central)
Euston (Northern/Victoria)
Leyton (Central)
Morden (Northern)
Pinner (Metropolitan)
Poplar (Docklands Light Railway)
Temple (Circle/District)

07 Aldgate (Circle/Metropolitan)
Archway (Northern)
Arsenal (Piccadilly)
Barking (District/Hammersmith and City)
Beckton (Docklands Light Railway)
Borough (Northern)
Bow Road (District/Hammersmith and City)

Brixton (Victoria)
Chesham (Metropolitan)
East Ham (District/Hammersmith and City)
Edgware (Northern)
Holborn (Central/Piccadilly)
Kilburn (Jubilee)
Mile End (Hammersmith and City/Central/ District)
Neasden (Jubilee)
Pimlico (Victoria)
Ruislip (Piccadilly/Metropolitan)
St Paul's (Central)
Wapping (East London)
Watford (Metropolitan)
West Ham (Hammersmith and City/District/ Jubilee)

08 Amersham (Metropolitan)
Barbican (Circle/Hammersmith and City/ Metropolitan)
Chigwell (Central)
Hainault (Central)

Heathrow (Piccadilly)
Highgate (Northern)
Lewisham (Docklands Light Railway)
Monument (Circle/District)
Moorgate (Northern/Circle/Metropolitan/
  Hammersmith and City)
Mudchute (Docklands Light Railway)
New Cross (East London)
Northolt (Central)
Perivale (Central)
Plaistow (Hammersmith and City/District)
Richmond (District)
Royal Oak (Hammersmith and City)
Shadwell (East London/Docklands Light
  Railway)
Stanmore (Jubilee)
Uxbridge (Piccadilly/Metropolitan)
Vauxhall (Victoria)
Victoria (Victoria/Circle/District)
Wanstead (Central)
Waterloo (Waterloo and City/Bakerloo/
  Northern/Jubilee)

09 Acton Town (District/Piccadilly)
All Saints (Docklands Light Railway)
Bayswater (Circle/District)
Blackwall (Docklands Light Railway)
Bow Church (Docklands Light Railway)
Chalk Farm (Northern)
Cutty Sark (Docklands Light Railway)
East Acton (Central)
East India (Docklands Light Railway)
Greenford (Central)
Green Park (Jubilee/Piccadilly/Victoria)
Greenwich (Docklands Light Railway)
Hampstead (Northern)
Harlesden (Bakerloo)
Kingsbury (Jubilee)
Limehouse (Docklands Light Railway)
Maida Vale (Bakerloo)
Old Street (Northern)
Park Royal (Piccadilly)
Queensway (Central)
South Quay (Docklands Light Railway)
Southwark (Jubilee)
Stockwell (Victoria/Northern)
Stratford (Jubilee/Central/Docklands Light
  Railway)
Tower Hill (Circle/District)
Upton Park (District/Hammersmith and City)
West Acton (Central)
Westferry (Docklands Light Railway)
White City (Central)
Wimbledon (District)
Wood Green (Piccadilly)

10 Bermondsey (Jubilee)
Bond Street (Central/Jubilee)
Brent Cross (Northern)

Camden Town (Northern)
Canons Park (Jubilee)
Devons Road (Docklands Light Railway)
Dollis Hill (Jubilee)
Earl's Court (District/Piccadilly)
East Putney (District)
Embankment (Bakerloo/Circle/District/
  Northern)
Farringdon (Circle/Metropolitan/
  Hammersmith and City)
Grange Hill (Central)
Hanger Lane (Central)
Heron Quays (Docklands Light Railway)
Hillingdon (Metropolitan/Piccadilly)
Hornchurch (District)
Kennington (Northern)
Kew Gardens (District)
Manor House (Piccadilly)
Marble Arch (Central)
Marylebone (Bakerloo)
North Acton (Central)
Paddington (Circle/District/Hammersmith
  and City/Bakerloo)
Queensbury (Jubilee)
Queen's Park (Bakerloo)
Shoreditch (East London)
Tooting Bec (Northern)

11 Aldgate East (District/Hammersmith and
  City)
Baker Street (Bakerloo/Circle/Hammersmith
  and City/Jubilee/Metropolitan)
Barons Court (District/Piccadilly)
Beckton Park (Docklands Light Railway)
Belsize Park (Northern)
Blackfriars (Circle/District)
Bounds Green (Piccadilly)
Canada Water (East London/Jubilee)
Canary Wharf (Docklands Light Railway/
  Jubilee)
Canning Town (Docklands Light Railway/
  Jubilee)
Chorleywood (Metropolitan)
Cockfosters (Piccadilly)
Custom House (Docklands Light Railway)
Edgware Road (Bakerloo/Circle/District/
  Hammersmith and City)
Gunnersbury (District)
Hammersmith (District/Hammersmith and
  City/Piccadilly)
Holland Park (Central)
Kensal Green (Bakerloo)
Kentish Town (Northern)
Kilburn Park (Bakerloo)
Latimer Road (Hammersmith and City)
Leytonstone (Central)
North Ealing (Piccadilly)
Northfields (Piccadilly)
Regent's Park (Bakerloo)

Rotherhithe (East London)
Royal Albert (Docklands Light Railway)
South Ealing (Piccadilly)
Southfields (District)
St John's Wood (Jubilee)
Surrey Quays (East London)
Tufnell Park (Northern)
Wembley Park (Jubilee/Metropolitan)
Westminster (Jubilee/Circle/District)
Whitechapel (East London/Hammersmith and City/District)

12 Bethnal Green (Circle)
Bromley-by-Bow (District/Hammersmith and City)
Cannon Street (Circle/District)
Chancery Lane (Central)
Charing Cross (Bakerloo/Northern)
Chiswick Park (District)
Clapham North (Northern)
Clapham South (Northern)
Colliers Wood (Northern)
Covent Garden (Piccadilly)
Dagenham East (District)
Ealing Common (District/Piccadilly)
East Finchley (Northern)
Elverson Road (Docklands Light Railway)
Euston Square (Circle/Hammersmith and City/Metropolitan)
Finchley Road (Jubilee/Metropolitan)
Finsbury Park (Piccadilly/Victoria)
Golders Green (Northern)
Goldhawk Road (Hammersmith and City)
Goodge Street (Northern)
Holloway Road (Piccadilly)
Lambeth North (Bakerloo)
London Bridge (Northern/Jubilee)
Mansion House (Circle/District)
New Cross Gate (East London)
Oxford Circus (Victoria/Bakerloo/Central)
Parsons Green (District)
Prince Regent (Docklands Light Railway)
Putney Bridge (District)
Seven Sisters (Victoria)
Sloane Square (Circle/District)
Stepney Green (Hammersmith and City/District)
St James's Park (Circle/District)
Swiss Cottage (Jubilee)
Tower Gateway (Docklands Light Railway)
Turnham Green (Piccadilly/District)
Turnpike Lane (Piccadilly)
Warren Street (Northern/Victoria)
West Brompton (District)

13 Clapham Common (Northern)
Gallions Reach (Docklands Light Railway)
Hendon Central (Northern)

Island Gardens (Docklands Light Railway)
Knightsbridge (Piccadilly)
Ladbroke Grove (Hammersmith and City)
Lancaster Gate (Central)
Rickmansworth (Metropolitan)
Royal Victoria (Docklands Light Railway)
Russell Square (Piccadilly)
Shepherd's Bush (Central/Hammersmith and City)
Stamford Brook (District)
Tottenham Hale (Victoria)
Warwick Avenue (Bakerloo)
West Hampstead (Jubilee)
West India Quay (Docklands Light Railway)
Wimbledon Park (District)

14 Blackhorse Road (Victoria)
Caledonian Road (Piccadilly)
Deptford Bridge (Docklands Light Railway)
Ealing Broadway (Central/District)
Fulham Broadway (District)
Gloucester Road (Circle/District/Piccadilly)
Hyde Park Corner (Piccadilly)
North Greenwich (Jubilee)
South Wimbledon (Northern)
Westbourne Park (Hammersmith and City)
West Kensington (District)
Willesden Green (Jubilee)

15 Finchley Central (Northern)
Harrow-on-the-Hill (Metropolitan)
Hounslow Central (Piccadilly)
Leicester Square (Piccadilly/Northern)
Liverpool Street (Central/Hammersmith and City/Circle/Metropolitan)
Notting Hill Gate (Circle/Central/District)
Pudding Mill Lane (Docklands Light Railway)
Ravenscourt Park (District)
South Kensington (Piccadilly/Circle/District)
Stonebridge Park (Bakerloo)
Tooting Broadway (Northern)

16 Piccadilly Circus (Piccadilly/Bakerloo)

17 Elephant and Castle (Bakerloo/Northern)
Kensington Olympia (District)
Willesden Junction (Bakerloo)

18 Chalfont and Latimer (Metropolitan)
Mornington Crescent (Northern)
Tottenham Court Road (Northern/Central)
Walthamstow Central (Victoria)

19 Great Portland Street (Circle/Hammersmith and City/Metropolitan)
King's Cross St Pancras (Circle/Hammersmith and City/Metropolitan/Northern/Piccadilly/Victoria)

20 Highbury and Islington (Victoria)
High Street Kensington (Circle/District)

See also **bridge; museum; palace**

lough *see* **lake**

lover

Lovers include:

04 Juan (Don; *Don Juan*, 1819–24, Lord Byron)

08 Casanova (Giacomo Girolamo; 1725–98, Italian)

Lothario (*The Fair Penitent*, 1703, Nicholas Rowe)

09 Valentino (Rudolph; 1895–1926, Italian/US)

Pairs of lovers include:

11 Rick and Ilsa (*Casablanca*, 1942)
Zeus and Hera (Greek mythology)

12 Darby and Joan (possibly from an 18c song)
Porgy and Bess (*Porgy*, 1925, DuBose Heyward)

13 Dido and Aeneas (Greek mythology)
Harry and Sally (*When Harry met Sally*, 1989)
Paris and Helen (Greek mythology)
Psyche and Eros (Greek mythology)

14 Bonnie and Clyde (Clyde Barrow; 1909–34, US/Bonnie Parker; 1911–34, US)
Hero and Leander (Greek mythology)
Romeo and Juliet (*Romeo and Juliet*, 1591–96, William Shakespeare)

16 Dante and Beatrice (Dante Alighieri; 1265–1321, Italian/Beatrice Portinari; c.1265–90, Italian)
Petrarch and Laura (Francesco Petrarca; 1304–74, Italian/possibly Laure de Noves, d.1348, Italian)
Pyramus and Thisbe (Greek mythology)
Rhiannon and Pwyll (Celtic mythology)
Samson and Delilah (Bible: Judges 16)
Tristan and Isolde (Celtic mythology)

17 Abelard and Héloïse (Peter Abelard; 1079–1142, French/Héloïse; c.1098–1164, French)

18 Antony and Cleopatra (Mark Antony; c.83–30 BC, Roman/Cleopatra; 69–30 BC, Egyptian)
Caesar and Cleopatra (Julius Caesar; 100 or 102–44 BC, Roman/Cleopatra; 69–30 BC, Egyptian)
Cathy and Heathcliff (*Wuthering Heights*, 1848, Emily Brontë)
Orpheus and Eurydice (Greek mythology)
Rosalind and Orlando (*As You Like It*, c.1600, William Shakespeare)
Troilus and Cressida (Greek mythology/medieval fiction)

19 Beatrice and Benedick (*Much Ado About Nothing*, 1598/1600, William Shakespeare)

Chopin and George Sand (Frédéric Chopin; 1810–49, Polish/George Sand; 1804–76, French)
Odysseus and Penelope (Greek mythology)

20 Charles II and Nell Gwyn (Charles II; 1630–85, English/Nell Gwyn; c.1650–1687, English)
Napoleon and Joséphine (Napoleon I; 1769–1821, French/Joséphine de Beauharnais; 1763–1814, French)

22 Adolf Hitler and Eva Braun (Adolf Hitler; 1889–1945; German/Eva Braun; 1912–45, German)
Jane Eyre and Mr Rochester (*Jane Eyre*, 1847, Charlotte Brontë)
Robin Hood and Maid Marian (English legend)

23 Edward VIII and Mrs Simpson (Edward VIII; 1894–1972, English/Wallis Simpson, Duchess of Windsor; 1896–1986, US)
Sir Lancelot and Guinevere (Arthurian legend)

24 Lady Chatterley and Mellors (*Lady Chatterley's Lover*, 1928, D H Lawrence)

25 Sid Vicious and Nancy Spungen (Sid Vicious; 1957–79, English/Nancy Spungen; 1958–78, US)

26 Elizabeth Bennett and Mr Darcy (*Pride and Prejudice*, 1813, Jane Austen)
Launcelot du Lac and Guinevere (Arthurian legend)

27 Anna Karenina and Count Vronsky (*Anna Karenina*, 1874–76, Leo Tolstoy)
Louis XV and Madame de Pompadour (Louis XV; 1710–74 , French/Madame de Pompadour; 1721–64, French)
Rhett Butler and Scarlett O'Hara (*Gone With the Wind*, 1939)

28 Arthur Rimbaud and Paul Verlaine (Arthur Rimbaud; 1854–91, French/Paul Verlaine; 1844–96, French)
Lord Byron and Lady Caroline Lamb (Lord

Byron; 1788–1824, English/Lady Caroline Lamb; 1795–1828, English)

29 Humphrey Bogart and Lauren Bacall (Humphrey Bogart; 1899–1957, US/Lauren Bacall; 1924– , US)
Lord Nelson and Lady Emma Hamilton (Lord Horatio Nelson; 1758–1805, English/Lady Emma Hamilton; c.1761–1815, English)

31 Katharine Hepburn and Spencer Tracy (Katharine Hepburn; 1907–2003, US/Spencer Tracy; 1900–67, US)
Richard Burton and Elizabeth Taylor (Richard Burton; 1925–84, Welsh/Dame Elizabeth Taylor; 1932– , English/US)

33 Elizabeth Barrett and Robert Browning (Elizabeth Barrett; 1806–61, English/Robert Browning; 1812–89, English)

Low Countries

Cities and notable towns in the Low Countries include:

05 Breda (The Netherlands)
Delft (The Netherlands)
Ghent (Belgium)
Liège (Belgium)
Namur (Belgium)

06 Arnhem (The Netherlands)
Bruges (Belgium)
Leiden (The Netherlands)

07 Antwerp (Belgium)
Haarlem (The Netherlands)
Tilburg (The Netherlands)

Utrecht (The Netherlands)

08 Brussels (Belgium)
The Hague (The Netherlands)

09 Amsterdam (The Netherlands)
Charleroi (Belgium)
Eindhoven (The Netherlands)
Groningen (The Netherlands)
Rotterdam (The Netherlands)

10 Luxembourg (Luxembourg)
Maastricht (The Netherlands)

luggage

Luggage includes:

03 bag
box
04 case
grip
05 chest
trunk
06 basket

hamper
kitbag
valise
07 holdall
satchel
08 backpack
knapsack

rucksack
suitcase
09 briefcase
flight bag
haversack
portfolio
travel bag

10 vanity case
11 attaché case
hand-luggage
portmanteau
12 Gladstone bag
overnight bag

lunar sea *see* **moon**

Luxembourg *see* **Low Countries**

lyricist *see* **libretto**

M

Macedonia *see* **Balkans**

machinery

Machinery includes:

03 Cat®
 JCB®
05 crane
 dozer
06 digger
 dumper
 grader
 jigger
07 dredger
 grapple
 gritter
 skidder
 tractor
08 dragline
 dustcart
 jib crane

09 bulldozer
 calfdozer
 dump truck
 excavator
10 angledozer
 earthmover
 pile-driver
 road roller
 snowplough
 tower crane
 tracklayer
 truck crane
 water crane
11 Caterpillar®
 dumper truck
 gantry crane
 road-sweeper

 wheel loader
12 cherry picker
 crawler crane
 luffing crane
 pick-up loader
13 concrete mixer
 floating crane
 fork-lift truck
 grabbing crane
 platform hoist
14 container crane
 crawler tractor
 tractor-scraper
15 hydraulic shovel
 luffing-jib crane
 walking dragline

See also **agriculture**

magazine *see* **newspaper**

magnate *see* **business; newspaper**

Mahler, Gustav (1860–1911)

Significant works include:

05 'Titan' (Symphony; 1885–88)
06 'Tragic' (Symphony; 1903–05)
12 'Resurrection' (Symphony; 1888–94)
15 *Das klagende Lied* (1880)
16 *Five Rückert Songs* (1905)
 Songs of a Wayfarer (1884–85)
 The Boy's Magic Horn (1888–99)
17 *Das Lied von der Erde* (1907–09)

 Kindertotenlieder (1901–04)
 The Song of the Earth (1907–09)
19 *Des Knaben Wunderhorn* (1888–99)
21 *Funf Lieder nach Rückert* (1905)
26 *Songs on the Deaths of Children* (1901–04)
28 *Lieder eines fahrenden Gesellen* (1884–85)
31 *Drei Lieder for tenor and pianoforte* (1880)

Major League *see* **baseball**

maker

People who make things include:

05 baker (bread)
roper (rope)
tawer (white leather)
tiler (tiles)
tyler (tiles)

06 bowyer (bows for archery)
coiner (coins)
cutler (cutlery)
fencer (fences)
framer (picture frames)
glover (gloves)
hatter (hats)
hosier (hosiery)
joiner (wooden components for buildings)
nailer (nails)
pinner (pins)
potter (pottery)
roofer (roofs)
tailor (clothes)

07 clogger (clogs)
dialist (dials)
girdler (girdles)
hurdler (hurdles)
lorimer (metal parts of a horse-harness)
loriner (metal parts of a horse-harness)
luthier (lutes, guitars, stringed instruments)
saddler (saddles)
wheeler (wheels)

08 armourer (arms and armour)
ceramist (ceramics)
chandler (candles)
clothier (clothes)
costumer (costumes)
fletcher (arrows)
glassman (glass)
gunsmith (guns)
jeweller (jewellery)
medalist (medals)
milliner (headgear)
optician (spectacles)
perfumer (perfumes)
spurrier (spurs)
wig-maker (wigs)

09 carpenter (wooden objects)
casemaker (book covers)

corsetier (corsets)
costumier (costumes)
horologer (clocks)
jacksmith (roasting jacks)
locksmith (locks)
medallist (medals)
outfitter (outfits)
pottinger (pottage)
robe maker (official robes)
shoemaker (shoes)
staymaker (corsets)
toolmaker (tools)
whittawer (saddles, harnesses, white leather)

10 blacksmith (iron objects)
butter-wife (butter)
cartwright (carts)
ceramicist (ceramics)
corsetière (corsets)
dressmaker (clothes)
file-cutter (metal files)
frame-maker (picture frames)
habit-maker (riding habits)
horseshoer (horseshoes)
mixologist (cocktails)
pastrycook (pastry)
perruquier (wigs)
shipwright (ships)
stockinger (stockings)
trunk maker (travelling trunks)
unguentary (unguents)
wainwright (wagons)
watchmaker (watches)
woodcutter (woodcuts)

11 butter-woman (butter)
chocolatier (chocolate sweets)
glass-blower (glassware)
mechanician (machines)
vitraillist (glass, stained glass)
wagonwright (wagons)
wax-chandler (wax candles)
wheelwright (wheels, wheeled carriages)

12 cabinet-maker (furniture)
confectioner (confectionery)
ploughwright (ploughs)
wood engraver (wood engravings)

See also **art**; **chef**; **footwear**; **furniture**; **motoring**; **occupation**; **pottery**; **sculpture**

male animal *see* animal

mammal

Mammals include:

03 ape
ass
bat
cat
cow
dog
elk
fox
gnu
pig
rat
yak

04 bear
boar
cavy
deer
goat
hare
ibex
kudu
lion
lynx
mink
mole
paca
puma
seal
soor
tahr
vole
wolf
zebu

05 aguti
bison
camel
civet
coney
coypu
dingo
eland
genet
horse
human
hyena
hyrax
koala
lemur
llama
loris
moose
mouse
okapi
otter
ounce

panda
potto
rhino
sheep
shrew
skunk
sloth
stoat
takin
tapir
tiger
whale
zebra

06 aye-aye
baboon
badger
beaver
beluga
bobcat
cattle
colugo
cougar
coyote
cuscus
dassie
dugong
duiker
ermine
ferret
galago
gerbil
gibbon
gopher
hacker
impala
jackal
jaguar
jerboa
langur
marmot
marten
monkey
numbat
ocelot
possum
rabbit
racoon
rhebok
sea cow
serval
tenrec
vicuña
walrus
wapiti

weasel
wombat

07 ant-bear
bosvark
buffalo
caracal
caribou
chamois
cheetah
dolphin
echidna
fur seal
gazelle
gerenuk
giraffe
gorilla
grampus
grizzly
guanaco
guereza
gymnura
hamster
lemming
leopard
macaque
manatee
meercat
meerkat
mole rat
muntjac
muskrat
narwhal
opossum
pack rat
panther
peccary
polecat
primate
raccoon
red deer
roe deer
sea lion
sun bear
tamarin
tarsier
wallaby
warthog
wild ass
wildcat

08 aardvark
aardwolf
anteater
antelope
bushbaby

bushbuck
capybara
chipmunk
dormouse
duckbill
elephant
fruit bat
grey wolf
harp seal
hedgehog
house bat
kangaroo
mandrill
mangabey
marmoset
mongoose
musk deer
oppossum
pacarana
pangolin
platypus
porpoise
reedbuck
reindeer
sea otter
sewer rat
squirrel
steenbok
steinbok
talapoin
wild goat

09 Arctic fox
armadillo
bamboo rat
bandicoot

black bear
blue sheep
blue whale
brown bear
dromedary
flying fox
grey whale
grindhval
guinea pig
jungle cat
mouse-deer
orang-utan
palm civet
phalanger
polar bear
porcupine
springbok
steinbuck
waterbuck
wolverine

10 Barbary ape
chevrotain
chimpanzee
chinchilla
coatimundi
common seal
fallow deer
field mouse
giant panda
hartebeest
house mouse
human being
jack rabbit
kodiak bear
pilot whale

pine marten
prairie dog
rhinoceros
sperm whale
springbuck
springhare
vampire bat
white whale
wildebeest

11 beaked whale
flying lemur
green monkey
grizzly bear
honey badger
killer whale
muntjac deer
pipistrelle
rat kangaroo
red squirrel
snow leopard

12 Arabian camel
barbary sheep
elephant seal
grey squirrel
harvest mouse
hippopotamus
leaf-nosed bat
mountain goat
mountain lion
rhesus monkey
river dolphin
spider monkey
two-toed sloth
vervet monkey
water buffalo

13 American bison
Bactrian camel
colobus monkey
dwarf antelope
elephant shrew
European bison
hanuman monkey
howling monkey
humpback whale
marsupial mole
mouse-eared bat
spiny anteater
Tasmanian wolf
thylacine wolf

14 capuchin monkey
edible dormouse
flying squirrel
Indian elephant
marsupial mouse
mountain beaver
Patagonian hare
squirrel monkey
Tasmanian devil
three-toed sloth

15 African elephant
black rhinoceros
brushtail possum
hamadryas baboon
humpbacked
  whale
proboscis monkey
ring-tailed lemur
Thomson's gazelle
white rhinoceros

See also **ape**; **bat**; **bear**; **carnivore**; **cat**; **cattle**; **deer**; **dog**; **horse**; **marsupial**; **monkey**; **pig**; **primate**; **rabbit**; **rodent**; **seal**; **sheep**; **whale**

mania

Manias include:

08 egomania (oneself)

09 cynomania (dogs)
demomania (crowds)
ergomania (work)
infomania (gathering information)
logomania (talking)
melomania (music)
monomania (single thought, idea or activity)
oenomania (alcohol)
opsomania (special kind of food)
pyromania (fire-raising)
theomania (God, religion)
tomomania (surgery)
xenomania (foreign things)

10 anthomania (flowers)

dipsomania (alcohol)
erotomania (sexual passion)
hippomania (horses)
hydromania (water)
methomania (alcohol)
metromania (writing verse)
mythomania (lying or exaggerating)
narcomania (drugs)
necromania (dead bodies)
nostomania (returning to familiar places)

11 ablutomania (personal cleanliness)
acronymania (forming acronyms)
ailuromania (cats)
bibliomania (books)
cleptomania (stealing)

demonomania (being possessed by devils)
etheromania (taking ether)
graphomania (writing)
hedonomania (pleasure)
kleptomania (stealing)
megalomania (power)
nymphomania (sexual desire)
technomania (technology)
toxicomania (poison)
tulipomania (tulip-growing)

12 arithmomania (numbers)
balletomania (ballet)
orchidomania (orchids)
potichomania (imitating Oriental porcelain)
pteridomania (ferns)
thanatomania (death)
theatromania (play-going)

13 flagellomania (beating and flogging)
morphinomania (morphine)

14 eleutheromania (freedom)

Maori

Maori leaders include:

05 Ngata (Sir Apirana Turupa; 1874–1950)

06 Cooper (Dame Whina; 1895–1994)
Mahuta (Sir Robert; 1897–1947)
O'Regan (Sir Tipene; 1939–)
Pomare (Sir Maui; 1876–1930)
Ratana (Tuhupotiki Wiremu; 1873–1939)

07 Te Kooti (Arikirangi Te Turuki; date
unknown–1893)

09 Heke Potai (Hone Wiremu; date
unknown–1850)
Hongi Hika (1772–1828)
Rua Kenana (Hepetipa; 1869–1937)

11 Te Rauparaha (date unknown–1849)

14 Te Heuheu Tukino (Sir Hepi; 1919–97)

See also **mythology**

marine biologist *see* biology

marketing

Terms used in marketing include:

03 ASA
B2B
CRM
CSI
dog
PLC
USP

04 AIDA
MVCs
star

05 ACORN
BOGOF
churn
FMCGs
R and D
viral

06 BOGOFF
DAGMAR
four p's
jingle
launch
mock-up
sell-in
slogan
upsell

07 adopter

canvass
cash cow
generic
gimmick
hit rate

08 call rate
campaign
cold call
coverage
footfall
free gift
giveaway
goody bag
hard sell
mailshot
own-brand
own-label
sales aid
up-market
wildcats

09 flash pack
frequency
heavy user

10 brand image
commercial
cover mount

data mining
direct mail
door-to-door
face-to-face
free sample
Gallup poll
Giffen good
halo effect
loss-leader
media buyer
normal good
sales drive
visualizer

11 aided recall
best of breed
cannibalism
dealer brand
demarketing
demographic
family brand
gap analysis
late adopter
loyalty card
market share
observation
point-of-sale
recognition

retail audit
sell-through
three-for-two
word of mouth
12 area sampling
brand loyalty
buyers' market
early adopter
field selling
house-to-house
key prospects
market demand
marketing mix
market leader
media planner
Nielsen index
party selling
response rate
solus mailing
static market
SWOT analysis
target market
13 buying motives
captive market
consumer panel
corner a market

impulse buying
island display
market profile
matched sample
merchandizing
necessity good
perceptual map
rolling launch
sales campaign
solus position
tachistoscope
test marketing
unaided recall
14 brand awareness
concept testing
corporate image
credibility gap
email marketing
filter question
inertia selling
lead generation
macro marketing
marketing audit
marketing board
market research
micro marketing

opinion leaders
prompted recall
pyramid selling
random sampling
reference group
target audience
viral marketing
15 blanket coverage
brand management
captive audience
cluster sampling
core positioning
customer profile
diversification
family life cycle
group discussion
journey planning
leading question
market potential
personal selling
problem children
public relations
saturation point
skimming pricing
social marketing
supply and demand

marriage

Terms to do with marriage and weddings include:

03 dot
vow
wed
04 ring
veil
wife
05 aisle
altar
banns
bride
dowry
elope
groom
in-law
jugal
piper
tiara
toast
usher
vicar
06 affair
affine
beenah
bigamy
digamy
favour
fiancé

garter
genial
huppah
pre-nup
priest
speech
spouse
the Mrs
07 best man
betroth
bouquet
chuppah
consort
divorce
espouse
exogamy
fiancée
flowers
husband
Ketubah
kirking
marital
merchet
Mr Right
nuptial
page boy
propose

punalua
trigamy
wedding
08 affiance
bedright
best maid
confetti
conjugal
endogamy
hen night
jointure
levirate
maritage
minister
monogamy
monogyny
polygamy
shidduch
09 annulment
best woman
coemption
common-law
communion
connubial
honeymoon
hope chest
horseshoe

hypergamy
love match
matrimony
other half
reception
registrar
stag night
threshold
trousseau

10 bridesmaid
buttonhole
consortium
consummate
engagement
first dance
first night
flower girl
her indoors
him indoors
honeymonth
intermarry
invitation
Lucy Stoner
maiden name
matrilocal

morganatic
patrilocal
separation
settlement
unfaithful
uxorilocal
wedding day

11 deuterogamy
dissolution
Gretna Green
handfasting
misalliance
morning gift
mother in-law
outmarriage
wedding cake
wedding list

12 bottom drawer
bridal shower
concubitancy
give one's hand
mariage blanc
open marriage
photographer

prothalamion
something new
something old
wedding dress
wedding march
wedding night

13 church service
civil marriage
fortune-hunter
hedge-marriage
holy matrimony
marriage-lines
seven-year itch
something blue
the better half

14 matron of honour
pop the question
special licence
steal a marriage

15 chief bridesmaid
decree of nullity
going-away outfit
marriage-licence
plight one's troth

See also **anniversary**

marshal

Marshals include:

03 Ney (Michel; 1769–1815, French)
04 Earp (Wyatt; 1848–1929, US)
Foch (Ferdinand; 1851–1929, French)
Saxe (Maurice, Comte de; 1696–1750, French)
Tito (Josip Broz; 1892–1980, Yugoslavian)

06 Hickok (Wild Bill; 1837–76, US)
Pétain (Philippe; 1856–1951, French)
Tedder (Arthur, Lord; 1890–1967, Scottish)
Zhukov (Georgi; 1896–1974, Russian)
08 MacMahon (Patrice de; 1808–93, French)

marsupial

Marsupials include:

04 euro
tuan
05 koala
quoll
06 boodie
cuscus
glider
numbat
possum
quokka
tammar
wombat
07 bettong
dasyure
dibbler
dunnart

opossum
potoroo
wallaby
08 kangaroo
macropod
tarsiped
wallaroo
09 bandicoot
boodie-rat
koala bear
native cat
pademelon
petaurist
phalanger
wambenger
10 native bear

Notoryctes
11 diprotodont
honey possum
rat kangaroo
rock wallaby
12 marsupial rat
pouched mouse
tree kangaroo
13 brush kangaroo
marsupial mole
Tasmanian wolf
14 marsupial mouse
Tasmanian devil
vulpine opossum
15 flying phalanger

martial art

Martial arts and forms of self-defence include:

04 judo
05 Iai-do
sambo
wushu
06 aikido
See also **karate**

karate
kung fu
t'ai chi
07 capuera
ju-jitsu

08 capoeira
jiu-jitsu
ninjitsu
ninjutsu
Shotokan

09 tae kwon do
10 kick boxing
11 self-defence
t'ai chi ch'uan

massacre

Massacres include:

04 Hama (1982, Syria)
Lari (1953, Kenya)

05 Ambon (1623, Dutch East Indies)
Katyn (1940, Russia)
My Lai (1968, Vietnam)
Paris (1871, France)
Sabra (1982, Lebanon)

06 Bezier (1209, France)
Boston (1770, America)
Cataví (1941, Bolivia)
Herrin (1922, USA)
Kanpur (1857, India)
Lidice (1942, Czechoslovakia)
Rishon (1991, Israel)

07 Amboyna (1623, Dutch East Indies)
Babi Yar (1941, Ukraine)
Badajoz (1936, Spain)
Baghdad (1258, now Iraq)
Chatila (1982, Lebanon)
Glencoe (1695, Scotland)
Halabja (1988, Iraq)
Nanking (1937–38, China)
Tianjin (1870, China)

08 Amritsar (1919, India)
Cawnpore (1857, India)
Drogheda (1649, Ireland)
El Mozote (1981, El Salvador)

Kishinev (1903, now Moldova)
Novgorod (1570, Russia)
Peterloo (1819, England)
Tientsin (1870, China)

09 Fetterman (1866, USA)
Innocents (c.1 AD, Bethlehem)
Jerusalem (1099)
Sand Creek (1864, USA)
September (1792, France)
Trebizond (1915, Turkey)

10 Addis Ababa (1937, Ethiopia)
Fort Pillow (1864, USA)
Myall Creek (1838, Australia)
Paxton Boys (1763, America)
Sack of Rome (1527, Italy)
Srebrenica (1995, Bosnia)
Tlatelolco (1968, Mexico)

11 Janissaries (1826, Turkey)
Sharpeville (1960, South Africa)
Wounded Knee (1890, USA)

12 Bloody Sunday (1905, Russia)
Sabra/Chatila (1982, Lebanon)

15 Oradour-sur-Glane (1944, France)
Sicilian Vespers (1282, Italy)
St Valentine's Day (1929, Chicago, USA)
Tiananmen Square (1989, Beijing, China)

material *see* **art**; **building**; **fabric**

mathematics

Branches of mathematics include:

06 conics
07 algebra
applied
fluxion
08 calculus
geometry

09 set theory
10 arithmetic
game theory
statistics
11 games theory
group theory

12 number theory
trigonometry
13 combinatorics
14 biomathematics
15 metamathematics
pure mathematics

Mathematicians include:

03 Dee (John; 1527–1608, English)
Lie (Sophus; 1842–99, Norwegian)

04 Abel (Niels Henrik; 1802–29, Norwegian)
Hopf (Heinz; 1894–1971, German)
Kerr (Roy; 1934– , New Zealand)
Pell (John; 1610–85, English)
Tait (Peter Guthrie; 1831–1901, Scottish)
Thom (René; 1923–2002, French)
Venn (John; 1834–1923, English)
Weil (André; 1906–98, French)
Weyl (Hermann; 1885–1955, German)

05 Aiken (Howard; 1900–73, US)
Artin (Emil; 1898–1962, Austrian)
Bayes (Thomas; 1702–61, English)
Blaeu (Willem; 1571–1638, Dutch)
Boole (George; 1815–64, English)
Borda (Jean Charles de; 1733–99, French)
Borel (Émile; 1871–1956, French)
Cotes (Roger; 1682–1716, English)
Craig (John; d.1731, Scottish)
Dirac (Paul; 1902–84, English)
Euler (Leonhard; 1707–83, Swiss)
Frege (Gottlob; 1848–1925, German)
Gauss (Carl Friedrich; 1777–1855, German)
Gödel (Kurt; 1906–78, US)
Green (Ben; 1977– , English)
Green (George; 1793–1841, English)
Hardy (Godfrey; 1877–1947, English)
Hoyle (Sir Fred; 1915–2001, English)
Klein (Felix; 1849–1925, German)
Mises (Richard von; 1883–1953, Austrian/
US)
Monge (Gaspard; 1746–1818, French)
North (John Dudley; 1893–1968, English)
Peano (Giuseppe; 1858–1932, Italian)
Pratt (John Henry; 1809–71, English)
Riesz (Frigyes; 1880–1956, Hungarian)
Schur (Issai; 1875–1941, Russian)
Serre (Jean-Pierre; 1926– , French)
Smith (Henry; 1826–83, Irish)
Snell (Willebrod; 1580–1626, Dutch)
Sturm (Charles François; 1803–55, French)
Vieta (Franciscus; 1540–1603, French)
Wiles (Sir Andrew; 1953– , English)

06 Agnesi (Maria; 1718–99, Italian)
Ampère (André; 1775–1836, French)
Argand (Jean-Robert; 1768–1822, Swiss)
Atiyah (Sir Michael; 1929– , English)
Banach (Stefan; 1892–1945, Polish)
Barrow (Isaac; 1630–77, English)
Bessel (Friedrich; 1784–1846, German)
Besson (Jacques; c.1535–c.1575, French)
Bidder (George Parker; 1806–78, English)
Bolyai (János; 1802–60, Hungarian)
Briggs (Henry; 1561–1630, English)

Bullen (Keith; 1906–76, New Zealand)
Cantor (Georg; 1845–1918, Russian/German)
Cartan (Élie Joseph; 1869–1951, French)
Cauchy (Augustin Louis, Lord; 1789–1857,
French)
Cayley (Arthur; 1821–95, English)
Ceulen (Ludolph van; 1540–1610, Dutch)
Digges (Leonard; 1520–c.1559, English)
Euclid (fl.300 BC, Greek)
Feller (William; 1906–70, Croatian/US)
Fermat (Pierre de; 1601–65, French)
Ferrel (William; 1817–91, US)
Fields (J C; 1863–1932, Canadian)
Fisher (Sir Ronald; 1890–1962, English)
Froude (William; 1810–79, English)
Galois (Évariste; 1811–32, French)
Goedel (Kurt; 1906–78, US)
Gunter (Edmund; 1581–1626, English)
Hadley (John; 1682–1744, English)
Halley (Edmond; 1656–1742, English)
Hariot (Thomas; c.1560–1621, English)
Jacobi (Carl; 1804–51, German)
Jordan (Camille; 1838–1922, French)
Kelvin (William Thomson, Lord; 1824–1907,
Scottish)
Keulen (Ludolph van; 1540–1610, Dutch)
Kummer (Ernst; 1810–93, German)
La Hire (Philippe de; 1640–1718, French)
Lorenz (Edward; 1917–2008, US)
Markov (Andrei; 1856–1922, Russian)
McCrea (Sir William; 1904–99, Irish)
Milnor (John; 1931– , US)
Möbius (August Ferdinand; 1790–1868,
German)
Moivre (Abraham de; 1667–1754, French)
Napier (John; 1550–1617, Scottish)
Newton (Sir Isaac; 1642–1727, English)
Pascal (Blaise; 1623–62, French)
Peirce (Benjamin; 1809–80, US)
Peirce (Charles; 1839–1914, US)
Picard (Émile; 1856–1941, French)
Ramsey (Frank Plumpton; 1903–30, English)
Robins (Benjamin; 1707–51, English)
Stevin (Simon; 1548–1620, Flemish)
Stokes (Sir George; 1819–1903, Irish)
Tarski (Alfred; 1902–83, US)
Taylor (Brook; 1685–1731, English)
Taylor (Sir Geoffrey; 1886–1975, English)
Turing (Alan; 1912–54, English)
Wallis (John; 1616–1703, English)
Werner (Wendelin; 1968– , German/French)
Wiener (Norbert; 1894–1964, US)
Zeeman (Sir Christopher; 1925– , English)

07 Alhazen (c.965–c.1040, Arab)
Arnauld (Antoine; 1612–94, French)
Babbage (Charles; 1791–1871, English)

Bolzano (Bernard; 1781–1848, Czech)
Borelli (Giovanni; 1608–79, Italian)
Brouwer (Luitzen; 1881–1966, Dutch)
Byrgius (Justus; 1552–1633, Swiss)
Cardano (Girolamo; 1501–76, Italian)
Carroll (Lewis; 1832–98, English)
Charney (Jule; 1917–81, US)
Courant (Richard; 1888–1972, German/US)
Dickson (Leonard; 1874–1954, US)
Fourier (Joseph, Baron de; 1768–1830, French)
Galileo (1564–1642, Italian)
Gelfand (Izrail; 1913–2009, Russian)
Germain (Sophie; 1776–1831, French)
Gregory (James; 1638–75, Scottish)
Guarini (Guarino; 1624–83, Italian)
Harriot (Thomas; c.1560–1621, English)
Hartree (Douglas; 1897–1958, English)
Hermite (Charles; 1822–1901, French)
Hilbert (David; 1862–1943, German)
Khazini (al-; fl.c.1115–30, Arab)
Lambert (Johann; 1728–77, Swiss)
Laplace (Pierre, Marquis de; 1749–1827, French)
Leibniz (Gottfried; 1646–1716, German)
Noether (Emmy; 1882–1935, German)
Pearson (Karl; 1857–1936, English)
Penrose (Sir Roger; 1931– , English)
Plücker (Julius; 1801–68, German)
Poisson (Siméon; 1781–1840, French)
Purbach (Georg von; 1423–61, Austrian)
Recorde (Robert; c.1510–58, English)
Riemann (Bernhard; 1826–66, German)
Russell (Bertrand, Earl; 1872–1970, English)
Shannon (Claude; 1916–2001, US)
Stibitz (George; 1904–95, US)
Størmer (Carl; 1874–1957, Norwegian)
Waerden (Bartel van der; 1903–96, Dutch)
Whiston (William; 1667–1752, English)
Zermelo (Ernst; 1871–1953, German)

08 Alembert (Jean le Rond d'; 1717–83, French)
Banneker (Benjamin; 1731–1806, US)
Birkhoff (George David; 1884–1944, US)
Bjerknes (Vilhelm; 1862–1951, Norwegian)
Bourbaki (Nicolas; 1930s pseudonym of several French mathematicians)
Burnside (William; 1852–1927, English)
Clairaut (Alexis Claude; 1713–65, French)
Clifford (William; 1845–79, English)
Dedekind (Julius; 1831–1916, German)
De Morgan (Augustus; 1806–71, English)
Guldberg (Cato; 1836–1902, Norwegian)
Hadamard (Jacques; 1865–1963, French)
Hamilton (Sir William Rowan; 1805–65, Irish)
Jeffreys (Sir Harold; 1891–1989, English)
Khinchin (Aleksandr; 1894–1959, Soviet)
Lagrange (Joseph de, Comte; 1736–1813, French)

Lebesgue (Henri; 1875–1941, French)
Legendre (Adrien-Marie; 1752–1833, French)
Lovelace (Ada, Countess of; 1815–52, English)
Lyapunov (Aleksandr; 1857–1918, Russian)
Margulis (Gregori; 1946– , Russian)
Mercator (Nicolaus; c.1620–1687, German)
Mersenne (Marin; 1588–1648, French)
Okounkov (Andrei Yuryevich; 1969– , Russian)
Oughtred (William; 1575–1660, English)
Perelman (Grigori; 1966– , Russian)
Playfair (John; 1748–1819, Scottish)
Poincaré (Jules; 1854–1912, French)
Poncelet (Jean Victor; 1788–1867, French)
Rheticus (1514–74, German)
Stirling (James; 1692–1770, Scottish)
Subbotin (Mikhail Fyodorovich; 1893–1966, Russian)
Volterra (Vito; 1860–1940, Italian)

09 Bartholin (Erasmus; 1625–98, Danish)
Bartholin (Thomas, the Elder; 1616–80, Danish)
Bernoulli (Daniel; 1700–82, Swiss)
Bernoulli (Jacques; 1654–1705, Swiss)
Bernoulli (Jakob; 1654–1705, Swiss)
Bernoulli (Jean; 1667–1748, Swiss)
Bernoulli (Johann; 1667–1748, Swiss)
Boscovich (Roger Joseph; 1711–87, Croatian)
Bronowski (Jacob; 1908–74, Polish)
Brouncker (William Brouncker, 2nd Viscount; 1620–84, Irish)
Cavalieri (Bonaventura; 1598–1647, Italian)
Chebyshev (Pafnutii; 1821–94, Russian)
Condorcet (Marie Jean Antoine Nicolas de Caritat, Marquis de; 1743–94, French)
Desargues (Gérard; 1591–1661, French)
Descartes (René; 1596–1650, French)
Dieudonné (Jean; 1906–92, French)
Dirichlet (Lejeune; 1805–59, German)
Fibonacci (Leonardo; c.1170–c.1250, Italian)
Frobenius (Georg; 1849–1917, German)
Grassmann (Hermann; 1809–77, German)
Hausdorff (Felix; 1868–1942, German)
Khwarizmi (Muhammad ibn Musa al; c.800–c.850, Arab)
Kronecker (Leopold; 1823–91, German)
Lefschetz (Solomon; 1884–1972, Russian/US)
Liouville (Joseph; 1809–82, French)
Maclaurin (Colin; 1698–1746, Scottish)
MacLaurin (Richard Cockburn; 1870–1920, Scottish/New Zealand)
Minkowski (Hermann; 1864–1909, Russian/German)
Peuerbach (Georg von; 1423–61, Austrian)

Ramanujan (Srinivasa; 1887–1920, Indian)
Silvester (James; 1814–97, English)
Sylvester (James; 1814–97, English)
Tartaglia (Niccolò; c.1500–57, Italian)
Whitehead (Alfred; 1861–1947, English)
Wilkinson (James; 1919–86, English)

10 Archimedes (c.287–212 BC, Greek)
Chi-Shen Tao (Terence; 1975–   , Australian)
Diophantus (fl.3 C AD, Greek)
Hipparchos (c.180–125 BC, Greek)
Hipparchus (c.180–125 BC, Greek)
Kolmogorov (Andrei; 1903–87, Soviet)
Levi-Civita (Tullio; 1873–1941, Italian)
Littlewood (John; 1885–1977, English)
Maupertuis (Pierre Louis de; 1698–1759, French)
Menaechmus (fl.4 C BC, Greek)
Pontryagin (Lev Semyonovich; 1908–88, Russian)
Pythagoras (c.580–c.500 BC, Greek)
Sacrobosco (Johannes de; fl.mid-13 C, English)
Sierpinski (Wacław; 1882–1969, Polish)
Somerville (Mary; 1780–1872, Scottish)
Theaetetus (c.414–c.369 BC, Greek)
Torricelli (Evangelista; 1608–47, Italian)
Von Neumann (John; 1903–57, Hungarian/US)

Wedderburn (Joseph; 1882–1948, Scottish/US)
Zeno of Elea (c.490–c.420 BC, Greek)

11 Aleksandrov (Pavel; 1896–1982, Russian)
Kantorovich (Leonid; 1912–86, Soviet)
Lacondamine (Charles Marie de; 1701–74, French)
Lobachevski (Nikolai; 1792–1856, Russian)
Omar Khayyám (c.1048–c.1122, Persian)
Shcharansky (Natan; 1948–   , Ukrainian)
Weierstrass (Karl; 1815–97, German)

12 Bougainville (Louis Antoine de; 1729–1811, French)
Carathéodory (Constantin; 1873–1950, Greek)
Eratosthenes (c.276–194 BC, Greek)
Grothendieck (Alexandre; 1928–   , German/French)
Kovalevskaya (Sofya; 1850–91, Russian)
Spottiswoode (William; 1825–83, English)

13 Regiomontanus (1436–76, German)

14 Châtelet-Lomont (Émilie, Marquise du; 1706–49, French)
Klingenstierna (Samuel; 1698–1765, Swedish)

15 Eudoxus of Cnidus (408–353 BC, Greek)

Terms used in mathematics include:

02 pi	equal	radian
03 arc	graph	radius
set	group	sample
04 apex	helix	secant
area	locus	sector
axes	minus	spiral
axis	ogive	square
base	point	subset
cube	ratio	vector
edge	solid	vertex
face	speed	volume
line	total	**07** algebra
mean	width	average
mode	**06** binary	bearing
plus	chance	bounded
root	convex	breadth
side	cosine	chaotic
sine	degree	concave
skew	factor	decimal
unit	height	divisor
zero	length	formula
05 angle	linear	fractal
chaos	matrix	integer
chord	median	mapping
curve	number	maximum
depth	origin	measure

minimum
modulus
oblique
product
segment
tangent

08 addition
analysis
antipode
argument
bar chart
bar graph
binomial
calculus
capacity
constant
converse
cube root
diagonal
diameter
discrete
dividend
division
equation
exponent
fraction
function
geometry
gradient
identity
infinity
latitude
less than
multiple
parabola
pie chart
quadrant
quartile
quotient
rotation
symmetry
variable
variance
velocity
vertical

09 algorithm
Cartesian
congruent
factorial

See also **measurement**

frequency
histogram
hyperbola
iteration
logarithm
longitude
numerator
odd number
operation
parameter
perimeter
remainder

10 acute angle
arithmetic
complement
continuous
coordinate
covariance
derivative
even number
horizontal
hypotenuse
percentage
percentile
place value
proportion
protractor
Pythagoras
real number
reciprocal
reflection
regression
right-angle
square root
statistics
subtractor

11 approximate
coefficient
combination
coordinates
correlation
denominator
determinant
enlargement
equidistant
exponential
greater than
integration
magic square

mirror image
Möbius strip
obtuse angle
permutation
plane figure
prime number
probability
Pythagorean
real numbers
reflex angle
translation
Venn diagram
whole number

12 asymmetrical
Bayes' theorem
cross section
distribution
random sample
straight line
trigonometry
universal set

13 circumference
complex number
Mandelbrot set
mixed fraction
natural number
ordinal number
parallel lines
perpendicular
quadrilateral
scalar segment
triangulation

14 axis of symmetry
cardinal number
common fraction
directed number
mirror symmetry
multiplication
negative number
parallel planes
positive number
rational number
transformation
vulgar fraction

15 conjugate angles
differentiation
imaginary number
scalene triangle

meal

Meals include:

03 BBQ	dinner	**08** barbecue	**10** fork supper
tea	nosh-up	cream tea	midday meal
04 bite	picnic	luncheon	slap-up meal
	repast	takeaway	**11** dinner party
05 feast	spread	tea break	evening meal
lunch	supper	tea party	**12** afternoon tea
snack	tiffin	TV dinner	safari supper
06 barbie	**07** banquet	**09** breakfast	**13** harvest supper
brunch	blow-out	cold table	
buffet	high tea	elevenses	

measurement

Measuring instruments include:

04 rule	voltmeter	pluviometer
05 gauge	volumeter	pyranometer
meter	wattmeter	salinometer
06 octant	wavemeter	seismograph
07 ammeter	**10** anemometer	seismometer
balance	audiometer	speedometer
burette	bathometer	spherometer
pipette	clinometer	tape measure
sextant	cyclometer	tensiometer
08 luxmeter	gravimeter	thermometer
odometer	hydrometer	vaporimeter
ohmmeter	hyetometer	velocimeter
quadrant	hygrometer	weighbridge
09 altimeter	hypsometer	**12** Breathalyser®
barometer	micrometer	densitometer
callipers	mileometer	evaporimeter
cryometer	multimeter	evaporometer
dosimeter	ombrometer	galvanometer
flowmeter	photometer	inclinometer
focimeter	planimeter	magnetometer
hodometer	protractor	psychrometer
hourglass	pulsimeter	respirometer
manometer	radiosonde	spectrometer
milometer	tachometer	sphygmometer
optometer	tachymeter	viscosimeter
pedometer	theodolite	**13** accelerometer
plumb line	vibrograph	decelerometer
pyrometer	vibrometer	Geiger counter
rheometer	viscometer	saccharometer
steelyard	**11** calorimeter	**14** geothermometer
stopwatch	chronometer	interferometer
vinometer	colorimeter	
	dynamometer	

SI units include:

04 mole (mol)	**06** ampere (A)	second (s)	**08** kilogram (kg)
05 metre (m)	kelvin (K)	**07** candela (cd)	**10** kilogramme (kg)

SI-derived units include:

03 lux (lx)
ohm (Ω)

04 gray (Gy)
volt (V)
watt (W)

05 farad (F)
henry (H)
hertz (Hz)
joule (J)
katal (kat)
lumen (lm)

tesla (T)
weber (Wb)

06 newton (N)
pascal (Pa)
radian (rad)

07 coulomb (C)
siemens (S)
sievert (Sv)
volt amp (VA)

09 becquerel (Bq)
steradian (sr)

10 cubic metre (m³)

11 newton metre (N m)
square metre (m²)

13 degree Celsius (°C)
volts per metre (V m⁻¹)

14 farads per metre (F m⁻¹)
henrys per metre (H m⁻¹)

15 metres per second (m s⁻¹)
newtons per metre (N m⁻¹)
volt amp reactive (VAr)

Metric units include:

03 are (a)

04 gram (g)

05 litre (l)
metre (m)
tonne (t)

06 gramme (g)

07 hectare (ha)

08 decigram (dg)
kilogram (kg)

09 centigram (cg)
decilitre (dl)

decimetre (dm)
hectogram (hg)
kilolitre (kl)
kilometre (km)
metric ton (t)
milligram (mg)

10 centilitre (cl)
centimetre (cm)
cubic metre (cu m)
decigramme (dg)
hectolitre (hl)
hectometre (hm)

kilogramme (kg)
millilitre (ml)
millimetre (mm)

11 centigramme (cg)
milligramme (mg)
square metre (sq m)

14 cubic decimetre (cu dm)

15 cubic centimetre (cu cm or
cc)
square decimetre (sq dm)
square kilometre (sq km)

Other units of measurement include:

02 as
em
en
li

03 bar
bel
cab
cor
cup
ell
erg
hin
kat
kin
kip
kos
lay
lea
ley
log
mil
mna
nit
oke
pin
rad

rod
tod
ton
tun
wey

04 acre (a)
aune
bath
baud
boll
bolt
butt
coss
cran
dram
dyne
epha
foot (ft)
gill
hand
inch (in)
kati
khat
mile (mi)
mina
muid

nail
obol
omer
peck (pk)
pica
pint (pt)
pipe
pole
pood
ream
rood
rope
rotl
seer
sone
span
thou
tola
torr
vara
yard (yd)

05 barye
cable
candy
caneh
carat

catty
chain
cubit
ephah
grain
kandy
kaneh
katti
maund
ounce (oz)
perch
picul
pikul
point
pound (lb)
quart (qt)
stere
stone (st)
therm
tical
todde

06 barrel
bushel (bu)
candie
cantar
carrat

degree
denier
drachm
fathom
firkin
fother
gallon (gal)
kantar
league
parsec
shekel
talent
07 calorie
centner

decibel
fresnel
furlong
lispund
long ton
megabar
quarter
scruple
08 angstrom
cord foot
hogshead
lispound
microbar
millibar

short ton
09 board foot
cubic foot (cu ft)
cubic inch (cu in)
cubic yard (cu yd)
decastere
decistere
light year
10 atmosphere
barleycorn
fluid ounce (fl oz)
hoppus foot
millistere

square foot (sq ft)
square inch (sq in)
square mile (sq mi)
square yard (sq yd)
12 cable's length
nautical mile
13 hundredweight
(cwt)

See also **angle**; **gauge**; **glass**; **paper**; **time**

meat

Cuts and joints of meat include:

03 leg
rib
04 chop
clod
hand
hock
loin
neck
rack
rump

shin
05 chine
chuck
flank
round
scrag
shank
06 breast
collar
cutlet

fillet
rib eye
saddle
07 best end
brisket
buttock
knuckle
sirloin
topside
08 escalope

forehock
noisette
popeseye
shoulder
spare rib
09 aitchbone
médaillon
10 silverside
11 filet mignon
porterhouse

Meats and meat products include:

03 ham
MRM
red
04 beef
duck
fowl
hare
lamb
pâté
pork
Spam®
spek
veal
05 bacon
brawn
goose
heart
liver
mince
offal

quail
speck
steak
tripe
vivda
white
06 brains
burger
faggot
gammon
grouse
haggis
haslet
kidney
mutton
oxtail
pigeon
polony
rabbit
tongue

turkey
07 biltong
chicken
fatback
griskin
harslet
long pig
pemican
poultry
rissole
sausage
variety
venison
08 bushmeat
escalope
foie gras
fricadel
meat loaf
pemmican
pheasant

scrapple
trotters
09 forcemeat
frikkadel
hamburger
partridge
rillettes
10 beefburger
horseflesh
minced beef
sweetbread
Weisswurst
11 pig's knuckle
sausage meat
12 black pudding
luncheon meat
13 shield of brawn
14 mousse de canard

Cold meats include:

03 ham

04 beef
game
pâté
pork
Spam®

06 salami
tongue
turkey

07 biltong
chicken
chorizo
game pie
kabanos
pork pie
sausage
terrine
venison

08 bresaola
Cervelat
cold cuts

cured ham
meat loaf
ox tongue
parma ham
pastrami
salt beef

09 Bierwurst
glazed ham
liver paté
Mettwurst
pepperoni
rillettes
roast beef
saucisson
scotch egg

10 breaded ham
corned beef
crispy duck
crumbed ham
liverwurst
mortadella
prosciutto

Serrano ham

11 crispy bacon
roast turkey
sausage roll

12 Ardennes pâté
Brunswick ham
Brussels pâté
Cajun chicken
jamón serrano
liver sausage
luncheon meat
peppered beef
roast chicken
Wiltshire ham

13 chicken breast
garlic sausage
honey roast ham
Schinkenwurst
smoked sausage

14 Chinese chicken

15 luncheon sausage

medical

Medical and surgical equipment includes:

03 ECG
MRI

05 clamp
swabs

06 canula
EpiPen®
scales

07 cannula
curette
dilator
forceps
inhaler
scalpel
scanner
syringe

08 catheter
iron lung
speculum
tweezers
X-ray unit

09 aspirator

auriscope
autoclave
CT scanner
dental dam
endoscope
incubator
inhalator
nebulizer
retractor

10 audiometer
CAT scanner
ear syringe
hypodermic
kidney dish
microscope
MRI scanner
oxygen mask
rectoscope
respirator
rhinoscope
sterilizer
ultrasound

11 body scanner
first aid kit
laparoscope
stethoscope
stomach pump
thermometer

12 bronchoscope
isolator tent
laryngoscope
resuscitator
surgical mask
urethroscope

13 aural speculum
defibrillator
specimen glass

14 oesophagoscope
operating table
ophthalmoscope
oxygen cylinder

15 instrument table
vaginal speculum

Medical specialists include:

07 dentist

08 optician

09 dietician
homeopath

10 homoeopath
oncologist
orthoptist
pharmacist

11 audiologist
chiropodist
neurologist
optometrist

pathologist
radiologist

12 anaesthetist
cardiologist
chiropractor
embryologist
geriatrician
immunologist
obstetrician

orthodontist
orthopaedist
psychiatrist
psychologist
toxicologist

13 dermatologist
gerontologist
gynaecologist
haematologist

paediatrician
vaccinologist

14 bacteriologist
microbiologist
pharmacologist
rheumatologist

15 endocrinologist
ophthalmologist
physiotherapist

Medical terms include:

03 CPR
HRT
IVF
MRI
STI

04 cure
gene
scan
X-ray

05 donor
enema
nurse
pulse
sling
virus

06 biopsy
clinic
CT scan
doctor
injury
labour
splint
stitch
suture
trauma
tumour

07 allergy
bandage
CAT scan
check-up
hospice
placebo
relapse
surgery
symptom
therapy
vaccine

08 abortion

casualty
compress
C-section
dialysis
hospital
recovery
specimen
syndrome

09 blood bank
blood test
Caesarean
diagnosis
dislocate
dressings
home visit
infection
injection
operation
pregnancy
prognosis
remission
smear test
treatment

10 amputation
barium meal
blood count
blood donor
blood group
childbirth
consultant
convulsion
dissection
incubation
paraplegia
post-mortem
prosthesis
quarantine
side effect
tourniquet

transplant

11 case history
catheterize
circulation
examination
inoculation
miscarriage
respiration
temperature
transfusion
vaccination

12 chemotherapy
circumcision
complication
consultation
immunization
implantation
inflammation
microsurgery
mouth-to-mouth
prescription
radiotherapy
thrombolysis

13 amniocentesis
blood pressure
cauterization
cervical smear
contraception
intensive care
psychosomatic
resuscitation
sterilization

14 defibrillation
keyhole surgery
laser treatment
rehabilitation

15 cardiotocograph
health screening

See also **doctor**; **nurse**; **surgery**

medicine

Medicines include:

04 pill	inhaler	pastille	gripe-water
05 tonic	linctus	polypill	nasal spray
	lozenge	sedative	painkiller
06 arnica	pessary	Ventolin®	penicillin
emetic	steroid	09 analgesic	11 suppository
gargle	08 ear drops	paregoric	13 anti-histamine
tablet	eye drops	10 antibiotic	cough medicine
07 antacid	laxative	antifungal	tranquillizer
capsule	ointment	antiseptic	

Branches of medicine include:

05 ob-gyn	pathology	diagnostics	radiotherapy
07 otology	radiology	gerontology	rheumatology
urology	10 cardiology	gynaecology	13 brachytherapy
08 nosology	embryology	haematology	cytopathology
obs/gynae	geriatrics	paediatrics	endocrinology
oncology	immunology	physiatrics	ophthalmology
pharmacy	obstetrics	12 anaesthetics	physiotherapy
09 andrology	osteopathy	bacteriology	psychotherapy
audiology	pediatrics	kinesiatrics	14 electrotherapy
chiropody	psychiatry	microbiology	neuropathology
dentistry	psychology	orthodontics	neuroradiology
neurology	toxicology	orthopaedics	sports medicine
optometry	11 dermatology	perinatology	15 neuropsychiatry
		pharmacology	

Branches of complementary medicine include:

04 yoga	iridology	aura therapy	hydrotherapy
05 reiki	10 art therapy	kinesiology	hypnotherapy
07 massage	autogenics	moxibustion	macrobiotics
Pilates	homeopathy	naturopathy	14 autosuggestion
Rolfing	meditation	reflexology	crystal healing
shiatsu	osteopathy	t'ai chi ch'uan	herbal medicine
08 Ayurveda	11 acupressure	12 aromatherapy	15 Chinese medicine
09 herbalism	acupuncture	Bach remedies	thalassotherapy
		chiropractic	

See also **anaesthetic**; **analgesic**; **antibiotic**; **antiseptic**; **drug**; **Nobel Prize**

melon

Melon varieties include:

04 musk	sweet	07 cassaba	10 cantaloupe
Ogen	water	08 honeydew	Charentais
rock	06 casaba	09 cantaloup	
05 galia	winter		

memorial *see* **monument**

metal

Metallic elements and their symbols:

03 tin (Sn)

04 gold (Au)
iron (Fe)
lead (Pb)
zinc (Zn)

06 barium (Ba)
cerium (Ce)
cobalt (Co)
copper (Cu)
curium (Cm)
erbium (Er)
indium (In)
nickel (Ni)
osmium (Os)
radium (Ra)
silver (Ag)
sodium (Na)

07 bismuth (Bi)
cadmium (Cd)
caesium (Cs)
calcium (Ca)
fermium (Fm)
gallium (Ga)
hafnium (Hf)
holmium (Ho)
iridium (Ir)
lithium (Li)

mercury (Hg)
niobium (Nb)
rhenium (Re)
rhodium (Rh)
terbium (Tb)
thorium (Th)
thulium (Tm)
uranium (U)
wolfram (W)
yttrium (Y)

08 actinium (Ac)
antimony (Sb)
chromium (Cr)
europium (Eu)
francium (Fr)
lutetium (Lu)
nobelium (No)
platinum (Pt)
polonium (Po)
rubidium (Rb)
samarium (Sm)
scandium (Sc)
tantalum (Ta)
thallium (Tl)
titanium (Ti)
tungsten (W)
vanadium (V)

09 aluminium (Al)

americium (Am)
berkelium (Bk)
beryllium (Be)
germanium (Ge)
lanthanum (La)
magnesium (Mg)
manganese (Mn)
neodymium (Nd)
neptunium (Np)
palladium (Pd)
plutonium (Pu)
potassium (K)
ruthenium (Ru)
strontium (Sr)
ytterbium (Yb)
zirconium (Zr)

10 dysprosium (Dy)
gadolinium (Gd)
lawrencium (Lr)
molybdenum (Mo)
promethium (Pm)
technetium (Tc)

11 californium (Cf)
einsteinium (Es)
mendelevium (Md)

12 praseodymium (Pr)
protactinium (Pa)

Metal alloys include:

03 pot

04 type

05 brass
Dutch
Invar®
Muntz
potin
steel
terne
white

06 Alnico®
billon
bronze
latten
occamy
ormolu
oroide

pewter
solder
tambac
tombac
tombak
Y-alloy

07 amalgam
Babbit's
chromel
Nitinol
prince's
shakudo
similor
tutania
tutenag

08 Babbitt's
cast iron

gunmetal
Manganin®
Nichrome®
orichalc
speculum
zircaloy
Zircoloy®

09 Britannia
Duralumin®
Dutch gold
Dutch leaf
magnalium
pinchbeck
shibuichi
white gold

10 constantan
ferro-alloy

iridosmine
iridosmium
mischmetal
Monel metal®
mosaic gold
osmiridium
white brass

11 chrome steel
cupro-nickel
nicrosilial
white copper

12 German silver
nickel silver

14 high-speed steel
phosphor-bronze
stainless steel

meteor

Meteor showers include:

06 Lyrids (19–25 Apr)
Ursids (19–24 Dec)

07 Leonids (14–20 Nov)
Taurids (25 Oct-25 Nov)

08 Geminids (8–14 Dec)
Orionids (15–25 Oct)

Perseids (27 Jul-17 Aug)

11 Quadrantids (1–6 Jan)

12 Eta Aquariids (1–8 May)

14 Alpha-Scorpiids (20 Apr-19 May)
Delta Aquariids (15 Jul-10 Aug)

meteorology

Terms used in meteorology include:

04 calm
eddy
flux
haar
haze
ITCZ
rime

05 flood
front
frost
lidar
polar
Q-code
radar
ridge
SIGWX
solar
taiga
virga

06 albedo
arctic
el Niño
flurry
haboob
ice fog
isobar
Kelvin
la Niña
oxygen
parcel
steppe
trough
zephyr

07 adiabat
air mass
ceiling
Celsius
chinook
climate
cyclone
density
drizzle

drought
graupel
isotach
mistral
monsoon
rainbow
thunder
tornado
typhoon
weather

08 acid rain
anabatic
blizzard
dewpoint
diabatic
doldrums
emission
föhn wind
forecast
humidity
isotherm
maritime
millibar
nitrogen
rainfall
sastrugi
semi-arid
wind rose
windsock
wind vane

09 accretion
adiabatic
advection
aerograph
altimeter
barograph
barometer
cold front
cut-off low
diffusion
exosphere
frequency
gust front

harmattan
heat index
hurricane
hyetology
ice nuclei
isotropic
jet stream
lapse rate
lightning
mesopause
mesoscale
Met Office
nephology
omega high
orography
radiation
rain gauge
reflected
satellite
scattered
stable air
sub-arctic
tephigram
trade wind
turbulent
upwelling
viscosity
vorticity
warm front
wind chill
wind field
wind shear
wind speed
zonal flow

10 absorption
aerography
air quality
anemometer
atmosphere
baroclinic
barotropic
cloud cover
conduction

convection
dart leader
depression
Fahrenheit
frost point
Hadley Cell
hemisphere
homosphere
hyetograph
hyetometer
hygrometer
ice pellets
insolation
ionosphere
isallobars
isothermal
Kelvin wave
latent heat
macroburst
macroscale
meridional
mesosphere
microburst
microscale
nephograph
nephoscope
nowcasting
ozone layer
radiosonde
rain shadow
rain shower
Rossby wave
saturation
squall line
storm track
streamline
subsidence
tropopause
valley wind
visibility
waterspout
wavelength
weather man

11 aggregation
air pressure
Aleutian Low
anticyclone
chemosphere
circulation
climatology
coalescence
continental
dissipation

Ekman spiral
entrainment
evaporation
frontolysis
Fujita scale
global scale
gravity wave
ground frost
hectapascal
hyetography
instability
mixing ratio
pollen count
pyranometer
satellitize
steady state
stratopause
supercooled
temperature
thermal belt
thermal wind
thermocline
thermograph
thermometer
thermopause
troposphere
ultra violet
unstable air
water vapour
wave cyclone
weather girl

12 advection fog
anabatic wind
cloud seeding
condensation
coupled model
cyclogenesis
heat capacity
heterosphere
meteorograph
microclimate
mountain wind
optical depth
pilot balloon
psychrometer
radiation fog
return stroke
seeder-feeder
sensible heat
Siberian High
station model
stratosphere
thermosphere

thunderstorm
transmission
water balance
weather chart
weather watch

13 ball lightning
Beaufort scale
boundary layer
carbon dioxide
climate change
cyclostrophic
fork lightning
freezing level
friction layer
frontogenesis
katabatic wind
magnetosphere
occluded front
onshore breeze
precipitation
radiant energy
remote sensing
scatterometer
stepped leader
synoptic chart
synoptic scale
thermodynamic
wind direction

14 air temperature
continentality
geostropic wind
horse latitudes
multicell storm
offshore breeze
orographic rain
prevailing wind
sheet lightning
supercell storm
transmissivity
twenty-foot wind
vapour pressure
weather station

15 contact freezing
hyetometrograph
polar easterlies
prognostic chart
stationary front
supersaturation
synoptic weather
water equivalent
weather forecast
wind-chill factor

See also **cloud**; **ice**; **precipitation**; **snow**; **storm**; **weather**; **wind**

metric unit *see* **measurement**

metro *see* **Underground**

Mexico

Cities and notable towns in Mexico include:

04 Léon	**07** Tijuana	**09** Chihuahua	**12** Ciudad Juárez
06 Mérida	Torréon	Monterrey	Villahermosa
Oaxaca	**08** Mazatlán	**10** Mexico City	**13** San Luis Potosí
Puebla	Veracruz	**11** Guadalajara	**14** Ciudad de México

Mexican landmarks include:

06 Cancún	**10** El Castillo	Jaguar Palace
Zócalo	Monte Albán	Popocatépetl
08 Acapulco	**11** Chichén Itzá	**14** Alameda Central
Palenque	La Ciudadela	**15** Avenue of the Dead
Río Bravo	Sierra Madre	Cerro del Tepeyac
	Teotihuacán	Palacio National
09 Ciudadela	**12** Citlaltépetl	Puebla Cathedral
Rio Grande	Ixtaccihuatl	Pyramid of the Sun

Middle East

Cities and notable towns in the Middle East include:

03 Qom (Iran)
   Sur (Lebanon)

04 Abha (Saudi Arabia)
   Acre (Israel)
   Aden (Yemen)
   Arak (Iran)
   Doha (Qatar)
   Gïza (Egypt)
   Hama (Syria)
   Hims (Syria)
   Homs (Syria)
   Ilam (Iran)
   Khoy (Iran)
   Kufa (Iraq)
   Qena (Egypt)
   Ruwi (Oman)
   Sari (Iran)
   Suez (Egypt)
   Taif (Saudi Arabia)
   Ta'iz (Yemen)
   Tyre (Lebanon)
   Yazd (Iran)

05 Ahvaz (Iran)
   Amman (Jordan)
   Aqaba (Jordan)
   Arbil (Iraq)
   Aswan (Egypt)
   Asyut (Egypt)
   Basra (Iraq)
   Cairo (Egypt)

   Dubai (United Arab Emirates)
   Haifa (Israel)
   Halab (Syria)
   Hilla (Iraq)
   Irbid (Jordan)
   Jedda (Saudi Arabia)
   Karaj (Iran)
   Karak (Jordan)
   Luxor (Egypt)
   Mecca (Saudi Arabia)
   Mosul (Iraq)
   Najaf (Iraq)
   Nazwa (Oman)
   Petra (Jordan)
   Rasht (Iran)
   Sana'a (Yemen)
   Sayda (Lebanon)
   Sidon (Lebanon)
   Tanta (Egypt)
   Zahle (Lebanon)
   Zarqa (Jordan)

06 Abadan (Iran)
   Aleppo (Syria)
   Ashdod (Israel)
   Beirut (Lebanon)
   Dammam (Saudi Arabia)
   Dezful (Iran)
   Gorgan (Iran)
   Hebron (Palestinian Autonomous Areas/West
     Bank)
   Jahrah (Kuwait)

Kerman (Iran)
Kirkuk (Iraq)
Manama (Bahrain)
Matrah (Oman)
Medina (Saudi Arabia)
Muscat (Oman)
Qazvin (Iran)
Ramadi (Iraq)
Riyadh (Saudi Arabia)
Semnan (Iran)
Shiraz (Iran)
Tabriz (Iran)
Tehran (Iran)
Zanjan (Iran)

07 Ardabil (Iran)
Baghdad (Iraq)
Baqubah (Iraq)
Bushehr (Iran)
El Minya (Egypt)
Esfahan (Iran)
Hamadan (Iran)
Hodeida (Yemen)
Isfahan (Iran)
Jericho (Palestinian Autonomous Areas/West Bank)
Karbala (Iraq)
Latakia (Syria)
Mashhad (Iran)
Netanya (Israel)
Salalah (Oman)
Samarra (Iraq)
Sharjah (United Arab Emirates)
Tel Aviv (Israel)
Tripoli (Lebanon)
Unayzah (Saudi Arabia)
Zagazig (Egypt)
Zahedan (Iran)

08 Abu Dhabi (United Arab Emirates)

Al Wafrah (Kuwait)
Ashqelon (Israel)
Beni Suef (Egypt)
Buraydah (Saudi Arabia)
Damanhur (Egypt)
Damascus (Syria)
El Faiyum (Egypt)
Fujairah (United Arab Emirates)
Gaza City (Palestinian Autonomous Areas/Gaza Strip)
Ismailia (Egypt)
Kazimayn (Iraq)
Orumiyeh (Iran)
Port Said (Egypt)
Ramallah (Palestinian Autonomous Areas/West Bank)
Sabzevar (Iran)
Sanandaj (Iran)
Tiberias (Israel)

09 Bakhtaran (Iran)
Beersheba (Israel)
El Mansura (Egypt)
Jerusalem (Israel)
Nahariyya (Israel)
Najafabad (Iran)
Nasiriyah (Iraq)
Neyshabur (Iran)
Tarabulus (Lebanon)

10 Alexandria (Egypt)
Al Muharraq (Bahrain)
Kuwait City (Kuwait)

11 Bandar Abbas (Iran)
Khorramabad (Iran)

12 Ras al-Khaimah (United Arab Emirates)
Sulaymaniyah (Iraq)

14 Rishon Le Ziyyon (Israel)

15 Shubra al-Khaymah (Egypt)

Middle Eastern landmarks include:

05 Kabaa
Petra

06 Masada
Qumran
Red Sea
Tigris

07 Baalbek

Dead Sea
Palmyra

09 Euphrates
The Sphinx

10 Persepolis

11 Grand Mosque
River Jordan

The Pyramids
Via Dolorosa
Wailing Wall
Western Wall

12 Sea of Galilee

13 Dome of the Rock

15 Elburz Mountains

military

Military ranks in the UK and US armies:

05 major

07 captain
colonel

general
private

08 corporal

sergeant

09 brigadier

10 lieutenant

12 field marshal
major-general
13 lance-corporal
staff sergeant
14 warrant officer

15 first lieutenant
16 brigadier general
general of the army
second lieutenant
17 lieutenant-colonel

lieutenant-general
private first class
20 company sergeant major
23 regimental sergeant major

Military ranks in the UK and US navies:

06 ensign
rating
seaman
07 admiral
captain
09 captain RN
commander

commodore
10 able seaman
lieutenant
midshipman
11 rear-admiral
vice-admiral
12 fleet admiral

petty officer
13 sub-lieutenant
14 warrant officer
17 admiral of the fleet
chief petty officer
19 lieutenant-commander
21 lieutenant junior grade

Military ranks in the UK and US air forces:

05 major
06 airman
07 captain
colonel
general
08 corporal
sergeant
10 air marshal
12 air commodore
group captain

major general
pilot officer
13 flying officer
staff sergeant
wing commander
14 air vice-marshal
flight sergeant
master sergeant
squadron leader
warrant officer

15 air chief marshal
first lieutenant
16 brigadier general
flight lieutenant
second lieutenant
17 lieutenant colonel
lieutenant general
20 general of the air force
25 marshal of the Royal Air
Force

Military decorations and honours include:

02 GC
GM
MC
MM
VC
03 AFC
AFM
BEM

CGM
CMH
DCM
DFC
DFM
DSC
DSM
DSO

09 Iron Cross
10 Bronze Star
Silver Star
11 George Cross
George Medal
Purple Heart
13 Air Force Cross

Air Force Medal
Croix de Guerre
Legion of Merit
Military Cross
Military Medal
Victoria Cross
14 Oak-leaf Cluster

Military units include:

04 file
post
wing
05 corps
flank
fleet
group
squad
troop
06 cohort

convoy
flight
legion
patrol
picket
07 battery
brigade
company
militia
phalanx

platoon
section
08 commando
division
flotilla
garrison
regiment
squadron
09 battalion
effective

task force
10 detachment
flying camp
rifle corps
11 battle group
flying party
12 flying column
Royal Marines
13 guard of honour

Military terms include:

03 ADC	charge	citation
arm	combat	conquest
foe	decamp	demotion
POW	defeat	division
van	detail	fatigues
WMD	disarm	flotilla
04 army	enlist	garrison
AWOL	ensign	infantry
base	flight	insignia
bomb	kit bag	invasion
camp	muster	last post
duty	mutiny	martinet
mess	orders	mobilize
navy	parade	ordnance
rank	parley	quarters
rear	parole	regiment
re-up	patrol	reveille
rout	ration	roll-call
tank	salute	skirmish
unit	sentry	squadron
wing	signal	standard
05 AWACS	sniper	strategy
corps	sortie	supplies
demob	stores	the front
depot	target	training
draft	tattoo	vanguard
drill	trench	**09** about turn
enemy	**07** air-drop	armistice
flank	arsenal	artillery
fleet	bivouac	attention
foray	black op	beachhead
force	brigade	bugle call
front	canteen	ceasefire
guard	colours	conscript
leave	command	crossfire
lines	company	desertion
march	defence	discharge
NAAFI	fall out	epaulette
padre	landing	excursion
radar	latrine	first post
range	liaison	front line
recce	mission	fusillade
shell	outpost	incursion
sonar	platoon	left wheel
squad	posting	logistics
troop	recruit	march past
truce	retreat	minefield
06 action	tactics	munitions
allies	victory	offensive
ambush	**08** adjutant	rearguard
attack	air cover	slow march
battle	air force	surrender
billet	barracks	task force
brevet	blockade	white flag
call up	briefing	**10** aide-de-camp
	campaign	blue-on-blue

bridgehead
camouflage
close ranks
commission
debriefing
decoration
demobilize
detachment
dispatches
encampment
evacuation
expedition
firing line
inspection
manoeuvres
operations
quick march
rifle range
route march

shell-shock
11 armed forces
bombardment
disarmament
forced march
requisition
12 conscription
court-martial
demilitarize
friendly fire
installation
intelligence
mission creep
parade ground
peacekeeping
13 assault course
atomic warfare
battle fatigue

counter-attack
prisoner of war
quartermaster
square-bashing
trench warfare
14 action stations
marching orders
nuclear warfare
pincer movement
reconnaissance
reinforcements
15 chemical warfare
insubordination
married quarters
national service
observation post
16 counterterrorism

See also **admiral**; **army**; **field marshal**; **general**; **missile**; **regiment**; **soldier**

Milton, John (1608–74)

Significant works include:

05 *Poems* (1645)
07 'Arcades' (c.1634)
    Lycidas (1637)
08 'L'Allegro' (c.1631)
10 'The Passion' (1645)
11 'Il Penseroso' (c.1631)
    Of Education (1644)
12 *Areopagitica* (1644)
    Comus: A Masque (1634)
    Paradise Lost (1667)
13 *Eikonoklastes* (1649)

15 *Defensio Secunda* (1654)
    Samson Agonistes (1671)
16 *Paradise Regained* (1671)
17 *Epitaphium Damonis* (1639)
19 *The History of Britain* (1670)
20 *De Doctrina Christiana* (unfinished)
26 *Pro Populo Anglicano Defensio* (1651)
30 *The Tenure of Kings and Magistrates* (1649)
33 *The Doctrine and Discipline of Divorce*
    (1643)

mineral

Main trace minerals include:

04 iron (liver, kidney, green leafy vegetables,
    egg yolk, dried fruit, potatoes, molasses)
    zinc (meat, whole grains, legumes, oysters,
    milk)
06 copper (green vegetables, fish, oysters,
    liver)
    iodine (seafood, saltwater fish, seaweed,
    iodized salt, table salt)
    sodium (table salt)
07 calcium (milk, butter, cheese, sardines,
    green leafy vegetables, citrus fruits)
08 chromium (brewer's yeast, black pepper,
    liver, wholemeal bread, beer)

fluorine (fluoridated drinking water, seafood,
    tea)
selenium (seafood, cereals, meat, egg yolk,
    garlic)
09 magnesium (green leafy vegetables (eaten
    raw), nuts, whole grains)
    manganese (legumes, cereal grains, green
    leafy vegetables, tea)
    potassium (fresh vegetables, meat, orange
    juice, bananas, bran)
10 molybdenum (legumes, cereal grains, liver,
    kidney, some dark green vegetables)
    phosphorus (meat, poultry, fish, eggs, dried
    beans and peas, milk products)

Minerals include:

03 jet

04 alum
mica
ruby
salt
spar
talc

05 beryl
borax
emery
flint
fluor
topaz
umber

06 albite
blende
cerite
galena
gangue
garnet
glance
gypsum
halite
haüyne
humite
illite
jasper
kermes
lithia
maltha
natron
nosean
pyrite
quartz
rutile
silica
sphene
spinel
talcum
zircon

07 anatase
apatite
axinite
azurite
barytes
biotite
bornite
brucite
calcite
cassite
crystal
cuprite
desmine
diamond

dysodil
epidote
jacinth
jadeite
jargoon
kandite
kyanite
leucite
nacrite
olivine
pennine
peridot
pyrites
realgar
syenite
thorite
uralite
uranite
zeolite
zincite
zoisite

08 allanite
ankerite
asbestos
autunite
blue john
boracite
brookite
calamine
calcspar
chlorite
chromite
cinnabar
corundum
crocoite
cryolite
diallage
diaspore
dolomite
dysodile
dysodyle
epsomite
erionite
euxenite
feldspar
fluorite
goethite
graphite
gyrolite
hematite
hyacinth
idocrase
ilmenite
iodyrite
lazulite

lazurite
lewisite
melilite
mimetite
nephrite
orpiment
plumbago
prehnite
pyroxene
rock salt
sanidine
sapphire
siderite
smaltite
sodalite
stannite
stibnite
stilbite
titanite
wurtzite

09 alabaster
amphibole
anhydrite
aragonite
atacamite
bentonite
blacklead
cairngorm
carnotite
celestite
chabazite
cheralite
cobaltite
columbite
covellite
dichroite
elaterite
enstatite
evaporite
fibrolite
fluorspar
fool's gold
goslarite
grossular
haematite
kaolinite
kermesite
kieserite
lodestone
magnesite
magnetite
malachite
marcasite
margarite
microlite

mispickel
muscovite
nepheline
niccolite
olivenite
ottrelite
pearl spar
phenacite
polianite
powellite
quartzite
rhodolite
rhodonite
rubellite
saltpetre
scheelite
scolecite
soapstone
sylvanite
tantalite
tremolite
turquoise
uraninite
variscite
vulpinite
wavellite
zinkenite

10 alabandite
andalusite
antimonite
aquamarine
argyrodite
aventurine
bastnäsite

See also **ore**

bloodstone
chalcedony
chalcocite
chrysolite
cordierite
cylindrite
dyscrasite
erubescite
glauberite
glauconite
halloysite
hornblende
Jamesonite
meerschaum
microcline
orthoclase
perovskite
polyhalite
pyrolusite
redruthite
samarskite
sapphirine
serpentine
smaragdite
sperrylite
sphalerite
tennantite
thaumasite
tourmaline
vanadinite

11 alexandrite
amblygonite
amphibolite
annabergite

apophyllite
baddeleyite
cassiterite
cerargyrite
chrysoberyl
clinochlore
crocidolite
franklinite
French chalk
greenockite
josephinite
lapis lazuli
molybdenite
piedmontite
pitchblende
sal ammoniac
sillimanite
smithsonite
tetradymite
vesuvianite
yttrocerite

12 chalcanthite
chalcopyrite
copper-nickel
hemimorphite
skutterudite

13 arsenopyrites
cummingtonite

14 hydroxyapatite
sodium chloride
yttro-columbite

15 gooseberry-stone
montmorillonite

mineral water *see* water

miser

Misers include:

05 Burns (Montgomery; *The Simpsons*, 1989– , Matt Groening)

06 Mammon (Bible)
Marner (Silas; *Silas Marner*, 1861, George Eliot)

07 Scrooge (Ebenezer; *A Christmas Carol*, 1843, Charles Dickens)

08 Nickleby (Ralph; *Nicholas Nickeby*,

See also **Eliot, George**; **Molière**

1838–39, Charles Dickens)
Trapbois (*The Fortunes of Nigel*, 1822, Sir Walter Scott)

10 Fardorough (*Fardorough the Miser*, 1939, William Carleton)
Van Swieten (Ghysbrecht; *The Cloister and the Hearth*, 1861, Charles Reade)

11 Earlforward (Henry; *Riceyman Steps*, 1923, Arnold Bennett)

missile

Missiles include:

02 MX	**04** ALCM	**05** smart	Tomahawk
V-2	ASBM	**06** AMRAAM	**09** ballistic
03 AAM	ICBM	cruise	Minuteman
ABM	IRBM	Exocet®	
AGM	MIRV	guided	**10** Sidewinder
ASM	MRBM	**07** Polaris	wire-guided
ATM	Scud	Trident	**11** heat-seeking
SAM	SLBM	**08** Maverick	**12** surface-to-air
SSM	TASM		

missionary

Missionaries and evangelists include:

03 Fox (George; 1624–91, English)
Huc (Evariste Régis; 1813–60, French)

04 Luke (St; 1c AD)
Mark (St; 1c AD)
Paul (St; d.c.64/68 AD)

05 Bliss (Philip; 1838–76, US)
Bruno (St; 970–1009, German)
Carey (William; 1761–1834, English)
David (Père Armand; 1826–1900, French)
Egede (Hans; 1686–1758, Norwegian)
Eliot (John; 1604–90, English)
Ellis (William; 1794–1872, English)
Grubb (Sir Kenneth; 1900–80, English)
Jones (Bob; 1883–1968, US)
Jones (Eli Stanley; 1884–1973, US)
Laval (François, de Montmorency; 1622–1708, French)
Legge (James; 1815–97, Scottish)
Moody (Dwight L; 1837–99, US)
Neill (Stephen; 1900–84, Scottish)
Niles (Daniel Thambyrajah; 1908–70, Tamil)
Paton (William; 1886–1943, Scottish)
Ricci (Matteo; 1552–1610, Italian)
Scott (Michael; 1907–83, English)
Serra (Junípero; 1713–84, Spanish)
Smith (Eli; 1801–57, US)
Smith (Rodney; 1860–1947, English)
Soong (Charlie; d.1927, Chinese)

06 Damien (Father Joseph; 1840–89, Belgian)
Graham (Billy; 1918– , US)
Judson (Adoniram; 1788–1850, US)
Kagawa (Toyohiko; 1888–1960, Japanese)
Martyn (Henry; 1781–1812, English)
Moffat (Robert; 1795–1883, Scottish)
Schall (Johann von; 1591–1669, German)
Teresa (Mother; 1910–97, Albanian)
Vieira (Antonio de; 1608–97, Portuguese)

Wesley (Charles; 1707–88, English)
Wesley (John; 1703–91, English)
Zwemer (Samuel; 1867–1952, US)

07 Andrews (Charles Freer; 1871–1940, English)
Aylward (Gladys; 1902–70, English)
Buchman (Frank; 1878–1961, US)
Columba (St; 521–97, Irish)
Falwell (Jerry; 1933–2007, US)
Laubach (Frank; 1884–1970, US)
Liddell (Eric; 1902–45, Scottish)
Roberts (Oral; 1918–2009, US)
Slessor (Mary; 1848–1915, Scottish)
ten Boom (Corrie; 1892–1983, Dutch)
Timothy (St; fl.c.50 AD)

08 Adalbert (St; d.981, German)
Boniface (St; c.680–c.754, Anglo-Saxon)
Brainerd (David; 1718–47, American)
Buchanan (Claudius; 1766–1815, Scottish)
Columban (St; 543–615, Irish)
Crowther (Samuel; 1809–91, African)
Cuthbert (St; c.635–87, Anglo-Saxon)
Duchesne (St Rose Philippine; 1769–1852, French)
Falconer (Ion Keith; 1856–87, Irish)
Grenfell (Sir Wilfred; 1865–1940, English)
Las Casas (Bartolomé de; 1474–1566, Spanish)
Morrison (Robert; 1782–1834, Scottish)
Newbigin (Lesslie; 1909–98, English)
Williams (John; 1796–1839, English)

09 Marquette (Jacques; 1637–75, French)
McPherson (Aimee Semple; 1890–1944, US)
Southwell (Robert; 1561–95, English)
Stapleton (Ruth; 1929–83, US)
Willibald (St; 700–86, Anglo-Saxon)

10 Columbanus (St; 543–615, Irish)
Hannington (James; 1847–85, English)

Huddleston (Trevor; 1913–98, English)
Macpherson (Annie; fl.1860s, Scottish)
Schweitzer (Albert; 1875–1965, Alsatian)
Whitefield (George; 1714–70, English)

11 Livingstone (David; 1813–73, Scottish)
   Vivekananda (1863–1902, Indian)
13 Francis Xavier (St; 1506–52, Spanish)
   Keith-Falconer (Ion; 1856–87, Irish)

Molière (1622–73)

Significant works include:

06 *L'Avare* (1668)
08 *L'Étourdi* (1658)
   Tartuffe (1664/1667)
   The Miser (1668)
09 *The Quacks* (1665)
10 *Amphitryon* (1668)
   Les Fâcheux (1662)
   Sganarelle (1660)
   The Picture (1660)
11 *The Dumb Lady* (1666)
12 *George Dandin* (1668)
13 *L'Amour médecin* (1665)
   Le Misanthrope (1665)
   The Blunderers (1658)
14 *L'Ecole des maris* (1662)
   Le Mariage forcé (1664)
   The Misanthrope (1665)
15 *L'Ecole des femmes* (1662)
   Le Dépit amoureux (1658)
   The Impertinents (1662)
16 *The Learned Ladies* (1672)
17 *La Princesse d'Élide* (1664)
   Les Femmes savantes (1672)
   The Amorous Quarrel (1658)

   The Cheats of Scapin (1671)
   The Forced Marriage (1664)
   The School for Wives (1662)
18 *Don Garcia of Navarre* (1661)
   Don Garcie de Navarre (1661)
   Le Malade imaginaire (1673)
   Le Médecin malgré lui (1666)
   The Female Virtuosos (1672)
19 *The Imaginary Cuckold* (1660)
   The Imaginary Invalid (1673)
   The Universal Passion (1664)
20 *The School for Husbands* (1662)
21 *Impromptu de Versailles* (1663)
   Les Fourberies de Scapin (1671)
   The Bourgeois Gentleman (1671)
22 *Don Juan or the Stone Guest* (1665)
   Le Bourgeois gentilhomme (1671)
   Les Précieuses ridicules (1659)
   Monsieur de Pourceaugnac (1669)
23 *The Conceited Young Ladies* (1659)
24 *School for Wives Criticised* (1663)
   The Impromptu of Versailles (1663)
25 *The Citizen turned Gentleman* (1671)
27 *La Critique de l'école des femmes* (1663)

Significant characters include:

05 Agnès
   Argan
   Célie
   Elise
   Lélie
   Orgon
06 Ariste
   Bélise
   Cathos
   Dorine
   Elmire
   Elvire
   Horace
   L'Avare

   Léonor
   Purgon
     (Monsieur)
   Vadius
   Valère
07 Alceste
   Anselme
   Armande
   Arsinoé
   Cléante
   Cléonte
   Dom Juan
   Don Juan
   Dorante

   Eliante
   Mariane
08 Arnolphe
   Célimène
   Chrysale
   Dimanche
     (Monsieur)
   Gorgibus
   Harpagon
   Isabelle
   Jourdain (Madame)
   Jourdain
     (Monsieur)
   Magdelon

   Philinte
   Tartuffe
   Toinette
09 Angélique
   Clitandre
   Diafoirus
     (Monsieur)
   Henriette
   Trissotin
10 Philaminte
   Sganarelle
13 Le Misanthrope

mollusc

Molluscs include:

04 clam
slug

05 conch
cowry
snail
spoot
squid
whelk

06 chiton
cockle
cowrie
cuttle
dodman
limpet

loligo
mussel
nerite
oyster
winkle

07 abalone
octopus
piddock
scallop
sea slug

08 escargot
nautilus
sea snail
shipworm

wallfish

09 cone shell
hodmandod
land snail
pond snail
razorclam
razorfish
tusk shell
wing shell
wing snail

10 cuttlefish
giant squid
nudibranch
periwinkle

razor shell
Roman snail

11 horse mussel
marine snail

12 sea butterfly

13 common octopus
great grey slug
keyhole limpet
ramshorn snail
slipper limpet

15 freshwater snail

monarch

Anglo-Saxon and English monarchs, with regnal dates:

04 Cnut ('the Great'; 1016–35)
Edwy (955–59)
Grey (Lady Jane; 1553)
John (Lackland; 1199–1216)
Mary (I, Tudor; 1553–58)
Offa (757–96)

05 Edgar (959–75)
Edred (946–55)
Henry (I; 1100–35)
Henry (II; 1154–89)
Henry (III; 1216–72)
Henry (IV; 1399–1413)
Henry (V; 1413–22)
Henry (VI; 1422–61/1470–71)
Henry (VII; 1485–1509)
Henry (VIII; 1509–47)
Svein (I Haraldsson, 'Fork-Beard'; 1013–14)

06 Alfred ('the Great'; 871–99)
Canute (1016–35)
Edmund (I; 939–46)
Edmund (II, 'Ironside'; 1016)
Edward (I; 1272–1307)
Edward (II; 1307–27)
Edward (III; 1327–77)
Edward (III, 'the Confessor'; 1042–66)

Edward (II, 'the Martyr'; 975–979)
Edward (IV; 1461–70/1471–83)
Edward ('the Elder'; 899–924)
Edward (V; 1483)
Edward (VI; 1547–53)
Egbert (802–39)
Harold (II; 1066)
Harold (I Knutsson, 'Harefoot'; 1035–40)

07 Richard (II; 1377–99)
Richard (III; 1483–85)
Richard (I, 'the Lion Heart'; 1189–99)
Stephen (1135–54)
William (II, 'Rufus'; 1087–1100)
William (I, 'the Conqueror'; 1066–87)

08 Ethelred (866–71)
Ethelred (II, 'the Unready'; 979–1013/1014–16)

09 Athelstan (924–39)
Elizabeth (I; 1558–1603)
Ethelbald (856–60)
Ethelbert (860–66)
Ethelwulf (839–56)

11 Hardicanute (1035–42)

13 Edgar Atheling (1066)
Knut Sveinsson (1016–35)

Scottish monarchs, with regnal dates:

03 Aed (877–78)

04 Dubh (962–66)
Duff (962–66)
Mary (Queen of Scots; 1542–67)

05 Bruce (Robert; 1306–29)

Culen (966–71)
David (I; 1124–53)
David (II; 1329–71)
Edgar (1097–1107)
Giric (878–89)
James (I; 1406–37)

James (II; 1437–60)
James (III; 1460–88)
James (IV; 1488–1513)
James (V; 1513–42)
James (VI; 1567–1625)

06 Baliol (Edward de; 1332)
Baliol (John de; 1292–96)
Donald (I; 858–62)
Donald (II; 889–900)
Donald (III, 'Bane'; 1093–94/1094–97)
Duncan (I; 1034–40)
Duncan (II; 1094)
Indulf (954–62)
Lulach (1057–58)
Robert (II; 1371–90)
Robert (III; 1390–1406)
Robert (I, 'the Bruce'; 1306–29)

07 Balliol (Edward de; 1332)

Balliol (John de; 1292–96)
Kenneth (I; 843–58)
Kenneth (II; 971–95)
Kenneth (III; 997–1005)
Macbeth (1040–57)
Malcolm (I; 943–54)
Malcolm (II; 1005–34)
Malcolm (III, 'Canmore'; 1058–93)
Malcolm (IV, 'the Maiden'; 1153–65)
William (I; 1165–1214)

08 Margaret ('Maid of Norway'; 1286–90)

09 Alexander (I; 1107–24)
Alexander (II; 1214–49)
Alexander (III; 1249–86)

11 Constantine (I; 862–77)
Constantine (II; 900–43)
Constantine (III; 995–97)

16 Mary, Queen of Scots (1542–67)

British monarchs, with regnal dates:

04 Anne (1702–14)
Mary (II; 1689–94)

05 James (VI and I; 1603–25)
James (VII and II; 1685–88)

06 Edward (VII; 1901–10)
Edward (VIII; 1936)
George (I; 1714–27)

George (II; 1727–60)
George (III; 1760–1820)
George (IV; 1820–30)
George (V; 1910–36)
George (VI; 1936–52)

07 Charles (I; 1625–49)
Charles (II; 1660–85)
William (II and III, of

Orange; 1689–1702)
William (IV; 1830–37)

08 Victoria (1837–1901)

09 Elizabeth (II; 1952–)

14 William and Mary (William
II and III and Mary II;
1689–94)

monastery, monk *see* **religious order**

money *see* **coin**; **currency**

monkey

Monkeys include:

03 ape
pug
sai

04 douc
leaf
mico
mona
saki
titi
zati

05 Diana
drill
green
magot
night

sajou
Satan
toque

06 baboon
bandar
bonnet
coaita
grivet
guenon
howler
langur
malmag
rhesus
sagoin
saguin
spider

tee-tee
uakari
vervet
woolly

07 cacajou
colobus
guereza
hanuman
macaque
sagouin
saimiri
sapajou
tamarin
tarsier

08 Capuchin

durukuli
entellus
mandrill
mangabey
marmoset
squirrel
talapoin
wanderoo

09 proboscis

10 Barbary ape
moustached

11 douroucouli
platyrrhine
white-eyelid

13 platyrrhinian

Monopoly®

Monopoly® properties:

06 Strand (red; £220)

07 Mayfair (dark blue; £400)

08 Pall Mall (pink; £140)
Park Lane (dark blue; £350)

09 Bow Street (orange; £180)
Whitehall (pink; £140)

10 Bond Street (green; £320)
Euston Road (light blue; £100)
Piccadilly (yellow; £280)
Vine Street (orange; £200)
Water Works (£150)

11 Fleet Street (red; £220)
Old Kent Road (brown; £60)
Whitechapel (brown; £60)

12 Oxford Street (green; £300)
Regent Street (green; £300)

14 Coventry Street (yellow; £260)

15 Electric Company (£150)
Leicester Square (yellow; £260)
Pentonville Road (light blue; £120)
Trafalgar Square (red; £240)

17 King's Cross Station (£200)
Marlborough Street (orange; £180)
Marylebone Station (£200)
The Angel Islington (light blue; £100)

20 Northumberland Avenue (pink; £160)

22 Fenchurch Street Station (£200)
Liverpool Street Station (£200)

Monopoly® terms include:

02 Go	turn	**07** auction	mortgaged
03 buy	**05** asset	circuit	penalties
own	board	doubles	play money
tax	bonus	low-rent	racing car
04 bank	hotel	race car	tax return
boot	house	repairs	throw dice
cash	money	rewards	title deed
deal	price	**08** bankrupt	utilities
debt	rules	birthday	**10** de-mortgage
dice	token	high-rent	raise money
fine	**06** banker	interest	Scottie dog
iron	bidder	mortgage	**11** Advance to Go
jail	borrow	opponent	collect rent
loan	Chance	property	colour group
rent	pewter	Super Tax	Free Parking
sell	salary	windfall	**12** 'Just Visiting'
ship	top hat	**09** Income Tax	**14** Community Chest

monster

Monster types include:

03 orc	bunyip	griffon	dinosaur
roc	gorgon	gryphon	lindworm
04 cete	kraken	prodigy	mooncalf
ogre	nicker	satyral	mushussu
05 gulon	ogress	taniwha	seahorse
harpy	sphinx	wendigo	**09** leviathan
lamia	wyvern	windigo	manticore
phoca	zombie	ziffius	marakihau
yowie	**07** cyclops	**08** basilisk	rosmarine
zombi	Grendel	behemoth	sea satyre
06 ajatar	griffin	bogeyman	wasserman

whirlpool
10 Black Annis
chupacabra

cockatrice
crio-sphinx
salamander

sea monster
sea serpent
11 amphisbaena

hippocampus

Monsters include:

03 orc (*The Lord of the Rings*, 1954–55, J R R Tolkien)

04 uruk (*The Lord of the Rings*, 1954–55, J R R Tolkien)

05 Alien (*Alien*, 1979, et seq)
Beast ('Beauty and the Beast' fairy tale)
Hydra (Greek mythology)
Smaug (*The Lord of the Rings*, 1954–55, J R R Tolkien)
snark (*The Hunting of the Snark*, 1876, Lewis Carroll)

06 Balrog (*The Lord of the Rings*, 1954–55, J R R Tolkien)
Duessa (*The Faerie Queene*, 1590–96, Sir Edmund Spenser)
Empusa (Greek mythology)
Fafnir (Norse mythology)
Geryon (Greek mythology)
Medusa (Greek mythology)
Nazgul (*The Lord of the Rings*, 1954–55, J R R Tolkien)
Python (Greek mythology)
Scylla (Greek mythology)
Shelob (*The Lord of the Rings*, 1954–55, J R R Tolkien)
Sphinx (Greek mythology)
Stheno (Greek mythology)
Typhon (Greek mythology)

07 Bathies (*The Kraken Wakes*, 1953, John Wyndham)
Caliban (*The Tempest*, 1611, William Shakespeare)
Cecrops (Greek mythology)
Chimera (Greek mythology)
Cyclops (Greek mythology)
Dracula (*Dracula*, 1897, Bram Stoker)

Echidna (Greek mythology)
Euryale (Greek mythology)
Grendel (*Beowulf*, 7c/8c, anon)
triffid (*The Day of the Triffids*, 1951, John Wyndham)

08 Cerberus (Greek mythology)
Chimaera (Greek mythology)
Godzilla (*Gojira*, 1954)
King Kong (*King Kong*, 1933/2005)
Minotaur (Greek mythology)
the Beast ('Beauty and the Beast' fairy tale)
Typhoeus (Greek mythology)

09 Charybdis (Greek mythology)

10 jabberwock (*Through the Looking-Glass*, 1872, Lewis Carroll)
Jormangund (Norse mythology)
jubjub bird (*Through the Looking-Glass*, 1872, Lewis Carroll)
Polyphemus (Greek mythology)

12 bandersnatch (*Through the Looking-Glass*, 1872, Lewis Carroll)
Blatant Beast (*The Faerie Queene*, 1590–96, Sir Edmund Spenser)
Count Dracula (*Dracula*, 1897, Bram Stoker)

13 Cookie Monster (*Sesame Street*, TV show)
Hecatonchires (Greek mythology)
Questing Beast (*Le Morte d'Arthur*, c.1469/70, Sir Thomas Malory)

14 Incredible Hulk (*The Incredible Hulk*, TV show)
Midgard serpent (Norse mythology)

15 Glatysaunt Beast (*Le Morte d'Arthur*, c.1469/70, Sir Thomas Malory)
Loch Ness monster (legend)

See also **mythology**

Montenegro *see* **Balkans**

month

Months:

03 May	**05** April	**07** January	February
04 July	March	October	November
June	**06** August	**08** December	**09** September

French month names with English translation:

03 mai (May)

04 août (August)
    juin (June)
    mars (March)

05 avril (April)

07 février (February)
    janvier (January)
    juillet (July)

octobre (October)

08 décembre (December)
    novembre (November)

09 septembre (September)

German month names with English translation:

03 Mai (May)

04 Juli (July)
    Juni (June)
    März (March)

05 April (April)

06 August (August)
    Januar (January)

07 Februar (February)

Oktober (October)

08 Dezember (December)
    November (November)

09 September (September)

Italian month names with English translation:

05 marzo (March)

06 agosto (August)
    aprile (April)
    giugno (June)

luglio (July)
maggio (May)

07 gennaio (January)
    ottobre (October)

08 dicembre (December)
    febbraio (February)
    novembre (November)

09 settembre (September)

Latin month names with English translation:

05 Maius (May)

06 Julius (July)
    Junius (June)

07 Aprilis (April)
    Martius (March)

October (October)

08 Augustus (August)
    December (December)
    November (November)
    Sextilis (August)

09 Januarius (January)
    Quintilis (July)
    September (September)

10 Februarius (February)

Spanish month names with English translation:

04 mayo (May)

05 abril (April)
    enero (January)
    julio (July)

junio (June)
marzo (March)

06 agosto (August)

07 febrero (February)

octubre (October)

09 diciembre (December)
    noviembre (November)

10 septiembre (September)

French Revolutionary calendar month names with English translation:

06 Nivôse (snow)

07 Floréal (blossom)
    Ventôse (wind)

08 Brumaire (mist)

Frimaire (frost)
Germinal (seed)
Messidor (harvest)
Pluviôse (rain)

Prairial (meadow)

09 Fructidor (fruits)
    Thermidor (heat)

11 Vendémiaire (vintage)

See also **calendar**

monument

Monuments and memorials include:

04 Eros (England)
    Homo (The Netherlands)

05 Grant (USA)
    Scott (Scotland)

06 Albert (England)

07 Lincoln (USA)
    Martyr's (Iraq)

08 Boadicea (England)
    Cenotaph (England)
    Taj Mahal (India)
    Victoria (England)

09 Charminar (India)
    Menin Gate (Belgium)

10 Broken Ring (Russia)

Marble Arch (England)
Mt Rushmore (USA)
Navigators' (Portugal)
Washington (USA)

11 Civil Rights (USA)
    Voortrekker (South Africa)

12 Great Pyramid (Egypt)

Statue of Zeus (Greece)

13 Admiralty Arch (England)
Arc de Triomphe (France)
Nelson's Column (England)
People's Heroes (China)

Trajan's Column (Italy)

14 Eleanor Crosses (England)
Gateway of India (India)
Hands of Victory (Iraq)
Hiroshima Peace (Japan)

Lenin Mausoleum (Russia)
Wright Brothers (USA)

15 Brandenburg Gate
(Germany)

See also **cemetery**

moon

Lunar seas:

08 Bay of Dew (Sinus Roris)

09 Moscow Sea (Mare Moscoviense)
Sea of Cold (Mare Frigoris)
Smyth's Sea (Mare Smythii)

10 Bay of Heats (Sinus Aestuum)
Central Bay (Sinus Medii)
Eastern Sea (Mare Orientale)
Foaming Sea (Mare Spumans)
Mare Nubium (Sea of Clouds)
Sea of Waves (Mare Undarum)
Sinus Medii (Central Bay)
Sinus Roris (Bay of Dew)

11 Lacus Mortis (Lake of Death)
Lake of Death (Lacus Mortis)
Mare Crisium (Sea of Crises)
Mare Humorum (Sea of Moisture)
Mare Imbrium (Sea of Showers)
Mare Ingenii (Sea of Geniuses)
Mare Smythii (Smyth's Sea)
Mare Spumans (Foaming Sea)
Mare Undarum (Sea of Waves)
Mare Vaporum (Sea of Vapours)
Marginal Sea (Mare Marginis)
Palus Somnii (Marsh of Sleep)
Sea of Clouds (Mare Nubium)
Sea of Crises (Mare Crisium)
Sea of Nectar (Mare Nectaris)
Sinus Iridum (Bay of Rainbows)
Southern Sea (Mare Australe)

12 Humboldt's Sea (Mare Humboldtianum)
Lake of Dreams (Lacus Somniorum)

Mare Australe (Southern Sea)
Mare Frigoris (Sea of Cold)
Mare Marginis (Marginal Sea)
Mare Nectaris (Sea of Nectar)
Marsh of Decay (Palus Putredinis)
Marsh of Mists (Palus Nebularum)
Marsh of Sleep (Palus Somnii)
Sea of Showers (Mare Imbrium)
Sea of Vapours (Mare Vaporum)
Sinus Aestuum (Bay of Heats)

13 Bay of Rainbows (Sinus Iridum)
Mare Orientale (Eastern Sea)
Ocean of Storms (Oceanus Procellarum)
Sea of Geniuses (Mare Ingenii)
Sea of Moisture (Mare Humorum)
Sea of Serenity (Mare Serenitatis)

14 Lacus Somniorum (Lake of Dreams)
Palus Nebularum (Marsh of Mists)
Sea of Fertility (Mare Fecunditatis)

15 Mare Moscoviense (Moscow Sea)
Mare Serenitatis (Sea of Serenity)
Palus Putredinis (Marsh of Decay)

16 Mare Fecunditatis (Sea of Fertility)
Marsh of Epidemics (Palus Epidemiarum)
Palus Epidemiarum (Marsh of Epidemics)

17 Mare Humboldtianum (Humboldt's Sea)
Sea of Tranquillity (Mare Tranquillitatis)

18 Oceanus Procellarum (Ocean of Storms)

19 Mare Tranquillitatis (Sea of Tranquillity)

Moons include:

02 Io (Jupiter)

04 Moon (Earth)
Rhea (Saturn)

05 Ariel (Uranus)
Dione (Saturn)
Mimas (Saturn)
Titan (Saturn)

06 Charon (Pluto)

Deimos (Mars)
Europa (Jupiter)
Nereid (Neptune)
Oberon (Uranus)
Phobos (Mars)
Tethys (Saturn)
Triton (Neptune)

07 Iapetus (Saturn)
Miranda (Uranus)

Proteus (Neptune)
Titania (Uranus)
Umbriel (Uranus)

08 Callisto (Jupiter)
Cruithne (Earth)
Ganymede (Jupiter)
Hyperion (Saturn)

09 Enceladus (Saturn)

Terms to do with the moon include:

05 lunar
phase

06 waning
waxing

07 far side
gibbous

new moon

08 blue moon
crescent
dark side
full moon
half-moon
lunation

near side

09 blood moon
moonlight
moonscape
moonshine

11 harvest moon

hunter's moon
last quarter
quarter moon

12 first quarter
man in the moon
synodic month
third quarter

Morrison, Toni (1931–)

Significant works include:

04 *Home* (2012)
Jazz (1992)
Love (2003)
Sula (1973)

06 *A Mercy* (2008)

07 *Beloved* (1987)

Tar Baby (1981)

08 *Paradise* (1998)

12 *The Bluest Eye* (1970)

13 *Song of Solomon* (1977)

Significant characters include:

01 L

03 Son

04 Dead (Macon 'Jake')
Dead (Macon 'Milkman')
Dead (Pilate)
Dear (Rose)

Gigi
Heed
Sosa (Consolata)

05 Bains (Guitar)
Belle (True)
Cosey (Bill)
Grace
Hagar

Peace (Sula)
Sethe
Trace (Joe)
Trace (Violet)

06 Childs (Jadine)
Connie
Junior
Seneca

Wright (Nel)

07 Beloved
Manfred (Dorcas)

08 Albright (Mavis)
Truelove (Pallas)

09 Breedlove (Pecola)
Consolata

moss

Mosses include:

03 bog
bur
cup
fog

04 burr
club

long
peat
tree

05 fairy
usnea

06 hypnum

07 acrogen
foggage
lycopod

08 sphagnum

staghorn

09 wolf's claw
wolf's foot

10 fontinalis
ground pine

moth

Moths include:

01 Y

02 Io

03 pug
wax

04 goat
hawk
luna
puss

05 ghost
gypsy

tiger

06 bogong
bugong
burnet
carpet
kitten
lackey
lappet
magpie
sphinx
turnip

winter

07 buff-tip
clothes
emerald
emperor
hook-tip
silver-Y
six-spot
tussock

08 cinnabar

peppered
silkworm

10 death's-head

11 garden tiger
pale tussock
swallowtail

12 Kentish glory
peach blossom
red underwing

13 processionary

See also **butterfly**

mother

Mothers include:

04 Joad (Ma; *The Grapes of Wrath*, 1939, John Steinbeck)
Mary (Bible)
Page (Mistress Margaret/Meg; *The Merry Wives of Windsor*, 1597–98, William Shakespeare)

05 Morel (Mrs; *Sons and Lovers*, 1913, D H Lawrence)
Niobe (Greek mythology)

06 Thaisa (*Pericles*, 1607, William Shakespeare)

07 Capulet (Lady; *Romeo and Juliet*, 1595, William Shakespeare)
Courage (Mother; *Mother Courage and her Children*, 1941, Bertolt Brecht)

Hubbard (nursery rhyme)

08 Gertrude (*Hamlet*, 1600–01, William Shakespeare)
Hermione (*The Winter's Tale*, 1609, William Shakespeare)

09 Agrippina (the Elder; c.14 BC–33 AD, Roman)
Elizabeth (Bible)
Pankhurst (Emmeline; 1857–1928, English)

10 Virgin Mary (Bible)

11 Queen Mother (1900–2002)
Worthington (Mrs; *Mrs Worthington*, 1935, Noël Coward)

15 Whistler's Mother (painting)

motor racing, motorcyclist *see* racing: motor racing

motoring

Motor vehicle parts include:

03 ABS	battery	brake shoe	windshield
04 axle	chassis	crankcase	wing mirror
boot	fog lamp	dashboard	**11** accelerator
door	gas tank	disc brake	anti-roll bar
gear	gearbox	drum brake	backup light
hood	kingpin	filler cap	exhaust pipe
horn	spoiler	fuel gauge	folding seat
jack	sunroof	gear-lever	ignition key
sill		gearshift	jockey wheel
tyre	**08** air brake	gear-stick	number plate
vent	air inlet	handbrake	parcel shelf
wing	bodywork	headlight	speedometer
	brake pad	indicator	
05 bezel	car phone	monocoque	**12** license plate
brake	car radio	overrider	parking-light
clock	door-lock	prop shaft	quarterlight
grill	fog light	rear light	transmission
shaft	headrest	reflector	
trunk	ignition	sidelight	**13** centre console
wheel	jump lead	spare tyre	courtesy light
	lift gate	stoplight	cruise control
06 airbag	oil gauge	wheel arch	flasher switch
bonnet	roof rack		pneumatic tyre
bumper	seat belt	**10** brake light	rack and pinion
clutch	silencer	drive shaft	radial-ply tyre
dimmer	solenoid	petrol tank	reclining seat
engine	sun visor	power brake	shock absorber
fender	swingarm	rev counter	side-impact bar
heater	track rod	side mirror	steering-wheel
hub-cap		stick shift	**14** air-conditioner
towbar	**09** bench seat	suspension	central locking
07 ashtray	brake drum	windscreen	electric window

		15	
emergency light	rear-view mirror	antiglare switch	instrument panel
four-wheel drive	reversing light	antitheft device	
hydraulic brake	steering-column	child-safety seat	windscreen-wiper

Motor manufacturers include:

02 MG (UK)

03 BMW (Germany)
Kia (South Korea)

04 Audi (Germany)
Fiat (Italy)
Ford (USA)
Jeep (USA)
Lada (Russia)
Mini (UK)
Saab (Sweden)
Seat (Spain)
Yugo (Yugoslavia)

05 Buick (USA)
Dodge (USA)
Honda (Japan)
Isuzu (Japan)
Lexus (Japan)
Lotus (UK)
Mazda (Japan)
Riley (UK)
Rover (UK)
Skoda (Czech Republic)
Smart (USA)

Volvo (Sweden)

06 Austin (UK)
Daewoo (South Korea)
Datsun (Japan)
Jaguar (UK)
Lancia (Italy)
Morgan (UK)
Morris (UK)
Nissan (Japan)
Proton (Malaysia)
Subaru (Japan)
Talbot (France)
Toyota (Japan)

07 Bentley (UK)
Bugatti (Italy)
Citroen (France)
Daimler (Germany)
Ferrari (Italy)
Hillman (UK)
Hyundai (South Korea)
Peugeot (France)
Pontiac (US)
Porsche (Germany)
Reliant (UK)

Renault (France)
Trabant (East Germany)
Triumph (UK)

08 Cadillac (USA)
Chrysler (USA)
Daihatsu (Japan)
De Lorean (US)
Maserati (Italy)
Mercedes (Germany)
Standard (UK)
Vauxhall (UK)
Wolseley (UK)

09 Alfa Romeo (Italy)
Chevrolet (USA)
Land Rover (UK)

10 Mitsubishi (Japan)
Oldsmobile (US)
Rolls Royce (UK)
Vanden Plas (UK)
Volkswagen (Germany)

11 Aston Martin (UK)
Lamborghini (Italy)

12 Mercedes-Benz (Germany)

Motor car types include:

03 cab
MPV
SUV

04 auto
jeep
limo
Mini®
taxi

05 buggy
coupé
sedan

06 banger

Beetle®
estate
hearse
hybrid
jalopy
kit-car
saloon

07 minivan

08 fastback
panda car
roadster
runabout

Smart car®
stock car

09 all-roader
automatic
bubble-car
cabriolet
hatchback
Land Rover®
limousine
muscle car
off-roader
patrol car

sports car

10 Model T Ford®
Range Rover®
Sinclair C5
veteran car
vintage car

11 convertible

12 station wagon

13 people carrier
shooting brake

14 four-wheel drive

Motor cars include:

04 FAB1 (*Thunderbirds, TV series*)

06 Herbie (*The Love Bug,* 1969)

08 Blue Bird (Malcolm Campbell/land speed
record)
De Lorean (*Back to the Future,* 1985, et seq)

09 Batmobile (*Batman* comic)
Christine (*Christine,* 1983, Stephen King)
Genevieve (*Genevieve,* 1953)

11 Flintmobile (*The Flintstones,* TV series)

Road signs include:

04 ford
stop

06 cattle
one-way

07 give way

08 clearway
keep left
no U-turns
red route
turn left

09 ahead only
keep right
no waiting
risk of ice
road works

side winds
T-junction
trams only
turn right

10 bend to left
crossroads
double bend
hump bridge
no left turn
roundabout
speed limit

11 no right turn
tunnel ahead

12 falling rocks
no overtaking

passing place
slippery road

13 end of clearway
end of motorway
level crossing
no through road
one-way traffic

14 mini-roundabout
road works ahead
stop and give way
traffic signals
turn right ahead

15 no motor vehicles
single-track road
start of motorway

Motoring terms include:

02 AA

03 ABS
dip
GPS
LRP
map
MOT
RAC
tow

04 exit
park
skid
SORN
stop

05 amber
brake
crash
cut up
flash
layby
on tow
prang
shunt

06 diesel
fill up
filter
garage
hold-up
L-plate
octane
petrol
pile-up
pull in

07 blowout
bollard
bus lane

car park
car wash
cat's-eye
give way
logbook
MOT test
neutral
pull out
reverse
road map
snarl-up
tax disc
traffic

08 accident
change up
coasting
declutch
fast lane
flat tyre
gridlock
indicate
junction
main beam
overtake
puncture
red light
road rage
services
slip road
slow lane
speeding
tailback
taxi rank
turn left
unleaded

09 blind spot
breakdown

collision
cycle lane
fifth gear
first gear
green card
hit-and-run
radar trap
road atlas
road studs
roadworks
sixth gear
third gear
T junction
turn right
wheelspin
white line

10 accelerate
amber light
arm signals
bottleneck
change down
change gear
change lane
contraflow
crossroads
fourth gear
green light
inside lane
middle lane
pedestrian
petrol pump
roundabout
screenwash
second gear
speed limit
stay in lane
straight on

tailgating
traffic jam
yellow line

11 box junction
crawler lane
drink-driver
driving test
hand signals
highway code
outside lane
speed camera
traffic cone
traffic cops
traffic news
zigzag lines

12 drink-driving
hard shoulder
left-hand lane
motorway toll
one-way system
parking meter
passing place

See also **vehicle**

road junction
speeding fine
tyre pressure

13 Belisha beacon
drink and drive
driving lesson
driving school
flashing amber
handbrake turn
jump the lights
left-hand drive
level crossing
no-claims bonus
parking ticket
pay and display
penalty points
petrol station
power steering
right-hand lane
super unleaded
traffic lights
traffic police

zebra crossing

14 cadence braking
double declutch
driver's license
driving licence
four-wheel drive
mini-roundabout
MOT certificate
motorway pile-up
overtaking lane
poor visibility
puffin crossing
right-hand drive
service station
speeding ticket
unleaded petrol

15 pelican crossing
put your foot down
road fund licence
test certificate
traction control
warning triangle

mountain

Mountains, mountain ranges and hills include:

02 K2 (Kashmir-Jammu/China)

03 Apo (Philippines)
Dom (Switzerland)
Tai (China)

04 Alai (Kyrgyzstan)
Alps (Switzerland/France/Germany/Austria/
 Liechtenstein/Italy/Slovenia/Croatia)
Blue (Australia)
Cook (New Zealand)
Etna (Italy)
Fuji (Japan)
Jura (France/Switzerland)
Meru (Hinduism/Buddhism)
Ossa (Australia)
Rila (Bulgaria)
Ural (Russia/Kazakhstan)

05 Altai (Russia/China/Mongolia)
Andes (Argentina/Chile/Bolivia/Peru/
 Ecuador/Colombia/Venezuela)
Atlas (Morocco/Algeria/Tunisia)
Coast (Canada/USA/Mexico)
Downs (England)
Eiger (Switzerland)
Ghats (India)
Halti (Finland)
Huang (China)
Kamet (India)
Kékes (Hungary)

Kenya (Kenya)
Logan (Canada)
Matra (Hungary)
Ozark (USA)
Qogir (Kashmir-Jammu/China)
Rocky (Mexico/USA/Canada)
Sinai (Egypt)
Snowy (Australia)
Table (South Africa)
Tatra (Poland/Slovakia)

06 Ararat (Turkey)
Cho Oyu (China/Nepal)
Denali (USA)
Egmont (New Zealand)
Elbert (USA)
Elbrus (Russia)
Haltia (Finland)
Hoggar (Algeria)
Lhotse (China/Nepal)
Makalu (China/Nepal)
Mendip (England)
Mourne (Northern Ireland)
Musala (Bulgaria)
Pindus (Greece)
Taurus (Turkey)
Vosges (France)
Zagros (Iran)

07 Ahaggar (Algeria)
Belukha (Russia/Kazakhstan)

Beskids (Poland/Slovakia)
Cascade (Canada/USA)
Cheviot (England/Scotland)
Darling (Australia)
Everest (China/Nepal)
Fuji-san (Japan)
Hua Shan (China)
Manaslu (Nepal)
Nilgiri (India)
Olympus (Cyprus)
Rainier (USA)
Rhodope (Bulgaria/Greece)
Rockies (Mexico/USA/Canada)
Roraima (Brazil/Guyana/Venezuela)
Ruapehu (New Zealand)
Skiddaw (England)
Snowdon (Wales)
Stanley (Democratic Republic of the Congo/ Uganda)
Tai Shan (China)
Troödos (Cyprus)

08 Ben Nevis (Scotland)
Cameroon (Cameroon)
Catskill (USA)
Caucasus (Russia/Georgia/Armenia/ Azerbaijan/Turkey/Iran)
Cévennes (France)
Chiltern (England)
Damavand (Iran)
Five Holy (China)
Flinders (Australia)
Fujiyama (Japan)
Heng Shan (China)
Jungfrau (Switzerland)
Kinabalu (Malaysia)
Mauna Kea (USA)
Mauna Loa (USA)
McKinley (USA)
Musgrave (Australia)
Pennines (England)
Pyrenees (France/Spain/Andorra)
Rushmore (USA)
Song Shan (China)
St Helens (USA)
Stirling (Australia)
Taranaki (New Zealand)

09 Aconcagua (Argentina)
Allegheny (USA)
Altai Shan (Russia/China/Mongolia)
Annapurna (Nepal)
Apennines (Italy)
Blue Ridge (USA)
Broad Peak (Kashmir-Jammu)
Cotswolds (England)
Dolomites (Italy)
Grampians (Australia/Scotland)
Hamersley (Australia)

Helvellyn (England)
Himalayas (central Asia)
Hindu Kush (central Asia)
Inyangani (Zimbabwe)
Karakoram (Kashmir-Jammu)
Kosciusko (Australia)
Lenin Peak (Tajikistan/Kyrgyzstan)
Mackenzie (Canada)
Mont Blanc (France/Italy)
Muz Tag Ata (China)
Nanda Devi (India)
Rakaposhi (Kashmir-Jammu)
Tirichmir (Pakistan)
Tirol Alps (Germany/Austria)
Zugspitze (Germany)

10 Adirondack (USA)
Cader Idris (Wales)
Cairngorms (Scotland)
Cantabrian (Spain)
Carpathian (Slovakia/Poland/Ukraine/ Romania)
Chimborazo (Ecuador)
Dhaulagiri (Nepal)
Gasherbrum (Kashmir-Jammu)
Gosainthan (China)
Great Smoky (USA)
MacDonnell (Australia)
Matterhorn (Switzerland)
Pobedy Peak (China/Kyrgyzstan)
Puncak Jaya (Indonesia)
Sagarmatha (China/Nepal)

11 Appalachian (Canada/USA)
Chomolungma (China/Nepal)
Drakensberg (South Africa)
Kilimanjaro (Tanzania)
Mongo-Ma-Loba (Cameroon)
Nanga Parbat (Kashmir-Jammu)
Pico Bolívar (Venezuela)
Scafell Pike (England)
Siula Grande (Peru)

12 Bavarian Alps (Germany/Austria)
Dufourspitze (Switzerland/Italy)
Kanchenjunga (India/Nepal)
Popocatepetl (Mexico)
Sierra Nevada (USA)
Southern Alps (New Zealand)
Tibet Plateau (China)
Ulugh Muztagh (China)
Vinson Massif (Antarctica)

13 Carrantuohill (Ireland)
Communism Peak (Tajikistan)
Great Dividing (Australia)
Haltiatunturi (Finland)
Kangchenjunga (India/Nepal)
Ojos del Salado (Argentina/Chile)

14 Australian Alps (Australia)

Bohemian Forest (Germany/Czech Republic)
Fichtelgebirge (Germany)
Qomolangma Feng (China/Nepal)
Thadentsonyane (Lesotho)

Trans-Antarctic (Antarctica)
15 Guiana Highlands (Venezuela/Brazil/
Guyana)
Nevado de Illampu (Bolivia)

Mountain passes include:

04 Ofen (Italy/Switzerland)
05 Haast (New Zealand)
Lewis (New Zealand)
South (USA)
06 Khyber (Pakistan/Afghanistan)
Lindis (New Zealand)
Shipka (Bulgaria)
07 Arthur's (New Zealand)
Brenner (Italy/Austria)
Oberalp (Switzerland)
Plöcken (Italy/Austria)
Simplon (Italy/Switzerland)

See also pike; **volcano**

Wrynose (England)
08 Hongshan (China)
Yangguan (China)
09 Khunjerab (China/Pakistan)
St Bernard (Italy/France/Switzerland)
10 St Gotthard (Switzerland)
12 Roncesvalles (Spain/France)
13 Cilician Gates (Turkey)
San Bernardino (Switzerland)
14 Grand St Bernard (Italy/Switzerland)
15 Little St Bernard (France/Italy)

mountaineering

Mountaineers include:

04 Hunt (John, Lord; 1910–98, English)
05 Brown (Joe; 1930– , English)
Bruce (C G; 1866–1939, English)
Meyer (Hans; 1858–1929, German)
Munro (Sir Hugh; 1856–1919, Scottish)
Scott (Doug; 1941– , English)
Tabei (Junko; 1939– , Japanese)
Wills (Sir Alfred; 1828–1912, English)
06 Haston (Dougal; 1940–77, Scottish)
Herzog (Maurice; 1919–2012, French)
Irvine (Andrew; 1902–24, English)
Smythe (Frank; 1900–49, English)
Tilman (Bill; 1898–1977, English)
Uemura (Naomi; 1942–84, Japanese)
07 Hillary (Sir Edmund; 1919–2008, New
Zealand)

Mallory (George; 1886–1924, English)
Messner (Reinhold; 1944– , Austrian)
Shipton (Eric; 1907–77, English)
Simpson (Myrtle; 1931– , Scottish)
Tazieff (Haroun; 1914–98, Polish/French)
Tenzing (Sherpa; 1914–86, Nepalese)
Whymper (Edward; 1840–1911, English)
08 Coolidge (W A B; 1850–1926, US/British)
MacInnes (Hamish; 1930– , Scottish)
Whillans (Don; 1933–85, English)
09 Bonington (Sir Chris; 1934– , English)
10 Eckenstein (Oscar; 1859–1921, English)
Freshfield (Douglas; 1845–1934, English)
Hargreaves (Alison; 1962–95, English)
12 Purtscheller (Ludwig; 1849–1900, Austrian)
13 Tenzing Norgay (1914–86, Nepalese)

Mountaineering and climbing terms include:

02	ax		rock		ridge		helmet
03	adz		rope		scree		ice axe
	axe		spur		sérac		piolet
	cam	**05**	arête		shunt		saddle
	col		belay		sling		Sherpa
	hut		chock		spike		summit
	nut		cleft		stack		top out
			gully	**06**	ascent		unrope
04	adze		Munro		corrie	**07**	belayer
	crag		pitch		étrier		bivouac
	pick		piton		Graham		bolting

chimney
cornice
crampon
descent
fissure
glacier
harness
ice step
Marilyn
tying in
wallnut

08 Alpinism
ascender
base camp
chalk bag
climbing
crevasse
hand hold

headwall
ice piton
ice ridge
ice screw
ice slope
overhang
rock face
rock wall
sea stack
traverse

09 abseiling
avalanche
carabiner
debolting
descender
hammer axe
karabiner
on the rope

rapelling
rock spike
rope sling
sling seat
trad route

10 bouldering
chalk cliff
chockstone
Dülfer seat
helmet lamp
non-belayer
prusik knot
prusik loop
sit harness
snow bridge
solo ascent
wrist sling

11 abseil piton
abseil sling
dynamic rope
ice climbing
ringed piton
snow cornice
snow gaiters
snow goggles

12 climbing wall
self-belaying
standing rope

13 abseil station
sport climbing

14 corkscrew piton
kernmantel rope

15 climbing harness
drive-in ice piton

mouth

Mouth parts include:

03 gum
jaw
lip

04 lips

05 uvula

06 tongue
tonsil

07 hare lip

08 lower lip
upper lip

10 hard palate
soft palate

11 cleft palate

13 alveolar ridge

15 isthmus of fauces

See also **teeth**

movement *see* **art**; **poetry**

Mozart, Wolfgang Amadeus (1756–91)

Significant works include:

04 'Hunt' (String Quartet; 1784)
'Linz' (Symphony; 1783)

05 'Paris' (Symphony; 1778)

06 'Lutzow' (Concerto; 1776)
'Prague' (Symphony; 1786)

07 *Don Juan* (1787)
'Haffner' (Symphony; 1782)
'Jupiter' (Symphony; 1788)

08 *Idomeneo* (1781)

10 'Coronation' (Concerto; 1788)
'Jeunehomme' (Concerto; 1777)
Lucio Silla (1772)

11 *Don Giovanni* (1787)
'Great G minor' (Symphony; 1788)

12 *Così fan tutte* (1790)
Little G minor' (Symphony; 1773)
Scipio's Dream (1772)

13 *Ascanio in Alba* (1771)
Missa in C minor (1783)

The Impresario (1786)
The Magic Flute (1791)

14 *Die Zauberflöte* (1791)

15 *La finta semplice* (1769)
Le nozze di Figaro (1786)
Requiem in D minor (1791)

16 *La Clemenza di Tito* (1791)

17 *Il dissoluto punito* (1787)
Il sogno di Scipione (1772)

18 *Apollo et Hyacinthus* (1767)
La finta giardiniera (1775)
Mitridate, Rè di Ponto (1770)
The School for Lovers (1790)

19 *Bastien und Bastienne* (1768)
La Scuola degli Amanti (1790)
The Marriage of Figaro (1786)

20 *Eine Kleine Nachtmusik* (1787)
The Dissolute Punished (1787)
The Pretended Gardener (1775)

21 *Der Schauspieldirektor* (1786)
   The Pretended Simpleton (1769)
23 *Mithridates, King of Pontus* (1770)

25 *Die Entführung aus dem Serail* (1782)
27 *The Abduction from the Seraglio* (1782)

Significant characters include:

04 Tito
06 Apollo
   Figaro
   Pamina
   Rosina
   Tamino
07 Bastien
   Susanna
08 Almaviva

Belmonte
Ferrando
Papagena
Papageno
Sarastro
Scipione
09 Bastienne
   Cherubino
   Constanze

Dorabella
Guglielmo
10 Fiordiligi
   Hyacinthus
   Monostatos
11 Don Giovanni
   Donna Elvira
15 Queen of the Night

murder

Murderers, alleged murderers and assassins include:

03 Ray (James Earl; 1928–98, US)
04 Aram (Eugene; 1704–59, English)
   Bell (Mary; 1957– , English)
   Edny (Clithero; *Edgar Huntly*, 1799, Charles Brockden Brown)
   Gacy (John Wayne; 1942–94, US)
   Gein (Edward; 1906–84, US)
   Hare (William; 1790–1860, Irish)
   Kray (Reggie; 1933–2000, English)
   Kray (Ronnie; 1933–95, English)
   Retz (Gilles de Laval, Baron; 1404–40, French)
   Ruby (Jack; 1911–67, US)
   Todd (Sweeney; late 18c, English)
   West (Fred; 1942–95, English)
   West (Rosemary; 1953– , English)
05 Beane (Sawney; fl.c.1600, Scottish)
   Booth (John Wilkes; 1839–65, US)
   Brady (Ian; 1938– , Scottish)
   Bundy (Ted; 1946–89, US)
   Burke (William; 1792–1829, Irish)
   Craig (Christopher; c.1936– , English)
   Ellis (Ruth; 1926–55, Welsh)
   Haigh (John; 1909–49, English)
   Havoc (Jack; *The Tiger in the Smoke*, 1952, Margery Allingham)
   Rudge (*Barnaby Rudge*, 1841, Charles Dickens)
06 Barrow (Clyde; 1909–34, US)
   Borden (Lizzie; 1860–1927, US)
   Corday (Charlotte; 1768–93, French)
   Dahmer (Jeffrey; 1960–94, US)
   Lecter (Dr Hannibal; *Red Dragon*, 1981, et seq, Thomas Harris)
   Manson (Charles; 1934– , US)
   Misfit (the; *A Good Man is Hard to Find*, 1948, Flannery O'Connor)

Nilsen (Dennis; 1945– , Scottish)
Oswald (Lee Harvey; 1939–63, US)
Parker (Bonnie; 1911–34, US)
Sirhan (Sirhan; c.1943– , Palestinian/US)
07 Bathori (Elizabeth; d.1614, Polish)
   Bentley (Derek; c.1933–1953, English)
   Bianchi (Kenneth; 1950– , US)
   Chapman (Mark; c.1955– , US)
   Crippen (Hawley Harvey; 1862–1910, US)
   DeSalvo (Albert; 1931–73, US)
   Hindley (Myra; 1942–2002, English)
   Macbeth (*Macbeth*, c.1606, William Shakespeare)
   Manston (Aeneas; *Desperate Remedies*, 1871, Thomas Hardy)
   Neilson (Donald; 1936–2011, English)
   Shipman (Harold; 1946–2004, English)
08 Barabbas (1c AD, Bible)
   Christie (John Reginald Halliday; 1898–1953, English)
   Claudius (*Hamlet*, 1601/2, William Shakespeare)
   Dominici (Gaston; 1877–1965, French)
   Hanratty (James; c.1936–1962, English)
   Son of Sam (David Berkowitz; c.1953– , US)
   Thompson (Edith; d.1923, English)
09 Berkowitz (David; c.1953– , US)
   Harmodius (d.514 BC, Athenian)
   McNaghten (Daniel; 19c, English)
   Sutcliffe (Peter; 1946– , English)
10 McNaughten (Daniel; 19c, English)
   Nirdlinger (Phyllis; *Double Indemnity*, 1944, James M Cain)
11 Anckarström (Johan Jakob; 1762–92, Swedish)
   Quare Fellow (the; *The Quare Fellow*, 1954, Brendan Behan)

12 Starkweather (Charles; 1938–59, US)
13 Jack the Ripper (19c, unknown)
14 Moors Murderers (Ian Brady; 1938– ,
Scottish/Myra Hindley; 1942–2002, English)
15 Yorkshire Ripper (Peter Sutcliffe; 1946– ,
English)

Murdoch, Dame Iris (1919–99)

07 *The Bell* (1958)
10 *A Word Child* (1975)
11 *Bruno's Dream* (1969)
Under the Net (1954)
12 *A Severed Head* (1961)
The Sea, The Sea (1978)
14 *The Black Prince* (1973)
The Green Knight (1993)
17 *The Good Apprentice* (1985)

The Red and the Green (1965)
18 *The Time of the Angels* (1966)
20 *The Philosopher's Pupil* (1983)
The Sovereignty of Good (1970)
21 *The Message to the Planet* (1989)
24 *The Book and the Brotherhood* (1987)
25 *Sartre: Romantic Rationalist* (1953)
27 *Metaphysics as a Guide to Morals* (1992)

03 Fox (Mischa)
Mor (William)
04 Duno (Stuart)
Finn (Peter O'Finney)
King (Julius)
Mead (Michael)
05 Blick (Calvin)
Burde (Hilary)
Gashe (Toby)
Keepe (Hunter)
Keepe (Rosa)
Klein (Honor)
Odell (Danby)
Sands (Emma)
06 Baffin (Arnold)
Browne (Morgan)
Browne (Tallis)
Carter (Rain)
Ducane (John)
Fawley (Catherine)
Fawley (Nick)
Forbes (Cato)

Foster (Hilda)
Foster (Rupert)
Foster (Simon)
Ludens (Alfred)
Saward (Peter)
Vallar (Marcus)
Watkin (Lisa)
07 Arrowby (Charles)
Baltram (Edward)
Baltram (Jesse)
Cavidge (Anne)
Crimond (David)
Fischer (Carel)
Fischer (Elizabeth)
Fischer (Marcus)
Fischer (Muriel)
Nilsson (Axel)
Pearson (Bradley)
Peshkov (Eugene)
Peshkov (Leo)
Rozanov (John Robert)
08 Cockeyne (Annette)

Donaghue (Jake James)
Openshaw (Gertrude)
Peronett (Hugh)
Tinckham (Mrs)
09 Lusiewicz (Jan)
Lusiewicz (Stefan)
McCaffrey (George)
O'Driscoll (Pattie)
10 Belfounder (Hugo)
Gibson Grey (Austin)
Greenfield (Dora)
Greenfield (Paul)
Marshalson (Henry)
Tayper Pace (James)
11 Greensleave (Bruno)
Greensleave (Diana)
Greensleave (Miles)
Lynch-Gibbon (Martin)
Magistretti (Maria 'Maggie')
Szczepanski (Wojciech
'Peter', the Count)

muscle

05 psoas
06 biceps
rectus
soleus
07 cardiac
deltoid
gluteus
iliacus
omohyid

triceps
08 detrusor
masseter
platysma
pronator
risorius
scalenus
splenius
09 abdominal

complexus
eye-string
perforans
sartorius
stapedius
supinator
trapezius
10 buccinator
quadriceps

11 ciliary body
rhomboideus
13 gastrocnemius
14 xiphihumeralis
15 latissimus dorsi
pectoralis major
pectoralis minor
peroneal muscles

muse

The Nine Muses of Greek mythology:

04 Clio (history and lyre-playing)

05 Erato (lyric poetry and hymns)

06 Thalia (comedy and idyllic poetry)
Urania (astronomy)

07 Euterpe (flute-playing)

08 Calliope (epic poetry)

09 Melpomene (tragedy)

10 Polyhymnia (dance, mime and acting)

11 Terpsichore (dance and lyric poetry)

museum

Museums and galleries include:

02 RA (England)

03 ICA (England)

04 MoMA (USA)
Tate (England)

05 Prado (Spain)
Terme (Italy)
V and A (England)

06 Correr (Italy)
London (England)
Louvre (France)
The Met (USA)
Uffizi (Italy)

07 British (England)
Fogg Art (USA)
Hayward (England)
Hofburg (Austria)
Mankind (England)
Pushkin (Russia)
Russian (Russia)
Science (England)
Vatican (Vatican City)
Whitney (USA)

08 Bargello (Italy)
Borghese (Italy)
National (various)
Pergamon (Germany)

09 Accademia (Italy)
Albertina (Austria)
Arnolfini (England)
Ashmolean (England)
Belvedere (Austria)
Deutsches (Germany)
Hermitage (Russia)
Holocaust (various)
Modern Art (various)
Sans Souci (Germany)
Tretyakov (Russia)
Whitworth (England)

10 Guggenheim (various)
Jeu de Paume (France)
Pinakothek (Germany)
Pitt-Rivers (England)
Serpentine (England)
Tate Modern (England)

11 Fitzwilliam (England)
Imperial War (England)
Mauritshuis (The Netherlands)
Musée d'Orsay (France)
Pitti Palace (Italy)
Rijksmuseum (The Netherlands)
Smithsonian (USA)
Tate Britain (England)

12 Royal Academy (England)
The Cloisters (USA)

13 Jean Paul Getty (USA)
Peace Memorial (Japan)
Royal Pavilion (England)

14 Barbican Centre (England)
Natural History (England)
Pompidou Centre (France)
State Hermitage (Russia)

15 Centre Beaubourg (France)
Frick Collection (USA)

mushroom

Mushrooms and toadstools include:

03 cep

04 base
ugly
wood

05 brain
field

gypsy
horse
magic
march
morel
naked

06 blewit
button
edible
elf cup
ink cap
meadow

mower's
oyster
satan's
winter

07 amanita
blewits
blusher
boletus
Caesar's
griping
parasol
porcini
truffle

08 chestnut
death cap
deceiver
hedgehog
inedible
penny bun
shiitake
sickener

09 cramp ball
earth ball
fairy ring
fly agaric
poisonous
St George's
stinkhorn

10 champignon
cultivated

See also **fungus**

false morel
lawyer's wig
liberty cap
panther cap
sweetbread
wood agaric

11 chanterelle
clean mycena
common morel
dingy agaric
honey fungus
stout agaric
sulphur tuft
the goat's lip
velvet shank

12 common ink cap
dryad's saddle
false blusher
horn of plenty
larch boletus
lurid boletus
purple blewit
shaggy ink cap
slippery jack
white truffle
winter fungus
wood hedgehog

13 buckler agaric
clouded agaric
copper trumpet

devil's boletus
emetic russula
firwood agaric
Jew's ear fungus
purple boletus
satan's boletus
shaggy milk cap
shaggy parasol
summer truffle
trumpet agaric
woolly milk cap
yellow stainer

14 common grisette
common laccaria
common puffball
fairies' bonnets
man on horseback
penny-bun fungus
saffron milk cap
yellow-staining

15 beefsteak fungus
chestnut boletus
common earthball
common stinkhorn
destroying angel
garlic marosmius
périgord truffle
Piedmont truffle
stinking parasol
stinking russula
verdigris agaric

music

Musical notes of the sol-fa scale:

02 do (first)
fa (fourth)
la (sixth)
me (third)
mi (third)

re (second)
si (seventh)
so (fifth)
te (seventh)
ti (seventh)

ut (first)

03 doh (first)
fah (fourth)
lah (sixth)
ray (second)

soh (fifth)
sol (fifth)

Music types include:

03 AOR
MOR
pop
rap
ska

04 folk
funk
jazz
jive
mood
rock
soul

05 bebop
blues
cajun
crunk
dance
disco
house
indie
krunk
muzak
R and B
salsa

samba
swing
world

06 atonal
ballet
choral
doo-wop
fusion
garage
gospel
grunge
hip-hop

jungle
lounge
popera
reggae
sacred
skronk
techno
trance

07 ambient
baroque
bhangra
Big Beat
calypso
chamber
country
gamelan
gangsta
jazz-pop
karaoke
nu-metal

ragtime
skiffle
trip-hop

08 acid jazz
ballroom
folk rock
glam rock
hardcore
hard rock
jazz-funk
jazz-rock
operatic
oratorio
punk rock
romantic
soft rock

09 acid house
bluegrass
classical
Dixieland

hard house
honky-tonk

10 electronic
electro-pop
heavy metal
incidental
orchestral
twelve-tone

11 country rock
drum and bass
rock and roll
thrash metal

12 boogie-woogie
electroclash
instrumental

13 easy listening

14 rhythm and blues

15 middle-of-the-road

Music compositions include:

03 jig
lay
rag

04 aria
hymn
lied
mass
opus
raga
reel
song
tune

05 canon
carol
étude
fugue
gigue
march
motet
opera
piece
polka
rondo
round
suite
tango
track

waltz

06 anthem
aubade
ballad
bolero
chorus
lament
lieder
masque
minuet
number
pavane
shanty
sonata

07 ballade
bourrée
cantata
chorale
fanfare
gavotte
mazurka
partita
prelude
requiem
scherzo
toccata

08 berceuse
cavatina
chaconne
concerto
fandango
fantasia
galliard
hornpipe
madrigal
nocturne
operetta
overture
rhapsody
saraband
serenade
sonatina
symphony
zarzuela

09 allemande
arabesque
bagatelle
cabaletta
capriccio
écossaise
farandole
impromptu
invention

pastorale
polonaise
sarabande
spiritual
voluntary

10 barcarolle
bergamasca
concertino
humoresque
intermezzo
opera buffa
strathspey
tarantella

11 bacchanalia
ballad opera
composition
pastourelle
sinfonietta

12 divertimento
extravaganza
nursery rhyme

13 Missa solemnis

14 chorale fantasy
chorale prelude
concerto grosso

Pieces of music include:

04 *Saul* (Handel, 1739)

05 *Rodeo* (Copland, 1942)

06 *Boléro* (Ravel, 1928)
Elijah (Mendelssohn, 1846)
Façade (Walton, 1920–21)

Images (Debussy, 1905–12)

07 *Epitaph* (Mingus, 1989)
Jephtha (Handel, 1751)
Mazeppa (Liszt, 1851)

08 *Creation* (Haydn, 1796–98)

Drum Mass (Haydn, 1796)
'Ode to Joy' (Beethoven, 1822–24)
Peer Gynt (Grieg, 1876)
09 *Finlandia* (Sibelius, 1899)
'Jerusalem' (Elgar, 1922)
10 'Nelson Mass' (Haydn, 1798)
Prozession (Stockhausen, 1967)
The Messiah (Handel, 1742)
The Planets (Holst, 1914–16)
The Seasons (Haydn, 1799–1801)
Water Music (Handel, c.1717)
11 *Curlew River* (Britten, 1964)
Gymnopédies (Satie, 1888)
'Minute Waltz' (Chopin, 1846–47)
Stabat Mater (unknown)
The Creation (Haydn, 1796–98)
Winterreise (Schubert, 1827)
12 *A Sea Symphony* (Vaughan Williams, 1910)
Danse Macabre (Saint-Saëns, 1874)
'Golden Sonata' (Purcell, 1697)
Karelia Suite (Sibelius, 1893)
Kinderscenen (Schumann, 1838)
'Linz Symphony' (Mozart, 1783)
Scheherazade (Rimsky-Korsakov, 1888)
'Trout Quintet' (Schubert, 1819)
13 *Alpensinfonie* (Richard Strauss, 1911–15)
Carmina Burana (Orff, 1937)

Ebony Concerto (Stravinsky, 1946)
'Faust Symphony' (Liszt, 1854–57)
Fêtes Galantes (Debussy, 1891–1904)
German Requiem (Brahms, 1857–68)
Israel in Egypt (Handel, 1739)
Metamorphosen (Richard Strauss, 1945)
On Wenlock Edge (Vaughan Williams, 1909)
The Art of Fugue (Bach, 1740s)
14 *Canticum Sacrum* (Stravinsky, 1956)
'Choral Symphony' (Beethoven, 1823–24)
Colour Symphony (Bliss, 1932)
'Eroica Symphony' (Beethoven, 1803–04)
Glagolitic Mass (Janácek, 1926)
'Prague Symphony' (Mozart, 1786)
Rhapsody in Blue (Gershwin, 1924)
Slavonic Dances (Dvorák, 1878–86)
The Four Seasons (Vivaldi, 1725)
15 *A Child of our Time* (Tippett, 1941)
Alexander's Feast (Handel, 1736)
Children's Corner (Debussy, 1908)
'Emperor Concerto' (Beethoven, 1809)
'Haffner Symphony' (Mozart, 1782)
Italian Concerto (Bach, 1735)
Judas Maccabaeus (Handel, 1747)
'Jupiter Symphony' (Mozart, 1788)
Manfred Symphony (Tchaikovsky, 1885)
Peter and the Wolf (Prokofiev, 1936)
Sicilian Vespers (Verdi, 1855)

Musical instruments include:

03	sax	flute	fiddle
04	bass	gusla	guitar
	bell	gusle	rattle
	drum	gusli	spinet
	erhu	hi-hat	tabour
	fife	kaval	tom-tom
	gong	kazoo	violin
	harp	mbira	zither
	horn	organ	**07** alphorn
	kora	piano	bagpipe
	koto	pipes	baryton
	lute	rebec	bassoon
	lyre	shalm	bodhran
	Moog®	shawm	buccina
	oboe	sitar	celeste
	pipe	tabla	cembalo
	tuba	tabor	cithara
	viol	vibes	cithern
	zeze	viola	cittern
05	Amati	zanze	clarion
	banjo	zirna	clavier
	bells	zurna	cowbell
	bongo	**06** cither	hautboy
	bugle	cornet	lyricon
	cello	cymbal	maracas
	chime	Fender	marimba

ocarina
pandora
Pianola®
piccolo
sackbut
sambuca
saxhorn
serpent
sistrum
tambura
theorbo
timpani
trumpet
ukulele
vihuela
whistle

08 angklung
bagpipes
barytone
bass drum
bouzouki
Calliope
carillon
cimbalom
clappers
clarinet
clarsach
cornpipe
crumhorn
dulcimer
handbell
hornpipe
humstrum
jew's harp
keyboard
mandolin
manzello
melodeon
Pan-pipes
polyphon
recorder

side-drum
spinette
Steinway
theramin
theremin
timbales
triangle
trombone
virginal
vocalion
zambomba

09 accordion
alpenhorn
balalaika
banjolele
bugle-horn
castanets
chime bars
decachord
euphonium
flageolet
harmonica
harmonium
Mellotron®
polyphone
saxophone
snare-drum
tenor-drum
wood block
Wurlitzer®
xylophone

10 bass guitar
bird-scarer
bongo-drums
bullroarer
clavichord
concertina
cor anglais
didgeridoo
double bass
eolian harp

flugelhorn
French horn
grand piano
hurdy-gurdy
kettle-drum
mouth organ
oboe d'amore
pentachord
pianoforte
sousaphone
squeeze-box
tambourine
thumb piano
tin whistle
vibraphone

11 aeolian harp
barrel organ
harpsichord
phonofiddle
player-piano
sleigh bells
synthesizer
violoncello

12 glockenspiel
harmonichord
penny whistle
stock and horn
Stradivarius
tubular bells
viola da gamba

13 contra-bassoon
Ondes Martenot
panharmonicon
slide trombone
Swanee whistle

14 acoustic guitar
electric guitar
jingling Johnny

15 Moog synthesizer®
wind synthesizer

Musical instrument parts include:

03 bag
bow
key
lug
rib

04 bell
butt
capo
foot
fret
frog
jack
mute

neck
pipe
reed
rose
skin
stop

05 belly
brace
crook
crown
drone
pedal
snare

spike
waist

06 beater
bridge
damper
end-pin
hammer
keybed
key rod
pegbox
pick-up
pillar
scroll

string
tom-tom
07 cup mute
peg hole
tail-pin
08 bass drum
blow hole
chin rest
drumhead
floor tom
hitch pin
keylever
ligature
lip plate
pedestal
pin block
plectrum
purfling
shoulder
tonehole
truss rod
water key
09 bass joint
bell joint
body joint
finger key
fretboard
head joint

headstock
pedal stop
resonator
scroll eye
snare drum
soft pedal
sound-hole
swell stop
tailpiece
tenor drum
tenor mute
thumb hook
toe piston
tuning peg
tuning pin
10 bass bridge
double reed
finger hole
finger ring
hammer rail
long bridge
mouthpiece
pedal board
ride cymbal
slide brace
soundboard
swell pedal
tenor joint
tension rod

touchpiece
tremolo bar
upper joint
valve slide
vibrato arm
wrest plank
11 choir manual
crash cymbal
damper pedal
fingerboard
great manual
hi-hat cymbal
keyboard lid
machine head
middle joint
piston valve
pressure bar
swell manual
tuning slide
12 scratchplate
treble bridge
13 right-hand rest
una corda pedal
14 lower octave key
sostenuto pedal
upper octave key
15 sustaining pedal

Terms used in music include:

03 bar
bis
cue
key
tie
04 a due
alto
arco
bass
beat
clef
coda
fine
flat
fret
hold
mode
mute
note
part
rest
root
slur
solo
tone
tune

turn
05 ad lib
breve
buffo
chord
dolce
drone
forte
grave
largo
lento
lyric
major
metre
minim
minor
molto
outro
pause
piano
piece
pitch
scale
score
senza
shake

sharp
staff
stave
swell
tacet
tanto
tempo
tenor
theme
triad
trill
tutti
06 adagio
al fine
a tempo
da capo
duplet
encore
finale
legato
manual
medley
melody
octave
phrase
presto

quaver
rhythm
sempre
subito
tenuto
timbre
treble
tuning
unison
upbeat
vivace

07 agitato
allegro
al segno
amoroso
andante
animato
attacca
bar line
cadence
con brio
concert
con moto
descant
harmony
langsam
marcato
mediant
middle C
mordent
natural
recital
refrain
soprano
tremolo
triplet
vibrato

08 acoustic
alto clef
arpeggio
baritone
bass clef
col canto
con fuoco
crotchet
diatonic
doloroso
dominant
downbeat
ensemble
interval
maestoso
moderato

movement
ostinato
perdendo
ritenuto
semitone
semplice
sequence
staccato
vigoroso
virtuoso

09 alla breve
altissimo
cantabile
cantilena
chromatic
contralto
crescendo
glissando
harmonics
imitation
larghetto
mezza voce
microtone
non troppo
obbligato
orchestra
pizzicato
semibreve
sextuplet
sforzando
smorzando
sostenuto
sotto voce
spiritoso
tablature
tenor clef

10 accidental
affettuoso
allargando
allegretto
consonance
diminuendo
dissonance
dotted note
dotted rest
double flat
expression
fortissimo
intonation
ledger line
mezzo forte
modulation
pedal point

pentatonic
pianissimo
quadruplet
quintuplet
resolution
semiquaver
simple time
submediant
supertonic
tonic sol-fa
treble clef
two-two time

11 accelerando
arrangement
capriccioso
decrescendo
double sharp
double trill
fingerboard
leading note
quarter tone
rallentando
rinforzando
subdominant
syncopation

12 acciaccatura
alla cappella
appoggiatura
compound time
counterpoint
four-four time
key signature
six-eight time

13 accompaniment
double bar line
fifth interval
improvisation
major interval
minor interval
orchestration
sixth interval
sul ponticello
third interval
three-four time
time signature
transposition

14 cross-fingering
demisemiquaver
fourth interval
second interval

15 perfect interval
seventh interval

See also **Bach, Johann Sebastian; Bartók, Béla; Beethoven, Ludwig van; Brahms, Johannes; Britten, Benjamin; composer; conductor; country and western; Debussy, Claude; Dvořák, Antonín; Elgar, Sir Edward; folk; Gilbert, Sir W S and Sullivan, Sir Arthur; Handel, George Frideric; Haydn, Joseph; jazz; key; Mahler, Gustav;**

Mozart, Wolfgang Amadeus; opera; organ stop; overture; pop; Prokofiev, Sergei; Puccini, Giacomo; Purcell, Henry; Ravel, Maurice; Rossini, Gioacchino; Schoenberg, Arnold; Schubert, Franz; Schumann, Robert; Shostakovich, Dmitri; song; Strauss, Richard; Stravinsky, Igor; Tchaikovsky, Pyotr Ilyich; Verdi, Giuseppe; Wagner, Richard

musical

Musicals include:

04 *Cats*
Fame
Gigi
Hair
Rent

05 *Annie*
Blitz
Chess
Evita
Queen
Zorba

06 *Grease*
Joseph
Kismet
Oliver!
The Wiz
Wicked

07 *Avenue Q*
Cabaret
Camelot
Chicago
Company
Follies
Matilda

08 *Carnival*
Carousel
Fiorello!
Godspell
Mamma Mia!
Oklahoma!
Peter Pan

Show Boat
Spamalot

09 *Brigadoon*
Funny Girl
Girl Crazy
Hairspray
On the Town

10 *42nd Street*
Hello Dolly!
Jersey Boys
Kiss Me Kate
Miss Saigon
My Fair Lady

11 *A Chorus Line*
Babes in Arms
Bitter Sweet
Carmen Jones
Mary Poppins
Me and My Girl
Sweeney Todd
The King and I
The Lion King
The Music Man

12 *Anything Goes*
Bombay Dreams
Bye Bye Birdie
Calamity Jane
Guys and Dolls
Martin Guerre
South Pacific
The Boy Friend

13 *Aspects of Love*
Blood Brothers
Les Misérables
Man of La Mancha
The Pajama Game
West Side Story

14 *Babes in Toyland*
Victor/Victoria

15 *Annie Get Your Gun*
La Cage aux Folles
Mister Wonderful
Singin' in the Rain
Sunset Boulevard
The Sound of Music
The Woman in White

16 *Fiddler on the Roof*
Starlight Express

17 *Matilda The Musical*

18 *Saturday Night Fever*
Whistle Down the Wind

19 *Little Shop of Horrors*

20 *Jesus Christ Superstar*
The Phantom of the Opera

21 *Jerry Springer: The Opera*

27 *Seven Brides for Seven Brothers*

39 *Joseph and the Amazing Technicolor Dreamcoat*

Songs from musicals include:

03 'One' *(A Chorus Line)*

04 'Fame' *(Fame)*
'Kids' *(Bye Bye Birdie)*

05 'Heart' *(Damn Yankees)*
'Hoops' *(The Band Wagon)*
'Maria' *(Sound of Music)*
'Maybe' *(Annie)*

06 'Anthem' *(Chess)*
'Do-Re-Mi' *(The Sound of Music)*
'Memory' *(Cats)*
'People' *(Funny Girl)*

07 'America' *(West Side Story)*
'Bali Ha'i' *(South Pacific)*
'Cabaret' *(Cabaret)*

'Camelot' *(Camelot)*
'Tonight' *(West Side Story)*

08 'All I Know' *(Martin Guerre)*
'Aquarius' *(Hair)*
'By My Side' *(Godspell)*
'Day by Day' *(Godspell)*
'Oklahoma!' *(Oklahoma!)*
'Time Warp' *(The Rocky Horror Picture Show)*
'Tomorrow' *(Annie)*

09 'Easy Terms' *(Blood Brothers)*
'Edelweiss' *(Sound of Music)*
'Evergreen' *(A Star is Born)*
'Footloose' *(Footloose)*
'Hymn to Him' *(My Fair Lady)*

'Somewhere' (*West Side Story*)
'Superstar' (*Jesus Christ Superstar*)
'Tradition' (*Fiddler on the Roof*)
'Windy City' (*Calamity Jane*)

10 '42nd Street' (*42nd Street*)
'Be Our Guest' (*Beauty and the Beast*)
'Big Spender' (*Sweet Charity*)
'Friendship' (*DuBarry Was a Lady*)
'Gimme, Gimme' (*Thoroughly Modern Millie*)
'Hello, Dolly' (*Hello, Dolly*)
'I Am What I Am' (*La Cage Aux Folles*)
'I Got Rhythm' (*Girl Crazy*)
'Matchmaker' (*Fiddler on the Roof*)
'Night Fever' (*Saturday Night Fever*)
'Ol' Man River' (*Show Boat*)
'Secret Love' (*Calamity Jane*)
'Small World' (*Gypsy*)
'Too Darn Hot' (*Kiss Me Kate*)
'Toot Sweets' (*Chitty Chitty Bang Bang*)
'Willkommen' (*Cabaret*)

11 '2 Good 2 Be Bad' (*The Goodbye Girl*)
'76 Trombones' (*The Music Man*)
'All That Jazz' (*Chicago*)
'Good Morning' (*Singin' in the Rain*)
'If I Loved You' (*Carousel*)
'I Love Louisa' (*The Band Wagon*)
'Luck, Be a Lady' (*Guys and Dolls*)
'Night and Day' (*Gay Divorce*)
'Old Man River' (*Show Boat*)
'Summer Lovin'' (*Grease*)
'Where is Love?' (*Oliver!*)
'You're the Top' (*Anything Goes*)

12 'All I Ask of You' (*The Phantom of the Opera*)
'Bosom Buddies' (*Mame*)
'Broadway Baby' (*Follies*)
'Circle of Life' (*The Lion King*)
'Dancing Queen' (*Mamma Mia!*)
'Easter Parade' (*As Thousands Cheer*)
'Endless Night' (*The Lion King*)
'Hakuna Matata' (*The Lion King*)
'I'd Do Anything' (*Oliver!*)
'It's a Fine Life' (*Oliver!*)
'Losing My Mind' (*Follies*)
'Mack the Knife' (*The Threepenny Opera*)
'Makin' Whoopee' (*Whoopee!*)
'No Matter What' (*Whistle Down the Wind*)
'Rich Man's Frug' (*Sweet Charity*)
'Shall We Dance?' (*The King and I*)
'Sound of Music' (*The Sound of Music*)
'Staying Alive' (*Saturday Night Fever*)
'Summer Nights' (*Grease*)
'There She Goes' (*Fame*)
'We Go Together' (*Grease*)

13 'All I Care About' (*Chicago*)
'American Dream' (*Miss Saigon*)

'Comedy Tonight' (*A Funny Thing Happened on the Way to the Forum*)
'Skimbleshanks' (*Cats*)
'Song of the King' (*Joseph and the Amazing Technicolour Dreamcoat*)
'Sunrise, Sunset' (*Fiddler on the Roof*)

14 'Ain't Misbehavin'' (*Ain't Misbehavin'*)
'A Man Doesn't Know' (*Damn Yankees*)
'Any Dream Will Do' (*Joseph and the Amazing Technicolour Dreamcoat*)
'Change Partners' (*Carefree*)
'Chim Chim Cher-ee' (*Mary Poppins*)
'Close Every Door' (*Joseph and the Amazing Technicolour Dreamcoat*)
'I Dreamed a Dream' (*Les Misérables*)
'I Know Him So Well' (*Chess*)
'Lonely Goatherd' (*Sound of Music*)
'Mr Mistoffelees' (*Cats*)
'New York, New York' (*It's a Wonderful Town*)
'So Long, Farewell' (*The Sound of Music*)
'The Trolley Song' (*Meet Me in St Louis*)
'They All Laughed' (*Shall We Dance*)
'This Can't Be Love' (*The Boys From Syracuse*)
'We're In the Money' (*42nd Street*)

15 'A Boy From Nowhere' (*Matador*)
'A Bushel and a Peck' (*Guys and Dolls*)
'A Lot of Livin' to Do' (*Bye Bye Birdie*)
'Bells Are Ringing' (*Bells Are Ringing*)
'Bring On Tomorrow' (*Fame*)
'Greased Lightnin'' (*Grease!*)
'Honeysuckle Rose' (*Ain't Misbehavin'*)
'I Am the Starlight' (*Starlight Express*)
'If I Were a Rich Man' (*Fiddler on the Roof*)
'Impossible Dream' (*Man of La Mancha*)
'Music of the Night' (*The Phantom of the Opera*)
'Put On a Happy Face' (*Bye Bye Birdie*)
'Send in the Clowns' (*A Little Night Music*)
'Singin' in the Rain' (*Singin' in the Rain*)
'Sunset Boulevard' (*Sunset Boulevard*)
'Tell Me on A Sunday' (*Song and Dance*)
'The Lady is a Tramp' (*Babes in Arms*)
'Till There Was You' (*The Music Man*)
'What I Did For Love' (*A Chorus Line*)

16 'A Heart Full of Love' (*Les Misérables*)
'Anything You Can Do' (*Annie Get Your Gun*)
'Consider Yourself' (*Oliver!*)
'Five Guys Named Moe' (*Five Guys Named Moe*)
'Food, Glorious Food' (*Oliver!*)
'Gee, Officer Krupke' (*West Side Story*)
'Getting to Know You' (*The King and I*)
'High Flying Adored' (*Evita*)
'My Funny Valentine' (*Babes in Arms*)

'Starlight Express' (Starlight Express)
'Tell Me It's Not True' (Blood Brothers)
'The Deadwood Stage (Whip-Crack-Away)' (Calamity Jane)
'Those Good Old Days' (Damn Yankees)
'Truly Scrumptious' (Chitty Chitty Bang Bang)
'Winner Takes It All' (Mamma Mia!)

17 'A Little Fall of Rain' (Les Misérables)
'Anything But Lonely' (Aspects of Love)
'As Long as He Needs Me' (Oliver!)
'Beauty and the Beast' (Beauty and the Beast)
'Ease on Down the Road' (The Wiz)
'Forget About the Boy' (Thoroughly Modern Millie)
'Hernando's Hideaway' (The Pajama Game)
'How Deep is Your Love' (Saturday Night Fever)
'I Get a Kick Out of You' (Anything Goes)
'Let Me Entertain You' (Gypsy)
'Lullaby of Broadway' (42nd Street)
'Miracle of Miracles' (Fiddler on the Roof)
'My Favourite Things' (The Sound of Music)
'My Heart Stood Still' (A Connecticut Yankee)
'One Night in Bangkok' (Chess)
'Someone Else's Story' (Chess)
'To Keep My Love Alive' (A Connecticut Yankee)
'Whatever Lola Wants' (Damn Yankees)
'What Kind of Fool Am I?' (Stop The World I Want to Get Off)
'Yankee Doodle Dandy' (George M!)

18 'Children Will Listen' (Into the Woods)
'Climb Every Mountain' (The Sound of Music)
'Don't Rain on My Parade' (Funny Girl)
'Holding Out For a Hero' (Footloose)
'Something Wonderful' (The King and I)
'Spring, Spring, Spring' (Seven Brides for Seven Brothers)
'Wouldn't It be Loverly?' (My Fair Lady)
'You Do Something to Me' (Can-Can)

19 'Beauty School Dropout' (Grease)
'It's the Hard-Knock Life' (Annie)
'Last Night of the World' (Miss Saigon)
'Let's Hear it For the Boy' (Footloose)
'Little Shop of Horrors' (Little Shop of Horrors)
'Look at Me, I'm Sandra Dee' (Grease)
'Springtime for Hitler' (The Producers)
'Thank You For the Music' (Mamma Mia!)
'Time Heals Everything' (Mack and Mabel)
'Tomorrow Belongs to Me' (Cabaret)
'Too Much In Love to Care' (Sunset Boulevard)

'You'll Never Walk Alone' (Carousel)

20 'Good Morning Starshine' (Hair)
'If Ever I Would Leave You' (Camelot)
'I've Got You Under My Skin' (Born to Dance)
'Kiss of the Spider Woman' (Kiss of the Spider Woman)
'Shuffle Off the Buffalo' (42nd Street)
'Some Enchanted Evening' (South Pacific)
'Someone to Watch Over Me' (Crazy For You)
'The Age of Not Believing' (Bedknobs and Broomsticks)
'The Music and the Mirror' (A Chorus Line)

21 'Almost Like Being in Love' (Brigadoon)
'Don't Cry For Me, Argentina' (Evita)
'Falling in Love With Love' (The Boys From Syracuse)
'Got to Pick a Pocket or Two' (Oliver!)
'I Don't Know How to Love Him' (Jesus Christ Superstar)
'Love Changes Everything' (Aspects of Love)
'The Black Hills of Dakota' (Calamity Jane)
'What's the Use of Wonderin'' (Carousel)
'Younger Than Springtime' (South Pacific)

22 'As If We Never Said Goodbye' (Sunset Boulevard)
'Brush Up Your Shakespeare' (Kiss Me Kate)
'Hopelessly Devoted to You' (Grease)
'I Loved You Once in Silence' (Camelot)
'June is Bustin' Out All Over' (Carousel)
'The First Man You Remember' (Aspects of Love)

23 'Another Op'nin', Another Show' (Kiss Me Kate)
'Bless Your Beautiful Bride' (Seven Brides for Seven Brothers)
'Give My Regards to Broadway' (George M!)
'Oh What a Beautiful Morning' (Oklahoma!)
'On The Street Where You Live' (My Fair Lady)
'People Will Say We're in Love' (Oklahoma!)
'Sixteen, Going on Seventeen' (The Sound of Music)
'Substitutiary Locomotion' (Bedknobs and Broomsticks)
'Take That Look Off Your Face' (Song and Dance)
'There is Nothing Like A Dame' (South Pacific)
'You'll Never Get Away from Me' (Gypsy)

24 'Can You Feel the Love Tonight?' (The Lion King)

'Everything's Coming Up Roses' *(Gypsy)*
'I Could Have Danced all Night' *(My Fair Lady)*
'Is You Is or Is You Ain't My Baby?' *(Five Guys Named Moe)*
'It's a Grand Night for Singing' *(State Fair)*
'Let's Call the Whole Thing Off' *(Shall We Dance)*

25 'How are Things in Glocca Morra?' *(Finian's Rainbow)*
'It's Harry I'm Planning To Marry' *(Calamity Jane)*
'Life is Just a Bowl of Cherries' *(Fosse)*
'Thank Heaven For Little Girls' *(Gigi)*

26 'Just Blew In From the Windy City' *(Calamity Jane)*
'They Can't Take That Away From Me' *(Shall We Dance)*

27 'Diamonds Are a Girl's Best Friend' *(Gentlemen Prefer Blondes)*
'On a Clear Day, You Can See Forever' *(On a Clear Day, You Can See Forever)*
'There are Worse Things I Could Do' *(Grease)*

28 'Another Suitcase in Another Hall' *(Evita)*
'Jellicle Songs for Jellicle Cats' *(Cats)*

30 'Bewitched, Bothered and Bewildered' *(Pal Joey)*

32 'There's No Business Like Show Business' *(Annie Get Your Gun)*

34 'I'm Gonna Wash That Man Right Outta My Hair' *(South Pacific)*
'Supercalifragilisticexpialidocious' *(Mary Poppins)*

36 'There's Gotta Be Something Better Than This' *(Sweet Charity)*

People associated with musicals include:

04 Ball (Michael; 1962– , English)
Bart (Lionel; 1930–99, English)
Cahn (Sammy; 1913–93, US)
Eddy (Nelson; 1901–67, US)
Grey (Joel; 1932– , US)
Hart (Lorenz; 1895–1943, US)
Hart (Moss; 1904–61, US)
Kaye (Danny; 1913–87, US)
Keel (Howard; 1917–2004, US)
Kern (Jerome; 1885–1945, US)
Lahr (Bert; 1895–1967, US)
Lane (Nathan; 1956– , US)
Nunn (Trevor; 1940– , English)
Rice (Tim; 1944– , English)

05 Black (Don; 1936– , English)
Brice (Fanny; 1891–1951, US)
Caird (John; 1948–, English)
Cohan (George; 1878–1942, US)
Donen (Stanley; 1924– , US)
Fosse (Bob; 1927–87, US)
Kelly (Gene; 1912–96, US)
Lenya (Lotte; 1898–1981, Austrian)
Loewe (Frederick; 1904–88, Austrian/US)
Paige (Elaine; 1948– , English)
Styne (Jule; 1905–94, US)

06 Berlin (Irving; 1888–1989, Russian/US)
Castle (Irene; 1893–1969, US)
Castle (Vernon; 1887–1918, English/US)
Coward (Sir Noel; 1899–1973, English)
Gaynor (Mitzi; 1931– , US)
Herman (Jerry; 1932– , US)
Jolson (Al; 1886–1950, US)
Lerner (Alan Jay; 1918–86, US)
MacRae (Gordon; 1921–86, US)
Martin (Mary; 1913–90, US)

Martin (Millicent; 1934– , English)
Merman (Ethel; 1909–84, US)
Miller (Ann; 1919–2004, US)
Newley (Anthony; 1931–99, English)
Peters (Bernadette; 1948– , US)
Porter (Cole; 1891–1964, US)
Prince (Hal; 1928– , US)
Rogers (Ginger; 1911–95, US)
Steele (Tommy; 1936– , English)
Tucker (Sophie; 1884–1966, Russian/US)

07 Astaire (Fred; 1899–1987, US)
Boublil (Alain; 1941– , Tunisian)
Burnett (Carol; 1933– , US)
Garland (Judy; 1922–69, US)
Grayson (Kathryn; 1922–2010, US)
Novello (Ivor; 1893–1951, Welsh)
O'Connor (Donald; 1925–2003, US)
Robbins (Jerome; 1918–98, US)
Rodgers (Richard; 1902–79, US)
Sharaff (Irene; 1910–93, US)
Sherman (Richard M; 1928– , US)
Sherman (Robert B; 1925–2012, US)
Ulvaeus (Björn; 1945– , Swedish)

08 Berkeley (Busby; 1895–1976, US)
Bricusse (Leslie; 1931– , English)
Buchanan (Jack; 1891–1957, Scottish)
Channing (Carol; 1921– , US)
Crawford (Michael; 1942– , English)
Gershwin (George; 1898–1937, US)
Gershwin (Ira; 1896–1983, US)
Lawrence (Gertrude; 1898–1952, English)
Matthews (Jessie; 1907–81, English)
McKenzie (Julia; 1941– , English)
Minnelli (Liza; 1946– , US)
Reynolds (Debbie; 1932– , US)

Robinson (Bill 'Bojangles'; 1878–1949, US)
Sondheim (Stephen; 1930– , US)
Ziegfeld (Florenz, Jnr; 1867–1932, US)
09 Andersson (Benny; 1946– , Swedish)
Bernstein (Leonard; 1918–90, US)
MacDonald (Jeanette; 1901–65, US)

Macintosh (Cameron; 1946– , Scottish)
Schönberg (Claude-Michel; 1944– , French)
Streisand (Barbra; 1942– , US)
11 Hammerstein (Oscar, II; 1895–1960, US)
Lloyd Webber (Andrew; 1948– , English)

musician

Musicians and musical groups include:

03 duo
04 band
bard
diva
duet
trio
05 choir
griot
group
nonet
octet
piper
06 bugler
busker
folkie
jazzer
oboist
player
sextet
singer

07 cellist
drummer
fiddler
harpist
maestro
Orphean
pianist
quartet
quintet
soloist
08 bluesman
clarsair
composer
ensemble
flautist
lutenist
minstrel
organist
virtuoso
vocalist

09 balladeer
conductor
guitarist
itinerant
orchestra
performer
trumpeter
violinist
10 one-man band
prima donna
trombonist
11 accompanist
saxophonist
12 backing group
clarinettist
13 percussionist
session singer
15 instrumentalist
session musician

Classical musicians, musicologists and instrument makers include:

02 Ma (Yo-Yo; 1955– , French/US)
03 Fou (Ts'ong; 1934– , Chinese)
Sax (Adolphe; 1814–94, Belgian)
Suk (Joseph; 1875–1935, Czech)
Tye (Christopher; c.1505–c.1572, English)
04 Adès (Thomas; 1971– , English)
Böhm (Theobald; 1794–1881, German)
Bush (Alan; 1900–95, English)
Hess (Dame Myra; 1890–1966, English)
Rosa (Carl, 1842–89, German)
Wood (Haydn; 1882–1959, English)
05 Alkan (1813–88, French)
Arrau (Claudio; 1903–91, Chilean)
Beach (Mrs H H A; 1867–1944, US)
Benda (Georg; 1722–95, Bohemian)
Boehm (Theobald; 1794–1881, German)
Bolet (Jorge; 1914–90, US)
Borge (Victor; 1909–2000, Danish/US)
Bream (Julian; 1933– , English)
Bülow (Hans, Baron von; 1830–94, German)
Busch (Adolf; 1891–1952, German/Swiss)
Chung (Kyung-Wha; 1948– , South Korean/US)

du Pré (Jacqueline; 1945–87, English)
Dupré (Marcel; 1886–1971, French)
Elman (Mischa; 1891–1967, Russian/US)
Field (John; 1782–1837, Irish)
Friml (Rudolf; 1879–1972, Czech/US)
Gould (Glenn; 1932–82, Canadian)
Grove (Sir George; 1820–1900, English)
Hallé (Sir Charles; 1819–95, German/British)
Harty (Sir Hamilton; 1880–1941, Northern Irish)
Joyce (Eileen; 1912–91, Australian)
Liszt (Franz; 1811–86, Hungarian)
Manns (Sir August; 1825–1907, German)
Nyman (Michael; 1944– , English)
Ogdon (John; 1937–89, English)
Sharp (Cecil; 1859–1924, English)
Spohr (Ludwig; 1784–1859, German)
Stern (Isaac; 1920–2001, Russian/US)
Szell (George; 1897–1970, Hungarian/US)
Tovey (Sir Donald Francis; 1873–1940, English)
Weber (Carl Maria von; 1786–1826, German)
Ysaye (Eugène; 1858–1931, Belgian)

06 Albert (Eugen d'; 1864–1932, German)
Alfvén (Hugo; 1872–1960, Swedish)
Busoni (Ferruccio; 1866–1924, Italian)
Casals (Pablo; 1876–1973, Spanish)
Chopin (Frédéric; 1810–49, Polish)
Cortot (Alfred; 1877–1962, French)
Cramer (Johann Baptist; 1771–1858,
German/British)
Curzon (Sir Clifford; 1907–82, English)
Czerny (Karl; 1791–1857, Austrian)
Dussek (Jan Ladislav; 1760–1812, Czech)
Galway (Sir James; 1939– , Northern Irish)
Godard (Benjamin; 1849–95, French)
Hummel (Johann; 1778–1837, Austrian)
Köchel (Ludwig von; 1800–77, Austrian)
Koppel (Herman D; 1908–98, Danish)
Lamond (Frederic; 1868–1948, Scottish)
Lassus (Orlandus; c.1532–94, Netherlandish)
Levine (James; 1943– , US)
Maazel (Lorin; 1930– , French/US)
Martin (Frank; 1890–1974, Swiss)
Mutter (Anne-Sophie; 1963– , German)
Quantz (Johann Joachim; 1697–1773,
German)
Riccio (David; c.1533–66, Italian)
Rizzio (David; c.1533–66, Italian)
Serkin (Rudolf; 1903–91, Hungarian/US)
Sitsky (Larry; 1934– , Chinese/Australian)
Stoker (Richard; 1938– , English)
Suggia (Guilhermina; 1888–1950,
Portuguese)
Turina (Joaquín; 1882–1949, Spanish)
Viotti (Giovanni Battista; 1753–1824,
Italian)
Wagner (Siegfried; 1869–1930, German)

07 Albéniz (Isaac; 1860–1909, Spanish)
Attwood (Thomas; 1765–1838, English)
Bennett (Sir William Sterndale; 1816–75,
English)
Bentzon (Niels Viggo; 1919–2000, Danish)
Blondel (fl.12c, French)
Brendel (Alfred; 1931– , Austrian)
Campoli (Alfredo; 1906–91, Italian)
Casella (Alfredo; 1883–1947, Italian)
Glennie (Evelyn; 1965– , Scottish)
Goodman (Isador; 1909–82, South African/
Australian)
Heifetz (Jascha; 1901–87, Russian/US)
Joachim (Joseph; 1831–1907, Hungarian)
Kennedy (Nigel; 1956– , English)
Kentner (Louis; 1905–87, Hungarian/British)
Leclair (Jean Marie; 1697–1764, French)
Lipatti (Dinu; 1917–50, Romanian)
Malcolm (George; 1917–97, English)
Marbeck (John; d.c.1585, English)
Mathias (William; 1934–92, Welsh)
Matthay (Tobias; 1858–1945, English)
McClary (Susan; 1946– , US)

McGuire (Edward; 1948– , Scottish)
Medtner (Nikolai; 1880–1951, Russian)
Menuhin (Yehudi, Lord; 1916–99, US/
British)
Perahia (Murray; 1947– , US)
Perlman (Itzhak; 1945– , Israeli)
Richter (Sviatoslav; 1915–97, Russian)
Segovia (Andrés; 1893–1987, Spanish)
Shankar (Ravi; 1920–2012, Indian)
Solomon (1902–88, English)
Sorabji (Kaikhosru Shapurji; 1892–1988,
English)
Stamitz (Carl; 1745–1801, German)
Stamitz (Johann; 1717–57, Bohemian)
Strauss (Johann, the Elder; 1804–49, Austrian)
Strauss (Johann, the Younger; 1825–99,
Austrian)
Szeryng (Henryk; 1918–88, Polish/
Mexican)
Taneyev (Sergei; 1856–1915, Russian)
Tartini (Giuseppe; 1692–1770, Italian)
Thibaud (Jacques; 1880–1953, French)
Vivaldi (Antonio; 1678–1741, Italian)
Zwilich (Ellen; 1939– , US)

08 Clementi (Muzio; 1752–1832, Italian)
Dohnanyi (Ernst von; 1877–1960,
Hungarian)
Fournier (Pierre; 1906–86, French)
Godowsky (Leopold; 1870–1938, Russian/
US)
Goossens (Eugène; 1867–1958, French/
Belgian)
Goossens (Léon; 1897–1988, English)
Grainger (Percy; 1882–1961, Australian/US)
Guarneri (fl.16–17c; Italian)
Henschel (Sir George; 1850–1934, Polish/
British)
Holliger (Heinz; 1939– , Swiss)
Horowitz (Vladimir; 1904–89, Russian/US)
Kreisler (Fritz; 1875–1962, Austrian/US)
Leighton (Kenneth; 1929–88, English)
Lhévinne (Josef; 1874–1944, Russian/US)
Lortzing (Albert; 1801–51, German)
Marriner (Sir Neville; 1924– , English)
Merbecke (John; d.c.1585, English)
Milstein (Nathan; 1904–92, Russian/US)
Oistrakh (David; 1908–74, Russian)
Pachmann (Vladimir de; 1848–1933,
Russian)
Paganini (Niccolò; 1782–1840, Italian)
Pfitzner (Hans; 1869–1949, German)
Richards (Henry Brinley; 1819–85, Welsh)
Sarasate (Pablo; 1844–1908, Spanish)
Schnabel (Artur; 1882–1951, Austrian)
Schumann (Clara; 1819–96, German)
Scriabin (Aleksandr; 1872–1915, Russian)
Skriabin (Aleksandr; 1872–1915, Russian)
Steinway (Henry; 1797–1871, German/US)

Thalberg (Sigismond; 1812–71, German or Austrian)
Williams (John; 1941– , Australian)
Zukerman (Pinchas; 1948– , Israeli)

09 Ashkenazy (Vladimir; 1937– , Russian/Icelandic)
Barenboim (Daniel; 1942– , Argentine/Israeli)
Bernstein (Leonard; 1918–90, US)
Bottesini (Giovanni; 1823–89, Italian)
Boulanger (Nadia; 1887–1979, French)
Broadwood (John; 1732–1812, Scottish)
Butterley (Nigel; 1935– , Australian)
Dolmetsch (Arnold; 1858–1940, French/British)
Gieseking (Walter; 1895–1956, German)
Guarnieri (fl.16–17c; Italian)
Landowska (Wanda; 1879–1959, Polish)
MacDowell (Edward; 1861–1908, US)
Moscheles (Ignaz; 1794–1870, Bohemian)
Stevenson (Ronald; 1928– , Scottish)
Tortelier (Paul; 1914–90, French)
Zimbalist (Efrem; 1889–1985, Russian/US)

10 Barbirolli (Sir John; 1899–1970, English)
Campenhout (François von; 1779–1849, Belgian)
Cristofori (Bartolommeo; 1655–1731, Italian)
Gottschalk (Louis Moreau; 1829–69, US)
Moszkowski (Moritz; 1854–1925, Polish)
Paderewski (Ignacy; 1860–1941, Polish)

Rubinstein (Anton; 1829–94, Russian)
Rubinstein (Artur; 1887–1982, Polish/US)
Scharwenka (Xaver; 1850–1924, Polish)
Stradivari (Antonio; c.1644–1737, Italian)
Vieuxtemps (Henri; 1820–81, Belgian)
Villa-Lobos (Heitor; 1887–1959, Brazilian)
Williamson (Malcolm; 1931–2003, Australian)

11 Cristofaloi (Bartolommeo; 1655–1731, Italian)
Dittersdorf (Karl Ditters von; 1739–99, Austrian)
Farren-Price (Ronald; 1930– , Australian)
Mitropoulos (Dimitri; 1896–1960, Greek/US)
Piatigorsky (Gregor; 1903–76, Russian/US)
Rachmaninov (Sergei; 1873–1943, Russian)
Rakhmaninov (Sergei; 1873–1943, Russian)
Reizenstein (Franz; 1911–68, German)
Theodorakis (Mikis; 1925– , Greek)

12 Guido d'Arezzo (c.990–1050, Italian)
Michelangeli (Arturo Benedetti; 1920–95, Italian)
Moiseiwitsch (Benno; 1890–1963, Russian/British)
Rostropovich (Mstislav; 1927–2007, Russian)
Shostakovich (Maxim Dmitriyevich; 1938– , Russian/US)
Stradivarius (Antonio; c.1644–1737, Italian)

14 Jaques-Dalcroze (Émile; 1865–1951, Swiss)
Orlando di Lasso (c.1532–94, Netherlandish)

See also **Bach, Johann Sebastian; Bartók, Béla; Beethoven, Ludwig van; Brahms, Johannes; Britten, Benjamin; composer; conductor; Debussy, Claude; Dvořák, Antonín; Elgar, Sir Edward; Gilbert, Sir W S and Sullivan, Sir Arthur; Handel, George Frideric; Haydn, Joseph; jazz; Mahler, Gustav; Mozart, Wolfgang Amadeus; pianist; pop; Prokofiev, Sergei; Puccini, Giacomo; Purcell, Henry; Ravel, Maurice; Rossini, Gioacchino; Schoenberg, Arnold; Schubert, Franz; Schumann, Robert; Shostakovich, Dmitri; song; Strauss, Richard; Stravinsky, Igor; Tchaikovsky, Pyotr Ilyich; Verdi, Giuseppe; Wagner, Richard**

musketeer *see* **Dumas, Alexandre**

muslim *see* **Islam**

mythology

Mythical animals and spirits include:

03 elf	**04** faun	**05** afrit
fay	fung	demon
fée	huma	devil
fum	jinn	djinn
hob	peri	dobby
imp	pixy	dryad
Mab	puck	dwarf
nis	yale	fairy
nix	yeti	genie

ghost
ghoul
giant
gnome
golem
jinni
kelpy
kylin
naiad
nisse
nixie
nymph
oread
pisky
pixie
pooka
pouke
satyr
shade
silky
Siren
sylph
troll
wight

06 afreet
dobbie
dragon
dybbuk
goblin
jinnee

kelpie
kobold
maelid
merman
nereid
Oberon
selkie
silkie
sprite
wyvern

07 banshee
Bigfoot
brownie
centaur
gremlin
griffin
incubus
Lorelei
mermaid
oceanid
Pegasus
phoenix
rusalka
rye wolf
sandman
unicorn
vampire

08 antelope
basilisk

Nibelung
succubus
werewolf
whistler

09 hamadryad
hobgoblin
impundulu
Julunggul
mermaiden
sasquatch
tokoloshe
tragelaph
water bull

10 hippogriff
hippogryph
leprechaun
salamander
sea serpent
tooth fairy

11 hircocervus
lubber fiend
scolopendra
thunderbird

12 little people
Rainbow Snake
shapeshifter

15 Lob-lie-by-the-fire
Robin Goodfellow

Mythical birds include:

03 fum
roc
rok

ruc
04 fung
huma

rukh
07 phoenix
08 whistler

09 impundulu
11 Thunderbird
12 bird of wonder

Mythical places include:

03 Dis
Hel
04 Hell
Styx
05 Argos
Babel
Hades
Lethe
Limbo
Pluto
Thule
06 Albion
Anghar
Asgard
Avalon
Heaven
Heorot

Nedyet
Utgard
Xanadu
07 Agartha
Alfheim
Alpheus
Arcadia
Bifrost
Boeotia
Camelot
Elysium
Lemuria
Nirvana
Pohjola
Tuonela
08 Amazonia
Archeron
Atlantis

El Dorado
Lyonesse
Niflheim
Paradise
Tlalocan
Valhalla
Vanaheim
09 Cockaigne
Fairyland
Purgatory
River Styx
Shangri-la
Yggdrasil
10 River Lethe
Stymphalos
11 Ultima Thule
12 River Alpheus

13 Jewel Mountain   14 Lake Stymphalos   The Isle of Avalon
   River Archeron   15 Cloudcuckooland   The Tower of Babel
   The Underworld   The Garden of Eden

Mythological rivers include:

04 Styx   Oceanus
05 Lethe   10 Phlegethon
07 Acheron

Babylonian gods include:

02 Ea (water/wisdom/spells/writing/building)   Enlil (air/land/earth/men's fates)
03 Anu (heavens/father of the gods)   Hadad (fertility/thunder)
   Bel (king of the gods/thunderstorms/light/life)   Mummu (mists)
   Sin (Moon)   06 Anshar (heaven/sky)
04 Adad (wind/storm/flood)   Dumuzi (animal/plant fertility)
   Apsu (primordial sweet-water ocean)   Marduk (king of the gods/thunderstorms/
   Baal (king of the gods/thunderstorms/light/   light/life)
   life)   Nergal (death/underworld)
   Enki (water/wisdom/spells/writing/building)   Tammuz (fertility/vegetation)
   Nabu (scribe/herald of the gods)   07 Ninurta (warrior)
05 Ellil (air/land/earth/men's fates)   Shamash (sun/justice)
                                                 Thammuz (fertility/vegetation)

Babylonian goddesses include:

03 Aja (the dawn)   Ningal (consort of Sin)
04 Antu (consort of Anu)   Ninlil (consort of Enlil)
05 Antum (mother of Ishtar)   Nintur (motherhood)
   Belit (wife of Bel/Baal/Marduk)   Tiamat (chaos/salt-water ocean/sky)
   Nintu (motherhood)   07 Anunitu (Moon)
06 Ishtar (love/fertility/war)   Damkina (Earth mother)
   Kishar (consort of Anshar)   10 Ereshkigal (underworld)

Celtic gods include:

03 Bel (sun/light/fire)   Goibniu (smithcraft)
   Don (chief/lord of the Otherworld)   Grannos (healing)
   Lug (sun/arts/healing)   Gwydion (enchantment/illusion)
04 Beli (sun/light/fire)   Pryderi (underworld)
   Lleu (hero/crafts/commerce/youth/games)   08 Gofannon (smiths/strength)
   Llyr (sea/water)   Silvanus (underworld)
   Ogma (eloquence/physical strength)   Sucellus (underworld)
05 Balor (death)   the Dagda (earth/fertility/prosperity)
   Dylan (sea)   09 Cernunnos (fertility/plenty/underworld/
   Mabon (youth/healing/music/hunting)   animals/lord of the Underworld)
   Nuada (harpers/healing/learning/warfare)   Manawydan (wisdom/patience)
   Nuadu (harpers/healing/learning/warfare)   10 Manawyddan (wisdom/patience)
   Ogmia (strength/eloquence)   11 Aengus Mac Og (youth/love/beauty)
   Pwyll (underworld)   Gwynn ap Nudd (underworld)
   Taran (thunder/war)   14 Bran the Blessed (prophecy/arts/war)
06 Merlin (guardian of the land)   Manannan Mac Lir (sea-god/regeneration)
   Ogmios (strength/eloquence)   15 Manawydan ap Llyr (sea/regeneration)
07 Belinus (sun/light/fire)

Celtic goddesses include:

03 Don (mother of the gods/rivers/wisdom/
magic)

04 Aine (love/fertility)
Anna (mother/fecundity/plenty)
Danu (mother/rivers/wisdom/magic)
Eriu (Ireland)

05 Badhb (battle/enlightenment)
Boann (river/water/fertility)
Édain (Otherworld)
Epona (horses/prosperity)
Étain (Otherworld)
Macha (warrior/horses/death/cunning)

06 Badhbh (battle/enlightenment)
Brigid (agriculture/smithcraft/inspiration)
Brigit (agriculture/smithcraft/inspiration)
Matres (Earth/fecundity/motherhood)
Medhbh (warrior/sexuality)

Modron (mother)

07 Branwen (love/beauty)
Brighid (midwifery/poetry/crafts)
Cliodna (peace/beauty)
Nemhain (war)

08 Cliodhna (peace/beauty)
Flidhais (wild animals)
Matronae (Earth/fecundity/motherhood)
Morrigan (war/lust/revenge/magic)
Rhiannon (horses/birds/the moon/wit)

09 Arianrhod (Earth)
Brigantia (livestock/agriculture)
Cerridwen (underworld)
Morríghan (war/lust/revenge/magic)

10 Blodeuwedd (love/generosity)

11 Dea Arduinna (wild animals)

Celtic mythological and legendary characters include:

03 Anu
Lug

04 Badb
Bran
Danu
Lugh
Medb
Ogma

05 Balor
Boann
Dagda
Macha
Maeve
Neman
Nuada
Oisin
Pwyll

06 Arthur
Brigit
Danaan
Deidre
Imbolc
Isolde
Ogmios
Ossian

07 banshee
Beltane
Branwen
Brighid
Deirdre
Samhain
Tristan

08 Manannan
Morrigan
Rhiannon
The Dagda
Tir nan-Og

09 Bean Sidhé
Cernunnos
Conchobar

10 Cú Chulainn
Lughnasadh

11 Finn mac Cool

13 Bendigeidfran
Finn mac Cumhal

14 Bran the Blessed
Finn mac Cumhail
Tuatha dé Danaan

Central and South American gods include:

04 Chac (Mayan; rain)
Inti (Inca; sun)

06 Tlaloc (Aztec; rain/mountains/springs)

07 Huang-ti (Aztec; war/protector of the
city)
Hunab Ku (Mayan; supreme creator)

Itzamma (Mayan; founder of culture/heaven/
maize/fertility/moon)

08 Catequil (Inca; thunder/lightning)
Kukulkan (Mayan; elements/creator)

09 the Bacabs (Mayan; wind)
Viracocha (Inca; supreme creator)

Xipe Totec (Aztec; springtime/renewal/
   nocturnal rain)

10 Apu Punchau (Inca; sun)
   Manco Capac (Inca; sun/father of Incans)
   Pachacamac (Inca; earth/creator)
   Xochipilli (Aztec; flowers/love/song/dance)

12 Quetzalcoatl (Aztec; creator/vegetation/
   wind)
   Tezcatlipoca (Aztec; trickster/sun)
   Xiuhtecuhtli (Aztec; hearth/fire/sun/
   volcanoes)

15 Huitzilopochtil (Aztec; war/sun)

Central and South American goddesses include:

05 Aknah (Mayan; birth)

06 Ixchel (Mayan; storm)

09 Coatlicue (Aztec; earth)
   Ixazaluoh (Mayan; water/inventor of
   weaving)
   Mama Oella (Inca; inventor of spinning)

Pachamama (Inca; earth)

10 Mama Quilla (Inca; moon)

11 Tlazolteotl (Aztec; lust)

12 Xochiquetzal (Aztec; flowers/love/childbirth)

15 Chalchiuhtlicue (Aztec; water)

Egyptian gods include:

02 Ra (Sun)
   Re (Sun)

03 Bes (home/childbirth/family)
   Geb (earth)
   Nut (sky)

04 Apis (fecundity/fertility/strength)
   Aten (unique god)
   Atum (ancestor of human race)
   Ptah (creation/protector of artists)

Seth (evil)

05 Horus (light/sun)
   Thoth (moon/learning/supreme scribe)

06 Amun-Re (universal)
   Anubis (funerals)
   Osiris (vegetation/death)

07 Khonsou (son of Amun-Re)
   Sarapis (compound of Osiris and Apis)
   Serapis (compound of Osiris and Apis)

Egyptian goddesses include:

04 Isis (magic/fertility/mother)

   Maat (order/law/justice)

05 Khnum (creation)

06 Hathor (love/fertility)
   Sakmet (might)
   Sekmet (might)

07 Nepthys (funerals)

Sakhmet (might)

Sekhmet (might)

08 Nephthys (funerals)

Greek gods include:

03 Pan (male sexuality/woods/
   shepherds)

04 Ares (war)
   Atys (vegetation)
   Eros (love)
   Zeus (king of the gods/sky/
   light/weather)

05 Atlas (Titan who bears
   Earth)
   Attis (vegetation)
   Hades (underworld)

06 Adonis (vegetation/rebirth)
   Aeolus (winds)
   Apollo (prophecy/music/
   youth/archery/healing)
   Boreas (north wind)
   Cronus (father of Zeus)
   Helios (sun)
   Hermes (messenger of the
   gods)
   Hypnos (sleep)
   Nereus (sea)

Plutus (wealth)

07 Oceanus (river Oceanus)

08 Dionysus (wine/vine)
   Ganymede (rain)
   Morpheus (dreams)
   Poseidon (sea)
   Thanatos (death)

09 Asclepius (healing)

10 Hephaestus (fire)

11 Aesculapius (healing)

Greek goddesses include:

03 Eos (dawn)
   Nyx (night)

04 Gaea (Earth)
   Gaia (Earth)
   Hebe (youth)

Hera (marriage/childbirth/
   queen of the gods)
Iris (rainbow)
Nike (victory)
Rhea (mother of Zeus)

05 Tyche (chance/luck)

06 Athene (prudence/wisdom/
   protectress of Athens)
   Cybele (earth)
   Hecate (moon)

Hestia (hearth/home)
Hygeia
Selene (moon)
Themis (established law/justice)
Thetis

07 Alphito (barley/goddess of Argos)

Artemis (fertility/chastity/hunting)
Demeter (corn/harvest)
Erinyes (vengeance)
Nemesis (destiny/moderation/vengeance)

08 Arethusa (springs/fountains)
the Fates (destiny)

the Horae (seasons)
the Muses (the liberal arts)

09 Aphrodite (love/beauty)
the Furies (vengeance)
the Graces (charm/beauty)

10 Persephone (underworld)

Greek mythological and legendary characters include:

02 Io

04 Ajax
Dido
Echo
Eris
Hero
Leda
Leto
Rhea

05 Atlas
Chloe
Circe
Creon
Danae
Helen
Horae
Hydra
Irene
Ixion
Jason
Kreon
Laius
Lamia
Medea
Midas
Minos
Niobe
Orion
Paris
Priam
Rheia

06 Aeneas
Aeolus
Alecto
Amazon
Atreus
Cadmus
Castor
Charon
Chiron
Cronus
Danaoi
Daphne
Dryads
Europa
Europe

Furies
Graiae
Hecabe
Hector
Hecuba
Hellen
Icarus
Iolaus
Kronos
Latona
Medusa
Megara
Memnon
Naiads
Nessus
Nestor
nymphs
Oreads
Peleus
Pelops
Phoebe
Pollux
Python
satyrs
Scylla
Semele
Sileni
Sirens
Stheno
Syrinx
Titans
Triton
Typhon

07 Actaeon
Alcyone
Arachne
Ariadne
Calchas
Calypso
Cecrops
Cepheus
Chimera
Cyclops
Danaans
Daphnis
Diomede
Echidna

Electra
Epigoni
Erinyes
Euryale
Galatea
Gorgons
Griffin
Gryphon
Harpies
Iapetus
Jocasta
Kekrops
Laocoon
Lapiths
Leander
Maenads
Marsyas
Nereids
Oceanus
Oedipus
Orestes
Orpheus
Pandora
Pegasus
Perseus
Phaedra
Silenus
Theseus
Titania
Troilus
Ulysses

08 Achilles
Alcestis
Alcmaeon
Anchises
Antigone
Arethusa
Atalanta
Basilisk
Centaurs
Cerberus
Chimaera
Cressida
Cyclopes
Daedalus
Diomedes
Endymion

Eteocles
Eurydice
Ganymede
Gigantes
Halcyone
Heracles
Hyperion
Iphicles
Lycurgus
Meleager
Menelaus
Minotaur
Nausicaa
Oceanids
Odysseus
Pasiphae
Penelope
Pentheus
Phaethon
Pleiades
Sarpedon
Sisyphus
Tantalus
Thyestes
Tiresias
Typhoeus

09 Aegisthus
Agamemnon
Andromeda
Argonauts
Autolycus
Cassandra
Charybdis
Deucalion
Idomeneus
Lotophagi
Mnemosyne
Myrmidons
Narcissus
Patroclus
Polynices
Pygmalion
Semiramis
Tisiphone

10 Amphitryon
Andromache

Cassiopeia	Hippolytus
Cockatrice	Iphigeneia
Erechtheus	Polyneices
Hamadryads	Polyphemus
Hesperides	Procrustes

Prometheus	Philoctetes
Telemachus	**12** Clytemnestra
11 Bellerophon	Hyperboreans
Lotus-eaters	Rhadamanthus
Neoptolemus	Rhadamanthys

Maori gods include:

02 Tu	**05** Rangi	**08** Ranginui	**11** Rongomatane
03 Uru	Rongo	Ruaumoko	Tumatauenga
04 Maui	**06** Haumia	Tangaroa	**12** Tawhiri Matea
Tane	**07** Tawhiri	**10** Tane Mahuta	

Maori goddesses include:

04 Papa	**11** Hinenuitepo
10 Hinetitama	Papatuanuku

Maori mythological and legendary characters include:

04 Kupe	**05** Pania	**09** Tutanekai
Maui	**07** Hinemoa	
Rona	Mahuika	

Norse gods include:

03 Bor (father of Odin)
Otr (otter god)
Tyr (battle/sky)
Ull (stepson of Thor/enchanter)

04 Frey (fertility/sunshine/growth)
Logi (fire)
Loki (mischief)
Odin (father/war/death/magic/law/poetic inspiration)
Thor (thunder/war/good crops)

05 Aegir (sea)
Aesir (warlike gods)
Alcis (sky)
Bragi (poetry)
Donar (thunder/war/good crops)
Freyr (fertility/fecundity)

Hoder (blind god who killed Balder)
Mimir (wisdom)
Njord (ships/the sea)
Vanir (benevolent gods)
Vidar (slayer of the wolf Fenrir)
Woden (father/war/death/magic/law/poetic inspiration)
Wotan (father/war/death/magic/law/poetic inspiration)

06 Balder (son of Odin/light/sovereignty/power)
Fafnir (dragon)
Hermod (son of Odin)
Hoenir (companion to Odin and Loki)
Kvasir (wise utterances)

07 Volundr (craftsman)

08 Heimdall (sentinel/dawn)

Norse goddesses include:

03 Hel (death; Queen of Niflheim/underworld)
Ran (sea)
Sif (wife of Thor)

04 Hela (death; Queen of Niflheim/underworld)

05 Frigg (fertility/wife of Odin)
Idunn (guardian of golden apples of youth)
Nanna (wife of Balder)
Norns (destiny)
Sigyn (wife of Loki)

06 Freyja (love/fertility/fecundity/victory/peace)
Gefion (received virgins after death)

07 Nerthus (earth)

08 Fjorgynn (mother of Thor)

09 Valkyries (warrior women/helpers of gods of war)

10 Nehallenia (plenty)

Norse mythological and legendary characters include:

03 Lif

06 Gudrun
Kraken
Sigurd
Weland

07 Beowulf
Grendel

Wayland
Weiland
Weyland

08 Brunhild

09 berserker

10 Lifthrasir

Roman gods include:

04 Mars (war)

05 Cupid (love)
Fides (honesty)
Janus (entrances/travel/dawn)
Lares (house)
Orcus (death)
Picus (woods)
Pluto (underworld)

06 Apollo (sun)
Consus (nature/agriculture)
Faunus (crops and herbs)
Genius (protector of individuals and the state)

Mithra (sun/regeneration)
Saturn (fertility/agriculture)
Vulcan (fire)

07 Bacchus (wine and ecstasy)
Jupiter (sky/sun/moon/thunder)
Mercury (messenger/merchants)
Mithras (sun/regeneration)
Neptune (sea)
Penates (food/drink)

08 Portunus (husbands)
Silvanus (trees/forests)

09 Vertumnus (fertility)

10 Liber Pater (fertility)

Roman goddesses include:

03 Ops (harvest)

04 Juno (marriage/childbirth/light)
Luna (moon)
Maia (fertility)

05 Ceres (corn/agriculture)
Diana (fertility/hunting/moon)
Fauna (fertility)
Flora (fruitfulness/flowers)
Pales (protectress of flocks)
Venus (spring/gardens/love)
Vesta (hearth)

06 Aurora (dawn)
Pomona (fruits)
Rumina (nursing mothers)

07 Bellona (war)
Egreria (fountains/childbirth)
Feronia
Fortuna (chance)
Minerva (war/craftsmen/education/arts)

08 Libitina
Victoria (victory)

10 Proserpina (underworld)

Roman mythological and legendary characters include:

05 Lamia
Lares
Manes
Remus
Sibyl

07 Latinus
Lemures
Lucrece
Penates
Romulus
Sibylla

Tarpeia

08 Anchises
Callisto
Hercules
Lucretia

Verginia

09 Androcles

10 Coriolanus
Rhea Silvia
Rhea Sylvia

Gods and goddesses of other regions and cultures include:

03 Anu (Sumerian)
Rod (Slavic)
Sin (Sumerian)
Wak (Ethiopian)

04 Adad (Mesopotamian)

Amma (Dogon)
Baal (Phoenician)
Enki (Sumerian)
Kane (Pacific islands)
Tane (Pacific islands)

05 Enlil (Sumerian)
Epona (Gallic)
Hadad (Assyrian)
Pan Gu (Chinese)
Perun (Slavic)

06 Adonis (Phoenician)
Cybele (Phrygian)
Guan Di (Chinese)
Inanna (Sumerian)
Ishtar (Mesopotamian)
Kuan Ti (Chinese)
Mithra (Indo-European)
Modimo (African)
Moloch (Canaanite)

Shango (African)
Svarog (Slavic)
Tengri (Mongol)
Teshub (Hurrian)
Tiamat (Akkadian)
Vahagn (Armenian)

07 Anahita (Persian)
Astarte (Mesopotamian)
Kumarbi (Hurrian)
Ninurta (Sumerian)
Taranis (Gallic)
Triglav (Slavic)
Zanhary (Madagascan)

08 Rosmerta (Gallo-Roman)

Skyamsen (Native
American)
Sucellus (Gallic)
Teutates (Gallic)

09 Amaterasu (Japanese)
Sventovit (Slavic)

10 Ahura Mazda (Indo-Iranian)

11 Thunderbird (Native
American)

15 Izanagi no Mikoto
(Japanese)
Izanami no Mikoto
(Japanese)

Mythological and legendary characters of other regions and cultures include:

03 Qat (Oceania)

04 Tell (William; Swiss)

05 Adapa (Akkadian)
El Cid (Spanish)
Faust (German)
Frost (Jack; Scandinavian)

06 Anansi (African)
Bunyan (Paul; American)
Enkidu (Sumerian)
George (St; English)
Godiva (Lady; English)
Merlin (British)
Roland (French)

07 Aladdin (Chinese)
Ali Baba (Arabian)

08 Baba Yaga (Russian/Slavic)

Hang Tuah (Malay)
Hiawatha (American)
Parsifal (European)

09 Appleseed (Johnny; American)
Bluebeard (French)
Lohengrin (Germanic)
Robin Hood (English)

10 King Arthur (British)
Yu the Great (Chinese)

11 Old King Cole (English)

12 Lemminkäinen (Finnish)
Rip Van Winkle (American)
Scheherazade (Middle Eastern)
Will-o'-the-Wisp (European)

14 Flying Dutchman (Dutch)

15 Father Christmas (universal)

See also **fairy tale; fate; Hinduism; Homer; horse; king; legend; lover; monster; muse; opera; pantomime; play; Shakespeare, William**

N

name

03 pen
pet
04 code
full
last
05 alias
brand
false
first

given
place
stage
06 anonym
eponym
exonym
family
maiden
middle
proper

second
07 agnomen
allonym
assumed
autonym
surname
toponym
08 nickname
09 baptismal

Christian
cryptonym
pseudonym
sobriquet
trademark
10 diminutive
nom de plume
soubriquet
11 nom de guerre

Boys' names include:

02 Al
Cy
Ed
Ik
Jo
03 Abe
Alf
Ali
Asa
Bat
Baz
Ben
Bob
Dai
Dan
Deb
Dee
Del
Den
Dev
Dob
Don
Gay
Gaz
Gil
Gus
Guy
Hew
Huw
Ian
Ike
Iky
Ira
Ivo
Jay

Jem
Jim
Joe
Jon
Jos
Ken
Kim
Kit
Lal
Lee
Len
Leo
Lew
Mat
Max
Nat
Ned
Nye
Pat
Pip
Rab
Rae
Ray
Reg
Rex
Rob
Rod
Roy
Sam
Sim
Sol
Tam
Ted
Tim
Tom

Val
Vic
Viv
Wat
Wyn
Zia
04 Adam
Adil
Alan
Alec
Aled
Alex
Algy
Alun
Amin
Andy
Anil
Arch
Arun
Bart
Bert
Bill
Bram
Bryn
Burt
Carl
Ceri
Chad
Chae
Chay
Clem
Colm
Dave
Davy
Dean

Dewi
Dick
Dirk
Doug
Drew
Eddy
Egon
Eoin
Eric
Eryl
Euan
Evan
Ewan
Ewen
Ezra
Finn
Fred
Gabi
Gary
Gaye
Gene
Glen
Glyn
Gwyn
Hani
Hank
Hari
Hope
Huey
Hugh
Hugo
Iain
Ifor
Ivan
Ivon

Ivor	Abd-al	Denis	Jared
Jack	Abdul	Denny	Jason
Jake	Abram	Denys	Jerry
Jeff	Adeel	Derek	Jesse
Jock	Adnan	Dicky	Jimmy
Joel	Ahmad	Dilip	Jools
Joey	Ahmed	Dipak	Kamal
John	Aidan	Donal	Kasim
Josh	Aiden	Duane	Keith
Joss	Alfie	Dwane	Kelly
Jude	Allan	Dylan	Kenny
Jule	Allen	Eddie	Kerry
Karl	Alwin	Edgar	Kevan
Kirk	Alwyn	Edwin	Kevin
Kurt	Amrit	Elroy	Kiran
Liam	Andie	Elton	Kumar
Luke	Angel	Elvis	Lance
Mark	Angus	Elwyn	Larry
Matt	Anwar	Emlyn	Leigh
Mick	Archy	Emrys	Lenny
Mike	Arran	Enoch	Leroy
Neal	Avril	Ernie	Lewie
Neil	Barry	Errol	Lewis
Nick	Basil	Farid	Linus
Noah	Bazza	Faruq	Lloyd
Noel	Benny	Felix	Logan
Omar	Billy	Fionn	Lorne
Owen	Bobby	Floyd	Louie
Ozzy	Boris	Frank	Louis
Paul	Brent	Gabby	Lucas
Pete	Brett	Gamal	Madoc
Phil	Brian	Garry	Manny
Rana	Bruce	Gavin	Micky
Ravi	Bruno	Geoff	Miles
Raza	Bryan	Gerry	Moray
René	Bunny	Giles	Moses
Reza	Cahal	Glenn	Moshe
Rhys	Calum	Gopal	Mungo
Rick	Cecil	Hamza	Murdo
Riza	Chaim	Harry	Myles
Rolf	Chris	Harun	Neale
Rory	Chuck	Hasan	Neddy
Ross	Claud	Haydn	Niall
Ryan	Clint	Henry	Nicky
Saul	Clive	Homer	Nicol
Sean	Clyde	Howel	Nigel
Seth	Colin	Humph	Ollie
Siôn	Colum	Husni	Orson
Theo	Conor	Hywel	Oscar
Toby	Corin	Idris	Ozzie
Tony	Cosmo	Ieuan	Paddy
Umar	Craig	Inigo	Percy
Walt	Cyril	Isaac	Perry
Will	Cyrus	Jacob	Peter
Yves	Damon	Jamal	Piers
Zach	Danny	James	Qasim
Zack	David	Jamie	Rajiv
05 Aaron	Davie	Jamil	Ralph

Randy	Barney	Faysal	Joshua
Ricky	Benjie	Fergus	Julian
Roald	Bernie	Finbar	Julius
Robin	Bertie	Fingal	Justin
Roddy	Bharat	Finlay	Kelvin
Roger	Billie	Finley	Kennie
Rowan	Blaise	Fintan	Kieran
Rufus	Bobbie	Freddy	Kieron
Sacha	Bunnie	Gareth	Kilian
Salim	Callum	Garret	Lachie
Samir	Calvin	George	Laurie
Sammy	Caspar	Georgy	Lawrie
Sandy	Cathal	Gerald	Lennie
Sasha	Cedric	Gerard	Leslie
Scott	Ciaran	Gerrie	Lester
Shane	Clancy	Gideon	Lionel
Shaun	Claude	Gobind	Lorcan
Shawn	Clovis	Gordon	Lucius
Silas	Colley	Govind	Luther
Simon	Connor	Graeme	Lynsey
Solly	Conrad	Graham	Magnus
Steve	Dafydd	Gussie	Mahmud
Sunil	Damian	Gwilym	Marcel
Taffy	Damien	Hamish	Marcus
Tariq	Daniel	Hamzah	Marlon
Teddy	Darren	Harold	Martin
Terry	Debdan	Haroun	Martyn
Tommy	Declan	Harvey	Marvin
Tudor	Deepak	Hassan	Melvin
Ulric	Delroy	Hayden	Melvyn
Ultan	Dennis	Haydon	Mervyn
Vijay	Denzil	Hector	Milton
Vinay	Dermot	Herbie	Morgan
Waldo	Deryck	Hervey	Morris
Walid	Devdan	Hilary	Murray
Wally	Dicken	Horace	Nathan
Wasim	Dickie	Howard	Neddie
Watty	Dickon	Howell	Nichol
Wayne	Dilwyn	Hubert	Ninian
Willy	Dobbin	Hughie	Norman
Wynne	Donald	Husain	Oliver
Zahir	Donnie	Husayn	Osbert
06 Adrian	Dougal	Isaiah	Oswald
Albert	Dudley	Iseult	Pascal
Alexei	Dugald	Ismail	Pearce
Alexej	Duggie	Israel	Philip
Alexis	Duncan	Jarvis	Pierce
Alfred	Dustin	Jasper	Rabbie
Andrew	Eamonn	Jemmie	Rajesh
Antony	Eamunn	Jeremy	Ramesh
Archie	Edmund	Jerome	Ranald
Arnold	Edward	Jervis	Randal
Arthur	Elijah	Jethro	Ranulf
Ashley	Ernest	Jimmie	Reggie
Ashraf	Esmond	Jockie	Reuben
Aubrey	Eugene	Jolyon	Richie
Austin	Faisal	Jordan	Robbie
Averil	Fareed	Joseph	Robert

Rodney
Roland
Ronald
Ruairi
Rudolf
Rupert
Rushdi
Saleem
Samuel
Sanjay
Seamas
Seamus
Seumas
Shamus
Sharif
Sidney
Sorley
Steven
Stevie
St John
Stuart
Suhayl
Sydney
Teddie
Thomas
Timmie
Tobias
Trevor
Tyrone
Vernon
Victor
Vikram
Virgil
Vivian
Vyvian
Vyvyan
Walter
Willie
Xavier
Zaheer
07 Abraham
Alister
Ambrose
Aneirin
Aneurin
Anthony
Auberon
Barnaby
Bernard
Bertram
Brendan
Brynmor
Chander
Chandra

Charles
Charley
Charlie
Christy
Clement
Crispin
Derrick
Desmond
Dominic
Douglas
Eustace
Feargal
Finbarr
Francie
Francis
Frankie
Freddie
Gabriel
Geordie
Georgie
Geraint
Gervase
Gilbert
Godfrey
Grahame
Gwillym
Herbert
Humphry
Hussain
Hussein
Ibrahim
Isadore
Isidore
Isodore
Jeffrey
Jocelin
Jocelyn
Johnnie
Kenneth
Killian
Krishna
Lachlan
Leonard
Leopold
Lindsay
Lindsey
Ludovic
Malcolm
Matthew
Maurice
Michael
Murdoch
Mustafa
Myrddin

Neville
Nicolas
Orlando
Patrick
Peredur
Phillip
Quentin
Quintin
Quinton
Randall
Randolf
Ranulph
Raymond
Reynold
Richard
Rowland
Rudolph
Russell
Shankar
Shelley
Solomon
Stanley
Stephen
Steuart
Stewart
Terence
Timothy
Torquil
Tristan
Vaughan
Vincent
Wilfred
Wilfrid
William
Winston
Zachary
08 Alasdair
Alastair
Algernon
Alistair
Ashleigh
Augustus
Barnabas
Benedick
Benedict
Benjamin
Beverley
Christie
Clarence
Clifford
Courtney
Crispian
Cuthbert
Dominick

Emmanuel
Frederic
Geoffrey
Humphrey
Jonathan
Jonathon
Joscelin
Kimberly
Kingsley
Lancelot
Laurence
Lawrence
Leontine
Leontyne
Llewelyn
Ludovick
Matthias
Meredith
Mordecai
Muhammad
Nicholas
Perceval
Percival
Randolph
Reginald
Roderick
Ruaidhri
Ruairidh
Ruaraidh
Rupinder
Terrance
Theodore
Tristram
09 Alexander
Archibald
Augustine
Christian
Ferdinand
Frederick
Gillespie
Kimberley
Launcelot
Nathaniel
Peregrine
Sebastian
Siegfried
Silvester
Somhairle
Sylvester
Valentine
10 Maximilian
11 Bartholomew
Christopher

Girls' names include:

02 Di	Pia	Gaea	Maev
Do	Rae	Gaia	Mary
Ib	Ray	Gail	Maud
Jo	Ria	Gale	Meta
Mo	Ros	Gaye	Mina
03 Ada	Roz	Gene	Moll
Ali	Sal	Gert	Mona
Amy	Sue	Gill	Myra
Ann	Tib	Gina	Nell
Bab	Una	Gita	Nina
Bea	Val	Gwen	Nita
Bee	Viv	Hope	Noel
Bel	Win	Ibby	Nola
Bet	Zoë	Ines	Nona
Cis	**04** Abby	Inez	Nora
Con	Abir	Inga	Olga
Deb	Addy	Inge	Page
Dee	Afra	Iona	Phyl
Die	Aggy	Iris	Poll
Dot	Alex	Irma	Prue
Edy	Ally	Isla	Rana
Emm	Alma	Jade	Rene
Ena	Angy	Jane	Rita
Eva	Anna	Jean	Romy
Eve	Anne	Jess	Rona
Fay	Asma	Jill	Rosa
Flo	Babs	Joan	Rose
Gay	Bell	Jodi	Ruby
Ida	Bess	Jody	Ruth
Ina	Beth	Joey	Sara
Isa	Cara	Joni	Sian
Ivy	Caro	Joss	Sìne
Jan	Cass	Jozy	Siri
Jay	Ceri	Jude	Sita
Jen	Cher	Judy	Suke
Joe	Cleo	June	Suky
Joy	Cora	Kate	Susy
Kay	Dana	Kath	Suzy
Kim	Dawn	Katy	Tess
Kit	Dian	Kaye	Thea
Lea	Dora	Kyra	Tina
Lee	Edel	Lala	Toni
Liv	Edie	Lara	Trix
Liz	Edna	Leah	Vera
Lou	Ella	Lena	Vita
Mae	Elma	Lian	Zara
Mag	Elva	Lily	Zena
Mat	Emma	Lina	Zola
May	Emmy	Lisa	**05** Addie
Meg	Enid	Lise	Adela
Mia	Erin	Livy	Adèle
Nan	Evie	Liza	Aggie
Pat	Faye	Lois	Agnes
Peg	Floy	Lola	Ailie
Pen	Fred	Lucy	Ailsa
	Gabi	Lynn	Aisha

Alexa	Doris	Jessy	Mercy
Alice	Edith	Jinny	Meryl
Allie	Effie	Jodie	Moira
Amber	Eliza	Joely	Molly
Amina	Ellen	Josie	Morag
Anaïs	Ellie	Joyce	Morna
Angel	Elsie	Judie	Moyra
Angie	Emily	Julia	Myrna
Anila	Emmie	Julie	Nabby
Anita	Erica	Kanta	Nadia
Annie	Essie	Karen	Nance
Annis	Ethel	Karin	Nancy
Annot	Ethna	Karla	Nelly
Aphra	Ethne	Kathy	Nerys
April	Faith	Katie	Nessa
Areta	Fanny	Katya	Nesta
Aruna	Farah	Kelly	Netta
Avril	Ffion	Kenna	Netty
Aysha	Fiona	Kerry	Ngaio
Becky	Fleur	Kiera	Niamh
Bella	Flora	Kitty	Nicky
Belle	Freda	Kylie	Noele
Beryl	Freya	Lalla	Norah
Bessy	Gabby	Lally	Norma
Betsy	Gauri	Laura	Nuala
Betty	Gayle	Leigh	Olive
Biddy	Geeta	Leila	Olwen
Bride	Gemma	Leona	Olwin
Brona	Gerda	Letty	Olwyn
Bunny	Ginny	Liana	Onora
Bunty	Golda	Libby	Oprah
Candy	Golde	Linda	Paddy
Carla	Grace	Lindy	Padma
Carly	Greta	Lorna	Paige
Carol	Haley	Lorne	Pansy
Carys	Hatty	Louie	Patsy
Cathy	Hazel	Lubna	Patty
Celia	Heidi	Lucia	Paula
Chère	Helen	Lydia	Pearl
Chloe	Helga	Lynda	Peggy
Chris	Hetty	Lynne	Penny
Ciara	Hilda	Mabel	Petra
Cindy	Holly	Madge	Pippa
Cissy	Honor	Maeve	Polly
Clara	Ilana	Magda	Priya
Clare	Ilona	Máire	Raine
Coral	Irena	Màiri	Rajni
Daisy	Irene	Mamie	Renée
Debby	Isbel	Mandy	Rhian
Debra	Isold	Margo	Rhoda
Delia	Ivana	Maria	Rhona
Della	Jaime	Marie	Robin
Diana	Jamie	Matty	Robyn
Diane	Janet	Maude	Rosie
Dilys	Janis	Maura	Sacha
Dinah	Jemma	Mavis	Sadie
Dolly	Jenna	Meena	Sally
Donna	Jenny	Megan	Sarah

Sasha	Audrey	Dulcie	Isobel
Senga	Auriel	Dympna	Isolda
Shona	Auriol	Eartha	Isolde
Shula	Aurora	Edwina	Jamila
Sibyl	Aurore	Eileen	Jancis
Sindy	Averil	Eilidh	Janice
Sonia	Ayesha	Eirian	Janina
Sonya	Babbie	Eirlys	Janine
Sophy	Barbie	Eithna	Jeanie
Stacy	Beatty	Eithne	Jemima
Sukie	Bertha	Elaine	Jennie
Susan	Bertie	Elinor	Jessie
Susie	Bessie	Eloisa	Joanie
Sybil	Bianca	Eloise	Joanna
Tamar	Biddie	Elspet	Joanne
Tammy	Blanch	Eluned	Joelle
Tania	Bonnie	Elvira	Joleen
Tanya	Brenda	Esther	Jolene
Terry	Bridie	Eunice	Judith
Tessa	Brigid	Evadne	Juliet
Thora	Brigit	Evelyn	Kamala
Tibby	Briony	Evonne	Karena
Tilda	Bryony	Fatima	Karina
Tilly	Bunnie	Fedora	Kathie
Tracy	Caddie	Felice	Kirsty
Trina	Candia	Finola	Kittie
Trish	Carina	Flavia	Kumari
Trixy	Carlie	Freddy	Lalage
Trudy	Carmel	Frieda	Lalita
Unity	Carmen	Gaynor	Lallie
Viola	Carola	Gertie	Laurel
Wanda	Carole	Gladys	Lauren
Wendy	Carrie	Glenda	Laurie
Wilma	Cassie	Glenys	Leanne
Zahra	Cathie	Gloria	Leonie
Zelda	Cecily	Glynis	Lesley
Zowie	Celina	Goldie	Lettie
	Cherie	Gracie	Lianna
06 Adella	Cherry	Grania	Lianne
Agatha	Cheryl	Granya	Lilian
Aileen	Cicely	Gudrun	Lilias
Alexia	Cissie	Gwenda	Linnet
Alexis	Claire	Hannah	Lisbet
Alicia	Connie	Hattie	Lizzie
Alison	Daphne	Hayley	Lolita
Althea	Davina	Helena	Lottie
Amabel	Deanna	Hermia	Louisa
Amanda	Deanne	Hester	Louise
Amelia	Debbie	Hilary	Lynsey
Andrea	Delyth	Honora	Madhur
Angela	Denise	Honour	Maggie
Anneka	Dervla	Imelda	Maisie
Annika	Dianne	Imogen	Marcia
Anthea	Dionne	Indira	Marian
Aphrah	Dolina	Ingrid	Marina
Aretha	Doreen	Isabel	Marion
Ashley	Dorrie	Iseult	Marsha
Astrid	Dottie	Ishbel	Martha

Mattie
Maxine
Melody
Meriel
Millie
Minnie
Miriam
Monica
Morven
Muriel
Myriam
Myrtle
Nabila
Nadine
Nellie
Nessie
Nettie
Nicola
Nicole
Noelle
Noreen
Odette
Olivia
Olwyne
Paloma
Pamela
Pattie
Petula
Phemie
Phoebe
Rachel
Rajani
Raquel
Regina
Renata
Rhonda
Robina
Rodney
Roisin
Roshan
Rosina
Rowena
Roxana
Roxane
Rubina
Sabina
Sabine
Salome
Sandra
Saskia
Selina
Seonag
Serena
Sharon
Shashi
Sheela
Sheena
Sheila

Sherry
Sheryl
Sidney
Sidony
Silvia
Simone
Sinéad
Sophia
Sophie
Sorcha
Stacey
Stella
Suhair
Sydney
Sylvia
Tamara
Tammie
Tamsin
Teenie
Teresa
Thelma
Tibbie
Tracey
Tricia
Trisha
Trixie
Ulrica
Ursula
Vanora
Verity
Vijaya
Vinaya
Violet
Vivian
Vivien
Vyvian
Vyvyan
Winnie
Winona
Wynona
Xanthe
Yasmin
Yvette
Yvonne
Zainab
Zaynab
07 Abigail
Aisling
Allegra
Allison
Andrina
Annabel
Annette
Antonia
Anushka
Ariadne
Augusta

Barbara
Beatrix
Belinda
Bernice
Bethany
Bettina
Bharati
Blanche
Bridget
Bronach
Bronagh
Bronwen
Caitlín
Camilla
Candace
Candice
Candida
Carleen
Carlene
Carolyn
Cecilia
Chandra
Chantal
Charity
Charley
Chelsea
Chelsey
Christy
Clarice
Claudia
Clodagh
Colette
Colleen
Corinna
Corinne
Crystal
Cynthia
Daniela
Deborah
Deepika
Deirdre
Demelza
Désirée
Dolores
Dorothy
Dymphna
Eiluned
Eleanor
Elspeth
Emerald
Estella
Estelle
Eugenia
Eugénie
Felicia
Fenella
Floella
Florrie

Flossie
Frances
Francie
Frankie
Freddie
Georgia
Georgie
Gillian
Giselle
Gráinne
Gwennie
Gwenyth
Gwyneth
Haniyya
Harriet
Heather
Heloise
Isadora
Iseabal
Isidora
Jacinta
Jacinth
Janetta
Janette
Jasmine
Jeannie
Jenifer
Jessica
Jillian
Jocasta
Jocelin
Jocelyn
Johanna
Jonquil
Josepha
Josette
Juliana
Justina
Justine
Kathryn
Katrina
Katrine
Khadija
Kirstie
Kirstin
Krystal
Krystle
Lakshmi
Laraine
Lavinia
Leonora
Letitia
Lettice
Lillian
Lillias
Lindsay
Lindsey
Linette

Lisbeth
Lisette
Lizbeth
Loretta
Lucilla
Lucille
Lucinda
Lynette
Madonna
Margery
Marilyn
Marjory
Marlene
Martina
Martine
Matilda
Maureen
Melanie
Melissa
Merriel
Mildred
Miranda
Myfanwy
Nanette
Natalia
Natalie
Natasha
Nichola
Nigella
Ninette
Ophelia
Ottilie
Pandora
Parvati
Pascale
Paulina
Pauline
Phyllis
Queenie
Rachael
Raelene
Rebecca
Roberta
Rosabel
Rosalie
Rosanna
Rosetta
Roxanne
Sabrina
Saffron
Seonaid
Sharifa
Shelagh
Shelley
Shirley
Sidonie
Silvana
Siobhán

Surayya
Susanna
Sybilla
Tabitha
Theresa
Tiffany
Valerie
Vanessa
Venetia
Wasimah
Wenonah
Yolanda
Zubaida
Zuleika

08 Adelaide
Adrianne
Adrienne
Angelica
Angelina
Angharad
Arabella
Ashleigh
Beatrice
Berenice
Beverley
Caroline
Catriona
Charlene
Charmian
Chrissie
Christie
Chrystal
Clarinda
Clarissa
Claudine
Cordelia
Cornelia
Courtney
Cressida
Daniella
Danielle
Dominica
Dorothea
Eleanore
Emmeline
Euphemia
Eustacia
Felicity
Florence
Francine
Georgina
Germaine
Gertrude
Gervaise
Griselda
Grizelda
Hermione

Isabella
Iseabail
Jacintha
Jacinthe
Jannetta
Jeanette
Jennifer
Joceline
Joscelin
Katerina
Kathleen
Kimberly
Kirsteen
Larraine
Lauretta
Leontine
Leontyne
Linnette
Lorraine
Madeline
Magdalen
Marcella
Marcelle
Margaret
Marianne
Marigold
Marjorie
Mathilda
Meredith
Michaela
Michelle
Morwenna
Ottoline
Patience
Patricia
Paulette
Penelope
Philippa
Primrose
Prudence
Prunella
Rhiannon
Rosalind
Rosamond
Rosamund
Roseanna
Roseanne
Rosemary
Samantha
Scarlett
Shakirah
Susannah
Theodora
Theresia
Tomasina
Veronica
Victoria
Virginia

Winifred
09 Albertina
Albertine
Alexandra
Anastasia
Annabella
Annabelle
Cassandra
Catharine
Catherina
Catherine
Charlotte
Charmaine
Christian
Christina
Christine
Claudette
Cleopatra
Constance
Elisabeth
Elizabeth
Fionnuala
Frederica
Gabrielle
Genevieve
Georgette
Georgiana
Geraldine
Ghislaine
Guinevere
Gwendolen
Gwenllian
Henrietta
Jackeline
Jacquelyn
Jacquetta
Jaqueline
Jeannette
Josephine
Katharine
Katherine
Kimberley
Madeleine
Magdalene
Mélisande
Millicent
Nicolette
Priscilla
Rosemarie
Serenella
Sharmaine
Sigourney
Silvestra
Stephanie
Sylvestra
Thomasina
Valentine

10 Antoinette	Christiana	Jacqueline	11 Constantine
Bernadette	Clementina	Shakuntala	
Christabel	Clementine	Wilhelmina	

See also **cinema; city; club; country; French; German; Irish; king; pseudonym; public house; queen; Scottish; Welsh**

narcotic

Narcotics include:

03 ava

04 bang
coca
dope
kava

05 bhang

dagga

06 charas
datura
pituri

07 churrus
narceen

08 narceine

10 belladonna

11 Indian berry
laurel-water

15 cocculus indicus

See also **drug**

National Football League see **American football**

national holiday see **holiday**

national park see **park**

nationality

Nationalities include:

03 Lao (Laos)

04 Kiwi (New Zealand)
Thai (Thailand)

05 Bajan (Barbados)
Congo (Congo/Democratic Republic of the Congo)
Cuban (Cuba)
Czech (Czech Republic)
Dutch (The Netherlands)
Greek (Greece)
Iraqi (Iraq)
Irish (Ireland)
Omani (Oman)
Saudi (Saudi Arabia)
Swazi (Swaziland)
Swiss (Switzerland)
Tajik (Tajikistan)
Uzbek (Uzbekistan)
Welsh (Wales)

06 Afghan (Afghanistan)
Danish (Denmark)
Fijian (Fiji)
French (France)

German (Germany)
Indian (India)
Kenyan (Kenya)
Korean (North Korea/South Korea)
Kyrgyz (Kyrgyzstan)
Libyan (Libya)
Malian (Mali)
Polish (Poland)
Qatari (Qatar)
Samoan (Samoa)
Somali (Somalia)
Syrian (Syria)
Tongan (Tonga)
Yapese (Federated States of Micronesia)
Yemeni (Yemen)

07 Angolan (Angola)
Basotho (Lesotho)
Belgian (Belgium)
Bosnian (Bosnia and Herzegovina)
British (United Kingdom)
Burmese (Myanmar)
Chadian (Chad)
Chilean (Chile)

Chinese (China)
Comoran (Comoros)
Cypriot (Cyprus)
Emirati (United Arab Emirates)
English (England)
Finnish (Finland)
Gambian (The Gambia)
Guinean (Guinea)
Haitian (Haiti)
Iranian (Iran)
Israeli (Israel)
Italian (Italy)
Ivorian (Côte d'Ivoire)
Kosraen (Federated States of Micronesia)
Kuwaiti (Kuwait)
Laotian (Laos)
Latvian (Latvia)
Maltese (Malta)
Mexican (Mexico)
Monacan (Monaco)
Mosotho (Lesotho)
Nauruan (Nauru)
Palauan (Palau)
Russian (Russia)
Rwandan (Rwanda)
Sahrawi (Western Sahara)
Serbian (Serbia)
Spanish (Spain)
Swedish (Sweden)
Tadzhik (Tajikistan)
Turkish (Turkey)
Turkmen (Turkmenistan)
Ugandan (Uganda)
Zambian (Zambia)

08 Albanian (Albania)
Algerian (Algeria)
American (United States of America)
Andorran (Andorra)
Antiguan (Antigua and Barbuda)
Armenian (Armenia)
Austrian (Austria)
Bahamian (The Bahamas)
Bahraini (Bahrain)
Barbudan (Antigua and Barbuda)
Batswana (Botswana)
Belizean (Belize)
Beninese (Benin)
Bolivian (Bolivia)
Bruneian (Brunei Darussalam)
Canadian (Canada)
Chuukese (Federated States of Micronesia)
Croatian (Croatia)
Egyptian (Egypt)
Eritrean (Eritrea)
Estonian (Estonia)
Filipina (Philippines)
Filipino (Philippines)
Gabonese (Gabon)

Georgian (Georgia)
Ghanaian (Ghana)
Grenadan (Grenada)
Guyanese (Guyana)
Honduran (Honduras)
Jamaican (Jamaica)
Japanese (Japan)
Lebanese (Lebanon)
Liberian (Liberia)
Malagasy (Madagascar)
Malawian (Malawi)
Moldovan (Moldova)
Moroccan (Morocco)
Motswana (Botswana)
Namibian (Namibia)
Nepalese (Nepal)
Nevisian (St Kitts and Nevis)
Nigerian (Nigeria)
Nigerien (Niger)
Peruvian (Peru)
Romanian (Romania)
Sahraoui (Western Sahara)
Scottish (Scotland)
St Lucian (St Lucia)
Sudanese (Sudan)
Timorese (East Timor)
Togolese (Togo)
Tunisian (Tunisia)
Tuvaluan (Tuvalu)

09 Argentine (Argentina)
Barbadian (Barbados)
Bhutanese (Bhutan)
Brazilian (Brazil)
Bulgarian (Bulgaria)
Burkinabé (Burkina Faso)
Burundian (Burundi)
Cambodian (Cambodia)
Colombian (Colombia)
Congolese (Congo/Democratic Republic of
   the Congo)
Dominican (Dominica/Dominican Republic)
Ethiopian (Ethiopia)
Grenadian (Grenada)
Hungarian (Hungary)
Icelandic (Iceland)
I-Kiribati (Kiribati)
Jordanian (Jordan)
Kittitian (St Kitts and Nevis)
Malaysian (Malaysia)
Maldivian (Maldives)
Mauritian (Mauritius)
Mongolian (Mongolia)
Ni-Vanuatu (Vanuatu)
Norwegian (Norway)
Pakistani (Pakistan)
Pohnpeian (Federated States of Micronesia)
Sahrawian (Western Sahara)
Santoméan (São Tomé and Príncipe)

São Toméan (São Tomé and Príncipe)
Singapore (Singapore)
Slovakian (Slovakia)
Slovenian (Slovenia)
Sri Lankan (Sri Lanka)
Taiwanese (Taiwan)
Tanzanian (Tanzania)
Ukrainian (Ukraine)
Uruguayan (Uruguay)

10 Australian (Australia)
Belarusian (Belarus)
Costa Rican (Costa Rica)
Djiboutian (Djibouti)
Ecuadorean (Ecuador)
Ecuadorian (Ecuador)
Guatemalan (Guatemala)
Indonesian (Indonesia)
Lithuanian (Lithuania)
Luxembourg (Luxembourg)
Macedonian (Macedonia)
Monégasque (Monaco)
Mozambican (Mozambique)
Myanmarese (Myanmar)
New Zealand (New Zealand)
Nicaraguan (Nicaragua)
Panamanian (Panama)
Paraguayan (Paraguay)
Philippine (Philippines)
Portuguese (Portugal)
Sahraouian (Western Sahara)
Salvadoran (El Salvador)
Senegalese (Senegal)
Surinamese (Suriname)
Tobagonian (Trinidad and Tobago)
Venezuelan (Venezuela)

Vietnamese (Vietnam)
Vincentian (St Vincent and the Grenadines)
Zimbabwean (Zimbabwe)

11 Argentinian (Argentina)
Azerbaijani (Azerbaijan)
Bangladeshi (Bangladesh)
Cameroonian (Cameroon)
Cape Verdean (Cape Verde)
Kazakhstani (Kazakhstan)
Marshallese (Marshall Islands)
Mauritanian (Mauritania)
Micronesian (Federated States of Micronesia)
Montenegrin (Montenegro)
North Korean (North Korea)
Sammarinese (San Marino)
Seychellois (Seychelles)
Singaporean (Singapore)
South Korean (South Korea)
Tajikistani (Tajikistan)
Trinidadian (Trinidad and Tobago)

12 Luxembourger (Luxembourg)
Saudi Arabian (Saudi Arabia)
South African (South Africa)
St Vincentian (St Vincent and the Grenadines)

13 Equatoguinean (Equatorial Guinea)
Herzegovinian (Bosnia and Herzegovina)
Liechtenstein (Liechtenstein)
Sierra Leonean (Sierra Leone)

14 Central African (Central African Republic)
Guinea-Bissauan (Guinea-Bissau)

15 Liechtensteiner (Liechtenstein)
Papua New Guinean (Papua New Guinea)
Solomon Islander (Solomon Islands)

See also **Africa**; **Asia**; **Europe**; **Scandinavia**

Native American *see* The Americas

NATO

North Atlantic Treaty Organization (NATO) members:

02 UK	Norway	Germany	09 Lithuania
03 USA	Poland	Hungary	10 Luxembourg
05 Italy	Turkey	Iceland	13 Czech Republic
Spain	07 Albania	Romania	United Kingdom
06 Canada	Belgium	08 Bulgaria	14 The Netherlands
France	Croatia	Portugal	21 United States of
Greece	Denmark	Slovakia	America
Latvia	Estonia	Slovenia	

See also **alphabet**

NATO phonetic alphabet *see* alphabet

natural history

Terms used in natural history include:

03 era	**06** animal	prairie	extinction
sea	botany	reserve	mineralogy
04 bird	desert	savanna	naturalist
bush	energy	species	population
cell	famine	wetland	rainforest
dune	flower	zoology	vertebrate
fish	forest	**08** acid rain	**11** archaeology
life	fossil	bacteria	circulation
moor	fungus	dinosaur	environment
park	garden	genetics	groundwater
reef	growth	hedgerow	living world
rock	insect	heredity	ornithology
soil	jungle	mountain	pollination
tree	mammal	savannah	reclamation
05 algae	nature	skeleton	respiration
atoll	period	wildlife	**12** anthropology
biome	phylum	woodland	biodiversity
coast	planet	**09** bacterium	conservation
Earth	**07** biology	behaviour	invertebrate
epoch	climate	breathing	national park
fungi	drought	digestion	paleontology
grass	ecology	evolution	reproduction
ocean	estuary	geography	**13** fertilization
plant	geology	grassland	global warming
river	habitat	pollution	palaeontology
swamp	mineral	**10** ecotourism	**14** photosynthesis
virus	peat bog	entomology	

See also **biology**; **zoology**

naturalist *see* **biology**

nature reserve *see* **park**

nautical

Nautical terms include:

03 aft	moor	haven	embark
jib	quay	jetty	jetsam
lee	reef	lay up	launch
row	roll	plane	marina
run	sink	put in	marine
yaw	tack	reach	maroon
04 beam	tide	refit	mayday
beat	trim	watch	mutiny
dock	wake	wharf	voyage
fore	wash	wreck	**07** ballast
gybe	wave	**06** afloat	bow-wave
heel	**05** cargo	broach	capsize
helm	ferry	convoy	cast off
knot	fleet	course	current
list	float	cruise	dry dock

ebb tide	slipway	windward	navigation
flotsam	weather	**09** amidships	run aground
foghorn	**08** bear away	disembark	seamanship
go about	becalmed	foreshore	shore leave
harbour	chandler	seafaring	slip anchor
heave to	dockyard	seaworthy	**11** harbour dues
leeward	flotilla	ship water	weigh anchor
low tide	high tide	shipwreck	**12** air-sea rescue
mooring	lee shore	stevedore	breeches-buoy
on board	life buoy	**10** coastguard	pitch and toss
ride out	life-raft	deadweight	shipping lane
riptide	make fast	harbour-bar	ship's company
salvage	neap tide	head to wind	**13** dead reckoning
sea lane	put to sea	heavy swell	harbour-master
sea legs	shipping	lay a course	**14** circumnavigate
seasick	shipyard	life-jacket	compass bearing
set sail	stowaway	life-rocket	
sheet in			

See also **navigation; sailing**

navigation

Navigational aids and systems include:

03 gee	pilot	**09** lightship	gyrocompass
GPS	radar	omnirange	**13** nautical table
INS	**07** compass	**10** depth gauge	parallel ruler
log	navarho	lighthouse	**15** astronavigation
Vor	sextant	marker buoy	flux-gate compass
04 GNSS	**08** bell buoy	**11** chronometer	magnetic compass
05 chart	dividers	conical buoy	
loran	VHF radio	echo-sounder	

See also **signal**

navigator *see* **exploration; sailing**

navy *see* **military**

nerve

Nerves include:

05 optic	phrenic	trochlear	thoracodorsal
sural	plantar	**10** oculomotor	**14** dorsal scapular
ulnar	sciatic	splanchnic	medial pectoral
vagus	**08** abducens	trigeminal	**15** iliohypogastric
06 facial	axillary	**11** hypoglossal	inferior gluteal
lumbar	peroneal	intercostal	lateral pectoral
median	thoracic	**12** ilioinguinal	lesser auricular
radial	**09** coccygeal	long thoracic	lesser occipital
sacral	obturator	suboccipital	spinal accessory
tibial	olfactory	**13** genitofemoral	superior gluteal
07 femoral	saphenous	suprascapular	

nest *see* **animal**

The Netherlands

Cities and notable towns in The Netherlands include:

05 Delft	Haarlem	**09** Amsterdam	**10** Leeuwarden
06 Arnhem	Utrecht	Eindhoven	Maastricht
	08 Nijmegen	Groningen	Middelburg
07 Den Haag	The Hague	Rotterdam	**11** 's-Gravenhage

Administrative divisions of The Netherlands, with regional capitals:

07 Drenthe (Assen)	Overijssel (Zwolle)
Limburg (Maastricht)	**11** Zuid-Holland (The Hague)
Utrecht (Utrecht)	
Zeeland (Middelburg)	**12** Noord-Brabant ('s-Hertogenbosch)
09 Flevoland (Lelijstad)	Noord-Holland (Haarlem)
Friesland (Leeuwarden)	North Brabant ('s-Hertogenbosch)
Groningen (Groningen)	North Holland (Haarlem)
10 Gelderland (Arnhem)	South Holland (The Hague)

Dutch landmarks include:

04 Maas	**08** Oude Kerk	**10** IJsselmeer	**13** Anne Frank Huis
06 Amstel	**09** Keukenhof	Nieuwe Kerk	**15** Ann Frank's house
07 Scheldt	Zuider Zee	**11** Afsluitdijk	Stedelijk Museum
		Rijksmuseum	

See also **Low Countries**

New York

New York boroughs:

05 Bronx	**08** Brooklyn	**12** Staten Island
06 Queens	**09** Manhattan	

Other districts of New York include:

04 Noho	El Barrio	The Bowery
Soho	Elmhurst	Turtle Bay
06 Corona	Flatbush	Woodhaven
Harlem	Flatiron	Yorkville
Hollis	Flushing	**10** Cobble Hill
Inwood	Gramercy	Douglaston
Nolita	Rego Park	Greenpoint
Queens	Steinway	Ground Zero
07 Astoria	The Bronx	Kew Gardens
Chelsea	West Side	Marble Hill
Clifton	**09** Briarwood	Sunset Park
Kips Bay	Chinatown	**11** Borough Park
Midtown	Flatlands	Central Park
Midwood	Manhattan	Coney Island
Tribeca	Ozone Park	East Village
08 Brooklyn	Park Slope	Ellis Island
Canarsie	Princeton	Forest Hills
East Side	Ridgewood	Howard Beach

Little Italy
Little Korea
New Brighton
West Village
12 Alphabet City
Crown Heights
Cypress Hills
Hell's Kitchen

South Jamaica
Staten Island
Williamsburg
13 Brighton Beach
Lower East Side
Spanish Harlem
Upper East Side
Upper West Side

14 Jackson Heights
Long Island City
Lower Manhattan
Manhattan Beach
Stuyvesant Town
15 Brooklyn Heights
Garment District
Roosevelt Island

New York streets include:

06 Bowery
07 Park Row
08 Broadway
FDR Drive
10 14th Street
21st Avenue
23rd Street
34th Street
36th Avenue
42nd Street
57th Street
79th Street
96th Street
Park Avenue
Wall Street
11 Canal Street
Fifth Avenue

First Avenue
Grand Street
Sixth Avenue
Third Avenue
Union Square
Vesey Street
12 Broome Street
Eighth Avenue
Fourth Avenue
Fulton Street
Hudson Street
Second Avenue
Spring Street
Varick Street
13 Houston Street
Jackson Avenue
JFK Expressway
Madison Square

Seventh Avenue
14 Bleecker Street
Columbus Circle
Delancey Street
East 42nd Street
Flatbush Avenue
Harrison Street
Riverside Drive
Sheridan Square
Sunrise Highway
West 42nd Street
15 Central Park West
Cortlandt Street
Greenwich Street
Lexington Avenue
Queens Boulevard
West Side Highway

New York landmarks include:

03 EWR
JFK
NYU
04 CBGB
MoMA
05 Macy's
06 The Met
07 Barneys
Factory
Whitney
08 Broadway
Bronx Zoo
Studio 54
09 East River
The Dakota
10 Bronx River
Cotton Club
FAO Schwarz
Ground Zero

Guggenheim
Rose Center
Wall Street
11 Battery Park
Central Park
Coney Island
Ellis Island
Federal Hall
Harlem River
Hudson River
Penn Station
Shea Stadium
Times Square
Union Square
12 Carnegie Hall
Chelsea Hotel
Hotel Chelsea
Prospect Park
Staten Island
The Cloisters

13 Apollo Theater
Bloomingdale's
Gracie Mansion
Lincoln Center
Lincoln Tunnel
Pan Am Building
St Paul's Church
Yankee Stadium
14 Brooklyn Bridge
Fraunces Tavern
Grand Army Plaza
Waldorf Astoria
Washington Arch
15 Flushing Meadows
Frick Collection
Manhattan Bridge
Metlife Building
Saks Fifth Avenue
Seagram Building
Statue of Liberty
Trump World Tower

New Zealand

Cities and notable towns in New Zealand include:

06 Napier
Nelson
Timaru

07 Dunedin
Manukau
Rotorua

08 Auckland
Gisborne
Hamilton
Hastings
Tauranga
Wanganui

09 Whangarei

10 Wellington

11 New Plymouth

12 Christchurch
Invercargill

15 Palmerston North

Regions and territories of New Zealand, with regional capitals:

04 Niue (Alofi)

05 Otago (Dunedin)

06 Nelson (Nelson)
Tasman (Richmond)

07 Tokelau
Waikato (Hamilton)

08 Auckland (Auckland)
Gisborne (Gisborne)
Taranaki (New Plymouth)

09 Hawke's Bay (Napier)

Northland (Whangarei)
Southland (Invercargill)
West Coast (Greymouth)

10 Canterbury (Christchurch)
Wellington (Wellington)

11 Bay of Plenty (Tauranga)
Cook Islands (Avarua)
Marlborough (Blenheim)

14 Chatham Islands

16 Manawatu-Wanganui (Palmerston North)

New Zealand electorates:

04 Ilam
Mana

05 Epsom
Otago
Otaki
Piako
Taupo

06 Aoraki
Napier
Nelson
Rakaia
Rodney
Tainui
Tamaki
Wigram

07 Mangere
New Lynn
Rotorua
Te Atatu

08 Clevedon
Manurewa
Mt Albert
Rimutaka

Rongotai
Tauranga
Tukituki
Waiariki

09 East Coast
Hutt South
Mt Roskill
Northcote
Northland
Pakuranga
Wairarapa
Waitakere
Whanganui
Whangarei

10 Coromandel
North Shore
Rangitikei
Te Tai Tonga

11 Bay of Plenty
Helensville
Manukau East
New Plymouth
Port Waikato

Waimakariri

12 Dunedin North
Dunedin South
Hamilton East
Hamilton West
Invercargill
Maungakiekie
Te Tai Hauauru
Te Tai Tokerau

13 East Coast Bays
Ikaora-Rawhiti
Ohariu-Belmont

14 Banks Peninsula
Tamaki Makaurau

15 Auckland Central
Clutha-Southland
Palmerston North
West Coast-Tasman

16 Christchurch East

17 Wellington Central

19 Christchurch Central
Taranaki-King Country

New Zealand landmarks include:

05 Hawea

06 Mt Cook
Te Anau

Wanaka

07 Aorangi
Rotorua

Ruapehu
Waikato

08 Mt Egmont

Wakatipu	**11** Rakaia Gorge	**15** Mangere Mountain
Wanganui	**12** Milford Sound	Ninety Mile Beach
09 Fiordland	Southern Alps	Whangaparaoa Bay
Lake Taupo	**13** Stewart Island	
10 Mt Victoria	**14** Otago Peninsula	

See also **Australasia**; **governor**; **mythology**; **prime minister**

news

News agencies include:

02 AP (Associated Press)
PA (Press Association)

03 AAP (Australian Associated Press)
AFP (Agence France-Presse)
UPI (United Press International)

04 NZPA (New Zealand Press Association)

Tass (Telegraph Agency of the Soviet Union)

07 Reuters

08 ITAR-Tass (Information Telegraph Agency of Russia)

15 Associated Press

newspaper

Newspapers and magazines include:

02 *GQ*
Ms
OK!
XL
Ya

03 *FHM*
NME
Red
She
TES
TLS
Viz

04 *Best*
Bild
Chat
Chic
Elle
Heat
Judy
Life
Lion
Look
Mind
Mizz
Mojo
More!
Puck
Time
Trud
TV21
Zest

05 *Arena*
Bella
Bliss

Bunty
Chips
Ebony
Globe
Hello!
Honey
Iskra
Jinty
Judge
Mandy
Maxim
Metro
Prima
Punch
Shoot
Stern
Tammy
Tiger
Vogue
Which?
Wired
Woman
World

06 *Avanti*
Buster
Cheeky
Closer
El Pais
Forbes
Granta
Herald
Hornet
Jackie
Lancet

Le Soir
Loaded
Nature
Pippin
Pravda
Scraps
Sparky
Tatler
The Sun
Topper
War Cry
Wonder

07 *Annabel*
Company
Die Welt
Esquire
Film Fun
Fortune
Glamour
Hotspur
Hustler
Jackpot
Journal
Kerrang!
La Libre
Le Monde
L'Equipe
Mayfair
Men Only
Newsday
Options
Playboy
Rainbow
Science

The Face
The Lady
The List
The Star
The Week
Time Out
Titbits
Tribune
TV Times
Twinkle
Valiant
Whizzer
Whoopee

08 Campaign
Decanter
Die Woche
European
Gay Times
Izvestia
Knockout
La Presse
La Stampa
Le Figaro
My Weekly
Newsweek
New Woman
Prospect
Scotsman
Smart Set
Sparkler
The Beano
The Dandy
The Eagle
The Field
The Idler
The Month
The Oldie
The Queen
The Times
USA Today

09 Adventure
Comic Cuts
Daily Mail
Daily News
Daily Star
Good Words
Home Notes
Ideal Home
Mirabelle
New Yorker
Penthouse
Petticoat
Q Magazine
Red Pepper
Smash Hits
The Beezer
The Friend

The Grocer
The Herald
The Lancet
The Mirror
The People
The Tablet
The Tatler
The Victor
Woman's Day
Woman's Own

10 Asian Times
Daily Sport
Der Spiegel
Eve's Weekly
Irish Times
Men's Health
New Society
Paris-Match
Private Eye
Racing Post
Radio Times
Sunday Post
The Courier
The Express
Vanity Fair
Weekly News

11 Church Times
Country Life
Daily Herald
Daily Mirror
Daily Record
Daily Sketch
Jack and Jill
Marie Claire
Melody Maker
Morning Star
New Republic
New York Post
Picture Post
Sunday Press
Sunday Sport
Sunday World
The Big Issue
The European
The Guardian
The Listener
The Observer
The Universe
Western Mail
Woman's Realm

12 Angling Times
Asahi Shimbun
Cosmopolitan
Daily Courant
Family Circle
Fortean Times
History Today

La Repubblica
Look and Learn
Mail on Sunday
New Scientist
New Statesman
New York Times
Nursing Times
Poetry Review
Rolling Stone
Sunday Mirror
Tagesspiegel
The Economist
The Pink Paper
The Spectator
Time Magazine
Woman and Home
Woman's Weekly

13 Catholic Times
Country Living
Daltons Weekly
Farmers Weekly
Financial News
Glasgow Herald
Harper's Bazaar
Harper's Weekly
Homes and Ideas
Horse and Hound
Just Seventeen
London Gazette
Mother and Baby
Penny Magazine
People's Friend
Reader's Digest
The Bookseller
The Sunday Post
The Watchtower
Wales on Sunday
Woman's Journal

14 Caribbean Times
Catholic Herald
Financial Times
House and Garden
House Beautiful
Literary Review
News of the World
Roy of the Rovers
Simplicissimus
The Boston Globe
The Gentlewoman
The Independent
The New York Post
The Suffragette
The Sunday Times
Washington Post

15 Evening Standard
Exchange and Mart
Express on Sunday

Harpers and Queen	Socialist Worker	The National Post
Homes and Gardens	Sunday Telegraph	The New York Times
Los Angeles Times	The Boston Herald	The Times of India
Picture Politics	The Boy's Own Paper	Whizzer and Chips
Press and Journal	The Mail on Sunday	

Newspaper proprietors and magnates include:

04 King (Cecil Harmsworth; 1901–87, English)
Ochs (Adolph Simon; 1858–1935, US)
Shah (Eddy; 1944–   , English)

05 Astor (John Jacob, Lord; 1886–1971, US/British)
Astor (William Waldorf, Viscount; 1848–1919, US/British)
Black (Conrad, Lord; 1944–   , Canadian/British)

06 Aitken (Sir Max; 1910–85, Canadian/British)
Graham (Katherine Meyer; 1917–2001, US)
Hearst (William Randolph; 1863–1951, US)
Packer (Sir Frank; 1906–74, Australian)
Ridder (Bernard H, Jnr; 1916–2002, US)
Walter (John; 1739–1812, English)
Walter (John; 1819–94, English)

07 Barclay (Sir David; 1934–   , English)
Barclay (Sir Frederick; 1934–   , English)
Camrose (William Ewert Berry, Viscount; 1879–1954, Welsh)

Kemsley (James Gomer Berry, Viscount; 1883–1968, Welsh)
Maxwell (Robert; 1923–91, Czech/British)
Murdoch (Rupert; 1931–   , Australian/US)
Pearson (Sir Cyril Arthur; 1866–1921, English)
Riddell (George, Lord; 1865–1934, Scottish)
Scripps (Edward Wyllis; 1854–1926, US)
Thomson (D C; 1861–1954, Scottish)
Thomson (Roy, Lord; 1894–1976, Canadian/British)

08 Pulitzer (Joseph; 1847–1911, US)

10 Berlusconi (Silvio; 1936–   , Italian)
Rothermere (Harold Harmsworth, Viscount; 1868–1940, English)

11 Beaverbrook (Max Aitken, Lord; 1879–1964, Canadian/British)
Northcliffe (Alfred Harmsworth, Viscount; 1865–1922, Irish/British)

See also **journalism**

nickname *see* **American football; Australia; Australian rules football; baseball; basketball; cricket; football; Rugby League; Rugby Union; United States of America**

Nine Muses *see* **muse**

Nobel Prize

Nobel Prize for Chemistry winners:

03 Lee (Yuan T; 1986)

04 Agre (Peter; 2003)
Berg (Paul; 1980)
Cech (Thomas R; 1989)
Cram (Donald J; 1987)
Curl (Robert F, Jnr; 1996)
Ertl (Gerhard; 2007)
Fenn (John B; 2002)
Hahn (Otto; 1944)
Heck (Richard, 2010)
Klug (Sir Aaron; 1982)
Kohn (Walter; 1998)
Kuhn (Richard; 1938)
Lehn (Jean-Marie; 1987)
Olah (George A; 1994)
Rose (Irwin; 2004)

Skou (Jens C; 1997)
Todd (Lord; 1957)
Urey (Harold C; 1934)

05 Alder (Kurt; 1950)
Aston (Francis W; 1922)
Bosch (Carl; 1931)
Boyer (Paul D; 1997)
Brown (Herbert C; 1979)
Corey (Elias James; 1990)
Curie (Marie; 1911)
Debye (Peter; 1936)
Diels (Otto; 1950)
Eigen (Manfred; 1967)
Ernst (Richard R; 1991)
Flory (Paul J; 1974)
Fukui (Kenichi; 1981)

Haber (Fritz; 1918)
Huber (Robert; 1988)
Karle (Jerome; 1985)
Kroto (Sir Harold; 1996)
Libby (Willard F; 1960)
Moore (Stanford; 1972)
Natta (Giulio; 1963)
Pople (John; 1998)
Pregl (Fritz; 1923)
Smith (Michael; 1993)
Soddy (Frederick; 1921)
Stein (William H; 1972)
Synge (Richard LM; 1952)
Taube (Henry; 1983)
Tsien (Roger Y; 2008)

06 Altman (Sidney; 1989)
Baeyer (Adolf von; 1905)
Barton (Sir Derek; 1969)
Calvin (Melvin; 1961)
Grubbs (Robert H; 2005)
Harden (Arthur; 1929)
Hassel (Odd; 1969)
Heeger (Alan; 2000)
Hevesy (George de; 1943)
Joliot (Frédéric; 1935)
Karrer (Paul; 1937)
Leloir (Luis; 1970)
Marcus (Rudolph A; 1992)
Martin (Archer JP; 1952)
Michel (Hartmut; 1988)
Molina (Mario J; 1995)
Mullis (Kary B; 1993)
Nernst (Walther; 1920)
Noyori (Ryoji; 2001)
Perutz (Max F; 1962)
Porter (George, Lord; 1967)
Prelog (Vladimir; 1975)
Ramsay (Sir William; 1904)
Sanger (Frederick; 1958, 1980)
Steitz (Thomas; 2009)
Sumner (James B; 1946)
Suzuki (Akira; 2010)
Tanaka (Koichi; 2002)
Walker (John E; 1997)
Werner (Alfred; 1913)
Wittig (Georg; 1979)
Yonath (Ada; 2009)
Zewail (Ahmed; 1999)

07 Bergius (Friedrich; 1931)
Buchner (Eduard; 1907)
Chalfie (Martin; 2008)
Chauvin (Yves; 2005)
Crutzen (Paul J; 1995)
Fischer (Emil; 1902)
Fischer (Ernst Otto; 1973)
Fischer (Hans; 1930)
Giauque (William F; 1949)

Gilbert (Walter; 1980)
Haworth (Sir Norman; 1937)
Hershko (Avram; 2004)
Hodgkin (Dorothy C; 1964)
Kendrew (Sir John C; 1962)
Knowles (William S; 2001)
Kobilka (Brian, 2012)
Moissan (Henri; 1906)
Negishi (Ei-ichi; 2010)
Norrish (Ronald GW; 1967)
Onsager (Lars; 1968)
Ostwald (Wilhelm; 1909)
Pauling (Linus; 1954)
Polanyi (John C; 1986)
Rowland (F Sherwood; 1995)
Ruzicka (Leopold; 1939)
Schrock (Richard R; 2005)
Seaborg (Glenn T; 1951)
Semenov (Nikolay; 1956)
Smalley (Richard E; 1996)
Stanley (Wendell M; 1946)
Wallach (Otto; 1910)
Wieland (Heinrich; 1927)
Windaus (Adolf; 1928)
Ziegler (Karl; 1963)

08 Anfinsen (Christian; 1972)
Grignard (Victor; 1912)
Hauptman (Herbert A; 1985)
Herzberg (Gerhard; 1971)
Hoffmann (Roald; 1981)
Kornberg (Roger D; 2006)
Langmuir (Irving; 1932)
Lipscomb (William; 1976)
McMillan (Edwin M; 1951)
Mitchell (Peter; 1978)
Mulliken (Robert S; 1966)
Northrop (John H; 1946)
Pedersen (Charles J; 1987)
Richards (Theodore W; 1914)
Robinson (Sir Robert; 1947)
Sabatier (Paul; 1912)
Svedberg (Theodor; 1926)
Tiselius (Arne; 1948)
van 't Hoff (Jacobus H; 1901)
Vigneaud (Vincent du; 1955)
Virtanen (Artturi; 1945)
Woodward (Robert B; 1965)
Wüthrich (Kurt; 2002)

09 Arrhenius (Svante; 1903)
Butenandt (Adolf; 1939)
Cornforth (Sir John; 1975)
Heyrovsky (Jaroslav; 1959)
Lefkowitz (Robert, 2012)
MacKinnon (Roderick; 2003)
Prigogine (Ilya; 1977)
Shechtman (Dan, 2011)
Sharpless (K Barry; 2001)

Shimomura (Osamu; 2008)
Shirakawa (Hideki; 2000)
Wilkinson (Sir Geoffrey; 1973)
Zsigmondy (Richard; 1925)

10 Herschbach (Dudley R; 1986)
MacDiarmid (Alan G; 2000)
Merrifield (Bruce; 1984)
Rutherford (Ernest, Lord; 1908)

Staudinger (Hermann; 1953)

11 Ciechanover (Aaron; 2004)
Deisenhofer (Johann; 1988)
Hinshelwood (Sir Cyril; 1956)
Joliot-Curie (Irène; 1935)
Willstätter (Richard; 1915)

12 Euler-Chelpin (Hans von; 1929)
Ramakrishnan (Venkatraman; 2009)

Nobel Prize for Economics winners:

03 Sen (Amartya; 1998)

04 Nash (John F, Jnr; 1994)
Roth (Alvin, 2012)
Sims (Christopher, 2011)

05 Arrow (Kenneth J; 1972)
Coase (Ronald H; 1991)
Engle (Robert F, III; 2003)
Fogel (Robert W; 1993)
Hayek (Friedrich August von; 1974)
Hicks (Sir John R; 1972)
Klein (Lawrence R; 1980)
Lewis (Sir Arthur; 1979)
Lucas (Robert E, Jnr; 1995)
Meade (James E; 1977)
North (Douglass C; 1993)
Ohlin (Bertil; 1977)
Simon (Herbert A; 1978)
Smith (Vernon L; 2002)
Solow (Robert M; 1987)
Stone (Sir Richard; 1984)
Tobin (James; 1982)

06 Allais (Maurice; 1988)
Aumann (Robert J; 2005)
Becker (Gary S; 1992)
Debreu (Gerard; 1984)
Frisch (Ragnar; 1969)
Maskin (Eric S; 2007)
Merton (Robert C; 1997)
Miller (Merton H; 1990)
Myrdal (Gunnar; 1974)
Ostrom (Elinor, 2009)
Phelps (Edmund S; 2006)
Selten (Reinhard; 1994)
Sharpe (William F; 1990)
Spence (A Michael; 2001)

07 Akerlof (George A; 2001)

Diamond (Peter, 2010)
Granger (Clive WJ; 2003)
Heckman (James J; 2000)
Hurwicz (Leonid; 2007)
Krugman (Paul; 2008)
Kuznets (Simon; 1971)
Kydland (Finn E; 2004)
Mundell (Robert A; 1999)
Myerson (Roger B; 2007)
Sargent (Thomas, 2011)
Scholes (Myron S; 1997)
Schultz (Theodore W; 1979)
Shapley (Lloyd, 2012)
Stigler (George J; 1982)
Vickrey (William; 1996)

08 Buchanan (James M, Jnr; 1986)
Friedman (Milton; 1976)
Haavelmo (Trygve; 1989)
Harsanyi (John C; 1994)
Kahneman (Daniel; 2002)
Koopmans (Tjalling C; 1975)
Leontief (Wassily; 1973)
McFadden (Daniel L; 2000)
Mirrlees (James A; 1996)
Prescott (Edward C; 2004)
Stiglitz (Joseph E; 2001)

09 Markowitz (Harry M; 1990)
Mortensen (Dale, 2010)
Samuelson (Paul A; 1970)
Schelling (Thomas C; 2005)
Tinbergen (Jan; 1969)

10 Modigliani (Franco; 1985)
Pissarides (Christopher; 2010)
Williamson (Oliver, 2009)

11 Kantorovich (Leonid Vitaliyevich; 1975)

Nobel Prize for Literature winners:

02 Fo (Dario; 1997)
Oe (Kenzaburo; 1994)

03 Paz (Octavio; 1990)

04 Böll (Heinrich; 1972)
Buck (Pearl; 1938)
Cela (Camilo José; 1989)

Gard (Roger Martin du; 1937)
Gide (André; 1947)
Mann (Thomas; 1929)
Shaw (George Bernard; 1925)

05 Agnon (Samuel; 1966)
Bunin (Ivan; 1933)
Camus (Albert; 1957)

Eliot (TS; 1948)
Grass (Günter; 1999)
Hesse (Hermann; 1946)
Heyse (Paul; 1910)
Lewis (Sinclair; 1930)
Mo Yan (2012)
Pamuk (Orhan; 2006)
Perse (Saint-John; 1960)
Sachs (Nelly; 1966)
Simon (Claude; 1985)
White (Patrick; 1973)
Yeats (W B; 1923)

06 Andric (Ivo; 1961)
Bellow (Saul; 1976)
Elytis (Odysseus; 1979)
Eucken (Rudolf; 1908)
France (Anatole; 1921)
Hamsun (Knut; 1920)
Heaney (Seamus; 1995)
Jensen (Johannes V; 1944)
Milosz (Czeslaw; 1980)
Müller (Herta, 2009)
Neruda (Pablo; 1971)
O'Neill (Eugene; 1936)
Pinter (Harold; 2005)
Sartre (Jean-Paul; 1964)
Singer (Isaac Bashevis; 1978)
Tagore (Rabindranath; 1913)
Undset (Sigrid; 1928)

07 Beckett (Samuel; 1969)
Bergson (Henri; 1927)
Brodsky (Joseph; 1987)
Canetti (Elias; 1981)
Coetzee (JM; 2003)
Deledda (Grazia; 1926)
Golding (William; 1983)
Jelinek (Elfriede; 2004)
Jiménez (Juan Ramón; 1956)
Johnson (Eyvind; 1974)
Kertész (Imre; 2002)
Kipling (Rudyard; 1907)
Laxness (Halldór; 1955)
Lessing (Doris; 2007)
Mahfouz (Naguib; 1988)
Márquez (Gabriel García; 1982)
Mauriac (François; 1952)
Mistral (Frédéric; 1904)
Mistral (Gabriela; 1945)
Mommsen (Theodor; 1902)

Montale (Eugenio; 1975)
Naipaul (VS; 2001)
Reymont (Wladyslaw; 1924)
Rolland (Romain; 1915)
Russell (Bertrand; 1950)
Seferis (Giorgos; 1963)
Seifert (Jaroslav; 1984)
Soyinka (Wole; 1986)
Walcott (Derek; 1992)

08 Asturias (Miguel Angel; 1967)
Bjørnson (Bjørnstjerne; 1903)
Carducci (Giosuè; 1906)
Faulkner (William; 1949)
Gordimer (Nadine; 1991)
Kawabata (Yasunari; 1968)
Lagerlöf (Selma; 1909)
Le Clézio (Jean-Marie Gustave; 2008)
Morrison (Toni; 1993)
Saramago (José; 1998)
Xingjian (Gao; 2000)

09 Benavente (Jacinto; 1922)
Churchill (Sir Winston; 1953)
Echegaray (José; 1904)
Gjellerup (Karl; 1917)
Hauptmann (Gerhart; 1912)
Hemingway (Ernest; 1954)
Karlfeldt (Erik Axel; 1931)
Martinson (Harry; 1974)
Pasternak (Boris; 1958)
Prudhomme (Sully; 1901)
Quasimodo (Salvatore; 1959)
Sholokhov (Mikhail; 1965)
Sillanpää (Frans Eemil; 1939)
Spitteler (Carl; 1919)
Steinbeck (John; 1962)

10 Aleixandre (Vicente; 1977)
Galsworthy (John; 1932)
Heidenstam (Verner von; 1916)
Lagerkvist (Pär; 1951)
Pirandello (Luigi; 1934)
Szymborska (Wislawa; 1996)

11 Maeterlinck (Maurice; 1911)
Pontoppidan (Henrik; 1917)
Sienkiewicz (Henryk; 1905)
Tranströmer (Tomas, 2011)
Vargas Llosa (Mario; 2010)

12 Solzhenitsyn (Alexander; 1970)

Nobel Peace Prize winners:

04 Belo (Carlos Filipe Ximenes; 1996)
Gore (Albert 'Al', Jnr; 2007)
Hull (Cordell; 1945)
Hume (John; 1998)
King (Martin Luther, Jnr, 1964)
Mott (John R; 1946)

Pire (Georges; 1958)
Root (Elihu; 1912)
Sato (Eisaku; 1974)
Tutu (Desmond; 1984)

05 Annan (Kofi; 2001)

Asser (Tobias; 1911)
Bajer (Fredrik; 1908)
Balch (Emily; 1946)
Begin (Menachem; 1978)
Cecil (Robert, Viscount; 1937)
Dawes (Charles G; 1925)
Ebadi (Shirin; 2003)
Fried (Alfred; 1911)
Gobat (Albert; 1902)
Lamas (Carlos Saavedra; 1936)
Lange (Christian; 1921)
Obama (Barack, 2009)
Passy (Frédéric; 1901)
Peres (Shimon; 1994)
Rabin (Yitzhak; 1994)
Yunus (Muhammad; 2006)

06 Addams (Jane; 1931)
Angell (Sir Norman; 1933)
Arafat (Yasser; 1994)
Brandt (Willy; 1971)
Briand (Aristide; 1926)
Bunche (Ralph; 1950)
Butler (Nicholas; 1931)
Carter (Jimmy; 2002)
Cassin (René; 1968)
Cremer (Randal; 1903)
Dunant (Henry; 1901)
Gbowee (Leymah, 2011)
Karman (Tawakkol, 2011)
Lutuli (Albert; 1960)
Moneta (Ernesto Teodoro; 1907)
Myrdal (Alva; 1982)
Nansen (Fridtjof; 1922)
Quidde (Ludwig; 1927)
Walesa (Lech; 1983)
Wiesel (Elie; 1986)
Wilson (Woodrow; 1919)

07 al-Sadat (Anwar; 1978)
Borlaug (Norman; 1970)
Boyd Orr (Lord; 1949)
Buisson (Ferdinand; 1927)
Dae-jung (Kim; 2000)
de Klerk (FW; 1993)
Jouhaux (Léon; 1951)
Kellogg (Frank B; 1929)
Maathai (Wangari; 2004)
Mandela (Nelson; 1993)
Pauling (Linus; 1962)
Pearson (Lester B; 1957)
Renault (Louis; 1907)
Rotblat (Joseph; 1995)
Sirleaf (Ellen Johnson, 2011)
Suttner (Bertha von; 1905)
Trimble (David; 1998)

08 Branting (Hjalmar; 1921)
Constant (Paul Henri d'Estournelles de; 1909)

Corrigan (Mairead; 1976)
Ducommun (Élie; 1902)
Le Duc Tho (1973)
MacBride (Seán; 1974)
Marshall (George C; 1953)
Sakharov (Andrei; 1975)
Williams (Betty; 1976)
Williams (Jody; 1997)

09 Ahtisaari (Martti; 2008)
Arnoldson (Klas; 1908)
Beernaert (Auguste; 1909)
Bourgeois (Léon; 1920)
Dalai Lama (14th; 1989)
ElBaradei (Mohamed; 2005)
Gorbachev (Mikhail; 1990)
Henderson (Arthur; 1934)
Kissinger (Henry; 1973)
Liu Xiaobo (2010)
Menchú Tum (Rigoberta; 1992)
Noel-Baker (Lord; 1959)
Ossietzky (Carl von; 1935)
Roosevelt (Theodore; 1906)
Söderblom (Nathan; 1930)

10 La Fontaine (Henri; 1913)
Ramos-Horta (José; 1996)
Schweitzer (Albert; 1952)
Stresemann (Gustav; 1926)

11 Chamberlain (Sir Austen; 1925)
Grameen Bank (2006)

12 Arias Sánchez (Oscar; 1987)
García Robles (Alfonso; 1982)
Hammarskjöld (Dag; 1961)
Mother Teresa (1979)

13 Aung San Suu Kyi (1991)
European Union (2012)
Pérez Esquivel (Adolfo; 1980)
United Nations (2001)

14 Johnson Sirleaf (Ellen, 2011)

20 Amnesty International (1977)

21 Friends Service Council (1947)

22 Médecins Sans Frontières (1999)

25 League of Red Cross Societies (1963)

26 United Nations Children's Fund (1965)

27 Institute of International Law (1904)

31 American Friends Service Committee (1947)
International Atomic Energy Agency (2005)
International Labour Organization (1969)
United Nations Peacekeeping Forces (1988)

33 Permanent International Peace Bureau (1910)

35 International Campaign to Ban Landmines (1997)
International Committee of the Red Cross (1917, 1944, 1963)

36 Nansen International Office for Refugees (1938)

37 Intergovernmental Panel on Climate Change (2007)

42 Pugwash Conferences on Science and World Affairs (1995)

51 International Physicians for the Prevention of Nuclear War (1985)
Office of the United Nations High Commissioner for Refugees (1954, 1981)

Nobel Prize for Physics winners:

03 Chu (Steven; 1997)
Kao (Charles Kuen, 2009)
Lee (David M; 1996)

04 Bohr (Aage N; 1975)
Bohr (Niels; 1922)
Born (Max; 1954)
Fert (Albert; 2007)
Geim (Andre, 2010)
Hall (John L; 2005)
Hess (Victor F; 1936)
Lamb (Willis E; 1955)
Laue (Max von; 1914)
Mott (Sir Nevill; 1977)
Néel (Louis; 1970)
Paul (Wolfgang; 1989)
Perl (Martin L; 1995)
Rabi (Isidor Isaac; 1944)
Ryle (Sir Martin; 1974)
Tamm (Igor Y; 1958)
Ting (Samuel CC; 1976)
Tsui (Daniel C; 1998)
Wien (Wilhelm; 1911)

05 Basov (Nicolay G; 1964)
Bethe (Hans; 1967)
Bloch (Felix; 1952)
Bothe (Walther; 1954)
Boyle (Willard, 2009)
Bragg (Lawrence; 1915)
Bragg (William; 1915)
Braun (Ferdinand; 1909)
Curie (Marie; 1903)
Curie (Pierre; 1903)
Dalén (Gustaf; 1912)
Davis (Raymond, Jnr; 2002)
Dirac (Paul AM; 1933)
Esaki (Leo; 1973)
Fermi (Enrico; 1938)
Fitch (Val; 1980)
Frank (Ilja M; 1958)
Gabor (Dennis; 1971)
Gross (David J; 2004)
Hertz (Gustav; 1925)
Hulse (Russell A; 1993)
Kilby (Jack S; 2000)
Kusch (Polykarp; 1955)
Nambu (Yoichiro; 2008)
Onnes (Heike Kamerlingh; 1913)
Pauli (Wolfgang; 1945)

Raman (Venkata; 1930)
Reiss (Adam, 2011)
Ruska (Ernst; 1986)
Salam (Abdus; 1979)
Segrè (Emilio; 1959)
Shull (Clifford G; 1994)
Smith (George, 2009)
Smoot (George F; 2006)
Stark (Johannes; 1919)
Stern (Otto; 1943)
Vleck (John H van; 1977)

06 Alfvén (Hannes; 1970)
Barkla (Charles G; 1917)
Binnig (Gerd; 1986)
Cooper (Leon N; 1972)
Cronin (James; 1980)
Fowler (William A; 1983)
Franck (James; 1925)
Glaser (Donald A; 1960)
Hänsch (Theodor W; 2005)
Hewish (Antony; 1974)
Jensen (J Hans D; 1963)
Landau (Lev; 1962)
Lenard (Philipp; 1905)
Mather (John C; 2006)
Müller (K Alex; 1987)
Perrin (Jean Baptiste; 1926)
Planck (Max; 1918)
Powell (Cecil; 1950)
Ramsey (Norman F; 1989)
Reines (Frederick; 1995)
Rohrer (Heinrich; 1986)
Rubbia (Carlo; 1984)
Taylor (Joseph H, Jnr; 1993)
Taylor (Richard E; 1990)
't Hooft (Gerardus; 1999)
Townes (Charles H; 1964)
Walton (Ernest TS; 1951)
Wieman (Carl E; 2001)
Wigner (Eugene; 1963)
Wilson (CTR; 1927)
Wilson (Kenneth G; 1982)
Wilson (Robert Woodrow; 1978)
Yukawa (Hideki; 1949)
Zeeman (Pieter; 1902)

07 Alferov (Zhores I; 2000)
Alvarez (Luis; 1968)
Bardeen (John; 1956, 1972)

Bednorz (J Georg; 1987)
Broglie (Louis de; 1929)
Charpak (Georges; 1992)
Compton (Arthur H; 1927)
Cornell (Eric A; 2001)
Dehmelt (Hans G; 1989)
Feynman (Richard P; 1965)
Giaever (Ivar; 1973)
Glashow (Sheldon; 1979)
Glauber (Roy J; 2005)
Haroche (Serge, 2012)
Kapitsa (Pyotr; 1978)
Kastler (Alfred; 1966)
Kendall (Henry W; 1990)
Koshiba (Masatoshi; 2002)
Kroemer (Herbert; 2000)
Leggett (Anthony J; 2003)
Lorentz (Hendrik A; 1902)
Marconi (Guglielmo; 1909)
Maskawa (Toshihide; 2008)
Penzias (Arno; 1978)
Purcell (E M; 1952)
Richter (Burton; 1976)
Röntgen (Wilhelm Conrad von; 1901)
Schmidt (Brian, 2011)
Störmer (Horst L; 1998)
Thomson (Sir George; 1937)
Thomson (JJ; 1906)
Veltman (Martinus JG; 1999)
Wilczek (Frank; 2004)
Zernike (Frits; 1953)

08 Anderson (Carl D; 1936)
Anderson (Philip W; 1977)
Appleton (Sir Edward; 1947)
Blackett (Patrick, Lord; 1948)
Brattain (Walter H; 1956)
Bridgman (Percy W; 1946)
Chadwick (Sir James; 1935)
Davisson (Clinton; 1937)
de Gennes (Pierre-Gilles; 1991)
Einstein (Albert; 1921)
Friedman (Jerome I; 1990)
Gell-Mann (Murray; 1969)
Giacconi (Riccardo; 2002)
Ginzburg (Vitaly L; 2003)
Grünberg (Peter; 2007)
Ketterle (Wolfgang; 2001)
Klitzing (Klaus von; 1985)
Laughlin (Robert B; 1998)

Lawrence (Ernest; 1939)
Lederman (Leon M; 1988)
Lippmann (Gabriel; 1908)
Millikan (Robert A; 1923)
Osheroff (Douglas D; 1996)
Phillips (William D; 1997)
Politzer (H David; 2004)
Rayleigh (Lord; 1904)
Schawlow (Arthur L; 1981)
Schwartz (Melvin; 1988)
Shockley (William B; 1956)
Siegbahn (Kai M; 1981)
Siegbahn (Manne; 1924)
Tomonaga (Sin-Itiro; 1965)
Weinberg (Steven; 1979)
Wineland (David, 2012)

09 Abrikosov (Alexei A; 2003)
Becquerel (Henri; 1903)
Cherenkov (Pavel A; 1958)
Cockcroft (Sir John; 1951)
Guillaume (Charles Edouard; 1920)
Josephson (Brian D; 1973)
Kobayashi (Makoto; 2008)
Michelson (Albert A; 1907)
Mössbauer (Rudolf; 1961)
Mottelson (Ben R; 1975)
Novoselov (Konstantin, 2010)
Prokhorov (Aleksandr M; 1964)
Rainwater (James; 1975)
Schwinger (Julian; 1965)

10 Brockhouse (Bertram N; 1994)
Heisenberg (Werner; 1932)
Hofstadter (Robert; 1961)
Perlmutter (Saul, 2011)
Richardson (Owen Willans; 1928)
Richardson (Robert C; 1996)
Schrieffer (Robert; 1972)
van der Meer (Simon; 1984)

11 Bloembergen (Nicolaas; 1981)
Chamberlain (Owen; 1959)
Schrödinger (Erwin; 1933)
Steinberger (Jack; 1988)
Tsung-Dao Lee (1957)
van der Waals (Johannes Diderik; 1910)

12 Chen Ning Yang (1957)

13 Chandrasekhar (Subramanyan; 1983)
Goeppert-Mayer (Maria; 1963)

14 Cohen-Tannoudji (Claude; 1997)

Nobel Prize for Physiology or Medicine winners:

03 Dam (Henrik; 1943)

04 Axel (Richard; 2004)
Buck (Linda B; 2004)
Cori (Carl; 1947)
Cori (Gerty; 1947)

Dale (Sir Henry; 1936)
Duve (Christian de; 1974)
Fire (Andrew Z; 2006)
Hess (Walter; 1949)
Hill (Archibald V; 1922)

Hunt (Tim; 2001)
Katz (Sir Bernard; 1970)
Koch (Robert; 1905)
Ross (Ronald; 1902)
Rous (Peyton; 1966)
Vane (Sir John; 1982)
Wald (George; 1967)

05 Arber (Werner; 1978)
Black (Sir James; 1988)
Bloch (Konrad; 1964)
Bovet (Daniel; 1957)
Brown (Michael S; 1985)
Chain (Sir Ernst; 1945)
Cohen (Stanley; 1986)
Crick (Francis; 1962)
Doisy (Edward A; 1943)
Elion (Gertrude B; 1988)
Euler (Ulf von; 1970)
Evans (Sir Martin; 2007)
Golgi (Camillo; 1906)
Hench (Philip S; 1950)
Hubel (David H; 1981)
Jacob (François; 1965)
Jerne (Niels K; 1984)
Krebs (Edwin G; 1992)
Krebs (Sir Hans; 1953)
Krogh (August; 1920)
Lewis (Edward B; 1995)
Loewi (Otto; 1936)
Luria (Salvador E; 1969)
Lwoff (André; 1965)
Lynen (Feodor; 1964)
Mello (Craig C; 2006)
Minot (George R; 1934)
Moniz (Egas; 1949)
Monod (Jacques; 1965)
Murad (Ferid; 1998)
Neher (Erwin; 1991)
Nurse (Sir Paul; 2001)
Ochoa (Severo; 1959)
Sharp (Phillip A; 1993)
Smith (Hamilton O; 1978)
Snell (George D; 1980)
Tatum (Edward; 1958)
Temin (Howard M; 1975)
Yalow (Rosalyn; 1977)

06 Adrian (Edgar; 1932)
Bárány (Robert; 1914)
Beadle (George; 1958)
Békésy (Georg von; 1961)
Bishop (J Michael; 1989)
Blobel (Günter; 1999)
Bordet (Jules; 1919)
Burnet (Sir F Macfarlane; 1960)
Carrel (Alexis; 1912)
Claude (Albert; 1974)
Domagk (Gerhard; 1939)
Eccles (Sir John; 1963)

Enders (John F; 1954)
Finsen (Niels Ryberg; 1903)
Florey (Howard, Lord; 1945)
Frisch (Karl von; 1973)
Gasser (Herbert S; 1944)
Gilman (Alfred G; 1994)
Granit (Ragnar; 1967)
Gurdon (Sir John, 2012)
Hausen (Harald zur; 2008)
Holley (Robert W; 1968)
Huxley (Sir Andrew; 1963)
Kandel (Eric R; 2000)
Kocher (Theodor; 1909)
Köhler (Georges JF; 1984)
Kossel (Albrecht; 1910)
Lorenz (Konrad; 1973)
Morgan (Thomas H; 1933)
Muller (Hermann J; 1946)
Müller (Paul; 1948)
Murphy (William P; 1934)
Murray (Joseph E; 1990)
Palade (George E; 1974)
Pavlov (Ivan; 1904)
Porter (Rodney R; 1972)
Richet (Charles; 1913)
Sperry (Roger W; 1981)
Thomas (E Donnall; 1990)
Varmus (Harold E; 1989)
Warren (J Robin; 2005)
Watson (James; 1962)
Weller (Thomas H; 1954)
Wiesel (Torsten N; 1981)

07 Axelrod (Julius; 1970)
Banting (Frederick G; 1923)
Behring (Emil von; 1901)
Beutler (Bruce, 2011)
Brenner (Sydney; 2002)
Cormack (Allan M; 1979)
Dausset (Jean; 1980)
Doherty (Peter C; 1996)
Edelman (Gerald M; 1972)
Edwards (Robert, 2010)
Ehrlich (Paul; 1908)
Eijkman (Christiaan; 1929)
Fibiger (Johannes; 1926)
Fischer (Edmond H; 1992)
Fleming (Sir Alexander; 1945)
Greider (Carol, 2009)
Hershey (Alfred D; 1969)
Heymans (Corneille; 1938)
Hodgkin (Sir Alan; 1963)
Hopkins (Sir Frederick; 1929)
Horvitz (H Robert; 2002)
Houssay (Bernardo; 1947)
Huggins (Charles B; 1966)
Ignarro (Louis J; 1998)
Kendall (Edward C; 1950)
Khorana (H Gobind; 1968)

Laveran (Alphonse; 1907)
Lipmann (Fritz; 1953)
Macleod (John; 1923)
Medawar (Sir Peter; 1960)
Nathans (Daniel; 1978)
Nicolle (Charles; 1928)
Robbins (Frederick C; 1954)
Roberts (Richard J; 1993)
Rodbell (Martin; 1994)
Sakmann (Bert; 1991)
Schally (Andrew V; 1977)
Spemann (Hans; 1935)
Sulston (John E; 2002)
Szostak (Jack, 2009)
Theiler (Max; 1951)
Waksman (Selman A; 1952)
Warburg (Otto; 1931)
Whipple (George H; 1934)
Wilkins (Maurice; 1962)

08 Blumberg (Baruch S; 1976)
Capecchi (Mario R; 2007)
Carlsson (Arvid; 2000)
Cournand (André F; 1956)
Delbrück (Max; 1969)
Dulbecco (Renato; 1975)
Erlanger (Joseph; 1944)
Gajdusek (D Carleton; 1976)
Hartline (Haldan K; 1967)
Hartwell (Leland H; 2001)
Hoffmann (Jules, 2011)
Kornberg (Arthur; 1959)
Marshall (Barry J; 2005)
Meyerhof (Otto; 1922)
Milstein (César; 1984)
Prusiner (Stanley B; 1997)
Richards (Dickinson W; 1956)
Smithies (Oliver; 2007)
Steinman (Ralph, 2011)

Theorell (Hugo; 1955)
Tonegawa (Susumu; 1987)
Yamanaka (Shinya, 2012)

09 Baltimore (David; 1975)
Bergström (Sune K; 1982)
Blackburn (Elizabeth, 2009)
Einthoven (Willem; 1924)
Forssmann (Werner; 1956)
Furchgott (Robert F; 1998)
Goldstein (Joseph L; 1985)
Greengard (Paul; 2000)
Guillemin (Roger; 1977)
Hitchings (George H; 1988)
Lauterbur (Paul C; 2003)
Lederberg (Joshua; 1958)
Mansfield (Sir Peter; 2003)
Mechnikov (Ilya; 1908)
Nirenberg (Marshall W; 1968)
Tinbergen (Nikolaas; 1973)
Wieschaus (Eric F; 1995)

10 Benacerraf (Baruj; 1980)
Gullstrand (Allvar; 1911)
Hounsfield (Godfrey N; 1979)
McClintock (Barbara; 1983)
Montagnier (Luc; 2008)
Reichstein (Tadeus; 1950)
Samuelsson (Bengt I; 1982)
Sutherland (Earl W, Jnr; 1971)

11 Landsteiner (Karl; 1930)
Ramón y Cajal (Santiago; 1906)
Sherrington (Sir Charles; 1932)
Zinkernagel (Rolf M; 1996)

12 Szent-Györgyi (Albert; 1937)

13 Barré-Sinoussi (Françoise; 2008)
Wagner-Jauregg (Julius; 1927)

14 Levi-Montalcini (Rita; 1986)

15 Nüsslein-Volhard (Christiane; 1995)

nobility

Ranks of the nobility include:

02 Bt	**05** baron	duchess	**09** grand duke
Kt	count	marquis	liege lord
03 Dom	laird	peeress	magnifico
Don	liege	vicomte	patrician
Duc	nawab	**08** baroness	**10** aristocrat
Sir	noble	countess	baronetess
04 Bart	thane	life peer	noblewoman
dame	**06** daimio	margrave	**11** marchioness
duke	Junker	marquess	viscountess
earl	knight	nobleman	**12** grand duchess
jarl	squire	seigneur	**13** grand seigneur
lady	vidame	starosta	**14** knight bachelor
lord	**07** baronet	vavasour	
peer	dowager	viscount	

See also **title**

non-alcoholic drink *see* drink

non-fiction

Non-fiction works include:

03 *OED* (1st edn, 1884–1928)

06 *Walden* (1854, Henry David Thoreau)

07 *Capital* (1867–94, Karl Marx)
Who's Who (annual; 1st edn, 1849)

08 *Self-Help* (1859, Samuel Smiles)

09 *Kama Sutra* (undated, Vatsyayana)
Leviathan (1651, Thomas Hobbes)
Mein Kampf (1925, Adolf Hitler)
On Liberty (1859, John Stuart Mill)
Table Talk (1821, William Hazlitt)
The Phaedo (4 c BC, Plato)

10 *Das Kapital* (1867–94, Karl Marx)
The Annales (3 c–2 c BC, Quintus Ennius)
The Gorgias (4 c BC, Plato)
The Poetics (4 c BC, Aristotle)
The Timaeus (4 c BC, Plato)

11 *Down the Mine* (1937, George Orwell)
Mythologies (1957, Roland Barthes)
The Agricola (1 c–2 c AD, Tacitus)
The Analects (5 c BC, Confucius)
The Germania (1 c–2 c AD, Tacitus)
The Phaedrus (4 c BC, Plato)
The Republic (4 c BC, Plato)

12 *Novum Organum* (1620, Francis Bacon)
Silent Spring (1962, Rachel Carson)
The City of God (413–26 AD, St Augustine of Hippo)
The Second Sex (1949, Simone de Beauvoir)
The Symposium (4 c BC, Plato)

13 *The Story of Art* (1950, Ernst Gombrich)

14 *A Room of One's Own* (1929, Virginia Woolf)
Birds of America (1827–38, John James Audubon)
Eudemian Ethics (4 c BC, Aristotle)
Inside the Whale (1940, George Orwell)
Modern Painters (1843–60, John Ruskin)

Sartor Resartus (1833–34, Thomas Carlyle)
The Age of Reason (1794–96, Tom Paine)
The Golden Bough (1890–1915, Sir James Frazer)
The Life of Jesus (1926, John Middleton Murry)
The Rights of Man (1791–92, Tom Paine)
The Selfish Gene (1976, Richard Dawkins)

15 *Lives of the Poets* (1779–81, Samuel Johnson)
The Essays of Elia (1823–33, Charles Lamb)
The Female Eunuch (1970, Germaine Greer)
The Sleepwalkers (1931–32, Hermann Broch)

16 *Pears Cyclopaedia* (annual; 1st edn, 1897)

17 *Whitaker's Almanack* (annual; 1st edn, 1868)

18 *The Origin of Species* (1859, Charles Darwin)

19 *A Brief History of Time* (1988, Stephen Hawking)
Eats, Shoots and Leaves (2003, Lynne Truss)

23 *Encyclopaedia Britannica* (1st edn, 1768)
Oxford English Dictionary (1st edn, 1884–1928)

25 *Schott's Original Miscellany* (2002, Ben Schott)

28 *Debrett's Peerage and Baronetage* (1st edn, 1769)

29 *National Dictionary of Biography* (1st edn, 1885–1900)

30 *Chambers Biographical Dictionary* (1st edn, 1897)
Dictionary of the English Language (1755, Samuel Johnson)

33 *Brewer's Dictionary of Phrase and Fable* (1st edn, 1870)

39 *Ecclesiastical History of the English People* (c.731, St Bede)

Non-fiction writers include:

04 Bede (St, 'the Venerable'; c.673–735, Anglo-Saxon)

05 Newby (Eric; 1919–2006, English)
Paine (Tom; 1737–1809, English)
Pliny (Gaius, the Younger; c.62–c.113 AD, Roman)

06 Beevor (Antony; 1946– , English)

Binyon (T J; 1936–2004, English)
Bryson (Bill; 1951– , US)
Carson (Rachel; 1907–64, US)
Fraser (Antonia; 1932– , English)
Gibbon (Edward; 1737–94, English)
Leavis (F R; 1895–1978, English)
Schama (Simon; 1945– , English)
Walton (Izaak; 1593–1683, English)

07 Boswell (James; 1740–95, Scottish)
Carlyle (Thomas; 1795–1881, Scottish)
Hazlitt (William; 1778–1830, English)

08 Plutarch (c.46–c.120 AD, Greek)
Strachey (Lytton; 1880–1932, English)

09 De Quincey (Thomas; 1785–1859, English)
Suetonius (c.69–c.140 AD, Roman)

10 Washington (Booker T; 1856–1915, US)

14 Chandrasekaran (Rajiv; 1969– , Indian/US)

Norse *see* fate; mythology

North Atlantic Treaty Organization *see* NATO

Northern Ireland *see* town; United Kingdom

Norway

Cities and notable towns in Norway include:

04 Oslo
06 Bergen
Drøbak
Tromsø

07 Drammen
Ølesund
09 Stavanger
Trondheim

10 Hammerfest
11 Lillehammer
12 Kristiansand

Administrative divisions of Norway, with regional capitals:

04 Oslo (Oslo)
05 Troms (Tromsø)
07 Hedmark (Hamar)
Oppland (Lillehammer)
Østfold (Moss)
08 Akershus
Buskerud (Drammen)

Finnmark (Vadsø)
Nordland (Bodø)
Rogaland (Stavanger)
Telemark (Skien)
Vestfold (Tønsberg)
09 Aust-Agder (Arendal)
Hordaland (Bergen)

Vest-Agder (Kristiansand)
12 Sør-Trøndelag (Trondheim)
13 Møre og Romsdal (Molde)
Nord-Trøndelag (Steinkjer)
14 Sogn og Fjordane
(Leikanger)

Norwegian landmarks include:

05 fjord
07 Bryggen
08 Snøhetta
Svalbard

09 Hardanger
10 Sognefjord
11 Jotunheimen
Royal Palace
Trollveggen

12 Galdhøpiggen
Gaustatoppen
Jiehkkevarri
Trollfjorden
Vigeland Park

13 Oslo Cathedral
14 Geirangerfjord
Jostedalsbreen
15 Svinesund Bridge

note *see* music

novel

Novels include:

01 *V* (1963, Thomas Pynchon)
03 *Kim* (1901, Rudyard Kipling)
She (1887, Sir H Rider Haggard)
04 *1984* (1949, George Orwell)
Emma (1816, Jane Austen)
Jazz (1992, Toni Morrison)
05 *Kipps* (1904, H G Wells)

Porgy (1925, DuBose Heyward)
Scoop (1938, Evelyn Waugh)
06 *Ben Hur* (1880, Lew Wallace)
Carrie (1974, Stephen King)
Herzog (1964, Saul Bellow)
Lanark (1981, Alasdair Gray)
Lolita (1955, Vladimir Nabokov)
Pamela (1740–41, Samuel Richardson)

Rob Roy (1817, Sir Walter Scott)
The Sea (1973, Edward Bond)
The Sea (2005, John Banville)
Trilby (1894, George Du Maurier)

07 Babbitt (1922, Sinclair Lewis)
Beloved (1988, Toni Morrison)
Catch-22 (1961, Joseph Heller)
Cat's Eye (1988, Margaret Atwood)
Dracula (1897, Bram Stoker)
Erewhon (1872, Samuel Butler)
Ivanhoe (1819, Sir Walter Scott)
Lord Jim (1900, Joseph Conrad)
Orlando (1928, Virginia Woolf)
Rebecca (1938, Daphne Du Maurier)
Shirley (1849, Charlotte Brontë)
The Bell (1958, Iris Murdoch)
Ulysses (1914, James Joyce)

08 Adam Bede (1859, George Eliot)
Birdsong (1993, Sebastian Faulks)
Clarissa (1748, Samuel Richardson)
Cranford (1853, Elizabeth Gaskell)
Disgrace (1999, J M Coetzee)
Germinal (1885, Émile Zola)
Jane Eyre (1847, Charlotte Brontë)
Lucky Jim (1954, Kingsley Amis)
Moby-Dick (1851, Herman Melville)
Nostromo (1904, Joseph Conrad)
Oroonoko (c.1688, Aphra Behn)
The Waves (1931, Virginia Woolf)
The Years (1937, Virginia Woolf)
Villette (1853, Charlotte Brontë)
Vineland (1990, Thomas Pynchon)
Waverley (1814, Sir Walter Scott)
Wolf Hall (2009, Hilary Mantel)

09 About a Boy (1998, Nick Hornby)
Amsterdam (1998, Ian McEwan)
Billy Budd (1924, Herman Melville)
Billy Liar (1959, Keith Waterhouse)
Brick Lane (2003, Monica Ali)
Hard Times (1854, Charles Dickens)
Kidnapped (1886, Robert Louis Stevenson)
On The Road (1957, Jack Kerouac)
The Egoist (1879, George Meredith)
The Hobbit (1937, J R R Tolkien)
The Warden (1855, Anthony Trollope)
White Fang (1906, Jack London)

10 A Man in Full (1998, Tom Wolfe)
Animal Farm (1945, George Orwell)
Bleak House (1853, Charles Dickens)
Cannery Row (1945, John Steinbeck)
Clayhanger (1910, Arnold Bennett)
East of Eden (1952, John Steinbeck)
Ethan Frome (1911, Edith Wharton)
Hotel du Lac (1984, Anita Brookner)
Howards End (1910, E M Forster)
Jamaica Inn (1936, Daphne du Maurier)
Kenilworth (1821, Sir Walter Scott)

Lorna Doone (1869, R D Blackmore)
Naked Lunch (1959, William Burroughs)
Parade's End (1924–28, Ford Madox Ford)
Persuasion (1818, Jane Austen)
Possession (1990, A S Byatt)
The Bell Jar (1963, Sylvia Plath)
The Leopard (1960, Giuseppe di Lampedusa)
The Rainbow (1915, D H Lawrence)
Titus Alone (1959, Mervyn Peake)
Uncle Remus (1880, Joel Chandler Harris)
Vanity Fair (1848, W M Thackeray)
Westward Ho! (1855, Charles Kingsley)
White Teeth (2000, Zadie Smith)

11 A Perfect Spy (1986, John Le Carré)
A Scots Quair (1946, Lewis Grassic Gibbon)
Black Beauty (1877, Anna Sewell)
Cakes and Ale (1930, W Somerset Maugham)
Daisy Miller (1878, Henry James)
Gormenghast (1950, Mervyn Peake)
Greenmantle (1916, John Buchan)
Heat and Dust (1975, Ruth Prawer Jhabvala)
Little Women (1868, Louisa M Alcott)
Mary Poppins (1934, P L Travers)
Middlemarch (1871–72, George Eliot)
Mrs Dalloway (1925, Virginia Woolf)
Night and Day (1919, Virginia Woolf)
Oliver Twist (1838, Charles Dickens)
Silas Marner (1861, George Eliot)
Small Island (2004, Andrea Levy)
Steppenwolf (1927, Hermann Hesse)
The Big Sleep (1939, Raymond Chandler)
The Crow Road (1992, Iain Banks)
The Hireling (1957, L P Hartley)
The Third Man (1950, Graham Greene)
War and Peace (1863–69, Count Leo Tolstoy)
Women in Love (1920, D H Lawrence)

12 Anna Karenina (1874–76, Count Leo Tolstoy)
A Severed Head (1961, Iris Murdoch)
A Suitable Boy (1993, Vikram Seth)
Barnaby Rudge (1841, Charles Dickens)
Brighton Rock (1938, Graham Greene)
Casino Royale (1954, Ian Fleming)
Cover Her Face (1962, P D James)
Dombey and Son (1848, Charles Dickens)
Enduring Love (1997, Ian McEwan)
Invisible Man (1952, Ralph Ellison)
Le Père Goriot (1835, Honoré de Balzac)
Little Dorrit (1857, Charles Dickens)
Madame Bovary (1857, Gustave Flaubert)
Manon Lescaut (1738, Abbé Prévost)
Moll Flanders (1722, Daniel Defoe)
Of Mice and Men (1937, John Steinbeck)
Rip Van Winkle (1819, Washington Irving)
The Dubliners (1914, James Joyce)

The Europeans (1878, Henry James)
The Ghost Road (1995, Pat Barker)
The Go-Between (1953, L P Hartley)
The Lost World (1912, Arthur Conan Doyle)
The Moonstone (1868, Wilkie Collins)
The Old Devils (1986, Kingsley Amis)
The Sea, The Sea (1978, Iris Murdoch)
Tortilla Flat (1935, John Steinbeck)
Whisky Galore (1947, Compton
  Mackenzie)

13 A Kind of Loving (1960, Stan Barstow)
Brave New World (1932, Aldous Huxley)
Carry On, Jeeves (1925, P G Wodehouse)
Charlotte Gray (1998, Sebastian Faulks)
Cousin Phillis (1864, Elizabeth Gaskell)
Daniel Deronda (1876, George Eliot)
Eyeless in Gaza (1936, Aldous Huxley)
Fahrenheit 451 (1953, Ray Bradbury)
Finnegans Wake (1939, James Joyce)
Les Misérables (1862, Victor Hugo)
Mansfield Park (1814, Jane Austen)
North and South (1854, Elizabeth Gaskell)
Right Ho, Jeeves (1934, P G Wodehouse)
Schindler's Ark (1982, Thomas Keneally)
Smiley's People (1980, John Le Carré)
Song of Solomon (1978, Toni Morrison)
Sons and Lovers (1913, D H Lawrence)
Tarka the Otter (1927, Henry Williamson)
The Awkward Age (1899, Henry James)
The Bone People (1985, Keri Hulme)
The Bostonians (1886, Henry James)
The Cancer Ward (1968–69, Aleksandr
  Solzhenitsyn)
The Golden Bowl (1904, Henry James)
The Jungle Book (1894, Rudyard Kipling)
Thérèse Raquin (1867, Émile Zola)
The Virginians (1857–59, W M Thackeray)
The White Tiger (2008, Aravind Adiga)
Watership Down (1972, Richard Adams)
Zuleika Dobson (1911, Max Beerbohm)

14 A Handful Of Dust (1934, Evelyn Waugh)
All the King's Men (1946, Robert Penn
  Warren)
American Psycho (1991, Bret Easton Ellis)
Another Country (1962, James Baldwin)
A Room With a View (1908, E M Forster)
A Town Like Alice (1950, Nevil Shute)
Between the Acts (1941, Virginia Woolf)
Cider With Rosie (1959, Laurie Lee)
Death on the Nile (1937, Dame Agatha
  Christie)
Decline and Fall (1928, Evelyn Waugh)
Goodbye, Mr Chips (1934, James Hilton)
Jude the Obscure (1895, Thomas Hardy)
Lord of the Flies (1954, William Golding)
My Cousin Rachel (1951, Daphne du
  Maurier)

Our Man in Havana (1958, Graham Greene)
Robinson Crusoe (1719, Daniel Defoe)
Tales of the City (1978, Armistead Maupin)
The Ambassadors (1903, Henry James)
The Caine Mutiny (1951, Herman Wouk)
The Color Purple (1983, Alice Walker)
The Corrections (2001, Jonathan Franzen)
The Forsyte Saga (1922, John Galsworthy)
The Good Soldier (1915, Ford Madox Ford)
The Great Gatsby (1925, F Scott Fitzgerald)
The Kraken Wakes (1953, John Wyndham)
The Lovely Bones (2002, Alice Sebold)
The L-Shaped Room (1960, Lynne Reid
  Banks)
The Secret Agent (1907, Joseph Conrad)
The Time Machine (1895, H G Wells)
The Wasp Factory (1984, Iain Banks)
The Woodlanders (1887, Thomas Hardy)
Treasure Island (1883, Robert Louis
  Stevenson)
Tristram Shandy (1759–67, Laurence Sterne)
Tropic of Cancer (1934, Henry Miller)
Uncle Tom's Cabin (1852, Harriet Beecher
  Stowe)
What Maisie Knew (1897, Henry James)

15 A Christmas Carol (1843, Charles Dickens)
A Farewell to Arms (1929, Ernest
  Hemingway)
A Passage to India (1924, E M Forster)
A Study in Scarlet (1887, Arthur Conan
  Doyle)
Bulldog Drummond (1920, 'Sapper')
Cold Comfort Farm (1932, Stella Gibbons)
Flaubert's Parrot (1984, Julian Barnes)
Frenchman's Creek (1942, Daphne Du
  Maurier)
Gone with the Wind (1936, Margaret
  Mitchell)
Gravity's Rainbow (1973, Thomas Pynchon)
Heart of Darkness (1902, Joseph Conrad)
Le Rouge et le noir (1830, Stendhal)
Northanger Abbey (1818, Jane Austen)
Oscar and Lucinda (1988, Peter Carey)
Our Mutual Friend (1865, Charles Dickens)
Slaughterhouse 5 (1969, Kurt Vonnegut)
Tarzan of the Apes (1914, Edgar Rice
  Burroughs)
The African Queen (1935, C S Forester)
The Famished Road (1991, Ben Okri)
The House of Mirth (1905, Edith Wharton)
The Invisible Man (1897, H G Wells)
The Old Wives' Tale (1908, Arnold Bennett)
The Shipping News (1993, Annie Proulx)
The Sun Also Rises (1926, Ernest
  Hemingway)
The Trumpet Major (1880, Thomas Hardy)
The Woman in White (1860, Wilkie Collins)
Things Fall Apart (1958, Chinua Achebe)

Three Men in a Boat (1889, Jerome K Jerome)
To the Lighthouse (1927, Virginia Woolf)
Vernon God Little (2003, D B C Pierre)
Where Eagles Dare (1967, Alistair MacLean)
Wide Sargasso Sea (1966, Jean Rhys)

16 *A Clockwork Orange* (1962, Anthony Burgess)
A Tale of Two Cities (1859, Charles Dickens)
Barchester Towers (1857, Anthony Trollope)
Bonjour tristesse (1954, Françoise Sagan)
Bring Up the Bodies (2012, Hilary Mantel)
David Copperfield (1850, Charles Dickens)
England, My England (1922, D H Lawrence)
Gulliver's Travels (1726, Jonathan Swift)
Martin Chuzzlewit (1844, Charles Dickens)
Memoirs of a Geisha (1997, Arthur Golden)
Mr Midshipman Easy (1836, Captain Frederick Marryat)
Nicholas Nickleby (1839, Charles Dickens)
Tender is the Night (1934, F Scott Fitzgerald)
The Blind Assassin (2000, Margaret Atwood)
The Call of the Wild (1903, Jack London)
The Crying of Lot 49 (1966, Thomas Pynchon)
The Grapes of Wrath (1939, John Steinbeck)
The Handmaid's Tale (1986, Margaret Atwood)
The Maltese Falcon (1930, Dashiell Hammett)
The Quiet American (1955, Graham Greene)
The Satanic Verses (1988, Salman Rushdie)
The Scarlet Letter (1850, Nathaniel Hawthorne)
To Have and Have Not (1937, Ernest Hemingway)
Wuthering Heights (1848, Emily Brontë)

17 *A Kestrel for a Knave* (1968, Barry Hines)
Anne of Green Gables (1925, L M Montgomery)
Fifty Shades of Grey (2011, E L James)
Fire on the Mountain (1977, Anita Desai)
Great Expectations (1861, Charles Dickens)
King Solomon's Mines (1885, Sir H Rider Haggard)
Midnight's Children (1981, Salman Rushdie)
Portnoy's Complaint (1969, Philip Roth)
Pride and Prejudice (1813, Jane Austen)
The Age of Innocence (1920, Edith Wharton)
The Day of the Jackal (1971, Frederick Forsyth)
The Diary of a Nobody (1892, George and Weedon Grossmith)
The End of the Affair (1951, Graham Greene)
The English Patient (1992, Michael Ondaatje)

The Lord of the Rings (1954–55, J R R Tolkien)
The Mill on the Floss (1860, George Eliot)
The Pickwick Papers (1837, Charles Dickens)
The Turn of the Screw (1898, Henry James)
The Wings of the Dove (1902, Henry James)
Travels With My Aunt (1969, Graham Greene)
Tropic of Capricorn (1938, Henry Miller)
Wives and Daughters (1866, Elizabeth Gaskell)

18 *A High Wind in Jamaica* (1929, Richard Hughes)
Bridget Jones's Diary (1996, Helen Fielding)
The Catcher in the Rye (1951, J D Salinger)
The Cider House Rules (1985, John Irving)
The Last Picture Show (1966, Larry McMurtry)
The Naked and the Dead (1949, Norman Mailer)
The Old Man and the Sea (1952, Ernest Hemingway)
The Portrait of a Lady (1881, Henry James)
The Prisoner of Zenda (1894, Anthony Hope)
The Sound and the Fury (1929, William Faulkner)
The Thirty-Nine Steps (1915, John Buchan)
The Three Musketeers (1844, Alexandre Dumas)
The Trials of Rumpole (1979, John Mortimer)
To Kill A Mockingbird (1960, Harper Lee)

19 *Breakfast at Tiffany's* 1958, Truman Capote)
Brideshead Revisited (1945, Evelyn Waugh)
For Whom the Bell Tolls (1940, Ernest Hemingway)
How Late It Was, How Late (1994, James Kelman)
Murder at the Vicarage (1930, Dame Agatha Christie)
Sense and Sensibility (1811, Jane Austen)
The Buddha of Suburbia (1995, Hanif Kureishi)
The Darling Buds of May (1958, H E Bates)
The Day of the Triffids (1951, John Wyndham)
The God of Small Things (1997, Arundhati Roy)
The Old Curiosity Shop (1841, Charles Dickens)
The Robber Bridegroom (1942, Eudora Welty)
The Scarlet Pimpernel (1905, Baroness Orczy)
The Talented Mr Ripley (1956, Patricia Highsmith)

The Well of Loneliness (1928, Radclyffe Hall)

Tom Brown's Schooldays (1857, Thomas Hughes)

20 Anthills of the Savanna (1987, Chinua Achebe)

Cry, the Beloved Country (1948, Alan Paton)

Lady Chatterley's Lover (1928, D H Lawrence)

Lark Rise to Candleford (1945, Flora Thompson)

Little Lord Fauntleroy (1885, Frances Hodgson Burnett)

The History of Tom Jones (1749, Henry Fielding)

The Last of the Mohicans (1826, James Fenimore Cooper)

The Optimist's Daughter (1972, Eudora Welty)

The Return of the Native (1878, Thomas Hardy)

The Silence of the Lambs (1988, Thomas Harris)

The Witches of Eastwick (1984, John Updike)

21 Girl With a Pearl Earring (1999, Tracy Chevalier)

Tess of the d'Urbervilles (1891, Thomas Hardy)

The Count of Monte Cristo (1844–45, Alexandre Dumas)

The Mysteries of Udolpho (1794, Ann Radcliffe)

The Snows of Kilimanjaro (1936, Ernest Hemingway)

The Tenderness of Wolves (2006, Stef Penney)

Under the Greenwood Tree (1872, Thomas Hardy)

22 A Dance to the Music of Time (12 volumes, 1951–75, Anthony Powell)

Far from the Madding Crowd (1874, Thomas Hardy)

Gentlemen Prefer Blondes (1925, Anita Loos)

Les Liaisons dangereuses (1782, Choderlos de Laclos)

Life and Times of Michael K (1983, J M Coetzee)

The Man with the Golden Arm (1949, Nelson Algren)

The Mayor of Casterbridge (1886, Thomas Hardy)

The Mystery of Edwin Drood (1870, Charles Dickens)

The Picture of Dorian Gray (1891, Oscar Wilde)

Tinker, Tailor, Soldier, Spy (1974, John Le Carré)

Where Angels Fear to Tread (1905, E M Forster)

23 Captain Corelli's Mandolin (1994, Louis de Bernières)

Keep the Aspidistra Flying (1936, George Orwell)

The Bonfire of the Vanities (1987, Tom Wolfe)

The Heart is a Lonely Hunter (1940, Carson McCullers)

The Island of Doctor Moreau (1896, H G Wells)

The Magnificent Ambersons (1918, Booth Tarkington)

The Murder of Roger Ackroyd (1926, Dame Agatha Christie)

The Tenant of Wildfell Hall (1848, Anne Brontë)

The World According to Garp (1976, John Irving)

24 Á la recherche du temps perdu 1913–27, Marcel Proust

Murder on the Orient Express (1934, Dame Agatha Christie)

The Adventures of Tom Sawyer (1876, Mark Twain)

The Fall of the House of Usher (1839, Edgar Allan Poe)

Their Eyes Were Watching God (1937, Zora Neale Hurston)

The Girl Who Played with Fire (2006, Stieg Larsson)

The Prime of Miss Jean Brodie (1961, Muriel Spark)

25 One Flew Over the Cuckoo's Nest (1962, Ken Kesey)

Oranges are Not the Only Fruit (1985, Jeanette Winterson)

The French Lieutenant's Woman (1969, John Fowles)

26 Around the World in Eighty Days (1873, Jules Verne)

The Girl with the Dragon Tattoo (2005, Stieg Larsson)

The Life and Loves of a She-Devil (1983, Fay Weldon)

The Postman Always Rings Twice (1934, James M Cain)

The Secret Life of Walter Mitty (1939, James Thurber)

The Spy Who Came in from the Cold (1963, John Le Carré)

27 The Mysterious Affair at Styles (1920, Dame Agatha Christie)

29 *A Journey to the Centre of the Earth* (1864, Jules Verne)

Saturday Night and Sunday Morning (1958, Alan Sillitoe)

30 *The Adventures of Huckleberry Finn* (1884, Mark Twain)

The Girl Who Kicked the Hornets' Nest (2007, Stieg Larsson)

The Hitch-Hiker's Guide to the Galaxy (1979, Douglas Adams)

31 *One Day in the Life of Ivan Denisovich* (1963, Aleksandr Solzhenitsyn)

32 *The Beastly Beatitudes of Balthazar B* (1968, J P Donleavy)

Twenty Thousand Leagues Under the Sea (1869, Jules Verne)

33 *Frankenstein, or, The Modern Prometheus* (1818, Mary Shelley)

The Strange Case of Dr Jekyll and Mr Hyde (1886, Robert Louis Stevenson)

34 *The Life and Opinions of Tristram Shandy* (1759–67, Laurence Sterne)

36 *The Loneliness of the Long Distance Runner* (1959, Alan Sillitoe)

40 *The Curious Incident of the Dog in the Night-Time* (2003, Mark Haddon)

41 *The Infernal Desire Machines of Doctor Hoffmann* (1972, Angela Carter)

Novels and books for children include:

04 *Junk* (1996, Melvin Burgess)

05 *Heidi* (1880, Johanna Spyri)
Noddy (series from 1949, Enid Blyton)
Smith (1967, Leon Garfield)

06 *Tehanu* (1972, Ursula Le Guin)
The BFG (1982, Roald Dahl)

07 *Forever* (1975, Judy Blume)
Matilda (1988, Roald Dahl)
Skellig (1998, David Almond)

08 *Peter Pan* (1904, J M Barrie)
The Twits (1980, Roald Dahl)
Twilight (2005, Stephenie Meyer)

09 *Kidnapped* (1886, Robert Louis Stevenson)
Pollyanna (1913, Eleanor H Porter)
The Hobbit (1937, J R R Tolkien)

10 *Dr Dolittle* (series from 1920, Hugh Lofting)
Goggle-Eyes (1989, Anne Fine)
The Witches (1983, Roald Dahl)
Uncle Remus (series from 1880–1906, Joel Chandler Harris)

11 *Artemis Fowl* (2001, Eoin Colfer)
Ballet Shoes (1936, Noel Streatfeild)
Just William (1922, Richmal Crompton)
Little Women (1868, Louisa May Alcott)
Mary Poppins (1934, P L Travers)
Now We Are Six (1927, A A Milne)
Tennis Shoes (1937, Noel Streatfeild)
The Sheep-Pig (1983, Dick King-Smith)
What Katy Did (1872, Susan Coolidge)

12 *The Borrowers* (1952, Mary Norton)

13 *Charlotte's Web* (1952, E B White)
Just So Stories (1902, Rudyard Kipling)
Stig of the Dump (1963, Clive King)
Struwwelpeter (1848, Heinrich Hoffman)
The Famous Five (series from 1942, Enid Blyton)
The Jungle Book (1894, Rudyard Kipling)

The Owl Service (1967, Alan Garner)
Watership Down (1972, Richard Adams)
Winnie-the-Pooh (1926, A A Milne)

14 *Lord of the Flies* (1954, William Golding)
Masterman Ready (1841–42, Captain Frederick Marryat)
National Velvet (1935, Enid Bagnold)
Northern Lights (1995, Philip Pullman)
Paddington Bear (series from 1958, Michael Bond)
Robinson Crusoe (1719, Daniel Defoe)
The Cat in the Hat (1957, Dr Seuss)
The Coral Island (1858, R M Ballantyne)
The Secret Seven (series from 1949, Enid Blyton)
The Subtle Knife (1997, Philip Pullman)
The Water-Babies (1863, Charles Kingsley)
Treasure Island (1883, Robert Louis Stevenson)
Uncle Tom's Cabin (1851–52, Harriet Beecher Stowe)

15 *A Gathering Light* (2003, Jennifer Donnelly)
A Little Princess (1905, Frances Hodgson Burnett)
Eagle of the Ninth (1954, Rosemary Sutcliff)
Madame Doubtfire (1987, Anne Fine)
The Chocolate War (1974, Robert Cormier)
The Secret Garden (1911, Frances Hodgson Burnett)
Tuck Everlasting (1975, Natalie Babbit)

16 *His Dark Materials* (1995–2000, Philip Pullman)
I Hate My Teddy Bear (1982, David McKee)
Outside Over There (1981, Maurice Sendak)
The Amber Spyglass (2000, Philip Pullman)
The Call of the Wild (1903, Jack London)
The Secret Passage (1963, Nina Bawden)

17 *Anne of Green Gables* (1908, L M Montgomery)
A Wizard of Earthsea (1967, Ursula Le Guin)
Diary of a Young Girl (1952, Anne Frank)
Pippi Longstocking (1945, Astrid Lindgren)
The Machine-Gunners (1975, Robert Westall)

18 *Goodnight Mister Tom* (1980, Michelle Magorian)
Swallows and Amazons (series from 1930–1947, Arthur Ransome)
The Railway Children (1906, Edith Nesbit)
The Tale of Tom Kitten (1907, Beatrix Potter)
Tom's Midnight Garden (1958, Philippa Pearce)

19 *Swiss Family Robinson* (1812, Johann Rudolf Wyss)
The Wind in the Willows (1908, Kenneth Grahame)
Tom Brown's Schooldays (1857, Thomas Hughes)
When We Were Very Young (1924, A A Milne)

20 *Little Lord Fauntleroy* (1886, Frances Hodgson Burnett)
The Great Gilly Hopkins (1978, Kathleen Paterson)
The House at Pooh Corner (1928, A A Milne)
The Tale of Peter Rabbit (1900, Beatrix Potter)

21 *James and the Giant Peach* (1961, Roald Dahl)
The Prince and the Pauper (1882, Mark Twain)
The Tailor of Gloucester (1902, Beatrix Potter)
Where the Wild Things Are (1963, Maurice Sendak)

22 *Seven Little Australians* (1894, Ethel Turner)
The Phoenix and the Carpet (1904, Edith Nesbit)
The Story of Tracey Beaker (1991, Jacqueline Wilson)
The Wonderful Wizard of Oz (1900, L Frank Baum)

Through the Looking-Glass (1871, Lewis Carroll)

24 *Little House in the Big Woods* (1932, Laura Ingalls Wilder)
The Adventures of Pinocchio (1883, Carlo Collodi)
The Adventures of Tom Sawyer (1876, Mark Twain)
The Very Hungry Caterpillar (1969, Eric Carle)

25 *The Children of the New Forest* (1847, Captain Frederick Marryat)

26 *Danny the Champion of the World* (1975, Roald Dahl)
How the Grinch Stole Christmas (1957, Dr Seuss)
The Weirdstone of Brisingamen (1960, Alan Garner)
The Wolves of Willoughby Chase (1963, Joan Aiken)

28 *Alice's Adventures in Wonderland* (1865, Lewis Carroll)
The Story of the Treasure Seekers (1899, Edith Nesbit)

29 *Charlie and the Chocolate Factory* (1964, Roald Dahl)
Harry Potter and the Goblet of Fire (2000, J K Rowling)
The Lion, the Witch and the Wardrobe (1950, C S Lewis)

30 *The Adventures of Huckleberry Finn* (1884, Mark Twain)

31 *Harry Potter and the Deathly Hallows* (2007, J K Rowling)

32 *Harry Potter and the Half-Blood Prince* (2005, J K Rowling)

33 *Harry Potter and the Chamber of Secrets* (1998, J K Rowling)

34 *Harry Potter and the Order of the Phoenix* (2003, J K Rowling)
Harry Potter and the Philosopher's Stone (1997, J K Rowling)
Harry Potter and the Prisoner of Azkaban (1999, J K Rowling)

Novelists and short-story writers include:

02 Mo (Timothy; 1950– , English)
Oë (Kenzaburo; 1935– , Japanese)

03 Abe (Kobo; 1924–93, Japanese)
Ali (Monica; 1967– , Bangladeshi/British)
Eco (Umberto; 1932– , Italian)
Eri (Vincent Serei; 1936–93, Papua New Guinean)

Fay (András; 1786–1864, Hungarian)
Gyp (1849–1932, French)
Han (Suyin; 1917–2012, Chinese/British)
Hay (Ian; 1876–1952, Scottish)
Kay (Jackie; 1961– , Scottish)
Kee (Robert; 1919–2013, English)
Lee (Harper; 1926– , US)

Lee (Laurie; 1914–97, English)
Lie (Jonas; 1833–1908, Norwegian)
Poe (Edgar Allan; 1809–49, US)
Pym (Barbara; 1913–80, English)
Rao (Raja; 1908–2006, Indian)
Roe (Edward Payson; 1838–88, US)
Roy (Arundhati; 1961– , Indian)
Sue (Eugène; 1804–57, French)
Tey (Josephine; 1897–1952, Scottish)

04 Adam (Paul; 1862–1920, French)
Agee (James; 1909–55, US)
Amis (Martin; 1949– , English)
Amis (Sir Kingsley; 1922–95, English)
Arlt (Roberto; 1900–42, Argentine)
Bage (Robert; 1728–1801, English)
Bahr (Hermann; 1863–1934, Austrian)
Baum (Vicki; 1888–1960, Austrian/US)
Behn (Aphra; 1640–89, English)
Bely (Andrei; 1880–1934, Russian)
Böll (Heinrich; 1917–85, German)
Boyd (Martin; 1893–1972, Australian)
Boyd (William; 1952– , Ghanaian/British)
Boye (Karin; 1900–41, Swedish)
Brod (Max; 1884–1968, Austrian)
Buck (Pearl S; 1892–1973, US)
Bury (Lady Charlotte; 1775–1861, Scottish)
Cain (James M; 1892–1977, US)
Cary (Joyce; 1888–1957, English)
Cela (Camilo José; 1916–2002, Spanish)
Dahl (Roald; 1916–90, Welsh/British)
Dane (Clemence; 1888–1965, English)
Dark (Eleanor; 1901–85, Australian)
Dell (Ethel M; 1881–1939, English)
Droz (Antoine Gustave; 1832–95, French)
Duun (Olav; 1876–1939, Norwegian)
Egge (Peter; 1869–1959, Norwegian)
Endo (Shusako; 1923–96, Japanese)
Fast (Howard; 1914–92, US)
Fine (Anne; 1947– , English)
Ford (Ford Madox; 1873–1939, English)
Ford (Richard; 1944– , US)
Gale (Zona; 1874–1938, US)
Galt (John; 1779–1839, Scottish)
Gass (William H; 1924– , US)
Gide (André; 1869–1951, French)
Glyn (Elinor; 1864–1943, British)
Gore (Catherine; 1799–1861, English)
Gray (Alasdair; 1934– , Scottish)
Grey (Zane; 1875–1939, US)
Gunn (Neil M; 1891–1973, Scottish)
Head (Bessie; 1937–86, South African)
Heym (Stefan; 1913–2001, German)
Hill (Reginald; 1936–2012, English)
Hill (Susan; 1942– , English)
Hogg (James; 1770–1835, Scottish)
Hope (Anthony; 1863–1933, English)
Huch (Ricarda; 1864–1947, German)
Hugo (Victor; 1802–85, French)

Hunt (E Howard; 1918–90, US)
Jane (Frederick Thomas; 1870–1916, English)
Karr (Alphonse; 1808–90, French)
King (Stephen; 1947– , US)
Kivi (Aleksis; 1834–72, Finnish)
Koch (C J; 1932– , Australian)
Kock (Charles Paul de; 1794–1871, French)
Laye (Camera; 1928–80, French Guinea)
Levi (Primo; 1919–87, Italian)
Levy (Andrea; 1956– , English)
Lily (John; c.1554–1606, English)
Loos (Anita; 1893–1981, US)
Lyly (John; c.1554–1606, English)
Mack (Louise; 1874–1935, Australian)
Mais (Roger; 1905–55, Jamaican)
Mann (Heinrich; 1871–1950, German)
Mann (Thomas; 1875–1955, German)
Muir (Willa; 1890–1970, Scottish)
Neal (John; 1793–1876, US)
Nexö (Martin Andersen; 1869–1954, Danish)
Okri (Ben; 1959– , Nigerian)
Page (Thomas Nelson; 1853–1922, US)
Prus (Boleslaw; 1847–1912, Polish)
Puig (Manuel; 1932–90, Argentine)
Puzo (Mario; 1920–99, US)
Reed (Ishmael; 1938– , US)
Renn (Ludwig; 1889–1979, German)
Rhys (Jean; 1894–1979, West Indian/British)
Rice (James; 1843–82, English)
Roth (Henry; 1906–95, Austrian/US)
Roth (Joseph; 1894–1939, Austrian)
Roth (Philip; 1933– , US)
Sade (Marquis de; 1740–1814, French)
Saki (Hector Hugh Munro; 1870–1916, British)
Sala (George; 1828–95, English)
Sand (George; 1804–76, French)
Seth (Vikram; 1952– , Indian)
Snow (C P, Lord; 1905–80, English)
Stow (Randolph; 1935–2010, Australian)
Vian (Boris; 1920–59, French)
Wain (John; 1925–94, English)
Wang (Meng; 1934– , Chinese)
Ward (Mary Augusta; 1851–1920, English)
Ward (Mrs Humphry; 1851–1920, English)
Webb (Mary; 1881–1927, English)
West (Dame Rebecca; 1892–1983, Irish)
West (Morris; 1916–99, Australian)
West (Nathanael; 1903–40, US)
Wolf (Christa; 1929–2011, German)
Wood (Mrs Henry; 1814–87, English)
Wouk (Herman; 1915– , US)
Wren (P C; 1885–1941, English)
Zola (Émile; 1840–1902, French)

05 About (Edmond; 1828–85, French)
Acker (Kathy; 1944–97, US)

Adams (Douglas; 1952–2001, English)
Adams (Richard; 1920–   , English)
Adiga (Aravind; 1974–   , Indian/Australian)
Agnon (S Y; 1888–1970, Israeli)
Aiken (Conrad; 1889–1973, US)
Akins (Zoë; 1886–1958, US)
Allen (Walter; 1911–95, English)
Amado (Jorge; 1912–2001, Brazilian)
Anand (Mulk Raj; 1905–2004, Indian)
Arlen (Michael; 1895–1956, Bulgarian/
   British)
Banks (Iain; 1954–2013, Scottish)
Banks (Lynne Reid; 1929–   , English)
Barke (James; 1905–58, Scottish)
Barth (John; 1930–   , US)
Bates (H E; 1905–74, English)
Bazin (René; 1853–1932, French)
Behan (Brendan; 1923–64, Irish)
Behan (Dominic; 1928–89, Irish)
Benet (Juan; 1927–93, Spanish)
Benét (Stephen Vincent; 1898–1943, US)
Berry (Wendell; 1934–   , US)
Bloch (Jean-Richard; 1884–1947, French)
Bowen (Elizabeth; 1899–1973, Irish)
Boyle (Kay; 1902–92, US)
Bragg (Melvyn, Lord; 1939–   , English)
Brand (Max; 1892–1944, US)
Brink (André; 1935–   , South African)
Broch (Hermann; 1886–1951, Austrian)
Brown (Charles Brockden; 1771–1810, US)
Brown (George Mackay; 1921–96, Scottish)
Bruce (Mary Grant; 1878–1958, Australian)
Buber (Martin; 1878–1965, Austrian)
Bunin (Ivan; 1870–1953, Russian)
Byatt (Dame A S; 1936–   , English)
Cahan (Abraham; 1860–1951, US)
Caine (Sir Hall; 1853–1931, English)
Camus (Albert; 1913–60, French)
Cantú (Cesare; 1804–95, Italian)
Capek (Karel; 1890–1938, Czech)
Carey (Peter; 1943–   , Australian)
Chase (James Hadley; 1906–85, English)
Clift (Charmian; 1923–69, Australian)
Crace (Jim; 1946–   , English)
Craik (Dinah Maria; 1826–87, English)
Crane (Stephen; 1871–1900, US)
Cross (Amanda; 1926–2003, US)
Davie (Elspeth; 1919–95, Scottish)
Davis (Richard Harding; 1863–1916, US)
Defoe (Daniel; 1660–1731, English)
Desai (Anita; 1937–   , Indian)
Doyle (Sir Arthur Conan; 1859–1930,
   Scottish)
Doyle (Roddy; 1958–   , Irish)
Dumas (Alexandre, père; 1802–70, French)
Duras (Marguerite; 1914–96, French)
Ebers (Georg Moritz; 1837–98, German)
Eliot (George; 1819–80, English)

Elkin (Stanley; 1930–95, US)
Ellis (Alice Thomas; 1932–2005, British)
Ellis (Bret Easton; 1964–   , US)
Elton (Ben; 1959–   , English)
Evans (Caradoc; 1878–1945, Welsh)
Faure (Edgar; 1908–88, French)
Féval (Paul; 1817–87, French)
Foote (Shelby; 1916–2005, US)
Frame (Janet; 1924–2004, New Zealand)
Frank (Leonhard; 1882–1961, German)
Frank (Waldo David; 1889–1967, US)
Frayn (Michael; 1933–   , English)
Friel (George; 1910–75, Scottish)
Genet (Jean; 1910–86, French)
Gogol (Nikolai; 1809–52, Russian)
Gorky (Maxim; 1868–1936, Russian)
Grand (Sarah; 1854–1943, British)
Grass (Günter; 1927–   , German)
Green (Henry; 1905–73, English)
Green (Julien; 1900–98, French)
Haley (Alex; 1921–92, US)
Hardy (Thomas; 1840–1928, English)
Harte (Bret; 1836–1902, US)
Hašek (Jaroslav; 1883–1923, Czech)
Hauff (Wilhelm; 1802–27, German)
Hearn (Lafcadio; 1850–1904, Greek)
Henry (O; 1862–1910, US)
Henty (G A; 1832–1902, English)
Hesse (Hermann; 1877–1962, German/
   Swiss)
Heyer (Georgette; 1902–74, English)
Himes (Chester; 1909–84, US)
Hines (Barry; 1939–   , English)
Hulme (Keri; 1947–   , New Zealand)
Innes (Hammond; 1913–98, English)
Jacob (Violet; 1863–1946, Scottish)
James (George Payne Rainsford; 1799–1860,
   English)
James (Henry; 1843–1916, US)
James (P D, Baroness; 1920–   , English)
Jesse (F Tennyson; 1888–1958, English)
Johns (Captain W E; 1893–1968, English)
Jókai (Maurus; 1825–1904, Hungarian)
Jókai (Mór; 1825–1904, Hungarian)
Jones (James; 1921–77, US)
Joyce (James; 1882–1941, Irish)
Kafka (Franz; 1883–1924, Austrian)
Keane (Molly; 1904–96, Irish)
Kesey (Ken; 1935–2001, US)
Kinck (Hans E; 1865–1926, Norwegian)
Laski (Marghanita; 1915–88, English)
Lavin (Mary; 1912–96, Irish)
Lever (Charles; 1806–72, Irish)
Lewis (C S; 1898–1963, British)
Lewis (M G; 1775–1818, English)
Lewis (Sinclair; 1885–1951, US)
Lewis (Wyndham; 1882–1957, English)
Linna (Väinö; 1920–92, Finnish)

Locke (William John; 1863–1930, English)
Lodge (David; 1935– , English)
Louÿs (Pierre; 1870–1925, Belgian/French)
Lowry (Malcolm; 1909–57, English)
Lurie (Alison; 1926– , US)
Marsé (Juan; 1933– , Spanish)
Marsh (Dame Ngaio; 1899–1982, New Zealand)
Mason (A E W; 1865–1948, English)
Mayor (F M; 1872–1931, English)
Meyer (Conrad; 1825–98, Swiss)
Milne (A A; 1882–1956, English)
Moore (Brian; 1921–99, Northern Irish/Canadian)
Moore (George; 1852–1933, Irish)
Moore (Thomas; 1779–1852, Irish)
Mo Yan (1955– , Chinese)
Munro (Alice; 1931– , Canadian)
Munro (Hector Hugh; 1870–1916, British)
Munro (Neil; 1864–1930, Scottish)
Musil (Robert; 1880–1942, Austrian)
Niven (Frederick; 1878–1944, Scottish)
Oates (Joyce Carol; 1938– , US)
O'Hara (John; 1905–70, US)
Orczy (Baroness; 1865–1947, Hungarian/British)
Ouida (1839–1908, English)
Ozick (Cynthia; 1928– , US)
Paton (Alan; 1903–88, South African)
Peake (Mervyn; 1911–68, English)
Pears (Tim; 1956– , English)
Percy (Walker; 1916–90, US)
Plath (Sylvia; 1932–63, US)
Potok (Chaim; 1929–2002, US)
Powys (John Cowper; 1872–1963, English)
Powys (T F; 1875–1953, English)
Praed (Rosa; 1851–1935, Australian)
Preda (Marin; 1922–80, Romanian)
Queen (Ellery; Frederick Dannay, 1905–82, US and Manfred B Lee, 1905–71, US)
Ramos (Graciliano; 1892–1953, Brazilian)
Reade (Charles; 1814–84, English)
Reeve (Clara; 1729–1807, English)
Rojas (Fernando de; c.1465–1541, Spanish)
Rolfe (Frederick William; 1860–1913, English)
Rulfo (Juan; 1918–86, Mexican)
Sagan (Françoise; 1935–2004, French)
Scott (Paul; 1920–78, English)
Scott (Sir Walter; 1771–1832, Scottish)
Selby (Hubert, Jnr; 1928–2004, US)
Serao (Matilde; 1856–1927, Greek/Italian)
Shute (Nevil; 1899–1960, English)
Silko (Leslie Marmon; 1948– , US)
Simms (William Gilmore; 1806–70, US)
Simon (Claude; 1913–2005, French)
Skram (Amalie; 1847–1905, Norwegian)
Smith (Alexander McCall; 1948– ,

Scottish)
Smith (Dodie; 1896–1990, English)
Smith (Iain Crichton; 1928–98, Scottish)
Smith (Stevie; 1902–71, English)
Smith (Wilbur; 1933– , Rhodesian/South African)
Smith (Zadie; 1975– , English)
Souza (Madame de; 1761–1836, French)
Spark (Dame Muriel; 1918–2006, Scottish)
Staël (Madame de; 1766–1817, French)
Stead (Christina; 1902–83, Australian)
Steel (Danielle; 1947– , US)
Stone (Irving; 1903–89, US)
Stout (Rex; 1886–1975, US)
Stowe (Harriet Beecher; 1811–96, US)
Svevo (Italo; 1861–1928, Italian)
Swift (Graham; 1949– , English)
Swift (Jonathan; 1667–1745, Irish)
Tam'si (Tchicaya U; 1931–88, Congolese)
Tartt (Donna; 1963– , US)
Toole (John Kennedy; 1937–69, US)
Torga (Miguel; 1907–90, Portuguese)
Turow (Scott; 1949– , US)
Twain (Mark; 1835–1910, US)
Tyler (Anne; 1941– , US)
Tynan (Katharine; 1861–1931, Irish)
Unruh (Fritz von; 1885–1970, German)
Verga (Giovanni; 1840–1922, Italian)
Verne (Jules; 1828–1905, French)
Viaud (Louis Marie Julien; 1850–1923, French)
Vidal (Gore; 1925–2012, US)
Waugh (Alec; 1898–1981, English)
Waugh (Auberon; 1939–2001, English)
Waugh (Evelyn; 1903–66, English)
Wells (H G; 1866–1946, English)
Welsh (Irvine; 1961– , Scottish)
Welty (Eudora; 1909–2001, US)
White (Antonia; 1899–1979, English)
White (E B; 1899–1985, US)
White (Patrick; 1912–90, English/Australian)
White (T H; 1906–64, English)
White (William Hale; 1831–1913, English)
Wilde (Oscar; 1854–1900, Irish)
Wolfe (Thomas; 1900–38, US)
Wolfe (Tom; 1931– , US)
Woolf (Virginia; 1882–1941, English)
Yates (Dornford; 1885–1960, English)
Yonge (Charlotte M; 1823–1901, English)
Young (Francis Brett; 1884–1954, English)
Zweig (Arnold; 1887–1968, German)

06 Achebe (Chinua; 1930–2013, Nigerian)
Alcott (Louisa M; 1832–88, US)
Aldiss (Brian W; 1925– , English)
Alemán (Mateo; 1547–1610 or 1620, Spanish)
Algren (Nelson; 1909–81, US)
Alvaro (Corrado; 1895–1956, Italian)

Ambler (Eric; 1909–98, English)
Amicis (Edmondo de; 1846–1908, Italian)
Aragon (Louis; 1897–1983, French)
Archer (Jeffrey, Lord; 1940–   , English)
Arenas (Reinaldo; 1943–90, Cuban)
Asimov (Isaac; 1920–92, Russian/US)
Atwood (Margaret; 1939–   , Canadian)
Austen (Jane; 1775–1817, English)
Auster (Paul; 1947–   , US)
Azorín (1873–1967, Spanish)
Balzac (Honoré de; 1799–1850, French)
Barham (R H; 1788–1845, English)
Barker (George Granville; 1913–91, English)
Barker (Pat; 1943–   , English)
Barnes (Djuna; 1892–1982, US)
Barnes (Julian; 1946–   , English)
Barrès (Maurice; 1862–1923, French)
Barrie (J M; 1860–1937, Scottish)
Bellow (Saul; 1915–2005, Canadian/US)
Berger (John; 1926–   , English)
Besant (Sir Walter; 1836–1901, English)
Binchy (Maeve; 1940–2012, Irish)
Blixen (Karen; 1885–1962, Danish)
Blunck (Hans Friedrich; 1888–1961, German)
Blyton (Enid; 1897–1968, English)
Borges (Jorge Luis; 1899–1986, Argentine)
Bowles (Paul; 1910–99, US)
Braine (John; 1922–86, English)
Bratby (John; 1928–92, English)
Brazil (Angela; 1868–1947, English)
Bremer (Fredrika; 1801–65, Swedish)
Brenan (Gerald; 1894–1987, English)
Brontë (Anne; 1820–49, English)
Brontë (Charlotte; 1816–55, English)
Brontë (Emily; 1818–48, English)
Brooks (Gwendolyn; 1917–2000, US)
Brophy (Brigid; 1929–95, English)
Buchan (John; 1875–1940, Scottish)
Bunyan (John; 1628–88, English)
Burney (Fanny; 1752–1840, English)
Butler (Samuel; 1835–1902, English)
Cabell (James Branch; 1879–1958, US)
Capote (Truman; 1924–84, US)
Carter (Angela; 1940–92, English)
Castro (Rosalía de; 1837–85, Spanish)
Cather (Willa; 1873–1947, US)
Céline (Louis-Ferdinand; 1894–1961, French)
Chabon (Michael; 1963–   , US)
Chopin (Katherine; 1851–1904, US)
Church (Richard Thomas; 1893–1972, English)
Clancy (Tom; 1947–   , US)
Clarke (Arthur C; 1917–2008, English)
Clarke (Marcus; 1846–81, Australian)
Cleary (Jon; 1917–2010, Australian)
Conrad (Joseph; 1857–1924, Polish/British)

Conway (Hugh; 1847–85, English)
Cooper (James Fenimore; 1789–1851, US)
Cooper (Jilly; 1937–   , English)
Cronin (A J; 1896–1981, Scottish)
Davies (Robertson; 1913–95, Canadian)
Dekker (Eduard Douwes; 1820–87, Dutch)
Desani (G V; 1909–2000, Kenyan/US)
Dexter (Colin; 1930–   , English)
Dibdin (Michael; 1947–2007, English)
Dickey (James; 1923–97, US)
Didion (Joan; 1934–   , US)
Döblin (Alfred; 1878–1957, German/French)
Donoso (José; 1928–96, Chilean)
Drezen (Youenn; 1899–1972, Breton)
Dutton (Geoffrey; 1922–98, Australian)
Faulks (Sebastian; 1953–   , English)
Fowles (John; 1926–2005, English)
France (Anatole; 1844–1924, French)
Fraser (George MacDonald; 1925–2008, English)
French (Marilyn; 1929–2009, US)
Frisch (Max; 1911–91, Swiss)
Fuller (Margaret; 1810–50, US)
Fuller (Roy; 1912–91, English)
Gaddis (William; 1922–98, US)
Garner (Alan; 1934–   , English)
Gibbon (Lewis Grassic; 1901–35, Scottish)
Godden (Rumer; 1907–98, English)
Godwin (William; 1756–1836, English)
Goethe (Johann Wolfgang von; 1749–1832, German)
Golden (Arthur; 1957–   , US)
Goudge (Elizabeth; 1900–84, English)
Graham (Winston; 1910–2003, English)
Graves (Robert; 1895–1985, English)
Greene (Graham; 1904–91, English)
Guzman (Martín Luis; 1887–1976, Mexican)
Haddon (Mark; 1962–   , English)
Hailey (Arthur; 1920–2004, English/Canadian)
Halévy (Ludovic; 1834–1908, French)
Hamsun (Knut; 1859–1952, Norwegian)
Hansen (Martin Alfred; 1909–55, Danish)
Harris (Thomas; 1940–   , US)
Harris (Wilson; 1921–   , British)
Heller (Joseph; 1923–99, US)
Heller (Zoë; 1965–   , English)
Hilton (James; 1900–54, English)
Holtby (Winifred; 1898–1935, English)
Hornby (Nick; 1957–   , English)
Hughes (Richard; 1900–76, English)
Hughes (Thomas; 1822–96, English)
Hunter (Evan; 1926–2005, US)
Huxley (Aldous; 1894–1963, English)
Huxley (Elspeth; 1907–97, English)
Ibáñez (Vicente Blasco; 1867–1928, Spanish)

Irving (John; 1942– , US)
Irving (Washington; 1783–1859, US)
Jensen (Johannes V; 1873–1950, Danish)
Jerome (Jerome K; 1859–1927, English)
Jewett (Sarah Orne; 1849–1909, US)
Jósika (Miklós, Baron von; 1794–1865,
  Hungarian)
Jünger (Ernst; 1895–1998, German)
Keller (Gottfried; 1819–90, Swiss)
Kelman (James; 1946– , Scottish)
Laclos (Pierre Choderlos de; 1741–1803,
  French)
La Guma (Alex; 1925–85, South African)
L'Amour (Louis; 1908–88, US)
Larkin (Philip; 1922–85, English)
Le Fanu (Sheridan; 1814–73, Irish)
Le Guin (Ursula; 1929– , US)
L'Engle (Madeleine; 1918–2007, US)
Lennox (Charlotte; c.1729–1804, American/
  British)
Lesage (Alain René; 1668–1747, French)
Lethem (Jonathan; 1964– , US)
Lewald (Fanny; 1811–89, German)
Lively (Penelope; 1933– , English)
London (Jack; 1876–1916, US)
Lytton (Edward Bulwer-Lytton, Lord;
  1803–73, English)
Machen (Arthur; 1863–1947, British)
Mahfuz (Naguib; 1911–2006, Egyptian)
Mailer (Norman; 1923–2007, US)
Mallea (Eduardo; 1903–82, Argentine)
Malouf (David; 1934– , Australian)
Martel (Yann; 1963– , Canadian)
Massie (Allan; 1938– , Scottish)
McCabe (Patrick; 1955– , Irish)
McEwan (Ian; 1948– , English)
Miller (Henry; 1891–1980, US)
Milosz (Czeslaw; 1911–2004, Russian/US)
Mistry (Rohinton; 1952– , Indian/
  Canadian)
Molnár (Ferenc; 1878–1952, Hungarian)
Moodie (Susanna; 1803–85, English)
Morgan (Charles Langbridge; 1894–1958,
  English)
Morgan (Lady Sydney; 1783–1859, Irish)
Moricz (Zsigmond; 1879–1942, Hungarian)
Mörike (Eduard; 1804–75, German)
Morley (Christopher; 1890–1957, US)
Müller (Herta; 1953– , Romanian/German)
Nesbit (E; 1858–1924, English)
Niland (D'Arcy; 1919–67, Australian)
Norris (Frank; 1870–1902, US)
Norton (Mary; 1903–92, English)
O'Brian (Patrick; 1914–2000, English)
O'Brien (Edna; 1932– , Irish)
O'Brien (Flann; 1911–66, Irish)
O'Brien (Kate; 1897–1974, Irish)
O'Duffy (Eimar; 1893–1935, Irish)

Onetti (Juan Carlos; 1909–94, Uruguayan)
Orwell (George; 1903–50, English)
Palmer (Vance; 1885–1959, Australian)
Pavese (Cesare; 1908–50, Italian)
Penney (Stef; 1969– , Scottish)
Pereda (José Maria de; 1833–1906, Spanish)
Peters (Ellis; 1913–95, English)
Piercy (Marge; 1936– , US)
Pierre (D B C; 1961– , Australian)
Porter (Eleanor; 1868–1920, US)
Porter (Katherine Anne; 1890–1980, US)
Powell (Anthony; 1905–2000, English)
Proulx (Annie; 1935– , US)
Proust (Marcel; 1871–1922, French)
Rankin (Ian; 1960– , Scottish)
Riding (Laura; 1901–91, US)
Rubens (Bernice; 1928–2004, Welsh)
Sábato (Ernesto; 1911–2011, Argentine)
Salten (Felix; 1869–1945, Austrian)
Sapper (1888–1937, English)
Sartre (Jean-Paul; 1905–80, French)
Sayers (Dorothy L; 1893–1957, English)
Sayles (John; 1950– , US)
Schlaf (Johannes; 1862–1941, German)
Sebold (Alice; 1963– , US)
Sewell (Anna; 1820–78, English)
Sharpe (Tom; 1928–2013, English)
Singer (Isaac Bashevis; 1904–91, Polish/US)
Spring (Howard; 1889–1965, Welsh)
Sterne (Laurence; 1713–68, Irish)
Stoker (Bram; 1847–1912, Irish)
Storey (David; 1933– , English)
Strong (L A G; 1896–1958, English)
Styron (William; 1925–2006, US)
Susann (Jacqueline; c.1926–74, US)
Tagore (Rabindranath; 1861–1941, Indian)
Taylor (Elizabeth; 1912–75, English)
Taylor (Peter; 1917–94, US)
Thomas (D M; 1935– , English)
Thomas (Leslie; 1931– , Welsh)
Traven (B; c.1890–1969, German)
Trevor (William; 1928– , Irish)
Turner (Ethel S; 1872–1958, English/
  Australian)
Undset (Sigrid; 1882–1949, Danish/
  Norwegian)
Updike (John; 1932–2009, US)
Valera (Don Juan; 1824–1905, Spanish)
Vesaas (Tarjei; 1897–1970, Norwegian)
Viebig (Clara; 1860–1952, German)
Walker (Alice; 1944– , US)
Warner (Alan; 1964– , Scottish)
Warner (Marina; 1946– , English)
Warner (Susan Bogert; 1819–85, US)
Warner (Sylvia Townsend; 1893–1978,
  English)
Warren (Robert Penn; 1905–89, US)
Waters (Sarah; 1966– , Welsh)

Weldon (Fay; 1931– , English)
Wesley (Mary; 1912–2002, English)
Weyman (Stanley John; 1855–1928, English)
Wiggin (Kate Douglas; 1856–1953, US)
Wilder (Thornton; 1897–1975, US)
Wilson (A N; 1950– , English)
Wilson (Jacqueline; 1945– , English)
Wilson (Sir Angus; 1913–91, English)
Wister (Owen; 1860–1938, US)
Wright (Richard; 1908–60, US)

07 Ackroyd (Peter; 1949– , English)
Aksakov (Sergei; 1791–1859, Russian)
Allende (Isabel; 1942– , Chilean)
Angelou (Maya; 1928– , US)
Arrabal (Fernando; 1932– , Spanish)
Ashford (Daisy; 1881–1972, English)
Bagnold (Enid; 1889–1981, English)
Baldwin (James; 1924–87, US)
Ballard (J G; 1930–2009, British)
Barnard (Marjorie; 1897–1987, Australian)
Barrios (Eduardo; 1884–1963, Chilean)
Barstow (Stan; 1928–2011, English)
Bassani (Giorgio; 1916–2000, Italian)
Beckett (Samuel; 1906–89, Irish)
Bellamy (Edward; 1850–98, US)
Bennett (Arnold; 1867–1931, English)
Bentine (Michael; 1921–96, English)
Bentley (Edmund Clerihew; 1875–1956,
  English)
Bergman (Hjalmar; 1883–1931, Swedish)
Bernard (Tristan; 1866–1947, French)
Biggers (Earl Derr; 1884–1933, US)
Blicher (Steen Steensen; 1782–1848,
  Danish)
Bogarde (Sir Dirk; 1921–99, English)
Bonnard (Abel; 1883–1968, French)
Bourget (Paul; 1852–1935, French)
Braddon (Mary Elizabeth; 1835–1915,
  English)
Branner (H C; 1903–66, Danish)
Burgess (Anthony; 1917–93, English)
Burnett (Frances Hodgson; 1849–1924,
  English/US)
Calvino (Italo; 1923–85, Italian)
Canetti (Elias; 1905–94, Bulgarian/British)
Carroll (Lewis; 1832–98, English)
Chatwin (Bruce; 1940–89, English)
Cheever (John; 1912–82, US)
Chekhov (Anton; 1860–1904, Russian)
Clavell (James; 1924–94, Australian/US)
Cleland (John; 1709–89, English)
Cocteau (Jean; 1889–1963, French)
Coetzee (J M; 1940– , South African)
Colette (1873–1954, French)
Collett (Camilla; 1813–95, Norwegian)
Collins (Wilkie; 1824–89, English)
Cookson (Dame Catherine; 1906–98,
  English)

Corelli (Marie; 1855–1924, English)
Cozzens (James Gould; 1903–78, US)
Deeping (Warwick; 1877–1950, English)
Deledda (Grazia; 1875–1936, Italian)
DeLillo (Don; 1936– , US)
Deutsch (Babette; 1895–1982, US)
De Vries (Peter; 1910–93, US)
Dickens (Charles; 1812–70, English)
Diderot (Denis; 1713–84, French)
Dinesen (Isak; 1885–1962, Danish)
Dorfman (Ariel; 1942– , Argentine/
  Chilean/US)
Douglas (Norman; 1868–1952, Scottish)
Drabble (Margaret; 1939– , English)
Dreiser (Theodore; 1871–1945, US)
Duhamel (Georges; 1884–1966, French)
Dunnett (Dorothy; 1923–2001, Scottish)
Dunsany (Edward Plunkett, Lord; 1878–
  1957, Irish)
Durrell (Gerald; 1925–95, English)
Durrell (Lawrence; 1912–90, English)
Edwards (Amelia; 1831–92, English)
Elliott (Sumner Locke; 1917–91, Australian/
  US)
Ellison (Ralph Waldo; 1914–94, US)
Enquist (Per Olov; 1934– , Swedish)
Enright (Anne; 1962– , Irish)
Fadeyev (Aleksandr; 1901–56, Russian)
Farrell (James T; 1904–79, US)
Farrell (J G; 1935–79, British)
Ferrier (Susan Edmonstone; 1782–1854,
  Scottish)
Feydeau (Ernest; 1821–73, French)
Firbank (Ronald; 1886–1926, English)
Fleming (Ian; 1908–64, English)
Fontane (Theodor; 1819–98, German)
Forster (E M; 1879–1970, English)
Forster (Margaret; 1938– , English)
Forsyth (Frederick; 1938– , English)
Francis (Dick; 1920–2010, English)
Frankau (Gilbert; 1884–1953, English)
Frankau (Pamela; 1908–67, English)
Franzen (Jonathan; 1959– , US)
Franzos (Karl Emil; 1848–1904, Austrian)
Frazier (Charles; 1950– , US)
Freytag (Gustav; 1816–95, German)
Fuentes (Carlos; 1928–2012, Mexican)
Gallant (Mavis; 1922– , Canadian)
Gallico (Paul; 1897–1976, US)
Ganivet (Angel; 1865–98, Spanish)
Gardner (Erle Stanley; 1889–1970, US)
Garnett (David; 1892–1981, English)
Gaskell (Mrs Elizabeth; 1810–65, English)
Gautier (Théophile; 1811–72, French)
Gibbons (Stella; 1902–89, English)
Gilbert (William; 1804–89, English)
Gippius (Zinaida; 1869–1945, Russian)
Gissing (George; 1857–1903, English)

Glasgow (Ellen; 1874–1945, US)
Golding (Sir William; 1911–93, English)
Grafton (Sue; 1940– , US)
Grahame (Kenneth; 1859–1932, Scottish)
Griffin (Gerald; 1803–40, Irish)
Grisham (John; 1955– , US)
Haggard (Sir H Rider; 1856–1925, English)
Hammett (Dashiell; 1894–1961, US)
Hansson (Ola; 1860–1925, Swedish)
Harland (Henry; 1861–1905, US)
Hartley (L P; 1895–1972, English)
Haywood (Eliza; c.1693–1756, English)
Hazzard (Shirley; 1931– , Australian/US)
Herbert (Xavier; 1901–84, Australian)
Herriot (James; 1916–95, English)
Hervieu (Paul; 1857–1915, French)
Hewlett (Maurice; 1861–1923, English)
Heyward (DuBose; 1885–1940, US)
Hiaasen (Carl; 1953– , US)
Hichens (Robert Smythe; 1864–1950, English)
Higgins (George V; 1939–99, US)
Hippius (Zinaida; 1869–1945, Russian)
Holland (Josiah Gilbert; 1819–81, US)
Hornung (E W; 1866–1921, English)
Housman (Laurence; 1865–1959, English)
Howells (William Dean; 1837–1920, US)
Hurston (Zora Neale; c.1901–1960, US)
Jameson (Storm; 1891–1986, English)
Jenkins (Robin; 1912–2005, Scottish)
Johnson (Dorothy M; 1905–84, US)
Johnson (Eyvind; 1900–76, Swedish)
Johnson (Pamela Hansford; 1912–81,
    English)
Keating (H R F; 1926–2011, English)
Kennedy (A L; 1965– , Scottish)
Kennedy (William; 1928– , US)
Kerouac (Jack; 1922–69, US)
Kincaid (Jamaica; 1949– , Antiguan/US)
Kipling (Rudyard; 1865–1936, English)
Klinger (Friedrich Maximilian von; 1752–
    1831, German)
Kretzer (Max; 1854–1941, German)
Kundera (Milan; 1929– , Czech/French)
La Farge (Oliver; 1901–63, US)
Lamming (George; 1927– , Barbadian)
Lardner (Ring; 1885–1933, US)
Laxness (Halldór; 1902–98, Icelandic)
Le Carré (John; 1931– , English)
Lehmann (Rosamond; 1901–90, English)
Leonard (Elmore; 1925– , US)
Lessing (Doris; 1919– , Rhodesian/
    British)
Lindsay (Jack; 1900–90, Australian)
Lindsay (Philip; 1906–58, Australian)
Lofting (Hugh; 1886–1947, English)
MacBeth (George; 1932–92, Scottish)
MacGill (Patrick; 1890–1963, Irish)
MacLean (Alistair; 1922–87, Scottish)

Mahfouz (Naguib; 1911–2006, Egyptian)
Maistre (Xavier, Comte de; 1763–1852,
    French)
Malamud (Bernard; 1914–86, US)
Malraux (André; 1901–76, French)
Manning (Olivia; 1908–80, English)
Manzoni (Alessandro; 1785–1873, Italian)
Márquez (Gabriel García; 1928– ,
    Colombian)
Marquis (Don; 1878–1937, US)
Marryat (Captain Frederick; 1792–1848,
    English)
Maturin (Charles Robert; 1782–1824, Irish)
Maugham (W Somerset; 1874–1965, British)
Mauriac (François; 1885–1970, French)
Maurois (André; 1885–1967, French)
Mérimée (Prosper; 1803–70, French)
Mirbeau (Octave; 1850–1917, French)
Mishima (Yukio; 1925–70, Japanese)
Mitford (Mary Russell; 1786–1855, English)
Mitford (Nancy; 1904–73, English)
Moravia (Alberto; 1907–90, Italian)
Murdoch (Dame Iris; 1919–99, Irish)
Nabokov (Vladimir; 1899–1977, Russian/
    US)
Naipaul (Sir V S; 1932– , Trinidadian)
Narayan (R K; 1906–2001, Indian)
Nemerov (Howard; 1920–91, US)
Novalis (1772–1801, German)
O'Connor (Flannery; 1925–64, US)
Ostenso (Martha; 1900–63, Norwegian/
    Canadian)
Parsons (Tony; 1955– , English)
Peacock (Thomas Love; 1785–1866,
    English)
Prévost (Abbé; 1697–1763, French)
Pullman (Philip; 1946– , English)
Pushkin (Alexander; 1799–1837, Russian)
Pynchon (Thomas; 1937– , US)
Queneau (Raymond; 1903–76, French)
Ransome (Arthur; 1884–1967, English)
Raphael (Frederic; 1931– , US/British)
Régnier (Henri de; 1864–1936, French)
Renault (Mary; 1905–83, English/South
    African)
Rendell (Ruth, Baroness; 1932– , English)
Reymont (Wladyslaw Stanislaw; 1867–1925,
    Polish)
Richler (Mordecai; 1931–2001, Canadian)
Richter (Conrad; 1890–1968, US)
Richter (Johann Paul Friedrich; 1763–1825,
    German)
Robbins (Harold; 1916–97, US)
Roberts (Kate; 1891–1985, Welsh)
Roberts (Kenneth; 1885–1957, US)
Rolland (Romain; 1866–1944, French)
Rowling (J K; 1965– , English)
Rushdie (Salman; 1947– , Indian/British)

Saroyan (William; 1908–81, US)
Sassoon (Siegfried; 1886–1967, English)
Scudéry (Madeleine de; 1608–1701, French)
Shelley (Mary Wollstonecraft; 1797–1851,
  English)
Shields (Carol; 1935–2003, Canadian)
Shvarts (Yevgeni; 1896–1958, Russian)
Simenon (Georges; 1903–89, Belgian/
  French)
Sitwell (Sir Osbert; 1892–1969, English)
Sologub (Fyodor; 1863–1927, Russian)
Soyinka (Wole; 1934– , Nigerian)
Spender (Sir Stephen; 1909–95, English)
Stewart (J I M; 1906–94, Scottish)
Stifter (Adalbert; 1805–68, Austrian)
Surtees (Robert Smith; 1803–64, English)
Suttner (Bertha von; 1843–1914, Czech)
Tennant (Emma; 1937– , English)
Tennant (Kylie; 1912–88, Australian)
Theroux (Paul; 1941– , US)
Thubron (Colin; 1939– , English)
Thurber (James; 1894–1961, US)
Tolkien (J R R; 1892–1973, South African/
  British)
Tolstoy (Count Aleksei; 1817–75, Russian)
Tolstoy (Count Leo; 1828–1910, Russian)
Tranter (Nigel; 1909–99, Scottish)
Tremain (Rose; 1943– , English)
Tutuola (Amos; 1920–97, Nigerian)
Upfield (Arthur; 1888–1964, Australian)
Vallejo (César; 1892–1938, Peruvian)
Van Dine (S S; 1887–1939, US)
Wallace (Lew; 1827–1905, US)
Walpole (Horace; 1717–97, English)
Walpole (Sir Hugh; 1884–1941, New
  Zealand/English)
Waltari (Mika Toimi; 1908–79, Finnish)
Wescott (Glenway; 1901–87, US)
Wharton (Edith; c.1861–1937, US)
Wyndham (John; 1903–69, English)
08 Andersen (Hans Christian; 1805–75, Danish)
Apuleius (Lucius; 2c AD, Roman)
Asturias (Miguel Angel; 1899–1974,
  Guatemalan)
Atherton (Gertrude; 1857–1948, US)
Auerbach (Berthold; 1812–82, German)
Banville (John; 1945– , Irish)
Barbusse (Henri; 1873–1935, French)
Beauvoir (Simone de; 1908–86, French)
Beckford (William; 1759–1844, English)
Beerbohm (Sir Max; 1872–1956, English)
Berryman (John; 1914–72, US)
Björnson (Björnstjerne; 1832–1910,
  Norwegian)
Bradbury (Ray; 1920–2012, US)
Bradbury (Sir Malcolm; 1932–2000, English)
Bradford (Barbara Taylor; 1933– , English)
Brentano (Clemens von; 1778–1842, German)

Brittain (Vera; 1893–1970, English)
Brookner (Anita; 1928– , English)
Buchanan (Robert Williams; 1841–1901,
  English)
Bukowski (Charles; 1920–94, US)
Bulgakov (Mikhail; 1891–1940, Russian)
Caldwell (Erskine; 1903–87, US)
Calisher (Hortense; 1911–2009, US)
Carleton (William; 1794–1869, Irish)
Cartland (Dame Barbara; 1901–2000,
  English)
Chandler (Raymond; 1888–1959, US)
Christie (Dame Agatha; 1890–1976, English)
Claretie (Jules; 1840–1913, French)
Cornwell (Bernard; 1944– , English)
Cornwell (Patricia; 1956– , US)
Couperus (Louis; 1863–1923, Dutch)
Crawford (F Marion; 1854–1909, Italian/US)
Crichton (Michael; 1942–2008, US)
Crockett (Samuel Rutherford; 1860–1914,
  Scottish)
Crompton (Richmal; 1890–1969, English)
Davidson (John; 1857–1909, Scottish)
Day-Lewis (Cecil; 1904–72, Irish)
Deighton (Len; 1929– , English)
de la Mare (Sir Walter; 1873–1956,
  English)
Disraeli (Benjamin, Earl of Beaconsfield;
  1804–81, English)
Doctorow (E L; 1931– , US)
Donleavy (J P; 1926– , Irish)
Emecheta (Buchi; 1944– , Nigerian/British)
Erenburg (Ilya; 1891–1967, Soviet)
Faulkner (William; 1897–1962, US)
Fielding (Helen; 1958– , English)
Fielding (Henry; 1707–54, English)
Flaubert (Gustave; 1821–80, French)
Forester (C S; 1899–1966, British)
Francome (John; 1952– , English)
Franklin (Miles; 1879–1954, Australian)
Frederic (Harold; 1856–98, US)
Freeling (Nicolas; 1927–2003, English)
Frenssen (Gustav; 1863–1945, German)
Gallegos (Rómulo; 1884–1969, Venezuelan)
Garfield (Leon; 1921–96, English)
Gerhardi (William; 1895–1977, English)
Gilliatt (Penelope; 1932–93, English)
Goncourt (Edmond de; 1822–96, French)
Goncourt (Jules de; 1830–70, French)
Gordimer (Nadine; 1923– , South African)
Gourmont (Rémy de; 1858–1915, French)
Gréville (Henry; 1842–1902, French)
Hahn-Hahn (Ida Gräfin; 1805–80, German)
Hamilton (Patrick; 1904–62, English)
Hochhuth (Rolf; 1931– , German)
Holcroft (Thomas; 1745–1809, English)
Huysmans (J K; 1848–1907, French)
Inchbald (Elizabeth; 1753–1821, English)

Ingemann (Bernhard Severin; 1789–1862, Danish)
Ishiguro (Kazuo; 1954– , Japanese/British)
Jacobsen (Jens Peter; 1847–85, Danish)
Jewsbury (Geraldine; 1812–80, English)
Jhabvala (Ruth Prawer; 1927–2013, German/British)
Karamzin (Nikolai; 1766–1826, Russian)
Kavanagh (Patrick; 1905–67, Irish)
Kawabata (Yasunari; 1899–1972, Japanese)
Keneally (Thomas; 1935– , Australian)
Kennaway (James; 1928–68, Scottish)
Kielland (Alexander L; 1849–1906, Norwegian)
Kingsley (Charles; 1819–75, English)
Kingsley (Henry; 1830–76, English)
Kingsley (Mary St Leger; 1852–1931, English)
Koestler (Arthur; 1905–83, Hungarian/British)
Kosinski (Jerzy; 1933–91, Polish/US)
Kureishi (Hanif; 1954– , English)
Lagerlöf (Selma; 1858–1940, Swedish)
Laurence (Margaret; 1926–87, Canadian)
Lawrence (D H; 1885–1930, English)
Leverson (Ada; 1865–1936, English)
Lindgren (Astrid; 1907–2002, Swedish)
Lockhart (John Gibson; 1794–1854, Scottish)
Macaulay (Dame Rose; 1881–1958, English)
Magorian (Michelle; 1948– , English)
Marquand (John P; 1893–1960, US)
McCarthy (Cormac, 1933– , US)
McCarthy (Mary; 1912–89, US)
McGahern (John; 1934–2006, Irish)
McMurtry (Larry; 1936– , US)
McNickle (D'Arcy; 1904–77, US)
Melville (Herman; 1819–91, US)
Meredith (George; 1828–1909, English)
Michener (James A; 1907–97, US)
Milligan (Spike; 1918–2002, Irish)
Mitchell (Margaret; 1900–49, US)
Mitchell (W O; 1914–98, Canadian)
Montague (Charles E; 1867–1928, English)
Moorcock (Michael; 1939– , English)
Morrison (Arthur; 1863–1945, English)
Morrison (Toni; 1931– , US)
Mortimer (Penelope; 1918–99, English)
Mortimer (Sir John; 1923–2009, English)
Murakami (Haruki; 1949– , Japanese)
Murasaki (Shikibu; c.970–c.1015, Japanese)
Naughton (Bill; 1910–92, English)
Nedreaas (Torborg; 1906–87, Norwegian)
Ó Cadhain (Máirtín; 1906–70, Irish)
Oliphant (Margaret; 1828–97, Scottish)
Ondaatje (Michael; 1943– , Ceylonese/Canadian)

Paretsky (Sara; 1947– , US)
Pasolini (Pier Paolo; 1922–75, Italian)
Petersen (Nis; 1897–1943, Danish)
Phillips (David Graham; 1867–1911, US)
Radiguet (Raymond; 1903–23, French)
Rawlings (Marjorie; 1896–1953, US)
Remarque (Erich Maria; 1898–1970, German/US)
Richards (Alun; 1929–2004, Welsh)
Richepin (Jean; 1849–1926, French)
Robinson (Marilynne; 1943– , US)
Robinson (Mary; 1758–1800, English)
Rosegger (Peter; 1843–1918, Austrian)
Rousseau (Jean Jacques; 1712–78, French)
Sabatini (Rafael; 1875–1950, Italian/British)
Salinger (J D; 1919–2010, US)
Sargeson (Frank; 1903–82, New Zealand)
Schaefer (Jack; 1907–91, US)
Scheffel (Joseph Victor von; 1826–86, German)
Sciascia (Leonardo; 1921–89, Sicilian)
Sedgwick (Catharine Maria; 1789–1867, US)
Sherriff (R C; 1896–1975, English)
Sillitoe (Alan; 1928–2010, English)
Sinclair (May; 1863–1946, English)
Sinclair (Upton; 1878–1968, US)
Smollett (Tobias; 1721–71, Scottish)
Spillane (Mickey; 1918–2006, US)
Stafford (Jean; 1915–79, US)
Stendhal (1783–1842, French)
Tanizaki (Junichiro; 1886–1965, Japanese)
Thirkell (Angela; 1891–1961, English)
Topelius (Zacharias; 1818–98, Finnish)
Townsend (Sue; 1945– , English)
Tressell (Robert; 1870–1911, Irish)
Trollope (Anthony; 1815–82, English)
Trollope (Frances; 1780–1863, English)
Trollope (Joanna; 1943– , English)
Turgenev (Ivan; 1818–83, Russian)
Unsworth (Barry; 1930–2012, English)
Urquhart (Fred; 1912–95, Scottish)
Voltaire (1694–1778, French)
Vonnegut (Kurt; 1922–2007, US)
Williams (Raymond; 1921–88, Welsh)
Williams (William Carlos; 1883–1963, US)
Zeromski (Stefan; 1864–1925, Polish)

09 Ainsworth (William Harrison; 1805–82, English)
Aldington (Richard; 1892–1962, English)
Allingham (Margery; 1904–66, English)
Andersson (Dan; 1888–1920, Swedish)
Bacchelli (Riccardo; 1891–1985, Italian)
Barthelme (Donald; 1931–89, US)
Benedetti (Mario; 1920–2009, Uruguayan)
Bergelson (David; 1884–1952, Russian)
Blackmore (Richard Doddridge; 1825–1900, English)
Blackwood (Algernon; 1869–1951, English)

Bromfield (Louis; 1896–1956, US)
Burroughs (Edgar Rice; 1875–1950, US)
Burroughs (William S; 1914–97, US)
Caballero (Fernán; 1797–1877, Swiss/
Spanish)
Callaghan (Morley Edward; 1903–90,
Canadian)
Cambridge (Ada; 1844–1926, Australian)
Cervantes (Miguel de; 1547–1616, Spanish)
Charteris (Leslie; 1907–93, US)
Chevalier (Tracy; 1962– , US)
Churchill (Winston; 1871–1947, US)
Crébillon (Claude Prosper Jolyot de;
1707–77, French)
Crnjanski (Milos; 1893–1977, Serbian)
d'Annunzio (Gabriele; 1863–1938, Italian)
Delafield (E M; 1890–1943, English)
de la Roche (Mazo; 1885–1961, Canadian)
De Quincey (Thomas; 1785–1859, English)
Dos Passos (John; 1896–1970, US)
du Maurier (Dame Daphne; 1907–89,
English)
du Maurier (George; 1834–96, French/
British)
Edgeworth (Maria; 1767–1849, Irish)
Ehrenburg (Ilya; 1891–1967, Soviet)
Findlater (Jane; 1866–1946, Scottish)
Findlater (Mary; 1865–1963, Scottish)
Fromentin (Eugène; 1820–76, French)
Futabatei (Shimei; 1864–1909, Japanese)
Gerhardie (William; 1895–1977, English)
Goldsmith (Oliver; 1730–74, Irish)
Goncharov (Ivan; 1812–91, Russian)
Goytisolo (Juan; 1931– , Spanish)
Greenwood (Walter; 1903–74, English)
Grossmith (George; 1847–1912, English)
Grossmith (Weedon; 1854–1919, English)
Guareschi (Giovanni; 1908–68, Italian)
Güiraldes (Ricardo; 1886–1927, Argentine)
Gütersloh (Albert Paris; 1887–1973,
Austrian)
Hauptmann (Gerhart; 1862–1946, German)
Hawthorne (Nathaniel; 1804–64, US)
Hemingway (Ernest; 1899–1961, US)
Highsmith (Patricia; 1921–95, US)
Hölderlin (Friedrich; 1770–1843, German)
Hopkinson (Sir Tom; 1905–90, English)
Humphreys (Emyr; 1919– , Welsh)
Immermann (Karl Leberecht; 1796–1840,
German)
Isherwood (Christopher; 1904–86, US)
Jefferies (Richard; 1848–87, English)
Johnstone (Isobel; 1781–1857, Scottish)
Jörgensen (Johannes; 1866–1956, Danish)
Kaye-Smith (Sheila; 1887–1956, English)
King-Smith (Dick; 1922–2011, English)
Korolenko (Vladimir; 1853–1921, Russian)
La Fayette (Madame de; 1634–93, French)

Lampedusa (Giuseppe di; 1896–1957,
Italian)
Lermontov (Mikhail; 1814–41, Russian)
Linklater (Eric; 1899–1974, Scottish)
Llewellyn (Richard; 1907–83, Welsh)
MacDonald (George; 1824–1905, Scottish)
Mackenzie (Sir Compton; 1883–1972,
English)
Maclennan (Hugh; 1907–90, Canadian)
Mankowitz (Wolf; 1924–98, English)
Mansfield (Katherine; 1888–1923, New
Zealand)
Marinetti (Filippo Tommaso; 1876–1944,
Italian)
Martinson (Harry; 1904–78, Swedish)
Masefield (John; 1878–1967, English)
McCullers (Carson; 1917–67, US)
Middleton (Stanley; 1919–2009, English)
Mitchison (Naomi; 1897–1999, Scottish)
Monsarrat (Nicholas; 1910–79, English)
Mukherjee (Bharati; 1940– , Indian/US)
Oppenheim (E Phillips; 1866–1946, English)
Palahniuk (Chuck; 1961– , US)
Pasternak (Boris; 1890–1960, Russian)
Pratchett (Sir Terry; 1948– , English)
Priestley (J B; 1894–1984, English)
Radcliffe (Ann; 1764–1823, English)
Roa Bastos (Augusto; 1917–2005,
Paraguayan)
Schreiner (Olive; 1855–1920, South African)
Sholokhov (Mikhail; 1905–84, Russian)
Sillanpää (Frans Eemil; 1888–1964, Finnish)
Söderberg (Hjalmar; 1869–1941, Swedish)
Spitteler (Carl; 1845–1924, Swiss)
Steinbeck (John; 1902–68, US)
Stevenson (Robert Louis; 1850–94, Scottish)
Streuvels (Stijn; 1871–1969, Flemish)
Sudermann (Hermann; 1857–1928, German)
Thackeray (William Makepeace; 1811–63,
English)
Vittorini (Elio; 1908–66, Italian)
Wentworth (Patricia; 1878–1961, English)
Whitehead (Charles; 1804–62, English)
Willeford (Charles; 1919–88, US)
Winterson (Jeanette; 1959– , English)
Wodehouse (Sir P G; 1881–1975, English)
Yourcenar (Marguerite; 1903–87, Belgian/
US/French)

10 Bainbridge (Dame Beryl; 1934– , English)
Ballantyne (Robert Michael; 1825–94,
Scottish)
Boldrewood (Rolf; 1826–1915, English/
Australian)
Carpentier (Alejo; 1904–80, Cuban)
Chatterjee (Bankim Chandra; 1838–94,
Indian)
Cherbuliez (Joel; 1806–70, Swiss)
Cherbuliez (Victor; 1829–99, Swiss/French)

Chesterton (G K; 1874–1936, English)
Chevallier (Gabriel; 1895–1969, French)
Conscience (Hendrik; 1812–83, Flemish)
Cunningham (Michael; 1952– , US)
Dostoevsky (Fyodor; 1821–81, Russian)
Fairbairns (Zoë; 1948– , English)
Falkberget (Johann; 1879–1967, Norwegian)
Fitzgerald (F Scott; 1896–1940, US)
Fitzgerald (Penelope; 1916–2000, English)
Galsworthy (John; 1867–1933, English)
Gombrowicz (Witold; 1904–69, Polish)
Gunnarsson (Gunnar; 1889–1975,
    Icelandic)
Kraszewski (Józef Ignacy; 1812–87, Polish)
Lagerkvist (Pär; 1891–1974, Swedish)
Lezama Lima (José; 1910–76, Cuban)
MacLaverty (Bernard; 1942– , Irish)
Manchester (William; 1922–2004, US)
Maupassant (Guy de; 1850–93, French)
McCullough (Colleen; 1937– , Australian)
McIlvanney (William; 1936– , Scottish)
Millhauser (Steven; 1943– , US)
Montemayor (Jorge de; c.1515–61,
    Portuguese)
Montgomery (L M; 1874–1942, Canadian)
Phillpotts (Eden; 1862–1960, English)
Pirandello (Luigi; 1867–1936, Italian)
Richardson (Dorothy M; 1873–1957,
    English)
Richardson (H H; 1870–1946, Australian)
Richardson (Samuel; 1689–1761, English)
Schnitzler (Arthur; 1862–1931, Austrian)
Somerville (Edith; 1858–1949, Irish)
Strindberg (August; 1849–1912, Swedish)
Tarkington (Booth; 1869–1946, US)
Thoroddsen (Jón; 1818–68, Icelandic)
van der Post (Sir Laurens; 1906–96, South
    African)
Wassermann (Jakob; 1873–1934, German)
Waterhouse (Keith; 1929–2009, English)
Williamson (Henry; 1895–1977, English)

11 Anzengruber (Ludwig; 1839–89, Austrian)
Auchincloss (Louis; 1917–2010, US)
Blessington (Marguerite Gardiner, Countess
    of; 1789–1849, Irish)
Bontempelli (Massimo; 1878–1960, Italian)
de Bernières (Louis; 1954– , English)
Dostoyevsky (Fyodor; 1821–81, Russian)
Eichendorff (Joseph, Freiherr von; 1788–
    1857, German)
Goldschmidt (Meïr; 1819–87, Danish)
Kazantzakis (Nikos; 1883–1957, Greek)
Matthiessen (Peter; 1927– , US)

Montherlant (Henri Millon de; 1896–1972,
    French)
Pérez Galdós (Benito; 1843–1920, Spanish)
Pontoppidan (Henrik; 1857–1944, Danish)
Sienkiewicz (Henryk; 1846–1916, Polish)
Valle-Inclán (Ramón del; 1869–1936,
    Spanish)
Vargas Llosa (Mario; 1936– , Peruvian)
Wildenbruch (Ernst von; 1845–1909,
    German)

12 Andrzejewski (Jerzy; 1909–83, Polish)
Ashton-Warner (Sylvia; 1908–84, New
    Zealand)
Eça de Queiros (José Maria de; 1845–1900,
    Portuguese)
Kovalevskaya (Sofya; 1850–91, Russian)
Martin du Gard (Roger; 1881–1958, French)
Martín-Santos (Luis; 1924–64, Spanish)
Merezhkovsky (Dmitri; 1865–1941, Russian)
Pérez de Ayala (Ramón; 1881–1962,
    Spanish)
Quiller-Couch (Sir Arthur; 1863–1944,
    English)
Robbe-Grillet (Alain; 1922–2008, French)
Saint-Exupéry (Antoine de; 1900–44,
    French)
Solzhenitsyn (Aleksandr; 1918–2008,
    Russian)

13 Aguilera Malta (Demetrio; 1909–81,
    Ecuadorean)
Alain-Fournier (Henri; 1886–1914, French)
Beresford-Howe (Constance; 1922– ,
    Canadian)
Castelo Branco (Camilo; 1825–90,
    Portuguese)
Guimarães Rosa (João; 1908–69, Brazilian)
Przybyszewski (Stanislaw; 1868–1927,
    Polish)
Sackville-West (Vita; 1892–1962, English)
Whyte-Melville (George; 1821–78, Scottish)

14 Cabrera Infante (Guillermo; 1929–2005,
    Cuban)
Compton-Burnett (Dame Ivy; 1884–1969,
    English)
Grimmelshausen (Hans Jacob Christoffel
    von; c.1622–1676, German)
Machado de Assis (Joaquim Maria; 1839–
    1908, Brazilian)

15 Hansford Johnson (Pamela; 1912–81,
    English)
Sergeyev-Tsensky (Sergei; 1875–1958,
    Russian)

See also **biography**; **essay**; **fable**; **history**; **literature**; **play**; **poetry**; **science fiction**

number

Numbers include:

03 nil
one
six
ten
two

04 five
four
half
nine
zero

05 eight
fifty
forty
seven
sixty
three

06 eighty
eleven
googol
nought
ninety
thirty
twelve
twenty

07 billion
chiliad
fifteen
hundred
million
seventy
sixteen

08 eighteen

fourteen
nineteen
thirteen
thousand
trillion

09 decillion
nonillion
octillion
seventeen

10 centillion
googolplex
one hundred
septillion
sextillion

11 quadrillion
quintillion

French numbers include:

02 un (1)

03 dix (10)
six (6)

04 cent (100)
cinq (5)
deux (2)
huit (8)
neuf (9)
onze (11)
sept (7)
zéro (0)

05 douze (12)
mille (1,000)
seize (16)
trois (3)
vingt (20)

06 quatre (4)
quinze (15)
treize (13)
trente (30)

07 dix-huit (18)
dix-neuf (19)
dix-sept (17)

million (1,000,000)

08 milliard (1,000,000,000)
quarante (40)
quatorze (14)
soixante (60)

09 cinquante (50)
deux mille (2,000)
un million (1,000,000)

10 un milliard (1,000,000,000)

11 soixante-dix (70)

12 quatre-vingts (80)

German numbers include:

03 elf (11)

04 acht (8)
drei (3)
eins (1)
fünf (5)
neun (9)
null (0)
vier (4)
zehn (10)
zwei (2)

05 sechs (6)
zwölf (12)

06 sieben (7)

07 achtzig (80)
Billion
fünfzig (50)
hundert (100)
Million (1,000,000)
neunzig (90)
sechzig (60)
siebzig (70)
tausend (1,000)
vierzig (40)
zwanzig (20)

08 achtzehn (18)
dreissig (30)
dreizehn (13)
fünfzehn (15)
neunzehn (19)
sechzehn (16)
siebzehn (17)
vierzehn (14)

09 Milliarde (1,000,000,000)

10 einhundert (100)
eintausend (1,000)

Italian numbers include:

03 due (2)
sei (6)
tre (3)
uno (1)

04 nove (9)

otto (8)

zero (0)

05 cento (100)
dieci (10)
sette (7)
venti (20)

06 cinque (5)
dodici (12)
sedici (16)
trenta (30)
undici (11)
07 novanta (90)

ottanta (80)
quattro (4)
tredici (13)
08 diciotto (18)
quaranta (40)
quindici (15)

sessanta (60)
settanta (70)
09 cinquanta (50)
10 diciannove (19)
11 diciassette (17)
quattordici (14)

Latin numbers include:

03 duo (2)
nil (0)
sex (6)
04 octo (8)
tres (3)
unus (1)
05 decem (10)
mille (1,000)
novem (9)
06 centum (100)

septem (7)
07 quinque (5)
sedecim (16)
undecim (11)
viginti (20)
08 duodecim (12)
quattuor (4)
tredecim (13)
trigenta (30)
09 nonaginta (90)

octoginta (80)
quindecim (15)
sexaginta (60)
11 quadraginta (40)
septendecim (17)
septuaginta (70)
undeviginti (19)
12 duodeviginti (18)
quinquaginta (50)
13 quattuordecim (14)

Spanish numbers include:

03 dos (2)
mil (1,000)
uno (1)
04 cero (0)
diez (10)
doce (12)
ocho (8)
once (11)
seis (6)
tres (3)
05 cinco (5)
nueve (9)
See also **numeral**

siete (7)
trece (13)
06 ciento (100)
cuatro (4)
millón (1,000,000)
quince (15)
veinte (20)
07 catorce (14)
noventa (90)
ochenta (80)
sesenta (60)
setenta (70)

treinta (30)
08 cuarenta (40)
un millón
09 cincuenta (50)
dieciocho (18)
dieciséis (16)
10 diecinueve (19)
diecisiete (17)
quinientos (500)
11 mil millones
(1,000,000,000)

numeral

Roman numerals include:

01 C (100)
D (500)
I (1)
L (50)
M (1,000)
V (5)

X (10)
02 II (2)
IV (4)
IX (9)
VI (6)
XI (11)

XV (15)
XX (20)
03 III (3)
VII (7)
XII (12)
XIV (14)

XIX (19)
XVI (16)
04 VIII (8)
XIII (13)
XVII (17)
05 XVIII (18)

nun *see* **religious order**

nurse

Nurse types include:

03 dry
wet

04 home
maid

sick

05 nanny
night

staff	**07** midwife	**10** consultant	**13** health visitor
tutor	nursery	Iain Rennie	State Enrolled
06 charge	**08** district	Marie Curie	theatre sister
dental	**09** auxiliary	ward sister	**15** locality manager
matron	children's	**11** night sister	State Registered
school	community	psychiatric	
sister	Macmillan	**12** practitioner	

Nurse grades include:

06 Grade A (Auxiliary/Assistant)
Grade B (Auxiliary/Assistant)
Grade C (Enrolled/Auxiliary)
Grade D (Newly Qualified Nurse)
Grade E (Experienced Staff Nurse)
Grade F (Senior Nurse)

Grade G (Senior/Charge Nurse)
Grade H (Modern Matron)
Grade H (Nurse Specialist)
Grade I (Modern Matron)
Grade I (Nurse Specialist)

Nurses include:

04 Gamp (Mrs Sarah; *Martin Chuzzlewit*, 1844, Charles Dickens)
Hana (*The English Patient*, 1992, Michael Ondaatje)
Nana (*Peter Pan*, 1904, J M Barrie)
Prig (Betsey; *Martin Chuzzlewit*, 1844, Charles Dickens)

05 Kenny (Elizabeth; 1886–1952, Australian)
Nurse (*Romeo and Juliet*, 1591–96, William Shakespeare)
Nurse (the; *Too True to be Good*, 1932, George Bernard Shaw)

06 Cavell (Edith; 1865–1915, English)
Glaucé (*The Faerie Queene*, 1590–96, Sir Edmund Spenser)
Purfoy (Sarah; *For the Term of His Natural Life*, 1874, Marcus Clarke)
Rayner (Claire; 1931–2010, English)
Sanger (Margaret; 1883–1966, US)
Toodle (Polly; *Dombey and Son*, 1848, Charles Dickens)
Wright (Vera; *Cabin Fever*, 1990, Elizabeth Jolley)

07 McMahon (Phyllis Jean/Fay; *Loot*, 1966, Joe

Orton)
Rachael (Mrs; *Bleak House*, 1853, Charles Dickens)
Ratched (Nurse Mildred; *One Flew Over the Cuckoo's Nest*, 1962, Ken Kesey)
Seacole (Mary; 1805–81, Jamaican)

08 Espinosa (Carla; *Scrubs*, TV sitcom, 2001–)
Fairhead (Charlie; *Casualty*, TV series, 1986–)
Houlihan (Margaret 'Hot Lips'; *MASH*, 1968, Richard Hooker)
Pattison (Dorothy; 1832–78, English)
Saunders (Cicely; 1918–2005, English)
Saunders (Daisy; *The Gate of Angels*, 1990, Penelope Fitzgerald)

10 Cunningham (Nurse; *The Ante-Room*, 1934, Kate O'Brien)
Flintwinch (Affery; *Little Dorrit*, 1857, Charles Dickens)
Ftatateeta (*Caesar and Cleopatra*, 1898, George Bernard Shaw)
Stephenson (Elsie; 1916–67, English)

11 Nightingale (Florence; 1820–1910, English)

nut

Nuts include:

04 pine	brazil	walnut	hazelnut
05 beech	cashew	**07** coconut	**09** groundnut
pecan	cobnut	filbert	macadamia
06 almond	monkey	**08** chestnut	pistachio
	peanut		

nutrition

Terms to do with nutrition include:

02 GI
03 BMI
fat
HDL
LDL
RDA
RDI
TPN
04 diet
iron
SACN
salt
05 fibre
lipid
obese
sugar
vegan
06 biotin
citrin
energy
enzyme
folate
gluten
iodine
low-fat
niacin
sodium
07 allergy
anaemic
bulimic
calorie
coeliac

glucose
mineral
organic
portion
protein
retinol
serving
vitamin
08 additive
anorexic
appetite
carotene
coenzyme
diabetic
eutrophy
glycemic
holozoic
lycopene
nutrient
roughage
thiamine
trans fat
trophesy
09 amino acid
anabolism
anorectic
dietician
diet sheet
digestion
dystrophy
fatty acid
folic acid
food group

glycaemic
kilojoule
probiotic
10 blood sugar
calciferol
catabolism
deficiency
low-calorie
metabolism
nut allergy
overweight
provitamin
riboflavin
supplement
tocopherol
trophology
vegetarian
weight gain
weight loss
11 antioxidant
axerophthol
bone density
cholesterol
dehydration
electrolyte
food allergy
growth chart
innutrition
kilocalorie
macrobiotic
mixotrophic
trigger food
underweight

12 ascorbic acid
balanced diet
bioflavonoid
carbohydrate
food aversion
lean body mass
malnutrition
multi-vitamin
nicotinamide
nutritionist
phytonadione
saturated fat
13 body mass index
macronutrient
malabsorption
micronutrient
nicotinic acid
phylloquinone
14 bad cholesterol
eating disorder
glycaemic index
HDL cholesterol
LDL cholesterol
monounsaturate
omega fatty acid
polyunsaturate
trophoneurosis
15 cholecalciferol
good cholesterol
malassimilation
obsessive eating

See also **diet; food**

O

observatory

Observatories include:

04 Keck (USA)

05 Royal (England)
Tower (England)

06 Gemini (USA/Chile)

07 Arecibo (Puerto Rico)

Palomar (USA)
Paranal (Chile)

08 Kitt Peak (USA)
Mauna Kea (USA)
Mt Wilson (USA)

09 Greenwich (England)

11 Jodrell Bank (England)

12 Herstmonceux (England)

13 Tower of London (England)

14 Royal Greenwich (England)

occult

Occult and supernatural terms include:

03 ESP
obi

04 jinx
juju
omen
rune

05 charm
coven
curse
dream
magic
relic
spell
totem
witch

06 amulet
déjà vu
fetish
garlic
hoodoo
mascot
medium
séance
shaman
spirit
trance

See also **witch**

vision
voodoo

07 bewitch
cabbala
conjure
diviner
evil eye
palmist
psychic
satanic
sorcery
warlock

08 black cat
exorcism
exorcist
familiar
illusion
magician
Satanism
Satanist
shamrock
sorcerer
talisman

09 astrology
black mass
ectoplasm

Hallowe'en
horoscope
horseshoe
influence
palmistry
pentagram
tarot card
telepathy

10 astrologer
black magic
chiromancy
divination
evil spirit
hydromancy
necromancy
Ouija board®
paranormal
planchette
possession
prediction
sixth sense
white magic
witchcraft

11 chiromancer
clairvoyant
crystal ball

divining-rod
hydromancer
incantation
necromancer
oneiromancy
poltergeist
premonition
psychometer
psychometry
rabbit's foot
second sight
telepathist
witch doctor

12 clairvoyance
oneiromancer
spiritualism
spiritualist
supernatural
superstition
tarot reading

13 fortune-teller
hallucination
witch's sabbath

14 Walpurgis Night

occupation

Occupations include:

02 AM
DJ
GP
MD
MP

PA

03 MSP
nun
spy
vet

04 aide
chef
cook
dean
dyer

hack
maid
monk
page
poet

05 abbot
actor
agent
baker
boxer
buyer
caddy
clerk
coach
diver
envoy
friar
guide
judge
juror
mason
mayor
medic
miner
model
nanny
nurse
pilot
slave
smith
tawer
tutor
usher
valet
vicar

06 abbess
artist
au pair
author
banker
barber
barman
bishop
bookie
bowyer
brewer
broker
butler
cabbie
cleric
cooper
copper
coster
cowboy
critic
curate
dancer
dealer

doctor
draper
driver
editor
eggler
factor
farmer
fitter
forger
gaffer
glazer
grocer
herald
hermit
hosier
hunter
jailer
jester
jockey
joiner
lawyer
mercer
miller
nannie
oilman
ostler
packer
parson
pastor
pig-man
pirate
player
porter
potter
priest
ragman
ranger
roofer
sailor
salter
server
singer
skater
skivvy
sniper
sparks
spicer
tailor
tanner
teller
tinner
trader
tycoon
typist
vendor
verger
waiter
warden

warder
weaver
welder
whaler
writer

07 acrobat
actress
actuary
admiral
adviser
almoner
analyst
artisan
artiste
athlete
attaché
auditor
aviator
bailiff
barista
barmaid
bellboy
bellhop
bottle-o
breeder
builder
butcher
cashier
chemist
cleaner
climber
coalman
cobbler
collier
coroner
courier
cowherd
crofter
curator
cyclist
dentist
doorman
dresser
drummer
equerry
farrier
fiddler
fighter
fireman
florist
footman
foreman
frogman
general
glazier
gymnast
hangman
haulier

hostess
janitor
junkman
lace-man
lineman
lorimer
luthier
magnate
manager
marshal
midwife
milkman
oculist
officer
orderly
painter
partner
pianist
planner
plumber
poacher
popstar
postman
prefect
printer
rancher
referee
saddler
scholar
senator
servant
shearer
sheriff
showman
soldier
spinner
stapler
steward
student
surgeon
teacher
trainee
trainer
trapper
vintner
warrior
woolman
workman

08 advocate
animator
armourer
attorney
banksman
botanist
bottle-oh
brakeman
callgirl
cardinal

chairman
chandler
chaplain
comedian
compiler
composer
conjurer
conjuror
corporal
costumer
coxswain
croupier
dairyman
deckhand
diplomat
director
druggist
educator
embalmer
engineer
engraver
essayist
executor
factotum
farmhand
ferryman
film star
fishwife
forester
gangster
gardener
goatherd
governor
gunsmith
handyman
henchman
herdsman
hireling
home help
hotelier
huntsman
inventor
jeweller
labourer
landlady
landlord
lecturer
linguist
lyricist
magician
maltster
mapmaker
masseuse
mechanic
merchant
milkmaid
milliner
minister

minstrel
muleteer
musician
novelist
operator
optician
organist
pardoner
perfumer
pig-woman
polisher
preacher
producer
promoter
publican
quarrier
recorder
reporter
retailer
reviewer
salesman
satirist
scrap-man
sculptor
seedsman
sergeant
shepherd
showgirl
smuggler
sorcerer
spaceman
spurrier
stockman
stripper
stuntman
supplier
surveyor
thatcher
upholder
waitress
watchman
wet nurse
wig-maker
woodsman
wrangler

09 alchemist
anatomist
announcer
antiquary
architect
archivist
art critic
art dealer
assistant
associate
astronaut
attendant
barperson

barrister
biologist
bodyguard
bookmaker
buccaneer
bus driver
cab driver
caretaker
carpenter
charwoman
chauffeur
clergyman
coal miner
collector
columnist
commander
concierge
conductor
constable
cosmonaut
costumier
couturier
cricketer
decorator
detective
dietician
dramatist
ecologist
economist
executive
facialist
financier
fisherman
fruiterer
gas fitter
geologist
goldsmith
governess
guitarist
gutter-man
harvester
herbalist
historian
homeopath
horologer
housemaid
hypnotist
innkeeper
inspector
ironsmith
jacksmith
landowner
launderer
laundress
librarian
lifeguard
locksmith
machinist

messenger
musketeer
navigator
newsagent
nursemaid
osteopath
outfitter
paralegal
paramedic
performer
physician
physicist
plasterer
ploughman
policeman
pop singer
poulterer
professor
publicist
publisher
puppeteer
registrar
robe maker
sailmaker
secretary
shoemaker
signaller
signalman
songsmith
spokesman
stagehand
stationer
staymaker
stevedore
subeditor
swineherd
therapist
towncrier
tradesman
traveller
trumpeter
usherette
van driver
violinist
volunteer
whittawer
yachtsman
zookeeper
zoologist

10 accountant
advertiser
air hostess
air steward
amanuensis
apothecary
apprentice
archbishop
astrologer

astronomer
auctioneer
baby sitter
bank teller
beautician
bellringer
bill-broker
biochemist
biographer
blacksmith
bookbinder
bookkeeper
bookseller
bricklayer
bureaucrat
campaigner
cartoonist
cartwright
chairmaker
clockmaker
coastguard
compositor
consultant
controller
copywriter
corn-dealer
corn-factor
councillor
counsellor
desk jockey
disc jockey
dishwasher
dramaturge
dressmaker
dry cleaner
equestrian
fellmonger
fishmonger
footballer
forecaster
frame-maker
fundraiser
gamekeeper
game warden
gangmaster
gatekeeper
geneticist
geochemist
geographer
glassmaker
handmaiden
headhunter
headmaster
highwayman
horologist
instructor
ironmonger
journalist

junk-dealer
keyboarder
legislator
librettist
lumberjack
magistrate
manageress
manicurist
manservant
midshipman
millwright
missionary
naturalist
negotiator
newscaster
newsmonger
nurseryman
obituarist
pallbearer
park ranger
pawnbroker
peltmonger
perruquier
pharmacist
piano tuner
playwright
podiatrist
politician
postmaster
private eye
programmer
proprietor
prospector
railwayman
removal man
researcher
ringmaster
roadmender
sales clerk
saleswoman
sempstress
shipbroker
shipwright
shopfitter
shopkeeper
signwriter
songstress
stewardess
stock agent
stockinger
stonemason
supervisor
taxi driver
technician
translator
typesetter
undertaker
unguentary

wainwright
wharfinger
whitesmith
wholesaler
woodcarver
woodcutter

11 accompanist
antiquarian
art director
astrologist
audio typist
bank manager
bingo caller
broadcaster
bullfighter
burn-the-wind
businessman
candlemaker
car salesman
chambermaid
cheerleader
chiropodist
clergywoman
commentator
coppersmith
delivery man
distributor
draughtsman
electrician
entertainer
estate agent
etymologist
executioner
firefighter
foot soldier
fund manager
glass blower
grave digger
greengrocer
haberdasher
hairdresser
hair stylist
head teacher
horse-dealer
illustrator
interpreter
interviewer
lifeboatman
linen-draper
lollipop man
lorry driver
metalworker
money broker
mountaineer
music-seller
neurologist
optometrist
panel beater

parlourmaid
pathologist
philatelist
philologist
philosopher
policewoman
proofreader
radiologist
relic-monger
secret agent
set designer
sharebroker
ship builder
silversmith
sociologist
steelworker
stockbroker
taxidermist
telephonist
ticket agent
tobacconist
travel agent
tree surgeon
truck driver
upholsterer
wagonwright
wax-chandler
web designer
wheelwright
wool-stapler
youth worker

12 anaesthetist
broker-dealer
cabinet maker
calligrapher
cartographer
cheesemonger
chimney sweep
chiropractor
churchwarden
civil servant
coal merchant
corn-merchant
costermonger
demonstrator
dramaturgist
entomologist
entrepreneur
event manager
fent-merchant
film director
garret-master
hotel manager
immunologist
IT consultant
longshoreman
maitre d'hotel
make-up artist

media planner
metallurgist
mineralogist
nutritionist
obstetrician
orthodontist
photographer
physiologist
ploughwright
postal worker
practitioner
PR consultant
press officer
prison warder
psychologist
radiographer
receptionist
sales manager
schoolmaster
screenwriter
scriptwriter
ship chandler
slink butcher
social worker
spokesperson
stage manager
statistician
stenographer
toxicologist
urban planner
veterinarian
wine merchant
wood engraver

13 administrator
antique dealer
archaeologist
charity worker

See also **maker**

choreographer
civil engineer
crane operator
criminologist
dental surgeon
food scientist
groundskeeper
gynaecologist
harbour master
health visitor
home economist
industrialist
lexicographer
lollipop woman
mathematician
meteorologist
nightwatchman
oceanographer
old-clothesman
police officer
prison officer
rag-and-bone-man
rent collector
retail manager
scrap merchant
security guard
ship's chandler
shop assistant
sound engineer
streetcleaner
streetsweeper
traffic warden
window cleaner
woollen-draper

14 anthropologist
camera operator
claims assessor

draughtsperson
gutter-merchant
market gardener
marriage-broker
merchant tailor
microbiologist
military member
music therapist
naval architect
pharmacologist
pharmacopolist
store detective
superintendent
systems analyst
tallow chandler

15 biotechnologist
business analyst
commission agent
computer analyst
conservationist
costume designer
dental hygienist
fashion designer
flight attendant
funeral director
graphic designer
marine biologist
military officer
ophthalmologist
personal trainer
physiotherapist
police constable
refuse collector
speech therapist
stock controller
ticket collector

ocean

Oceans include:

06 Arctic
Indian

07 Pacific

08 Atlantic
Southern

12 North Pacific

South Pacific

13 North Atlantic
South Atlantic

Ocean trenches include:

03 Yap (Pacific)

04 Java (Indian)

05 Japan (Pacific)
Kuril (Pacific)
Palau (Pacific)
Tonga (Pacific)

06 Cayman (Atlantic)

Ryukyu (Pacific)

07 Atacama (Pacific)
Mariana (Pacific)

08 Aleutian (Pacific)
Izu Bonin (Pacific)
Kermadec (Pacific)
Marianas (Pacific)
Mindanao (Pacific)

Romanche (Atlantic)

09 Peru-Chile (Pacific)

10 Philippine (Pacific)
Puerto Rico
(Atlantic)

11 Nansei Shoto
(Pacific)

12 Bougainville
(Pacific)
West Caroline
(Pacific)

13 Middle America
(Pacific)
South Sandwich
(Southern)

See also **sea**

Oceania *see* Australasia

office

Offices include:

02 CO
FO
PO
TO
WO

03 box
COI
CRO
DLO
EPO
FCO
GAO
GPO
IIP
IRO
Met
NAO
OFT
OME
ONS
OPW
ORR
OSS
OST
pay
PRO
RLO
SFO
War

04 back

BFPO
fire
HMSO
Holy
Home
land
loan
Pipe
Post

05 Assay
Crown
front
Ofcom
Offer
Ofgas
Ofgem
Oflot
Oftel
Ofwat
paper
press
stamp

06 Ofsted
Patent
Pat Off
police
Record
ticket

07 booking
Foreign

sorting

08 Chancery
Colonial
Eurostat
incident
printing
register
registry
Scottish

09 personnel
receiving
telegraph

10 dead-letter
employment
Quai d'Orsay
registered
Stationery

11 general post
left-luggage
victualling

12 Commonwealth
Serious Fraud

13 Inland Revenue
National Audit

14 European Patent
Meteorological
returned letter

15 Criminal Records

Office furniture includes:

04 desk
safe

07 lectern

08 desk lamp
fire safe

09 partition
plan chest
stepstool
work table

11 storage unit
swivel chair
workstation

12 computer desk
drawing-board
fire cupboard
printer stand
typist's chair

13 executive desk

filing cabinet
filing trolley

14 boardroom table
display cabinet
executive chair
filing cupboard
reception chair

15 conference table
secretarial desk

Office equipment includes:

03 fax
OHP
VDU

05 mouse

06 inkpad

screen
tacker

07 cash box
monitor
planner

printer
scanner
stapler
trimmer

08 computer

intercom
keyboard
mouse mat
plan file
shredder

09 date-stamp
dust cover
laminator
telephone
textphone
time clock
wages book

10 calculator
comb binder
copy holder
Dictaphone®
duplicator
fax machine
guillotine

letter tray
monitor arm
paper punch
printwheel
ring binder
typewriter

11 comb binding
hole puncher
noticeboard
photocopier
switchboard

12 acoustic hood
letter opener
letter scales
message board
parcel scales
screen filter
telex machine
visitors' book

wire bindings

13 data cartridge
desk organizer
lever arch file
microcassette
planning board
reference book
staple-remover
thermal binder
waste-paper bin
word processor

14 adhesive binder
diskette mailer
flip-chart easel
laptop computer
slide projector
telephone index

15 terminal trolley

See also **government**; **stationery**

official

Officials include:

02 JP
MP
03 MEP
05 agent
chief
clerk
elder
envoy
hakim
mayor
usher
06 consul
Euro-MP
notary
07 bailiff
captain

coroner
equerry
manager
marshal
monitor
prefect
proctor
senator
sheriff
steward
08 alderman
chairman
delegate
diplomat
director
Eurocrat

executor
governor
mandarin
mayoress
minister
overseer
09 commander
commissar
executive
Gauleiter
inspector
ombudsman
president
principal
registrar
10 ambassador

bureaucrat
chairwoman
chancellor
councillor
magistrate
proprietor
supervisor
11 chairperson
congressman
12 civil servant
commissioner
13 administrator
congresswoman
14 representative
superintendent

oil

Oils include:

03 ben
gas
nim
nut
til
04 baby
bone
cade
coal
corn
crab

derv
dika
fish
fuel
hair
palm
poon
rape
rock
rose
rusa

seed
tall
tung
wood
wool
yolk
zest
05 attar
beech
benne
carap

crude
fusel
grass
heavy
joint
macaw
niger
olive
poppy
pulza
rosin
salad
savin
shale
shark
snake
sperm
spike
stand
sweet
thyme
train
whale
06 ajowan
almond
banana
butter
canola
carron
castor
chrism
cloves
cohune
croton
diesel
garlic

illipe
jojoba
macoya
neroli
peanut
savine
Seneca
sesame
07 arachis
cajuput
camphor
coconut
gingili
jinjili
linseed
lumbang
mineral
mirbane
mustard
myrrhol
retinol
rhodium
spindle
verbena
vitriol
08 ambrosia
bergamot
camphine
cinnamon
cod-liver
creosote
gingelly
kerosene
kerosine
lavender

macahuba
macassar
North Sea
paraffin
pristane
rapeseed
rosewood
09 black gold
candlenut
grapeseed
neat's-foot
patchouli
patchouly
safflower
sassafras
spikenard
sunflower
vanaspati
vegetable
10 citronella
eucalyptus
peppermint
petit grain
turpentine
ylang-ylang
11 camphorated
chaulmoogra
wintergreen
12 benzaldehyde
brilliantine
13 bitter almonds
14 glutaraldehyde
15 evening primrose

See also **refining**

Olympic Games

Summer Olympic venues:

04 Rome (Italy; 1960)
05 Paris (France; 1900/1924)
Seoul (South Korea; 1988)
Tokyo (Japan; 1964)
06 Athens (Greece; 1896/1906/2004)
Berlin (Germany; 1936)
London (UK; 1908/1948/2012)
Moscow (USSR; 1980)
Munich (West Germany; 1972)
Sydney (Australia; 2000)
07 Antwerp (Belgium; 1920)

Atlanta (USA; 1996)
Beijing (China; 2008)
St Louis (USA; 1904)
08 Helsinki (Finland; 1952)
Montréal (Canada; 1976)
09 Amsterdam (The Netherlands; 1928)
Barcelona (Spain; 1992)
Melbourne (Australia; 1956)
Stockholm (Sweden; 1912)
10 Los Angeles (USA; 1932/1984)
Mexico City (Mexico; 1968)

Summer Olympic events include:

03 BMX

04 beam
judo
trap

05 rings
skeet
vault

06 boxing
dinghy
discus
diving
hammer
hockey
keirin
omnium
rowing
sprint
tennis

07 archery
cycling
fencing
javelin
jumping
sailing
shot put

08 20km walk
50km walk
50m rifle
baseball
canoeing
dressage
eventing
football
handball
high jump

keelboat
long jump
marathon
shooting
softball
swimming

09 100 metres
200 metres
25m pistol
400 metres
50m pistol
800 metres
athletics
badminton
decathlon
multihull
pole vault
tae kwon do
triathlon
water polo
wrestling

10 1,500 metres
5,000 metres
basketball
double trap
equestrian
gymnastics
heptathlon
points race
team sprint
trampoline
triple jump
uneven bars
volleyball

11 10,000 metres

100m hurdles
10m air rifle
10m platform
110m hurdles
4×100m relay
4×400m relay
400m hurdles
discus throw
hammer throw
pommel horse
table tennis
team pursuit
windsurfing

12 10m air pistol
1km time trial
50m freestyle
cross-country
javelin throw
parallel bars

13 100m butterfly
100m freestyle
200m butterfly
200m freestyle
3m springboard
400m freestyle
500m time trial
50m rifle prone
800m freestyle
horizontal bar
weightlifting

14 100m backstroke
1,500m freestyle
200m backstroke
floor exercises

15 beach volleyball

Winter Olympic venues:

04 Oslo (Norway; 1952)

05 Turin (Italy; 2006)

06 Nagano (Japan; 1998)

07 Calgary (Canada; 1988)
Cortina (Italy; 1956)
Sapporo (Japan; 1972)

08 Chamonix (France; 1924)
Grenoble (France; 1968)
Sarajevo (Yugoslavia; 1984)

St Moritz (Switzerland; 1928/1948)

09 Innsbruck (Austria; 1964/1976)
Vancouver (Canada; 2010)

10 Lake Placid (USA; 1932/1980)

11 Albertville (France; 1992)
Lillehammer (Norway; 1994)
Squaw Valley (USA; 1960)

12 Salt Lake City (USA; 2002)

21 Garmisch-Partenkirchen (Germany; 1936)

Winter Olympic events include:

04 luge

05 pairs

06 moguls

skiing
slalom
super-G
two-man

07 aerials
curling
four-man
skating

08 biathlon
downhill
halfpipe
skeleton
09 500 metres
bobsleigh
ice hockey
snowboard
10 1,000 metres
1,500 metres
1.5km sprint
3,000 metres
3,000m relay

4×5km relay
5,000 metres
5,000m relay
ice dancing
individual
ski jumping
11 10,000 metres
4×10km relay
giant slalom
12 alpine skiing
snowboarding
speed skating
13 10km classical

15km classical
15km freestyle
30km classical
30km freestyle
50km classical
figure skating
relay biathlon
14 alpine combined
Nordic combined
snowboard cross
15 combined pursuit
freestyle skiing
pursuit biathlon

Olympians include:

03 Coe (Sebastian, Lord; 1956–   ; English, athletics)
Hoy (Sir Chris; 1976–   , Scottish, cycling)

04 Bolt (Usain; 1986–   , Jamaican, athletics)
Clay (Cassius; 1942–   ; US, boxing)
Dean (Christopher; 1958–   ; English, figure skating)
Ewry (Ray; 1873–1937; US, athletics)
Otto (Kristin; 1966–   ; German, swimming)
Papp (Laszlo; 1926–2003; Hungarian, boxing)
Todd (Mark; 1956–   ; New Zealand, equestrianism)
Witt (Katarina; 1965–   ; German, figure skating)

05 Blair (Bonnie; 1964–   ; US, speed skating)
Bubka (Sergei; 1963–   ; Soviet/Ukrainian, athletics)
Chand (Dhyan; 1905–79; Indian, hockey)
Cranz (Christl; 1914–2004; German, alpine skiing)
Curry (John; 1949–94; English, figure skating)
Ennis (Jessica; 1986–   ; English, athletics)
Farah (Mo; 1983–   ; Somali/English, athletics)
Henie (Sonja; 1912–69; Norwegian, figure skating)
Killy (Jean-Claude; 1943–   ; French, alpine skiing)
Lewis (Carl; 1961–   ; US, athletics)
Lewis (Denise; 1972–   ; English, athletics)
Longo (Jeannie; 1958–   ; French, cycling)
Meade (Richard; 1938–   ; English, equestrianism)
Nurmi (Paavo; 1897–1973; Finnish, athletics)
Ottey (Merlene; 1960–   ; Jamaican/Slovenian, athletics)
Owens (Jesse; 1913–80; US, athletics)
Popov (Aleksandr; 1971–   ; Russian, swimming)
Savon (Felix; 1967–   ; Cuban, boxing)

Spitz (Mark; 1950–   ; US, swimming)
Tomba (Alberto; 1966–   ; Italian, alpine skiing)

06 Aamodt (Kjetil; 1971–   ; Norwegian, alpine skiing)
Beamon (Bob; 1946–   ; US, athletics)
Bikila (Abebe; 1932–73; Ethiopian, athletics)
Biondi (Matt; 1965–   ; US, swimming)
Button (Dick; 1929–   ; US, figure skating)
D'Inzeo (Raimondo; 1925–   ; Italian, equestrianism)
Fraser (Dawn; 1937–   ; Australian, swimming)
Heiden (Eric; 1958–   ; US, speed skating)
Holmes (Dame Kelly; 1970–   ; English, athletics)
Korbut (Olga; 1955–   ; Belarussian, gymnastics)
Oerter (Al; 1936–2007; US, athletics)
Phelps (Michael; 1985–   ; US, swimming)
Ritola (Ville; 1896–1982; Finnish, athletics)
Sailer (Toni; 1936–2009; Austrian, alpine skiing)
Thorpe (Ian; 1982–   ; Australian, swimming)
Thorpe (Jim; c.1888–1953; US, athletics)

07 Ainslie (Ben; 1977–   , English, sailing)
Boitano (Brian; 1963–   ; US, figure skating)
Cousins (Robin; 1957–   ; English, figure skating)
Daehlie (Bjorn; 1967–   ; Norwegian, Nordic skiing)
Edwards (Jonathan; 1966–   , English, triple jump)
Fischer (Birgit; 1962–   ; German; canoeing)
Johnson (Michael; 1967–   ; US, athletics)
Klammer (Franz; 1953–   ; Austrian, alpine skiing)
Mathias (Bob; 1930–2006; US, athletics)
Nykänen (Matti; 1963–   ; Finnish, ski-jumping)

Pinsent (Sir Matthew; 1970– ; English, rowing)

Rodnina (Irina; 1949– ; Soviet, pairs skating)

Scherbo (Vitaly; 1972– ; Soviet/ Belarussian, gymnastics)

Schmidt (Birgit; 1962– ; German, canoeing)

Torvill (Jayne; 1957– ; English, figure skating)

Voronin (Mikhail; 1945–2004; Soviet, gymnastics)

Zatopek (Emil; 1922–2000; Czech, athletics)

Zelezny (Jan; 1966– ; Czech, athletics)

08 Christie (Linford; 1960– , English, athletics)

Comaneci (Nadia; 1961– ; Romanian, gymnastics)

Cuthbert (Betty; 1938– ; Australian, athletics)

de Bruijn (Inge; 1973– ; Dutch, swimming)

Dityatin (Aleksandr; 1957– ; Russian, gymnastics)

Elvstrøm (Paul; 1928– ; Danish, sailing)

Gerevich (Aladár; 1910–91; Hungarian, fencing)

Jernberg (Sixten; 1929–2012; Swedish, Nordic skiing)

Latynina (Larissa; 1934– ; Ukrainian, gymnastics)

Louganis (Greg; 1960– ; US, diving)

Ohuruogu (Christine; 1984– , British, 400m)

Redgrave (Sir Steve; 1962– ; English, rowing)

Stenmark (Ingemar; 1956– ; Swedish, alpine skiing)

Thompson (Daley; 1958– ; English, athletics)

Zijlaard (Leontien; 1970– ; Dutch, cycling)

09 Adlington (Rebecca; 1989– , English, swimming)

Andrianov (Nikolay; 1952– ; Russian, gymnastics)

Babashoff (Shirley; 1957– ; US, swimming)

Cáslavská (Vera; 1942– ; Czech, gymnastics)

Egerszegi (Krisztina; 1974– ; Hungarian, swimming)

Ennis-Hill (Jessica; 1986– ; English, athletics)

Gräfström (Gillis; 1893–1938; Swedish, figure skating)

Pendleton (Victoria; 1980– , English, cycling)

Schneider (Vreni; 1964– ; Swiss, alpine skiing)

Seizinger (Katja; 1972– ; German, alpine skiing)

Stevenson (Teófilo; 1952– ; Cuban, boxing)

10 Linsenhoff (Liselott; 1927–99; German, equestrianism)

Moser-Proll (Annemarie; 1953– ; Austrian, alpine skiing)

van Moorsel (Leontien; 1970– ; Dutch, cycling)

11 Mangiarotti (Edouardo; 1919–2012; Italian, fencing)

Weissmuller (Johnny; 1904–84; US, swimming)

12 Blankers-Koen (Fanny; 1918–2004; Dutch, athletics)

Gebrselassie (Haile; 1973– ; Ethiopian, athletics)

Germeshausen (Bernhard; 1951– ; German, bobsledding)

Joyner-Kersee (Jackie; 1962– ; US, athletics)

Suleymanoglu (Naim; 1967– ; Bulgarian/ Turkish, weightlifting)

13 Longo-Ciprelli (Jeannie; 1958– ; French, cycling)

14 Griffith-Joyner (Florence; 1959–98; US, athletics)

O'Neill, Eugene (1888–1953)

Significant works include:

11 *The Fountain* (1925)
The Hairy Ape (1922)

12 *Ah, Wilderness* (1933)
Anna Christie (1921)

13 *Marco Millions* (1928)

14 *Days Without End* (1934)
Lazarus Laughed (1928)

15 *The Emperor Jones* (1920)
The Iceman Cometh (1946)

16 *Beyond the Horizon* (1920)

Strange Interlude (1928)
The Great God Brown (1926)

18 *Desire Under the Elms* (1924)
Moon of the Caribbees (1918)

19 *Bound East for Cardiff* (1916)

21 *Moon for the Misbegotten* (1947)

22 *All God's Chillun Got Wings* (1924)
Mourning Becomes Electra (1931)

24 *Long Day's Journey Into Night* (1956)

Significant characters include:

03 Lem

04 Mayo (Andrew)
Mayo (Robert)
Yank

05 Brant (Captain Adam)
Brown (William A)
Burke (Mat)
Cabot (Eben)
Cabot (Ephraim)

Jones (Brutus)
Leeds (Nina)

06 Downey (Ella)
Mannon (Brigadier-General
Ezra)
Mannon (Christine)
Mannon (Lavinia)
Mannon (Orin)
Putnam (Abbie)

Tyrone (Edmund)
Tyrone (James)
Tyrone (Jamie)
Tyrone (Mary)

07 Anthony (Dion)
Douglas (Mildred)

08 Smithers (Henry)

14 Christopherson (Anna)
Christopherson (Chris)

OPEC

Organization of Petroleum Exporting Countries (OPEC) members:

04 Iran
Iraq

05 Libya
Qatar

06 Angola
Kuwait

07 Algeria
Ecuador

Nigeria

09 Venezuela

11 Saudi Arabia

18 United Arab
Emirates

opera

Operas and operettas include:

04 *Aïda* (Verdi, 1871)
Lulu (Berg, 1937)

05 *Faust* (Gounod, 1859)
Manon (Massenet, 1884)
Norma (Bellini, 1831)
Tosca (Puccini, 1900)

06 *Carmen* (Bizet, 1875)
Jenufa (Janácek, 1904)
Otello (Verdi, 1887)
Salome (Richard Strauss, 1911)

07 *Elektra* (Richard Strauss, 1909)
Fidelio (Beethoven, 1814)
Macbeth (Verdi, 1847)
Nabucco (Verdi, 1842)
The Ring (Wagner, 1876)
Thespis (Gilbert & Sullivan, 1871)
Werther (Massenet, 1892)
Wozzeck (Berg, 1925)

08 *Falstaff* (Verdi, 1893)
Idomeneo (Mozart, 1781)
La bohème (Puccini, 1896)
Parsifal (Wagner, 1882)
Patience (Gilbert & Sullivan, 1881)
Turandot (Puccini, 1926)

09 *Billy Budd* (Britten, 1951)
Capriccio (Richard Strauss, 1942)
Don Carlos (Verdi, 1867)
King Priam (Tippett, 1962)
Lohengrin (Wagner, 1850)
Pagliacci (Leoncavallo, 1892)
Rigoletto (Verdi, 1851)
Ruddigore (Gilbert & Sullivan, 1887)

Siegfried (Wagner, 1876)
The Mikado (Gilbert & Sullivan, 1885)
Véronique (Andre Messager, 1898)

10 *Cendrillon* (Massenet, 1899)
Cinderella (Rossini, 1817; Massenet, 1899)
Die Walküre (Wagner, 1870)
I Pagliacci (Leoncavallo, 1892)
La traviata (Verdi, 1853)
Oedipus Rex (Stravinsky, 1928)
Tannhäuser (Wagner, 1845)

11 *Don Giovanni* (Mozart, 1787)
Don Pasquale (Donizetti, 1843)
HMS Pinafore (Gilbert & Sullivan, 1878)
Il trovatore (Verdi, 1853)
La Périchole (Offenbach, 1868)
Peter Grimes (Britten, 1945)
Princess Ida (Gilbert & Sullivan, 1884)
The Sorceror (Gilbert & Sullivan, 1877)
Trial by Jury (Gilbert & Sullivan, 1875)
William Tell (Rossini, 1829)

12 *Boris Godunov* (Mussorgsky, 1874)
Così fan tutte (Mozart, 1790)
Das Rheingold (Wagner, 1869)
Eugene Onegin (Tchaikovsky, 1879)
La sonnambula (Bellini, 1831)
Manon Lescaut (Puccini, 1893)
Moses und Aron (Schönberg, 1954)
Nixon in China (John Adams, 1990)
Porgy and Bess (Gershwin, 1935)
The Grand Duke (Gilbert & Sullivan, 1896)
The Huguenots (Meyerbeer, 1836)
The Rhinegold (Wagner, 1869)

The Valkyries (Wagner, 1870)

13 Albert Herring (Britten, 1947)
Andrea Chénier (Umberto Giordano, 1896)
Der Freischütz (Carl Maria von Weber, 1821)
Dido and Aeneas (Purcell, 1689)
Die Fledermaus (Johann Strauss, 1874)
La Belle Hélène (Offenbach, 1864)
La Cenerentola (Rossini, 1819)
Moses and Aaron (Schönberg, 1954)
Powder Her Face (Ades, 1995)
The Fairy Queen (Purcell, 1692)
The Gondoliers (Gilbert & Sullivan, 1889)
The Gypsy Baron (Johann Strauss, 1885)
The Knot Garden (Tippett, 1970)
The Magic Flute (Mozart, 1791)
Utopia Limited (Gilbert & Sullivan, 1893)

14 Die Zauberflöte (Mozart, 1791)
Le Grand Macabre (Ligeti, 1978)
Samson et Dalila (Saint-Saëns, 1877)

15 Ariadne auf Naxos (Richard Strauss, 1916)
Götterdämmerung (Wagner, 1876)
Hansel and Gretel (Humperdinck, 1893)
Le nozze di Figaro (Mozart, 1786)
Madama Butterfly (Puccini, 1904)
Madame Butterfly (Puccini, 1904)
Orfeo ed Euridice (Gluck, 1762)
Simon Boccanegra (Verdi, 1857)
The Beggar's Opera (Gay, 1728)
The Pearl Fishers (Bizet, 1863)

16 Der Rosenkavalier (Richard Strauss, 1911)
Der Zigeunerbaron (Johann Strauss, 1885)
The Bartered Bride (Smetana, 1866)

The Rake's Progress (Stravinsky, 1951)
Tristan und Isolde (Wagner, 1865)

17 La Fille du régiment (Donizetti, 1840)
Lucia di Lammermoor (Donizetti, 1835)
The Flying Dutchman (Wagner, 1843)
The Tales of Hoffman (Offenbach, 1881)
The Turn of the Screw (Britten, 1954)
Un ballo in maschera (Verdi, 1859)

18 Einstein on the Beach (Philip Glass, 1976)
La Damnation de Faust (Berlioz, 1846)
Pelléas et Mélisande (Debussy, 1902)
The Barber of Seville (Rossini, 1816)
The Threepenny Opera (Weill, 1928)

19 Cavalleria rusticana (Mascagni, 1890)
The Marriage of Figaro (Mozart, 1786)
The Yeoman of the Guard (Gilbert &
Sullivan, 1888)

20 Der Ring des Nibelungen (Wagner, 1876)
Duke Bluebeard's Castle (Bartók, 1918)
Il barbiere di Siviglia (Rossini, 1816)
Lady Macbeth of Mtsensk (Shostakovich,
1934)
The Midsummer Marriage (Tippett, 1955)
The Pirates of Penzance (Gilbert & Sullivan,
1879)
The Twilight of the Gods (Wagner, 1876)

21 The Cunning Little Vixen (Janácek, 1924)

22 Orpheus in the Underworld (Offenbach,
1858)
The Love for Three Oranges (Prokofiev, 1920)
The Merry Wives of Windsor (Otto Nicolai,
1849)

Opera characters include:

03 Cis *(Albert Herring)*
Eva *(The Mastersingers of Nuremberg)*
Ida *(Die Fledermaus)*
Jim *(Porgy and Bess)*
Liu *(Turandot)*
Sid *(Albert Herring)*

04 Aïda *(Aïda)*
Bess *(Porgy and Bess)*
Budd (Billy; *Billy Budd)*
Budd *(Superintendent; Albert Herring)*
Doxy *(Betty; The Beggar's Opera)*
Erda *(Der Ring des Nibelungen)*
Erik *(The Flying Dutchman)*
Ford *(Alice; Falstaff)*
Ford *(Frank; Falstaff)*
Froh *(Der Ring des Nibelungen)*
Goro *(Madame Butterfly)*
Gzak *(Prince Igor)*
Iago *(Otello)*
Ines *(Il Trovatore)*
Jake *(Porgy and Bess)*

John *(Peter Grimes)*
Lily *(Porgy and Bess)*
Loge *(Der Ring des Nibelungen)*
Lola *(Cavalleria rusticana)*
Luna (The Count/Il Conte de; *Il Trovatore)*
Mary *(The Flying Dutchman)*
Mime *(Der Ring des Nibelungen)*
Mimì *(La bohème)*
Ochs *(Baron; Der Rosenkavalier)*
Olga *(Eugene Onegin)*
Page *(Meg; Falstaff)*
Pang *(Turandot)*
Pike *(Florence; Albert Herring)*
Ping *(Turandot)*
Pong *(Turandot)*
Ruiz *(Il trovatore)*
Vere *(Captain; Billy Budd)*
Zorn *(Balthasar; The Mastersingers of
Nuremberg)*

05 Adele *(Die Fledermaus)*
Alfio *(Cavalleria rusticana)*

Alice *(Lucia di Lammermoor)*
Alisa *(Lucia di Lammermoor)*
Annie *(Porgy and Bess)*
Berta *(The Barber of Seville)*
Blind (Doctor; *Die Fledermaus)*
Boles (Bob; *Peter Grimes)*
Borsa (Matteo; *Rigoletto)*
Budge (Ben; *The Beggar's Opera)*
Caius (Doctor; *Falstaff)*
Calaf *(Turandot)*
Canio *(I Pagliacci)*
Clara *(Porgy and Bess)*
Colas *(Bastien und Bastienne)*
Creon *(Oedipus Rex)*
Crown *(Porgy and Bess)*
David *(The Mastersingers of Nuremberg)*
Diver (Jenny; *The Beggar's Opera)*
Emmie *(Albert Herring)*
Falke (Doctor; *Die Fledermaus)*
Faust *(Faust/La Damnation de Faust)*
Filch *(The Beggar's Opera)*
Flora (Bervoix; *La traviata)*
Foltz (Hans; *The Mastersingers of Nuremberg)*
Frank *(Die Fledermaus)*
Freia *(Der Ring des Nibelungen)*
Gedge (Mr; *Albert Herring)*
Gilda *(Rigoletto)*
Harry *(Albert Herring)*
Herod *(Salome)*
Jeník *(The Bartered Bride)*
Jones (Arthur; *Billy Budd)*
Kecal *(The Bartered Bride)*
Keene (Ned; *Peter Grimes)*
Lucia (Mama; *Cavalleria rusticana)*
Lucia *(The Rape of Lucretia)*
Maria *(Porgy and Bess)*
Marie *(Wozzeck)*
Marke (King; *Tristan und Isolde)*
Melot *(Tristan und Isolde)*
Mícha (Tobia; *The Bartered Bride)*
Mingo *(Porgy and Bess)*
Moser (Augustin; *The Mastersingers of Nuremberg)*
Nancy *(Albert Herring)*
Nedda *(I Pagliacci)*
Ortel (Hermann; *The Mastersingers of Nuremberg)*
Peppe *(I Pagliacci)*
Peter *(Hansel and Gretel)*
Peter *(Porgy and Bess)*
Pimen *(Boris Godunov)*
Porgy *(Porgy and Bess)*
Rocco *(Fidelio)*
Sachs (Hans; *The Mastersingers of Nuremberg)*
Senta *(The Flying Dutchman)*
Timur *(Turandot)*

Titus *(La clemenza di Tito)*
Tonio *(I Pagliacci)*
Tosca (Floria; *Tosca)*
Trull (Dolly; *The Beggar's Opera)*
Vasek *(The Bartered Bride)*
Venus *(Tannhäuser)*
Vixen (Miss; *The Beggar's Opera)*
Wotan *(Der Ring des Nibelungen)*
Xenia *(Boris Godunov)*

06 Alcina *(Alcina)*
Altoum (Emperor; *Turandot)*
Alvaro *(Alzira)*
Alzira *(Alzira)*
Annina *(Der Rosenkavalier)*
Annina *(La traviata)*
Annius *(La clemenza di Tito)*
Ashton (Lucy/Lucia; *Lucia di Lammermoor)*
Ashton (Sir Henry/Enrico; *Lucia di Lammermoor)*
Benoît *(La bohème)*
Bianca *(The Rape of Lucretia)*
Brazen (Molly; *The Beggar's Opera)*
Carmen *(Carmen)*
Cassio *(Otello)*
Coaxer (Mrs; *The Beggar's Opera)*
Daland *(The Flying Dutchman)*
Donald *(Billy Budd)*
Donner *(Der Ring des Nibelungen)*
Emilia *(Otello)*
Fafner *(Der Ring des Nibelungen)*
Fasolt *(Der Ring des Nibelungen)*
Fenton *(Falstaff)*
Feodor *(Boris Godunov)*
Figaro *(The Barber of Seville/The Marriage of Figaro)*
Frantz *(The Tales of Hoffmann)*
Fricka *(Der Ring des Nibelungen)*
Frosch *(Die Fledermaus)*
Fyodor *(Boris Godunov)*
Golaud *(Pelléas et Mélisande)*
Gremin (Prince; *Eugene Onegin)*
Gretel *(Hansel and Gretel)*
Grimes (Peter; *Peter Grimes)*
Hänsel *(Hansel and Gretel)*
Isolde *(Tristan und Isolde)*
Junius *(The Rape of Lucretia)*
Kundry *(Parsifal)*
Larina (Marina; *Eugene Onegin)*
Lensky *(Eugene Onegin)*
Lockit (Lucy; *The Beggar's Opera)*
Lockit (Lucy; *The Beggar's Opera)*
Lockit *(The Beggar's Opera)*
Luther *(The Tales of Hoffmann)*
Mantua (Duke of; *Rigoletto)*
Nelson *(Porgy and Bess)*
Norman *(Lucia di Lammermoor)*
Oberto *(Alcina)*
Onegin (Eugene; *Eugene Onegin)*

Orford (Ellen; *Peter Grimes*)
Oronte *(Alcina)*
Ortrud *(Lohengrin)*
Otello *(Otello)*
Otumbo *(Alzira)*
Ovando *(Alzira)*
Ovlour *(Prince Igor)*
Pamina *(The Magic Flute)*
Pastia (Lillas; *Carmen)*
Pogner (Veit; *The Mastersingers of Nuremberg)*
Ramfis *(Aïda)*
Rosina *(The Barber of Seville)*
Salome *(Salome)*
Serena *(Porgy and Bess)*
Sextus *(La clemenza di Tito)*
Siebel *(Faust)*
Silvio *(I Pagliacci)*
Sophie *(Der Rosenkavalier)*
Squeak *(Billy Budd)*
Stella *(The Tales of Hoffmann)*
Suzuki *(Madame Butterfly)*
Tamino *(The Magic Flute)*
Tawdry (Suky; *The Beggar's Opera)*
Trapes (Mrs; *The Beggar's Opera)*
Upfold (Mr; *Albert Herring)*
Valery (Violetta; *La traviata)*
Wagner *(Faust)*
Yniold *(Pelléas et Mélisande)*
Zamoro *(Alzira)*
Zuniga *(Carmen)*

07 Alfredo (Germont; *La traviata)*
Amneris *(Aïda)*
Antonio *(The Marriage of Figaro)*
Ataliba *(Alzira)*
Azucena *(Il trovatore)*
Bartolo *(The Barber of Seville/The Marriage of Figaro)*
Basilio *(The Barber of Seville)*
Bastien *(Bastien und Bastienne)*
Bervoix (Flora; *La traviata)*
Billows (Lady; *Albert Herring)*
Bucklow (Lord Arturo/Arthur; *Lucia di Lammermoor)*
Colline *(La bohème)*
Crab Man *(Porgy and Bess)*
Dansker *(Billy Budd)*
Despina *(Così fan tutte)*
Don José *(Carmen)*
Douphol (Baron; *La traviata)*
Eroshka *(Prince Igor)*
Faninal *(Der Rosenkavalier)*
Frazier *(Porgy and Bess)*
Gastone *(La traviata)*
Germont (Alfredo; *La traviata)*
Germont (Giorgio; *La traviata)*
Godfrey *(Lohengrin)*
Godunov (Boris; *Boris Godunov)*

Gunther *(Der Ring des Nibelungen)*
Gusmano *(Alzira)*
Gutrune *(Der Ring des Nibelungen)*
Heraldo *(Lohengrin)*
Hermann *(Tannhäuser)*
Hermann *(The Tales of Hoffmann)*
Herring (Albert; *Albert Herring)*
Herring (Mrs; *Albert Herring)*
Hunding *(Der Ring des Nibelungen)*
Jaquino *(Fidelio)*
Jocasta *(Oedipus Rex)*
Kothner (Fritz; *The Mastersingers of Nuremberg)*
Leonora *(Fidelio)*
Leonora *(Il trovatore)*
Lindorf *(The Tales of Hoffmann)*
Mahomet *(Der Rosenkavalier)*
Manrico *(Il trovatore)*
Marenka *(The Bartered Bride)*
Marullo (Cavaliere; *Rigoletto)*
Masetto *(Don Giovanni)*
Melisso *(Alcina)*
Micaëla *(Carmen)*
Miracle (Doctor; *The Tales of Hoffmann)*
Missail *(Boris Godunov)*
Mnishek (Marina; *Boris Godunov)*
Montano *(Otello)*
Morales *(Carmen)*
Morgana *(Alcina)*
Musetta *(La bohème)*
Oedipus *(Oedipus Rex)*
Olympis *(The Tales of Hoffmann)*
Peachum (Polly; *The Beggar's Opera)*
Peachum *(The Beggar's Opera)*
Pelléas *(Pelléas et Mélisande)*
Pistola *(Falstaff)*
Publius *(La clemenza di Tito)*
Quickly (Mistress; *Falstaff)*
Radamès *(Aïda)*
Rangoni *(Boris Godunov)*
Redburn (Mr; *Billy Budd)*
Robbins *(Porgy and Bess)*
Rodolfo *(La bohème)*
Rofrano (Octavian; *Der Rosenkavalier)*
Scarpia (Baron; *Tosca)*
Schwarz (Hans; *The Mastersingers of Nuremberg)*
Susanna *(The Marriage of Figaro)*
Tatiana *(Eugene Onegin)*
Titurel (King; *Parsifal)*
Triquet (Monsieur; *Eugene Onegin)*
Tristan *(Tristan und Isolde)*
Trouble *(Madame Butterfly)*
Turiddu *(Cavalleria rusticana)*
Varlaam *(Boris Godunov)*
Walther (von Stolzing; *The Mastersingers of Nuremberg)*
Wozzeck *(Wozzeck)*

Zerlina *(Don Giovanni)*

08 Alberich *(Der Ring des Nibelungen)*
Almaviva *(Count/Il Conte d'; The Barber of Seville/The Marriage of Figaro)*
Almaviva *(Countess/Il Contessa di; The Marriage of Figaro)*
Ambrogio *(The Barber of Seville)*
Amfortas *(Parsifal)*
Amonasro *(Aïda)*
Archdale *(Mr; Porgy and Bess)*
Bardolfo *(Falstaff)*
Bidebent *(Raymond/Raimondo; Lucia di Lammermoor)*
Biterolf *(Tannhäuser)*
Brangäne *(Tristan und Isolde)*
Claggart *(Billy Budd)*
Falstaff *(Sir John; Falstaff)*
Fernando *(Fidelio)*
Ferrando *(Così fan tutte)*
Ferrando *(Il trovatore)*
Fiorello *(The Barber of Seville)*
Galitsky *(Prince; Prince Igor)*
Gerhilde *(Der Ring des Nibelungen)*
Gertrude *(Hansel and Gretel)*
Giovanna *(Rigoletto)*
Giuseppe *(La traviata)*
Grigorij *(Boris Godunov)*
Grigoriy *(Boris Godunov)*
Helmwige *(Der Ring des Nibelungen)*
Herodias *(Salome)*
Hoffmann *(The Tales of Hoffmann)*
Jacquino *(Fidelio)*
Klingsor *(Parsifal)*
Kontchak *(Prince Igor)*
Kurvenal *(Tristan und Isolde)*
Kurwenal *(Tristan und Isolde)*
Lodovico *(Otello)*
Lucretia *(The Rape of Lucretia)*
Macheath *(Captain; The Beggar's Opera)*
Marcello *(La bohème)*
Mercédès *(Carmen)*
Nannetta *(Falstaff)*
Nicklaus *(The Tales of Hoffmann)*
Nikitich *(Boris Godunov)*
Normando *(Lucia di Lammermoor)*
Octavian *(Rofrano; Der Rosenkavalier)*
Orlofsky *(Prince; Die Fledermaus)*
Orlovsky *(Prince; Die Fledermaus)*
Ortlinde *(Der Ring des Nibelungen)*
Papagena *(The Magic Flute)*
Papageno *(The Magic Flute)*
Parsifal *(Parsifal)*
Rhadames *(Aïda)*
Roderigo *(Otello)*
Ruggiero *(Alcina)*
Santuzza *(Cavalleria rusticana)*
Sarastro *(The Magic Flute)*
Servilia *(La clemenza di Tito)*

Siegmund *(Der Ring des Nibelungen)*
Spoletta *(Tosca)*
Stolzing *(Walter von; The Mastersingers of Nuremberg)*
The Bonze *(Madame Butterfly)*
The Witch *(Hansel and Gretel)*
Tiresias *(Oedipus Rex)*
Turandot *(Princess; Turandot)*
Twitcher *(Jemmy; The Beggar's Opera)*
Valentin *(Faust)*
Violetta *(Valery; La traviata)*
Vitellia *(La clemenza di Tito)*
Woglinde *(Der Ring des Nibelungen)*
Yamadori *(Prince; Madame Butterfly)*
Zaretski *(Eugene Onegin)*

09 Alcindoro *(La bohème)*
Angelotti *(Cesare; Tosca)*
Barbarina *(The Marriage of Figaro)*
Bastienne *(Bastien und Bastienne)*
Butterfly *(Madame; Madame Butterfly)*
Chelkalov *(Andrey/Andrei; Boris Godunov)*
Cherubino *(The Marriage of Figaro)*
Cio-Cio-San *(Madame Butterfly)*
Coppelius *(The Tales of Hoffmann)*
Desdemona *(Otello)*
Don Curzio *(The Marriage of Figaro)*
Donna Anna *(Don Giovanni)*
Dorabella *(Così fan tutte)*
Elisabeth *(Tannhäuser)*
Escamillo *(Carmen)*
Esmerelda *(The Bartered Bride)*
Florestan *(Fidelio)*
Frasquita *(Carmen)*
Genevieve *(Pelléas et Mélisande)*
Grimgerde *(Der Ring des Nibelungen)*
Guglielmo *(Così fan tutte)*
Gurnemanz *(Parsifal)*
Leporello *(Don Giovanni)*
Lohengrin *(Lohengrin)*
Maddalena *(Rigoletto)*
Magdalena *(The Mastersingers of Nuremberg)*
Magdalene *(The Mastersingers of Nuremberg)*
Mélisande *(Pelléas et Mélisande)*
Narraboth *(Salome)*
Nathanael *(The Tales of Hoffmann)*
Parpignol *(La bohème)*
Pinkerton *(Kate; Madame Butterfly)*
Pinkerton *(Lieutenant Benjamin; Madame Butterfly)*
Red Indian *(The Bartered Bride)*
Rigoletto *(Rigoletto)*
Rosalinda *(Die Fledermaus)*
Sacristan *(Tosca)*
Schaunard *(La bohème)*
Sciarrone *(Tosca)*
Sharpless *(Madame Butterfly)*

Siegfried *(Der Ring des Nibelungen)*
Sieglunde *(Der Ring des Nibelungen)*
Telramund *(*Frederick/Frederico;
  Lohengrin)
The Dewman *(Hansel and Gretel)*
Valzacchi *(Der Rosenkavalier)*
Vogelsang *(*Kunz; *The Mastersingers of*
  Nuremberg)
Von Zweter (Reinmar; *Tannhäuser)*
Waltraute *(Der Ring des Nibelungen)*
Wellgunde *(Der Ring des Nibelungen)*

10 Beckmesser *(*Sixtus; *The Mastersingers of*
  Nuremberg)
Bradamante *(Alcina)*
Brünnhilde *(Der Ring des Nibelungen)*
Collatinus *(The Rape of Lucretia)*
Dapertutto *(The Tales of Hoffmann)*
Don Alfonso *(Cosí fan tutte)*
Don Basilio *(The Marriage of Figaro)*
Don Ottavio *(Don Giovanni)*
Don Pizarro *(Fidelio)*
Eisenstein *(*Gabriel von; *Die Fledermaus)*
Eisslinger *(*Ulrich; *The Mastersingers of*
  Nuremberg)
El Dancairo *(Carmen)*
Filipievna *(Eugene Onegin)*
Fiordiligi *(Cosí fan tutte)*
Flosshilde *(Der Ring des Nibelungen)*
Igorevitch *(*Vladimir; *Prince Igor)*
Jaroslavna *(Prince Igor)*
La Contessa *(Rigoletto)*
Marcellina *(Fidelio)*
Marcellina *(The Marriage of Figaro)*
Marguérite *(Faust/La Damnation de*
  Faust)
Marzelline *(Fidelio)*
Monostatos *(The Magic Flute)*
Nachtigall *(*Konrad; *The Mastersingers of*
  Nuremberg)
Nimming Ned *(The Beggar's Opera)*
Paddington *(*Harry; *The Beggar's Opera)*
Prince Igor *(Prince Igor)*
Ravenswood *(*Sir Edgar/Edgardo; *Lucia di*
  Lammermoor)

Rey Enrique *(Lohengrin)*
Rossweisse *(Der Ring des Nibelungen)*
Schwerlein *(*Marthe; *Faust)*
Spalanzani *(The Tales of Hoffmann)*
Tannhäuser *(*Heinrich; *Tannhäuser)*
The Sandman *(Hansel and Gretel)*
The Speaker *(The Magic Flute)*
Wordsworth *(*Miss; *Albert Herring)*
Yaroslavna *(Prince Igor)*

11 Cavaradossi *(*Mario; *Tosca)*
Chochenille *(The Tales of Hoffmann)*
Don Giovanni *(Don Giovanni)*
Donna Elvira *(Don Giovanni)*
El Remendado *(Carmen)*
King of Egypt *(Aïda)*
Marschallin *(Der Rosenkavalier)*
Red Whiskers *(Billy Budd)*
Sparafucile *(Rigoletto)*
Sportin' Life *(Porgy and Bess)*
Taumännchen *(Hansel and Gretel)*
The Dutchman *(The Flying Dutchman)*
Vogelgesang *(*Kunz; *The Mastersingers of*
  Nuremberg)

12 Der Schreiber *(*Heinrich; *Tannhäuser)*
Kontchakovna *(Prince Igor)*
Leitmetzerin *(*Marianne; *Der*
  Rosenkavalier)
Mat of the Mint *(The Beggar's Opera)*
Sandmännchen *(Hansel and Gretel)*
The Steersman *(The Flying Dutchman)*

13 Elsa of Brabant *(Lohengrin)*
Von Eschenbach *(*Wolfram; *Tannhäuser)*

14 Customs Officer *(La Bohème)*
Henry the Fowler *(Lohengrin)*
John the Baptist *(Salome)*
Mephistopheles *(Faust/La Damnation de*
  Faust)
Pittichinaccio *(The Tales of Hoffmann)*
Usciere di Corte *(Rigoletto)*
Yaroslavovitch *(*Vladimir; *Prince Igor)*

15 Il duca di Mantova *(Rigoletto)*
Ochs von Lercheau *(*Baron; *Der*
  Rosenkavalier)

Opera houses include:

04 Lyon (France)

05 Cairo (Egypt)
Lyric (USA)
Royal (England)
State (Czech Republic)

06 De Munt (Belgium)
Semper (Germany)
Sydney (Australia)
Zurich (Switzerland)

07 La Scala (Italy)

Leipzig (Germany)

08 Bastille (France)
La Fenice (Italy)
San Carlo (Italy)

09 La Monnaie (Belgium)

10 Gothenburg (Sweden)
Monte-Carlo (Monaco)
Mussorgsky (Russia)

11 Teatro Liceo (Spain)

Verona Arena (Italy)
Vienna State (Austria)

12 Glyndebourne (England)
Hamburg State (Germany)
Komische Oper
  (Germany)
Metropolitan (USA)
Opéra-Comique (France)

13 Kennedy Center (USA)
Lincoln Center (USA)

Muziektheater (The
Netherlands)
Palais Garnier (France)
Teatro Massimo (Italy)
14 Bolshoi Theatre (Russia)

Estates Theatre (Czech
Republic)
Hungarian State (Hungary)
Kungliga Operan (Sweden)
London Coliseum (England)

Unter den Linden (Germany)
15 Royal Opera House
(England)
Teatro alla Scala (Italy)

Opera singers include:

03 Mei (Lanfang; 1894–1961, Chinese)
04 Butt (Dame Clara; 1872–1936, English,
contralto)
Lind (Jenny; 1820–87, Swedish, soprano)
Nash (Heddle; 1896–1961, English, tenor)
Pons (Lily; 1898–1976, French/US, soprano)
Popp (Lucia; 1939–93, Czech, soprano)
Prey (Hermann; 1929–98, German, baritone)
Tear (Robert; 1939–2011, Welsh, tenor)
Ward (David; 1922–83, Scottish, bass)
05 Allen (Sir Thomas; 1944– , English,
baritone)
Baker (Dame Janet; 1933– , English,
mezzo-soprano)
Bonci (Alessandro; 1870–1940, Italian, tenor)
Craig (Charles; 1922–97, English, tenor)
Evans (Sir Geraint; 1922–92, Welsh, baritone)
Ewing (Maria; 1950– , US, mezzo-soprano)
Field (Helen; 1951– , Welsh, soprano)
Freni (Mirella; 1936– , Italian, soprano)
Gedda (Nicolai; 1925– , Swedish, tenor)
Gigli (Beniamino; 1890–1957, Italian, tenor)
Gobbi (Tito; 1913–84, Italian, baritone)
Grisi (Giuditta; 1805–40, Italian, mezzo-
soprano)
Grisi (Giulia; 1811–69, Italian, soprano)
Horne (Marilyn; 1934– , US, mezzo-
soprano)
Jones (Dame Gwyneth; 1936– , Welsh,
soprano)
Kollo (René; 1937– , German, tenor)
Kraus (Alfredo; 1927–99, Spanish, tenor)
Lanza (Mario; 1921–59, US, tenor)
Luxon (Benjamin; 1937– , English, baritone)
Major (Dame Malvina; 1943– , New
Zealand, soprano)
Meier (Johanna; 1938– , US, soprano)
Melba (Dame Nellie; 1861–1931,
Australian, soprano)
Patti (Adelina; 1843–1919, Italian, soprano)
Pears (Sir Peter; 1910–86, English, tenor)
Pinza (Ezio; 1892–1957, Italian, bass)
Price (Leontyne; 1927– , US, soprano)
Siepi (Cesare; 1923–2010, Italian, bass)
Sills (Beverly; 1929–2007, US, soprano)
Teyte (Dame Maggie; 1888–1976, English,
soprano)
06 Bowman (James; 1941– , English, counter-
tenor)

Braham (John; 1774–1856, English, tenor)
Callas (Maria; 1923–77, US/Greek, soprano)
Carden (Joan; 1937– , Australian, soprano)
Caruso (Enrico; 1873–1921, Italian, tenor)
Davies (Arthur; 1950– , Welsh, tenor)
Davies (Ryland; 1943– , Welsh, tenor)
Dawson (Peter; 1882–1961, Australian,
bass-baritone)
Deller (Alfred; 1912–79, English, counter-
tenor)
de Luca (Giuseppe; 1876–1950, Italian,
baritone)
Farrar (Geraldine; 1882–1967, US, soprano)
García (Manuel; 1775–1832, Spanish, tenor)
Garden (Mary; 1874–1967, Scottish, soprano)
Harper (Heather; 1930– , Northern Irish,
soprano)
Hislop (Joseph; 1884–1977, Scottish, tenor)
Hotter (Hans; 1909–2003, German, bass-
baritone)
Ludwig (Christa; 1928– , German, mezzo-
soprano)
Mangin (Noel; 1931–95, New Zealand,
bass)
Minton (Yvonne; 1938– , Australian,
mezzo-soprano)
Norman (Jessye; 1945– , US, soprano)
Reszke (Edouard de; 1856–1917, Polish,
bass)
Reszke (Jean de; 1850–1925, Polish, tenor)
Reszke (Joséphine de; 1855–91, Polish,
soprano)
Scotto (Renata; 1934– , Italian, soprano)
Studer (Cheryl; 1955– , US, soprano)
Tauber (Richard; 1892–1948, Austrian/
British, tenor)
Terfel (Bryn; 1965– , Welsh, bass-baritone)
Turner (Dame Eva; 1892–1990, English,
soprano)
Upshaw (Dawn; 1960– , US, soprano)
van Dam (José; 1940– , Belgian, bass-
baritone)
Wiener (Otto; 1911–2000, Austrian,
baritone)
07 Austral (Florence; 1894–1968, Australian,
soprano)
Baillie (Dame Isobel; 1895–1983, Scottish,
soprano)
Barstow (Dame Josephine; 1940– , English,
soprano)

Bartoli (Cecilia; 1966– , Italian, mezzo-soprano)
Bocelli (Andrea; 1958– , Italian, tenor)
Caballé (Montserrat; 1933– , Spanish, soprano)
Collier (Maria; 1926–71, Australian, soprano)
Corelli (Franco; 1921–2003, Italian, tenor)
De Lucia (Fernando; 1860–1925, Italian, tenor)
Domingo (Placido; 1941– , Spanish, tenor)
Farrell (Eileen; 1920–2002, US, soprano)
Ferrier (Kathleen; 1912–53, English, contralto)
Garrett (Lesley; 1955– , English, soprano)
Hammond (Dame Joan; 1912–96, New Zealand/Australian, soprano)
Jurinac (Sena; 1921–2011, Yugoslav/Bosnian, soprano)
Lehmann (Lilli; 1848–1929, German, soprano)
Lehmann (Lotte; 1888–1976, US, soprano)
Migenes (Julia; 1945– , US, soprano)
Milanov (Zinka; 1906–89, Croatian, soprano)
Nilsson (Birgit; 1918–2005, Swedish, soprano)
Santley (Sir Charles; 1834–1922, English, baritone)
Smirnov (Dimitri; 1882–1944, Russian, tenor)
Stratas (Teresa; 1938– , Canadian, soprano)
Tebaldi (Renata; 1922–2004, Italian, soprano)
Tibbett (Lawrence; 1896–1960, US, baritone)
Tinsley (Pauline; 1928– , English, soprano)
Traubel (Helen; 1899–1972, US, soprano)
Vickers (Jon; 1926– , Canadian, tenor)

08 Anderson (Marian; 1902–93, US, contralto)
Berganza (Teresa; 1935– , Spanish, mezzo-soprano)
Bergonzi (Carlo; 1924– , Italian, tenor)
Björling (Jussi; 1911–60, Swedish, tenor)
Borgatti (Giuseppe; 1871–1950, Italian, tenor)
Borgioli (Dino; 1891–1960, Italian, tenor)
Bronhill (June; 1929–2005, Australian, soprano)
Brownlee (John; 1900–69, Australian, baritone)
Carreras (José; 1946– , Spanish, tenor)
Crossley (Ada; 1871–1929, Australian, contralto)
Dernesch (Helga; 1939– , Austrian, soprano)
Flagstad (Kirsten; 1895–1962, Norwegian, soprano)

Fremstad (Olive; 1871–1951, US, soprano)
Ghiaurov (Nicolai; 1929–2004, Bulgarian, bass)
Lablache (Luigi; 1794–1858, Italian, bass)
Lawrence (Marjorie; 1908–79, Australian, soprano)
Malibran (Marie; 1808–36, Spanish, mezzo-soprano)
Melchior (Lauritz; 1890–1973, Danish/US, tenor)
Piccaver (Alfred; 1884–1958, English, tenor)
Ponselle (Rosa; 1897–1981, US, soprano)
Schumann (Elisabeth; 1889–1952, US, soprano)
Seefried (Irmgard; 1919–88, Austrian, soprano)
Te Kanawa (Dame Kiri; 1944– , New Zealand, soprano)
Williams (Harold; 1893–1976, Australian, baritone)

09 Berberian (Cathy; 1925–83, US, soprano)
Brannigan (Owen; 1908–73, English, bass-baritone)
Chaliapin (Feodor; 1873–1938, Russian, bass)
Christoff (Boris; 1914–93, Bulgarian, bass-baritone)
della Casa (Lisa; 1919–2012, Swiss, soprano)
Del Monaco (Mario; 1915–82, Italian, tenor)
Forrester (Maureen; 1930–2010, Canadian, contralto)
Hendricks (Barbara; 1948– , US, soprano)
McCormack (John; 1884–1945, Irish/US, tenor)
McCracken (James; 1927–88, US, tenor)
Pavarotti (Luciano; 1935–2007, Italian, tenor)
Tomlinson (Sir John; 1946– , English, bass)

10 Battistini (Mattia; 1856–1928, Italian, baritone)
Galli-Curci (Amelita; 1882–1963, Italian, soprano)
Galli-Marie (Celestine; 1840–1905, French, mezzo-soprano)
Los Angeles (Victoria de; 1923–2005, Spanish, soprano)
Martinelli (Giovanni; 1885–1969, Italian, tenor)
Söderström (Elisabeth; 1927–2009, Swedish, soprano)
Sutherland (Dame Joan; 1926–2010, Australian, soprano)
Tetrazzini (Luisa; 1871–1940, Italian, soprano)

11 Schwarzkopf (Dame Elisabeth; 1915–2006, Austrian/British, soprano)

12 de los Angeles (Victoria; 1923–2005, Spanish, soprano)

Shirley-Quirk (John; 1931–   , English, bass-baritone)

13 Viardot-García (Pauline; 1821–1910, Spanish, mezzo-soprano)

14 Fischer-Dieskau (Dietrich; 1925–2012, German, baritone)

See also **Bartók, Béla; Beethoven, Ludwig van; Britten, Benjamin; Gilbert, Sir W S and Sullivan, Sir Arthur; Handel, George Frideric; libretto; Mozart, Wolfgang Amadeus; overture; Prokofiev, Sergei; Puccini, Giacomo; Purcell, Henry; Ravel, Maurice; Rossini, Gioacchino; Schubert, Franz; Shostakovich, Dmitri; Strauss, Richard; Stravinsky, Igor; Tchaikovsky, Pyotr Ilyich; Verdi, Giuseppe; Wagner, Richard**

optics

Optical instruments and devices include:

05 laser	telescope	stereocamera
06 camera	**10** binoculars	**13** film projector
07 sextant	microscope	**14** slide projector
08 spyglass	opera-glass	**15** magnifying glass
09 endoscope	theodolite	photomicroscope
periscope	**12** field-glasses	telescopic sight

See also **observatory**

orange

Orange varieties include:

04 mock	sweet	naartje	mandarin
Ruta	topaz	nartjie	
sour		satsuma	**09** Clockwork
05 blood	**06** bitter	Seville	mandarine
Jaffa	**07** cumquat	**08** bergamot	tangerine
navel	kumquat	bigarade	**10** clementine

Shades of orange include:

04 gold	**06** anatta	tawney	**08** croceate
05 amber	anatto	**07** annatta	croceous
chica	aurora	annatto	mandarin
chico	chicha	apricot	**09** bilirubin
coral	kamala	arnotto	tangerine
henna	kamela	jacinth	**13** cadmium yellow
tawny	kamila	nacarat	canthaxanthin
tenné	roucou	paprika	
tenny	salmon	saffron	

See also **fruit**

oratorio

Oratorios include:

04 *Saul* (1739, Handel)

06 *Elijah* (1846, Mendelssohn)
Esther (1732, Handel)
Joshua (1747, Handel)
Samson (1743, Handel)

Semele (1743, Handel)
St Paul (1836, Mendelssohn)

07 *Athalia* (1733, Handel)
Deborah (1733, Handel)
Jephtha (1751, Handel)

Messiah (1742, Handel)
Solomon (1749, Handel)
Susanna (1748, Handel)
08 Christus (1866, Liszt)
Hercules (1744, Handel)
Theodora (1749, Handel)
09 Christmas (1734, J S Bach)
10 Belshazzar (1744, Handel)
Oedipus Rex (1927, Stravinsky)

The Seasons (1801, Haydn)
11 The Creation (1798, Haydn)
13 Israel in Egypt (1739, Handel)
14 Alexander Balus (1747, Handel)
La Resurrezione (1708, Handel)
15 Judas Maccabaeus (1747, Handel)
16 Belshazzar's Feast (1931, Walton)
L'enfance du Christ (1854, Berlioz)

See also **music**; **musician**

orchestra

Common orchestra names include:

07 Chamber
08 National

Sinfonia
Symphony

12 Philharmonic

orchid

Orchids include:

03 bee
bog
bug
fen
fly
man
sun
04 blue
frog
king
kite
lady
moth
musk
wasp
05 burnt
clown
comet
ghost
giant
pansy

queen
tiger
tulip
06 lizard
monkey
spider
07 leopard
slipper
vanilla
08 crucifix
fragrant
military
09 birds-nest
chocolate
Christmas
coralroot
false musk
pyramidal
10 early marsh
late spider

small white
11 cockleshell
dancing lady
early purple
early spider
green-winged
12 black vanilla
heath spotted
Lapland marsh
narrow-leaved
one-leaved bog
western marsh
13 Chinese ground
common spotted
dense-flowered
elder-flowered
loose-flowered
orange blossom
southern marsh
15 lesser butterfly
violet birds-nest

order *see* **religious order**

orders of angel *see* **angel**

ore

Ores include:

03 wad (manganese)
04 wadd (manganese)
wadt (manganese)

06 bog ore (iron)
coltan (tantalum)
galena (lead)

rutile (titanium)
07 bauxite (aluminium)
bog iron (iron)

bornite (copper)
cuprite (copper)
iron ore (iron)
oligist (iron)
wood tin (tin)

08 beauxite (aluminium)
braunite (manganese)
calamine (zinc)
enargite (copper)
hematite (iron)
limonite (iron)
siderite (iron)
sinopite (iron)
taconite (iron)
tenorite (copper)

See also **mineral**

09 anglesite (lead)
blackband (iron)
coffinite (uranium)
haematite (iron)
hedyphane (lead)
ironstone (iron)
kidney ore (iron)
lodestone (iron)
magnetite (iron)
manganite (manganese)
morass ore (iron)
proustite (silver)
tantalite (tantalum)

10 erubescite (copper)
melaconite (copper)

peacock ore (copper)
sphalerite (zinc)
stephanite (silver)

11 cassiterite (tin)
chloanthite (nickel)
pyrargyrite (silver)
tetradymite (tellurium)

12 babingtonite (iron)
chalcopyrite (copper)
pyromorphite (lead)
tetrahedrite (copper)

13 copper pyrites (copper)
horseflesh ore (copper)
ruby silver ore (silver)

15 stilpnosiderite (iron)

organ

Organs include:

03 ear
eye

04 nose
skin

05 bowel
brain
colon
liver
lungs
lymph
penis
vulva

06 cervix
rectum
spleen
testes
throat
thymus
ureter

uterus
vagina

07 bladder
kidneys
ovaries
oviduct
pharynx
scrotum
stomach
tonsils
trachea
urethra

08 adenoids
appendix
bronchus
clitoris
pancreas
prostate
windpipe

09 diaphragm
pituitary
taste buds

10 epididymis
intestines
lymph nodes
oesophagus
spinal cord

11 gall bladder
vas deferens

12 hypothalamus
thymus glands
thyroid gland

13 adrenal glands

14 fallopian tubes
large intestine
small intestine

15 ejaculatory duct
seminal vesicles

See also **anatomy**

organ stop

Organ stops include:

04 echo
oboe
sext
tuba

05 dolce
gamba
quint

06 cornet
nasard

octave
tierce

07 bombard
bourdon
clarino
clarion
fagotto
mixture
piccolo

salicet
trumpet

08 carillon
crumhorn
diapason
diaphone
dulciana
gemshorn
krumhorn

register
waldhorn

09 fifteenth
furniture
krummhorn
principal

pyramidon
vox humana
waldflute

10 clarabella
fourniture
salicional

11 superoctave
voix céleste

12 sesquialtera

15 corno di bassetto

organism *see* **classification**

Organization of Petroleum Exporting Countries *see* OPEC

Orwell, George (1903–50)

Significant works include:

10 *Animal Farm* (1945)

11 *Burmese Days* (1934)

14 *Coming up for Air* (1939)
Critical Essays (1946)
Inside the Whale (1940)

17 *Homage to Catalonia* (1938)

18 *Nineteen Eighty-Four* (1949)

Shooting an Elephant (1936)
The Road to Wigan Pier (1937)

19 *A Clergyman's Daughter* (1935)
Such, Such Were The Joys (1953)

20 *The Lion and the Unicorn* (1941)

23 *Keep the Aspidistra Flying* (1936)

26 *Down and Out in Paris and London* (1933)

Significant characters include:

04 Hare (Dorothy)

05 Boxer
Jones (Farmer)
Julia
Moses
Smith (Winston)

06 Clover

Mollie
O'Brien

07 Bowling (George)
Whymper

08 Benjamin
Comstock (Gordon)
Napoleon

Old Major
Snowball
Squealer

09 Frederick (Mr)

10 Big Brother
Pilkington (Mr)

11 Charrington (Mr)

outlaw *see* **crime**

overture

Overtures include:

05 *Cuban* (Gershwin)
Herod (Hadley)

06 *Choral* (Beethoven)
Comedy (Harty)
Esther (d'Albert)
French (Lully)
Heroic (Panufnik)
Solemn (Sallinen)
Spring (Sibelius)
Thalia (Chadwick)
Tragic (Brahms)

07 *Adonais* (Chadwick)
Aladdin (Nielsen)
Euterpe (Chadwick)
Festive (Shostakovich)

Holiday (Carter)
Idyllic (Reznicek)
Jubilee (von Weber)
Leonora (Beethoven)
Maytime (Phillips)
Othello (Dvorak)

08 *Carnival* (Dvorak)
Columbus (Wagner)
Coriolan (Beethoven)
Hebrides (Mendelssohn)
Hyperion (Schubert)
In Autumn (Sibelius)
King Lear (Berlioz)
Romantic (Bruckner)
The Wasps (Vaughan Williams)
Waverley (Berlioz)

09 *Britannia* (Wagner)
  Children's (Quilter)
  Fairy Land (Mendelssohn)
  In Bohemia (Balakirev)
  Pinocchio (Toch)
  The Naiads (Schumann)

10 *Amid Nature* (Dvorak)
  In the South (Elgar)
  Salutatory (Myaskovsky)

11 *East and West* (Bach)
  'Fingal's Cave' (Mendelssohn)
  Pickwickian (Gal)
  Shéhérazade (Ravel)
  William Tell (Rossini)

12 *Fair Melusina* (Mendelssohn)

  In London Town (Elgar)
  Rip van Winkle (Chadwick)
  Street Corner (Rawsthorne)

13 *Shadowy Waters* (Seeger)
  The Wood-Nymphs (Sterndale Bennett)

14 *Eighteen Twelve* (Tchaikovsky)
  Eighteen-Twelve (Tchaikovsky)
  In Nature's Realm (Dvorak)
  In the Highlands (Loewe)
  In the Mountains (Berlioz)
  Romeo and Juliet (Tchaikovsky)
  Venus and Adonis (Blow)

15 *Comes Autumn Time* (Sowerby)
  Portsmouth Point (Walton)
  The Fair Melusina (Mendelssohn)

Oxford University *see* college

P

paint

Paints include:

03 oil	fabric	masonry	**09** distemper
04 matt	pastel	scumble	undercoat
oils	poster	stencil	whitewash
05 glaze	primer	varnish	**10** colourwash
gloss	**07** acrylic	**08** eggshell	**11** boot-topping
06 enamel	gouache	emulsion	watercolour
	lacquer		

Paintings, drawings and other images include:

04 *Fall* (1963; Bridget Riley)
Flag (1954; Jasper Johns)

05 *Manga* (15 vols, from 1814; Hokusai)
Pietà (1573–76; Titian)

07 *Bubbles* (1886; Sir John Everett Millais)
Erasmus (1523; Hans Holbein the Younger)
Olympia (1865; Édouard Manet)
Targets (from c.1954; Jasper Johns)
The Kiss (1907–08; Gustav Klimt)

08 *Guernica* (1937; Pablo Picasso)
L'Estaque (c.1888; Paul Cézanne)
Maja Nude (c.1797–1800; Goya)
Mona Lisa (c.1504; Leonardo da Vinci)
The Dream (1910; Henri Rousseau)

09 *Bacchanal* (c.1518; Titian)
Black Iris (1949; Georgia O'Keefe)
Haystacks (1890–91; Claude Monet)
Henry VIII (1698; Hans Holbein the Younger)
L'Escargot (1953; Henri Matisse)
Night Café (1888; Vincent Van Gogh)
Primavera (c.1478; Sandro Botticelli)
The Scream (1893; Edvard Munch)
The Tailor (16c; Giovanni Battista Moroni)

10 *Assumption* (1516–18; Titian)
Blue Horses (1911; Franz Marc)
Las Meninas (1655; Diego Velázquez)
Sunflowers (1888; Vincent Van Gogh)
The Angelus (1859; Jean François Millet)
The Hay Wain (1821; John Constable)

11 *100 Soup Cans* (1962; Andy Warhol)
A Shrimp Girl (c.1759; William Hogarth)
Crucifixion (1565; Tintoretto/17c; Diego Velázquez)
Limp Watches (1931; Salvador Dalí)
Maja Clothed (c.1797–1800; Goya)

Starry Night (1889; Vincent Van Gogh)
The Gleaners (1857; Jean François Millet)
View of Delft (c.1660; Jan Vermeer)
Water Lilies (1899–1926; Claude Monet)

12 *Autumn Rhythm* (1950; Jackson Pollock)
Beata Beatrix (1863; Dante Gabriel Rossetti)
Black on Black (1918; Alexander Rodchenko)
Los Caprichos (1799; Goya)
Peasant Dance (c.1568; Pieter Breughel)
Rape of Europa (1573–76; Titian/c.1632; Rembrandt)
The Scapegoat (1856; William Holman Hunt)
The Umbrellas (c.1881–84; Pierre Auguste Renoir)

13 *Composition VI* (1913; Wassily Kandinsky)
Man with a Glove (c.1520; Titian)
Sleeping Gypsy (1897; Henri Rousseau)
The Last Supper (completed c.1498; Leonardo da Vinci)
The Night Watch (1642; Rembrandt)

14 *A Rake's Progress* (1733–35; William Hogarth)
Random Sketches (15 vols, from 1814; Hokusai)
Rouen Cathedral (1892–94; Claude Monet)
Sistine Madonna (c.1512–13; Raphael)
The Ambassadors (1533; Hans Holbein the Younger)
The Card Players (1890–92; Paul Cézanne)
The Four Seasons (1660–64; Nicolas Poussin)
The Rokeby Venus (c.1651; Diego Velázquez)
The Turkish Bath (1859–62; Jean Auguste Dominique Ingres)

View on the Stour (1819; John Constable)

15 *Absinthe Drinker* (1859; Édouard Manet)
Commodore Keppel (1753; Sir Joshua Reynolds)
Flight into Egypt (1753; Giandomenico Tiepolo)
Madonna del Prato (c.1505; Raphael)
Marriage à la Mode (1743–45; William Hogarth)
The Annunciation (1333; Simone Martini/1423–24; Antonio Pisanello)
The Birth of Venus (c.1482–84; Sandro Botticelli)
The Charnel House (1945; Pablo Picasso)
The Death of Marat (1793; Jacques Louis David)
The Flagellation (c.1456–57; Piero della Francesca)
The Potato Eaters (1885; Vincent Van Gogh)
Triumph of Caesar (c.1486; Andrea Mantegna)

16 *Agony in the Garden* (c.1450; Andrea Mantegna/c.1465; Giovanni Bellini)
At the Moulin Rouge (1895; Henri de Toulouse-Lautrec)
Monarch of the Glen (1851; Sir Edwin Landseer)
The Artist's Mother (1871–72; James Abbott McNeill Whistler)
The Harvest Waggon (1767; Thomas Gainsborough)
The Last Judgement (1536–41; Michelangelo)
The Toilet of Venus (1647–51; Diego Velázquez)
The Watering Place (1777; Thomas Gainsborough)
Women in the Garden (1866–67; Claude Monet)

17 *Bacchus and Ariadne* (c.1523; Titian)
Campbell's Soup Cans (1962; Andy Warhol)
Child Holding a Dove (1902–04; Pablo Picasso)
Family of Charles IV (1800; Goya)
Grande Odalisque, La (1814; Jean Auguste Dominique Ingres)
Rain, Steam and Speed (1844; J M W Turner)
The Human Condition (1934/35; René Magritte)
The Jewish Cemetery (17c; Jacob van Ruisdael)
The School of Athens (1509–11; Raphael)
The Windmill at Wijk (c.1665; Jacob van Ruïsdael)

18 *36 Views of Mount Fuji* (c.1826–33; Hokusai)
Adoration of the Magi (1481–c.1482;

Leonardo da Vinci/1573; Paolo Veronese/1619; Diego Velázquez)
Salisbury Cathedral (1823; John Constable)
The Football Players (1908; Henri Rousseau)
The Light of the World (1854; William Holman Hunt)
The Menaced Assassin (1926; René Magritte)
The Mills of Gardanne (1885–86; Paul Cézanne)
The Raft of the Medusa (1819; Théodore Géricault)
The Seven Sacraments (1640s; Nicolas Poussin)
The Triumph of Venice (c.1535; Paolo Veronese)
White on White square (1915; Kazimir Malevich)
Woman with a Water Jug (c.1658–60; Jan Vermeer)

19 *Dancer Lacing Her Shoe* (c.1878; Edgar Degas)
Impression: Rising Sun (1872; Claude Monet)
Le Déjeuner sur l'herbe (1863; Édouard Manet)
Peasant Wedding Dance (1566; Pieter Breughel)
The Blinding of Samson (1636; Rembrandt)
The Boyhood of Raleigh (1870; Sir John Everett Millais)
The Fate of the Animals (1913; Franz Marc)
The Judgement of Paris (c.1914; Pierre Auguste Renoir)
The Laughing Cavalier (1624; Frans Hals)
Une Baignade, Asnières (1883–84; Georges Seurat)

20 *Broadway Boogie-Woogie* (1942–43; Piet Mondrian)
Crucifixion of St Peter (1542–50; Michelangelo)
Madonna of the Long Neck (c.1535; Parmigiano)
Sacred and Profane Love (c.1515; Titian)
St George and the Dragon (c.1460; Paolo Uccello)
The Fighting Téméraire (1839; J M W Turner)

21 *Assumption of the Virgin* (1577; El Greco)
Feast in the House of Levi (1573; Paolo Veronese)
Girl with a Pearl Earring (17c; Jan Vermeer)
Madonna of the Goldfinch (c.1505; Raphael)
Temptation of St Anthony (c.15–16c; Hieronymus Bosch)
The Burial of Count Orgaz (1586; El Greco)
Un Bar aux Folies-Bergère (1881–82; Édouard Manet)

22 *Impression: soleil levant* (1872; Claude Monet)
Les Demoiselles d'Avignon, (1906–07; Pablo Picasso)
The Marriage Feast at Cana (1562–63; Paolo Veronese)
The Old Woman Cooking Eggs (1618; Diego Velázquez)
The Persistence of Memory (1931; Salvador Dalí)
The Resurrection: Cookham (1922–27; Sir Stanley Spencer)

23 *On the Threshold of Liberty* (1930; René Magritte)
The Avenue at Middelharnis (1689; Meindert Hobbema)
The Girlhood of Mary Virgin (1849; Dante Gabriel Rossetti)
The Legend of the Holy Cross (c.1452–c.1466; Piero della Francesca)

24 *Between the Clock and the Bed* (1940; Edvard Munch)
Christ in the House of Martha (c.1618; Diego Velázquez)
Christ of St John of the Cross (1951; Salvador Dalí)
Courtyard of a House in Delft (1658; Pieter de Hooch)
Experiment with the Air Pump (1768; Joseph Wright)
The Anatomy Lesson of Dr Tulp (1632; Rembrandt)
Virgin and Child with St Anne (c.1501–12; Leonardo da Vinci)

25 *Madonna of Burgomaster Meyer* (1526; Hans Holbein the Younger)

The Return of the Prodigal Son (1669; Rembrandt)
The Rev Robert Walker Skating (1784; Henry Raeburn)

26 *Christ Reproved by His Parents* (1342; Simone Martini)
The Garden of Earthly Delights (c.15–16c; Hieronymus Bosch)
The Resurrection: Port Glasgow (1950; Sir Stanley Spencer)

27 *Sarah Siddons as the Tragic Muse* (1784; Sir Joshua Reynolds)
The Adoration of the Golden Calf (c.1560; Tintoretto/c.1635; Nicolas Poussin)

28 *Christ in the House of His Parents* (1850; Sir John Everett Millais)
King Cophetua and the Beggar Maid (1884; Sir Edward Burne-Jones)
Regents of the Old Men's Alms House (1664; Frans Hals)

30 *L'Embarquement pour l'île de Cythère* (1717; Jean-Antoine Watteau)

32 *The Battle of the Lapiths and Centaurs* (1486; Piero de Cosimo)

34 *Joshua Commanding the Sun to Stand Still* (1816; John Martin)

41 *Arrangement in Grey and Black: the Artist's Mother* (1871–72; James Abbott McNeill Whistler)

44 *Reverend Robert Walker Skating on Duddingston Loch* (1784; Henry Raeburn)

50 *The Banquet of the Officers of the St George Militia Company* (Frans Hals)

Painters, printmakers and other artists include:

03 Arp (Jean; 1887–1966, Alsatian)
Dix (Otto; 1891–1969, German)
Ray (Man; 1890–1976, US)

04 Bell (Vanessa; 1879–1961, English)
Dalí (Salvador; 1904–89, Spanish)
Doré (Gustave; 1832–83, French)
Dufy (Raoul; 1877–1953, French)
Emin (Tracey; 1963– , English)
Eyck (Jan van; c.1389–1441, Flemish)
Goya (Francisco de; 1746–1828, Spanish)
Gris (Juan; 1887–1927, Spanish)
Hals (Frans; c.1580–1666, Dutch)
Hunt (Holman; 1827–1910, English)
John (Augustus; 1878–1961, Welsh)
John (Gwen; 1876–1939, Welsh)
Kent (William; 1684–1748, English)
Klee (Paul; 1879–1940, Swiss)
Lely (Sir Peter; 1618–1680, British)

Long (Richard; 1945– , English)
Marc (Franz; 1880–1916, German)
Miró (Joán; 1893–1983, Spanish)
Nash (Paul; 1889–1946, English)
Watt (Alison; 1965– , Scottish)

05 Bacon (Francis; 1909–92, British)
Bakst (Léon; 1866–1924, Russian)
Blake (Peter; 1932– , English)
Blake (William; 1757–1827, English)
Bosch (Hieronymus; c.1450–1516, Dutch)
Brown (Ford Madox; 1821–93, British)
Burra (Edward; 1905–76, English)
Clark (Kenneth, Lord; 1903–83, English)
Corot (Camille; 1796–1875, French)
David (Jacques Louis; 1748–1825, French)
Degas (Edgar; 1834–1917, French)
Dürer (Albrecht; 1471–1528, German)
Ernst (Max; 1891–1976, German)

Freud (Lucian; 1922–2011, British)
Gorky (Arshile; 1905–48, US)
Greco (El; 1541–1614, Spanish)
Grosz (George; 1893–1959, US)
Hirst (Damien; 1965– , English)
Homer (Winslow; 1836–1910, US)
Hooch (Pieter de; c.1629–1684, Dutch)
Johns (Jasper; 1930– , US)
Kahlo (Frida; 1907–54, Mexican)
Kitaj (R B; 1932–2007, US)
Klimt (Gustav; 1862–1918, Austrian)
Kline (Franz; 1910–62, US)
Léger (Fernand; 1881–1955, French)
Lewis (Wyndham; 1882–1957, English)
Lippi (Filippino; c.1458–1504, Italian)
Lippi (Fra Filippo; c.1406–69, Italian)
Lowry (L S; 1887–1976, English)
Lucas (Sarah; 1962– , English)
Manet (Édouard; 1832–83, French)
Monet (Claude; 1840–1926, French)
Mucha (Alphonse; 1860–1939, Czech)
Munch (Edvard; 1863–1944, Norwegian)
Nolan (Sir Sidney; 1917–92, Australian)
Peake (Mervyn; 1911–68, English)
Piper (John; 1903–92, English)
Riley (Bridget; 1931– , English)
Sarto (Andrea del; 1486–1531, Italian)

06 Braque (Georges; 1882–1963, French)
Bratby (John; 1928–92, English)
Cadell (Francis C B; 1883–1937, Scottish)
Claude (Claude Le Lorrain; 1600–82,
  French)
Derain (André; 1880–1954, French)
Escher (Maurits Cornelis; 1898–1972,
  Dutch)
Fuseli (Henry; 1741–1825, British)
Giotto (di Bondone; c.1267–1337, Italian)
Howson (Peter; 1958– , Scottish)
Gordon (Douglas; 1967– , Scottish)
Hunter (Leslie; 1879–1931, Scottish)
Ingres (Jean; 1780–1867, French)
Jarman (Derek; 1942–94, English)
Knight (Dame Laura; 1877–1970, English)
Lavery (Sir John; 1856–1941, British)
Mabuse (Jan; c.1470–1532, Flemish)
Marini (Marino; 1901–80, Italian)
Martin (John; 1789–1854, English)
Massys (Quentin; c.1466–c.1531, Flemish)
Millet (Jean François; 1814–75, French)
Morley (Malcolm; 1931– , English)
Moroni (Giovanni Battista; 1525–78, Italian)
Morris (William; 1834–96, English)
Newman (Barnett; 1905–70, US)
Orozco (José; 1883–1949, Mexican)
Palmer (Samuel; 1805–81, English)
Peploe (Samuel John; 1871–1935, Scottish)
Pisano (Nicola; c.1225–c.1284, Italian)
Ramsay (Allan; 1713–84, Scottish)

Renoir (Pierre Auguste; 1841–1919, French)
Rivera (Diego; 1886–1957, Mexican)
Rothko (Mark; 1903–70, US)
Rubens (Peter Paul; 1577–1640, Flemish)
Scarfe (Gerald; 1936– , English)
Searle (Ronald; 1920–2011, English)
Seurat (Georges; 1859–91, French)
Sisley (Alfred; 1839–99, French)
Strong (Sir Roy; 1935– , English)
Stubbs (George; 1724–1806, English)
Tanguy (Yves; 1900–55, US)
Tissot (James; 1836–1902, French)
Titian (c.1488–1576, Venetian)
Turner (J M W; 1775–1851, English)
Warhol (Andy; 1928–87, US)
Wilkie (Sir David; 1785–1841, Scottish)
Wright (Joseph; 1734–97, English)

07 Attwell (Mabel Lucie; 1879–1964, English)
Bellini (Giovanni; c.1430–1516, Venetian)
Bonnard (Pierre; 1867–1947, French)
Boucher (François; 1703–70, French)
Cassatt (Mary; 1844–1926, US)
Cézanne (Paul; 1839–1906, French)
Chagall (Marc; 1887–1985, French)
Chapman (Dinos; 1962– , English)
Chapman (Jake; 1966– , English)
Chirico (Giorgio de; 1888–1978, Italian)
Christo (1935– , US)
Cimabué (Giovanni; c.1240–c.1302, Italian)
Courbet (Gustave; 1819–77, French)
Cranach (Lucas, the Elder; 1472–1553,
  German)
Daumier (Honoré; 1808–78, French)
Delvaux (Paul; 1897–1994, Belgian)
Duchamp (Marcel; 1887–1968, US)
El Greco (1541–1614, Spanish)
Gauguin (Paul; 1848–1903, French)
Guthrie (Sir James; 1859–1930, Scottish)
Hobbema (Meindert; 1638–1709, Dutch)
Hockney (David; 1937– , English)
Hodgkin (Sir Howard; 1932– , English)
Hogarth (William; 1697–1764, English)
Hokusai (Katsushika; 1760–1849, Japanese)
Holbein (Hans, the Younger; 1497–1543,
  German)
Keating (Tom; 1917–84, English)
Martini (Simone; c.1284–1344, Italian)
Matisse (Henri; 1869–1954, French)
Millais (Sir John Everett; 1829–96, English)
Morisot (Berthe; 1841–95, French)
O'Keeffe (Georgia; 1887–1986, US)
Pevsner (Antoine; 1886–1962, French)
Picabia (Francis; 1879–1953, French)
Picasso (Pablo; 1881–1973, Spanish)
Pollock (Jackson; 1912–56, US)
Poussin (Nicolas; 1594–1665, French)
Rackham (Arthur; 1867–1939, English)
Raeburn (Sir Henry; 1756–1823, Scottish)

Raphael (Raffaello Sanzio; 1483–1520, Italian)
Sargent (John Singer; 1856–1925, US)
Saville (Jenny; 1970– , English)
Schiele (Egon; 1890–1918, Austrian)
Sickert (Walter; 1860–1942, British)
Spencer (Sir Stanley; 1891–1959, English)
Tenniel (Sir John; 1820–1914, English)
Thurber (James; 1894–1961, US)
Tiepolo (Giovanni; 1696–1770, Italian)
Uccello (Paolo; c.1396–1475, Florentine)
Utrillo (Maurice; 1883–1955, French)
Van Dyck (Sir Anthony; 1599–1641, Flemish)
Vandyke (Sir Anthony; 1599–1641, Flemish)
van Eyck (Jan; c.1389–1441, Flemish)
Van Gogh (Vincent; 1853–90, Dutch)
Vermeer (Jan; 1632–75, Dutch)
Watteau (Antoine; 1684–1721, French)
Wearing (Gillian; 1963– , English)

08 Angelico (Fra; c.1387–1455, Italian)
Annigoni (Pietro; 1910–88, Italian)
Auerbach (Frank; 1931– , British)
Breughel (Jan, the Elder; 1568–1625, Flemish)
Breughel (Pieter, the Younger; c.1564–1638, Flemish)
Brueghel (Jan, the Elder; 1568–1625, Flemish)
Brueghel (Pieter, the Younger; c.1564–1638, Flemish)
Campbell (Steven; 1953–2007, Scottish)
cummings (e e; 1894–1962, US)
Delaunay (Robert; 1885–1941, French)
Dubuffet (Jean; 1901–85, French)
Goncourt (Edmond de; 1822–96, French)
Gossaert (Jan; c.1470–1532, Flemish)
Hamilton (Richard; 1922–2011, English)
Hilliard (Nicholas; c.1547–1619, English)
Landseer (Sir Edwin; 1802–73, English)
Magritte (René; 1898–1967, Belgian)
Malevich (Kasimir; 1878–1935, Russian)
Mantegna (Andrea; 1431–1506, Italian)
Masaccio (1401–c.1428, Italian)
Mondrian (Piet; 1872–1944, Dutch)
Munnings (Sir Alfred; 1878–1959, English)
Perugino (Pietro; c.1450–1523, Italian)
Piranesi (Giambattista; 1720–78, Italian)
Pissarro (Camille; 1830–1903, French)
Reynolds (Sir Joshua; 1723–92, English)
Rossetti (Dante Gabriel; 1828–82, English)
Rousseau (Henri, 'Le Douanier'; 1844–1910, French)
Rousseau (Théodore; 1812–67, French)
Ruïsdael (Jacob van; c.1628–1682, Dutch)
Ruysdael (Jacob van; c.1628–1682, Dutch)
Topolski (Feliks; 1907–89, British)
Vasarely (Viktor; 1908–97, French)

Veronese (Paolo Caliari; c.1528–88, Venetian)
Vlaminck (Maurice de; 1876–1958, French)
Whistler (James McNeill; 1834–1903, US)

09 Beardsley (Aubrey; 1872–98, English)
Canaletto (1697–1768, Italian)
Carpaccio (Vittore; c.1455–1522, Italian)
Constable (John; 1776–1837, English)
Correggio (Antonio Allegri da; c.1494–1534, Italian)
De Kooning (Willem; 1904–97, US)
Delacroix (Eugène; 1798–1863, French)
Fergusson (John Duncan; 1874–1961, Scottish)
Fragonard (Jean; 1732–1806, French)
Friedrich (Caspar David; 1774–1840, German)
Géricault (Théodore; 1791–1824, French)
Giorgione (c.1478–1511, Italian)
Greenaway (Kate; 1846–1901, English)
Greenaway (Peter; 1942– , English)
Grünewald (Matthias; c.1475–1528, German)
Hiroshige (Ando; 1797–1858, Japanese)
Kandinsky (Wassily; 1866–1944, French)
Kokoschka (Oskar; 1886–1980, British)
Lancaster (Sir Osbert; 1908–86, English)
Nicholson (Ben; 1894–1982, English)
Nollekens (Joseph; 1737–1823, English)
Pisanello (Antonio; 1395–1455, Italian)
Rembrandt (van Rijn; 1606–69, Dutch)
Rodchenko (Aleksandr; 1891–1956, Russian)
Velázquez (Diego; 1599–1660, Spanish)
Vettriano (Jack; 1951– , Scottish)

10 Alma-Tadema (Sir Lawrence; 1836–1912, British)
Botticelli (Sandro; 1445–1510, Florentine)
Burne-Jones (Sir Edward; 1833–98, English)
Caravaggio (Michelangelo Merisi da; 1573–1610, Italian)
Caravaggio (Polidoro da; c.1492–1543, Italian)
Giacometti (Alberto; 1901–66, Swiss)
Modigliani (Amedeo; 1884–1920, Italian)
Motherwell (Robert; 1915–91, US)
Parmigiano (Girolamo Mazzola; 1503–40, Italian)
Sutherland (Graham; 1903–80, English)
Tintoretto (1518–94, Italian)

11 Domenichino (1581–1641, Italian)
Ghirlandaio (Domenico; 1449–94, Italian)

12 Bairnsfather (Bruce; 1888–1959, British)
Fantin-Latour (Henri; 1836–1904, French)
Gainsborough (Thomas; 1727–88, English)
Lichtenstein (Roy; 1923–97, US)

Michelangelo (1475–1564, Italian)
13 Piero di Cosimo (c.1462–c.1521, Italian)
14 Andrea del Sarto (1486–1531, Italian)
Claude Lorraine (1600–82, French)

Lucas Van Leyden (1494–1533, Dutch)
15 Leonardo da Vinci (1452–1519, Italian)
Toulouse-Lautrec (Henri de; 1864–1901, French)

Painting terms include:

04 icon
tint
tone
wash

05 bloom
brush
easel
gesso
mural
paint
pietà
secco
tondo

06 canvas
fresco
frieze
primer
sketch

07 atelier
aureola
aureole
cartoon
collage
diptych
drawing
facture
gallery
gouache

impasto
limning
montage
palette
pastels
paysage
picture
pigment
scumble
sfumato
stipple
tempera
08 abstract
aquatint
bleeding
charcoal
esquisse
fixative
frottage
hard edge
hatching
oil paint
paintbox
pastoral
portrait
seascape
skyscape
thinners
triptych

vignette
09 alla prima
aquarelle
brushwork
capriccio
encaustic
flat brush
grisaille
grotesque
landscape
lay figure
mahlstick
maulstick
miniature
oil colour
polyptych
scumbling
sgraffito
still life

10 art gallery
craquelure
dead colour
figurative
hair-pencil
monochrome
paintbrush
pentimento
pochade box

round brush
sable brush
silhouette
turpentine
11 canvas board
chiaroscuro
composition
fête galante
foreshorten
found object
illusionism
objet trouvé
oil painting
perspective
pointillism
trompe l'oeil
watercolour
12 anamorphosis
brush strokes
camera lucida
filbert brush
illustration
palette knife
pencil sketch
13 fête champêtre
genre painting
underpainting
14 foreshortening

See also **art**; **picture**

palace

Palaces include:

05 Pitti (Italy)
Royal (The Netherlands)
Savoy (England)

06 Louvre (France)
Mirror (Iran)
Potala (Tibet)
Winter (Russia)

07 Bishop's (England)
Crystal (England)
People's (Scotland)
Vatican (Vatican City)

08 Alhambra (Spain)
Blenheim (England)
Borghese (Italy)

Imperial (Japan)
National (Portugal)
St James's (England)

09 Episcopal (Portugal)
Maharaja's (India)
Sans Souci (Germany)
Tuileries (France)
Whitehall (England)

10 Buckingham (England)
El Escorial (Spain)
Fishbourne (England)
Generalife (Spain)
Kensington (England)
Linlithgow (Scotland)
President's (Poland)

Qusayr Amra (Jordan)
Quseir Amra (Jordan)
Schönbrunn (Austria)
Versailles (France)
11 Archbishop's (Portugal)
Umaid Bhawan (India)
Westminster (England)

13 Forbidden City (China)
Holyrood House (Scotland)
Royal Pavilion (England)
Tower of London (England)
Windsor Castle (England)
14 Charlottenburg (Germany)
15 Palais de l'Elysée (France)

palaeontology

Palaeontologists include:

04 Cope (Edward Drinker; 1840–97, US)
Hall (James; 1811–98, US)
Owen (Sir Richard; 1804–92, English)

05 Boule (Marcellin; 1861–1942, French)
Broom (Robert; 1866–1951, South African)
Dollo (Louis; 1857–1931, Belgian)
Foote (Michael J; 1963–   , US)
Gould (Stephen Jay; 1941–2002, US)
Leidy (Joseph; 1823–91, US)
Marsh (O C; 1831–99, US)
Romer (Alfred Sherwood; 1894–1973, US)

06 Dubois (Eugène; 1858–1940, Dutch)
Forbes (Edward; 1815–54, British)
Foulke (William Parker; 1816–65, US)
Hallam (Tony; 1933–   , English)
Kurtén (Björn; 1924–88, Finnish)
Lartet (Édouard; 1801–71, French)
Leakey (Louis; 1903–72, British)

Leakey (Mary; 1913–96, English)
Leakey (Richard; 1944–   , Kenyan)
Osborn (Henry Fairfield; 1857–1935, US)
Zittel (Karl von; 1839–1904, German)

07 Colbert (Edwin 'Ned'; 1905–2001, US)
Mantell (Gideon; 1790–1852, English)
Simpson (George Gaylord; 1902–84, US)

08 Eldredge (Niles; 1943–   , US)
Falconer (Hugh; 1808–65, Scottish)
Guettard (Jean Étienne; 1715–86, French)
Johanson (Donald; 1943–   , US)
Sepkoski (J John; 1948–99, US)

09 Parkinson (James; 1755–1824, English)
Seilacher (Adolf 'Dolf'; 1925–   , German)

10 Williamson (William Crawford; 1816–95, English)

11 Schindewolf (Otto Heinrich; 1896–1971, German)

Terms used in palaeontology include:

03 eon
era
04 Lucy
06 Eocene
Eryops
fossil
ice age
period
tar pit
07 Baltica
bivalve
carpoid
crinoid
hominid
ichnite
Java man
mammoth
Miocene
mollusc
Neogene
Pangaea
Permian
protist

remains
saurian
Vendian
08 agnathan
ammonite
ammonoid
bacteria
Cambrian
Cenozoic
conodont
cromlech
cruziana
Devonian
dinosaur
echinoid
Eoraptor
Gondwana
Jurassic
mastodon
Mesozoic
nautilus
Pliocene
Ponginae

primeval
sauropod
Silurian
skeleton
Tertiary
theropod
Triassic
09 acritarch
arthropod
belemnite
bryophyte
chondrite
coccolith
coprolite
Cro-Magnon
cubichnia
Ediacaran
eukaryote
eumetazoa
fodichnia
homalozoa
ichnolite
ichnology

Iguanodon
Lepidotes
marsupial
Oligocene
ostraderm
Oviraptor
Peking man
placoderm
pterosaur
reliquiae
repichnia
Rhabdodon
sea urchin
subfossil
taphonomy
thecodont
therapsid
trilobite

10 Allosaurus
Archeozoic
Barosaurus
bilaterian
bipedalism
brachiopod
Cretaceous
Diplodocus
echinoderm
graptolite
nanofossil
Nodosaurus
Ordovician
ornithopod
Palaeocene
Palaeogene

Palaeozoic
pascichnia
prokaryote
protohuman
Pteranodon
Quaternary
saurischia
Utahraptor
vertebrate

11 acanthodian
Apatosaurus
Archaeozoic
Archosaurus
asteriacite
ceratopsian
chlorophyte
guide fossil
Hadrosaurus
Homo erectus
Homo habilis
Homo sapiens
ichnofossil
index fossil
macrofossil
microfossil
Microraptor
Neanderthal
Phanerozoic
Precambrian
Protocardia
Stegosaurus
titanothere
trace fossil
Triceratops

12 Ankylosaurus
Burgess shale
chalicothere
Gondwanaland
Homo ergaster
invertebrate
Megalosaurus
palaeobotany
Palaeolithic
Plesiosaurus
stromatolite
type locality
Velociraptor

13 Archaeopteryx
Brachiosaurus
Carboniferous
ornithischian
palaeobiology
palaeoecology
palaeontology
palaeozoology
phytoplankton
Pterodactylus
sedimentology
Thalassinoide
Tyrannosaurus
Zephyrosaurus

14 Giganotosaurus

15 Argentinosaurus
biostratigraphy
Homo rudolfensis
lophotrochozoan
palaeomagnetism

See also **fossil**; **geology**

palm

Palms include:

03 dum
ita
oil
wax

04 atap
coco
date
doom
doum
hemp
nipa
sago

05 areca
assai
bussu

macaw
nikau
peach
royal
Sabal
sugar
toddy

06 buriti
cohune
corozo
Elaeis
gomuti
gru-gru
jupati
kentia

kittul
miriti
raffia
Raphia
rattan
troely

07 babassu
cabbage
calamus
coconut
coquito
Corypha
Euterpe
moriche
palmyra

paxiuba
pupunha
talipat
talipot
troelie
troolie

08 carnauba
coco-tree
date-tree
groo-groo
palmetto

10 Chamaerops

12 chiquichiqui
Washingtonia

15 cabbage-palmetto

pantomime

Pantomimes include:

07 *Aladdin*
   Cinders
08 *Peter Pan*
   Rapunzel
09 *Pinocchio*
   Robin Hood
10 *Cinderella*
11 *Mother Goose*
   Old King Cole
   Puss in Boots
12 *The Snow Queen*
14 *Babes in the Wood*
   Robinson Crusoe
   Sleeping Beauty
   Treasure Island
15 *Hansel and Gretel*
   Rumpelstiltskin

Sinbad the Sailor
The Swan Princess
17 *Alice in Wonderland*
   Beauty and the Beast
18 *Jack the Giant Killer*
   The Three Musketeers
19 *Jack and the Beanstalk*
   Little Red Riding Hood
21 *The Pied Piper of Hamelin*
24 *Dick Whittington and His Cat*
   Stromboli the Puppet Master
25 *Ali Baba and the Forty Thieves*
   Robin Hood and the Singing Nun
26 *Goldilocks and the Three Bears*
   Snow White and the Seven Dwarfs
28 *Alice's Adventures in Wonderland*

Pantomime characters include:

04 Jack *(Babes in the Wood)*
   Jack *(Jack and the Beanstalk)*
   Jill *(Babes in the Wood)*
05 Giant *(Jack and the Beanstalk)*
   Wendy *(Peter Pan)*
06 Beauty *(Beauty and the Beast)*
   Gretel *(Hansel and Gretel)*
   Hansel *(Hansel and Gretel)*
07 Buttons *(Cinderella)*
   Dandini *(Cinderella)*
   Emperor *(Aladdin)*
   King Rat *(Dick Whittington)*
08 Abanazer *(Aladdin)*
   Idle Jack *(Dick Whittington)*
   Peter Pan *(Peter Pan)*
   The Beast *(Beauty and the Beast)*
09 Alan-a-Dale *(Babes in the Wood/Robin Hood)*
   Friar Tuck *(Babes in the Wood/Robin Hood)*
   Robin Hood *(Babes in the Wood/Robin Hood)*
10 Billy Goose *(Mother Goose)*
   Cinderella *(Cinderella)*
   Little John *(Babes in the Wood/Robin Hood)*
   Maid Marian *(Babes in the Wood/Robin Hood)*
   Maid Marion *(Babes in the Wood/Robin Hood)*
   Prince John *(Babes in the Wood/Robin Hood)*

Tinkerbell *(Peter Pan)*
11 Baron Hardup *(Cinderella)*
   Captain Hook *(Peter Pan)*
   Daisy the Cow *(Jack and the Beanstalk)*
   Jack's Mother *(Jack and the Beanstalk)*
   King Richard *(Babes in the Wood/Robin Hood)*
   Mother Goose *(Mother Goose)*
   Simple Simon *(Jack and the Beanstalk)*
   Will Scarlet *(Babes in the Wood/Robin Hood)*
12 Pantomime Cow
   Principal Boy
   Sarah the Cook *(Dick Whittington)*
   Widow Twankey *(Aladdin)*
   Will Scarlett *(Babes in the Wood/Robin Hood)*
   Wishee Washee *(Aladdin)*
13 Principal Girl
14 Baroness Hardup *(Cinderella)*
   Fairy Godmother *(Cinderella/Sleeping Beauty)*
   Pantomime Horse
   Prince Charming *(Cinderella/Sleeping Beauty)*
   Princess Aurora *(Sleeping Beauty)*
   Slave of the Ring *(Aladdin)*
   The Ugly Sisters *(Cinderella)*
15 Alice Fitzwarren *(Dick Whittington)*
   Princess Jasmine *(Aladdin)*
   Rumpelstiltskin *(Rumpelstiltskin)*

See also **mythology**

paper

Papers include:

03 art	**05** crêpe	vellum	recycled
rag	graph	**07** manilla	wrapping
04 bank	sugar	papyrus	**09** cardboard
bond	**06** carbon	tracing	cartridge
card	manila	writing	parchment
note	silver	**08** acid-free	**10** pasteboard
rice	tissue	blotting	**11** greaseproof
wall	toilet	handmade	

Paper sizes include:

02 A0	**04** demy	legal	**08** elephant
A1	post	royal	foolscap
A2	pott	**06** letter	imperial
A3	**05** atlas	medium	**09** antiquary
A4	crown	quarto	music-demy
A5	folio	**07** emperor	**10** super-royal
03 pot	jésus		

See also **Japan**

Paralympic Games

Summer Paralympic venues:

04 Rome (Italy; 1960)

05 Seoul (South Korea; 1988)
Tokyo (Japan; 1964)

06 Arnhem (The Netherlands; 1980)
Athens (Greece; 2004)
London (UK; 2012)
Sydney (Australia; 2000)

07 Atlanta (USA; 1996)

Beijing (China; 2008)
New York (USA; 1984)
Tel Aviv (Israel; 1968)
Toronto (Canada; 1976)

09 Barcelona (Spain; 1992)

10 Heidelberg (West Germany; 1972)

15 Stoke Mandeville (UK; 1952/1984)

Summer Paralympic events include:

04 epée	marathon		4×100m relay
foil	road race		4×400m relay
judo	shooting		table tennis
05 sabre	swimming		**12** 10m air pistol
06 boccia	**09** 100 metres		1km time trial
discus	200 metres		50m butterfly
rowing	400 metres		50m free rifle
07 archery	800 metres		50m freestyle
cycling	athletics		double sculls
javelin	coxed four		powerlifting
sailing	**10** 1500 metres		single sculls
shot put	3000 metres		tandem sprint
08 dressage	5000 metres		**13** 100m butterfly
goalball	equestrian		100m freestyle
high jump	pentathlon		200m freestyle
keelboat	triple jump		400m freestyle
long jump	volleyball		50m backstroke
	11 10,000 metres		50m free pistol

50m sport rifle	football 5-a-side	**15** 50m breaststroke
14 100m backstroke	football 7-a-side	wheelchair rugby
25m sport pistol	tandem road race	

Winter Paralympic venues:

05 Geilo (Norway; 1980)
Turin (Italy; 2006)

06 Nagano (Japan; 1998)

09 Innsbruck (Austria; 1984/1988)
Vancouver (Canada; 2010)

11 Albertville (France; 1992)
Lillehammer (Norway; 1994)

12 Örnsköldsvik (Sweden; 1976)
Salt Lake City (USA; 2002)

Winter Paralympic events include:

05 relay	**10** sled hockey	Nordic skiing
06 slalom	**11** giant slalom	sledge hockey
super-G	**12** alpine skiing	**13** short distance
08 biathlon	cross-country	**14** middle distance
downhill	long distance	**15** ice sledge hockey

Paralympic athletes include:

04 Toit (Natalie du; 1984– , South African)
Weir (David; 1979– , English)

05 Innes (Caroline; 1974– , Scottish)

06 Holmes (Chris; 1971– , English)

07 Jackson (Simon; 1972– , English)
McEleny (Maggi; 1965– , Scottish)
Sauvage (Louise; 1973– , Australian)

08 Anderson (James 'Jim the Swim'; 1963– , Scottish)
Simmonds (Eleanor; 1994– , English)
Thatcher (Noel; 1966– , English)

09 Tesoriero (Paula; 1975– , New Zealand)

12 Grey-Thompson (Dame Tanni; 1969– , Welsh)

parasite

Parasites include:

03 bot	**07** argulus	strongyl	trematode
ked	ascarid	tapeworm	**10** Guinea worm
nit	ascaris	toxocara	Plasmodium
04 bott	Babesia	whipworm	threadworm
chat	bonamia	**09** Bilharzia	**11** biting louse
crab	cestode	bird louse	sarcocystis
flea	chalcid	crab louse	scabies mite
kade	chigger	fish louse	trichomonad
mite	Giardia	fluke-worm	trypanosome
tick	pinworm	head louse	**12** echinococcus
05 fluke	**08** hookworm	pediculus	ectoparasite
06 chigoe	itch-mite	roundworm	endoparasite
chigre	lungworm	sheep tick	semiparasite
cootie	nematode	sporozoan	**13** hyperparasite
jigger	sheep ked	strongyle	

parasol *see* **umbrella**

Paris

Paris districts include:

05 Bercy
Opéra
06 Étoile
Louvre
Marais
07 Pigalle
08 Bastille
Chaillot
Left Bank
Sorbonne

09 Chinatown
La Défense
Les Halles
Right Bank
Trocadero
Tuileries
10 Belleville
La Villette
Montmartre
Rive Droite
Rive Gauche

Tour Eiffel
11 Batignolles
12 Latin Quarter
Les Invalides
Montparnasse
Place d'Italie
13 Champs Élysées
Quartier Latin
15 Butte-aux-cailles
Neuilly-sur-Seine

Paris streets include:

07 Pigalle
09 Port Royal
Rue de Buci
Rue de Rome
10 Avenue Foch
Quai d'Orsay
Rue d'Alésia
11 Rue Dauphine
Rue de Clichy
Rue de Rennes
Rue de Rivoli

Rue de Sèvres
Rue des Levis
Rue Mazarine
Rue St-Honoré
12 périphérique
Place d'Italie
Place Vendôme
Quai de la Gare
Quai du Louvre
Quai Voltaire
Rue de Paradis

Rue François I
Rue St-Antoine
13 Avenue George V
Place du Tertre
Rue des Rosiers
Rue Mouffetard
14 Place des Vosges
Rue de Chevalier
Rue de Richelieu
15 Avenue Montaigne
Quai d'Austerlitz

Paris landmarks include:

04 Dôme
05 Géode
Seine
06 Bourse
Louvre
07 Pyramid
08 Bastille
Panthéon
Pont Neuf
Sorbonne
09 Beaubourg
Bon Marché
Invalides
Madeleine
Notre-Dame
Orangerie
St-Severin
St-Sulpice
Trocadero
Tuileries
10 Carnavalet
Gare du Nord

Île St-Louis
Longchamps
Montmartre
Musée Rodin
Sacré Coeur
11 Champ de Mars
Eiffel Tower
Grande Arche
Grand Palais
Île de la Cité
Moulin Rouge
Musée d'Orsay
Palais Royal
Parc Monceau
Petit Palais
Pont des Arts
12 Conciergerie
Église du Dôme
Hôtel de Rohan
Hôtel de Ville
Musée de Cluny
Musée Picasso
Opéra Garnier
Porte Maillot

13 Arc de Triomphe
Champs-Élysées
Les Catacombes
Napoleon's tomb
Opéra Bastille
Pont Alexandre
14 Arènes de Lutèce
Bois de Boulogne
École Militaire
Forum des Halles
Hôtel de Soubise
Maison de Balzac
Palais du Louvre
Parc des Princes
Parc Montsouris
Place de l'Étoile
Pompidou Centre
Sainte Chapelle
15 Bois de Vincennes
Cité des Sciences
Le Stade de France
Musée Carnavalet
Palais de Justice

park

Park types include:

03 car	**06** oyster	hunting	**09** adventure
fun	pocket	science	amusement
04 ball	public	terrain	**10** industrial
deer	retail	trailer	skateboard
wind	safari	**08** business	technology
05 coach	**07** caravan	national	vest-pocket
theme	country	research	zoological
water	holiday	wildlife	**14** multistorey car

Parks include:

04 Hyde (England/Australia)
West (South Africa)

05 Green (England)
Güell (Spain)
Kings (Australia)

06 Albert (Australia)
Domain (Australia)

07 Battery (USA)

Central (USA)
Phoenix (Ireland)
Regent's (England)
Stanley (Canada)

08 Gramercy (USA)
Richmond (England)
St James's (England)
Victoria (Australia)

09 Battersea (England)

Tuileries (France)

10 Tiergarten (Germany)

11 Champ de Mars (France)
Vienna Woods (Austria)

13 Madison Square (USA)
Tivoli Gardens (Denmark)

14 Bois de Boulogne (France)

15 Bois de Vincennes (France)

National parks in the UK:

06 Exmoor (1954; moorland/coastline)

08 Dartmoor (1951; moorland)

09 New Forest (2005; woodland)
Snowdonia (1951; mountains/valleys)
The Broads (1989; waterways/fens)

10 Cairngorms (2003; mountains/moorland/
forest)
Loch Lomond (2002; lochs/mountains)

12 Lake District (1951; mountains/valleys/

glaciated lakes)
Peak District (1951; moorland/dales)

13 Brecon Beacons (1957; mountains/valleys)
The South Downs (2010; woodland/heathland)

14 Northumberland (1956; hills)
North York Moors (1952; woodland/
moorland)
Yorkshire Dales (1954; dales)

18 Pembrokeshire Coast (1952/1995; cliffs/
moorland/islands)

National parks and nature reserves worldwide include:

03 Gir (India)

04 Manu (Peru)
Waza (Cameroon)
Yoho (Canada)
Zion (USA)

05 Banff (Canada)
Chaco (Argentina)
El Rey (Argentina)
Fundy (Canada)
Kafue (Zambia)
Mt Apo (Philippines)
Royal (Australia)
Sarek (Sweden)
Swiss (Switzerland)
Tatra (Czech Republic/Poland)
Tikal (Guatemala)

Tsavo (Kenya)
Uluru (Australia)

06 Abisko (Sweden)
Acadia (USA)
Angkor (Cambodia)
Arches (USA)
Burren (Ireland)
Denali (USA)
Doñana (Spain)
Egmont (New Zealand)
Etosha (Namibia)
Iguaçu (Brazil/Argentina)
Iguazú (Brazil/Argentina)
Jasper (Canada)
Kakadu (Australia)
Katmai (USA)
Kruger (South Africa)

Mt Cook (New Zealand)
Muddus (Sweden)
Phu Rua (Thailand)
Wolong (China)

07 Bicayne (USA)
Big Bend (USA)
Canaima (Venezuela)
Chitwan (Nepal)
Corbett (India)
Gemsbok (Botswana)
Glacier (USA)
Khao Yai (Thailand)
Nairobi (Kenya)
Olympic (USA)
Paparoa (New Zealand)
Rakiura (New Zealand)
Redwood (USA)
Saguaro (USA)
Sequoia (USA)
Toubkal (Morocco)
Urewera (New Zealand)
Virunga (Democratic Republic of the Congo)

08 Amazonia (Brazil)
Badlands (USA)
Camargue (France)
Kinabalu (Malaysia)
Kootenay (Canada)
Rwenzori (Uganda)
Taranaki (New Zealand)
Westland (New Zealand)
Wind Cave (USA)
Yosemite (USA)

09 Carnarvon (Australia)
Connemara (Ireland)
Fiordland (New Zealand)
Galápagos (Ecuador)
Glenveagh (Ireland)
Kahurangi (New Zealand)
Kaziranga (India)
Killarney (Ireland)
Kosciusko (Australia)
Lake Clark (USA)
Mesa Verde (USA)
Mt Olympus (Greece)
Mt Rainier (USA)
Ruwenzori (Uganda)
Serengeti (Tanzania)
The Burren (Ireland)
Tongariro (New Zealand)
Voyageurs (USA)
Whanganui (New Zealand)

10 Abel Tasman (New Zealand)
Crater Lake (USA)
Everglades (USA)

Glacier Bay (USA)
Hoge Veluwe (The Netherlands)
Hot Springs (USA)
Joshua Tree (USA)
Mercantour (France)
Mt Aspiring (New Zealand)
Ngorongoro (Tanzania)
Sagarmatha (Nepal)
Shenandoah (USA)
Tai Poutini (New Zealand)
Ujung-Kulon (Indonesia)

11 Arthur's Pass (New Zealand)
Bialowieski (Poland)
Bryce Canyon (USA)
Canyonlands (USA)
Daisetsuzan (Japan)
Death Valley (USA)
Grand Canyon (USA)
Heron Island (Australia)
Kenai Fjords (USA)
Kilimanjaro (Tanzania)
Kobuk Valley (USA)
Mammoth Cave (USA)
Nelson Lakes (New Zealand)
Pfälzerwald (Germany)
Tumucumaque (Brazil)
Wood Buffalo (Canada)
Yellowstone (USA)

12 Gammon Ranges (Australia)
Gran Paradiso (Italy)
Komodo Island (Indonesia)
Los Glaciares (Argentina/Chile)
Popocatépetl (Mexico)
Warrumbungle (Australia)
Wooroonooran (Australia)

13 Blue Mountains (Australia)
Fuji-Hakone-Izu (Japan)
Namib-Naukluft (Namibia)
North Cascades (USA)
Rocky Mountain (USA)
Royal National (Australia)
Victoria Falls (Zimbabwe/Zambia)
Virgin Islands (USA)
Waterton Lakes (Canada)

14 Altos de Campana (Panama)
Great Sand Dunes (USA)
Hardangervidda (Norway)
Lassen Volcanic (USA)
Tierra del Fuego (Argentina)
Uluru-Kata Tjuta (Australia)

15 Carlsbad Caverns (USA)
Hawaii Volcanoes (USA)
Petrified Forest (USA)
Wrangell-St Elias (USA)

See also **World Heritage site**

parliament

Parliament types include:

04 diet
duma
moot

05 boule
douma
gemot
jirga

06 majlis
senate

07 commons

08 assembly
congress

09 volksraad

10 consistory
lower house
upper house

12 lower chamber
upper chamber

14 Council of State

15 House of Assembly

Parliaments, political assemblies and venues include:

02 EP
HK
HP

04 Dáil (Ireland)
Diet (Japan)
Duma (Russia)
Keys (Isle of Man)
Long (England)
Pnyx (Ancient Athens)
Rump (England)
Sejm (Poland)

05 boule (Greece)
gemot (Anglo-Saxons)
Lords (UK)
Porte (Turkey)

06 Cortes (Portugal/Spain)
kgotla (Botswana)
Majlis (Iran)
Mejlis (Iran)
Seanad (Ireland)
Senate (Australia/Canada/France/USA)
Senato (Italy)
Senedd (Wales)

07 Althing (Iceland)
comitia (Ancient Rome)
Commons (UK)
Knesset (Israel)
Lagting (Norway/Faroe Islands)
Landtag (Germany)
Rigsdag (Denmark)
Riksdag (Sweden)
Tynwald (Isle of Man)
zemstvo (Russia)

08 Congress (USA)
ecclesia (Ancient Athens)
European (European Union)
folkmoot (Anglo-Saxons)
Imperial (UK)
Lagthing (Norway/Faroe Islands)
Lok Sabha (India)
Scottish (Scotland)

See also **politics**

Sobranje (Bulgaria)
Sobranye (Bulgaria)
Stannary (Cornish tinners)
Storting (Norway)

09 Bundesrat (Austria/Germany/Switzerland)
Bundestag (Germany)
Eduskunta (Finland)
Folketing (Denmark)
Landsting (Denmark)
Loya Jirga (Afghanistan)
Odelsting (Norway)
Reichsrat (Germany)
Reichstag (Germany)
Skupstina (Serbia/Montenegro/Yugoslavia)
Ständerat (Switzerland)
State Duma (Russia)

10 Bundesrath (Austria/Germany/Switzerland)
Landsthing (Denmark)
Odelsthing (Norway)
Oireachtas (Ireland)
Rajya Sabha (India)
Reichsrath (Germany)
Skupshtina (Serbia/Montenegro/Yugoslavia)
St Stephen's (UK)

11 Dáil Eireann (Ireland)
House of Keys (Isle of Man)
Nationalrat (Austria/Switzerland)
Volkskammer (German Democratic
Republic)
Westminster (UK)

12 House of Lords (UK)

13 House of States (India)
Seanad Eireann (Ireland)
States General (The Netherlands)
Supreme Soviet (USSR)
Welsh Assembly (Wales)

14 House of Commons (UK/Canada)
Staten-Generaal (The Netherlands)

15 Council of States
House of Assembly (South Africa)
People's Assembly (Egypt)

parrot

Parrots include:

03 fig	conure	paroquet	Psittacus
kea	kakapo	Pesquet's	Stringops
04 grey	Nestor	Strigops	**10** budgerigar
kaka	**07** corella	**09** cockateel	ring-necked
lory	hanging	cockatiel	**11** African grey
05 galah	rosella	green leek	night-parrot
macaw	**08** cockatoo	owl-parrot	shell-parrot
pygmy	lorikeet	paraquito	**13** Major Mitchell
06 Amazon	lovebird	parrakeet	shell parakeet
budgie	parakeet	parroquet	zebra parakeet
		parrotlet	

particle *see* **atom**

parts of speech *see* grammar

party

Parties include:

02 do	hangi	New Year	reception
03 hen	**06** dinner	potluck	sleepover
key	drinks	slumber	stag night
tea	garden	**08** barbecue	welcoming
04 bash	grog-on	birthday	**10** baby shower
foam	hooley	bunfight	fancy dress
orgy	picnic	cocktail	hootenanny
rave	pyjama	farewell	**11** discotheque
stag	social	surprise	flat-warming
toga	soirée	**09** acid-house	**12** bridal shower
wrap	supper	beanfeast	house-warming
05 beano	**07** ceilidh	Christmas	**13** cheese and wine
disco	knees-up	Hallowe'en	
	leaving	hootnanny	

Political parties in the UK include:

03 BNP	UKIP	**09** Communist	Parliamentary
DUP	**05** Green	**10** Democratic	Scottish Green
PLP	**06** Labour	Plaid Cymru	**14** Militant Labour
PUP	Lib Dem	Republican	UK Independence
SNP	**07** Liberal	UK Unionist	Ulster Unionist
SSP	Veritas	**11** Co-operative	**15** British National
SWP	**08** Alliance	**12** Conservative	Popular Alliance
04 SDLP	Sinn Féin	**13** National Front	

Political parties worldwide include:

02 AN (Italy)	FDP (Germany)	**05** Green (Ireland)
FN (France)	NDP (Canada)	Green (USA)
PP (Spain)	NPD (Canada)	**06** Labour (Ireland)
03 ALP (Australia)	UMP (France)	**08** Batasuna (Spain)
CDU (Germany)	**04** PSOE (Spain)	Democrat (USA)

Fine Gael (Ireland)
Sinn Féin (Ireland)

09 One Nation (Australia)
Socialist (Ireland)

See also **game**; **politics**

10 Fianna Fáil (Ireland)
Republican (USA)

12 Workers' Party (Ireland)

13 Bloc Québécois (Canada)

Front National (France)
National Front (France)

14 Partido Popular (Spain)

party game *see* **game**

pass *see* **mountain**

passage

Passages include:

04 Mona (Puerto Rico/Dominican Republic)

05 Drake (Antarctica)
Gaspé (Canada)
Umnak (Aleutian Islands, USA)

06 Akutan (Aleutian Islands, USA)
Amukta (Aleutian Islands, USA)
Burias (Philippines)
Caicos (The Bahamas)
Colvos (USA)
Mompog (Philippines)
Seguam (Aleutian Islands, USA)
Unimak (Aleutian Islands, USA)

07 Oronsay (Scotland)
Palawan (Philippines)

08 Amchitka (Aleutian Islands, USA)
Dominica (Dominica/Martinique)

Fenimore (Aleutian Islands, USA)
Mouchoir (The Bahamas)
Saratoga (USA)
Windward (Cuba/Haiti)

09 Deception (USA)
Mayaguana (The Bahamas)
St Vincent (St Vincent/St Lucia)

10 Backstairs (Australia)
Guadeloupe (Guadeloupe/Montserrat)
Martinique (Martinique/Dominica)
Mira Por Vos (The Bahamas)
Silver Bank (The Bahamas)

11 Turks Island (The Bahamas)
Verde Island (Philippines)

13 Crooked Island (The Bahamas)

14 Jacques Cartier (Canada)

pasta

Pasta includes:

04 orza
zite
ziti

05 penne
ruoti

06 anelli
ditali
noodle
trofie

07 fusilli
gnocchi
lasagna
lasagne
lumache
mafalde
maruzze
mezzani
noodles

pennine
ravioli

08 bucatini
farfalle
fedelini
linguine
linguini
macaroni
rigatoni
stelline

09 agnolotti
angel hair
casarecci
crescioni
fettucine
fettucini
fiochetti
manicotti
spaghetti

10 angel's hair
bombolotti
cannelloni
conchiglie
farfalline
fettuccine
strangozzi
tagliarini
taglierini
tortellini
vermicelli

11 cappelletti
orecchiette
pappardelle
tagliatelle

12 lasagne verde
noodle farfel

13 elbow macaroni

pastime

Pasta dishes include:

07 lasagna	**08** marinara	manicotti	puttanesca
lasagne	tortelli	spaghetti	**14** macaroni cheese
ravioli	**09** arrabiata	**10** cannelloni	
spag bol	carbonara	minestrone	

pastime *see* **hobby**

pastry

Pastry includes:

04 filo	sweet	suetcrust	**12** biscuit-crumb
flan	**06** cheese	**10** pâte brisée	pâte à savarin
puff	Danish	pâte frolle	**13** American crust
05 choux	**07** pork-pie	pâte sablée	hot-water crust
flaky	**08** one-stage	pâte sucrée	**14** rich shortcrust
plain	**09** rough-puff	shortcrust	
short		wholewheat	

See also **cake**

patriarch

Patriarchs include:

04 Levi	Abram	Jacob	Ishmael
Noah	Enoch	**06** Joseph	**10** Methuselah
05 Aaron	Isaac	**07** Abraham	Theophilus

patron saint *see* **saint**

peace *see* **Nobel Prize**

pear

Pear varieties include:

04 musk	poprin	blanquet	poppering
05 nelis	seckel	muscadel	**10** conference
06 beurré	seckle	muscatel	jargonelle
Colmar	warden	Williams	**11** bon chrétien
comice	**07** poperin	**09** Catherine	queez-maddam
nelies	**08** bergamot	muscadine	**12** cuisse-madame

peninsula

Peninsulas include:

04 Ards (Northern Ireland)	Gower (Wales)
Cape (South Africa)	Italy (Italy)
Eyre (Australia)	Lleyn (Wales)
Gyda (Russia)	Malay (Malaysia)
Huon (Papua New Guinea)	Otago (New Zealand)
Kola (Russia)	Qatar (Qatar)
05 Gaspé (Canada)	Sinai (Egypt)

06 Alaska (USA)
Avalon (Canada)
Azuero (Panama)
Balkan (Eastern Europe)
Carnac (France)
Crimea (Ukraine)
Iberia (Portugal/Spain)
Istria (Croatia/Slovenia)
Jaffna (Sri Lanka)
Korean (North Korea/South Korea)
Recife (Brazil)
Seward (USA)
Taymyr (Russia)
Wirral (England)

07 Alaskan (USA)
Arabian (Middle East)
Cape Cod (USA)
Chukchi (Russia)
Florida (USA)
Furness (England)
Iberian (Portugal/Spain)
Jiulong (Hong Kong)
Jutland (Denmark)
Kintyre (Scotland)
Kowloon (Hong Kong)

See also **cape**

Olympic (USA)
Yucatán (Mexico)

08 Apsheron (Azerbaijan)
Cape York (Australia)
Cotentin (Normandy)
Musandam (Oman)
Pinellas (USA)
Sorrento (Italy)
Yorktown (USA)

09 Cape Verde (Senegal)
Gallipoli (Turkey)
Kamchatka (Russia)
Paraguana (Venezuela)
Peary Land (Greenland)

10 Arnhem Land (Australia)
Graham Land (Antarctica)
Isle of Dogs (England)
Nova Scotia (Canada)

11 Peloponnese (Greece)

12 Scandinavian (Scandinavia)

14 Baja California (Mexico)
Isle of Portland (England)

15 Rinns of Galloway (Scotland)

people

Peoples include:

03 Han (China)
Ibo (Nigeria)
Jat (India/Pakistan)
Kru (Liberia)
Mam (Guatemala)
Mon (Myanmar/Thailand)
San (South Africa)
Tiv (Nigeria)
Twi (Ghana)

04 Ainu (Japan)
Cham (Vietnam/Cambodia)
Efik (Nigeria)
Goth (Germanic)
Hutu (Rwanda/Burundi)
Igbo (Nigeria)
Jute (Germanic)
Kroo (Liberia)
Lett (Latvia)
Moor (North Africa)
Motu (Papua New Guinea)
Nair (India)
Nupe (Nigeria)
Roma (Europe)
Saba (Yemen)
Shan (Asia)
Sulu (Philippines)

Susu (West Africa)
Tshi (Ghana)
Zulu (South Africa)

05 Bajau (Malaysia)
Bantu (Africa)
Hausa (Nigeria)
Iceni (Britain)
Inuit (Arctic)
Karen (Myanmar)
Khmer (Cambodia)
Maori (New Zealand)
Masai (Africa)
Nayar (India)
Nguni (South/East Africa)
Oriya (India)
Saxon (German)
Swazi (Swaziland)
Taino (West Indies)
Tamil (India/Sri Lanka)
Temne (Sierra Leone)
Tonga (Africa)
Tutsi (Rwanda/Burundi)
Vedda (Sri Lanka)
Wolof (West Africa)
Yakut (Russia)
Yupik (Arctic)

06 Angles (Germanic)
Aymara (South America)
Griqua (South Africa)
Gurkha (Nepal)
Herero (Namibia)
Innuit (Arctic)
Kabyle (North Africa)
Kalmyk (China/Russia)
Kikuyu (Kenya)
Manchu (China)
Nyanja (Malawi)
Ostiak (Russia)
Ostyak (Russia)
Sherpa (Nepal)
Tswana (Botswana)
Tungus (Russia)
Yoruba (West Africa)
Zyrian (Russia)

07 Barotse (Zambia)
Basotho (Lesotho)
Calmuck (China/Russia)
Cossack (Russia)

Goorkha (Nepal)
Hittite (Syria)
Kalmuck (China/Russia)
Manchoo (China)
Maratha (India)
Pashtun (Afghanistan)
Quechua (Peru)
Quichua (Peru)
Samoyed (Russia)
Swahili (Africa)
Tagálog (Philippines)
Walloon (Belgium)

08 Khoikhoi (South Africa)
Mahratta (India)
Polabian (Slavonic)
Yanomami (Brazil/Venezuela)

09 Himyarite (Yemen)
Ostrogoth (Germanic)
Ruthenian (Ukraine)
Sinhalese (Sri Lanka)
Tocharian (Asia)
Tokharian (Asia)

See also **aborigine**; **Africa**; **The Americas**; **Asia**

pepper

Pepper and peppercorns include:

03 red
04 bird
pink
05 black
chile
chili

green
sweet
white
06 cherry
chilli
yellow

07 cayenne
Jamaica
paprika
pimento
08 allspice
capsicum

habañero
jalapeño
pimiento
piquillo
12 Scotch bonnet

period *see* **geology**; **history**; **time**

pet

Pets include:

03 cat
cow
dog
pig
rat
04 bird
fish
goat
newt
pony

05 goose
horse
llama
mouse
sheep
06 alpaca
canary
donkey
ferret
gerbil

jerboa
lizard
parrot
rabbit
turtle
07 chicken
hamster
08 chipmunk
cyberpet
goldfish

parakeet
terrapin
tortoise
09 guinea pig
tarantula
10 budgerigar
chinchilla
salamander
virtual pet
11 stick insect

See also **cat**; **dog**; **fish**; **horse**; **parrot**; **rabbit**

Petrarch (1304–74)

Significant works include:

06 *Africa* (1338–42)
08 *Secretum* (c.1343–58)
10 *Canzoniere* (1327–74)

15 *De vita solitaria* (c.1346–56)
27 *De remediis utriusque fortunae* (c.1354–60)

philately

Famous and rare stamps include:

08 Bull's eye
Penny Red
09 Basel dove
Penny Blue
10 Mount Athos

Penny Black
Red Mercury
Scinde Dawk
VR official
11 Jenny invert

St Louis bear
12 Inverted swan
13 Black Honduras
Inverted Jenny
Uganda Cowries

Philately terms include:

02 NH
OC
OG
03 gum
NVI
04 coil
pair
pane
used
05 block
cover
flown
grill
hinge
mount
stamp
06 cachet
cancel
cliché
crease
entire
gutter
invert

matrix
unused
07 Machins
perfins
selvage
Smilers
tagging
08 centring
line pair
multiple
postmark
selvedge
se-tenant
stamp pen
thematic
09 approvals
backstamp
catalogue
face value
handstamp
regionals
watermark
10 gutter pair

rouletting
semipostal
stamp album
stamp tongs
stocksheet
11 imperforate
maximaphily
never hinged
original gum
12 cancellation
denomination
13 commemorative
first day cover
generic stamps
mint condition
original cover
souvenir sheet
14 controlled mail
miniature sheet
15 greetings stamps
magnifying glass
stamp collecting

philosophy

Branches of philosophy include:

03 law
04 mind
05 logic
moral
06 ethics
07 biology
eastern

history
science
08 axiology
language
medicine
ontology
politics
religion

09 bioethics
economics
education
semiotics
10 aesthetics
literature
psychology

11 informatics
mathematics
metaphysics
12 epistemology
13 applied ethics
jurisprudence
phenomenology

Philosophical schools, doctrines and theories include:

05 deism
06 egoism
    monism
    Taoism
    theism
07 atheism
    atomism
    dualism
    fideism
    Marxism
    realism
    Thomism
08 altruism
    ascetism
    cynicism
    fatalism
    feminism
    hedonism
    humanism
    idealism
    nihilism
    Stoicism
    womanism
09 dogmatism
    pantheism
    Platonism

    pluralism
    solipsism
10 absolutism
    Eleaticism
    empiricism
    gnosticism
    Kantianism
    naturalism
    nominalism
    positivism
    pragmatism
    Pyrrhonism
    relativism
    scepticism
11 agnosticism
    determinism
    Hegelianism
    historicism
    materialism
    objectivism
    rationalism
    Sankhya-Yoga
12 behaviourism
    Cartesianism
    Confucianism
    Epicureanism
    essentialism

    Neoplatonism
    reductionism
    subjectivism
13 antinomianism
    conceptualism
    descriptivism
    immaterialism
    Neo-Kantianism
    occasionalism
    phenomenalism
    scholasticism
    structuralism
14 existentialism
    interactionism
    intuitionalism
    libertarianism
    Nyaya-Vaisesika
    prescriptivism
    Pythagoreanism
    sensationalism
    utilitarianism
    Vedanta-Mimamsa
15 Aristotelianism
    experimentalism
    Frankfurt School
    instrumentalism

Philosophers include:

04 Ayer (Sir A J; 1910–89, English)
Bain (Alexander; 1818–1903, Scottish)
Hick (John; 1922–2012, English)
Hook (Sidney; 1902–89, US)
Hume (David; 1711–76, Scottish)
Joad (C E M; 1891–1953, English)
Kant (Immanuel; 1724–1804, German)
Kuhn (Thomas; 1922–96, US)
Marx (Karl; 1818–83, German)
Mill (Harriet Taylor; 1807–58, English)
Mill (James; 1773–1836, Scottish)
Mill (John Stuart; 1806–73, English)
More (Henry; 1614–87, English)
Otto (Rudolf; 1869–1937, German)
Reid (Thomas; 1710–96, Scottish)
Ryle (Gilbert; 1900–76, English)
Vico (Giambattista; 1668–1744, Italian)
Weil (Simone; 1909–43, French)
Wolf (Christian von; 1679–1754, German)

05 Amiel (Henri Frédéric; 1821–81, Swiss)
Bacon (Francis, Lord; 1561–1626, English)
Bacon (Roger; c.1214–92, English)
Bayle (Pierre; 1647–1706, French)
Benda (Julien; 1867–1956, French)
Bodin (Jean; c.1530–96, French)
Broad (Charlie Dunbar; 1887–1971, English)

Bruno (Giordano; 1548–1600, Italian)
Buber (Martin; 1878–1965, Austrian)
Burke (Edmund; 1729–97, Irish)
Burke (Kenneth; 1897–1992, US)
Burks (Arthur; 1915–2008, US)
Cohen (Hermann; 1842–1912, German)
Comte (Auguste; 1798–1857, French)
Croce (Benedetto; 1866–1952, Italian)
Dewey (John; 1859–1952, US)
Duhem (Pierre; 1861–1916, French)
Dunne (John William; 1875–1949, English)
Frege (Gottlob; 1848–1925, German)
Gödel (Kurt; 1906–78, Czech/US)
Hegel (Georg Wilhelm Friedrich; 1770–1831, German)
Hulme (T E; 1883–1917, English)
Iqbal (Sir Muhammad; 1875–1938, Indian)
James (William; 1842–1910, US)
Kames (Henry Home, Lord; 1696–1782, Scottish)
Kindi (al-; c.800–c.870, Arab)
Laozi (6c BC, Chinese)
Lewis (Hywel; 1910–92, Welsh)
Locke (John; 1632–1704, English)
Lotze (Rudolf; 1817–81, German)
Moore (G E; 1873–1958, English)

Nagel (Ernest; 1901–85, Czech/US)
Nagel (Thomas; 1937– , Yugoslav/US)
Occam (William of; c.1285–c.1349, English)
Plato (c.428–c.348 BC, Greek)
Price (H H; 1899–1985, Welsh)
Price (Richard; 1723–91, Welsh)
Quine (William Van Orman; 1908–2000, US)
Rawls (John; 1921–2002, US)
Rhees (Rush; 1905–89, US)
Rorty (Richard McKay; 1931–2007, US)
Royce (Josiah; 1855–1916, US)
Smith (Adam; 1723–90, Scottish)
Sorel (Georges; 1847–1922, French)
Stein (Edith; 1891–1942, German)
Stout (George Frederick; 1860–1944, English)
Taine (Hippolyte Adolphe; 1828–93, French)
Vives (Juan Luis; 1492–1540, Spanish)
Wolff (Christian von; 1679–1754, German)

06 Adorno (Theodor; 1903–69, German)
Anselm (St; 1033–1109, Italian)
Arendt (Hannah; 1906–75, German/US)
Austin (J L; 1911–60, English)
Baader (Franz von; 1765–1841, German)
Berlin (Sir Isaiah; 1907–97, Latvian/British)
Bonnet (Charles; 1720–93, Swiss)
Butler (Joseph; 1692–1752, English)
Carnap (Rudolf; 1891–1970, German/US)
Celsus (2cAD, Roman)
Clarke (Samuel; 1675–1729, English)
Cousin (Victor; 1792–1867, French)
Eliade (Mircea; 1907–86, Romanian)
Engels (Friedrich; 1820–95, German)
Eucken (Rudolf; 1846–1926, German)
Farabi (Abu Nasr al-; 878–c.950, Islamic)
Fichte (Johann Gottlieb; 1762–1814, German)
Ficino (Marsilio; 1433–99, Italian)
Gehlen (Arnold; 1904–76, German)
Gilson (Étienne; 1884–1978, French)
Goedel (Kurt; 1906–78, Czech/US)
Halevi (Jehuda; 1075–1141, Spanish)
Hamann (Johann; 1730–88, German)
Herder (Johann; 1744–1803, German)
Hobbes (Thomas; 1588–1679, English)
Kaplan (Mordecai; 1881–1983, Lithuanian/US)
Kripke (Saul; 1940– , US)
Langer (Susanne K; 1895–1985, US)
Lao Tzu (6c BC, Chinese)
Littré (Émile; 1801–81, French)
Lukacs (Georg; Hungarian)
Madhva (14c, Indian)
Marcel (Gabriel; 1889–1973, French)
Ockham (William of; c.1285–c.1349, English)
Peirce (Charles; 1839–1914, US)
Popper (Sir Karl; 1902–94, Austrian/British)

Putnam (Hilary; 1926– , US)
Pyrrho (c.365–270 BC, Greek)
Ramsey (Frank; 1903–30, English)
Ramsey (Ian; 1915–72, English)
Sa'adia (ben Joseph; 882–942, Egyptian-Babylonian)
Sartre (Jean-Paul; 1905–80, French)
Schutz (Alfred; 1899–1959, Austrian/US)
Searle (John; 1932– , US)
Seneca (Lucius Annaeus; c.4 BC–c.65 AD, Roman)
Simmel (Georg; 1858–1918, German)
Suárez (Francisco; 1548–1617, Spanish)
Tagore (Rabindranath; 1861–1941, Indian)
Tarski (Alfred; 1902–83, Polish)
Thales (c.620–c.555 BC, Greek)
Vanini (Lucilio; 1584–1619, Italian)
Wright (Georg Henrik von; 1916–2003, Finnish)

07 Abelard (Peter; 1079–1142, French)
Adelard (12c, English)
Aquinas (St Thomas; 1225–74, Italian)
Arnauld (Antoine; 1612–94, French)
Bentham (Jeremy; 1748–1832, English)
Bergson (Henri; 1859–1941, French)
Bolzano (Bernard; 1781–1848, Czech)
Bradley (Francis Herbert; 1846–1924, Welsh)
Buridan (Jean; c.1300–c.1358, French)
Collier (Arthur; 1680–1732, English)
Deleuze (Gilles; 1925–95, French)
Dennett (Daniel; 1942– , US)
Derrida (Jacques; 1930–2004, French)
Diderot (Denis; 1713–84, French)
Dilthey (Wilhelm; 1833–1911, German)
Driesch (Hans; 1867–1941, German)
Dummett (Sir Michael; 1925–2011, English)
Edwards (Jonathan; 1703–58, American)
Erasmus (Desiderius; c.1466–1536, Dutch)
Erigena (John Scotus; c.810–c.877, Irish)
Ferrier (James Frederick; 1808–64, Scottish)
Gadamer (Hans-Georg; 1900–2002, German)
Gassend (Pierre; 1592–1655, French)
Gautama (1cAD, Indian)
Gentile (Giovanni; 1875–1944, Italian)
Ghazali (al-; 1058–1111, Persian)
Gorgias (c.490–c.385 BC, Greek)
Gracian (Baltasar; 1601–58, Spanish)
Haldane (Richard, Viscount; 1856–1928, Scottish)
Hartley (David; 1705–57, English)
Herbart (Johann; 1776–1841, German)
Herbert (Edward, Lord; 1583–1648, English)
Holberg (Ludvig, Baron; 1684–1754, Norwegian)
Husserl (Edmund; 1859–1938, German)
Hypatia (c.370–415 AD, Greek)

Ibn Daud (Abraham; c.1100–c.1180, Spanish)
Jaspers (Karl; 1883–1969, German)
Johnson (Alexander Bryan; 1786–1867, English/US)
Lakatos (Imre; 1922–74, Hungarian)
Lambert (Johann Heinrich; 1728–77, Swiss)
Leibniz (Gottfried Wilhelm; 1646–1716, German)
Lovejoy (Arthur O; 1873–1963, German/US)
Maistre (Joseph Marie, Comte de; 1753–1821, French)
Marcuse (Herbert; 1898–1979, German/US)
Meinong (Alexius von; 1853–1920, Austrian)
Mencius (c.372–c.289 BC, Chinese)
Murdoch (Dame Iris; 1919–99, Irish)
Neurath (Otto; 1882–1945, Austrian)
Polanyi (Michael; 1891–1976, Hungarian/ British)
Proclus (c.410–485 AD, Greek)
Pyrrhon (c.365–270 BC, Greek)
Rickert (Heinrich; 1863–1936, German)
Ricoeur (Paul; 1913–2005, French)
Russell (Bertrand, Earl; 1872–1970, English)
Sanchez (Francisco; c.1550–1623, Portuguese or Spanish)
Sankara (c.700–750, Indian)
Scheler (Max; 1874–1928, German)
Schlick (Moritz; 1882–1936, German)
Scruton (Roger; 1944– , British)
Spencer (Herbert; 1820–1903, English)
Spinoza (Benedict de; 1632–77, Dutch)
Steiner (Rudolf; 1861–1925, Austrian)
Stewart (Dugald; 1753–1828, Scottish)
Tillich (Paul; 1886–1965, German/US)
Tolstoy (Count Leo; 1828–1910, Russian)
Unamuno (Miguel de; 1864–1936, Spanish)
Warnock (Mary, Baroness; 1924– , English)

08 Alembert (Jean le Rond d'; 1717–83, French)
Ammonius (c.160–242 AD, Greek)
Anderson (John; 1893–1962, Scottish/ Australian)
Anscombe (Elizabeth; 1919–2001, Irish)
Antiphon (5c BC, Greek)
Averroës (1126–98, Spanish)
Avicenna (980–1037, Persian)
Beauvoir (Simone de; 1908–86, French)
Beccaria (Cesare, Marchese de; 1738–94, Italian)
Berdyaev (Nikolai; 1874–1948, Russian)
Berkeley (George; 1685–1753, Irish)
Boethius (Anicius Manlius Severinus; c.475–524 AD, Roman)
Brentano (Franz; 1838–1917, German)
Buchanan (George; c.1506–82, Scottish)
Bulgakov (Sergei; 1871–1944, Russian)
Campbell (Charles; 1897–1974, Scottish)

Cassirer (Ernst; 1874–1945, Polish/German)
Cudworth (Ralph; 1617–88, English)
Davidson (Donald; 1917–2003, US)
Epicurus (c.341–270 BC, Greek)
Ferguson (Adam; 1723–1816, Scottish)
Foucault (Michel; 1926–84, French)
Gassendi (Pierre; 1592–1655, French)
Geulincx (Arnold; 1624–69, Belgian)
Glanvill (Joseph; 1636–80, English)
Habermas (Jürgen; 1929– , German)
Hamilton (Sir William; 1788–1856, Scottish)
Harrison (Frederic; 1831–1923, English)
Hintikka (Jaakko; 1929– , Finnish)
Hobhouse (Leonard Trelawney; 1864–1929, English)
Lonergan (Bernard; 1904–85, Canadian)
Longinus (1c AD, Greek)
Maritain (Jacques; 1882–1973, French)
Melissus (5c BC, Greek)
M'Taggart (John M'Taggart Ellis; 1866–1925, English)
Passmore (John; 1914–2004, Australian)
Plessner (Helmuth; 1892–1985, German)
Plotinus (c.205–270 AD, Greek)
Plutarch (c.46–c.120 AD, Greek)
Porphyry (c.232–c.305 AD, Greek)
Ramanuja (11c–12c, Tamil)
Ram Singh (1816–85, Indian)
Rousseau (Jean Jacques; 1712–78, French)
Sidgwick (Henry; 1838–1900, English)
Socrates (469–399 BC, Greek)
Soloviev (Vladimir; 1853–1900, Russian)
Spengler (Oswald; 1880–1936, German)
Strawson (Sir Peter Frederick; 1919–2006, English)
Waismann (Friedrich; 1896–1959, Austrian)
Williams (Sir Bernard; 1929–2003, English)

09 Alexander (Samuel; 1859–1938, Australian)
Althusser (Louis; 1918–90, French)
Arcesilas (c.316–c.241 BC, Greek)
Aristotle (384–322 BC, Greek)
Aurobindo (Sri; 1872–1950, Indian)
Averrhoës (1126–98, Spanish)
Avicebrón (c.1020–c.1070,Spanish)
Bachelard (Gaston; 1884–1962, French)
Basilides (fl.c.125 AD, Syrian)
Bosanquet (Bernard; 1848–1923, English)
Carneades (c.214–129 BC, Greek)
Cleánthes (c.331–232 BC, Greek)
Condillac (Étienne Bonnot de; 1715–80, French)
Condorcet (Marie Jean Antoine Nicolas de Caritat, Marquis de; 1743–94, French)
Confucius (551–479 BC, Chinese)
Copleston (Frederick; 1907–93, English)
Cratippus (1c BC, Greek)
Descartes (René; 1596–1650, French)
Epictetus (1c AD, Greek)

Euhemerus (fl.c.300 BC, Greek)
Feuerbach (Ludwig; 1804–72, German)
Heidegger (Martin; 1889–1976, German)
Helvétius (Claude-Adrien; 1715–71, French)
Hutcheson (Francis; 1694–1746, British)
La Mettrie (Julien de; 1709–51, French)
Leucippus (5c BC, Greek)
Lévy-Bruhl (Lucien; 1857–1939, French)
Lucretius (c.99–55 BC, Roman)
MacIntyre (Alasdair Chalmers; 1929– ,
  Scottish)
Mackinnon (Donald; 1913–94, Scottish)
Nagarjuna (c.150–c.250 AD, Indian)
Nietzsche (Friedrich; 1844–1900, German)
Oakeshott (Michael; 1901–90, English)
Ouspensky (Peter; 1878–1947, Russian)
Panaetius (c.185–c.110 BC, Greek)
Plantinga (Alvin; 1932– , US)
Plekhanov (Georgi; 1856–1918, Russian)
Rothacker (Erich; 1888–1965, German)
Santayana (George; 1863–1952, Spanish/
  US)
Schelling (Friedrich; 1775–1854, German)
Whichcote (Benjamin; 1609–83, English)

10 Anaxagoras (500–428 BC, Ionian)
Anaximenes (d.c.500 BC, Greek)
Arcesilaus (c.316–c.241 BC, Greek)
Aristippus (410–350 BC, Greek)
Baumgarten (Alexander; 1714–62, German)
Campanella (Tommaso; 1568–1639, Italian)
Chrysippus (c.280–c.206 BC, Greek)
Cumberland (Richard; 1631–1718, English)
Democritus (c.460–c.370 BC, Greek)
Duns Scotus (John; c.1265–1308, Scottish)
Empedocles (fl.c.450 BC, Greek)
Heraclitus (d.460 BC, Greek)
Horkheimer (Max; 1895–1973, German)
Ibn Khaldun (1332–1406; Arab)
Maimonides (Moses; 1135–1204, Spanish)
Pashukanis (Yevgeni; 1894–c.1937, Russian)
Posidonius (c.135–c.51 BC, Greek)
Protagoras (c.490–c.420 BC, Greek)
Pythagoras (c.580–c.500 BC, Greek)
Schweitzer (Albert; 1875–1965, Alsatian)
Windelband (Wilhelm; 1848–1915,
  German)
Xenocrates (c.395–314 BC, Greek)

Xenophanes (c.570–c.480 BC, Greek)
Zeno of Elea (c.490–c.420 BC, Greek)

11 Aenesidemus (1c BC, Greek)
Anaximander (611–547 BC, Ionian)
Antisthenes (c.455–c.360 BC, Greek)
Collingwood (R G; 1889–1943, English)
Kierkegaard (Søren; 1813–55, Danish)
Lévi-Strauss (Claude; 1908–2009, French)
Machiavelli (Niccolò; 1469–1527, Italian)
Malebranche (Nicolas; 1638–1715, French)
Mendelssohn (Moses; 1729–86, German)
Montesquieu (Charles-Louis de Secondat,
  Baron de; 1689–1755, French)
Reichenbach (Hans; 1891–1953, German/
  US)
Shaftesbury (Anthony Ashley Cooper, 3rd
  Earl of; 1671–1713, English)

12 Frohschammer (Jakob; 1821–93, German)
Merleau-Ponty (Maurice; 1908–61, French)
Philo Judaeus (c.20 BC–c.40 AD, Hellenistic)
Royer-Collard (Pierre Paul; 1763–1845,
  French)
Schopenhauer (Arthur; 1788–1860,
  German)
Theophrastus (c.372–c.286 BC, Greek)
Wittgenstein (Ludwig; 1889–1951, Austrian/
  British)
Zeno of Citium (c.334–c.265 BC, Greek)

13 Arete of Cyrene (5c–4c BC, Greek)
Dio Chrysostom (c.40–c.112 AD, Greek)
Ortega y Gasset (José; 1883–1955, Spanish)
Radhakrishnan (Sir Sarvepalli; 1888–1975,
  Indian)
Timon of Phlius (c.325–c.235 BC, Greek)

14 Albertus Magnus (St, Graf von Bollstädt;
  c.1200–80, German)
Crates of Athens (early 3c BC, Greek)
Dion Chrysostom (c.40–c.112 AD, Greek)
Marcus Aurelius (AD121–80, Roman)
Nicholas of Cusa (1401–64, German)
Rosmini-Serbati (Antonio; 1797–1855,
  Italian)
Schleiermacher (Friedrich Ernst Daniel;
  1768–1834, German)

15 Sextus Empiricus (2c AD, Greek)

Terms used in philosophy include:

07 a priori	**09** deduction	substance	entailment
falsafa	induction	syllogism	**11** a posteriori
08 identity	intuition	teleology	**13** jurisprudence
ontology	sense data	**10** deontology	phenomenology

See also **belief**

phobia

Phobias include:

08 euphobia (good news)

09 apiphobia (bees)
atephobia (ruin)
ecophobia (one's home surroundings)
neophobia (newness/novelty)
panphobia (everything)
zoophobia (animals)

10 acrophobia (heights)
aerophobia (draughts/air)
algophobia (pain)
aquaphobia (water)
aulophobia (flutes)
autophobia (being by oneself)
barophobia (gravity)
basophobia (walking)
canophobia (dogs)
cynophobia (dogs)
demophobia (crowds)
dikephobia (injustice)
doraphobia (fur)
eosophobia (dawn)
ergophobia (work)
genophobia (sex)
gynophobia (women)
hadephobia (hell)
hodophobia (travel)
ideophobia (ideas)
kenophobia (empty spaces/voids)
kopophobia (fatigue)
logophobia (words)
misophobia (contamination)
monophobia (one thing/being alone)
musophobia (mice)
mysophobia (contamination)
nelophobia (glass)
nosophobia (disease)
ochophobia (vehicles)
oikophobia (home)
polyphobia (many things)
potophobia (alcoholic drink)
pyrophobia (fire)
rypophobia (soiling)
selaphobia (flashes)
sitophobia (food)
theophobia (God)
toxiphobia (poison)
xenophobia (strangers/foreigners)
zelophobia (jealousy)

11 acerophobia (sourness)
agoraphobia (open spaces)
amakaphobia (carriages)
androphobia (men)
anemophobia (wind/draughts)

antlophobia (flood)
astraphobia (lightning)
bathophobia (falling from a high place)
cnidophobia (stings)
cyberphobia (computers)
dromophobia (crossing streets)
emetophobia (vomiting)
eremophobia (solitude)
eretephobia (pins)
erotophobia (sexual involvement)
geumaphobia (taste)
gymnophobia (nudity)
haphephobia (touch)
hierophobia (sacred objects)
hippophobia (horses)
hormephobia (shock)
hydrophobia (water)
hypnophobia (sleep)
laliophobia (stuttering)
lyssophobia (insanity)
maniaphobia (insanity)
necrophobia (corpses)
nephophobia (clouds)
nyctophobia (night/darkness)
ochlophobia (crowds)
ophiophobia (snakes)
pantophobia (everything)
pathophobia (disease)
peniaphobia (poverty)
phagophobia (eating)
phobophobia (fears)
phonophobia (noise/speaking aloud)
photophobia (light)
poinephobia (punishment)
scopophobia (being looked at)
scotophobia (darkness)
sitiophobia (food)
stasiphobia (standing)
tachophobia (speed)
taphephobia (being buried alive)
taphophobia (being buried alive)
tremophobia (trembling)

12 achluophobia (darkness)
aichmophobia (sharp/pointed objects)
ailurophobia (cats)
amathophobia (dust)
anginophobia (narrowness)
apeirophobia (infinity)
auroraphobia (Northern Lights)
belonephobia (needles)
bibliophobia (books)
brontophobia (thunder)
cancerphobia (cancer)
cheimaphobia (cold)

chionophobia (snow)
chromophobia (colour)
chronophobia (duration)
cometophobia (comets)
demonophobia (demons)
entomophobia (insects)
graphophobia (writing)
hedonophobia (pleasure)
kinesophobia (motion)
kleptophobia (stealing)
linonophobia (string)
musicophobia (music)
odontophobia (teeth)
ommatophobia (eyes)
oneirophobia (dreams)
ouranophobia (heaven)
phasmophobia (ghosts)
phengophobia (daylight)
satanophobia (the Devil)
scoptophobia (being looked at)
siderophobia (stars)
spermaphobia (germs)
stygiophobia (hell)
technophobia (technology)
thaasophobia (sitting)
thermophobia (heat)
toxicophobia (poison)

13 aichurophobia (points)
arachnophobia (spiders)
arithmophobia (numbers)
asthenophobia (weakness)
astrapophobia (lightning)
bacilliphobia (microbes)
cancerophobia (cancer)
dermatophobia (skin)
electrophobia (electricity)
ergasiophobia (work)
erythrophobia (blushing)

haematophobia (blood)
harpaxophobia (robbers)
herpetophobia (reptiles)
hypegiaphobia (responsibility)
keraunophobia (thunder)
mastigophobia (flogging)
mechanophobia (machinery)
metallophobia (metals)
meteorophobia (meteors)
olfactophobia (smell)
ophidiophobia (snakes)
ornithophobia (birds)
patroiophobia (heredity)
pnigerophobia (smothering)
pteronophobia (feathers)
syphilophobia (syphilis)
thanatophobia (death)
tonitrophobia (thunder)

14 anthropophobia (people/society)
batrachophobia (frogs/toads/newts)
chrometophobia (money)
claustrophobia (closed spaces)
eisoptrophobia (mirrors)
ereuthrophobia (blushing)
hamartiophobia (sin)
homichlophobia (fog)
katagelophobia (ridicule)
parthenophobia (girls)
spermatophobia (germs)
symmetrophobia (symmetry)
thalassophobia (sea)

15 akousticophobia (sound)
dysmorphophobia (personal physical
  deformity)
eleutherophobia (freedom)
helminthophobia (worms)
kristallophobia (ice)
ophthalmophobia (being stared at)

photography

Photographic equipment includes:

05 easel	long lens	**13** developer bath
stand	stop bath	enlarger timer
06 camera		film projector
screen	**09** camcorder	flash umbrella
tripod	safelight	**14** contact printer
viewer	**10** fixing bath	developing tank
07 boom arm	paper drier	focus magnifier
	Vertoscope®	slide projector
08 enlarger	**11** print washer	**15** negative carrier
light-box	slide viewer	print-drying rack

Photographic accessories include:

04 film	**05** snoot	filter
lens	**06** eye-cup	**07** battery

hot shoe
lens cap
08 diffuser
disc film
film pack
flashgun
lens hood
zoom lens
09 barn doors
camera bag
flashbulb
flash card
flashcube
flash unit
macro lens

polarizer
spot meter
10 afocal lens
heat filter
lens shield
light meter
memory card
slide mount
video light
video mixer
viewfinder
11 close-up lens
fish-eye lens
sepia filter
video editor

12 cable release
cassette film
colour filter
memory reader
13 auxiliary lens
cartridge film
exposure meter
remote control
teleconverter
telephoto lens
wide-angle lens
14 skylight filter
15 cassette adaptor

Photographers include:

03 Ray (Man; 1890–1976, US)
04 Bing (Ilse; 1899–1998, German)
Capa (Robert; 1913–54, US)
Chim (US; 1911–56, US)
Gill (Sir David; 1843–1914, Scottish)
Gray (Gustave Le; 1820–82, French)
Haas (Ernst; 1921–86, Austrian)
Hill (David Octavius; 1802–70, Scottish)
Hine (Lewis W; 1874–1940, US)
Hiro (1930– , Japanese/US)
Penn (Irving; 1917–2009, US)

05 Adams (Ansel; 1902–84, US)
Adams (Eddie; 1933–2004, US)
Adams (Marcus Algernon; 1875–1959, English)
Annan (James Craig; 1864–1946, Scottish)
Annan (Thomas; 1829–87, Scottish)
Arbus (Diane; 1923–71, US)
Atget (Eugène; 1857–1927, French)
Beals (Jessie Tarbox; 1870–1942, US)
Brady (Mathew B; 1823–96, US)
Evans (Frederick; 1853–1943, English)
Evans (Walker; 1903–75, US)
Firth (Francis; 1822–98, English)
Frank (Robert; 1924– , Swiss)
Frith (Francis; 1822–98, English)
Hardy (Bert; 1913–95, English)
Henri (Florence; 1893–1982, US)
Karsh (Yousuf; 1908–2002, Canadian)
Keith (Thomas; 1827–95, Scottish)
Lange (Dorothea; 1895–1965, US)
Marey (Étienne Jules; 1830–1903, French)
Maude (Clementina, Lady Hawarden; 1822–65, Scottish)
Model (Lisette; 1901–83, US)
Nadar (1820–1910, French)
Parer (Damien; 1912–44, Australian)
Parks (Gordon; 1912–2006, US)
Ritts (Herb; 1952–2002, US)

Smith (W Eugene; 1918–78, US)
White (Minor; 1908–76, US)
06 Abbott (Berenice; 1898–1991, US)
Arnold (Eve; 1913–2012, US)
Atkins (Anna; 1799–1871, English)
Avedon (Richard; 1923–2004, US)
Bailey (David; 1938– , English)
Beaton (Sir Cecil; 1904–80, English)
Boubat (Édouard; 1923–99, French)
Brandt (Bill; 1904–83, English)
Burgin (Victor; 1941– , English)
Coburn (Alvin Langdon; 1882–1966, British)
Curtis (Edward; 1868–1952, US)
Draper (Henry; 1837–82, US)
Du Camp (Maxime; 1822–94, French)
Eakins (Thomas; 1844–1916, US)
Erwitt (Elliott; 1928– , US)
Fenton (Roger; 1819–69, English)
Genthe (Arnold; 1869–1942, US)
Gilpin (Laura; 1891–1979, US)
Godwin (Fay; 1931–2005, English)
Halász (Gyula; 1899–1984, French)
Jacobi (Lotte; 1896–1990, US)
Levitt (Helen; 1913–2009, US)
Martin (Paul; 1864–1942, Anglo-French)
McBean (Angus Rowland; 1904–90, Welsh)
Miller (Lee; 1907–77, US)
Morgan (Barbara Brooks; 1900–92, US)
Newman (Arnold; 1918–2006, US)
Newton (Helmut; 1920–2004, Australian)
Niepce (Joseph; 1765–1833, French)
Notman (William; 1826–91, Canadian)
Porter (Eliot; 1901–90, US)
Rankin (1966– , Scottish)
Rodger (George; 1908–95, English)
Sander (August; 1876–1964, German)
Sawada (Kyoichi; 1936–70, Japanese)
Smythe (Frank; 1900–49, English)
Strand (Paul; 1890–1976, US)

Szymin (David; 1911–56, US)
Talbot (William Henry Fox; 1800–77, English)
Warhol (Andy; 1926–87, US)
Weston (Edward; 1886–1958, US)
Wilson (George Washington; 1823–93, Scottish)

07 Adamson (Robert; 1821–48, Scottish)
Akiyama (Shotaro; 1920–2003, Japanese)
Bischof (Werner; 1916–54, Swiss)
Brassaï (1899–1984, French)
Bullock (Wynn; 1902–75, US)
Cameron (Julia Margaret; 1815–79, British)
Carroll (Lewis; 1832–98, English)
Clergue (Lucien; 1934– , French)
Dodgson (Charles Lutwidge; 1832–98, English)
Donovan (Terence; 1936–96, English)
Eastman (George; 1854–1932, US)
Gardner (Alexander; 1821–82, US)
Halsman (Philippe; 1906–79, US)
Jackson (William Henry; 1843–1942, US)
Kertész (André; 1894–1985, Hungarian/US)
Lumière (Auguste; 1862–1954, French)
Lumière (Louis; 1865–1948, French)
McCurry (Steve; 1950– , US)
Modotti (Tina; 1896–1942, Mexican)
Nilsson (Lennart; 1922– , Swedish)
Plummer (Edith; 1893–1975, English)
Salgado (Sebastião; 1944– , Brazilian)
Salomon (Erich; 1886–1944, German)
Seymour (David; 1911–56, US)
Sheeler (Charles; 1883–1965, US)
Siskind (Aaron; 1903–91, US)
Snowdon (Antony Armstrong-Jones, Lord; 1930– , English)
Thomson (John; 1837–1921, Scottish)
Waddell (Rankin; 1966– , Scottish)
Watkins (Carleton E; 1829–1916, US)
Watkins (Margaret; 1884–1969, Canadian)
Yevonde (Madame/Philonie; 1893–1975, English)

08 Anschütz (Ottomar; 1846–1907, German)
Biermann (Aenne; 1898–1933, German)
Chadwick (Helen; 1953–96, English)
Cosindas (Marie; 1925– , US)
Crawford (Osbert Guy Stanhope; 1886–1957, British)
Daguerre (Louis; 1787–1851, French)
Davidson (Bruce; 1933– , US)
DeCarava (Roy; 1919–2009, US)
Doisneau (Robert; 1912–94, French)
Edgerton (Harold; 1903–90, US)

Johnston (Frances Benjamin; 1864–1952, US)
Käsebier (Gertrude; 1852–1934, US)
Lartigue (Jacques-Henri; 1894–1986, French)
Lavenson (Alma; 1897–1989, US)
McCullin (Don; 1935– , English)
Robinson (Henry Peach; 1830–1901, English)
Sielmann (Heinz; 1917–2006, German)
Steichen (Edward; 1879–1973, US)

09 Feininger (Andreas; 1906–99, US)
Friedmann (Andrei; 1913–54, US)
Leibovitz (Annie; 1949– , US)
Lichfield (Patrick, 5th Earl of; 1939– , English)
Mountford (Charles Percy; 1890–1976, Australian)
Muybridge (Eadweard; 1830–1904, Anglo-US)
O'Sullivan (Timothy H; 1840–82, US)
Parkinson (Norman; 1913–90, English)
Rodchenko (Alexander; 1891–1956, Russian)
Rosenblum (Walter; 1919–2006, US)
Rothstein (Arthur; 1915–85, US)
Stieglitz (Alfred; 1864–1946, US)
Sutcliffe (Frank Meadow; 1853–1941, English)
Winogrand (Garry; 1928–84, US)

10 Blumenfeld (Erwin; 1897–1969, US)
Cunningham (Imogen; 1883–1976, US)
Macpherson (Robert; d.1872, Scottish)
Moholy-Nagy (László; 1895–1946, US)
Muggeridge (Edward James; 1830–1904, Anglo-US)
Rabinovich (Emanuel; 1890–1976, US)
Tournachon (Gaspard-Felix; 1820–1910, French)

11 Bourke-White (Margaret; 1904–71, US)
Eisenstaedt (Alfred; 1898–1995, US)
Saint Joseph (John Kenneth Sinclair; 1912–94, English)
Wakabayashi (Yasuhiro; 1930– , Japanese/US)

12 Friese-Greene (William; 1855–1921, English)
Mapplethorpe (Robert; 1946–1989, US)
Van der Elsken (Ed; 1925–90, Dutch)

13 Ducos du Hauron (Louis; 1837–1920, French)

14 Armstrong-Jones (Antony; 1930– , English)
Cartier-Bresson (Henri; 1908–2004, French)

See also **camera**

physics

03 Cox (Brian; 1968– , English)
Kao (Charles; 1933– , Chinese)
Lee (David; 1931– , US)
Ohm (Georg; 1787–1854, German)

04 Abbe (Ernst; 1840–1905, German)
Bohr (Niels; 1885–1962, Danish)
Born (Max; 1882–1970, German)
Bose (Satyendra Nath; 1894–1974, Indian)
Bose (Sir Jagadis Chandra; 1858–1937, Indian)
Fert (Albert; 1938– , French)
Geim (Andre; 1958– , Russian)
Hall (John L; 1934– , US)
Hess (Victor; 1883–1964, Austrian/US)
Katz (Sir Bernard; 1911–2003, German/British)
Kerr (John; 1824–1907, Scottish)
Kohn (Walter; 1923– , Austrian/US)
Lamb (Willis; 1913–2008, US)
Laue (Max von; 1879–1960, German)
Mach (Ernst; 1838–1916, Austrian)
Mott (Sir Nevill; 1905–96, English)
Néel (Louis; 1904–2000, French)
Paul (Wolfgang; 1913–93, German)
Rabi (Isidor Isaac; 1898–1988, Austrian/US)
Snow (C P, Lord; 1905–80, English)
Ting (Samuel C C; 1936– , US)
Wien (Wilhelm; 1864–1928, German)
Yang (Chen Ning; 1922– , Chinese/US)

05 Adams (Sir John; 1920–84, English)
Allen (Sir Geoffrey; 1928– , English)
Aston (Francis; 1877–1945, English)
Auger (Pierre; 1899–1993, French)
Basov (Nikolai; 1922–2001, Russian)
Bethe (Hans; 1906–2005, German/US)
Bloch (Felix; 1905–83, Swiss/US)
Bondi (Sir Hermann; 1919–2005, Austrian/British)
Bothe (Walther; 1891–1957, German)
Boyle (Robert; 1627–91, Irish)
Boyle (Willard; 1924–2011, Canadian)
Bragg (Sir Lawrence; 1890–1971, Australian/British)
Bragg (Sir William; 1862–1942, English)
Braun (Ferdinand; 1850–1918, German)
Curie (Marie; 1867–1934, Polish/French)
Curie (Pierre; 1859–1906, French)
Debye (Peter; 1884–1966, Dutch/US)
Dewar (Sir James; 1842–1923, Scottish)
Dirac (Paul; 1902–84, English)
Dyson (Freeman; 1923– , English/US)
Esaki (Leo; 1925– , Japanese)
Ewing (Sir Alfred; 1855–1935, Scottish)
Fabry (Charles; 1867–1945, French)

Fermi (Enrico; 1901–54, Italian/US)
Fuchs (Klaus; 1912–88, German/British)
Gauss (Carl Friedrich; 1777–1855, German)
Gibbs (J Willard; 1839–1903, US)
Grove (Sir William; 1811–96, Welsh)
Henry (Joseph; 1797–1878, US)
Hertz (Gustav; 1887–1975, German)
Hertz (Heinrich; 1857–94, German)
Higgs (Peter; 1929– , English)
Hooke (Robert; 1635–1703, English)
Jeans (Sir James; 1877–1946, English)
Joule (James Prescott; 1818–89, English)
Kusch (Polykarp; 1911–93, German/US)
Lodge (Sir Oliver; 1851–1940, English)
Nambu (Yoichiro; 1921– , Japanese/US)
Pauli (Wolfgang; 1900–58, Austrian/Swiss/US)
Popov (Aleksandr; 1859–1905, Russian)
Porta (Giovanni; 1535–1615, Italian)
Segrè (Emilio; 1905–89, Italian/US)
Smith (George; 1930– , US)
Smoot (George F; 1946– , US)
Stark (Johannes; 1874–1957, German)
Stern (Otto; 1888–1969, German/US)
Tesla (Nikola; 1856–1943, Austro-Hungarian/US)
Volta (Alessandro, Count; 1745–1827, Italian)
Waals (Johannes van der; 1837–1923, Dutch)
Young (Thomas; 1773–1829, English)

06 Alfvén (Hannes; 1908–96, Swedish)
Ampère (André Marie; 1775–1836, French)
Barkla (Charles Glover; 1877–1944, English)
Barlow (Peter; 1776–1862, English)
Binnig (Gerd; 1947– , German)
Bunsen (Robert; 1811–99, German)
Carnot (Sadi; 1796–1832, French)
Cooper (Leon N; 1930– , US)
Cronin (James; 1931– , US)
Dalton (John; 1766–1844, English)
Edison (Thomas Alva; 1847–1931, US)
Franck (James; 1882–1964, German/US)
Frisch (Otto; 1904–79, Austrian/British)
Geiger (Hans; 1882–1945, German)
Glaser (Donald; 1926–2013, US)
Hänsch (Theodor W; 1941– , German)
Jensen (Hans; 1907–73, German)
Kelvin (William Thomson, Lord; 1824–1907, Scottish)
Landau (Lev; 1908–68, Soviet)
Leslie (Sir John; 1766–1832, Scottish)
Lorenz (Ludwig Valentin; 1829–91, Danish)
Mather (John C; 1945– , US)
Newton (Sir Isaac; 1642–1727, English)
Pascal (Blaise; 1623–62, French)

Perrin (Jean Baptiste; 1870–1942, French)
Planck (Max; 1858–1947, German)
Powell (Cecil; 1903–69, English)
Stroud (William; 1860–1938, English)
Talbot (William Fox; 1800–77, English)
Townes (Charles; 1915– , US)
Walton (Ernest; 1903–95, Irish)
Wigner (Eugene; 1902–95, Hungarian/US)
Wilson (Charles Thomson Rees; 1869–1959, Scottish)
Wilson (Robert Woodrow; 1936– , US)
Yukawa (Hideki; 1907–81, Japanese)
Zwicky (Fritz; 1898–1974, Swiss/US)

07 Alferov (Zhores; 1930– , Russian)
Alvarez (Luis; 1911–88, US)
Babinet (Jacques; 1794–1872, French)
Bardeen (John; 1908–91, US)
Bednorz (Georg; 1950– , German)
Broglie (Louis, Duc de; 1892–1987, French)
Charles (Jacques; 1746–1823, French)
Compton (Arthur; 1892–1962, US)
Coulomb (Charles Augustin de; 1736–1806, French)
Crookes (Sir William; 1832–1919, English)
Doppler (Christian; 1803–53, Austrian)
Faraday (Michael; 1791–1867, English)
Fechner (Gustav; 1801–87, German)
Feynman (Richard; 1918–88, US)
Fresnel (Augustin; 1788–1827, French)
Galileo (1564–1642, Italian)
Gilbert (William; 1544–1603, English)
Glauber (Roy J; 1925– , US)
Goddard (Robert; 1882–1945, US)
Haroche (Serge; 1944– , Moroccan)
Hawking (Stephen; 1942– , English)
Huygens (Christiaan; 1629–93, Dutch)
Kapitza (Peter; 1894–1984, Soviet)
Langley (Samuel; 1834–1906, US)
Lebedev (P N; 1866–1912, Russian)
Leggett (Anthony J; 1938– , English)
Lorentz (Hendrik; 1853–1928, Dutch)
Marconi (Guglielmo, Marchese; 1874–1937, Italian)
Maskawa (Toshihide; 1940– , Japanese)
Mauchly (John W; 1907–80, US)
Maxwell (James Clerk; 1831–79, Scottish)
Meitner (Lise; 1878–1968, Austrian)
Moseley (Harry; 1887–1915, English)
Oersted (Hans Christian; 1777–1851, Danish)
Peierls (Sir Rudolf; 1907–95, German/British)
Piccard (Auguste; 1884–1962, Swiss)
Purcell (Edward Mills; 1912–97, US)
Réaumur (René; 1683–1757, French)
Richter (Burton; 1931– , US)
Röntgen (Wilhelm; 1845–1923, German)
Rotblat (Sir Joseph; 1908–2005, Polish/British)

Seaborg (Glenn; 1912–99, US)
Szilard (Leo; 1898–1964, Hungarian/US)
Thomson (Sir George Paget; 1892–1975, English)
Thomson (Sir J J; 1856–1940, English)
Tyndall (John; 1820–93, Irish)
Wheeler (John; 1911–2008, US)
Wilkins (Maurice; 1916–2004, New Zealand/British)

08 Anderson (Carl; 1905–91, US)
Anderson (Philip W; 1923– , US)
Ångström (Anders Jonas; 1814–74, Swedish)
Appleton (Sir Edward; 1892–1965, English)
Avogadro (Amedeo; 1776–1856, Italian)
Beaufort (Sir Francis; 1774–1857, British)
Blackett (Patrick Stuart, Lord; 1897–1974, English)
Brattain (Walter; 1902–87, US)
Brewster (Sir David; 1781–1868, Scottish)
Bridgman (P W; 1882–1961, US)
Chadwick (Sir James; 1891–1974, English)
Cherwell (Frederick Lindemann, Viscount; 1886–1957, English)
Clausius (Rudolf; 1822–88, German)
Davisson (Clinton; 1881–1958, US)
Einstein (Albert; 1879–1955, German/Swiss/US)
Foucault (Léon; 1819–68, French)
Gell-Mann (Murray; 1929– , US)
Ginzburg (Vitaly L; 1916–2009, Russian)
Grünberg (Peter; 1939– , German)
Ketterle (Wolfgang; 1957– , German)
Lawrence (Ernest; 1901–58, US)
Mulliken (Robert S; 1896–1986, US)
Oliphant (Sir Mark; 1901–2000, Australian)
Rayleigh (John William Strutt, Lord; 1842–1919, English)
Roentgen (Wilhelm; 1845–1923, German)
Sakharov (Andrei; 1921–89, Soviet)
Shockley (William; 1910–89, US)
Siegbahn (Kai M; 1918–2007, Swedish)
Van Allen (James; 1914–2006, US)
Weinberg (Steven; 1933– , US)
Wineland (David; 1944– , US)
Zworykin (Vladimir; 1889–1982, Russian/US)

09 Abrikosov (Alexei A; 1928– , Russian)
Atanasoff (John; 1903–95, US)
Bartholin (Erasmus; 1625–98, Danish)
Becquerel (Henri; 1852–1908, French)
Boltzmann (Ludwig; 1844–1906, Austrian)
Cavendish (Henry; 1731–1810, English)
Cherenkov (Pavel; 1904–90, Soviet)
Cockcroft (Sir John; 1897–1967, English)
Gay-Lussac (Joseph; 1778–1850, French)
Heaviside (Oliver; 1850–1925, English)
Helmholtz (Hermann von; 1821–94, German)
Josephson (Brian; 1940– , Welsh)

Kirchhoff (Gustav; 1824–87, German)
Kobayashi (Makoto; 1944– , Japanese)
Kurchatov (Igor; 1903–60, Soviet)
Michelson (Albert; 1852–1931, Polish/US)
Mössbauer (Rudolf; 1929–2011, German)
Novoselov (Konstantin; 1974– , Russian)
Uhlenbeck (George; 1900–88, Dutch/US)
Waterston (John James; 1811–83, Scottish)

10 Barkhausen (Heinrich; 1881–1956, German)
Fahrenheit (Daniel; 1686–1736, German)
Fraunhofer (Joseph von; 1787–1826, German)
Glazebrook (Sir Richard; 1854–1935, English)
Heisenberg (Werner; 1901–76, German)
Richardson (Sir Owen Willans; 1879–1959, English)
Rutherford (Ernest, Lord; 1871–1937, New Zealand)
Torricelli (Evangelista; 1608–47, Italian)

Watson-Watt (Sir Robert; 1892–1973, Scottish)
Weizsäcker (Carl, Freiherr von; 1912–2007, German)
Wheatstone (Sir Charles; 1802–75, English)

11 Chamberlain (Owen; 1920–2006, US)
Joliot-Curie (Frédéric; 1900–58, French)
Joliot-Curie (Irène; 1897–1956, French)
Leeuwenhoek (Antoni van; 1632–1723, Dutch)
Oppenheimer (Robert; 1904–67, US)
Schrödinger (Erwin; 1887–1961, Austrian)
Van de Graaff (Robert J; 1901–67, US)

12 Lennard-Jones (Sir John; 1894–1954, English)
Spottiswoode (William; 1825–83, English)

13 Chandrasekhar (Subrahmanyan; 1910–95, Indian/US)
Goeppert-Mayer (Maria; 1906–72, German/US)

Terms used in physics include:

03 gal
gas
GeV
GUT
ion
law
QCD
QED
SHM
TOE

04 area
atom
barn
flux
heat
lens
mass
node
rule
spin
torr
wave
WIMP
work
X-ray

05 chaos
crith
fermi
field
focus
force
henry
laser
lever
light
phase

power
quark
ratio
sabin
sound
speed
SQUID
state

06 albedo
atomic
charge
couple
dipole
energy
engine
exergy
Kelvin
liquid
mirror
moment
motion
optics
phonon
photon
plasma
proton
quench
scalar
SI unit
string
theory
vacuum
volume
weight

07 astatic
capture

carrier
chronon
density
digital
dynamic
entropy
formula
gravity
inertia
isotope
kinetic
lambert
maxwell
neutron
nuclear
nucleus
oersted
orbital
poundal
process
singlet
speckle
statics
tension

08 absorber
adhesion
adynamic
alpha ray
antinode
critical
electron
ensemble
enthalpy
equation
friction
gamma ray

graviton
half-life
harmonic
infrared
molecule
momentum
monopole
neutrino
nutation
particle
periodic
polarity
pressure
rest mass
spectrum
velocity
vibronic
wormhole

09 abundance
acoustics
amplitude
aperiodic
atmolysis
black body
collision
conductor
cosmology
deviation
dimension
elastance
frequency
hyperfine
incidence
induction
insulator
isenergic
magnetism
mechanics
Mohs scale
multiplet
potential
principle
radiation
radio wave
resonance
schlieren
sound wave
sparticle
subatomic
substance
transient
vibration
viscosity
weak force
white heat
world line

10 anharmonic
annihilate

athermancy
attraction
Cooper pair
cryogenics
degenerate
diacaustic
efficiency
elasticity
flash point
focal plane
force field
gauge boson
heavy water
Higgs boson
hydraulics
isentropic
Kerr effect
latent heat
Mach number
microwaves
multiplier
pulsatance
quadrupole
reflection
refraction
relativity
relaxation
resistance
resolution
scattering
separation
shear force
spallation
straggling
ultrasound
wavelength
world sheet

11 Auger effect
backscatter
catacaustic
diffraction
electricity
equilibrium
evaporation
homocentric
illuminance
light source
mode-locking
ordinary ray
oscillation
periodic law
sensitivity
spintronics
steady state
strong force
temperature
ultraviolet

12 absolute zero

acceleration
apochromatic
Balmer series
beta particle
boiling point
caustic curve
centre of mass
critical mass
Fresnel zones
hydrostatics
impenetrable
interference
Kelvin effect
laws of motion
Lorentz force
luminescence
nanoparticle
pyro-electric
radioisotope
recalescence
spectroscopy
speed of light
standing wave
string theory
time dilation
wave equation
wave property
work function
Zeeman effect

13 alpha particle
Appleton layer
Big Bang theory
binding energy
chain reaction
change of state
freezing point
hydrodynamics
incandescence
kinetic energy
kinetic theory
light emission
magnetic field
nuclear fusion
optical centre
photonegative
photopositive
Poisson's ratio
potential well
quantum theory
radioactivity
self-shielding
semiconductor
stopping power
strange matter
supersymmetry
Thomson effect
transmittance
transmutation

twistor theory
wave mechanics
14 analogue signal
applied physics
bremsstrahlung
caustic surface
Coriolis effect
Dirac's constant
interferometry
internal energy
light intensity
Meissner effect
nuclear fission
nuclear physics
parallel motion
See also **Nobel Prize**

Schottky defect
states of matter
superconductor
surface tension
thermodynamics
transverse wave
viscous damping
15 angular momentum
capillary action
centre of gravity
charged particle
conservation law
degree of freedom
electric current
electrodynamics

Fourier analysis
impact parameter
moment of inertia
Mössbauer effect
optical activity
optical spectrum
perpetual motion
Planck's constant
potential energy
renormalization
specific gravity
thermal capacity
visible spectrum
weak interaction
zero-point energy

physiology

Physiologists include:

04 Bert (Paul; 1833–86, French)
Best (Charles; 1899–1978, Canadian)
Dale (Sir Henry; 1875–1968, English)
Fick (Adolph; 1829–1901, German)
Hall (Marshall; 1790–1857, English)
Hess (Walter; 1881–1973, Swiss)
Hill (A V; 1886–1977, English)
Hyde (Ida; 1857–1945, US)
Loeb (Jacques; 1859–1924, German/US)
Roux (Wilhelm; 1850–1924, German)

05 Beale (Lionel; 1828–1906, English)
Crile (George; 1864–1943, US)
Hubel (David; 1926– , US)
Krogh (August; 1874–1949, Danish)
Kühne (Wilhelm; 1837–1900, German)
Lower (Richard; 1631–91, English)
Marey (Etienne-Jules; 1830–1904, French)
Mayow (John; 1640–79, English)
Weber (Ernst Heinrich; 1795–1878, German)
Wundt (Wilhelm; 1832–1920, German)

06 Adrian (Edgar, Lord; 1889–1977, English)
Békésy (Georg von; 1899–1972, Hungarian/US)
Bordet (Jules; 1870–1961, Belgian)
Cannon (Walter B; 1871–1945, US)
Foster (Sir Michael; 1836–1907, English)
Gasser (Herbert; 1888–1963, US)
Gmelin (Leopold; 1788–1853, German)
Granit (Ragnar; 1900–91, Swedish)
Haller (Albrecht von; 1708–77, Swiss)
Harvey (William; 1578–1657, English)
Hensen (Viktor; 1835–1924, German)
Hogben (Lancelot; 1895–1975, English)
Hunter (John; 1728–93, Scottish)
Huxley (Sir Andrew; 1917–2012, English)
Ludwig (Karl; 1816–95, German)
Müller (Johannes; 1801–58, German)
Pavlov (Ivan; 1849–1936, Russian)

Pincus (Gregory; 1903–67, US)
Richet (Charles; 1850–1935, French)
Waller (Augustus; 1816–70, English)

07 Banting (Sir Frederick; 1891–1941, Canadian)
Bayliss (Sir William; 1860–1924, English)
Beddoes (Thomas Lovell; 1803–49, English)
Bernard (Claude; 1813–78, French)
Beutler (Bruce; 1957– , US)
Borelli (Giovanni; 1608–79, Italian)
Diamond (Jared; 1937– , US)
Driesch (Hans; 1867–1941, German)
Edwards (Robert; 1925–2013, British)
Galvani (Luigi; 1737–98, Italian)
Gaskell (Walter; 1847–1914, English)
Greider (Carol; 1961– , US)
Guthrie (Charles; 1880–1963, US)
Haldane (John Scott; 1860–1936, Scottish)
Helmont (Jan Baptista van; 1579–1644, Flemish)
Heymans (Corneille; 1892–1968, Belgian)
Hodgkin (Sir Alan; 1914–98, English)
Horsley (Sir Victor; 1857–1916, English)
Houssay (Bernardo; 1887–1971, Argentine)
Langley (John; 1852–1925, English)
Macleod (John; 1876–1935, Scottish)
Purkyne (Jan; 1787–1869, Czech)
Robbins (Frederick; 1916–2003, US)
Rudbeck (Olof; 1630–1702, Swedish)
Schwann (Theodor; 1810–82, German)
Szostak (Jack; 1952– , English)

08 Barcroft (Sir Joseph; 1872–1947, Irish)
Bowditch (Henry; 1840–1911, US)
Erlanger (Joseph; 1874–1965, US)
Flourens (Pierre; 1794–1867, French)
Hartline (Haldan K; 1903–83, US)
Hoffmann (Jules; 1941– , Luxembourger)
Magendie (François; 1783–1855, French)

Mariotte (Edmé; c.1620–1684, French)
Purkinje (Jan; 1787–1869, Czech)
Senebier (Jean; 1742–1809, Swiss)
Starling (Ernest Henry; 1866–1927, English)
Steinman (Ralph; 1943–2011, Canadian)
Voronoff (Serge; 1866–1951, Russian)

09 Blackburn (Elizabeth; 1948– , Australian)
Blakemore (Colin; 1944– , British)
Cesalpino (Andrea; 1519–1603, Italian)
Dutrochet (Henri; 1776–1847, French)
Einthoven (Willem; 1860–1927, Dutch)
Guillemin (Roger; 1924– , French/US)
Helmholtz (Hermann von; 1821–94, German)

11 Bois-Reymond (Emil du; 1818–96, German)
Sherrington (Sir Charles; 1857–1952, English)

12 Brown-Séquard (Édouard; 1817–94, French)
Papanicolaou (George; 1883–1962, Greek/US)

13 Du Bois-Reymond (Emil; 1818–96, German)

14 Schmidt-Nielsen (Knut; 1915–2007, Norwegian)
Sharpey-Schäfer (Sir Edward; 1850–1935, English)

Terms used in physiology include:

04 bone
cell
skin
05 blood
brain
gland
nerve
organ
sleep
06 enzyme
growth
muscle
tissue
torpor
07 anatomy
fatigue
hormone
ketosis

vitamin
08 dormancy
genetics
reflexes
skeleton
09 digestion
endocrine
lymphatic
pathology
secretion
urination
10 estivation
excitation
immunology
metabolism
motor nerve
psychology
salivation

11 blood typing
circulation
contraction
hibernation
homeostasis
respiration
12 homoeostasis
immune system
reproduction
sensory nerve
13 fertilization
14 cardiovascular
photosynthesis
15 circadian rhythm
neurophysiology
plant physiology

See also **anatomy**; **doctor**; **Nobel Prize**; **surgery**

pianist

Pianists include:

02 Ax (Emmanuel; 1949– , US)

03 Fou (Ts'ong; 1934– , Chinese)

04 Bush (Alan; 1900–95, English)
Cole (Nat 'King'; 1919–65, US)
Hess (Dame Myra; 1890–1966, English)
John (Sir Elton; 1947– , English)
Lupu (Radu; 1945– , Romanian)
Monk (Thelonious; 1917–82, US)
Wild (Earl; 1915–2010, US)

05 Alkan (Valentin; 1813–88, French)
Arrau (Claudio; 1903–91, Chilean)
Basie (Count; 1904–84, US)
Beach (Amy 'Mrs H H A'; 1867–1944, US)
Blake (James Hubert 'Eubie'; 1887–1983, US)
Bolet (Jorge; 1914–90, Cuban)

Borge (Victor; 1909–2000, Danish/US)
Bülow (Hans von; 1830–94, German)
Corea (Chick; 1941– , US)
Evans (Bill; 1929–80, US)
Evans (Gil; 1912–88, Canadian)
Field (John; 1782–1837, Irish)
Friml (Rudolf; 1879–1972, Czech/US)
Gould (Glenn; 1932–82, Canadian)
Hallé (Sir Charles; 1819–95, German/British)
Harty (Sir Hamilton; 1880–1941, Northern Irish)
Hines (Earl; 1903–83, US)
Joyce (Eileen; 1912–91, Australian)
Lewis (Jerry Lee; 1935– , US)
Liszt (Franz; 1811–86, Hungarian)
Nyman (Michael; 1944– , English)
Ogdon (John; 1937–89, English)

Szell (George; 1897–1970, Hungarian/US)
Tatum (Art; 1910–56, US)
Tovey (Sir Donald Francis; 1873–1940, English)
Weber (Carl Maria von; 1786–1826, German)

06 Albert (Eugen d'; 1864–1932, German)
Arnaud (Yvonne; 1892–1958, French)
Atwell (Winifred; 1914–83, Trinidadian)
Busoni (Ferruccio; 1866–1924, Italian)
Chopin (Frédéric; 1810–49, Polish)
Cortot (Alfred; 1877–1962, French)
Cramer (Johann Baptist; 1771–1858, German/British)
Curzon (Sir Clifford; 1907–82, English)
Czerny (Karl; 1791–1857, Austrian)
Domino (Fats; 1928– , US)
Dussek (Jan Ladislav; 1760–1812, Czech)
Garner (Errol; 1921–77, US)
Hummel (Johann; 1778–1837, Austrian)
Joplin (Scott; 1868–1917, US)
Kenton (Stan; 1912–79, US)
Kissin (Evgeny; 1971– , Russian)
Koppel (Herman D; 1908–98, Danish)
Lamond (Frederic; 1868–1948, Scottish)
Levine (James; 1943– , US)
Martin (Frank; 1890–1974, Swiss)
Morton (Jelly Roll; 1890–1941, US)
Powell (Bud; 1924–66, US)
Schiff (András; 1953– , Hungarian/British)
Serkin (Rudolf; 1903–91, Hungarian/US)
Sitsky (Larry; 1934– , Chinese/Australian)
Stoker (Richard; 1938– , English)
Taylor (Cecil; 1933– , US)
Tracey (Stan; 1926– , English)
Turina (Joaquín; 1882–1949, Spanish)
Waller (Fats; 1904–43, US)
Wilson (Teddy; 1912–86, US)

07 Albéniz (Isaac; 1860–1909, Spanish)
Bennett (Sir William Sterndale; 1816–75, English)
Bentzon (Niels; 1919–2000; Danish)
Brendel (Alfred; 1931– , Czech)
Brubeck (Dave; 1920–2012, US)
Charles (Ray; 1930–2004, US)
Goodman (Isador; 1909–82, South African/Australian)
Hancock (Herbie; 1940– , US)
Ibrahim (Abdullah; 1934– , South African)
Johnson (James P; 1894–1955, US)
Kentner (Louis; 1905–87, Hungarian/British)
Malcolm (George; 1917–97, English)
Mathias (William; 1934–92, Welsh)
Matthay (Tobias; 1858–1945, English)
Medtner (Nikolai; 1880–1951, Russian)
Perahia (Murray; 1947– , US)

Richter (Sviatoslav; 1915–97, Russian)
Solomon (1902–88, English)
Sorabji (Kaikhosru Shapurji; 1892–1988, English)
Taneyev (Sergei; 1856–1915, Russian)
Vaughan (Sarah; 1924–90, US)

08 Argerich (Martha; 1941– , Argentine)
Bronfman (Yefim; 1958– , Russian/US)
Browning (John; 1933–2003, US)
Clementi (Muzio; 1752–1832, Italian)
Dohnányi (Ernst von; 1877–1960, Hungarian)
Franklin (Aretha; 1942– , US)
Godowsky (Leopold; 1870–1938, Russian/US)
Grainger (Percy; 1882–1961, Australian/US)
Henschel (Sir George; 1850–1934, Polish/British)
Horowitz (Vladimir; 1904–89, Russian/US)
Leighton (Kenneth; 1929–88, English)
Lhévinne (Josef; 1874–1944, Russian/US)
Pachmann (Vladimir de; 1848–1933, Russian)
Peterson (Oscar; 1925–2007, Canadian)
Richards (Henry Brinley; 1819–85, Welsh)
Schnabel (Artur; 1882–1951, Austrian)
Schumann (Clara; 1819–96, German)
Scriabin (Aleksandr; 1872–1915, Russian)
Skriabin (Aleksandr; 1872–1915, Russian)
Thalberg (Sigismond; 1812–71, German or Austrian)
Williams (Mary Lou; 1910–81, US)

09 Ashkenazy (Vladimir; 1937– , Icelandic)
Barenboim (Daniel; 1942– , Israeli)
Bernstein (Leonard; 1918–90; US)
Butterley (Nigel; 1935– , Australian)
Ellington (Duke; 1899–1974, US)
Gieseking (Walter; 1895–1956, German)
Henderson (Fletcher; 1897–1952, US)
Landowska (Wanda; 1879–1959, Polish)
MacDowell (Edward; 1861–1908, US)
Moscheles (Ignaz; 1794–1870, Bohemian)
Stevenson (Ronald; 1928– , Scottish)
Westbrook (Mike; 1936– , English)

10 de Larrocha (Alicia; 1923–2009, Spanish)
Gottschalk (Louis Moreau; 1829–69, US)
Moszkowski (Moritz; 1854–1925, Polish)
Paderewski (Ignacy; 1860–1941, Polish)
Rubinstein (Anton; 1829–94, Russian)
Rubinstein (Artur; 1887–1982, Polish/US)
Scharwenka (Xaver; 1850–1924, Polish)

11 Farren-Price (Ronald; 1930– , Australian)
Mitropoulos (Dimitri; 1896–1960, Greek/US)
Reizenstein (Franz; 1911–68, German)

12 Michelangeli (Arturo Benedetti; 1920–95, Italian)
Moiseiwitsch (Benno; 1890–1963, Russian/ British)

Shostakovich (Maxim Dmitriyevich; 1938– , Russian/US)

13 Little Richard (Penniman; 1932– , US)

See also **jazz**; **pop**

picture

Pictures include:

04 icon
snap

05 cameo
image
mural
pin-up
plate
print
slide
still
study

06 bitmap
canvas
design
doodle
effigy
fresco
Kit-Cat
mosaic
sketch
veduta

07 cartoon
collage
diptych
drawing

etching
modello
montage
mugshot
tableau
tracing
vanitas

08 abstract
anaglyph
graffiti
graphics
kakemono
likeness
monotype
negative
painting
Photofit®
portrait
snapshot
tapestry
transfer
triptych
vignette

09 bricolage
engraving

identikit
landscape
miniature
old master
oleograph
still life

10 altarpiece
caricature
photograph
silhouette

11 oil painting
trompe l'oeil
watercolour

12 illustration
photogravure
reproduction
self-portrait
transparency

13 passport photo

14 action painting
cabinet picture
representation

15 acrylic painting

See also **art**; **paint**; **photography**

pig

Pigs include:

05 Duroc
07 Old Spot
warthog
08 landrace
Pietrain

Tamworth
wild boar

09 Berkshire
Hampshire
Yorkshire

10 Large White
potbellied
saddleback

11 Middle White

14 Chinese Meishan

pigment

Pigments include:

03 hem
04 haem
heme
05 henna
ochre
sepia

smalt
umber

06 bister
bistre
cobalt
cyanin

lutein
madder
sienna
zaffer
zaffre

07 carmine

etiolin
gamboge
melanin
sinopia
turacin
08 cinnabar
luteolin
orpiment
rose-pink
verditer
viridian
09 anthocyan
bilirubin
colcothar
Indian red
lamp-black
lithopone
phycocyan
quercetin
vermilion
See also **dye**

zinc white
10 Berlin blue
biliverdin
Chinese red
chlorophyl
green earth
lipochrome
madder-lake
Paris-green
pearl white
rhodophane
terre verte
11 anthochlore
anthocyanin
chlorophyll
King's-yellow
phycocyanin
phycophaein
phytochrome
ultramarine

Venetian red
12 anthoxanthin
Cappagh-brown
Chinese white
chrome yellow
Naples-yellow
phaeomelanin
phycoxanthin
Prussian blue
turacoverdin
Tyrian purple
xanthopterin
13 cadmium yellow
phycoerythrin
Scheele's green
titanium white
xanthopterine
15 purple of Cassius

pike

Pikes include:

03 Esk
Red
04 Cold
High
05 Heron
Rispa

06 Causey
Kidsty
Ullock
07 Rossett
Scafell
08 Kentmere

Langdale
09 Angletarn
Grisedale
Sheffield
10 Dollywagon
Nethermost

pine

Pine trees include:

03 nut
red
04 blue
Huon
jack
pond
05 beach
black
Chile
kauri
piñon
Scots
shore
slash
stone
sugar
swamp
Swiss
white

06 Aleppo
arolla
Bhutan
bishop
celery
cembra
cowdie
cowrie
Jersey
Korean
limber
Norway
Paraná
pinyon
Scotch
spruce
Yunnan
07 Amboina
ancient
Armand's

Bosnian
Chilean
cluster
hickory
Jeffrey
Mexican
prickly
radiata
Turkish
08 Austrian
Corsican
Holford's
Japanese
Jeffrey's
knobcone
lacebark
loblolly
longleaf
maritime
Monterey

mountain
Pandanus
pinaster
Scots fir
Sumatran
umbrella
Virginia
Weymouth

09 Jerusalem
Korean nut
lodgepole
ponderosa
Scotch fir
shortleaf

whitebark

10 Macedonian
Swiss stone

11 bristlecone
Canadian red
Japanese red
Siberian nut

12 Canary island
Chinese white
eastern white
frankincense
Mexican white
monkey puzzle

Western white

13 dwarf mountain
European black
Japanese black
Japanese white
Norfolk Island
northern pitch
Siberian cedar
Siberian dwarf
Table Mountain
western yellow

14 Mexican weeping
three-leaved nut

pink

Shades of pink include:

04 puce
rose
05 coral
peach

06 oyster
salmon
shrimp
07 old rose

08 cyclamen
09 carnation
pompadour
shell pink

12 mushroom pink
shocking pink

pipe *see* **tobacco**

piracy

Pirates, privateers and buccaneers include:

03 Tew (Thomas; d.1695, American)

04 Bart (Jean; 1651–1702, French)
Gunn (Ben; *Treasure Island*, 1883, Robert
Louis Stevenson)
Hook (Captain; *Peter Pan*, 1904, J M Barrie)
Kidd (Captain William; c.1645–1701,
Scottish)
Otto (*A High Wind in Jamaica*, 1929,
Richard Hughes)
Read (Mary; b.c.1675, English)
Smee (*Peter Pan*, 1904, J M Barrie)

05 Barth (Jean; 1651–1702, French)
Bones (Billy; *Treasure Island*, 1883, Robert
Louis Stevenson)
Bonny (Anne; b.c.1697, Irish)
Bunce (Jack; *The Pirate*, 1821, Sir Walter
Scott)
Drake (Sir Francis; c.1540–96, English)
Every (Henry; b.c.1653, English)
Ewart (Nanty; *Redgauntlet*, 1824, Sir Walter
Scott)
Flint (Captain; *Swallows and Amazons*,
1930, Arthur Ransome)
Selim (*The Bride of Abydos: A Turkish Tale*,
1813, Lord Byron)
Tache (Edward; d.1718, English)
Teach (Edward; d.1718, English)

06 Aubery (Jean-Benoit; *Frenchman's Creek*,
1942, Daphne Du Maurier)
Butler (Nathaniel; c.1577–date unknown,
English)
Conrad (*The Corsair: A Tale*, 1814, Lord
Byron)
Fleury (Jean; d.1527, French)
Jonsen (Captain; *A High Wind in Jamaica*,
1929, Richard Hughes)
Morgan (Sir Henry; c.1635–88, Welsh)
Silver (Long John; *Treasure Island*, 1883,
Robert Louis Stevenson)
Thatch (Edward; d.1718, English)
Walker (William; 1824–60, US)

07 Bellamy (Samuel 'Black Sam'; c.1689–1717,
English)
Dampier (William; 1652–1715, English)
Lafitte (Jean; c.1780–c.1826, French)
O'Malley (Grace; c.1530–1603, Irish)
Rackham (John; d.1720)
Roberts (Bartholomew; c.1682–1722, Welsh)
Sparrow (Captain Jack; *Pirates of the
Caribbean*, 2003)
Surcouf (Robert; 1773–1827, French)
Trumpet (Solomon; *Jack Holborn*, 1964,
Leon Garfield)
Zheng Yi (d.1807; Chinese)

08 Altamont (Frederick; *The Pirate*, 1821, Sir Walter Scott)
Black Dog (*Treasure Island*, 1883, Robert Louis Stevenson)
Blackett (Nancy; *Swallows and Amazons*, 1930, Arthur Ransome)
Blackett (Peggy; *Swallows and Amazons*, 1930, Arthur Ransome)
Blind Pew (*Treasure Island*, 1883, Robert Louis Stevenson)

Redbeard (Khair-ed-din Barbarossa; d.1546, Barbary)
Ringrose (Basil; c.1653–86, English)
09 Black Bart (Bartholomew Roberts; c.1682–1722, Welsh)
Cleveland (Clement; *The Pirate*, 1821, Sir Walter Scott)
10 Barbarossa (Khair-ed-din; d.1546, Barbary)
Blackbeard (Edward Teach; d.1718, English)
Calico Jack (John Rackham; d.1720)

plague

The ten Biblical plagues:

04 lice	**07** locusts	**18** disease of livestock
05 boils	**08** darkness	**19** death of the firstborn
flies	**09** hailstorm	**21** Nile waters turn to blood
frogs		

plain

Plains include:

04 vega	**06** maidan	tundra	sabkhat
05 carse	pampas	**07** lowland	**08** savannah
lande	sabkha	prairie	
llano	steppe	sabkhah	

planet

Planets of the solar system:

04 Mars	Venus	**07** Jupiter
05 Earth	**06** Saturn	Mercury
Pluto	Uranus	Neptune

Terms to do with planets include:

04 axis	Jovian	gas giant	perihelion
body	Saturn	prograde	retrograde
Mars	Uranus	rotation	revolution
moon	**07** gravity	**09** axial tilt	**11** Jovian winds
05 Earth	Jupiter	celestial	morning star
orbit	Martian	magnitude	planetology
Pluto	Mercury	red planet	sidereal day
rings	Neptune	satellite	solar system
Venus	red spot	**10** atmosphere	**12** Great Red Spot
06 crater	**08** aphelion	blue planet	perturbation

See also **satellite**

plant

Plants include:

04 bulb	herb	vine	grass
bush	moss	weed	shrub
fern	tree	**05** algae	**06** annual

cactus	**07** climber	pot plant	vegetable
cereal	sapling	seedling	**10** house plant
flower			water plant
fungus	**08** air-plant	**09** evergreen	wild flower
hybrid	biennial	perennial	**15** herbaceous plant
lichen	cultivar	succulent	

Terms to do with plants include:

03 bud
ear
set

04 bark
base
bast
bine
bulb
corm
curl
gall
germ
leaf
node
root
rust
seed
shaw
soma
stem
twig
wart

05 arrow
crown
floss
frond
fruit
gemma
graft
kinin
scion
shoot
stalk
stele
stoma
thorn
trunk
tuber

06 blotch
branch
bulbel
bulbil
caulis
collar
collet

cortex
cyanin
embryo
enarch
flower
inarch
phloem
phyton
runner
stolon
succus
sucker

07 clasper
crenate
crosier
crozier
cutting
foliage
pot-sick
prickle
rhizome
sapling
soft rot
tendril
thallus

08 abscisin
blastema
brown rot
crenated
domatium
endogamy
epicotyl
etiolate
leaf curl
leaf spot
plantule
pot-bound
root ball
seedling
tegument
trichome
white rot

09 acropetal
chlorosis
cotyledon

cytokinin
diandrous
emergence
epidermis
hypocotyl
internode
pericycle
porphyrin
propagule
rootstock
subentire

10 abscission
calmodulin
distichous
fungus-gall
monoecious
perfoliate
phytotoxin
propagulum
protoplast
root nodule
starveling

11 allelopathy
chlorophyll
downy mildew
inoculation
phytochrome
pollination
sinistrorse
xeromorphic
xerophilous
xerothermic

12 monadelphous
phytohormone
sclerenchyma
xeromorphous

13 hermaphrodite
inflorescence
phytoestrogen
phytonutrient
powdery mildew

14 gynomonoecious
photosynthesis
sudden oak death

15 andromonoecious

See also **algae**; **bulb**; **cactus**; **crop**; **disease**; **emblem**; **fern**; **flower**; **fruit**; **fungus**; **garden**;
grass; **hybrid**; **insectivorous plant**; **leaf**; **lily**; **moss**; **mushroom**; **nut**; **orchid**; **palm**;
pine; **poison**; **seaweed**; **sedge**; **shrub**; **tree**; **vegetable**; **weed**; **wood**

plastic

Plastics include:

03 PVC	Teflon®	Plexiglas®	**12** polyethylene
04 PTFE	**07** Perspex®	polyester	polyurethane
UPVC	**08** Bakelite®	polythene	**13** phenolic resin
05 vinyl	silicone	**10** epoxy resin	polypropylene
06 Biopol®	**09** Celluloid®	plexiglass	**14** polynorbornene
		11 polystyrene	

play

Plays include:

04 *Loot* (1966; Joe Orton)
Not I (1972; Samuel Beckett)

05 *Eh Joe* (1965; Samuel Beckett)
Equus (1973; Peter Schaffer)
Faust (c.1775–1832; Johann Wolfgang von Goethe)
Le Cid (1637; Pierre Corneille)
Medea (2000; Liz Lochhead)
Medea (431 BC; Euripides)
Médée (1946; Jean Anouilh)
Roots (1959; Arthur Wesker)
Yerma (1934; Federico García Lorca)

06 *Becket* (1959; Jean Anouilh)
Luther (1961; John Osborne)
Phèdre (1677; Jean Racine)
St Joan (1923; George Bernard Shaw)

07 *Amadeus* (1979; Peter Schaffer)
Candida (1897; George Bernard Shaw)
Electra (c.418–410 BC; Sophocles)
Endgame (1958; Samuel Beckett)
Galileo (1938; Bertolt Brecht)
La Ronde (1900; Arthur Schnitzler)
Oedipus (c.429 BC; Sophocles)
Oleanna (1992; David Mamet)
Orestes (408 BC; Euripides)
Our Town (1938; Thornton Wilder)
Volpone (1606; Ben Jonson)
Woyzeck (1837; Georg Büchner)

08 *Antigone* (1946; Jean Anouilh)
Antigone (441 BC; Sophocles)
Betrayal (1978; Harold Pinter)
Edward II (1594; Christopher Marlowe)
Everyman (15c)
Hay Fever (1925; Noël Coward)
Huis Clos (1944; Jean-Paul Sartre)
Oresteia (c.458 BC; Aeschylus)
Peer Gynt (1867; Henrik Ibsen)
Tartuffe (1667; Molière)
The Birds (c.414 BC; Aristophanes)
The Flies (1943; Jean-Paul Sartre)
The Frogs (405 BC; Aristophanes)
The Miser (1668; Molière)
The Price (1968; Arthur Miller)

The Visit (1958; Friedrich Dürrenmatt)
The Wasps (422 BC; Aristophanes)
War Horse (2007; Nick Stafford/Michael Morpurgo)

09 *All My Sons* (1947; Arthur Miller)
Come and Go (1965; Samuel Beckett)
Happy Days (1961; Samuel Beckett)
Jerusalem (2010; Jez Butterworth)
L'Alouette (1953; Jean Anouilh)
Miss Julie (1888; August Strindberg)
Party Time (1991; Harold Pinter)
Pygmalion (1913; George Bernard Shaw)
The Chairs (1952; Eugène Ionesco)
The Clouds (423 BC; Aristophanes)
The Father (1887; August Strindberg)
The Rivals (1775; Richard Brinsley Sheridan)
The Vortex (1924; Noël Coward)

10 *A Dream Play* (1902; August Strindberg)
All for Love (1677; John Dryden)
Andromache (425 BC; Euripides)
Andromaque (1667; Jean Racine)
Lysistrata (411 BC; Aristophanes)
Misery Guts (2002; Liz Lochhead)
No Man's Land (1975; Harold Pinter)
The Bacchae (405 BC; Euripides)
The Robbers (1781; Friedrich von Schiller)
The Seagull (1912; Anton Chekhov)
Uncle Vanya (1896; Anton Chekhov)

11 *A Doll's House* (1879; Henrik Ibsen)
Blood and Ice (1982; Liz Lochhead)
Hedda Gabler (1890; Henrik Ibsen)
Love for Love (1695; William Congreve)
Maria Stuart (1800; Friedrich von Schiller)
Restoration (1981; Edward Bond)
The Blue Bird (1908; Maurice Maeterlinck)
The Crucible (1953; Arthur Miller)
The Hairy Ape (1922; Eugene O'Neill)
The Wild Duck (1884; Henrik Ibsen)
Trojan Women (415 BC; Euripides)

12 *Anna Christie* (1922; Eugene O'Neill)
Blithe Spirit (1941; Noël Coward)
Blood Wedding (1933; Federico García Lorca)
Boris Godunov (1825; Alexander Pushkin)

Cabal and Love (1783; Friedrich von Schiller)
Major Barbara (1905; George Bernard Shaw)
Private Lives (1930; Noël Coward)
Punch and Judy (traditional)
Speed-the-Plow (1988; David Mamet)
The Alchemist (1610; Ben Jonson)
The Apple Cart (1929; George Bernard Shaw)
The Caretaker (1958; Harold Pinter)
The Litigants (1715; Jean Racine)
The Mousetrap (1952; Agatha Christie)
Translations (1980; Brian Friel)

13 A Patriot for Me (1965; John Osborne)
Arms and the Man (1898; George Bernard Shaw)
A Taste of Honey (1958; Shelagh Delaney)
Bailegangaire (1986; Tom Murphy)
Doctor Faustus (1594–1601; Christopher Marlowe)
Educating Rita (1979; Willy Russell)
The Cryptogram (1994; David Mamet)
The Homecoming (1965; Harold Pinter)
The Jew of Malta (c.1592–94; Christopher Marlowe)
The Physicists (1962; Friedrich Dürrenmatt)
The Shaughraun (1876; Dion Boucicault)
The White Devil (1612; John Webster)
The Winslow Boy (1946; Terence Rattigan)

14 Can't Pay? Won't Pay! (1974; Dario Fo)
Krapp's Last Tape (1958; Samuel Beckett)
Man and Superman (1902; George Bernard Shaw)
Orlando Furioso (1594; Robert Greene)
Riders to the Sea (1904; J M Synge)
Separate Tables (1954; Terence Rattigan)
The Country Wife (1675; William Wycherley)
The Entertainer (1957; John Osborne)
The Misanthrope (1666; Molière)
The Plain Dealer (1676/7; William Wycherley)
The Silent Woman (1609; Ben Jonson)
Venice Preserv'd (1682; Thomas Otway)

15 American Buffalo (1975; David Mamet)
Angels in America (1991–92; Tony Kushner)
Bartholomew Fair (1614; Ben Jonson)
Heartbreak House (1919; George Bernard Shaw)
Look Back in Anger (1956; John Osborne)
Prometheus Bound (c.430 BC; Aeschylus)
Spring Awakening (1909; Frank Wedekind)
The Beggar's Opera (1728; John Gay)
The Emperor Jones (1920; Eugene O'Neill)
The Gigli Concert (1984; Tom Murphy)
The Iceman Cometh (1946; Eugene O'Neill)
The Three Sisters (1901; Anton Chekhov)

Too Late for Logic (1990; Tom Murphy)
Waiting for Godot (1955; Samuel Beckett)

16 Back to Methuselah (1921; George Bernard Shaw)
Beyond the Horizon (1920; Eugene O'Neill)
Cat on a Hot Tin Roof (1955; Tennessee Williams)
Death of a Salesman (1949; Arthur Miller)
Lettice and Lovage (1987; Peter Schaffer)
One Man, Two Guvnors (2011; Richard Bean)
Shirley Valentine (1986; Willy Russell)
Strange Interlude (1928; Eugene O'Neill)
Sweet Bird of Youth (1959; Tennessee Williams)
The Birthday Party (1959; Harold Pinter)
The Cherry Orchard (1904; Anton Chekhov)
The Great God Brown (1926; Eugene O'Neill)
The Sanctuary Lamp (1976; Tom Murphy)
The Way of the World (1700; William Congreve)
When We Dead Awaken (1899; Henrik Ibsen)

17 Dancing at Lughnasa (1990; Brian Friel)
Glengarry Glen Ross (1983; David Mamet)
Juno and the Paycock (1924; Sean O'Casey)
Orpheus Descending (1958; Tennessee Williams)
The Beaux Stratagem (1707; George Farquhar)
The Duchess of Malfi (1623; John Webster)
The Glass Menagerie (1945; Tennessee Williams)
'Tis Pity She's a Whore (c.1631; John Ford)

18 An Enemy of the People (1882; Henrik Ibsen)
A View from the Bridge (1955; Arthur Miller)
Desire under the Elms (1924; Eugene O'Neill)
Suddenly Last Summer (1958; Tennessee Williams)
The Threepenny Opera (1928; Bertolt Brecht)

19 Androcles and the Lion (1912; George Bernard Shaw)
The Night of the Iguana (1961; Tennessee Williams)
The School for Scandal (1777; Richard Brinsley Sheridan)

20 Inadmissible Evidence (1964; John Osborne)
In the Shadow of the Glen (1903; J M Synge)
John Bull's Other Island (1904; George Bernard Shaw)
Mrs Warren's Profession (1898; George Bernard Shaw)
The Plough and the Stars (1926; Sean O'Casey)

The School for Husbands (1662; Molière)

21 Chicken Soup with Barley (1957; Arthur Wesker)

Philadelphia, Here I Come! (1964; Brian Friel)

The Cripple of Inishmaan (1996; Martin McDonagh)

The Lady's Not for Burning (1949; Christopher Fry)

22 Mourning Becomes Electra (1931; Eugene O'Neill)

The Good Person of Setzuan (1943; Bertolt Brecht)

The Government Inspector (1836; Nikolai Gogol)

23 I'm Talking About Jerusalem (1958–59; Arthur Wesker)

Someone Who'll Watch Over Me (1992; Frank McGuinness)

Tales from the Vienna Woods (1931; Ödön von Horváth)

The Beauty Queen of Leenane (1996; Martin McDonagh)

The Caucasian Chalk Circle (1947; Bertolt Brecht)

24 Long Day's Journey Into Night (1956; Eugene O'Neill)

The Lieutenant of Inishmore (2001; Martin McDonagh)

25 Sexual Perversity in Chicago (1977; David Mamet)

26 Conversations on a Homecoming (1985; Tom Murphy)

27 Mother Courage and her Children (1941; Bertolt Brecht)

The Playboy of the Western World (1907; J M Synge)

Playwrights, dramatists and screenwriters include:

02 Fo (Dario; 1926– , Italian)

03 Ade (George; 1866–1944, US)
Box (Muriel; 1905–91, English)
Day (John; 1574–1640, English)
Fry (Christopher; 1907–2005, English)
Gay (John; 1685–1732, English)
Hay (Ian; 1876–1952, Scottish)
Kyd (Thomas; 1558–94, English)
Lee (Nathaniel; c.1649/53–1692, English)
May (Elaine; 1932– , US)

04 Bahr (Hermann; 1863–1934, Austrian)
Bale (John; 1495–1563, English)
Behn (Aphra; 1640–89, English)
Bolt (Robert; 1924–95, English)
Bond (Edward; 1934– , English)
Coen (Ethan; 1957– , US)
Coen (Joel; 1954– , US)
Cruz (Ramón de la; 1731–94, Spanish)
Dahl (Roald; 1916–90, British)
Daly (Augustin; 1838–99, US)
Dane (Clemence; 1888–1965, English)
Fast (Howard; 1914–2003, US)
Ford (John; c.1586–c.1640, English)
Gale (Zona; 1874–1938, US)
Gems (Pam; 1925–2011, English)
Gray (Simon; 1936–2008, English)
Hall (Willis; 1929–2005, English)
Hare (Sir David; 1947– , English)
Hart (Moss; 1904–61, US)
Hill (Aaron; 1685–1750, English)
Home (John; 1722–1808, Scottish)
Inge (William; 1913–73, US)
Jouy (Étienne; 1764–1846; French)
Kivi (Aleksis; 1834–72, Finnish)
Lily (John; c.1554–1606, English)

Lyly (John; c.1554–1606, English)
More (Hannah; 1745–1833, English)
Munk (Kaj; 1898–1944, Danish)
Rice (Elmer; 1892–1967, US)
Rowe (Nicholas; 1674–1718, English)
Shaw (George Bernard; 1856–1950, Irish)
Tate (Nahum; 1652–1715, Irish)
Ts'ao (Yü; 1910–96, Chinese)
Vega (Lope de; 1562–1635, Spanish)
Vian (Boris; 1920–59, French)
West (Morris; 1916–99, Australian)

05 Abell (Kjeld; 1901–61, Danish)
Akins (Zoë; 1886–1958, US)
Albee (Edward, III; 1928– , US)
Allen (Woody; 1935– , US)
Arden (John; 1930–2012, English)
Ayrer (Jacob; 1543–1605, German)
Barry (Philip; 1896–1949, US)
Behan (Brendan; 1923–64, Irish)
Betti (Ugo; 1892–1953, Italian)
Bhasa (fl.3CAD, Sanskrit)
Boker (George Henry; 1823–90, US)
Brome (Richard; c.1590–1652, English)
Byrne (John; 1940– , Scottish)
Canth (Minna; 1844–97, Finnish)
Cao Yu (1910–96, Chinese)
Čapek (Karel; 1890–1938, Czech)
Colum (Pádraic; 1881–1972, Irish)
Čsiky (Gregor; 1842–91, Hungarian)
Cueva (Juan de la; c.1550–1610, Spanish)
Dumas (Alexandre; 1802–70, French)
Edgar (David; 1948– , English)
Eliot (T S; 1888–1965, US/British)
Esson (Louis; 1879–1943, Scottish/Australian)

Ewald (Johannes; 1743–81, Danish)
Field (Nathan; 1587–c.1620, English)
Foote (Horton; 1916–2009, US)
Frayn (Michael; 1933– , English)
Friel (Brian; 1929– , Northern Irish)
Genet (Jean; 1910–86, French)
Gogol (Nikolai; 1809–52, Russian)
Gozzi (Count Carlo; 1720–1806, Italian)
Greif (Andreas; 1616–64, German)
Grieg (Nordahl; 1902–43, Norwegian)
Guare (John; 1938– , US)
Hardy (Alexandre; c.1570–c.1631, French)
Havel (Václav; 1936–2011, Czech)
Hayes (Alfred; 1911–85, English/US)
Ibsen (Henrik; 1828–1906, Norwegian)
Jesse (F Tennyson; 1888–1958, English)
Jones (Henry Arthur; 1851–1929, English)
Kinck (Hans E; 1865–1926, Norwegian)
Laube (Heinrich; 1806–84, German)
Lewis (Saunders; 1893–1985, Welsh)
Lillo (George; 1693–1739, English)
Lodge (Thomas; c.1558–1625, English)
Mamet (David; 1947– , US)
Moody (William Vaughn; 1869–1910, US)
Moore (Edward; 1712–57, English)
Nashe (Thomas; 1567–1601, English)
Odets (Clifford; 1906–63, US)
Orton (Joe; 1933–67, English)
Otway (Thomas; 1652–85, English)
Payne (John Howard; 1791–1852, US)
Peele (George; c.1558–96, English)
Piron (Alexis; 1689–1773, French)
Reade (Charles; 1814–84, English)
Rueda (Lope de; c.1510–65, Spanish)
Sachs (Hans; 1494–1576, German)
Sachs (Nelly; 1891–1970, German/Swedish)
Sheil (Richard Lalor; 1791–1851, Irish)
Simon (Neil; 1927– , US)
Smith (Dodie; 1896–1990, English)
Stone (Oliver; 1946– , US)
Sutro (Alfred; 1863–1933, English)
Synge (J M; 1871–1909, Irish)
Udall (Nicholas; 1504–56, English)
Unruh (Fritz von; 1885–1970, German)
Weiss (Peter; 1916–82, German)
Wells (John; 1936–98, English)
Wilde (Oscar; 1854–1900, Irish)
Wills (William Gorman; 1828–91, Irish)
Wolfe (George C; 1954– , US)
Yeats (W B; 1865–1939, Irish)
Young (Douglas; 1913–73, Scottish)

06 Abbott (George; 1887–1995, US)
Adamov (Arthur; 1908–70, Russian/French)
Artaud (Antonin; 1896–1948, French)
Augier (Émile; 1820–89, French)
Baraka (Amiri; 1934– , US)
Barker (Howard; 1946– , English)
Barnes (Peter; 1931–2004, English)

Barrie (J M; 1860–1937, Scottish)
Baxter (James K; 1926–72, New Zealand)
Becque (Henry; 1837–99, French)
Belloy (Dormont de; 1727–75, French)
Binchy (Maeve; 1940–2012, Irish)
Bowles (Jane; 1918–73, US)
Brecht (Bertolt; 1898–1956, German)
Bridie (James; 1888–1951, Scottish)
Brieux (Eugène; 1858–1932, French)
Bryden (Bill; 1942– , Scottish)
Casona (Alejandro; 1903–65, Spanish)
Cibber (Colley; 1671–1757, English)
Clarke (Austin; 1896–1974, Irish)
Colman (George, the Elder; 1732–94,
   English)
Colman (George, the Younger; 1762–1836,
   English)
Cooney (Ray; 1932– , English)
Cooper (Giles; 1918–66, Irish)
Coward (Sir Noël; 1899–1973, English)
Cowley (Hannah; 1743–1809, English)
Dantas (Julio; 1876–1962, Portuguese)
Davies (Terence; 1945– , English)
Dekker (Thomas; c.1570–1632, English)
Donnay (Maurice; 1859–1945, French)
Drezen (Youenn; 1899–1972, Breton)
Druten (John van; 1901–57, US)
Dryden (John; 1631–1700, English)
D'Urfey (Tom; 1653–1723, English)
Encina (Juan del; c.1469–c.1530, Spanish)
Enzina (Juan del; c.1469–c.1530, Spanish)
Ephron (Nora; 1941–2012, US)
Ervine (St John; 1883–1971, Irish)
Favart (Charles Simon; 1710–92, French)
Frisch (Max; 1911–91, Swiss)
Fugard (Athol; 1932– , South African)
Fuller (Charles H, Jnr; 1939– , US)
Gibson (Wilfrid; 1878–1962, English)
Godber (John; 1956– , English)
Goethe (Johann Wolfgang von; 1749–1832,
   German)
Grabbe (Christian; 1801–36, German)
Greene (Robert; 1558–92, English)
Guerra (Tonino; 1920–2012, Italian)
Guitry (Sacha; 1885–1957, Russian/French)
Halévy (Ludovic; 1834–1908, French)
Handke (Peter; 1942– , Austrian)
Hebbel (Friedrich; 1813–63, German)
Herzog (Werner; 1942– , German)
Hewett (Dorothy; 1923–2002, Australian)
Hilton (James; 1900–54, English)
Howard (Sidney; 1891–1939, US)
Huston (John; 1906–87, US)
Jonson (Ben; 1572–1637, English)
Kaiser (Georg; 1878–1945, German)
Kelman (James; 1946– , Scottish)
Kleist (Heinrich von; 1777–1811, German)
Kneale (Nigel; 1922–2006, Manx)

Lawler (Ray; 1921– , Australian)
Lerner (Alan Jay; 1918–86, US)
Lesage (Alain René; 1668–1747, French)
Linney (Romulus; 1930–2011, US)
Lytton (Bulwer; 1803–73, English)
Maffei (Francesco Scipione, Marchese di; 1675–1755, Italian)
Marcel (Gabriel; 1889–1973, French)
Marion (Frances; 1887–1973, US)
Mercer (David; 1928–80, English)
Miller (Arthur; 1915–2005, US)
Miller (Henry; 1891–1980, US)
Molnár (Ferenč; 1878–1952, Hungarian)
Morton (John Maddison; 1811–91, English)
Morton (Thomas; 1764–1838, English)
Murphy (Arthur; 1727–1805, Irish)
Musset (Alfred de; 1810–57, French)
Oakley (Barry; 1931– , Australian)
O'Brien (Kate; 1897–1974, Irish)
O'Casey (Sean; 1884–1964, Irish)
O'Duffy (Eimar; 1893–1935, Irish)
O'Neill (Eugene; 1888–1953, US)
Pagnol (Marcel; 1895–1974, French)
Patten (Brian; 1946– , English)
Pinero (Sir Arthur Wing; 1855–1934, English)
Pinter (Harold; 1930–2008, English)
Plater (Alan; 1935–2010, English)
Porter (Hal; 1911–84, Australian)
Potter (Dennis; 1935–94, English)
Powell (Michael; 1905–90, English)
Racine (Jean; 1639–99, French)
Riskin (Robert; 1897–1955, US)
Rotrou (Jean de; 1609–50, French)
Rowley (William; c.1585–c.1626, English)
Sardou (Victorien; 1831–1908, French)
Sartre (Jean-Paul; 1905–80, French)
Sayles (John; 1950– , US)
Scribe (Eugène; 1791–1861, French)
Seneca (Lucius Annaeus; c.4 BC–AD65, Roman)
Settle (Elkanah; 1648–1724, English)
Storey (David; 1933– , English)
Tagore (Rabindranath; 1861–1941, Indian)
Taylor (Tom; 1817–80, Scottish)
Thomas (Brandon; 1849/56–1914, English)
Trevor (William; 1928– , Irish)
Ts'ao Yü (1910–96, Chinese)
Usigli (Rodolfo; 1905–79, Mexican)
Vitrac (Roger; 1899–1952, French)
Vondel (Joost van den; 1587–1679, Dutch)
Werner (Zacharias; 1768–1823, German)
Wesker (Arnold; 1932– , English)
Wilder (Thornton; 1897–1975, US)
Wilson (August; 1945–2005, US)
07 Akerman (Chantal; 1950– , Belgian)
Alarcón (Juan Ruiz de; c.1580–1639, Spanish)

Alfieri (Vittorio, Count; 1749–1803, Italian)
Anouilh (Jean; 1910–87, French)
Arbuzov (Aleksei; 1908–86, Soviet)
Arrabal (Fernando; 1932– , Spanish)
Barbier (Jules; 1825–1901, French)
Barlach (Ernst; 1870–1938, German)
Beckett (Samuel; 1906–89, Irish)
Behrman (S N; 1893–1973, US)
Belasco (David; 1853–1931, US)
Benelli (Sem; 1877–1949, Italian)
Bennett (Alan; 1934– , English)
Bergman (Hjalmar; 1883–1931, Swedish)
Berkoff (Steven; 1937– , English)
Bernard (Tristan; 1866–1947, French)
Branner (H C; 1903–66, Danish)
Brenton (Howard; 1942– , English)
Büchner (Georg; 1813–37, German)
Burnand (Sir Francis; 1836–1917, English)
Césaire (Aimé; 1913–2008, West Indian)
Chapman (George; c.1559–1634, English)
Chekhov (Anton; 1860–1904, Russian)
Chettle (Henry; c.1560–c.1607, English)
Claudel (Paul; 1868–1955, French)
Cocteau (Jean; 1889–1963, French)
Coppola (Francis Ford; 1939– , US)
Delaney (Shelagh; 1939–2011, English)
Dennery (Adolphe; 1811–99, French)
D'Errico (Ezio; 1892–1973, Italian)
Diamond (I A L; 1920–88, Romanian/US)
Diderot (Denis; 1713–84, French)
Dodsley (Robert; 1704–64, English)
Dorfman (Ariel; 1942– , Argentine/Chilean)
Dunsany (Edward Plunkett, Lord; 1878–1957, Irish)
Elliott (Sumner Locke; 1917–91, Australian/US)
Enquist (Per Olov; 1934– , Swedish)
Ferrari (Paolo; 1822–89, Italian)
Feydeau (Georges; 1862–1921, French)
Freytag (Gustav; 1816–95, German)
Garnier (Robert; 1534–90, French)
Giacosa (Giuseppe; 1847–1906, Italian)
Goldoni (Carlo; 1707–93, Italian)
Gregory (Augusta, Lady; 1852–1932, Irish)
Guevara (Luis Vélez de; 1570–1644, Spanish)
Guimerá (Ángel; 1849–1924, Catalan)
Hampton (Christopher; 1946– , English)
Harwood (Harold Marsh; 1874–1959, English)
Heiberg (Gunnar; 1857–1929, Norwegian)
Heiberg (Johan; 1791–1860, Danish)
Hellman (Lillian; 1907–84, US)
Hervieu (Paul; 1857–1915, French)
Heywood (John; c.1497–c.1580, English)
Heywood (Thomas; c.1574–1641, English)
Hibberd (Jack; 1940– , Australian)

Holberg (Ludvig, Baron; 1684–1754, Norwegian)
Horváth (Ödön von; 1901–38, Austro-Hungarian)
Housman (Laurence; 1865–1959, English)
Ionesco (Eugène; 1912–94, Romanian/French)
Jerrold (Douglas; 1803–57, English)
Jodelle (Étienne, Sieur de Lymodin; 1532–73, French)
Kaufman (George S; 1889–1961, US)
Klinger (Friedrich M von; 1752–1831, German)
Knowles (Sheridan; 1784–1862, Irish)
Kubrick (Stanley; 1928–99, US)
Kushner (Tony; 1956– , US)
Labiche (Eugène; 1815–88, French)
La Motte (Antoine Houdar de; 1672–1731, French)
Lardner (Ring; 1885–1933, US)
Larivey (Pierre; c.1550–1612, French)
Marlowe (Christopher; 1564–93, English)
Marquis (Don; 1878–1937, US)
Marston (John; 1576–1634, English)
Maturin (Charles; 1782–1824, Irish)
McGough (Roger; 1937– , English)
Medwall (Henry; 1462–c.1505, English)
Meilhac (Henri; 1831–97, French)
Mirbeau (Octave; 1850–1917, French)
Mishima (Yukio; 1925–70, Japanese)
Molière (1622–73, French)
Moratin (Leandro de; 1760–1828, Spanish)
Naevius (Gnaeus; c.264–c.201 BC, Roman)
Nestroy (Johann; 1801–62, Austrian)
Osborne (John; 1929–94, English)
Patrick (John; 1905–95, US)
Planché (James Robinson; 1795–1880, English)
Plautus (Titus Maccius; c.250–184 BC, Roman)
Prévert (Jacques; 1900–77, French)
Rastell (John; 1475–1536, English)
Regnard (Jean François; 1655–1709, French)
Richler (Mordecai; 1931–2001, Canadian)
Romeril (John; 1945– , Australian)
Rostand (Edmond; 1868–1918, French)
Russell (Willy; 1947– , English)
Saroyan (William; 1908–81, US)
Serling (Rod; 1924–75, US)
Seymour (Alan; 1927– , Australian)
Shaffer (Peter Levin; 1926– , English)
Shepard (Sam; 1943– , US)
Shirley (James; 1596–1666, English)
Shvarts (Yevgeni; 1896–1958, Russian)
Soyinka (Wole; 1934– , Nigerian)
Speight (Johnny; 1920–98, English)
Sturges (Preston; 1898–1959, US)
Terence (c.195–159 BC, Roman)

Tolstoy (Count Aleksei Konstantinovich; 1817–75, Russian)
Travers (Ben; 1886–1980, English)
Ustinov (Sir Peter; 1921–2004, English)
Uvedale (Nicholas; 1504–56, English)
Vicente (Gil; c.1470–c.1537, Portuguese)
Walcott (Derek; 1930– , West Indian)
Webster (John; c.1580–c.1625, English)
Welland (Colin; 1934– , English)
Whiting (John; 1917–63, English)

08 Andersen (Hans Christian; 1805–75, Danish)
Anderson (Maxwell; 1888–1959, US)
Banville (Théodore de; 1823–91, French)
Beaumont (Francis; c.1584–1616, English)
Bjørnson (Bjørnstjerne; 1832–1910, Norwegian)
Brentano (Clemens von; 1778–1842, German)
Bulgakov (Mikhail; 1891–1940, Russian)
Burgoyne (John; 1722–92, English)
Congreve (William; 1670–1729, English)
Connelly (Marc; 1890–1980, US)
Dancourt (Florent; 1661–1725, French)
D'Avenant (Sir William; 1606–68, English)
Etherege (Sir George; c.1635–1691, English)
Farquhar (George; c.1677–1707, Irish)
Fielding (Henry; 1707–54, English)
Fitzball (Edward; 1792–1873, English)
Fletcher (John; 1579–1625, English)
Gilliatt (Penelope; 1932–93, English)
Gryphius (Andreas; 1616–64, German)
Hochhuth (Rolf; 1931– , German)
Holcroft (Thomas; 1745–1809, English)
Houghton (Stanley; 1881–1913, English)
Inchbald (Elizabeth; 1753–1821, English)
Johnston (Denis; 1901–84, Irish)
Kálidása (fl.450 BC, Indian)
Kotzebue (August von; 1761–1819, German)
Lemaître (Jules; 1853–1914, French)
Lissauer (Ernst; 1882–1937, German)
Lochhead (Liz; 1947– , Scottish)
Lonsdale (Frederick; 1881–1954, British)
Marivaux (Pierre de; 1688–1763, French)
Menander (c.343–c.291 BC, Greek)
Mortimer (Sir John; 1923–2009, English)
Pasolini (Pier Paolo; 1922–75, Italian)
Polanski (Roman; 1933– , French/Polish)
Randolph (Thomas; 1605–35, English)
Rattigan (Sir Terence; 1911–77, English)
Richards (Alun; 1929–2004, Welsh)
Robinson (Lennox; 1886–1958, Irish)
Ruzzante (1502–42, Italian)
Salacrou (Armand; 1899–1990, French)
Schiller (Friedrich von; 1759–1805, German)
Schröder (Friedrich; 1744–1816, German)
Shadwell (Thomas; c.1642–1692, English)
Sheridan (Richard Brinsley; 1751–1816, Irish)

Sherriff (R C; 1896–1975, English)
Sherwood (Robert E; 1896–1955, US)
Stoppard (Sir Tom; 1937–   , Czech/British)
Suckling (Sir John; 1609–42, English)
Tourneur (Cyril; c.1575–1626, English)
Vanbrugh (Sir John; 1664–1726, English)
von Trier (Lars; 1956–   , Danish)
Wedekind (Frank; 1864–1918, German)
Wildgans (Anton; 1881–1932, Austrian)
Williams (Emlyn; 1905–87, Welsh)
Williams (Tennessee; 1911–83, US)

09 Aeschylus (c.525–c.456 BC, Greek)
Ayckbourn (Sir Alan; 1939–   , English)
Bleasdale (Alan; 1946–   , English)
Bottomley (Gordon; 1874–1948, English)
Brighouse (Harold; 1882–1958, English)
Centlivre (Susannah; c.1667–c.1723, English)
Charteris (Leslie; 1907–93, US)
Chayefsky (Paddy; 1923–81, US)
Chiarelli (Luigi; 1884–1947, Italian)
Churchill (Caryl; 1938–   , English)
Corneille (Pierre; 1606–84, French)
Corneille (Thomas; 1625–1709, French)
Crébillon (Prosper Jolyot de; 1674–1762,
   French)
d'Annunzio (Gabriele; 1863–1938, Italian)
Delavigne (Casimir; 1793–1843, French)
Euripides (484/480–406 BC, Greek)
Fierstein (Harvey; 1954–   , US)
Giraudoux (Jean; 1882–1944, French)
Goldsmith (Oliver; 1730–74, Irish)
Griffiths (Trevor; 1935–   , English)
Hansberry (Lorraine; 1930–65, US)
Hauptmann (Gerhart; 1862–1946, German)
Immermann (Karl; 1796–1840, German)
Isherwood (Christopher; 1904–86, US)
Killigrew (Thomas; 1612–83, English)
Kisfaludy (Karoly; 1788–1830, Hungarian)
Lenormand (Henri-René; 1882–1951,
   French)
MacArthur (Charles; 1895–1956, US)
MacDonagh (Donagh; 1912–68, Irish)
Mankowitz (Wolf; 1924–98, English)
Marinetti (Tommaso; 1876–1944, Italian)
Massinger (Philip; 1583–1640, English)
Middleton (Thomas; c.1580–1627, English)
Minghella (Anthony; 1954–2008, English)
Ostrovsky (Aleksandr; 1823–86, Russian)
Poliakoff (Stephen; 1952–   , English)
Priestley (J B; 1894–1984, English)
Robertson (T W; 1829–71, English)
Rosenthal (Jack; 1931–2004, English)
Sackville (Thomas; 1553–1608, English)
Söderberg (Hjalmar; 1869–1941, Swedish)
Sophocles (c.496–405 BC, Greek)
Southerne (Thomas; 1660–1746, Irish)
Sudermann (Hermann; 1857–1928,
   German)

Tarantino (Quentin; 1963–   , US)
Wergeland (Hendrik; 1808–45, Norwegian)
Whitehead (William; 1715–85, English)
Wycherley (William; c.1640–1716, English)
Zavattini (Cesare; 1902–89, Italian)
Zuckmayer (Carl; 1896–1977, German)

10 Bhavabhûti (fl.8c, Indian)
Boucicault (Dion; 1820–90, Irish)
Cartwright (William; 1611–43, English)
Courteline (Georges; 1860–1929, French)
Cumberland (Richard; 1732–1811, English)
Destouches (Philippe; 1680–1754, French)
Drinkwater (John; 1882–1937, English)
Galsworthy (John; 1867–1933, English)
La Chaussée (Pierre Claude Nivelle de;
   1692–1754, French)
Lagerkvist (Pär; 1891–1974, Swedish)
Mankiewicz (Herman; 1897–1953, US)
Mayakovsky (Vladimir; 1894–1930,
   Russian)
Mnouchkine (Ariane; 1938–   , French)
Phillpotts (Eden; 1862–1960, English)
Pirandello (Luigi; 1867–1936, Italian)
Porto-Riche (Georges de; 1849–1930,
   French)
Schnitzler (Arthur; 1862–1931, Austrian)
Strindberg (August; 1849–1912, Swedish)
Vörösmarty (Michael; 1800–55, Hungarian)
Waterhouse (Keith; 1929–2009, English)
Williamson (David; 1942–   , Australian)

11 Anzengruber (Ludwig; 1839–89, Austrian)
Bontempelli (Massimo; 1878–1960, Italian)
Douglas-Home (William; 1912–92, Scottish)
García Lorca (Federico; 1898–1936,
   Spanish)
Hasenclever (Walter; 1890–1940, German)
Maeterlinck (Maurice, Count; 1862–1949,
   Belgian)
Montherlant (Henri de; 1896–1972, French)
Núñez de Arce (Gaspar; 1834–1903,
   Spanish)
Pérez Galdós (Benito; 1843–1920, Spanish)
Pixérécourt (Guilbert de; 1773–1844,
   French)
Pressburger (Emeric; 1902–88, Hungarian)
Shakespeare (William; 1564–1616, English)
Valle-Inclán (Ramón del; 1869–1936,
   Spanish)
Wildenbruch (Ernst von; 1845–1909,
   German)

12 Aristophanes (c.448–c.385 BC, Greek)
Beaumarchais (Pierre de; 1732–99, French)
Bickerstaffe (Isaac; c.1735–c.1812, Irish)
Campton, David (1924–2006, English)
Cecchi d'Amico (Suso; 1914–2010, Italian)
Hofmannsthal (Hugo von; 1874–1929,
   Austrian)

Sigurjónsson (Jóhann; 1880–1919, Icelandic)
13 Gonçalves Dias (António; 1823–64, Brazilian)
Przybyszewski (Stanisław; 1868–1927, Polish)
Tirso de Molina (c.1571–1648, Spanish)
14 Castro y Bellvis (Guillén de; 1569–1631, Spanish)

Oehlenschläger (Adam; 1779–1850, Danish)
Zorrilla y Moral (José; 1817–93, Spanish)
15 Fabre d'Églantine (Philippe; 1750–94, French)
García Gutiérrez (Antonio; 1813–84, Spanish)
Granville-Barker (Harley; 1877–1946, English)

See also **Brecht, Bertolt; Chekhov, Anton; Coward, Noël; Ibsen, Henrik; Molière; O'Neill, Eugene; Racine, Jean; Shakespeare, William; theatre; Wilde, Oscar**

player see baseball; basketball; chess; darts; football; ice hockey; Rugby League; Rugby Union; snooker; tennis

plum

Plum varieties include:

03	egg	**06**	cherry	**07**	quetsch
04	gage		damask	**08**	victoria
	musk		damson	**09**	greengage
05	prune		French		mirabelle
			mussel		

plumbing

Plumbing fittings and equipment include:

02	WC		geyser	**09**	ball valve
03	pan		hopper		blowtorch
	tap		nipple		draincock
	tee		shower		gate valve
04	bath		solder		mains pipe
	bend		toilet		nipple key
	bowl		urinal		waste pipe
	flux		washer	**10**	back boiler
	hose	**07**	cistern		bottle trap
	pipe		coupler		check valve
	plug		plunger		copper pipe
	pump		reducer		copper tube
	sink		stop end		elbow joint
	tank		Y-branch		flare joint
	trap	**08**	ballcock		header tank
05	auger		cylinder		pipe bender
	basin		drain rod		pipe cutter
	bidet		lavatory		pipe wrench
	float		lever tap		programmer
	joint		mixer tap		septic tank
	P-trap		pedestal		shower head
	U-bend		pipe clip		Teflon® tape
	union		radiator		thermostat
	valve		soil vent		tube cutter
06	boiler		stopcock	**11**	water closet
	faucet		sump pump	**12**	basin spanner
	gasket		valve key		monkey wrench

overflow bend	expansion tank	**15** immersion heater
pipe coupling	lavatory chain	lockshield valve
siphon washer	**14** gas water heater	tube flaring tool
13 deburring tool	Stillson® wrench	

Poe, Edgar Allan (1809–49)

Significant works include:

05 *Poems* (1831)

08 *Al Aaraaf* (1829)
'The Raven' (1845)

10 'Annabel Lee' (1849)
'The Gold Bug' (1843)

13 'William Wilson' (1839)

14 'The Balloon-Hoax' (1844)

18 'The Purloined Letter' (1844)

20 'The Cask of Amontillado' (1847)

'The Pit and the Pendulum' (1842)

22 *Tamerlane and Other Poems* (1827)
'The Masque of the Red Death' (1842)

24 'The Fall of the House of Usher' (1839)
'The Murders in the Rue Morgue' (1841)

26 *The Philosophy of Composition* (1846)

28 'The Facts in the Case of M Valdemar' (1845)

31 *Tales of the Grotesque and Arabesque*
(1840)

poetry

Poetry includes:

03 lay
ode

04 epic
song

05 ditty
elegy
epode
haiku
idyll
lyric
rhyme

tanka
verse

06 ballad
epopee
monody
sonnet

07 bucolic
couplet
eclogue
epigram
georgic

pantoum
rondeau
sestina
triolet
virelay

08 cinquain
clerihew
limerick
lipogram
madrigal
palinode

pastoral
thin poem
verselet
versicle

09 roundelay
shape poem

10 villanelle

12 concrete poem
epithalamium
nursery rhyme
prothalamion

Poems and poetry collections include:

02 'If' (1910, Rudyard Kipling)

04 *Crow* (1970, Ted Hughes)
'Days' (1964, Philip Larkin)
Edda (c.1000–1300, anon)
'Hope' (1815, John Keats)
'Howl' (1956, Allen Ginsberg)
'Maud' (1855, Alfred, Lord Tennyson)
Odes (23 BC, Horace)

05 *Comus* (1637, John Milton)
'Lamia' (1819, John Keats)

06 *Façade* (1923, Dame Edith Sitwell)
'Heaven' (1915, Rupert Brooke)
Hellas (1822, Percy Bysshe Shelley)
'The Fly' (1732, William Oldys)

07 'A Vision' (1881, Oscar Wilde)
Beowulf (c.1000, anon)
Don Juan (1819, Lord Byron)
Lycidas (1637, John Milton)

'Mariana' (1830, Alfred, Lord Tennyson)
Marmion (1808, Sir Walter Scott)
'Requiem' (1887, Robert Louis Stevenson)
'Rondeau' (1838, Leigh Hunt)
'The Quip' (1633, George Herbert)

08 'Bermudas' (1686–87, Andrew Marvell)
Endymion (1818, John Keats)
Georgics (c.29 BC, Virgil)
'Gunga Din' (1892, Rudyard Kipling)
Hiawatha (1855, Henry Wadsworth
Longfellow)
Hudibras (1663–78, Samuel Butler)
'Insomnia' (1881, Dante Gabriel Rossetti)
Kalevala (1835, Elias Lönnrot)
Lupercal (1960, Ted Hughes)
Queen Mab (1813, Percy Bysshe Shelley)
Ramayana (c.250 BC, Valmiki)
The Iliad (c.8c BC, Homer)
The Pearl (c.1400, anon)

'The Tyger' (1794, William Blake)
'Tithonus' (1833–59, Alfred, Lord Tennyson)
'To Autumn' (1819, John Keats)

09 *Decameron* (1358, Giovanni Boccaccio)
Human Life (1815, Samuel Taylor Coleridge)
Jerusalem (1804–20, William Blake)
'Kubla Khan' (1816, Samuel Taylor Coleridge)
The Aeneid (c.19 BC, Virgil)
The Cantos (1917, Ezra Pound)

10 'Cherry Ripe' (Thomas Campion)
'Christabel' (1816, Samuel Taylor Coleridge)
Dream Songs (1955–68, John Berryman)
In Memoriam (1850, Alfred, Lord Tennyson)
Lalla Rookh (1817, Thomas Moore)
The Dunciad (1728, Alexander Pope)
The Odyssey (c.8c BC, Homer)
The Poetics (c.330 BC, Aristotle)
The Prelude (1805, William Wordsworth)
The Village (1783, George Crabbe)
'View of a Pig' (1960, Ted Hughes)

11 'A Red, Red Rose' (1787–1803, Robert Burns)
Ars Amatoria (c.1 BC, Ovid)
'Empty Vessel' (1926, Hugh MacDiarmid)
High Windows (1974, Philip Larkin)
Holy Sonnets (17c, John Donne)
'Jabberwocky' (1872, Lewis Carroll)
Mahabharata (c.350 AD, Vyasa)
'Memorabilia' (1855, Robert Browning)
'Remembrance' (1845, Emily Brontë)
Song of My Cid (12c, Juan Ruiz)
'Sudden Light' (1863, Dante Gabriel Rossetti)
'Tam O'Shanter' (1790, Robert Burns)
The Eclogues (37 BC, Virgil)
'The Exstasie' (1896, John Donne)
'The Retreate' (1650, Henry Vaughan)
'The Sick Rose' (1794, William Blake)
'The Sluggard' (c.1700, Isaac Watts)

12 *A Glass of Beer* (17c, Dáibhidh Ó Bruadair)
'Ash Wednesday' (1930, T S Eliot)
'A Song to Celia' (1616, Ben Jonson)
A Song to David (1763, Christopher Smart)
'Auld Lang Syne' (1787–1803, Robert Burns)
Bhagavad Gita (c.400 BC)
Eugene Onegin (1828, Alexander Pushkin)
'Faith Healing' (1960, Philip Larkin)
Four Quartets (1935, T S Eliot)
Goblin Market (1862, Christina Rossetti)
'Hawk Roosting' (1957, Ted Hughes)
Homage to Clio (1960, W H Auden)
Jubilate Agno (1939, Christopher Smart)
Mercian Hymns (1971, Geoffrey Hill)
Morte d'Arthur (1469–70, Sir Thomas Malory)
'Ode to Evening' (1747, William Collins)

Paradise Lost (1667, John Milton)
Piers Plowman (14c, William Langland)
The Lucy Poems (1801, William Wordsworth)
The Visionary (1870, Jonas Lie)
The Waste Land (1922, T S Eliot)
'The Windhover' (1877, Gerard Manley Hopkins)

13 'Arms and the Boy' (1918, Wilfred Owen)
Gilgamesh Epic (1942–53, Willi Baumeister)
Leaves of Grass (1855, Walt Whitman)
Metamorphoses (8c AD, Ovid)
'Missing the Sea' (1965, Derek Walcott)
'Naming of Parts' (1942, Henry Reed)
Roman de la Rose (13c, Guillaume de Lorris and Jean de Meung)
'September Song' (1968, Geoffrey Hill)
'Song by Isbrand' (1825–50, Thomas Lovell Beddoes)
The Book of Thel (1789, William Blake)

14 *A Shropshire Lad* (1896, A E Housman)
Divina Commedia (c.1307, Dante Alighieri)
Elegiac Sonnets (1784, Charlotte Smith)
'Leda and the Swan' (1928, W B Yeats)
Les Fleurs du mal (1857, Charles Baudelaire)
'Love Songs in Age' (1964, Philip Larkin)
Lyrical Ballads (1798, Samuel Taylor Coleridge and William Wordsworth)
Orlando Furioso (1516, Ludovico Ariosto)
Song of Hiawatha (1855, Henry Wadsworth Longfellow)
'Strange Meeting' (1918, Wilfred Owen)
'The Divine Image' (1789, William Blake)
'The Feel of Hands' (1973, Thom Gunn)
'The Lotus-Eaters' (1833, Alfred, Lord Tennyson)
'The Ship of Death' (1929–30, D H Lawrence)

15 *Canterbury Tales* (c.1387–1400, Geoffrey Chaucer)
Cautionary Tales (1907, Hilaire Belloc)
'Love without Hope' (1925, Robert Graves)
'Magna Est Veritas' (1975, Stevie Smith)
'Ode on Melancholy' (1820, John Keats)
Summoned by Bells (1960, Sir John Betjeman)
The Age of Anxiety (1948, W H Auden)
The Divine Comedy (c.1307, Dante Alighieri)
'The Eve of St Agnes' (1819, John Keats)
The Faerie Queene (1590/1596, Edmund Spenser)
'The Garden of Love' (1794, William Blake)
'The Grauballe Man' (1975, Seamus Heaney)
'The Second Coming' (1920, W B Yeats)
'The Sorrow of Love' (1893, W B Yeats)

Poetry movements include:

04 Beat

07 Acmeism
digital
epitaph
imagism

08 concrete
medieval
pastoral
Trouvère

09 modernism

symbolism
Troubador
Victorian

10 Parnassian

11 found poetry
Minnesinger
objectivist
Romanticism
sound poetry
The Movement

traditional

12 metaphysical

13 Black Mountain
erasure poetry
New York School
non-conformism
post-modernism

14 chanson de geste

15 automatic poetry

Poets include:

03 Gay (John; 1685–1732, English)
Key (Francis Scott; 1780–1843, US)
Paz (Octavio; 1914–98, Mexican)
Poe (Edgar Allan; 1809–49, US)
Pye (Henry; 1745–1813, English)

04 Agee (James; 1909–55, US)
Amis (Sir Kingsley; 1922–95, English)
Benn (Gottfried; 1886–1956, German)
Blok (Aleksandr; 1880–1921, Russian)
Bold (Alan; 1943–1998, Scottish)
Cope (Wendy; 1945– , English)
Cory (William Johnson; 1823–92, English)
Cruz (Sor Juana Inés de la; 1648–95, Mexican)
Dunn (Douglas; 1942– , Scottish)
Dyer (Sir Edward; c.1545–1607, English)
Gray (Thomas; 1716–71, English)
Gunn (Thom; 1929–2004, English)
Hill (Geoffrey; 1932– , English)
Hogg (James; 1770–1835, Scottish)
Hood (Thomas; 1799–1845, English)
Hugo (Victor; 1802–85, French)
Hunt (Leigh; 1784–1859, English)
Muir (Edwin; 1887–1959, Scottish)
Okri (Ben; 1959– , Nigerian)
Ovid (43 BC–AD17, Roman)
Owen (Wilfred; 1893–1918, English)
Pope (Alexander; 1688–1744, English)
Read (Sir Herbert; 1893–1968, English)
Rich (Adrienne; 1929–2010, US)
Rowe (Nicholas; 1674–1718, English)
Sádi (c.1184–c.1292, Persian)
Tate (Allen; 1899–1979, US)
Tate (Nahum; 1652–1715, Irish)
Vega (Lope de; 1562–1635, Spanish)

05 Aiken (Conrad; 1889–1973, US)
Arany (János; 1817–82, Hungarian)
Auden (W H ; 1907–73, English/US)
Basho (Matsuo; 1644–94, Japanese)
Benét (Stephen Vincent; 1898–1943, US)
Blair (Robert; 1699–1746, Scottish)
Blake (William; 1757–1827, English)

Brant (Sebastian; 1458–1521, German)
Burns (Robert; 1759–96, Scottish)
Byron (George Gordon, Lord; 1788–1824, English)
Carew (Thomas; 1595–1639, English)
Clare (John; 1793–1864, English)
Colum (Pádraic; 1881–1972, Irish)
Crane (Hart; 1899–1932, US)
Darío (Rubén; 1867–1916, Nicaraguan)
Donne (John; c.1572–1631, English)
Duffy (Carol Ann; 1955– , Scottish)
Eliot (T S; 1888–1965, US/British)
Ewald (Johannes; 1743–81, Danish)
Frost (Robert; 1874–1963, US)
Gower (John; c.1325–1408, English)
Hafiz (c.1326–90, Persian)
Hardy (Thomas; 1840–1928, English)
Harry (Blind; fl.1470–92, Scottish)
Heine (Heinrich; 1797–1856, German)
Henri (Adrian; 1932–2000, English)
Hesse (Hermann; 1877–1962, German/Swiss)
Homer (c.8c BC; Greek)
Hulme (T E; 1883–1917, English)
Iqbal (Sir Muhammad; 1875–1938, Indian)
Joyce (James; 1882–1941, Irish)
Keats (John; 1795–1821, English)
Keble (John; 1792–1866, English)
Keyes (Sidney; 1922–43, English)
Lodge (Thomas; c.1558–1625, English)
Lucan (AD39–65, Roman)
Marot (Clément; c.1497–1544, French)
Meyer (Conrad; 1825–98, Swiss)
Moore (Marianne; 1887–1972, US)
Moore (Thomas; 1779–1852, Irish)
Myers (Frederic; 1843–1901, English)
Noyes (Alfred; 1880–1958, English)
Péguy (Charles; 1873–1914, French)
Plath (Sylvia; 1932–63, US)
Pound (Ezra; 1885–1972, US)
Prior (Matthew; 1664–1721, English)
Pulci (Luigi; 1432–84, Italian)
Reyes (Alfonso; 1889–1959, Mexican)

Rilke (Rainer Maria; 1875–1926, Austrian)
Sachs (Hans; 1494–1576, German)
Sachs (Nelly; 1891–1970, German/Swedish)
Scott (Sir Walter; 1771–1832, Scottish)
Smart (Christopher; 1722–71, English)
Smith (Charlotte; 1749–1806, English)
Smith (Stevie; 1902–71, English)
Tasso (Torquato; 1544–95, Italian)
Tynan (Katharine; 1861–1931, Irish)
Wilde (Oscar; 1854–1900, Irish)
Wolfe (Charles; 1791–1823, Irish)
Wyatt (Sir Thomas; 1503–42, English)
Yeats (W B; 1865–1939, Irish)
Young (Edward; 1683–1765, English)

06 Achebe (Chinua; 1930–2013, Nigerian)
Adcock (Fleur; 1934– , New Zealand)
Arnold (Matthew; 1822–88, English)
Austin (Alfred; 1835–1913, English)
Barnes (William; 1801–86, English)
Belloc (Hilaire; 1870–1953, French/British)
Bishop (Elizabeth; 1911–79, US)
Brooke (Rupert; 1887–1915, English)
Camões (Luís de; 1524–80, Portuguese)
Brooks (Gwendolyn; 1917–2000, US)
Carver (Raymond; 1939–88, US)
Cibber (Colley; 1671–1757, English)
Clough (Arthur Hugh; 1819–61, English)
Cowper (William; 1731–1800, English)
Crabbe (George; 1754–1832, English)
Dowson (Ernest; 1867–1900, English)
Dryden (John; 1631–1700, English)
Dunbar (William; c.1460–c.1520, Scottish)
Dutton (Geoffrey; 1922–98, Australian)
Éluard (Paul; 1895–1952, French)
Empson (Sir William; 1906–84, English)
Ennius (Quintus; c.239–169 BC; Roman)
Eusden (Laurence; 1688–1730, English)
George (Stefan; 1868–1933, German)
Goethe (Johann Wolfgang von; 1749–1832,
  German)
Graves (Robert; 1895–1985, English)
Heaney (Seamus; 1939–2013, Northern Irish)
Hegley (John; 1953– , English)
Hesiod (c.8c BC; Greek)
Horace (65–8 BC; Roman)
Hughes (Langston; 1902–67, US)
Hughes (Ted; 1930–98, English)
Jonson (Ben; 1572–1637, English)
Larkin (Philip; 1922–85, English)
Lowell (Amy; 1874–1925, US)
Lowell (Robert, Jnr; 1917–77, US)
Millay (Edna St Vincent; 1892–1950, US)
Milosz (Czeslaw; 1911–2004, Lithuanian/
  US)
Milton (John; 1608–74, English)
Morgan (Edwin; 1920–2010, Scottish)
Morris (Sir Lewis; 1833–1907, Welsh)
Motion (Andrew; 1952– , English)

Neruda (Pablo; 1904–73, Chilean)
O'Brien (Sean; 1952– , English)
Ossian (c.3c AD, Irish)
Patten (Brian; 1946– , English)
Pindar (c.518–c.438 BC; Greek)
Porter (Peter; 1929– , Australian)
Racine (Jean; 1639–99, French)
Riding (Laura; 1901–91, US)
Sappho (c.610–c.580 BC; Greek)
Sidney (Sir Philip; 1554–86, English)
Snyder (Gary; 1930– , US)
Soutar (William; 1898–1943, Scottish)
Tagore (Rabindranath; 1861–1941, Indian)
Thomas (Dylan; 1914–53, Welsh)
Thomas (Edward; 1878–1917, British)
Thomas (R S; 1913–2000, Welsh)
Trench (Richard Chenevix; 1807–86, Irish)
Vergil (70–19 BC; Roman)
Villon (François; 1431–after 1463, French)
Virgil (70–19 BC; Roman)
Waller (Edmund; 1606–87, English)
Warton (Thomas; 1728–90, English)
Wright (Judith; 1915–2000, Australian)

07 Alcaeus (c.620–after 580 BC; Greek)
Aneirin (fl.6c–7c; British)
Aneurin (fl.6c–7c; British)
Angelou (Maya; 1928– , US)
Aretino (Pietro; 1492–1556, Italian)
Ariosto (Ludovico; 1474–1533, Italian)
Beddoes (Thomas Lovell; 1803–49, English)
Belleau (Rémy; 1528–77, French)
Bennett (Louise; 1919–2006, Jamaican)
Blunden (Edmund; 1896–1974, English)
Bridges (Robert; 1844–1930, English)
Brodsky (Iosif; 1940–96, Russian/US)
Caedmon (7c; Anglo-Saxon)
Camoëns (Luis de; 1524–80, Portuguese)
Campion (Thomas; 1567–1620, English)
Causley (Charles; 1917–2003, English)
Chaucer (Geoffrey; c.1345–1400, English)
Collins (William; 1721–59, English)
Emerson (Ralph Waldo; 1803–82, US)
Flecker (James Elroy; 1884–1915, English)
Herbert (George; 1593–1633, English)
Heredia (José María; 1803–39, Cuban)
Herrick (Robert; 1591–1674, English)
Hodgson (Ralph; 1871–1962, English)
Hopkins (Gerard Manley; 1844–89, English)
Housman (A E; 1859–1936, English)
Johnson (Linton Kwesi; 1952– , Jamaican)
Layamon (fl. early 13c; English)
Lazarus (Emma; 1849–87, US)
Leonard (Tom; 1944– , Scottish)
MacCaig (Norman; 1910–96, Scottish)
MacLean (Sorley; 1911–96, Scottish)
Martial (c.40–c.104 AD; Roman)
Marvell (Andrew; 1621–78, English)
McGough (Roger; 1937– , English)

Mistral (Frédéric; 1830–1914, French)
Newbolt (Sir Henry; 1862–1938, English)
Peacock (Thomas Love; 1785–1866, English)
Pushkin (Alexander; 1799–1837, Russian)
Rexroth (Kenneth; 1905–82, US)
Rimbaud (Arthur; 1854–91, French)
Roethke (Theodore; 1908–63, US)
Ronsard (Pierre de; 1524–85, French)
Russell (George; 1867–1935, Irish)
Sassoon (Siegfried; 1886–1967, English)
Seifert (Jaroslav; 1901–86, Czech)
Service (Robert; 1874–1958, English/
    Canadian)
Shelley (Percy Bysshe; 1792–1822, English)
Sitwell (Dame Edith; 1887–1964, English)
Skelton (John; c.1460–1529, English)
Southey (Robert; 1774–1843, English)
Soyinka (Wole; 1934–   , Nigerian)
Spender (Sir Stephen; 1909–95, English)
Spenser (Edmund; c.1552–99, English)
Statius (Publius Papinius; c.45–96 AD;
    Roman)
Stevens (Wallace; 1879–1955, US)
Szirtes (George; 1948–   , Hungarian)
Vaughan (Henry; 1622–95, Welsh)
Walcott (Derek; 1930–   , West Indian)
Whitman (Walt; 1819–92, US)

08 Anacreon (c.570–c.475 BC; Greek)
Berryman (John; 1914–72, US)
Betjeman (Sir John; 1906–84, English)
Browning (Elizabeth Barrett; 1806–61,
    English)
Browning (Robert; 1812–89, English)
Bukowski (Charles; 1920–94, German/US)
Campbell (Thomas; 1777–1844, Scottish)
Catullus (Gaius Valerius; c.84–c.54 BC;
    Roman)
Congreve (William; 1670–1729, English)
Cynewulf (c.700–c.800, Anglo-Saxon)
D'Avenant (Sir William; 1606–68, English)
Day-Lewis (Cecil; 1904–72, Irish)
de la Mare (Walter; 1873–1956, English)
Fanshawe (Richard; 1608–66, English)
Ginsberg (Allen; 1926–97, US)
Hamilton (William; 1704–54, Scottish)
Hatfield (Jen; 1958–   , English)
Henryson (Robert; c.1425–c.1508, Scottish)
Jennings (Elizabeth; 1926–2001, English)
Kavanagh (Patrick; 1905–67, Irish)
Langland (William; c.1332–c.1400, English)
Lawrence (D H; 1885–1930, English)
Leopardi (Giacomo; 1798–1837, Italian)
Lochhead (Liz; 1947–   , Scottish)
Lovelace (Richard; 1618–57, English)
MacNeice (Louis; 1907–63, Northern Irish)
Mallarmé (Stéphane; 1842–98, French)
Menander (c.343–c.291 BC; Greek)
Petrarch (Francesco; 1304–74, Italian)

Rossetti (Christina; 1830–94, English)
Rossetti (Dante Gabriel; 1828–82, English)
Schiller (Friedrich; 1759–1805, German)
Shadwell (Thomas; c.1642–1692, English)
Stephens (James; 1882–1950, Irish)
Suckling (Sir John; 1609–42, English)
Tennyson (Alfred, Lord; 1809–92, English)
Thompson (Francis; 1859–1907, English)
Traherne (Thomas; c.1636–1674, English)
Tyrtaeus (fl.c.685–668 BC; Greek)
Verlaine (Paul; 1844–96, French)
Whittier (John Greenleaf; 1807–92, US)
Williams (William Carlos; 1883–1963, US)

09 Coleridge (Samuel Taylor; 1772–1834,
    English)
Dickinson (Emily; 1830–86, US)
Doolittle (Hilda; 1886–1961, US)
Fanthorpe (U A; 1929–2009, English)
Goldsmith (Oliver; 1730–74, Irish)
Lamartine (Alphonse de; 1790–1869,
    French)
Lovecraft (H P; 1890–1937, US)
Lucretius (c.99–55 BC; Roman)
Masefield (John; 1878–1967, English)
Quasimodo (Salvatore; 1901–68, Italian)
Rochester (John Wilmot, 2nd Earl of;
    1647–80, English)
Rosenberg (Isaac; 1890–1918, English)
Shenstone (William; 1714–63, English)
Swinburne (Algernon; 1837–1909, English)
Whitehead (William; 1715–85, English)
Zephaniah (Benjamin; 1958–   , British)

10 Baudelaire (Charles; 1821–67, French)
Chatterton (Thomas; 1752–70, English)
Drinkwater (John; 1882–1937, English)
Fitzgerald (Edward; 1809–83, English)
Gawain Poet (The; fl.c.1370, English)
Longfellow (Henry Wadsworth; 1807–82,
    US)
MacDiarmid (Hugh; 1892–1978, Scottish)
McGonagall (William; 1830–1902, Scottish)
Propertius (Sextus; c.48–c.15 BC; Roman)
Szymborska (Wislawa; 1923–2012, Polish)
Tannhäuser (Der; c.1210–c.1270, German)
Theocritus (c.310–250 BC; Greek)
Wordsworth (William; 1770–1850, English)

11 Apollinaire (Guillaume; 1880–1918, Italian/
    French)
Callimachus (c.305–c.240 BC; Hellenistic)
Omar Khayyám (c.1048–c.1122, Persian)
Shakespeare (William; 1564–1616, English)
Tranströmer (Tomas; 1931–   , Swedish)

12 Ferlinghetti (Lawrence; 1919–   , US)

14 Dafydd ap Gwilym (c.1315–c.1370, Welsh)
Dante Alighieri (1265–1321, Italian)

15 Thomas the Rhymer (c.1220–c.1297, Scottish)

Poets Laureate, with date of appointment:

03 Pye (Henry; 1745–1813, English; 1790)

04 Rowe (Nicholas; 1674–1718, English; 1715)
Tate (Nahum; 1652–1715, Irish; 1692)

05 Duffy (Carol Ann; 1955– , English; 2009)

06 Austin (Alfred; 1835–1913, English; 1896)
Cibber (Colley; 1671–1757, English; 1730)
Dryden (John; 1631–1700, English; 1668)
Eusden (Laurence; 1688–1730; English)
Hughes (Ted; 1930–98, English; 1984)
Jonson (Ben; 1572–1637, English; 1617)
Motion (Andrew; 1952– , English; 1999)
Warton (Thomas; 1728–90, English; 1785)

07 Bridges (Robert Seymour; 1844–1930,
English; 1913)
Southey (Robert; 1774–1843, English; 1813)

08 Betjeman (Sir John; 1906–84, English; 1972)
D'Avenant (Sir William; 1606–68, English; 1638)
Day-Lewis (Cecil; 1904–72, Irish; 1968)
Shadwell (Thomas; c.1642–1692, English; 1689)
Tennyson (Alfred, Lord; 1809–92, English; 1850)

09 Masefield (John; 1878–1967, English; 1930)
Whitehead (William; 1715–85, English; 1757)

10 Wordsworth (William; 1770–1850, English; 1843)

Poetry terms include:

03 bob	tercet	**09** free verse	short metre
04 slam	**07** sapphic	terza rima	**12** ballad stanza
05 rubai	sestina	**10** blank verse	**13** Italian sonnet
06 sonnet	**08** bobwheel	end-stopped	**14** Miltonic sonnet
stanza	cinquain	ottava rima	Sicilian octave
	quatrain	poetry slam	

See also **Betjeman, Sir John; Blake, William; Burns, Robert; Byron, George Gordon, Lord; Clare, John; Dante Alighieri; Eliot, T S; Frost, Robert; Goethe, Johann Wolfgang von; Heaney, Seamus; Homer; Hughes, Ted; Keats, John; Milton, John; Petrarch; Poe, Edgar Allan; prosody; rhyme; Shakespeare, William; Tennyson, Alfred, Lord; Virgil; Whitman, Walt; Wordsworth, William; Yeats, W B**

points of a horse *see* horse

poison

Poisoning types include:

04 food	**08** botulism	mephitism	strychnism
lead	ergotism	sapraemia	
05 algae	plumbism	saturnism	**11** phosphorism
blood	ptomaine	zinc colic	septicaemia
06 iodism	toxaemia	**10** alcoholism	**12** hydrargyrism
07 bromism	**09** brominism	molybdosis	intoxication
gassing	crotalism	salicylism	strychninism
pyaemia	fluorosis	salmonella	
sausage	lead colic	stibialism	**13** mycotoxicosis

Poisons and toxic substances include:

03 BHC	ricin	curare
04 bane	sarin	dioxin
lead	toxin	G-agent
05 abrin	venin	iodine
conin	venom	ketene
lysol	VX gas	V-agent
ozone	**06** arsine	wabain

war gas
07 arsenic
bromine
cacodyl
coniine
cyanide
digoxin
dioxane
mercury
mineral
neurine
ouabain
stibine
tanghin
08 antimony
atropine
chlordan
chlorine
cyanogen
cytisine
fluorine
gossypol
lobeline

melittin
nerve gas
Paraquat®
phosgene
ptomaine
ratsbane
rotenone
thebaine
urushiol
09 aflatoxin
amygdalin
chaconine
chlordane
muscarine
mycotoxin
nux vomica
saxitoxin
white damp
10 acrylamide
aqua Tofana
bufotenine
ciguatoxin
domoic acid

heptachlor
mustard gas
neurotoxin
oxalic acid
phosphorus
phytotoxin
picrotoxin
strychnine
tetrotoxin
11 enterotoxin
hyoscyamine
nitric oxide
prussic acid
sugar of lead
12 strophanthin
tetrodotoxin
13 Scheele's green
silver nitrate
14 carbon monoxide
glutaraldehyde
15 alpha-chloralose
hydrogen cyanide
nitrogen dioxide

Poisonous plants include:

05 dwale
07 aconite
amanita
anemone
cowbane
hemlock
lantana
08 banewort
foxglove
laburnum
mandrake
oleander

wild arum
09 digitalis
monkshood
naked boys
naked lady
poison ivy
stinkweed
wake-robin
wolfsbane
10 belladonna
cuckoo pint
jimson weed

nightshade
stramonium
thorn apple
windflower
12 giant hogweed
helmet flower
13 meadow saffron
14 castor oil plant
lords-and-ladies
15 black nightshade

Poisonous creatures include:

03 asp
04 fugu
gila
seps
weta
05 adder
cobra
viper
06 dugite
katipo
taipan
07 redback

sea wasp
08 blowfish
cerastes
jararaca
jararaka
mocassin
moccasin
ringhals
rinkhals
scorpion
sea snake
09 berg-adder
boomslang

funnel-web
globe fish
hamadryad
king cobra
puff adder
stonefish
tarantula
10 bandy-bandy
black snake
black widow
bushmaster
copperhead
coral snake

death adder
puffer fish
11 cottonmouth
gaboon viper
gila monster
rattlesnake
12 box jellyfish
scorpion fish
sea porcupine
violin spider
13 water moccasin
15 funnel-web spider

See also **insect**; **insecticide**; **narcotic**; **snake**

poker

Poker terms include:

03 pat	stud	suited	full house
shy	**05** blind	**08** hole card	**10** royal flush
04 ante	bluff	showdown	**11** busted flush
call	check	stand pat	pass the buck
flop	flush	straight	**13** community card
pair	**06** kicker	**09** four-flush	straight flush
stay			

police

Police ranks in the UK:

08 Sergeant		**18** Deputy Commissioner
09 Commander		**19** Chief Superintendent
Constable		**20** Deputy Chief Constable
Inspector		**21** Assistant Commissioner
12 Commissioner		**23** Assistant Chief Constable
14 Chief Constable		**27** Deputy Assistant Commissioner
Chief Inspector		
Superintendent		

Police forces and branches include:

02 AP	Stasi	**11** flying squad
KP	**07** Europol	gendarmerie
MP	Gestapo	strike force
PD	sweeney	sweeney todd
SS	the Yard	Yardie squad
03 CIB	**08** Interpol	**12** mobile police
CID	Mounties	Scotland Yard
KGB	**09** Air Police	secret police
Met	bomb squad	Texas Rangers
MGB	drug squad	**13** Garda Siochana
RMP	porn squad	mounted police
04 Ogpu	riot squad	Schutzstaffel
PSNI	task force	Special Branch
RCMP	vice squad	traffic police
SWAT	**10** riot police	**14** military police
05 cheka	Securitate	**15** New Scotland Yard
Garda	water guard	

Terms to do with the police include:

02 PC	fuzz	baton
PD	nark	beast
PS	nick	bobby
03 cop	plod	cheka
WPC	raid	cuffs
04 ACPO	rank	filth
beat	shop	fit-up
book	tana	force
bust	tank	frame
cell	**05** ACPOS	garda

go off
grass
jawan
manor
plant
polis
pound
set-up
snout
squad
sting
tanna
thana
tunic

06 arrest
batoon
charge
copper
cordon
curfew
fisgig
fizgig
helmet
line-up
patrol
peeler
Q-train
rozzer
rumble
sbirro
search
tannah
thanah
thanna
wanted

07 captain
caution
copshop
custody
dragnet
epaulet
Europol
jemadar
manhunt
marshal
mugshot
officer
Old Bill
pentito

round-up
station
stinger
stoolie
sweeney
thannah
the Bill
the Yard
trooper
uniform
warrant

08 evidence
gendarme
Interpol
mouchard
panda car
precinct
prowl car
sergeant
serjeant
speed gun
squad car

09 blue light
bomb squad
centenier
commander
constable
detective
drug squad
handcuffs
identikit
inspector
meat wagon
on the beat
police dog
policeman
porn squad
radar trap
riot squad
shakedown
speed trap
task force
truncheon
vice squad

10 body armour
boys in blue
carabinero
gangbuster

lieutenant
police cell
police trap
supergrass
tenderloin
tracker dog
watch house

11 carabiniere
fingerprint
flying squad
jam sandwich
Judges' Rules
police force
policewoman
stool pigeon
strike force
sweeney todd
utility belt
warrant card
Yardie squad

12 bertillonage
constabulary
incident room
mobile police
peace officer
police escort
police-manure
Scotland Yard
secret police
surveillance
walkie-talkie

13 branch officer
mounted police
police station
rogues' gallery
search warrant
Special Branch
stop-and-search
traffic police

14 catch red-handed
Chief Constable
chief inspector
criminal record
police sergeant

15 bullet-proof vest
long arm of the law
New Scotland Yard
scene of the crime

See also **detective**

political party *see* **party**

politics

Political ideologies include:

06 holism
Maoism
Nazism
07 fascism
Marxism
08 third way
Whiggism
09 anarchism
communism
democracy
neo-Nazism

pluralism
socialism
theocracy
10 absolutism
Bolshevism
federalism
liberalism
neo-fascism
Trotskyism
11 imperialism
nationalism

syndicalism
Thatcherism
12 collectivism
conservatism
13 individualism
republicanism
unilateralism
14 egalitarianism
neocolonialism
15 social democracy
totalitarianism

Politicians and political leaders include:

02 Nu (U; 1907–95, Burmese)

03 Coe (Sebastian, Lord; 1956– , English)
Doe (Samuel; 1951–90, Liberian)
Lie (Trygve; 1896–1968, Norwegian)
Moi (Daniel arap; 1924– , Kenyan)
Rao (P V Narasimha; 1921–2004, Indian)
Rau (Johannes; 1931–2006, German)
Sun (Yat-sen; 1866–1925, Chinese)
Zia (Khaleda; 1945– , Bangladeshi)

04 Amin (Idi; 1925–2003, Ugandan)
Benn (Tony; 1925– , English)
Bird (Vere Cornwall; 1910–99, Antiguan)
Blum (Léon; 1872–1950, French)
Bush (George Herbert Walker; 1924– , US)
Bush (George W; 1946– , US)
Coty (René; 1882–1962, French)
Deng (Xiaoping; 1904–97, Chinese)
Dole (Bob; 1923– , US)
Eden (Sir Anthony, 1st Earl of Avon; 1897–1977, English)
Foot (Michael; 1913–2010, English)
Ford (Gerald R; 1913–2006, US)
Gore (Al, Jnr; 1948– , US)
Hays (Will; 1879–1954, US)
Hess (Rudolf; 1894–1987, German)
Home (Alec Douglas-Home, Lord; 1903–95, English)
Hoon (Geoff; 1953– , English)
Howe (Geoffrey, Lord; 1926– , British)
Hume (John; 1937– , Northern Irish)
Hurd (Douglas, Lord; 1930– , English)
King (Mackenzie; 1874–1950, Canadian)
King (William; 1786–1853, US)
Kohl (Helmut; 1930– , German)
Meir (Golda; 1898–1978, Russian/US/Israeli)
More (Sir Thomas, St; 1478–1535, English)
Nagy (Imre; 1895–1958, Hungarian)
Owen (David, Lord; 1938– , English)
Peel (Sir Robert; 1788–1850, English)

Pitt (William; 1759–1806, English)
Polk (James K; 1795–1849, US)
Reid (John; 1947– , Scottish)
Reno (Janet; 1938– , US)
Rice (Condoleezza; 1954– , US)
Röhm (Ernst; 1887–1934, German)
Taft (William; 1857–1930, US)
Tito (1892–1980, Yugoslav)

05 Adams (Gerry; 1948– , Northern Ireland)
Adams (John; 1735–1826, US)
Adams (John Quincy; 1767–1848, US)
Agnew (Spiro T; 1918–96, US)
Ahern (Bertie; 1951– , Irish)
Amory (Derick Heathcoat Amory, 1st Viscount; 1899–1981, English)
Arens (Moshe; 1925– , Lithuanian/Israeli)
Astor (Nancy, Viscountess; 1879–1964, US/British)
Astor (Waldorf, Viscount; 1879–1952, US/British)
Bacon (Francis, Lord; 1561–1626, English)
Baker (James, III; 1930– , US)
Baker (Kenneth, Lord; 1934– , English)
Banda (Hastings; 1898–1997, Malawian)
Barak (Ehud; 1942– , Israeli)
Barre (Mohamed Siad; 1919–95, Somali)
Begin (Menachem; 1913–92, Polish/Israeli)
Bevan (Aneurin; 1897–1960, Welsh)
Biden (Joe; 1942– , US)
Blair (Tony; 1953– , British)
Botha (Louis; 1862–1919, South African)
Botha (P W; 1916–2006, South African)
Brown (Gordon; 1951– , Scottish)
Burke (Edmund; 1729–97, Irish)
Byers (Stephen; 1953– , English)
Cecil (Robert, Marquis of Salisbury; 1830–1903, English)
Clark (Alan; 1928–99, English)
Clark (Helen; 1950– , New Zealand)
Clegg (Nick; 1967– , English)

Cowen (Brian; 1960– , Irish)
Craxi (Bettino; 1934–2000, Italian)
Dacko (David; 1930–2003, Central African
Republic)
Dayan (Moshe; 1915–81, Israeli)
Dewar (Donald; 1937–2000, Scottish)
Ewing (Winnie; 1929– , Scottish)
Grant (Bernie; 1944–2000, British)
Grant (Ulysses S; 1822–85, US)
Hácha (Emil; 1872–1945, Czechoslovak)
Hague (William; 1961– , English)
Havel (Václav; 1936–2011, Czech)
Hawke (Bob; 1929– , Australian)
Hayes (Rutherford B; 1822–93, US)
Heath (Sir Edward; 1916–2005, English)
Hoxha (Enver; 1908–85, Albanian)
Juppé (Alain; 1945– , French)
Khama (Sir Seretse; 1921–80, African)
Klima (Viktor; 1947– , Austrian)
Krenz (Egon; 1937– , German)
Lenin (Vladimir Ilyich; 1870–1924, Russian)
Le Pen (Jean-Marie; 1928– , French)
Major (John; 1943– , English)
Mbeki (Thabo; 1942– , South African)
Menem (Carlos; 1935– , Argentine)
Mogae (Festus; 1939– , Botswana)
Nehru (Jawaharlal; 1889–1964, Indian)
Ne Win (U; 1911–2002, Burmese)
Nixon (Richard; 1913–94, US)
Obama (Barack; 1961– , US)
Obote (Milton; 1924–2005, Ugandan)
Palme (Olof; 1927–86, Swedish)
Peres (Shimon; 1923– , Polish/Israeli)
Perón (Isabelita; 1931– , Argentine)
Perón (Juan; 1895–1974, Argentine)
Perot (Ross; 1930– , US)
Prodi (Romano; 1939– , Italian)
Putin (Vladimir; 1952– , Russian)
Rabin (Yitzhak; 1922–95, Israeli)
Roehm (Ernst; 1887–1934, German)
Sadat (Anwar el-; 1918–81, Egyptian)
Short (Clare; 1946– , English)
Smith (Ian; 1919–2007, Rhodesian)
Smuts (Jan; 1870–1950, South African)
Steel (David, Lord; 1938– , Scottish)
Straw (Jack; 1946– , English)
Tambo (Oliver; 1917–93, South African)
Vance (Cyrus R; 1917–2002, US)

06 Abacha (Sani; 1943–98, Nigerian)
Abbott (Diane; 1953– , English)
Ancram (Michael; 1945– , English)
Antony (Mark; c.83–30 BC, Roman)
Aquino (Benigno; 1932–83, Philippine)
Aquino (Cory; 1933–2009, Philippine)
Archer (Jeffrey, Lord; 1940– , English)
Attlee (Clement, Earl; 1883–1967, English)
Bhutto (Benazir; 1953–2007, Pakistani)
Bhutto (Zulfikar; 1928–79, Pakistani)

Brandt (Willy; 1913–92, German)
Briand (Aristide; 1862–1932, French)
Caesar (Julius; 100/102–44 BC, Roman)
Carter (Jimmy; 1924– , US)
Castle (Barbara, Baroness; 1910–2002,
English)
Castro (Fidel; 1926– , Cuban)
Cheney (Dick; 1941– , US)
Chirac (Jacques; 1932– , French)
Cicero (Marcus Tullius; 106–43 BC, Roman)
Clarke (Kenneth; 1940– , English)
Delors (Jacques; 1925– , French)
Dönitz (Karl; 1891–1980, German)
Dubček (Alexander; 1921–92,
Czechoslovak)
Dulles (John Foster; 1888–1959, US)
Ecevit (Bülent; 1925–2006, Turkish)
Engels (Friedrich; 1820–95, German)
Fillon (François, 1955– , French)
Franco (Francisco; 1892–1975, Spanish)
Gandhi (Indira; 1917–84, Indian)
Gandhi (Rajiv; 1944–91, Indian)
Giroud (Françoise; 1916–2003, French)
Göring (Hermann Wilhelm; 1893–1946,
German)
Gummer (John; 1939– , English)
Hardie (Keir; 1856–1915, Scottish)
Harman (Harriet; 1950– , English)
Healey (Denis, Lord; 1917– , English)
Hitler (Adolf; 1889–1945, German)
Hoover (Herbert; 1874–1964, US)
Howard (John; 1939– , Australian)
Howard (Michael; 1941– , British)
Hun Sen (1952– , Cambodian)
Jospin (Lionel; 1937– , French)
Kabila (Joseph; 1970– , Congolese)
Kabila (Laurent-Désiré; 1939–2001,
Congolese)
Kaunda (Kenneth; 1924– , Zambian)
Kruger (Paul; 1825–1904, South African)
Lamont (Norman, Lord; 1942– , Scottish)
Lawson (Nigel, Lord; 1932– , English)
Lilley (Peter; 1943– , English)
Machel (Samora; 1933–86, Mozambique)
Marcos (Ferdinand; 1917–89, Philippine)
Marcos (Imelda; c.1930– , Philippine)
Merkel (Angela; 1954– , Germany)
Mobutu (Sese Seko; 1930–97, Zairean)
Mowlam (Mo; 1949–2005, English)
Mugabe (Robert; 1924– , Zimbabwean)
Nasser (Gamal Abd al-; 1918–70, Egyptian)
Norris (Steven; 1945– , English)
Patten (Chris, Lord; 1944– , English)
Pétain (Philippe; 1856–1951, French)
Pol Pot (1925–98, Cambodian)
Powell (Colin; 1937– , US)
Powell (Enoch; 1912–98, English)
Prasad (Rajendra; 1884–1963, Indian)

Quayle (Dan; 1947– , US)
Reagan (Ronald; 1911–2004, US)
Rhodes (Cecil; 1853–1902, South African)
Seneca (Lucius Annaeus; c.4 BC–c.65 AD,
   Roman)
Sharon (Ariel; 1928– , Israeli)
Stalin (Joseph; 1879–1953, Soviet)
Tebbit (Norman, Lord; 1931– , English)
Truman (Harry S; 1884–1972, US)
Walesa (Lech; 1943– , Polish)
Wilson (Harold, Lord; 1916–95, English)
Wilson (Woodrow; 1856–1924, US)
Wolsey (Thomas; c.1475–1530, English)

07 Acheson (Dean; 1893–1971, US)
Akihito (1933– , Japanese)
Allende (Salvador; 1908–73, Chilean)
Ashdown (Paddy, Lord; 1941– , English)
Asquith (H H, 1st Earl of Oxford and
   Asquith; 1852–1928, English)
Atatürk (Mustapha Kemal; 1881–1938,
   Turkish)
Baldwin (Stanley Baldwin, 1st Earl; 1867–
   1947, English)
Balfour (Arthur James Balfour, 1st Earl of;
   1848–1930, Scottish)
Beckett (Dame Margaret; 1943– , English)
Bingham (Hiram; 1875–1956, US)
Boateng (Paul; 1951– , British)
Bokassa (Jean Bédel; 1921–96, Central
   African Republic)
Chalker (Lynda, Baroness; 1942– , English)
Chatham (William Pitt, Earl of; 1708–78,
   English)
Clinton (Bill; 1946– , US)
Clinton (Hillary; 1947– , US)
Collins (Michael; 1890–1922, Irish)
Cresson (Edith; 1934– , French)
Dalyell (Tam; 1932– , Scottish)
Darling (Alistair; 1953– , Scottish)
de Klerk (F W; 1936– , South African)
Dukakis (Michael; 1933– , US)
Göbbels (Joseph; 1897–1945, German)
Goering (Hermann; 1893–1946, German)
Halonen (Tarja; 1943– , Finnish)
Harding (Warren G; 1865–1923, US)
Haughey (Charles; 1925–2006, Irish)
Hussein (Saddam; 1937–2006, Iraqi)
Iliescu (Ion; 1930– , Romanian)
Jackson (Andrew; 1767–1845, US)
Jackson (Glenda; 1936– , English)
Jenkins (Roy, Lord; 1920–2003, Welsh)
Johnson (Boris; 1964– , English)
Johnson (Lyndon B; 1908–73, US)
Keating (Paul; 1944– , Australian)
Kennedy (Edward; 1932–2009, US)
Kennedy (John F; 1917–63, US)
Kennedy (Robert F; 1925–68, US)
Khatami (Mohammad; 1943– , Iranian)
Kinnock (Neil; 1942– , Welsh)

Klestil (Thomas; 1932–2004, Austrian)
Koizumi (Junichiro; 1942– , Japanese)
Kosygin (Aleksei; 1904–80, Soviet)
Liddell (Helen; 1950– , Scottish)
Lincoln (Abraham; 1809–65, US)
Mandela (Nelson; 1918– , South African)
Mazarin (Jules; 1602–61, Italian/French)
McLeish (Henry; 1948– , Scottish)
Mondale (Walter F; 1928– , US)
Mubarak (Hosni; 1928– , Egyptian)
Nkrumah (Kwame; 1909–72, Ghanaian)
Noriega (General Manuel; 1940– ,
   Panamanian)
Nyerere (Julius; 1922–99, Tanzanian)
Paisley (Ian; 1926– , Northern Irish)
Parnell (Charles Stewart; 1846–91, Irish)
Pearson (Lester; 1897–1972, Canadian)
Profumo (John Dennis; 1915–2006, English)
Rifkind (Sir Malcolm; 1946– , Scottish)
Salazar (Antonio; 1889–1970, Portuguese)
Salmond (Alex; 1955– , Scottish)
Sarkozy (Nicolas; 1955– , French)
Shipley (Jenny; 1952– , New Zealand)
Suharto (Thojib N J; 1921–2008, Indonesian)
Sukarno (Ahmed; 1902–70, Indonesian)
Swinney (John; 1964– , Scottish)
Trimble (David; 1944– , Northern Irish)
Trudeau (Pierre; 1919–2000, Canadian)
Tudjman (Franjo; 1922–99, Croatian)
Walpole (Sir Robert, 1st Earl of Orford;
   1676–1745, English)
Whitlam (Gough; 1916– , Australian)
Wilhelm (II, Kaiser; 1859–1941, Prusso-
   German)
Yeltsin (Boris; 1931–2007, Russian)

08 Adenauer (Konrad; 1876–1967, German)
Andropov (Yuri; 1914–84, Soviet)
Ashcroft (John; 1942– , US)
Balladur (Edouard; 1929– , Turkish/French)
Banerjea (Sir Surendranath; 1848–1925,
   Indian)
Ben Bella (Ahmed; 1916–2012, Algerian)
Bismarck (Prince Otto von; 1815–98,
   Prusso-German)
Blunkett (David; 1947– , English)
Brezhnev (Leonid; 1906–82, Soviet)
Campbell (Kim; 1947– , Canadian)
Chamorro (Violetta; 1919– , Nicaraguan)
Chrétien (Jean; 1934– , Canadian)
Coolidge (Calvin; 1872–1933, US)
Cromwell (Oliver; 1599–1658, English)
de Gaulle (Charles; 1890–1970, French)
de Valera (Éamon; 1882–1975, Irish)
Disraeli (Benjamin, 1st Earl of Beaconsfield;
   1804–81, English)
Franklin (Benjamin; 1706–90, US)
Fujimori (Alberto; 1939– , Peruvian)
Galtieri (Leopoldo; 1926–2003, Argentine)
Garfield (James A; 1831–81, US)

Gingrich (Newt; 1943– , US)
Giuliani (Rudolph 'Rudy', 1944– , US)
Goebbels (Joseph; 1897–1945, German)
Hailsham (Quintin Hogg, 2nd Viscount;
   1907–2001, English)
Harrison (Benjamin; 1833–1901, US)
Harrison (William Henry; 1773–1841, US)
Hirohito (1901–89, Japanese)
Honecker (Erich; 1912–94, German)
Iturbide (Agustín de; 1783–1824, Mexican)
Karadjic (Radovan; 1945– , Bosnian-Serb)
Karadžić (Radovan; 1945– , Bosnian-Serb)
Kenyatta (Jomo; c.1889–1978, Kenyan)
Le Duc Tho (1911–90, Vietnamese)
McAleese (Mary; 1951– , Irish)
McCarthy (Joseph; 1909–57, US)
McKinley (William; 1843–1901, US)
Medvedev (Dmitry Anatolyevich; 1965– ,
   Russian)
Mengistu (Haile Mariam; 1941– ,
   Ethiopian)
Mulroney (Brian; 1939– , Canadian)
Napoleon (I, Bonaparte; 1769–1821,
   French)
Nicholas (I, Tsar; 1868–1918, Russian)
Obasanjo (Olusegun; 1937– , Nigerian)
Pericles (c.490–429 BC, Athenian)
Pinochet (Augusto; 1915–2006, Chilean)
Pompidou (Georges; 1911–74, French)
Portillo (Michael; 1953– , English)
Prescott (John; 1938– , English)
Robinson (Mary; 1944– , Irish)
Rumsfeld (Donald; 1932– , US)
Schröder (Gerhard; 1944– , German)
Schüssel (Wolfgang; 1945– , Austrian)
Sihanouk (King Norodom; 1922–2012,
   Cambodian)
Thatcher (Margaret, Baroness; 1925–2013,
   English)
Van Buren (Martin; 1782–1862, US)
Verwoerd (Hendrik; 1901–66, Dutch/South
   African)
Waldheim (Kurt; 1918–2007, Austrian)
Whitelaw (Willie Whitelaw, 1st Viscount;
   1918–99, Scottish)
Williams (Shirley, Baroness; 1930– ,
   English)
Zia ul-Haq (Mohammed; 1924–88,
   Pakistani)

09 Aristides (c.550–c.467 BC, Athenian)
Ben-Gurion (David; 1886–1973, Polish/
   Israeli)
Boothroyd (Betty, Baroness; 1929– ,
   English)
Bottomley (Virginia; 1948– , British)
Buthelezi (Chief Mangosuthu; 1928– ,
   South African)
Callaghan (James, Lord; 1912–2005, English)

Ceauşescu (Nicolae; 1918–89, Romanian)
Churchill (Lord Randolph; 1849–95, English)
Churchill (Sir Winston; 1874–1965, English)
Clarendon (Edward Hyde, 1st Earl of;
   1609–74, English)
Clarendon (George William Frederick
   Villiers, 4th Earl of; 1800–70, English)
Cleveland (Grover; 1837–1908, US)
Garibaldi (Giuseppe; 1807–82, Italian)
Gladstone (William; 1809–98, English)
Gorbachev (Mikhail; 1931– , Russian)
Heseltine (Michael; 1933– , English)
Ho Chi Minh (1890–1969, Vietnamese)
Jefferson (Thomas; 1743–1826, US)
Kim-Il Sung (1912–94, North Korean)
Kim Jong Il (1942–2011, North Korean)
La Guardia (Fiorello H; 1882–1947, US)
Mao Zedong (1893–1976, Chinese)
Mawhinney (Brian, Lord; 1940– , British)
McConnell (Jack; 1960– , Scottish)
Melbourne (William Lamb, 2nd Viscount;
   1779–1848, English)
Milošević (Slobodan; 1941–2006, Serbian)
Musharraf (Pervaiz; 1943– , Pakistani)
Mussolini (Benito; 1883–1945, Italian)
Netanyahu (Binyamin; 1949– , Israeli)
Parkinson (Cecil, Lord; 1932– , English)
Pretorius (Marthinus; 1819–1901, Afrikaner)
Richelieu (Armand Jean Duplessis, Duc de;
   1585–1642, French)
Roosevelt (Franklin D; 1882–1945, US)
Roosevelt (Theodore; 1858–1919, US)
Sun Yat-Sen (1866–1925, Chinese)

10 Berlusconi (Silvio; 1936– , Italian)
Clemenceau (Georges; 1841–1929, French)
Eisenhower (Dwight D; 1890–1969, US)
Enver Pasha (1881–1922, Turkish)
Fox Quesada (Vicente; 1942– , Mexican)
Hattersley (Roy, Lord); 1932– , English)
Jiang Zemin (1926– , Chinese)
Khrushchev (Nikita; 1894–1971, Soviet)
Kim Dae-Jung (1925–2009, South Korean)
Mitterrand (François; 1916–96, French)
Palmerston (Henry John Temple, 3rd
   Viscount; 1784–1865, English)
Rafsanjani (Hojatoleslam Ali Akbar
   Hashemi; 1934– , Iranian)
Talleyrand (Charles Maurice de, Prince of
   Benevento; 1754–1838, French)
Tsvangirai (Morgan; 1952– , Zimbabwean)
Waldegrave (William, Lord; 1946– ,
   English)
Walsingham (Sir Francis; c.1530–90,
   English)
Washington (George; 1732–99, US)
Wellington (Arthur, Duke of; 1769–1852,
   Irish)
Widdecombe (Ann; 1947– , English)

11 Chamberlain (Neville; 1869–1940, English)
Duncan Smith (Iain; 1954– , English)
Kumaratunga (Chandrika; 1945– , Sri
Lankan)
Livingstone (Ken; 1945– , English)
Lloyd-George (David Lloyd George, 1st Earl;
1863–1945, Welsh)
Machiavelli (Niccolò; 1469–1527, Italian)
Mountbatten (Louis, Earl; 1900–79, English)
Robespierre (Maximilien; 1758–94, French)
Rockefeller (Nelson; 1908–79, US)
Verhofstadt (Guy; 1953– , Belgian)

12 Bandaranaike (Sirimavo; 1916–2000, Sri
Lankan)
Bandaranaike (S W R D; 1899–1959,
Ceylonese)
Boutros-Ghali (Boutros; 1922– , Egyptian)
Chernomyrdin (Viktor; 1938–2010, Russian)

Hammarskjöld (Dag; 1905–61, Swedish)
Shevardnadze (Eduard; 1928– , Georgian/
Soviet)

13 Belaúnde Terry (Fernando; 1913–2002,
Peruvian)
Chateaubriand (René, Vicomte de; 1768–
1848, French)
Chiang Kai-shek (1887–1975, Chinese)

14 Bjelke-Petersen (Sir Joh; 1911–2005, New
Zealand/Australian)
Finnbogadóttir (Vígdis; 1930– , Icelandic)
Pinochet Ugarte (Augusto; 1915–2006,
Chilean)

15 Giscard d'Estaing (Valéry; 1926– ,
French)
Macapagal-Arroyo (Gloria; 1948– ,
Philippine)

Terms used in politics include:

04 bill	election	trade union
FPTP	left wing	wedge issue
veto	majority	white paper
vote	sanction	
whip	**09** apartheid	**11** ginger group
05 lobby	coalition	sovereignty
party	coup d'état	**12** civil service
state	judiciary	constitution
06 ballot	manifesto	term of office
neocon	party line	welfare state
summit	right wing	**13** electoral roll
07 cabinet	**10** devolution	privatization
council	filibuster	shadow cabinet
détente	focus group	three-line whip
Hansard	government	**14** go to the country
mandate	green paper	hung parliament
08 alliance	parliament	**15** general election
blockade	propaganda	local government
campaign	referendum	nationalization

See also **economics**; **parliament**; **party**; **president**; **prime minister**; **republic**

pony *see* **horse**

pop

Pop and rock music groups include:

02 U2	INXS	Slade
03 ABC	Pulp	Texas
REM	T-Rex	ZZ Top
Yes	Wham!	**06** Boney M
04 ABBA	**05** Bread	The Jam
AC/DC	Cream	The Who
Blur	Oasis	Travis
Free	Queen	**07** Bee Gees

Blondie
Bon Jovi
Boyzone
Genesis
Madness
Nirvana
Rainbow
Santana
Strawbs
The Band
The Cure
The Move
Traffic
Wizzard

08 Coldplay
Hawkwind
Ink Spots
New Order
Platters
Take That
The Byrds
The Clash
The Doors
The Faces
The Kinks

09 Aerosmith
Buzzcocks
Catatonia
Marillion
Motorhead
Pink Floyd
Roxy Music
Status Quo
Steely Dan
The Damned
The Eagles
The Pogues
The Police

The Smiths
The Troggs
Thin Lizzy
Uriah Heep
Wet Wet Wet
Yardbirds

10 Bad Company
Deep Purple
Def Leppard
Duran Duran
Eurythmics
Iron Maiden
Jamiroquai
Jethro Tull
Moody Blues
New Seekers
Sex Pistols
Small Faces
Spice Girls
The Animals
The Beatles
The Hollies
The Monkees
The Osmonds
The Ramones
The Seekers
The Shadows

11 Culture Club
Depeche Mode
Dire Straits
Four Seasons
Jackson Five
Judas Priest
Led Zeppelin
Manfred Mann
Procol Harum
Simple Minds
The Drifters

The Four Tops
The Scaffold
The Supremes
Wishbone Ash

12 Black Sabbath
Boomtown Rats
Fleetwood Mac
Talking Heads
The Bachelors
The Beach Boys
The Searchers
The Tremeloes
Three Degrees

13 Dave Clark Five
Isley Brothers
Lynyrd Skynyrd
Mott the Hoople
Rolling Stones
Spandau Ballet
The Carpenters
The Chieftains
The Commodores
The Communards
The Stone Roses
The Stranglers

14 Adam and the Ants
Bay City Rollers
Everly Brothers
Herman's Hermits
Tangerine Dream
The Foundations
The Temptations
Walker Brothers

15 Neville Brothers
The Grateful Dead
The Style Council
The White Stripes

Pop and rock musicians and singers include:

03 Eno (Brian; 1948– , English)
Lee (Peggy; 1920–2002, US)
Pop (Iggy; 1947– , US)
Ray (Johnnie; 1927–90, US)

04 Bush (Kate; 1958– , English)
Cher (1946– , US)
Crow (Sheryl; 1962– , US)
Dion (Céline; 1968– , Canadian)
Dury (Ian; 1942–2000, English)
Gaye (Marvin; 1939–84, US)
Gray (David; 1970– , English)
Joel (Billy; 1949– , US)
John (Sir Elton; 1947– , English)
Khan (Chaka; 1953– , US)
King (B B; 1925– , US)
King (Ben E; 1938– , US)

King (Carole; 1942– , US)
Lulu (1948– , Scottish)
Page (Jimmy; 1944– , English)
Reed (Lou; 1944– , US)
Ross (Diana; 1944– , US)
Sade (1959– , Nigerian/British)
Shaw (Sandie; 1947– , English)
Vega (Suzanne; 1959– , US)

05 Adams (Bryan; 1959– , Canadian)
Berry (Chuck; 1926– , US)
Black (Cilla; 1943– , English)
Blunt (James; 1974– , English)
Bowie (David; 1947– , English)
Brown (James; 1928–2006, US)
Byrne (David; 1952– , Scottish/US)
Carey (Mariah; 1969– , US)

Cohen (Leonard; 1934– , Canadian)
Cooke (Sam; 1935–64, US)
Davis (Sammy, Jnr; 1925–90, US)
Dylan (Bob; 1941– , US)
Ferry (Bryan; 1945– , English)
Flack (Roberta; 1939– , US)
Green (Al; 1946– , US)
Haley (Bill; 1925–81, US)
Harry (Deborah; 1945– , US)
Holly (Buddy; 1936–59, US)
Jarre (Jean-Michel; 1948– , French)
Jones (Grace; 1952– , Jamaican)
Jones (Sir Tom; 1940– , Welsh)
Lewis (Jerry Lee; 1935– , US)
Moyet (Alison; 1961– , English)
Plant (Robert; 1948– , English)
Simon (Carly; 1945– , US)
Simon (Paul; 1941– , US)
Smith (Patti; 1946– , US)
Sting (1951– , English)
Tormé (Mel; 1925–99, US)
Twain (Shania; 1965– , Canadian)
Waits (Tom; 1949– , US)
White (Barry; 1944–2003, US)
Wills (Bob; 1905–75, US)
Young (Neil; 1945– , Canadian)
Young (Will; 1979– , English)
Zappa (Frank; 1940–93, US)

06 Cocker (Joe; 1944– , English)
Cooper (Alice; 1948– , US)
Domino (Fats; 1928– , US)
Easton (Sheena; 1959– , Scottish)
Joplin (Janis; 1943–70, US)
Knight (Gladys; 1944– , US)
Lauper (Cyndi; 1953– , US)
Lennon (John; 1940–80, English)
Lennox (Annie; 1954– , Scottish)
Marley (Bob; 1945–81, Jamaican)
Mayall (John; 1933– , English)
Midler (Bette; 1945– , US)
Miller (Steve; 1943– , US)
Nelson (Ricky; 1940–85, US)
Newman (Randy; 1944– , US)
Palmer (Robert; 1949–2003, English)
Pitney (Gene; 1941–2006, US)
Prince (1958– , US)
Richie (Lionel; 1949– , US)
Sedaka (Neil; 1939– , US)
Simone (Nina; 1933–2003, US)
Spears (Britney; 1981– , US)
Summer (Donna; 1948–2012, US)
Taylor (James; 1948– , US)
Turner (Tina; 1938– , US)
Valens (Ritchie; 1941–59, US)
Watson (Doc; 1923–2012, US)
Weller (Paul; 1958– , English)
Wilson (Brian; 1942– , US)
Wonder (Stevie; 1950– , US)

Yoakam (Dwight; 1956– , US)

07 Bennett (Tony; 1926– , US)
Charles (Ray; 1930–2004, US)
Clapton (Eric; 1945– , English)
Cochran (Eddie; 1938–60, US)
Collins (Phil; 1951– , English)
Diamond (Neil; 1941– , US)
Diddley (Bo; 1928–2008, US)
Gabriel (Peter; 1950– , English)
Hendrix (Jimi; 1942–70, US)
Holland (Jools; 1958– , English)
Houston (Whitney; 1963–2012, US)
Jackson (Janet; 1966– , US)
Jackson (Michael; 1958–2009, US)
Madonna (1958– , US)
Manilow (Barry; 1946– , US)
Michael (George; 1963– , English)
Minogue (Kylie; 1968– , Australian)
O'Connor (Sinéad; 1966– , Irish)
Orbison (Roy; 1936–88, US)
Pickett (Wilson; 1941–2006, US)
Presley (Elvis; 1935–77, US)
Redding (Otis; 1941–67, US)
Richard (Sir Cliff; 1940– , English)
Rodgers (Jimmie; 1897–1933, US)
Santana (Carlos ; 1947– , Mexican)
Shannon (Del; 1939–90, US)
Stevens (Cat; 1947– , English)
Stewart (Rod; 1945– , English)
Vincent (Gene; 1935–71, US)
Warwick (Dionne; 1940– , US)

08 Costello (Elvis; 1955– , English)
Franklin (Aretha; 1942– , US)
Harrison (George; 1943–2001, English)
Knopfler (Mark; 1949– , British)
Lady Gaga (1986– , US)
Morrison (Van; 1945– , Northern Irish)
Oldfield (Mike; 1953– , English)
Robinson (Smokey; 1940– , US)
Thompson (Richard; 1949– , English)
Vandross (Luther; 1951–2005, US)
Williams (Robbie; 1974– , English)

09 Boy George (1961– , English)
Etheridge (Melissa; 1962– , US)
Faithfull (Marianne; 1946– , English)
McCartney (Sir Paul; 1942– , English)
Morrissey (Steven; 1959– , English)
Streisand (Barbra; 1942– , US)
Winehouse (Amy; 1983–2011, English)

10 Fitzgerald (Ella; 1917–96, US)
Morissette (Alanis; 1974– , Canadian)

11 Armatrading (Joan; 1950– , West Indian/
British)
Springfield (Dusty; 1939–99, English)
Springsteen (Bruce; 1949– , US)

13 Little Richard (1935– , US)

Pop songs include:

03 'Bad' (Michael Jackson)

04 '1999' (Prince)
'Gold' (Spandau Ballet)
'Help!' (The Beatles)
'Sing' (Travis)
'True' (Spandau Ballet)

05 'Clair' (Gilbert O'Sullivan)
'Crazy' (Patsy Cline)
'Diana' (Paul Anka)
'Ernie' (Benny Hill)
'Faith' (George Michael)
'Fever' (Peggy Lee)
'Layla' (Derek & the Dominoes)
'My Way' (Elvis Presley/Frank Sinatra)
'Relax' (Frankie Goes to Hollywood)
'Shout' (Lulu)
'Smile' (Lily Allen)

06 'Apache' (Shadows)
'Atomic' (Blondie)
'Exodus' (Bob Marley & the Wailers)
'Rock DJ' (Robbie Williams)
'The End' (The Doors)
'Vienna' (Ultravox)
'Volare' (Dean Martin)
'Yellow' (Coldplay)

07 'Delilah' (Tom Jones)
'D.I.V.O.R.C.E.' (Tammy Wynette)
'Grandad' (St Winifred's School Choir)
'Hey Jude' (The Beatles)
'Holiday' (Madonna)
'I Like it' (Gerry & the Pacemakers)
'Imagine' (John Lennon)
'Jamming' (Bob Marley & the Wailers)
'La Bamba' (Richie Valens)
'Let It Be' (The Beatles)
'Rat Trap' (Boomtown Rats)
'Respect' (Aretha Franklin)
'Sailing' (Rod Stewart)
'Starman' (David Bowie)

08 'Answer Me' (Frankie Laine)
'Antmusic' (Adam & the Ants)
'At the Hop' (Danny & the Juniors)
'Baby Love' (Supremes)
'Downtown' (Petula Clark)
'I Want You' (Bob Dylan)
'Love Me Do' (The Beatles)
'Mamma Mia' (Abba)
'Mony Mony' (Tommy James & the Shondells)
'Our House' (Madness)
'Paranoid' (Black Sabbath)
'Parklife' (Blur)
'Peggy Sue' (Buddy Holly)
'The Boxer' (Simon & Garfunkel)
'The Model' (Kraftwerk)

'Thriller' (Michael Jackson)
'Wannabee' (Spice Girls)
'Waterloo' (Abba)

09 'Albatross' (Fleetwood Mac)
'Born to Run' (Bruce Springsteen)
'Dance Away' (Roxy Music)
'Glory Days' (Bruce Springsteen)
'I Feel Love' (Donna Summer)
'Jean Genie' (David Bowie)
'Maggie May' (Rod Stewart)
'Metal Guru' (T Rex)
'Penny Lane' (The Beatles)
'Praise You' (Fatboy Slim)
'Release Me' (Engelbert Humperdinck)
'Something' (The Beatles)
'Stand by Me' (Ben E King)
'Two Tribes' (Frankie Goes to Hollywood)
'Wild Thing' (The Troggs)
'Yesterday' (The Beatles)

10 'All Shook Up' (Elvis Presley)
'Annie's Song' (John Denver)
'Band of Gold' (Freda Payne)
'Billie Jean' (Michael Jackson)
'Blue Monday' (New Order)
'Bye Bye Baby' (Bay City Rollers)
'Close to You' (Carpenters)
'House of Fun' (Madness)
'Jealous Guy' (John Lennon)
'King Creole' (Elvis Presley)
'Lay, Lady, Lay' (Bob Dylan)
'Lazy Sunday' (Small Faces)
'Living Doll' (Cliff Richard)
'Millennium' (Robbie Williams)
'Moving On Up' (Primal Scream)
'Night Fever' (Bee Gees)
'Perfect Day' (Lou Reed)
'Purple Haze' (Jimi Hendrix)
'Purple Rain' (Prince)
'Reet Petite' (Jackie Wilson)
'Ring of Fire' (Johnny Cash)
'Sex Machine' (James Brown)
'Sugar Sugar' (The Archies)
'Wonderwall' (Oasis)

11 'All Right Now' (Free)
'American Pie' (Don McLean)
'Back for Good' (Take That)
'Baker Street' (Gerry Rafferty)
'Cathy's Clown' (Everly Brothers)
'Firestarter' (Prodigy)
'From Me to You' (The Beatles)
'Glad All Over' (Dave Clark Five)
'Golden Brown' (The Stranglers)
'Greatest Day' (Take That)
'I Got You Babe' (Sonny & Cher)
'I Have a Dream' (Abba)

'I'm Not in Love' (10CC)
'Light My Fire' (The Doors)
'Like a Prayer' (Madonna)
'Like a Virgin' (Madonna)
'Lily the Pink' (The Scaffold)
'Mrs Robinson' (Simon and Garfunkel)
'Oliver's Army' (Elvis Costello & The Attractions)
'She Loves You' (The Beatles)
'Space Oddity' (David Bowie)
'Tainted Love' (Soft Cell)
'Venus as a Boy' (Bjork)
'Voodoo Chile' (Jimi Hendrix)

12 'A Boy Named Sue' (Johnny Cash)
'All Or Nothing' (Small Faces)
'Ashes to Ashes' (David Bowie)
'Bat out of Hell' (Meatloaf)
'Born in the USA' (Bruce Springsteen)
'Born to Be Wild' (Steppenwolf)
'Come on Eileen' (Dexys Midnight Runners)
'Common People' (Pulp)
'Dancing Queen' (Abba)
'Eleanor Rigby' (The Beatles)
'God Only Knows' (The Beach Boys)
'Heart of Glass' (Blondie)
'How Do You Do It?' (Gerry & the Pacemakers)
'It Ain't Me, Babe' (Bob Dylan)
'I Walk the Line' (Johnny Cash)
'Johnny B Goode' (Chuck Berry)
'Material Girl' (Madonna)
'No Woman No Cry' (Bob Marley & the Wailers)
'Paint It Black' (Rolling Stones)
'Pretty Vacant' (Sex Pistols)
'The Birdy Song' (The Tweets)
'The Passenger' (Iggy Pop)
'West End Girls' (Pet Shop Boys)

13 'Blueberry Hill' (Fats Domino)
'Brass in Pocket' (The Pretenders)
'Can't Buy Me Love' (The Beatles)
'Chantilly Lace' (The Big Bopper)
'Club Tropicana' (Wham)
'Design for Life' (Manic Street Preachers)
'Don't You Want Me' (Human League)
'Get off My Cloud' (Rolling Stones)
'Into the Groove' (Madonna)
'It's Not Unusual' (Tom Jones)
'It's Now Or Never' (Elvis Presley)
'Jailhouse Rock' (Elvis Presley)
'Last Christmas' (Wham!)
'London Calling' (The Clash)
'Long Tall Sally' (Little Richard)
'Mary's Boy Child' (Boney M)
'Mull of Kintyre' (Wings)
'Oh, Pretty Woman' (Roy Orbison)
'Only the Lonely' (Roy Orbison)

'Pinball Wizard' (The Who)
'Road to Nowhere' (Talking Heads)
'Rock the Casbah' (The Clash)
'Summer Holiday' (Cliff Richard)
'Tears in Heaven' (Eric Clapton)
'Urban Spaceman' (Bonzo Dog Doodah Band)

14 '20th Century Boy' (T Rex)
'A Hard Day's Night' (The Beatles)
'Always on My Mind' (Elvis Presley)
'Blue Suede Shoes' (Elvis Presley/Carl Perkins)
'Good Vibrations' (Beach Boys)
'Just Like a Woman' (Bob Dylan)
'Karma Chameleon' (Culture Club)
'Spirit in the Sky' (Norman Greenbaum)
'Stand by Your Man' (Tammy Wynette)
'Sunny Afternoon' (Kinks)
'That'll Be the Day' (Buddy Holly & the Crickets)
'The Mighty Quinn' (Bob Dylan)
'The Power of Love' (Huey Lewis & the News)
'Waterloo Sunset' (Kinks)
'White Christmas' (Bing Crosby)
'Wonderful World' (Louis Armstrong)
'You're Beautiful' (James Blunt)

15 'Baby One More Time' (Britney Spears)
'Begin the Beguine' (Julio Iglesias)
'Blowin' in the Wind' (Bob Dylan)
'Candle in the Wind' (Elton John)
'Careless Whisper' (George Michael)
'Congratulations' (Cliff Richard)
'God Save the Queen' (Sex Pistols)
'Heartbreak Hotel' (Elvis Presley)
'Hotel California' (Eagles)
'In the Name of Love' (U2)
'I Shot the Sheriff' (Bob Marley & the Wailers)
'Jumpin' Jack Flash' (Rolling Stones)
'Killing Me Softly' (Roberta Flack)
'Living on a Prayer' (Bon Jovi)
'Love Is All Around' (Troggs/Wet Wet Wet)
'Me and Bobby McGee' (Kris Kristofferson)
'Money for Nothing' (Dire Straits)
'Money, Money, Money' (Abba)
'Mr Tambourine Man' (Bob Dylan)
'Paperback Writer' (The Beatles)
'Puppet on a String' (Sandie Shaw)
'Rivers of Babylon' (Boney M)
'Silence Is Golden' (The Tremeloes)
'Smoke on the Water' (Deep Purple)
'This Charming Man' (The Smiths)
'Unchained Melody' (Righteous Brothers)
'When I Fall in Love' (Nat King Cole)
'Yellow Submarine' (The Beatles)

16 '24 Hours from Tulsa' (Gene Pitney)

'All You Need Is Love' (The Beatles)
'Bohemian Rhapsody' (Queen)
'Dancing in the Dark' (Bruce Springsteen)
'Going Underground' (Jam)
'Great Balls of Fire' (Jerry Lee Lewis)
'I Don't Like Mondays' (Boomtown Rats)
'I Should Be So Lucky' (Kylie Minogue)
'The Real Slim Shady' (Eminem)
'The Tears of a Clown' (Smokey Robinson &
  the Miracles)
'With Or Without You' (U2)
'Wuthering Heights' (Kate Bush)

17 'California Dreamin'' (Mamas & the Papas)
'Folsom Prison Blues' (Johnny Cash)
'Here Comes the Night' (Them)
'Like a Rolling Stone' (Bob Dylan)
'Nothing Compares 2 U' (Sinead O'Connor)
'Walk on the Wild Side' (Lou Reed)
'We Are the Champions' (Queen)
'Your Cheating Heart' (Hank Williams)

18 'Anyone Who Had a Heart' (Cilla Black)
'Dancing in the Street' (Martha & the
  Vandellas)
'Good Golly Miss Molly' (Little Richard)
'Merry Xmas Everybody' (Slade)
'Nights in White Satin' (Moody Blues)
'Rock around the Clock' (Bill Haley & the
  Comets)
'Stranger in Paradise' (Tony Bennett)
'The Air That I Breathe' (Hollies)
'Three Steps to Heaven' (Eddie Cochran)

19 'All I Have to Do Is Dream' (Everly Brothers)
'Don't Look Back in Anger' (Oasis)
'Ferry Cross the Mersey' (Gerry & the
  Pacemakers)
'House of the Rising Sun' (Animals)
'I Want to Hold Your Hand' (The Beatles)
'Knowing Me Knowing You' (Abba)
'Stop in the Name of Love' (Supremes)
'Strangers in the Night' (Frank Sinatra)
'What a Wonderful World' (Louis Armstrong)
'When a Man Loves a Woman' (Percy Sledge)
'You'll Never Walk Alone' (Gerry & the
  Pacemakers)

20 'Don't Stand So Close to Me' (Police)
'I Only Want to Be with You' (Dusty
  Springfield)
'Knockin' on Heaven's Door' (Bob Dylan)
'Make It Easy on Yourself' (Walker Brothers)
'My Baby Just Cares for Me' (Nina Simone)
'Smells Like Teen Spirit' (Nirvana)
'Why Do Fools Fall in Love' (Frankie Lymon
  & the Teenagers)

21 'All along the Watchtower' (Bob Dylan)
'Another Brick in the Wall' (Pink Floyd)

'Are You Lonesome Tonight?' (Elvis Presley)
'Can't Get You out of My Head' (Kylie
  Minogue)
'Can't Help Falling in Love' (Andy Williams)
'Don't Go Breaking My Heart' (Elton John &
  Kiki Dee)
'Green Green Grass of Home' (Tom Jones)
'It's All Over Now, Baby Blue' (Bob Dylan)
'River Deep Mountain High' (Ike & Tina
  Turner)
'The Wind beneath My Wings' (Lee
  Greenwood/Bette Midler)
'Wake Me Up before You Go-Go' (Wham)

22 'All Day and All of the Night' (Kinks)
'Do They Know It's Christmas' (Band Aid)
'(I Can't Get No) Satisfaction' (Rolling
  Stones)
'Should I Stay Or Should I Go' (The Clash)

23 'Bridge over Troubled Water' (Simon &
  Garfunkel)
'Donald Where's Yer Troosers' (Andy
  Stewart)
'Do You Really Want to Hurt Me' (Culture
  Club)
'He Ain't Heavy, He's My Brother' (Hollies)
'I Wanna Dance with Somebody' (Whitney
  Houston)
'(Sittin' on) The Dock of the Bay' (Otis
  Redding)
'The Times They Are A-Changin'' (Bob
  Dylan)

24 'Ain't No Mountain High Enough' (Diana
  Ross)
'(Everything I Do) I Do It for You' (Bryan
  Adams)
'Hit Me with Your Rhythm Stick' (Ian Dury &
  the Blockheads)
'You've Lost That Lovin' Feelin'' (Righteous
  Brothers)

25 'Heaven Knows I'm Miserable Now' (The
  Smiths)
'Subterranean Homesick Blues' (Bob Dylan)
'You Don't Have to Say You Love Me' (Dusty
  Springfield)

26 'I Left My Heart in San Francisco' (Tony
  Bennett)
'These Boots Are Made for Walkin'' (Nancy
  Sinatra)

27 'I Heard It through the Grapevine' (Marvin
  Gaye)
'The Sun Ain't Gonna Shine Any More'
  (Walker Brothers)

28 'With a Little Help from My Friends' (The
  Beatles)

See also **jazz**

pope

Gregory (IV; 827–44)
Gregory (IX; 1227–41)
Gregory (V; 996–99)
Gregory (VI; 1045–46)
Gregory (VII; 1073–85)
Gregory (VIII; 1187)
Gregory (X; 1271–76)
Gregory (XI; 1370–78)
Gregory (XII; 1406–15)
Gregory (XIII; 1572–85)
Gregory (XIV; 1590–91)
Gregory (XV; 1621–23)
Gregory (XVI; 1831–46)
Hadrian (I; 772–95)
Hadrian (II; 867–72)
Hadrian (III; 884–85)
Hadrian (IV; 1154–59)
Hadrian (V; 1276)
Hadrian (VI; 1522–23)
Hilarus (461–68)
Hyginus (c.137–c.140)
Marinus (I; 882–84)
Marinus (II; 942–46)
Paschal (I; 817–24)
Paschal (II; 1099–1118)
Pontian (230–35)
Romanus (897)
Sergius (I; 687–701)
Sergius (II; 844–47)
Sergius (III; 904–11)
Sergius (IV; 1009–12)
Stephen (I; 254–57)
Stephen (II; 752)
Stephen (II; III; 752–57)
Stephen (III; IV; 768–72)
Stephen (IV; V; 816–17)
Stephen (V; VI; 885–91)
Stephen (VI; VII; 896–97)
Stephen (VII; VIII; 928–31)
Stephen (VIII; IX; 939–42)
Stephen (IX; X; 1057–58)
Zosimus (417–18)

08 Agapetus (I; 535–36)
Agapetus (II; 946–55)
Anicetus (c.154–c.166)
Benedict (I; 575–79)
Benedict (II; 684–85)
Benedict (III; 855–58)
Benedict (IV; 900–03)
Benedict (IX; 1032–44/1045/1047–48)
Benedict (V; 964)
Benedict (VI; 973–74)
Benedict (VII; 974–83)
Benedict (VIII; 1012–24)
Benedict (XI; 1303–04)
Benedict (XII; 1334–42)
Benedict (XIII; 1724–30)
Benedict (XIV; 1740–58)

Benedict (XV; 1914–22)
Benedict (XVI; 2005–13)
Boniface (I; 418–22)
Boniface (II; 530–32)
Boniface (III; 607)
Boniface (IV; 608–15)
Boniface (IX; 1389–1404)
Boniface (V; 619–25)
Boniface (VI; 896)
Boniface (VIII; 1294–1303)
Eugenius (I; 654–57)
Eugenius (II; 824–27)
Eugenius (III; 1145–53)
Eugenius (IV; 1431–47)
Eusebius (310)
Formosus (891–96)
Gelasius (I; 492–96)
Gelasius (II; 1118–19)
Honorius (I; 625–38)
Honorius (II; 1124–30)
Honorius (III; 1216–27)
Honorius (IV; 1285–87)
Innocent (I; 402–17)
Innocent (II; 1130–43)
Innocent (III; 1198–1216)
Innocent (IV; 1243–54)
Innocent (IX; 1591)
Innocent (V; 1276)
Innocent (VI; 1352–62)
Innocent (VII; 1404–06)
Innocent (VIII; 1484–92)
Innocent (X; 1644–55)
Innocent (XI; 1676–89)
Innocent (XII; 1691–1700)
Innocent (XIII; 1721–24)
John Paul (I; 1978)
John Paul (II; 1978–2005)
Liberius (352–66)
Nicholas (I; 858–67)
Nicholas (II; 1059–61)
Nicholas (III; 1277–80)
Nicholas (IV; 1288–92)
Nicholas (V; 1447–55)
Pelagius (I; 556–61)
Pelagius (II; 579–90)
Siricius (384–99)
Theodore (I; 642–49)
Theodore (II; 897)
Vigilius (537–55)
Vitalian (657–72)

09 Adeodatus (I; 615–18)
Adeodatus (II; 672–76)
Alexander (I; c.105–c.117)
Alexander (II; 1061–73)
Alexander (III; 1159–81)
Alexander (IV; 1254–61)
Alexander (VI; 1492–1503)
Alexander (VII; 1655–67)

Alexander (VIII; 1689–91)
Anacletus (c.76–c.90)
Callistus (I; 217–22)
Callistus (II; 1119–24)
Callistus (III; 1455–58)
Celestine (I; 422–32)
Celestine (II; 1143–44)
Celestine (III; 1191–98)
Celestine (IV; 1241)
Celestine (V; 1294)
Cornelius (251–53)
Deusdedit (615–18)
Dionysius (259–68)
Evaristus (c.99–c.105)
Hormisdas (514–23)
Marcellus (I; 308–09)
Marcellus (II; 1555)
Miltiades (311–14)
Severinus (640)
Silverius (536–37)

Sisinnius (708)
Sylvester (I; 314–35)
Sylvester (II; 999–1003)
Sylvester (III; 1045)
Symmachus (498–514)
Valentine (827)
Zacharias (741–52)

10 Anastasius (I; 399–401)
Anastasius (II; 496–98)
Anastasius (III; 911–13)
Anastasius (IV; 1153–54)
Sabinianus (604–06)
Simplicius (468–83)
Zephyrinus (198–217)

11 Constantine (708–15)
Eleutherius (175–89)
Eutychianus (275–83)
Marcellinus (296–304)
Telesphorus (c.127–c.137)

Antipopes, with regnal dates (all AD) include:

03 Leo (VIII; 963–65)
04 John (844)
John (XVI; 997–98)
John (XXIII; 1410–15)
05 Felix (II; 355–65)
Felix (V; 1439–49)
06 Albert (1102)
Philip (768)
Victor (IV; 1138)
Victor (IV; 1159–64)
07 Clement (III; 1080/1084–1100)
Clement (VII; 1378–94)
Clement (VIII; 1423–29)
Gregory (1012)
Gregory (VIII; 1118–21)
Paschal (687–92)
Paschal (III; 1164–68)
Ursinus (366–67)
08 Benedict (X; 1058–59)

Benedict (XIII; 1394–1423)
Benedict (XIV; 1425–30)
Boniface (VII; 974/984–85)
Eulalius (418–19)
Honorius (II; 1061–72)
Innocent (III; 1179–80)
Nicholas (V; 1328–30)
Novatian (251–c.258)
Theodore (687)

09 Alexander (V; 1409–10)
Anacletus (II; 1130–38)
Callistus (III; 1168–78)
Celestine (II; 1124)
Dioscorus (530)
Sylvester (IV; 1105–11)
Theodoric (1100–02)

10 Hippolytus (217–c.235)
Laurentius (498/501–05)

11 Christopher (903–04)
Constantine (II; 767–69)

porcelain

Porcelain includes:

05 Imari
Kraak
06 bisque
Canton
Parian
07 biscuit

faience
nankeen
08 eggshell
kakiemon
Yingqing
09 bone china

copper red
hard paste
soft paste
10 salt-glazed
11 Capodimonte
chinoiserie

famille-rose
12 blue and white
famille-verte
14 soapstone paste

Porcelain makes include:

03 Bow	**06** Minton	Meissen	Davenport
04 Ming	Sèvres	Nanking	Worcester
Noke	Vienna	Satsuma	**10** Cookworthy
Wade	**07** Belleek	**08** Caughley	Crown Derby
05 Arita	Bristol	Coalport	Rockingham
Delft	Chelsea	Copeland	
Derby	Dresden	Wedgwood	**12** Royal Doulton
Spode	Limoges	**09** Chantilly	**14** Royal Worcester

Porcelain makers include:

04 Noke (Charles John; 1858–1941, English)

05 Spode (Josiah; 1754–1827, English)

06 Lladró (Juan/José/Vicente; Spanish)
   Minton (Thomas; 1765–1836, English)

See also **pottery**

07 Böttger (Johann Friedrich; 1682–1719, German)

08 Copeland (William Taylor; 1797–1868, English)
   Wedgwood (Josiah; 1730–95, English)

10 Cookworthy (William; 1705–80, English)

port

Ports include:

04 Aden (Yemen)
   Apia (Samoa)
   Baku (Azerbaijan)
   Bari (Italy)
   Caen (France)
   Cebu (Philippines)
   Cork (Ireland)
   Doha (Qatar)
   Elat (Israel)
   Faro (Portugal)
   Hull (England)
   Kiel (Germany)
   Kobe (Japan)
   Lomé (Togo)
   Lüda (China)
   Nice (France)
   Oran (Algeria)
   Oslo (Norway)
   Oulu (Finland)
   Pula (Croatia)
   Riga (Latvia)
   Safi (Morocco)
   Sfax (Tunisia)
   Suez (Egypt)
   Suva (Fiji)
   Tyre (Lebanon)
   Vigo (Spain)

05 Accra (Ghana)
   Aqaba (Jordan)
   Arica (Chile)
   Beira (Mozambique)
   Belem (Brazil)
   Brest (France)
   Busan (South Korea)

Cadiz (Spain)
Chiba (Japan)
Colón (Panama)
Dakar (Senegal)
Davao (Philippines)
Dover (England)
Dubai (United Arab Emirates)
Emden (Germany)
Gavle (Sweden)
Genoa (Italy)
Ghent (Belgium)
Gijon (Spain)
Goole (England)
Haifa (Israel)
Ibiza (Ibiza)
Izmir (Turkey)
Koper (Slovenia)
Lagos (Nigeria)
Larne (Northern Ireland)
Leith (Scotland)
Liège (Belgium)
Macao (China)
Malmö (Sweden)
Masan (South Korea)
Miami (USA)
Nampo (North Korea)
Natal (Brazil)
Osaka (Japan)
Palma (Majorca)
Paris (France)
Poole (England)
Pusan (South Korea)
Rouen (France)
Sakai (Japan)

Sitra (Bahrain)
Split (Croatia)
Tampa (USA)
Tanga (Tanzania)
Tokyo (Japan)
Tunis (Tunisia)
Turku (Finland)
Ulsan (South Korea)
Vaasa (Finland)
Varna (Bulgaria)

06 Aarhus (Denmark)
Abadan (Iran)
Agadir (Morocco)
Ancona (Italy)
Annaba (Algeria)
Ashdod (Israel)
Aveiro (Portugal)
Aviles (Spain)
Balboa (Panama)
Banjul (The Gambia)
Basrah (Iraq)
Batumi (Georgia)
Beirut (Lebanon)
Bergen (Norway)
Bilbao (Spain)
Bissau (Guinea-Bissau)
Boston (USA)
Bremen (Germany)
Calais (France)
Callao (Peru)
Cannes (France)
Cochin (India)
Dalian (China)
Dammam (Saudi Arabia)
Darwin (Australia)
Dieppe (France)
Douala (Cameroon)
Dublin (Ireland)
Duluth (USA)
Dundee (Scotland)
Durban (South Africa)
Durres (Albania)
Galway (Ireland)
Gdánsk (Poland)
Gdynia (Poland)
Havana (Cuba)
Hobart (Australia)
Inchon (South Korea)
Jarrow (England)
Jeddah (Saudi Arabia)
Juneau (USA)
Kalmar (Sweden)
Kandla (India)
Khulna (Bangladesh)
Kuwait (Kuwait)
Lisbon (Portugal)
Lobito (Angola)
London (England)

Luanda (Angola)
Lübeck (Germany)
Malaga (Spain)
Manama (Bahrain)
Manaus (Brazil)
Manila (Philippines)
Maputo (Mozambique)
Mersin (Turkey)
Mobile (USA)
Mumbai (India)
Muscat (Oman)
Nacala (Mozambique)
Nagoya (Japan)
Nantes (France)
Napier (New Zealand)
Naples (Italy)
Narvik (Norway)
Nassau (The Bahamas)
Nelson (New Zealand)
Noumea (New Caledonia)
Nyborg (Denmark)
Odense (Denmark)
Odessa (Ukraine)
Oporto (Portugal)
Ostend (Belgium)
Penang (Malaysia)
Quebec (Canada)
Recife (Brazil)
Rijeka (Croatia)
Rimini (Italy)
Samsun (Turkey)
Santos (Brazil)
Sasebo (Japan)
Savona (Italy)
Sittwe (Myanmar)
Sousse (Tunisia)
St John (Canada)
St Malo (France)
Sydney (Australia)
Sydney (Canada)
Tacoma (USA)
Timaru (New Zealand)
Toledo (USA)
Toulon (France)
Toyama (Japan)
Velsen (The Netherlands)
Venice (Italy)
Yangon (Myanmar)

07 Aalborg (Denmark)
Abidjan (Côte d'Ivoire)
Ajaccio (Corsica)
Alcudia (Majorca)
Algiers (Algeria)
Almeria (Spain)
Antwerp (Belgium)
Bangkok (Thailand)
Belfast (Northern Ireland)
Bizerta (Tunisia)

Bourgas (Bulgaria)
Bristol (England)
Buffalo (USA)
Cabinda (Angola)
Calabar (Nigeria)
Caldera (Costa Rica)
Calicut (India)
Cardiff (Wales)
Catania (Sicily)
Cayenne (French Guiana)
Chennai (India)
Chicago (USA)
Cologne (Germany)
Colombo (Sri Lanka)
Conakry (Guinea)
Corinth (Greece)
Corinto (Nicaragua)
Cotonou (Benin)
Dampier (Australia)
Detroit (USA)
Douglas (Isle of Man)
Dunedin (New Zealand)
Dunkirk (France)
Esbjerg (Denmark)
Funchal (Madeira)
Geelong (Australia)
Glasgow (Scotland)
Grimsby (England)
Halifax (Canada)
Hamburg (Germany)
Harstad (Norway)
Harwich (England)
Hodeida (Yemen)
Honiari (Solomon Islands)
Houston (USA)
Jakarta (Indonesia)
Karachi (Pakistan)
Kolkata (India)
Kowloon (Hong Kong)
Kuching (Malaysia)
Kushiro (Japan)
La Plata (Argentina)
Larnaca (Cyprus)
La Union (El Salvador)
Le Havre (France)
Livorno (Italy)
Marsala (Sicily)
Messina (Sicily)
Mindelo (Cape Verde)
Mombasa (Kenya)
Newport (Wales)
New York (USA)
Oakland (USA)
Palermo (Sicily)
Papeete (Tahiti)
Paradip (India)
Pasajes (Spain)
Piraeus (Greece)

Rangoon (Myanmar)
Ravenna (Italy)
Rosaria (Argentina)
Rostock (Germany)
Salerno (Italy)
San José (Guatemala)
San Juan (Puerto Rico)
San Remo (Italy)
Santa Fé (Argentina)
São Tomé (São Tomé and Príncipe)
Seattle (USA)
Seville (Spain)
Shimizu (Japan)
St John's (Antigua)
St John's (Canada)
Swansea (Wales)
Tallinn (Estonia)
Tampico (Mexico)
Tangier (Morocco)
Taranto (Italy)
Tianjin (China)
Toronto (Canada)
Trieste (Italy)
Tripoli (Lebanon)
Tripoli (Libya)
Valetta (Malta)
Vitoria (Brazil)
Xingang (China)
Zhdanov (Ukraine)

08 Aberdeen (Scotland)
Abu Dhabi (United Arab Emirates)
Acajutla (El Salvador)
Acapulco (Mexico)
Adelaide (Australia)
Alicante (Spain)
Asunción (Paraguay)
Auckland (New Zealand)
Benghazi (Libya)
Bordeaux (France)
Boulogne (France)
Brindisi (Italy)
Brisbane (Australia)
Cagliari (Sardinia)
Cape Town (South Africa)
Djibouti (Djibouti)
Duisburg (Germany)
Flushing (The Netherlands)
Freeport (The Bahamas)
Freeport (USA)
Freetown (Sierra Leone)
Godthaab (Greenland)
Greenock (Scotland)
Hakodate (Japan)
Halmstad (Sweden)
Hamilton (Bermuda)
Hamilton (Canada)
Hay Point (Australia)
Helsinki (Finland)

Holyhead (Wales)
Hong Kong (Hong Kong)
Honolulu (Hawaii)
Istanbul (Turkey)
Kawasaki (Japan)
Kingston (Jamaica)
Klaipeda (Lithuania)
La Coruña (Spain)
La Guaira (Venezuela)
La Spezia (Italy)
Lattakia (Syria)
Limassol (Cyprus)
Limerick (Ireland)
Mannheim (Germany)
Matanzas (Cuba)
Monrovia (Liberia)
Montreal (Canada)
Mormugao (India)
Moulmein (Myanmar)
Murmansk (Russia)
Nagasaki (Japan)
New Haven (USA)
Pago Pago (Samoa)
Plymouth (England)
Portland (USA)
Port Said (Egypt)
Ramsgate (England)
Richmond (USA)
Salonica (Greece)
Salvador (Brazil)
San Diego (USA)
San Pedro (Côte d'Ivoire)
Savannah (USA)
Shanghai (China)
St Helier (Jersey)
Stockton (USA)
Surabaya (Indonesia)
Syracuse (Sicily)
Szczecin (Poland)
Takoradi (Ghana)
Tauranga (New Zealand)
Torshavn (Faroes)
Valencia (Spain)
Veracruz (Mexico)
Yokohama (Japan)
Zanzibar (Tanzania)

09 Algeciras (Spain)
Amsterdam (The Netherlands)
Anchorage (USA)
Archangel (Russia)
Baltimore (USA)
Barcelona (Spain)
Cartagena (Colombia)
Cartagena (Spain)
Cherbourg (France)
Cleveland (USA)
Constanta (Romania)
Dordrecht (The Netherlands)

Dubrovnik (Croatia)
Europoort (The Netherlands)
Famagusta (Cyprus)
Flensburg (Germany)
Fortaleza (Brazil)
Frankfurt (Germany)
Fremantle (Australia)
Galveston (USA)
Gateshead (England)
Gibraltar (Gibraltar)
Gravesend (England)
Guayaquil (Ecuador)
Hiroshima (Japan)
Kagoshima (Japan)
Kaohsiung (Taiwan)
Kirkcaldy (Scotland)
Langesund (Norway)
Las Palmas (Grand Canary)
Liverpool (England)
Long Beach (USA)
Lowestoft (England)
Maracaibo (Venezuela)
Mariehamn (Finland)
Melbourne (Australia)
Milwaukee (USA)
Mizushima (Japan)
Mogadishu (Somalia)
Newcastle (Australia)
Newcastle (England)
Nukualofa (Tonga)
Palm Beach (USA)
Paranagua (Brazil)
Phnom Penh (Cambodia)
Port Limon (Costa Rica)
Port Louis (Mauritius)
Port Sudan (Sudan)
Reykjavik (Iceland)
Rio Grande (Brazil)
Rotterdam (The Netherlands)
Santander (Spain)
Sassandra (Côte d'Ivoire)
Singapore (Singapore)
Stavanger (Norway)
St George's (Grenada)
St Nazaire (France)
Stockholm (Sweden)
Stralsund (Germany)
Sundsvall (Sweden)
Takamatsu (Japan)
Tarragona (Spain)
Toamasina (Madagascar)
Trebizond (Turkey)
Trondheim (Norway)
Tuticorin (India)
Vancouver (Canada)
Volgograd (Russia)
Walvis Bay (Namibia)
Zamboanga (Philippines)

Zeebrugge (Belgium)
10 Alexandria (Egypt)
Belize City (Belize)
Bridgetown (Barbados)
Cap Haitian (Haiti)
Casablanca (Morocco)
Charleston (USA)
Chittagong (Bangladesh)
Cienfuegos (Cuba)
Copenhagen (Denmark)
East London (South Africa)
Felixstowe (England)
Folkestone (England)
Fray Bentos (Uruguay)
Fredericia (Denmark)
Georgetown (Cayman Islands)
Georgetown (Guyana)
Gothenburg (Sweden)
Hartlepool (England)
Iskenderun (Turkey)
Kitakyushu (Japan)
Kompong Som (Cambodia)
Launceston (Australia)
Libreville (Gabon)
Los Angeles (USA)
Manzanillo (Mexico)
Marseilles (France)
Mina Qaboos (Oman)
Mina Sulman (Bahrain)
Montego Bay (Jamaica)
Montevideo (Uruguay)
New Orleans (USA)
Nouakchott (Mauritania)
Paramaribo (Suriname)
Pork Kelang (Malaysia)
Port Gentil (Gabon)
Port Kembla (Australia)
Portsmouth (England)
Port Talbot (Wales)
Providence (USA)
Sacramento (USA)
Salina Cruz (Mexico)
San Lorenzo (Argentina)
Santa Marta (Colombia)
Sevastopol (Ukraine)
Sunderland (England)
Thunder Bay (Canada)
Townsville (Australia)
Valparaíso (Chile)
Wellington (New Zealand)
Willemstad (Netherlands Antilles)
Wilmington (USA)
11 Antofagasta (Chile)
Bahia Blanca (Argentina)
Bandar Abbas (Iran)
Brazzaville (Congo)

Buenos Aires (Argentina)
Dar es Salaam (Tanzania)
Fredrikstad (Norway)
Grangemouth (Scotland)
Helsingborg (Sweden)
Livingstone (Guatemala)
Mar del Plata (Argentina)
New Plymouth (New Zealand)
Panama Canal (Panama)
Pasir Gudang (Malaysia)
Point-a-Pitre (Guadeloupe)
Pointe-Noire (Congo)
Pondicherry (India)
Port Cartier (Canada)
Port Hedland (Australia)
Port Moresby (Papua New Guinea)
Porto Alegre (Brazil)
Port of Spain (Trinidad)
Punta Arenas (Chile)
Richards Bay (South Africa)
Southampton (England)
Vlaardingen (The Netherlands)
Vladivostok (Russia)
12 Barranquilla (Colombia)
Buena Ventura (Colombia)
Fort de France (Martinique)
Jacksonville (USA)
Kota Kinabalu (Malaysia)
Kristiansand (Norway)
New Amsterdam (Guyana)
New Mangalore (India)
Novorossiysk (Russia)
Philadelphia (USA)
Ponta Delgada (Azores)
Port Adelaide (Australia)
Port-au-Prince (Haiti)
Port Harcourt (Nigeria)
Port Victoria (Seychelles)
Prince Rupert (Canada)
Puerto Cortés (Honduras)
Rio de Janeiro (Brazil)
San Francisco (USA)
San Sebastián (Spain)
Santo Domingo (Dominican Republic)
St Petersburg (Russia)
13 Coatzacoalcos (Mexico)
Frederikshavn (Denmark)
Great Yarmouth (England)
Ho Chi Minh City (Vietnam)
Middlesbrough (England)
Port Elizabeth (South Africa)
San Juan del Sur (Nicaragua)
Trois Rivières (Canada)
Visakhapatnam (India)
14 Port Georgetown (Guyana)
Santiago de Cuba (Cuba)

Portugal

Cities and notable towns in Portugal include:

04 Faro

05 Braga
Porto

06 Lisboa
Lisbon
Oporto

Sintra

07 Coimbra

Administrative divisions of Portugal, with regional capitals:

04 Beja (Beja)
Faro (Faro)

05 Braga (Braga)
Évora (Évora)
Porto (Porto)
Viseu (Viseu)

06 Aveiro (Aveiro)
Guarda (Guarda)
Leiria (Leiria)
Lisboa (Lisboa (Lisbon))

07 Coimbra (Coimbra)
Madeira (Funchal)
Setúbal (Setúbal)

08 Bragança (Bragança)
Santarém (Santarém)
Vila Real (Vila Real)

09 The Azores (Ponta Delgada)

10 Portalegre (Portalegre)

13 Castelo Branco (Castelo Branco)

14 Viana do Castelo (Viana do Castelo)

Portuguese landmarks include:

04 Fóia

05 Douro
Tagus

06 Azores

Fátima

07 Algarve
Batalha
Madeira

08 Cruz Alta

09 Cristo Rei

10 Pena Palace

12 Torre de Belém

Tower of Belém

13 Serra de Sintra

position *see* sport

potato

Potatoes include:

03 new

04 aloo
chat
seed
spud

ware

05 praty
sweet
tater
tatie

06 batata
camote
kidney
kumara
murphy

pratie
tattie

Potato dishes and cooking methods include:

04 chip
mash
soup

05 boxty
champ
chips
crisp
fluke
fries
rösti
scone

06 boiled
crisps
jacket

mashed
roesti
spirit

07 chippie
pancake
sautéed
scallop
scollop
stovies

08 duchesse

09 colcannon
croquette
French fry

game chips
hash brown
home fries
oven chips

10 hash browns
peel-and-eat
tattie-claw

11 dauphinoise
French fried
French fries

13 rumbledethump

14 rumbledethumps

15 bubble and squeak

Potter, Beatrix (1866–1943)

Significant works include:

14 *The Tale of Mr Tod* (1912)

18 *The Roly-Poly Pudding* (1908)
The Tale of Tom Kitten (1907)

19 *The Tale of Two Bad Mice* (1904)

20 *The Tale of Peter Rabbit* (1902)

21 *The Tailor of Gloucester* (1903)
The Tale of Pigling Bland (1913)
The Tale of Timmy Tiptoes (1911)

22 *The Tale of Benjamin Bunny* (1904)
The Tale of Mr Jeremy Fisher (1905)

The Tale of Mrs Tiggy-Winkle (1905)
The Tale of Mrs Tittlemouse (1910)
The Tale of Samuel Whiskers (1908)
The Tale of Squirrel Nutkin (1903)

24 *The Tale of Johnny Town-Mouse* (1918)
The Tale of the Faithful Dove (1956)

25 *The Tale of Ginger and Pickles* (1909)
The Tale of Jemima Puddle-Duck (1908)
The Tale of the Flopsy Bunnies (1909)

26 *The Tale of Little Pig Robinson* (1930)

29 *The Tale of the Pie and the Patty-pan* (1905)

Significant characters include:

03 Tod (Mr)

05 Lucie
Mopsy
Peter

06 Fisher (Mr Jeremy)
Flopsy

08 McGregor (Mr)

Old Brown
Whiskers (Samuel)

09 Tom Kitten

10 Cotton-tail
Hunca Munca
Puddle-Duck (Jemima)

11 Peter Rabbit

Tiggy-Winkle (Mrs)
Tittlemouse (Mrs)

12 Pigling Bland
Timmy Tiptoes

13 Benjamin Bunny
Flopsy Bunnies

14 Squirrel Nutkin

pottery

Pottery includes:

04 Ming
Wade

05 Bizen
china
delft
Poole

06 basalt
bisque
Dunoon
flambé
Hummel
jasper
Parian
Sèvres

07 biscuit
ceramic
Dresden
faience
Meissen
redware

08 ceramics
Coalport

crockery
maiolica
majolica
rakuware
Rookwood
slipware

09 agateware
bone china
creamware
Davenport
Delftware
ironstone
Jackfield
pearlware
porcelain
red figure
stoneware
Worcester

10 jasperware
lustreware
Parian ware
Queen's ware

terracotta
Wemyss ware

11 black figure
earthenware
Florian ware
pâte-sur-pâte
Portmeirion
soufflé ware
spatter ware

12 Royal Doulton
transfer ware
Wedgwood ware

13 Claremont ware
Hazledene ware
Staffordshire
tortoiseshell
willow pattern

14 ironstone china

15 cauliflower ware
Royal Crown Derby
Wedgwood pottery

Pottery makers include:

03 Fry (Laura; 1857–1943, US)
Rie (Dame Lucie; 1902–95, Austrian)

04 Boyd (Arthur; 1920–99, Australian)
Boyd (Merric; 1888–1959, Australian)
Vyse (Charles; 1882–1971, English)
Wood (Aaron; 1717–85, English)
Wood (Enoch; 1759–1840, English)
Wood (John; 1746–97, English)
Wood (Ralph; 1715–72, English)
Wood (Ralph, Jnr; 1748–95, English)
Wyse (Henry Taylor; 1870–1951, Scottish)

05 Adams (Truda; 1890–1958, English)
Adams (William; 1745–1805, English)
Adams (William; 1748–1831, English)
Adams (William; 1772–1829, English)
Amour (Elizabeth; 1885–1945, Scottish)
Cliff (Clarice; 1899–1972, English)
Coper (Hans; 1920–81, British)
Finch (Alfred William; 1854–1930, Finnish)
Korin (Ogata; 1658–1716, Japanese)
Leach (Bernard; 1887–1979, English)
Mason (Miles; 1752–1822, English)
Moore (Bernard; 1850–1935, English)
Perry (Grayson; 1960– , English)
Spira (Rupert; 1960– , English)

06 Cardew (Michael; 1901–82, English)
Carter (Truda; 1890–1958, English)
de Waal (Edmund; 1964– , English)
Dwight (John; c.1637–1703, English)

Hamada (Shoji; 1894–1978, Japanese)
Kenzan (Ogata; 1663–1743, Japanese)
Murray (William Staite; 1881–1962, English)
Taylor (William Howson; 1876–1935, English)

07 Astbury (John; 1688–1743, English)
Britton (Alison; 1948– , English)
Doulton (Sir Henry; 1820–97, English)
Execias (fl.late 6c BC, Greek)
Exekias (fl.late 6c BC, Greek)
Forsyth (Gordon; 1879–1953, Scottish)
Fritsch (Elizabeth; 1940– , English)
Gardner (Peter; 1836–1902, Scottish)
Grotell (Maija; 1899–1973, Finnish)
Palissy (Bernard; c.1509–89, French)
Twyford (Joshua; 1640–1729, English)

08 Fujiwara (Kei; 1899–1983, Japanese)
Overbeck (Elizabeth; 1875–1936, US)
Overbeck (Hannah; 1870–1931, US)
Overbeck (Margaret; 1863–1911, US)
Overbeck (Mary; 1878–1955, US)
Robineau (Adelaide; 1865–1929, US)
Wedgwood (Josiah; 1730–95, English)
Whieldon (Thomas; 1719–95, English)
Yamamoto (Toshu; 1906–94, Japanese)

09 Kaneshige (Toyo; 1896–1967, Japanese)
Moorcroft (William; 1872–1945, English)

10 Euphronios (fl.late 6c–5c BC, Greek)

Pottery terms include:

04 kiln
raku
slip

05 delft
glaze
model

06 basalt
enamel
figure
firing
flambé
ground
jasper
lustre
sagger

07 celadon

ceramic
crazing
faience
fairing

08 armorial
bronzing
flatback
maiolica
majolica
monogram
slip-cast

09 china clay
cloisonné
creamware
grotesque
ironstone
overglaze

porcelain
sgraffito
stoneware

10 art pottery
maker's mark
spongeware
terracotta
underglaze

11 crackleware
earthenware
scratch blue

12 blanc-de-chine

13 Staffordshire
willow pattern

15 mandarin palette

See also **porcelain**

poultry

Poultry include:

03 hen
04 duck
05 goose
06 bantam
turkey
07 chicken
10 guinea fowl

See also **chicken**; **duck**; **goose**

power station

Power stations include:

06 Huntly (New Zealand)
07 Benmore (New Zealand)
08 Bankside (England)
   Dounreay (Scotland)
   Sizewell (England)
   Yallourn (Australia)
09 Battersea (England)
   Chernobyl (Ukraine)

Dungeness (England)
Manapouri (New Zealand)
Windscale (England)
10 Sellafield (England)
11 Wallerawang (Australia)
12 Marsden Point (New Zealand)
14 Snowy Mountains (Australia)
15 Three Mile Island (USA)

prayer

Prayers include:

02 Om
05 adhan
   Ardas
   grace
   salat
   Shema
06 Amidah
   Gloria
   rosary
   Yizkor
07 angelus

khotbah
khutbah
08 Agnus Dei
   Ave Maria
   Habdalah
   Hail Mary
   Havdalah
   Kaddhish
   Kol Nidre
   shahadah
09 Confiteor
   Our Father

10 Benedictus
   Lychnapsia
   Magnificat
   requiescat
11 Lord's Prayer
   Paternoster
   Sursum Corda
12 Divine Office
   Kyrie eleison
   Nunc Dimittis
15 Act of Contrition

precipitation

Precipitation includes:

03 dew
   fog
04 hail
   mist
rain
snow
05 sleet
06 shower
07 drizzle
08 downpour
   rainfall
   snowfall
09 rainstorm
   snowflake

See also **ice**; **meteorology**; **snow**; **weather**

prefix *see* **science**

presenter *see* **radio**; **television**

president

04 Bush (George; 1989–93)
Bush (George W; 2001–09)
Ford (Gerald; 1974–77)
Polk (James K; 1845–49)
Taft (William H; 1909–13)

05 Adams (John; 1797–1801)
Adams (John Quincy; 1825–29)
Buren (Martin van; 1837–41)
Grant (Ulysses S; 1869–77)
Hayes (Rutherford B; 1877–81)
Nixon (Richard M; 1969–74)
Obama (Barack; 2009–)
Tyler (John; 1841–45)

06 Arthur (Chester A; 1881–85)
Carter (Jimmy; 1977–81)
Hoover (Herbert; 1929–33)
Monroe (James; 1817–25)
Pierce (Franklin; 1853–57)
Reagan (Ronald; 1981–89)
Taylor (Zachary; 1849–50)
Truman (Harry S; 1945–53)
Wilson (Woodrow; 1913–21)

07 Clinton (Bill; 1993–2001)
Harding (Warren G; 1921–23)
Jackson (Andrew; 1829–37)
Johnson (Andrew; 1865–69)
Johnson (Lyndon B; 1963–69)
Kennedy (John F; 1961–63)
Lincoln (Abraham; 1861–65)
Madison (James; 1809–17)

08 Buchanan (James; 1857–61)
Coolidge (Calvin; 1923–29)
Fillmore (Millard; 1850–53)
Garfield (James A; 1881)
Harrison (Benjamin; 1889–93)
Harrison (William Henry; 1841)
McKinley (William; 1897–1901)

09 Cleveland (Grover; 1885–89, 1893–97)
Jefferson (Thomas; 1801–09)
Roosevelt (Franklin D; 1933–45)
Roosevelt (Theodore; 1901–09)

10 Eisenhower (Dwight D; 1953–61)
Washington (George; 1789–97)

03 Doe (Samuel; 1951–90, Liberian)
Moi (Daniel arap; 1924– , Kenyan)
Rau (Johannes; 1931–2006, German)
Sun (Yat-sen; 1866–1925, Chinese)
Zia (Khaleda; 1945– , Bangladeshi)

04 Amin (Idi; 1925–2003, Ugandan)
Díaz (Porfirio; 1830–1915, Mexican)
Khan (Ayub; 1907–1974, Pakistani)
Ozal (Turgut; 1927–93, Turkish)
René (France-Albert; 1935– , Seychelles)
Rhee (Syngman; 1875–1965, Korean)
Tito (Josip Broz; 1892–1980, Yugoslav)
Zuma (Jacob; 1942– , South African)

05 Ahmed (Shehabuddin; 1930, Bangladeshi)
Assad (Bashar al-; 1965– , Syrian)
Assad (Hafez al-; 1928–2000, Syrian)
Banda (Hastings; 1898–1997, Malawian)
Botha (P W; 1916–2006, South African)
Havel (Václav; 1936–2011, Czech)
Heuss (Theodor; 1884–1963, German)
Mbeki (Thabo; 1942– , South African)
Menem (Carlos; 1935– , Argentine)
Obote (Milton; 1924–2005, Ugandan)
Perón (Juan; 1895–1974, Argentine)
Perón (Maria Estela Martínez de 'Isabelita';
1931– , Argentine)
Putin (Vladimir; 1952– , Russian)
Ramos (Fidel; 1928– , Philippine)
Sadat (Anwar el-; 1918–81, Egyptian)

06 Aideed (Mohammed; 1934–96, Somalian)
Aquino (Cory; 1933–2009, Philippine)
Banana (Canaan; 1936–2003, Zimbabwean)
Bao Dai (1913–97, Indo-Chinese/Vietnamese)
Bhutto (Zulfikar; 1928–79, Pakistani)
Biswas (Abdur Rahman; 1926– , Bangladeshi)
Calles (Plutarco Elías; 1877–1945, Mexican)
Castro (Fidel; 1926– , Cuban)
Castro (Raúl; 1931– , Cuban)
Chirac (Jacques; 1932– , French)
Ciampi (Carlo Azeglio; 1920– , Italian)
Gaulle (Charles de; 1890–1970, French)
Geisel (Ernesto; 1908–96, Brazilian)
Herzog (Chaim; 1918–1997, Israeli)
Juárez (Benito; 1806–72, Mexican)
Karzai (Hamid; 1957– , Afghan)
Kruger (Paul; 1825–1904, South African)
Kuchma (Leonid; 1938– , Ukrainian)
Lahoud (Émile; 1936– , Lebanese)
Marcos (Ferdinand; 1917–89, Philippine)
Mobutu (Sese Seko; 1930–97, Zairean)
Mugabe (Robert; 1924– , Zimbabwean)
Nasser (Gamal Abd al-; 1918–70, Egyptian)
Nathan (Sellapan Ramanathan; 1924– ,
Singaporean)
Ortega (Daniel; 1945– , Nicaraguan)
Préval (René; 1943– , Haitian)
Rahman (Ziaur; 1936–1981, Bangladeshi)
Renner (Karl; 1870–1950, Austrian)

Santos (José Eduardo dos; 1942– , Angolan)
Somoza (Anastasio 1896–1956, Nicaraguan)
Somoza (Luis; 1922–1967, Nicaraguan)
Valera (Éamon de; 1882–1975, Irish)
Vargas (Getúlio; 1883–1954, Brazilian)
Walesa (Lech; 1943– , Polish)

07 Atatürk (Mustapha Kemal; 1881–1938, Turkish)
Batista (Fulgencio; 1901–73, Cuban)
Bolívar (Simón; 1783–1830, Colombian/
  South American)
Cardoso (Fernando Henrique; 1931– ,
  Brazilian)
de Klerk (F W; 1936– , South African)
Demirel (Süleyman; 1924– , Turkish)
Estrada (Joseph Ejercito; 1937– , Philippine)
Gaddafi (Muammar; 1942–2011, Libyan)
Gemayel (Amin; 1942– , Lebanese)
Gromyko (Andrei; 1909–89, Soviet)
Habibie (Jusuf; 1936– , Indonesian)
Hussein (Saddam; 1937–2006, Iraqi)
Iliescu (Ion; 1930– , Romanian)
Khatami (Mohammad; 1943– , Iranian)
Mancham (James; 1939– , Seychelles)
Mandela (Nelson; 1918– , South African)
Masaryk (Thomás; 1850–1937,
  Czechoslovak)
Mubarak (Hosni; 1928– , Egyptian)
Nkrumah (Kwame; 1909–72, Ghanaian)
Parnell (Charles Stewart; 1846–91, Irish)
Sampaio (Jorge; 1939– , Portuguese)
Sarkozy (Nicolas; 1955– , French)
Sirleaf (Ellen Johnson; 1938– , Liberian)
Suharto (Thojib N J; 1921–2008, Indonesian)
Sukarno (Ahmed; 1902–70, Indonesian)
Tudjman (Franjo; 1922–99, Croatian)
Weizman (Ezer; 1924–2005, Israeli)
Yanayev (Gennady; 1937–2010, Russian)
Yeltsin (Boris; 1931–2007, Russian)
Zhivkov (Todor; 1911–98, Bulgarian)

08 Andropov (Yuri; 1914–84, Soviet)
Aristide (Jean-Bertrand; 1953– , Haitian)
Bani-Sadr (Abolhassan; 1935– , Iranian)
Brezhnev (Leonid; 1906–82, Soviet)
Chamorro (Violetta; 1919– , Nicaraguan)
Childers (Erskine; 1905–74, Irish)
Cosgrave (William Thomas; 1880–1965, Irish)
de Gaulle (Charles; 1890–1970, French)
de Valera (Éamon; 1882–1975, Irish)
Duvalier (François 'Papa Doc'; 1907–71,
  Haitian)
Duvalier (Jean-Claude 'Baby Doc'; 1951– ,
  Haitian)
Fujimori (Alberto; 1939– , Peruvian)
Galtieri (Leopoldo; 1926–2003, Argentine)
Hollande (François; 1954– , French)

Karadžić (Radovan; 1945– , Bosnian-Serb)
Kenyatta (Jomo; c.1889–1978, Kenyan)
Khamenei (Sayed Ali; 1939– , Iranian)
Kravchuk (Leonid; 1934– , Ukrainian)
MacMahon (Patrice de; 1808–93, French)
Makarios (Cyprus Enosis; 1913–77, Cypriot)
McAleese (Mary; 1951– , Irish)
Medvedev (Dmitry; 1965– , Russian)
Mengistu (Haile Mariam; 1941– , Ethiopian)
Museveni (Yoweri; 1944– , Ugandan)
Napoleon (I, Bonaparte; 1769–1821, French)
Pinochet (Augusto; 1915–2006, Chilean)
Poincaré (Raymond; 1860–1934, French)
Pompidou (Georges; 1911–74, French)
Rawlings (Jerry; 1947– , Ghanaian)
Robinson (Mary; 1944– , Irish)
Waldheim (Kurt; 1918–2007, Austrian)
Weizmann (Chaim; 1874–1952, Israeli)
Zia ul-Haq (Muhammad; 1924–88, Pakistani)

09 Ceauşescu (Nicolae; 1918–89, Romanian)
Chernenko (Konstantin; 1911–85, Soviet)
Gorbachev (Mikhail; 1931– , Russian)
Ho Chi Minh (1890–1969, Vietnamese)
Kim-Il Sung (1912–94, North Korean)
Kim Jong Il (1942–2011, North Korean)
Kim Jong-un (1983/4– , North Korean)
Mao Zedong (1893–1976, Chinese)
Milošević (Slobodan; 1941–2006, Serbian)
Motlanthe (Kgalema Petrus; 1949– , South
  Africa)
Narayanan (Kocheril Raman; 1920–2005 ,
  Indian)
Pilsudski (Józef; 1867–1935, Polish)

10 Alessandri (Arturo; 1868–1950, Chilean)
Betancourt (Rómulo; 1908–81, Venezuelan)
Bouteflika (Abdelaziz; 1937– , Algerian)
Hindenburg (Paul von; 1847–1934, German)
Jaruzelski (Wojciech; 1923– , Polish)
Jiang Zemin (1926– , Chinese)
Khrushchev (Nikita; 1894–1971, Soviet)
Kubitschek (Juscelino; 1902–76, Brazilian)
Lukashenko (Alexander; 1954– , Belorusian)
Mannerheim (Carl Gustav, Baron von;
  1867–1951, Finnish)
Mitterrand (François; 1916–96, French)
Najibullah (Mohammad; 1947–96, Afghan)
Rafsanjani (Hojatoleslam Ali Akbar
  Hashemi; 1934– , Iranian)
Stroessner (Alfredo; 1912–2006, Paraguayan)
Voroshilov (Kliment; 1881–1969, Soviet)
Yushchenko (Viktor; 1954– , Ukrainian)

13 Paz Estenssoro (Víctor; 1907–2001, Bolivian)

14 Johnson Sirleaf (Ellen; 1938– , Liberian)

15 Giscard d'Estaing (Valéry; 1926– , French)

prey *see* **bird**

priest

Priests include:

04 lama (Buddhism)
papa (Greek Orthodox)
pope (Greek Orthodox)

05 bonze (Buddhism)
druid (Celtic)
magus (Ancient Persia)
mambo (voodoo)
rabbi (Judaism)

06 flamen (Ancient Rome)
Levite (Judaism)

lucumo (Etruscan)
pujari (Hindu)

07 Brahman (Hindu)
Pythian (Ancient Greece)
tohunga (Maori)

08 bacchant (Bacchus)
corybant (Ancient Greece)

09 bacchanal (Bacchus)
presbyter (Episcopal churches)

10 arch-flamen (Ancient Rome)

primate

Primates include:

03 ape

05 human
lemur
loris
pongo

06 galago
gibbon
monkey

07 gorilla

08 bushbaby

great ape
night-ape

09 catarhine
orang-utan
prosimian

10 catarrhine
chimpanzee
protohuman

11 Homo sapiens
orang-outang

See also **ape**

prime minister

Prime ministers of Australia, with dates of office:

04 Cook (Joseph; 1913–14, Liberal)
Holt (Harold; 1966–67, Liberal)
Page (Earle; 1939, Country)
Reid (George; 1904–05, Free Trade)
Rudd (Kevin; 2007– 2010, 2013– , Labor)

05 Bruce (Stanley; 1923–29, Nationalist)
Forde (Francis Michael; 1945, Labor)
Hawke (Bob; 1983–91, Labor)
Lyons (Joseph; 1932–39, United)

06 Barton (Edmund; 1901–03, Protectionist)
Curtin (John; 1941–45, Labor)
Deakin (Alfred; 1903–04/1905–08,
Protectionist/1909–10, Fusion)
Fadden (Arthur; 1941, Country)
Fisher (Andrew; 1908–09/1910–13/
1914–15, Labor)

Fraser (Malcolm; 1975–83, Liberal)
Gorton (John; 1968–71, Liberal)
Howard (John; 1996–2007, Liberal)
Hughes (Billy; 1915–17, National
Labor/1917–23, Nationalist)
McEwen (John; 1967–68, Country)
Watson (Chris; 1904, Labor)

07 Chifley (Ben; 1945–49, Labor)
Gillard (Julia; 2010–13, Labor)
Keating (Paul; 1991–96, Labor)
McMahon (William; 1971–72, Liberal)
Menzies (Robert; 1939–41,
United/1949–66, Liberal)
Scullin (James; 1929–32, Labor)
Whitlam (Gough; 1972–75, Labor)

Prime ministers of Canada, with dates of office:

04 King (William Lyon Mackenzie; 1921–
26/1926–30/1935–48, Liberal)

05 Abbot (John J C; 1891–92, Conservative)
Clark (Joseph; 1979–80, Conservative)

06 Borden (Robert; 1911–20, Conservative/
Unionist)
Bowell (Mackenzie; 1894–96, Conservative)
Harper (Stephen; 2006– , Conservative)

Martin (Paul; 2003–06, Liberal)
Tupper (Charles; 1896, Conservative)
Turner (John; 1984, Liberal)

07 Bennett (R B; 1930–35, Conservative)
Laurier (Wilfrid; 1896–1911, Liberal)
Meighen (Arthur; 1920–21, Unionist/
Conservative/1926, Conservative)
Pearson (Lester B; 1963–68, Liberal)

Trudeau (Pierre; 1968–79/1980–84, Liberal)

08 Campbell (Kim; 1993, Conservative)
Chrétien (Jean; 1993–2003, Liberal)
Mulroney (Brian; 1984–93, Conservative)
Thompson (John S D; 1892–94, Conservative)

09 Macdonald (John A; 1867–73/1878–91, Conservative)
Mackenzie (Alexander; 1873–78, Liberal)
St Laurent (Louis; 1948–57, Liberal)

11 Diefenbaker (John G; 1957–63, Conservative)

Prime ministers of New Zealand, with dates of office:

03 Key (John; 2008–   , National)

04 Bell (Francis; 1925, Reform)
Kirk (Norman Eric; 1972–74, Labour)
Nash (Walter; 1957–60, Labour)
Ward (Joseph; 1906–12/1928–30, Liberal/National)

05 Clark (Helen; 1999–2008, Labour)
Lange (David; 1984–89, Labour)
Moore (Mike; 1990, Labour)

06 Bolger (James; 1990–97, National)
Coates (Gordon; 1925–28, Reform)
Forbes (George William; 1930–35, United)
Fraser (Peter; 1940–49, Labour)

Massey (William; 1912–25, Reform)
Palmer (Geoffrey; 1989–90, Labour)
Savage (Michael Joseph; 1935–40, Labour)
Seddon (Richard; 1893–1906, Liberal)

07 Holland (Sidney; 1949–57, National)
Muldoon (Robert; 1975–84, National)
Rowling (Wallace; 1974–75, Labour)
Shipley (Jenny; 1997–99, National)

08 Holyoake (Keith; 1957/1960–72, National)
Marshall (John Ross; 1972, National)

09 Hall-Jones (William; 1906, Liberal)
Mackenzie (Thomas; 1912, National)

Prime ministers of the United Kingdom, with dates of office:

04 Bute (John Stuart, Earl of; 1762–63, Tory)
Eden (Anthony; 1955–57, Conservative)
Grey (Charles Grey, Earl; 1830–34, Whig)
Home (Alec Douglas-Home, Earl of; 1963–64, Conservative)
Peel (Robert; 1834–35/1841–46, Conservative)
Pitt (William; 1783–1801/1804–06, Tory)

05 Blair (Tony; 1997–2007, Labour)
Brown (Gordon; 2007–10, Labour)
Derby (Edward Stanley, Earl of; 1852/1858–59/1866–68, Conservative)
Heath (Ted; 1970–74, Conservative)
Major (John; 1990–97, Conservative)
North (Frederick North, Lord; 1770–82, Tory)

06 Attlee (Clement; 1945–51, Labour)
Pelham (Henry; 1743–54, Whig)
Wilson (Harold; 1964–70/1974–76, Labour)

07 Asquith (Herbert; 1908–15, Liberal/1915–16, Coalition)
Baldwin (Stanley; 1923–24/1924–29, Conservative/1935–37, Nationalist)
Balfour (Arthur; 1902–05, Conservative)
Cameron (David; 2010– , Conservative)
Canning (George; 1827, Tory)
Grafton (Augustus Henry Fitzroy, Duke of; 1766–70, Whig)
Russell (John, Lord; 1846–52/1865–66, Liberal)
Walpole (Robert; 1721–42, Whig)

08 Aberdeen (George Hamilton-Gordon, Lord; 1852–55, Peelite)

Bonar Law (Andrew; 1922–23, Conservative)
Disraeli (Benjamin; 1868/1874–80, Conservative)
Goderich (Frederick John Robinson, Viscount; 1827–28, Tory)
Perceval (Spencer; 1809–12, Tory)
Portland (William Henry Cavendish Bentinck, Duke of; 1783, Coalition/1807–09, Tory)
Rosebery (Archibald Philip Primrose, Earl of; 1894–95, Liberal)
Thatcher (Margaret; 1979–90, Conservative)

09 Addington (Henry; 1801–04, Tory)
Callaghan (James; 1976–79, Labour)
Churchill (Winston; 1940–45, Coalition/1951–55, Conservative)
Gladstone (William; 1868–74/1880–85/1886/1892–94, Liberal)
Grenville (George; 1763–65, Whig)
Grenville (William Wyndham, Lord; 1806–07, Whig)
Liverpool (Robert Jenkinson, Earl of; 1812–27, Tory)
MacDonald (Ramsay; 1924/1929–31, Labour/1931–35, Nationalist)
Macmillan (Harold; 1957–63, Conservative)
Melbourne (William Lamb, Viscount; 1834/1835–41, Whig)
Newcastle (Thomas Pelham-Holles, Duke of; 1754–56/1757–62, Whig)
Salisbury (Robert Gascoyne-Cecil,

Marquess of; 1885–86/1886–92/
1895–1902, Conservative)
Shelburne (William Petty-Fitzmaurice, Earl
of; 1782–83, Whig)

10 Devonshire (William Cavendish, Duke of;
1756–57, Whig)
Palmerston (Henry John Temple, Viscount;
1855–58/1859–65, Liberal)
Rockingham (Charles Watson Wentworth,
Marquess of; 1765–66/1782, Whig)

Wellington (Arthur Wellesley, Duke of;
1828–30, Tory)
Wilmington (Spencer Compton, Earl;
1742–43, Whig)

11 Chamberlain (Neville; 1937–40, Nationalist)
Douglas-Home (Alec; 1963–64,
Conservative)
Lloyd George (David; 1916–22, Coalition)

17 Campbell-Bannerman (Henry; 1905–08,
Liberal)

Prime ministers of other countries include:

02 Nu (U; 1907–95, Burmese)

03 Ito (Hirobumi; 1838–1909, Japanese)

04 Meir (Golda; 1898–1978, Russian/US/Israeli)
Moro (Aldo; 1916–78, Italian)
Tojo (Hideki; 1885–1948, Japanese)

05 Ahern (Bertie; 1951– , Irish)
Assad (Hafez al-; 1928–2000, Syrian)
Azaña (Manuel; 1880–1940, Spanish)
Aznar (José María; 1953– , Spanish)
Banda (Hastings; 1898–1997, Malawian)
Barak (Ehud; 1942– , Israeli)
Barre (Raymond; 1924–2007, French)
Begin (Menachem; 1913–92, Polish/Israeli)
Botha (Louis; 1862–1919, South African)
Botha (P W; 1916–2006, South African)
Cowen (Brian; 1960– , Irish)
Craxi (Bettino; 1934–2000, Italian)
Desai (Morarji; 1896–1995, Indian)
Faure (Edgar; 1908–88, French)
Hoxha (Enver; 1908–85, Albanian)
Juppé (Alain; 1945– , French)
Khama (Sir Seretse; 1921–80, African)
Laval (Pierre; 1883–1945, French)
Lynch (John 'Jack'; 1917–99, Irish)
Malan (Daniel; 1874–1959, South African)
Nehru (Jawaharlal; 1889–1964, Indian)
Obote (Milton; 1924–2005, Ugandan)
Pasić (Nikola; c.1846–1926, Serbian)
Peres (Shimon; 1923– , Polish/Israeli)
Prodi (Romano; 1939– , Italian)
Putin (Vladimir; 1952– , Russian)
Rabin (Yitzhak; 1922–95, Israeli)
Sadat (Anwar el-; 1918–81, Egyptian)
Singh (V P; 1931–2008, Indian)
Smith (Ian; 1919–2007, Rhodesian)
Smuts (Jan; 1870–1950, South African)
Spaak (Paul Henri; 1899–1972, Belgian)

06 Bhutto (Benazir; 1953–2007, Pakistani)
Bhutto (Zulfikar; 1928–79, Pakistani)
Briand (Aristide; 1862–1932, French)
Bruton (John; 1947– , Irish)
Castro (Fidel; 1926– , Cuban)
Chirac (Jacques; 1932– , French)

Ecevit (Bülent; 1925–2006, Turkish)
Fabius (Laurent; 1946– , French)
Gandhi (Indira; 1917–84, Indian)
Gandhi (Rajiv; 1944–91, Indian)
Hun Sen (1952– , Cambodian)
Jospin (Lionel; 1937– , French)
Li Peng (1928– , Chinese)
Manley (Michael; 1924–97, Jamaican)
Mugabe (Robert; 1924– , Zimbabwean)
Neguib (Mohammed; 1901–84, Egyptian)
O'Neill (Terence, Lord; 1914–90, Northern
Irish)
Pétain (Philippe; 1856–1951, French)
Pol Pot (1925–98, Cambodian)
Pombal (Sebastião de Carvalho e Mello,
Marques de; 1699–1782, Portuguese)
Rahman (Sheikh Mujibur; 1920–75,
Bangladeshi)
Rhodes (Cecil; 1853–1902, South African)
Shamir (Yitzhak; 1915–2012, Israeli)
Sharif (Mian Muhammad Nawaz; 1941– ,
Pakistani)
Sharon (Ariel; 1928– , Israeli)
Thiers (Adolphe; 1797–1877, French)

07 Berisha (Sali; 1944– , Albanian)
Bingham (Hiram; 1875–1956, US)
Cresson (Edith; 1934– , French)
Gasperi (Alcide de; 1881–1954, Italian)
Halifax (Charles Montagu, 1st Earl of;
1661–1715, English)
Haughey (Charles; 1925–2006, Irish)
Hertzog (J B M; 1866–1942, South African)
Kosygin (Aleksei; 1904–80, Soviet)
Lubbers (Ruud; 1939– , Dutch)
Molotov (Vyacheslav; 1890–1986, Soviet)
Nkrumah (Kwame; 1909–72, Ghanaian)
Nyerere (Julius; 1922–99, Tanzanian)
Vorster (John; 1915–83, South African)
Yeltsin (Boris; 1931–2007, Russian)

08 Ben Bella (Ahmed; 1916–2012, Algerian)
Bismarck (Prince Otto von; 1815–98,
Prusso-German)
Bulganin (Nikolai; 1895–1975, Russian)
Daladier (Édouard; 1884–1970, French)

de Gaulle (Charles; 1890–1970, French)
de Valera (Éamon; 1882–1975, Irish)
González (Felipe; 1942– , Spanish)
Kenyatta (Jomo; c.1889–1978, Kenyan)
Nakasone (Yasuhiro; 1917– , Japanese)
Poincaré (Raymond; 1860–1934, French)
Pompidou (Georges; 1911–74, French)
Quisling (Vidkun; 1887–1945, Norwegian)
Reynolds (Albert; 1932– , Irish)
Vajpayee (Atal Bihari; 1926– , Indian)
Verwoerd (Hendrik; 1901–66, Dutch/South African)
Zapatero (José Luis Rodríguez; 1960– , Spanish)

09 Andreotti (Giulio; 1919–2013, Italian)
Ben-Gurion (David; 1886–1973, Polish/Israeli)
Hashimoto (Ryutaro; 1937–2006, Japanese)

Kim-Il Sung (1912–94, North Korean)
Kim Jong Il (1942–2011, North Korean)
Mussolini (Benito; 1883–1945, Italian)
Netanyahu (Binyamin; 1949– , Israeli)
Stanishev (Sergei; 1966– , Bulgarian)

10 Balkenende (Jan Peter; 1956– , Dutch)
Berlusconi (Silvio; 1936– , Italian)
Clemenceau (Georges; 1841–1929, French)
Fitzgerald (Garrett; 1926–2011, Irish)
Jaruzelski (Wojciech; 1923– , Polish)
Lee Kuan Yew (1923– , Singaporean)

11 Verhofstadt (Guy; 1953– , Belgian)

12 Bandaranaike (S W R D; 1899–1959, Ceylonese)
Chernomyrdin (Viktor; 1938–2010, Russian)

13 Brookeborough (Basil Brooke, Viscount; 1888–1973, Northern Irish)

prince

Princes include:

03 Hal (*Henry IV Part I*, 1596/7, William Shakespeare)

04 Ivan (I; c.1304–41, Russian)
John (*Ivanhoe*, 1819, Sir Walter Scott)
John (of Gaunt, Duke of Lancaster; 1340–99, English)
John (of Lancaster; *Henry IV Part I*, 1596/7, William Shakespeare)
York (Andrew, Duke of; 1960– , British)
York (Richard, Duke of; 1470–83, English)

05 Bulbo (*The Rose and the Ring*, 1855, W M Thackeray)
Canty (Tom; *The Prince and the Pauper*, 1881, Mark Twain)
Cyrus (the Younger; 424–401 BC, Persian)
Harry (1984– , British)
Henry (1594–1612, Scottish)
Henry (*King John*, 1590/1, William Shakespeare)
Henry (of Wales; *Henry IV Part I*, 1596/7, William Shakespeare)
Madoc (fl.1150–80, Welsh)
Wales (Charles, Prince of; 1948– , British)

06 Albert (1819–61, German)
Albert (II, 1958– ; Monaco)
Andrew (1960– , British)
Aragon (*The Merchant of Venice*, 1594–5, William Shakespeare)
Arthur (1486–1502, English)
Arthur (*The Faerie Queene*, 1590–96, Sir Edmund Spenser)
Ben Hur (*Ben Hur*, 1880, Lew Wallace)
Carlos (Don; 1545–68, Spanish)
Dmitri (1583–91, Russian)

Edward (1964– , British)
Edward ('the Black Prince'; 1330–76, English)
Edward (*The Prince and the Pauper*, 1881, Mark Twain)
Egmond (Lamoraal, Graf van; 1522–68, Flemish)
Egmont (Lamoraal, Graf van; 1522–68, Flemish)
Giglio (*The Rose and the Ring*, 1855, W M Thackeray)
Haakon (1973– ; Norwegian)
Hamlet (*Hamlet*, 1601/2, William Shakespeare)
Philip (1921– , Greek)
Stuart (Charles; 1720–88, British)
Stuart (James; 1688–1766, British)
Ulrich (Crown Prince of Evarchia; *Palace without Chairs*, 1978, Brigid Brophy)
Wessex (Edward, Earl of; 1964– , British)

07 Amerigo (*The Golden Bowl*, 1904, Henry James)
Arragon (*The Merchant of Venice*, 1594/5, William Shakespeare)
Bedford (John of Lancaster, Duke of; 1389–1435, English)
Charles (Prince of Wales; 1948– , British)
Charles (*The Fortunes of Nigel*, 1822, Sir Walter Scott)
Escalus (Prince of Verona; *Romeo and Juliet*, 1591–96, William Shakespeare)
Manfred (Prince of Otranto; *The Castle of Otranto*, 1764, Horace Walpole)
Maurice (1567–1625, Nassau)
Michael (of Kent; 1942– , British)

Morocco (*The Merchant of Venice*, 1594/5,
William Shakespeare)
Orléans (Louis Philippe Joseph, Duc d';
1747–93, French)
Rainier (III; 1923–2005, Monaco)
Richard (1470–83, English)
Rothsay (David of Scotland, Duke of; *The
Fair Maid of Perth, or St Valentine's Day*,
1828, Sir Walter Scott)
Stewart (Charles; 1720–88, British)
Stewart (James; 1688–1766, British)
William (1982– , British)
William (I; the Silent; 1533–84, Dutch)
Yakimov (*The Balkan Trilogy*, 1960–65,
Olivia Manning)

08 Berthier (Alexandre; 1753–1815, French)
Bohemond (I; c.1056–1111, Antioch)
Bohemond (II; c.1108–31, Antioch)
Carloman (751–71, Frankish)
Don Pedro (*Much Ado about Nothing*,
1598/1600, William Shakespeare)
Florizel (Prince of Bohemia; *The Suicide
Club*, 1878, Robert Louis Stevenson)
Florizel (*The Winter's Tale*, 1611, William
Shakespeare)
Hans-Adam (II; 1945– ; Liechtenstein)
Pericles (*Pericles*, c.1608, William
Shakespeare)
Pyrocles (*The Countess of Pembroke's
Arcadia*, 1581–84, Sir Philip Sidney)
Queequeg (*Moby-Dick*, 1851, Herman
Melville)
Rasselas (*The History of Rasselas, Prince of
Abissinia*, 1759, Samuel Johnson)
Ulugh-Beg (1394–1449, Tatar)
Vladimir (II, Monomakh; 1053–1125, Russian)
Volscius (*The Rehearsal*, 1671, George
Villiers, 2nd Duke of Buckingham)

09 Abu al-Fida (1273–1331, Syrian)
Antipater (d.4 BC, Judean)
Balthazar (*The Spanish Tragedy*, 1592,
Thomas Kyd)
Bonaparte (Lucien; 1775–1840, Italian)
Bras-Coupé (*The Grandissimes*, 1880,
George Washington Cable)
Connaught (Arthur, Duke of; 1850–1942,
English)
Demetrius (1583–91, Russian)
Edinburgh (Philip, Duke of; 1921– , British)
Ferdinand (I; 1861–1948, Austrian)
Musidorus (*The Countess of Pembroke's
Arcadia*, 1581–84, Sir Philip Sidney)
Pretty-man (*The Rehearsal*, 1671, George
Villiers, 2nd Duke of Buckingham)
Vincentio (*The Gentleman Usher*, 1602/3,
George Chapman)

10 Anacharsis (6c BC, Scythian)
Battenberg (Alexander of; 1857–93, Austrian)
Battenberg (Henry of; 1858–96, German)
Gloucester (Henry, Duke of; 1900–74, English)
Gloucester (Humphrey, Earl of Pembroke
and Duke of; 1391–1447, English)
Gloucester (Richard, Duke of; 1944– ,
English)
Gloucester (Robert, Earl of; d.1147, English)

11 Happy Prince ('The Happy Prince', 1888,
Oscar Wilde)

14 Frederick Louis (1707–51, German)

15 Alexander Nevsky (c.1220–63, Russian)
Alexis Petrovich (1690–1718, Russian)
Bernhard Leopold (1911–2004, Dutch)
Lewis the Dauphin (*Henry V*, 1599, William
Shakespeare)
Owain ap Gruffydd (c.1109–70, Welsh)
Saxe-Coburg-Gotha (Alfred Ernest Albert,
Prince of; 1844–1900, English)

princess

Princesses include:

03 Bee (St; 7c, Irish)

04 Anne (1950– , English)
Bega (St; 7c, Irish)
Begh (St; 7c, Irish)
Ebba (St; d.683, Northumbrian)
Olga (St; c.890–968, Russian)

05 Alice (1843–78, English)
Diana (Princess of Wales; 1961–97, English)
Grace (1929–82, US)
Irene (*The Princess and the Goblin*, 1871,
George MacDonald)
Wales (Diana, Princess of; 1961–97, English)

06 Albany (Louisa Caroline, Countess of;

1752–1824, Italian)
Audrey (St; c.630–79, Anglo-Saxon)
Dympna (c.9c, Irish)
France (*Love's Labour's Lost*, c.1594,
William Shakespeare)
Lieven (Dorothea; 1784–1857, Russian)
Salome (1c AD, Judean)

07 Arsinoë (c.316–270 BC, Macedonian)
Eudocia (AD401–65, Byzantine)
Eugenie (1990– , English)
Jezebel (d.842 BC, Phoenician)
Matilda (1102–67, English)
Rosalba (*The Rose and the Ring*, 1855, W M
Thackeray)

08 Angelica (*The Rose and the Ring*, 1855, W M Thackeray)
Beatrice (1988– , English)
Berenice (1c BC, Judean)
Berenice (c.28–c.79 AD, Judean)
Berenice (I; fl.c.317–c.275 BC, Macedonian)
Berenice (II; c.269–221 BC, Cyrene)
Berenice (III; d.c.80 BC, Egyptian)
Berenice (IV; d.55 BC, Egyptian)
Caroline (1957– , Monacan)
Dashkova (Yekaterina Romanovna; 1743–1810, Russian)
Glorvina (Lady; *The Wild Irish Girl*, 1806, Lady Morgan)
Grimaldi (Grace, of Monaco; 1929–82, US)
Margaret (1930–2002, British)
Victoria (1977– , Swedish)
Volupine ('Burbank with a Baedeker; Bleistein with a Cigar', 1920, T S Eliot)

09 Alexandra (1936– , English)
Bacciochi (Maria Anna Elisa; 1777–1820, Corsican)

Bonaparte (Pauline; 1780–1825, Corsican)
Charlotte (1796–1817, English)
Katharine (Princess of France; *Henry V*, 1599, William Shakespeare)
Stephanie (1965– , Monacan)
Theophano (c.955–991, Byzantine)

10 Etheldreda (St; c.630–79, Anglo-Saxon)
Mette-Marit (1973– , Norwegian)
Pocahontas (1595–1617, American)

11 Anna Comnena (1083–1148, Byzantine)
Anna Comnena (*Count Robert of Paris*, 1831, Sir Walter Scott)
Casamassima (*The Princess Casamassima*, 1886, Henry James)

12 Aethelthryth (St; c.630–79, Anglo-Saxon)
Anne of Cleves (1515–57, German)

13 Anne of Denmark (1574–1619, Danish)
Henrietta Anne (Duchesse d'Orleans; 1644–70, English)

14 Henrietta Maria (1609–69, French)

printing

Printing methods include:

03	CTP	**11**	die-stamping
05	litho		duplicating
07	etching		flexography
	gravure		letterpress
08	intaglio		lithography
09	collotype		rotary press
	engraving		stencilling
10	xerography		twin-etching
		12	lino blocking

thermography
13 laser printing
14 ink-jet printing
offset printing
photoengraving
screen printing
15 computer-to-plate
copper engraving

Printing terms include:

03 CTP
TLS
TPS
04 bulk
case
CYMK
demi
laid
logo
sewn
tint
trim
05 bleed
chase
cloth
cover
flong
forme

litho
moiré
press
proof
quoin
spine
zinco
06 batter
coated
cut-off
galley
jacket
mackle
matrix
octavo
Ozalid®
quarto
spread
unsewn

web-fed
07 bromide
carding
compose
dampers
dot gain
end even
foiling
leading
opacity
Pantone®
strip in
woodcut
08 art paper
book wove
flatback
foolscap
half-tone

hardback
headband
Linotype®
logotype
misprint
Monotype®
mottling
offprint
press run
print run
sheet fed
slipcase
softback
spoilage
strike-on
tailband
thumb cut
uncoated
wood-free

09 backing-up
book-block
case cover
duodecimo
dust cover
endpapers
finishing
flexi-bind
front flap
gilt edges
half bound
hard-bound
ink spread
Intertype®
letterset
make-ready
Monophoto®

newsprint
overprint
paperback
signature
soft-bound
trim marks
UV varnish
watermark
web offset

10 back margin
collograph
compositor
dot-etching
dustjacket
feathering
imposition
impression
lamination
mechanical
perfecting
see-through
shrink-wrap
silk screen
spot colour
stereotype

11 drum printer
electrotype
French bound
letter press
line printer
Oxford bound
show through
slot binding

12 black printer
brass artwork
burst binding

flat-bed press
inking roller
keep standing
machine proof
marker ribbon
non-image area
one-piece case
planographic
quarter bound
registration

13 anodized plate
base alignment
bonded leather
composing room
cylinder press
image printing
pantone colour
printing press
process colour
reader's spread
wood engraving

14 imitation cloth
kiss impression
part-mechanical
printer's spread
relief printing
thermal printer
transparencies

15 camera-ready copy
cold composition
composition size
digital printing
marble endpapers
trimmed leaf size
trimmed page size

See also **book**; **paint**; **publishing**

prison

Prisons include:

04 Maze (Northern Ireland)
05 Fleet (England)
Hoa Lo (Vietnam)
Pozzi (Italy)
06 Albany (England)
Attica (USA)
Folsom (USA)
07 Brixton (England)
Feltham (England)
Newgate (England)
08 Alcatraz (USA)
Bastille (France)
Belmarsh (England)
Dartmoor (England)

Holloway (England)
Long Kesh (Northern Ireland)
Lubyanka (Russia/USSR)
Mountjoy (Ireland)
Saughton (Scotland)
Sing Sing (USA)

09 Barlinnie (Scotland)
Fremantle (Australia)
Parkhurst (England)
Peterhead (Scotland)
the Scrubs (England)

10 Portlaoise (Ireland)
San Quentin (USA)
Wandsworth (England)

11 Hanoi Hilton (Vietnam)
Pentonville (England)
Strangeways (England)
12 Devil's Island (French Guiana)

Rikers Island (USA)
Robben Island (South Africa)
13 Tower of London (England)
14 Wormwood Scrubs (England)

prize *see* **award; literature; Nobel Prize**

probe *see* **space travel**

producer *see* **director**

programme *see* **television**

programming language *see* **computer**

Prokofiev, Sergei (1891–1953)

Significant works include:

05 *Chout* (1921)
09 'Classical' (Symphony; 1918)
'Zdravitsa' (Cantata; 1939)
10 *Cinderella* (1945)
The Buffoon (1921)
The Gambler (1915–16)
11 *Le Pas d'acier* (1927)
War and Peace (1944/1952)
12 *The Steel Step* (1927)
13 *Scythian Suite* (1916)
The Fiery Angel (1919–27)

14 *Lieutenant Kijé* (1934)
Romeo and Juliet (1936)
The Prodigal Son (1929)
15 *Alexander Nevsky* (1938)
Ivan the Terrible (1945)
Peter and the Wolf (1936)
18 *The Story of a Real Man* (1948)
19 'Sinfonia Concertante' (1952)
20 *Tale of the Stone Flower* (1954)
22 *The Love for Three Oranges* (1921)

prophet

Prophets and prophetesses include:

02 Is
03 Dan
Hag
Hos
Isa
Jer
Jon
Mic
Nah
Sam
04 Amos

Ezek
Joel
Obad
Zeph
05 Hosea
Jonah
Micah
Moses
Nahum
06 Daniel
Elijah

Elisha
Haggai
Isaiah
Nathan
Samuel
St John
07 Ezekiel
Malachi
Obadiah
08 Jeremiah
Mohammed

Muhammad
Nehemiah
09 al-Mokanna
Zephaniah
Zoroaster
11 Zarathustra
12 the Nun of Kent
13 the Maid of Kent
14 John the Baptist

prosody

Prosody terms include:

04 foot
iamb

05 canto
envoy

epode
ictus

Ionic
metre

paeon	triolet	hexameter	linked verse
06 choree	tripody	macaronic	long-measure
dactyl	triseme	monometer	septenarius
dipody	trochee	monorhyme	**12** alliteration
dizain	virelay	rime riche	antibacchius
laisse	**08** anapaest	tetrapody	Leonine rhyme
miurus	choriamb	**10** amphibrach	Pythian verse
rondel	cinquain	amphimacer	sprung rhythm
sonnet	eye rhyme	blank verse	**13** abstract verse
07 ballade	Pindaric	consonance	feminine rhyme
caesura	quatrain	enjambment	heroic couplet
couplet	tribrach	galliambic	hypermetrical
distich	trimeter	heptameter	internal rhyme
elision	**09** anacrusis	pentameter	**14** feminine ending
pantoum	assonance	rhyme royal	masculine rhyme
pyrrhic	catalexis	tetrameter	rime suffisante
rondeau	dispondee	villanelle	**15** feminine caesura
Sapphic	ditrochee	**11** Alcaic verse	masculine ending
spondee	free verse	alexandrine	poulters' measure
strophe	half-rhyme	broken rhyme	

protein

Proteins include:

03 TSP	insulin	complement
TVP	plasmin	dystrophin
04 zein	sericin	factor VIII
05 actin	trypsin	fibrinogen
opsin	tubulin	huntingtin
prion	**08** aleurone	interferon
renin	amandine	polymerase
06 avidin	collagen	**11** angiostatin
casein	Copaxone®	angiotensin
cyclin	ferritin	haemoglobin
enzyme	globulin	hydrogenase
fibrin	integrin	interleukin
globin	lysozyme	lactalbumin
gluten	protease	lipoprotein
kinase	thrombin	myoglobulin
lectin	**09** fibrillin	phosphatase
leptin	hydrolase	plasminogen
ligase	invertase	transferrin
myosin	isomerase	tropomyosin
papain	luciferin	**12** endonuclease
pepsin	myostatin	neurotrophin
rennin	phaseolin	serum albumin
07 albumin	prolamine	**13** lactoglobulin
elastin	protamine	**14** clotting factor
histone	sclerotin	immunoglobulin
hordein	**10** calmodulin	**15** intrinsic factor

Proust, Marcel (1871–1922)

Significant works include:

12 Jean Santeuil (1927)
17 Contre Sainte-Beuve (1954)
18 On Art and Literature (1954)
19 Pastiches et mélanges (1919)

Pleasures and Regrets (1896)
21 Les Plaisirs et les jours (1896)
23 Remembrance of Things Past (1913–27)
24 À la recherche du temps perdu (1913–27)

À la recherche du temps perdu comprises:

09 Swann's Way (1913)
10 La Fugitive (1925)
11 The Fugitive (1925)
    The Prisoner (1923)
12 Time Regained (1927)
13 La Prisonnière (1923)
15 Le Temps retrouvé (1927)
16 Sodom and Gomorrah (1921–22)

Sodome et Gomorrhe (1921–22)
The Guermantes Way (1920)
17 Albertine disparue (1925)
    Du côté de chez Swann (1913)
    The Sweet Cheat Gone (1925)
18 Le Côté de Guermantes (1920)
19 Within a Budding Grove (1919)
29 À l'ombre des jeunes filles en fleur (1919)

Significant characters include:

05 Bloch
    Morel (Charles)
    Swann (Charles)
    Swann (Gilberte)
06 Jupien
    Leonie (Aunt)
    Marcel
    Rachel
07 Adolphe
    Charlus (Baron Palamède de 'Mémé')

de Crécy (Odette)
Simonet (Albertine)
08 Verdurin (Madame)
    Vinteuil (Mlle)
09 Françoise
    Saint-Loup (Robert Marquis de)
12 de Guermantes (Duchesse Oriane)
13 de Forcheville (Comte)
14 de Villeparisis (Madame)

province *see* **Canada; Ireland; New Zealand; South Africa**

pseudonym

Pseudonyms and stage names include:

03 Day (Doris: Doris Kappelhoff)
    Pop (Iggy; James Osterberg)
    Tey (Josephine; Elizabeth Mackintosh)
04 Alda (Alan; Alphonso d'Abruzzo)
    Bell (Acton; Anne Brontë)
    Bell (Currer; Charlotte Brontë)
    Bell (Ellis; Emily Brontë)
    Cage (Nicolas; Nicholas Coppola)
    Dors (Diana; Diana Fluck)
    Ford (Ford Madox; Ford Hueffer)
    Gish (Lillian Diana; Lilian de Guiche)
    Hite (Shere; Shirley Gregory)
    Holm (Sir Ian; Ian Holm Cuthbert)
    John (Sir Elton; Reginald Dwight)
    Lulu (Marie Lawrie)
    Lynn (Dame Vera; Vera Welch)

Piaf (Edith; Edith Gassion)
Reed (Lou; Louis Firbank)
Rhys (Jean; Gwen Williams)
Ross (Diana; Diane Earle)
Saki (Hector Munro)
Sand (George; Amandine Aurore Lucile
    Dupin)
West (Dame Rebecca; Cecily Andrews)
West (Nathanael; Nathan Wallenstein)
Wood (Natalie; Natasha Gurdin)
York (Susannah; Susannah Yolande-Fletcher)
05 Allen (Woody; Allen Konigsberg)
    Bizet (Georges; Alexandre César Léopold
    Bizet)
    Black (Cilla; Priscilla White)
    Bowie (David; David Jones)

Caine (Sir Michael; Maurice Micklewhite)
Cline (Patsy; Virginia Patricia Hensley)
Dylan (Bob; Robert Zimmerman)
Eliot (George; Mary Ann Evans)
Flynn (Errol; Leslie Flynn)
Garbo (Greta; Greta Gustafsson)
Gorky (Maxim; Aleksei Maksimovich Peshkov)
Grant (Cary; Archibald Leach)
Grant (Richard E; Richard Grant Esterhuysen)
Hardy (Oliver; Norvell Hardy Junior)
Henry (O; William Porter)
Holly (Buddy; Charles Hardin)
Jason (David; David White)
Keith (Penelope; Penelope Hatfield)
Lanza (Mario; Alfredo Coccozza)
Leigh (Vivien; Vivian Hartley)
Loren (Sophia; Sofia Scicolone)
Moore (Demi; Demi Guynes)
Moore (Julianne; Julie Anne Smith)
Niven (David; James Nevins)
Queen (Ellery; Frederick Dannay)
Ryder (Winona; Winona Horowitz)
Scott (Ronnie; Ronald Schatt)
Seuss (Dr; Theodor Seuss Geisel)
Smith (Stevie; Florence Smith)
Solti (Sir Georg; Gyorgy Stern)
Stern (Daniel; Marie de Flavigny, Comtesse d'Agoult)
Sting (Gordon Sumner)
Twain (Mark; Samuel Clemens)
Wayne (John; Marion Michael Morrison)
Welch (Raquel; Raquel Tejada)

06 Bacall (Lauren; Betty Perske)
Bardot (Brigitte; Camille Javal)
Berlin (Irving; Israel Baline)
Brooks (Mel; Melvin Kaminsky)
Burton (Richard; Richard Jenkins)
Conrad (Joseph; Józef Teodor Konrad Korzeniowski)
Crosby (Bing; Harry Lillis Crosby)
Curtis (Tony; Bernard Schwartz)
Fields (Dame Gracie; Grace Stansfield)
Foster (Jodie; Alicia Foster)
France (Anatole; Anatole Thibault)
Gibbon (Lewis Grassic; James Leslie Mitchell)
Harlow (Jean; Harlean Carpentier)
Heston (Charlton; Charles Carter)
Irving (Sir Henry; John Henry Brodribb)
Jolson (Al; Asa Yoelson)
Keaton (Diane; Diane Hall)
Laurel (Stan; Arthur Stanley Jefferson)
London (Jack; John Chaney)
Lugosi (Bela; Bela Blasko)
McBain (Ed; Salvatore Albert Lombino)
Mirren (Helen; Helen Mironoff)

Monroe (Marilyn; Norma Jean Mortenson)
Morton (Jelly Roll; Ferdinand La Menthe)
Neeson (Liam; William John Neeson)
Orwell (George; Eric Blair)
Peters (Ellis; Edith Pargeter)
Rogers (Ginger; Virginia McMath)
Salten (Felix; Siegmund Salzmann)
Sapper (Herman McNeile)
Scales (Prunella; Prunella Illingworth)
Simone (Nina; Eunice Waymon)
Spacey (Kevin; Kevin Fowler)
Steele (Tommy; Thomas Hicks)
Turner (Lana; Julia Turner)
Turner (Tina; Annie Mae Bullock)
Waters (Muddy; McKinley Morganfield)
Weldon (Fay; Franklin Birkinshaw)
Wesley (Mary; Mary Siepmann)
Wonder (Stevie; Steveland Judkins)

07 Andrews (Dame Julie; Julia Wells)
Bachman (Richard; Stephen King)
Bennett (Tony; Anthony Benedetto)
Bogarde (Sir Dirk; Derek van den Bogaerde)
Bronson (Charles; Charles Buchinsky)
Carroll (Lewis; Charles Dodgson)
Deneuve (Catherine; Catherine Dorleac)
Dinesen (Isak; Baroness Karen von Blixen)
Douglas (Kirk; Issur Danielovich)
Gardner (Ava; Lucy Johnson)
Garland (Judy; Frances Gumm)
Hepburn (Audrey; Edda Van Heemstra Hepburn-Ruston)
Higgins (Jack; Harry Patterson)
Holiday (Billie; Eleanora Fagan)
Jacques (Hattie; Josephine Jacques)
Karloff (Boris; William Pratt)
Kincaid (Jamaica; Elaine Richardson)
Le Carré (John; David Cornwell)
Lindsay (Robert; Robert Lindsay Stevenson)
Lombard (Carole; Jane Peters)
Matthau (Walter; Walter Matuschanskavasky)
Mercury (Freddie; Frederick Bulsara)
Michael (George; Georgios Panayiotou)
Miranda (Carmen; Maria do Carmo Miranda da Dunha)
Molière (Jean Baptiste Poquelin)
Montand (Yves; Ivo Livi)
Novello (Ivor; David Ivor Davies)
Richard (Sir Cliff; Harry Webb)
Robbins (Harold; Francis Kane)
Russell (Lillian; Helen Leonard)
Shepard (Sam; Samuel Shepard Rogers)
Swanson (Gloria; Gloria Svensson)
Wyndham (John; John Wyndham Parkes Lucas Beynon Harris)
Wynette (Tammy; Virginia Wynette Pugh)

08 Bancroft (Anne; Anna Maria Italiano)

Coltrane (Robbie; Anthony Robert McMillan)
Coolidge (Susan; Sarah Woolsey)
Costello (Elvis; Declan McManus)
Crawford (Joan; Lucille le Sueur)
Dietrich (Marlene; Maria Magdalena von Losch)
Gershwin (George; Jacob Gershvin)
Gershwin (Ira; Israel Gershvin)
Goldberg (Whoopi; Caryn Johnson)
Hayworth (Rita; Margarita Cansino)
Kingsley (Ben; Krishna Bhanji)
MacLaine (Shirley; Shirley Maclean Beaty)
Ma Rainey (Gertrude Rainey)
Pickford (Mary; Gladys Mary Smith)
Robinson (Edward G; Emanuel Goldenberg)
Sly Stone (Sylvester Stewart)
Stanwyck (Barbara; Ruby Stevens)

Stoppard (Tom; Thomas Straussler)
Voltaire (François Marie Arouet)
Williams (Tennessee; Thomas Lanier)
09 Bernhardt (Sarah; Sara-Marie-Henriette Bernard)
Bo Diddley (Ellas Bates)
Charteris (Leslie; Leslie Bowyer-Yin)
Fairbanks (Douglas; Douglas Ullman)
Lancaster (Burt; Stephen Burton Lancaster)
Leadbelly (Huddie William Ledbetter)
Offenbach (Jacques; Jakob Eberst)
Streisand (Barbra; Barbara Rosen)
Valentino (Rudolph; Rodolfo Guglielmi)
10 Howlin' Wolf (Chester Arthur Burnett)
Washington (Dinah; Ruth Jones)
Westmacott (Mary; Agatha Christie)
11 Springfield (Dusty; Mary O'Brien)

psychiatry

Psychiatrists and psychoanalysts include:

04 Beck (Aaron; 1921– , US)
Jung (Carl; 1875–1961, Swiss)
Rank (Otto; 1884–1939, Austrian)
05 Adler (Alfred; 1870–1937, Austrian)
Clare (Anthony; 1942–2007, Irish)
Crane (Frasier; *Cheers* 1982–93/*Frasier* 1993–2004, TV sitcoms, NBC)
Freud (Anna; 1895–1982, Austrian/British)
Freud (Sigmund; 1856–1939, Austrian)
Fromm (Erich; 1900–80, German/US)
Jones (Ernest; 1879–1958, Welsh)
Klein (Melanie; 1882–1960, Austrian/British)
Lacan (Jacques; 1901–81, French)
Laing (R D; 1927–89, Scottish)
Laing (Ronald David; 1927–89, Scottish)
Meyer (Adolf; 1866–1950, Swiss/US)
Reich (Wilhelm; 1897–1957, Austrian)
Szasz (Thomas; 1920–2012, Hungarian/US)
06 Berger (Hans; 1873–1941, German)
Bowlby (John; 1907–90, English)
Dysart (Martin; *Equus*, 1973, Peter Shaffer)

Hitzig (Julius; 1838–1907, German)
Snyder (Solomon; 1938– , US)
07 Bleuler (Eugen; 1857–1939, Swiss)
Erikson (Erik; 1902–94, US)
Persaud (Raj; 1963– , English)
08 Halfrunt (Gag; *The Hitchhiker's Guide to the Galaxy*, 1978 et seq, Douglas Adams)
Maudsley (Henry; 1835–1918, English)
Sullivan (Harry Stack; 1892–1949, US)
Wernicke (Carl; 1848–1905, German)
09 Alexander (Franz; 1891–1964, Hungarian/US)
Alzheimer (Alois; 1864–1915, German)
Kraepelin (Emil; 1856–1926, German)
Menninger (Karl; 1893–1990, US)
Rorschach (Hermann; 1884–1922, Swiss)
11 Krafft-Ebing (Richard, von; 1840–1902, German)
13 Wagner-Jauregg (Julius; 1857–1940, Austrian)

Terms used in psychiatry include:

02 id	psyche	paranoia
03 ECT	shrink	superego
ego	**07** Jungian	syndrome
04 mind	symptom	**09** acting out
05 angst	therapy	behaviour
brain	**08** alienist	catharsis
drugs	delusion	cognition
06 déjà vu	dementia	diagnosis
denial	Freudian	neurology
	neurosis	**10** abreaction

alienation
depression
11 suppression
12 psychiatrist
transference

13 conscious mind
mental illness
psychosurgery
psychotherapy
schizophrenia

14 psychoanalysis
15 bipolar disorder
personality test
unconscious mind

psychology

Branches of psychology include:

03 bio
04 para
05 child
depth
neuro
sport
06 health
social
08 abnormal

clinical
criminal
forensic
hedonics
09 cognitive
narrative
10 industrial
structural
11 educational
12 evolutionary

experimental
occupational
13 developmental
environmental
psychobiology
psychometrics
transpersonal
14 organizational
psychoanalysis
15 psychopathology

Psychology theories include:

07 atomism
Gestalt
Jungian
08 Adlerian
Freudian
Jamesian
Lacanian

09 cognitive
Pavlovian
10 attachment
functional
humanistic
Skinnerian
structural

11 behavioural
personality
13 connectionism
functionalism
structuralism
14 associationism
psychoanalytic

Psychological conditions and disorders include:

04 PTSD
06 autism
manias
07 agnosia
bulimia
phobias
08 dementia
neurosis
paranoia
09 addiction

anhedonia
Asperger's
psychosis
Tourette's
10 abreaction
Alzheimer's
blindsight
depression
dysmorphia
sociopathy
11 Huntington's

kleptomania
Munchausen's
psychopathy
12 hypochondria
13 acatamathesia
battle fatigue
schizophrenia
15 anorexia nervosa
bipolar disorder

Psychological therapies include:

03 art
05 drama
group
hypno
06 colour
psycho

07 Gestalt
08 aversion
09 cognitive
10 regression
11 behavioural

counselling
12 electroshock
13 interpersonal
person-centred
psychodynamic

Psychologists include:

04 Bain (Alexander; 1818–1903, Scottish)
Burt (Sir Cyril; 1883–1971, English)
Hall (G Stanley; 1844–1924, US)
Hebb (Donald O; 1904–85, Canadian)
King (Sir Truby; 1858–1938, New Zealand)
Mead (George Herbert; 1863–1931, US)
Ward (James; 1843–1925, English)

05 Beach (Frank; 1911–88, US)
Binet (Alfred; 1857–1911, French)
Clark (Kenneth B; 1914–2005, US)
Craik (Kenneth; 1914–45, Scottish)
Forel (Auguste; 1848–1931, Swiss)
James (William; 1842–1910, US)
Janet (Pierre; 1859–1947, French)
Kelly (George A; 1905–66, US)
Lange (Carl; 1834–1900, Danish)
Luria (Aleksandr; 1902–77, Soviet)
Pratt (J Gaither; 1910–79, US)
Rhine (Joseph Banks; 1895–1980, US)
Simon (Herbert; 1916–2001, US)
Stout (George Frederick; 1860–1944, English)
Wundt (Wilhelm; 1832–1920, German)

06 Bruner (Jerome; 1915– , US)
de Bono (Edward; 1933– , Maltese/British)
Gesell (Arnold; 1880–1961, US)
Gibson (James; 1904–79, US)
Harlow (Harry; 1905–81, US)
Kinsey (Alfred; 1894–1956, US)
Koffka (Kurt; 1886–1941, German)
Köhler (Wolfgang; 1887–1967, German)
Milner (Brenda; 1918–2008, Canadian)
Morris (Robert L; 1942–2004, US)
Murphy (Gardner; 1895–1979, US)
Piaget (Jean; 1896–1980, Swiss)
Pinker (Steven; 1954– , Canadian/US)
Terman (Lewis; 1877–1956, US)
Tolman (Edward C; 1886–1959, US)
Wallas (Graham; 1858–1932, English)

Watson (John B; 1878–1958, US)

07 Baldwin (James Mark; 1861–1934, US)
Cattell (Raymond B; 1905–98, English)
Eysenck (Hans; 1916–97, German/British)
Fechner (Gustav Theodor; 1801–87, German)
Hartley (David; 1705–57, English)
Johnson (Virginia E; 1925– , US)
Lashley (Karl Spencer; 1890–1958, US)
Meinong (Alexius von; 1853–1920, Austrian)
Milgram (Stanley; 1933–84, US)
Neisser (Ulric; 1928–2012, German/US)
Pringle (Mia Kellmer; 1920–83, Austrian)
Skinner (B F; 1904–90, US)
Stevens (Stanley S; 1906–73, US)

08 Bartlett (Sir Frederic C; 1886–1969, English)
Brentano (Franz; 1838–1917, German)
Gilligan (Carol; 1936– , US)
Vygotsky (Lev; 1896–1934, Soviet)

09 Broadbent (Donald; 1926–93, English)
Claparède (Édouard; 1873–1940, Swiss)
Condillac (Étienne Bonnot de; 1715–80, French)
Festinger (Leon; 1919–89, US)
Macgregor (Douglas; 1906–64, US)
McDougall (William; 1871–1938, English/US)
Sternberg (Robert J; 1949– , US)
Thorndike (Edward L; 1874–1949, US)
Thurstone (L L; 1887–1955, US)
Titchener (Edward Bradford; 1867–1927, English/US)

10 Bettelheim (Bruno; 1903–90, US)
Ebbinghaus (Hermann; 1850–1909, German)
Wertheimer (Max; 1880–1943, German)

11 Tranströmer (Tomas; 1931– , Swedish)

Terms used in psychology include:

02 id
03 cue
ego
04 self
05 anima
horme
image
imago
limen
06 affect
animus
denial
libido

schema
symbol
07 anxiety
bonding
complex
phallic
08 cathexis
chunking
delusion
ego ideal
fixation
illusion
superego

09 anal stage
body image
catharsis
death wish
extrovert
introvert
mechanism
penis envy
puerilism
word salad
10 paragnosis
perception
projection
regression

repression
Zener cards

11 unconscious

12 co-dependency
cognitive map
conditioning
displacement
dissociation
preconscious

psychosexual
role reversal
subconscious
transference

13 configuration
consciousness
metacognition
primal therapy
psychosomatic

Rorschach test

14 Electra complex
identification
Oedipus complex
Phaedra complex
wish fulfilment

15 escape mechanism
externalization

See also **therapy**

public house

Public house names include:

04 Bell
Bull
Ship
Swan

05 Crown
Globe

06 Anchor
Castle
George
New Inn
Plough

07 Railway

Red Lion

08 Green Man
Nags Head
Royal Oak
Victoria

09 Black Bull
Cross Keys
King's Arms
King's Head
White Hart
White Lion
White Swan

10 Black Horse
Golden Lion
Queen's Head
Wheatsheaf
White Horse

12 Fox and Hounds
Rose and Crown

13 Hare and Hounds
Prince of Wales

14 Coach and Horses

15 George and Dragon

public transport

Public transport includes:

03 bus
cab

04 taxi
tram
tube

05 coach
ferry

metro
train

07 omnibus
railway
trolley

08 bendy-bus

10 stagecoach
trolleybus

11 mass transit
park-and-ride
underground

12 cable railway
light railway

See also **railway**; **ship**; **underground**

publishing

Publishers and imprints include:

02 DK

03 CUP
OUP
Pan

05 Corgi
Orion
T and F

06 Puffin
Viking
Virago

07 Berlitz

Cassell
Collins
Longman
Merriam
Methuen
Pearson
Penguin
Picador
Pimlico
Usborne

08 BBC Books
Chambers

Everyman
Flamingo
Gollancz
Ladybird
Larousse
Michelin
Palgrave

09 Allen Lane
Black Swan
Blackwell
Doubleday
Heinemann

Macmillan
Routledge

10 A and C Black
Bloomsbury
Bodley Head
Hutchinson
McGraw-Hill
Paul Hamlyn
Scholastic
Times Books
Transworld

11 Bantam Press

Bertelsmann
Fodor Guides
Rand McNally
Random House
Rough Guides
12 André Deutsch
Butterworths
Edward Arnold

Fourth Estate
Jonathan Cape
Lonely Planet
Mills and Boon
Penguin Books
Reed Elsevier
13 Allen and Unwin
AOL/Time Warner

Atlantic Books
Faber and Faber
Hachette Livre
HarperCollins
Reader's Digest
14 Canongate Books
Chambers Harrap
Chrysalis Books

Hodder Headline
Springer-Verlag
15 Chatto and Windus
Houghton Mifflin
Mitchell Beazley
Sweet and Maxwell
Thames and
Hudson

Publishing terms include:

02 em
en
PA
03 IPA
IPC
NBA
NPA
04 body
bold
copy
dupe
font
ISBN
kern
pica
rule
stet
text
typo
05 agent
blurb
caret
colon
comma
flush
folio
fount
index
point
proof
recto
roman
run-in
run on
serif
title
verso
widow
06 author
banner
byline
centre
cliché
column
delete
editor

em dash
em rule
en dash
en rule
errata
format
galley
gutter
hyphen
indent
insert
italic
margin
non-net
orphan
ragged
reader
rights
serial
series
take in
taster
07 binding
caption
cast-off
chapter
close up
concise
copyfit
drop cap
edition
excerpt
fair use
flat fee
imprint
leaders
library
literal
oblique
pen name
preface
prelims
reprint
subhead
typeset
upright
x-height

08 appendix
ascender
back flap
backlist
bad break
base line
body copy
bold face
book fair
colophon
ellipsis
endpaper
epilogue
foreword
glossary
Greeking
hackwork
headline
ligature
portrait
prepress
prologue
take back
take over
template
typeface
type spec
09 afterword
ampersand
anthology
catchword
character
clean copy
condensed
copyright
descender
duplicate
expert set
half title
justified
landscape
lower-case
paragraph
press date
pseudonym
publicist
pull quote

royalties
run-around
sans-serif
semicolon
strapline
tailpiece
title page
transpose
upper-case

10 apostrophe
back matter
bestseller
bookseller
column inch
commission
dedication
divider tab
facing page
first proof
hard hyphen
house style
journalism
journalist
large print
leader dots
manuscript
out of print

See also **book**; **printing**

pagination
periodical
plagiarism
ragged left
review copy
royalty fee
soft hyphen
substitute
typescript
typography
undertaker
white space

11 circulation
composition
copy editing
copyfitting
front matter
ghost writer
initial caps
ragged right
running foot
running head
running text
typesetting
typographer
word spacing

12 author's proof

bastard title
bibliography
character set
contents page
divider sheet
expanded type
first edition
illustration
introduction
proofreading
public domain
specimen page

13 bestsellerdom
expert reading
hanging indent
justification
letter spacing
off-press proof
raised initial
small capitals

14 capital letters
content editing
nanopublishing
library edition
quotation marks

15 proof correction
table of contents

Puccini, Giacomo (1858–1924)

Significant works include:

05 *Edgar* (1889)
Tosca (1900)

07 *Le Villi* (1884)

08 *La Bohème* (1896)
The Cloak (1918)
Turandot (1926)

09 *Il Tabarro* (1918)

La Rondine (1917)

10 *Crisantemi* (1890)
Il Trittico (1918)
The Swallow (1917)
The Witches (1884)

12 *Manon Lescaut* (1893)
Suor Angelica (1918)

13 *Messa di Gloria* (1880)

14 *Gianni Schicchi* (1918)
Sister Angelica (1918)

15 *Madama Butterfly* (1904)

17 *Preludio sinfonico* (1876)

18 *Capriccio sinfonico* (1883)
La fanciulla del West (1910)

Significant characters include:

03 Liu
Zia (Principessa La)

04 Goro
Mimì
Pang
Ping
Pong

05 Calaf
Civry (Magda de)
Luigi
Talpa
Timur
Tinca

Tosca (Floria)

06 Altoum (Emperor)
Benoît
Minnie
Ravoir (Geronte di)
Suzuki

07 A Jailer
Colline
Edmondo
Frugola
Lastouc (Ruggero)
Lescaut
Lescaut (Manon)

Lisette
Michele
Musetta
Prunier
Rodolfo
Scarpia (Baron)
The Mole
Trouble

08 Marcello
Rinuccio
Schicchi (Gianni)
Schicchi (Lauretta)
Spoletta

The Bonze
The Tench
Turandot (Princess)
Yakuside
Yamadori (Prince)
09 Alcindoro
A Mandarin
Angelotti (Cesare)
Butterfly (Madame)

Cio-Cio-San
Des Grieux (Chevalier)
Fernandez (Rambaldo)
Giorgetta
Parpignol
Pinkerton (Kate)
Pinkerton (Lieutenant Benjamin)
Sacristan

Schaunard
Sciarrone
Sharpless
11 Cavaradossi (Mario)
The Rummager
14 Customs Officer
Sister Angelica

pudding *see* **cake**; **dessert**

pulse *see* **bean**

punctuation

Punctuation marks include:

04 dash
star
05 colon
comma
06 hyphen
period

quotes
07 solidus
08 asterisk
brackets
ellipsis
full stop

09 backslash
semicolon
10 apostrophe
11 parentheses
speech marks
12 question mark

13 oblique stroke
14 inverted commas
quotation marks
square brackets
15 exclamation mark

punishment

Punishments include:

04 fine
gaol
jail
05 exile
lines
06 gating
hiding
prison
07 beating
belting
borstal
capital
flaying
hitting
jankers
lashing

the cane
the rack
08 corporal
demotion
flogging
slapping
smacking
spanking
the birch
whipping
09 chain gang
detention
exclusion
execution
expulsion
grounding

larruping
probation
scourging
strappado
the stocks
thrashing
torturing
10 banishment
cashiering
decimation
defrocking
internment
leathering
suspension
the slipper
unfrocking

11 confinement
deportation
house arrest
keelhauling
knee-capping
mastheading
penal colony
12 confiscation
dressing-down
imprisonment
13 horsewhipping
incarceration
sequestration
14 transportation
15 excommunication
walking the plank

See also **execution**; **prison**

Purcell, Henry (c.1659–95)

Significant works include:

05 *Circe* (c.1690)

07 *Bonduca* (1695)
Oedipus (c.1692)
Regulus (1692)

08 *Oroonoko* (1695)

09 *Abdelazer* (1695)
Cleomenes (1692)

10 *Amphitryon* (1690)

Aureng-Zebe (c.1692)
Don Quixote (1695)
Epsom Wells (1693)
King Arthur (1691)
Sophonisba (c.1685)
The Tempest (c.1695)
11 Old Bachelor (1691)
12 The Libertine (c.1692)
Tyrannic Love (1694)
13 Dido and Aeneas (1689)
The Fairy Queen (1689)
The Prophetess (1690)
The Theodosius (1680)
Timon of Athens (1694)
14 Love Triumphant (1693)
Sir Anthony Love (1690)
The Indian Queen (1695)
The Married Beau (1694)
The Wife's Excuse (1691)
15 Come, Ye Sons of Art (1694)
Female Virtuosos (1693)
Sir Barnaby Whigg (1681)
The Double Dealer (1693)
The Mock Marriage (1695)
The Rival Sisters (1695)
The Spanish Friar (1695)
The Virtuous Wife (c.1694)
16 A Fool's Preferment (1688)

The English Lawyer (1685)
The Fatal Marriage (1694)
The Indian Emperor (1691)
The Knight of Malta (1691)
17 Hail Bright Cecilia (1692)
My Heart is Inditing (1685)
Thy Word is a Lantern (c.1694)
18 Nymphs and Shepherds (c.1692)
The Canterbury Guest (1694)
The Maid's Last Prayer (1693)
The Massacre of Paris (1690)
The Richmond Heiress (1693)
19 Distressed Innocence (1694)
History of Dioclesian (1690)
The Gordian Knot Unty'd (1691)
20 Henry II, King of England (1692)
What Hope for Us Remains (1679)
21 Rule a Wife and Have a Wife (1693)
22 History of King Richard II (1681)
The Marriage-Hater Match'd (1692)
24 Arise, Ye Subterranean Winds (1695)
26 Remember Not, Lord, our Offences (1682)
28 High on a Throne of Glittering Ore (1690)
29 They that go Down to the Sea in Ships (1685)
29 The Pausanius Betrayer of His Country (1695)

purple

Shades of purple include:

04 anil	prune	heather	mulberry
plum	**06** cerise	magenta	**09** aubergine
puce	damson	purpure	**11** royal purple
puke	indigo	**08** amethyst	
05 lilac	maroon	burgundy	
mauve	violet	hyacinth	
pansy	**07** fuchsia	lavender	

See also **dye**; **pigment**

puzzle

Puzzles include:

04 maze	kakuro	tangram	Rubik's Cube®
quiz	sudoku	**08** acrostic	wordsearch
05 logic	**07** anagram	wordgame	**12** magic pyramid
rebus	cidouri	**09** crossword	
06 hitori	hangman	**10** alphametic	
jigsaw	sorites	cryptogram	

See also **crossword**; **game**

qualification

02 BA
MA

03 BSc
MSc
PhD

04 GCSE

05 Lower

06 A level
degree
Higher
O grade
O level

07 AS level

10 eleven-plus
Lower grade

11 Higher grade
Legum doctor

12 Doctor of Laws
Master of Arts
Master of Laws

13 Advanced level
Bachelor of Law
Doctor of Music
Legum magister
Master of Music
Ordinary grade
Ordinary level

Standard grade

14 Advanced Higher
Artium Magister
Bachelor of Arts
Bachelor of Laws
Magister Artium

15 Bachelor of Music
Doctor of Letters
Doctor of Science
Doctor of Surgery
Master of Letters
Master of Science
Master of Surgery
Medicinae Doctor

queen

04 Anne
Emma
Jane
Joan
Mary

05 Maria
Marie

06 Esther
Isabel
Louisa

07 Beatrix
Eleanor
Juliana

08 Caroline
Isabella
Margaret
Philippa
Victoria

09 Catherine
Charlotte

Cleopatra
Elizabeth
Katherine
Margrethe

12 Maria Theresa

14 Henrietta Maria

15 Charlotte Sophia
Marie Antoinette

03 Min (1851–95, Korea)

04 Anne (1665–1714, Great Britain and Ireland)
Anne (of Austria; 1601–66, France)
Anne (of Bohemia; 1366–94, England)
Anne (of Brittany; 1476–1514, France)
Anne (of Cleves; 1515–57, England)
Anne (of Denmark; 1574–1619, Scotland and England)
Emma (d.1052, England)
Grey (Lady Jane; 1537–54, England)
Joan (of Navarre; c.1370–1437, England)
Leda (Greek mythology, Sparta)
Lucy (*The Lion, the Witch and the Wardrobe*, 1950, C S Lewis)

Mary (II; 1662–94, Great Britain and Ireland)
Mary (I, Tudor; 1516–58, England and Ireland)
Mary (of Guise; 1515–60, Scotland)
Mary (of Hungary; 1505–58, Hungary and Bohemia)
Mary (of Modena; 1658–1718, Great Britain and Ireland)
Mary (of Teck; 1867–1953, Great Britain and Northern Ireland)
Mary (Queen of Scots; 1542–87, Scotland)
Mary (Queen of Scots; *The Abbot*, 1820, Sir Walter Scott)
Medb (Celtic mythology, Connaught)
Noor (of Jordan; 1951– , US)

Parr (Catherine; 1512–48, England)
Parr (Katherine; 1512–48, England)

05 Juana (1479–1555, Castile)
Maeve (Celtic mythology, Connaught)
Maria (II; 1819–53, Portugal)
Marie (de Médicis; 1573–1642, France)
Rania (of Jordan; 1970– , Kuwaiti)
Sheba (1c BC, Sabeans)
Susan (*The Lion, the Witch and the Wardrobe*, 1950, C S Lewis)

06 Boleyn (Anne; 1501–36, England)
Esther (5c BC, Persia)
Hautia (*Mardi*, 1849, Herman Melville)
Hearts (Queen of; *Alice's Adventures in Wonderland*, 1865, Lewis Carroll)
Hecuba (Greek mythology, Troy)
Himiko (d.247 AD, Japan)
Howard (Catherine; d.1542, England)
Isabel (*Henry V*, 1599, William Shakespeare)
Louisa (1776–1810, Prussia)
Mbande (Jinga; c.1582–1663, Jaga)
Nzinga (c.1582–1663, Jaga)
Salote (1900–65, Tonga)
Silvia (1943– , Sweden)
Soraya (1932–2001, Persia)
Tamara (c.1160–1212, Georgia)
Tamora (*Titus Andronicus*, c.1589, William Shakespeare)
Videna (*Gorboduc*, 1561, Thomas Norton and Thomas Sackville)

07 Beatrix (1938– , The Netherlands)
Bonduca (*Bonduca*, 1613–14, Francis Beaumont and John Fletcher)
Eleanor (of Aquitaine; c.1122–1204, France and England)
Eleanor (of Castile; c.1245–90, England)
Jocasta (Greek mythology; Thebes)
Juliana (1909–2004, The Netherlands)
Macbeth (Lady; *Macbeth*, c.1606, William Shakespeare)
Panthea (*A King and No King*, 1611, Francis Beaumont and John Fletcher)
Phaedra (Greek mythology, Athens)
Seymour (Jane; c.1509–37, England)
Titania (*A Midsummer Night's Dream*, 1595–96, William Shakespeare)
Zenobia (3c AD, Palmyra)

08 Adelaide (1792–1849, Great Britain)
Berenice (c.280–c.246 BC, Syria)
Berenice (I; fl.c.317–c.275 BC, Egypt)
Boadicea (d.61 AD, Iceni)
Boudicca (d.61 AD, Iceni)
Caroline (of Ansbach; 1683–1737, Great Britain and Ireland)
Caroline (of Brunswick; 1768–1821, Great Britain and Ireland)
Clotilda (St; AD474–545, Franks)

Cordelia (British legend, England)
Gertrude (*Hamlet*, 1601/2, William Shakespeare)
Gloriana (*The Faerie Queene*, 1590–96, Sir Edmund Spenser)
Hermione (*The Winter's Tale*, 1611, William Shakespeare)
Isabella (*Edward II*, 1594, Christopher Marlowe)
Isabella (II; 1830–1904, Spain)
Isabella (I; of Castile; 1451–1504, Spain)
Isabella (of Angoulême; c.1188–1246, England)
Isabella (of France; 1292–1358, England)
Jane Grey (Lady; 1537–54, England)
Margaret ('Maid of Norway'; 1283–90, Scotland)
Margaret (of Angoulême; 1492–1549, Navarre)
Margaret (of Anjou; 1430–82, England)
Margaret (of Valois; 1553–1615, Navarre)
Margaret (*Richard III*, 1592/3, William Shakespeare)
Margaret (St; c.1046–93, Scotland)
Mercilla (*The Faerie Queene*, 1590–96, Sir Edmund Spenser)
Olympias (d.316 BC, Epirus)
Pasiphae (Greek mythology, Crete)
Philippa (of Hainault; c.1314–69, England)
Radigund (*The Faerie Queene*, 1590–96, Sir Edmund Spenser)
Victoria (1819–1901, Great Britain and Ireland)

09 Alexandra (1844–1925, Great Britain and Northern Ireland)
Artemisia (II; d.c.350 BC, Caria)
Bonaparte (Caroline; 1782–1839, Naples)
Brunhilde (c.534–613, Franks)
Catherine (de Médicis; 1519–89, France)
Catherine (de Valois; 1401–37, England)
Catherine (of Aragon; 1485–1536, England)
Catherine (of Braganza; 1638–1705, Great Britain and Ireland)
Christina (1626–89, Sweden)
Cleopatra (69–30 BC, Egypt)
Cleopatra (*Antony and Cleopatra*, 1606/7, William Shakespeare)
Cleopatra (*Caesar and Cleopatra*, 1898, George Bernard Shaw)
Elizabeth (1596–1662, Bohemia)
Elizabeth (1843–1916, Romania)
Elizabeth (I; 1533–1603, England and Ireland)
Elizabeth (II; 1926– , Great Britain and Northern Ireland)
Elizabeth (I; Queen of England; *Kenilworth*, 1821, Sir Walter Scott)
Elizabeth (of Portugal; St; 1271–1336, Portugal)

Elizabeth (*Richard III*, 1592/3, William Shakespeare)

Elizabeth (the Queen Mother; 1900–2002, Great Britain and Northern Ireland)

Fredegond (d.598, Franks)

Guinevere (Arthurian legend, Britain)

Hippolyta (Greek mythology, Amazons)

Maintenon (Françoise d'Aubigné, Marquise de; 1635–1719, France)

Margrethe (I; 1353–1412, Denmark, Norway and Sweden)

Margrethe (II; 1940– , Denmark)

Nefertiti (14c BC, Egypt)

Semiramis (Greek mythology, Assyria)

Tanaquill (*The Faerie Queene*, 1590–96, Sir Edmund Spenser)

Woodville (Elizabeth; c.1437–92, England)

10 Anne Boleyn (1501–36, England)

Berengaria (*The Talisman: A Tale of the Crusaders*, 1825, Sir Walter Scott)

Hatshepsut (c.1540–c.1481 BC, Egypt)

Lakshmi Bai (1835–58, Jhansi)

Marguerite (of Angoulême; 1492–1549, Navarre)

Persephone (Greek mythology, underworld)

Proserpina (Greek mythology, underworld)

Wilhelmina (of Orange-Nassau; 1880–1962, The Netherlands)

11 Beauharnais (Hortense Eugénie Cécile; 1783–1837, Holland)

Jane Seymour (c.1509–1537, England)

12 Clytemnestra (Greek mythology, Argos)

Maria Theresa (1717–80, Hungary and Bohemia)

13 Catherine Parr (1512–48, England)

Katherine Parr (1512–48, England)

Margaret Tudor (1489–1541, Scotland)

14 Henrietta Maria (1609–69, England)

Ulrika Eleonora (1688–1741, Sweden)

15 Catherine Howard (d.1542, England)

Charlotte Sophia (1744–1818, Great Britain and Ireland)

Marie Antoinette (1755–93, France)

quiz

Radio and television quiz shows and hosts include:

02 *QI* (Stephen Fry)

03 *3–2–1* (Ted Rogers)

05 *Dotto* (Robert Gladwell/Jimmy Hanley/Shaw Taylor)

06 *Gambit* (Fred Dineage)

07 *Pop Quiz* (Mike Read)

Wipeout (Paul Daniels)

08 *Bullseye* (Jim Bowen)

Mr and Mrs (Alan Taylor/Derek Batey/Julian Clary)

Quiz Ball (David Vine/Barry Davies/Stuart Hall)

Whispers (Gyles Brandreth)

09 *Brainwave* (Andy Craig)

Countdown (Richard Whiteley/Des Lynam/ Des O'Connor/Jeff Stelling/Nick Hewer)

Odd One Out (Paul Daniels)

Small Talk (Ronnie Corbett)

10 *Mastermind* (Magnus Magnusson/John Humphrys)

Masterteam (Angela Rippon/Peter Snow)

Screen Test (Michael Rodd/Brian Trueman/ Mark Curry)

11 *Call My Bluff* (Robert Robinson/Bob Holness/Fiona Bruce)

Catchphrase (Roy Walker/Nick Weir/Mark Curry)

Give Us a Clue (Michael Aspel/Michael Parkinson)

Just a Minute (Nicholas Parsons)

Mock the Week (Dara Ó Briain)

Only Connect (Victoria Coren Mitchell)

Spot the Tune (Ken Platt/Ted Ray/Jackie Rae/ Pete Murray)

The Food Quiz (Jay Rayner)

The News Quiz (Barry Norman/Barry Took/ Simon Hoggart/Sandi Toksvig)

What's My Line? (Eamonn Andrews/David Jacobs/Penelope Keith/Angela Rippon/ Emma Forbes)

12 *Ask the Family* (Robert Robinson)

Blockbusters (Bob Holness)

Bognor or Bust (Angus Deayton)

Face the Music (Joseph Cooper)

Fifteen to One (William G Stewart)

Going for Gold (Henry Kelly)

Lucky Numbers (Shane Richie)

Name That Tune (Tom O'Connor/Lionel Blair)

Strike It Rich (Michael Barrymore)

Take Your Pick (Michael Miles/Des O'Connor)

Telly Addicts (Noel Edmonds)

Winning Lines (Phillip Schofield)

13 *Blankety Blank* (Terry Wogan/Les Dawson/ Lily Savage)

Bob's Full House (Bob Monkhouse)

Going for a Song (Max Robertson/Michael Parkinson)

Public Opinion (Gyles Brandreth)
Strike It Lucky (Michael Barrymore)
Test the Nation (Anne Robinson & Phillip Schofield/Danny Wallace)
The Travel Quiz (Andi Peters)

14 Brain of Britain (Robert Robinson/Russell Davies)
Criss Cross Quiz (Jeremy Hawk)
Family Fortunes (Bob Monkhouse/Max Bygraves/Les Dennis)
Going, Going, Gone (Andy Craig)
Quotation Marks (Vanessa Feltz)
The Weakest Link (Anne Robinson)
Wheel of Fortune (Nicky Campbell/Bradley Walsh/John Leslie)
Winner Takes All (Jimmy Tarbuck)
Would I Lie to You? (Angus Deayton/Rob Brydon)

15 Double Your Money (Hughie Green)
The Price Is Right (Leslie Crowther)

16 A Question of Sport (David Vine/David Coleman/Sue Barker)
Celebrity Squares (Bob Monkhouse)
Cheggers Plays Pop (Keith Chegwin)
Round Britain Quiz (Gordon Clough/Nick Clarke/Tom Sutcliffe)

Sale of the Century (Nicholas Parsons)
Supermarket Sweep (Dale Winton)

17 Every Second Counts (Paul Daniels)
The $64,000 Question (Bob Monkhouse)

18 Bruce's Price Is Right (Bruce Forsyth)
Have I Got News for You (Angus Deayton/various)
Play Your Cards Right (Bruce Forsyth)

19 I'm Sorry I Haven't a Clue (Humphrey Lyttelton/Jack Dee)
It's Only TV … But I Like It (Jonathan Ross)
The Great British Quiz (Janice Long)
They Think It's All Over (Nick Hancock)
University Challenge (Bamber Gascoigne/Jeremy Paxman)

21 Never Mind the Buzzcocks (Mark Lamarr/Simon Amstell/various)

22 Animal, Vegetable, Mineral? (Glyn Daniel)

23 Talking Telephone Numbers (Phillip Schofield & Emma Forbes)

24 Who Wants to Be a Millionaire? (Chris Tarrant)

R

rabbi *see* **chief rabbi**

rabbit

Rabbits and hares include:

03 fox	hotot	Polish	snowshoe
lop	sable	silver	**09** harlequin
Rex	satin	tapeti	Himalayan
tan	swamp	Vienna	**10** chinchilla
04 jack	water	**07** Argente	cottontail
pika	**06** Alaska	Belgian	New Zealand
rock	Angora	Flemish	Van Beveren
sage	Arctic	**08** European	**11** black silver
05 brown	Havana	lionhead	English spot
Dutch	oar-lap	riverine	Rhinelander

race

Race types include:

03 ski	slalom	scramble	Formula One
04 dash	sprint	speedway	motorcycle
road	**07** harness	stock car	track event
sack	hurdles	swimming	**11** egg-and-spoon
05 cycle	pancake	trotting	three-legged
horse	pursuit	**09** Grand Prix	wheelbarrow
motor	regatta	greyhound	**12** cross-country
relay	walking	motocross	steeplechase
yacht	**08** autotest	time trial	**14** snowboard cross
06 keirin	downhill	walkathon	
rowing	marathon	**10** cyclo-cross	

Races include:

02 TT	**09** Grand Prix	Grand National
04 Oaks	**11** Admiral's Cup	Kentucky Derby
05 Derby	America's Cup	**14** Greyhound Derby
06 Le Mans	Breeder's Cup	London Marathon
07 St Leger	Giro d'Italia	**15** Indianapolis 500
08 Boat Race	the Classics	Monte Carlo Rally
Milk Race	**12** Melbourne Cup	New York Marathon
RAC Rally	Tour de France	
	13 Diamond Sculls	

See also **racing: horse racing; racing: motor racing**

racehorse *see* **racing: horse racing**

Racine, Jean (1639–99)

Significant works include:

06 *Esther* (1689)
Phèdre (1677)
07 *Athalie* (1691)
Bajazet (1672)
08 *Bérénice* (1670)
09 *Iphigénie* (1675)

10 *Andromache* (1667)
Andromaque (1667)
Mithridate (1673)
11 *Britannicus* (1669)
Mithridates (1673)
12 *Les Plaideurs* (1668)

16 *Alexandre le grand* (1665)
17 *La Nymphe de la Seine* (1660)
28 *La Thébaïde ou Les Frères ennemis* (1664)

Significant characters include:

04 Aman
Nero
05 Joash
06 Aricia
Attale
Dandin
Esther
Monima

Phèdre
Roxane
07 Atalide
Athalie
Bajazet
Leander
Orestes
Pyrrhus
Theseus

08 Assureus
Berenice
Hermione
09 Agrippina
Alexander
Iphigénie
Petit-Jean
10 Andromache

Andromaque
Chicanneau
Hippolytus
Mithridate
11 Britannicus
Mithridates

racing: horse racing

Racehorses include:

05 Arkle
Cigar
Pinza
06 Nearco
Red Rum
Sir Ken
07 Alleged
Dawn Run
Eclipse

Pharlap
Sceptre
Shergar
Sir Ivor
08 Aldaniti
Best Mate
Corbiere
Esha Ness
Hyperion

Istabraq
Mill Reef
Nijinsky
09 John Henry
L'Escargot
Oh So Sharp
10 Night Nurse
Persian War
See You Then

Sun Chariot
11 Cottage Rake
Never Say Die
Pretty Polly
12 Dancing Brave
Desert Orchid
Golden Miller
Hattons Grace

Racecourses include:

03 Ayr (Scotland)
04 York (England)
05 Ascot (England)
Epsom (England)
Kelso (Scotland)
07 Aintree (England)
Chester (England)
Curragh (Ireland)
Newbury (England)
Pimlico (USA)
Sandown (England)

Warwick (England)
08 Goodwood (England)
Wetherby (England)
09 Chantilly (France)
Doncaster (England)
Leicester (England)
Newcastle (England)
Newmarket (England)
Towcester (England)
Uttoxeter (England)
10 Cheltenham (England)
Epsom Downs (England)

Flemington (Australia)
Longchamps (France)
Pontefract (England)
The Curragh (Ireland)
11 Belmont Park (USA)
Haydock Park (England)
Kempton Park (England)
Musselburgh (Scotland)
Sandown Park (England)
Thistledown (USA)
12 Hamilton Park (Scotland)
14 Churchill Downs (USA)

Jockeys and associated figures include:

04 Hern (Major Dick; 1921–2002, English)
Pipe (Martin; 1945– , English)

05 Cecil (Henry; 1943–2013, Scottish)
Krone (Julie; 1963– , US)

Lukas (D Wayne; 1935–   , US)
McCoy (Tony; 1974–   , Irish)
Moore (Ryan; 1983–   , English)
Smith (Robyn; 1943–   , US)
Walsh (Ruby; 1979–   , Irish)

06 Arcaro (Eddie; 1916–97, US)
Archer (Fred; 1857–86, English)
Carson (Willie; 1942–   , Scottish)
Eddery (Pat; 1952–   , Irish)
Fallon (Kieren; 1965–   , Irish)
Knight (Henrietta; 1946–   , English)
Mellor (Stan; 1937–   , British)
O'Brien (Aidan; 1969–   , Irish)
O'Brien (Vincent; 1917– 2009, Irish)
O'Neill (Jonjo; 1952–   , Irish)
Pitman (Jenny; 1946–   , English)
Stoute (Sir Michael; 1945–   , Barbadian)
Winter (Fred; 1926–2004, English)

07 Cauthen (Steve; 1960–   , US)
Cordero (Angel, Jnr; 1942–   , Puerto Rican)
Dettori (Frankie; 1970–   , Italian)

Fordham (George; 1837–87, English)
Francis (Dick; 1920–2010, English)
Gifford (Josh; 1941–   , English)
Piggott (Lester; 1935–   , English)
Sanders (Seb; 1971–   , English)
Spencer (Jamie; 1980–   , Irish)

08 Breasley (Scobie; 1914–2006, Australian)
Champion (Bob; 1948–   , English)
Donoghue (Steve; 1884–1945, English)
Dunwoody (Richard; 1964–   , Northern Irish)
Francome (John; 1952–   , English)
Geraghty (Barry; 1979–   , Irish)
Richards (Sir Gordon; 1904–86, English)

09 Scudamore (Peter; 1958–   , English)
Shoemaker (Willie; 1931–2003, US)

10 Desormeaux (Kent; 1970–   , US)
Fitzgerald (Mick; 1970–   , Irish)
Williamson (Norman; 1969–   , Irish)

11 Saint-Martin (Yves; 1941–   , French)

Horse racing terms include:

03 dam
nap
net

04 colt
face
firm
foal
form
good
hand
hard
head
mare
nose
odds
rouf
sire
soft
stud
tips
trip
turf
yard

05 evens
fence
field
filly
going
heavy
neves
owner
place
silks

stake
wrist

06 bottle
carpet
chaser
faller
jockey
length
novice
odds-on
pull up
raider
sprint
stable
stayer
tic-tac
weight

07 classic
earhole
furlong
gelding
meeting
mudlark
tipster
trainer

08 ante-post
Bismarck
blinkers
handicap
hurdling
juvenile
outsider
racecard

shoulder
stallion
standard
stewards
yearling
yielding

09 favourite
group race
non-runner
pacemaker
Polytrack®
short head
shoulders

10 all-weather
bumper race
flat racing
listed race
parade ring
stakes race

11 accumulator
connections
handicapper
hunter chase
pattern race
photo finish
Triple Crown
winning post

12 double carpet
handicap race
National Hunt
starting gate
steeplechase
thoroughbred

top of the head	**14** conditions race	stewards' enquiry
weighing room	**15** levels you devils	

See also **equestrian sport; horse**

racing: motor racing

Formula One motor racing teams include:

03 BAR	Toyota	Minardi	**13** Red Bull Racing
06 Jordan	**07** Ferrari	Renault	
Sauber	McLaren	**08** Williams	

Formula One Grand Prix circuits include:

05 Imola (Imola, Italy; 'San Marino' GP)
Monza (Monza, Italy)

06 Sakhir (Manama, Bahrain)
Sepang (Kuala Lumpur, Malaysia)
Suzuka (Suzuka, Japan)

08 Shanghai (Shanghai, China)

10 Albert Park (Melbourne, Australia)

Hockenheim (Hockenheim, Germany)
Interlagos (São Paulo, Brazil)
Magny-Cours (Magny-Cours, France)
Monte Carlo (Monte Carlo, Monaco)

11 Hungaroring (Budapest, Hungary)
Nurburgring (Nurburg, Germany; 'Europe'
GP)
Silverstone (Silverstone, England)

Motor racing drivers, motorcyclists and associated figures include:

04 Foyt (A J, Jnr; 1935– , US)
Hill (Damon; 1960– , English)
Hill (Graham; 1929–75, English)
Hunt (James; 1947–93, English)
Ickx (Jacky; 1945– , Belgian)
Loeb (Sébastien; 1974– , French)
Moss (Sir Stirling; 1929– , English)

05 Alesi (Jean; 1964– , French)
Clark (Jim; 1936–68, Scottish)
Clark (Roger; 1939–98, English)
Hulme (Denny; 1936–94, New Zealand)
Lauda (Niki; 1949– , Austrian)
McRae (Colin; 1968–2007, Scottish)
Petty (Richard; 1937– , US)
Prost (Alain; 1955– , French)
Rossi (Valentino; 1979– , Italian)
Sainz (Carlos; 1962– , Spanish)
Senna (Ayrton; 1960–94, Brazilian)
Unser (Al; 1939– , US)
Unser (Bobby; 1934– , US)

06 Ascari (Alberto; 1918–55, Italian)
Berger (Gerhard; 1959– , Austrian)
Briggs (Barry; 1934– , New Zealand)
Button (Jensen; 1980– , English)
Doohan (Mick; 1965– , Australian)
Dunlop (Joey; 1952–2000, Northern Irish)
Fangio (Juan Manuel; 1911–95, Argentine)
Irvine (Eddie; 1965– , Northern Irish)
Lawson (Eddie; 1958– , US)
Mauger (Ivan; 1939– , New Zealand)
Piquet (Nelson; 1952– , Brazilian)
Sheene (Barry; 1950–2003, English)

Vettel (Sebastian; 1987– , German)
Walker (Murray; 1923– , English)

07 Brabham (Sir Jack; 1926– , Australian)
Brundle (Martin; 1959– , English)
Ferrari (Enzo; 1898–1988, Italian)
Fogarty (Carl; 1965– , English)
Guthrie (Janet; 1938– , US)
Mäkinen (Tommi; 1964– , Finnish)
Mansell (Nigel; 1953– , English)
McLaren (Bruce; 1937–70, New Zealand)
Mikkola (Hannu; 1942– , Finnish)
Roberts (Kenny; 1951– , US)
Segrave (Sir Henry; 1896–1930, US/British)
Stewart (Sir Jackie; 1939– , Scottish)
Surtees (John; 1934– , English)

08 Agostini (Giacomo; 1943– , Italian)
Andretti (Mario; 1940– , Italian/US)
Campbell (Donald; 1921–67, English)
Campbell (Sir Malcolm; 1885–1948, English)
Hailwood (Mike; 1940–81, English)
Hakkinen (Mika; 1968– , Finnish)
Hamilton (Lewis; 1985– , English)
Oldfield (Barney; 1878–1946, US)
Williams (Sir Frank; 1942– , Scottish)

09 Blomqvist (Stig; 1946– , Swedish)
Chevrolet (Louis; 1878–1941, Swiss/US)
Coulthard (David; 1971– , Scottish)
Earnhardt (Dale; 1951–2001, US)
Hawthorne (Mike; c.1930–1959, English)
Kankkunen (Juha; 1959– , Finnish)

10 Ecclestone (Bernard; 1930– , English)
Fittipaldi (Emerson; 1946– , Brazilian)

Schumacher (Michael; 1969– , German)
Schumacher (Ralf; 1975– , German)

Villeneuve (Jacques; 1971– , Canadian)
12 Rickenbacker (Eddie; 1890–1973, US)

Motor racing terms include:

03 lap
off
pit

04 apex
grid
oval
pits
pole
T-car

05 apron
Armco
in lap
Nomex®
plank
shunt

06 out lap
slicks
tifosi

07 chicane
cockpit
hairpin
marshal
pace car
paddock
pit babe
pit lane

pit stop
pit wall
stagger
steward
traffic

08 diffuser
dirty air
drafting
fishtail
fuel load
lollipop
outbrake
pit board
scuderia
sidepods
straight
tyre wall

09 Brickyard
down force
monocoque
oversteer
parade lap
parc fermé
safety car
telemetry
warm-up lap

10 back marker

barge board
gravel trap
qualifying
racing line
run-off area
slipstream
team orders
understeer

11 braking zone
pit straight
shut the door
tyre blanket
victory lane

12 formation lap
ground effect
podium finish
pole position
straightaway

13 intermediates
launch control
scrutineering
start straight
stop-go penalty
superspeedway

14 finish straight

15 traction control

radiation

Radiation includes:

04 beta
hard
heat
soft

05 alpha
gamma
light
X-rays

06 cosmic

07 Hawking
visible

08 Cerenkov
gamma ray
infrared
ionizing

09 black body

10 background
insolation

microwaves
radio waves
synchroton

11 ultraviolet

12 beta particle

13 alpha particle

14 bremsstrahlung

15 electromagnetic

radio

Radio stations include:

03 LBC
XFM

04 Kiss

05 1Xtra

06 6 Music

Jazz FM
Kiss FM
Radio 1
Radio 2
Radio 3
Radio 4

08 BBC 1Xtra
Five Live

09 BBC 6 Music
BBC London
BBC Radio 1
BBC Radio 2

BBC Radio 3　　　　Radio Five　　　　**13** Radio Caroline
BBC Radio 4　　　　Talksport　　　　　　Radio Scotland
Capital FM　　　**11** Virgin Radio　　**15** BBC World Service
Classic FM　　　**12** World Service　　　　Radio Luxembourg

Radio shows include:

02 PM
04 ITMA
05 Today
07 Midweek
　　The Verb
08 Front Row
　　Money Box
　　Sport on 5
　　Whispers
09 Loose Ends
10 Any Answers?
　　Home Truths
　　The Archers
　　Week Ending
　　Woman's Hour
11 Dead Ringers
　　Just a Minute
　　The Food Quiz
　　The Goon Show
　　The Navy Lark
　　The News Quiz
　　You and Yours
12 100 Best Tunes
　　Any Questions?
　　Beyond Our Ken
　　Farming Today
　　Poetry Please
　　Quote … Unquote
　　Start the Week
　　Sunday Papers
　　The Moral Maze
　　Top of the Form
13 Absolute Power
　　Afternoon Play
　　Book at Bedtime
　　Book of the Week
　　Classic Serial
　　Mrs Dale's Diary

　　One Big Weekend
　　Pick of the Pops
　　Pick of the Week
　　Round the Horne
　　The Friday Play
　　The World at One
　　Waggoners' Walk
14 Brain of Britain
　　Changing Places
　　Melodies for You
　　Performance on 3
　　The Brains Trust
15 Educating Archie
　　It's That Man Again
　　The Saturday Play
　　Through the Night
　　Workers' Playtime
16 Family Favourites
　　Housewives' Choice
　　Listen with Mother
　　Lunchtime Concert
　　Round Britain Quiz
　　Shipping Forecast
　　The Food Programme
　　The Smith Lectures
17 Composer of the Week
　　Desert Island Discs
　　Letter from America
　　Today in Parliament
　　Weekend Woman's Hour
19 I'm Sorry I Haven't a Clue
　　Trevor's World of Sport
20 The Mark Steel Lectures
　　The Week in Westminster
21 Smooth Classics at Seven
　　Yesterday in Parliament
23 Friday Night Is Music Night
　　From Our Own Correspondent
　　I'm Sorry, I'll Read That Again

Radio presenters include:

03 Cox (Sara; 1974– , English)
04 Dunn (John; 1934–2004, Scottish)
　　Mayo (Simon; 1958– , English)
　　Peel (John; 1939–2004, English)
　　Ross (Jonathan; 1960– , English)
　　Tong (Pete; 1960– , English)

05 Clare (Anthony Ward; 1942–2007, Irish)
　　Cooke (Alistair; 1908–2004, English/US)
　　Evans (Chris; 1966– , English)
　　Jones (Aled; 1970– , Welsh)
　　Stern (Howard; 1954– , US)
　　Wogan (Terry; 1938– , Irish)

Young (Kirsty; 1968– , Scottish)
Young (Sir Jimmy; 1921– , English)

06 Harris (Bob; 1950– , English)
Lamacq (Steve; 1965– , English)
Lamarr (Mark; 1967– , English)
Lawley (Sue; 1946– , English)
Moyles (Chris; 1974– , English)
Murray (Jenni; 1950– , English)
Savile (Sir Jimmy; 1926–2011, English)
Walker (Johnnie; 1945– , English)
Whiley (Jo; 1965– , English)
Wright (Steve; 1954– , English)

07 De Manio (Jack; 1914–88, British)
Edmonds (Noel; 1948– , English)
Everett (Kenny; 1944–95, English)
Freeman (Alan 'Fluff'; 1927–2006, Australian)
Jackson (Jack; 1906–78, English)
Keillor (Garrison; 1942– , US)

See also **quiz**

Kershaw (Andy; 1959– , English)
Pickles (Wilfred; 1904–1978, English)
Plomley (Roy; 1914–85, English)
Redhead (Brian; 1929–94, English)
Tarrant (Chris; 1946– , English)

08 Anderson (Marjorie; 1913–99, English)
Campbell (Nicky; 1961– , Scottish)
Humphrys (John; 1943– , Welsh)
Metcalfe (Jean; 1923–2000, English)
Naughtie (James; 1952– , Scottish)
Westwood (Tim; 1958– , English)

09 Blackburn (Tony; 1943– , English)
MacGregor (Sue; 1941– , English)
Radcliffe (Mark; 1958– , English)

10 Gambaccini (Paul; 1949– , US)
Hardcastle (William; 1918–75, English)

11 Nightingale (Annie; 1942– , English)

railway

Railways include:

04 rack	subway	monorail	feeder line
tube	**07** cutting	mountain	**11** narrow gauge
05 cable	express	**09** funicular	underground
light	freight	goods line	**13** high-speed line
metro	tramway	Intercity®	passenger line
model	**08** electric	trunk line	rack-and-pinion
06 garden	elevated	**10** branch line	standard gauge
siding	main line	broad gauge	**15** marshalling yard

Railway stations include:

04 Ueno (Japan)

05 Crewe (England)
Odéon (France)
Passy (France)

06 Atocha (Spain)
Egmore (India)
Euston (England)
Howrah (India)

07 Bath Spa (England)
Shibuya (Japan)
Sirkeci (Turkey)
Termini (Italy)
Varenne (France)

08 Charbagh (India)
Châtelet (France)
Concorde (France)
Mirabeau (France)
Pont-Neuf (France)
Shinjuku (Japan)
Victoria (England)
Waterloo (England)

Waverley (Scotland)

09 Carnforth (England)
Chamartin (Spain)
Haymarket (Scotland)
Ikebukuro (Japan)
Invalides (France)
Madeleine (France)
Shinagawa (Japan)
St Pancras (England)
Tuileries (France)

10 Gare de Lyon (France)
Gare du Nord (France)
Kings Cross (England)
Lime Street (England)
Marylebone (England)
Ostbahnhof (Germany)
Paddington (England)
Piccadilly (England)
Südbahnhof (Austria)

11 Hull Paragon (England)
Lille Europe (France)

Penn Station (USA)
Roma Termini (Italy)
Westbahnhof (Austria)

12 Brussels Midi (Belgium)
Charing Cross (England)
Gare St Lazare (France)
Grand Central (USA)
Hauptbahnhof (Germany)
Louvre Rivoli (France)

13 Calais Fréthun (France)

14 Cardiff Central (Wales)
Exeter St Davids (England)
Flinders Street (Australia)
Glasgow Central (Scotland)
London Victoria (England)

15 Clapham Junction (England)
Cluny La Sorbonne (France)
Fenchurch Street (England)
Gare d'Austerlitz (France)
Watford Junction (England)

Train types include:

- **01** Q
- **02** up
- **03** APT
  HST
  owl
  TGV
  way
- **04** boat
  down
  loco
  mail
  milk
- **05** goods

  hover
  mixed
  paddy
  steam
- **06** bullet
  diesel
  Maglev
- **07** baggage
  express
  freight
  through
  tilting
- **08** cable-car
  corridor

  monorail
  push-pull
- **09** aerotrain
  excursion
  high-speed
  Intercity®
  manriding
  Pendolino®
- **10** locomotive
- **12** Freightliner®
- **13** accommodation
- **14** shuttle service
- **15** steam locomotive

Famous trains include:

03 TGV	The Ghan	**13** Indian Pacific	**15** Hogwarts Express
06 Rocket	**08** Eurostar	Orient Express	
Thomas	**09** The A-Train	Trans-Siberian	
07 Mallard	**11** Bullet Train	**14** Flying Scotsman	

Railway terms include:

- **01** L
- **02** el
  Ry
- **03** ABC
  APT
  ATC
  ATP
  bay
  cab
  car
  cog
  HST
  lie
  lye
  rly
  RMT
  rod
  RPC
  Rwy
  SRA
  Sta
  TGV
  tie
  TOC
  van
- **04** APEX
  bank
  crew
  dock
  dome
  frog

  halt
  line
  loco
  rail
  RUCC
  slot
  SPAD
  spur
  stay
  TPWS
  tube
- **05** aisle
  berth
  bogey
  bogie
  brake
  brute
  cabin
  chair
  coach
  coupé
  crank
  depot
  diner
  grate
  guard
  local
  lorry
  metro
  Mogul
  rivet
  shunt

  staff
  track
  T-rail
  train
  truck
  trunk
  valve
  wagon
- **06** balise
  banker
  boiler
  branch
  buffer
  buffet
  bumper
  coaler
  derail
  diesel
  engine
  flange
  fogger
  fogman
  gantry
  gricer
  hopper
  maglev
  piston
  points
  porter
  Q-train
  redcap
  reefer

saloon
siding
stoker
subway
target
tender
tunnel
up-line
waggon
Y-track

07 axle-box
ballast
banking
bay-line
booking
buckeye
bulgine
butcher
caboose
cocopan
cutting
detrain
drag-bar
drawbar
entrain
fettler
firebox
fireman
flatcar
flyover
gondola
handcar
hostler
lineman
locoman
network
off-peak
Pullman
railage
railbed
railbus
railcar
railman
roadbed
signals
sleeper
station
tank car
turnout
up-train
viaduct
whistle
yardman

08 box-wagon
Bradshaw
brakeman
brake van

bullgine
cable-car
cant-rail
carriage
catenary
choo-choo
corridor
coupling
crosstie
down-line
draw-gear
firehole
fire-tube
fly-under
horse box
junction
live-rail
loop-line
main line
manrider
monorail
motorail
motorman
overpass
owl-train
pilotman
platform
puff-puff
rack rail
railcard
railhead
railroad
roomette
side-line
smokebox
subgrade
terminus
trackage
trackbed
wagon-lit
way train

09 aerotrain
alignment
blastpipe
boat train
brakesman
buffet car
checkrail
concourse
conductor
container
couchette
crossover
cross-sill
day return
dining-car
down-train
drag-chain

fishplate
footboard
footplate
funicular
goods line
goods yard
guardrail
guard's van
Intercity®
interrail
iron horse
jerkwater
lengthman
mail-train
milk train
non-smoker
overshoot
palace-car
parlor car
plate rail
pointsman
rail-borne
rail-motor
railwoman
second man
sidetrack
signal box
signalman
slip-coach
steam pipe
tank wagon
third rail
train mile
trunk line
turntable
vestibule
wheelbase

10 baggage-car
brake block
branch line
broad-gauge
centre-rail
cog railway
cowcatcher
disentrain
draught-bar
embankment
Eurotunnel
feeder line
free on rail
goods train
griddle car
home-signal
hovertrain
lengthsman
locomotive
luggage-van
mini-buffet

mixed train
paddy train
parlour car
platelayer
Pullman car
railroader
railwayman
smokestack
steam brake
steam train
supersaver
surfaceman
switchback
tank engine
train ferry
zone-ticket

11 bay platform
block-system
bullet train
catch points
compartment
conductress
crémaillère
drawing room
gandy dancer
goods engine
lodging turn
mail-catcher
narrow-gauge
people mover
pilot engine
rack railway
railroad car
ship railway

side cutting
sleeping car
strap-hanger
throatplate
track-walker
underbridge
underground
vacuum brake
whistle stop

12 baggage-train
cable railway
coachbuilder
dormitory-car
double-header
driving wheel
engine-driver
euroterminal
express train
footplateman
Freightliner®
freight-train
light railway
loading gauge
omnibus train
permanent way
rolling stock
running board
shunting yard
slip-carriage
station house
throttle pipe
through train
ticket porter
trainspotter

13 brake cylinder
conductor rail
corridor-train
dead man's pedal
distant-signal
garden railway
level crossing
push-pull train
scenic railway
sleeping coach
standard gauge
stationmaster

14 dead man's handle
excursion train
expansion joint
footplatewoman
high-speed train
limited express
manriding train
observation car
regulator valve
saloon carriage
shuttle service
station-manager
superelevation

15 fellow traveller
marshalling yard
mountain railway
railway carriage
railway crossing
smoking carriage
steam locomotive
third-rail system

See also **London**; **underground**

rainbow

Colours of the rainbow:

03 red	**05** green	orange	yellow
04 blue	**06** indigo	violet	

range *see* **mountain**

rank *see* **military**; **nobility**; **police**

Ravel, Maurice (1875–1937)

Significant works include:

06 *Boléro* (1928)	**09** *Fountains* (1902)
07 *Miroirs* (1906)	**10** *Ma mère l'oye* (1910)
Mirrors (1906)	**11** *Mother Goose* (1910)
Tzigane (1924)	**12** *Schéhérazade* (1898)
08 *Jeux d'eau* (1902)	**14** *Daphnis et Chloé* (1912)

The Spanish Hour (1911)

15 Gaspard de la nuit (1909)
L'Heure espagnole (1911)
Spanish Rhapsody (1908)

16 Natural Histories (1907)

17 Phantom of the Night (1909)
The Tomb of Couperin (1917)

18 Chansons madécasses (1926)
Rhapsodie espagnole (1908)

19 Histoires Naturelles (1907)
Le Tombeau de Couperin (1917)

21 Don Quichotte à Dulcinée (1934)

22 L'enfant et les sortilèges (1925)
Pavane for a Dead Princess (1902/1911)

26 Noble and Sentimental Waltzes (1911/1914)
The Child and the Enchantments (1925)

27 Pavane pour une infante défunte
(1902/1911)
Valses nobles et sentimentales (1911/1914)

28 Fanfare pour l'Éventail de Jeanne (1929)
Three Poems by Stéphane Mallarmé (1914)

29 Trois poèmes de Stéphane Mallarmé (1914)

rebellion

Rebellions include:

03 Rum (1808, Australia)

07 Fifteen (1715, Scotland)
Whiskey (1794, US)

08 Jacobite (1715/1745, Scotland)

09 Forty-Five (1745, Scotland)

10 The Fifteen (1715, Scotland)

11 Boxer Rising (1898–1900, China)

12 Easter Rising (1916, Ireland)
The Forty-Five (1745, Scotland)

13 The Arab Spring (2010–, North Africa and
the Middle East)

14 Eureka Stockade (1854, Australia)

See also **revolutionary**; **war**

record

Recordings include:

02 CD	mono	single	videotape
EP	tape	stereo	**11** compact disc
LP	tele	**07** digital	long-playing
03 DAT	**05** album	**08** cassette	**12** extended play
DVD	video	MiniDisc®	magnetic tape
MP3	vinyl	**09** audiotape	
04 disc	**06** record	video disc	**13** video cassette

red

Shades of red include:

04 guly	damask	crimson
pink	ginger	fuchsia
rose	maroon	lobster
ruby	minium	nacarat
rust	modena	scarlet
wine	murrey	stammel
05 brick	rufous	vermeil
gules	russet	**08** beetroot
henna	Titian	blood-red
ruddy	tomato	brick-red
06 auburn	Tyrian	burgundy
cerise	**07** carmine	cardinal
cherry	carroty	chestnut
claret	cramesy	cinnabar

cramoisy		vermilion	terracotta
sanguine	**10**	Chinese red	**11** burnt sienna
09 carnation		coccineous	incarnadine
solferino		coquelicot	sang-de-boeuf

See also **dye**; **pigment**

refining

Products and by-products of refining include:

03 tar	**07** asphalt		treacle	**11** golden syrup
05 sugar		bitumen	**08** molasses	

reformer

Reformers include:

03 Hus (Jan; c.1369–1415, Bohemian/Czech)

04 Huss (John; c.1369–1415, Bohemian/Czech)
Knox (John; c.1513–1572, Scottish)
Mill (John Stuart; 1806–73, English)
Owen (Robert; 1771–1858, Welsh)

05 Perón (Evita; 1919–52, Argentine)

06 Calvin (John; 1509–64, French)
Luther (Martin; 1483–1546, German)
Wiclif (John; c.1329–84, English)

Wyclif (John; c.1329–84, English)

07 Stanton (Elizabeth Cady; 1815–1902)
Wycliff (John; c.1329–84, English)
Zwingli (Huldreich; 1484–1531, Swiss)
Zwingli (Ulrich; 1484–1531, Swiss)

08 Wicliffe (John; c.1329–84, English)
Wycliffe (John; c.1329–84, English)

10 Pestalozzi (Johann; 1746–1827, Swiss)

11 Wilberforce (William; 1759–1833, English)

See also **heroism**; **religion**

regiment

Army regiments include:

02 RA	**11** Highlanders	**13** Artists' Rifles
RE	Horse Guards	Kings Regiment
TA	Irish Guards	Light Dragoons
03 SAS	Scots Guards	Light Infantry
	Welsh Guards	**14** London Regiment
04 REME	**12** Army Air Corps	Royal Engineers
05 Paras	Green Howards	**15** Grenadier Guards
10 Black Watch	Rifle Brigade	Rifle Volunteers
Life Guards	Royal Hussars	
Royal Scots	Royal Lancers	

region see **geography**

reindeer see **Christmas**

relative

Relatives include:

02 ex	mum	gran	wife
03 bro	sis	heir	**05** aunty
dad	son	nana	daddy
mom	**04** aunt	twin	mummy

nanna	spouse	grandkid	twin-sister
nanny	**07** brother	grandson	**11** first cousin
niece	grandad	**09** ex-husband	foster-child
uncle	grandma	godfather	goddaughter
06 auntie	grandpa	godmother	grandfather
cousin	husband	great aunt	grandmother
ex-wife	partner	stepchild	grandparent
father	sibling	**10** grandchild	half-brother
german	stepdad	great uncle	stepbrother
godson	stepmum	half-sister	twin-brother
granny	stepson	stepfather	**12** foster-parent
mother	**08** daughter	stepmother	second cousin
nephew	godchild	step-parent	stepdaughter
parent	granddad	stepsister	**13** granddaughter
sister			

See also **aunt**; **daughter**; **father**; **genealogy**; **mother**; **son**; **uncle**

religion

Religions and religious groups include:

03 Bon	Druidism	Creationism
Zen	Hasidism	Freemasonry
04 Shi'a	Hinduism	Hare Krishna
05 Amish	paganism	Lutheranism
Baha'i	Tantrism	Manichaeism
Druze	Wahhabis	Scientology
Islam	**09** Ahmadiyya	Zen Buddhism
Sunni	Cabbalism	**12** Albigensians
06 Sufism	Calvinism	Christianity
Taoism	Methodism	Confucianism
voodoo	Mithraism	Nestorianism
07 animism	Mormonism	Unitarianism
Baha'ism	occultism	**13** Church in Wales
Essenes	Parseeism	Protestantism
Jainism	shamanism	Reform Judaism
Jesuits	Shintoism	Salvation Army
Judaism	Vedantism	**14** Fundamentalism
Lamaism	Waldenses	Oxford Movement
Moonies	**10** Adventists	Pentecostalism
Opus Dei	Brahmanism	Rastafarianism
Orphism	Evangelism	Rosicrucianism
Quakers	Gnosticism	Society of Jesus
Saivism	iconoclasm	Ultramontanism
Saktism	Puritanism	Zoroastrianism
Sikhism	Soka Gakkai	**15** ancestor-worship
08 Baptists	**11** Anabaptists	Church of England
Buddhism	Anglicanism	Presbyterianism
	Catholicism	

Religious officers include:

03 nun	pope	kohen	**06** abbess
04 dean	**05** abbot	padre	bishop
guru	canon	prior	clergy
imam	elder	rabbi	curate
monk	friar	vicar	deacon

father	**07** muezzin	**09** ayatollah	archdeacon
mullah	prelate	clergyman	chancellor
parson	proctor	Dalai Lama	Pachen Lama
pastor	**08** cardinal	deaconess	
priest	chaplain	Monsignor	**11** clergywoman
rector	minister	**10** archbishop	**14** mother superior

Religious writings include:

02 NT	**07** epistle	Lotus Sutra
OT	Li Ching	Nohon Shoki
05 Bayan	Puranas	Pentateuch
Bible	Shari'ah	Svetambara
Koran	**08** Haft Wadi	Tao-te-ching
Qur'an	Halakhah	Upanishads
sutra	Ramayana	Zend-Avesta
Torah	Shu Ching	**11** Bardo Thodol
Vedas	**09** Adi Granth	Mahabharata
Zohar	Apocrypha	**12** Bhagavad Gita
06 Gemara	Chuang-tzu	Kitab al-Aqdas
gospel	Chu'un Ch'iu	Milindapanha
Granth	Decalogue	New Testament
Hadith	Digambara	Old Testament
I Ching	Hexateuch	**14** Dead Sea Scrolls
Kojiki	scripture	Mahayana Sutras
Mishna	Shih Ching	Revised Version
Talmud	Tripitaka	**15** Ten Commandments
Tantra	**10** Heptateuch	

Religious services include:

04 Mass	**09** communion	**12** confirmation
07 baptism	Eucharist	Midnight Mass
evening	**10** bar mitzvah	thanksgiving
funeral	bat mitzvah	**13** Holy Communion
morning	dedication	Holy Matrimony
wedding	**11** christening	**14** First Communion
08 evensong	Lord's Supper	morning prayers
High Mass	nuptial Mass	**15** harvest festival
marriage	remembrance	
memorial	Requiem Mass	

Religious building types include:

03 wat	gompa	pagoda	**08** gurdwara
04 fane	**06** bethel	shrine	**09** cathedral
kirk	church	temple	synagogue
shul	mandir	vihara	**10** tabernacle
05 abbey	masjid	**07** chantry	**12** meeting-house
	mosque	minster	

Religious buildings and sites include:

05 Kaaba (Saudi Arabia)	Parthenon (Greece)
08 Pantheon (Italy)	**10** Blue Mosque (Turkey)
09 Acropolis (Greece)	Erechtheum (Greece)

Harimandir (India)
Sacré Coeur (France)

11 Ajanta caves (India)
Ellora caves (India)
Erechtheion (Greece)
Great Mosque (Syria)
Great Sphinx (Egypt)
Hagia Sophia (Turkey)
Temple Mount (Israel)
Wailing Wall (Israel)
Western Wall (Israel)

12 Golden Temple (India)
Great Pyramid (Egypt)
Monte Cassino (Italy)
Temple of Hera (Italy)
Temple of Isis (Egypt)

13 Cordoba Mosque (Spain)
Dome of the Rock (Israel)
Horyuji Temple (Japan)
Kailasa Temple (India)
Mt Grace Priory (England)
Muhammad's Tomb (Saudi Arabia)
Pattan Somnath (India)
Prabhas Pattan (India)
Rila Monastery (Bulgaria)
Sistine Chapel (Vatican City)
Umayyad Mosque (Syria)
Vézelay Church (France)

14 Abu Bakar Mosque (Malaysia)

Belém Monastery (Brazil)
Certosa of Pavia (Italy)
Dilwara temples (India)
Golden Pavilion (Japan)
Great Synagogue (Israel)
Mahamuni Pagoda (Myanmar)
My Son Sanctuary (Vietnam)
Sagrada Familia (Spain)
Selimiye Mosque (Cyprus)
Suleiman Mosque (Turkey)
Temple of Amon-Ra (Egypt)
Temple of Apollo (Greece)
Temple of Athena (Greece)
Temple of Hathor (Egypt)
Temple of Heaven (China)

15 Chavín de Huantar (Peru)
Decani Monastery (Kosovo)
Ggantija temples (Malta)
Ketchaoua Mosque (Algeria)
Mahabodhi Temple (India)
Maisel Synagogue (Czech Republic)
Mont-Saint-Michel (France)
Pyramid of Cheops (Egypt)
Pyramid of the Sun (Mexico)
Shwe Dagon Pagoda (Myanmar)
Shwezigon Pagoda (Myanmar)
Temple of Artemis (Turkey)
Temple of Solomon (Israel)
Temple of Somnath (India)
Thousand Temples (Indonesia)

Religious festivals and holidays include:

02 Id
03 Eid
04 Holi
Lent
Lots
Obon
Oram
Yule

05 Litha
Pesah
Purim
Vesak

06 Advent
Bakrid
Basant
Dhamma
Divali
Diwali
Easter
Imbolc
Lammas
Pesach
Sangha
Sukkot

07 Baisaki
Beltane
matsuri
New Year
Ramadan
Samhain
Shavuot
Sukkoth

08 All Souls
Baisakhi
Dipavali
Dusserah
Epiphany
Hanukkah
Id al-Adha
Id al-Fitr
Id ul-Zuha
Muharram
Passover

09 All Saints
Ascension
Candlemas
Christmas
Deepavali

Dolayatra
Durga-puja
Easter Day
Eid al-Adha
Eid al-Fitr
Mardi Gras
Navaratri
Oshogatsu
Pentecost
Up-Helly-Aa
Yom Kippur

10 All Hallows
Assumption
Good Friday
Lughnasadh
Lupercalia
Michaelmas
Palm Sunday
Ramanavami
Rathayatra
Saturnalia
Vulcanalia
Whit Sunday

11 All Souls' Day

Bacchanalia
Lakshmi-puja
Milad-un-Nabi
Panathenaea
Rosh Hashana
12 All Saints' Day
Annunciation
Ascension Day
Ash Wednesday
Christmas Day
Easter Sunday
Holy Saturday
Holy Thursday

Hoshi Matsuri
Night of Power
Ohinamatsuri
Prakash Utsav
Rosh Hashanah
Simchat Torah
Star Festival
Tango no Sekku
13 Buddha Purnima
Corpus Christi
Holy Innocents
Night of Ascent
Passion Sunday

spring equinox
Trinity Sunday
vernal equinox
14 Chinese New Year
Day of Atonement
Easter Saturday
Maundy Thursday
summer solstice
winter solstice
15 autumnal equinox
Lantern Festival
Tanabata Matsuri
Transfiguration

Religious symbols include:

02 Om
03 IHC
IHS
04 ankh
fish

yoni
05 cross
linga
06 chakra
filfot

fylfot
lingam
07 Ik Onkar
mandala
menorah

yin-yang
08 crescent
swastika
11 Christingle
star of David

Religious figures and leaders include:

03 Ali (d.661, Arab)
Fox (George; 1624–91, English)
Fry (Elizabeth; 1780–1845, English)
Hus (Jan; c.1369–1415, Bohemian)
04 Bede (St, 'the Venerable'; c.673–735, Anglo-Saxon)
Boff (Leonardo; 1938– , Brazilian)
Eddy (Mary; 1821–1910, US)
Hick (John; 1922–2012, English)
Huss (John; c.1369–1415, Bohemian)
King (Martin Luther; 1929–68, US)
Knox (John; c.1513–72, Scottish)
Küng (Hans; 1928– , Swiss)
Mani (c.215–276 AD, Persian)
Otto (Rudolf; 1869–1937, German)
Penn (William; 1644–1718, English)
Pire (Dominique; 1910–69, Belgian)
Tutu (Desmond; 1931– , South African)
Weil (Simone; 1909–43, French)
05 Alban (St; 3 CAD, Roman)
Amman (Jakob; c.1645–c.1730, Swiss)
Arius (c.250–336 AD, Libyan)
Askew (Anne; 1521–46, English)
Barth (Karl; 1886–1968, Swiss)
Booth (William; 1829–1912, English)
Buber (Martin; 1878–1965, Austrian/Israeli)
Keble (John; 1792–1866, English)
Lao Zi (6 CBC, Chinese)
Mahdi (al-; 1844–85, Arab)
Mbiti (John; 1931– , Kenyan)
Moses (15–13 CBC; Bible)
Paley (William; 1743–1805, English)

Paris (Matthew; c.1200–59, English)
Smith (Joseph; 1805–44, US)
Soper (Donald, Lord; 1903–98, English)
Waite (Terry; 1939– , English)
Young (Brigham; 1801–77, US)
06 Agatha (St; d.251 AD, Sicilian)
Anselm (St; 1033–1109, Italian)
Baxter (Richard; 1615–91, English)
Becket (St Thomas à; 1118–70, English)
Besant (Annie; 1847–1933, English)
Browne (Robert; c.1550–c.1633, English)
Buddha (Prince Siddhartha Gautama; c.560–c.480 BC, Nepali)
Bunyan (John; 1628–88, English)
Calvin (John; 1509–64, French)
Cupitt (Don; 1934– , English)
Gandhi (Mahatma; 1869–1948, Indian)
Garvey (Marcus; 1887–1940, Jamaican)
Graham (Billy; 1918– , US)
Hillel (1 CBC–1 CAD, Babylonian)
Hutter (Jakob; d.1536, Swiss)
Jansen (Cornelius; 1585–1638, Dutch)
Kempis (Thomas à; 1379–1471, German)
Lao-tzu (6 CBC, Chinese)
Luther (Martin; 1483–1546, German)
Mather (Cotton; 1662–1728, American)
Newman (John Henry; 1801–90, English)
Olcott (Colonel Henry Steel; 1832–1907, US)
Origen (c.185–c.254 AD, Greek)
Rahner (Karl; 1904–84, German)
Raikes (Robert; 1735–1811, English)
Ramsey (Ian; 1915–72, English)
Ridley (Nicholas; c.1500–55, English)

Rogers (John; c.1500–55, English)
Sieyès (the Abbé; 1748–1836, French)
Teresa (Mother; 1910–97, Albanian)
Tetzel (Johann; c.1465–1519, German)
Wesley (John; 1703–91, English)
07 Abelard (Peter; 1079–1142, French)
Aga Khan (III; 1877–1957, Pakistani)
Aga Khan (IV, Karim; 1936– , Pakistani)
Aquinas (St Thomas; 1225–74, Italian)
Ayeshah (c.613–678, Arab)
Brunner (Emil; 1889–1966, Swiss)
Buchman (Frank; 1878–1961, US)
Cranmer (Thomas; 1489–1556, English)
Eckhart (Johannes; c.1260–c.1327, German)
Erasmus (Desiderius; 1466–1536, Dutch)
Falwell (Jerry; 1933–2007, US)
Fénelon (François; 1651–1715, French)
Ghazali (Abu Hamid al-; 1058–1111, Persian)
Hubbard (L Ron; 1911–86, US)
Jenkins (David; 1925– , English)
Latimer (Hugh; c.1485–1555, English)
Mencius (c.372–c.298 BC, Chinese)
Müntzer (Thomas; c.1488–1525, German)
Niebuhr (Reinhold; 1892–1971, US)
Paisley (Rev. Ian; 1926– , Northern Irish)
Photius (c.820–91, Byzantine)
Ruether (Rosemary Radford; 1936– , US)
Russell (Pastor; 1852–1916, US)
Sankara (c.700–c.750, Indian)
Steiner (Rudolf; 1861–1925, Austrian)
Strauss (David; 1808–74, German)
Tillich (Paul; 1886–1965, German)
Tyndale (William; c.1494–1536, English)
Wishart (George; c.1513–46, Scottish)
Zwingli (Huldreich; 1484–1531, Swiss)
08 Agricola (Johann; 1492–1566, German)
Andrewes (Lancelot; 1555–1626, English)
Bultmann (Rudolf; 1884–1976, German)
Hamilton (Patrick; 1503–28, Scottish)
Irenaeus (St; c.130–c.200 AD, Greek)
Khomeini (Ayatollah Ruhollah; 1900–89, Iranian)
Mahavira (Vardhamana; c.540–468 BC, Indian)
Moltmann (Jürgen; 1926– , German)
Muhammad (c.570–c.632, Arab)
Muhammad (Elijah; 1897–1975, US)
Patteson (John; 1827–71, English)
Pelagius (c.360–c.420 AD, British)
Rajneesh (Bhagwan Shree; 1931–90, Indian)
Rasputin (Grigoriy; 1871–1916, Russian)
Robinson (J A T; 1919–83, English)
Selassie (Emperor Haile; 1891–1975, Ethiopian)

Williams (John; 1796–1839, English)
Williams (Roger; c.1604–83, American)
Wycliffe (John; c.1330–84, English)
09 Baha-Allah (1817–92, Persian)
Blavatsky (H P; 1831–91, Russian)
Clitherow (St Margaret; c.1556–86, English)
Confucius (551–479 BC, Chinese)
Dalai Lama (1935– , Tibetan)
Guru Nanak (1469–1539, Indian)
Gutiérrez (Gustavo; 1928– , Peruvian)
Joan of Arc (St; c.1412–31, French)
K'ung Fu-tse (551–479 BC, Chinese)
McPherson (Aimee Semple; 1890–1944, US)
Nagarjuna (c.150–c.250 AD, Indian)
Niemöller (Martin; 1892–1984, German)
Zoroaster (c.630–c.553 BC, Iranian)
10 Athanasius (St; c.296–373 AD, Greek)
Bonhoeffer (Dietrich; 1906–45, German)
Fateh Singh (Sant; 1911–72, Indian)
Huddleston (Trevor; 1913–98, English)
Huntingdon (Selina Hastings, Countess of; 1707–91, English)
Manichaeus (c.215–276 AD, Persian)
Pannenberg (Wolfhart; 1928– , German)
Savonarola (Girolamo; 1452–98, Italian)
Schweitzer (Albert; 1875–1965, German)
Swedenborg (Emmanuel; 1688–1772, Swedish)
Tertullian (c.160–220 AD, North African)
Torquemada (Tomás de; 1420–98, Spanish)
Whitefield (George; 1714–70, English)
11 Bodhidharma (6c, Indian)
Gobind Singh (1666–1708, Indian)
Jesus Christ (c.4 BC–c.30 AD, Judean)
Melanchthon (Philip; 1497–1560, German)
Wilberforce (William; 1759–1833, English)
Zarathustra (c.630–c.553 BC, Iranian)
12 John of Leyden (1509–36, Dutch)
Krishnamurti (Jiddu; 1895–1986, Indian)
Mother Teresa (of Calcutta; 1910–97, Albanian)
Tenzin Gyatso (1935– , Tibetan)
13 Muhammad Ahmed (1844–85, Arab)
Teresa of Ávila (St; 1515–82, Spanish)
William of Tyre (c.1130–85, Syrian)
14 Ignatius Loyola (St; 1491–1556, Spanish)
John of the Cross (St; 1542–91, Spanish)
Schleiermacher (Friedrich; 1768–1834, German)
15 Francis of Assisi (St; c.1181–1226, Italian)
Jesus of Nazareth (c.4 BC–c.30 AD, Judean)
Julian of Norwich (c.1342–c.1413, English)

Terms to do with religion include:

03 God
haj
Jew

04 cult
hadj
hajj
Holi
imam
kara
kesh
Magi
Mass
myth
pope
puja
Rama
saum
sect
umra
wudu

05 Allah
Amish
Arhat
Bahai
Bible
Druze
Flood
Islam
kacha
kanga
Koran
Mahdi
Mecca
Qur'an
sabha
salah
Shiva
subha
Sunni
Sutra
Torah
umrah
zakat

06 Babism
Brahma
chapel
church
Daoism
dharma
Diwali
Easter
Five Ks
kippah
kirpan
mandir
moksha

mosque
Nevi'im
Pesach
Ratana
sangha
Shiism
Shinto
Sufism
Taoism
tasbih
temple
Tenakh
Vishnu

07 Abraham
Amoraim
apostle
atheism
Baptist
Brahman
Cluniac
deities
Gabriel
Gospels
Gurpurb
Holy Ark
Jainism
Jesuits
Jibrail
Judaism
Ketuvim
Krishna
Moonies
muezzin
nirvana
Parsees
prasada
Quakers
Ramadan
Ranters
Rig-Veda
Ringatu
Sabbath
Saivism
samsara
Shabbat
shahada
shaheed
Shakers
Shingon
Sikhism
Vatican
Wahhabi
Zealots

08 Arianism
Beghards
Beguines
bhikkhus

Buddhism
cardinal
Creation
disciple
Druidism
Falashas
Gurdwara
Hanukkah
Hinduism
Id ul-Adha
Id ul-Fitr
Ismailis
Lollards
Mohammad
Muhammad
nativity
paganism
Passover
Ramayana
religion
Santería
tefillin

09 Adventism
Arya Samaj
Ascension
Bethlehem
Calvinism
Capuchins
cathedral
Christmas
Eucharist
Guru Nanak
Huguenots
Maronites
Methodism
Mithraism
Mormonism
Pharisees
Sadducees
Sephardim
Shamanism
synagogue
The Buddha
Trappists
Tripitaka
Waldenses

10 Adam and Eve
Albigenses
Anabaptism
Ashkenazim
Avatamsaka
bar mitzvah
bat mitzvah
Carmelites
Confucians
Dissenters
Dominicans

Good Friday
Holy Spirit
Mennonites
Soka Gakkai

11 agnosticism
Carthusians
Catholicism
Cistercians
Covenanters
Creationism
Crucifixion
Franciscans
Hare Krishna
Jesus Christ
Lord's Prayer
Lutheranism
Scientology
Three Jewels
Vaishnavism

Vijnanavada
Wheel of Life
Zen Buddhism

12 Augustinians
Benedictines
Christianity
Confucianism
Coptic Church
New Testament
Old Testament
Resurrection
Three Wise Men
Unitarianism

13 Nonconformism
Protestantism
Salvation Army
The Last Supper

14 Anglican Church

Armenian Church
Fundamentalism
Knights Templar
Millenarianism
Moravian Church
Orthodox Church
Rastafarianism
Society of Jesus
Zoroastrianism

15 Assemblies of God
Avatamsaka Sutra
Bhagavata-Purana
Branch Davidians
Episcopal Church
Four Noble Truths
Nestorian Church
Pentecostalists
Presbyterianism

See also **abbey**; **angel**; **apostle**; **archbishop**; **Bible**; **Buddhism**; **cardinal**; **cathedral**; **celebration**; **ceremony**; **chief rabbi**; **Christianity**; **Christmas**; **church**; **clerical vestment**; **cross**; **Dalai Lama**; **diocese**; **fast**; **Hinduism**; **Islam**; **Judaism**; **missionary**; **mythology**; **patriarch**; **plague**; **pope**; **prayer**; **priest**; **prophet**; **reformer**; **religious order**; **saint**; **Sikhism**; **theology**

religious order

Religious orders include:

04 Sufi
05 Taizé
06 Culdee
Essene
Jesuit
Loreto
Marist
07 Jesuits
Marists
Rifaite
08 Buddhist
Capuchin
Grey nuns
Minorite

Trappist
Ursuline
09 Barnabite
Capuchins
Carmelite
Dominican
Marianist
Mawlawite
mendicant
Salesians
Trappists
Ursulines
10 Bernardine
Carmelites

Carthusian
Celestines
Cistercian
Conventual
Dominicans
Franciscan
Gilbertine
Grey friars
Norbertine
Oratorians
Poor Clares
11 Augustinian
Benedictine
Black friars

Camaldolite
Carthusians
Cistercians
Franciscans
Ignorantine
Sylvestrine
White friars
12 Augustinians
Austin friars
Benedictines
13 Society of Mary
14 Knights Templar
Sisters of Mercy
Society of Jesus

Monasteries and convents include:

04 Iona (Scotland)
05 Cluny (France)
07 Mt Athos (Greece)
Shaolin (China)
08 Hilandar (Greece)
Sénanque (France)
09 Melk Abbey (Austria)
Tengboche (Nepal)
10 Douai Abbey (England)
El Escorial (Spain)
Ettal Abbey (Germany)

San Lorenzo (various)
Santa Croce (Italy)
Worth Abbey (England)
11 Ealing Abbey (England)
Glendalough (Ireland)
Lindisfarne (England)
Parkminster (England)
Simonopetra (Greece)
Val-Duchesse (Belgium)
Whitby Abbey (England)
12 Belmont Abbey (England)
Colwich Abbey (England)

Monte Cassino (Italy)
Mont St Michel (France)
St John's Abbey (USA)

13 Buckfast Abbey (England)
Donglin Temple (China)
Downside Abbey (England)
Monasterboice (Ireland)
Rievaulx Abbey (England)

Tyburn Convent (England)

14 Fountains Abbey (England)
Stanbrook Abbey (England)

15 Ampleforth Abbey (England)
Curzon Park Abbey (England)
Portsmouth Abbey (England)
St Cecilia's Abbey (England)

Monks and nuns include:

02 Fa (Hsien; fl.400 AD, Chinese)
Fa (Xian; fl.400 AD, Chinese)

03 Orm (fl.1200, English)

04 Gall (St; c.550–645, Irish)
Hume (Basil; 1923–99, English)
Rule (St; 4CAD)
Sava (St; c.1174–1235/6, Serbian)

05 Aidan (St; d.651, Irish)
Barat (St Madeleine Sophie; 1779–1865, French)
Borde (Andrew; c.1490–1549, English)
Jacob (Max; 1876–1944, French)
Ormin (fl.1200, English)
Rancé (Armand Jean de; 1626–1700, French)
Sabas (St; c.1174–1235/6, Serbian)

06 Arnulf (1040–1124, French)
Boorde (Andrew; c.1490–1549, English)
Colman (St; d.676, Irish)
Eadmer (d.c.1124, English)
Ernulf (1040–1124, French)
Gildas (St; c.493–570 AD, Roman-British)
Gyatso (Geshe Kelsang; 1931– , Tibetan)
Merton (Thomas; 1915–68, US)
Teresa (Mother; 1910–97, Albanian)
Tetzel (Johann; c.1465–1519, German)
Turgot (d.1115, Anglo-Saxon)

07 Adamnan (St; c.625–704, Irish)
Adomnan (St; c.625–704, Irish)
Arnauld (Angélique; 1624–84, French)
Arnauld (Marie-Angélique; 1591–1661, French)
Beckett (Sister Wendy; 1930– , South African/British)
Cabrini (St Francesca Xavier; 1850–1917, US)
Carpini (John of Plano; c.1182–c.1253, Italian)
Cassian (St John; c.360–c.435 AD, Romanian)

Gratian (12c, Italian)
Lydgate (John; c.1370–c.1451, English)
Mortara (Edgar; 1852–1940, Italian)
Regulus (St; 4c AD)
Schwarz (Berthold; fl.1320, German)

08 Alacoque (St Marguerite Marie; 1647–90, French)
Bonivard (François de; 1493–1570, Swiss)
Duchesne (St Rose Philippine; 1769–1852, French)
Foucauld (Charles de; 1858–1916, French)
Houedard (Dom Sylvester; 1924–92, British)
Pelagius (c.360–c.420 AD, British)
Rabelais (François; 1483 or 1494–1553, French)

09 Bonnivard (François de; 1493–1570, Swiss)
MacKillop (Mary; 1842–1909, Australian)
Skobtsova (Maria; 1891–1945, Russian)

10 Bernadette (St; 1844–79, French)
Fra Diavolo (1760–1806, Italian)
Montfaucon (Bernard de; 1655–1741, French)
Torquemada (Tomás de; 1420–98, Spanish)
Walsingham (Thomas; d.c.1422, English)
Willibrord (St; 658–739, English)

11 Bodhidharma (6c, Indian)
Ponce de León (Luis; 1527–91, Spanish)
Scholastica (St; c.480–c.543 AD, Italian)

12 Guido d'Arezzo (c.990–1050, Italian)
Mother Teresa (of Calcutta; 1910–97, Albanian)

13 The Singing Nun (Jeanne Deckers; 1933–85, Belgian)

14 Francis of Paola (St; 1416–1507, Italian)
Marianus Scotus (d.c.1088, Irish)
Peter the Hermit (c.1050–c.1115, French)

15 Bernard of Morval (12c, French)

See also **abbey**; **Buddhism**; **Christianity**; **Hinduism**; **Judaism**; **Sikhism**

reptile

Reptiles include:

04 croc
05 gator

06 caiman
cayman

garial
gavial

mugger
turtle
07 gharial
hicatee
snapper
tuatara
08 aligarta
galapago
hiccatee
matamata
See also **lizard**; **snake**

stinkpot
synapsid
terrapin
tortoise
09 alligarta
alligator
crocodile
hawksbill
mud turtle
sea turtle

10 loggerhead
musk turtle
11 green turtle
leatherback
13 giant tortoise
water tortoise
14 leathery turtle
snapping turtle
15 hawksbill turtle

republic

Republics include:

03 USA
04 Chad
Cuba
Fiji
Iran
Iraq
Laos
Mali
Peru
Togo
05 Benin
Chile
China
Congo
Egypt
Gabon
Ghana
Haiti
India
Italy
Kenya
Malta
Nauru
Nepal
Niger
Palau
Sudan
Syria
Yemen
06 Angola
Brazil
Cyprus
France
Greece
Guinea
Guyana
Israel
Latvia
Malawi
Mexico
Panama

Poland
Russia
Rwanda
Taiwan
Turkey
Uganda
Zambia
07 Albania
Algeria
Armenia
Austria
Belarus
Bolivia
Burundi
Croatia
Ecuador
Estonia
Finland
Georgia
Germany
Hungary
Iceland
Ireland
Lebanon
Liberia
Moldova
Myanmar
Namibia
Nigeria
Romania
Senegal
Somalia
Tunisia
Ukraine
Uruguay
Vanuatu
Vietnam
08 Botswana
Bulgaria
Cameroon
Colombia
Djibouti

Ethiopia
Honduras
Kiribati
Maldives
Mongolia
Pakistan
Paraguay
Portugal
Slovakia
Slovenia
Sri Lanka
Suriname
Tanzania
Zimbabwe
09 Argentina
Cape Verde
Costa Rica
East Timor
Guatemala
Indonesia
Lithuania
Macedonia
Mauritius
Nicaragua
San Marino
Singapore
The Gambia
Venezuela
10 Azerbaijan
Bangladesh
El Salvador
Kazakhstan
Kyrgyzstan
Madagascar
Mauritania
Mozambique
North Korea
Seychelles
South Korea
South Sudan
Tajikistan
Uzbekistan

11 Burkina Faso
Côte d'Ivoire
Philippines
Sierra Leone

South Africa
Switzerland
12 Guinea-Bissau
Turkmenistan

13 Czech Republic
Western Sahara
15 Marshall Islands

resort

Resorts include:

04 Nice (France)
Rhyl (Wales)
05 Aspen (USA)
Davos (Switzerland)
06 Cairns (Australia)
Cancún (Mexico)
Cannes (France)
St Ives (England)
St-Malo (France)
Whitby (England)
07 Funchal (Portugal)
Margate (England)
Newquay (England)
Torquay (England)
Ventnor (England)
Zermatt (Switzerland)
08 Acapulco (Mexico)
Alicante (Spain)
Aviemore (Scotland)
Benidorm (Spain)
Biarritz (France)
Chamonix (France)
Honolulu (USA)
Klosters (Switzerland)
Marbella (Spain)
Montreux (Switzerland)
Penzance (England)
Skegness (England)
St Helier (Channel Islands)
St Moritz (Switzerland)
St-Tropez (France)
Weymouth (England)
09 Albufeira (Portugal)
Blackpool (England)

See also **spa**

Galveston (USA)
Gold Coast (Australia)
Kitzbühel (Austria)
Lanzarote (Spain)
Morecambe (England)
Nantucket (USA)
10 Baden Baden (Germany)
Bondi Beach (Australia)
Costa Brava (Spain)
Eastbourne (England)
Lake Placid (USA)
Long Island (USA)
Miami Beach (USA)
Monte Carlo (Monaco)
Windermere (England)
11 Bognor Regis (England)
Bournemouth (England)
Bridlington (England)
Cleethorpes (England)
Coney Island (USA)
Costa Blanca (Spain)
Costa del Sol (Spain)
Costa Dorada (Spain)
Gran Canaria (Spain)
Grand Bahama (The Bahamas)
Palm Springs (USA)
Scarborough (England)
12 San Sebastian (Spain)
Santa Barbara (USA)
Waikiki Beach (USA)
13 Great Yarmouth (England)
Southend-on-Sea (England)
15 Martha's Vineyard (USA)
Weston-super-Mare (England)

restaurant

Restaurant types include:

04 café
05 diner
grill
NAAFI
06 bistro
buffet
chippy

pull-in
07 carvery
chipper
milk bar
taverna
tea room
tea shop

08 creperie
pizzeria
snack-bar
sushi bar
taqueria
teahouse
09 brasserie

burger bar	rotisserie	Internet café
cafeteria	steakhouse	luncheonette
coffee bar	**11** eating-house	motorway café
dining-car	greasy spoon	**13** transport café
grill room	sandwich bar	**15** fish-and-chip shop
trattoria	self-service	ice-cream parlour
10 dining room	**12** drivethrough	

Restaurants include:

03 Umu (England)
04 Nahm (England)
Nobu (England)
05 Arzak (Spain)
Boyer (France)
Craft (USA)
Per Se (USA)
Spago (USA)
06 Arpège (France)
Daniel (USA)
Le Cinq (France)
Orrery (England)
Sketch (England)
St John (England)
The Ivy (England)
07 Assaggi (England)
Bukhara (India)
Capital (England)
Cote d'Or (France)
El Bulli (Spain)
Foliage (England)
Ledoyen (France)
Louis XV (Monaco)
08 Al Mahara (Dubai)
Guy Savoy (France)
Hakkasan (England)
Hibiscus (England)
La Tupina (France)
Rockpool (Australia)
Tamarind (England)
Tetsuya's (Australia)
The Cliff (Barbados)
Yauatcha (England)
09 Al Sorriso (Italy)
Aubergine (England)
Balthazar (USA)
Chez Bruce (England)
De Librije (The Netherlands)
Lameloise (France)
L'Ami Louis (France)
Le Meurice (France)
L'Escargot (England)
Mirabelle (England)
The Square (England)
Thornton's (Ireland)
Tom Aikens (England)

Troisgros (France)
Zafferano (England)
10 Club Gascon (England)
Flower Drum (Australia)
L'Ambroisie (France)
L'Arnsbourg (France)
Le Calandre (Italy)
Le Gavroche (England)
L'Espérance (France)
Michel Bras (France)
Park Heuvel (The Netherlands)
Paul Bocuse (France)
Pied à terre (England)
Roussillon (England)
Savoy Grill (England)
Taillevent (France)
The Fat Duck (England)
11 Au Crocodile (France)
Buerehiesel (France)
Chez Panisse (California)
De Karmeliet (Belgium)
Grand Vefour (France)
Jean Georges (USA)
Lucas Carton (France)
The Wolseley (England)
12 Comme Chez Soi (Belgium)
Dal Pescatore (Italy)
Dieter Muller (Germany)
Gambero Rosso (Italy)
Georges Blanc (France)
Gidleigh Park (England)
Gordon Ramsay (England)
Heinz Winkler (Germany)
Hotel de Ville (Switzerland)
Im Schiffchen (Germany)
Plaza Athénée (France)
Putney Bridge (England)
The River Café (England)
Waterside Inn (England)
13 Auberge de l'Ill (France)
Cote St Jacques (France)
Jardins de Sens (France)
Le Pont de Brent (Switzerland)
Le Tour d'Argent (France)
Martin Wishart (Scotland)
The Greenhouse (England)

14 1 Lombard Street (England)
Charlie Trotter (USA)
Ferme de mon Père (France)
Gramercy Tavern (USA)

Pierre Gagnaire (France)

15 Les Prés d'Eugénie (France)
Patrick Guilbaud (Ireland)

Fast food restaurant chains include:

03 KFC
06 Wendy's
08 Pizza Hut
Taco Bell
Wagamama
09 Harvester

McDonald's
Spud U Like
Starbucks
10 Burger King
Dairy Queen
Little Chef

Red Rooster
TGI Friday's
11 Hungry Jacks
Krispy Kreme
12 Domino's Pizza
Dunkin' Donuts

Hard Rock Café
Pizza Express
13 Baskin-Robbins
Harry Ramsden's
14 Subway Sandwich

restaurateur *see* **chef**

revolution

Revolutions include:

04 July (1830, France)
06 French (1830, France)
Orange (2004–05, Ukraine)
Velvet (1989,
Czechoslovakia)

07 October (1917, Russia)
Russian (1917, Russia)
Singing (1988, Estonia/
Latvia/Lithuania)
08 American (1775–83)

Cultural (1966–76, China)
February (1917, Russia)
Glorious (1688, Britain)
10 Industrial (18c–19c, Britain)
12 Agricultural (18c, Britain)

revolutionary

Revolutionaries, rebels and terrorists include:

02 He (Xiangning; 1880–1972, Chinese)
Ho (Hsiang-ning; 1880–1972, Chinese)
Li (Dazhao; 1888–1927, Chinese)
Li (Ta-chao; 1888–1927, Chinese)

03 Cai (Chang; 1900–90, Chinese)
Guo (Morno; 1892–1978, Chinese)
Kim (Ok-kyun; 1851–94, Korean)
Kun (Béla; 1886–c.1937, Hungarian)
Kuo (Mo-jo; 1892–1978, Chinese)
Lee (Richard Henry; 1732–94, American)
Mao (Tse-tung; 1893–1976, Chinese)
Mao (Zedong; 1893–1976, Chinese)
Qiu (Jin; 1875–1907, Chinese)
Sun (Chung-shan; 1866–1925, Chinese)
Sun (Yat-sen; 1866–1925, Chinese)
Sun (Yixian; 1866–1925, Chinese)
Sun (Zhongshan; 1866–1925, Chinese)

04 Aske (Robert; d.1537, English)
Ball (John; d.1381, English)
Biko (Steve; 1946–77, South African)
Cade (Jack; d.1450, Irish)
Chen (Duxiu; 1879–1942, Chinese)
Ch'en (Tu-hsiu; 1879–1942, Chinese)
Ch'iu (Chin; 1875–1907, Chinese)
Hong (Xiuquan; 1813–64, Chinese)
Hung (Hsiu-ch'üan; 1813–64, Chinese)
Kett (Robert; d.1549, English)

Marx (Karl; 1818–83, German)
Páez (José Antonio; 1790–1873, Venezuelan)
Peng (Pai; 1896–1929, Chinese)
Popé (c.1630–c.1690, American)
Pyat (Félix; 1810–89, French)
Song (Jiaoren; 1882–1913, Chinese)
Sung (Chiao-jen; 1882–1913, Chinese)
Ts'ai (Ch'ang; 1900–90, Chinese)

05 Allen (Ethan; 1738–89, American)
Botev (Khristo; 1848–76, Bulgarian)
Fanon (Frantz; 1925–61, French West
Indian)
Gorky (Maxim; 1868–1936, Russian)
Henry (Patrick; 1736–99, American)
Huang (Hsing; 1871–1916, Chinese)
Huang (Xing; 1871–1916, Chinese)
Jiang (Jieshi; 1887–1975, Chinese)
Kirov (Sergei; 1886–1934, Russian)
Lenin (Vladimir Ilyich; 1870–1924, Russian)
Marat (Jean Paul; 1743–93, French)
Paine (Thomas; 1737–1809, English)
Radek (Karl; 1885–1939, Russian)
Razin (Stenka; c.1630–1671, Russian)
Rykov (Aleksei; 1881–1938, Russian)
Sands (Bobby; 1954–81, Irish)
Sucre (Antonio José de; 1793–1830, South
American)

Tyler (Wat; d.1381, English)
Villa (Pancho; 1877–1923, Mexican)
06 Arafat (Yasser; 1929–2004, Palestinian)
Baader (Andreas; 1943–77, German)
Barère (Bertrand; 1755–1841, French)
Barras (Paul, Comte de; 1755–1829, French)
Cambon (Joseph; 1756–1820, French)
Carnot (Lazare; 1753–1823, French)
Castro (Fidel; 1927– , Cuban)
Clarke (Thomas; 1858–1916, Irish)
Cloots (Jean Baptiste, Baron de; 1755–94, French)
Corday (Charlotte; 1768–93, French)
Danton (Georges; 1759–94, French)
Farini (Luigi Carlo; 1812–66, Italian)
Fawkes (Guy; 1570–1606, English)
Fouché (Joseph, Duc d'Otrante; 1763–1829, French)
Frunze (Mikhail; 1885–1925, Russian)
Fuller (Margaret, Marchioness Ossoli; 1810–50, US)
Görgey (Artúr; 1818–1916, Hungarian)
Hébert (Jacques; 1757–94, French)
Kassem (Abdul Karim; 1914–63, Iraqi)
Madero (Francisco; 1873–1913, Mexican)
Misley (Enrico; 1801–63, Italian)
Moreno (Mariano; 1778–1811, Argentine)
O'Neill (Hugh, Earl of Tyrone; c.1540–1616, Irish)
Orsini (Felice; 1819–58, Italian)
Pétion (Alexandre; 1770–1818, Haitian)
Qassim (Abd al-Krim; 1914–63, Iraqi)
Stalin (Joseph; 1879–1953, Soviet)
St-Just (Louis Antoine; 1767–94, French)
Travis (William; 1809–36, American)
Zapata (Emiliano; 1879–1919, Mexican)
07 Artigas (José; 1774–1850, Spanish American)
Astorga (Nora; 1949–88, Nicaraguan)
Attucks (Crispus; c.1723–1770, American)
Bakunin (Mikhail; 1814–76, Russian)
Barnave (Antoine; 1761–93, French)
Blanqui (Auguste; 1805–81, French)
Bolívar (Simón; 1783–1830, South American)
Brissot (Jacques Pierre; 1754–93, French)
Carrier (Jean Baptiste; 1756–94, French)
Carroll (Charles; 1737–1832, American)
Catesby (Robert; 1573–1605, English)
Couthon (Georges; 1756–94, French)
Durruti (Buenaventura; 1896–1936, Spanish)
Gadsden (Christopher; 1724–1805, American)
Goldman (Emma; 1869–1940, US)
Guevara (Che; 1928–67, Argentine)
Hancock (John; 1737–93, American)
Hidalgo (Miguel; 1753–1811, Mexican)

Horváth (Mihály; 1809–78, Hungarian)
Kamenev (Lev; 1883–1936, Russian)
Kossuth (Lajos; 1802–94, Hungarian)
Laurens (Henry; 1724–92, American)
Leisler (Jacob; 1640–91, American)
Mandela (Nelson; 1918– , South African)
Meinhof (Ulrike; 1934–76, German)
Menotti (Ciro; 1798–1831, Italian)
Miranda (Francisco de; 1750–1816, Venezuelan)
Modotti (Tina; 1896–1942, Mexican)
Morelos (José; 1765–1815, Mexican)
Nechaev (Sergei; 1847–82, Russian)
Padilla (Juan de; 1490–1521, Spanish)
Padmore (George; 1902–59, Trinidadian)
Princip (Gavrilo; 1895–1918, Serbian)
Rákóczi (Francis II; 1676–1735, Hungarian)
Sandino (Augusto; 1895–1934, Nicaraguan)
Savimbi (Jonas; 1934–2002, Angolan)
Tallien (Jean Lambert; 1767–1820, French)
Trotsky (Leon; 1879–1940, Russian)
Wallace (Sir William; c.1274–1305, Scottish)
08 Abu Nidal (1937–2002, Palestinian)
bin Laden (Osama; c.1957– 2011, Saudi Arabian)
Bukharin (Nikolai; 1888–1938, Russian)
Cadoudal (Georges; 1771–1804, French)
Catilina (Lucius Sergius; c.108–62 BC, Roman)
Catiline (c.108–62 BC, Roman)
Grégoire (Henri; 1750–1831, French)
Hereward (fl.1070, Anglo-Saxon)
Kerensky (Aleksandr; 1881–1970, Russian)
La Farina (Giuseppe; 1815–63, Italian)
Lassalle (Ferdinand; 1825–64, German)
Lilburne (John; c.1614–1657, English)
Litvinov (Maxim; 1876–1951, Soviet)
Mirabeau (Honoré Gabriel Riqueti, Comte de; 1749–91, French)
Museveni (Yoweri Kaguta; 1944– , Ugandan)
O'Donnell (Peadar; 1893–1986, Irish)
O'Higgins (Bernardo; 1778–1842, Chilean)
Paterson (William; 1745–1806, American)
Pisacane (Carlo; 1818–57, Italian)
Proudhon (Pierre Joseph; 1809–65, French)
Santerre (Antoine Joseph; 1752–1809, French)
Stepnyak (1852–95, Russian)
Zinoviev (Grigori; 1883–1936, Russian)
09 Aguinaldo (Emilio; 1870–1964, Philippine)
Bonifacio (Andres; 1863–97, Philippine)
Chaumette (Pierre; 1763–94, French)
Chicherin (G V; 1872–1936, Russian)

Christian (Fletcher; c.1764–c.1794, English)
Garibaldi (Giuseppe; 1807–82, Italian)
Glendower (Owen; c.1350–c.1416, Welsh)
Guillotin (Joseph; 1738–1814, French)
Karavelov (Lyuben; 1835–79, Bulgarian)
Kobayashi (Takaji; 1903–33, Japanese)
Kollontai (Aleksandra; 1872–1952, Russian)
Kropotkin (Prince Peter; 1842–1921, Russian)
Krupskaya (Nadezhda; 1869–1939, Russian)
Lafayette (Marquis de; 1757–1834, French)
Luxemburg (Rosa; 1871–1919, German)
Nana Sahib (c.1820–1859, Indian)
Plekhanov (Georgi; 1856–1918, Russian)
Saint-Just (Louis Antoine; 1767–94, French)
Spartacus (d.71 BC, Roman)

10 Buonarroti (Filippo; 1761–1837, Italian)
Choibalsan (d.1952, Mongolian)
Christophe (Henri; 1767–1829, Haitian)
Delescluze (Charles; 1809–71, French)
Desmoulins (Camille; 1760–94, French)
Engelbrekt (c.1390–1436, Swedish)
Espronceda (José de; 1808–42, Spanish)

See also **month**; **rebellion**; **war**

Kovalskaya (Yelizaveta; 1851–1943, Russian)
Liebknecht (Karl; 1871–1919, German)
Pasvanoglu (Osman Pasha; 1758–1807, Balkan)
Tiradentes (1748–92, Brazilian)
Tupac Amarú (c.1742–1781, Peruvian)

11 Dzerzhinsky (Felix; 1877–1926, Russian)
Lunacharsky (Anatoli; 1875–1933, Russian)
MacDiarmada (Seán; 1884–1916, Irish)
Robespierre (Maximilien; 1758–94, French)
Tantia Topee (d.1859, Indian)
Velestinlis (Rigas; 1757–98, Greek)

13 Chiang Kai-Shek (1887–1975, Chinese)
Muhammad Ahmed (1844–85, Arab)
Paz Estenssoro (Víctor; 1907–2001, Bolivian)

14 Billaud-Varenne (Jean Nicolas; 1756–1819, French)
Collot d'Herbois (Jean Marie; 1751–96, French)
Engelbrektsson (c.1390–1436, Swedish)
García y Iñigues (Calixto; 1839–98, Cuban)

15 Hereward the Wake (fl.1070, Anglo-Saxon)

rhetoric

Rhetorical devices include:

03 pun
05 irony
trope
06 aporia
bathos
climax
simile
zeugma
07 auxesis
epigram
erotema
litotes
meiosis
paradox
08 anaphora
chiasmus
diallage
diegesis
ellipsis
epanodos
erotetic
innuendo
metaphor
metonymy
oxymoron
parabole

symploce
09 asyndeton
cataphora
dissimile
epizeuxis
euphemism
hendiadys
hypallage
hyperbole
increment
prolepsis
syllepsis
tautology
10 abscission
anastrophe
anticlimax
antithesis
apostrophe
dysphemism
enantiosis
epanaphora
epiphonema
epistrophe
metalepsis
synchrysis
synecdoche
11 anacoluthon

anadiplosis
antiphrasis
antonomasia
catachresis
enumeration
epanalepsis
hypostrophe
hypotyposis
paraleipsis
parenthesis
synchoresis
synoeciosis
12 alliteration
antimetabole
epanorthosis
onomatopoeia
13 amplification
dramatic irony
epanadiplosis
mixed metaphor
vicious circle
14 antimetathesis
double entendre
figure of speech
15 pathetic fallacy
personification

rhizome *see* bulb

rhyme

Rhymes include:

03 end
eye
04 half
head
male
near
rich
tail
05 slant
vowel
06 female
riding
tailed
08 feminine
internal
09 assonance
identical
masculine
pararhyme
rime riche
10 apocopated
cynghanedd
rhyme royal
14 rime suffisante

river

River and watercourse types include:

02 ea
03 cut
pow
sny
04 beck
burn
flow
kill
lake
lane
nala
rill
snye
wadi
wady
05 bourn
brook
canal
creek
delta
firth
fresh
frith
inlet
mouth
nalla
nulla
06 broads
influx
nallah
nullah
rapids
rillet
runnel
source
stream
07 channel
estuary
freshet
riveret
rivulet
torrent
08 affluent
brooklet
effluent
influent
waterway
09 anabranch
backwater
billabong
confluent
headwater
streamlet
tributary
10 confluence
head-stream
millstream
streamling
11 trout stream
water splash
12 distributary
embranchment
14 mountain stream

Rivers include:

02 Li (China)
Ob (Russia)
Po (Italy)
03 Ahr (Germany)
Ain (France)
Axe (England)
Bug (Ukraine/Poland)
Cam (England)
Dal (Sweden)
Dee (Scotland; England/Wales)
Don (Russia; Scotland; England)
Ems (Germany)
Esk (Scotland)
Exe (England)
Fly (Papua New Guinea)
Han (China)
Hsi (China)
Ill (Finland)
Lea (England)
Lee (England)
Lek (The Netherlands)
Lim (Albania/Serbia/Montenegro/Bosnia and Herzegovina)
Lot (France)
Lys (France/Belgium)
Mun (Thailand)
Mur (Austria)
Nid (Norway)
Olt (Romania)
Oti (Burkina Faso/Togo/Ghana)
Our (Belgium/Luxembourg)
Pra (Ghana)
Red (Vietnam/USA)
San (Poland)
Sau (Slovakia/Croatia/Bosnia and Herzegovina/Serbia)
Sil (Spain)
Taw (England)
Tay (Scotland)
Tua (Portugal)
Ume (Sweden)
Una (Croatia/Bosnia and Herzegovina)

Usk (Wales)
Váh (Slovakia)
Wey (England)
Wye (Wales/England)

04 Aare (Switzerland)
Aire (England)
Alta (Norway)
Amur (China/Russia)
Arno (Italy)
Arun (England)
Aube (France)
Aude (France)
Avon (England)
Bann (Ireland)
Beni (Bolivia)
Cher (France)
Coco (Nicaragua)
Dart (England)
Drin (Albania)
Ebbw (Wales)
Ebro (Spain)
Eden (England)
Eems (Germany)
Elbe (Czech Republic/Germany)
Enns (Austria)
Eure (France)
Gail (Austria)
Gers (France)
Gurk (Austria)
Hong (Vietnam)
Ibar (Serbia/Montenegro)
Kamp (Austria)
Kemi (Finland)
Krka (Croatia)
Kupa (Croatia)
Kymi (Finland)
Labe (Czech Republic/Germany)
Lahn (Germany)
Lech (Austria/Germany)
Leie (France/Belgium)
Lena (Russia)
Lima (Spain/Portugal)
Lule (Sweden)
Lune (England)
Maas (France/Belgium/The Netherlands)
Main (Germany)
Mino (Spain/Portugal)
Mira (Portugal)
Mole (England)
Mono (Togo)
Mürz (Austria)
Naab (Germany)
Nams (Norway)
Napa (USA)
Nene (England)
Nile (Uganda/South Sudan/Sudan/Egypt)
Nith (Scotland)
Oder (Czech Republic/Poland/Germany)

Odra (Czech Republic/Poland/Germany)
Ohio (USA)
Oise (Belgium/France)
Omme (Denmark)
Orne (France)
Oste (Germany)
Otra (Norway)
Ouse (England)
Oxus (Afghanistan/Turkmenistan/
  Uzbekistan)
Ping (Thailand)
Prut (Romania)
Raab (Hungary)
Rába (Hungary)
Ramu (Papua New Guinea)
Ravi (Pakistan)
Reno (Italy)
Ruhr (Germany)
Saar (France/Germany)
Sado (Portugal)
Sava (Slovakia/Croatia/Bosnia and
  Herzegovina/Serbia)
Save (Slovakia/Croatia/Bosnia and
  Herzegovina/Serbia)
Soar (England)
Spey (Scotland)
Sûre (Belgium/Luxembourg)
Svir (Russia)
Swan (Australia)
Taff (Wales)
Tajo (Spain/Portugal)
Tana (Kenya; Norway)
Tano (Ghana)
Tarn (France)
Taro (Italy)
Tees (England)
Tejo (Spain/Portugal)
Teme (Wales/England)
Test (England)
Towy (Wales)
Tyne (England)
Tywi (Wales)
Ulúa (Honduras)
Ural (Russia/Kazakhstan)
Vaal (South Africa)
Waal (The Netherlands)
Yaik (Russia/Kazakhstan)
Yalu (North Korea)
Yare (England)
Ybbs (Austria)

05 Adige (Italy)
Adour (France)
Aguán (Honduras)
Aisne (France)
Aldan (Russia)
Arges (Romania)
Argun (China/Russia)
Benue (Cameroon/Nigeria)

Black (Canada; USA)
Boyne (Ireland)
Cauca (Colombia)
Chari (Chad)
Clerf (Belgium/Luxembourg)
Clwyd (Wales)
Clyde (Scotland)
Congo (Zambia/Democratic Republic of the Congo)
Conwy (Wales)
Demer (Belgium)
Desna (Ukraine)
Dnepr (Russia/Ukraine)
Donau (Germany/Austria/Slovakia/Hungary/Croatia/Serbia/Bulgaria/Romania/Moldova)
Doubs (France)
Douro (Spain)
Drina (Bosnia and Herzegovina/Serbia)
Drôme (France)
Duero (Spain)
Eider (Germany)
Fleet (England)
Forth (Scotland)
Fulda (Germany)
Ganga (India)
Genil (Spain)
Glåma (Norway)
Gogra (China/Nepal/India)
Harut (Afghanistan)
Hugli (India)
Hunte (Germany)
Indre (France)
Indus (Pakistan)
Isère (France)
Ishim (Kazakhstan/Russia)
Iskur (Bulgaria)
Jalon (Spain)
Júcar (Spain)
Jumna (India)
Kalix (Sweden)
Körös (Hungary)
Kuban (Russia)
Lågen (Norway)
Lajta (Austria/Hungary)
Leine (Germany)
Lempa (Guatemala/El Salvador)
Liard (Canada)
Loing (France)
Loire (France)
Manas (China/Bhutan/India)
March (Serbia)
Marne (France)
Memel (Belarus/Lithuania)
Meric (Bulgaria/Greece/Turkey)
Meuse (France/Belgium/The Netherlands)
Minho (Spain/Portugal)
Mosel (France/Luxembourg/Germany)
Mulde (Germany)

Mures (Romania/Hungary)
Narew (Poland)
Negro (Argentina)
Neman (Belarus/Lithuania)
Newry (Northern Ireland)
Niger (Guinea/Mali/Niger/Nigeria)
Notec (Poland)
Onega (Russia)
Ouémé (Benin)
Ounas (Finland)
Peace (Canada)
Pearl (China)
Pecos (USA)
Perak (Malaysia)
Piave (Italy)
Plata (Argentina)
Plate (Uruguay/Argentina)
Purus (Peru/Brazil)
Rhein (Switzerland/France/Germany/The Netherlands)
Rhine (Switzerland/France/Germany/The Netherlands)
Rhône (Switzerland/France)
Rille (France)
Risle (France)
Saale (Germany)
Sabor (Portugal)
Saône (France)
Sarre (France/Germany)
Sauer (Belgium/Luxembourg)
Segre (France/Spain)
Seine (France)
Siret (Romania)
Snake (USA)
Somes (Romania)
Somme (France)
Spree (Germany)
Stour (England)
Stura (Italy)
Tagus (Spain/Portugal)
Tamar (England)
Teifi (Wales)
Thame (England)
Tiber (Italy)
Tirso (Italy)
Tisza (Hungary)
Tobol (Kazakhstan/Russia)
Traun (Austria)
Trave (Germany)
Trent (England)
Tumen (North Korea)
Turia (Spain)
Tweed (Scotland/England)
Varde (Denmark)
Volga (Russia)
Volta (Ghana)
Vouga (Portugal)
Vrbas (Bosnia and Herzegovina)

Warta (Poland)
Werra (Germany)
Weser (Germany)
Wisla (Poland)
Woleu (Gabon/Equatorial Guinea)
Xingu (Brazil)
Yonne (France)
Yukon (Canada)
Zújar (Spain)

06 Alfiós (Greece)
Allier (France)
Amazon (Peru/Brazil)
Angara (Russia)
Ariège (France)
Barrow (Ireland)
Belize (Guatemala/Belize)
Bénoué (Cameroon/Nigeria)
Brazos (USA)
Calder (England)
Chenab (India/Pakistan)
Clerve (Belgium/Luxembourg)
Clutha (New Zealand)
Coquet (England)
Creuse (France)
Danube (Germany/Austria/Slovakia/
    Hungary/Croatia/Serbia/Bulgaria/Romania/
    Moldova)
Dender (Belgium)
Dendre (Belgium)
Devoll (Albania)
Dnestr (Ukraine/Moldova)
Donets (Ukraine/Russia)
Escaut (France/Belgium/The Netherlands)
Fraser (Canada)
Gambia (Guinea/Senegal/The Gambia)
Gambie (The Gambia)
Gandak (Nepal/India)
Ganges (India)
Glomma (Norway)
Grande (Nicaragua)
Guayas (Ecuador)
Gudenå (Denmark)
Hevros (Bulgaria/Greece/Turkey)
Hudson (USA)
Humber (England)
Iijoki (Finland)
Ijoälv (Finland)
Irtysh (China/Kazakhstan/Russia)
Jantra (Bulgaria)
Jhelum (India/Pakistan)
Jordan (Syria/Israel/Jordan)
Kennet (England)
Khabur (Turkey/Syria)
Kistna (India)
Kolyma (Russia)
Lavant (Austria)
Leitha (Austria/Hungary)
Liffey (Ireland)

Litani (Lebanon)
Ljusna (Sweden)
Logone (Chad)
Marica (Bulgaria/Greece/Turkey)
Medway (England)
Mekong (China/Myanmar/Thailand/Laos/
    Cambodia/Vietnam)
Meping (Thailand)
Mersey (England)
Moldau (Czech Republic)
Morava (Serbia)
Murray (Australia)
Mystic (USA)
Namsen (Norway)
Neckar (Germany)
Nelson (Canada)
Nidelv (Norway)
Ogooué (Congo/Gabon)
Olenëk (Russia)
Orange (Lesotho/South Africa/Namibia)
Ottawa (Canada)
Ourthe (Belgium)
Pahang (Malaysia)
Paraná (Brazil/Paraguay/Argentina)
Patuca (Honduras)
Piniós (Greece)
Pripet (Ukraine/Belarus)
Rajang (Malaysia)
Ribble (England)
Rideau (Canada)
Rovuma (Tanzania/Mozambique)
Rudall (Australia)
Ruvuma (Tanzania/Mozambique)
Salado (Argentina)
Sambre (France)
Sanaga (Cameroon)
Sarthe (France)
Sárviz (Hungary)
Segura (Spain)
Severn (England)
Seyhan (Turkey)
Struma (Bulgaria)
Sutlej (Pakistan)
Taieri (New Zealand)
Tâmega (Portugal)
Tevere (Italy)
Thames (England)
Tigris (Turkey/Iraq)
Tornio (Sweden)
Ubangi (Democratic Republic of the Congo/
    Central African Republic)
Vienne (France)
Vijosa (Albania)
Vijosë (Albania)
Vltava (Czech Republic)
Vyatka (Russia)
Wabash (USA)
Warthe (Poland)

Wharfe (England)
Wieprz (Poland)
Witham (England)
Yakima (USA)
Yamuna (India)
Yantra (Bulgaria)
Yellow (China)
Zezere (Portugal)
Zhayyq (Russia/Kazakhstan)

07 Alpheus (Greece)
Alzette (Luxembourg)
Ardèche (France)
Aveyron (France)
Biferno (Italy)
Cabriel (Spain)
Caledon (Lesotho/South Africa)
Charles (USA)
Cubango (Angola/Namibia/Botswana)
Darling (Australia)
Derwent (England)
Dnieper (Russia/Ukraine)
Dniestr (Ukraine/Moldova)
Drammen (Norway)
Durance (France)
Garonne (France)
Glommen (Norway)
Guayape (Honduras)
Hangang (South Korea)
Helmand (Afghanistan)
Hérault (France)
Hooghly (India)
Huang He (China)
Huang Ho (China)
Ilmenau (Germany)
Kavengo (Angola/Namibia/Botswana)
Kemiälv (Finland)
Kilkeel (Ireland)
Krishna (India)
Lachlan (Australia)
Limpopo (South Africa/Botswana/Zimbabwe/
　Mozambique)
Ljusnan (Sweden)
Lualaba (Democratic Republic of the
　Congo)
Madeira (Brazil)
Marañón (Peru)
Maritsa (Bulgaria/Greece/Turkey)
Mataura (New Zealand)
Mayenne (France)
Meurthe (France)
Mondego (Portugal)
Moselle (France/Luxembourg/Germany)
Motagua (Guatemala)
Narbada (India)
Narmada (India)
Neretva (Bosnia and Herzegovina)
Niagara (USA/Canada)
Nu Jiang (China/Myanmar)

Orinoco (Venezuela)
Orontes (Lebanon/Syria/Turkey)
Parrett (England)
Passaic (USA)
Pechora (Russia)
Potomac (USA)
Pripyat (Ukraine/Belarus)
Rabnitz (Austria)
Sakarya (Turkey)
Salween (China/Myanmar)
Salzach (Austria)
San Juan (Nicaragua)
Schelde (France/Belgium/The Netherlands)
Scheldt (France/Belgium/The Netherlands)
Segovia (Nicaragua)
Selenga (Mongolia)
Selenge (Mongolia)
Sénégal (Guinea/Mali/Senegal)
Shannon (Ireland)
Sittang (Myanmar)
Sorraia (Portugal)
Staaten (Australia)
Strimon (Bulgaria)
Sukhona (Russia)
Tapajós (Brazil)
Tarim He (China)
Thiamis (Greece)
Traisen (Austria)
Ucayali (Peru)
Uruguay (Brazil/Argentina/Uruguay)
Vilaine (France)
Vistula (Poland)
Voiussa (Albania)
Waikato (New Zealand)
Waveney (England)
Welland (England)
Yangtze (China)
Yenisei (Russia)
Yenisey (Russia)
Zambesi (Zambia/Angola/Botswana/
　Zimbabwe/Mozambique)
Zambezi (Zambia/Angola/Botswana/
　Zimbabwe/Mozambique)

08 Abay Wenz (Sudan)
Achelous (Greece)
Akhelóös (Greece)
Aliákmon (Greece)
Altaelva (Norway)
Amazonas (Peru/Brazil)
Amudar'ya (Afghanistan/Turkmenistan/
　Uzbekistan)
Amu Darya (Afghanistan/Turkmenistan/
　Uzbekistan)
Angerman (Sweden)
Araguaia (Brazil)
Arkansas (USA)
Berounka (Czech Republic)
Blue Nile (Sudan)

Brisbane (Australia)
Canadian (USA)
Charente (France)
Chu-Kiang (China)
Clarence (Australia; New Zealand)
Colorado (USA)
Columbia (Canada/USA)
Cuyahoga (USA)
Dalälven (Sweden)
Delaware (USA)
Dniester (Ukraine/Moldova)
Dordogne (France)
Drysdale (Australia)
Ghaghara (China/Nepal/India)
Godavari (India)
Godaveri (India)
Guadiana (Spain/Portugal)
Ialomiţa (Romania)
Kemijoki (Finland)
Kymijoki (Finland)
Mahanadi (India)
Mahaveli (Sri Lanka)
Mahaweli (Sri Lanka)
Mazaruni (Guyana)
Missouri (USA)
Okavango (Angola/Namibia/Botswana)
Orhon Gol (Mongolia)
Paraguay (Brazil/Paraguay/Argentina)
Parnaíba (Brazil)
Pisuerga (Spain)
Polochic (Guatemala)
Río Bravo (USA)
Río Negro (Argentina)
Santa Ana (USA)
Shkumbin (Albania)
Solimões (Peru/Brazil)
Syr Darya (Uzbekistan/Tajikistan/
   Kazakhstan)
Tunguska (Russia)
Vychegda (Russia)
Wanganui (New Zealand)
Zhu Jiang (China)

09 Almanzora (Spain)
Athabasca (Canada)
Churchill (Canada)
Crocodile (South Africa/Botswana/
   Zimbabwe/Mozambique)
Dangme Chu (China/Bhutan/India)
Essequibo (Guyana)
Euphrates (Turkey/Syria/Iraq)
Great Ouse (England)
Indigirka (Russia)
Irrawaddy (Myanmar)
Katherine (Australia)
Kuskokwim (USA)
Mackenzie (Canada)
Magdalena (Colombia)
Nahr el Asi (Lebanon/Syria/Turkey)

Ounasjoki (Finland)
Río Balsas (Mexico)
Rio Grande (USA)
Río Paraná (Brazil/Paraguay/Argentina)
San Carlos (Costa Rica)
Schwechat (Austria)
St Laurent (Canada)
Tennessee (USA)
Tocantins (Brazil)
Vistritsa (Greece)
White Nile (Ethiopia)
Yuan Jiang (Vietnam)

10 Albert Nile (Uganda)
Alto Paraná (Brazil/Paraguay/Argentina)
Chang Jiang (China)
Chao Phraya (Thailand)
Chateaugay (USA/Canada)
Des Plaines (USA)
Hackensack (USA)
Kizil Irmak (Turkey)
Little Ouse (England)
Rangitikei (New Zealand)
Río Uruguay (Brazil/Argentina/Uruguay)
Sacramento (USA)
San Antonio (USA)
San Joaquin (USA)
Santa Maria (USA)
Shenandoah (USA)
St Lawrence (Canada)
Usumacinta (Guatemala/Mexico)
Walla Walla (USA)

11 Assiniboine (Canada)
Bahr el Ablad (Ethiopia)
Bahr el Azraq (Sudan)
Brahmaputra (China/India/Bangladesh)
Châteauguay (USA/Canada)
Mississippi (USA)
Nyamyang Chu (China/Bhutan/India)
Río Paraguay (Paraguay)
Shatt al-Arab (Iraq)
Yellowknife (Canada)

12 Guadalquivir (Spain)
Heilong Jiang (China/Russia)
Kinabatangan (Malaysia)
Murrumbidgee (Australia)
Oranjerivier (Lesotho/South Africa/Namibia)
Río de la Plata (Uruguay/Argentina)
São Francisco (Brazil)
Saskatchewan (Canada)
Victoria Nile (Uganda)
Western Dvina (Russia/Belarus/Latvia)

13 Ångermanälven (Sweden)
Langcang Jiang (China/Myanmar/Thailand/
   Laos/Cambodia/Vietnam)
Lower Tunguska (Russia)
Mahaveli Ganga (Sri Lanka)
Mahaweli Ganga (Sri Lanka)

Northern Dvina (Russia)
Río Usumacinta (Guatemala/Mexico)

Severnaya Dvina (Russia)
Zapadnaya Dvina (Russia/Belarus/Latvia)

14 Northern Donets (Ukraine/Russia)
Río de las Balsas (Mexico)

15 Dramsvassdraget (Norway)
Severskiy Donets (Ukraine/Russia)

road

Road types include:

01 A		strand	bridleway
B		street	cart track
C		subway	dirt track
E			esplanade
03 way	**07**	beltway	green lane
04 drag		dead end	promenade
high		flyover	unadopted
lane		freeway	underpass
mews		highway	**10** autostrada
pass		off ramp	bridlepath
ring		parkway	cloverleaf
side		private	expressway
slip		through	interstate
toll	**08**	alleyway	unmetalled
05 alley		autobahn	**11** gravel track
byway		causeway	scenic route
close		clearway	single track
gated		crescent	**12** holiday route
Roman		cul-de-sac	mountain pass
route		metalled	superhighway
strip		motorway	thoroughfare
track		overpass	unclassified
trunk		red route	**14** divided highway
06 avenue		short cut	gyratory system
bypass		speedway	**15** dual carriageway
parade		trackway	elevated section
rat run		turnpike	European highway
relief	**09**	autoroute	
		boulevard	

Roads include:

02 A1 (England/Scotland)
M1 (England)
M2 (England)
M3 (England)
M4 (England/Wales)
M5 (England)
M6 (England)
M8 (Scotland)
M9 (Scotland)

03 M11 (England)
M25 (England)
M40 (England)
M62 (England)

06 Big Dig (USA)

07 Route 66 (USA)
Westway (England)

08 Fern Pass (Austria)

Fosse Way (England)
Highway 1 (Australia/USA)
Silk Road (Italy–China)

09 Appian Way (Italy)
Burma Road (China/Myanmar)
Furka Pass (Switzerland)
Highway 61 (USA)
Snake Pass (England)

10 Cassian Way (Italy)
Dere Street (England/Scotland)
Flexen Pass (Austria)
Flüela Pass (Switzerland)
Gioffo Pass (Italy)
Hanger Lane (England)
Highway 401 (Canada)
Highway 407 (Canada)
Jaufen Pass (Italy)

Julier Pass (Switzerland)
Khyber Pass (Pakistan/Afghanistan)
Maloja Pass (Switzerland)
Mendel Pass (Italy)
Spluga Pass (Switzerland/Italy)
Susten Pass (Switzerland)

11 Aemilian Way (Italy)
Arlberg Pass (Austria)
Aurelian Way (Italy)
Bealach Na Ba (Scotland)
Bernina Pass (Italy/Switzerland)
Brenner Pass (Austria/Italy)
Gardena Pass (Italy)
Grimsel Pass (Switzerland)
Hume Highway (Australia)
Icknield Way (England)
Klausen Pass (Switzerland)
Mendola Pass (Italy)
Oberalp Pass (Switzerland)
Old Post Road (USA)
Oregon Trail (USA)
Salarian Way (Italy)
Simplon Pass (Switzerland/Italy)
Splügen Pass (Switzerland/Italy)
Stane Street (England)
Stelvio Pass (Italy)

12 Akeman Street (England)
Alcan Highway (Canada/USA)
Cat and Fiddle (England)
Dixie Highway (USA)
El Camino Real (USA/Mexico)
Ermine Street (England)
Flaminian Way (Italy)
King's Highway (Arabia–Mediterranean)
King's Highway (USA)
Maloggia Pass (Switzerland)
National Road (USA)

Périphérique (France)
Santa Fe Trail (USA)
Sempione Pass (Switzerland/Italy)
Sturt Highway (Australia)
Tre Croci Pass (Italy)

13 Alaska Highway (Canada/USA)
Cairnwell Pass (Scotland)
Cumberland Gap (USA)
Great West Road (England)
Lancaster Road (USA)
Mont Cenis Pass (France/Italy)
North Circular (England)
Pass of Glen Coe (Scotland)
South Circular (England)
Stuart Highway (Australia)
Uspallata Pass (Argentina/Chile)
Watling Street (England)

14 Boston Post Road (USA)
Capital Beltway (USA)
Cumberland Road (USA)
Eastern Parkway (USA)
Grand Trunk Road (India/Pakistan)
Great Ocean Road (Australia)
Great River Road (USA)
Le Périphérique (France)
Lincoln Highway (USA)
Merritt Parkway (USA)
Moncenisio Pass (France/Italy)
Pacific Highway (Australia)
St Gotthard Pass (Italy/Switzerland)
Tauernhöhe Pass (Austria)
Wilderness Road (USA)
Zirlerberg Pass (Austria)

15 Great Valley Road (USA)
Grödner Joch Pass (Italy)
Magic Roundabout (England)
Overseas Highway (USA)

See also **London**; **motoring**; **New York**; **Paris**

road sign *see* **motoring**

robber *see* **thief**

Robin Hood *see* **legend**

rock

Rocks include:

02 aa	**05** chalk	**06** basalt
03 ore	chert	gabbro
04 coal	flint	gneiss
lava	shale	gravel
marl	slate	marble

		10 greenstone
schist	obsidian	serpentine
07 breccia	porphyry	**11** pumice stone
granite	**09** greywacke	**12** conglomerate
08 dolerite	limestone	
hornfels	sandstone	

Terms to do with rocks include:

05 basic	**08** dioritic	concretion	pyroclastic
darcy	**09** schistose	gabbroitic	sedimentary
fault	siliceous	miarolitic	**12** argillaceous
07 clastic	silicious	stratified	carbonaceous
igneous	**10** arenaceous	**11** cataclastic	conglomerate
outcrop	calcareous	metamorphic	**13** argentiferous

See also **geology**; **pop**

rodent

Rodents include:

03 rat	rabbit	viscacha
04 cavy	**07** cane rat	water rat
cony	hamster	**09** bandicoot
degu	lemming	groundhog
hare	meerkat	guinea pig
pika	muskrat	porcupine
vole	ondatra	water vole
05 aguti	potoroo	woodchuck
coney	**08** black rat	**10** chinchilla
coypu	brown rat	fieldmouse
mouse	capybara	prairie dog
06 agouti	chipmunk	springhaas
beaver	dormouse	springhase
ferret	hampster	**11** kangaroo rat
gerbil	hedgehog	red squirrel
gopher	musquash	spermophile
hog-rat	sewer rat	**12** grey squirrel
jerboa	squirrel	harvest mouse
marmot	tucutuco	

See also **rabbit**

roll see **bread**

Roman numeral see **numeral**

Romania see **Balkans**

Rome

The seven hills of Rome:

07 Caelian	Palatine	**10** Capitoline
Viminal	Quirinal	
08 Aventine	**09** Esquiline	

Roman emperors, with regnal dates:

03 Leo (I; AD457–74)
Leo (II; AD474)

04 Geta (AD209–12)
Nero (AD54–68)
Otho (AD69)
Zeno (AD474–91)

05 Carus (AD282–83)
Gaius (AD12–41)
Galba (AD68–69)
Nerva (AD96–98)
Titus (AD79–81)

06 Avitus (AD455–56)
Decius (AD249–51)
Gallus (AD251–53)
Julian (AD360–63)
Philip (AD244–49)
Probus (AD276–82)
Trajan (AD98–117)
Valens (AD364–78)

07 Carinus (AD283–85)
Florian (AD276)
Gordian (I; AD238)
Gordian (II; AD238)
Gordian (III; AD238–44)
Gratian (AD375–83)
Hadrian (AD117–38)
Marcian (AD450–57)
Maximin (AD235–38)
Maximus (AD238)
Severus (AD306–07)
Tacitus (AD275–76)

08 Aemilian (AD253)
Arcadius (AD395–408)
Augustus (31 BC–AD14)
Aurelian (AD270–75)
Balbinus (AD238)
Caligula (AD37–41)
Claudius (II; AD268–69)
Commodus (AD176–92)
Constans (I; AD337–50)
Domitian (AD81–96)
Galerius (AD305–11)

Honorius (AD395–423)
Licinius (AD308–24)
Macrinus (AD217–18)
Majorian (AD457–61)
Maximian (AD286–305)
Numerian (AD283–84)
Olybrius (AD472–73)
Pertinax (AD193)
Tiberius (AD14–37)
Valerian (AD253–60)

09 Anthemius (AD467–72)
Caracalla (AD198–217)
Gallienus (AD253–68)
Hostilian (AD251)
Maxentius (AD306–12)
Procopius (AD365–66)
Vespasian (AD69–79)
Vitellius (AD69)

10 Diocletian (AD284–305)
Elagabalus (AD218–22)
Magnentius (AD350–51)
Quintillus (AD269–70)
Theodosius (I; AD379–95)
Theodosius (II; AD408–50)

11 Constantine (I; AD306–37)
Constantine (II; AD337–40)
Constantius (I; AD305–06)
Constantius (II; AD337–61)
Constantius (III; AD421–23)
Julius Nepos (AD474–80)
Lucius Verus (AD161–69)
Valentinian (I; AD364–75)
Valentinian (II; AD375–92)
Valentinian (III; AD423–55)

13 Antoninus Pius (AD138–61)
Libius Severus (AD461–67)

14 Didius Julianus (AD193)
Marcus Aurelius (AD161–80)

15 Romulus Augustus (AD475–76)

16 Alexander Severus (AD222–35)
Petronius Maximus (AD455)
Septemius Severus (AD193–211)

Roman kings:

07 Romulus (753–715 BC)

12 Ancus Marcius (642–616 BC)

13 Numa Pompilius (715–673 BC)

14 Servius Tullius (578–534 BC)

15 Tullus Hostilius (673–642 BC)

17 Tarquinius Priscus (616–578 BC)

18 Tarquinius Superbus (534–509 BC)

Romans include:

04 Cato (Marcius Porcius, the Elder; 234–149 BC, statesman, orator)

Cato (Marcius Porcius, the Younger; 95–46 BC, statesman, orator)

Livy (Titus Livius; 59 BC–AD 17, historian)
Ovid (Publius Ovidius Naso; 43 BC–AD 17, poet)

05 Lucan (Marcus Annaeus Lucanus; 39–65 AD, poet)
Pliny (Gaius Plinius Caecilius Secundus, the Elder; 62–c.113 AD, writer, orator)
Pliny (Gaius Plinius Secundus, the Elder; 23–79 AD, scholar)

06 Antony (Mark; c.83–30 BC, politician, soldier)
Brutus (Marcus Junius; c.85–42 BC, politician)
Cicero (Marcus Tullius; 106–43 BC, orator, statesman, man of letters)
Horace (Quintus Horatius Flaccus; 65–8 BC, poet, satirist)
Pilate (Pontius; d.c.36 AD, prefect of Judea and Samaria)
Pompey (Gnaeus Pompeius Magnus; 106–48 BC, soldier, politician)
Seneca (Lucius Annaeus; c.4 BC–c.65 AD, Stoic philosopher, statesman, tragedian)
Vergil (Publius Vergilius Maro; 70–19 BC, poet)
Virgil (Publius Vergilius Maro; 70–19 BC, poet)

07 Atticus (Titus Pomponius; 110–32 BC, intellectual, businessman, writer)
Cassius (Gaius Cassius Longinus; d.42 BC, conspirator)
Juvenal (Decimus Junius Juvenalis; c.55–c.140 AD, lawyer, satirist)
Martial (Marcus Valerius Martialis; c.40–104 AD, poet, epigrammatist)

See also **mythology**; **play**; **poetry**; **satire**; **Virgil**

Plautus (Titus Maccius; c.250–184 BC, comic dramatist)
Roscius (Quintus Roscius Gallus; c.134–62 BC, comic actor)
Tacitus (Publius Cornelius; c.55–120 AD, historian)
Terence (Publius Terentius Afer; c.195–159 BC, comic dramatist)

08 Agricola (Gnaeus Julius; c.63–12 BC, general, imperial administrator)
Catilina (Lucius Sergius 'Catiline'; c.108–62 BC, conspirator)
Catiline (c.108–62 BC, conspirator)
Catullus (Gaius Valerius; c.84–54 BC, poet)
Claudian (Claudius Claudianus; 340–410 AD, poet)
Gracchus (Tiberius Sempronius; 168–133 BC, statesman)
Lucretia (6c BC, matron, legendary rape victim)

09 Agrippina (the Elder; c.14 BC–AD 33, noblewoman)
Agrippina (the Younger; 15–59 AD, empress, wife of Claudius, mother of Nero)
Lucretius (Titus Lucretius Carus; c.99–55 BC, poet, philosopher)
Spartacus (d.71 BC, gladiator, rebel)
Suetonius (Gaius Suetonius Tranquillus; c.69–140 AD, biographer, antiquary)

10 Coriolanus (Gaius; 5c BC, folk hero)
Quintilian (Marcus Fabius Quintilianus; c.35–c.100 AD, rhetorician)

14 Marcus Antonius (c.83–30 BC, politician, soldier)

roof

Roofs include:

03 hip	**05** gable	monitor	**10** imbricated
04 bell	**06** cupola	pitched	saucer dome
dome	French	**08** imperial	**12** geodesic dome
flat	lean-to	pavilion	sloped turret
helm	saddle	sawtooth	**13** conical broach
ogee	**07** gambrel	thatched	**14** gable-and-valley
span	mansard	**09** onion dome	pendentive dome

room

Rooms include:

02 WC	loo	hall	tack
03 bed		loft	wash
box	**04** ante	play	work
day	bath	rest	**05** attic
den	cell	sick	board
	dark		

cabin	common	drawing		chambers
class	dining	en suite		changing
cloak	engine	fitting		dressing
court	family	kitchen		lavatory
foyer	larder	landing		scullery
front	living	laundry		workshop
games	locker	lecture	**09**	breakfast
green	lounge	library		dormitory
guard	lumber	meeting		mezzanine
guest	office	morning		reception
lobby	pantry	nursery		sun lounge
music	rumpus	parlour	**10**	consulting
porch	saddle	reading		laboratory
salon	strong	seminar		recreation
spare	studio	sitting	**11**	kitchenette
staff	toilet	smoking		lounge-diner
state	**07** boudoir	utility	**12**	conservatory
stock	buttery	waiting		kitchen-diner
store	chamber	wet room	**15**	en suite bathroom
study	control	**08** assembly		
06 cellar	cubicle	basement		

rope

Ropes include:

03 guy	cable	string		outhaul
tow	lasso	tackle		painter
04 cord	noose	tether		ratline
drag	sheet	**07** bobstay	**08**	buntline
head	widdy	bowline		clew-line
line	**06** bridle	cordage		dockline
stay	halter	cringle		downhaul
tack	hawser	halyard		dragline
vang	hobble	lanyard		gantline
warp	lariat	lashing	**09**	hackamore
05 brace	runner	marline		
	strand	mooring		

Rossini, Gioacchino (1792–1868)

Significant works include:

06 *Armida* (1817)
Otello (1816)

07 *Ermione* (1819)
Zelmira (1822)

08 *Count Ory* (1828)
Tancredi (1813)

09 *La gazetta* (1816)

10 *Le Comte Ory* (1828)
Semiramide (1823)
Sigismondo (1814)

11 *Stabat Mater* (1842)
William Tell (1829)

12 *La gazza ladra* (1817)
Mosè in Egitto (1818)

Moses in Egypt (1818)
Sins of Old Age (1863)

13 *Guillaume Tell* (1829)
La Cenerentola (1817)
La scala di seta (1812)

14 *La donna del lago* (1819)
L'inganno felice (1812)
Matilde Shabran (1821)
Moïse et Pharaon (1827)
The Turk in Italy (1814)

15 *Bianca e Falliero* (1819)
Ciro in Babilonia (1812)
Il turco in Italia (1814)
Il viaggio a Reims (1825)
Maometto secondo (1820)

The Silken Ladder (1812)

16 Demetrio e Polibio (1812)
Eduardo e Cristinà (1819)

17 Il Signor Bruschino (1813)
Le Siège de Corinthe (1826)
L'italiana in Algeri (1813)
Ricciardo e Zoraide (1818)
The Thieving Magpie (1817)
Torvaldo e Dorliska (1815)

18 Adelaide di Borgogna (1817)
Aureliano in Palmira (1813)
Péchés de vieillesse (1863)

The Barber of Seville (1816)

19 La pietra del paragone (1812)
L'Occasione fa il ladro (1812)

20 Il barbiere di Siviglia (1816)
L'equivoco stravagante (1811)

21 Petite Messe Solennelle (1863)

22 La cambiale di matrimonio (1810)

23 Adina, o Il califfo di Bagdad (1818)
The Italian Girl in Algiers (1813)

26 Otello, ossia Il Moro di Venezia (1816)

28 Elisabetta Regina d'Inghilterra (1815)

Round Table *see* **legend**

rowing

Rowers include:

04 Reed (Peter; 1981– , English)

05 Tufte (Olaf; 1976– , Norway)

06 Foster (Tim; 1970– , English)
Ivanov (Vyacheslav; 1938– , Russian)

07 Pinsent (Sir Matthew; 1970– , English)
Waddell (Rob; 1975– , New Zealand)

08 Nickalls (Guy; 1866–1935, English)
Redgrave (Sir Steve; 1962– , English)
Ridgeway (John; 1938– , English)

09 Beresford (Jack; 1899–1977, English)
Cracknell (James; 1972– , English)
Karpinnen (Pertti; 1953– , Finnish)

Rowing terms include:

03 bow	coxed	skying	repechage
cox	drive	stroke	slide seat
rig	eight	**07** bowside	stretcher
04 crew	pitch	coxless	**10** catch a crab
easy	scull	give way	feathering
four	shell	gunwale	pivot point
gate	stern	regatta	strokeside
keel	**06** boatie	row over	**11** double scull
loom	button	sculler	single scull
pair	canvas	**08** coxswain	the Boat Race
quad	collar	paddling	toss the oars
rate	finish	recovery	**12** missing water
skeg	gunnel	rowlocks	shortening up
span	length	**09** ergometer	**13** getting spoons
wash	puddle	head races	**15** jumping the slide
05 blade	rating	outrigger	
catch	rigger		

Rowling, J K (1965–)

Significant works include:

16 The Casual Vacancy (2012)

17 The Cuckoo's Calling (2013)

23 Quidditch Through the Ages (2001)
The Tales of Beedle the Bard (2008)

29 Harry Potter and the Goblet of Fire (2000)

31 Harry Potter and the Deathly Hallows (2007)
Harry Potter and the Sorcerer's Stone (1998)

32 Harry Potter and the Half-Blood Prince (2005)

33 Fantastic Beasts and Where to Find Them (2001)

Harry Potter and the Chamber of Secrets (1998)

34 Harry Potter and the Order of the Phoenix (2003)

Harry Potter and the Philosopher's Stone (1997)

Harry Potter and the Prisoner of Azkaban (1999)

Significant characters include:

05 Black (Sirius)
Snape (Professor Severus)

06 Hagrid (Rubeus)
Malfoy (Draco)
Potter (Harry)

07 Granger (Hermione)
Weasley (Fred)
Weasley (George)

Weasley (Ginny)
Weasley (Ron)

09 Voldemort (Lord)

10 Dumbledore (Professor Albus)
Longbottom (Neville)
McGonagall (Professor Minerva)

11 Crookshanks
Death Eaters

rubber

Rubber types and trees include:

03 ule

04 buna
cold
foam
hard
hule
pará
root

05 butyl
crêpe
hevea
India
Lagos
sorbo

06 Panama
sponge

07 ebonite
guayule
seringa

08 castilla
Funtumia
neoprene
Silastic®

09 camelback

vulcanite

10 caoutchouc
gum elastic
mangabeira

14 high-hysteresis

rug *see* **carpet**

Rugby League

Rugby League teams and nicknames:

04 Eels (Parramatta)
Reds (Salford City)

05 Bears (Coventry; North
Sydney)
Bulls (Bradford)
Kiwis (New Zealand)
Lions (Great Britain)
Quins (Greater London)
Storm (Melbourne)

06 Eagles (Sheffield)
Giants (Huddersfield)
Hull FC
Kumuls (Papua New
Guinea)
Rhinos (Leeds)
Sharks (Cronulla-
Sutherland)
Tigers (Castleford; Wests)

Wolves (Warrington)

07 Blue Sox (Halifax)
Broncos (Brisbane)
Cowboys (North
Queensland)
Dragons (Catalans; St
George Illawarra)
Knights (Newcastle)
Raiders (Canberra)

08 Bulldogs (Batley)
Panthers (Penrith)
Roosters (Sydney)
Warriors (Wigan)
Wildcats (Wakefield)

09 Kangaroos (Australia)
Rabbitohs (South Sydney)
Tomahawks (USA)

10 Harlequins (Greater
London)
Lionhearts (England)

11 Bravehearts (Scotland)
Leeds Rhinos
St Helens RFC

13 Bradford Bulls
Widnes Vikings
Wigan Warriors

15 Irish Wolfhounds (Boston)
Leigh Centurions
Les Chanticleers (France)
Salford City Reds

16 Warrington Wolves

18 Huddersfield Giants

24 Wakefield Trinity Wildcats

Rugby League players and associated figures include:

03 Fox (Neil; 1939– , English)

04 Roby (James; 1985– , English)

05 Bevan (Brian; 1924–91, Australian/British)

06 Boston (Billy; 1934– , Welsh)
Hanley (Ellery; 1961– , English)
Murphy (Alex; 1939– , English)
Offiah (Martin; 1966– , English)

07 Edwards (Shaun; 1966– , English)
Farrell (Andy; 1975– , English)
Gregory (Andy; 1961– , English)
Meninga (Mal; 1960– , Australian)
Wellens (Paul; 1980– , English)

08 Millward (Roger; 1948– , English)
Sullivan (Jim; 1903–77, Welsh)

Rugby League terms include:

03 try

04 back
feed
lock
pack
prop
punt
Test

05 dummy
put-in
scrum

06 centre
hooker
in-goal
sin-bin
tackle
winger

07 dropout
forward
hand-off
knock on
offload
See also **sport**

offside
penalty
try line

08 40/20 rule
blood bin
drop goal
free-kick
front row
full back
gain line
goal line
halfback
handover
open side
scissors
sidestep
stand-off
turnover

09 advantage
blind side
dummy half
field goal
place kick

scrum half

10 charge down
conversion
five-eighth
penalty try
up and under
yellow card
zero tackle

11 forward pass
grubber kick
play-the-ball
sixth tackle
spear tackle
touch-in-goal

12 dead-ball line
loose forward
three-quarter
video referee

13 loose-head prop

14 acting halfback

15 twenty-metre line

Rugby Union

Rugby Union teams and nicknames:

04 Oaks (Romania)
Reds (Queensland)

05 Lelos (Georgia)
Lions (British; Irish)
Pumas (Argentina)
Wasps (London)

06 Eagles (USA)

07 Canucks (Canada)
Dragons (Gwent)

08 Brumbies (Canberra)
Les Bleus (France)

Los Teros (Uruguay)
Saracens (Watford)
Waratahs (New South
Wales)

09 All Blacks (New Zealand)
Bath Rugby
Wallabies (Australia)

10 Barbarians (invitation)
Gli Azzurri (Italy)
Gloucester
Harlequins (Greater London)

Leeds Tykes
Sale Sharks
Springboks (South Africa)

11 London Irish

13 Brave Blossoms (Japan)

14 Cherry Blossoms (Japan)

15 Leicester Tigers

16 Newcastle Falcons

17 Northampton Saints
Worcester Warriors

Rugby Union players and associated figures include:

04 Hare (Dusty; 1952– , English)
Hill (Richard; 1973– , English)

John (Barry; 1945– , Welsh)
Lomu (Jonah; 1975– , New Zealand)

Sole (David; 1962– , Scottish)
Wood (Keith; 1972– , Irish)

05 Batty (Grant; 1951– , New Zealand)
Botha (Naas; 1958– , South African)
Meads (Colin; 1936– , New Zealand)
Price (Graham; 1951– , Welsh)
Rives (Jean-Pierre; 1952– , French)
Sella (Philippe; 1962– , French)

06 Andrew (Rob; 1963– , English)
Blanco (Serge; 1958– , Venezuelan/French)
Brooke (Zinzan; 1965– , New Zealand)
Calder (Finlay; 1957– , Scottish)
Cotton (Fran; 1947– , English)
Craven (Danie; 1910–93, South African)
Davies (Jonathan; 1962– , Welsh)
Gibson (Mike; 1947– , Northern Irish)
Gregan (George; 1973– , Australian)
Irvine (Andy; 1951– , Scottish)
Kirwan (John; 1964– , New Zealand)
Lynagh (Michael; 1963– , Australian)

07 Bennett (Phil; 1948– , Welsh)
Campese (David; 1962– , Australian)
Carling (Will; 1965– , English)
Duckham (David; 1946– , English)
Edwards (Gareth; 1947– , Welsh)

Guscott (Jeremy; 1965– , English)
Jeffrey (John; 1959– , Scottish)
Jenkins (Neil; 1972– , Welsh)
Johnson (Martin; 1970– , English)
McBride (Willie John; 1940– , Northern Irish)
McLaren (Bill; 1923–2010, Scottish)
O'Reilly (Tony; 1936– , Irish)
Pienaar (François; 1967– , South African)
Tindall (Michael; 1978– , English)
Vickery (Philip; 1976– , English)

08 Beaumont (Bill; 1952– , English)
Hastings (Gavin; 1962– , Scottish)
Richards (Dean; 1963– , English)
Slattery (Fergus; 1949– , Irish)
Williams (J P R; 1949– , Welsh)
Woodward (Sir Clive; 1956– , English)

09 Dallaglio (Lawrence; 1972– , English)
Farr-Jones (Nick; 1962– , Australian)
McGeechan (Ian; 1946– , Scottish)
Underwood (Rory; 1963– , English)
Wilkinson (Jonny; 1979– , English)

10 Rutherford (John; 1955– , Scottish)

11 Fitzpatrick (Sean; 1963– , New Zealand)

12 Starmer-Smith (Nigel; 1944– , English)

Rugby Union terms include:

03 gas
tee
try

04 back
cite
feed
hack
lock
mark
maul
pack
ping
prop
ruck

05 clear
drive
dummy
girls
Lions
loose
phase
Pumas
put-in
scrum
tight
touch
wheel

06 centre

hooker
in-goal
jumper
sevens
sin-bin
tackle
uglies
winger

07 Baa-Baas
back row
binding
box kick
dropout
flanker
fly hack
fly-half
forward
hand-off
knock on
lifting
line-out
offload
offside
penalty
recycle
restart
try line

08 blood bin

collapse
crossing
drop goal
free-kick
front row
full back
gain line
goal line
halfback
handbags
miss move
open side
scissors
scrum cap
set piece
sidestep
stand-off
turnover
Twickers

09 advantage
All Blacks
back three
blind side
breakdown
crash ball
front five
garryowen
grand slam

place kick
scrum half
second row
tap tackle
third half
tight five
touchline
twenty-two
Wallabies

10 Barbarians
charge down
conversion
pack leader
penalty try
Six Nations

See also **sport**

Springboks
tap penalty
touch judge
up and under

11 Calcutta Cup
cover tackle
forward pass
grubber kick
number eight
outside half
pushover try
spear tackle
ten-man rugby
triple crown
up the jumper

wing forward

12 Bledisloe Cup
dead-ball line
inside centre
loose forward
three-quarter
video referee

13 dummy scissors
loose-head prop
outside centre
tight-head prop

14 against the head

15 truck and trailer

ruler

Rulers include:

03 aga
04 czar
duce
emir
head
khan
king
lord
rani
shah
tsar
05 begum
nawab
nizam
queen
rajah
06 Caesar

caliph
consul
Führer
kaiser
leader
mikado
prince
regent
sheikh
shogun
sultan
07 czarina
emperor
empress
monarch
pharaoh
sultana
tsarina

viceroy

08 governor
maharaja
maharani
overlord
princess
suzerain

09 commander
maharajah
maharanee
potentate
president
sovereign

10 controller

11 head of state

15 governor-general

See also **Byzantine empire**; **despot**; **Egypt**; **empire**; **governor**; **king**; **monarch**; **politics**; **president**; **prime minister**; **queen**; **Rome**

ruminant

Ruminants include:

02 ox
03 cow
04 goat

05 camel
sheep
06 musk ox

07 giraffe
08 antelope
cavicorn

09 pronghorn

Stomachs of ruminants include:

05 bible
rumen
06 bonnet

fardel
omasum
paunch

08 abomasum
09 king's-hood
manyplies

rennet-bag
reticulum
10 psalterium

See also **antelope**; **cattle**; **sheep**

Russia

Cities and notable towns in Russia include:

04 Omsk	**09** Archangel	Vladivostok
05 Kazan	Volgograd	**12** Ekaterinburg
06 Moscow	**11** Archangelsk	St Petersburg
Moskva	Chelyabinsk	**13** Yekaterinburg
Samara	Novosibirsk	
08 Novgorod	Rostov-on-Don	**15** Nizhniy Novgorod

Russian landmarks include:

03 Don	**08** Caucasus	**12** Palace Square
04 Neva	Mt Elbrus	Summer Garden
05 Urals	**09** Gorky Park	Summer Palace
Volga	Red Square	Winter Palace
07 Kremlin	**10** Lenin's tomb	**13** Ural Mountains
Siberia	**11** Mt Narodnaya	**14** Bolshoi Theatre
Steppes	Sheremetevo	**15** Hermitage Museum

Russians include:

05 Khant	Ostyak	**08** Siberian
White	**07** Bashkir	**09** Muscovite
06 Buryat	Cossack	**10** Volga Tatar

S

sage

The Seven Sages:

04 Bias (of Priene in Caria)
05 Solon (of Athens)
06 Chilon (of Sparta)
Thales (of Miletus)

08 Pittacus (of Mitylene)
09 Cleobulus (tyrant of Lindus in Rhodes)
Periander (tyrant of Corinth)

sailing

Sails include:

03 jib	kite	lateen	studding
lug	main	mizzen	**09** foreroyal
rig	stay	square	moonraker
sky	**05** genoa	**07** foretop	spinnaker
top	royal	gaff-top	**10** Bermuda rig
try	sprit	jury rig	main course
04 fore	**06** canvas	maintop	topgallant
gaff	course	spanker	**13** fore-and-aft rig
head	jigger	**08** forestay	**14** fore-topgallant

Sailor types include:

02 AB	**06** bargee	crewman	**09** boatswain
03 cox	hearty	Jack tar	buccaneer
gob	lascar	matelot	fisherman
tar	marine	oarsman	galiongee
04 mate	master	sculler	navigator
salt	pirate	skipper	yachtsman
Wren	purser	**08** cabin boy	**10** able seaman
05 bosun	rating	coxswain	bluejacket
limey	seadog	deck hand	**11** leatherneck
pilot	**07** boatman	helmsman	tarry-breeks
rower	captain	water rat	yachtswoman

Sailors and navigators include:

04 Ahab (Captain; *Moby-Dick*, 1851, Herman Melville)
Bass (George; 1771–1803/12, English)
Budd (Billy; *Billy Budd, Foretopman*, 1924, Herman Melville)
Byng (George, Viscount Torrington; 1663–1733, English)
Byng (John; 1704–57, English)
Cano (Juan Sebastian del; d.1526, Basque)
Cook (Captain James; 1728–79, English)
Dias (Bartolomeu; c.1450–1500, Portuguese)

Diaz (Bartolomeu; c.1450–1500, Portuguese)
Easy (Jack; *Mr Midshipman Easy*, 1836, Captain Frederick Marryat)
Eden (Martin; *Martin Eden*, 1909, Jack London)
Gama (Vasco da; c.1469–1525, Portuguese)
Heyn (Piet; 1578–1629, Dutch)
Home (Captain Alexander; 'Five Visions of Captain Cook', 1931, Kenneth Slessor)
Hood (Alexander, Viscount Bridport; 1727–1814, English)

Hood (Samuel, Viscount; 1724–1816, English)
Hope (*Two Years Before the Mast*, 1840, R H Dana Jnr)
Hull (Isaac; 1773–1843, US)
Jake (Congo; *Manhattan Transfer*, 1925, John Dos Passos)
Jarl (*Mardi*, 1849, Herman Melville)
King (Ernest; 1878–1956, US)
Kirk (Alan; 1888–1963, US)
Riou (Vincent; 1972– , French)
Rose (Sir Alec; 1908–91, English)
Ross (Sir James; 1800–62, Scottish)
Ross (Sir John; 1777–1856, Scottish)
Sims (W S; 1858–1936, US)
Spee (Count Maximilian von; 1861–1914, German)
Taji (*Mardi*, 1849, Herman Melville)
Toby (*Typee*, 1846, Herman Melville)
Togo (1848–1934, Japanese)
Vere (Captain Edward Fairfax; *Billy Budd, Foretopman*, 1924, Herman Melville)
Vian (Sir Philip; 1894–1968, English)

05 Acton (Sir John; 1736–1811, English)
Adams (John; c.1760–1829, English)
Adams (Will; 1564–1620, English)
Anson (George, Lord; 1697–1762, English)
Blake (Richard; *Offshore*, 1979, Penelope Fitzgerald)
Blake (Robert; 1599–1657, English)
Blake (Sir Peter; 1948–2001, New Zealand)
Bligh (Captain William; 1754–c.1817, English)
Blyth (Sir Chay; 1940– , Scottish)
Broke (Sir Philip; 1776–1841, English)
Burke (Mat; *Anna Christie*, 1922, Eugene O'Neill)
Byron (John; 1723–86, English)
Cabot (John; 1425–c.1500, Italian)
Cabot (Sebastian; 1474–1557, Venetian)
Chase (Jack; *White-Jacket*, 1850, Herman Melville)
Davis (John; c.1550–1605, English)
Davys (John; c.1550–1605, English)
Drake (Sir Francis; c.1540–96, English)
Foote (Andrew H; 1806–63, US)
Greig (Sir Samuel; 1735–88, Scottish)
Hanno (5cBC, Carthaginian)
Heijn (Piet; 1578–1629, Dutch)
Honda (Toshiaki; 1744–1821, Japanese)
Jones (John Paul; 1747–92, Scottish/ American)
Joyon (Francis; 1956– , French)
Keyes (Roger, Lord; 1872–1945, English)
Leigh (Amyas; *Westward Ho!*, 1855, Charles Kingsley)
Lyons (Edmund, Lord; 1790–1858, English)
Mahan (Alfred Thayer; 1840–1914, US)

Maryk (Lieutenant Steve; *The Caine Mutiny*, 1951, Herman Wouk)
Nares (Sir George; 1831–1915, Scottish)
Parry (Sir William Edward; 1790–1855, English)
Peary (Robert; 1856–1920, US)
Perry (Commodore Matthew; 1794–1858, US)
Perry (Oliver; 1785–1819, US)
Pound (Sir Dudley; 1877–1943, English)
Ready (Masterman; *Masterman Ready*, 1842, Captain Frederick Marryat)
Scott (Sir Percy, Baronet; 1853–1924, English)
Smith (Sir Sidney; 1764–1840, English)
Stark (Harold; 1880–1972, US)
Tommo (*Typee*, 1846, Herman Melville)
Tovey (John, Lord; 1885–1971, English)
Tromp (Cornelis; 1629–91, Dutch)
Tryon (Sir George; 1832–93, English)
Viaud (Julien; 1850–1923, French)
Yonai (Mitsumasa; 1880–1948, Japanese)

06 Aubrey (Jack; *Master and Commander*, 1970, Patrick O'Brian)
Baffin (William; c.1584–1622, English)
Barrow (Sir John; 1764–1848, English)
Beatty (David, Earl; 1871–1936, English)
Behaim (Martin; 1440–1507, German)
Benbow (John; 1653–1702, English)
Bering (Vitus; 1681–1741, Danish)
Bolton (Harry; *Redburn*, 1849, Herman Melville)
Cabral (Pedro Álvarez; c.1467–c.1520, Portuguese)
Castro (João de; 1500–48, Portuguese)
Cereno (Captain Benito; *The Piazza Tales*, 1856, Herman Melville)
Claret (Captain; *White-Jacket*, 1850, Herman Melville)
Colomb (Philip; 1831–99, Scottish)
Conner (Denis; 1942– , US)
Coutts (Russell; 1962– , New Zealand)
Cuttle (Captain Ned; *Dombey and Son*, 1848, Charles Dickens)
Dönitz (Karl; 1891–1980, German)
Duncan (Adam, Viscount; 1731–1804, Scottish)
du Pont (Samuel; 1803–65, US)
Elcano (Juan Sebastian del; d.1526, Basque)
Fisher (John, Lord; 1841–1920, English)
Fraser (Bruce, Lord; 1888–1981, English)
Guzman (Don; *Westward Ho!*, 1855, Charles Kingsley)
Halsey (William F, Jnr; 1884–1959, US)
Harris (Tom; *Two Years Before the Mast*, 1840, R H Dana Jnr)
Hipper (Franz von; 1863–1932, German)
Hornby (Sir Geoffrey; 1825–95, English)
Hornby (Sir Phipps; 1785–1867, English)

Hudson (Henry; c.1550–1611, English)
Hunter (John; 1737–1821, Scottish)
Keppel (Augustus, Viscount; 1725–86, English)
Keppel (Sir Henry; 1809–1904, English)
Mapple (Father; *Moby-Dick*, 1851, Herman Melville)
Monson (Sir William; 1569–1643, English)
Morgan (Mr; *The Adventures of Roderick Random*, 1748, Tobias Smollett)
Nagano (Osami; 1880–1947, Japanese)
Napier (Sir Charles; 1786–1860, Scottish)
Nelson (Horatio, Lord; 1758–1805, English)
Nimitz (Chester; 1885–1966, US)
Osborn (Sherard; 1822–75, English)
Porter (David; 1780–1843, US)
Porter (David Dixon; 1813–91, US)
Quiros (Pedro Fernandez de; 1565–1615, Portuguese)
Raeder (Erich; 1876–1960, German)
Ralegh (Sir Walter; 1552–1618, English)
Ramsay (Sir Bertram; 1883–1945, Scottish)
Random (Roderick; *The Adventures of Roderick Random*, 1748, Tobias Smollett)
Rodney (George, Lord; c.1718–1792, English)
Rogers (Woodes; c.1679–1732, English)
Ruyter (Michiel de; 1607–76, Dutch)
Scheer (Reinhard; 1863–1928, German)
Semmes (Raphael; 1809–77, US)
Shovel (Sir Cloudesley; 1650–1707, English)
Tasman (Abel; 1603–c.1659, Dutch)
Torres (Luis de; fl.1605–13, Spanish)
Tyrone (Edmund; *Long Day's Journey Into Night*, 1956, Eugene O'Neill)
Vernon (Edward; 1684–1757, English)
Wallis (Samuel; 1728–95, English)
Wilkes (Charles; 1798–1877, US)
Winter (Jan Willem de; 1750–1812, Dutch)

07 Ainslie (Ben; 1977– , English)
Apraxin (Fyodor, Count; 1671–1728, Russian)
Barents (Willem; d.1597, Dutch)
Belcher (Sir Edward; 1799–1877, English)
Borough (Steven; 1525–84, English)
Borough (William; 1536–99, English)
Bowling (Lieutenant Tom; *The Adventures of Roderick Random*, 1748, Tobias Smollett)
Cabrera (Pedro Álvarez; c.1467–c.1520, Portuguese)
Canaris (Wilhelm; 1887–1945, German)
Cartier (Jacques; 1491–1557, French)
Dampier (William; 1652–1715, English)
Decatur (Stephen; 1779–1820, US)
Estaing (Charles Hector, Comte d'; 1729–94, French)
Exmouth (Edward Pellew, Viscount; 1757–1833, English)
Fitzroy (Robert; 1805–65, English)

Francis (Clare; 1946– , English)
Freneau (Philip; 1752–1832, US)
Gambier (James, Lord; 1756–1833, English)
Gilbert (Sir Humphrey; 1537–83, English)
Harwood (Sir Henry; 1888–1959, English)
Hawkins (Sir John; 1532–95, English)
Hawkyns (Sir John; 1532–95, English)
Kanaris (Constantine; 1790–1877, Greek)
Kolchak (Aleksandr; 1874–1920, Russian)
Leggatt (*The Secret Sharer*, 1912, Joseph Conrad)
Lingard (Captain Tom; *Almayer's Folly*, 1895, Joseph Conrad)
Lord Jim (*Lord Jim*, 1900, Joseph Conrad)
Loveday (Bob; *The Trumpet Major*, 1880, Thomas Hardy)
Marryat (Captain Frederick; 1792–1848, English)
Maturin (Stephen; *Master and Commander*, 1970, Patrick O'Brian)
Moresby (John; 1830–1922, English)
Phillip (Arthur; 1738–1814, English)
Raleigh (Sir Walter; 1552–1618, English)
Redburn (Wellingborough; *Redburn*, 1849, Herman Melville)
Selkirk (Alexander; 1676–1721, Scottish)
Sturdee (Sir F C Doveton, Baronet; 1859–1925, English)
Weddell (James; 1787–1834, English)
Zheng He (1371–1433, Chinese)

08 Alcester (Beauchamp Seymour, Lord; 1821–95, English)
Apraksin (Fyodor, Count; 1671–1728, Russian)
Beaufort (Sir Francis; 1774–1857, British)
Boscawen (Edward; 1711–61, English)
Carteret (Philip; d.1796, English)
Cochrane (Thomas, Earl of Dundonald; 1775–1860, Scottish)
Columbus (Christopher; 1451–1506, Genoese)
Cousteau (Jacques; 1910–97, French)
Dahlgren (John; 1809–70, US)
Duquesne (Abraham, Marquis of; 1610–88, French)
Elvström (Paul; 1928– , Danish)
Eriksson (Leif; fl.1000, Icelandic)
Farragut (David; 1801–70, US)
Kotzebue (Otto von; 1787–1846, Russian)
Lysander (d.395 BC, Spartan)
Magellan (Ferdinand; c.1480–1521, Portuguese)
Pitcairn (Robert; c.1745–1770, English)
Rickover (Hyman; 1900–86, Russian/US)
Sandwich (Edward Montagu, Earl of; 1625–72, English)
Saumarez (James, Lord de; 1757–1836, British)
Spruance (Raymond; 1885–1969, US)

Vespucci (Amerigo; 1451–1512, Italian/ Spanish)
Vlamingh (Willem de; fl.1690s; Dutch)
Williams (Joe; *The 42nd Parallel*, 1930, John Dos Passos)
Yamamoto (Isoroku; 1884–1943, Japanese)

09 Beresford (Charles, Lord; 1846–1919, Irish)
Christian (Fletcher; c.1764–c.1794, English)
Duckworth (Sir John Thomas; 1748–1817, English)
Fernández (Juan; c.1536–c.1604, Spanish)
Frobisher (Sir Martin; c.1535–94, English)
Grenville (Sir Richard; c.1541–91, English)
Hindmarsh (Sir John; c.1782–1860, English)
Hythloday (Raphael; *Utopia*, 1516, Thomas More)
Joinville (François, Prince de; 1818–1900, French)
Lancaster (Sir James; c.1554–1618, English)
La Pérouse (Jean François, Comte de; 1741–88, French)
MacArthur (Dame Ellen; 1977– , English)
Selacraig (Alexander; 1676–1721, Scottish)
St Vincent (John Jervis, Earl of; 1735–1823, English)
Tourville (Anne Hilarion de Cotentin, Comte de; 1642–1701, French)
Vancouver (George; 1757–98, English)
Verrazano (Giovanni da; c.1480–1527, Italian)

10 Antalcidas (4c BC, Spartan)
Caracciolo (Francesco, Duca di Brienza; 1752–99, Neapolitan)
Chancellor (Richard; d.1556, English)
Chichester (Sir Francis; 1901–72, English)
Codrington (Sir Edward; 1770–1851, English)
Codrington (Sir Henry; 1808–77, English)
Cunningham (Andrew Browne, Viscount; 1883–1963, British)
Erik the Red (10c, Norwegian)

Hatteraick (Captain Dirk; *Guy Mannering*, 1816, Sir Walter Scott)
Hornblower (Horatio; *The Happy Return*, 1937, C S Forester)
Kempenfelt (Richard; 1718–82, English)
Mountevans (Edward, Lord; 1881–1957, English)
Poindexter (John; 1936– , US)
Shackleton (Sir Ernest; 1874–1922, Irish)
Somerville (Sir James; 1882–1949, English)
Villeneuve (Pierre de; 1763–1806, French)

11 Butterworth (Bradley; 1959– , New Zealand)
Collingwood (Cuthbert, Lord; 1750–1810, English)
Elphinstone (George Keith, Viscount Keith; 1746–1823, Scottish)
Hobart Pasha (1822–86, English)
Mountbatten (Louis, Earl; 1900–79, English)
Mountbatten (Prince Louis; 1854–1921, Austrian/British)
Thrasybulus (d.388 BC; Athenian)
White-Jacket (*White-Jacket*, 1850, Herman Melville)

12 Bougainville (Louis Antoine de; 1729–1811, French)
Knox-Johnston (Sir Robin; 1939– , English)
Nordenskjöld (Nils, Baron; 1832–1901, Swedish)
Saint Vincent (John Jervis, Earl of; 1735–1823, English)
Themistocles (c.523–c.458 BC, Athenian)

13 Carrero Blanco (Luis; 1903–73, Spanish)
La Bourdonnais (Bertrand François Mahé, Comte de; 1699–1753, French)
Medina-Sidonia (Alonzo Pérez de Gusmàn, Duque de; 1550–1619, Spanish)
Pincher Martin (*Pincher Martin*, 1956, William Golding)

14 Dumont d'Urville (Jules; 1790–1842, French)

Sailing terms include:

04 beat	**07** backing	reaching
gybe	bearing	stepping
lift	beating	under way
port	bending	windward
veer	handing	
	heeling	**09** alongside
05 abaft	in irons	beam reach
fetch	in stays	knockdown
lay up	lee helm	laying off
lee-oh!	running	letting go
	tacking	starboard
06 astern		unbending
leeway	**08** downwind	
upwind	gennaker	**10** broad reach
yawing	port tack	casting off

close reach
fitting-out
going about
ready about!
standing on
unstepping
weathering
11 breaking out
close-hauled

coming about
steerage way
weather helm
12 handing a sail
sail trimming
spilling wind
13 across the wind
hard on the wind
starboard tack

veer the anchor
14 bending on a sail
unbending a sail
15 fixing a position
points of sailing
sailing by the lee
sheeting in a sail
stepping the mast
taking soundings

See also **admiral**; **ship**

saint

Patron saints include:

03 Ivo (lawyers)
04 Adam (gardeners)
Anne (miners)
Lucy (glassworkers/writers)
Luke (artists/butchers/doctors/glassworkers/
sculptors/surgeons)
Zita (servants)
05 Agnes (girls/virgins)
Amand (brewers/hotelkeepers)
David (Wales; poets)
James (labourers)
Louis (sculptors)
Paula (widows)
Peter (fishermen)
Vitus (actors/comedians/dancers)
06 Andrew (Scotland; fishermen)
Dismas (undertakers)
Fiacre (gardeners/taxi drivers)
George (England; soldiers)
Jerome (librarians)
Joseph (carpenters/workers)
Martha (cooks/housewives/servants/waiters)
Monica (widows)
07 Barbara (builders/miners)
Cecilia (musicians/poets/singers)
Crispin (shoemakers)
Dominic (astronomers)
Dorothy (florists)
Eligius (blacksmiths/jewellers/metalworkers)
Erasmus (sailors)
Florian (firemen)
Gabriel (messengers/postal workers/radio
workers/television workers)
Gregory (singers)
Isidore (farmers)

Leonard (prisoners)
Matthew (accountants/bookkeepers/tax
collectors)
Michael (grocers/police)
Pancras (children)
Patrick (Ireland)
08 Angelico (artists)
Genesius (actors/secretaries)
Lawrence (cooks)
Nicholas (children)
09 Apollonia (dentists)
Augustine (theologians)
Homobonus (tailors)
Honoratus (bakers)
Joan of Arc (soldiers)
John Bosco (labourers)
John of God (book trade/nurses/printers)
Sebastian (athletes/soldiers)
Wenceslas (brewers)
10 Crispinian (shoemakers)
Thomas More (lawyers)
11 Christopher (motorists/sailors/travellers)
13 Martin of Tours (soldiers)
Thomas Aquinas (philosophers/scholars/
students/theologians)
14 Albert the Great (scientists)
Francis de Sales (authors/editors/journalists)
Francis of Paola (sailors)
15 Cosmas and Damian (barbers/chemists/
doctors/surgeons)
Francis of Assisi (merchants)
Gregory the Great (musicians/teachers)
Our Lady of Loreto (aviators)
Raymond Nonnatus (midwives)

Other saints include:

03 Leo
04 Anne
Bede

Gall
Joan (of Arc)
John

John (Chrysostom)
John (of the Cross)
John (the Baptist)

Jude
Lucy
Luke
Mark
Mary
Mary (Magdalene)
Paul

05 Agnes
Aidan
Alban
Basil (the Great)
Bruno (of Cologne)
Clare
Cyril
Cyril (of Alexandria)
David
Denis
Edwin
Giles
James
Peter
Titus
Vitus

06 Albert (the Great)
Andrew
Anselm
Antony
Antony (of Padua)
Aquila
Cosmas
Damian
Edmund
Edmund (Campion)
Edward (the Martyr)
George
Helena
Hilary (of Poitiers)
Jerome
Joseph
Joseph (of Arimathea)
Justin
Martha

Martin
Monica
Oliver
Oliver (Plunket)
Oswald
Philip
Prisca
Robert
Simeon
Teresa (of Avila)
Thomas
Thomas (à Becket)
Thomas (Aquinas)
Thomas (Becket)
Thomas (More)
Ursula

07 Adamnan
Ambrose
Anthony
Anthony (of Padua)
Bernard
Bernard (of Clairvaux)
Bernard (of Menthon)
Bridget
Cecilia
Clement
Columba
Crispin
Cyprian
Dominic
Dunstan
Francis (de Sales)
Francis (of Assisi)
Francis (Romulus)
Francis (Xavier)
Gregory (of Nazianzus)
Gregory (of Tours)
Gregory (the Great)
Isidore (of Seville)
Matthew
Michael
Pancras
Patrick

Stephen
Swithin
Theresa (of Lisieux)
Timothy
Vincent (de Paul)
Wilfrid

08 Albertus (Magnus)
Barnabas
Benedict (of Nursia)
Boniface
Cuthbert
Ignatius (of Loyola)
Irenaeus
Lawrence
Margaret
Matthias
Nicholas
Polycarp
Veronica
Walpurga

09 Alexander
Alexander (Nevsky)
Augustine (of Canterbury)
Augustine (of Hippo)
Catherine
Genevieve
Kentigern
Ladislaus
Methodius
Sebastian
Valentine

10 Athanasius
Bernadette
John Fisher
Stanislaus
Wenceslaus

11 Bonaventure
Christopher

12 Justin Martyr

15 Aquila and Prisca
Cosmas and Damian

salad

Salads include:

04 herb
rice
slaw

05 fruit
Greek
green
pasta

06 Caesar

potato
tomato

07 Florida
mesclum
mesclun
Niçoise
Russian
seafood
tabouli

Waldorf

08 coleslaw
couscous

09 mixed leaf
tabbouleh
three bean

11 bulgar wheat

15 mustard and cress

Salad ingredients include:

03 egg
ham
nut

04 meat
tuna

05 bacon
chard
cress
olive

06 borage
carrot
celery

endive
lovage
potato
rocket
tomato

07 anchovy
arugula
chicken
chicory
crouton

08 bacon bit
beetroot

cold meat
coleslaw
cucumber

09 boiled egg
corn-salad
green bean
new potato
radicchio
sweetcorn

10 cos lettuce
lollo rosso
mayonnaise

salad cream
watercress

11 salad burnet
spring onion

12 cherry tomato
lamb's lettuce
round lettuce

13 hard-boiled egg
roasted pepper
salad dressing

14 iceberg lettuce
sundried tomato

Salad dressings include:

06 Caesar
French

07 Italian

Russian

09 Marie Rose

10 blue cheese

mayonnaise
salad cream

11 vinaigrette

14 Thousand Island

See also **lettuce**; **vegetable**

sale

Sales include:

04 boot
fair
work

06 autumn
bazaar
forced
garage
jumble
market
online
public
spring
summer
winter

07 auction
car-boot
charity
January

private
rummage
warrant

08 bazumble
clearing
cold call
e-auction
tabletop

09 clearance
end-of-line
mail order
mid-season
pre-season
remainder
telesales
trade show

10 exhibition
exposition

fleamarket
open market
second-hand

11 bring-and-buy
closing-down
end-of-season
on-promotion
stocktaking

12 bargain offer
church bazaar
grand opening
of the century
special offer

13 online auction

14 pyramid selling

15 of bankrupt stock

salt

Salts include:

05 azide

06 aurate
borate
folate
halite
iodate
iodide

malate
oleate

07 bay salt
caprate
citrate
cyanate
ferrate

formate
lactate
maleate
nitrate
nitrite
oxalate
sorbate

tannate
toluate
viscose

08 arsenite
benzoate
butyrate
caproate

chlorate
chloride
chromate
plumbate
pyruvate
rock salt
silicate
stearate
sulphate
sulphide
sulphite

tartrate
vanadate
xanthate

09 ascorbate
bath salts
carbamate
carbonate
glutamate
manganate
molybdate

periodate
phosphate
phthalate
solar salt
succinate
table salt

10 antimonite
bichromate
dichromate
Epsom salts

liver salts
salicylate

11 bicarbonate
health salts
persulphate
sal volatile

12 borosilicate
permanganate
Rochelle-salt

13 smelling salts

satellite

Planetary satellites include:

02 Io (Jupiter)

03 Mab (Uranus)
Nix (Pluto)
Pan (Saturn)
Sao (Neptune)

04 Hati (Saturn)
Kale (Jupiter)
Kari (Saturn)
Kore (Jupiter)
Leda (Jupiter)
Loge (Saturn)
Moon (Earth)
Neso (Neptune)
Puck (Uranus)
Rhea (Saturn)
Ymir (Saturn)

05 Aegir (Saturn)
Aitne (Jupiter)
Anthe (Saturn)
Aoede (Jupiter)
Arche (Jupiter)
Ariel (Uranus)
Atlas (Saturn)
Carme (Jupiter)
Carpo (Jupiter)
Cupid (Uranus)
Dione (Saturn)
Elara (Jupiter)
Greip (Saturn)
Hydra (Pluto)
Janus (Saturn)
Metis (Jupiter)
Mimas (Saturn)
Mneme (Jupiter)
Naiad (Neptune)
Narvi (Saturn)
Skoll (Saturn)
Thebe (Jupiter)
Titan (Saturn)

06 Ananke (Jupiter)
Bestla (Saturn)

Bianca (Uranus)
Charon (Pluto)
Diemos (Mars)
Europa (Jupiter)
Fenrir (Saturn)
Helene (Saturn)
Helike (Jupiter)
Ijiraq (Saturn)
Isonoe (Jupiter)
Juliet (Uranus)
Kalyke (Jupiter)
Kiviuq (Saturn)
Nereid (Neptune)
Oberon (Uranus)
Phobos (Mars)
Phoebe (Saturn)
Portia (Uranus)
Sinope (Jupiter)
Skathi (Saturn)
Sponde (Jupiter)
Surtur (Saturn)
Tarqeq (Saturn)
Tarvos (Saturn)
Tethys (Saturn)
Thrymr (Saturn)
Thyone (Jupiter)
Triton (Neptune)

07 Autonoe (Jupiter)
Belinda (Uranus)
Caliban (Uranus)
Calypso (Saturn)
Cyllene (Jupiter)
Daphnis (Saturn)
Despina (Neptune)
Erinome (Jupiter)
Erriapo (Saturn)
Euanthe (Jupiter)
Euporie (Jupiter)
Fornjot (Saturn)
Galatea (Neptune)
Himalia (Jupiter)
Iapetus (Saturn)

Iocaste (Jupiter)
Larissa (Neptune)
Methone (Saturn)
Miranda (Uranus)
Ophelia (Uranus)
Paaliaq (Saturn)
Pallene (Saturn)
Pandora (Saturn)
Perdita (Uranus)
Proteus (Neptune)
Setebos (Uranus)
Siarnaq (Saturn)
Sycorax (Uranus)
Taygete (Jupiter)
Telesto (Saturn)
Titania (Uranus)
Umbriel (Uranus)

08 Adrastea (Jupiter)
Albiorix (Saturn)
Amalthea (Jupiter)
Bebhionn (Saturn)
Callisto (Jupiter)
Chaldene (Jupiter)
Cordelia (Uranus)
Cressida (Uranus)
Erriapus (Saturn)
Eukelade (Jupiter)
Eurydome (Jupiter)
Farbauti (Saturn)
Ganymede (Jupiter)
Halimede (Neptune)
Hegemone (Jupiter)
Hermippe (Jupiter)

Hyperion (Saturn)
Jarnsaxa (Saturn)
Lysithea (Jupiter)
Margaret (Uranus)
Orthosie (Jupiter)
Pasiphae (Jupiter)
Pasithee (Jupiter)
Prospero (Uranus)
Psamathe (Neptune)
Rosalind (Uranus)
Stephano (Uranus)
Suttungr (Saturn)
Thalassa (Neptune)
Themisto (Jupiter)
Trinculo (Uranus)

09 Bergelmir (Saturn)
Desdemona (Uranus)
Enceladus (Saturn)
Ferdinand (Uranus)
Francisco (Uranus)
Harpalyke (Jupiter)
Hyrrokkin (Saturn)
Laomedeia (Neptune)
Megaclite (Jupiter)
Praxidike (Jupiter)
Thelxinoe (Jupiter)

10 Callirrhoe (Jupiter)
Epimetheus (Saturn)
Kallichore (Jupiter)
Mundilfari (Saturn)
Polydeuces (Saturn)
Prometheus (Saturn)

Man-made satellites include:

03 CAT	Rohini	**08** Explorer	Long March
04 ECHO	**07** Asterix	Inmarsat	**11** Black Knight
05 Astra	Horizon	Intelsat	
TIROS	Sputnik	Prospero	
06 Oshumi	Transit	**09** Early Bird	

satire

Satirists include:

04 Isla (José Francisco de; 1703–81, Spanish)

05 Börne (Ludwig; 1786–1838, German)
Brown (Thomas; 1663–1704, English)
Ellis (George; 1753–1815, British)
Larra (Mariano José de; 1809–37, Spanish)
Meung (Jean de; c.1250–1305, French)
Nashe (Thomas; 1567–1601, English)
Swift (Jonathan; 1667–1745, Anglo-Irish)

06 Butler (Samuel; 1612–80, English)
Giusti (Giuseppe; 1809–50, Italian)
Horace (65–8 BC, Roman)

Lucian (c.117–c.180 AD, Greek)
Pindar (Peter; 1738–1819, English)
Wolcot (John; 1738–1819, English)

07 Barclay (John; 1582–1621, Scottish)
Juvenal (c.55–c.140 AD, Roman)
Marston (John; 1576–1634, English)
Persius (AD 34–62, Roman)
Régnier (Mathurin; 1573–1613, French)

08 Apuleius (Lucius; 2c AD, Roman)
Fischart (Johann; c.1545–90, German)
Lucilius (Gaius; c.180–c.102 BC, Roman)

Rabelais (François; 1483 or 1494–1553, French)

09 Churchill (Charles; 1731–64, English)
Delavigne (Casimir; 1793–1843, French)
Junqueiro (Ablio Manuel Guerra; 1850–

1923, Portuguese)
Whitehead (Paul; 1710–74, English)

10 Mandeville (Bernard; 1670–1733, British)

12 Konstantinov (Aleko; 1863–97, Bulgarian)

sauce

Sauces include:

02 HP®	salsa	ketchup	demi-glace
03 BBQ	satay	nuoc mam	espagnole
jus	shoyu	passata	Marie Rose
red	white	rouille	remoulade
soy	**06** catsup	sabayon	Worcester
04 fish	cheese	soubise	**10** avgolemono
hard	chilli	supreme	chaudfroid
mint	coulis	Tabasco®	Cumberland
mole	fondue	tartare	mayonnaise
ragu	fu yung	velouté	mousseline
soja	hoisin	**08** barbecue	salad cream
soya	mornay	béchamel	salsa verde
wine	nam pla	bigarade	stroganoff
05 apple	oxymel	chasseur	**11** bourguignon
bread	oyster	marinara	buerre blanc
brown	panada	piri-piri	hollandaise
caper	reform	salpicon	horseradish
cream	tamari	yakitori	vinaigrette
curry	tartar	**09** béarnaise	**12** brandy butter
fudge	tomato	black bean	sweet-and-sour
garum	tommy K	bolognese	**13** crème anglaise
gravy	**07** catchup	carbonara	salad dressing
melba	custard	chocolate	tomato ketchup
pesto	harissa	cranberry	**14** Worcestershire

sausage

Sausages include:

04 beef	salami	**08** cervelat	loukanika
lamb	square	chaurice	pepperoni
lola	summer	chourico	saucisson
pork	weenie	cocktail	**10** bauerwurst
05 blood	Wiener	drisheen	boudin noir
liver	wienie	kielbasa	cervellata
Lorne	**07** Abruzzo	linguica	Cumberland
Lyons	baloney	peperoni	knackwurst
snags	Bologna	Toulouse	knockwurst
weeny	boloney	**09** andouille	liverwurst
wurst	cabanos	bierwurst	mortadella
06 banger	chorizo	blutwurst	**11** boudin blanc
bumbar	corn dog	bockwurst	boudin rouge
garlic	kabanos	boerewors	frankfurter
kishke	klobasa	bratwurst	Wienerwurst
lolita	merguez	chipolata	**12** andouillette
mumbar	saveloy	cotechino	black pudding
polony	zampone	lap cheong	**14** braunschweiger

saw

Saws include:

03 jig		hand	**06** coping	**08** circular
rip	**05** bench		rabbet	crosscut
04 band		chain	scroll	**09** radial-arm
fret		panel	**07** compass	
hack		tenon	pruning	**11** power-driven

scale *see* music

Scandinavia

Scandinavians include:

04 Dane	**05** Swede	**08** Norseman	Varangian
Finn	**06** Norman	**09** Icelander	
Lapp	Viking	Norwegian	

See also **Denmark; Finland; Norway; Sweden**

scanner

Scanners include:

02 CT	PET	SPET	flatbed
03 CAT	**04** body	**07** barcode	**10** Emi-Scanner®

scarf

Scarfs, veils and other headcloths include:

04 caul	whisk	chuddah	kalyptra
doek	**06** chadar	chuddar	keffiyeh
haik	chador	dopatta	kerchief
hyke	cravat	dupatta	mantilla
rail	haique	foulard	neckatee
sash	khimar	kufiyah	puggaree
05 curch	kiss-me	modesty	vexillum
fichu	madras	muffler	**09** comforter
haick	rebozo	orarium	headcloth
hejab	tippet	puggery	headscarf
hijab	turban	puggree	muffettee
nikab	weeper	whimple	**10** fascinator
niqab	wimple	yashmak	lambrequin
pagri	**07** belcher	**08** babushka	**11** kiss-me-quick
patka	chaddar	chrismal	neckerchief
volet	chaddor	kaffiyeh	nightingale

Schoenberg, Arnold (1874–1951)

Significant works include:

09 *Erwartung* (1924)	*Songs of Gurre* (1910)
11 *Expectation* (1924)	*The Lucky Hand* (1924)
Gurrelieder (1910)	**14** *Pierrot Lunaire* (1912)
12 *Herzgewächse* (1923)	*Verklärte Nacht* (1902)
Moses und Aron (1957)	**17** *Die Glückliche Hand* (1924)

Foliage of the Heart (1923)
Transfigured Night (1902)
Von Heute auf Morgen (1930)
18 Six Orchestral Songs (1914)
19 A Survivor From Warsaw (1948)
Four Orchestral Songs (1932)

From Today to Tomorrow (1930)
Pelleas und Melisande (1905)
20 Five Orchestral Pieces (1912)
22 Variations for Orchestra (1928)
23 Ode to Napoleon Buonaparte (1944)

school

Schools include:

03 day	Harrow	boarding	**11** city academy
04 dame	public	Hogwarts	faith school
Eton	**07** Loretto	**09** finishing	Giggleswick
05 Rugby	primary	secondary	Gordonstoun
Slade	private	**10** Ampleforth	Marlborough
state	Roedean	Shrewsbury	Westminster
06 church	St Paul's	Stonyhurst	**12** Charterhouse
Fettes	**08** Bluecoat	Winchester	**15** Merchant Taylors'

See also **art**; **education**; **economics**; **philosophy**; **university**

Schubert, Franz (1797–1828)

Significant works include:

05 Bliss (1816)
06 Adrast (1819)
  'Tragic' (Symphony; 1816)
07 Erl King (1815)
  'Forelle' (Piano Quintet; 1819)
08 Erlkönig (1815)
  Fernando (1815)
  Swan Song (1828)
  The Diver (1813/1815)
  'The Great' (Symphony; 1825)
  'The Trout' (Piano Quintet; 1819)
09 Fierabras (1823)
  Rosamunde (1823)
  Seligkeit (1816)
  The Pledge (c.1816)
10 Der Taucher (1813/1815)
  Einsamkeit (1818)
  Loneliness (1818)
  'Unfinished' (Symphony; 1822)
11 Hagars Klage (1811)
  'The Wanderer' (Piano Fantasy; 1822)
12 Hagar's Lament (1811)
  The Magic Harp (1820)
  The Patricide (1811)
13 Das Marienbild (1818)
  Die Bürgschaft (c.1816)
  Picture of Mary (1818)
  Tantum Ergo in E (1828)

14 Der Vatermörder (1811)
  Die Winterreise (1827)
  Die Zauberharfe (1820)
  Schwanengesang (1828)
  Winter's Journey (1827)
15 Four-Year Posting (1815)
  Lazarus oratorio (1820)
  Shepherd's Lament (1815)
  The Conspirators (1823)
  The Twin Brothers (c.1820)
16 Die Verschworenen (1823)
17 'Death and the Maiden' (String Quartet; 1824)
  Die Schöne Müllerin (1823)
  Schäfers Klagelied (1815)
18 Alfonso und Estrella (1822/1854)
  Die Zwillingsbrüder (c.1820)
19 Gretchen am Spinnrade (1814)
20 Der vierjährige Posten (1815)
21 Claudine von Villabella (1815)
  Des Teufels Lustschloss (1815/1879)
  The Friends of Salamanca (c.1815)
22 Die Freunde von Salamanka (c.1815)
23 The Devil's Pleasure-Castle (1815/1879)
26 Gretchen at the Spinning Wheel (1814)
27 The Miller's Beautiful Daughter (1823)

Schumann, Robert (1810–56)

Significant works include:

06 'Spring' (Symphony; 1841)

07 *Myrthen* (1840)
'Rhenish' (Symphony; 1850)

08 *Carnaval* (1835)
Genoveva (1850)

09 *Papillons* (1832)
Poet's Love (1840)
Song Cycle (1840)

10 *Intermezzi* (1832)

11 *Butterflies* (1832)
Liederkreis (1840)
Novelletten (1838)

12 *Bunte Blätter* (1849)
Dichterliebe (1840)
Kinderszenen (1838)
Kreisleriana (1838)

13 *Fantasy Pieces* (1837)

14 *Coloured Leaves* (1849)

15 *Phantasiestücke* (1837)

16 *Album for the Young* (1848)
Spanish Love Songs (1849)

17 *Album für die Jugend* (1848)
Woman's Love and Life (1840)

18 *Davidsbündlertänze* (1837)
Études Symphoniques (1834/1852)
Paradise and the Peri (1843)

19 *Frauenliebe und Leben* (1840)
Scenes from Childhood (1838)

21 *Das Paradies und die Peri* (1843)
Spanische Liebeslieder (1849)

24 *Dances of the League of David* (1837)

science

Sciences include:

04 agri
food
life

05 earth

06 botany

07 anatomy
biology
ecology
geology
medical
natural
physics
zoology

08 chemurgy
computer
domestic
dynamics
genetics

robotics

09 acoustics
astronomy
chemistry
dietetics
economics
materials
mechanics
pathology
political
sociology

10 biophysics
entomology
geophysics
graphology
hydraulics
metallurgy
mineralogy

morphology
physiology
psychology
toxicology
veterinary

11 aeronautics
archaeology
behavioural
climatology
cybernetics
diagnostics
electronics
engineering
linguistics
mathematics
meteorology
ornithology
ultrasonics

12 aerodynamics
agricultural
anthropology
astrophysics
biochemistry
geochemistry
geographical
macrobiotics
microbiology
pharmacology

13 environmental

14 geoarchaeology
nuclear physics
radiochemistry
thermodynamics

15 electrodynamics
space technology

Scientific concepts include:

04 area (A, a)
heat (Q)
mass (m)
time (t)
work (W)

05 force (F)
power (P)

06 energy (E)
length (l)

stress
torque (T)
volume (V, v)

07 density

08 enthalpy (H)
momentum (p)
pressure
velocity (v, u)

09 frequency (f)

impedance (Z)
reactance (X)
viscosity

10 admittance (Y)
plane angle
solid angle

11 capacitance (C)
conductance (G)
power factor (pf)

susceptance (B)	permeability	self inductance (L)
temperature (T)	permittivity	surface tension
12 acceleration (a)	**13** electric force (E)	**15** angular momentum (l)
electric flux	kinetic energy	electric current (I)
illumination (E)	moment of force (M)	moment of inertia (I)
luminous flux	**14** electric charge (Q)	potential energy (V)
magnetic flux	mass rate of flow (m, M)	velocity of light (c)

Scientific instruments include:

06 strobe	telemeter	radarscope	electrosonde
07 coherer	tesla coil	radiosonde	Geissler tube
vernier	thyratron	tachograph	oscillograph
08 barostat	zymoscope	teinoscope	oscilloscope
cryostat	**10** centrifuge	thermostat	spectroscope
rheocord	collimator	**11** chronograph	**13** dipleidoscope
rheostat	eudiometer	fluoroscope	phonendoscope
09 decoherer	heliograph	Fresnel lens	tachistoscope
heliostat	humidistat	stactometer	
hodoscope	hydrophone	stauroscope	**14** absorptiometer
hydrostat	hydroscope	stroboscope	image converter
hygrostat	hygrograph	transformer	interferometer
image tube	iconoscope	transponder	torsion balance
microtome	nephograph	tunnel diode	**15** electromyograph
slide rule	pantograph	**12** dephlegmator	telethermoscope

SI prefixes include:

03 exa (10^{18}; E)	kilo (10^3; k)	tera (10^{12}; T)	milli (10^{-3}; m)
04 atto (10^{-18}; a)	mega (10^6; M)	**05** centi (10^{-2}; c)	yocto (10^{-24}; y)
deca (10^1; da)	nano (10^{-9}; n)	femto (10^{-15}; f)	yotta (10^{24}; Y)
deci (10^{-1}; d)	peta (10^{15}; P)	hecto (10^2; h)	zepto (10^{-21}; z)
giga (10^9; G)	pico (10^{-12}; p)	micro (10^{-6}; μ)	zetta (10^{21}; Z)

See also **acid**; **amino acid**; **anatomy**; **astronomy**; **atom**; **bacteria**; **biochemistry**; **biology**;
     botany; **chemistry**; **classification**; **electricity**; **engine**; **engineering**; **gas**; **gauge**;
     genetics; **geology**; **hydrocarbon**; **laboratory**; **law**; **measurement**; **medical**;
     medicine; **meteorology**; **oil**; **optics**; **ore**; **plastic**; **psychiatry**; **psychology**; **radiation**;
     study; **zoology**

science fiction

Science fiction works include:

03 *Air* (2004; Geoff Ryman)
     RUR (1921; Karel Capek)

04 *Dune* (1965; Frank Herbert)

06 *Brasyl* (2007; Ian McDonald)
     I, Robot (1950; Isaac Asimov)
     N-Space (1990; Larry Niven)
     Sirius (1940; Olaf Stapledon)

07 *Erewhon* (1872; Samuel Butler)
     Solaris (1961; Stanislaw Lem)

10 *The Last Man* (1826; Mary Wollstonecraft
     Shelley)

11 *Neuromancer* (1984; William Gibson)

Off on a Comet (1877; Jules Verne)
Rainbows End (2006; Vernor Vinge)
The Naked Sun (1957; Isaac Asimov)

12 *Frankenstein* (1818; Mary Wollstonecraft
     Shelley)
     The Lost World (1912; Arthur Conan Doyle)

13 *Brave New World* (1932; Aldous Huxley)
     Childhood's End (1953; Arthur C Clarke)
     Fahrenheit 451 (1953; Ray Bradbury)
     The Chrysalids (1955; John Wyndham)

14 *Children of Dune* (1976; Frank Herbert)
     The Kraken Wakes (1953; John Wyndham)
     The Time Machine (1895; H G Wells)

15 *Last and First Men* (1930; Olaf Stapledon)
    The Caves of Steel (1953; Isaac Asimov)
    The Drowned World (1962; J G Ballard)
    The Invisible Man (1897; H G Wells)

16 *Island of Dr Moreau* (1896; H G Wells)
    The Scarlet Plague (1912; Jack London)

17 *Rushing to Paradise* (1994; J G Ballard)
    The Midwich Cuckoos (1957; John Wyndham)
    The War of the Worlds (1898; H G Wells)

18 *Nineteen Eighty-Four* (1949; George Orwell)
    The Andromeda Strain (1968; Michael Crichton)

19 *The Day of the Triffids* (1961; John Wyndham)
    When the Sleeper Wakes (1899; H G Wells)

20 *Out of the Silent Planet* (1938; C S Lewis)
    The First Men in the Moon (1901; H G Wells)
    The Green Hills of Earth (1951; Robert Heinlein)
    The Martian Chronicles (1950; Ray Bradbury)

21 *From the Earth to the Moon* (1865; Jules Verne)
    The Left Hand of Darkness (1969; Ursula Le Guin)
    The Man in the High Castle (1962; Philip K Dick)

22 *Stranger in a Strange Land* (1961; Robert Heinlein)

23 *20,000 Leagues Under the Sea* (1870; Jules Verne)
    The Unparalleled Invasion (1910; Jack London)

28 *Journey to the Centre of the Earth* (1864; Jules Verne)

30 *Do Androids Dream of Electric Sheep?* (1968; Philip K Dick)
    The Hitchhiker's Guide to the Galaxy (1979; Douglas Adams)

33 *Frankenstein or the Modern Prometheus* (1818; Mary Wollstonecraft Shelley)
    The Strange Case of Dr Jekyll and Mr Hyde (1886; Robert Louis Stevenson)

Science fiction and fantasy writers include:

04 Dick (Philip K; 1928–82, US)
    Pohl (Frederik; 1919– , US)

05 Adams (Douglas; 1952–2001, English)
    Banks (Iain M; 1954–2013, Scottish)
    Capek (Karel; 1890–1938, Czech)
    Hoyle (Sir Fred; 1915–2001, English)
    Lewis (C S; 1898–1963, British)
    Simak (Clifford D; 1904–88, US)
    Smith (E E; 1890–1965, US)
    Verne (Jules; 1828–1905, French)
    Wells (H G; 1866–1946, English)
    White (T H; 1906–64, English)

06 Aldiss (Brian; 1925– , English)
    Asimov (Isaac; 1920–92, Russian/US)
    Atwood (Margaret; 1939– , Canadian)
    Bishop (Michael; 1945– , US)
    Brooks (Terry; 1944– , US)
    Clarke (Sir Arthur C; 1917–2008, English)
    Gaiman (Neil; 1960– , English)
    Kneale (Nigel; 1922–2006, Manx)
    Le Guin (Ursula K; 1929– , US)
    Orwell (George; 1903–50, English)

07 Ballard (J G; 1930–2009, Chinese/British)
    Herbert (Frank; 1920–86, US)
    Hubbard (L Ron; 1911–86, US)
    Pullman (Philip; 1946– , English)
    Resnick (Michael; 1942– , US)
    Serling (Rod; 1924–75, US)
    Tolkien (J R R; 1892–1973, South African/British)
    Wyndham (John; 1903–69, English)

08 Bradbury (Ray; 1920–2012, US)
    Crichton (Michael; 1942–2008, US)
    Hamilton (Edmond; 1904–77, US)
    Harrison (M John; 1945– , English)
    Heinlein (Robert; 1907–88, US)
    McDonald (Ian; 1960– , Northern Irish)
    Moorcock (Michael; 1939– , English)
    Vonnegut (Kurt; 1922–2007, US)

09 Lovecraft (H P; 1890–1937, US)
    Pratchett (Terry; 1948– , English)

11 Tsiolkovsky (Konstantin; 1857–1935, Russian)

Scott, Sir Walter (1771–1832)

Significant works include:

06 *Rob Roy* (1817)
    Rokeby (1813)

07 *Ivanhoe* (1819)

Marmion (1808)

08 *The Abbot* (1820)
    Waverley (1814)

09 *The Pirate* (1821)
   Woodstock (1826)

10 *Kenilworth* (1821)

11 *Halidon Hill* (1822)
   Redgauntlet (1824)
   The Talisman (1825)

12 *Guy Mannering* (1815)
   St Ronan's Well (1823)
   The Antiquary (1816)
   The Betrothed (1825)
   The Monastery (1820)

13 *Macduff's Cross* (1823)
   The Black Dwarf (1816)

14 *Quentin Durward* (1823)

15 *Castle Dangerous* (1831)

16 *Anne of Geierstein* (1829)
   Peveril of the Peak (1823)
   The Highland Widow (1827)
   The Lady of the Lake (1810)

17 *A Legend of Montrose* (1819)
   History of Scotland (1829–30)

The Lord of the Isles (1815)

18 *Count Robert of Paris* (1831)
   Harold the Dauntless (1817)
   The Fair Maid of Perth (1828)
   The Fortunes of Nigel (1822)

19 *Lives of the Novelists* (1821)
   Tales of the Crusaders (1825)

20 *The Bridal of Triermain* (1813)
   The Bride of Lammermoor (1819)
   The Heart of Midlothian (1818)

21 *The Tale of Old Mortality* (1816)

22 *The Tales of a Grandfather* (1827–30)

23 *The Lay of the Last Minstrel* (1805)

24 *Chronicles of the Canongate* (1827–28)
   Paul's Letters to His Kinfolk (1816)

27 *The Life of Napoleon Buonaparte* (1827)

29 *Minstrelsy of the Scottish Border* (1802–03)

31 *Provincial Antiquities of Scotland* (1819–26)

32 *Letters on Demonology and Witchcraft*
   (1830)

Significant characters include:

03 Lee (Alice)
   Lee (Colonel)
   Lee (Sir Henry)

04 Dods (Mistress Meg)
   Gray (Menie)
   John (Prince)
   Lyle (Annot)
   Tuck (Friar)

05 Balue (Cardinal John of)
   Binks (Sir Bingo)
   Blood (Colonel Thomas)
   Bunce (Jack)
   Deans (Davie 'Douce Davie')
   Deans ('Effie' Euphemia)
   Deans (Jeanie)
   Ewart (Nanty)
   Gurth (the Swineherd)
   James (King of England)
   Lesly (Ludovic 'le Balafre')
   Liege (Bishop of)
   Louis (King of France)
   Lovel
   Nixon (Cristal)
   Oates (Titus)
   Smith (Henry)
   Smith (Wayland)
   Troil (Brenda)
   Troil (Magnus)
   Troil (Minna)
   Wamba

06 Albany (Duke of)

Argyle (Archibald, Duke of)
Ashton (Lady)
Ashton (Lucy)
Ashton (Sir William, Lord Keeper)
Avenel (Julian)
Avenel (Mary)
Avenel (White Lady of)
Baliol (Mrs Martha Bethune)
Butler (Reuben)
de Lacy (Damian)
de Lacy (Hugo)
de Lacy (Randal)
Geddes (Joshua)
Glover (Catharine)
Glover (Simon)
Graeme (Magdalen)
Graeme (Roland)
Halcro (Claud)
Heriot (George 'Jinglin' Geordie)
Hudson (Sir Geoffrey)
James I (King of England)
Jarvie (Bailie Nicol)
Le Dain (Oliver)
Morton (Henry)
Murray (Regent)
Philip (King of France and Navarre)
Ramsay (David)
Ramsay (Margaret)
Robert (King of Scotland)
Rob Roy
Rowena (Lady)
Seyton (Catherine)

Sludge (Dickie 'Flibbertigibbet')
Tyrrel (Frank)
Ulrica (Dame Urfried)
Varney (Sir Richard)
Vernon (Diana 'Di')
Warden (Henry)
Wilson (Alison)

07 Ambrose (Father, Abbot of Kennaquhair)
Austria (Leopold, Grand Duke of)
Bertram (Harry)
Charles (King of England)
Charles (Prince)
Clement (Father)
de Clare (Lady Clare)
de Croye (Isabelle)
Dinmont (Dandie)
Durward (Quentin)
Elliott ('Hobbie' Halbert)
Eustace (Father)
Everard (Colonel Markham)
Fenella
Glossin (Gilbert)
Hartley (Dr Adam)
Ivanhoe (Wilfred of Ivanhoe)
Kenneth (Sir)
Langley (Sir Frederick)
Latimer (Darsie)
Louis XI (King of France)
MacIvor (Fergus)
MacIvor (Flora)
MacTurk (Captain Hector)
Marmion (Lord)
Mertoun (Basil)
Mertoun (Mordaunt)
Mowbray (Clara)
Mowbray (John, Laird of St Ronan's)
Oldbuck (Jonathan)
Peebles (Peter)
Peveril (Julian)
Peveril (Sir Geoffrey)
Ramorny (Sir John)
Rebecca
Richard (King of England)
Robsart (Amy)
Robsart (Sir Hugh)
Rothsay (Duke of Rothsay, Prince David of
   Scotland)
Sampson (Dominie Abel)
Shafton (Sir Piercie)
Tomkins (Joseph)
Wardour (Sir Arthur)
Wilfred (of Ivanhoe)

08 Bean Lean (Donald)
Berenger (Eveline)
Boniface (Abbot)
Bothwell (Sargent)
Burgundy (Charles the Bold, Duke of)

Charles I
Conachar
Cromwell (Oliver)
Dalgarno (Lord)
Dennison (Jenny)
de Wilton (Sir Ralph)
Evandale (Lord)
Fairford (Alan)
Fairford (Saunders)
Galeotti (Martius/Marti/Martivalle)
Gardiner (Colonel)
Headrigg (Cuthbert 'Cuddie')
Headrigg (Mause)
Hereward
Locksley
MacBriar (Ephraim)
M'Combich (Robin Oig)
Menteith (Lord)
Montrose (Earl of)
Musgrave (Sir Richard)
Olifaunt (Nigel, Lord Glenvarloch)
Philip II (King of France and Navarre)
Pleydell (Paulus)
Porteous (Captain John)
Richard I (Richard, Coeur-de-Lion)
Staunton (Sir George)
Steenson (Willie 'Wandering Willie')
Trapbois
Trapbois (Martha)
Waverley (Edward)
Waverley (Sir Everard)
Wildfire (Madge)
Wildrake (Roger)

09 Armstrong (Grace)
Bellenden (Edith)
Biederman (Arnold)
Brenhilda (Countess of Paris)
Briennius (Nicephorus)
Charles II
Chiffinch
Christian (Edward)
Cleveland (Captain Clement)
Cranstoun (Lord)
de la Marck (William)
Deloraine (Sir William)
Elizabeth (Queen of England)
Ellieslaw (Laird of)
Gellatley (Davie)
Hagenbach (Archibald von)
Henderson (Elias)
Leicester (Robert Dudley, Earl of)
Lochinvar
Lochleven (Lady of)
Macgregor (Rob Roy)
MacTavish ('Elspat' Elspeth)
Mannering (Colonel Guy)
Mannering (Julia)
Maugrabin (Hayraddin)

Merrilies (Meg)
Moniplies (Richie)
Ochiltree (Edie)
Pattieson (Peter)
Philipson (Arthur)
Plumdamas (Peter)
Proudfute (Oliver)
Ratcliffe (James 'Daddy Rat')
Robert III (King of Scotland)
Touchwood (Peregrine)
Wakefield (Harry)
Yellowley (Barbara 'Baby')
Yellowley (Triptolemus)

10 Berengaria (Queen)
Black Dwarf
Buckingham (George Villiers, Duke of)
Campo-Basso (Count of)
Croftangry (Chrystal)
de Beverley (Constance)
des Comines (Philip)
Dryfesdale
Elizabeth I (Queen of England)
Geierstein
Geierstein (Anne of)
Hatteraick (Captain Dirk)
Holdenough (Reverend Nehemiah)
Humgudgeon
Lowestoffe (Reginald)
Macwheeble (Bailie Duncan)
Middlemass (Richard)
Montserrat (Conrade, Marquis of)
Murdockson (Meg)
Nectabanus
Penfeather (Lady Penelope)
Quackleben (Dr Quentin)
Ravenswood (Edgar, Master of Ravenswood)
Rintherout (Jenny)
Saddletree (Bartoline)
Snailsfoot (Bryce)
Suddlechop (Benjamin)
Suddlechop (Dame Ursula/Dame Ursley)

11 Anna Comnena
Balchristie (Jenny)

Balderstone (Caleb)
Blattergowl (Mr)
Bradwardine (Baron of)
Bradwardine (Rose)
Bridgenorth (Alice)
Bridgenorth (Major)
Donnerhugel (Rudolph)
Dumbiedikes (John 'Jock' Dumbie, Laird of)
Etherington (Earl of)
Fairservice (Andrew)
Glendinning (Simon)
Glendinning (Sir Halbert)
Isaac of York
Mucklewrath (Habbakkuk)
Plantagenet (Edith)
Redgauntlet (Lilias)
The Minstrel
Tressillian (Edmund)

12 Balmawhapple (Laird of)
Bois-Guilbert (Sir Brian de)
Buonaventure (Father)
Cleishbotham (Jedediah)
Front-de-Boeuf (Sir Reginald)
Hob the Miller
Malagrowther (Sir Mungo)
Mucklebackit (Saunders)
Old Mortality
Osbaldistone ('Frank' Francis)
Osbaldistone (Rashleigh)
Osbaldistone (Sir Hildebrand)

13 Dousterswivel (Herman)
Kettledrummle (Reverend Gabriel)

14 Cedric the Saxon
Charles the Bold (Duke of Burgundy)
Mysie of the Mill
Saladin the Turk

15 Abbot of Unreason
Alexius Comnenus
Balfour of Burley (John)
Margaret of Anjou
Torquil of the Oak
Tristan l'Hermite

Scottish

Scottish clans include:

03 Gow	Shaw	Logan	Eliott
Hay	**05** Agnew	Monro	Elliot
04 Boyd	Baird	Munro	Forbes
Gunn	Boyle	Scott	Fraser
Haig	Bruce		Gordon
Home	Durie	**06** Bisset	Graeme
Hume	Eliot	Brodie	Graham
Kerr	Grant	Buchan	Hannay
Rose	Innes	Dunbar	Hunter
Ross	Keith	Duncan	Irvine
		Dundas	

Irving
Lamond
Lamont
Lauder
Lennox
Leslie
Macfie
Mackay
Macnab
Macrae
Moffat
Monroe
Murray
Napier
Ogilvy
Ramsay
Stuart

07 Balfour
Barclay
Burnett
Cameron
Cumming
Douglas
Erskine
Guthrie
Hopkirk
Jardine
Kennedy
Lindsay
MacBain
MacBean

MacColl
Macduff
MacEwen
MacIver
Maclean
Macleod
Macneil
Macphee
Malcolm
Maxwell
Menzies
Ogilvie
Stewart
Wallace

08 Anderson
Buchanan
Campbell
Carnegie
Cathcart
Chisholm
Crawford
Crichton
Cummings
Davidson
Drummond
Ferguson
Hamilton
Johnston
Lockhart
Macaulay
MacInnes

MacLaine
MacLaren
Macneill
Macnicol
MacQueen
Maitland
Matheson
Morrison
Oliphant
Sinclair
Stirling
Urquhart

09 Armstrong
Colquhoun
Fergusson
Henderson
Johnstone
MacAlpine
MacAndrew
MacArthur
MacCallum
Macdonald
Macdonell
Macdowall
Macduffie
Macgregor
Macintosh
Macintyre
Mackenzie
Mackinnon
MacLaurin

MacLennon
Macmillan
Macquarie
Mathieson
Nicholson
Robertson

10 Anstruther
Arbuthnott
Carmichael
Clanranald
Cunningham
MacAlister
Macdonnell
Macdougall
Macfarlane
Mackintosh
MacLachlan
Macpherson
Macquarrie
Moncrieffe
Sutherland

11 Clan Chattan
Farquharson
MacAllister
MacKendrick
MacLauchlan
MacLaughlan
Macnaughton

12 MacGillivray

Scottish boys' names include:

03 Ian
Rab
04 Doug
Euan
Ewan
Ewen
Greg
Iain

Jock
05 Angus
Arran
Blair
Calum
Clyde
Colin
Craig

Logan
Lorne
Sandy
06 Callum
Dougie
Gordon
Gregor
Hamish

Kelvin
Rabbie
Ranald
07 Cameron
Douglas
Malcolm
08 Campbell

Scottish girls' names include:

03 Rae
04 Iona
Isla
Jess

05 Ailsa
Isbel
Lorna
Morag

06 Aileen
Elspet
Ishbel
Lilias

Mhàiri
Vanora
07 Elspeth
08 Catriona

See also **football**; **monarch**; **town**; **United Kingdom**

screenwriter see play

sculpture

Sculpture types include:

04 bust
cast
head
herm
kore
05 group
06 bronze

effigy
figure
kouros
marble
relief
statue
07 carving

kinetic
telamon
waxwork
08 caryatid
Daibutsu
figurine
maquette

moulding
09 bas-relief
death mask
statuette
10 high-relief
11 plaster cast

Sculptures and statues include:

04 *Eros* (Alfred Gilbert; 1892–93)
Zeus (Phidias; c.430 BC)

05 *David* (Michelangelo; 1504)
Moses (Michelangelo; c.1513–15)
Pietà (Michelangelo; 1499)

06 *Balzac* (Auguste Rodin; 1898)
Hermes (Praxiteles; 4c BC)

07 *Anteros* (Alfred Gilbert; 1892–93)
Bacchus (Michelangelo; 1496–97)
Liberty (Auguste Bartholdi; 1886)
Lincoln (Daniel Chester French; 1918–22)
Perseus (Benvenuto Cellini; 1545–54)
The Kiss (Auguste Rodin; 1888–89)

08 *Mahamuni* (2c AD; Myanmar)

10 *Discobolus* (Myron; 5c BC)
Doryphorus (Myron; 5c BC)
Single Form (Dame Barbara Hepworth; 1963)

The Thinker (Auguste Rodin; 1881)

11 *Gomateswara* (983; India)
Pierced Form (Dame Barbara Hepworth; 1931)
Spear Bearer (Myron; 5c BC)
Venus de Milo (unknown; c.100 BC)

12 *Elgin Marbles* (ancient; Athens)

13 *Discus Thrower* (Myron; 5c BC)

14 *The Age of Bronze* (Auguste Rodin; 1877)
The Gates of Hell (Auguste Rodin; 1880–1917)
The Three Graces (Antonio Canova; 1814)

15 *Angel of the North* (Antony Gormley; 1998)
Buddhas of Bamian (ancient; Afghanistan)
Christ in Majesty (Sir Jacob Epstein; 1957)
Madonna and Child (Henry Moore; 1943–4)

19 *The Burghers of Calais* (Auguste Rodin; 1886–95)

Sculptors include:

03 Arp (Hans; 1887–1966, Alsatian)
Arp (Jean; 1887–1966, Alsatian)
Ray (Man; 1890–1976, US)

04 Bell (John; 1811–95, English)
Bone (Phyllis; 1896–1972, Scottish)
Boyd (Arthur; 1920–99, Australian)
Cano (Alonso; 1601–67, Spanish)
Caro (Sir Anthony; 1924– , English)
Eldh (Carl; 1873–1954, Swedish)
Gabo (Naum; 1890–1977, US)
Gill (Eric; 1882–1940, English)
King (Phillip; 1934– , British)
Mach (David; 1956– , Scottish)
Rude (François; 1784–1855, French)
Vyse (Charles; 1882–1971, English)
Zorn (Anders; 1860–1920, Swedish)

05 Akers (Benjamin Paul; 1825–61, US)
Andre (Carl; 1935– , US)
Appel (Karel; 1921–2006, Dutch)
Bacon (John; 1740–99, English)
Baily (Edward Hodges; 1788–1867, English)

Banco (Nanni di; c.1384–1421, Italian)
Banks (Thomas; 1735–1805, English)
Barye (Antoine Louis; 1796–1875, French)
Beuys (Joseph; 1921–86, German)
Boehm (Sir Joseph Edgar; 1834–90, Austrian/ British)
Bosio (François Joseph, Baron; 1769–1845, French)
Boyle (Jimmy; 1944– , Scottish)
César (1921–1998, French)
Cragg (Tony; 1949– , English)
Dalou (Jules; 1838–1902, French)
Davey (Grenville; 1961– , English)
Drury (Alfred; 1857–1944, English)
Ernst (Max; 1891–1976, German)
Foley (John Henry; 1818–74, Irish)
Frink (Dame Elisabeth; 1930–93, English)
Hesse (Eva; 1936–70, German/US)
Johns (Jasper; 1930– , US)
Jones (Allen; 1937– , English)
Koons (Jeff; 1955– , US)
Leoni (Leone; 1509–90, Italian)

Manzú (Giacomo; 1908–91, Italian)
Moore (Henry; 1898–1986, English)
Myron (5c BC, Greek)
Notke (Bernt; c.1440–1509, German)
Pilon (Germain; 1537–90, French)
Puget (Pierre; 1622–94, French)
Quinn (Marc; 1964– , English)
Rauch (Christian Daniel; 1777–1857,
  German)
Rodin (Auguste; 1840–1917, French)
Segal (George; 1924–2000, US)
Serra (Richard; 1939– , US)
Smith (David; 1906–65, US)
Stead (Tim; 1952–2000, English)
Story (William Wetmore; 1819–95, US)
Stoss (Veit; 1447–1533, German)
Stozz (Veit; 1447–1533, German)
Theed (William; 1804–91, English)

06 Akeley (Carl; 1864–1926, US)
Alonso (Mateo; 1878–1955, Argentine)
Ayrton (Michael; 1921–75, English)
Barton (Glenys; 1944– , English)
Butler (Reg; 1913–81, English)
Calder (Alexander; 1898–1976, US)
Canova (Antonio; 1757–1822, Italian)
Cousin (Jean; 1501–c.1590, French)
Deacon (Richard; 1949– , British)
Dobson (Frank; 1888–1963, English)
Floris (Cornelis; c.1514/1520–75, Dutch)
French (Daniel Chester; 1850–1931, US)
Gibson (John; 1790–1866, British)
Goujon (Jean; c.1510–c.1568, French)
Hanson (Duane; 1925–96, US)
Hatoum (Mona; 1952– , Lebanese/British)
Hermes (Gertrude; 1901–83, English)
Houdon (Jean Antoine; 1741–1828, French)
Jagger (Charles Sargeant; 1885–1934, English)
Kapoor (Anish; 1954– , Indian/British)
Keyser (Hendrik de; 1565–1621, Dutch)
Marini (Marino; 1901–80, Italian)
Martin (Kenneth; 1905–84, English)
Martin (Mary; 1907–69, English)
Michel (Claude; 1738–1814, French)
Milles (Carl; 1875–1955, Swedish/US)
Nauman (Bruce; 1941– , US)
Pisano (Andrea; c.1270–1349, Italian)
Pisano (Giovanni; c.1250–c.1320, Italian)
Pisano (Nicola; c.1225–c.1284, Italian)
Powers (Hiram; 1805–73, US)
Rogers (Randolph; 1825–92, US)
Schotz (Benno; 1891–1986, Estonian)
Scopas (4c BC, Greek)
Sluter (Claus; c.1350–1405, Flemish)
Steell (Sir John; 1804–91, Scottish)
Walker (Dame Ethel; 1861–1951, Scottish)
Wright (Patience; 1725–86, American)
Wyllie (George; 1921–2012, Scottish)
Zorach (William; 1887–1966, Lithuanian/US)

07 Algardi (Alessandro; 1598–1654, Italian)
Álvarez (José; 1768–1827, Spanish)
Antenor (6c BC, Greek)
Barlach (Ernst; 1870–1938, German)
Bernini (Gian Lorenzo; 1598–1680, Italian)
Bologna (Giovanni; 1524–1608, Flemish)
Bonheur (Rosa; 1822–99, French)
Borglum (Gutzon; 1867–1941, US)
Brisley (Stuart; 1933– , English)
Cellini (Benvenuto; 1500–71, Italian)
Christo (1935– , Bulgarian/US)
Claudel (Camille; 1864–1943, French)
Coustou (Guillaume; 1678–1746, French)
Coustou (Guillaume; 1716–77, French)
Coustou (Nicolas; 1658–1733, French)
da Vinci (Leonardo; 1452–1519, Italian)
Despiau (Charles; 1874–1946, French)
Duchamp (Marcel; 1887–1968, French/US)
Epstein (Sir Jacob; 1880–1959, US/British)
Flaxman (John; 1755–1826, English)
Gibbons (Grinling; 1648–1721, English)
Gilbert (Sir Alfred; 1854–1934, English)
Gormley (Antony; 1950– , English)
Hoffman (Malvina; 1887–1966, US)
Jónsson (Einar; 1874–1954, Icelandic)
Klinger (Max; 1857–1920, German)
Lambert (George; 1873–1930, Australian)
Laurens (Henri; 1885–1954, French)
Le Sueur (Hubert; c.1580–c.1670, French)
Longman (Evelyn; 1874–1954, US)
Maillol (Aristide; 1861–1944, French)
Manship (Paul; 1885–1966, US)
Millett (Kate; 1934– , US)
Noguchi (Isamu; 1904–88, US)
Orcagna (c.1308–68, Italian)
Permeke (Constant; 1886–1951, Belgian)
Pevsner (Antoine; 1886–1962, Russian/
  French)
Phidias (b.c.500 BC, Greek)
Pigalle (Jean Baptiste; 1714–85, French)
Quercia (Jacopo della; c.1367–1438, Italian)
Richier (Germaine; 1904–59, French)
Samaras (Lucas; 1936– , Greek/US)
Schadow (Gottfried; 1764–1850, Prussian)
Schadow (Rudolf; 1786–1822, Prussian)
Stevens (Alfred; 1818–75, English)
Turrell (James; 1943– , US)
Vischer (Peter; 1455–1529, German)
Whitney (Anne; 1821–1915, US)
Whitney (Gertrude Vanderbilt; 1875–1942,
  US)
Wilding (Alison; 1948– , English)
Woolner (Thomas; 1826–92, English)
Zadkine (Ossip; 1890–1967, Russian/French)

08 Aaltonen (Wäinö; 1894–1966, Finnish)
Ammanati (Bartolommeo; 1511–92, Italian)
Armitage (Kenneth; 1916–2002, English)
Armstead (Henry Hugh; 1828–1905, English)

Boccioni (Umberto; 1882–1916, Italian)
Brancusi (Constantin; 1876–1957,
 Romanian)
Carpeaux (Jean Baptiste; 1827–75, French)
Chadwick (Lynn; 1914–2003, English)
Chantrey (Sir Francis; 1781–1841, English)
Coysevox (Antoine; 1640–1720, French)
Crawford (Thomas; 1814–57, US)
Davidson (Jo; 1883–1952, US)
Falconet (Étienne Maurice; 1716–91,
 French)
Filarete (Antonio; c.1400–c.1469,
 Florentine)
Flanagan (Barry; 1941–2009, British)
Frampton (Sir George; 1860–1928, English)
Ghiberti (Lorenzo; 1378–1455, Italian)
Girardon (François; 1630–1715, French)
González (Julio; 1876–1942, Spanish)
Hepworth (Dame Barbara; 1903–75,
 English)
Kollwitz (Käthe; 1867–1945, German)
Lachaise (Gaston; 1882–1935, US)
Landseer (Sir Edwin; 1802–73, English)
Lipchitz (Jacques; 1891–1973, Lithuanian/
 French)
Lombardo (Pietro; c.1433–1515, Italian)
Marshall (William Calder; 1813–94, Scottish)
Nadelman (Elie; 1882–1946, Polish/US)
Nevelson (Louise; 1900–88, US)
Paolozzi (Sir Eduardo; 1924–2005, Scottish)
Pheidias (b.c.500 BC, Greek)
Rysbrack (Michael; c.1693–1770, Flemish)
Stebbins (Emma; 1815–82, US)
St-Phalle (Niki de; 1930–2002, French)
Tinguely (Jean; 1925–91, Swiss)

09 Alcamenes (5 C BC, Greek)
Bartholdi (Auguste; 1834–1904, French)
Bartolini (Lorenzo; 1777–1850, Italian)
Borromini (Francesco; 1599–1667, Italian)
Bourdelle (Antoine; 1861–1929, French)
Bourgeois (Louise; 1911–2010, French/US)
Donatello (c.1386–1466, Florentine)
Euphranor (4 C BC, Greek)
Falguière (Alexandre; 1831–1900, French)
Greenough (Horatio; 1805–52, US)
Houshiary (Shirazeh; 1955– , Iranian/
 British)
Leochares (fl.c.350–330 BC, Greek)
McWilliam (F E; 1909–92, Northern Irish)
Nollekens (Joseph; 1737–1823, English)
Oldenburg (Claes; 1929– , Swedish/US)
Rietschel (Ernst; 1804–61, German)
Roubiliac (Louis François; 1702/1705–1762,
 French)
Roubillac (Louis François; 1702/1705–1762,
 French)

See also **monument**

Sansovino (1460–1529, Italian)
Sansovino (Jacopo; 1486–1570, Italian)
Schlemmer (Oskar; 1888–1943, German)
St-Gaudens (Augustus; 1848–1907, US)
Sveinsson (Ásmundur; 1893–1982,
 Icelandic)
Whiteread (Rachel; 1963– , English)
Willumsen (J F; 1863–1958, Danish)

10 Antokolski (Mark; 1843–1902, Russian)
Archipenko (Alexander; 1880–1964, US)
Bandinelli (Baccio; 1493–1560, Italian)
Bartholomé (Albert; 1848–1928, French)
Berruguete (Alonso; c.1489–1561, Spanish)
della Robia (Luca; c.1400–82, Italian)
Giacometti (Alberto; 1901–66, Swiss)
Hildebrand (Adolf; 1847–1921, German)
Kennington (Eric; 1888–1960, English)
Marochetti (Carlo, Baron; 1805–67, Italian)
Michelozzi (Michelozzo di Bartolommeo;
 1396–1472, Italian)
Modigliani (Amedeo; 1884–1920, Italian)
Polyclitus (5c BC, Greek)
Praxiteles (4c BC, Greek)
Rossellino (Antonio; 1427–c.1479, Italian)
Rossellino (Bernardo; 1409–64, Italian)
Schwitters (Kurt; 1887–1948, German)
Torrigiano (Pietro; c.1472–1522, Italian)
Verrocchio (Andrea del; c.1435–c.1488,
 Italian)

11 Abakanowicz (Magdalena; 1930– , Polish)
della Robbia (Luca; c.1400–82, Italian)
Goldsworthy (Andy; 1956– , English)
Saint-Phalle (Niki de; 1930–2002, French)
Scheemakers (Pieter; 1691–1781, Flemish)
Thornycroft (Sir Hamo; 1850–1925, English)
Thorvaldsen (Bertel; 1770–1844, Danish)

12 Brunelleschi (1377–1446, Italian)
David d'Angers (Pierre Jean; 1789–1856,
 French)
Francheville (Pierre; 1548–1616, French)
Franqueville (Pierre; 1548–1616, French)
Jeanne-Claude (1935–2009, French/US)
MacGillivray (James Pittendrigh; 1856–
 1938, Scottish)
Michelangelo (1475–1564, Italian)
Saint-Gaudens (Augustus; 1848–1907, US)

13 Duchamp-Villon (Raymond; 1876–1918,
 French)
Tino di Camaino (c.1285–1337, Italian)

14 Gaudier-Brzeska (Henri; 1891–1915, French)

15 Arnolfo di Cambio (1232–1302, Italian)
Leonardo da Vinci (1452–1519, Italian)
Riemenschneider (Tilman; 1460–1531,
 German)

sea

Seas include:

03 Red (Egypt/Eritrea/Israel/Jordan/Saudi Arabia/
Sudan/Yemen)

04 Aral (Kazakhstan/Uzbekistan)
Azov (Russia/Ukraine)
Dead (Israel/Jordan)
East (Japan/North Korea/Russia/South Korea)
Java (Indonesia)
Kara (Russia)
Ross (Antarctica)
Sulu (Philippines)

05 Banda (East Timor/Indonesia)
Black (Bulgaria/Georgia/Romania/Russia/
Turkey/Ukraine)
Coral (Australia/Papua New Guinea/
Solomon Islands/Vanuatu)
Crete (Greece)
Irish (Ireland/Isle of Man/England/Scotland/
Wales)
Japan (Japan/North Korea/Russia/South
Korea)
North (Denmark/Germany/The Netherlands/
Norway/England/Scotland)
Timor (Australia/East Timor/Indonesia)
White (Russia)

06 Aegean (Greece/Turkey)
Baltic (Denmark/Estonia/Finland/Germany/
Latvia/Lithuania/Poland/Russia/Sweden)
Bering (Russia/USA)
Celtic (Ireland/Wales/England)
Flores (Indonesia)
Inland (Japan)
Ionian (Greece/Italy)
Laptev (Russia)
Nan Hai (Brunei/Cambodia/China/Malaysia/
Philippines/Taiwan/Thailand/Vietnam)
Scotia (Antarctica/Argentina/Falkland
Islands)
Tasman (Australia/New Zealand)
Yellow (China/Japan/North Korea/South
Korea)

07 Andaman (Indonesia/Myanmar/Thailand)
Arabian (India/Iran/Oman/Pakistan/Somalia/
Yemen)
Arafura (Australia/East Timor/Indonesia)
Barents (Norway/Russia)
Caspian (Azerbaijan/Iran/Kazakhstan/Russia/
Turkmenistan)

Celebes (Indonesia/Malaysia/Philippines)
Chukchi (Russia/USA)
Dong Hai (China/Japan/South Korea/Taiwan)
Galilee (Israel)
Marmara (Turkey)
Okhotsk (Japan/Russia)
Solomon (Papua New Guinea/Solomon
Islands)
Weddell (Antarctica)

08 Adriatic (Albania/Croatia/Italy/Montenegro/
Slovenia)
Amundsen (Antarctica)
Beaufort (Canada/USA)
Bismarck (Papua New Guinea)
Hebrides (Scotland)
Huang Hai (China/Japan/North Korea/South
Korea)
Labrador (Canada/Greenland)
Ligurian (France/Italy/Monaco)
McKinley (Greenland/Russia)
Sargasso (The Bahamas/USA)

09 Caribbean (Antigua/Barbados/Belize/
Colombia/Costa Rica/Cuba/Dominica/
Dominican Republic/Grenada/Guatemala/
Haiti/Honduras/Jamaica/Mexico/
Nicaragua/Panama/St Kitts and Nevis/
St Lucia/St Vincent and the Grenadines/
Trinidad and Tobago/Venezuela)
East China (China/Japan/South Korea/
Taiwan)
Greenland (Greenland/Norway)
Norwegian (Greenland/Iceland/Norway)

10 Philippine (Philippines)
Setonaikai (Japan)
South China (Brunei/Cambodia/China/
Malaysia/Philippines/Taiwan/Thailand/
Vietnam)
Tyrrhenian (France/Italy)

11 Yam Kinneret (Israel)

12 East Siberian (Russia)

13 Mediterranean (Algeria/Cyprus/Egypt/France/
Greece/Israel/Italy/Lebanon/Libya/Malta/
Monaco/Morocco/Spain/Syria/Tunisia/
Turkey)

14 Bellingshausen (Antarctica)

See also **ocean**

seabird *see* **bird**

seafood

Seafood and seafood dishes include:

04 bisk	paella	**08** calamari	**11** clam-chowder
clam	scampi	coquille	Dublin prawn
crab	shrimp	crawfish	fritto misto
05 prawn	winkle	crevette	fruits de mer
squid	**07** abalone	marinara	langoustine
sushi	lobster	zarzuela	tiger shrimp
whelk	octopus	**09** jambalaya	**13** bouillabaisse
	risotto	king prawn	Norway lobster
06 bisque	scallop	surf'n'turf	prawn cocktail
mussel	tempura	**10** tiger prawn	**14** Dublin Bay prawn
oyster	toheroa		

seal

Seals include:

03 fur	ribbon	sea calf	whitecoat
04 grey	sea dog	sea lion	
hair	sealch	Weddell	**10** common seal
harp	sealgh	**08** Atlantic	saddleback
monk	selkie	elephant	sea leopard
05 phoca	silkie	seecatch	
silky	**07** harbour	**09** crab-eater	**11** sea elephant
06 hooded	sea bear	Greenland	

season

Seasons include:

03 dry	silly	winter	shooting
wet	**06** autumn	**07** festive	**12** Indian summer
04 high	closed	holiday	
05 close	spring	monsoon	
rainy	summer	**08** breeding	

seaweed

Seaweeds include:

03 ore	laver	porphyra
red	vraic	rockweed
04 alga	wrack	sargasso
kelp	**06** fucoid	sea wrack
kilp	tangle	whipcord
nori	wakame	**09** carrageen
tang	**07** oarweed	coralline
ulva	oreweed	coral weed
ware	redware	drift-weed
05 arame	sea lace	Irish moss
domoi	sea moss	Laminaria
dulse	seaware	nullipore
fucus	**08** bull kelp	sargassum
kombu	gulfweed	seabottle
		sea girdle

sea tangle
thongweed
10 badderlock
carragheen
Ceylon moss
green laver

sea lettuce
sea whistle
tangleweed
11 purple laver
sea furbelow
12 bladderwrack

peacock's tail
Phaeophyceae
Rhodophyceae
13 Chlorophyceae
15 channelled wrack

See also **algae**

sedative

Sedatives and tranquillizers include:

06 Amytal®
Ativan®
Valium®
07 codeine
Librium®
lupulin
08 diazepam

Nembutal®
Rohypnol®
tetronal
thridace
09 barbitone
clozapine
lorazepam

Temazepam
10 clonazepam
11 amobarbital
deserpidine
laurel-water
scopalamine
thalidomide

12 meprobramate
methaqualone
promethazine
14 chloral hydrate
cyclobarbitone
pentobarbitone
phenobarbitone

See also **drug**

sedge

Sedges include:

04 star
05 Carex
chufa

starr
07 bulrush
papyrus

08 clubrush
sawgrass
tiger nut

09 deergrass
13 umbrella plant
water chestnut

self-defence *see* **martial art**

Serbia *see* **Balkans**

servant

Servants include:

03 fag
04 char
chef
cook
maid
page
05 boots
carer
daily
groom
nanny
slave
valet
wench
06 au pair
barman
batman
butler

chokra
drudge
garçon
haiduk
lackey
menial
ostler
skivvy
tweeny
waiter
07 barmaid
bellboy
bellhop
cleaner
equerry
flunkey
footman
gossoon

pageboy
steward
tapsman
08 charlady
coachman
dogsbody
domestic
factotum
gardener
handmaid
henchman
home help
house boy
retainer
scullion
servitor
waitress
wet nurse

09 chauffeur
errand boy
governess
housemaid
lady's maid
major-domo
seneschal

10 chauffeuse
handmaiden

henchwoman
manservant
stewardess

11 body servant
boot-catcher
chambermaid
henchperson
housekeeper
kitchen-maid

maidservant
parlour-maid

12 domestic help
scullery maid

13 care assistant
lady-in-waiting
livery-servant

14 commissionaire

service *see* **religion**

session *see* **term**

setter *see* **crossword**

Seven Against Thebes

The Seven Greek champions who attacked Thebes:

06 Tydeus

Capaneus

10 Amphiaraus

13 Parthenopaeus

08 Adrastus

09 Polynices

Hippomedon

Seven Deadly Sins *see* **sin**

Seven Dwarfs *see* **dwarf**

seven hills *see* **Rome**

Seven Sages *see* **sage**

Seven Sisters colleges *see* **university**

Seven Wonders of the World *see* **wonder**

Shakespeare, William (1564–1616)

Shakespeare's plays:

06 *Hamlet* (1600–01)
Henry V (1598–99)

07 *Macbeth* (1606)
Othello (1603–04)

08 *King John* (1596)
King Lear (1605–06)
Pericles (1607)

09 *All Is True* (1613)
Cymbeline (1610)
Henry VIII (1613)
Richard II (1595)

10 *Coriolanus* (1608)
Richard III (1592–93)

The Tempest (1611)

11 *As You Like It* (1599–1600)
What You Will (1601)

12 *Julius Caesar* (1599)
Twelfth Night (1601)

13 *Timon of Athens* (1605)

14 *Henry IV Part One* (1596–97)
Henry IV Part Two (1597–98)
Henry VI Part One (1592)
Henry VI Part Two (1592)
Romeo and Juliet (1595)
The Winter's Tale (1609)

15 *Titus Andronicus* (1592)

16 *Henry VI Part Three* (1592)
Love's Labours Lost (1594–95)

17 *Measure for Measure* (1603)
The Comedy of Errors (1594)

18 *Antony and Cleopatra* (1606)
Troilus and Cressida (1602)

19 *Much Ado About Nothing* (1598)
The Merchant of Venice (1596–97)
The Taming of the Shrew (1593)
The Tragedy of Macbeth (1606)

20 *All's Well That Ends Well* (1604–05)
Pericles, Prince of Tyre (1607)
The Tragedy of King Lear (1605–06)

21 *A Midsummer Night's Dream* (1595)

22 *Cymbeline, King of Britain* (1610)
The Life of Henry the Fifth (1598–99)
The Life of Timon of Athens (1605)

The Merry Wives of Windsor (1597–98)
The Tragedy of Coriolanus (1608)

23 *The Two Gentlemen of Verona* (1590–91)

24 *The Tragedy of Julius Caesar* (1599)

25 *The Life and Death of King John* (1596)

26 *The History of Henry the Fourth* (1596–97)

30 *The Tragedy of Antony and Cleopatra* (1606)

31 *The Tragedy of King Richard the Third* (1592–93)

32 *The Tragedy of King Richard the Second* (1595)

33 *The Tragedy of Hamlet, Prince of Denmark* (1600–01)

34 *The Tragedy of Othello, the Moor of Venice* (1603–04)

Shakespeare's poems include:

07 *Sonnets* (1609)

14 *Venus and Adonis* (1593)

16 *'A Lover's Complaint'* (1609)

The Rape of Lucrece (1594)

22 *'The Phoenix and the Turtle'* (1601)

Significant characters in All's Well That Ends Well include:

05 Diana
Lafeu

06 France (King of)
Helena

07 Bertram

Capilet (Widow)
Lavatch
Mariana

08 Florence (Duke of)
Parolles

Reynaldo

09 Rousillon (Count of/
Countess of)

Significant characters in A Midsummer Night's Dream include:

04 Moth
Puck
Snug

05 Egeus
Flute (Francis)
Snout (Tom)

06 Bottom (Nick)
Cobweb

Helena
Hermia
Oberon
Quince (Peter)
Thisbe

07 Pyramus
Theseus
Titania

08 Lysander

09 Demetrius
Hippolyta

10 Starveling (Robin)

11 Mustardseed

12 Peaseblossom

15 Robin Goodfellow

Significant characters in Antony and Cleopatra include:

04 Iras

06 Caesar (Octavius)
Pompey

07 Lepidus (Marcus Aemilius)

Octavia

08 Charmian
Pompeius (Sextus)

09 Cleopatra

Enobarbus (Domitius)

10 Mark Antony

14 Marcus Antonius

Significant characters in As You Like It include:

05 Celia
Corin
Hymen

Phebe

06 Aliena
Audrey

Le Beau
Oliver
Senior (Duke)

07 Charles
Jacques
Martext (Sir Oliver)
Orlando

Silvius
William
08 Ganymede
Rosalind

09 Frederick (Duke)
10 Touchstone

Significant characters in Coriolanus include:

06 Brutus (Junius)
07 Agrippa (Menenius)
Velutus (Sicinius)

08 Aufidius (Tullus)
Cominius
Virgilia

Volumnia
10 Coriolanus (Gaius Martius)

Significant characters in Cymbeline include:

05 Queen
06 Cadwal
Cloten
Imogen
Lucius (Caius)
Morgan

07 Filario
Giacomo
Iachimo
Pisario
08 Belarius
Leonatus (Posthumus)

Leonatus (Sicilius)
Polydore
09 Arviragus
Cornelius
Cymbeline
Guiderius

Significant characters in Hamlet include:

05 Clown
Ghost (the)
06 Hamlet
07 Horatio

Laertes
Ophelia
08 Claudius
Gertrude

Polonius
10 Fortinbras
11 Gravedigger
Rosencrantz

12 Guildenstern

Significant characters in Henry IV Part I include:

03 Hal (Prince)
04 Peto
05 Blunt (Sir Walter)
Harry (Prince)
Percy (Henry)
Percy (Lady)
Percy (Thomas)

Poins
07 Henry IV
Hotspur (Henry Percy)
08 Bardolph
Falstaff (Sir John)
Gadshill
Mortimer (Edmund)

Mortimer (Lady)
09 Glendower (Owen)
13 Prince of Wales
15 Earl of Worcester
John of Lancaster (Prince)
Mistress Quickly

Significant characters in Henry IV Part II include:

05 Harry (Prince)
Percy (Henry)
Percy (Lady)
Poins
06 Henry V

Pistol
07 Henry IV
Shallow (Justice)
08 Bardolph
Falstaff (Sir John)

13 Doll Tearsheet
14 Northumberland (Lady)
15 John of Lancaster (Prince)
Mistress Quickly

Significant characters in Henry V include:

03 Nym
04 Jamy
05 Gower
06 Chorus (the)
Henry V
Isabel

Pistol
08 Bardolph
Burgundy (Duke of)
Fluellen
Mountjoy
09 Charles VI
Katharine

Macmorris
10 Canterbury (Archbishop of)
12 King of France
13 Queen of France
15 Lewis the Dauphin
Mistress Quickly

Significant characters in Henry VI Part I include:

04 Cade (Jack)	**07** Henry VI	**13** Joan la Pucelle	**15** Margaret of Anjou
York (Duke of)	**09** Joan of Arc	Queen Margaret	

Significant characters in Henry VI Part II include:

04 York (Duke of)	Richard	**13** Queen Margaret
06 Edward	**08** Edward IV	**15** Margaret of Anjou
07 Henry VI	**11** Earl of March	

Significant characters in Henry VI Part III include:

04 York (Duke of)	Henry VII	**13** Queen Margaret
06 Edward	Richmond (Henry, Earl of)	**14** Duke of Clarence
George	**09** Woodville (Anthony)	Queen Elizabeth
07 Henry VI	Woodville (Elizabeth)	**15** Margaret of Anjou
Richard	**10** Earl Rivers	
08 Edward IV	**11** Earl of March	

Significant characters in Henry VIII (All is True) include:

06 Boleyn (Anne)	**07** Cranmer (Thomas)	Katherine
Wolsey (Cardinal Thomas)	**09** Henry VIII	**14** Queen of England

Significant characters in Julius Caesar include:

05 Casca	Caesar (Octavius)	**09** Calpurnia
06 Brutus (Decius)	Portia	**10** Mark Antony
Brutus (Marcus)	**07** Cassius (Caius)	Soothsayer
Caesar (Julius)	Lepidus (Marcus Aemilius)	**14** Marcus Antonius

Significant characters in King John include:

04 John (King)	Lymoges
05 Henry (Prince)	**08** Brittany (Duke of/Duchess of)
06 Arthur	Pandulph
France (King of)	**09** Constance
Philip	**12** Falconbridge (Philip)
07 Austria (Duke of)	Falconbridge (Robert)
Blanche	**14** Peter of Pomfret
de Burgh (Hubert)	**15** Lewis the Dauphin
Eleanor	

Significant characters in King Lear include:

04 Fool (the)	**06** Albany (Duke of)	**08** Burgundy (Duke of)
Kent (Earl of)	Edmund	Cordelia
Lear (King)	France (King of)	Cornwall (Duke of)
05 Edgar	Oswald	**10** Gloucester (Earl of)
Regan	**07** Goneril	

Significant characters in Love's Labour's Lost include:

04 Dull	Maria	France (Princess of)
05 Boyet	**06** Armado (Don Adriano del)	**07** Berowne

Costard
Dumaine
08 Rosaline

09 Ferdinand (King)
Katharine
Nathanael (Sir)

10 Holofernes
Jaquenetta
Longaville

Significant characters in Macbeth include:

06 Banquo
Duncan (King)
Hecate

Porter (the)
07 Fleance
Macbeth

Macbeth (Lady)
Macduff
Macduff (Lady)

Malcolm
09 Donalbain
12 three witches (the)

Significant characters in Measure for Measure include:

05 Lucio
06 Angelo

Pompey
07 Claudio

08 Isabella
Marianna

09 Vincentio (Duke)

Significant characters in Much Ado About Nothing include:

04 Hero
06 Ursula
Verges
07 Claudio

Conrade
Don John
Leonato
08 Beatrice

Benedick
Borachio
Dogberry
Don Pedro

Margaret
12 Friar Francis

Significant characters in Othello include:

04 Iago
06 Bianca

Cassio
Emilia

07 Othello
08 Roderigo

09 Desdemona

Significant characters in Pericles include:

05 Cleon
06 Marina

Thaisa
07 Dionyza

08 Pericles
09 Antiochus

Helicanus
Simonides

Significant characters in Richard II include:

04 York (Duke of)
05 Bagot
Bushy
Green
Percy (Henry)

Queen (the)
07 Hotspur (Henry
Percy)
Mowbray (Thomas)
Norfolk (Duke of)

Richard (King)
08 Gardener (the)
Isabella
09 Lancaster (Duke of)
Richard II (King)

11 Bolingbroke
John of Gaunt
13 Pierce of Exton (Sir)
14 Northumberland
(Earl of)

Significant characters in Richard III include:

04 Anne (Lady)
05 Henry
March (Earl of)
06 Edward
George
07 Henry VI
Richard (Duke of York)

Richard (King)
08 Clarence (Duke of)
Edward IV
Hastings (Lord)
Henry VII
Richmond (Earl of)
09 Woodville (Anthony)
Woodville (Elizabeth)

10 Buckingham (Duke of)
Earl Rivers
Gloucester (Duke of)
Richard III
13 Queen Margaret
14 Queen Elizabeth
15 Margaret of Anjou

Significant characters in Romeo and Juliet include:

05 Nurse
Paris
Romeo

06 Juliet
Tybalt
07 Capulet

Capulet (Lady)
08 Benvolio
Mercutio

Montague
13 Friar Lawrence

Significant characters in The Comedy of Errors include:

06 Aegeon
Dromio (of Ephesus)
Dromio (of Syracuse)

07 Adriana
Aemilia
Luciana

10 Antipholus (of Ephesus)
Antipholus (of Syracuse)

Significant characters in The Merchant of Venice include:

05 Gobbo (Launcelot)
06 Portia
07 Antonio

Arragon (Prince of)
Jessica
Lorenzo

Morocco (Prince
of)
Nerissa

Shylock
08 Bassanio
Gratiano

Significant characters in The Merry Wives of Windsor include:

03 Nym
04 Ford (Frank)
Ford (Mistress Alice)
Page (Anne)
Page (George)
Page (Mistress Margaret)

05 Caius (Dr)
Evans (Sir Hugh)
Robin
Rugby (John)
06 Fenton
Pistol

Simple (Peter)
07 Shallow (Justice)
Slender (Abraham)
08 Falstaff (Sir John)
15 Mistress Quickly

Significant characters in The Taming of the Shrew include:

03 Sly (Christopher)
06 Bianca
Curtis
Gremio
Grumio

Tranio
08 Lucentio
09 Biondello
Hortensio
Katharina (Kate)

Petruchio
Vincentio
11 Bartholomew
14 Baptista Minola

Significant characters in The Tempest include:

05 Ariel
06 Adrian
Alonso
07 Antonio

Caliban
Gonzalo
Miranda
Sycorax

08 Prospero
Stephano
Trinculo
09 Ferdinand

Francisco
Sebastian

Significant characters in The Winter's Tale include:

07 Camillo
Leontes
Paulina

Perdita
08 Florizel
Hermione

09 Antigonus
Autolycus
Polixenes

Significant characters in Timon of Athens include:

07 Flavius
09 Apemantus

Ventidius
10 Alcibiades

13 Timon of Athens

Significant characters in Titus Andronicus include:

05 Aaron (the Moor)
06 Tamora (Queen)
07 Lavinia

09 Bassianus
10 Andronicus (Lucius)
Andronicus (Marcus)

Andronicus (Quintus)
Andronicus (Titus)
Saturninus

Significant characters in Troilus and Cressida include:

04 Ajax
05 Helen

Paris
Priam

06 Hector
07 Calchas

Helenus
Troilus

Ulysses

08 Achilles

Cressida

Diomedes

Pandarus

09 Agamemnon

Cassandra

Patroclus

Thersites

10 Andromache

Significant characters in Twelfth Night include:

05 Belch (Sir Toby)

Feste

Maria

Viola

06 Olivia

Orsino

07 Antonio

Cesario

08 Malvolio

09 Aguecheek (Sir
Andrew)

Sebastian

Significant characters in Two Gentlemen of Verona include:

05 Julia

Milan (Duke of)

Speed

06 Launce

Silvia

Thurio

07 Antonio

Proteus

08 Eglamour (Sir)

09 Valentine

Terms to do with Shakespeare include:

03 act

RSC

set

04 fame

hero

line

love

play

plot

poem

poet

role

05 actor

aside

clown

court

death

drama

genre

Greek

Latin

meter

scene

stage

theme

witch

06 chorus

climax

comedy

editor

jester

masque

patron

plague

simile

See also **fool**

sonnet

source

speech

Thames

troupe

07 costume

couplet

edition

English

Fortune

players

scholar

tragedy

trochee

08 director

epilogue

Jacobean

King's Men

language

metaphor

New Place

prologue

quatrain

rhetoric

violence

09 character

dramatist

Folio text

interlude

Queen's Men

soliloquy

Stratford

universal

10 adaptation

Bard of Avon

bardolatry

blank verse

bowdlerize

chronology

dark comedy

First Folio

groundling

literature

malcontent

manuscript

playwright

production

Quarto text

11 bear baiting

Elizabethan

masterpiece

protagonist

Rose Theatre

Swan Theatre

12 Globe Theatre

history plays

Scottish play

St George's Day

13 acting company

collaboration

Lord of Misrule

narrative poem

Shakespearean

Shakespearian

14 King's New School

revenge-tragedy

stage direction

15 Sweet Swan of Avon

shape

Shapes include:

04 cone
cube
kite
oval
05 prism
06 circle
cuboid
oblong
sector
sphere
square
07 decagon
diamond
ellipse

hexagon
nonagon
octagon
polygon
pyramid
rhombus
08 crescent
cylinder
heptagon
pentagon
quadrant
tetragon
triangle
09 chiliagon
dodecagon

rectangle
trapezium
undecagon
10 hemisphere
hendecagon
octahedron
polyhedron
quadrangle
semicircle
11 pentahedron
tetrahedron
13 parallelogram
quadrilateral
15 scalene triangle

See also **circle**; **leaf**; **triangle**

shark

Sharks include:

03 cat
fox
saw
04 blue
bull
mako
05 blind
dusky
ghost
lemon
night
nurse
sagre

swell
tiger
whale
zebra
06 beagle
carpet
goblin
salmon
school
sea cat
07 basking
bramble
dogfish

leopard
requiem
sleeper
soupfin
08 blacktip
grey reef
mackerel
thresher
whitetip
09 angelfish
epaulette
Greenland
man-eating

porbeagle
sand tiger
sevengill
sharpnose
wobbegong
10 Colclough's
great white
hammerhead
Portuguese
shovelhead
11 ragged-tooth
smooth-hound

sheep

Sheep include:

03 Rya
04 Dala
Gute
Soay
05 ammon
ancon
aodad
Jacob
Lleyn
Lonck
Masai
Rygja
Texel
Tunis

urial
06 aoudad
Arcott
argali
Awassi
Balwen
Beltex
bharal
burhel
burrel
Dorper
Galway
Masham
merino

muflon
Romney
07 Barbary
bighorn
burrell
burrhel
caracul
Cheviot
Colbred
Gotland
karakul
Karaman
Lincoln
mouflon

Romanov
Roussin
Ryeland
St Croix
Steigar
Suffolk
Tibetan
Vendeen

08 Columbia
Cotentin
Cotswold
Herdwick
Katahdin
Loaghtan
Meatlinc
moufflon
Ouessant
Peliquey
Polwarth
Portland
Shetland
thinhorn
Troender

09 blackface
blue sheep
Cambridge
Charmoise
Charolais
Coopworth

Dalesbred
Dall Sheep
Finn Sheep
Fuglestad
Greenland
Hebridean
Icelandic
Kerry Hill
Leicester
Llanwenog
Marco Polo
Montadale
Perendale
Rough Fell
snow sheep
Southdown
Swaledale
Teeswater
Welsh Mule
Zwartbles

10 Borderdale
Charollais
Clun Forest
Corriedale
Dorset Down
Dorset Horn
Exmoor Horn
Hill Radnor
Morada Nova
Oxford Down

Poll Dorset
Scotch Mule
Shropshire
stone sheep

11 Ile de France
Manx Loghtan
Norfolk Horn
Rambouillet
Wensleydale

12 Bleu du Marine
East Friesian
Faroe Islands
Navajo-Churro

13 Desert Bighorn
Hampshire Down
Rouge de l'Ouest
Tyrol Mountain
Welsh Halfbred
Wiltshire Horn

14 Danish Landrace
Devon Closewool
North Ronaldsay
Scotch Halfbred
Wicklow Cheviot

15 Berrichon du Cher
Border Leicester
Est A Laine Merino
Shetland-Cheviot
White Faced Marsh

ship

Ship and boat types include:

01 E
Q
U

02 MV
NS
SS
TB

03 air
ark
bum
cat
cog
cot
day
dow
fly
gig
gun
HMS
hoy
ice
jet

kit
MTB
mud
pig
row
tow
tub
tug
USS
war

04 bark
brig
buss
cock
cott
dhow
dory
falt
fire
flag
flat
fold
four

grab
HMAS
HMCS
hulk
hush
junk
keel
koff
life
long
mail
maxi
pair
pink
pont
post
pram
prau
proa
prow
punt
saic
scow

show
snow
surf
tall
tilt
Turk
waka
well
wind
yawl
zulu

05 aviso
barca
barge
botel
butty
cabin
canal
canoe
casco
coble
coper
crare
dandy
dingy
drake
ferry
funny
guard
gulet
hatch
horse
house
jolly
kayak
ketch
laker
light
liner
motor
oiler
peter
pilot
plate
power
praam
prahu
prore
razee
river
rotor
saick
scout
scull
seine
shell
shore
skiff

slave
sloop
smack
speed
stake
steam
store
swamp
tanka
track
tramp
troop
umiak
wager
waist
whale
whiff
xebec
yacht
zabra

06 advice
argosy
banker
barque
bateau
battle
bethel
bireme
caique
carvel
castle
coaler
cobble
cockle
codder
coffin
convoy
cooper
crayer
cutter
dingey
dinghy
dogger
dragon
droger
dromon
drover
dugout
flying
galiot
galley
gay-you
hooker
hopper
jigger
lateen
launch
lorcha

lugger
masula
monkey
mother
narrow
nuggar
oomiac
oomiak
packet
paddle
pedalo
pirate
prison
puffer
pulwar
puteli
randan
reefer
rowing
runner
sailer
saique
sampan
sandal
sanpan
school
schuit
schuyt
settee
slaver
tanker
tartan
torpid
trader
turret
wangan
wangun
wherry

07 assault
Berthon
birlinn
budgero
capital
caravel
clipper
coaster
collier
consort
coracle
corsair
cruiser
currach
curragh
dredger
drifter
drogher
dromond
factory

felucca
four-oar
frigate
gabbard
gabbart
galleon
galliot
Geordie
gondola
landing
liberty
lighter
lymphad
man-o'-war
mistico
mudscow
mystery
nacelle
oomiack
pair-oar
passage
patamar
pearler
pinnace
piragua
pirogue
polacca
pontoon
sailing
scooter
shallop
sharpie
sponger
steamer
tartane
torpedo
trawler
trireme
vedette
victory
wanigan
warship
weather
Yngling

08 bilander
billyboy
budgerow
car ferry
corocore
corocoro
corvette
dahabieh
dispatch
eight-oar
galleass
galliass
gallivat
hospital

hoveller
Indiaman
ironclad
johnboat
log-canoe
longship
mackinaw
man-of-war
masoolah
massoola
merchant
monohull
montaria
periagua
pleasure
repeater
row barge
runabout
sally-man
schooner
skipjack
smuggler
Spaniard
training
trimaran
water bus
woodskin

09 bomb-ketch
Bucentaur
catamaran
commodore
container
dahabeeah
dahabiyah
dahabiyeh
daysailer
daysailor
destroyer
firefloat
flying jib
freighter
herringer
Hollander
hydrofoil
klondiker
klondyker
lapstrake
lapstreak
leviathan
long-liner
minelayer
monoxylon
motoscafo
multihull
Norwegian
oil-burner
oil tanker
outrigger

privateer
randan gig
receiving
sallee-man
speedster
steamship
store ship
submarine
surf canoe
transport
two-decker
two-master
vaporetto
well smack

10 armour-clad
bomb-vessel
brigantine
free-trader
hovercraft
icebreaker
minehunter
quadrireme
seal-fisher
tea clipper
trekschuit
triaconter
victualler
windjammer

11 bulk carrier
cockleshell
dreadnought
galley-foist
merchantman
minesweeper
motor launch
penteconter
purse-seiner
quinquereme
sallee-rover
salmon coble
side-wheeler
steam launch
steam packet
steam vessel
submersible
three-decker
three-master
victualling
wooden horse

12 cabin cruiser
deepwaterman
double-decker
East-Indiaman
line-of-battle
screw steamer
single-decker
square-rigger

stern-wheeler
tangle-netter
tramp steamer
troop carrier
13 Canadian canoe

paddle steamer
revenue cutter
roll-on roll-off
14 Flying Dutchman
ocean-greyhound

turbine steamer
15 aircraft-carrier
floating battery
logistics vessel

Ship parts include:

03 bow
box
oar
rig
04 beam
brig
brow
bunk
cant
deck
eyes
head
hold
keel
mast
port
prow
sail
05 berth
bilge
cabin
cable
chimb
chime
chine
cleat
coach
davit
hatch
hawse
stern
wheel
winch
06 anchor
bridge
buffer
dodger

fender
fo'c'sle
funnel
galley
gunnel
hawser
rigger
rudder
tiller
07 bollard
caboose
capstan
channel
counter
fardage
gangway
gun deck
gunwale
hammock
landing
quarter
rowlock
top deck
transom
08 binnacle
boat deck
boom-iron
bulkhead
bulwarks
cutwater
foot-rope
forepeak
garboard
hatchway
main deck
poop deck
porthole
wardroom

09 afterdeck
billboard
breadroom
chart room
crosstree
crow's nest
floorhead
forecabin
gangplank
goose-wing
hawsehole
hawsepipe
lower deck
radio room
stanchion
starboard
stateroom
waterline
10 boiler room
engine room
fiddlehead
figurehead
flight deck
forecastle
pilot house
stabilizer
11 boot-topping
chain locker
floor timber
paddle wheel
quarter deck
12 companionway
Plimsoll line
13 promenade deck
14 garboard strake
superstructure
15 companion ladder

Ships include:

03 *QE2*
04 *Ajax*
Argo
Hood
Nina
05 *Argus*
Maine
Pinta

06 *Beagle*
Bounty
Cathay
Oriana
Pequod
Renown
07 *Alabama*
Amistad

Belfast
Blücher
Olympic
Pelican
Potomac
Repulse
Tirpitz
Titanic

Victory
08 Ark Royal
Bismarck
Canberra
Fearless
Graf Spee
Intrepid
Iron Duke
Mary Rose
Royal Oak
09 Adventure
Aquitania
Brittania
Brittanic
Carinthia
Cutty Sark

Discovery
Endeavour
Gneisenau
Lexington
Lusitania
Mayflower
Normandie
Queen Mary
Sheffield
Téméraire
Terranova
10 Golden Hind
Hispaniola
Invincible
Mauretania
Prinz Eugen
Resolution

Santa Maria
Washington
11 Dawn Treader
Dreadnought
Illustrious
Scharnhorst
12 Great Britain
Great Eastern
Great Western
Marie Celeste
13 Prince of Wales
14 Flying Dutchman
Queen Elizabeth
15 Admiral Graf Spee
General Belgrano
Queen Elizabeth 2

Ships' crewmen and officers include:

02 AB	purser	**08** cabin-boy	**10** able rating
04 mate	**07** captain	ship's boy	able seaman
06 master	steward	**09** first mate	**12** first officer

Shipping forecast areas:

04 Sole	Biscay	FitzRoy	Portland
Tyne	Dogger	Forties	**09** Trafalgar
05 Dover	Faroes	Rockall	**10** Finisterre
Forth	Fisher	Shannon	**11** German Bight
Lundy	Humber	**08** Cromarty	North Utsire
Malin	Thames	Fair Isle	South Utsire
Wight	Viking	Hebrides	
06 Bailey	**07** Faeroes	Irish Sea	**16** South-East Iceland
	Fastnet	Plymouth	

See also **sailing**

shop

Shop types include:

01 e	sweet	butcher	
02 op	video	charity	
03 toy	**06** barber	chemist	
04 book	bazaar	chipper	
chip	bookie	clothes	
farm	bottle	florist	
grog	chippy	saddler	
shoe	corner	**08** boutique	
tuck	draper	hardware	
05 baker	grocer	jeweller	
dairy	market	milliner	
dress	online	pharmacy	
offie	record	takeaway	
phone	tailor	**09** bookmaker	
stall	thrift	drugstore	
	07 betting	newsagent	

outfitter
stationer
superette
10 candy store
chain store
electrical
fishmonger
health-food
ironmonger
mini-market
off-licence
pawnbroker

post office
radio and TV
second-hand
superstore
11 bottle store
fish and chip
five-and-dime
greengrocer
haberdasher
hairdresser
hypermarket
launderette

online store
opportunity
supermarket
tobacconist
12 cash-and-carry
confectioner
delicatessen
general store
indoor market
13 computer store
farmers' market
15 department store

Shops include:

03 BHV (France)
04 Tati (France)
05 Macy's (USA)
07 Hamleys (England)
Harrods (England)
Jenners (Scotland)
Liberty (England)
09 Century 21 (USA)
Printemps (France)
10 FAO Schwarz (USA)

Selfridge's (England)
11 Le Bon Marché (France)
12 Tiffany and Co (USA)
13 Bloomingdale's (USA)
Harvey Nichols (England/Scotland)
La Samaritaine (France)
Lord and Taylor (USA)
15 Bergdorf Goodman (USA)
Fortnum and Mason (England)
Saks Fifth Avenue (USA)

French shops include:

05 tabac
08 boutique
épicerie
09 boucherie

librairie
10 bijouterie
confiserie
fromagerie

parfumerie
pâtisserie
rôtisserie
11 boulangerie

charcuterie
12 chocolaterie
grand magasin
poissonnerie

Shopping terms include:

03 VAT
04 EPOS
mall
rail
till
05 aisle
cabas
chain
plaza
price
sales
shelf
stand
06 branch
browse
change
cheque
EFTPOS
fascia
market

markup
refund
retail
ring up
07 barcode
bargain
cashier
counter
display
dump bin
étalage
in-store
mall rat
receipt
reduced
service
spinner
tote bag
trolley
08 checkout

consumer
customer
discount
exchange
galleria
messages
precinct
price tag
purchase
salesman
sales tax
shop bell
warranty
09 brand name
debit card
dump table
guarantee
mail order
mannequin
midinette
strip mall

10 carrier bag
channel-hop
charge card
credit card
credit note
department
floor limit
high street
impulse buy
outlet mall
saleswoman
shop around
shop window

11 dump display
fitting room
loyalty card
merchandise

See also **business**

salesperson
security tag
shopping bag
supermarket

12 cash register
early closing
hire purchase
home delivery
home shopping
January sales
opening hours
profit margin
shopping list
teleshopping

13 bargain-hunter
counter-jumper

credit voucher
outlet village
retail therapy
security guard
shop assistant
value-added tax

14 consumer rights
counter-skipper
sales assistant
shopping basket
shopping centre
window-shopping

15 bargain basement
express checkout
shopping trolley
statutory rights

short story *see* **novel**

Shostakovich, Dmitri (1906–75)

Significant works include:

03 *Nos* (1930)

07 'Babi-Yar' (Symphony; 1962)
'October' (Symphony; 1927)
The Bolt (1931)
The Nose (1930)

09 'Leningrad' (Symphony; 1942)

10 'Stalingrad' (Symphony; 1943)

11 'The Year 1905' (Symphony; 1957)
'The Year 1917' (Symphony; 1961)

12 *The Golden Age* (1930)

13 'The First of May' (Symphony; 1930)

14 *The Limpid Brook* (1935)

17 *Katerina Izmailova* (1963)

31 *Lady Macbeth of the Mtsensk District* (1934)

shotokan belt *see* **karate**

shout

Shouts and cries include:

02 io
oi!
yo!

03 hey
hup
nix

04 euoi
evoe
fall
fore
haro
I-spy

rivo
shoo
sola

05 chevy
chivy
evhoe
evohe
havoc
heigh
holla
hollo
hooch
huzza

06 banzai
chivvy
eureka
halloa
halloo
harrow
hoicks
what ho!
yoicks

07 glory be
heigh-ho
heureka
kamerad

tally-ho
tantivy

08 alleluia
gardyloo
Geronimo
harambee

09 scaldings
stop thief!

10 halleluiah
hallelujah
view-halloo
westward ho!

show *see* **quiz**; **radio**; **television**

showjumper *see* equestrian sport

shrub

Shrubs include:

03 ivy		mallow	**08** berberis		wisteria
04 hebe		mimosa	buddleia	**09** eucryphia
rose		privet	camellia	firethorn
05 broom	**07** arbutus	clematis	forsythia
holly		dogwood	euonymus	hydrangea
lilac		fuchsia	japonica	**10** mock orange
peony		heather	laburnum	witch hazel
yucca		jasmine	lavender	**11** cotoneaster
06 azalea		phlomis	magnolia	honeysuckle
daphne		spiraea	musk rose	**12** rhododendron
laurel		weigela	tamarisk	**15** Siberian ginseng

03 ivy — mallow — 08 berberis — wisteria
04 hebe — mimosa — buddleia — 09 eucryphia
rose — privet — camellia — firethorn
05 broom — 07 arbutus — clematis — forsythia
holly — dogwood — euonymus — hydrangea
lilac — fuchsia — japonica — 10 mock orange
peony — heather — laburnum — witch hazel
yucca — jasmine — lavender — 11 cotoneaster
06 azalea — phlomis — magnolia — honeysuckle
daphne — spiraea — musk rose — 12 rhododendron
laurel — weigela — tamarisk — 15 Siberian ginseng

See also **tree**

SI prefix *see* science

SI unit *see* measurement

siege

Sieges include:

04 Acre (ended 1191)
Metz (1552)
Waco (1993)

05 Alamo (1836)
Derry (1688–89)
Kuito (1992–94)
Paris (ended 1590; 1870–71)
Rouen (ended 1592)

06 Janina (1821–22)
London (1016)
Quebec (1759; 1775)
Toulon (1793)
Vienna (1529; 1683)

07 Antioch (1097–98)
Bristol (1643)
Granada (1490–92)
Lucknow (1857)
Orléans (1428–29)

08 Damascus (1148)
Limerick (1691)
Mafeking (1899–1900)
Roxburgh (1460)

Sarajevo (1992–95)
Syracuse (213–212 BC)
The Alamo (1836)
Yorktown (1781)

09 Barcelona (ended 1652; 1713–14)
Kimberley (1899–1900)
Ladysmith (1899–1900)
Leningrad (1941–44)
Silistria (1809)
Vicksburg (1863)

10 Charleston (1780)
Kut al-amara (1915–16)
Sevastopol (1854–55)

12 Tenochtitlán (1521)

14 Constantinople (1391–98; 1422; 1453)
Entebbe Airport (1976)
Iranian Embassy (1980)
Munich Olympics (1972)

15 Bourj al-Barajneh (1987)
Japanese Embassy (1996–97)
Palace of Culture (2002)

sight impairment *see* blindness

sign *see* motoring; zodiac

signal

Signals and warnings include:

03 cue
SOS

04 bell
buoy
fire
flag
gong
honk
horn
pips
toot

05 alarm
bugle
flare
knell
larum
pager
shout
siren
vigia

06 beacon
buzzer
hooter
klaxon
mayday
rocket
tattoo

tocsin
winker

07 bleeper
car horn
foghorn
go-ahead
red card
red flag
whistle

08 car alarm
drumbeat
password
red alert
red light
reveille

09 alarm-bell
fire alarm
indicator
larum-bell
Morse code
signal box
storm cone
Very light

10 alarm clock
amber light
curfew bell
green light

hand signal
heliograph
Lutine bell
smoke alarm
time signal
yellow card
yellow flag

11 bicycle bell
gale warning
smoke signal
starter's gun
storm signal
trafficator

12 burglar alarm
final warning
storm warning
warning light

13 Belisha beacon
flashing light
personal alarm
police whistle
security alarm
signal letters
traffic lights

14 distress signal
written warning

15 semaphore signal

See also **navigation**

Sikhism

Sikh groups and movements include:

05 Akali
Udasi

07 Nihangs
Nirmala

08 Namdhari

09 Nirankari

See also **religion**

simile

Similes include:

11 as dry as bone
as ugly as sin

12 as clear as mud
as good as gold
as often as not
as sick as a dog

13 as bald as a coot
as blind as a bat
as bold as brass
as dead as a dodo
as deaf as a post

as free as a bird
as hard as nails
as high as a kite
as large as life
as right as rain
as thin as a rake
as warm as toast
as white as snow
as wise as an owl

14 as black as pitch
as clear as a bell
as daft as a brush

as drunk as a lord
as fit as a fiddle
as happy as a lark
as happy as Larry
as mad as a hatter
as merry as a grig
as safe as houses
as sound as a bell

15 as brown as a berry
as cold as charity
as fresh as a daisy
as keen as mustard

as old as the hills	as sharp as a razor	as stiff as a poker
as quiet as a mouse	as sick as a parrot	as thick as a plank
as rich as Croesus	as sober as a judge	as weak as a kitten
as ripe as a cherry	as steady as a rock	as white as a sheet

sin

The Seven Deadly Sins:

04 envy	pride	**06** acedia	**08** gluttony
lust	sloth	**07** accidie	**12** covetousness
05 anger	wrath	avarice	

singer

Singer types include:

03 pop	treble	falsetto	sopranist
04 alto	**07** crooner	minstrel	**10** prima donna
bass	pop star	songster	songstress
diva	soloist	vocalist	troubadour
folk	soprano	**09** balladeer	**11** Heldentenor
05 carol	warbler	chanteuse	**12** counter-tenor
mezzo	**08** baritone	choirgirl	mezzo-soprano
opera	barytone	chorister	**13** basso profondo
tenor	castrato	contralto	basso profundo
06 chorus	choirboy	precentor	

Singers include:

03 Day (Doris; 1924– , US)

04 Cole (Nat 'King'; 1919–65, US)
Lynn (Dame Vera; 1917– , English)
Piaf (Edith; 1915–63, French)

05 Jones (Aled; 1970– , Welsh)
Lloyd (Marie; 1870–1922, English)
Paige (Elaine; 1951– , English)

06 Atwell (Winifred; 1914–83, Trinidadian)
Bassey (Dame Shirley; 1937– , Welsh)
Church (Charlotte; 1986– , Welsh)
Crosby (Bing; 1903–77, US)
Fields (Dame Gracie; 1898–1979, English)
Jolson (Al; 1886–1950, US)
Lauder (Sir Harry; 1870–1950, Scottish)

Lillie (Beatrice; 1894–1989, Canadian)
Steele (Tommy; 1936– , English)

07 Andrews (Dame Julie; 1935– , English)
Dickson (Barbara; 1947– , Scottish)
Garland (Judy; 1922–69, US)
Jenkins (Katherine; 1980– , Welsh)
Miranda (Carmen; 1909–55, Brazilian)
Robeson (Paul; 1898–1976, US)
Secombe (Sir Harry; 1921–2001, Welsh)
Sinatra (Frank; 1915–98, US)

08 Bygraves (Max; 1922–2012, English)
Liberace (1919–87, US)

09 Belafonte (Harry; 1927– , US)
Chevalier (Albert; 1861–1923, English)

See also **country and western**; **folk**; **jazz**; **opera**; **pop**

skating see **ice skating**

skiing

Skiing events include:

05 grass	nordic	**08** combined	snowboard
mogul	slalom	downhill	**11** giant slalom
relay	sprint	halfpipe	**12** cross-country
speed	super-g	**09** classical	
06 aerial	**07** jumping	dual mogul	
alpine	pursuit	freestyle	

Skiers include:

04 Hess (Erica; 1962– , Swiss)
Vonn (Lindsey; 1984– , US)

05 Cranz (Christl; 1914–2004, Belgian)
Killy (Jean-Claude; 1943– , French)
Maier (Hermann; 1972– , Austrian)
Raich (Benjamin; 1978– , Austrian)
Tomba (Alberto; 1966– , Italian)

06 Dahlie (Bjørn; 1967– , Norwegian)
Figini (Michela; 1966– , Swiss)
Miller (Bode; 1977– , US)
Sailer (Toni; 1935–2009, Austrian)
Wenzel (Hanni; 1956– , German/
Liechtenstein)

07 Edwards (Eddie 'the Eagle'; 1963– , English)
Klammer (Franz; 1953– , Austrian)
Nykänen (Matti; 1963– , Finnish)
Simpson (Myrtle; 1931– , Scottish)
Svindal (Aksel Lund; 1982– , Norwegian)

08 Stenmark (Ingemar; 1956– , Swedish)
Walliser (Maria; 1963– , Swiss)

09 Schneider (Vreni; 1964– , Swiss)
Smetanina (Raisa; 1952– , Russian)

10 Girardelli (Marc; 1963– , Austrian/
Luxembourg)
Moser-Pröll (Annemarie; 1953– , Austrian)
Zurbriggen (Pirmin; 1963– , Swiss)

Skiing terms include:

04 gate
05 daffy
glide
inrun
piste
split
06 basket
big air
edging
kicker
k point
outrun

p point
schuss
07 grip wax
hairpin
harries
kick wax
takeoff
08 freeride
glide wax
off-piste
start hut
table top

09 aerialist
large hill
mass start
Steilhang
V-position
10 Hahnenkamm
helicopter
normal hill
11 carving skis
egg position
scramble leg
spread eagle

12 starting gate
tuck position
vertical gate
13 backscratcher
critical point
herringboning
safety netting
14 freeride skiing
outjump the hill
safety bindings
staggered start

skin

Skin parts include:

04 derm
hair
hide
pore

05 cutis
derma
06 corium
dermis

07 cuticle
papilla
09 epidermis
10 sweat gland

11 lower dermis
12 hair follicle
14 sebaceous gland

Skin diseases and conditions include:

02 EB
XP
04 acne
boba
buba
rash
wart
yaws

05 favus
tinea
ulcer
06 eczema
herpes
07 anthrax
bedsore
gum rash

leprosy
rosacea
scabies
08 dandruff
melanoma
ringworm
09 keratosis
psoriasis

10 dermatitis
dermatosis
framboesia
11 prickly heat
12 athlete's foot
button scurvy

See also **hair**; **inflammation**

smell

Smells include:

03 hum	nose	sniff	perfume
04 funk	pong	stink	**08** malodour
fust	reek	whiff	mephitis
guff	**05** aroma	**06** miasma	pungency
ming	fetor	stench	**09** fragrance
must	odour	**07** bouquet	redolence
niff	scent		

Particular smells include:

02 BO	smoke	**07** alcohol	**09** body odour
04 feet	spice	camphor	patchouli
musk	**06** cheese	incense	pot pourri
rose	coffee	menthol	woodsmoke
05 basil	garlic	perfume	**10** eucalyptus
booze	nutmeg	vanilla	peppermint
ozone	pepper	**08** bergamot	**11** wintergreen
		lavender	

snake

Snakes include:

03 asp	blind	rattle	hamadryas
boa	brown	ribbon	king cobra
rat	cobra	smooth	puff adder
sea	coral	taipan	river-jack
04 boma	Elaps	**07** diamond	**10** bandy-bandy
bull	grass	hognose	bushmaster
corn	green	langaha	copperhead
file	krait	rattler	death adder
hoop	mamba	**08** anaconda	dendrophis
king	racer	cerastes	fer-de-lance
milk	tiger	colubrid	Gabon viper
naga	viper	cylinder	massasauga
Naia	water	jararaca	sidewinder
Naja	**06** carpet	jararaka	**11** constrictor
pine	dipsas	mocassin	cottonmouth
pipe	dugite	moccasin	diamondback
ring	elapid	pit viper	gaboon viper
rock	ellops	ringhals	horned viper
sand	flying	rinkhals	massasauger
seps	gaboon	sucurujú	**12** carpet python
tree	garter	water boa	**13** diamond python
whip	gopher	**09** berg-adder	water moccasin
worm	indigo	boomslang	**14** boa constrictor
05 adder	karait	coachwhip	river-jack viper
black	python	hamadryad	

See also **poison**

snooker

Snooker players include:

03 Meo (Tony; 1959– , English)

05 Davis (Fred; 1913–98, English)
Davis (Joe; 1901–78, English)
Davis (Steve; 1957– , English)
Ebdon (Peter; 1970– , English)
Virgo (John; 1946– , English)
White (Jimmy; 1962– , English)

06 Fisher (Allison; 1968– , English)
Hendry (Stephen; 1969– , Scottish)
Taylor (Dennis; 1949– , Northern Irish)

07 Doherty (Ken; 1975– , Irish)

Higgins (Alex; 1949–2010, Northern Irish)
Higgins (John; 1975– , Scottish)
Maguire (Stephen; 1981– , Scottish)
Parrott (John; 1964– , English)
Reardon (Ray; 1932– , Welsh)
Stevens (Matthew; 1977– , Welsh)

08 Charlton (Eddie; 1929–2004, Australian)
Thorburn (Cliff; 1948– , Canadian)
Williams (Mark; 1975– , Welsh)

09 Griffiths (Terry; 1947– , Welsh)
O'Sullivan (Ronnie; 1975– , English)

Snooker terms include:

01 D	side	cannon	free ball
03 bed	sink	colour	full ball
cue	spot	double	half ball
pot	stun	miscue	half-butt
set	**05** angle	pocket	**09** baulk line
tip	baize	safety	check side
04 ball	baulk	spider	extension
butt	break	**07** century	screw shot
drag	chalk	cue ball	**10** object ball
foul	fluke	cushion	push stroke
jaws	frame	English	safety shot
kick	in-off	feather	**11** half-century
kiss	massé	maximum	running side
miss	plant	snooker	**12** maximum break
pack	screw	topspin	touching ball
rail	table	**08** backspin	**13** follow-through
rest	**06** bridge	break-off	shot to nothing

See also **sport**

snow

Snow types and formations include:

03 red	**05** drift	sludge	**09** avalanche
04 corn	flake	yellow	spindrift
crud	sleet	**07** cornice	
firn	slush	flaught	
névé	**06** powder	**08** sastruga	

See also **ice**

Snow White *see* **dwarf**

soap

Soaps include:

03 Lux®	hard	**05** glass	sugar
04 Dove®	soft	Pears®	**06** liquid

marine	**07** Castile	Windsor	olive-oil
saddle	coal-tar		**09** Palmolive®
toilet	shaving	**08** carbolic	
yellow	Spanish	mountain	**10** coconut-oil

soap opera

Soap operas include:

06 *Dallas*	**08** *Casualty*	*Hollyoaks*	*The Archers*
07 *Dynasty*	**09** *Brookside*	*River City*	**11** *Home and Away*
The Bill	*Emmerdale*	**10** *EastEnders*	
	Holby City	*Neighbours*	

See also **radio**; **television**

social media

SMS/texting abbreviations include:

01 U (you)

02 CU (see you)
PW (parents are watching)

03 ATM (at the moment)
BFN (bye for now)
BRB (be right back)
HAK (hugs and kisses)
LOL (laughing out loud)
LUV (love)
MSG (message)
OMG (Oh, my god)

PAW (parents are watching)
PLS (please)
POV (point of view)
RAK (random act of kindness)
THX (thanks)
TXT (text)

04 ASAP (as soon as possible)
BCNU (be seeing you)
HAND (have a nice day)
MYOB (mind your own business)

ROFL (rolling on the floor laughing)
SWYP (so what's your problem?)
THNX (thanks)
TTYL (talk to you later)
WDYT (what do you think?)
WKND (weekend)
XOXO (hugs and kisses)

05 AFAIR (as far as I remember)

Social media terms include:

03 app
MMS
SMS

04 Bebo®
blog
chat
like
poke
post
sext
spam
text
vlog
wall
wiki

05 flame
share
Skype®
splog
troll
tweet
Weibo

06 follow
friend

mobile
moblog
QR code
selfie
tablet
texter
upload
webcam
web log

07 blogger
hashtag
message
Mumsnet
podcast
profile
retweet
roaming
setting
SMS chat
textese
texting
Twitter
vlogger
YouTube

08 blogging
blogring
blogroll
chat room
emoticon
Facebook®
Flash SMS
follower
LinkedIn®
smart mob
spam blog
timeline
unfriend
vlogging

09 cellphone
Geocities
meat world
messaging
microblog
Sino Weibo
video clip
Wikipedia

10 Blackberry®
cyber bully

moblogging
selfie fail
smartphone
smiley face
ugly selfie
WAP-enabled
11 application
blogosphere
file-sharing
interactive
mobile phone

social media
text message
Twitterfeed
12 photo-sharing
video-sharing
virtual world
13 bulletin board
crowdsourcing
cyber bullying
microblogging
mobile network

social network
text messaging
user-generated
14 group messaging
hosting service
internet dating
predictive text
privacy setting
social software
15 Friends Reunited
social media site

See also **computer; Internet; video game**

society

Societies include:

03 BCS
BPS
CSP
ENS
04 BNES

BRCS
05 ASLEF
Royal
06 burial

choral
Dorcas
07 benefit
Camorra

08 affluent
building
friendly
Red Cross

sociology

Terms used in sociology include:

06 family
gender
07 culture
in-group
10 demography
matriarchy
patriarchy
subculture
underclass

11 dysfunction
gender roles
megalopolis
12 assimilation
primary group
13 class conflict
ethnocentrism
nuclear family

14 achieved status
ascribed status
extended family
life expectancy
secondary group
social mobility
stratification
tertiary sector
15 absolute poverty

sofa

Sofas include:

05 couch
divan
futon
squab
06 canapé
day bed
litter

lounge
settee
sunbed
07 bergère
casting
dos-à-dos
lounger

sofa bed
09 banquette
bed-settee
davenport
tête-à-tête
twoseater
10 sun lounger

11 studio couch
12 chaise-longue
chesterfield

See also **chair**

solar system *see* **planet**

soldier

Soldier types include:

02 GI	sentry	trooper	irregular
03 NCO	sniper	warrior	mercenary
05 cadet	troops	**08** commando	minuteman
tommy	**07** dragoon	fusilier	**10** cavalryman
06 ensign	fighter	partisan	serviceman
gunner	officer	rifleman	**11** infantryman
hussar	orderly	**09** centurion	legionnaire
lancer	private	conscript	paratrooper
marine	recruit	guardsman	Territorial
sapper	regular	guerrilla	**12** sharpshooter
	terrier		

Soldiers include:

02 Li (Hongzhang; 1823–1901, Chinese)

03 Chu (Te; 1886–1976, Chinese)
Chu (Teh; 1886–1976, Chinese)
Cid (El; c.1043–99, Spanish)
Lee (Charles; 1731–82, English/American)
Lee (Henry; 1756–1818, American)
Lee (Robert E; 1807–70, US)
Lin (Biao; 1908–71, Chinese)
Lin (Piao; 1908–71, Chinese)
Mac (*Rusty Bugles*, 1948, Sumner Locke Elliott)
Odd (Sgt Fred; *Keep the Home Guard Turning*, 1943, Compton Mackenzie)
Wet (Christiaan de; 1854–1922, Boer)
Zhu (De; 1886–1976, Chinese)

04 Alba (Ferdinand Alvarez de Toledo, Duke of; 1508–82, Spanish)
Alva (Ferdinand Alvarez de Toledo, Duke of; 1508–82, Spanish)
Amin (Idi; 1925–2003, Ugandan)
Byng (Julian, Viscount; 1862–1935, English)
Cade (Jack; d.1450, Irish)
Cope (Sir John; d.1760, English)
Díaz (Porfirio; 1830–1915, Mexican)
Foch (Ferdinand; 1851–1929, French)
Gage (Thomas; 1721–87, English)
Haig (Alexander; 1924–2010, US)
Haig (Douglas, Earl, 1861–1928, Scottish)
Hood (John B; 1831–79, US)
Howe (William, Viscount; 1729–1814, English)
Hull (William; 1753–1825, American)
Jamy (*Henry V*, 1599, William Shakespeare)
Knox (Henry; 1750–1806, US)
Mack (Karl, Freiherr von; 1752–1828, Austrian)
Monk (George, Duke of Albemarle; 1608–70, English)
Pile (Sir Frederick, Baronet; 1884–1976, English)
Polk (Leonidas; 1806–64, US)
Rich (Brackenbury; *The Suicide Club*, 1878, Robert Louis Stevenson)
Saxe (Maurice, Comte de; 1696–1750, French)
Slim (William, Viscount; 1891–1970, English)
Tojo (Hideki; 1885–1948, Japanese)
Troy (Sgt Francis; *Far from the Madding Crowd*, 1874, Thomas Hardy)
York (Sergeant; 1887–1964, US)

05 Aidid (Mohamed Farah; c.1930–1996, Somali)
Allen (Ethan; 1738–89, American)
André (John; 1751–80, English)
Arnim (Hans Georg von; 1581–1641, German)
Arnim (Jürgen, Baron von; 1891–1971, German)
Barak (Ehud; 1942– , Israeli)
Bixio (Girolamo; 1821–73, Italian)
Botha (Louis; 1862–1919, South African)
Bowie (Jim; 1790–1836, US/Mexican)
Boyle (Roger, Earl of Orrery; 1621–79, Irish)
Bruce (Robert; 1274–1329, Scottish)
Brune (Guillaume Marie Anne; 1762–1815, French)
Cecil (Thomas, Earl of Exeter; 1542–1623, English)
Chard (John; 1847–97, English)
Cimon (c.507–c.450 BC, Athenian)
Clark (Mark; 1896–1984, US)
Cleon (d.422 BC, Athenian)
Condé (Louis I de Bourbon, Prince de; 1530–69, French)
Conté (Lansana; 1934–2008, Guinean)
Coote (Sir Eyre; 1726–83, Anglo-Irish)
Craig (Sir James; 1748–1812, British)
Crook (George; 1829–90, US)
Dayan (Moshe; 1915–81, Israeli)

Derby (James Stanley, Earl of; 1606–51, English)

Early (Jubal; 1816–94, US)

Essex (Robert Devereux, Earl of; 1591–1646, English)

Evans (Lance-Bombardier; *Events While Guarding the Bofors Gun*, 1966, John McGrath)

Ewell (Richard; 1817–72, US)

Glubb (Sir John; 1897–1986, English)

Gough (Hugh, Viscount; 1779–1869, Anglo-Irish)

Gower (*Henry V*, 1599, William Shakespeare)

Gowon (Yakubu; 1934– , Nigerian)

Grant (Ulysses S; 1822–85, US)

Guise (Claude of Lorraine, Duke of; 1496–1550, French)

Guise (Francis, Duke of; 1519–63, French)

Heros (*The Woman*, 1978, Edward Bond)

Hicks (William; 1830–83, English)

Inönü (Ismet; 1884–1973, Turkish)

Ismay (Hastings, Lord; 1887–1965, English)

Junot (Andoche, Duc d'Abrantès; 1771–1813, French)

Kluge (Günther von; 1882–1944, German)

Konev (Ivan; 1897–1973, Soviet)

Lebed (Alexander; 1950–2002, Russian)

Leese (Sir Oliver; 1894–1978, English)

Meade (George G; 1815–72, US)

Monck (George, Duke of Albemarle; 1608–70, English)

Moore (Sir Jeremy; 1928–2007, English)

Moore (Sir John; 1761–1809, Scottish)

Mosby (John S; 1833–1916, US)

Murat (Joachim; 1767–1815, French)

Nolan (Des; *Rusty Bugles*, 1948, Sumner Locke Elliott)

North (Oliver; 1943– , US)

Perón (Juan; 1895–1974, Argentine)

Pride (Thomas; d.1658, English)

Rabin (Itzhak; 1922–95, Israeli)

Rabin (Yitzhak; 1922–95, Israeli)

Sadat (Anwar el-; 1918–81, Egyptian)

San Yu (U; 1919–96, Burmese)

Sawin (Birdofredum; *The Biglow Papers*, 1848, James Russell Lowell)

Smuts (Jan; 1870–1950, South African)

Stack (Lee; d.1924, British)

Stark (John; 1728–1822, American)

Sucre (Antonio José de; 1793–1830, South American)

Sully (Maximilien de Béthune, Duc de; 1560–1641, French)

Tilly (Johann Tserklaes, Count von; 1559–1632, Bavarian)

Timur (1336–1405, Tatar)

Wayne (Anthony; 1745–96, American)

Wyatt (Sir Thomas, the Younger; c.1520–54, English)

06 Abacha (Sani; 1943–98, Nigerian)

Abboud (Ibrahim; 1900–83, Sudanese)

Abrams (Creighton; 1914–74, US)

Anders (Wladyslaw; 1892–1970, Polish)

Angelo (Private; *Private Angelo*, 1946, Eric Linklater)

Antony (Mark; c.83–30 BC, Roman)

Aumale (Duc d'; 1822–97, French)

Baldry (Captain Chris; *The Return of the Soldier*, 1918, Rebecca West)

Barton (David; *Strange Meeting*, 1971, Susan Hill)

Bayard (Pierre du Terrail, Chevalier de; 1476–1524, French)

Baynes (Gen; *The Adventures of Philip*, 1861–62, W M Thackeray)

Blamey (Sir Thomas; 1884–1951, Australian)

Blount (Charles, Earl of Devonshire; 1563–1606, English)

Borgia (Cesare; c.1476–1507, Italian)

Bosola (Daniel de; *The Duchess of Malfi*, 1623, John Webster)

Brooke (Sir James; 1803–68, English)

Brooks (Sgt; *Rusty Bugles*, 1948, Sumner Locke Elliott)

Browne (Sir Sam; 1824–1901, British)

Buhari (Muhammadu; 1942– , Nigerian)

Cortés (Hernán; 1485–1547, Spanish)

Cortés (Hernando; 1485–1547, Spanish)

Crerar (Harry; 1888–1965, Canadian)

Cronje (Piet; 1835–1911, South African)

Custer (George; 1839–76, US)

Davies (Christian; 1667–1739, Irish)

Dobbie (Sir William; 1879–1964, English)

Drouet (Jean Baptiste, Comte d'Erlon; 1765–1844, French)

Dufour (Guillaume Henri; 1787–1875, Swiss)

Dundee (John Graham, Viscount; c.1649–1689, Scottish)

Egmond (Lamoraal, Graf van; 1522–68, Flemish)

Egmont (Lamoraal, Graf van; 1522–68, Flemish)

Ershad (Hossain; 1930– , Bangladeshi)

Fabius (d.203 BC, Roman)

Falcon (Ken; *Rusty Bugles*, 1948, Sumner Locke Elliott)

Frunze (Mikhail; 1885–1925, Russian)

Fuller (John; 1878–1966, English)

Gatsby (Jay; *The Great Gatsby*, 1925, F Scott Fitzgerald)

Ginkel (Godert de, Earl of Athlone; 1630–1703, Dutch/British)

Giraud (Henri; 1879–1949, French)

Görgey (Artúr; 1818–1916, Hungarian)

Granby (John Manners, Marquis of; 1721–70, English)
Greene (Nathanael; 1742–86, American)
Haynau (Julius, Baron von; 1786–1853, Austrian)
Hooker (Joseph; 1814–79, US)
Howard (Oliver O; 1830–1909, US)
Howard (Thomas, Duke of Norfolk and Earl of Surrey; 1443–1524, English)
Joffre (Joseph; 1852–1931, French)
Keitel (Wilhelm; 1882–1946, German)
Lovell (Lord; *A New Way to Pay Old Debts*, 1633, Philip Massinger)
Moltke (Helmuth; 1848–1916, German)
Moltke (Helmuth, Count von; 1800–91, Prussian)
Monash (Sir John; 1865–1931, Australian)
Murphy (Audie; 1924–71, US)
Murray (Lord George; c.1700–1760, Scottish)
Napier (Robert, Lord; 1810–90, British)
Nasser (Gamal Abd al-; 1918–70, Egyptian)
Neguib (Mohammed; 1901–84, Egyptian)
Nicias (d.413 BC, Athenian)
Ojukwu (Chukwuemeka; 1933–2011, Nigerian)
Otford (Eric; *Rusty Bugles*, 1948, Sumner Locke Elliott)
Patton (George; 1885–1945, US)
Paulus (Friedrich; 1890–1957, German)
Pétain (Philippe; 1856–1951, French)
Pierre (*Venice Preserv'd*, 1682, Thomas Otway)
Plumer (Herbert, Viscount; 1857–1932, English)
Pompey (106–48 BC, Roman)
Powell (Colin; 1937–   , US)
Procop (Andrew; c.1380–1434, Bohemian)
Prokop (Andrew; c.1380–1434, Bohemian)
Putnam (Israel; 1718–90, American)
Raglan (Fitzroy Somerset, Lord; 1788–1855, English)
Rahman (Ziaur; 1935–81, Bangladeshi)
Revere (Paul; 1735–1818, American)
Rommel (Erwin; 1891–1944, German)
Rupert (Prince; 1619–82, English)
Sevier (John; 1745–1815, US)
Sharpe (Richard; *Sharpe's Eagle*, et seq, 1981, Bernard Cornwell)
Smalls (Robert; 1839–1915, US)
Stalky (*Stalky & Co*, 1899, Rudyard Kipling)
Stuart (Jeb; 1833–64, US)
Sumter (Thomas; 1734–1832, American)
Talbot (Mary Anne; 1778–1808, English)
Talbot (Sir John, Earl Shrewsbury; c.1390–1453, English)
Turvey (*Turvey: a Military Picaresque*, 1949, Earle Birney)

Vauban (Sebastien le Prestre de; 1633–1707, French)
Waller (Sir William; c.1597–1688, English)
Wavell (Archibald, Earl; 1883–1950, English)
Wilson (Henry, Lord; 1881–1964, English)

07 Allenby (Edmund, Viscount; 1861–1936, English)
Almagro (Diego de; 1475–1538, Spanish)
Amherst (Jeffrey, Lord; 1717–97, English)
Apraxin (Stepan, Count; 1702–58, Russian)
Artigas (José; 1764–1850, Uruguayan)
Bazaine (Achille François; 1811–88, French)
Bedford (John of Lancaster, Duke of; 1389–1435, English)
Blücher (Gebhard von, Prince of Wahlstadt; 1742–1819, Prussian)
Bokassa (Jean Bédel; 1921–96, Central African Republic)
Bourbon (Charles; 1490–1527, French)
Brandon (Charles, Duke of Suffolk; 1484–1545, English)
Buckner (Simon B, Jnr; 1886–1945, US)
Budenny (Semyon; 1883–1973, Russian)
Bugeaud (Thomas; 1784–1849, French)
Bullock (John; *A Patriot's Progress*, 1930, Henry Williamson)
Cadogan (William, Earl; 1675–1726, English)
Caprivi (Leo, Graf von; 1831–99, German)
Catroux (Georges; 1877–1969, French)
Clinton (James; 1736–1812, American)
Clinton (Sir Henry; c.1738–1795, Canadian/British)
Coligny (Gaspard de, Duc; 1519–72, French)
Crillon (Louis de; 1541–1615, French)
Dalyell (Thomas; c.1615–1685, Scottish)
Dalzell (Thomas; c.1615–1685, Scottish)
Denikin (Anton; 1872–1947, Russian)
Dreyfus (Alfred; c.1859–1935, French)
Edmonds (Sarah; 1841–98, Canadian)
Enghien (Louis Antoine Henri de Bourbon, Duc d'; 1772–1804, French)
Farnese (Alessandro; 1546–92, Italian/Spanish)
Gaddafi (Muammar; 1942–2011, Libyan)
Gamelin (Maurice; 1872–1958, French)
Gemayel (Bashir; 1947–82, Lebanese)
Grenfel (Henry; *The Fox*, 1923, D H Lawrence)
Grouchy (Emmanuel, Marquis de; 1766–1847, French)
Hackett (Sir John; 1910–97, Australian/British)
Halleck (Henry W; 1815–72, US)
Hampton (Wade; 1818–1902, US)
Hancock (Winfield Scott; 1824–86, US)

Hunyady (János; c.1387–1456, Hungarian)
Hunyady (John; c.1387–1456, Hungarian)
Jackson (Sir W G F; 1917–99, English)
Jackson (Thomas 'Stonewall'; 1824–63, US)
Joubert (Piet; 1834–1900, Afrikaner)
Jourdan (Jean-Baptiste, Comte; 1762–1833, French)
Kérékou (Mathieu; 1933– , Benin)
Kolchak (Aleksandr; 1874–1920, Russian)
Kutuzov (Mikhail, Prince of Smolensk; 1745–1813, Russian)
Lambert (Gen; *The Virginians*, 1857–59, W M Thackeray)
Leclerc (Jacques Philippe; 1902–47, French)
Le Clerc (Jacques Philippe; 1902–47, French)
Le Fever (Lieutenant; *The Life and Opinions of Tristram Shandy*, 1759–67, Laurence Sterne)
MacTurk (Captain Hector; *St Ronan's Well*, 1823, Sir Walter Scott)
Marmont (Auguste de; 1774–1852, French)
Mastern (Cass; *All the King's Men*, 1946, Robert Penn Warren)
Metaxas (Yanni; 1870–1941, Greek)
Narváez (Ramón María; 1800–68, Spanish)
Nimeiri (Gaafar; 1930–2009, Sudanese)
Nivelle (Robert; 1857–1924, French)
Noriega (Manuel; 1940– , Panamanian)
Phocion (c.397–318 BC, Athenian)
Pizarro (Francisco; c.1478–1541, Spanish)
Pizarro (Gonzalo; c.1506–48, Spanish)
Prewitt (Robert E Lee; *From Here to Eternity*, 1951, James Jones)
Ptolemy (I; c.367–283 BC, Egyptian)
Qaddafi (Muammar; 1942–2011, Libyan)
Ritchie (Sir Neil; 1897–1983, Scottish)
Roberts (Frederick, Earl; 1832–1914, English)
Sankara (Thomas; 1950–87, Burkina Faso)
Sarrail (Maurice; 1856–1929, French)
Savimbi (Jonas; 1934–2002, Angolan)
Searing (Private Jerome; 'One of the Missing', 1888, Ambrose Bierce)
Sherman (William; 1820–91, US)
Skinner (James; 1778–1841, Indian)
Speidel (Hans; 1897–1984, German)
Spinola (Ambrogio, Marquis of Los Balbases; 1539–1630, Genoese)
St Clair (Arthur; 1736–1818, Scottish/American)
Steuben (Frederick, Baron; 1730–94, German/American)
Strozzi (Piero; 1510–58, Italian)
Suharto (Thojib N J; 1921–2008, Indonesian)
Suvorov (Aleksandr, Count; 1729–1800, Russian)
Svoboda (Ludvík; 1895–1979, Czech)
Tancred (1078–1112, Norman)

Templer (Sir Gerald; 1898–1979, English)
Turenne (Henri de la Tour d'Auvergne, Vicomte de; 1611–75, French)
Vendôme (Louis Joseph, Duc de; 1654–1712, French)
Villars (Claude, Duc de; 1653–1734, French)
Warwick (Richard Neville, Earl of; 1428–71, English)
Weygand (Maxime; 1867–1965, Belgian/French)
Wingate (Orde; 1903–44, English)
Yolland (Lieutenant George; *Translations*, 1981, Brian Friel)
Zapolya (Stephen; d.1499, Hungarian)

08 Absolute (Captain Jack; *The Rivals*, 1775, R B Sheridan)
Alvarado (Pedro de; c.1485–1541, Spanish)
Anderson (Robert; 1806–71, US)
Anglesey (Henry Paget, Marquis of; 1768–1854, English)
Apraksin (Stepan, Count; 1702–58, Russian)
Arminius (d.19 AD, German/Roman)
Aubusson (Pierre d'; 1423–1503, French)
Augereau (Pierre, Duc de Castiglione; 1757–1816, French)
Ayub Khan (Mohammed; 1907–74, Pakistani)
Bamforth (*The Long and the Short and the Tall*, 1958, Willis Hall)
Bobadill (Captain; *Every Man in his Humour*, 1598, Ben Jonson)
Bothwell (Sgt; *Old Mortality*, 1816, Sir Walter Scott)
Braddock (Edward; 1695–1755, Scottish)
Brusilov (Aleksei; 1856–1926, Russian)
Burgoyne (John; 1722–92, English)
Burnside (Ambrose; 1824–81, US)
Campbell (Sir Colin; 1792–1863, Scottish)
Castaños (Francisco de, Duke of Bailen; 1756–1852, Spanish)
Colleoni (Bartolommeo; 1400–75, Italian)
Cromwell (Oliver; 1599–1658, English)
Dalgetty (Captain Dugald, of Drumthwacket; *A Legend of Montrose*, 1819, Sir Walter Scott)
Eichmann (Adolf; 1906–62, Austrian)
Endicott (John; 'The Maypole of Merry Mount', 1836, Nathaniel Hawthorne)
Fielding (Sgt; *Too True to be Good*, 1932, George Bernard Shaw)
Fluellen (*Henry V*, 1599, William Shakespeare)
Freyberg (Bernard, Lord; 1889–1963, English/New Zealand)
Galliéni (Joseph; 1849–1916, French)
Galtieri (Leopoldo; 1926–2003, Argentine)
Gilligan (Joe; *Soldier's Pay*, 1926, William

Faulkner)

Ginckell (Godert de, Earl of Athlone; 1630–1703, Dutch/British)

Graziani (Rodolfo, Marchese di Neghelli; 1882–1955, Italian)

Guesclin (Bertrand du; c.1320–80, French)

Guiscard (Robert; c.1015–85, Norman)

Hamilcar (c.270–228 BC, Carthaginian)

Hamilton (James, Duke of; 1606–49, Scottish)

Hannibal (247–182 BC, Carthaginian)

Hardinge (Henry, Viscount; 1785–1856, English)

Harrison (Thomas; 1606–60, English)

Harrison (William Henry; 1773–1841, US)

Hastings (Francis, Marquis of; 1754–1826, English)

Havelock (Sir Henry; 1795–1857, English)

Horrocks (Sir Brian; 1895–1985, English)

Hyder Ali (1728–82, Indian)

Ironside (William Edmund, Lord; 1880–1959, Scottish)

Lawrence (T E; 1888–1935, Anglo-Irish)

Lucullus (c.110–57 BC, Roman)

MacMahon (Patrice de; 1808–93, French)

Manstein (Erich von; 1887–1973, German)

Marcello (*The White Devil*, 1612, John Webster)

Marrable (Captain Walter; *The Vicar of Bullhampton*, 1870, Anthony Trollope)

Marshall (George; 1880–1959, US)

Montcalm (Louis Joseph, Marquis de; 1712–59, French)

Montfort (Simon de, Earl of Leicester; c.1208–65, English)

Morshead (Sir Leslie; 1889–1959, Australian)

Museveni (Yoweri; 1944– , Ugandan)

Nicholas (Grand-Duke; 1856–1929, Russian)

Obasanjo (Olusegun; 1937– , Nigerian)

O'Donnell (Leopoldo; 1809–67, Spanish)

Pershing (John; 1860–1948, US)

Pinochet (Augusto; 1915–2006, Chilean)

Randolph (Sir Thomas; d.1332, Scottish)

Richards (Vic; *Rusty Bugles*, 1948, Sumner Locke Elliott)

Sanjurjo (José; 1872–1936, Spanish)

Scarlett (Sir James Yorke; 1799–1871, English)

Sheridan (Philip; 1831–88, US)

Shrapnel (Henry; 1761–1842, English)

Sikorski (Władysław; 1881–1943, Polish)

Skorzeny (Otto; 1908–75, Austrian)

Soeharto (Thojib N J; 1921–2008, Indonesian)

Standish (Miles; *The Courtship of Miles Standish*, 1858, Henry Wadsworth Longfellow)

Stanhope (Dennis; *Journey's End*, 1928, R C Sherriff)

Stanhope (James, Earl; 1673–1721, English)

Stilicho (Flavius; c.365–408 AD, Roman)

Stilwell (Joseph W; 1883–1946, US)

Stirling (Sir David; 1915–90, Scottish)

Sullivan (John; 1740–95, American)

Tarleton (Sir Banastre; 1754–1833, English)

Tokugawa (Ieyasu; 1543–1616, Japanese)

Valdivia (Pedro de; c.1510–59, Spanish)

Wauchope (Sir Arthur; 1874–1947, Scottish)

Williams (Leslie; *The Hostage*, 1957, Brendan Behan)

Williams (Private Ellgee; *Reflections in a Golden Eye*, 1941, Carson McCullers)

Winthrop (John; 1639–1707, Anglo-American)

Wolseley (Garnet, Viscount; 1833–1913, British)

Xenophon (c.435–c.354 BC, Greek)

Yamagata (Aritomo; 1838–1922, Japanese)

Zia ul-Haq (Mohammed; 1924–88, Pakistani)

09 Alexander (Harold, Earl; 1891–1969, Anglo-Irish)

Angoulême (Louis Antoine de Bourbon, Duc d'; 1775–1844, French)

Babangida (Ibrahim; 1941– , Nigerian)

Bellenden (Major Miles, of Charnwood; *Old Mortality*, 1816, Sir Walter Scott)

Bennigsen (Levin, Count; 1745–1826, German)

Beresford (William Carr Beresford, Viscount; 1768–1854, British)

Bonaparte (Jérôme; 1784–1860, French)

Bonaparte (Napoleon; 1769–1821, French)

Carausius (d.293 AD, Roman)

Castelnau (Noël, Vicomte de; 1851–1944, French)

Cavaignac (Louis Eugène; 1802–57, French)

Cavendish (William, Duke of Newcastle; 1592–1676, English)

Dalhousie (James Ramsay, Marquis of; 1812–60, Scottish)

Fergusson (Bernard, Lord Ballantrae; 1911–80, Scottish)

Fleetwood (Charles; c.1618–1692, English)

Garibaldi (Giuseppe; 1807–82, Italian)

Gneisenau (August, Graf von; 1760–1831, Prussian)

Gondarino (*The Woman Hater*, 1605, Francis Beaumont)

Gorchakov (Prince Mikhail; 1795–1861, Russian)

Grenville (Sir Bevil; 1596–1643, English)

Haidar Ali (1728–82, Indian)

Hideyoshi (Toyotomi; 1536–98, Japanese)

Kim-Il Sung (1912–94, North Korean)

Kitchener (Horatio, Earl; 1850–1916, British)
La Marmora (Alfonso; 1804–78, Italian)
Lismahago (Lieutenant Obadiah; *The Expedition of Humphry Clinker*, 1771, Tobias Smollett)
MacArthur (Douglas; 1880–1964, US)
Macdonald (Jacques, Duc de Tarente; 1765–1840, French)
Macdonald (Sir Hector; 1857–1903, Scottish)
Macmorris (*Henry V*, 1599, William Shakespeare)
Musharraf (Pervaiz; 1943– , Pakistani)
Napoleon I (1769–1821, French)
Oldcastle (Sir John; c.1378–1417, English)
Pausanias (5c BC, Spartan)
Pelopidas (d.364 BC, Theban)
Peniakoff (Vladimir; 1897–1951, Belgian)
Pilsudski (Józef; 1867–1935, Polish)
Rawlinson (Henry, Lord; 1864–1925, English)
Rosecrans (William S; 1819–98, US)
Rundstedt (Karl von; 1875–1953, German)
San Martin (José de; 1778–1850, Argentine)
Santa Anna (Antonio López de; 1797–1876, Mexican)
Sarsfield (Patrick, Earl of Lucan; c.1645–1693, Irish)
Schofield (John; 1831–1906, US)
Schomberg (Frederick Hermann, Duke of; 1615–90, German/French)
Sertorius (123–72 BC, Roman)
Spartacus (d.71 BC, Roman)
Trenchard (Hugh, Viscount; 1873–1956, English)
Waldstein (Albrecht von; 1583–1634, Austrian)
Worcester (Sir Thomas Percy, Earl of; 1344–1403, English)
Yahya Khan (Agha Muhammad; 1917–80, Pakistani)
Yamashita (Tomoyuki; 1885–1946, Japanese)

10 Abd-el-Kader (1807–83, Algerian)
Acheampong (Ignatius; 1931–79, Ghanaian)
Ahmed Arabi (1839–1911, Egyptian)
Alanbrooke (Alan Brooke, Lord; 1883–1963, British)
Alcibiades (c.450–404 BC, Athenian)
Amr ibn al-'As (d.664, Arab)
Auchinleck (Sir Claude; 1884–1981, English)
Bluntschli (*Arms and the Man*, 1894, George Bernard Shaw)
Clausewitz (Karl von; 1780–1831, Prussian)
Cornwallis (Charles; 1738–1805, English)
Cumberland (William Augustus, Duke of; 1721–65, English)
Enver Pasha (1881–1922, Turkish)
Falkenhayn (Erich von; 1861–1922,

German)
Frundsberg (Georg von; 1473–1528, German)
Heathfield (George Augustus Eliott, Lord; 1717–90, Scottish)
Hindenburg (Paul von; 1847–1934, German)
Humgudgeon (*Woodstock*, 1826, Sir Walter Scott)
Jaruzelski (Wojciech; 1923– , Polish)
Kellermann (François Christophe, Duc de Valmy; 1735–1820, French)
Kościuszko (Tadeusz; 1746–1817, Polish/US)
Kuropatkin (Aleksei; 1848–1925, Russian)
Longstreet (James; 1821–1904, US)
Ludendorff (Erich; 1865–1937, German)
Luxembourg (François Henri de Montmorency-Bouteville, Duc de; 1628–95, French)
Malinovsky (Rodion; 1898–1967, Russian)
Manchester (Edward Montagu, Earl of; 1602–71, English)
Mannerheim (Carl Gustav, Baron; 1867–1951, Finnish)
McNaughton (Andrew; 1887–1966, Canadian)
Montgomery (Bernard, Viscount; 1887–1976, English)
Rochambeau (Jean Baptiste Donatien de Vimeur, Comte de; 1725–1807, French)
Saint Clair (Arthur; 1736–1818, Scottish/American)
Schlieffen (Alfred, Count von; 1833–1913, Prussian)
Sébastiani (Horace, Count; 1772–1851, French)
Stroessner (Alfredo; 1912–2006, Paraguayan)
Urabi Pasha (1839–1911, Egyptian)
Voroshilov (Kliment; 1881–1969, Soviet)
Washington (George; 1732–99, US)
Wellington (Arthur Wellesley, Duke of; 1769–1852, Anglo-Irish)
William III (1650–1702, Dutch)

11 Baden-Powell (Robert, Lord; 1857–1941, English)
Cincinnatus (Lucius Quinctius; fl.460 BC, Roman)
Demosthenes (d.413 BC, Athenian)
Genghis Khan (c.1162–1227, Mongol)
Habyarimana (Juvenal; 1937–94, Rwandan)
Marlborough (John Churchill, Duke of; 1650–1722, English)
Mihailovich (Draza; 1893–1946, Serbian)
Montmorency (Anne, Duc de; 1493–1567, French)
Philopoemen (c.253–182 BC, Greek)
Poniatowski (Joseph; 1762–1813, Polish)
Rokossovsky (Konstantin; 1896–1968,

Russian)
Scharnhorst (Gerhard von; 1755–1813,
 German)
Tantia Topee (d.1859, Indian)
Wallenstein (Albrecht von; 1583–1634,
 Austrian)
Ziaur Rahman (1935–81, Bangladeshi)

12 Aguiyi-Ironsi (Johnson; 1925–66, Nigerian)
de Chastelain (John; 1937– , British/
 Canadian)
Papadopoulos (George; 1919–99, Greek)
Tukhachevsky (Mikhail; 1893–1937,
 Russian)
Westmoreland (William; 1914–2005, US)

13 Charles Martel (c.688–741, Frankish)
Eugène of Savoy (Prince; 1663–1736,
 French/Austrian)
John of Austria (Don; 1547–78, Spanish)
Komorowski-Bór (Tadeusz; 1895–1966,

Polish)
Musa ibn Nosair (640–717, Arab)
Musa ibn Nusayr (640–717, Arab)
Queipo de Llano (Gonzalo; 1875–1951,
 Spanish)
Van Rensselaer (Stephen; 1765–1839,
 American)

14 Chadli Benjedid (1929–2012, Algerian)
Nguyen Van Thieu (1923–2001, Vietnamese)

15 Desaix de Veygoux (Louis; 1768–1800,
 French)
Díaz del Castillo (Bernal; c.1492–1581,
 Spanish)
Eumenes of Cardia (c.360–316 BC,
 Macedonian)
La Tour d'Auvergne (Théophile Malo Corret
 de; 1743–1800, French)
Scipio Africanus (236–183 BC, Roman)

See also **general**

son

Sons include:

04 Abel (Bible)
Amis (Martin; 1949– , English)
Bush (George W; 1946– , US)
Cain (Bible)
Esau (Bible)
Pitt (William; 1759–1806, English)

05 Dumas (Alexandre; 1824–95, French)
Groan (Titus; *Gormenghast* trilogy, 1946–59,
 Mervyn Peake)
Harry (Prince; 1984– , English)
Isaac (Bible)
Jacob (Bible)
Milne (Christopher Robin; 1920–96,
 English)
Morel (Paul; *Sons and Lovers*, 1913, D H
 Lawrence)
Waugh (Auberon; 1939–2001, English)

06 Andrew (Prince; 1960– , English)
Edward (Prince; 1964– , English)
Gandhi (Rajiv; 1944–91, Indian)
Hamlet (*Hamlet*, 1600–01, William
 Shakespeare)
Joseph (Bible)

07 Absalom (Bible)
Charles (Prince; 1948– , English)
Douglas (Michael; 1944– , US)
Hotspur (*Henry IV Part I*, 1596–97, William
 Shakespeare)
Laertes (*Hamlet*, 1600–01, William
 Shakespeare)
Oedipus (Greek mythology)
Simpson (Bart; *The Simpsons*, TV show)
William (Prince; 1982– , English)

08 Benjamin (Bible)
Dimbleby (David; 1938– , English)
Dimbleby (Jonathan; 1944– , English)
Florizel (*The Winter's Tale*, 1609, William
 Shakespeare)
Pontifex (Ernest; *The Way of All Flesh*, 1903,
 Samuel Butler)

09 Dumas fils (Alexandre; 1824–95, French)

10 Duke of York (1960– , English)

11 Jesus Christ (c.6 BC–c.30 AD)

13 Prince of Wales (1948– , English)

14 Pitt the Younger (William; 1759–1806, English)

song

Song types include:

03		**04**	
air	pop	aria	lied
art		bird	lilt
lay	pub	folk	love
ode	war	hymn	rock

tune	anthem	descant	dithyramb
05 blues	ballad	lullaby	epinikion
carol	chorus	refrain	roundelay
chant	gospel	requiem	spiritual
dirge	jingle	wassail	**10** plainchant
ditty	lyrics	**08** birdcall	recitative
elegy	melody	canticle	**11** bothy ballad
lyric	number	canzonet	chansonette
plain	shanty	madrigal	rock and roll
psalm	**07** calypso	serenade	**12** epithalamium
torch	cantata	threnody	nursery rhyme
yodel	canzone	**09** barcarole	**14** Negro spiritual
06 amoret	chanson	cantilena	

Songwriters include:

03 Gow (Niel; 1727–1807, Scottish)
Pop (Iggy; 1947– , US)

04 Bush (Kate; 1958– , English)
Cahn (Sammy; 1913–93, US)
Cash (Johnny; 1932–2003, US)
Hill (Joe; c.1872–1915, Swedish/US)
John (Sir Elton; 1947– , English)
Kern (Jerome; 1885–1945, US)
Reed (Lou; 1944– , US)

05 Allen (Lily; 1985– , English)
Arlen (Harold; 1905–86, US)
Berry (Chuck; 1926– , US)
Blunt (James; 1974– , English)
Brown (James; 1928–2006, US)
Brown (Nacio Herb; 1896–1954, US)
Burns (Robert; 1759–96, Scottish)
Cohan (George M; 1878–1942, US)
Davis (Miles; 1926–91, US)
Dylan (Bob; 1941– , US)
Gordy (Berry, Jnr; 1929– , US)
Holly (Buddy; 1936–59, US)
Loewe (Frederick; 1904–88, German/US)
Lover (Samuel; 1797–1868, Irish)
Melua (Ketevan (Katie); 1984– , Georgian/
English)
Simon (Paul; 1941– , US)
Smith (Tommy; 1967– , Scottish)
Sousa (John Philip; 1854–1932, US)
Sting (1951– , English)
Styne (Jule; 1905–94, English/US)
Tormé (Mel; 1925–99, US)
Waits (Tom; 1949– , US)
Weill (Kurt; 1900–50, US)
Young (Neil; 1945– , Canadian)

06 Berlin (Irving; 1888–1989, Russian/US)
Coward (Sir Noël; 1899–1973, English)
Dibdin (Charles; 1745–1814, English)
D'Urfey (Tom; 1653–1723, English)
Foster (Stephen; 1826–64, US)
Herman (Jerry; 1932– , US)
Jagger (Mick; 1943– , English)

Jensen (Adolf; 1837–79, German)
Joplin (Scott; 1868–1917, US)
Lennon (John; 1940–80, English)
Lovett (Lyle; 1956– , US)
Marley (Bob; 1945–81, Jamaican)
McHugh (Jimmy; 1896–1969, US)
Mercer (Johnny H; 1909–76, US)
Morton (Jelly Roll; 1890–1941, US)
Nairne (Lady Carolina; 1766–1845,
Scottish)
Nelson (Willie; 1933– , US)
Oliver (King; 1885–1938, US)
Parker (Charlie; 1920–55, US)
Parton (Dolly; 1946– , US)
Porter (Cole; 1891–1964, US)
Seeger (Pete; 1919– , US)
Waller (Fats; 1904–43, US)
Warren (Harry; 1893–1981, US)

07 Boswell (Alexander, Baronet; 1775–1822,
Scottish)
Britten (Benjamin, Lord; 1913–76, English)
Collins (Phil; 1951– , English)
Dickson (Barbara; 1947– , Scottish)
Donovan (Leitch; 1946– , Scottish)
Dowland (John; 1563–1626, English)
Gabriel (Peter; 1950– , English)
Guthrie (Woody; 1912–67, US)
Haggard (Merle; 1937– , US)
Hendrix (Jimi; 1942–70, US)
Loesser (Frank Henry; 1910–69, US)
MacColl (Ewan; 1915–89, Scottish)
Mancini (Henry; 1924–94, US)
Michael (George; 1963– , English)
Novello (Ivor; 1893–1951, Welsh)
Orbison (Roy; 1936–88, US)
Rodgers (Jimmie; 1897–1933, US)
Rodgers (Richard; 1902–79, US)
Romberg (Sigmund; 1887–1951, US)
Ulvaeus (Björn; 1945– , Swedish)

08 Coltrane (John; 1926–67, US)
Costello (Elvis; 1955– , English)

Gershwin (George; 1898–1937, US)
Griffith (Nanci; 1954– , US)
Harrison (George; 1943–2001, English)
Jennings (Waylon; 1937–2002, US)
Mitchell (Joni; 1943– , Canadian)
Morrison (Van; 1945– , Northern Irish)
Schubert (Franz; 1797–1828, Austrian)
Schumann (Robert; 1810–56, German)
Sondheim (Stephen; 1930– , US)
Thompson (Richard; 1949– , English)
Vandross (Luther; 1951–2005, US)
Williams (Hank; 1923–53, US)

09 Andersson (Benny; 1946– , Swedish)
Bernstein (Leonard; 1918–90, US)
Carpenter (Mary Chapin; 1959– , US)
Ellington (Duke; 1899–1974, US)

See also **musical; pop**

Etheridge (Melissa; 1962– , US)
Faithfull (Marianne; 1946– , English)
Gillespie (Dizzy; 1917–93, US)
McCartney (Sir Paul; 1942– , English)
Winehouse (Amy; 1983–2011, English)

10 Carmichael (Hoagy; 1899–1981, US)
Livingston (Jay; 1915–2001, US)
Wainwright (Loudon, III; 1946– , US)

11 Armatrading (Joan; 1950– , West Indian/
British)
Lloyd-Webber (Andrew, Lord; 1948– ,
English)
Sainte-Marie (Buffy; 1941/42– , US)
Springsteen (Bruce; 1949– , US)

12 Spottiswoode (Alicia Anne; 1810–1900,
Scottish)

sound

Audible sounds include:

03 cry	sigh	drone	murmur
hum	slam	grate	patter
pip	snap	groan	rattle
pop	thud	knock	report
sob	tick	skirl	rumble
tap	ting	slurp	rustle
04 bang	toot	smack	scrape
beep	wail	sniff	scream
boom	yell	snore	sizzle
buzz	**05** blare	snort	splash
chug	blast	swish	squeak
clap	bleep	throb	squeal
echo	chime	thump	tinkle
fizz	chink	twang	**07** clatter
hiss	clack	whine	crackle
honk	clang	whirr	explode
hoot	clank	whoop	grizzle
moan	clash	**06** bubble	screech
peal	click	crunch	squelch
ping	clink	gurgle	thunder
plop	crack	hiccup	whimper
ring	crash	jangle	whistle
roar	creak	jingle	**08** splutter

Geographical sounds include:

03 Hoy (Scotland)	King (Australia)	Inner (Scotland)
Rum (Scotland)	Mull (Scotland)	Islay (Scotland)
04 Bute (Scotland)	Papa (Scotland)	Luing (Scotland)
Calf (Isle of Man)	Rock (The Bahamas)	Puget (USA)
Crow (Scilly Isles)	Yell (Scotland)	Sanda (Scotland)
Deer (Scotland)		Shuna (Scotland)
Eigg (Scotland)	**05** Barra (Scotland)	Sleat (Scotland)
Holm (Scotland)	Canna (Scotland)	
Iona (Scotland)	Cross (USA)	**06** Breton (USA)
Jura (Scotland)	Exuma (The Bahamas)	Harris (Scotland)
	Gigha (Scotland)	Norton (USA)

Pabbay (Scotland)
Raasay (Scotland)
Ramsey (Wales)
Sanday (Scotland)
Shiant (Scotland)
Turner (The Bahamas)
07 Arisaig (Scotland)
Bardsey (Wales)
Caswell (New Zealand)
Cuillin (Scotland)
Gairsay (Scotland)
McMurdo (Antarctica)
Milford (New Zealand)
Pamlico (USA)

St Mary's (Scilly Isles)
08 Auskerry (Scotland)
Bluemull (Scotland)
Breaksea (New Zealand)
Colgrave (Scotland)
Doubtful (New Zealand)
Kotzebue (USA)
Taransay (Scotland)
09 Albemarle (USA)
Casiguran (Philippines)
Currituck (USA)
Eynhallow (Scotland)
Lancaster (Canada)

Shapinsay (Scotland)
10 Chandeleur (USA)
Cumberland (Canada)
Kilbrannan (Scotland)
King George (Australia)
Long Island (USA)
New Georgia (Solomon
Islands)
Possession (USA)
11 Mississippi (USA)
Roes Welcome (Canada)
12 Prince Albert (Canada)
13 Prince William (USA)

See also **animal**

soup

Soups include:

03 dal
pea
pho
04 cawl
crab
dhal
game
miso
05 adrak
blaff
broth
egusi
gumbo
locro
misua
rasam
snert
06 ajiaco
asapao
barley
birria
cocido
congee
fennel
guacho
harira
lentil
noodle
oxtail
pazole
posole
potage
potato
reuben
sambar

tomato
turtle
won ton
07 borscht
chicken
chowder
tarator
turbana
08 borschch
broccoli
callaloo
chirmole
consommé
ful nabed
gazpacho
halászlé
mondongo
mushroom
okroshka
sancocho
solianka
split pea
09 bird's nest
cacciucco
Clanallen
escabeche
fasolatha
pea and ham
pepperpot
picadillo
quimbombo
royal game
rozsolnyk
shark's fin
tom kha gai

white foam
10 avgolemono
caldo verde
minestrone
mock turtle
mole de olla
sauerkraut
superkanja
watercress
11 clam chowder
cock-a-leekie
cullen skink
fish chowder
French onion
gaeng som kai
gaeng som pla
Scotch broth
tom yam goong
vichyssoise
12 beef consommé
bouneschlupp
brown Windsor
chicken broth
guriltai shul
mulligatawny
seafood gumbo
13 bouillabaisse
chicken noodle
cream of tomato
lobster bisque
potato and leek
stracciatella
14 lentil and bacon
15 Queen Anne's broth

South Africa

Cities and notable towns in South Africa include:

06 Benoni
Durban
Soweto
08 Cape Town
Pretoria

09 Kimberley
Ladysmith
Polokwane
10 East London
Klerksdorp

Rustenburg
Simonstown
11 Vereeniging
12 Bloemfontein
Johannesburg

Stellenbosch
13 Port Elizabeth

South African provinces, with regional capitals:

07 Gauteng (Johannesburg)
Limpopo (Polokwane)
09 Free State (Bloemfontein)
North-West (Mmabatho)
10 Mpumalanga (Nelspruit)

11 Eastern Cape (Bisho)
Western Cape (Cape Town)
12 KwaZulu-Natal (Pietermaritzburg)
Northern Cape (Kimberley)

South African landmarks include:

05 Karoo
07 Sun City
10 Mapungubwe
11 Orange River
12 Gold Reef City

Limpopo River
Robben Island
13 Table Mountain
14 Cape of Good Hope
Crocodile River

Rhodes Memorial
The Garden Route

South America *see* The Americas

South-East Asia

Cities and notable towns in South-East Asia include:

03 Hué (Vietnam)

04 Cebu (Philippines)
Dili (East Timor)
Ipoh (Malaysia)
Pegu (Myanmar)
Vinh (Vietnam)

05 Ambon (Indonesia)
Dà Lat (Vietnam)
Davao (Philippines)
Hanoi (Vietnam)
Medan (Indonesia)
My Tho (Vietnam)
Pakse (Laos)

06 Can Tho (Vietnam)
Da Nang (Vietnam)
Ha Long (Vietnam)
Hat Yai (Thailand)
Iloilo (Philippines)
Malang (Indonesia)
Manila (Philippines)
Mérida (Philippines)
Padang (Indonesia)

07 Bacolod (Philippines)
Bandung (Indonesia)

Bangkok (Thailand)
Bien Hoa (Vietnam)
Henzada (Myanmar)
Jakarta (Indonesia)
Kuantan (Malaysia)
Kuching (Malaysia)
Malacca (Malaysia)
Pathein (Myanmar)
Qui Nhon (Vietnam)
Rangoon (Myanmar)
Vung Tàu (Vietnam)

08 Caloocan (Philippines)
Chon Buri (Thailand)
Haiphong (Vietnam)
Jayapura (Indonesia)
Khon Kaen (Thailand)
Mandalay (Myanmar)
Myingyan (Myanmar)
Nha Trang (Vietnam)
Pyinmana (Myanmar)
Semarang (Indonesia)
Seremban (Malaysia)
Siem Reap (Cambodia)
Songkhla (Thailand)
Surabaya (Indonesia)

09 Alor Setar (Malaysia)
Chiang Mai (Thailand)
Chiang Rai (Thailand)
Naypyidaw (Myanmar)
Palembang (Indonesia)
Phnom Penh (Cambodia)
Pontianak (Indonesia)
Putrajaya (Malaysia)
Singapore (Singapore)
Surakarta (Indonesia)
Udon Thani (Thailand)
Vientiane (Laos)

10 Battambang (Cambodia)
George Town (Malaysia)
Kâmpŏng Som (Cambodia)
Kota Baharu (Malaysia)

Mawlamyine (Myanmar)
Nonthaburi (Thailand)
Quezon City (Philippines)
Surat Thani (Thailand)
Yogyakarta (Indonesia)

11 Banjarmasin (Indonesia)
Johor Baharu (Malaysia)
Kuala Lumpur (Malaysia)

12 Kota Kinabalu (Malaysia)
Luang Prabang (Laos)
Petaling Jaya (Malaysia)
Ujung Pandang (Indonesia)

13 Ho Chi Minh City (Vietnam)
Zamboanga City (Philippines)

14 Kuala Trengganu (Malaysia)

spa

Spas include:

03 Dax (France)
04 Bath (England)
05 Baden (Germany)
Baños (Ecuador)
Epsom (England)
Sochi (Russia)
Vichy (France)
06 Aachen (Germany)
Buxton (England)
Ilkley (England)
Trebon (Czech Republic)

07 Lourdes (France)
Malvern (England)
Matlock (England)
08 Carlsbad (Czech Republic)
Shearsby (England)
09 Bad Elster (Germany)
Boston Spa (England)
Droitwich (England)
Harrogate (England)
Marienbad (Czech Republic)
Velingrad (Bulgaria)

10 Baden Baden (Germany)
Cheltenham (England)
11 Bad Dürrheim (Germany)
Scarborough (England)
Woodhall Spa (England)
12 Strathpeffer (Scotland)
13 Aix-la-Chapelle (France)
Knaresborough (England)
Leamington Spa (England)
14 Tunbridge Wells (England)

space travel

Spacecraft include:

03 Mir (Soviet space station)
06 Skylab (US space station)
Tardis (*Doctor Who* films/TV series)
07 Gemini 4 (US spacecraft)
Vostok 1 (Soviet spacecraft)
Vostok 5 (Soviet spacecraft)
Vostok 6 (Soviet spacecraft)
08 Apollo 11 (US spacecraft)
Apollo 13 (US spacecraft)
Apollo 17 (US spacecraft)
Columbia (US space shuttle)
Freedom 7 (US spacecraft)
Nostromo (*Alien* films)
Red Dwarf (*Red Dwarf* TV series)
Serenity (*Firefly* TV series)
Sputnik 1 (Soviet spacecraft)
Sputnik 2 (Soviet spacecraft)
Voskhod 1 (Soviet spacecraft)
Voskhod 2 (Soviet spacecraft)

09 Discovery (US space shuttle)
Endeavour (US space shuttle)
Galactica (*Battlestar Galactica* TV series)
Liberator (*Blake's 7* TV series)
Pioneer 10 (US spacecraft)
Shenzhou V (Chinese spacecraft)
10 Challenger (US space shuttle)
USS Voyager (*Star Trek* films/TV series)
11 Fireball XL5 (*Fireball XL5* TV series)
Heart of Gold (*The Hitchhiker's Guide to the Galaxy*, Douglas Adams, 1979)
12 SS Discovery 1 (*2001: A Space Odyssey*, Sir Arthur C Clarke, 1968)
Thunderbird 3 (*Thunderbirds* TV series)
Thunderbird 5 (*Thunderbirds* TV series)
13 Deep Space Nine (*Star Trek* TV series)
Moonbase Alpha (*Space 1999* TV series)
USS Enterprise (*Star Trek* films/TV series)

Space probes include:

04 Luna	Pioneer	**09** Messenger
06 Viking	Ulysses	**10** Deep Impact
07 Galileo	Voyager	**15** Cassini–Huygens
Mariner	**08** Magellan	

Terms to do with space travel include:

03 bus	**08** ablation	**11** aerobraking
ELV	aerozine	declination
ESA	aimpoint	inclination
ISS	attitude	lunar module
LOX	blast-off	solar system
LRV	downlink	thermal tile
MCC	free-fall	zero gravity
04 NASA	fuel cell	**12** ascent module
05 abort	fuel tank	launch window
flyby	impactor	liquid oxygen
orbit	lunanaut	lunar landing
06 albedo	moonwalk	man on the moon
CAPCOM	nose cone	microgravity
drogue	sloshing	space station
G force	**09** astronaut	**13** angle of attack
hydyne	cosmonaut	ascending node
launch	hydrazine	command module
module	launch pad	descent engine
parsec	light year	descent module
rocket	lunarnaut	entry corridor
shroud	spaceship	jet propulsion
07 booster	space suit	space sickness
coolant	taikonaut	**14** escape velocity
docking	**10** heat shield	geosynchronous
lift-off	pogo effect	horizon scanner
mission	propellant	mission control
nominal	rendezvous	weightlessness
payload	spacecraft	**15** re-entry corridor
re-entry	space probe	solid propellant
shuttle	trajectory	
vidicon	vomit comet	

See also **astronaut**; **astronomy**

Spain

Cities and notable towns in Spain include:

06 Bilbao	**07** Córdoba	Pamplona	**10** Valladolid
Madrid	Granada	Valencia	
Málaga	Seville	Zaragoza	
Toledo	**08** Alicante	**09** Barcelona	

Administrative divisions of Spain, with regional capitals:

04 Jaén (Jáen)
León (León)
Lugo (Lugo)

05 Álava (Vitoria Gasteiz)
Ávila (Ávila)
Cádiz (Cádiz)
Soria (Soria)

06 Burgos (Burgos)
Cuenca (Cuenca)
Girona (Gerona; Girona)
Huelva (Huelva)
Huesca (Huesca)
Lérida (Lérida)
Madrid (Madrid)
Málaga (Málaga)
Murcia (Murcia)
Orense (Orense)
Teruel (Teruel)
Toledo (Toledo)
Zamora (Zamora)

07 Almería (Almería)
Badajoz (Badajoz)
Cáceres (Cáceres)
Córdoba (Córdoba)
Granada (Granada)
La Rioja (Logrono)

Navarra (Pamplona)
Segovia (Segovia)
Sevilla (Sevilla)
Vizcaya (Bilbao)

08 Albacete (Albacete)
Alicante (Alicante)
Asturias (Oviedo)
Baleares (Palma)
La Coruña (La Coruña)
Palencia (Palencia)
Valencia (Valencia)
Zaragoza (Zaragoza)

09 Barcelona (Barcelona)
Cantabria (Santander)
Castellón (Castellón)
Guipúzcoa (San Sebastián)
Las Palmas (Las Palmas)
Salamanca (Salamanca)
Tarragona (Tarragona)

10 Ciudad Real (Ciudad Real)
Pontevedra (Vigo)
Valladolid (Valladolid)

11 Guadalajara (Guadalajara)

19 Santa Cruz de Tenerife (Santa Cruz de Tenerife)

Spanish landmarks include:

04 Ebro

05 Ibiza
Prado

08 Alhambra
Canaries
Pyrenees

Tenerife

09 Balearics
Lanzarote
Parc Güell

10 Guggenheim
Montserrat

11 Pico de Teide

12 Guadalquivir

13 Canary Islands
Museo del Prado

14 Sagrada Familia

15 Balearic Islands

spaniel

Spaniels include:

03 toy
04 land
05 field
water

06 cocker
Sussex

07 clumber

08 Blenheim

papillon
springer

10 Irish water
Maltese dog

11 King Charles

Spanish

Spanish words and expressions include:

03 olé! ('bravo!')

05 adobe (sun-dried bricks)
costa (coast)

guano (sea bird excrement)
junta (military ruling faction)
playa (beach)

tapas (savoury snacks)
06 barrio (community)
bodega (wine shop)
bolero (dance)
El Niño (southward current in the Pacific Ocean)
gaucho (South American mounted herdsman)
gitana (female Spanish gypsy)
gringo (foreigner)
hombre (man)
mañana (tomorrow; an unspecified time in the future)
pelota (racket-and-ball game)
07 chicano (Mexican or a Mexican-American)
corrida (bullfighting)
infanta (princess)
matador (bullfighter)
picador (bullfighter)
qué pasa? (what's up?)
vaquero (cowboy or cattle-driver)
08 compadre (companion, friend)
El Dorado (golden land or city imagined by the Spanish explorers in America)

frijoles (beans)
habanera (Cuban dance)
hacienda (house and estate)
mariachi (itinerant Mexican folk band)
nunca más (never again)
por favor (please)
toreador (bullfighter)
09 ay caramba! (expression of surprise or dismay)
bandolero (bandit)
guerrilla (person fighting an irregular war)
10 àdios amigo (goodbye, my friend)
aficionado (fan)
carabinero (frontier guard or customs officer)
peccadillo (small fault)
viva España! (long live Spain)
11 como siempre (as always)
embarcadero (wharf)
12 hasta la vista! (see you!)
13 incommunicado (deprived of the right to communicate with others)
14 mi casa es su casa (make yourself at home)

See also **day**; **month**; **number**

specialist *see* **medical**

spice *see* **herb**

spider

Spiders and arachnids include:

03	red	**06**	diadem	**08**	attercop	cheesemite
04	bird		epeira		huntsman	harvestman
	mite		katipo		scorpion	saltigrade
	tick		mygale		trapdoor	**11** harvest mite
	wolf		violin	**09**	funnel-web	harvest tick
05	bolas	**07**	araneid		harvester	**12** bird-catching
	money		harvest		phalangid	book-scorpion
	water		hunting		tarantula	money-spinner
	zebra		jumping	**10**	black widow	whip scorpion
			redback			

See also **poison**

spirit

Spirits include:

03	gin	**04**	feni		sake
	kir		grog		
	rum		ouzo	**05**	fenny
	rye		raki		Pimm's®

pisco
vodka

06 brandy
cognac
eggnog
geneva
grappa
kirsch
mescal
mezcal
pastis
Pernod®
poteen
Scotch
whisky

07 aquavit
Bacardi®
bitters

bourbon
Campari
dark rum
genever
pink gin
sloe gin
tequila
whiskey

08 armagnac
calvados
eau de vie
Hollands
hot toddy
sambucca
schnapps
vermouth
white rum
witblits

09 apple-jack
aqua vitae
framboise
golden rum
mirabelle
slivovitz
spiced rum

10 malt whisky
usquebaugh

11 gold tequila
Hollands gin
peach brandy

12 añejo tequila

13 peach schnapps
silver tequila

15 reposado tequila

See also **drink**; **liqueur**; **mythology**

sport

Sports include:

04 golf
judo
polo
pool

05 bowls
darts
fives
rugby

06 boules
boxing
discus
diving
futsal
hockey
karate
kung fu
luging
Nascar®
pelota
quoits
rowing
shinty
skiing
slalom
soccer
squash
tennis

07 angling
archery
camogie
cricket
croquet
curling

fencing
fishing
gliding
hunting
hurling
javelin
jogging
jujitsu
keep-fit
netball
Parkour
putting
running
sailing
shot put
snooker
surfing
walking

08 aerobics
baseball
canoeing
climbing
football
handball
high-jump
hurdling
lacrosse
long-jump
marathon
pétanque
ping-pong
ringette
rounders
shooting

swimming
trotting
yachting

09 badminton
billiards
bobsleigh
decathlon
go-karting
ice-hockey
pole vault
pot-holing
sky-diving
tae kwon do
water polo
wrestling

10 basketball
drag-racing
gymnastics
ice-skating
motorsport
pentathlon
skin-diving
triple-jump
volleyball

11 cycle racing
free running
hang-gliding
horse racing
kitesurfing
motor racing
paragliding
show-jumping
skeleton bob

table-tennis
tobogganing
water-skiing
windsurfing
12 aqua aerobics
cross-country
kiteboarding
lifeboarding

orienteering
pitch and putt
rock-climbing
snowboarding
speed skating
trampolining
13 roller-skating
tenpin bowling

weightlifting
14 downhill skiing
Gaelic football
mountaineering
speedway racing
stock-car racing
15 greyhound-racing

Sporting competitions include:

02 TT (motorcycle racing)

05 Ashes (cricket)
Derby (horseracing)
FA Cup (football)

06 Le Mans (motor racing)

07 Grey Cup (Canadian football)
Masters (golf/snooker)
Uber Cup (badminton)
UEFA Cup (football)

08 Rose Bowl (American football)
Ryder Cup (golf)
Speedway (motorcycle racing)
World Cup (various)

09 Grand Prix (motor racing)
Motocross (motorcycle racing)
Super Bowl (American football)
Thomas Cup (badminton)

World Bowl (American football)

10 Asian Games
Formula One (motor racing)
Solheim Cup (golf)
Stanley Cup (ice hockey)

11 Admiral's Cup (sailing)
America's Cup (sailing)
Kinnaird Cup (Eton fives)
World Series (baseball)

12 Iditarod Race (sled dog racing)
Olympic Games
Tour de France (cycling)

13 Grand National (horseracing)
Kentucky Derby (horseracing)
Leonard Trophy (bowls)

15 Paralympic Games

Sports positions include:

04 lock
slip
wing

05 cover
gully
mid-on
point
rover

06 batter
centre
goalie
hooker
libero
long on
mid-off
setter
winger

07 batsman
catcher
fine leg
flanker
fly-half
fly slip
forward

leg slip
long leg
long off
number 8
pitcher
ruckman
sweeper
torpedo

08 attacker
backstop
defender
fullback
halfback
left back
left wing
long stop
short leg
split end
third man
tight end
wing back

09 deep cover
deep point
first base
first slip

left field
left guard
leg gulley
mid-wicket
right back
right wing
ruck rover
scrum-half
short stop
square leg
third base
third slip

10 back pocket
cover point
defenceman
extra cover
goal attack
goalkeeper
goaltender
inside left
left tackle
midfielder
point guard
right field
right guard

second base
second slip
silly mid-on
silly point
wing attack

11 centre field
deep fine leg
full-forward
goal defence
goal shooter
inside right
left forward
prop forward
quarterback

right tackle
silly mid-off
wing defence

12 left half-back
power forward
right forward
short fine leg
small forward
stand-off half
wicketkeeper

13 backward point
centre-forward
deep mid-wicket
deep square leg

forward pocket
half-back flank
loosehead prop
right half-back
shooting guard
tighthead prop

14 centre half-back
deep extra cover
left corner-back
short mid-wicket

15 left half-forward
right corner-back
short extra cover

Sports equipment includes:

03 bow
cue
fly
jig
mat
net
oar
ski
tee

04 bail
bait
beam
bolt
bowl
épée
foil
gaff
hook
jack
lure
mask
mitt
nets
pins
puck
rack
reel
rest
rope
shot
wood

05 arrow
boule
brush
caman
chalk
float
rings
sabre
stump
table

trace

06 bridge
discus
fly rod
hammer
hurley
priest
spider
wicket

07 cue ball
fly reel
javelin
keep-net
netball
snorkel

08 aqualung
baseball
crossbow
football
gang-hook
golfball
golf club
ice-skate
punch-bag
ski stick
toboggan
water-ski

09 disgorger
face-guard
grind rail
gum shield
kiteboard
longboard
punch-ball
rugby ball
sailboard
snow board
surfboard

10 basketball
cricket bat

fishing-rod
hockey ball
roller boot
skateboard
speed skate
tennis ball
trampoline
volleyball

11 balance beam
baseball bat
bowling ball
boxing glove
cricket ball
fishing-line
hockey skate
hockey stick
in-line skate
paternoster
pommel horse
racket press
rollerblade
roller-skate
shuttlecock
snooker ball
spinning rod
springboard

12 billiard ball
curling stone
golfing glove
grinding rail
isometric bar
parallel-bars
tennis racket

13 catcher's glove
horizontal bar
mountainboard
vaulting horse

14 ice-hockey stick

15 badminton racket

Sportspeople include:

03 Fox (Richard; 1960– , English, canoeing)
Lin (Ma; 1980– , Chinese, table tennis)
Nan (Wang; 1978– , Chinese, table tennis)

04 Hall (Lars; 1927–1991, Swedish, modern pentathlon)
Mota (Rosa; 1958– , Portuguese, marathon)
Ring (Christy; 1920–79, Irish, hurling)
Wood (Willie; 1938– , Scottish, bowls)

05 Barna (Viktor; 1911–72 , Hungarian, table tennis)
Howey (Kate; 1973– , English, judo)
Ngugi (John; 1962– , Kenyan, cross-country running)
Sipos (Anna; 1908–1972 , Hungarian, table tennis)
Waitz (Grete; 1953– , Norwegian, cross-country running/marathon)

06 Balczó (András; 1938– , Hungarian, modern pentathlon)
Briggs (Karen; 1963– , English, judo)
Bryant (David; 1931– , English, bowls)
Mackey (Mick; 1912–82, Irish, hurling)
Slater (Kelly; 1972– , US, surfing)
Tamura (Ryoko; 1975– , Japanese, judo)
Tergat (Paul; 1969– , Kenyan, cross-country running)

07 Allcock (Tony; 1955– , English, bowls)
Baldini (Stefano; 1971– , Italian, marathon)
Fischer (Birgit; 1962– , German, canoeing)

Geesink (Anton; 1934–2010, Dutch, judo)
Rackard (Billy, 1930–2009, Irish, hurling)
Rackard (Bobby, 1927–96, Irish, hurling)
Rackard (Nicky, 1922–90, Irish, hurling)
Rodgers (Bill; 1947– , US, marathon)
Rozeanu (Angelica; 1921–2006, Romanian, table tennis)
Wanjiru (Samuel; 1986– , Kenyan, marathon)

08 Beachley (Layne; 1972– , Australian, surfing)
Bergmann (Richard; 1920–70 , Austrian, table tennis)
Douillet (David; 1969– , French, judo)
Farrelly (Bernard; 1943– , Australian, surfing)
Guoliang (Liu; 1976– , Chinese, table tennis)
Marshall (Alex; 1967– , Scottish, bowls)
Martikán (Michal; 1979– , Slovakian, canoeing)

09 Berghmans (Ingrid; 1961– , Belgian, judo)

10 Kahanamoku (Duke;1890–1968 , Hawaiian, surfing)

11 Fredriksson (Gert; 1919–2006, Swedish, canoeing)
Kristiansen (Ingrid; 1956– , Norwegian, marathon)
Mednyánszky (Mária; 1901–78 , Hungarian, table tennis)

Terms to do with sport include:

02 do	nut	dojo
ET	obi	draw
gi	rig	dyno
RU	tee	faja
03 air	tip	fins
bas	two	fire
bos	uke	foot
cam	**04** back	foul
cue	bank	gate
cúl	bogu	goal
dam	boom	gybe
dan	bout	hack
end	bull	hail
fin	bump	head
gie	butt	hook
hog	cant	iona
jam	card	jack
kyo	chop	jibe
kyu	chui	juez
let	clew	kata
lob	curl	kiai
mat	dead	koka
men	deck	kote
		lane

lead	court	arrows
limb	dachi	attack
loop	ditch	barrel
lure	dohyo	batten
mast	drive	bisque
mène	fakie	bounce
nage	field	bowl-in
nock	frame	bridle
nose	green	button
peel	grind	cannon
pips	guard	canopy
pits	gyoji	carpet
post	hit-in	carrot
pull	house	centre
punt	ikkyo	course
push	ippon	cradle
rack	judge	crosse
rail	kayak	dedans
rest	leash	double
rink	leave	drop in
shot	leech	dumper
side	matte	enduro
sire	nikyo	entice
skeg	ollie	footer
skip	pitch	freeze
snap	piton	grille
spot	pivot	hajime
tare	place	hakama
test	point	hammer
tice	rails	hazard
topo	raise	hot-dog
trap	recce	hurley
tube	reigi	iomain
vent	resin	judogi
vert	round	judoka
wake	rover	kennel
wall	sheet	kumite
wire	shiai	length
wood	shido	maiden
yuko	shiko	mallet
yump	skeet	marker
05 basho	smash	McHawk
belay	solid	muzzle
belly	spare	noda-wa
biter	split	nollie
blade	stick	parade
block	third	pasaka
blunt	three	pebble
brace	throw	peg out
break	tirer	pocket
broom	traps	prusik
caman	truck	quiver
camán	tsuki	raider
casco	tzuki	rappel
cesta	yoshi	rebote
chase	**06** abseil	roquet
chute	airgun	rouler
cinta	anchor	sankyo

second
seiken
sensei
shinai
slalom
street
strike
stripe
tattoo
top out
trench
trials
turkey
umpire
uphaul
upshot
upwind
uraken
wazari
yonkyo

07 aerials
armlock
banzuke
barmaid
blanket
blocker
booking
burnout
carreau
carving
chimney
chukker
coaming
cockpit
cornice
counter
cue ball
cushion
cutback
defence
English
face-off
flagman
floater
free hit
frontis
frontón
goal-hit
grommet
gutters
haragei
head pin
hog line
jai alai
judoist
jump cue
keikogi
keikoku

kendoka
kentsui
kingpin
knock in
layback
lead-out
leeward
leg rope
luffing
main nue
mawashi
McTwist
measure
offside
paddock
penalty
pin hole
plomber
pointer
push out
regatta
rikishi
ripcord
sighter
sliotar
spotter
takeout
tambour
tee-line
throw-in
toprope
topspin
toucher
trainer
waza-ari
wheelie
wipe-out
zaguero

08 aikidoka
alley-oop
ascender
ashi-tori
backhand
back line
back shot
backspin
bindings
body drop
bonspiel
bowsight
break cue
bullseye
chistera
chon-mage
co-driver
crampons
dead ball
dead draw

dead hang
dead heat
diamonds
dohyo-iri
downhaul
downwind
drop ball
drop shot
encho-sen
fall line
foot spot
forehand
foul line
free fall
free gate
free pass
funny car
glissade
goal area
griptape
half-pipe
handicap
handpass
jack high
jump shot
karateka
kata-tori
ketaguri
kickflip
kick-nose
kick shot
kick-tail
kick-turn
kimarite
lollipop
low house
main wall
methanol
nearside
neck shot
pass line
pelotari
perfecta
pivoting
play line
pony goal
pro-stock
quiniela
road book
run a hoop
seoi-nage
shoot-off
shot bowl
side line
sidespin
snowdome
sode-tori
sono-mama

speedway
sumotori
tail shot
third man
throw-off
traverse
trinquet
tsuppari
uchi mata
windward
yokozuna
yorikiri

09 appealing
awasewaza
baulk line
bodyboard
body-check
carabiner
cat stance
check side
choke hold
cochonnet
Croke Park
delantero
descender
dock start
duck drive
fault line
finger tab
first home
fixed rope
flatwater
free throw
galleries
goofy foot
high house
karabiner
kneeboard
koshi-nage
leech-line
longboard
makekoshi
morozashi
motocross
oicho-mage
open table
pace notes
parc fermé
passivity
penholder
penthouse
petit bois
petticoat
pivot ball
quickdraw
repêchage
Robin Hood
rover ball
rover hoop

ryote-tori
shakedown
short head
skydiving
snowcross
sore matte
speed trap
spray deck
superbike
supermoto
tai-otoshi
third home
washboard
wave board
wing balls

10 baulk lines
bouldering
centre pass
chanko nabe
classic bow
cover point
crosscourt
dead weight
double trap
draw weight
Eskimo roll
firing line
fletchings
gargu kamae
goal attack
goal circle
goal crease
goalkeeper
hailkeeper
half-strike
harai goshi
hataki-komi
head string
juji-gatame
kachikoshi
kaiten-nage
katate-tori
line player
losing cant
mono skiing
morote-tori
nose riding
object ball
petit final
pin spotter
place libre
post weight
power break
recurve bow
road racing
second home
shakehands
shomen-uchi
sideboards

spray skirt
stabilizer
static line
supercross
tachi-mochi
travelling
tsuyu-harai
whitewater
wing attack

11 anti-raiders
base jumping
boogie board
broadsiding
centreboard
combination
compound bow
court player
croquet shot
down the line
elapsed time
goal defence
goal shooter
handicapper
hanso-kumake
lag for break
natural foot
obstruction
passive play
penalty line
penalty pass
penalty shot
perfect game
photo finish
pioneer ball
quarter-pipe
Roman candle
running shot
running side
ryokata-tori
service line
service park
shroud lines
time control
udekime-nage
western grip
wing defence
yokomen-uchi

12 angle of split
back paddling
boundary line
cleek the shot
climbing wall
flying finish
free climbing
goal-area line
kesho mawashi
nitromethane
podium finish

powersliding
reaction time
referee throw
running belay
six-metre line
special stage
standing shot
starting gate
stranglehold
striker's ball
Telemark turn
trail the jack
trapshooting
trick release
upstream gate

13 airborne throw
Canadian canoe

Christmas tree
double-wake cut
expansion bolt
four-metre line
free-throw line
hare and hounds
high toss serve
neko-ashi-dachi
nine-metre line
Olympic trench
running target
scrutineering
shortmat bowls
starting boxes
step-over turns
terminal speed
waiting blocks

14 deepwater start
downstream gate
killing the ball
non-combativity
seven-metre line
shooting circle
universal joint
winning gallery

15 feathered paddle
longtrack racing
reclining dragon
seven-metre throw
third-ball attack
top fuel dragster
transverse lines
winning openings

See also **American football**; **archery**; **athletics**; **Australian rules football**; **award**; **badminton**; **baseball**; **basketball**; **boxing**; **cricket**; **cycling**; **darts**; **equestrian sport**; **exercise**; **fencing**; **football**; **golf**; **gymnastics**; **hockey**; **ice hockey**; **ice skating**; **karate**; **martial art**; **Olympic Games**; **Paralympic Games**; **race**; **racing: horse racing**; **racing: motor racing**; **rowing**; **Rugby League**; **Rugby Union**; **skiing**; **snooker**; **squash**; **stadium**; **swimming**; **tennis**; **trophy**; **volleyball**; **weightlifting**; **wrestling**

spread

Spreads include:

03 jam

04 marg
oleo
pâté

05 honey

marge

06 butter

07 Marmite®
Nutella®

08 dripping

sandwich
Vegemite®

09 butterine
lemon curd
margarine

marmalade

11 lemon cheese

12 peanut butter

13 oleomargarine

spring *see* **well**

spy

Spies, double agents and turncoats include:

03 Pym (Magnus; *A Perfect Spy*, 1986, John le Carré)

04 Blee (David Henry; 1916–2000, US)
Bond (James; *Casino Royale*, 1954, et seq, Ian Fleming)
Boyd (Belle; 1844–1900, US)
Hale (Nathan; 1755–76, American)

05 André (John; 1751–80, English)
Bazna (Elyesa; 1904–70, Albanian)
Blair (Barley; *The Spy Who Came in from the Cold*, 1963, John le Carré)
Blake (George; 1922– , Dutch/British)
Blunt (Anthony; 1907–83, English)
Fuchs (Klaus; 1911–88, German/British)
Karla (*Tinker, Tailor, Soldier, Spy*, 1974, et seq, John le Carré)

Mundy (Ted; *Absolute Friends*, 2003, John le Carré)
Sorge (Richard; 1895–1944, German/Soviet)
Wynne (Greville; 1919–90, British)

06 Arnold (Benedict; 1741–1801, American)
Cicero (1904–70, Albanian)
Haydon (Bill; *Tinker, Tailor, Soldier, Spy*, 1974, John le Carré)
Kelway (Robert; *The Heat of the Day*, 1949, Elizabeth Bowen)
Leamas (Alec; *The Spy Who Came in from the Cold*, 1963, John le Carré)
Philby (Kim; 1911–88, British)
Reilly (Sidney; 1874–1925, Russian/British)
Ricard (Marthe; 1889–1982, French)
Smiley (George; *Call for the Dead*, 1961, et

seq, John le Carré)
Vidocq (Eugène François; 1775–1857, French)
Werner (Ruth; 1907–2000, German)

07 Biggles (*The Camels are Coming*, 1932, et
seq, Captain W E Johns)
Burgess (Guy; 1910–63, English)
Defarge (Madame; *A Tale of Two Cities*,
1859, Charles Dickens)
Edmonds (Sarah Emma; 1841–98, Canadian)
Maclean (Donald Duart; 1913–83, English)
Nunn May (Alan; 1911–2003, British)

08 Greenhow (Rose O'Neal; 1817–64, US)

See also **espionage**

Lonsdale (Gordon; 1924–c.1970, Canadian/
Russian)
Mata Hari (1876–1917, Dutch)
Westerby (Jerry; *The Honourable Schoolboy*,
1977, John le Carré)

09 Carstares (William; 1649–1715, Scottish)
Philbrick (Herbert Arthur; 1915–93, US)
Rosenberg (Ethel; 1915–53, US)
Rosenberg (Julius; 1918–53, US)

10 Cairncross (John; 1913–95, Scottish)
Litvinenko (Alexander; 1962–2006, Russian)

square

Squares include:

03 Red (Russia)
05 Times (USA)
06 Sloane (England)
07 Central (USA)
Madison (USA)
People's (China)
08 Berkeley (England)

Victoria (England/Northern Ireland)
09 Leicester (England)
Tiananmen (China)
Trafalgar (England)
10 Bloomsbury (England)
Washington (USA)
12 Covent Garden (England)

squash

Squash terms include:

01 T	**04** drop	rally	**10** service box
03 ace	nick	tight	**12** boast for nick
get	rail	**06** stroke	quarter court
let	**05** alley	volley	**13** half-court line
lob	angle	**08** telltale	
set	boast	**09** short line	
tin	not up		

stadium

Sporting stadia and venues include:

05 Ascot (horse racing)
Epsom (horse racing)
Ibrox (football)
Imola (motor racing)
Lords (cricket)
Monza (motor racing)
Texas (American football)
Troon (golf)

06 Azteca (football)
Henley (rowing)
Heysel (football)
Le Mans (motor racing)

07 Aintree (horse racing)
Anaheim (baseball)

Anfield (football)
Daytona (motor racing)
San Siro (football)
The Oval (cricket)
Wembley (football)

08 Bernabau (football)
Highbury (football)
Maracana (football)
Sandwich (golf)

09 Cresta Run (tobogganing)
Edgbaston (cricket)
Longchamp (horse racing)
Muirfield (golf)
Newmarket (horse racing)

St Andrews (golf)
The Belfry (golf)
Turnberry (golf)
Villa Park (football)
Wimbledon (tennis)
10 Brooklands (motor racing)
Carnoustie (golf)
Celtic Park (football)
Cheltenham (horse racing)
Elland Road (football)
Fairyhouse (horse racing)
Headingley (cricket/rugby)
Hockenheim (motor racing)
Interlagos (motor racing)
Monte Carlo (motor racing)
Twickenham (rugby)
11 Belmont Park (horse racing)
Brands Hatch (motor racing)
Hampden Park (football)

Murrayfield (rugby)
Old Trafford (football)
Royal Lytham (golf)
Sandown Park (horse racing)
Silverstone (motor racing)
The Crucible (snooker)
The Rose Bowl (cricket)
Trent Bridge (cricket)
Windsor Park (football)
12 Goodison Park (football)
13 Crystal Palace (athletics/football)
Lansdowne Road (rugby)
Royal Birkdale (golf)
White Hart Lane (football)
14 Churchill Downs (horse racing)
Flushing Meadow (tennis)
Stamford Bridge (football)

See also **football; golf; racing: motor racing**

stamp *see* **philately**

star

Stars include:

03 Dog	Sirius	Alderamin
04 Mira	**07** Alphard	Fomalhaut
nova	Antares	supernova
Pole	Canopus	**10** Beta Crucis
Vega	Capella	Betelgeuse
05 Deneb	falling	brown dwarf
Dubhe	neutron	supergiant
Merak	Polaris	white dwarf
North	**08** Arcturus	**11** Alpha Boötis
Spica	Barnard's	Alpha Crucis
06 Castor	red dwarf	Delta Cephei
Pollux	red giant	**12** Alpha Doradus
pulsar	shooting	**13** Alpha Centauri
quasar	**09** Aldebaran	**15** Proxima Centauri

See also **constellation**

star sign *see* **zodiac**

state *see* **Australia; India; United States of America**

station *see* **radio; railway**

stationery

Stationery items include:

03 ink	file tab	**10** calculator	printer label
pen	Filofax®	drawing pin	printer paper
pin	memo pad	filing tray	writing paper
04 file		floppy disk	**13** expanding file
05 diary	**08** calendar	graph paper	lever arch file
label	cash book	paper knife	paper fastener
ruler	envelope	ring binder	printer ribbon
toner	Jiffy bag®	rubber band	tape dispenser
	notebook		
06 eraser	scissors	**11** account book	**14** document folder
folder	stamp pad	address book	document wallet
marker		bulldog clip	manila envelope
pencil	**09** card index	carbon paper	spiral notebook
Post-it®	clipboard	elastic band	suspension file
rubber	desk diary	rubber stamp	window envelope
staple	flip chart	treasury tag	**15** cartridge ribbon
Tipp-Ex®	index card	**12** adhesive tape	correcting paper
07 blotter	notepaper	computer disk	correction fluid
Blu-Tack®	paper clip	copying paper	headed notepaper
divider	Sellotape®	pocket folder	pencil-sharpener
	wall chart		

statue *see* **sculpture**

stealing

Ways of stealing include:

03 bag	pull	finger	highjack
cly	smug	hijack	knock off
dip	whip	pickle	liberate
lag		pilfer	peculate
mag	**05** annex	pocket	scrounge
nap	boost	rip off	shoplift
nim	bribe	rustle	souvenir
nip	filch	scrump	
rob	heist	skrimp	**09** condiddle
	hoist	skrump	duckshove
04 blag	miche	snitch	
crib	mooch	thieve	**10** burglarize
duff	mouch	twitch	plagiarize
glom	pinch		run off with
knap	purse	**07** cabbage	
lift	sneak	purloin	**11** appropriate
mill	swipe	snaffle	pick a pocket
nick			walk off with
pick	**06** burgle	**08** abstract	
	convey	half-inch	**12** make away with

step *see* **dance**

Stevenson, Robert Louis (1850–94)

Significant works include:

06 *St Ives* (1898)	**09** *Kidnapped* (1886)
08 *Catriona* (1893)	**10** *The Ebb-Tide* (1894)
'Markheim' (1886)	*The Wrecker* (1892)

11	*The Wrong Box* (1889)		21	*A Child's Garden of Verses* (1885)
	'Thrawn Janet' (1881)			*The Master of Ballantrae* (1889)
12	*Inland Voyage* (1878)			*The Silverado Squatters* (1884)
13	*The Black Arrow* (1888)		26	*Island Nights' Entertainments* (1893)
14	*Treasure Island* (1883)		28	*Familiar Studies of Men and Books* (1882)
15	*Weir of Hermiston* (1896)		31	*Travels with a Donkey in the Cévennes* (1879)
16	*New Arabian Nights* (1882)			*The Merry Men and Other Tales and Fables*
	'The Beach of Falesá' (1892)			(1887)
19	*Virginibus Puerisque* (1881)			*The Strange Case of Dr Jekyll and Mr Hyde*
				(1886)

Significant characters include:

03 Uma

04 Case
Gunn (Ben)
Hyde (Mr Edward)
Rich (Brackenbury)
Weir (Adam)
Weir (Archie)

05 Breck (Alan)
Davis
Durie (Henry)
Durie (James)
Hyish
Innes (Frank)

06 Jekyll (Dr Henry)
McLour (Janet)
Red Fox (the)
Silver (Long John)
Soulis (Murdoch)
St Ives (Vicomte de)

07 Balfour (David)

Balfour (Ebenezer)
Elliott (Andrew 'Dand')
Elliott (Christina)
Elliott (Clement 'Clem')
Elliott (Gilbert 'Gib')
Elliott (Kirstie)
Elliott (Robert 'Rob')
Hawkins (Jim)
Herrick
Randall (Captain)
Skelton (Richard 'Dick')

08 Drummond (Catriona)
Drummond (James More)
Florizel (Prince of Bohemia)
Markheim
Tarleton

09 Mackellar (Mr)
Wiltshire (Mr)

10 Scuddamore (Silas Q)

15 James of the Glens

stick

Sticks include:

03	lug			stake	07	sceptre
	rod			waddy		walking
		wand				woomera
04	cane	whip	06	alpeen	08	bludgeon
	club			crutch		
	cosh	**05** baton		cudgel	09	truncheon
	pike	billy		hockey	10	alpenstock
	pole	birch		kierie		knobkerrie
	post	crook		tripod		shillelagh
		lathi				
		staff				

stitch *see* **embroidery**

stomach *see* **ruminant**

stone *see* **birth symbol**

storm

Storms include:

03 ice
sea
sun

04 dust
gale
hail
line
rain
sand

snow

05 buran
devil

06 baguio
calima
haboob
meteor
pelter
squall

07 cyclone
monsoon
Shaitan
tempest
thunder
tornado
typhoon
violent

08 blizzard

downpour
magnetic

09 bourasque
dust devil
hurricane
whirlwind

10 cloudburst
electrical

strait

Straits include:

03 Rae (Canada)

04 Adak (Aleutian Islands, USA)
Bass (Australia)
Cook (New Zealand)
Haro (Canada/USA)
Irbe (Estonia)
Kara (Russia)
Palk (India/Sri Lanka)
Pitt (New Zealand)
Soya (Japan)

05 Banks (Australia)
Bohai (China)
Cabot (Canada)
Canso (Canada)
Davis (Canada/Greenland)
Dease (Canada)
Dover (England)
Kerch (Ukraine)
Korea (Japan/South Korea)
Luzon (Philippines)
Menai (Wales)
Osumi (Japan)
Sunda (Indonesia)
Tatar (Russia)

06 Bering (Russia/USA)
Dundas (Australia)
Etolin (USA)
Fisher (Canada)
Hecate (Canada)
Hormuz (Iran)
Hudson (Canada)
Lombok (Indonesia)
Solent (England)
Sunday (Australia)
Tablas (Philippines)
Taiwan (Taiwan)
Tokara (Japan)
Torres (Australia/Papua New Guinea)
Vitiaz (Papua New Guinea)

07 Balabac (Malaysia/Philippines)
Chatham (USA)
Dampier (Indonesia)
Denmark (Greenland/Iceland)
Florida (USA)
Formosa (Taiwan)
Foveaux (New Zealand)
Georgia (Canada/USA)
Le Maire (Argentina)
Makasar (Indonesia)
Malacca (Malaysia)
McClure (Canada)
Messina (Italy)
Mindoro (Philippines)
Otranto (Albania/Italy)
Polillo (Philippines)
Rosario (USA)
Tsugaru (Japan)

08 Bosporus (Turkey)
Clarence (Australia)
Karimata (Indonesia)
Kattegat (Denmark/Sweden)
Mackinac (USA)
Magellan (Argentina/Chile)
Makassar (Indonesia)
Shelikof (USA)
Tsushima (Japan/South Korea)
Victoria (Canada)

09 Belle Isle (Canada)
Bonifacio (Corsica/Sardinia)
Bosphorus (Turkey)
Gibraltar (Spain)
Great Belt (Denmark)
La Pérouse (Japan)
Linapacan (Philippines)
Van Diemen (Japan)

10 Juan de Fuca (Canada/USA)
Little Belt (Denmark)

11 Dardanelles (Turkey)

12 Bougainville (Papua New Guinea)
Investigator (Australia)

13 San Bernardino (Philippines)

14 Northumberland (Canada)
Queen Charlotte (Canada)

15 Dolphin and Union (Canada)

Strauss, Richard (1864–1949)

Significant works include:

06 *Daphne* (1938)
Morgen (1894)
Salome (1905)

07 *Don Juan* (1889)
Elektra (1909)
Guntram (1894)
Macbeth (1888)
Morning (1894)

08 *Arabella* (1933)
Peace Day (1938)

09 *Capriccio* (1942)
Feuersnot (1911)
From Italy (1887)
Zueignung (1885)

10 *A Hero's Life* (1898)
Dedication (1885)
Don Quixote (1897)
Festmarsch (1881)
Fire Famine (1911)
Intermezzo (1924)

11 *Friedenstag* (1938)
Schlagobers (1922)

12 *Festive March* (1881)
Whipped Cream (1922)

13 *Four Last Songs* (1948)
Metamorphosen (1945)

14 *Alpine Symphony* (1915)
Ein Heldenleben (1898)
Josephslegende (1914)
Legend of Joseph (1914)
The Love of Danae (1952)
The Silent Woman (1935)

15 *Ariadne auf Naxos* (1912)

16 *Der Rosenkavalier* (1911)
Die Liebe der Danae (1952)
The Egyptian Helen (1928)
Tod und Verklärung (1889)

17 *Eine Alpensinfonie* (1915)

18 *Die Schweigsame Frau* (1935)
Symphonia Domestica (1904)
The Knight of the Rose (1911)

19 *Die Frau ohne Schatten* (1919)

20 *Die Aegyptische Helena* (1928)
Thus Spake Zarathustra (1896)

21 *Also sprach Zarathustra* (1896)

22 *The Woman Without a Shadow* (1919)

23 *Death and Transfiguration* (1889)

26 *Aus Italien Symphonic Fantasy* (1887)

28 *Till Eulenspiegel's Merry Pranks* (1895)

32 *Till Eulenspiegels lustige Streiche* (1895)

Stravinsky, Igor (1882–1971)

Significant works include:

04 *Agon* (1957)
Mass (1948)

05 *Babel* (1944)
Mavra (1922)

06 *Renard* (1922)
Septet (1953)
Threni (1958)

07 *Orpheus* (1948)
Ragtime (1918)

08 *Concerto* (1924)
Les Noces (1923)
The Flood (1962)

09 *Fireworks* (1908)
Introitus (1965)
Petrushka (1911)
Wind Octet (1923)

10 *Oedipus Rex* (1927)
Perséphone (1934)
Pulcinella (1920)
Tarantella (1898)
The Wedding (1923)

11 *Circus Polka* (1942)
Jeu de cartes (1937)
Le Rossignol (1914)
The Card Game (1937)
The Firebird (1910)

12 *Feu d'Artifice* (1908)

13 *Der Feuervogel* (1910)
'Dumbarton Oaks'
(Concerto; 1938)
Faun et bergère (1907)
Piano Rag-Music (1919)
The Fairy's Kiss (1928)

14 *Canticum Sacrum* (1955)
The Nightingale (1914)

15 *Abraham and Isaac* (1963)
Apollon Musagète (1928)
Le Baiser de la Fée (1928)
Le roi des étoiles (1912)
The Rite of Spring (1913)
The Soldier's Tale (1918)

16 *Dylan Thomas Elegy* (1954)
Requiem Canticles (1966)
The Rake's Progress (1951)

17 *L'Histoire du soldat* (1918)
The King of the Stars (1912)

18 *Faun and Shepherdess* (1907)
Scherzo fantastique (1902)

street *see* **London; New York; Paris; road**

stroke *see* **swimming**

study

Subjects of study include:

02 IT

03 art
ICT
law
PSE

04 PHSE

05 craft
dance
D and T
drama
music
sport

06 botany
design

07 anatomy
biology
driving
ecology
fashion
fitness
geology
history
physics
pottery
science
zoology

08 Classics
commerce
eugenics
genetics
heraldry
medicine
penology
politics
theology

09 astrology
astronomy
chemistry
cosmology
economics
education
erotology
ethnology
forensics
geography
languages
logistics
marketing
mechanics
mythology
pathology
shorthand
sociology
surveying
web design

10 humanities
journalism
literature
metallurgy
philosophy
physiology
psychology
publishing
statistics
technology
visual arts

11 accountancy
agriculture
archaeology
calligraphy
citizenship
dressmaking

electronics
engineering
linguistics
mathematics
metaphysics
meteorology
ornithology
photography
the Classics
typewriting

12 anthropology
architecture
astrobiology
horticulture
lexicography
media studies
oceanography
pharmacology

13 gender studies
home economics
librarianship
marine studies
nutrigenomics
women's studies

14 food technology
leisure studies
natural history
quantum physics
social sciences
toxicogenomics
word processing

15 building studies
business studies
computer studies
creative writing
hotel management

subatomic particle *see* **atom**

sugar

Sugars include:

03 gur

04 beet
cane

date
goor
loaf
lump

milk
palm
spun
wood

05 brown
fruit
grape
icing

maple
syrup
white
06 aldose
barley
caster
castor
golden
hexose
invert
ketose

xylose
07 glucose
glycose
jaggery
lactose
maltose
mannose
pentose
refined
sucrose
treacle

08 demerara
dextrose
fructose
levulose
molasses
powdered
09 arabinose
galactose
laevulose
muscovado
raffinose

sucralose
trehalose
unrefined
10 granulated
saccharose
11 glucosamine
12 crystallized
13 confectioner's

suit

Suits include:

01 g
03 cat
dry
Mao
NBC
sun
wet
04 body
Eton
jump
play

swim
zoot
05 drape
dress
noddy
pants
shell
siren
sleep
space
sweat

track
union
06 boiler
diving
flying
lounge
monkey
riding
safari
sailor
tsotsi

07 bathing
leisure
morning
penguin
trouser
08 birthday
business
pressure
skeleton
sleeping

Summer Olympics *see* Olympic Games

Summer Paralympics *see* Paralympic Games

superhero

Superheroes include:

04 Hulk (Bruce Banner; comic/TV/film)
Thor (Thor Odinson; comic)

05 Robin (Dick Grayson; comic/TV/film)
Rogue (Marie D'Ancanto; comic/film)
Storm (Ororo Munroe; comic/film)

06 Batman (Bruce Wayne; comic/TV/film)
Iceman (Bobby Drake; comic/film)
Xavier (Professor Charles; comic/film)

07 Batgirl (comic/film)
Blossom (TV)
Bubbles (TV)
Cyclops (Scott Summers; comic/film)
Elektra (comic/film)
Frozone (Lucius Best; film)
Hellboy (Anung Un Rama; comic/film)
Iron Man (Tony Stark; comic/film)
Nite Owl (Dan Dreiberg; comic/film)
Phoenix (Jean Grey; comic/film)

The Atom (Albert Pratt; comic)
The X-Men (comic/film)

08 Batwoman (Kathy Kane; comic)
Catwoman (Selina Kyle; comic/film)
Superman (Clark Kent; comic/TV/film)
The Thing (Ben Grimm; comic/film)

09 Buttercup (TV)
Daredevil (Matthew Murdock; comic/film)
Firestorm (Jason Rusch; comic)
Nighthawk (Kyle Richmond; comic)
Nightwing (comic)
Spiderman (Peter Parker; comic/film)
Supergirl (Kara Zor-El; comic/film)
Wolverine (Logan/James Howlett; comic/film)

10 Cannonball (Samuel Zachery Guthrie; comic)
Elastigirl (Helen Parr; film)

Freakazoid (TV)
Ghost Rider (John Blaze; comic/film)
Human Torch (Johnny Storm; comic/film)
Kamen Rider (TV/film)
Moon Knight (Marc Spector; comic)
Ozymandias (Adrian Veidt; comic/film)
Sailor Moon (TV/film)

11 Dr Manhattan (Dr Jonathan

Osterman; comic/film)
Kim Possible (TV)
Mr Fantastic (Reed Richards; comic/film)
Wonder Woman (Princess Diana; comic/TV)

12 Black Panther (T'Challa; comic)
Mr Incredible (Robert Parr; film)
Silver Surfer (Norrin Radd; comic)

13 Captain Planet (TV)
Silk Spectre II (Laurie Juspeczyk; comic/film)

14 Captain America (Steve Rogers; comic)
Invisible Woman (Susan Storm Richards; comic/film)
Power Puff Girls (TV)
The Cheerleader (Claire Bennet; TV)

supernatural *see* **occult**

surgery

Surgery types include:

06 biopsy

07 keyhole
nose job

08 cosmesis
C-section
facelift
lobotomy
tenotomy
vagotomy

09 amniotomy
Caesarean
colectomy
colostomy
cordotomy
cystotomy
ileostomy
iridotomy
leucotomy
lipectomy
lithotomy
lobectomy
necrotomy
neurotomy
osteotomy
sex change
tubectomy
tummy tuck

10 adenectomy
autoplasty
chordotomy
cordectomy
cystectomy
cystostomy
discectomy
herniotomy
iridectomy
keratotomy
laparotomy

lumpectomy
mastectomy
neurectomy
nip and tuck
ovariotomy
phlebotomy
strabotomy
thymectomy
tuboplasty
varicotomy
vitrectomy

11 angioplasty
cosmetology
craniectomy
cryosurgery
embolectomy
enterectomy
enterostomy
gastrectomy
glossectomy
hepatectomy
hysterotomy
laparoscopy
mammoplasty
nephrectomy
osteoplasty
ovariectomy
rhinoplasty
splenectomy
syringotomy
tracheotomy
uranoplasty

12 appendectomy
arthroplasty
circumcision
cluster graft
corneal graft
hysterectomy
laryngectomy

meniscectomy
microsurgery
neurosurgery
oophorectomy
patellectomy
pinealectomy
tonsilectomy
tracheoscopy
tracheostomy

13 adenoidectomy
pneumonectomy
prostatectomy
psychosurgery
salpingectomy
sigmoidectomy
stomatoplasty
sympathectomy
symphyseotomy
symphysiotomy
thoracentesis
thoracoplasty
thyroidectomy
tonsillectomy

14 abdominoplasty
appendicectomy
blepharoplasty
cholecystotomy
clitoridectomy
coronary bypass
endarterectomy
fundoplication
hypophysectomy
pancreatectomy
plastic surgery
staphyloplasty

15 cholecystectomy
cholecystostomy
cosmetic surgery
thoracocentesis

Surgeons include:

03 eye	heart	**07** general
04 oral	house	plastic
tree	neuro	**08** cosmetic
05 brain	**06** dental	**10** veterinary

Terms to do with surgery include:

02 op
04 CABG
seam
05 couch
curet
donor
stoma
taxis
truss
06 canula
curare
curari
domino
dossil
garrot
hobday
lancet
post-op
reduce
stitch
trepan
trocar
07 cadaver
cannula
catling
curette
forceps
garotte
heparin
myotome
operate
patient
pessary
scalpel
section
torsion
08 ablation
adhesion
bistoury
cannular
capeline
centesis

clinical
compress
cosmesis
crow-bill
curarine
écraseur
elective
garrotte
incision
incisure
invasive
operable
plastics
trephine
09 abduction
autograft
cannulate
capelline
collodion
crow's-bill
curettage
depressor
dermatome
diastasis
donor card
enucleate
operation
osteotome
piggyback
resection
retractor
tamponade
tamponage
tenaculum
10 atracurium
deligation
diorthosis
discussion
guillotine
inoperable
lithotrite
lithotrity
obstetrics

osteoclast
11 anaesthetic
arthrodesis
autoplastic
cannulation
curettement
decapsulate
exteriorize
incarnation
laparoscope
lithotripsy
lithotritor
prosthetics
trepanation
12 azathioprine
circumcision
cluster graft
corneal graft
cyclosporin A
fenestration
lithotripter
lithotriptor
lunar caustic
paracentesis
scarificator
short circuit
tissue-typing
trephination
13 cyclodialysis
decompression
herniorrhaphy
incarceration
lithontriptor
operating room
post-operative
premedication
thoracentesis
under the knife
14 embryo transfer
operating table
15 thoracocentesis

See also **anaesthetic**; **medical**

swan

Swans include:

04 mute	**07** Bewick's	**08** whooping	whistling
05 black	whooper	**09** trumpeter	**11** black-necked

Sweden

Cities and notable towns in Sweden include:

05 Borås	**06** Kalmar	**09** Gällivare	**10** Gothenburg
Luleå	Kiruna	Jönköping	
Malmö	**07** Uppsala	Stockholm	
Visby	**08** Göteborg	Sundsvall	

Administrative divisions of Sweden, with regional capitals:

05 Skåne (Malmö)
06 Kalmar (Kalmar)
Örebro (Örebro)
07 Dalarna (Falun)
Gotland (Visby)
Halland (Halmstad)
Uppsala (Uppsala)
08 Blekinge (Karlskrona)
Jämtland (Östersund)
Värmland (Karlstad)
09 Gävleborg (Gävle)

Jönköping (Jönköping)
Kronoberg (Växjö)
Stockholm (Stockholm)
10 Norrbotten (Lulece)
11 Västmanland (Västeraces)
12 Östergötland (Linköping)
Södermanland (Nyköping)
Västerbotten (Umeå)
14 Västernorrland (Härnösand)
15 Västra Götalands (Gothenburg)

Swedish landmarks include:

05 Öland
Sarek
06 Globen
08 Haga Park
09 Gamla Stan

Njupeskär
10 Stadshuset
Storkyrkan
11 Fulufjället
Lake Vättern

Royal Palace
Trollhättan
12 Örebro Castle
15 Kungliga Slottet

sweet

Sweets and confectionery include:

04 jube
Mars®
rock
05 fudge
halva
jelly
06 bonbon
confit
humbug
jujube
nougat
tablet
toffee
07 alcorza

caramel
fondant
gumdrop
lozenge
pomfret
praline
truffle
wine gum
08 acid drop
bull's eye
confetti
lollipop
marzipan
noisette

pear drop
09 chocolate
jelly baby
jelly bean
lemon drop
liquorice
10 chewing-gum
gobstopper
peppermint
11 aniseed ball
barley sugar
marshmallow
toffee apple

12 butterscotch
dolly mixture

13 Edinburgh rock
fruit pastille

14 pineapple chunk
Turkish delight

swimming

Swimming strokes include:

05 crawl

07 trudgen

09 back-crawl
butterfly

dog-paddle
freestyle

10 backstroke
front crawl

11 doggy-paddle

12 breaststroke

15 Australian crawl

Swimmers and divers include:

04 Klim (Michael; 1977– , Polish/Australian)
Otto (Kristin; 1966– , German)
Rice (Stephanie; 1988– , Australian)
Rose (Murray; 1939–2012, Scottish/
Australian)
Webb (Matthew; 1848–83, English)

05 Crapp (Lorraine; 1938– , Australian)
Curry (Lisa; 1962– , Australian)
Daley (Thomas; 1994– , English)
Ender (Kornelia; 1958– , German)
Evans (Janet; 1971– , US)
Gould (Shane; 1956– , Australian)
Gross (Michael; 1964– , German)
Jones (Leisel; 1985– , Australian)
Lewis (Hayley; 1974– , Australian)
Riley (Samantha; 1972– , Australian)
Spitz (Mark; 1950– , US)

06 Biondi (Matt; 1965– , US)
Davies (Sharron; 1962– , English)
Durack (Fanny; 1891–1956, Australian)
Ederle (Gertrude; 1906–2003, US)
Fraser (Dawn; 1937– , Australian)
Loader (Danyon; 1975– , New Zealand)
O'Neill (Susie; 1973– , Australian)
Phelps (Michael; 1985– , US)

Thorpe (Ian; 1982– , Australian)
Wilkie (David; 1954– , Scottish)

07 Goodhew (Duncan; 1957– , English)
Hackett (Grant; 1980– , Australian)
Perkins (Kieren; 1973– , Australian)
Wickham (Tracey; 1962– , Australian)

08 Champion (Malcolm; 1883–1939, New
Zealand)
Charlton (Boy; 1907–75, Australian)
de Bruijn (Inge; 1973– , Dutch)
Louganis (Greg; 1960– , US)
Manoudou (Laure; 1986– , French)
Streeter (Alison; 1964– , English)
van Wisse (Tammy; 1968– , Australian)
Williams (Esther; 1923–2013, US)

09 Adlington (Rebecca; 1989– , English)
Armstrong (Duncan; 1968– , Australian)
Kellerman (Annette; 1887–1975,
Australian)
Klochkova (Yana; 1982– , Ukrainian)

11 Beaurepaire (Sir Frank; 1891–1956,
Australian)
Weissmuller (Johnny; 1903–84, Hungarian-
German/US)

Swimming and diving terms include:

02 IM

03 fly
rip

04 pike
tuck

05 block
boost
entry
scull
split

06 inward
layout
length
medley

07 forward
reverse

08 armstand
backward
flamingo

09 ballet leg
eggbeater

elevation

10 tumble turn

11 dolphin kick
flutter kick
rocket split

12 combined spin

13 negative split

14 continuous spin

15 backstroke flags
ballet leg double

Switzerland

sword

See also **dagger**; **knife**

symbol

Symbols include:

04 icon
ikon
logo
05 badge
brand
crest
motif

token
totem
06 cipher
emblem
smiley
uraeus

08 caduceus
ideogram
insignia
logogram
monogram
swastika
09 pentagram

trademark
watermark
10 coat of arms
hieroglyph
pictograph
12 yellow ribbon

See also **birth symbol**; **religion**

symptom *see* disease

T

table

See also **cutlery**

tack *see* **horse**

taste

pungent
savoury

08 vinegary

11 bittersweet

taxation

Taxes include:

03 GST
sur
VAT

04 PAYE
poll
toll

05 rates
tithe

06 excise
income

07 airport
council
customs

08 green tax
property

09 death duty
insurance

10 capitation
estate duty
value added

11 corporation
inheritance

12 capital gains
pay as you earn

15 capital transfer
community charge

Tchaikovsky, Pyotr Ilyich (1840–93)

Significant works include:

06 'Polish' (Symphony; 1873)
Undine (1870)

07 *Iolanta* (1891)
Mazeppa (1884)

08 *Swan Lake* (1877/1895)

10 'Mozartiana' (Suite; 1887)
'Pathétique' (Symphony; 1893)

11 *Cherevichki* (1887)
Marche Slave (1876)
The Slippers (1887)
The Voyevoda (1868)
The Year 1812 (1882)

12 *1812 Overture* (1882)
Eugene Onegin (1879)
The Oprichnik (1874)
The Sorceress (1887)
Valse-Scherzo (1877)

13 'Little Russian' (Symphony; 1873)
Slavonic March (1876)
The Nutcracker (1892)

14 *Romeo and Juliet* (1870/80)
Vakula the Smith (1876)

15 *Concert Fantasia* (1884)
Manfred Symphony (1885)
'Winter Daydreams' (Symphony; 1868)

16 *Andante and Finale* (1893)
Capriccio Italien (1880)
Pezzo capriccioso (1887)
The Maid of Orleans (1882)
The Queen of Spades (1890)

17 *Francesca da Rimini* (1876)
The Sleeping Beauty (1890)

18 *The Nutcracker Suite* (1892)

20 *Sérénade mélancolique* (1875)

tea

Teas and herbal teas include:

03 ice

04 beef
bush
chai
herb
iced
mate
mint
sage

05 Assam
black
bohea

brick
caper
China
congo
fruit
green
hyson
lemon
pekoe
senna
white
yerba

06 Ceylon

congou
herbal
oolong
oulong

07 cambric
instant
jasmine
lapsang
redbush
rooibos
rosehip
Russian
twankay

08 camomile
Earl Grey
Lady Grey
souchong

09 chamomile
gunpowder

10 Darjeeling

11 orange pekoe

13 decaffeinated

15 lapsang souchong

teaching

Teacher types include:

03 don
NQT
04 dean
form
guru
head
05 coach
tutor
06 doctor
duenna
fellow
master
mentor
pedant
pundit
reader
school
supply

07 adviser
crammer
student
trainer
08 lecturer
mistress
09 governess
maharishi
pedagogue
preceptor
principal
professor
reception
10 counsellor
deputy head
headmaster
head of year
instructor

schoolmarm
11 housemaster
preceptress
upper school
12 demonstrator
headmistress
middle school
pastoral head
private tutor
schoolmaster
13 housemistress
nursery school
primary school
14 schoolmistress
senior lecturer
15 college lecturer
secondary school

Teaching methods include:

06 lesson
theory
07 seminar
tuition
08 briefing
coaching
drilling
guidance
role-play
training
tutelage

tutorial
09 grounding
lecturing
practical
preaching
schooling
shadowing
11 counselling
instruction
job training
master-class

12 home-learning
rote learning
13 demonstration
14 apprenticeship
indoctrination
private tuition
special tuition
work experience
15 familiarization
hands-on training

Teachers include:

04 Beck (Madame; *Villette*, 1853, Charlotte Brontë)
Eyre (Jane; *Jane Eyre*, 1847, Charlotte Brontë)
Hart (Sheba; *Notes on a Scandal*, 2003, Zoë Heller)
Howe (Joseph; *Of This Time, Of That Place*, 1943, Lionel Trilling)
King (Anna; *Only Children*, 1979, Alison Lurie)
Lamb (Michael; *Lamb*, 1980, Bernard MacLaverty)
Nunn (Sir Percy; 1870–1944, English)
Wilt (Henry; *Wilt*, 1976, Tom Sharpe)

05 Brill (Miss; *Miss Brill*, 1922, Katherine Mansfield)
Chips (Mr; *Goodbye Mr Chips*, 1934, James Hilton)

Crane (Edwina; *The Raj Quartet*, 1966–75, Paul Scott)
Crick (Tom; *Waterland*, 1983, Graham Swift)
Dixon (Jim; *Lucky Jim*, 1954, Kingsley Amis)
Doyle (Patrick; *A Disaffection*, 1989, James Kelman)
Handy (Charles Brian; 1932– , Irish)
Henri (Frances; *The Professor*, 1857, Charlotte Brontë)
Irwin (*The History Boys*, 2004, Alan Bennett)
Levin (Sam; *A New Life*, 1961, Bernard Malamud)
Lloyd (Teddy; *The Prime of Miss Jean Brodie*, 1961, Muriel Spark)
Odili (*A Man of the People*, 1966, Chinua Achebe)

Snape (Severus; *Harry Potter and the Philosopher's Stone*, 1997, et seq, J K Rowling)

06 Alcott (Bronson; 1799–1888, US)
Angelo (Albert; *Albert Angelo*, 1964, B S Johnson)
Arnold (Thomas; 1795–1842, English)
Brodie (Miss Jean; *The Prime of Miss Jean Brodie*, 1961, Muriel Spark)
Coppin (Fanny Marion Jackson; 1837–1913, US)
Cotton (George Edward Lynch; 1813–66, English)
Covett (Barbara; *Notes on a Scandal*, 2003, Zoë Heller)
Graham (Martha; 1894–1991, US)
Grimes (Captain; *Decline and Fall*, 1928, Evelyn Waugh)
Gyatso (Geshe Kelsang; 1931– , Tibetan)
Hagrid (Rubeus; *Harry Potter and the Philosopher's Stone*, 1997, et seq, J K Rowling)
Harris (Crocker; *The Browning Version*, 1948, Terence Rattigan)
Hector (*The History Boys*, 2004, Alan Bennett)
Hillel (1 c BC–1 c AD)
Hornby (A S; 1898–1978, English)
Ramsay (Dunstan; *The Deptford Trilogy*, 1983, Robertson Davies)
Solent (Wolf; *Wolf Solent*, 1929, John Cowper Powys)

07 Darling (Sir James Ralph; 1899–1995, Australian)
Eckhart (Miss; *The Golden Apples*, 1949, Eudora Welty)
Edwards (James; *Whack-o!*, 1950s, TV sitcom)
Enketei (Mira; *Amalgamemnon*, 1984, Christine Brooke-Rose)
Fischer (Marcus; *The Time of the Angels*, 1966, Iris Murdoch)
Keating (John; *Dead Poets Society*, 1989)
Krishna (*The English Teacher*, 1945, R K Narayan)
Lowther (Gordon; *The Prime of Miss Jean Brodie*, 1961, Muriel Spark)
Matthay (Tobias; 1858–1945, English)
Mr Chips (*Goodbye Mr Chips*, 1934, James Hilton)
Mulcahy (Henry; *The Groves of Academe*, 1952, Mary McCarthy)

See also **education; school**

Peecher (Emma; *Our Mutual Friend*, 1865, Charles Dickens)
Porpora (Nicola; 1686–1766, Italian)
Saville (Colin; *Saville*, 1976, David Storey)
Squeers (Wackford; *Nicholas Nickleby*, 1838–39, Charles Dickens)
Vaughan (Barbara; *The Mandelbaum Gate*, 1965, Muriel Spark)
Wackles (Sophy; *The Old Curiosity Shop*, 1841, Charles Dickens)

08 Bridgman (Laura Dewey; 1829–89, US)
Caldwell (George; *The Centaur*, 1963, John Updike)
Chipping (Mr; *Goodbye Mr Chips*, 1934, James Hilton)
Doubloon (Maggie; *Slouching Towards Kalamazoo*, 1983, Peter De Vries)
Lewisham (George; *Love and Mr Lewisham*, 1900, H G Wells)
Prodicus (5c, Greek)
Sullivan (Anne; 1866–1936, US)

09 Batchelor (Barbie; *The Raj Quartet*, 1966–75, Paul Scott)
Bellgrove (Professor; *Gormenghast* trilogy, 1946–59, Mervyn Peake)
Braidwood (Thomas; 1715–1806, Scottish)
Hartright (Walter; *The Woman in White*, 1860, Wilkie Collins)
Headstone (Bradley; *Our Mutual Friend*, 1865, Charles Dickens)
Strasberg (Lee; 1901–82, US)

10 Dumbledore (Albus; *Harry Potter and the Philosopher's Stone*, 1997, et seq, J K Rowling)
Leadbetter (David; 1955– , English)
Madame Beck (*Villette*, 1853, Charlotte Brontë)
Madam Hooch (*Harry Potter and the Philosopher's Stone*, 1997, et seq, J K Rowling)
McGonagall (Minerva; *Harry Potter and the Philosopher's Stone*, 1997, et seq, J K Rowling)
Protagoras (c.490–c.420 BC, Greek)

12 Pennyfeather (Paul; *Decline and Fall*, 1928, Evelyn Waugh)
Stanislavsky (1863–1938, Russian)

13 M'Choakumchild (Mr; *Hard Times*, 1854, Charles Dickens)

---

team *see* **American football; Australian rules football; baseball; basketball; cricket; football; Rugby League; Rugby Union**

teeth

Teeth include:

03 cap	tush	chisel	permanent
dog	tusk	corner	sectorial
egg	wang	cuspid	serration
eye	wolf	wisdom	**10** carnassial
gag	**05** cheek	**07** denture	first molar
gam	colt's	grinder	masticator
jaw	crown	incisor	molendinar
04 baby	false	scissor	third molar
back	first	snaggle	**11** multicuspid
buck	molar	**08** bicuspid	second molar
fang	plate	dentures	**13** first premolar
fore	store	impacted	**14** central incisor
gold	sweet	premolar	lateral incisor
milk	**06** bridge	**09** milk-molar	second premolar
mill	canine		

television

Television programme types include:

04 news	sitcom	chat show	soap opera
soap	**07** cartoon	docusoap	**11** documentary
05 anime	phone-in	game show	**12** makeover show
drama	reality	quiz show	mockumentary
06 repeat	**08** bulletin	**09** panel game	

Television channels include:

02 E4	ITV1	Living TV
FX	ITV2	Sky Arts 1
03 ABC	ITV3	
CNN	ITV4	**09** al-Jazeera
Fox		BBC News 24
HBO	**05** Bravo	Bloomberg
MTV	More4	Eurosport
NBC	Sci-Fi	Sky Movies
QVC	Watch	Sky Sports
S4C		**11** Nickelodeon
TCM	**06** Sky One	**12** Adult Channel
VH1	The Box	Animal Planet
04 BBC1	**07** Fantasy	Sky Box Office
BBC2	Fox News	**13** Discovery Kids
BBC3	Playboy	Disney Channel
BBC4	Sky News	Extreme Sports
CBBC	Virgin1	**14** Cartoon Network
CNBC	**08** BBC World	Fox Kids Network
Dave	Cbeebies	History Channel
Five	Channel 4	ITV News Channel
GOLD	Channel 9	**15** Paramount Comedy
	FilmFour	

Television shows include:

02 ER	TW3	GMTV
QI	**04** CDUK	Look
03 3-2-1	Chef!	M*A*S*H
CSI	Fame	NCIS
QED	Glee	Soap

Taxi

05 Arena
Bread
Hotel
House
Joe 90
Kojak
LA Law
Lewis
Rhoda
Shaft
Sorry!
Sykes
Tenko
The OC
Wogan
Z Cars

06 Angels
Batman
Bottom
Callan
Cheers
Dallas
DIY SOS
Hannay
Harry O
Hi-De-Hi
Lassie
Magpie
Mannix
Merlin
Minder
Mr Bean
Quincy
Sharpe
Shogun
Tiswas
Trisha
Whack-o!

07 24 Hours
Airline
Airport
Bagpuss
Blake's 7
Bonanza
Cadfael
Chigley
Colditz
Columbo
Compact
Cracker
Daktari
Doctors
Dragnet
Dynasty
Flipper
Frasier
Friends

Hancock
Holiday
Horizon
Laramie
Laugh-In
Lovejoy
Maigret
McCloud
Miranda
Misfits
Monitor
Mr Magoo
Omnibus
Poldark
Pop Idol
Rainbow
Rawhide
Room 101
Serpico
Shelley
Spender
Taggart
The Bill
The Hour
The Wire
The Word
Tonight
Top Gear
Warship

08 'Allo 'Allo
Aquarius
Ask Aspel
Bad Girls
Baywatch
Benidorm
Bergerac
Casualty
Cheyenne
Clangers
Cold Feet
Dad's Army
Due South
Eldorado
Faking It
Hadleigh
Hugh and I
Lou Grant
Maverick
Mister Ed
Mr and Mrs
My Family
New Faces
NYPD Blue
On Safari
Panorama
Peep Show
Play Away
Porridge
Pot Black

Red Dwarf
Roseanne
Seinfeld
Sgt Bilko
Sherlock
Star Trek
Stingray
Survival
The A-Team
The Royal
The Saint
The Voice
This Life
This Week
Time Team
Triangle
Trumpton
Vision On
Watchdog
Wife Swap

09 60 Minutes
Andy Pandy
Bewitched
Blind Date
Blue Peter
Brookside
Catweazle
Chronicle
Countdown
Danger Man
Danger UXB
Dark Angel
Did You See ...?
Doctor Who
Doomwatch
Dr Kildare
Emmerdale
Endeavour
Eurotrash
Family Guy
Father Ted
Going Live!
Happy Days
Heartbeat
Holby City
Hollyoaks
I Love Lucy
Jackanory
Jason King
Love Hurts
Miami Vice
Naked City
News at Ten
Newsnight
Newsround
Oh Brother!
Parkinson
Please Sir!
Public Eye

Real Lives
Scooby-Doo
Shameless
South Park
Strangers
TFI Friday
That's Life
The Expert
The Lovers
The Office
The X Files
Torchwood
Twin Peaks
Up Pompeii!
Whodunnit?

10 Ally McBeal
Big Brother
Blackadder
Byker Grove
Crossroads
Deputy Dawg
Dispatches
Dragon's Den
EastEnders
Elizabeth R
Full Circle
Gladiators
Grandstand
Grange Hill
Hart to Hart
Howards' Way
Jim'll Fix It
Kavanagh QC
Life on Mars
Loose Women
Masterchef
Mastermind
Miss Marple
Naked Video
Nationwide
Neighbours
On the Buses
Pebble Mill
Perry Mason
Play School
Pole to Pole
Police Five
Postman Pat
Quatermass
Rentaghost
Rising Damp
Robin's Nest
Screen Test
Secret Army
Shoestring
The Goodies
The Jetsons
The Killing

The Monkees
The One Show
The Sweeney
The Waltons
The Wombles
The X-Factor
Van der Valk
Wacky Races
Wagon Train
Wells Fargo
Who Do You Do?
Why Don't You?

11 Animal Magic
Bargain Hunt
Born and Bred
Butterflies
Call My Bluff
Catchphrase
Come Dancing
Comic Relief
Crackerjack
Dangerfield
Dangermouse
Daniel Boone
Dead Ringers
Falcon Crest
Fame Academy
Give Us a Clue
Ground Force
Hawaii Five-O
Home and Away
Juke Box Jury
Juliet Bravo
Just William
Life on Earth
Lost in Space
Outnumbered
Peyton Place
Picture Book
Pie in the Sky
Rab C Nesbitt
Rock Follies
St Elsewhere
Sunset Beach
Teletubbies
The Avengers
The Brothers
The Day Today
The Fast Show
The Fugitive
The Good Life
The Invaders
The Lucy Show
The Munsters
The Prisoner
The Rag Trade
The Simpsons
The Sopranos

The Third Man
This Morning
Tom and Jerry
What's My Line?
Whirlybirds
Whistle Test
Wonder Woman
Yes, Minister

12 A Family at War
A Fine Romance
A Life of Grime
Ashes to Ashes
Ask the Family
As Time Goes By
Blockbusters
Candid Camera
Citizen Smith
Crimewatch UK
Dawson's Creek
dinnerladies
Downton Abbey
Face the Music
Fawlty Towers
Fifteen to One
Food and Drink
Forty Minutes
Grand Designs
Hector's House
It's a Knockout
Kaleidoscope
Knots Landing
Melrose Place
Moonlighting
Mork and Mindy
Open All Hours
Peak Practice
Play for Today
Points of View
Preston Front
Prime Suspect
Question Time
Sesame Street
Softly, Softly
Strike It Rich
Take Your Pick
Telly Addicts
Terry and June
The Champions
The Comedians
The Newcomers
The Power Game
The Sullivans
The Thick of It
The Virginian
The Young Ones
Three of a Kind
Thunderbirds
Top of the Form

Top of the Pops
Treasure Hunt
Weekend World
Who Dares, Wins ...
Will and Grace
Working Lunch
World of Sport

13 77 Sunset Strip
A Touch of Frost
Blankety Blank
Bob the Builder
Breakfast Time
Changing Rooms
Emmerdale Farm
Family Affairs
Fantasy Island
Fortunes of War
Game for a Laugh
Going for a Song
Hamish Macbeth
Ivor the Engine
Jonathan Creek
Little Britain
Marcus Welby, MD
Match of the Day
May to December
Muffin the Mule
Pinky and Perky
Ready, Steady, Go!
Sex and the City
Silent Witness
Songs of Praise
Special Branch
Spitting Image
Steptoe and Son
Strike It Lucky
The Apprentice
The Golden Shot
The Likely Lads
The Liver Birds
The Lone Ranger
The Main Chance
The Muppet Show
The Onedin Line
The Persuaders
The Protectors
The Sky at Night
The Two Ronnies
The Woodentops
The World at War
Waiting for God
What Not to Wear
Whicker's World
World in Action

14 Animal Hospital
Ballykissangel
Cagney and Lacey
Call The Midwife

Captain Pugwash
Cash in the Attic
Charlie and Lola
Come Dine With Me
Charlie's Angels
Criss Cross Quiz
Family Fortunes
Gardener's World
Gavin and Stacey
Happy Ever After
In at the Deep End
Inspector Morse
London's Burning
Murder, She Wrote
My Friend Flicka
Not Only ... But Also ...
Only When I Laugh
Property Ladder
Record Breakers
Six-Five Special
Soldier, Soldier
Surgical Spirit
Take Three Girls
The Ascent of Man
The Crystal Maze
The Flintstones
The Forsyte Saga
The Frost Report
The Golden Girls
The Good Old Days
The Lotus Eaters
The New Avengers
The Outer Limits
The Royle Family
The Weakest Link
This Is Your Life
Three Up, Two Down
Tomorrow's World
To the Manor Born
Wheel of Fortune
Winner Takes All
Worzel Gummidge

15 2 Point 4 Children
Armchair Theatre
Birds of a Feather
Camberwick Green
Challenge Anneka
Comedy Playhouse
Double Your Money
General Hospital
Hill Street Blues
It's a Square World
Just Good Friends
Late Night Line-Up
Lord Peter Wimsey
Midsomer Murders
Noel's House Party
No Place Like Home

One Man and His Dog
Ready Steady Cook
Remington Steele
Starsky and Hutch
The Addams Family
The Big Breakfast
The Flying Doctor
The Inbetweeners
The Invisible Man
The Kumars at No 42
The Late Late Show
The Living Planet
The Man from UNCLE
The New Statesman
The Price is Right
The Twilight Zone
The Untouchables
The World About Us
Thirtysomething
Watch with Mother
Where the Heart Is
Wish You Were Here ...?
You've Been Framed

16 All Gas and Gaiters
All Our Yesterdays
Antiques Roadshow
A Question of Sport
Can't Cook, Won't Cook
Celebrity Squares
Coronation Street
Dalziel and Pascoe
Dixon of Dock Green
Doctor in the House
Footballers' Wives
Hancock's Half Hour
Harry Hill's TV Burp
In the Night Garden
It Ain't Half Hot Mum
Jeeves and Wooster
Love Thy Neighbour
Man about the House
Men Behaving Badly
Monarch of the Glen
Murder Most Horrid
Northern Exposure
Rag Tag and Bobtail
Sale of the Century
Sapphire and Steel
Stars in Their Eyes
Surprise, Surprise
The Big Bang Theory
The Dick Emery Show
The High Chaparral
The House of Eliott
The Krypton Factor
The Professionals
The Rockford Files
The South Bank Show

The Vicar of Dibley
The Wednesday Play
What the Papers Say
Within These Walls
Yes, Prime Minister

17 Alas Smith and Jones
Are You Being Served?
Auf Wiedersehen, Pet
Beggar My Neighbour
Beverly Hills 90210
Britain's Got Talent
Dr Finlay's Casebook
Drop the Dead Donkey
Every Second Counts
French and Saunders
Mission: Impossible
Nearest and Dearest
One Foot in the Grave
Opportunity Knocks
Shine On Harvey Moon
The $64,000 Question
The Dukes of Hazzard
The Generation Game
The Incredible Hulk
The Only Way Is Essex
The Tomorrow People
Through the Keyhole
Till Death Us Do Part

18 Absolutely Fabulous
Alias Smith and Jones
A Man Called Ironside
Do Not Adjust Your Set
Goodness Gracious Me
Have I Got News for You
How to Look Good Naked
I Didn't Know You Cared
Jeux sans Frontières
Old Grey Whistle Test
Only Fools and Horses
Play Your Cards Right
Prisoner: Cell Block H
Rumpole of the Bailey

Some Mothers Do 'Ave 'Em
The Dick Van Dyke Show
The Magic Roundabout
The Partridge Family
The Phil Silvers Show
The Troubleshooters
Upstairs, Downstairs
When the Boat Comes In

19 Desperate Housewives
Goodnight Sweetheart
How Clean Is Your House?
Last of the Summer Wine
Strictly Come Dancing
Tales of the Riverbank
Thank Your Lucky Stars
The Chinese Detective
The Lenny the Lion Show
The White Heather Club
They Think It's All Over
University Challenge
Who Do You Think You Are?
Whose Line Is It Anyway?
Xena: Warrior Princess

20 Harry Enfield and Chums
John Craven's Newsround
Keeping Up Appearances
Not the Nine O'Clock News
Tales of the Unexpected
The League of Gentlemen
Your Life in Their Hands

21 Agatha Christie's Poirot
A Very Peculiar Practice
Buffy the Vampire Slayer
Eurovision Song Contest
Ever Decreasing Circles
Multi-Coloured Swap Shop
Mystery and Imagination
Never Mind the Buzzcocks
Oh No It's Selwyn Froggitt
Skippy, the Bush Kangaroo
That Was the Week That Was
The Beverly Hillbillies

22 Around the World in 80 Days
Rowan and Martin's Laugh-In
Television Top of the Form
The Duchess of Duke Street
The Six Million Dollar Man
The Six Wives of Henry VIII

23 It'll Be Alright on the Night
Little House on the Prairie
Not in Front of the Children
Royal Variety Performance
The Ruth Rendell Mysteries

24 Location, Location, Location
Monty Python's Flying Circus
Ramsay's Kitchen Nightmares
Rutland Weekend Television
The Adventures of Rin-Tin-Tin
The Late, Late Breakfast Show
The Streets of San Francisco
Who Wants to Be a
Millionaire?

25 All Creatures Great and Small
Queer Eye for the Straight Guy
Randall and Hopkirk
(Deceased)

26 I'm a Celebrity - Get Me out
of Here!

28 The Black and White
Minstrel Show

29 Thomas the Tank Engine
and Friends

30 The Fall and Rise of
Reginald Perrin
The Hitch-Hiker's Guide to
the Galaxy

31 Never Mind the Quality,
Feel the Width
Sunday Night at the London
Palladium
Whatever Happened to the
Likely Lads?

TV characters include:

02 C J (*The Fall And Rise Of Reginald Perrin*)

04 Best (Dave; *The Royle Family*)
Best (Denise; *The Royle Family*)
Bing (Chandler; *Friends*)
Bird (Ronald 'Budgie'; *Budgie*)
Buck (Rose; *Upstairs, Downstairs*)
Cage (John; *Ally McBeal*)
Cook (Edgar 'Egg'; *This Life*)
Fish (Richard; *Ally McBeal*)
Gale (Cathy; *The Avengers*)
Good (Barbara; *The Good Life*)
Good (Tom; *The Good Life*)
Hope (Viv; *Emmerdale*)

Hunt (Gene; *Life on Mars/Ashes to Ashes*)
King (Sadie; *Emmerdale*)
King (Tara; *The Avengers*)
Kirk (Captain James Tiberius; *Star Trek*)
Mike (*The Young Ones*)
Moon (Alfie; *EastEnders*)
Moon (Daphne; *Frasier*)
Mork (*Mork and Mindy*)
Neil (*The Young Ones*)
Peck (Lieutenant Templeton 'Faceman'; *The
A-Team*)
Peel (Mrs Emma; *The Avengers*)
Pike (Private Frank; *Dad's Army*)

Rick (*The Young Ones*)
Ross (Dr Doug; *ER*)
Ryan (Sam; *Silent Witness*)
Solo (Napoleon; *The Man from UNCLE*)
Sulu (Hikaru; *Star Trek*)
Tate (Kim; *Emmerdale*)
York (Charlotte; *Sex and the City*)

05 Angel (*Buffy The Vampire Slayer/Angel*)
Batty (Nora; *Last of the Summer Wine*)
Bauer (Jack; *24*)
Beale (Ian; *EastEnders*)
Bilko (Sgt Ernest G, 'Ernie'; *The Phil Silvers Show*)
Birch (Edna; *Emmerdale*)
Blake (Inspector Cyril, 'Blakey'; *On The Buses*)
Bodie (William; *The Professionals*)
Brent (David; *The Office*)
Brian (*Family Guy*)
Briss (Hilary; *The League of Gentlemen*)
Burns (Charles Montgomery 'Monty'; *The Simpsons*)
Clegg (Norman; *Last of the Summer Wine*)
Crane (Dr Frasier; *Cheers/Frasier*)
Crane (Dr Niles; *Frasier*)
Crane (Martin; *Frasier*)
Daley (Arthur; *Minder*)
Dixon (PC George; *Dixon of Dock Green*)
Doyle (Mrs; *Father Ted*)
Doyle (Raymond; *The Professionals*)
Evans (Pat; *EastEnders*)
Ewing (Bobby; *Dallas*)
Ewing (John Ross, 'J R'; *Dallas*)
Frost (DI Jack; *A Touch of Frost*)
Gates (Amber; *Footballers' Wives*)
Grant (Bobby; *Brookside*)
Grant (Sheila; *Brookside*)
Green (Rachel; *Friends*)
Jones (Lance-Corporal Jack; *Dad's Army*)
Jones (Martha; *Doctor Who*)
Jones (Miss Ruth; *Rising Damp*)
Jones (Samantha; *Sex and the City*)
Kojak (Lieutenant Theo; *Kojak*)
Lewis (Robbie; *Morse/Lewis*)
Lynch (Bet; *Coronation Street*)
Mayer (Susan; *Desperate Housewives*)
McCoy (Dr Leonard, 'Bones'; *Star Trek*)
Morse (Endeavour; *Morse/Endeavour*)
McFee (Shughie; *Crossroads*)
Noble (Donna; *Doctor Who*)
Ogden (Hilda; *Coronation Street*)
Percy (*Blackadder*)
Platt (Gail; *Coronation Street*)
Polly (*Fawlty Towers*)
Regan (DI Jack; *The Sweeney*)
Roach (Megan; *Casualty*)
Rolfe (Jack; *Howard's Way*)
Royle (Antony; *The Royle Family*)
Royle (Barbara; *The Royle Family*)

Royle (Jim; *The Royle Family*)
Rudge (Olive; *On The Buses*)
Scavo (Lynette; *Desperate Housewives*)
Scott (Montgomery, 'Scotty'; *Star Trek*)
Smith (Colonel John 'Hannibal'; *The A-Team*)
Smith (Sarah Jane; *Doctor Who*)
Solis (Gabrielle; *Desperate Housewives*)
Spock (Mr; *Star Trek*)
Steed (John; *The Avengers/The New Avengers*)
Stone (Patsy; *Absolutely Fabulous*)
Tubbs (*The League of Gentlemen*)
Tyler (Rose; *Doctor Who*)
Tyler (Sam; *Life on Mars*)
Uhura (Lieutenant; *Star Trek*)
Watts (Angie; *EastEnders*)
Watts ('Dirty' Den; *EastEnders*)
Weber (Warren 'Potsie'; *Happy Days*)
Wicks (Simon 'Wicksy'; *EastEnders*)
Wilde (Danny; *The Persuaders!*)

06 Arcola (Charles 'Chachi'; *Happy Days*)
Austin (Steve; *The Six Million Dollar Man*)
Barlow (Deirdre; *Coronation Street*)
Barlow (Ken; *Coronation Street*)
Barnes (Cliff; *Dallas*)
Benton (Dr Peter; *ER*)
Bishop (Emily; *Coronation Street*)
Bishop (Harold; *Neighbours*)
B'Stard (Alan; *The New Statesman*)
Bubble (*Absolutely Fabulous*)
Bucket (Hyacinth; *Keeping Up Appearances*)
Buffay (Phoebe; *Friends*)
Butler (Stan; *On The Buses*)
Carter (Dr John; *ER*)
Carter (DS George; *The Sweeney*)
Chekov (Pavel; *Star Trek*)
Cooper (Gwen; *Torchwood*)
Cooper (Special Agent Dale; *Twin Peaks*)
Cotton (Dot; *EastEnders*)
Cowley (George; *The Professionals*)
Crilly (Father Ted; *Father Ted*)
Denton (Harvey; *The League of Gentlemen*)
Denton (Val; *The League of Gentlemen*)
Dingle (Mandy; *Emmerdale*)
Dingle (Marlon; *Emmerdale*)
Duffin (Lisa 'Duffy'; *Casualty*)
Edward (*The League of Gentlemen*)
Fawlty (Basil; *Fawlty Towers*)
Fawlty (Sybil; *Fawlty Towers*)
Ferris (Bob; *The Likely Lads*)
Forbes (Anna; *This Life*)
Fowler (Pauline; *EastEnders*)
Frazer (Private James; *Dad's Army*)
Gambit (Mike; *The New Avengers*)
Geller (Monica; *Friends*)
Geller (Ross; *Friends*)
Glover (Kathy; *Emmerdale*)
Godber (Lennie; *Porridge*)

Greene (Dr Mark; *ER*)
Hacker (Jim; *Yes Minister/Yes, Prime Minister*)
Hobbes (Miranda; *Sex and the City*)
Howard (Jan; *Howard's Way*)
Howard (Tom; *Howard's Way*)
Hudson (Mr Angus; *Upstairs, Downstairs*)
Hughes (Yosser; *Boys from the Blackstuff*)
Hunter (David; *Crossroads*)
Lurcio (*Up Pompeii*)
Mackay (Mr; *Porridge*)
Malone (Sam; *Cheers*)
Mangel (Nell; *Neighbours*)
Manuel (*Fawlty Towers*)
McBeal (Ally; *Ally McBeal*)
McCann (Terry; *Minder*)
Nassim (Milly; *This Life*)
Palmer (Laura; *Twin Peaks*)
Perrin (Reginald Iolanthe, 'Reggie'; *The Fall and Rise of Reginald Perrin*)
Purdey (*The New Avengers*)
Ramsay (Madge; *Neighbours*)
Rigsby (Rupert; *Rising Damp*)
Slater (Kat; *EastEnders*)
Sugden (Annie; *Emmerdale*)
Sugden (Jack; *Emmerdale*)
Turner (Alan; *Emmerdale*)
Turner (Tanya; *Footballers' Wives*)
Turtle (Amy; *Crossroads*)
Vassal (Elaine; *Ally McBeal*)
Vyvyan (*The Young Ones*)
Weaver (Dr Kerry; *ER*)
Wilson (Sergeant Arthur; *Dad's Army*)

07 Appleby (Sir Humphrey; *Yes Minister/Yes, Prime Minister*)
Baldwin (Mike; *Coronation Street*)
Baracus (Sgt Bosco 'B A'; *The A-Team*)
Boswell (Carol; *The Liver Birds*)
Brearly (Amos; *Emmerdale*)
Bridges (Mrs Kate; *Upstairs, Downstairs*)
Butcher (Frank; *EastEnders*)
Collier (Terry; *The Likely Lads*)
Columbo (Lieutenant; *Columbo*)
Daniels (Helen; *Neighbours*)
Garnett (Alf; *Till Death Us Do Part*)
Godfrey (Private Charles; *Dad's Army*)
Griffin (Peter; *Family Guy*)
Griffin (Stewie; *Family Guy*)
Hackett (Father Jack; *Father Ted*)
Hawkeye (Benjamin Franklin Pierce; *M*A*S*H*)
Hawkins (Benny; *Crossroads*)
Hopkirk (Marty; *Randall and Hopkirk (Deceased)*)
Jackson (Arnold; *Diff'rent Strokes*)
MacBeth (Hamish; *Hamish MacBeth*)
Maguire (Father Dougal; *Father Ted*)
Masters (Ken; *Howard's Way*)
Meldrew (Margaret; *One Foot in the Grave*)

Meldrew (Victor; *One Foot in the Grave*)
Monsoon (Edina 'Eddy'; *Absolutely Fabulous*)
Monsoon (Saffron 'Saffy'; *Absolutely Fabulous*)
Murdock (Captain H M 'Howling Mad'; *The A-Team*)
Nesbitt (Rab C; *Rab C Nesbitt*)
Pauline (*The League of Gentlemen*)
Queenie (*Blackadder*)
Randall (Jeff; *Randall and Hopkirk (Deceased)*)
Ricardo (Lucy; *I Love Lucy*)
Ricardo (Ricky; *I Love Lucy*)
Roberts (Audrey; *Coronation Street*)
Rumpole (Horace; *Rumpole of the Bailey*)
Simpson (Bart; *The Simpsons*)
Simpson (Homer; *The Simpsons*)
Simpson (Lisa; *The Simpsons*)
Simpson (Marge; *The Simpsons*)
Soprano (Tony; *The Sopranos*)
Spencer (Betty; *Some Mothers Do 'Ave 'Em*)
Spencer (Frank; *Some Mothers Do 'Ave 'Em*)
Starsky (Detective Dave; *Starsky and Hutch*)
Steptoe (Albert; *Steptoe and Son*)
Steptoe (Harold; *Steptoe and Son*)
Stewart (Miles; *This Life*)
Summers (Buffy; *Buffy The Vampire Slayer*)
The Fonz (*Happy Days*)
Tilsley (Gail; *Coronation Street*)
Trotter (Derek 'Del Boy'; *Only Fools and Horses*)
Trotter (Rodney; *Only Fools and Horses*)

08 Baldrick (*Blackadder*)
Bradshaw (Carrie; *Sex and the City*)
Corkhill (Billy; *Brookside*)
Dewhurst (Walter 'Foggy'; *Last of the Summer Wine*)
Fairhead (Charlie; *Casualty*)
Flanders (Ned; *The Simpsons*)
Fletcher (Norman Stanley; *Porridge*)
Harkness (Captain Jack; *Doctor Who/Torchwood*)
Hathaway (Nurse Carol; *ER*)
Houlihan (Margaret 'Hotlips'; *M*A*S*H*)
Jordache (Beth; *Brookside*)
Kavanagh (James; *Kavanagh QC*)
Kuryakin (Illya; *The Man from UNCLE*)
McDonald (Steve; *Coronation Street*)
Milligan (Bruno; *Footballers' Wives*)
Mitchell (Grant; *EastEnders*)
Mitchell (Peggy; *EastEnders*)
Mitchell (Phil; *EastEnders*)
Mortimer (Meg; *Crossroads*)
Robinson (Charlene; *Neighbours*)
Robinson (Scott; *Neighbours*)
Simonite (William 'Compo'; *Last of the Summer Wine*)

Sinclair (Lord Brett; *The Persuaders!*)
Skilbeck (Dolly; *Emmerdale*)
Speakman (Norma, 'Nana'; *The Royle Family*)
Sullivan (Rita; *Coronation Street*)
Tennison (DCI Jane; *Prime Suspect*)
Tortelli (Carla; *Cheers*)
Urquhart (Francis; *House of Cards*)

09 Arkwright (Albert; *Open All Hours*)
Armstrong (Seth; *Emmerdale*)
Carpenter (Lou; *Neighbours*)
Duckworth (Jack; *Coronation Street*)
Duckworth (Vera; *Coronation Street*)
Gallagher (Frank; *Shameless*)
Granville (*Open All Hours*)
Griffiths (Josh; *Casualty*)
Hennessey (Beryl; *The Liver Birds*)
Huggy Bear (*Starsky and Hutch*)
McConnell (Mindy; *Mork and Mindy*)
Number Six (*The Prisoner*)
Partridge (Danny; *The Partridge Family*)

Partridge (Keith Douglas; *The Partridge Family*)
The Doctor (*Doctor Who*)
Tribbiani (Joey; *Friends*)
Van De Kamp (Bree; *Desperate Housewives*)

10 Blackadder (Edmund; *Blackadder*)
Cunningham (Joanie; *Happy Days*)
Cunningham (Richard 'Richie'; *Happy Days*)
Fitzgerald (Dr Eddie, 'Fitz'; *Cracker*)
Fonzarelli (Arthur 'Fonzie'; *Happy Days*)
Hutchinson (Detective Ken 'Hutch'; *Starsky and Hutch*)
Hutchinson (Sandra; *The Liver Birds*)
Lane-Pascoe (Chardonnay; *Footballers' Wives*)
Leadbetter (Jerry; *The Good Life*)
Leadbetter (Margot; *The Good Life*)
Mainwaring (Captain George; *Dad's Army*)
Penhaligon (DS Jane, 'Panhandle'; *Cracker*)

14 Krusty the Clown (*The Simpsons*)

15 Fletcher-Dervish (Piers; *The New Statesman*)

Television presenters include:

03 Ant (Anthony McPartlin; 1975– , English)
Dec (Declan Donnelly; 1975– , English)

04 Marr (Andrew; 1959– , Scottish)
Muir (Frank; 1920–98, English)
Ross (Jonathan; 1960– , English)

05 Aspel (Michael; 1933– , Welsh)
Baker (Matt; 1977– , English)
Black (Cilla; 1943– , English)
Bragg (Melvyn, Lord; 1939– , English)
Evans (Chris; 1966– , English)
Fogle (Ben; 1973– , English)
Frost (Sir David; 1939–2013, English)
James (Clive; 1939– , Australian)
Jones (Alex; 1977– , Welsh)
Kelly (Lorraine; 1959– , Scottish)
Moore (Sir Patrick; 1923–2012, English)
Negus (Arthur; 1903–85, English)
Wogan (Terry; 1938– , Irish)

06 Carson (Johnny; 1925–2005, US)
Chiles (Adrian; 1967– , English)
McCall (Davina; 1967– , English)
Norden (Denis; 1922– , English)
Norman (Barry; 1933– , English)
Norton (Graham; 1963– , Irish)
Paxman (Jeremy; 1950– , English)
Rayner (Claire; 1931–2010, English)
Savile (Sir Jimmy; 1926–2011, English)

07 Andrews (Eamon; 1922–87, Irish)
Balding (Clare; 1971– , English)
Bellamy (David; 1933– , English)

Britton (Fern; 1957– , English)
Edmonds (Noel; 1948– , English)
Forsyth (Bruce; 1928– , English)
Kennedy (Sir Ludovic; 1919–2009, Scottish)
Madeley (Richard; 1956– , English)
Rantzen (Esther; 1940– , English)
Starkey (David; 1945– , English)
Tarrant (Chris; 1946– , English)
Wheldon (Sir Huw; 1916–86, Welsh)
Whicker (Alan; 1925–2013, English)
Winfrey (Oprah; 1954– , US)

08 Bakewell (Joan; 1933– , English)
Bleakley (Christine; 1980– , Northern Irish)
Campbell (Nicky; 1961– , Scottish)
Clarkson (Jeremy; 1960– , English)
Finnigan (Judy; 1948– , English)
Springer (Jerry; 1944– , US)
Stoppard (Miriam; 1937– , English)
Sullivan (Ed; 1902–74, US)

09 Ant and Dec (Anthony McPartlin; 1975– , English/Declan Donnelly; 1975– , English)
Magnusson (Magnus; 1929–2007, Icelandic/Scottish)
Parkinson (Michael; 1935– , English)
Schofield (Phillip; 1962– , English)
Vorderman (Carol; 1960– , English)

10 Titchmarsh (Alan; 1949– , English)

12 Attenborough (Sir David; 1926– , English)

14 Richard and Judy (Richard Madeley; 1956– , English/Judy Finnigan; 1948– , English)

See also **broadcasting**; **comedy**; **quiz**; **soap opera**

tennis

Tennis players include:

04 Ashe (Arthur; 1943–93, US)
Borg (Björn; 1956– , Swedish)
Cash (Pat; 1965– , Australian)
Graf (Steffi; 1969– , German)
Hoad (Lew; 1934–94, Australian)
King (Billie Jean; 1943– , US)
Ryan (Elizabeth; 1892–1979, US)
Wade (Virginia; 1945– , English)

05 Budge (Don; 1915–2000, US)
Bueno (Maria; 1939– , Brazilian)
Court (Margaret; 1942– , Australian)
Durie (Jo; 1960– , English)
Evert (Chris; 1954– , US)
Henin (Justine; 1982– , Belgian)
Jones (Ann; 1938– , English)
Laver (Rod; 1938– , Australian)
Lendl (Ivan; 1960– , Czech/US)
Lloyd (Chris; c.1951– , English)
Nadal (Rafael; 1986– , Spanish)
Perry (Fred; 1909–95, English/US)
Seles (Monica; 1973– , Yugoslav/US)
Stich (Michael; 1968– , German)
Vilas (Guillermo; 1952– , Argentine)

06 Agassi (Andre; 1970– , US)
Austin (Tracy; 1962– , US)
Barker (Sue; 1956– , English)
Becker (Boris; 1967– , German)
Cawley (Evonne; 1951– , Australian)
Drobny (Jaroslav; 1921–2001, Czech/British)
DuPont (Margaret; 1918–2012, US)
Edberg (Stefan; 1966– , Swedish)
Gibson (Althea; 1927–2003, US)
Henman (Tim; 1974– , English)
Hewitt (Lleyton; 1981– , Australian)
Hingis (Martina; 1980– , Czech/Swiss)
Hopman (Harry; 1906–85, Australian)
Kramer (Jack; 1921–2009, US)
Murray (Andrew; 1987– , Scottish)
Rafter (Pat; 1972– , Australian)
Tilden (Bill; 1893–1953, US)

07 Borotra (Jean; 1898–94, French)
Brookes (Sir Norman; 1877–1968, Australian)
Connors (Jimmy; 1952– , US)

Emerson (Roy; 1936– , Australian)
Federer (Roger; 1981– , Swiss)
Godfree (Kitty; 1896–1992, English)
LaCoste (Rene; 1904–96, French)
Lenglen (Suzanne; 1899–1938, French)
Maskell (Dan; 1908–92, English)
McEnroe (John; 1959– , US)
Nastase (Ilie; 1946– , Romanian)
Novotna (Jana; 1968– , Czech)
Renshaw (Willie; 1861–1904, English)
Roddick (Andrew; 1982– , US)
Sampras (Pete; 1971– , US)
Sedgman (Frank; 1927– , Australian)
Shriver (Pam; 1962– , US)
Zvereva (Natasha; 1971– , Belarus)

08 Capriati (Jennifer; 1976– , US)
Connolly (Maureen; 1934–69, US)
Djokovic (Novak; 1987– , Serbian)
Gonzales (Pancho; 1928–95, US)
Janković (Jelena; 1985– , Serbian)
Krajicek (Richard; 1971– , Dutch)
Mauresmo (Amélie; 1979– , French)
Newcombe (John; 1944– , Australian)
Rosewall (Ken; 1934– , Australian)
Rusedski (Greg; 1973– , Canadian/British)
Sabatini (Gabriela; 1970– , Argentine)
Wightman (Hazel Hotchkiss; 1886–1974, US)
Williams (Serena; 1981– , US)
Williams (Venus; 1980– , US)

09 Davenport (Lindsay; 1976– , US)
Goolagong (Evonne; 1951– , Australian)
Sharapova (Maria; 1987– , Russian)
Woodforde (Mark; 1965– , Australian)

10 Ivanisevic (Goran; 1971– , Croatian)
Kafelnikov (Yevgeny; 1974– , Russian)
Kournikova (Anna; 1981– , Russian)
Mandlikova (Hana; 1962– , Czech/Australian)
Wills Moody (Helen; 1905–98, US)
Woodbridge (Todd; 1971– , Australian)

11 Navratilova (Martina; 1956– , Czech/US)

15 Goolagong Cawley (Evonne; 1951– , Australian)

Tennis terms include:

03	ace		WTA	break		slice
	ATP	**04**	love	deuce		smash
	let		pass	drive	**06**	return
	lob		tape	fault		umpire
	LTA	**05**	AELTC	rally		volley
	set		alley	serve		winner

07 ballboy
net cord
runback

08 backhand
ballgirl
baseline
drop shot
forehand
line call
love game
midcourt
net judge

See also **sport**

overhead
overrule
set point
tie-break
wood shot

09 advantage
backcourt
baseliner
break back
foot fault
forecourt
hold serve

line judge
mini-break
shotmaker
sweet spot
tramlines
two-handed

10 break point
cross court
deuce court
match point

11 block volley

double fault
service game
service line

12 approach shot
ground stroke
mixed doubles
service court

13 second service

14 advantage court
serve and volley

Tennyson, Alfred, Lord (1809–92)

Significant works include:

04 *Maud* (1855)

06 *Becket* (1884)
Harold (1876)
Oenone (1833)
The Cup (1881)

07 *Mariana* (1830)
Ulysses (1842)

08 *The Brook* (1855)
The Daisy (1855)
Tithonus (1881)

09 *Queen Mary* (1875)
The Falcon (1879)
The Voyage (1881)
Timbuctoo (1829)

10 *In Memoriam* (1850)
St Agnes Eve (1842)
The Mermaid (1833)

11 *Edwin Morris* (1842)

The Princess (1847)

12 *Locksley Hall* (1842)
Morte d'Arthur (1842)

14 *The Lotos-Eaters* (1833)

15 *Break, Break, Break* (1842)
Idylls of the King (1859–85)

16 *The Lady of Shalott* (1833)

17 *A Dream of Fair Women* (1833)
Maud and Other Poems (1855)
Poems in Two Volumes (1842)

19 *Poems Chiefly Lyrical* (1830)

20 *Ballads and Other Poems* (1880)
The Gardener's Daughter (1842)

21 *Tiresias and Other Poems* (1885)

25 *The Holy Grail and Other Poems* (1869)

26 *The Charge of the Light Brigade* (1855)

31 *Recollections of the Arabian Nights* (1830)

tense *see* **grammar**

tent

Tents include:

03 box
mat

04 bell
dome
kata
yurt

05 bivvy

black
frame
lodge
ridge
tepee
tupik

06 big top
canopy

canvas
tunnel
wigwam

07 conical
marquee
touring
trailer
yaranga

10 single hoop
tabernacle

11 hooped bivvy

12 sloping ridge
sloping wedge

13 barrel-vaulted
crossover pole

term

Terms and sessions include:

04 Lent   Hilary   **08** Epiphany
06 Easter   **07** Trinity   **10** Michaelmas

terrier

Terriers include:

03 fox
 toy
04 bull
 Skye
05 cairn
 foxie
 Irish
 Welsh
06 Border
 Boston
 Scotch

 Scotty
 Westie
 Yorkie
07 pit bull
 Scottie
 Tibetan
08 Aberdeen
 Airedale
 Doberman
 Scottish
 Sealyham
 wire-hair

09 Kerry blue
 schnauzer
 Yorkshire
10 Australian
 Bedlington
 Manchester
 wire-haired
11 Jack Russell
12 West Highland
13 Dandie Dinmont
15 American pit bull

territory *see* **Australia; Canada**

terrorist *see* **revolutionary**

theatre

Theatrical forms include:

03 Noh
04 mime
 play
05 farce
 opera
 revue
06 Absurd
 ballet
 circus
 comedy
 fringe
 kabuki
 masque
 puppet

 street
07 cabaret
 Cruelty
 mummery
 musical
 pageant
 tableau
 tragedy
08 duologue
 operetta
09 burlesque
 melodrama
 monologue
 music hall

 pantomime
10 in-the-round
11 black comedy
 kitchen-sink
 miracle play
 mystery play
12 Grand Guignol
 morality play
 Punch and Judy
13 musical comedy
14 comedy of menace
15 comedy of humours
 comedy of manners

Theatre parts include:

03 box
 pit
 set
04 flat
 grid
 loge
05 apron

 decor
 flies
 house
 logum
 spots
 stage
 wings

06 border
 bridge
 circle
 floats
 floods
 lights
 loggia
 scruto

stalls
07 balcony
catwalk
curtain
cut drop
gallery
leg drop
rostrum
the gods
upstage
08 backdrop
coulisse

trapdoor
09 backstage
cyclorama
downstage
forestage
green room
mezzanine
open stage
tormentor
10 auditorium
footlights
fourth wall

ghost light
prompt side
proscenium
11 upper circle
12 orchestra pit
13 safety curtain
14 opposite prompt
proscenium arch
revolving stage
15 proscenium doors

Theatres include:

03 Pit (England)
04 Rose (England)
Swan (England)
05 Abbey (Ireland)
Globe (England)
Lyric (England)
Savoy (England)
06 Albery (England)
Lyceum (England)
Old Vic (England)
Queen's (England)
07 Adelphi (England)
Aldwych (England)
Almeida (England)
Garrick (England)
Olivier (England)
08 Coliseum (England)
Crucible (England)
Dominion (England)
National (England)

Young Vic (England)
Ziegfeld (USA)
09 Cambridge (England)
Cottesloe (England)
Criterion (England)
Drury Lane (England)
Haymarket (England)
Lyttelton (England)
Palladium (England)
11 Comedy Store (England)
Duke of York's (England)
Moulin Rouge (France)
12 Sadler's Wells (England)
Theatre Royal (England)
13 Folies Bergère (France)
Prince of Wales (England)
The Other Place (England)
The Roundhouse (England)
14 Barbican Centre (England)
15 Donmar Warehouse (England)

Terms to do with the theatre include:

02 BS
LX
OB
OP
PS
03 act
cue
fée
fly
gel
mug
rep
run
vis
yok
04 call
cast
flat

grid
juve
loge
plot
pong
rake
tabs
wash
yock
05 actor
ad lib
angel
aside
cameo
derig
dry up
fit-up
genre

get-in
lines
lodge
props
re-rig
scene
spike
usher
06 baffle
chorus
corpse
critic
double
dry ice
Equity
flyman
fringe
get-out

make-up
miscue
places
prompt
review
script
walk-on

07 actress
costume
curtain
dresser
dry tech
matinee
pittite
preview
project
rhubarb
rigging
scenery
tableau
upstage
West End

08 audience
audition
blackout
block out
Broadway
business
coulisse
dialogue
director
duologue
entr'acte
interval
libretto
overture
pass door
play-goer
producer
ring down
thespian
wardrobe
white out

09 backlight
backstage
beginners
box office
break a leg
chaperone
curtain up
cyclorama
double act
downstage
footlight
full house
happening
limelight
monologue
periaktos
programme
rehearsal
repertory
skin money
soliloquy
soubrette
spotlight
stage crew
stage door
stage hand
stage left
usherette
visual cue

10 book-holder
dénouement
first night
followspot
fourth wall
get the bird
in the wings
piano dress
prompt book
prompt copy
prompt desk
prompt side
stagecraft
stage right

understudy
walk-around

11 bastard side
bums on seats
centre stage
curtain call
curtain time
die the death
greasepaint
house lights
iron curtain
leading lady
off-Broadway
quick change
read-through
stage fright
top one's part
wind machine

12 breeches part
breeches role
first-nighter
front of house
intermission
jeune premier
juvenile lead
monstre sacré
principal boy
prompt corner
prompt script
stage manager
travesty role

13 bastard prompt
curtain-raiser
curtain speech
grande vedette
jeune première
safety curtain

14 dress rehearsal
opposite prompt
special effects

15 genteel business
opposite bastard

See also **cinema**; **director**

theology

Cyril (St, of Alexandria; AD376–444, Greek)
Henry (Carl F H; 1913–2003, US)
Mbiti (John S; 1931– , Kenyan)
Occam (William of; c.1285–c.1349, English)
Pusey (E B; 1800–82, English)
Rainy (Robert; 1826–1906, Scottish)
Sarpi (Pietro, Fra Paolo; 1552–1623, Italian)
Tracy (David; 1939– , US)

06 Anselm (St; 1033–1109, Italian)
Calvin (John; 1509–64, French)
Cupitt (Don; 1934– , English)
Eckart (Johannes; c.1260–1327, German)
Ferrar (Nicholas; 1592–1637, English)
Jansen (Cornelius; 1585–1638, Dutch)
Jüngel (Eberhard; 1934– , German)
Mather (Increase; 1639–1723, American)
Ockham (William of; c.1285–c.1349, English)
Origen (c.185–c.254 AD, Greek)
Pagels (Elaine; 1943– , US)
Suárez (Francisco; 1548–1617, Spanish)
Taylor (Jeremy; 1613–67, English)

07 Altizer (Thomas J J; 1927– , US)
Aquinas (St Thomas; 1225–74, Italian)
Barclay (William; 1907–78, Scottish)
Bernard (St, of Clairvaux; 1090–1153, French)
Brunner (Emil; 1889–1966, Swiss)
Eckhart (Johannes; c.1260–1327, German)
Edwards (Jonathan; 1703–58, American)
Erigena (John Scotus; c.810–c.877, Irish)
Forsyth (P T; 1848–1921, Scottish)
Ghazali (al-; 1058–1111, Islamic)
Gregory (of Nazianzus; c.330–c.389 AD, Greek)
Gregory (of Nyssa; AD331–95, Greek)
Jenkins (David E; 1925– , English)
Lombard (Peter; c.1100–1160, Italian)
Niebuhr (H Richard; 1894–1962, US)
Niebuhr (Reinhold; 1892–1971, US)
Quesnel (Pasquier; 1634–1719, French)

See also **reformer**

Ruether (Rosemary Radford; 1936– , US)
Sankara (c.700–750, Indian)
Strauss (David; 1808–74, German)
Tillich (Paul; 1886–1965, US)
William (of Auvergne; c.1180–1249, French)
William (of Auxerre; c.1140–1231, French)

08 Arminius (Jacobus; 1560–1609, Dutch)
Bulgakov (Sergei; 1871–1944, Russian)
Bultmann (Rudolf; 1884–1976, German)
Cudworth (Ralph; 1617–88, English)
Cullmann (Oscar; 1902–99, German)
Eusebius (of Caesarea; c.264–340 AD, Palestinian)
Hamilton (Patrick; 1503–28, Scottish)
Irenaeus (St; c.130–c.200 AD, Greek)
Moltmann (Jürgen; 1926– , German)
Robinson (John; 1919–83, English)
Torrance (Thomas F; 1913–2007, Scottish)

09 Gurdjieff (Georgei; c.1865–1949, Armenian)
Gutiérrez (Gustavo; 1928– , Peruvian)
Niemöller (Martin; 1892–1984, German)
Thielicke (Helmut; 1908–86, German)
Whichcote (Benjamin; 1609–83, English)

10 Athanasius (St; c.296–373 AD, Greek)
Bellarmine (St Francis; 1542–1621, Italian)
Duns Scotus (John; c.1265–1308, Scottish)
Mackintosh (H R; 1870–1936, Scottish)
Macquarrie (John; 1919–2007, Scottish)
Rosenzweig (Franz; 1886–1929, German)
Swedenborg (Emanuel; 1688–1772, Swedish)
Tertullian (c.160–c.220 AD, North African)

11 Witherspoon (John; 1723–94, American)

14 Eboussi-Boulaga (Fabien; 1934– , Cameroonian)
Rosmini-Serbati (Antonio; 1797–1855, Italian)
Schleiermacher (Friedrich; 1768–1834, German)

theory

Theories include:

03 GUT
TOE
04 game
05 chaos
06 atomic
number
string

07 Big Bang
quantum
09 collision
Darwinism
evolution
10 panspermia
relativity

11 catastrophe
12 Grand Unified
Milankovitch
14 plate tectonics
15 butterfly effect

See also **astronomy**; **economics**; **mathematics**; **philosophy**; **physics**; **psychology**

therapy

Therapies include:

03 art
CST
ECT
HRT
LDT
sex

04 drug
play
zone

05 chemo
drama
group
music
photo
reiki

06 beauty
family
Gerson
primal
retail

speech

07 Gestalt
Rolfing
shiatsu

08 aversion

09 behaviour
cognitive
herbalism

10 homeopathy
osteopathy
regression
ultrasound

11 acupressure
acupuncture
biofeedback
irradiation
mesotherapy
moxibustion
naturopathy

reflexology

12 aromatherapy
chemotherapy
chiropractic
craniosacral
electroshock
faith healing
horticulture
hydrotherapy
hypnotherapy
occupational
radiotherapy
reminiscence

13 confrontation
dream analysis
heat treatment
physiotherapy
psychotherapy

14 electrotherapy

See also **psychology**

thief

Thieves and robbers include:

03 dip
pad

04 bung
file
prig
Tory
wire
yegg

05 crook
diver
heist
kiddy
rover
sneak

06 bandit
bulker
chummy
con man
dacoit
dakoit
dipper
hotter
ice man
latron
lifter
limmer
looter
magpie

mugger
nicker
nipper
pirate
raider
robber

07 abactor
blagger
booster
brigand
burglar
cateran
cosh boy
filcher
footpad
hoister
ladrone
land-rat
nobbler
nut-hook
pandoor
pandour
poacher
prigger
rustler
stealer
tea leaf
twoccer

whizzer
yeggman

08 cly-faker
cutpurse
hijacker
huaquero
larcener
pilferer
rapparee
river-rat
swindler

09 area-sneak
Autolycus
cracksman
embezzler
fraudster
larcenist
pick-purse
plunderer
ram-raider
sea robber

10 cat-burglar
gully-raker
highjacker
highwayman
horse-thief
land-pirate
man-stealer

pickpocket	safe-breaker	housebreaker
roberdsman	safe-cracker	kleptomaniac
robertsman	snatch-purse	sheep-stealer
shoplifter	snow-dropper	snow-gatherer
sneak thief	**12** appropriator	**13** highway robber
water thief	baby-snatcher	**15** resurrectionist
11 motor-bandit	cattle-lifter	resurrection man

Three Graces *see* grace

Three Musketeers *see* Dumas, Alexandre

tie

Ties include:

03 bow	**06** cravat	soubise	steenkirk
04 bolo	kipper	**08** bootlace	waterfall
neck	string	kerchief	**10** tawdry lace
05 ascot	**07** overlay	**09** neckcloth	**11** neckerchief
stock	owrelay	solitaire	

time

Time zones:

02 AT	**04** AKST	**18** Alaska Standard Time
CT	CYST	Daylight Saving Time
ET	HAST	Hawaii Standard Time
MT	WAST	**19** British Standard Time
PT	WEST	Central European Time
03 AST	**08** Zulu time	Central Standard Time
BST	**10** Alaska Time	Eastern European Time
CET	**11** Central Time	Eastern Standard Time
CST	Eastern Time	Pacific Standard Time
EET	Pacific Time	Western European Time
EST	**12** Atlantic Time	Western Standard Time
GMT	Mountain Time	**20** Atlantic Standard Time
HST	**13** Greenwich Time	Mountain Standard Time
MST	**17** British Summer Time	**26** Hawaii-Aleutian Standard
PST	Greenwich Mean Time	Time
WET		

Times and periods of time include:

02 am	morn	decade	winter
pm	noon	midday	**07** bedtime
03 age	week	minute	century
day	year	moment	chiliad
eon	**05** epoch	morrow	daytime
era	month	period	evening
04 dawn	night	season	instant
dusk	sun-up	second	midweek
fall	today	spring	morning
hour	**06** autumn	summer	quarter
		sunset	sunrise

teatime
tonight
weekday
weekend
08 eternity
high noon
lifetime

tomorrow
twilight
09 afternoon
decennium
fortnight
light-year
midsummer

nightfall
night-time
10 generation
millennium
nanosecond
yesteryear
11 long weekend

microsecond
millisecond
12 quinquennium
13 the early hours
wee small hours

Terms to do with time include:

02 AD
BC
03 ago
ere
ETA
fix
now
old
TAI
UTC
yet
04 date
late
past
term
then
05 about
after
again
alarm
clock
count
dated
early
flash
jiffy
meter
metre
never
often
spell
still
tardy
tempo
watch
while
06 always
before
behind

for now
future
heyday
in time
o'clock
old hat
on time
pre-war
rhythm
07 airtime
current
delayed
diurnal
forever
history
measure
overdue
present
session
stretch
08 duration
in a flash
in a jiffy
instance
interval
juncture
mean time
on and off
on the dot
promptly
schedule
temporal
09 aforehand
aftertime
diuturnal
extra time
nocturnal
out of date
prime time

programme
sometimes
timetable
10 afterwards
beforehand
behind time
common time
frequently
in good time
injury time
now and then
on occasion
previously
punctually
repeatedly
simple time
11 at the moment
closing time
now and again
recurrently
12 apparent time
borrowed time
compound time
every so often
for the moment
occasionally
once in a while
periodically
time and again
13 again and again
for the present
in the meantime
mean solar time
14 drinking-up time
from time to time
intermittently
15 ahead of schedule
every now and then
with time to spare

See also **calendar**; **day**; **geology**; **hour**; **month**; **year**

title

Titles include:

01	M		Miss		Signor
	U		Prof		Sister
02	Dr		sama		Tuanku
	Mr		Sant		07 Bahadur
	Ms		Shri		Brother
03	bey		tuan		Captain
	Dan	05	baboo		Colonel
	Dom		begum		effendi
	Don		ghazi		esquire
	Mrs		hodja		Majesty
	Pir		khoja		Signior
	Rav		Madam		Signora
	Reb		Mirza		Signore
	Rev		molla		08 Alderman
	Rex		padre		Fräulein
	san		pasha		Highness
	Sir		Rebbe		memsahib
	Sri		Señor		Mistress
	Ven		Swami		Monsieur
04	amir		Uncle		Reverend
	Aunt	06	Doctor		Señorita
	babu		Father		Viscount
	bhai		khodja		09 Monsignor
	Capt		kumari		Professor
	Dame		Madame		Signorina
	Devi		Master		Signorino
	Doña		Milord		Your Grace
	emir		Mister		10 burra sahib
	Frau		mollah		11 Monseigneur
	Herr		moolah		Your Majesty
	Imam		Mother		Your Worship
	Lady		mullah		12 Mademoiselle
	Lord		Regina		15 Right Honourable
	Ma'am		Señora		

See also **nobility**

toadstool *see* **mushroom**

tobacco

Tobacco and tobacco preparations include:

04	capa		snout	07	caporal		short-cut
	chaw		snuff		chewing		Virginia
	chew		snush		Latakia		
	plug		twist		nail-rod	09	broad-leaf
	quid	06	burley		perique		cavendish
	shag		dottle		pigtail		flue-cured
	weed		rappee		sheesha		mundungus
05	bacco		return	08	bird's-eye		strip-leaf
	baccy		shisha		canaster		
	régie		sneesh		honeydew		

Tobacco pipes include:

03 cob	water	dudheen	**09** chibouque
04 bong	**06** dudeen	nargile	narghilly
clay	hookah	nargily	**10** meerschaum
05 briar	kalian	**08** calabash	**12** churchwarden
brier	**07** calumet	narghile	hubble-bubble
cutty	chibouk	narghily	**13** woodcock's-head
hooka	chillum	nargileh	
peace	corncob	nargilly	

Cigarettes and cigars include:

03 cig	segar	low-tar	**08** king-size
fag	smoke	manila	long-nine
tab	snout	reefer	perfecto
04 bidi	stogy	roll-up	**09** cigarillo
burn	whiff	spliff	filter tip
05 beedi	**06** beedie	stogey	panatella
blunt	biftah	stogie	**10** coffin nail
ciggy	bifter	**07** cheroot	tailor-made
claro	bomber	high-tar	**11** cancer stick
joint	ciggie	manilla	corona lucis
paper	concha	menthol	roll-your-own
roach	gasper	regalia	
	Havana		

Tolkien, J R R (1892–1973)

Significant works include:

09 *The Hobbit* (1937)
12 *Silmarillion* (1977)
The Two Towers (1954)
17 *The Lord of the Rings* (1954–55)

18 *The Return of the King* (1955)
22 *The Fellowship of the Ring* (1954)
26 *The Adventures of Tom Bombadil* (1962)

Significant characters include:

04 Took (Peregrin 'Pippin')
05 Balin
Gimli
Smaug
06 Elrond
Gamgee (Samwise 'Sam')
Gollum
Sauron
Shelob
07 Aragorn

Baggins (Bilbo)
Baggins (Frodo)
Boromir
Gandalf
Legolas
Saruman
Sméagol
Strider
08 Bombadil (Tom)
Evenstar (Lady Arwen)

09 Galadriel
Treebeard
10 Brandybuck (Meriadoc 'Merry')
11 Black Riders
Oakenshield (Thorin)
Ringwraiths (the)
14 Gandalf the Grey
15 Gandalf the White

Tolstoy, Count Leo (1828–1910)

Significant works include:

05 *Youth* (1855–57)
07 *Boyhood* (1854)
The Raid (1852)
09 *Childhood* (1852)
10 *Confession* (1879)

Hadji Murat (1911)
Sebastopol (1854–55)
11 *The Cossacks* (1861)
War and Peace (1863–69)
12 *Anna Karenina* (1874–76)

Master and Man (1894)
Resurrection (1899)
15 *Family Happiness* (1859)

17 *The Kreutzer Sonata* (1889)
21 *The Death of Ivan Ilyitch* (1886)

Significant characters include:

04 Lvov (Prince 'Arseny')
05 Levin (Konstantin Dmitrich 'Kostya')
Levin (Nicholas)
Lvova (Princess Natalie Alexandrovna)
06 Levina (Catherine Alexandrovna 'Kitty')
Rostov (Count Ilya Andreyevich)
07 Gerasim
Ilyitch (Ivan)
Ivanich (Valadimir)
Karenin (Alexey Alexandrovich)
Karenin (Sergey Alexeyich 'Seriozha')
Kuragin (Prince Anatol)
Kuragin (Prince Ippolit)
Kuragin (Prince Vasily Sergeyevich)
Rostova (Countess Natalya Ilyinichna
'Natasha')
Vronsky (Count Alexey Kirilich)
08 Bezukhov (Pyotor Kirilovich 'Pierre')
Fedorona (Praskovya)

Ivanovna (Countess Lydia)
Karenina (Anna Arkadyevna)
Kuragina (Princess Elena Vasilyevna)
Oblonsky (Prince Stepan Arkadyevich
'Stiva')
09 Bolkonsky (Prince Andrei Nikolayevich)
Bolkonsky (Prince Nikolai Andreyevich
'Nikolushka')
Tverskaya (Princess Elizabeth Fedorovna
'Betsy')
Vronskaya (Countess)
10 Nikolaevna (Mary 'Masha')
Oblonskaya (Princess Darya Alexandrovna
'Dolly')
11 Bolkonskaya (Princess Lisa)
Bolkonskaya (Princess Marya Nikolayevna)
12 Shcherbatsky (Prince Alexander)
14 Shcherbatskaya (Princess)

tool

Tools include:

03 awl	steel	cleaver	**09** box cutter
axe	tongs	crowbar	grass-rake
hod	**06** bodkin	forceps	jack-plane
hoe	chaser	fretsaw	pitchfork
saw	chisel	hacksaw	plumb-line
04 adze	dibber	handsaw	secateurs
file	gimlet	hay fork	set-square
fork	hammer	jointer	**10** jackhammer
jack	jig-saw	mattock	paper-knife
mace	mallet	pick-axe	protractor
pick	mortar	pincers	**11** brace and bit
rake	needle	scalpel	crochet hook
rasp	pestle	scriber	paper-cutter
rule	pliers	stapler	pocket-knife
vice	plough	T-square	screwdriver
05 auger	sander	**08** billhook	spirit level
bevel	scythe	chainsaw	**12** caulking-iron
clamp	shears	dividers	pruning-knife
dolly	shovel	penknife	sledgehammer
drill	sickle	scissors	socket-wrench
level	trowel	spraygun	**13** pinking-shears
plane	wrench	tenon-saw	pruning-shears
punch	**07** bolster	thresher	soldering-iron
snips	bradawl	tommy bar	
spade	chopper	tweezers	

See also **agriculture**; **key**; **machinery**; **saw**

torture

Torture forms and instruments include:

03 saw

04 boot
cage
pear
rack

05 brank
irons
jougs
wheel

06 carcan
harrow
picana
shabeh
spider
stocks
turcas

07 bilboes
boiling
cat's paw
hooding
picquet
pillory
pincers
scourge
stoning

08 bootikin
branding
garrotte
knotting
pendulum
pressing
shin vice

09 bastinado
gauntlets
gridirons
picketing
scarpines
strappado
treadmill

10 brazen bull
cattle prod
impalement
iron collar
iron maiden
Judas scale
pilliwinks
spiked hare
starvation
suspension
treadwheel

11 cave of roses

forcipation
German chair
head crusher
Judas cradle
keelhauling
knee-capping
squassation
thumbscrews
wooden horse

12 ball and chain
ducking-stool
flesh tearers
scold's bridle
shrew's fiddle
skull crusher
Spanish chair
water torture

13 cat-o'-nine-tails
electric shock
heretic's forks
Spanish mantle

14 Austrian ladder
devil-on-the-neck
disembowelment
drunkard's cloak

15 confession chair

tower

Tower types include:

04 bell
fort
gate
keep
peel

05 block
minar
spire
watch
water

06 belfry
castle
church
column
donjon
pagoda
turret

07 bastion
citadel
lookout

minaret
mirador
steeple

08 barbican
bastille
fortress
high-rise
hill-fort
martello
scaffold

09 belvedere
campanile
smock mill
tower mill

10 skyscraper
stronghold

11 demi-bastion

13 fortification

Towers include:

02 CN (Canada)

03 AMP (Australia)
Sky (New Zealand)

04 Pisa (Italy)

05 Babel (Bible)
Clock (England)
Macau (China)
Sears (USA)
Seoul (South Korea)

Tokyo (Japan)

06 Big Ben (England)
Dragon (China)
Eiffel (France)
Kiev TV (Ukraine)
Riga TV (Latvia)
Tahoto (Japan)

07 Alma-Ata (Kazakhstan)
Leaning (Italy)

Olympic (Canada)
Praha TV (Czech Republic)
Yueyang (China)

08 Tashkent (Uzbekistan)
Tengwang (China)

09 Blackpool (England)
Donauturm (Austria)
Ostankino (Russia)
Tallinn TV (Estonia)
Tianjin TV (China)

10 Collserola (Spain)
Liberation (Kuwait)

11 Fernsehturm (Germany)
Space Needle (USA)
The Euromast (The Netherlands)
Yellow Crane (China)

12 Stratosphere (USA)

13 Oriental Pearl (China)
Petronas Twins (Malaysia)

town

County towns and administrative headquarters include:

03 Ayr (Ayrshire/South Ayrshire)

04 Mold (Clwyd/Flintshire)
Wick (Caithness)
York (North Yorkshire/Yorkshire)

05 Banff (Banffshire)
Cupar (Fife)
Derby (Derbyshire)
Derry (County Londonderry)
Elgin (Elginshire/Moray)
Lewes (East Sussex)
Nairn (Nairnshire)
Omagh (Tyrone)
Perth (Perthshire/Perth and Kinross)
Truro (Cornwall)

06 Armagh (County Armagh)
Brecon (Brecknockshire)
Durham (County Durham)
Exeter (Devon)
Forfar (Angus/Forfarshire)
Kendal (Westmorland)
Lanark (Lanarkshire)
London (Greater London/Middlesex)
Oakham (Rutland)
Oxford (Oxfordshire)

07 Bedford (Bedfordshire)
Belfast (County Antrim)
Bristol (Avon)
Cardiff (Glamorgan)
Chester (Cheshire)
Denbigh (Denbighshire)
Dornoch (Sutherland)
Glasgow (Lanark/Strathclyde)
Ipswich (Suffolk)
Kinross (Ross-shire)
Lerwick (Shetland/Zetland)
Lincoln (Lincolnshire)
Matlock (Derbyshire)
Morpeth (Northumberland)
Newport (Isle of Wight)
Norwich (Norfolk)
Peebles (Peeblesshire)
Preston (Lancashire)

Reading (Berkshire)
Renfrew (Renfrewshire)
Selkirk (Selkirkshire)
Swansea (West Glamorgan)
Taunton (Somerset)
Warwick (Warwickshire)
Wigtown (Wigtownshire)

08 Aberdeen (Grampian/Aberdeenshire)
Barnsley (South Yorkshire)
Beverley (Humberside/East Riding of
Yorkshire)
Cardigan (Cardiganshire)
Carlisle (Cumberland/Cumbria)
Cromarty (Cromartyshire)
Dingwall (Ross-shire)
Dumfries (Dumfriesshire/Dumfries and
Galloway)
Greenlaw (Berwickshire)
Hereford (Herefordshire)
Hertford (Hertfordshire)
Jedburgh (Roxburghshire)
Kirkwall (Orkney)
Monmouth (Monmouthshire)
Pembroke (Pembrokeshire)
Rothesay (Buteshire)
Stafford (Staffordshire)
Stirling (Stirlingshire/Stirling)

09 Aylesbury (Buckinghamshire)
Beaumaris (Anglesey)
Cambridge (Cambridgeshire)
Dolgellau (Merioneth)
Dumbarton (Dunbartonshire/
Dumbartonshire/West Dunbartonshire)
Edinburgh (Edinburghshire/Midlothian/
Lothian)
Inveraray (Argyllshire)
Inverness (Inverness-shire/Highland)
Lancaster (Lancashire)
Leicester (Leicestershire)
Liverpool (Merseyside)
Maidstone (Kent)
Newcastle (Tyne & Wear/Northumberland)

Wakefield (West Yorkshire/West Riding of
Yorkshire)
Worcester (Hereford and Worcester/
Worcestershire)

10 Birmingham (West Midlands)
Caernarfon (Caernarfonshire/Gwynedd)
Carmarthen (Dyfed/Carmarthenshire)
Chelmsford (Essex)
Chichester (Sussex/West Sussex)
Dorchester (Dorset)
Gloucester (Gloucestershire)
Haddington (East Lothian/Haddingtonshire)
Huntingdon (Huntingdonshire)
Linlithgow (West Lothian/Linlithgowshire)
Manchester (Greater Manchester)

Montgomery (Montgomeryshire)
Nottingham (Nottinghamshire)
Presteigne (Radnorshire)
Shrewsbury (Shropshire)
Stonehaven (Kincardineshire)
Trowbridge (Wiltshire)
Winchester (Hampshire)

11 Clackmannan (Clackmannanshire)
Downpatrick (County Down)
Enniskillen (County Fermanagh)
Northampton (Northamptonshire)

12 Kircudbright (Kircudbrightshire)

13 Middlesbrough (Cleveland)
Northallerton (North Yorkshire/North Riding
of Yorkshire)

English towns include:

03 Ely

04 Bath
Bury
Hove
Hull
York

05 Ascot
Corby
Cowes
Crewe
Derby
Dover
Epsom
Ewell
Hythe
Leeds
Lewes
Luton
Otley
Poole
Ripon
Rugby
Truro
Wells
Wigan

06 Bexley
Bodmin
Bolton
Bootle
Boston
Buxton
Darwen
Dudley
Durham
Exeter
Harlow
Harrow
Ilkley

Jarrow
Kendal
London
Ludlow
Oakham
Oldham
Oundle
Oxford
Ramsey
Slough
St Ives
Stroud
Torbay
Warley
Whitby
Widnes
Woking
Yeovil

07 Andover
Arundel
Ashford
Bedford
Berwick
Bristol
Brixham
Burnley
Chatham
Cheddar
Chester
Crawley
Croydon
Dorking
Evesham
Exmouth
Gosport
Grimsby
Halifax
Harwich
Haworth

Helston
Horsham
Ipswich
Keswick
Lincoln
Malvern
Margate
Matlock
Morpeth
Newport
Norwich
Padstow
Preston
Reading
Redruth
Reigate
Runcorn
Salford
Stilton
Sudbury
Swindon
Taunton
Telford
Tilbury
Torquay
Walsall
Wantage
Warwick
Watford
Windsor

08 Abingdon
Barnsley
Basildon
Beverley
Bradford
Brighton
Carlisle
Coventry
Dartford

Falmouth
Grantham
Hastings
Hatfield
Hereford
Hertford
Kingston
Knowsley
Minehead
Nantwich
Newhaven
Nuneaton
Penzance
Plymouth
Ramsgate
Redditch
Richmond
Rochdale
Sandwell
Solihull
Spalding
Stafford
St Albans
Stamford
St Helens
Thetford
Westbury
Weymouth
Worthing

09 Aldeburgh
Aldershot
Ambleside
Ashbourne
Axminster
Aylesbury
Blackburn
Blackpool
Bletchley
Bracknell
Cambridge
Dartmouth
Doncaster
Gateshead
Gravesend
Greenwich
Guildford
Harrogate
King's Lynn
Lancaster
Leicester
Lichfield
Liverpool

Lowestoft
Lyme Regis
Maidstone
Morecambe
Newcastle
Newmarket
Rochester
Rotherham
Salisbury
Sheerness
Sheffield
Sherborne
Southport
St Austell
Stevenage
Stockport
Stratford
Wakefield
Worcester

10 Birkenhead
Birmingham
Bridgwater
Bromsgrove
Buckingham
Canterbury
Chelmsford
Cheltenham
Chichester
Colchester
Darlington
Dorchester
Eastbourne
Felixstowe
Folkestone
Gillingham
Gloucester
Hartlepool
Huntingdon
Kenilworth
Kensington
Launceston
Letchworth
Maidenhead
Manchester
Nottingham
Pontefract
Portsmouth
Scunthorpe
Shrewsbury
Sunderland
Tewkesbury
Warrington

Washington
Whitehaven
Winchester

11 Bognor Regis
Bournemouth
Cirencester
Cleethorpes
Farnborough
Glastonbury
High Wycombe
Northampton
Scarborough
Shaftesbury
Southampton

12 Chesterfield
Clacton-on-Sea
Great Malvern
Huddersfield
Loughborough
Macclesfield
Milton Keynes
North Shields
Peterborough
South Shields
Stoke-on-Trent
West Bromwich

13 Bury St Edmunds
Ellesmere Port
Great Yarmouth
Kidderminster
Leamington Spa
Littlehampton
Lytham St Anne's
Middlesbrough
Saffron Walden
Southend-on-Sea
West Bridgford
Wolverhampton

14 Ashby-de-la-Zouch
Bishop Auckland
Chipping Norton
Hemel Hempstead
Henley-on-Thames
Stockton-on-Tees
Tunbridge Wells

15 Ashton-under-Lyne
Barrow-in-Furness
Burton upon Trent
Sutton Coldfield
Weston-super-Mare

Northern Irish towns include:

05 Derry
Larne
Newry

Omagh
06 Antrim
Armagh

Bangor
Lurgan
07 Belfast

Lifford
Lisburn
08 Limavady

Portrush	Cookstown	**11** Downpatrick	Portstewart
Strabane	Dungannon	Enniskillen	**13** Carrickfergus
09 Ballymena	Portadown	Londonderry	
Banbridge	**10** Ballyclare	Magherafelt	
Coleraine	Ballymoney	Newtownards	

Scottish towns include:

03 Ayr	Mallaig	St Andrews
04 Oban	Paisley	Stornoway
Tain	Peebles	Stranraer
Wick	Portree	**10** Coatbridge
05 Alloa	Selkirk	Dalbeattie
Banff	**08** Aberdeen	Galashiels
Elgin	Arbroath	Glenrothes
Keith	Banchory	Kilmarnock
Kelso	Dalkeith	Kincardine
Nairn	Dingwall	Linlithgow
Perth	Dumfries	Livingston
Scone	Dunblane	Motherwell
Troon	Fortrose	Newtonmore
06 Alness	Giffnock	Stonehaven
Dunbar	Greenock	**11** Blairgowrie
Dundee	Hamilton	Campbeltown
Dunoon	Jedburgh	Cowdenbeath
Forfar	Kirkwall	Crianlarich
Girvan	Montrose	Cumbernauld
Glamis	Stirling	Dunfermline
Hawick	Ullapool	Fort William
Huntly	**09** Ardrossan	Fraserburgh
Irvine	Callander	Grangemouth
Lanark	Clydebank	Gretna Green
Thurso	Dumbarton	Invergordon
07 Airdrie	Edinburgh	John o'Groats
Alloway	Inverness	Port Glasgow
Braemar	Inverurie	**12** Auchterarder
Dornoch	Kingussie	East Kilbride
Falkirk	Kirkcaldy	Lochgilphead
Glasgow	Lockerbie	**13** Castle Douglas
Golspie	Peterhead	Kirkcudbright
Gourock	Pitlochry	Kirkintilloch
Lerwick	Prestwick	**14** Grantown-on-Spey

Welsh towns include:

04 Bala	Cwmbrân	Chepstow
Mold	Denbigh	Ebbw Vale
Rhyl	Harlech	Hay-on-Wye
05 Barry	Newport	Holyhead
Conwy	Newtown	Lampeter
Tenby	Swansea	Llanelli
Tywyn	Wrexham	Monmouth
06 Bangor	**08** Aberdare	Pembroke
Brecon	Barmouth	Pwllheli
Ruthin	Bridgend	Rhayader
07 Cardiff	Cardigan	St David's
		Treorchy

09 Aberaeron
Carnarvon
Colwyn Bay
Dolgellau
Fishguard
Llandudno
Llangefni
Pontypool
Prestatyn

Welshpool
10 Caernarfon
Caerphilly
Carmarthen
Llandovery
Llangollen
Pontypridd
Porthmadog
Port Talbot

11 Abergavenny
Abertillery
Aberystwyth
Builth Wells
Machynlleth
12 Milford Haven
13 Haverfordwest
Merthyr Tydfil

See also **Australia; Austria; Belgium; Canada; China; city; Czech Republic; Denmark; Finland; France; Germany; Greece; India; Ireland; Italy; Japan; Mexico; The Netherlands; New Zealand; Norway; Portugal; resort; Russia; Spain; Sweden; Switzerland**

toxin *see* **poison**

toy

Toys include:

03 gun
04 ball
bike
doll
farm
fort
game
kite
Lego®
Sega®
XBox®
yo-yo
05 slide
swing
trike
06 cap-gun
garage
go-kart
guitar
paints
pop-gun
puzzle
rattle
rocker
seesaw
tea set
07 balloon
bicycle
box-kite
crayons
Digimon®
dreidel
drum set
Frisbee®
Game Boy®
marbles
Meccano®

ocarina
Play-Doh®
Pokémon®
rag doll
sandpit
scooter
soft-toy
Turtles®
08 catapult
doll's cot
football
GameCube®
golliwog
hula-hoop
Matchbox®
model car
model kit
Nintendo®
pedal-car
Subbuteo®
train set
tricycle
09 Action Man®
aeroplane
Care Bears
doll's pram
gyroscope
playhouse
pogo stick
Sindy doll®
swingball
teddy bear
video game
10 baby-walker
Barbie doll®
doll's buggy
doll's house

fivestones
hobby-horse
kewpie doll
musical box
pantograph
peashooter
Plasticene®
Rubik's Cube®
Scalextric®
skateboard
Steiff bear
Super Mario®
toy soldier
trampoline
typewriter
Wendy house
11 baby-bouncer
glove puppet
PlayStation®
shape-sorter
silly string
spacehopper
spinning top
tiddly winks
water pistol
12 action figure
boxing-gloves
computer game
executive toy
jack-in-the-box
jigsaw puzzle
kaleidoscope
model railway
mountain bike
My Little Pony
paddling-pool
Power Rangers®
rocking-horse

skipping-rope
walkie-talkie
13 Bob the Builder®
climbing-frame
modelling clay

See also **doll**

sewing machine
Space Invaders®
Tiny-Tears doll®
14 activity centre
building-blocks

building-bricks
electronic game
Paddington Bear
Powerpuff Girls®

trace mineral *see* **mineral**

train *see* **railway**

tranquillizer *see* **sedative**

travel

Travel methods and forms include:

03	bus		trip	06	aviate		mission
	fly		walk		cruise		shuttle
	row	05	cycle		flight	09	excursion
	ski		drive		outing		freewheel
04	bike		jaunt		paddle		hitch-hike
	hike		march		ramble		migration
	punt		motor		safari		orienteer
	ride		pilot		voyage	10	expedition
	sail		skate	07	commute		pilgrimage
	tour		steam		holiday	11	exploration
	trek		visit		journey		

See also **air travel**; **aircraft**; **aviation**; **bicycle**; **carriage**; **London**; **motoring**; **public transport**; **railway**; **road**; **sailing**; **underground**; **vehicle**

treaty

Treaties and agreements include:

03	Edo	06	Amiens		Rapallo
	INF		Berlin		Rastatt
	NPT		Bruges		Tianjin
04	GATT		Harris		Trianon
	Iasi		London		Wichale
	Jay's		Madrid	08	Alinagar
	NATO		Passau		Brussels
	Rome		Tilsit		Gulistan
05	Baden		Vienna		Kanagawa
	Basic	07	Barrier		Lausanne
	Basle		Beijing		Nijmegen
	CENTO		Cambrai		Rijswijk
	Dover		Dresden		Tientsin
	Ghent		Erzerum		Waitangi
	Jassy		Kanghwa	09	Andrusovo
	Lyons		Kiakhta		Bucharest
	Paris		Münster		Hay-Herrán
	SEATO		Nanjing		Karlowitz
	START		Neuilly		Nerchinsk
	Union		Nystadt		Pressburg

St Germain
10 Adrianople
Anglo-Iraqi
Greenville
Maastricht
Magna Carta
Paris Pacts
Portsmouth
San Stefano
Tlatelolco
Versailles
Warsaw Pact
Washington
11 Campo Formio
Finkenstein
Fort Stanwix

Locarno Pact
Passarowitz
Shimonoseki
The Pyrenees
Turkmanchai
Westminster
12 Brest-Litovsk
British-Iraqi
Campoformido
Grundvertrag
Lateran Pacts
Rio de Janeiro
San Francisco
13 Anglo-Egyptian
Austrian State
Clayton-Bulwer

Hay-Pauncefote
Social Chapter
Triple Entente
14 Constantinople
Hague Agreement
Hoare-Laval Pact
Kuchuk Kainarji
Nuclear Test-Ban
Peace of Utrecht
Unkiar-Skelessi
15 Cateau-Cambrésis
Entente Cordiale
Hay-Bunau-Varilla
Munich Agreement
US-Japan Security

tree

Tree types include:

03 nut	citron	**08** hardwood	**10** ornamental
04 palm	citrus	softwood	
05 covin	forest	**09** broad-leaf	
fruit	timber	Christmas	
06 bonsai	**07** conifer	deciduous	
	dwarfed	evergreen	

Trees include:

02 bo	cola	upas	
ti	dali	**05** abele	
03 ash	dhak	abies	
bay	dika	ackee	
bel	dita	afara	
ben	holm	alder	
box	hule	apple	
elm	ilex	areca	
fig	jack	argan	
fir	kina	aspen	
gum	kola	balsa	
jak	lime	bania	
koa	mako	beech	
may	neem	belah	
nim	nimb	birch	
oak	ombu	bodhi	
sal	palm	bunya	
tea	pear	cacao	
ule	pine	carap	
yew	plum	carob	
04 acer	poon	cedar	
akee	rata	ceiba	
amla	rimu	china	
arar	shea	ebony	
bael	sorb	elder	
bhel	tawa	ficus	
bito	teak	genip	
coco	titi	guava	
	toon		

hazel
hevea
holly
iroko
jambu
jarul
karri
kauri
khaya
kiaat
kokum
larch
lemon
lichi
lilac
lotus
mahoe
mahua
mahwa
mamee
mamey
mango
maple
marri
matai
mvule
neemb
ngaio
nikau
nyssa
olive
opepe
osier
palas
palay
panax
papaw
peach
pecan
piñon
pipal
pipul
plane
quina
ramin
raoul
roble
rowan
salix
saman
thuja
thuya
toyon
wahoo
wicky
wilga
zaman

06 acacia

acajou
almond
angico
antiar
arolla
balata
bamboo
banana
banian
banyan
baobab
bilian
bombax
bo tree
cashew
cassia
cembra
cerris
chenar
cherry
chicha
cornel
damson
deodar
durian
durion
emblic
feijoa
gingko
ginkgo
guango
gurjun
illipe
illupi
jambul
jarool
jarrah
jujube
kamala
kamela
kamila
karaka
karite
kermes
kowhai
laurel
lebbek
lichee
linden
litchi
locust
longan
loquat
lucuma
lychee
mallee
mammee
manuka

mastic
medlar
mimosa
mopane
mopani
myrtle
nutmeg
obeche
padauk
padouk
papaya
pawpaw
peepul
platan
pomelo
poplar
prunus
quince
redbud
red fir
red gum
red oak
sallow
samaan
sandal
sapele
sapota
saxaul
she-oak
sissoo
souari
spruce
tamanu
titoki
ti tree
totara
tupelo
waboom
walnut
wicken
willow
witgat
zamang

07 ailanto
apricot
avocado
Banksia
bebeeru
big tree
bilimbi
blue gum
brownea
bubinga
buckeye
bullace
canella
catalpa
champac

champak
cork oak
corylus
cowtree
cumquat
cypress
davidia
dogwood
durmast
fig tree
fir tree
geebung
genipap
gum tree
hemlock
hickory
hog-plum
holm-oak
hoop-ash
jambool
jipyapa
kumquat
leechee
lentisc
lentisk
live oak
logwood
lumbang
madrona
madrone
madrono
manjack
margosa
mastich
may tree
mesquit
nut pine
oil-tree
pereira
pimento
platane
quassia
quicken
quillai
radiata
red pine
redwood
rock elm
saksaul
saouari
satsuma
sequoia
seringa
service
shittah
snow gum
soursop
sundari

talipat
talipot
tanghin
tea tree
wallaba
wax tree
wych elm
yew tree

08 basswood
bauhinia
bead tree
bean tree
bergamot
boortree
bourtree
buddleia
calabash
cecropia
chestnut
cider gum
cinchona
cinnamon
coco-palm
cocoplum
coco-tree
Cook pine
coolabah
coolibah
coolibar
coprosma
crab tree
date palm
dhak tree
dividivi
Dutch elm
euonymus
garcinia
gardenia
ghost gum
gold tree
guaiacum
hawthorn
Hibiscus
holly-oak
hornbeam
Huon pine
ironbark
ironwood
jack pine
jambolan
jelutong
kalumpit
kinakina
kingwood
lacebark
loblolly
magnolia
mahogany

mako-mako
mandarin
mangrove
manna-ash
meal-tree
mesquite
milk-tree
mulberry
neem tree
oiticica
oleaster
palm tree
pandanus
pear-tree
piassaba
piassava
pichurim
pinaster
pine tree
plantain
podocarp
pyinkado
quandang
quandong
quantong
rain tree
rambutan
rewarewa
sack tree
sapucaia
Scots fir
sebesten
shaddock
shagbark
shea tree
silky oak
simaruba
soapbark
soap tree
sourwood
swamp oak
sycamine
sycamore
sycomore
tamarack
tamarind
teak tree
tung tree
upas-tree
zizyphus

09 ailanthus
angophora
araucaria
arrowwood
Asian pear
balsam fir
berg-cedar
black bean

black butt
blackwood
bloodwood
bodhi tree
bolletrie
Brazil nut
bread tree
bulletrie
bully-tree
butternut
candlenut
carambola
casuarina
Chile pine
chincapin
chinkapin
cigar tree
clove-tree
coachwood
combretum
common ash
common oak
common yew
coral tree
cordyline
courbaril
cowdie-gum
crab apple
currajong
curry-leaf
doornboom
eaglewood
eucryphia
fever tree
flame tree
forest-oak
grapetree
greengage
hackberry
Indian fig
ivory-tree
jacaranda
jackfruit
jambolana
Judas tree
kahikatea
kapok tree
kauri-pine
kermes oak
kurrajong
lancewood
leylandii
macadamia
mahwa tree
melaleuca
mirabelle
mockernut
monkey pod

naseberry
nectarine
nikau palm
nux vomica
ohi' a lehua
paloverde
paperbark
paulownia
peach-tree
pecan tree
persimmon
pitch-tree
poinciana
prickwood
quebracho
quickbeam
quinquina
rose apple
rowan tree
royal palm
sapodilla
saskatoon
sassafras
satinwood
Scotch elm
Scotch fir
Scots pine
screw pine
silver fir
simarouba
sour-gourd
spruce fir
star anise
sterculia
stone pine
sugar pine
sweetwood
tangerine
terebinth
thorntree
tonga-bean
tonka-bean
torchwood
tulip tree
turkey oak
wagenboom
wax myrtle
whitebeam
white pine
white teak
whitewood
wild mango
winged elm
wych-hazel
zebrawood
10 afrormosia
balata tree
bitterwood

blackthorn
bottle tree
breadfruit
bullet-tree
bunya-bunya
butter-tree
buttonball
buttonwood
calamondin
candle-tree
cannonball
celery pine
cembra pine
chaste tree
chaulmugra
cheesewood
chinaberry
chinachina
chinquapin
coffee tree
corylopsis
cotton tree
cottonwood
cowdie-pine
cowrie-pine
Douglas fir
dragon tree
durmast oak
English elm
English oak
eucalyptus
fiddlewood
field maple
flindersia
gean cherry
goat willow
golden rain
grapefruit
greenheart
jippi-jappa
Joshua-tree
kaffirboom
letter-wood
lilly-pilly
locust tree
macrocarpa
manchineel
mangabeira
mangosteen
manna-larch
missel-tree
nettle-tree
noble beech
Norway pine
orange tree
pagoda-tree
paper-birch
Parana pine

pepper tree
pohutukawa
powderpuff
prickly ash
quercitron
quinaquina
red sanders
rubber tree
sandalwood
sessile oak
shillelagh
silver bell
silver tree
sneezewood
sorrel tree
sour cherry
spiceberry
spruce pine
sugar maple
tallow tree
tiger's claw
valonia oak
violet-wood
weeping elm
white birch
white cedar
wild cherry
wild cotton
witch hazel
witgatboom
wooden pear
woollybutt
ylang-ylang

11 African teak
agnus castus
Amboina pine
bastard teak
black poplar
black walnut
bottle brush
bristlecone
burning bush
chaulmoogra
Chilean pine
cluster pine
coconut palm
common alder
common beech
common hazel
common maple
copper beech
coral shower
cotoneaster
crape myrtle
dawn cypress
dipterocarp
false acacia
golden larch

honey locust
lacquer tree
leatherwood
leopard-wood
London plane
maceranduba
mammoth-tree
metasequoia
monkey bread
mountain ash
mulberry fig
Norway maple
octopus tree
Osage orange
pomegranate
pussy willow
quicken-tree
radiata pine
sandbox tree
sausage tree
saw palmetto
service tree
shittah tree
silver birch
silver maple
sitka spruce
slippery elm
sweet orange
sweet willow
sycomore fig
tonquin-bean
trumpet tree
trumpet wood
umbrella fir
varnish tree
white laurel
white poplar
white willow
wild service

12 Austrian pine
balsam poplar
benjamin-tree
calabash tree
Christ's-thorn
common walnut
Corsican pine
cucumber tree
dead rat's tree
elephant's ear
evergreen oak
golden shower
lipstick tree
liriodendron
loblolly pine
loblolly tree
longleaf pine
macadamia nut
massaranduba

masseranduba
monkey puzzle
Monterey pine
Norway spruce
red quebracho
sallow willow
serviceberry
snowdrop tree
soapbark tree
swamp cypress
tree of heaven
umbrella pine
umbrella tree
weeping birch
Wellingtonia
yellow poplar

13 angel's trumpet
autograph tree
common dogwood
common juniper
cranberry tree
European larch
hemlock spruce
horse chestnut
Japanese cedar
Japanese maple
Lawson cypress
lodgepole pine
marmalade tree
morello cherry
Moreton Bay fig
Oriental plane
paperbark tree
paper mulberry
peacock-flower
rose apple tree
sandarach tree
Siberian cedar
soapberry tree
Surinam cherry
sweet chestnut
toothache tree
weeping willow
white mulberry

14 alligator apple
cannonball-tree
Castanospermum
cedar of Lebanon
Christmas-berry
common laburnum
common mulberry
flamboyant-tree
granadilla tree
Leyland cypress
Lombardy poplar
maidenhair-tree
strawberry tree

Swiss stonepine	yellow oleander	flamboyante-tree
traveller's tree	**15** beach heliotrope	gutta-percha tree
tropical almond	bristlecone pine	horseradish tree
turpentine tree	candelabrum tree	small-leafed lime
western hemlock	common silver fir	Spanish chestnut
white quebracho	emblic myrobalan	true service tree

See also **palm**; **pine**; **rubber**; **shrub**

trench *see* ocean

triangle

Triangles include:

05 right	scalene	congruent	equilateral
07 Bermuda	similar	isosceles	right-angled
eternal	warning	spherical	
Pascal's	**09** cocked hat	**11** acute-angled	**12** obtuse-angled

Trollope, Anthony (1815–82)

Significant works include:

09 *Orley Farm* (1861–62)
The Warden (1855)

11 *Ayala's Angel* (1880–81)
Phineas Finn (1867–68)
The Bertrams (1859)

12 *Doctor Thorne* (1858)
Phineas Redux (1873–74)

13 *The Claverings* (1866–67)

14 *The Three Clerks* (1858)

15 *An Autobiography* (1883)
Dr Wortle's School (1880)
The Belton Estate (1865–66)
The Way We Live Now (1874–75)

16 *Barchester Towers* (1857)

Can You Forgive Her? (1864–65)
Framley Parsonage (1860–61)
He Knew He Was Right (1868–69)
The Duke's Children (1879–80)
The Prime Minister (1875–76)

17 *The Palliser Novels* (1864–80)

18 *The American Senator* (1876–77)
The Eustace Diamonds (1871–73)

20 *Mr Scarborough's Family* (1882–83)

21 *The Vicar of Bullhampton* (1869–70)

24 *The Last Chronicle of Barset* (1866–67)
The Small House at Allington (1862–64)

26 *The MacDermots of Ballycloran* (1847)

Significant characters include:

04 Bold (John)
Dale (Isabella 'Bella')
Dale (Lilian 'Lily')
Fawn (Viscount Frederick)
Finn (Phineas)
Grex (Lady Mabel)
Grey (John)
Monk (Lady)

05 Eames (John)
Guest (Lady Julia de)
Guest (Lord de)
Lopez (Ferdinand)
Maule (Gerard)
Slope (Reverend Obadiah)
Tifto (Major)

Tulla (Earl of)

06 Arabin (Reverend Francis)
Bozzle (Samuel)
Burton (Florence)
Courcy (Lady Amelia de)
Crofts (Dr James)
Fisker (Hamilton K)
Lufton (Lady)
Lufton (Lord Ludovic)
Morris (Lucy)
Neroni (Signora Madeline Vesey)
Omnium (Duke of)
Petrie (Miss Wallachia)
Rowley (Emily)
Rowley (Nora)

Thorne (Dr Thomas)
Thorne (Mary)

07 Bonteen (Mr)
Brattle (Carry)
Carbury (Lady Matilda)
Carbury (Roger)
Carbury (Sir Felix)
Crawley (Grace)
Crawley (Mrs)
Crawley (Reverend Josiah)
Crosbie (Adolphus)
Daubeny (Mr)
Emilius (Reverend Joseph)
Eustace (Lady Lizzie)
Eustace (Sir Florian)
Fenwick (Reverend Frank)
Gilmore (Harry)
Goesler (Marie)
Gotobed (Elias)
Grantly (Dr Theophilus)
Grantly (Griselda)
Grantly (Major Henry)
Greenow (Mrs Arabella)
Gresham (Frank Newbold)
Gresham ('Old' Frank Newbold)
Harding (Eleanor)
Harding (Reverend Septimus)
Kennedy (Lady Laura)
Kennedy (Robert)
Lowther (Mary)
Osborne (Colonel Frederic)
Proudie (Dr)
Proudie (Mrs)
Robarts (Lucy)
Robarts (Reverend Mark)
Sowerby (Nathaniel)
Trefoil (Arabella)
Tregear (Francis Oliphant 'Frank')
Vavasor (Alice)

Vavasor (George)
Wharton (Emily)

08 Brabazon (Julia)
Chiltern (Lord Oswald Standish)
Dumbello (Lord)
Glascock (Charles)
Marrable (Captain Walter)
Melmotte (Augustus)
Melmotte (Marie)
Palliser (Adelaide)
Palliser (Lady Glencora)
Palliser (Lady Mary)
Palliser (Lord Gerald)
Palliser (Plantagenet)
Pateroff (Count)
Spalding (Caroline)
Stanbury (Aunt Jemima)
Stanbury (Hugh)
Trumbull (Farmer)

09 Boncassen (Ezekiel)
Boncassen (Isabel)
Clavering (Harry)
Demolines (Madalina)
Dunstable (Miss Martha)
Effingham (Violet)
Gordeloup (Sophie)
Greystock (Frank)
Quiverful (Mr)
Quiverful (Mrs)
Scatcherd (Sir Louis Philippe)
Scatcherd (Sir Roger)
Trevelyan (Louis)

10 Carruthers (Lord George de Bruce)
Fitzgerald (Burgo)
Flood Jones (Mary)
Nidderdale (Lord)
Trowbridge (Marquis of)

12 Chaffanbrass (Mr)
Silverbridge (Lord)

trophy

Trophies include:

05 FA Cup (football)

06 Fed Cup (tennis)

07 Auld Mug (America's Cup/sailing)
Gold Cup (horse racing)
Grey Cup (Canadian football)
Uber Cup (badminton)

08 Davis Cup (tennis)
Ryder Cup (golf)
The Ashes (cricket)
World Cup (various)

09 Aresti Cup (aerobatics)
Curtis Cup (golf)

Thomas Cup (badminton)
Walker Cup (golf)

10 Masters Cup (tennis)
Solheim Cup (golf)
Stanley Cup (ice hockey)
Winston Cup (motor racing)

11 Admiral's Cup (sailing)
America's Cup (sailing)
Eschborn Cup (race walking)
Kinnaird Cup (Eton fives)
McCarthy Cup (hurling)

12 Camanachd Cup (shinty)
Lugano Trophy (race walking)

13 Heisman trophy (American football)
Leonard Trophy (bowls)
Sam Maguire Cup (Gaelic football)
14 Continental Cup (ice hockey)
Jesters' Club Cup (Rugby fives)
See also **award**

15 Champions Trophy (hockey)
Lilienthal Medal (gliding)
Louis Vuitton Cup (sailing)
Nascar Nextel Cup (motor racing)
Scotch Whisky Cup (curling)

tuber *see* **bulb**

tumour

Tumours include:

05 gumma	**07** adenoma	teratoma	rodent ulcer
myoma	angioma	xanthoma	**12** glioblastoma
Wilm's	fibroma	**09** carcinoma	mesothelioma
06 epulis	myeloma	papilloma	osteosarcoma
glioma	sarcoma	syphiloma	
lipoma	**08** lymphoma	**10** meningioma	**13** neuroblastoma
myxoma	melanoma	**11** astrocytoma	**14** retinoblastoma

See also **disease**

tunnel

Tunnels include:

03 Aki (Japan; rail)
Box (England; rail)
05 Keijo (Japan; rail)
Rokko (Japan; rail)
06 FATIMA (Norway; road)
Fréjus (France/Italy; rail)
Fucino (Italy; drainage)
Haruna (Japan; rail)
Hoosac (USA; rail)
Kanmon (Japan; rail)
Mersey (England; road)
Moffat (USA; rail)
Seikan (Japan; rail)
Thames (England; pedestrian and rail)
07 Arlberg (Austria; rail)
Cascade (USA; rail)
Channel (England/France; rail)
Holland (USA; road)
Laerdal (Norway; road)
Øresund (Denmark/Sweden; road-rail)
Simplon (Switzerland/Italy; rail)
Vereina (Switzerland; rail)
08 Apennine (Italy; rail)
Flathead (USA; rail)
Hokuriku (Japan; rail)
Hyperion (USA; sewer)
Lierasen (Norway; rail)
Nakayama (Japan; rail)
Posilipo (Italy; road)

Tronquoy (France; canal)
09 Blackwall (England; road)
Dayaoshan (China; rail)
Eupalinus (Greece; water supply)
Furka Base (Switzerland; rail)
Mont Blanc (France/Italy; road)
Standedge (England; canal)
10 Chesbrough (USA; water supply)
Dai-shimizu (Japan; rail)
Gorigamine (Japan; rail)
Lotschberg (Switzerland; rail)
Qinling I-II (China; rail)
Rogers Pass (Canada; rail)
St Gotthard (Switzerland/Italy; road and rail)
11 Kilsby Ridge (England; rail)
Mt MacDonald (Canada; rail)
Shin-shimizu (Japan; rail)
Tower Subway (England; rail)
12 Detroit River (USA/Canada; rail)
Moscow subway (Russia; rail)
13 Great Apennine (Italy; rail)
Iwate Ichinohe (Japan; rail)
Severomuyskiy (Russia; rail)
14 NEAT St Gotthard (Switzerland; rail)
Romeriksporten (Norway; rail)
15 Monte Santomarco (Italy; rail)
Orange-Fish River (South Africa; irrigation)

turncoat *see* **spy**

Twain, Mark (1835–1910)

Significant works include:

10 *Roughing It* (1872)
18 *The Innocents Abroad* (1869)
20 *Life on the Mississippi* (1883)
21 *The Mysterious Stranger* (1916)

The Prince and the Pauper (1882)
24 *The Adventures of Tom Sawyer* (1876)
27 *Adventures of Huckleberry Finn* (1885)
29 *The Man That Corrupted Hadleyburg* (1900)

Significant characters include:

03 Jim
04 Finn (Huckleberry 'Huck')
Roxy (Roxana)
05 Canty (Tom)
Polly (Aunt)
Selby (Colonel George)
Smith (Hank)
06 Edward (Prince)
Hendon (Miles)
Sawyer (Tom)
Smiley (Jim)

Wilson (David
  'Pudd'nhead')
07 Brierly (Henry 'Harry')
Goodson (Barclay)
Hawkins (Clay)
Hawkins (Laura)
Hawkins (Si 'Squire')
Sellers (Colonel Beriah)
Webster (Dan'l)
08 Chambers
Driscoll (Judge York

Leicester)
Driscoll (Percy
  Northumberland)
Driscoll (Tom)
Halliday (Jack)
Injun Joe
Richards (Edward)
Richards (Mary)
Thatcher (Becky)
09 Dilworthy (Senator Abner)
10 Stephenson (Howard L)

Twelve Days of Christmas *see* Christmas

twin

Twins include:

12 Jacob and Esau (Bible)
Weasley twins (*Harry Potter and the Philosopher's Stone*, 1997, et seq, J K Rowling)
14 Apollo and Diana (Roman mythology)
15 Castor and Pollux (Greek mythology)
Romulus and Remus (Roman mythology)
16 Apollo and Artemis (Greek mythology)
Thomas the Apostle (Bible)
17 Eng and Chang Bunker (1811–74, Siamese)
Mark and Steve Waugh (1965– , Australian)
Sebastian and Viola (*Twelfth Night*, c.1601, William Shakespeare)
19 Hercules and Iphicles (Greek legend)
Maurice and Robin Gibb (Maurice Gibb, 1949–2003/Robin Gibb, 1949–2012; English)
Ronnie and Reggie Kray (Ronald Kray, 1933–95/Reginald Kray, 1933–2000; English)
21 Pat and Isabel O'Sullivan (*The Twins at St*

Clare's, 1941, et seq, Enid Blyton)
23 King Louis XIV and Philippe (*The Man in the Iron Mask*, Alexandre Dumas)
Tweedledum and Tweedledee (*Alice's Adventures in Wonderland*, 1865, Lewis Carroll)
24 Freelon and Francis Stanley (Francis Stanley, 1849–1918/Freelon Stanley, 1849–1940; US)
26 Jean-Felix and Auguste Piccard (Jean-Felix Piccard, 1884–1963/Auguste Piccard, 1884–1962; US)
28 Jessica and Elizabeth Wakefield (*Sweet Valley High* books, Francine Pascal)
34 Dromio of Syracuse and Dromio of Ephesus (*Comedy of Errors*, c.1594, William Shakespeare)
42 Antipholus of Syracuse and Antipholus of Ephesus (*Comedy of Errors*, c.1594, William Shakespeare)

typeface

Typefaces include:

04 Bell
bold
font
Gill

05 Arial
fount
roman
Times

06 Gothic
Impact
italic
Lucida
Modern
serif
Tahoma

07 Calibri
Courier
Curlz MT
Georgia
Marlett
Verdana

08 Franklin
Garamond
Jokerman
Perpetua
Playbill
Rockwell
Webdings

09 Colonna MT
Helvetica
sans serif

Wide Latin
Wingdings

10 Courier New
Lucida Sans

11 Baskerville
Book Antiqua
Comic Sans MS
Poor Richard
Trebuchet MS

13 Century Gothic
Lucida Console
Times New Roman

14 Franklin Gothic

15 Bookman Old Style

U

umbrella

uncle

underground

underwear

Underwear includes:

03 bra	briefs	Y-fronts	wyliecoat
04 body	corset	**08** bloomers	**10** suspenders
jump	garter	camisole	underdress
slip	girdle	chuddies	underlinen
vest	knicks	frillies	underpants
05 bania	semmit	knickers	undershirt
cimar	skivvy	lingerie	underskirt
cymar	smalls	scanties	
jupon	teddie	subucula	**11** boxer shorts
pants	undies	thermals	undershorts
shift	**07** chemise	underset	**12** body stocking
teddy	drawers	**09** brassière	camiknickers
thong	G-string	crinoline	combinations
tunic	hosiery	jockstrap	**13** liberty bodice
06 banian	linings	long johns	suspender-belt
banyan	panties	petticoat	**14** French knickers
basque	singlet	stockings	unmentionables
	spencer	union suit	

union

Unions include:

02 AU	FBU	RMT	T and G
CU	GMB	**04** BIFU	Unite
EU	ITU	CCCP	**06** Amicus
03 AUT	NFU	TGWU	NUMAST
CDU	NUJ	UEFA	Soviet
CGT	NUM	USSR	UNISON
CWU	NUS	ZANU	**07** African
EIS	NUT	ZAPU	**08** European
EMU	RFU	**05** BECTU	

See also **Africa**; **Europe**; **party**

unit *see* **measurement**; **military**

United Kingdom

Cities and notable towns in the UK include:

03 Ely	**06** Armagh	Lisburn	St Davids
04 Bath	Bangor	Newport	Stirling
Hull	Dundee	Norwich	**09** Cambridge
York	Durham	Preston	Edinburgh
05 Derby	Exeter	Salford	Inverness
Derry	London	Swansea	Lancaster
Leeds	Oxford	**08** Aberdeen	Leicester
Newry	**07** Belfast	Bradford	Lichfield
Ripon	Bristol	Carlisle	Liverpool
Stoke	Cardiff	Coventry	Newcastle
Truro	Chester	Hereford	Salisbury
Wells	Glasgow	Plymouth	Sheffield
	Lincoln	St Albans	Wakefield

Worcester

10 Birmingham
Canterbury
Chichester

Gloucester
Manchester
Nottingham
Portsmouth

Sunderland
Winchester

11 Southampton
Westminster

12 Peterborough

13 Wolverhampton

15 Brighton and Hove

English counties and administrative areas:

04 Kent
York

05 Derby
Devon (Dev)
Essex (Ess)
Luton
Poole

06 Dorset (Dors)
Durham (Dur)
Halton
London
Medway
Slough
Surrey (Sur)
Torbay

07 Bristol
Cumbria (Cumb)
Norfolk
Reading
Rutland
Suffolk (Suff)
Swindon

08 Cheshire (Ches)
Cornwall (Corn)
Plymouth
Somerset (Som)
Thurrock

09 Blackpool
Hampshire (Hants)
Leicester
Wiltshire (Wilts)

Wokingham

10 Darlington
Derbyshire
East Sussex (E Suss)
Hartlepool
Lancashire (Lancs)
Merseyside
Nottingham
Portsmouth
Shropshire (Shrops)
Warrington
West Sussex

11 Bournemouth
Isle of Wight
Oxfordshire (Oxon)
Southampton
Tyne and Wear

12 Bedfordshire (Beds)
Lincolnshire (Lincs)
Milton Keynes
Peterborough
Stoke-on-Trent
Warwickshire (War)
West Midlands

13 Herefordshire
Hertfordshire (Herts)
Isles of Scilly
Middlesbrough
North Somerset
Southend-on-Sea
Staffordshire (Staffs)

West Berkshire
West Yorkshire

14 Cambridgeshire (Cambs)
Leicestershire (Leics)
Northumberland
(Northumb)
North Yorkshire
South Yorkshire
Stockton-on-Tees
Worcestershire (Worcs)

15 Bracknell Forest
Brighton and Hove
Buckinghamshire (Bucks)
Gloucestershire (Glos)
Nottinghamshire

16 Kingston upon Hull
Northamptonshire
(Northants)
Telford and Wrekin

17 Greater Manchester
North Lincolnshire

18 Redcar and Cleveland

19 Blackburn with Darwen

20 South Gloucestershire
Windsor and Maidenhead

21 East Riding of Yorkshire
North East Lincolnshire

24 Bath and North East
Somerset

Northern Irish districts:

04 Ards
Down

05 Derry
Larne
Moyle
Omagh

06 Antrim

Armagh

07 Belfast
Lisburn

08 Limavady
Strabane

09 Ballymena
Banbridge

Coleraine
Cookstown
Craigavon
Fermanagh
North Down

10 Ballymoney

11 Castlereagh

Magherafelt

12 Newtownabbey

13 Carrickfergus

14 Newry and Mourne

23 Dungannon and
South Tyrone

Scottish council areas:

04 Fife

05 Angus
Moray

06 Dundee

07 Falkirk
Glasgow

08 Aberdeen
Highland

Stirling

10 Eilean Siar
Inverclyde
Midlothian

11 East Lothian
   West Lothian
12 East Ayrshire
   Renfrewshire
   Western Isles
13 Aberdeenshire
   Argyll and Bute

North Ayrshire
Orkney Islands
South Ayrshire
15 City of Edinburgh
   Perth and Kinross
   Scottish Borders
   Shetland Islands

16 Clackmannanshire
   East Renfrewshire
   North Lanarkshire
   South Lanarkshire
18 East Dunbartonshire
   West Dunbartonshire
19 Dumfries and Galloway

Welsh council areas:

05 Conwy
   Powys
07 Cardiff
   Gwynedd
   Newport
   Swansea
   Torfaen
   Wrexham
   Ynys Mon

08 Bridgend
10 Caerphilly
   Ceredigion
   Flintshire
12 Blaenau Gwent
   Denbighshire
13 Merthyr Tydfil
   Monmouthshire

   Pembrokeshire
14 Isle of Anglesey
15 Carmarthenshire
   Neath Port Talbot
   Vale of Glamorgan
16 Rhondda, Cynon, Taff

UK landmarks include:

04 Fens
   Tyne
06 Big Ben
   Exmoor
   Mersey
   Severn
   Thames
07 Avebury
   Glencoe
   Needles
   Snowdon
   St Paul's
08 Balmoral
   Bass Rock
   Ben Nevis
   Dartmoor
   Land's End
   Loch Ness
09 Cape Wrath
   Chilterns
   Cotswolds
   Helvellyn
   London Eye
   New Forest
   Offa's Dyke
   Royal Mile
   Snowdonia
   Tay Bridge
10 Beachy Head
   Cader Idris
   Holy Island

   Ironbridge
   Kew Gardens
   Loch Lomond
   Lough Earne
   Lough Neagh
   Stonehenge
   The Gherkin
   Windermere
11 Arthur's Seat
   Canary Wharf
   Forth Bridge
   Hever Castle
   Isle of Wight
   John O'Groats
   Leeds Castle
   Lizard Point
   Menai Bridge
   Old Man of Hoy
   Scafell Pike
   York Minster
12 Antonine Wall
   Brighton Pier
   Castle Howard
   Cheddar Gorge
   Forest of Dean
   Hadrian's Wall
   Hampton Court
   Humber Bridge
   Lake District
   Peak District
   Seven Sisters
   Severn Bridge

13 Arundel Castle
   Blue John Caves
   Brecon Beacons
   Bridge of Sighs
   Hatfield House
   Liver Building
   Norfolk Broads
   Robin Hood's Bay
   Royal Pavilion
   Tower of London
   Warwick Castle
   Windsor Castle
14 Blackpool Tower
   Blenheim Palace
   Giant's Causeway
   Holyrood Palace
   Inverary Castle
   Isle of Anglesey
   Sherwood Forest
   Stirling Castle
   Wells Cathedral
15 Angel of the North
   Bodleian Library
   Caledonian Canal
   Cerne Abbas Giant
   Chatsworth House
   Edinburgh Castle
   Flamborough Head
   Grand Union Canal
   Post Office Tower
   St Michael's Mount

See also **city**; **monarch**; **Prime Minister**; **town**

United Nations

United Nations members:

04 Chad
Cuba
Fiji
Iran
Iraq
Laos
Mali
Oman
Peru
Togo

05 Benin
Chile
China
Congo
Egypt
Gabon
Ghana
Haiti
India
Italy
Japan
Kenya
Libya
Malta
Nauru
Nepal
Niger
Palau
Qatar
Samoa
Spain
Sudan
Syria
Tonga
Yemen

06 Angola
Belize
Bhutan
Brazil
Canada
Cyprus
France
Greece
Guinea
Guyana
Israel
Jordan
Kuwait
Latvia
Malawi
Mexico
Monaco
Norway
Panama

Poland
Russia
Rwanda
Serbia
Sweden
Turkey
Tuvalu
Uganda
Zambia

07 Albania
Algeria
Andorra
Armenia
Austria
Bahrain
Belarus
Belgium
Bolivia
Burundi
Comoros
Croatia
Denmark
Ecuador
Eritrea
Estonia
Finland
Georgia
Germany
Grenada
Hungary
Iceland
Ireland
Jamaica
Lebanon
Lesotho
Liberia
Moldova
Morocco
Myanmar
Namibia
Nigeria
Romania
Senegal
Somalia
St Lucia
Tunisia
Ukraine
Uruguay
Vanuatu
Vietnam

08 Barbados
Botswana
Bulgaria
Cambodia

Cameroon
Colombia
Djibouti
Dominica
Ethiopia
Honduras
Kiribati
Malaysia
Maldives
Mongolia
Pakistan
Paraguay
Portugal
Slovakia
Slovenia
Sri Lanka
Suriname
Tanzania
Thailand
Zimbabwe

09 Argentina
Australia
Cape Verde
Costa Rica
East Timor
Guatemala
Indonesia
Lithuania
Macedonia
Mauritius
Nicaragua
San Marino
Singapore
Swaziland
The Gambia
Venezuela

10 Azerbaijan
Bangladesh
El Salvador
Kazakhstan
Kyrgyzstan
Luxembourg
Madagascar
Mauritania
Montenegro
Mozambique

New Zealand
North Korea
Seychelles
South Korea
South Sudan
Tajikistan
The Bahamas
Timor-Leste
Uzbekistan

11 Afghanistan
Burkina Faso
Côte d'Ivoire
Philippines
Saudi Arabia
Sierra Leone
South Africa
Switzerland

12 Guinea-Bissau
Turkmenistan

13 Czech Republic
Liechtenstein
United Kingdom

14 Papua New Guinea
Solomon Islands
The Netherlands

15 Marshall Islands
St Kitts and Nevis

16 Brunei Darussalam
Equatorial Guinea

17 Antigua and Barbuda
Dominican Republic
Trinidad and Tobago

18 São Tomé and Príncipe
United Arab Emirates

20 Bosnia and Herzegovina

21 United States of America

22 Central African Republic

25 St Vincent and the Grenadines

27 Federated States of Micronesia

28 Democratic Republic of the Congo

32 Democratic People's Republic of Korea

United Nations organs:

11 Secretariat

15 General Assembly
Security Council

18 Trusteeship Council

24 Economic and Social Council

27 International Court of Justice

United Nations specialized agencies:

03 FAO	IFC	IMF	ITU
IDA	ILO	IMO	UPU

WHO	ICAO	WIPO	UNWTO
WMO	IFAD	**05** ICSID	**06** UNESCO
04 IBRD	MIGA	UNIDO	**09** World Bank

United Nations' Secretaries-General, with term of office:

03 Lie (Trygve; 1896–1968, Norwegian; 1946–53)

05 Annan (Kofi; 1938– , Ghanaian; 1997–2006)
Thant (U; 1909–74, Burmese; 1961–71)

06 Ki-moon (Ban; 1944– , South Korean; 2007–)

08 Waldheim (Kurt; 1918–2007, Austrian; 1972–81)

12 Boutros-Ghali (Boutros; 1922– , Egyptian; 1992–96)
Hammarskjöld (Dag; 1905–61, Swedish; 1953–61)

14 Pérez de Cuéllar (Javier; 1920– , Peruvian; 1982–91)

United States of America

US states, with abbreviations, state capitals and order of entry into the union:

04 Iowa (Iowa; Des Moines, 29th)
Ohio (Ohio; Columbus, 17th)
Utah (Utah; Salt Lake City, 45th)

05 Idaho (Idaho; Boise, 43rd)
Maine (Maine; Augusta, 23rd)
Texas (Tex; Austin, 28th)

06 Alaska (Alaska; Juneau, 49th)
Hawaii (Hawaii; Honolulu, 50th)
Kansas (Kans; Topeka, 34th)
Nevada (Nev; Carson City, 36th)
Oregon (Oreg; Salem, 33rd)

07 Alabama (Ala; Montgomery, 22nd)
Arizona (Ariz; Phoenix, 48th)
Florida (Fla; Tallahassee, 27th)
Georgia (Ga; Atlanta, 4th)
Indiana (Ind; Indianapolis, 19th)
Montana (Mont; Helena, 41st)
New York (NY; Albany, 11th)
Vermont (Vt; Montpelier, 14th)
Wyoming (Wyo; Cheyenne, 44th)

08 Arkansas (Ark; Little Rock, 25th)
Colorado (Colo; Denver, 38th)
Delaware (Del; Dover, 1st)
Illinois (Ill; Springfield, 21st)
Kentucky (Ky; Frankfort, 15th)
Maryland (Md; Annapolis, 7th)

Michigan (Mich; Lansing, 26th)
Missouri (Mo; Jefferson City, 24th)
Nebraska (Nebr; Lincoln, 37th)
Oklahoma (Okla; Oklahoma City, 46th)
Virginia (Va; Richmond, 10th)

09 Louisiana (La; Baton Rouge, 18th)
Minnesota (Minn; St Paul, 32nd)
New Jersey (NJ; Trenton, 3rd)
New Mexico (N Mex; Santa Fe, 47th)
Tennessee (Tenn; Nashville, 16th)
Wisconsin (Wis; Madison, 30th)

10 California (Calif; Sacramento, 31st)
Washington (Wash; Olympia, 42nd)

11 Connecticut (Conn; Hartford, 5th)
Mississippi (Miss; Jackson, 20th)
North Dakota (N Dak; Bismarck, 39th)
Rhode Island (RI; Providence, 13th)
South Dakota (S Dak; Pierre, 40th)

12 New Hampshire (NH; Concord, 9th)
Pennsylvania (Pa; Harrisburg, 2nd)
West Virginia (W Va; Charleston, 35th)

13 Massachusetts (Mass; Boston, 6th)
North Carolina (NC; Raleigh, 12th)
South Carolina (SC; Columbia, 8th)

18 District of Columbia (DC; Washington)

US state zip codes:

02 AK (Alaska)
AL (Alabama)
AR (Arkansas)
AZ (Arizona)

CA (California)
CO (Colorado)
CT (Connecticut)
DC (District of Columbia)

DE (Delaware)
FL (Florida)
GA (Georgia)
HI (Hawaii)

IA (Iowa)
ID (Idaho)
IL (Illinois)
IN (Indiana)
KS (Kansas)
KY (Kentucky)
LA (Louisiana)
MA (Massachusetts)
MD (Maryland)
ME (Maine)
MI (Michigan)
MN (Minnesota)
MO (Missouri)

MS (Mississippi)
MT (Montana)
NC (North Carolina)
ND (North Dakota)
NE (Nebraska)
NH (New Hampshire)
NJ (New Jersey)
NM (New Mexico)
NV (Nevada)
NY (New York)
OH (Ohio)
OK (Oklahoma)
OR (Oregon)

PA (Pennsylvania)
RI (Rhode Island)
SC (South Carolina)
SD (South Dakota)
TN (Tennessee)
TX (Texas)
UT (Utah)
VA (Virginia)
VT (Vermont)
WA (Washington)
WI (Wisconsin)
WV (West Virginia)
WY (Wyoming)

US state nicknames:

08 Bay State (Massachusetts)
Gem State (Idaho)

09 Beef State (Nebraska)
Corn State (Iowa)
Free State (Maryland)
Old Colony (Massachusetts)

10 Aloha State (Hawaii)
First State (Delaware)
Peach State (Georgia)
Sioux State (North Dakota)

11 Beaver State (Oregon)
Coyote State (South Dakota)
Creole State (Louisiana)
Empire State (New York)
Garden State (New Jersey)
Golden State (California)
Gopher State (Minnesota)
Little Rhody (Rhode Island)
Nutmeg State (Connecticut)
Show Me State (Missouri)
Silver State (Nevada)
Sooner State (Oklahoma)
Sunset State (Oklahoma)

12 Beehive State (Utah)
Buckeye State (Ohio)
Bullion State (Missouri)
Chinook State (Washington)
Diamond State (Delaware)
Granite State (New Hampshire)
Hawkeye State (Indiana)
Heart of Dixie (Alabama)
Hoosier State (Indiana)
Old Line State (Maryland)
Prairie State (Illinois)
Tar Heel State (North Carolina)

13 Big Sky Country (Montana)
Camellia State (Alabama)
Equality State (Wyoming)
Keystone State (Pennsylvania)
Land of Lincoln (Illinois)
Lone Star State (Texas)
Magnolia State (Mississippi)
Mainland State (Alaska)
Mountain State (West Virginia)
Old North State (North Carolina)
Palmetto State (South Carolina)
Pine Tree State (Maine)
Sunshine State (Florida/New Mexico/
 South Carolina)
Treasure State (Montana)

14 Bluegrass State (Kentucky)
Evergreen State (Washington)
Great Lake State (Michigan)
Jayhawker State (Kansas)
North Star State (Minnesota)
Panhandle State (West Virginia)
Sagebrush State (Nevada)
Volunteer State (Tennessee)
Wolverine State (Michigan)

15 Centennial State (Colorado)
Plantation State (Rhode Island)
The Last Frontier (Alaska)

16 Flickertail State (North Dakota)
Grand Canyon State (Arizona)
Peace Garden State (North Dakota)

17 America's Dairyland (Wisconsin)
Constitution State (Connecticut)
Land of Enchantment (New Mexico)
Land of Opportunity (Arkansas)

18 Green Mountain State (Vermont)
Mother of Presidents (Virginia)

Cities and notable towns in the USA include:

02 LA	Houston	San Diego	San Antonio
03 NYC	Memphis	**09** Baltimore	**11** New York City
05 Miami	New York	Milwaukee	
06 Boston	Phoenix	Nashville	**12** Philadelphia
Dallas	Seattle	**10** Los Angeles	Salt Lake City
07 Chicago	**08** Las Vegas	New Orleans	San Francisco
Detroit	Portland	Pittsburgh	Washington DC

US landmarks include:

05 Yukon	Milwaukee	Pearl Harbor
07 Capitol	Mt Rainier	Space Needle
Rockies	**10** Everglades	Yellowstone
08 Colorado	Great Lakes	**12** Appalachians
Lake Erie	Joshua Tree	Carnegie Hall
Missouri	Mt McKinley	Lake Michigan
Mt Elbert	Mt Rushmore	Lake Superior
Mt Vernon	Mt St Helens	**13** Great Salt Lake
Pentagon	Sears Tower	**14** Brooklyn Bridge
Yosemite	White House	Monument Valley
09 Graceland	**11** Grand Canyon	Rocky Mountains
Hollywood	Lake Ontario	**15** Lincoln Memorial
Hoover Dam	Liberty Bell	Statue of Liberty
Lake Huron	Mississippi	

See also **The Americas**; **president**

university

Universities in the UK include:

03 ICL	Surrey	Leicester
LSE	Sussex	Liverpool
UCL	Ulster	Sheffield
04 Bath	**07** Bristol	St Andrews
City	Cardiff	**10** Birmingham
Hull	Glasgow	Buckingham
Kent	Lincoln	De Montfort
SOAS	Paisley	East Anglia
York	Reading	East London
05 Aston	Salford	Heriot-Watt
Derby	Warwick	Manchester
Essex	**08** Aberdeen	Nottingham
Keele	Bradford	Portsmouth
Leeds	Brighton	Sunderland
Luton	Coventry	**11** Bournemouth
Wales	Plymouth	King Alfred's
06 Bolton	Stirling	Southampton
Brunel	Teesside	Strathclyde
Dundee	**09** Cambridge	Westminster
Durham	Edinburgh	**12** Huddersfield
Exeter	Glamorgan	Loughborough
Napier	Greenwich	Robert Gordon
Oxford	Lancaster	Thames Valley

Wales Swansea
13 Abertay Dundee
Hertfordshire
Oxford Brookes

Royal Holloway
West of England
Wolverhampton
14 Wales Institute

15 Gloucestershire
London South Bank
Nottingham Trent
Sheffield Hallam

Ivy League universities:

04 Yale	**07** Cornell	**08** Columbia	**12** Pennsylvania
05 Brown	Harvard	**09** Princeton	**16** Dartmouth College

Seven Sisters colleges:

05 Smith	**07** Barnard	**09** Radcliffe	**12** Mount Holyoke
06 Vassar	**08** Bryn Mawr	Wellesley	

Universities worldwide include:

03 CIT	**07** Caltech	**10** California
MIT	**08** Ann Arbor	**14** Trinity College
04 CUNY	Berkeley	**15** California State
UCLA	Sorbonne	Juilliard School
06 Leiden	Stanford	

Terms to do with university include:

02 2:1	unit	master
2:2	viva	module
BA	**05** chair	pennal
MA	crest	porter
03 BSc	essay	reader
COP	grace	rector
don	grant	school
gyp	major	sconce
JCR	minor	senate
lab	scout	syndic
law	sizar	tenure
LLB	sizer	thesis
MCR	staff	tosher
MSc	study	tripos
NUS	third	**07** academy
SCR	tutor	alumnus
04 arts	union	bursary
blue	**06** agrégé	buttery
club	alumni	college
dean	beadle	council
exam	bursar	diploma
fail	Bursch	Erasmus
fees	campus	faculty
gown	course	fresher
hood	credit	great go
pass	degree	gyp room
PGCE	docent	honours
poll	fellow	lecture
term	finals	library
test	incept	live out
UCAS	lector	marshal
		NUS card

procter
proctor
rag week
scholar
science
seminar
society
student
subfusc
subject
varsity

08 academic
accredit
ad eundem
bachelor
calendar
classics
clearing
cum laude
divinity
encaenia
examiner
freshman
graduate
half-blue
half term
lecturer
magister
medicine
Oxbridge
redbrick
research
semester
send down
servitor
Socrates
sorority
theology
tutorial

09 alma mater
apparitor
catalogue
commorant

doctorate
education
Ivy League
moderator
practical
principal
professor
refectory
semi-bajan
sophomore
top-up fees

10 assessment
chancellor
curriculum
department
exhibition
extramural
fellowship
fraternity
graduation
humanities
laboratory
management
non-gremial
pass degree
philosophy
praelector
prospectus
readership

11 application
certificate
convocation
double first
engineering
examination
lectureship
lower second
mathematics
mortarboard
scholarship
student loan
town and gown
tuition fees

upper second

12 access course
dissertation
exhibitioner
freshers' ball
freshers' fair
freshers' week
joint honours
long vacation
Phi Beta Kappa
postgraduate
self-catering
sport one's oak
summer school

13 academic dress
baccalaureate
honours degree
magna cum laude
matriculation
mature student
personal chair
societies fair
summa cum laude
undergraduate

14 Bachelor of Arts
graduate school
graduation ball
sandwich course
seat of learning
social sciences
vice-chancellor

15 combination room
hall of residence
higher education
modern languages

See also **college**; **education**; **institute**

utensil *see* **cookery**

V

valve

04 ball
blow
gate
side
tube
05 bleed
choke
clack
diode
heart
slide

06 escape
mitral
mixing
needle
poppet
puppet
safety
triode
ventil
07 exhaust
petcock

seacock
snifter
tetrode
08 bicuspid
bistable
cylinder
dynatron
snifting
throttle
turncock

09 air-intake
butterfly
induction
injection
magnetron
non-return
semilunar
thyratron
10 Eustachian
thermionic

See also **bicycle**; **heart**

variety *see* **fruit**; **wine**

vegetable

03 yam
04 kale
leek
okra
spud
05 chard
choko
cress
gumbo
laver
mooli
onion
swede
06 carrot
celery
chives
chocho
daikon
endive
fennel
garlic
manioc
marrow
mibuna

mizuna
pepper
potato
radish
rocket
sorrel
squash
tomato
turnip
07 avocado
bok choy
cabbage
cardoon
cassava
chayote
chicory
lettuce
pak choi
parsnip
pumpkin
salsify
shallot
spinach
tapioca

08 baby corn
beetroot
borecole
broccoli
capsicum
celeriac
cucumber
eggplant
finochio
kohlrabi
leaf beet
mushroom
red onion
rutabaga
zucchini
09 artichoke
asparagus
aubergine
bean shoot
calabrese
courgette
finnochio
finocchio
red pepper
sweetcorn

10 bean sprout
lollo rosso
red cabbage
swiss chard
Tuscan kale
watercress
11 cauliflower
chinese leaf
green pepper
lady's finger
spring onion
sweet potato
12 marrow-squash
savoy cabbage
summer squash
turnip greens
winter squash
yellow pepper
13 ladies' fingers
14 Brussels sprout
Chinese cabbage
globe artichoke
15 vegetable marrow

See also **lettuce**

vehicle

Vehicles include:

03 bus
cab
car
gig
HGV
HOV
van

04 bike
boat
dray
ship
sled
tank
taxi
tram
trap
Tube

05 coach
cycle
lorry
plane
sulky
train

truck
Vespa®
wagon

06 bakkie
camper
hansom
Humvee®
jinker
landau
litter
maglev
matatu
sledge
sleigh
surrey
tandem
troika

07 bicycle
blokart
caravan
crew cab
dog-cart
minibus

minivan
omnibus
phaeton
Pullman
scooter
sleeper
tractor
trailer
Transit®

08 barouche
brougham
Cape cart
golf cart
minimoto
monorail
rickshaw
toboggan
tricycle
wagon-lit

09 bobsleigh
buck-wagon
charabanc
motorbike

Winnebago®

10 boneshaker
four-in-hand
juggernaut
motorcycle
pocket bike
post-chaise
Scotch cart
sedan-chair
service car
stagecoach
trolleybus

11 caravanette
steam-roller

12 double-decker
pantechnicon

13 fork-lift truck
penny-farthing

15 hackney-carriage
recovery vehicle

Countries with their International Vehicle Registration (IVR) codes:

04 Chad (TCH)
Cuba (C)
Fiji (FJI)
Iran (IR)
Iraq (IRQ)
Laos (LAO)
Mali (RMM)
Peru (PE)
Togo (TG)

05 Benin (DY)
Chile (RCH)
Congo (RCB)
Egypt (ET)
Gabon (G)
Ghana (GH)
Haiti (RH)
India (IND)
Italy (I)
Japan (J)
Kenya (EAK)
Libya (LAR)
Malta (M)
Nauru (NAU)
Nepal (NEP)
Niger (RN)
Qatar (Q)
Samoa (WS)
Spain (E)

Sudan (SUD)
Syria (SYR)
Yemen (YAR)

06 Belize (BZ)
Brazil (BR)
Canada (CDN)
Cyprus (CY)
France (F)
Greece (GR)
Guinea (RG)
Guyana (GUY)
Israel (IL)
Jersey (GBJ)
Jordan (HKJ)
Kuwait (KWT)
Latvia (LV)
Malawi (MW)
Mexico (MEX)
Monaco (MC)
Norway (N)
Panama (PA)
Poland (PL)
Russia (RUS)
Rwanda (RWA)
Serbia (SRB)
Sweden (S)
Taiwan (RC)
Turkey (TR)

Uganda (EAU)
Zambia (Z)

07 Albania (AL)
Algeria (DZ)
Andorra (AND)
Armenia (AM)
Austria (A)
Bahrain (BRN)
Belarus (BY)
Belgium (B)
Bolivia (BOL)
Burundi (RU)
Croatia (HR)
Denmark (DK)
Ecuador (EC)
Estonia (EST)
Finland (FIN)
Georgia (GE)
Germany (D)
Grenada (WG)
Hungary (H)
Iceland (IS)
Ireland (IRL)
Jamaica (JA)
Lebanon (RL)
Lesotho (LS)
Liberia (LB)
Moldova (MD)
Morocco (MA)
Namibia (NAM)
Nigeria (NGR)
Romania (RO)
Senegal (SN)
Somalia (SO)
St Lucia (WL)
Tunisia (TN)
Ukraine (UA)
Uruguay (ROU)
Vietnam (VN)

08 Alderney (GBA)
Barbados (BDS)
Botswana (RB)
Bulgaria (BG)
Cambodia (K)
Cameroon (CAM)
Colombia (CO)
Dominica (WD)
Ethiopia (ETH)
Guernsey (GBG)
Hong Kong (HK)
Malaysia (MAL)
Mongolia (MGL)
Pakistan (PK)
Paraguay (PY)
Portugal (P)
Slovakia (SK)
Slovenia (SLO)

Sri Lanka (CL)
Suriname (SME)
Tanzania (EAT)
Thailand (T)
Zanzibar (EAZ)
Zimbabwe (ZW)

09 Argentina (RA)
Australia (AUS)
Costa Rica (CR)
Gibraltar (GBZ)
Guatemala (GCA)
Indonesia (RI)
Isle of Man (GBM)
Lithuania (LT)
Macedonia (MK)
Mauritius (MS)
Nicaragua (NIC)
San Marino (RSM)
Singapore (SGP)
Swaziland (SD)
The Gambia (WAG)
Venezuela (YV)

10 Azerbaijan (AZ)
Bangladesh (BD)
El Salvador (ES)
Kazakhstan (KZ)
Kyrgyzstan (KS)
Luxembourg (L)
Madagascar (RM)
Mauritania (RIM)
Montenegro (MNE)
Mozambique (MOC)
New Zealand (NZ)
Seychelles (SY)
South Korea (ROK)
Tajikistan (TJ)
The Bahamas (BS)
Uzbekistan (UZ)

11 Afghanistan (AFG)
Burkina Faso (BF)
Côte d'Ivoire (CI)
Philippines (RP)
Saudi Arabia (SA)
Sierra Leone (WAL)
South Africa (ZA)
Switzerland (CH)
Vatican City (V)

12 Faroe Islands (FO)
Guinea-Bissau (RGB)
Turkmenistan (TM)

13 Czech Republic (CZ)
Liechtenstein (FL)
United Kingdom (GB)

14 Papua New Guinea (PNG)
The Netherlands (NL)

16 Brunei Darussalam (BRU)

17 Dominican Republic (DOM)
Trinidad and Tobago (TT)

18 United Arab Emirates (UAE)

20 Bosnia and Herzegovina (BIH)
See also **carriage**; **motoring**

21 United States of America (USA)

22 Central African Republic (RCA)

25 St Vincent and the Grenadines (WV)

28 Democratic Republic of the Congo (ZRE)

veil *see* **scarf**

vein

Veins include:

06 portal
thread
07 basilic
jugular
See also **artery**

organic
precava
saphena
08 postcava

praecava
varicose
vena cava
10 innominate

15 brachiocephalic

venue *see* **Olympic Games**; **Paralympic Games**; **parliament**; **stadium**

Verdi, Giuseppe (1813–1901)

Significant works include:

04 *Aïda* (1871)

06 *Alzira* (1845)
Aroldo (1857)
Attila (1846)
Ernani (1844)
Oberto (1839)
Otello (1887)

07 *Macbeth* (1847)
Nabucco (1842)

08 *Ave Maria* (1879–80)
Falstaff (1893)
Libera me (1869)

09 *Don Carlos* (1867)
Il corsaro (1848)
Jerusalem (1847)
Rigoletto (1851)
Stiffelio (1850)

10 *La traviata* (1853)
Tantum Ergo (1836)
The Corsair (1848)
The Robbers (1847)

11 *A Masked Ball* (1859)
I due foscari (1844)
Il trovatore (1853)
I masnadieri (1847)
King for a Day (1840)

Luisa Miller (1849)
Pater Noster (1879–80)
Pietà, Signor (1894)
Requiem Mass (1874)

13 *Giovanna d'Arco* (1845)
Suona la tromba (1848)
The Two Foscari (1844)

14 *Messa da Requiem* (1874)

15 *Sicilian Vespers* (1855)
Simon Boccanegra (1857)
Un giorno di regno (1840)

16 *Hymn of the Nations* (1862)
Inno delle Nazioni (1862)
Quatro Pezzi sacri (1898)

17 *La forza del destino* (1862)
Quattro pezzi sacri (1897–98)
The Force of Destiny (1862)
Un ballo in maschera (1859)

18 *Romanza senza parole* (1865)
The Battle of Legnano (1849)

19 *Sei romanze song cycle* (1838/1845)

20 *La battaglia di Legnano* (1849)
Les vêpres siciliennes (1855)

22 *Stornello for Album Piave* (1869)

25 *Lombards at the First Crusade* (1843)

Significant characters include:

03 Tom

04 Aïda
Anna
Ezio
Ford (Alice)
Ford (Frank)
Horn
Iago
Ines
Jorg
Lina
Mina
Page (Meg)
Ruiz
Seid
Wurm
Zuma

05 Banco
Béarn (Viscount of)
Borsa (Matteo)
Caius (Dr)
Carlo
Curra
Delil
Eboli (Princess)
Egypt (King of)
Elena
Gilda
Laura
Leone
Lerma (Count of)
Moser
Oscar
Pirro
Ramla (Emir of)
Roger
Rolla
Sofia

06 Adorno (Gabriele)
Alcade
Alvaro
Alzira
Amalia
Amelia
Annina
Aroldo
Arrigo
Arvino
Attila
Banquo
Briano
Cassio
Cuniza
Elvira
Emilia
Enrico
Ernani

Fenena
Fenton
Fiesco (Jacopo)
Gaston
Hélène
Imelda
Isaure
Kelbar (Baron)
Mantua (Duke of)
Medora
Miller
Miller (Luisa)
Oberto
Oronte
Otello
Otumbo
Ovando
Pagano
Pietro
Pisana
Pistol (Pistola)
Poggio (La Marchesa del)
Ramfis
Renato
Samuel
Sanval (Edoardo di)
Selimo
Talbot
Uldino
Ulrica
Valéry (Violetta)
Valois (Elisabetta di)
Vargas (Don Carlo di)
Walter (Count)
Zamoro

07 Abdallo
Acciano
Albiani (Paolo)
Amneris
Arminio
Ataliba
Azucena
Bervoix (Flora)
Bethune
Ceprano (Countess)
Corrado
Daniele
d'Obigny (Marchese)
Dorotea
Douphol (Baron)
Egberto
Foresto
Foscari (Francesco)
Foscari (Jacopo)
Frengel (Federico di)
Germont (Alfredo)
Germont (Giorgio)

Giacomo
Giselda
Godvino
Grenvil (Doctor)
Gulnara
Gusmano
Ismaele
La Rocca
Leonora
Macbeth
Macduff
Malcolm
Manrico
Marullo (Cavaliere)
Montano
Montova (Il Duca di)
Nabucco
Ninetta
Ostheim (Duchess of)
Quickly (Mistress)
Radamès
Raymond
Ribbing
Roberto
Rodolfo
Rodrigo
Rolando
Silvano
Stankar
Tebaldo
Trabuco

08 Amonasro
Arvidson (Mlle)
Bardolph (Bardolfo)
Belfiore (Il Cavaliere di)
Carlo VII
Delmonte
Don Carlo
Falstaff (Sir John)
Federica
Ferrando
Giovanna
Giovanni
Giuseppe
Herreros (Don Federico)
Leuthold (Raffaele di)
Lodovico
Loredano (Jacopo)
Manfredo
Melitone (Brother/Fra)
Monforte (Guido di)
Montfort (Guy de)
Montheil (Ademar de)
Nannetta
Odabella
Old Gypsy
Philip II

Rhadames
Riccardo
Roderigo
The Abbot
Thibault
Toulouse (Count of)
Viclinda
Zaccaria
09 Abigaille
Barbarigo
Calatrava (Marquis of/
Marchese di)
Contarini (Lucrezia)
Desdemona
Don Alvaro
Don Carlos

Filippo II
Francesco
Giulietta
Grenville (Dottore)
Maddalena
Monterone (Count)
Rigoletto
Stiffelio
Vaudemont (Comte)
10 Barbarossa (Federico)
Boccanegra (Simon)
Gustavo III
Letorières (Viscount
Gaston/Gastone de)
11 Count de Luna

Don Riccardo
Lady Macbeth
Preziosilla
Salinguerra (Conte de/
Conte di)
Sparafucile
12 Anckarstroem
Doge of Venice
Gomez de Silva (Don Ruy)
Massimiliano (Count)
San Bonifacio (Conte de/
Conte di)
13 High Priestess
Nabucodonosor
15 Guido di Monforte

vermin

Vermin include:

03 fox
rat
04 crow
hare

lice
mice
moth
05 louse

mouse
06 pigeon
rabbit
weevil

09 cockroach

See also **beetle**; **insect**; **moth**; **parasite**; **plague**; **rodent**

vessel *see* **container**; **ship**

vestment *see* **clerical vestment**

video game

Significant games and games series include:

03 Nim
OXO
Wii
04 Doom
Halo
Lego
Pong
06 Diablo
Driver
Pac-Man
Pikmin
Tetris
07 Pokémon

SimCity
The Sims
08 Spacewar
Warcraft
09 Asteroids
Mario Bros
Minecraft
10 Angry Birds
Call of Duty
Donkey Kong
Fruit Ninja
Second Life
Super Mario

Tomb Raider
11 Gran Turismo
12 Final Fantasy
Mortal Kombat
Resident Evil
Tennis for Two
13 Space Invaders
Street Fighter
14 Grand Theft Auto
15 Flight Simulator
World of Warcraft

Significant characters include:

04 Link (*The Legend of Zelda*)
05 Eevee (*Pokémon*)
Gutsu (*Fruit Ninja*)
Luigi (*Mario Bros*; *Super Mario*)
Mario (*Donkey Kong*; *Mario Bros*;
Super Mario)

Sonic (*Sonic the Hedgehog*)
Zelda (*The Legend of Zelda*)
06 Pac-Man
Pikmin
07 Arbiter (*Halo*)
Pauline (*Donkey Kong*)

Pikachu (*Pokémon*)

08 resident (*Second Life*)
Squirtle (*Pokémon*)

09 Bulbasaur (*Pokémon*)
Lara Croft (*Tomb Raider*)

10 Charmander (*Pokémon*)

11 Ivo Robotnik (*Sonic the Hedgehog*)
Master Chief (*Halo*)
power ranger (*Mighty Morphin Power Rangers*)

13 Dr Ivo Robotnik (*Sonic the Hedgehog*)
Gordon Freeman (*Half-Life*)
Princess Zelda (*The Legend of Zelda*)

Terms to do with video gaming include:

02 IM

03 mod
sim

04 chat
grid
port
Sega
Xbox

05 Atari
gamer

06 avatar
MMORPG
modder
PC game
sprite

07 Android
buy mode
console
Game Boy

in-world
sim game
Simlish

08 core game
game code
GameCube
gameplay
joystick
live mode
mini-game
Nintendo
platform
Simoleon
universe

09 build mode
Commodore
group chat
interface
local chat
open-world

PvP combat
video game

10 arcade game
stand-alone

11 console game
game console
multiplayer
PlayStation

12 computer game
Linden dollar
mobile gaming

13 expansion pack

14 game controller
instant message
life simulation
virtual reality

15 multiplayer game
role-playing game

See also **computer***;* **Internet***;* **social media**

villain

Villains include:

04 Case ('The Beach of Falesá', 1892, Robert Louis Stevenson)
Cass (Dunstan; *Silas Marner*, 1861, George Eliot)
Hyde (Mr; *The Strange Case of Dr Jekyll and Mr Hyde*, 1886, Robert Louis Stevenson)
Iago (*Othello*, 1603–04, William Shakespeare)

05 Bates (Norman; *Psycho*, 1960)
Doone (Carver; *Lorna Doone*, 1869, R D Blackmore)
Queeg (Captain; *The Caine Mutiny*, 1951, Herman Wouk)
Regan (*King Lear*, c.1605–06, William Shakespeare)

06 Lecter (Dr Hannibal; *The Silence of the Lambs*, 1988, Thomas Harris)
Oswald (*King Lear*, c.1605–06, William Shakespeare)

Silver (Long John; *Treasure Island*, 1883, Robert Louis Stevenson)

07 Antonio (*The Tempest*, 1611, William Shakespeare)
Bateman (Patrick; *American Psycho*, 1991, Bret Easton Ellis)
Blofeld (Ernst; *Thunderball*, 1961, Ian Fleming)
Goneril (*King Lear*, c.1605–06, William Shakespeare)

08 Cornwall (Duke of; *King Lear*, c.1605–06, William Shakespeare)
Injun Joe (*The Adventures of Tom Sawyer*, 1876, Mark Twain)
The Queen (*Snow White and the Seven Dwarfs*, fairytale)

09 Voldemort (Lord; *Harry Potter and the Philosopher's Stone*, 1997, et seq, J K Rowling)

10 Darth Vader (*Star Wars*, 1977, et seq)

Goldfinger (Auric; *Goldfinger*, 1959, Ian
Fleming)

Richard III (*Richard III*, 1592–93, William
Shakespeare)

12 Aaron, the Moor (*Titus Andronicus*, 1592,
William Shakespeare)

14 Sauron the Great (*The Lord of the Rings*,
1954–55, J R R Tolkien)

Virgil (70–19 BC)

Significant works include:

06 *Aeneid* (c.29–19 BC; twelve books)

08 *Bucolics* (37 BC; ten books)
Eclogues (37 BC; ten books)

Georgics (36–29 BC; four books)

14 *Art of Husbandry* (36–29 BC; four books)

virtue

The Virtues:

04 hope	**07** charity	**08** prudence	**10** temperance
05 faith	justice	**09** fortitude	

virus

Viruses include:

03 CDV	hanta	influenza
DNA	irido	mimivirus
EBV	lenti	norovirus
flu	parvo	papilloma
FLV	phage	**10** hepatitis A
HIV	retro	hepatitis B
HPV	rhino	hepatitis C
pox	**06** baculo	Lassa fever
pro	calici	leaf mosaic
RNA	cowpox	**11** chikungunya
04 arbo	herpes	coronavirus
cold	papova	Epstein-Barr
ECHO	**07** oncorna	**13** bacteriophage
filo	picorna	West Nile virus
HTLV	polyoma	parainfluenza
myxo	variola	**14** human papilloma
rota	**08** morbilli	**15** canine distemper
05 Ebola	Vaccinia	feline leukaemia
flavi	**09** Coxsackie	

vitamin

Vitamins include:

01 A	**06** biotin	**09** folic acid
B	citrin	menadione
C	niacin	**10** calciferol
D	**07** adermin	pyridoxine
E	aneurin	riboflavin
G	retinol	tocopherol
H	thiamin	**11** menaquinone
K	**08** carotene	pteroic acid
P	thiamine	

12 ascorbic acid
    bioflavonoid
    linoleic acid
13 linolenic acid
    nicotinic acid

    phylloquinone
14 cyanocobalamin
    dehydroretinol
    ergocalciferol
    phytomenadione

15 cholecalciferol
    pantothenic acid
    vitamin B complex

volcano

Volcanoes and extinct volcanoes include:

03 Apo (Philippines)
    Awu (Indonesia)
    Usu (Japan)
04 Etna (Italy)
    Fuji (Japan)
    Laki (Iceland)
    Taal (Philippines)
05 Hekla (Iceland)
    Kenya (Kenya)
    Mayon (Philippines)
    Pelée (Martinique)
    Thera (Greece)
    Thira (Greece)
    Unzen (Japan)
06 Ararat (Turkey)
    Erebus (Antarctica)
    Hudson (Chile)
    Katmai (Alaska)
    Sangay (Ecuador)
07 Jurullo (Mexico)
    Kilauea (USA)
    Rainier (USA)
    Ruapehu (New Zealand)
    Surtsey (Iceland)
    Tambora (Indonesia)
    Vulcano (Italy)
08 Cotopaxi (Ecuador)
    Krakatoa (Indonesia)
    Mauna Kea (USA)
    Mauna Loa (USA)
    Pinatubo (Philippines)
    St Helens (USA)

    Tarawera (New Zealand)
    Vesuvius (Italy)
09 Aconcagua (Argentina)
    Coseguina (Nicaragua)
    El Chichón (Mexico)
    Helgafell (Iceland)
    Karisimbi (Rwanda)
    Lamington (Papua New Guinea)
    Paricutín (Mexico)
    Pichincha (Ecuador)
    Santorini (Greece)
    Stromboli (Italy)
    Tongariro (New Zealand)
10 Bezymianny (Russia)
    Chimborazo (Ecuador)
    Galunggung (Java)
    Lassen Peak (USA)
    Tungurahua (Ecuador)
11 Kilimanjaro (Tanzania)
    La Soufrière (St Vincent)
    Nyamuragira (Democratic Republic of the
      Congo)
12 Citlaltépetl (Mexico)
    Ixtaccihuatl (Mexico)
    Klyuchevskoy (Russia)
    Popocatèpetl (Mexico)
13 Nevado del Ruiz (Colombia)
    Ojos del Salado (Argentina/Chile)
    Volcán El Misti (Peru)
14 Soufrière Hills (Montserrat)
15 Haleakala Crater (USA)

See also **crust**

volleyball

Volleyball terms include:

03 ace
    dig
04 dump
    kill

05 block
    spike
06 libero
    screen

    setter
    volley
08 rotation
    shoot set

10 attack line
11 double-touch

Voltaire (1694–1778)

05 *Irène* (1778)
  Zadig (1747)
  Zaïre (1732)
06 *Mérope* (1743)
  Oedipe (1718)
07 *Candide* (1759)
  Mahomet (1741)
18 *Princesse de Navarre* (1745)
20 *Philosophical Letters* (1734)
  The Century of Louis XIV (1751)
  Traité de métaphysique (1748)
21 *La Ligue ou Henri le Grand* (1732)
  Siècle de Louis Quatorze (1751)

23 *Philosophical Dictionary* (1764)
  Poem on the Lisbon Disaster (1756)
25 *Dictionnaire philosophique* (1764)
  Letters on the English Nation (1734)
27 *Elements of Newton's Philosophy* (1737)
28 *Les Moeurs et l'esprit des nations* (1756)
  Poème sur le désastre de Lisbonne (1756)
31 *Eléments de la philosophie de Newton*
  (1738)
33 *Dictionnaire philosophique portatif* (1764)
36 *Lettres écrites de Londres sur les Anglais*
  (1734)

06 Farmer (the)
  Martin
  Sailor (the)
07 Cacambo
  Candide
  Jacques
08 Fernando (Don)
  Giroflée (Brother/Friar)
  Issachar (Don)
  Old woman (the)

  Pangloss (Dr)
  Paquette
  Perigord (Abbé of)
09 Baron's son (the)
  Cunégonde
10 Inquisitor (My Lord the/The Grand)
  Maximilian
  Parolignac (Marquis de)
11 Pococurante (Count/Lord)
12 Vanderdendur (Mynheer)

W

wading bird *see* **bird**

Wagner, Richard (1813–83)

Significant works include:

07 *Die Feen* (1888)
08 *Parsifal* (1882)
09 *Lohengrin* (1850)
    Siegfried (1876)
10 *Die Walküre* (1870)
    The Fairies (1888)
11 *The Valkyrie* (1870)
12 *Das Rheingold* (1869)
    The Rhinegold (1869)
14 *Siegfried Idyll* (1870)
15 *Das Liebesverbot* (1836)
    Götterdämmerung (1876)
16 *The Forbidden Love* (1836)
    Tristan und Isolde (1865)
    Wesendonck Lieder (1858)
17 *The Flying Dutchman* (1843)
19 *Die Novize von Palermo* (1836)

20 *Der Ring des Nibelungen* (1876)
    The Twilight of the Gods (1876)
21 *Der fliegende Holländer* (1843)
    The Ring of the Nibelungs (1876)
22 *Arrival of the Black Swans* (1861)
23 *Rienzi, Last of the Tribunes* (1842)
24 *Five Songs for a Female Voice* (1858)
26 *Rienzi, der letzte der Tribunen* (1842)
    Seven songs from Goethe's Faust (1832)
27 *Die Meistersinger von Nürnberg* (1868)
    The Mastersingers of Nuremberg (1868)
28 *Albumblatt für Frau Betty Schott* (1875)
30 *Ankunft bei den schwarzen Schwänen*
    (1861)
40 *Tannhäuser and the Song Contest on the
    Wartburg* (1845)

Significant characters include:

03 Eva
04 Elsa
    Erda
    Erik
    Froh
    Loge
    Mime
05 David
    Freia
    Irene
    Marke (King)
    Melot
    Sachs (Hans)
    Senta
    Venus
    Wotan
06 Daland
    Fafner
    Fasolt
    Fricka
    Isolde
    Kundry

Orsini (Paolo)
Ortrud
Pogner (Veit)
Rienzi (Cola)
07 Adriano
    Colonna (Stefano)
    Gunther
    Gutrune
    Hermann
    Hunding
    Kothner (Fritz)
    Tristan
    Wolfram
08 Alberich
    Amfortas
    Brangäne
    Dutchman (The)
    Gerhilde
    Klingsor
    Kurvenal
    Kurwenal
    Ortlinde

Parsifal
Raimondo
Siegmund
Stolzing (Walter von)
Woglinde
09 Elisabeth
    Friedrich
    Grimgerde
    Gurnemanz
    Lohengrin
    Magdalena
    Magdalene
    Siegfried
    Sieglinde
    Steersman (The)
    Telramund (Frederick of/
        Federico)
    Waltraute
    Wellgunde
10 Beckmesser (Sixtus)
    Brünnhilde
    Flosshilde

Rossweisse
Tannhäuser (Heinrich)
12 Rhine-maidens

13 Elsa of Brabant
Von Eschenbach
(Wolfram)

14 Henry the Fowler (King)

wall

Wall types include:

03 dam
sea
04 dike
dyke
05 block
brick
death
fence
hedge
inner
mural

party
06 bailey
cavity
garden
paling
screen
shield
07 barrier
bulwark
curtain
divider

parapet
rampart
08 abutment
bulkhead
buttress
obstacle
palisade
stockade
09 barricade
enclosure
partition

retaining
10 embankment
11 breeze-block
load-bearing
outer bailey
13 fortification
stud partition
14 flying buttress

Walls include:

05 Great (China)
06 Berlin (Germany)
07 Wailing (Israel)

Western (Israel)
08 Antonine (Scotland)
Hadrian's (England)

war

War and warfare types include:

03 hot
04 cold
germ
holy
05 blitz
civil
jihad
total
trade
world

06 ambush
attack
battle
jungle
nerves
trench
07 assault
limited
nuclear
private

08 chemical
intifada
invasion
skirmish
struggle
09 attrition
guerrilla
10 asymmetric
biological
biowarfare

blitzkrieg
engagement
manoeuvres
resistance
11 bombardment
12 asymmetrical
state of siege
13 armed conflict
counter-attack

Wars include:

03 Cod
04 Boer
Gulf
Iraq
Sikh
Zulu
05 Chaco
Civil
Dutch
Great
Maori
Opium
Punic
Roses

World
06 Afghan
Balkan
Barons'
Gallic
Indian
Korean
Six-Day
Trojan
Vendée
Winter
07 Bishops'
Crimean
Italian

Mexican
Pacific
Persian
Servile
Vietnam
08 Crusades
Football
Iran-Iraq
Peasants'
Religion
Ten Years'
09 Black Hawk
Falklands
Yom Kippur

10 Devolution
Jenkins' Ear
Napoleonic
Peninsular
Queen Anne's
Seven Years'
Suez Crisis
11 Arab-Israeli
Eighty Years'
Indian Civil

King Philip's
Thirty Years'
12 English Civil
Hundred Years'
Independence
King William's
Russian Civil
Russo-Finnish
Russo-Turkish
Spanish Civil

13 American Civil
Grand Alliance
Russo-Japanese
14 Boxer Rebellion
Franco-Prussian
Indian Uprising
July Revolution
Triple Alliance
15 Easter Rebellion

See also **battle; massacre; rebellion; siege**

warning *see* signal

watch *see* clock

water

Mineral water brands include:

05 Evian®
06 Buxton®
Ty Nant®

Vittel®
Volvic®
07 Deeside®

Perrier®
08 Aqua Pura®
10 Strathmore®

13 Pennine Spring®
San Pellegrino®
14 Highland Spring®

water source *see* well

watercourse *see* river

waterfall

Waterfalls include:

05 Angel (Venezuela)
Della (Canada)
Glass (Brazil)
Pilao (Brazil)
Tysse (Norway)
06 Boyoma (Congo)
Iguaçu (Brazil/Argentina)
Krimml (Austria)
Ormeli (Norway)
Ribbon (USA)
Tugela (South Africa)
07 Mtarazi (Zimbabwe)
Niagara (Canada/USA)
Stanley (Congo)
Thukela (South Africa)
08 Cuquenán (Guyana/Venezuela)
Gavarnie (France)
Itatinga (Brazil)
Kaieteur (Guyana)
Takkakaw (Canada)

Victoria (Zambia/Zimbabwe)
Wallaman (Australia)
Yosemite (USA)
09 Churchill (Canada)
Giessbach (Norway)
Multnomah (USA)
Staubbach (Switzerland)
10 Cleve-Garth (New Zealand)
Skjeggedal (Norway)
Sutherland (New Zealand)
Wollomombi (Australia)
11 Reichenbach (Switzerland)
Trummelbach (Switzerland)
12 Cusiana River (Colombia)
Paulo Alfonso (Brazil)
Silver Strand (USA)
13 Mardalsfossen (Norway)
Tyssetrengane (Norway)
Upper Yosemite (USA)
Vestre Mardola (Norway)

weapon

03 bow
gas
gun
IED
Uzi
WMD

04 bomb
Colt®
cosh
dirk
épée
foil
Mace®
mine
pike
Scud

05 arrow
billy
bolas
CS gas
H-bomb
knife
lance
Luger®
panga
rifle
sabre
sling
spear
sword
taser
vouge

06 airgun
cannon
cudgel
dagger
Exocet®
glaive
jambok
magnum
Mauser
mortar
musket
pistol
rapier

rocket
six-gun
taiaha
tomboc

07 assegai
balista
bayonet
bazooka
bomblet
Bren gun
caltrap
caltrop
carbine
halberd
harpoon
longbow
machete
poleaxe
poniard
shotgun
sjambok
sten gun
stun gun
tear-gas
torpedo

08 air rifle
atom bomb
ballista
blowpipe
calthrop
catapult
claymore
crossbow
field gun
howitzer
landmine
nail bomb
nerve gas
nunchaku
partisan
revolver
scimitar
shuriken
stiletto
threshel

time-bomb
tomahawk
tommy-gun

09 automatic
battleaxe
boomerang
Mills bomb
smart bomb
truncheon
turret-gun

10 bowie knife
broadsword
flick-knife
gatling-gun
machine-gun
mustard gas
napalm bomb
shillelagh
six-shooter

11 Agent Orange
anti-tank gun
blunderbuss
bow and arrow
cluster-bomb
daisy-cutter
depth-charge
elephant gun
hand grenade
kalashnikov
submunition

12 binary weapon
bunker buster
flame-thrower
quarterstaff

13 Cruise missile
knuckleduster
maurikigusari
submachine-gun

14 binary munition
incendiary bomb
rocket-launcher

15 thermobaric bomb
Winchester® rifle

03 aim
cap
dog
fan
wad

04 ball

bead
bore
cock
fire
fuse
head
hilt

kick
land
load
sear
slug
vizy

05 arrow
blade
chape
chase
flint
forte
guard
mouth
point
prime
range
rifle
shaft
shell
sight
steel
stock
train
visie

06 barrel
breech
bullet
casing
charge
cocked
delope
gunner
hammer
handle
muzzle
pommel
ramrod

random
recoil
sheath
target
uncock
vizzie
volley

07 battery
caliber
calibre
chamber
chassis
dispart
quillon
rifling
tampion
tompion
trigger
warhead

08 carriage
full-cock
half-cock
kick back
pike-head
unlimber

09 bowstring
cartridge
chokebore
discharge
flechette
fléchette
foresight

hilt-guard
hindsight
proof-mark
reinforce
sword-hilt
wheel lock

10 barleycorn
basket-hilt
black Maria
cross guard
knuckle-bow
projectile
self-cocker
spear-point
spear-shaft
sword-guard

11 fingerguard
hair trigger
safety catch
self-loading

12 rubber bullet

13 ball cartridge
gauntlet-guard
percussion cap
scouring stick

14 blank cartridge
cross batteries
panoramic sight
percussion-fuse
percussion-lock

15 telescopic sight

See also **bomb**; **dagger**; **gun**; **knife**; **missile**; **sword**

weather

Weather phenomena include:

03 fog
ice

04 gale
hail
haze
mist
rain
smog
snow
thaw

wind

05 cloud
frost
sleet
slush
storm

06 breeze
deluge
shower
squall

07 chinook
cyclone
drizzle
drought
mistral
monsoon
rainbow
tempest
thunder
tornado
twister

typhoon

08 black ice
downpour
heatwave
sunshine

09 hoar frost
hurricane
lightning
snowstorm
whirlwind

See also **cloud**; **ice**; **meteorology**; **precipitation**; **snow**; **storm**; **wind**

wedding *see* **anniversary**; **marriage**

weed

Weeds include:

04 dock
moss
05 daisy
vetch
06 fat hen
oxalis
spurge
yarrow
07 bracken
ragweed
ribwort
08 bindweed
duckweed
knapweed
self-heal
09 chickweed
coltsfoot
dandelion
ground ivy

groundsel
horsetail
knotgrass
liverwort
pearlwort
snakeweed
speedwell
sun spurge
10 cinquefoil
common reed
couch grass
curled dock
deadnettle
sow thistle
thale cress
11 ground elder
meadow grass
petty spurge
salad burnet
white clover

12 annual nettle
rough hawkbit
sheep's sorrel
13 common burdock
field wood rush
large bindweed
pineapple weed
small bindweed
14 common plantain
shepherd's purse
15 broad-leaved dock
burnet saxifrage
common chickweed
creeping thistle
greater plantain
lesser celandine
perennial nettle
stemless thistle

week *see* **day**

weight division *see* boxing

weightlifting

Weightlifters include:

03 Cao (Lei; 1983– , Chinese)
04 Jang (Mi-Ran; 1983– , South Korean)
Kono (Tommy; 1930– , US)
05 Davis (John; 1921–84, US)
Vinci (Charles; 1933– , US)
06 Xiexia (Chen; 1983– , Chinese)
07 Hongmei (Qiu; 1983– , Chinese)

08 Aramanau (Andrei; 1988– , Belarussian)
Guozheng (Zhang; 1974– , Chinese)
Slivenko (Oxana; 1986– , Russian)
09 Alekseyev (Vasily; 1942–2011, Russian)
11 Zakharevich (Yuriy; 1963– , Russian)
Zhabotinsky (Leonid; 1938– , Soviet)
12 Suleymanoglu (Naim; 1967– , Bulgarian/
Turkish)

Weightlifting terms include:

03 bar
04 jerk
05 chalk
class

clean
06 collar
no lift
snatch

07 barbell
08 good lift
press-out
10 bench press

down signal
simple grip
11 disc weights

well

Wells, springs and water sources include:

03 eye
spa
04 font

pool
05 fount
06 geyser

source
spring
supply

07 aquifer
hot well
mickery

08 artesian
draw-well
fountain
pump-well
wellhead

09 hot spring

reservoir
water hole

10 wellspring

11 groundwater
mineral well
wishing well

12 dropping-well
watering hole

13 weeping spring

Wells, H G (1866–1946)

Significant works include:

05 *Kipps* (1905)

10 *Tono-Bungay* (1909)

11 *Ann Veronica* (1909)
Men Like Gods (1923)

14 *The Time Machine* (1895)

15 *The Invisible Man* (1897)

17 *Love and Mr Lewisham* (1900)
The New Machiavelli (1911)
The War of the Worlds (1898)
The Wonderful Visit (1895)

19 *The History of Mr Polly* (1910)
The Island of Dr Moreau (1896)
The Outline of History (1920)
When the Sleeper Wakes (1899)

20 *The First Men in the Moon* (1901)

22 *The Shape of Things to Come* (1933)

23 *A Short History of the World* (1922)
Mind at the End of Its Tether (1945)
Mr Britling Sees It Through (1916)

25 *Experiment in Autobiography* (1934)
The World of William Clissold (1926)

Significant characters include:

04 Eloi (the)

05 Kipps (Arthur)
Polly (Alfred)

06 Moreau (Doctor)

07 Griffin (John)

Stanley (Ann Veronica)

08 Britling (Mr)
Clissold (William)
Lewisham (George)
Morlocks (the)
Prendick (Edward)

09 Ponderevo (Edward)

10 Montgomery (Doctor)

12 Invisible Man (the)

13 Time Traveller (the)

Welsh

Welsh boys' names include:

03 Dai
Huw
Nye
Wyn

04 Aled
Alun
Bryn
Dewi
Eryl
Evan
Glyn
Ifor
Ioan

Owen
Rees
Rhys
Siôn

05 Dylan
Elwyn
Emlyn
Emrys
Gavin
Haydn
Howel
Hywel
Idris

Ieuan
Lloyd
Madoc
Tudor

06 Dafydd
Dilwyn
Eirian
Gareth
Gwilym
Howell
Mervyn
Morgan
Rhodri

07 Aneirin
Aneurin
Brynmor
Geraint
Gwillym
Myrddin
Peredur
Vaughan

08 Llewelyn
Llywelyn
Meredith

Welsh girls' names include:

04 Ceri
Enid
Gwen
Gwyn
Mair

Siân

05 Carys
Cerys
Dilys
Ffion

Megan
Nerys
Olwen
Olwin
Olwyn

Rhian
06 Delyth
Eirlys
Eluned
Gaynor
Gladys
Glenda
Glenys

Glynis
Gwenda
Morgan
Olwyne
07 Bronwen
Eiluned
Gwenyth
Gwyneth

Myfanwy
08 Angharad
Morwenna
Rhiannon
09 Gwendolen
Gwenllian

See also **town**; **United Kingdom**

whale

Whales and dolphins include:

03 fin
04 blue
grey
orca
05 black
minke
pigmy
piked
pilot
right
sperm
white
06 baleen
beaked
beluga

caa'ing
finner
killer
07 bowhead
dolphin
finback
grampus
Layard's
narwhal
rorqual
toothed
wholpin
08 humpback
porpoise
09 Greenland

grindhval
razorback
whalebone
10 bottlenose
humpbacked
11 bottle-nosed
false killer
12 river dolphin
strap-toothed
13 common rorqual
Risso's dolphin
sulphur-bottom
15 gangetic dolphin
harbour porpoise

wheel

Wheels include:

03 big
cog
fly
04 buff
cart
gear
idle
mill

worm
05 crown
drive
wagon
water
06 castor
charka
escape

Ferris
paddle
prayer
07 balance
driving
fortune
potter's
ratchet

08 roulette
spinning
sprocket
spur gear
steering
09 Catherine
13 spinning jenny

whisky

Whiskies include:

03 rye
04 dram
half
malt
05 blend
hooch
06 hootch
poteen
red-eye

Scotch
07 blended
Bourbon
potheen
spunkie
08 peat-reek
sour mash
09 aqua vitae
good stuff

the cratur
10 barley-bree
barley-broo
cornbrandy
corn whisky
single malt
tanglefoot
usquebaugh
11 barley-broth

mountain dew
the Auld Kirk
water of life
12 the real McCoy
13 the real Mackay
14 chain lightning
tarantula juice

white

Shades of white include:

04 ecru
grey
lily
opal
whey
05 cream
ivory
milky
snowy
06 argent
creamy
pearly
silver
08 magnolia
09 champagne
lily-white
snow-white
11 silver-white

See also **pigment**

Whitman, Walt (1819–92)

Significant works include:

08 *Drum-Taps* (1865)
12 'Song of Myself' (1881)
13 *Leaves of Grass* (1855)
16 *Sequel to Drum-Taps* (1866)
17 'O Captain! My Captain!' (1865–66)
'Pioneers! O, Pioneers!'

20 'I Sing the Body Electric'
21 *Memoranda During the War* (1875–76)
30 'Out of the Cradle Endlessly Rocking'
33 'When Lilacs Last in the Dooryard Bloom'd'
(1865–66)

wild flower *see* flower

Wilde, Oscar (1854–1900)

Significant works include:

06 *Salomé* (1896)
11 *De Profundis* (1905)
14 *An Ideal Husband* (1895)
17 *The Duchess of Padua* (1891)
18 *Lady Windermere's Fan* (1892)
Vera; or The Nihilists (1883)

20 *A Woman of No Importance* (1893)
22 *Lord Arthur Savile's Crime* (1891)
The Ballad of Reading Gaol (1898)
The Picture of Dorian Gray (1891)
27 *The Happy Prince and Other Tales* (1888)
The Importance of Being Earnest (1895)

Significant characters include:

04 Gray (Dorian)
05 Prism (Miss)
06 Cardew (Cecily)
Goring (Viscount)
Salomé
Savile (Lord Arthur)
Wooton (Lord Henry)
07 Erlynne (Mrs)
08 Chiltern (Sir Robert)

Worthing (John 'Jack') [aka Ernest]
09 Arbuthnot (Gerald)
Arbuthnot (Mrs Rachel)
Bracknell (Lady)
Moncrieff (Algernon)
10 Windermere (Lady)
11 Happy Prince (the)
Illingworth (Lord)

wind

Winds include:

04 berg
bise
bora
east
föhn
helm
05 north
trade
zonda

06 buster
doctor
El Niño
levant
samiel
simoom
zephyr

07 austral
chinook
cyclone
etesian

gregale
khamsin
meltemi
mistral
monsoon
pampero
sirocco

08 Favonian
libeccio
westerly
williwaw

09 harmattan
nor'wester
snow eater
southerly

10 Cape doctor
prevailing
tramontana
wet chinook
willy-willy

11 anticyclone

15 southerly buster

Literary winds include:

05 Eurus
Notus

06 Auster
Boreas

07 Aquilon
08 Argestes

Favonius
10 Euroclydon

Terms to do with the wind include:

04 calm
flaw
gale
veer

05 blore
storm

06 upwind

07 aeolian
bluster
cutting
leeward

08 downwind
forewind
headwind
landwind
light air
near gale
periodic
sidewind
tailwind
windward

09 crosswind
katabatic

10 cool change
strong gale

11 fresh breeze
light breeze
surface wind

12 gentle breeze
strong breeze
violent storm

13 following wind

14 moderate breeze

window

Windows include:

03 bay
bow

04 pane
rose
sash
shop

05 Jesse
Judas
oriel
ox-eye
Velux®

06 dormer
French
lancet
louvre
Norman
oculus
rosace

screen
ticket

07 compass
guichet
lattice
lucarne
luthern
sexfoil
sliding
ventana
windock
windore
winnock

08 astragal
bull's eye
casement
fanlight
porthole
skylight

09 decorated
jut-window
mezzanine
mullioned
patio door

10 fenestella

11 lychnoscope
oeil-de-boeuf

12 double-glazed
early English
quarterlight
stained glass

13 batement light
double-glazing
perpendicular

14 Catherine wheel

15 secondary-glazed

wine

Wine-bottle sizes include:

06 flagon	rehoboam	salmanazar
magnum	**09** balthazar	**11** Marie-Jeanne
08 jeroboam	**10** methuselah	**14** nebuchadnezzar

Wine types, varieties and grapes include:

03 Dao
dry
red
sec

04 Asti
brut
Cava
fino
hock
port
rosé
Sekt
Tent

05 blush
bombo
Douro
Durif
Fitou
Gamay
house
Mâcon
Médoc
plonk
Rioja
Soave
straw
sweet
Syrah
table
Tavel
Tokay
tonic
white

06 Alsace
Barolo
Barsac
Beaune
canary
claret
grappa
Graves
Malaga
Malbec
Merlot
mulled
Muscat
Pontac

sherry
Shiraz

07 alicant
Aligoté
Amarone
Auslese
Barbera
Bunyuls
Chablis
Chianti
Cinsaut
demi-sec
Madeira
Malmsey
Margaux
Marsala
moselle
oloroso
Orvieto
Pomerol
retsina
Rhenish
sangria
vintage
Vouvray

08 Alicante
Bordeaux
Brunello
bucellas
Burgundy
Carignan
Cinsault
Dolcetto
Frascati
Garnacha
glühwein
Grenache
house red
jerepigo
Kabinett
Malvasia
Marsanne
Montilla
Muscadet
muscatel
Nebbiolo
New World
Palomino

Pauillac
Pinotage
prosecco
Riesling
Rousanne
ruby port
Sancerre
Sauterne
Sémillon
Spätlese
spumante
St Julien
Sylvaner
Tinta Cão
vermouth
vin santo
Viognier

09 bacharach
Bardolino
Carignane
Carmenère
champagne
Colombard
dry sherry
fortified
frizzante
Hermitage
Lambrusco
Langue d'oc
Minervois
Mourvèdre
Pinot Gris
Pinot Noir
Rhine wine
Sauternes
Scheurebe
sparkling
St-Émilion
Tarragona
tawny port
Trebbiano
Ugni Blanc
white port
Zinfandel

10 Barbaresco
Beaujolais
Chambertin
Chardonnay

Constantia
Grignolino
house white
manzanilla
Mateus Rosé
Monastrell
Muscadelle
Petit Syrah
Piesporter
Pinot Blanc
Sangiovese
Tinta Roriz
Verdicchio
vinho verde
11 alcohol-free
amontillado
Chenin Blanc
cream sherry
Niersteiner
Petite Sirah

Petit Verdot
Pinot Grigio
Portugieser
Pouilly-Fumé
Rüdesheimer
scuppernong
Steinberger
sweet sherry
Tempranillo
vintage port
12 Blanc de Noirs
Côtes du Rhône
Folle Blanche
Johannisberg
Marcobrunner
medium sherry
Pedro Ximénez
Pinot Meunier
Ruby Cabernet
Tinta Barroca

Valpolicella
13 Blanc de Blancs
Cabernet Franc
Château Lafite
Liebfraumilch
Montepulciano
Müller-Thurgau
Pouilly-Fuissé
14 Crémant d'Alsace
Crémant de Loire
Gewürztraminer
Lacryma Christi
Sauvignon Blanc
15 Crozes-Hermitage
Gewürtztraminer
Grüner Veltliner
Lachryma Christi
Touriga Nacional

Terms to do with wine include:

03 big
cru
DOC
dry
fat
hot
sec
tun
04 body
brut
DOCG
fine
full
hard
hock
lees
legs
long
marc
mull
must
nose
pipe
port
race
rack
racy
rape
ripe
rosé
sack
Sekt
soft
stum

tart
thin
VDQs
vine
vino
05 argol
clean
crisp
fresh
green
heavy
light
mirin
nutty
oaked
plonk
sharp
short
spicy
sweet
tears
vault
white
woody
06 acetic
cépage
claret
coarse
common
corked
decant
earthy
finish
flabby

flinty
fruity
grapey
grappa
hearty
honest
length
lively
magnum
mature
medium
mellow
palate
robust
severe
sherry
smooth
stalky
supple
tannin
tartar
tierce
ullage
vinous
winery
yeasty
07 acidity
balance
bouquet
breathe
chambré
château
clarity
finesse

flowery
fortify
lay down
malmsey
piquant
remuage
retsina
Rhenish
unoaked
velvety
vintage
vintner
weighty
08 demijohn
generous
glühwein
grand cru
hanepoot
muscatel
noble rot
oenology
prädikat
red biddy
spritzig
spumante
vermouth
vineyard
vinosity
vin rouge
wine list
wineskin
09 character
en primeur
frizzante

malic acid	Rhine wine	full-bodied	**11** viniculture
oenophile	vin de pays	maceration	viticulture
oxidation	winepress	madeirized	**12** vin ordinaire
pétillant	wine vault	vinho verde	well-balanced
quaffable	**10** aftertaste	wine cellar	**14** sulphurous acid

Winter Olympics *see* Olympic Games

Winter Paralympics *see* Paralympic Games

witch

Witches, witch doctors and wizards include:

03 hag	mganga	conjurer	**10** besom-rider
hex	shaman	magician	reim-kennar
04 mage	voodoo	marabout	**11** enchantress
05 Hecat	wisard	night-hag	gyre-carline
lamia	zendik	**09** enchanter	medicine man
magus	**07** angekok	galdragon	necromancer
sibyl	carline	occultist	thaumaturge
weird	sangoma	pythoness	**12** Weird Sisters
06 Hecate	warlock	sorceress	**13** thaumaturgist
magian	wise man	wise woman	
	08 angekkok	witch-wife	

Witches include:

04 Nitt (Agnes; *Lords and Ladies*, 1993, et seq, Terry Pratchett)

Tick (Perspicacia; *The Wee Free Men*, 2003, et seq, Terry Pratchett)

Yoop (Mrs; *The Tin Woodman of Oz*, 1918, L Frank Baum)

05 Circe (Greek mythology)

Jadis (*The Lion, the Witch, and the Wardrobe*, 1950, et seq, C S Lewis)

Medea (Greek mythology)

Mombi (*The Marvelous Land of Oz*, 1904, L Frank Baum)

Orddu (*The Black Cauldron*, 1965, Lloyd Alexander)

Orwen (*The Black Cauldron*, 1965, Lloyd Alexander)

Owens (Gillian; *Practical Magic*, 1996, Alice Hoffman)

Owens (Sally; *Practical Magic*, 1996, Alice Hoffman)

Price (Eglantine; *Bedknobs and Broomsticks*, 1971)

Smart (Jane; *The Witches of Eastwick*, 1984, John Updike)

06 Aching (Tiffany; *The Wee Free Men*, 2003, et seq, Terry Pratchett)

Achren (*The Book of Three*, 1964, et seq, Lloyd Alexander)

Alcina (*Alcina*, 1735, G F Handel)

Aradia (mythology)

Cackle (Miss; *The Worst Witch*, 1974, et seq, Jill Murphy)

Endora (*Bewitched*, 1964–72, TV series)

Glinda (the Good Witch of the South; *The Wonderful Wizard of Oz*, 1900, et seq, L Frank Baum)

Hallow (Ethel; *The Worst Witch*, 1974, et seq, Jill Murphy)

Hecate (Greek mythology)

Hubble (Mildred; *The Worst Witch*, 1974, et seq, Jill Murphy)

Maclay (Tara; *Buffy the Vampire Slayer*, 1997–2003, TV series)

Nutter (Agnes; *Good Omens*, 1990, Neil Gaiman and Terry Pratchett)

Orgoch (*The Black Cauldron*, 1965, Lloyd Alexander)

Potter (Lily; *Harry Potter and the Philosopher's Stone*, 1997, et seq, J K Rowling)

Sprout (Pomona; *Harry Potter and the Philosopher's Stone*, 1997, et seq, J K Rowling)

Ursula (*The Little Mermaid*, 1989)

Yubaba (*Spirited Away*, 2001)

Zeniba (*Spirited Away*, 2001)

07 Blinkie (*The Scarecrow of Oz*, 1915, L Frank Baum)

de Passe (Bianca; *Bell, Book and Candle*, 1958, film)

Garlick (Magrat; *Wyrd Sisters*, 1989, et seq, Terry Pratchett)

Granger (Hermione; *Harry Potter and the Philosopher's Stone*, 1997, et seq, J K Rowling)

Holroyd (Gillian; *Bell, Book and Candle*, 1950, John van Druten)

Madison (Amy; *Buffy the Vampire Slayer*, 1997–2003, TV series)

Pekkala (Serafina; *Northern Lights*, 1995, et seq, Philip Pullman)

Repulsa (Rita; *Mighty Morphin' Power Rangers*, 1993–96, TV series)

Sycorax (*The Tempest*, 1611, William Shakespeare)

Weasley (Ginevra 'Ginny'; *Harry Potter and the Philosopher's Stone*, 1997, et seq, J K Rowling)

Weasley (Molly; *Harry Potter and the Philosopher's Stone*, 1997, et seq, J K Rowling)

08 Baba Yaga (Russian folklore)

Calendar (Jenny; *Buffy the Vampire Slayer*, 1997–2003, TV series)

Madam Mim (*The Sword in the Stone*, 1963)

Matthews (Paige; *Charmed*, 1998–2006, TV series)

Nanny Ogg (*Wyrd Sisters*, 1989, et seq, Terry Pratchett)

Rowlands (Morgan; *The Book of Shadows*, 2002, et seq, Cate Tiernan)

Spellman (Sabrina; *Sabrina, the Teenage Witch*, 1996–2003, TV series)

Spofford (Alexandra; *The Witches of Eastwick*, 1984, John Updike)

Stephens (Samantha; *Bewitched*,1964–72, TV series)

Stephens (Tabitha; *Bewitched*, 1964–72, TV series)

Wizadora (*Wizadora*, 1993–2000, TV series)

09 Aunt Clara (*Bewitched*, 1964–72, TV series)

Frau Trude (Grimm Brothers fairytale)

Gayelette (the Good Witch of the North; *The Wonderful Wizard of Oz*, 1900, L Frank Baum)

Halliwell (Phoebe; *Charmed*, 1998–2006, TV series)

Halliwell (Piper; *Charmed*, 1998–2006, TV series)

Halliwell (Prue; *Charmed*, 1998–2006, TV series)

Hardbroom (Miss; *The Worst Witch*, 1974, et seq, Jill Murphy)

Lestrange (Bellatrix; *Harry Potter and the Goblet of Fire*, 2000, et seq, J K Rowling)

Moonshine (Maud; *The Worst Witch*, 1974, et seq, Jill Murphy)

Ravenclaw (Rowena; *Harry Potter and the Philosopher's Stone*, 1997, et seq, J K Rowling)

Rosenburg (Willow; *Buffy the Vampire Slayer*, 1997–2003, TV series)

Rougemont (Sukie; *The Witches of Eastwick*, 1984, John Updike)

Sanderson (Mary; *Hocus Pocus*, 1993)

Sanderson (Sarah; *Hocus Pocus*, 1993)

Sanderson (Winifred 'Winnie'; *Hocus Pocus*, 1993)

10 Hufflepuff (Helga; *Harry Potter and the Philosopher's Stone*, 1997, et seq, J K Rowling)

Madam Hooch (*Harry Potter and the Philosopher's Stone*, 1997, et seq, J K Rowling)

McGonagall (Minerva; *Harry Potter and the Philosopher's Stone*, 1997, et seq, J K Rowling)

Nightshade (Enid; *The Worst Witch*, 1974, et seq, Jill Murphy)

11 Morgan Le Fay (Arthurian legend)

12 Rhea Dubativo (*The Gunslinger: The Dark Tower I*, 1982, et seq, Stephen King)

Scarlet Witch (comic)

The Snow Queen (Hans Christian Andersen fairytale)

13 Rhea of the Coös (*The Gunslinger: The Dark Tower I*, 1982, et seq, Stephen King)

The White Witch (*The Lion, the Witch, and the Wardrobe*, 1950, et seq, C S Lewis)

15 Princess Eilonwy (*The Book of Three*, 1964, et seq, Lloyd Alexander)

The Weird Sisters (*Macbeth*, 1606, William Shakespeare)

Terms to do with witches and wizards include:

03 hex		goety	wicca
04 mojo	**05** charm	magic	**06** cackle
muti	coven	spell	potion

	wart		

Sabbat	**08** black art	enchanted	**11** apotropaism
voodoo	black cat	occultism	conjuration
voudou	cauldron	the occult	enchantment
07 cantrip	diablery	witch's hat	incantation
gramary	familiar	**10** black magic	thaumaturgy
hag-seed	gramarye	broomstick	the black art
pricker	pishogue	divination	witch-finder
Sabbath	wizardry	necromancy	**12** witching hour
sorcery	**09** diablerie	witchcraft	**14** Walpurgis night

See also **fairy tale**; **legend**; **Rowling, J K**; **Shakespeare, William**

wizard

Wizards include:

04 Howl (*Howl's Moving Castle*, 1986, Diana Wynne Jones)
Math (*The Mabinogion*)

05 Black (Sirius; *Harry Potter and the Prisoner of Azkaban*, 1999, et seq, J K Rowling)
Moody (Alastor 'Mad-Eye'; *Harry Potter and the Goblet of Fire*, 2000, et seq, J K Rowling)
Smith (Eskarina; *Equal Rites*, 1987, Terry Pratchett)
Snape (Severus; *Harry Potter and the Philosopher's Stone*, 1997, et seq, J K Rowling)

06 Alatar (*The Lord of the Rings*, 1954–5, J R R Tolkien)
Malfoy (Draco; *Harry Potter and the Philosopher's Stone*, 1997, et seq, J K Rowling)
Merlin (Arthurian legend)
Mordru (comic)
Potter (Harry; *Harry Potter and the Philosopher's Stone*, 1997, et seq, J K Rowling)
Zordon (*Mighty Morphin' Power Rangers*, 1993–6, TV series)

07 Calatin (Irish mythology)
Gandalf (*The Lord of the Rings*, 1954–5, J R R Tolkien)
Gwydion (*The Mabinogion*)
Saruman (*The Lord of the Rings*, 1954–5, J R R Tolkien)
Scratch (Nicholas; comic)
Weasley (Ron; *Harry Potter and the Philosopher's Stone*, 1997, et seq, J K Rowling)

08 Coriakin (*The Voyage of the Dawn Treader*, 1952, C S Lewis)
Lockhart (Gilderoy; *Harry Potter and the Chamber of Secrets*, 1998, J K Rowling)
Pallando (*The Lord of the Rings*, 1954–5, J R R Tolkien)
Prospero (*The Tempest*, 1611, William Shakespeare)
Radagast (*The Lord of the Rings*, 1954–5, J R R Tolkien)

09 Archimago (*The Faerie Queene*, 1590, Edmund Spenser)
Jack o' Kent (English folklore)
Rincewind (*The Colour of Magic*, 1985, et seq, Terry Pratchett)
Slytherin (Salazar; *Harry Potter and the Philosopher's Stone*, 1997, et seq, J K Rowling)

10 Doctor Fate (comic)
Dumbledore (Albus; *Harry Potter and the Philosopher's Stone*, 1997, et seq, J K Rowling)
Gryffindor (Godric; *Harry Potter and the Philosopher's Stone*, 1997, et seq, J K Rowling)

13 Lord Voldemort (*Harry Potter and the Philosopher's Stone*, 1997, et seq, J K Rowling)
The Wizard King (French fairytale)

15 Mustrum Ridcully (*Moving Picture*, 1990, et seq, Terry Pratchett)

Wodehouse, Sir P G (1881–1975)

Significant works include:

11 *My Man Jeeves* (1919)

12 *Quick Service* (1940)

13 *Carry On, Jeeves* (1925)
Right Ho, Jeeves (1934)

15 *The Mating Season* (1949)

20 *The Code of the Woosters* (1938)

21 *The Man with Two Left Feet* (1916)

Significant characters include:

06 Jeeves (Reginald)
Psmith (Ronald)

07 Travers (Aunt Dahlia)
Wooster (Bertram Wilberforce 'Bertie')

08 Emsworth (Lord)
Mulliner (Mr)

09 Uncle Fred
Aunt Agatha
Aunt Dahlia

10 Fink-Nottle (Augustus 'Gussie')

15 The Oldest Member

womanizer

Womanizers and libertines include:

04 goat
lech
rake
roué
wolf

05 letch
Romeo

06 gay dog
lecher

07 Don Juan
seducer
wastrel

08 Casanova
Lothario

Lovelace
palliard
rakehell

09 debauchee
ladies' man
libertine
reprobate
voluptary

womanizer

10 Corinthian
lady-killer
profligate
sensualist

11 gay deceiver
philanderer

wonder

The Seven Wonders of the World:

15 Pyramids of Egypt

16 Colossus of Rhodes

18 Pharos of Alexandria

21 Statue of Zeus at Olympia

23 Hanging Gardens of Babylon

24 Mausoleum of Halicarnassus
Temple of Artemis at Ephesus

wood

Woods include:

03 ash
box
cam
elm
fir
nut
oak
ply
red
sap
yew

04 bass
cord
cork
deal
fire
hard
iron
lime
pine
pink
pulp
rose

sasa
soft
teak

05 alder
apple
balsa
beech
black
brush
cedar
drift
ebony
green
hazel
heart
kauri
larch
maple
match
olive
peach
plane
ramin

satin
tiger
torch
tulip
utile
white
zebra

06 acacia
bamboo
bitter
brazil
candle
cherry
cotton
linden
lumber
obeche
orange
padauk
pedauk
poplar
rubber
sandal

sapele
spruce
timber
veneer
walnut
willow

07 Amboina
bubinga
hickory
palmyra
quassia

08 amaranth
chestnut
cocobolo
hornbeam
mahogany
red lauan
seasoned
silky oak
sycamore

09 chipboard
hardboard

jacaranda	paper birch	purple heart	yellow birch
quebracho	**11** black cherry	tulip poplar	**13** sweet chestnut
10 afrormosia	lignum vitae	white walnut	

See also **forest**

Woolf, Virginia (1882–1941)

Significant works include:

05 *Flush* (1933)

07 *Orlando* (1928)

08 *The Waves* (1931)
The Years (1937)

10 *Jacob's Room* (1922)

11 *Mrs Dalloway* (1925)
Night and Day (1919)

12 *The Voyage Out* (1915)

Three Guineas (1938)

13 *A Haunted House* (1943)

14 *A Room of One's Own* (1929)
Between the Acts (1941)

15 *To the Lighthouse* (1927)

17 *Granite and Rainbow* (1958)
The Death of the Moth (1942)

19 *The Captain's Death Bed* (1950)

Significant characters include:

05 Flush
Hewet (Terence)
Hirst (St John)
Jinny
Louis
Seton (Sally)
Susan
Walsh (Peter)

06 Denham (Ralph)

Ramsay (Mr)
Ramsay (Mrs)
Rodney (William)

07 Ambrose (Helen)
Briscoe (Lily)
Datchet (Mary)
Hilbery (Katharine)
La Trobe (Miss)
Neville

Orlando
Swithin (Mrs)
Vinrace (Rachel)

08 Dalloway (Clarissa)
Dalloway (Richard)
Flanders (Jacob)
Pargiter (Colonel Abel)
Pargiter (Eleanor)
Percival

word

Words and expressions from foreign languages include:

03 cwm (Welsh; valley or mountain hollow)
kop (Afrikaans; hill/football terrace)
obi (Japanese; sash)

04 agar (Malay; jelly used to grow bacteria cultures)
bint (Arabic; girl)
dhow (Arabic, sailing vessel)
dojo (Japanese; place where martial arts take place)
duma (Russian; Russian parliament)
guru (Hindi; a spiritual leader)
hajj (Arabic; the Muslim pilgrimage to Mecca)
haka (Maori; ceremonial war dance)
jiva (Sanskrit; the soul)
khat (Arabic; narcotic shrub leaves)
luau (Hawaiian; party or feast)
veld (Afrikaans; open grassland)

05 aloha (Hawaiian; a salutation)
bagel (Yiddish; ring-shaped bread roll)
balti (Urdu; type of cuisine)
basho (Japanese; sumo wrestling tournament)
batik (Javanese; painted form of decoration)
bhaji (Hindi; fried vegetables)
blini (Russian; stuffed pancakes)
burka (Urdu; yashmak)
cooee (Aboriginal; called to attract attention)
dacha (Russian; small country house)
dekko (Hindustani; look)
dhobi (Hindustani; washerman or washerwoman)
dhoti (Hindustani; cloth worn by Hindu males)
fakir (Arabic; religious mendicant)
fatwa (Arabic; ruling given on a point of Islamic law by an expert)
haiku (Japanese; a short poem)
halal (Arabic; meat from an animal killed in accordance with Islamic law)
jihad (Arabic; holy war against unbelievers)
kanzu (Kiswahili; a long white robe worn by East African men)
karma (Sanskrit; the concept that actions determine future conditions)

kayak (Inuit; covered canoe)
kippa (Hebrew; a skullcap worn by orthodox male Jews)
manga (Japanese; comic book or strip)
pasha (Turkish; officer of high rank)
pukka (Hindi; genuine, true)
samfu (Chinese; suit of jacket and trousers worn mainly by women)
wushu (Chinese; the Chinese martial arts)

06 anorak (Inuit; hooded jacket)
avatar (Sanskrit; manifestation)
banzai (Japanese; a battle cry, salute or exclamation of joy)
bonsai (Japanese; art of growing miniature trees in pots)
bunyip (Aboriginal; swamp monster)
datcha (Russian; small country house)
dim sum (Chinese; snack)
eureka (Greek; cry of triumph at a discovery)
favela (Portuguese; a shack or shanty)
fellah (Arabic; peasant)
kaftan (Turkish; long loose dress or shirt)
kirpan (Punjabi; ceremonial dagger worn by Sikhs)
kosher (Hebrew; pure or clean according to Jewish law)
kvetch (Yiddish; complain, whine)
loofah (Arabic; sponge for bathing)
muu-muu (Hawaiian; loose, brightly coloured dress)
punkah (Hindi; a large cooling fan)
salaam (Arabic; a greeting meaning 'peace')
shogun (Japanese; ruler of feudal Japan)
t'ai chi (Chinese; system of exercise and self-defence)
yakusa (Japanese; gangsters)

07 baklava (Turkish; a dessert)
basmati (Hindi; fragrant rice)
bhangra (Punjabi; folk dance/music)
biltong (Afrikaans; dried meat strips)
bortsch (Russian; soup containing beetroot)
crannog (Irish; ancient fortified settlement)
dashiki (West African; loose, brightly coloured shirt)
dervish (Turkish; a holy man)
falafel (Arabic; ball of spiced minced pulses)
ikebana (Japanese; the art of flower arrangement)
jellaba (Arabic; a loose, hooded, long-sleeved cloak)
karaoke (Japanese; singing a solo to a recorded backing)
karoshi (Japanese; death by overwork)
Kashrut (Hebrew; Jewish religious laws relating to food etc)
khamsin (Arabic; hot southerly wind)
kibbutz (Hebrew; a communal agricultural settlement in Israel)
lambada (Portuguese; a dance)
menorah (Hebrew; candelabrum)
namaste (Hindi; gesture of greeting by bringing palms together and bowing)
netsuke (Japanese; a small carved ornament)
nirvana (Sanskrit; state of enlightenment, bliss)
origami (Japanese; art of folding paper)
schlock (Yiddish; inferior, shoddy)
schmuck (Yiddish; stupid person)
tsunami (Japanese; a wave generated by movement of the Earth's surface underwater)

08 auto-da-fé (Portuguese; public declaration or carrying out of a sentence imposed on heretics)
babushka (Russian; granny)
boondock (Tagalog; remote parts of the country)
chutzpah (Yiddish; nerve to do or say outrageous things)
clarsach (Gaelic; harp)
djellaba (Arabic; a loose, hooded, long-sleeved robe)
feng-shui (Chinese; study and system of environmental harmony)
glasnost (Russian; policy of openness and forthrightness)
kamikaze (Japanese; any reckless, potentially self-destructive act)
kielbasa (Polish; highly seasoned sausage)
mazel tov (Hebrew; good luck, congratulations)
samizdat (Russian; secret printing and distribution of banned literature)
schmaltz (Yiddish; showy sentimentality)

09 apartheid (Afrikaans; enforced separation of races)
baksheesh (Persian; a gift or present of money)
balalaika (Russian; a musical instrument)
billabong (Aboriginal; backwater)
boomerang (Aboriginal; curved wooden missile)
bossa nova (Portuguese; a dance)
catamaran (Tamil; a raft, now a twin-hulled boat)
djellabah (Arabic; a loose, hooded, long-sleeved robe)
hoi polloi (Greek; the rabble)
inshallah (Arabic; if Allah wills)
maharishi (Sanskrit; a Hindu sage or spiritual leader)

10 bar mitzvah (Hebrew; religious initiation ceremony for boys)
tamagotchi (Japanese; electronic toy pet)

11 apparatchik (Russian; any bureaucratic hack)
bath mitzvah (Hebrew; religious initiation
ceremony for girls)

perestroika (Russian; restructuring of an
organization)

See also **The Americas**; **French**; **German**; **Italian**; **Latin**; **Spanish**

Wordsworth, William (1770–1850)

Significant works include:

07 'Michael' (1801)
09 *Peter Bell* (1819)
10 *The Prelude* (1850)
The Recluse (1800)
11 *The Waggoner* (1819)
12 *The Excursion* (1814)
13 *An Evening Walk* (1793)
14 *Lyrical Ballads* (1798)

17 *Poems in Two Volumes* (1807)
19 *Descriptive Sketches* (1793)
20 *The Borderers: A Tragedy* (1796)
21 *The White Doe of Rylstone* (1815)
'Upon Westminster Bridge' (1801)
27 'Ode: Intimations of Immortality' (1807)
29 'Lines Written Above Tintern Abbey' (1798)

World Heritage site

World Heritage sites include:

03 Bam (Iran)
04 Bath (England)
Graz (Austria)
Lima (Peru)
Pisa (Italy)
Riga (Latvia)
Troy (Turkey)
05 Aksum (Ethiopia)
Berne (Switzerland)
Bosra (Syria)
Cuzco (Peru)
Delos (Greece)
Kandy (Sri Lanka)
Lyons (France)
Paris (France)
Petra (Jordan)
Quito (Ecuador)
Siena (Italy)
Sucre (Bolivia)
06 Aleppo (Syria)
Amazon (Brazil)
Angkor (Cambodia)
Assisi (Italy)
Brugge (Belgium)
Cyrene (Libya)
Delphi (Greece)
Kracow (Poland)
Naples (Italy)
Oporto (Portugal)
Potosi (Bolivia)
Prague (Czech Republic)
Puebla (Mexico)
Sintra (Portugal)
Thebes (Egypt)

Toledo (Spain)
Venice (Italy)
Verona (Italy)
Vienna (Austria)
Warsaw (Poland)
07 Abu Mena (Egypt)
Avignon (France)
Caracas (Venezuela)
Caserta (Italy)
Cordoba (Spain)
Holy See (Vatican City)
Kremlin (Russia)
Olympia (Greece)
Pompeii (Italy)
St Kilda (Scotland)
Vicenza (Italy)
08 Agra Fort (India)
Alhambra (Spain)
Brasilia (Brazil)
Budapest (Hungary)
Damascus (Syria)
Florence (Italy)
Istanbul (Turkey)
Pyrénées (France/Spain)
Salzburg (Austria)
Shark Bay (Australia)
Taj Mahal (India)
Timbuktu (Mali)
Valletta (Malta)
Yosemite (USA)
09 Acropolis (Greece)
Agrigento (Italy)
Auschwitz (Poland)
Ayutthaya (Thailand)

Dubrovnik (Croatia)
Galapagos (Ecuador)
Jerusalem (Israel)
Mesa Verde (USA)
New Lanark (Scotland)
Purnululu (Australia)
Red Square (Russia)

10 Everglades (USA)
Herculaneum (Italy)
Lake Baikal (Russia)
Lake Malawi (Malawi)
Luxembourg (Luxembourg)
Mexico City (Mexico)
Safranbolu (Turkey)
Stonehenge (England)
The Rockies (Canada)
Versailles (France)

11 Ajanta Caves (India)
Ancient Nara (Japan)
Danube Delta (Romania)
Ellora Caves (India)
Grand Canyon (USA)
Kilimanjaro (Tanzania)
Leptis Magna (Libya)
Machu Picchu (Peru)
Medina of Fez (Morocco)
Parque Güell (Spain)

Quedlinburg (Germany)
Vatican City (Holy See)
Yellowstone (USA)

12 Altamira Cave (Spain)
Ancient Kyoto (Japan)
Anuradhapura (Sri Lanka)
Fraser Island (Australia)
Hadrian's Wall (England)
Hué Monuments (Vietnam)
Koguryo Tombs (North Korea)
Los Glaciares (Argentina)
Robben Island (South Africa)
Santo Domingo (Dominican Republic)
The Great Wall (China)

13 Bamiyan Valley (Afghanistan)
Tower of London (England)

14 Blenheim Palace (England)
Elephanta Caves (India)
Giant's Causeway (Northern Ireland)
Rocky Mountains (Canada)

15 Aachen Cathedral (Germany)
Amiens Cathedral (France)
Classical Weimar (Germany)
Ironbridge Gorge (England)
Kasbah of Algiers (Algeria)
Kathmandu Valley (Nepal)
Statue of Liberty (USA)

worm

Worms include:

03 eel	hook	leech	**07** annelid
lug	tape	round	bristle
pin	**05** arrow	**06** peanut	**08** sea mouse
rag	earth	ribbon	**10** blood fluke
04 flat	fluke	thread	liver fluke

wrestling

Wrestling holds and throws include:

03 hug	hip-lock	full nelson
04 lock	**08** arm throw	hammerlock
06 grovet	body lock	**11** backbreaker
nelson	headlock	scissor hold
souple	scissors	**12** cross-buttock
suplex	**09** ankle lace	scissors hold
07 bear hug	body throw	stranglehold
buttock	**10** Boston crab	**14** grand amplitude

Wrestling terms include:

03 mat	fall	**05** judge
pin	hold	**06** action
04 bout	open	bridge

souple
07 default
referee

08 arm throw
body lock
chairman
exposing
reversal
takedown

09 ankle lace
body throw
bridge out
freestyle
grapevine
gut wrench
passivity

10 arm control
Greco-Roman

13 central circle
cross-body ride
passivity zone

14 danger position
grand amplitude
protection area

15 double-leg tackle
single leg tackle
technical points

writing

Writings include:

03 ode
04 blog
book
epic
news
play
poem
tale

05 diary
drama
essay
fable
lyric
novel
paper
story
study

06 annals
column
fanfic
letter
memoir
record
report
review

satire
script
sketch
sonnet
thesis
weblog

07 account
apology
article
epistle
feature
fiction
history
journal
novella
parable
profile

08 apologia
critique
tip sheet
treatise
yearbook

09 biography
chronicle
criticism

discourse
editorial
life story
monograph
narrative
statement
technical

10 commentary
journalism
literature
non-fiction
propaganda
scientific
travelogue

11 confessions
copywriting
documentary

12 dissertation

13 autobiography
legal document

14 correspondence

15 advertising copy
curriculum vitae
newspaper column

Writing instruments include:

03 pen
04 Biro®
reed
05 quill
06 crayon
dip pen
pencil
stylus
07 cane pen
08 brailler

CD marker
steel pen

09 ballpoint
eraser pen
ink pencil
marker pen

10 felt-tip pen
lead-pencil
typewriter

11 board marker

fountain pen
highlighter

12 cartridge pen
writing brush

13 laundry marker
Roman metal pen
word-processor

14 calligraphy pen
coloured pencil

15 permanent marker

Writers include:

04 bard
hack
poet
05 clerk
06 author
editor
fabler
penman
pen-pal
rhymer
scribe
07 copyist
diarist
08 annalist
composer
essayist

lyricist
novelist
penwoman
reporter
satirist
09 columnist
dramatist
historian
pen-friend
penpusher
scribbler
sonneteer
web author
10 biographer
chronicler
copywriter
journalist

librettist
playwright
11 contributor
ghost writer
storyteller
12 leader-writer
poet laureate
scriptwriter
stenographer
13 calligraphist
correspondent
court reporter
fiction writer
lexicographer
14 autobiographer
15 technical writer

See also **alphabet; Austen, Jane; Blyton, Enid; Brontë, Anne; Brontë, Charlotte; Brontë, Emily; Carroll, Lewis; Chaucer, Geoffrey; Christie, Dame Agatha; Defoe, Daniel; Dickens, Charles; Dostoevsky, Fyodor; Doyle, Sir Arthur Conan; Dumas, Alexandre; Eliot, George; fable; Hardy, Thomas; Hemingway, Ernest; James, Henry; Joyce, James; Kipling, Rudyard; Lawrence, D H; Morrison, Toni; Murdoch, Dame Iris; Nobel Prize; non-fiction; novel; Orwell, George; poetry; Potter, Beatrix; Proust, Marcel; religion; Rowling, J K; science fiction; Scott, Sir Walter; Stevenson, Robert Louis; Tolkien, J R R; Tolstoy, Count Leo; Trollope, Anthony; Twain, Mark; Voltaire; Wells, H G; Wodehouse, Sir P G; Woolf, Virginia; Zola, Émile**

XYZ

year

Yeats, W B (1865–1939)

yellow

yoga

Yoga types include:

03 Dru	Karma	Yantra	Saptanga
hot	Kaula	**07** Iyengar	Shadanga
04 Agni	Kriya	Kripalu	**09** Ghatastha
Japa	Nidra	Samkhya	Kundalini
Laya	**06** Abhava	Samputa	Pashupata
Maha	Bhakti	Tantric	Patanjala
Nada	Bikram	Vinyasa	Patanjali
Raja	Buddhi	**08** Adhyatma	Sivananda
Vini	Mantra	Ashtanga	
05 Hatha	Sahaja	Asparsha	**12** Yoga-Darshana
Jñāna	Taraka	Ayurveda	**13** Hiranyagarbha

Yoga terms and positions include:

02 om	Monkey	Dog and Cat
03 Bow	niyama	Happy Baby
Cat	Pigeon	Headstand
	Prayer	One-legged
04 anga	Secret	pranayama
Boat	shakti	Side Crane
Easy	siddha	Side Plank
Fish	siddhi	
Hero	Throne	**10** Flying Crow
Lion		Head to Knee
Plow	**07** Compass	meditation
Tree	Cow Face	pratyahara
yama	dharana	Salutation
yogi	Diamond	shatkarmas
	drishti	tongue lock
05 Angle	Firefly	
asana	Garland	**11** Raised Hands
Camel	Goddess	Thunderbolt
Child	Peacock	yogic flying
Cobra	Pendant	yogi toe lock
Crane	Pyramid	**12** Accomplished
Eagle	samadhi	Awkward Chair
Lotus	Warrior	Forearm Stand
mudra		
mukti	**08** chin lock	**13** abdominal lock
prana	Cobbler's	Cat-Cow Stretch
Staff	Cockerel	Legs up the Wall
Wheel	ekāgrata	Shoulder stand
yogin	Half Moon	Sun Salutation
	Mountain	Wind-releasing
06 asanas	Palm Tree	
Bridge	Powerful	**14** Hand-foot-big toe
chakra	Scorpion	King of the Dance
Corpse	Tortoise	Reclined Big Toe
dhyana	Triangle	Sleeping Vishnu
Lizard		**15** Four Limbed Staff
Locust	**09** alignment	Turned Side-Angle
mantra	Crocodile	Upward Facing Dog

York *see* **archbishop**

young *see* **animal**

zip code *see* **United States of America**

zodiac

Signs of the zodiac:

03 Leo (Lion; 24 Jul-23 Aug; fire)

05 Aries (Ram; 21 Mar-20 Apr; fire)
Libra (Balance; 24 Sep-22 Oct; air)
Virgo (Virgin; 24 Aug-23 Sep; earth)

06 Cancer (Crab; 22 Jun-23 Jul; water)
Gemini (Twins; 21 May-21 Jun; air)

See also **astrology**

Pisces (Fishes; 20 Feb-20 Mar; water)
Taurus (Bull; 21 Apr-20 May; earth)

07 Scorpio (Scorpion; 23 Oct-22 Nov; water)

08 Aquarius (Water Bearer; 21 Jan-19 Feb; air)

09 Capricorn (Goat; 23 Dec-20 Jan; earth)

11 Sagittarius (Archer; 23 Nov-22 Dec; fire)

Zola, Émile (1840–1902)

Significant works include:

04 *Rome* (1896)

05 *Paris* (1898)

06 *Vérité* (1903)

07 '*J'accuse*' (1898)
Lourdes (1894)
Travail (1901)

09 *Fécondité* (1899)

13 *Thérèse Raquin* (1867)

14 *Les Trois Villes* (1894–98)

17 *Les Rougon-Macquart* (1871–93)

18 *Les Quatre Évangiles* (1899–1903)

19 *Le roman expérimental* (1880)

Les Rougon-Macquart comprises:

04 *Nana* (1880)

06 *Le Rêve* (1888)

07 *La Curée* (1872)
L'Argent (1891)
La Terre (1887)
L'Oeuvre (1886)

08 *Germinal* (1885)

09 *La Débâcle* (1892)

10 *L'Assommoir* (1877)
Pot-Bouille (1882)

13 *La Bête humaine* (1890)
La Joie de vivre (1884)
Une Page d'amour (1878)

15 *Le Docteur Pascal* (1893)
Le Ventre de Paris (1873)

17 *Au Bonheur des dames* (1883)

18 *La Fortune des Rougon* (1871)

20 *La Conquête de Plassans* (1874)
La Faute de l'Abbé Mouret (1875)

25 *Son Excellence Eugène Rougon* (1876)

Significant characters include:

04 Dide (Aunt)

05 Baudu (Denise)
Hugon (Georges)
Hugon (Philippe)
Maheu (Toussaint)
Puech (Félicité)
Quenu
Quenu (Pauline)
Weiss

06 Buteau
Chaval

Fouque (Adélaïde)
Mouret
Mouret (Désirée)
Mouret (François)
Mouret (Hélène)
Mouret (Octave)
Mouret (Serge)
Mouret (Silvère)
Pascal (Le Docteur)
Rougon
Rougon (Angélique)

Rougon (Aristide)
Rougon (Charles)
Rougon (Clotilde)
Rougon (Eugène)
Rougon (Marthe)
Rougon (Maxime)
Rougon (Pascal)
Rougon (Pierre)
Rougon (Sidonie)
Rougon (Victor)
Sandoz (Pierre)

07 Coupeau
Coupeau (Anna 'Nana')
Coupeau (Louis 'Louiset')
Deleuze (Caroline)
Hedouin (Mme)
Lantier (Auguste)
Lantier (Claude)
Lantier (Étienne)
Lantier (Jacques)
Lantier (Jacques-Louis)
Laurent
Levaque
Mareuil (Louise de)
Racquin (Camille)
Racquin (Laurent)

Racquin (Mme)
Racquin (Thérèse)
Rambaud
Steiner
Vineuil (Colonel de)

08 Fauchéry (Léon)
Gavaudan (Joséphine)
Macquart
Macquart (Antoine)
Macquart (Gervaise)
Macquart (Jean)
Macquart (Lisa)
Macquart (Ursule)
Sicardot
Sicardot (Angèle)

09 Bordenave
Catherine
Chavaille (Rosalie)
Grandjean
Grandjean (Jeanne)
Souvarine

10 Hallegrain (Christine)
Hautecoeur (Angélique de)
Hautecoeur (Felicien VII de)
Vandeuvres (Comte Xavier de)

14 Angélique Marie
Béraud du Châtel (Renée)

15 Beulin d'Orchères (Véronique)

zoology

Branches of zoology include:

07 ecology
zoonomy
zootaxy

08 cetology
oecology

09 acarology
hippology
mammalogy
ophiology
therology

10 autecology

conchology
embryology
entomology
limacology
malacology
morphology
nematology

11 arachnology
herpetology
ichthyology
insectology
myrmecology

ornithology

12 gnotobiology
parasitology
protozoology
zoopathology

13 helminthology
neuroethology
palaeozoology
zoophysiology

14 archaeozoology

15 lepidopterology

Zoologists include:

03 Pye (John David; 1932– , English)

04 Gray (John Edward; 1800–75, English)
Gray (Sir James; 1891–1975, English)
Mayr (Ernst Walter; 1904–2005, German/US)
Owen (Sir Richard; 1804–92, English)
Savi (Paolo; 1798–1871, Italian)

05 Blyth (Edward; 1810–73, English)
Ewart (James Cossar; 1851–1933, Scottish)
Fabre (Jean Henri; 1823–1915, French)
Hinde (Robert; 1923– , English)
Hyman (Libbie Henrietta; 1888–1969, US)
Krebs (John, Lord; 1945– , English)
Yonge (Charles Maurice; 1899–1986, English)

06 Darwin (Charles; 1809–82, English)
de Beer (Sir Gavin; 1899–1972, English)
Flower (Sir William Henry; 1831–99, English)
Fossey (Dian; 1932–85, US)
Frisch (Karl von; 1886–1982, Austrian)
Hooker (Sir Joseph; 1817–1911, English)

Kinsey (Alfred; 1894–1956, US)
Lorenz (Konrad; 1903–89, Austrian)
Morris (Desmond; 1928– , English)
Newton (Alfred; 1829–1907, English)
Osborn (Henry Fairfield; 1857–1935, US)
Rensch (Bernhard; 1900–90, German)
Sloane (Sir Hans; 1660–1753, British)
Thorpe (William Homan; 1902–86, English)
Wilson (Edmund Beecher; 1856–1939, US)

07 Agassiz (Alexander; 1835–1910, US)
Agassiz (Louis; 1807–73, US)
Audubon (John James; 1785–1851, US)
Dawkins (Richard; 1941– , British)
Durrell (Gerald; 1925–95, English)
Griffin (Donald; 1915–2003, US)
Hediger (Heini; 1908–1992, Swiss)
Hertwig (Oscar; 1849–1922, German)
Mantell (Gideon; 1790–1852, English)
Medawar (Sir Peter; 1915–87, British)
Merriam (Clinton Hart; 1885–1942, US)
Rüppell (Eduard; 1794–1884, German)

Siebold (Karl Theodor Ernst von; 1804–65, German)
Spemann (Hans; 1869–1941, German)
Wallace (Alfred Russel; 1823–1913, English)

08 Brünnich (Morten Thrane; 1737–1827, Danish)
Hamilton (William Donald; 1936–2000, English)
Jennings (Herbert Spencer; 1868–1947, US)
Kammerer (Paul; 1880–1926, Austrian)
Leuckart (Karl Georg Friedrich Rudolf; 1822–98, German)
Linnaeus (Carolus; 1707–78, Swedish)
Mitchell (Sir Peter Chalmers; 1864–1945, Scottish)
Schultze (Max Johann Sigismund; 1825–74, German)
Thompson (John Vaughan; 1779–1847, English)
Thompson (Sir D'Arcy; 1860–1948, Scottish)

09 Aristotle (384–322 BC, Greek)
Lankester (Sir Edwin; 1847–1929, English)
Schaudinn (Fritz; 1871–1906, German)
Southwood (Sir Richard; 1931–2005, English)
Tinbergen (Nikolaas; 1907–88, Dutch)
Zuckerman (Solly, Lord; 1904–93, South African/British)

10 Kettlewell (Henry Bernard David; 1907–79, English)
Rothschild (Lionel Walter, Lord; 1868–1937, English)
Rothschild (Dame Miriam; 1908–2005, English)
Steenstrup (Johannes Iapetus Smith; 1813–97, Danish)
Williamson (William Crawford; 1816–95, English)

12 Attenborough (Sir David; 1926–   , English)
Wynne-Edwards (Vero; 1906–97, English)

Terms used in zoology include:

04 host
05 biped
clade
morph
06 aliped
atocia
07 habitat
mimicry
oestrus
08 gastrula
holotype
startle colours
See also **classification**

monogamy
ommateum
parasite
polygamy
ungulate
09 anoestrus
didelphic
oviparous
piscivore
quadruped
refection

taligrade
10 alloparent
camouflage
gressorial
nucivorous
omnivorous
prehensile
viviparous
11 aestivation
artiodactyl
carnivorous

granivorous
herbivorous
hibernation
iteroparous
multiparous
noctilucent
plantigrade
12 carpophagous
exteroceptor
13 hermaphrodite
14 autocoprophagy